INSIDE DREAMW[...]

BY
Laura Gutman
Patricia J. Ayers
Donald S. Booth

201 West 103rd Street, Indianapolis, Indiana 46290

An Imprint of Pearson Education

Boston • Indianapolis • London • Munich • New York • San Francisco

Inside Dreamweaver® MX

International Standard Book Number: 0-7357-1181-X

Library of Congress Catalog Card Number: 752064711810

06 05 04 03 02   7 6 5 4 3 2 1

Interpretation of the printing code: The rightmost double-digit number is the year of the book's printing; the rightmost single-digit number is the number of the book's printing. For example, the printing code 02-1 shows that the first printing of the book occurred in 2002.

Printed in the United States of America

Trademarks

Warning and Disclaimer

Publisher
David Dwyer

Associate Publisher
Stephanie Wall

Production Manager
Gina Kanouse

Managing Editor
Kristy Knoop

Acquisitions Editors
Linda Anne Bump
Deborah Hittel-Shoaf

Senior Development Editor
Lisa Thibault

Product Marketing Manager
Tammy Detrich

Publicity Manager
Susan Nixon

Project Editor
Suzanne Pettypiece

Copy Editor
Keith Cline

Indexer
Lisa Stumpf

Manufacturing Coordinator
Jim Conway

Book Designer
Louisa Klucznik

Cover Designer
Aren Howell

Proofreader
Linda Seifert

Composition
Jeff Bredensteiner
Gloria Schurick

Media Developer
Jay Payne

Contents at a Glance

Introduction

Part IV   Site Management with Dreamweaver

21   Development Issues: Planning Your Site   697

22   Local Site Management   715

About the Authors

Laura Gutman works as a multimedia developer, web application developer, and educator in the fields of multimedia, programming, and design. Her first experience in computer science was at an IBM training school in 1983, where she learned how to punch cards, dissect mainframes, and program in COBOL. In the intervening years, she earned her doctorate in English from the University of St. Andrews (Scotland) and has worked as a graphic designer and illustrator (for print and multimedia), technical writer, and multimedia developer. Currently, Laura lives with her dog, parakeets, and hundreds of computer toys in Albuquerque, New Mexico. In addition to her development and consulting work, she teaches a range of courses in multimedia and graphic design at the University of New Mexico. You can visit her online at `www.rocketlaura.com`.

Patricia J. Ayers has been producing web sites professionally for more than 6 years, with more than 20 sites successfully completed in the past year. She is the owner of Carolina Web Solutions (`www.carolinawebsolutions.com`), a web design company specializing in small business web sites, and uses Dreamweaver and Fireworks as her primary design tools.

Patty attended the State University of New York at New Paltz and Pace University, and is currently an avid student of marketing, advertising, and graphic design, in addition to web development.

As a Macromedia Certified web developer and regular volunteer on the Dreamweaver user forums, Patty maintains a Dreamweaver resources site featuring original tutorials at `www.thepattysite.com` and is involved in the beta testing of Dreamweaver extensions. She is also a member of the Carolina ColdFusion User Group.

Patty lives in Chapel Hill, North Carolina with her family, and depends on such occupations as biking, gardening, and playing guitar as antidotes to too much computer time.

Donald S. Booth currently works as a team lead on the Dreamweaver Technical Support Team at Macromedia. He has been working at Macromedia for two and a half years. He also works on the Authorware Support team as a technician and trainer. He has degrees in art and philosophy from the University of Rhode Island.

When not building web pages, Don likes to build other things such as guitars, cameras, and a good library. He likes taking photographs and collecting cameras. Don loves music and has a fascination with spacecraft that borders on plain silly.

He currently resides in San Francisco. Learn more about him at `www.dbooth.net`.

About the Technical Reviewers

These reviewers contributed their considerable hands-on expertise to the entire development process for *Inside Dreamweaver MX*. As the book was being written, these dedicated professionals reviewed all the material for technical content, organization, and flow. Their feedback was critical to ensuring that *Inside Dreamweaver MX* fits our readers' need for the highest quality technical information.

Brad Halstead started out in the computer industry as a sales representative for a local company and moved up quickly to senior technician, where he performed service contracts for companies such as IBM, PC Service Partners, Xerox, and Olivetti for several years. In 1994, he became interested in web design and hasn't looked back since. Brad is very lucky and thankful for the support of his partner, Brenda, and children (Amanda, Aaron, and Megan) through his endeavors in this field.

Julie Hallstrom is a team lead for the Macromedia Dreamweaver technical support team. She came to her love of Dreamweaver after hand coding HTML for a year and designing web sites for small companies. She sees her job of supporting Dreamweaver users as an opportunity to share her enthusiasm for a really wonderful product.

Elaine Montoya is a principal of Zocoloco Studios—a graphic design firm specializing in web development, motion graphics, and print. Founded in 1985, Zocoloco Studios has won numerous awards and has been published in *HOW Magazine*.

From a young age, Elaine began to pursue her career in the creative field. At age 14, she started working in printing and graphics and has worked in advertising, graphic design, and multimedia since. Currently she has over 25 years of experience in the field of graphic design and multimedia. She has a degree in liberal arts from the University of NM as well as a degree in advertising design from the Colorado Institute of Art.

Elaine uses a combination of Macromedia products in her daily work with Zocoloco Studios. She finds the combination of Flash, Dreamweaver, and ColdFusion (or PHP) to be an excellent means to create rich media sites with database connectivity for her clients.

Dedications

To Caroline. She kick-started my career all those years ago, and has been a haven of sanity for me ever since.

—*Laura Gutman*

This is for my parents, Donald and Lynn Ayers, who have always been confident that I would amount to something, despite some evidence to the contrary.

—*Patricia J. Ayers*

I dedicate this book to my parents, who have supported me in everything I have done.

—*Donald S. Booth*

Acknowledgments

Laura Gutman:

Hats off to our terrific editors at New Riders—Deb, Lisa, and Linda—for getting us all together and keeping us afloat through all the dragon-filled waters of writing this big book. My technical knowledge was expanded and supported by my colleagues at the University of New Mexico and by Elaine, Jen, Becky, and the rest of the Girl Geeks. Lots of people's skill and experience got tucked into the pages herein!

Patricia J. Ayers:

I would like to thank David Pickens, who first suggested the wild idea that I could work at web design as more than a hobby and then helped and supported me every step of the way.

Many thanks to all of my dear friends and colleagues from the Macromedia user forums, who have helped, taught, supported, and amused me throughout this project, especially Martina Kosloff, Corey Eiges, Murray Summers, Jag Sidhu, Marion Kaltenschnee, Adrian (JoJo) Senior, John Waller, Bob Haroche, Becky Tench, Laurie Casolino, Colm Gallagher, John Tucker, and all the rest.

Donald S. Booth:

Thanks to Julie Hallstrom for her excellent technical editing and for providing daily laughs.

Thanks to Eric Lerner for recommending me for this project.

Thanks to my co-authors, Laura and Patty, for their help and insight with this project. You both made it more enjoyable for me.

Tell Us What You Think

As the reader of this book, you are the most important critic and commentator. We value your opinion and want to know what we're doing right, what we could do better, what areas you'd like to see us publish in, and any other words of wisdom you're willing to pass our way.

As the Associate Publisher for New Riders Publishing, I welcome your comments. You can fax, email, or write me directly to let me know what you did or didn't like about this book—as well as what we can do to make our books stronger.

Please note that I cannot help you with technical problems related to the topic of this book, and that due to the high volume of mail I receive, I might not be able to reply to every message.

When you write, please be sure to include this book's title and author as well as your name and phone or fax number. I will carefully review your comments and share them with the author and editors who worked on the book.

Fax: 317-581-4663

Email: stephanie.wall@newriders.com

Mail: Stephanie Wall
         Associate Publisher
         New Riders Publishing
         201 West 103rd Street
         Indianapolis, IN 46290 USA

Visit Our Web Site: www.newriders.com

On our web site, you'll find information about our other books, the authors we partner with, book updates and file downloads, promotions, discussion boards for online interaction with other users and with technology experts, and a calendar of trade shows and other professional events with which we'll be involved. We hope to see you around.

Email Us from Our Web Site

Go to www.newriders.com and click on the Contact Us link if you

- Have comments or questions about this book.

- Want to report errors that you have found in this book.

- Have a book proposal or are interested in writing for New Riders.

- Would like us to send you one of our author kits.

- Are an expert in a computer topic or technology and are interested in being a reviewer or technical editor.

- Want to find a distributor for our titles in your area.

- Are an educator/instructor who wants to preview New Riders books for class-room use. In the body/comments area, include your name, school, department, address, phone number, office days/hours, text currently in use, and enrollment in your department, along with your request for either desk/examination copies or additional information.

Introduction

Welcome to *Inside Dreamweaver MX*! It's an exciting place to be. Your authors have combined all their knowledge and diverse experience to provide you with a rich resource for learning all about the new Dreamweaver and learning how to apply your knowledge to deal with real-world web-authoring issues.

What (and Whom) This Book Is For

Our goal in writing this book was to give you a more in-depth experience of Dreamweaver, and of web page creation, than you'll find in the program manual or beginner-level books. If you've never fired up a copy of Dreamweaver before, you'll find plenty of good fundamental information about where things are and how they work. If you're already a Dreamweaver user, but aren't satisfied that you're taking full advantage of the software, or want to take your knowledge to the next level, there's plenty here for you as well. If you're a web developer just itching to wrap your brain around database-driven web sites, XHTML, DHTML, and other cutting-edge technologies, we have sections on each of those topics to help you play technology catch-up.

Dreamweaver in the Larger Scheme of Things

Working with web development software isn't like working with any other kind of program. Before you can use Dreamweaver effectively, you need to know how browsers work, and how HTML, JavaScript, and other web technologies function within the browser to create web experiences. One of our goals in this book is to help you look beyond the software, to start thinking about what's possible on the web and how Dreamweaver can help you accomplish that.

To that end, this book examines every topic as it relates to browsers and HTML standards, as well as how it's implemented in Dreamweaver. Instead of just learning how to format type in Dreamweaver, you want to know what all the possibilities are for type formatting in HTML, how they work, and what their relative advantages are. Then you want to know how to use Dreamweaver to make that formatting happen. That's the emphasis throughout this book.

Dreamweaver in the Real World

We also know that no one becomes a pro by memorizing program features. To really master any software, you have to know not only what the program can do, but also how to use its capabilities creatively to solve real problems and build real projects. This book teaches you how to use various program features. However, it also explains why to use them—and how to use them well. Each chapter includes our own professional tips and strategies, as well as exercises showing you how to apply program features. We've also included several interviews with web professionals so you can see how Dreamweaver works in the trenches.

Dreamweaver and Live Data

The most dramatic change in Dreamweaver MX is the incorporation of UltraDev's dynamic data features into the main Dreamweaver program. If you're not yet versed in this aspect of web development but want to learn, we have some special features for you. In addition to a section of the book devoted to creating data-driven web sites (Part V, "Dreamweaver and Dynamic Data"), we've placed relevant dynamic data topics throughout the book's other chapters. They're marked with a special icon, so they'll be easy to identify. And for those of you who aren't interested in this aspect of web development, Dreamweaver hasn't abandoned you and we haven't either. You can ignore Part V and skip right past the dynamic data topics—there's plenty of other information to absorb.

Other New Features

There's more new to Dreamweaver MX than just database connectivity. The program sports a new, streamlined interface, organized around dockable panel groups. Dreamweaver now offers XML and XHTML support, including **DocType** declarations and validation. Cascading Style Sheet (CSS) support has been beefed up. Dreamweaver now makes it easier to write accessible code. And for the hand-coders among you, many HomeSite features have been integrated into Dreamweaver. Integration with Flash MX is a joy to behold. And that's just the highlights! Throughout the book, keep your eye out for the special "new features" icon. Wherever we show off a new feature, you'll see that icon in the margin.

How This Book Is Organized

Each of the book's 36 chapters contains explanatory text, lots of pictures, and several hands-on exercises. The chapters are grouped into six sections:

Part I: Web Page Construction with Dreamweaver

These chapters cover the nuts and bolts of creating web pages with Dreamweaver, including setting up the workspace, creating documents, working with text and images, setting up links and navigation systems, and adding head content. Just because these are fundamentals doesn't mean this section is only for beginners! There's a lot to learn here about good, solid work skills for creating good foundation documents.

Part II: Design with Dreamweaver

This section looks at Dreamweaver as a design tool. This includes creating good page layout with tables and layers, using CSS, creating frame-based layouts, and designing forms. The focus is on creating attractive, functional and communicative page designs, and on developing good coding skills to create well-structured pages that will display well across browsers and platforms.

Part III: Interactivity, DHTML, and Multimedia

Web pages don't have to be static. An important part of the web experience is interactivity, whether it's for user engagement, efficient presentation of information, or entertainment value. The chapters in this section examine all the tools for making things hop and pop, turning the static web experience into something interactive. This includes JavaScript behaviors, DHTML (what it is and how you can use it), as well as working beyond HTML with Flash and other rich media content.

Part IV: Site Management with Dreamweaver

No web page is an island. This section covers Dreamweaver as an organizational tool for working with the dozens or hundreds of files that comprise a web site. This section covers creating a local site and taking advantage of Dreamweaver file management resources, working with remote sites, and using Dreamweaver tools for team-based or large-scale web development.

Part V: Dreamweaver and Dynamic Data

Dynamic data is the future of web development. Read this section of the book to start using Dreamweaver to work with ASP and ASP.NET, ColdFusion, PHP, and JSP. These chapters get you going from the ground up, explaining how dynamic web pages work and how to set up a workstation for dynamic development. One chapter is devoted to each of the major development environments Dreamweaver supports.

Part VI: Dreamweaver Under the Hood

Think of this section as Dreamweaver for geeks. Starting with an overview of the web from a coder's point of view, these chapters cover Dreamweaver as a coding tool; customizing the Dreamweaver workspace; working with extensions and the Extension Manager; and finally, using a bit of scripting to write your own extensions.

How to Use This Book

How you use this book depends on who you are and how *you* want to use it.

- **Reading front to back.** You could read this book from front to back, like a good novel—the topics are generally arranged from simpler to more challenging, and from small-scale (working with individual pages) to large-scale (working with sites and servers). Or you could pick any section or chapter you like, and start reading there. Each chapter contains enough cross-references that you should be able to pick up the story anywhere you like, and still be oriented.

- **Doing the exercises or not.** The exercises are provided to give you practice with various Dreamweaver topics and examples of how to put different Dreamweaver functions to use. You'll gain a lot by doing them. Sometimes, however, you just don't have time to do exercises—you need answers *now*. All topics are fully covered outside the exercises; so if you want to use the book as a reference only, you can find everything you're looking for in the text.

- **Getting started with dynamic data.** If you're ready to enter the brave new world of live data, you should start by reading Part V. Then go through the book's other chapters. Look out for the "dynamic data" icons; they'll point out aspects of each chapter's subject matter that relates to dynamic data web sites.

What to Take Away from This Book

We hope you enjoy learning about Dreamweaver as much as we have enjoyed writing about it. We want you to close the covers of this book with a greater understanding of how web development works, and how to use Dreamweaver to work with it, than when you started. But remember, no one ever became a better web designer just by reading books. Read the book. Then go create some web sites. Then come back and read more of the book. Then go make more web sites. And just about the time you think you've got everything mastered, it'll be time for a new book!

Chapter 1

What's New with Dreamweaver MX?

Dreamweaver MX represents a huge advance in the power and functionality of Dreamweaver. It combines fantastic new improvements to the user interface, a more robust code-editing environment, and the power of application servers and database-driven live data pages to make it a tremendous upgrade from the preceding version. This will even further solidify its place as the clear choice for web developers.

From the Tag Library Editor, which gives users complete control over the formatting of every tag to support for development languages such as ASP.NET, JSP, ColdFusion and XHTML, Dreamweaver MX gives web developers an easy-to-use yet powerful tool to create complex, dynamic web sites that are easy to maintain.

This chapter covers the many new features of Dreamweaver MX.

Note

MX   Be on the lookout for this icon throughout the book, wherever a new Dreamweaver MX feature is covered.

Improved Interface

Many improvements have been made to the basic usability of the program. For Mac users, Dreamweaver MX now runs natively in OS X as well as OS 9.1. For Windows users, it offers native Windows XP support. For both platforms, the look and feel of the program is streamlined and improved.

Integrated Workspace

For Dreamweaver/Windows users, the new integrated workspace presents one large application window, with dockable panels, inspectors, and report windows (see Figure 1.1). (Don't worry—you can still choose the Classic Dreamweaver 4 workspace, if you prefer.)

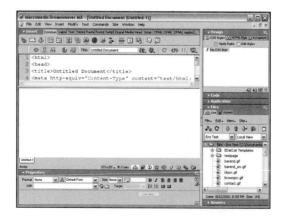

Figure 1.1   The new, integrated workspace for Dreamweaver MX/Windows.

Dockable Panel Groups

Panels have a new look and functionality. They are now stacked on the right or left of the window and will cascade as needed. This new look will keep the panels from covering up your Document window—no longer will you have to shuffle panels around just to see your page! As always, you can still group panels to your preference.

Customizable Insert Bar

The Objects panel, now called the *Insert bar*, has been moved to the top of the page a la ColdFusion Studio and HomeSite+. Still customizable from the **Configuration** folder, it will no longer clutter up your design space. It also has been expanded to include more common objects, more frameset options, and even editable regions for templates. And it's context-sensitive, showing different categories and objects depending on the kind of document you're working on, and whether you're in Code or Design view.

Customizable Toolbars

In addition to the familiar Document toolbar, a *Standard toolbar* offers quick icon-based access to basic file operations (Save, New, Open, and more). The toolbar functionality in Dreamweaver MX is also now extensible, which opens the door to third-party developers adding specialized toolbars for different purposes.

Answers Panel

A new concept in software connectivity, the *Answers panel* lets you connect directly to Macromedia online support resources. Get tips and tricks, tutorials, and the latest news from Macromedia, all without leaving Dreamweaver (see Figure 1.2).

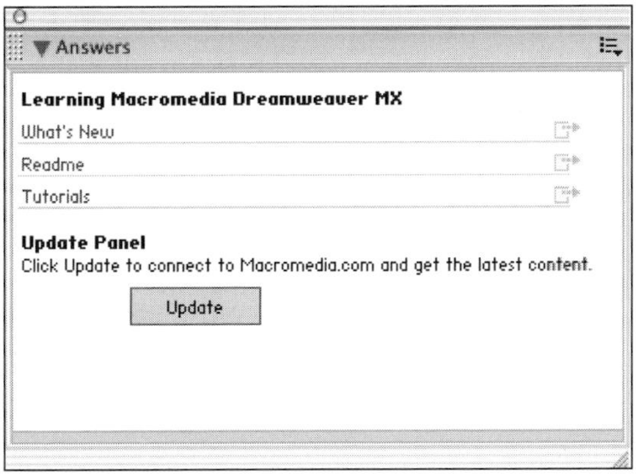

Figure 1.2   The Answers panel in action.

And More...

And those are only the big changes. Lots of little changes make your working life easier, too. Functions and keyboard commands are now coordinated across all Macromedia programs. Right-click options have been increased. Copy HTML and paste HTML are back! And, for those of you who are extension-happy, the interface is more open to customizing and extending than ever.

Page Design

As a page design tool, Dreamweaver MX offers a lot of new features that will help you quickly build professional pages.

Improved Document Creation

The New Document dialog box now enables you to choose from a range of file types as you're creating your file, and also to see a small preview of all your template files (see Figure 1.3). Whatever file type you choose, the proper code framework will be put in place for you. You also can preview and choose from a selection of professionally designed stationery (prebuilt pages).

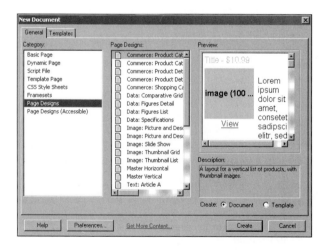

Figure 1.3   The New Document dialog box showing choices for file type and stationery.

Snippets

Snippets are small pieces of code used frequently in your sites. Any piece of code that you use often can be saved as a snippet. After you've saved the snippet, whenever you need that code again, just go to the Snippets panel and insert it. Snippets are similar to library items in that they are reusable; unlike library items, they do not update automatically.

Dreamweaver MX comes with a hefty selection of prebuilt snippets for you to use. It includes things such as common header and footer elements and even a Close Window button to use with the Open Browser Window behavior! Basic navigation schemes and table settings can be dropped into your documents and customized to suit every situation.

Enhanced CSS Support

The new, improved CSS panel shows all CSS elements, including redefined tags and CSS selectors (see Figure 1.4). The panel includes a description of each style. All classes can be applied from a drop-down menu. The CSS Style Creator has been streamlined to make setting up borders and colors easier.

Figure 1.4   The new, improved CSS panel in action.

Design time styles have been introduced. This feature enables you to use and hide different styles during design time. These can be different styles from those used for the live site.

Accessibility Options

You can now set a preference that will prompt you to add accessibility parameters when you insert items such as images, tables, or forms. The UsableNet Accessibility Guide has been added to the Reference panel.

You also can make Dreamweaver itself more accessible by using large fonts for the panels and setting dialog boxes to automatically accept default values after a set time. Dreamweaver MX supports the JAWS and Window Eyes screen readers. You also can use operating system features such as high-contrast color schemes for developing. (In Code view, the code-coloring scheme is disabled; in Design view, coded colors used will match the look of the page in the browser.)

Site Design

Dreamweaver has always provided excellent site management tools, from file management to built-in FTP to sophisticated synchronization. Dreamweaver MX offers even more tools to help you keep your files organized, and your design team coordinated, on even the most extensive site projects.

Enhanced Template Functionality

Templates can do a lot more than they've ever done before. With *template inheritance*, you can define one template based on another. *Nested templates* allow you to embed one template inside another. In addition to editable regions, templates can now contain repeating regions, optional regions, and even editable tag attributes, allowing template users to edit the parameters of a tag while the tag itself remains locked.

Dreamweaver MX also gives you a series of prebuilt templates that you can use and customize.

Integrated Site Panel

You can now have the Site panel grouped with all your other panels! This makes it easier to see your list of site files while working in documents (see Figure 1.5). It also makes functions such as linking with Point-to-File very easy. If you don't want your Site panel integrated, you can choose to leave it as a separate window, as it was in Dreamweaver 4.

The Site files pane of the Site panel now includes a *file explorer* (see Figure 1.5). In addition to showing all the files within your site, it lists the entire contents of your hard drive, in an expandable format similar to Windows Explorer or the Mac Finder's list view. With the file explorer, you can easily locate files anywhere on your computer, open them, and move them into your site folder—all without leaving Dreamweaver.

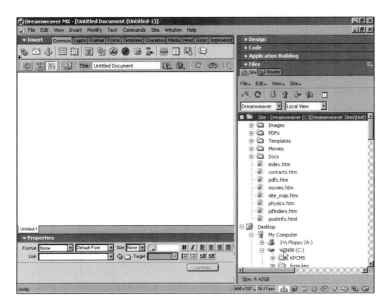

Figure 1.5   The new, integrated Site panel showing the new file explorer in action.

Site Definition Wizard

Setting up site definitions has always been confusing to many new users, and with the addition of dynamic features in Dreamweaver MX, the process of setting up a site is now more complex than ever. The new *Site Definition Wizard* will walk you through every step of setting up the site, from choosing your local root folder to setting up your FTP connection. It helps you set up your application server for live data pages and gives a clear explanation of the required information at every step. For more advanced users, the Site Definition dialog box offers an Advanced setting based on the familiar Dreamweaver 4 interface.

Cloaking

A new and welcome feature, *cloaking* allows you to specify certain folders or files types to *not* be considered during site operations such as putting, getting, and synchronizing. Cloaking is a real lifesaver, especially if you work with programs like Fireworks or Flash that create authoring files that don't need to be uploaded to the web server. Tell Dreamweaver to cloak all PNG and FLA files, and you can happily synchronize your site without worrying that those files will be uploaded (see Figure 1.6).

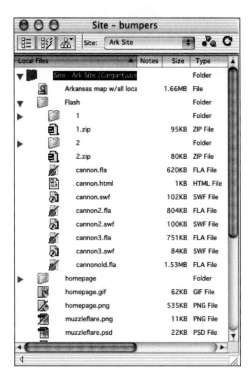

Figure 1.6   Cloaked media in the Site panel.

Site Definition Importing and Exporting

With *site export*, you can now export site definition information as an XML file. With *site import*, you can turn that XML file back into a site definition. Use site import/export to move site definitions from one computer to another, to share definitions between computers in a workgroup, or just to back up your definition in case disaster strikes your computer.

And More…

What else is there? Macromedia Sitespring tasks and files can be edited and completed with built-in Sitespring integration. SSH encryption has been added to the FTP functionality. An improved Reports interface makes creating site reports easier than ever. Site management has never been better.

DHTML and Multimedia

Dreamweaver MX increases your ability to use multimedia within your web sites. Improved integration with other Macromedia MX programs, new DHTML behaviors, and improved layer control all add up to a smoother workflow for rich media pages of all kinds.

Improved Flash MX Integration

If you're using Flash MX, you now have *launch-and-edit* capabilities between Dreamweaver and Flash. Select an embedded SWF file in a Dreamweaver document, click a button, and Flash MX launches, opening your original FLA file for editing. Make your changes, save and close, and Flash automatically generates a new SWF and sends you back to Dreamweaver.

If your embedded SWF file contains links, you can even update those links without ever leaving Dreamweaver. Changed links are logged in a Design Note, and passed to the FLA file the next time you launch-and-edit. Now you don't need to recompile the Flash files in your document every time you change a link.

Enhanced Fireworks Integration

The integration between Fireworks and Dreamweaver has been improved to make life a bit easier. Dreamweaver can differentiate between Fireworks 4 and Fireworks MX files.

With the new Image Placeholder feature in Dreamweaver, you can insert a placeholder image onto your page and resize it however you like. In the Property inspector, you will see a Create button with the Fireworks MX logo. Click this button and Fireworks MX will launch with a new document open with the image placeholder size ready to go. Create the image in Fireworks and click the Done button. Fireworks will prompt you to save the source PNG file and automatically create a GIF or JPEG (whatever is set in the Optimize panel) and insert it into your Dreamweaver page!

There also has been an enhancement with the pop-up menus that Fireworks creates. In previous versions, it would show up in Dreamweaver as Custom JavaScript in the Behaviors panel. Dreamweaver will now recognize it as a pop-up menu in the Behaviors panel. You will be able to edit it directly in Dreamweaver or use Roundtrip HTML to update the menu in Fireworks. Creating the menus in Fireworks will give you the option of using images in the background. You can then update these images and Dreamweaver will know to update the scripts correctly.

Pop-Up Menus

This great behavior, available in Macromedia Fireworks 4, is now built into Dreamweaver MX. You can now create pop-up menus, in all sizes, types, and colors, directly from the Behaviors panel (see Figure 1.7).

Figure 1.7   A menu created with the new Pop-Up Menu behavior.

Code Editing

Dreamweaver MX has many new features that will be a boon to hand coding productivity. Many new coding features will make hand coding, coloring, and formatting easier than ever.

Tag Completion and Code Hints

For those developers who like to write code, but don't like to type, Dreamweaver MX now has several automatic code writing features. With *tag completion*, type the opening tag in a pair, and Dreamweaver automatically enters the closing tag for you. Type <**table**> and get an automatic </table>. With *code hints*, Dreamweaver helps you type by guessing what tag you're typing next, and providing easily navigable lists of attributes and values—as you type. It makes writing code that much easier, even if you're all thumbs!

Tag Chooser, Tag Editor, and Tag Library Editor

Several new commands and dialog boxes help you set up tag functionality (see Figure 1.8).

The *Tag Chooser* lets you examine every tag Dreamweaver understands, including its attributes and their supported values, and correct syntax.

Inserting a tag from the tag chooser opens the *tag editor*, enabling you to set general properties, browser-specific attributes, and style sheet information for that tag.

Finally, the *tag library editor* determines what information appears in the other tag editors. From here, you can set the code formatting and syntax coloring for every tag, specify default settings for all the standard attributes, and even add your own attributes and tags as HTML develops or your coding needs expand.

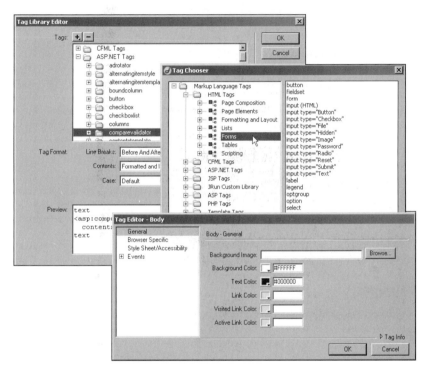

Figure 1.8 The new tag dialog boxes.

Tag Inspector

The new *Tag Inspector panel* is a great way to set attributes, and it offers two great tools for examining and editing code (see Figure 1.9). The top half of the panel presents a collapsible tree structure view of all the tags in the current document and their contents. Selecting a tag from the tree view displays a Tag Inspector in the bottom half of the panel, listing all the attributes for that tag and its values. From here, you can select and edit any of these attributes. Drop-down menus will list all the standard values for the attribute; Browse and Live Data buttons appear where appropriate, to help you set filenames and dynamic data sources as attribute values. It's a great way to have access to the attributes beyond the Property inspector! And it's a great learning tool for visually minded web designers who want to understand the logical structure of their HTML pages.

Figure 1.9   The Tag Inspector showing tree view and the Tag Attribute inspector.

Printing Code

It's a minor feature to some; to others, it's a lifesaver. You can now print source code directly from Code view. No more having to print through the browser, or open your documents in a stand-alone text editor, just for the privilege of printing.

XML/XHTML Support

XML is becoming more popular, and a working knowledge of XML is now vital for large, dynamic web sites. Dreamweaver MX incorporates features that make sure your pages are compliant with XML and XHTML standards.

XML Validation

Dreamweaver can now validate your XML, going through the code to make sure you have set up your XML page correctly. The Results report will let you know about any invalid XML (see Figure 1.10).

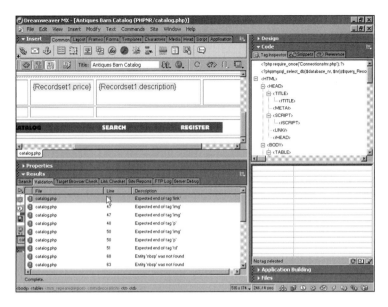

Figure 1.10   A document validation report.

XHTML Code Writing and Validation

As part of its XML support, Dreamweaver now gives you the ability to convert any HTML page into XHTML. The `DocType` declaration will be added; non-paired tags like `<img>` will be properly closed. The New Document dialog box also gives you the option of making all new files XHTML compliant.

Default File Type

You can now choose a default document type when you set up your site. This can be different for every site definition.

Dynamic Data

This is the quantum jump in Dreamweaver. Dreamweaver MX now contains all the database power of UltraDev and extends it with support for ASP.NET and PHP, in addition to ASP, JSP, and ColdFusion. For users new to dynamic web sites, the Site Wizard and other little interface touches help smooth the way to understanding a new technology. For power users migrating from UltraDev, there's plenty of new power here as well. Part V of this book is all about this new facet to Dreamweaver. (If you're brand new to dynamic data, start by reading Chapter 26, "Introduction to Dynamic Dreamweaver.")

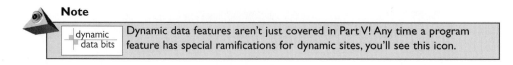

Note

dynamic data bits | Dynamic data features aren't just covered in Part V! Any time a program feature has special ramifications for dynamic sites, you'll see this icon.

Improved ColdFusion and JSP Support

There has been a big increase in the ColdFusion support in Dreamweaver MX. Not only have some of the interface features of ColdFusion Studio been incorporated, but you also can now automatically insert ColdFusion basic, flow, and advanced objects.

For JSP users, Dreamweaver MX offers full JavaBean introspection and improved JSP Tag Library support.

New ASP.NET and PHP Support

Dreamweaver MX provides support for the new Microsoft .NET initiative with support for ASP.NET documents and sites, including custom tag support, rendering of web forms, and DataGrid and DataList objects (see Figure 1.11).

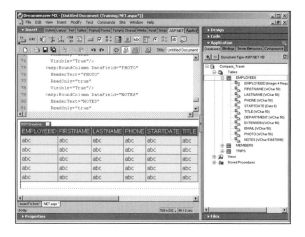

Figure 1.11   Working on an ASP.NET document in Dreamweaver MX.

Dreamweaver MX also provides support for the open source PHP language. With PHP you can make dynamic sites that use simple, easy-to-understand code; and it has the added benefit of being free! Used with a MySQL database (also free), PHP can get you up and running with a database-driven web site in no time at all.

New Dynamic Objects

The Insert bar now includes an Application objects category, as well as context-specific categories for JSP, ColdFusion, and other supported languages (see Figure 1.12). New dynamic form objects simplify the creation of database-driven pop-up menus and other form elements.

Figure 1.12   The Insert bar showing objects available for working on ColdFusion documents.

Integrated Database Explorer

Much like the Site panel's integrated file explorer, the Databases panel allows you to browse all connected databases from within the Dreamweaver interface. Tables, views, and schemas are all available in a handy expandable tree view.

Multi-Language Reference Panels

To help you work with the coding side of dynamic data, the Reference panel now includes ASP and JSP reference sections, both based on the popular Wrox programming books.

Summary

As you can see, Dreamweaver MX represents a huge leap in the functionality of Dreamweaver. From stem to stern, the program has been beefed up, tightened up, polished up, and fully integrated into Macromedia's line of MX version software. This chapter has covered the highlights—but there's plenty more, tucked into every corner of the program. Whether you're a graphic designer focusing on page layout; a team coordinator trying to maximize workflow efficiency; a code junkie looking for the best way to manage all your HTML, JS, and CSS; or a web applications developer who needs to harness the power of dynamic data and server-side scripting; Dreamweaver MX has what you need.

Chapter 2

Setting Up the Dreamweaver Workspace

A big part of what makes Dreamweaver so efficient and intuitive to work with, for web design newbies as well as seasoned professionals, is the flexible and streamlined workspace. If you've been using Dreamweaver for years, you already know this—but you might be having a bit of culture shock wandering around the new, improved Dreamweaver MX interface. If you're new to Dreamweaver, it's all new and wonderful. Whoever you are, it's a good idea to take a few minutes to explore the environment, learn where things are, and see how you can set it up to suit your working style and level of expertise.

This chapter introduces the basic concepts of working with Dreamweaver, explores the new Dreamweaver MX interface (including the integrated workspace for Windows) and takes you on a guided tour through the major items you'll see therein, including docked panel groups, the document and site panels, the Insert bar, Property inspector and other miscellaneous windows. You'll also learn where to get help when you need it, using the Reference panel, the Help menu, and the new Answers panel.

How Dreamweaver Thinks

Dreamweaver was built on the premise that it would write code for you, but if you wanted to edit your code by hand, the program would not change it. This made Dreamweaver very different from the other WYSIWYG applications of the day. This means that, while working in Dreamweaver, you can develop a file in one of two ways: in a visual interface (Design view), or a coding interface (Code view). If you choose to work entirely in Design view, Dreamweaver creates all of your code for you and is completely in charge of creating valid, workable documents for browser display. If you choose to do any of your own coding—either coding pages from scratch or editing the code that Dreamweaver has created—you can also choose how Dreamweaver will treat your code. You can set Dreamweaver to fix invalid code automatically, to highlight invalid code but not touch it, or to leave you alone and let you code in peace. (This is in contrast to many other WYSIWYG editors that automatically "correct" what they perceive as invalid code, causing much gnashing of teeth among savvy HTML coders.)

Note

WYSIWYG means "What You See Is What You Get." Technically, Dreamweaver has never called itself a WYSIWYG editor as other editors like Page Mill, FrontPage, and GoLive have. (The acronym WYSIWYG doesn't appear once in the Dreamweaver documentation.) By providing a visual design interface, however, which attempts to render HTML code similarly to how a browser renders, Dreamweaver invites comparison to the WYSIWYG editors.

At its most basic, a web page is a text file. This text file is read by the browser and displays the information therein according to the instructions in the HTML page. As an example, a basic tag in HTML is the `<font>` tag. A typical `<font>` tag looks like this:

```
<font face="Arial" size="2">This is the actual text. </font>
```

The browser reads this as "Use the Arial font and set the font size to 2 and display the text between the opening and closing tag." Then in the window, the browser displays the following:

```
This is the actual text.
```

What Dreamweaver does is write this code for you as you create the page. As you type in the actual text, Dreamweaver writes all the tags. The Dreamweaver Interface provides an intuitive, graphical way to write all the code required to display a web page. When it comes to, say, choosing the color of the text, you don't have to know the six-digit code for the particular color you want for your page background. All you have to do is select it in the color picker and Dreamweaver will fill in the code. Of course, if you happen to know that particular color code, you can enter it manually.

With Dreamweaver *behaviors*, which are combinations of HTML and JavaScript that enable you to do things that go beyond strict HTML, you can open a new browser window with a click, or easily create a pop-up menu navigation scheme.

dynamic
data bits

With the advent of Dreamweaver MX, you can now create dynamic, database-driven web sites through this graphical interface. Dreamweaver will write the required functions for you, and through the application server, enable you to see this dynamic content within the Design window rather than just through the browser. Using dynamic data, it is possible to display a wide array of information and actually have to design only a couple of pages. (Chapter 26, "Introduction to Dynamic Dreamweaver," discusses dynamic sites.)

Some developers like to write their code by hand. Because an HTML document is really a text document, this can be done in any text editor, such as Notepad or Simple Text. You can certainly use Dreamweaver to write the code and then use its other features, but letting Dreamweaver do the work for you is the whole idea of it. With the introduction of tag completion and code hints, writing by hand is even easier in Dreamweaver MX.

The New Dreamweaver Workspaces

Whether or not you're new to Dreamweaver, launching Dreamweaver MX for the first time and seeing the new interface will be a new experience for you. If you're working on Dreamweaver/Windows, you're seeing the new integrated interface that Macromedia is introducing with all of its MX software (Dreamweaver, Fireworks, Flash). If you're working on Dreamweaver/Mac, you're seeing the non-integrated but still brand-new Dreamweaver Macintosh interface (Aqua-fied, if you're on Mac OS X). No matter which platform you're on, you have new choices to make about how you want your workspace set up so you can do your best work.

Note

In a panic after upgrading? Relax! Although the interface looks quite a bit different than in previous versions of Dreamweaver, only the layout has changed. All the same features are there, along with a few more.

The Dreamweaver Workspace for Windows

For Windows users, Dreamweaver MX presents a big change over previous versions of the program and offers you several different ways to set up your workspace. The first time you launch the program, you'll be looking at the new integrated workspace. To see your workspace options and choose between them, do this (see Figure 2.1):

1. Choose Edit > Preferences.

2. When the Preferences dialog box opens, go to the General category.

3. Click the Change Workspace button.

4. When the Change Workspace dialog box appears, you'll see that you have the choice of the Integrated Workspace (with or without HomeSite style) or the Classic Dreamweaver 4 Workspace. Make your choice and click OK.

5. Dreamweaver will alert you that you need to restart for any workspace change to take effect. Click OK to close the alert window, then OK again to close the Preferences dialog box.

6. Quit and relaunch Dreamweaver to see and start using your new workspace.

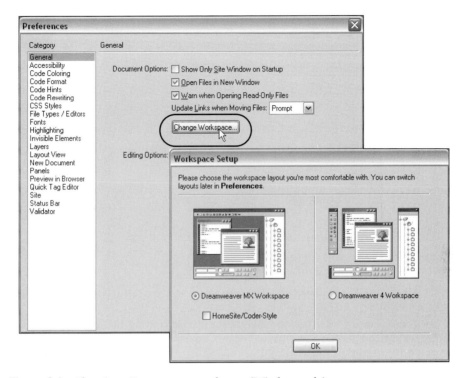

Figure 2.1   Choosing a Dreamweaver workspace (Windows only).

The following sections describe each of the workspace options, and why you might want to choose it.

The Integrated Workspace (Windows)

The *Integrated Workspace* for Windows is an exciting new development in all Macromedia MX programs (Dreamweaver, Fireworks, and Flash). Following the trend of many Windows applications, the entire interface is built into one large application window, which is then subdivided to hold different docked panels and windows. The main panel dock is on the right; on the left, the Insert bar and Property inspector frame the Document window (see Figure 2.2).

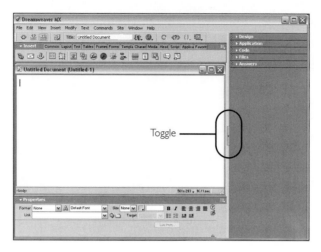

Figure 2.2   The integrated workspace for Dreamweaver MX (Windows).

Making Room

For horizontal spacing adjustments, the vertical bar separating the left and right segments of the window can be adjusted to give you more document room or more panel-viewing room. If you're on a smaller monitor, and are feeling a bit cramped in there with all of those window divisions taking up space, you also can click the triangle in that vertical bar to toggle the panels portion of the interface on and off as needed (see Figure 2.3). To get more space vertically around the Document window, you can collapse or expand the Insert bar and Property inspector by clicking on their expand/collapse triangles (see Figure 2.3).

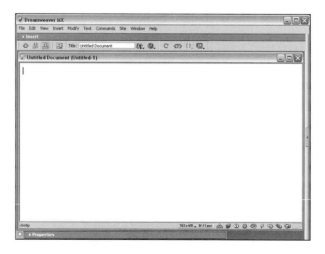

Figure 2.3   Minimizing the Insert bar and Property inspector in the integrated workspace.

Creating Free-Standing Panels

Docked panels and windows can be very efficient to work with because all parts of the interface are right there in front of you and nothing is ever hidden behind something else. If, however, you prefer to work with one or more of your panels as free-standing, you can undock any panel or panel group from the main application window. (See the section on "The Docked Panel Layout," later in this chapter for complete directions on working with docked panels.) A free-standing panel will never go behind the application window, but it might get hidden behind other free-standing panels. Free-standing panels can even be positioned outside the bounds of the application window (see Figure 2.4)—a great help if your workstation includes side-by-side monitors.

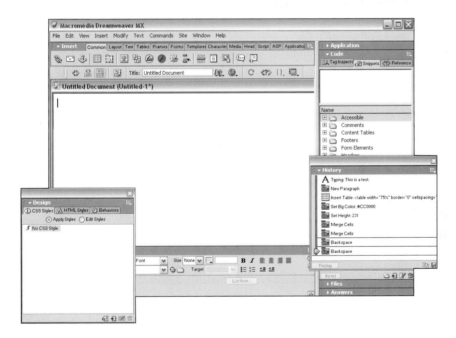

Figure 2.4   The integrated workspace showing free-standing panels floating outside the application window.

Dealing with the Document Window

In the integrated workspace, the only window that isn't docked by default is the Document window. Instead, it floats as a free-standing window surrounded by docked panels. While you can't dock this window in the same way panels are docked, you can dock it by maximizing it (see Figure 2.5). A maximized Document window has no title bar and no status bar, but it does have a bottom tab (for switching between multiple open documents) and an information area at the bottom that contains the same information normally found in the status bar.

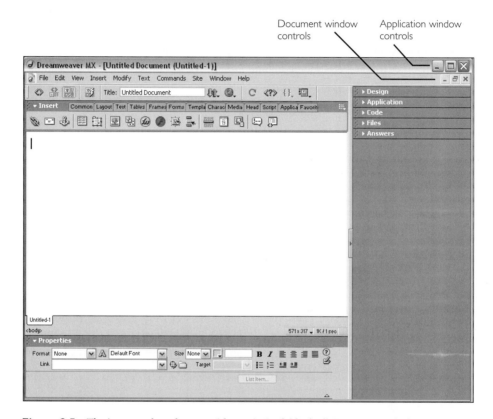

Figure 2.5   The integrated workspace with maximized (docked) Document window.

Panels on the Left: HomeSite/Coder-Style

If you like the integrated workspace but it seems backward to you with panels on the right, you can put the panel dock on the left instead. Just open the Choose Workspace dialog box, as described earlier, and choose the Dreamwaver MX Workspace with the HomeSite/Coder-Style option enabled. (When you enable this option, the dialog box will show a preview image of the left-panel-sided workspace.) The next time you launch Dreamweaver, your workspace will be rearranged with panels on the left (see Figure 2.6).

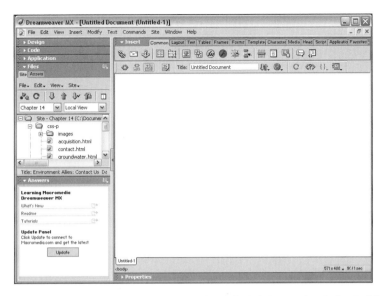

Figure 2.6   The integrated workspace with panels on the left (HomeSite/Coder-Style).

The Classic Dreamweaver 4 Workspace (Windows)

Versions of Dreamweaver/Windows before MX presented an interface consisting of various free-standing windows and panels with no application window holding them together. This kind of interface—which is familiar to Mac and UNIX users—makes it simple to move between open programs on the computer, because you can see and access all programs from within any program. But for Windows users it was unfamiliar territory. It also meant that the program could not continue running unless either the Site panel or one Document window was open.

The glory of the new integrated workspace is that it does away with this multi-window interface in favor of one large application window, which is much more comfortable for most Windows users. However, if you're an old Dreamweaver pro who still likes the old interface, or if you're a cross-platform user who likes multi-window interfaces, you can still have this experience in Dreamweaver MX—it's called the Dreamweaver 4 Workspace (see Figure 2.7), and it's all yours for the taking. The Document window, Property inspector, and Site panel are all free-standing. The horizontal Insert bar is free-standing and has been restored to its "classic" vertical appearance. The only modernization that has occurred is that the panels are docked into one main panel window.

Note

To give yourself a complete Dreamweaver 4 retrofit, you can undock the panels so they're all free-standing. (See the section on "The Docked Panel Layout" later in this chapter for details on doing this.)

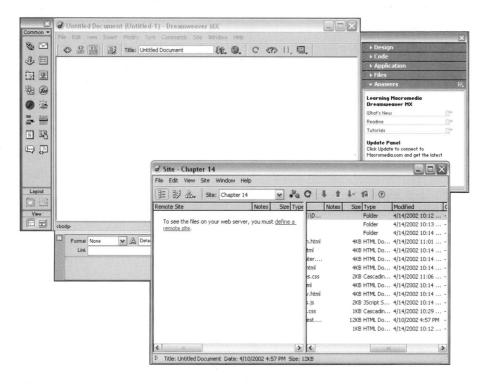

Figure 2.7   The Classic Dreamweaver 4 workspace

The Dreamweaver MX Interface (Macintosh)

There is no equivalent to the Windows integrated workspace for Dreamweaver/Mac, which means that Mac users don't have the overwhelming set of workspace choices that your Windows compatriots have. If you're upgrading from an earlier version of Dreamweaver, you also won't have nearly the interface shock as they will. Feeling left out? Don't take it personally! The whole reason for the new, integrated setup on Windows is that the old (Classic) interface with its multiple windows and lack of an application window was not very Windows-like. But it has always been Mac-like. And now, for those of you using OS X, it's also Aqua-fied, complete with anti-aliased text in dialog boxes and panels, translucent effects, and a Dreamweaver application menu (see Figure 2.8).

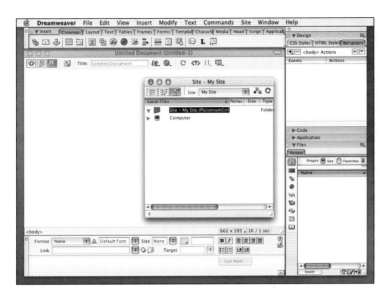

Figure 2.8   The aqua Dreamweaver/Mac interface for Mac OS X.

Though the Mac interface isn't integrated into one large application window, it does have docked panels—one central floating window containing most of the Dreamweaver panels. Like the Dreamweaver/Windows integrated workspace, it also has a horizontal Insert bar in place of the vertical Objects panel found in previous versions of Dreamweaver—though, if you don't like the new tabbed Insert bar, you can restore it to its old vertical appearance by clicking the horizontal/vertical toggle located in the panel's lower-right corner (see Figure 2.9).

Toggle

Figure 2.9   Toggling the Insert bar to a vertical structure like the old Objects panel (Mac only).

Using the Vertical Insert Bar

The purpose of the Insert bar is to help you insert objects into your documents; because there are a lot of kinds of objects available, the bar is divided into categories that appear as tabs. But when the Insert bar is in its vertical position (in Dreamweaver/Windows Classic Workspace or Dreamweaver/Mac regular workspace), it has no tabs! In vertical mode, the category appears as a title bar at the top of the panel. To switch between categories, click the title and choose from the pop-up menu of categories that appears (see Figure 2.10).

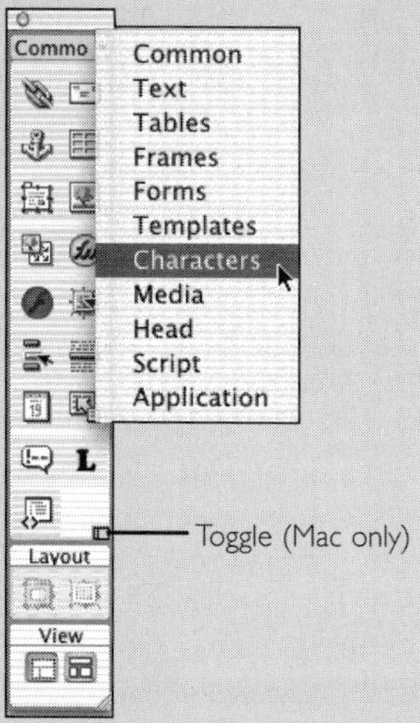

Figure 2.10   Switching between categories of objects using the Insert bar in its vertical (Classic) mode.

Touring the Dreamweaver Interface

Whichever Dreamweaver workspace you're using, and whichever platform and OS you're working on, the same major interface elements are present. The following sections present an overview of all the windows and toolbars and such that you're looking at as you're working in Dreamweaver. Use this section as a way to get the lay of the land if you're brand-new to the program, or as a refresher and introduction to new features if you're upgrading.

Standard Toolbar

In their never-ending effort to provide the most graphic and efficient workspace for you, Macromedia has beefed up the toolbar presence in Dreamweaver MX. Following the trend in much software, the new Standard toolbar gives you easy access to frequently used commands from the File and Edit menus (see Figure 2.11). The Standard toolbar can be toggled on and off by choosing View > Toolbars > Standard. In Dreamweaver/Windows, the Standard toolbar can be undocked by dragging it into the center of the Document window; after it's undocked, redock it by double-clicking on its title bar.

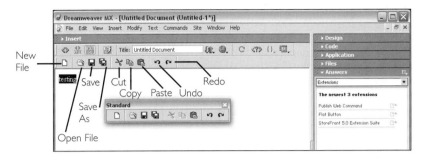

Figure 2.11 The new Standard toolbar in its docked and undocked states.

Panels, Inspectors, and Windows

Panels provide access to almost all the components of Dreamweaver. Although you can usually do something in Dreamweaver in more than one way, panels give you a graphical interface to almost all program functions. Panels can be shown or hidden together, collected into panel groups, resized, and docked and undocked.

The Docked Panel Layout

Dreamweaver MX introduces *cascading panels*. Whether or not you're working in the integrated workspace, most of the program's panels appear docked together in a single unit—either a free-standing panel window or a segment of the application window. Within the panel window, individual panels appear in groups; the groups are docked together in the panel window; and each group can be expanded or contracted to show or hide its contents. It's a very space-efficient setup that means you'll never again have to worry about, "Did I hide the Behaviors panel behind the CSS panel or did I close it, or where did it go?"

Panels and Panel Groups

To save space and reduce interface clutter, Dreamweaver collects panels into panel groups related by function. Within a group, the individual panels appear as tabbed layers—click the panel's tab to bring it to the front of the group. Table 2.1 lists the Dreamweaver panels, which panel groups each belongs to, how that panel can be opened (or expanded), and whether the panel is normally part of the panel window.

Table 2.1   The Dreamweaver Panels

Panel Group	Panel Name	To Open (Expand)	Part of Default Panel Layout
Design	Behaviors	Window > Behaviors	Yes
	CSS Styles	Window > CSS Styles	Yes
	HTML Styles	Window > HTML Styles	Yes
Code	Tag Inspector	Window > Tag Inspector	Yes
	Snippets	Window > Snippets	Yes
	Reference	Window > Reference	Yes
Application	Databases	Window > Databases	Yes
	Bindings	Window > Bindings	Yes
	Server Behaviors	Window > Server Behaviors	Yes
	Components	Window > Components	Yes
Files	Site (integrated workspace only)	Window > Site	Yes
	Assets	Window > Assets	Yes
Answers	Answers	Window > Others > Answers	Yes
Advanced Layout	Frames	Window > Others> Frames	No
	Layers	Windows > Others > Layers	No
History	History	Window > Others > History	No

Expanding, Contracting, Docking, and Undocking

Working with a clump of cascading panel groups involves a lot of expanding and contracting and general adjusting. Because you can't possibly have all of the panel groups showing in the docked window at the same time (unless your monitor is four feet tall), you'll always be tinkering with your groups as you work. Figure 2.12 shows the panel window and its main options.

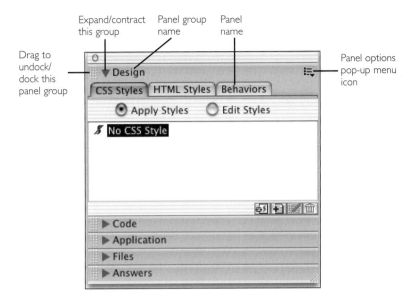

Figure 2.12   The docked panel window with cascading options highlighted.

- To expand or contract a panel group, click the expand/contract arrow in the panel group's title bar. If necessary, the panel window will stretch out to accommodate expanded panels.

- To adjust the relative height of two panel groups within the window, position the cursor between the two. The cursor will turn into a two-headed arrow. Drag up or down to resize.

- To close a panel group (for example, remove it from the docked window entirely), access its options menu and choose Close Panel Group.

- To expand a panel group and resize it to be as tall as possible, access its options menu and choose Maximize Panel Group.

- To undock a panel group, press the grabber edge at the left edge of the panel's title bar and drag it out of the panel window.

- To undock a specific panel, expand its group, click the panel's title tab, access its options menu, and choose Group With > New Panel Group.

- To redock a panel, grab the panel's title tab and drag it back into a docked group.

- To redock a panel, click the panel's title bar, access its options menu, and choose Group With, selecting the panel group with which to dock it.

- To resize the panel window (when it's undocked), drag its lower-right corner.

The Horizontal Panels

Various Dreamweaver panels have horizontal layouts and dock in different ways than the others. These include the Insert bar, Property inspector, Timelines panel, Code inspector, Results window, and Sitespring panel. In the integrated workspace, they function much the same as other panels: they can be expanded or contracted, and can be docked with each other (along the top and/or bottom edge of the application window). In the other workspaces, they aren't dockable and don't function as cascading panels.

> **Note**
> Sitespring is a new Macromedia product geared toward project management and versioning. It integrates with Dreamweaver through the Sitespring panel.

The Insert Bar

The Insert bar is one of the most often-used panels, containing all the objects that will insert code chunks into your document. It isn't part of the panel window. In the integrated workspace, by default it docks along the top edge of the application window above the Document window. The Insert bar is divided into tabs representing different categories of objects.

The Property Inspector

In the integrated workspace, the Property inspector docks along the bottom edge of the application window. In the non-integrated workspaces, the Property inspector is always free-standing but can be expanded or contracted using the triangle at its lower-right corner (see Figure 2.13).

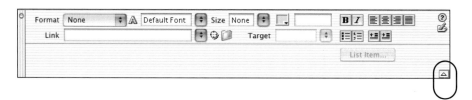

Figure 2.13   Expanding and contracting the undocked Property inspector.

Docking Horizontal Panels

In the integrated workspace, if several horizontal panels are docked together, they start to behave like the vertical panel dock, complete with a movable divider line and toggle button for hiding and showing the docked panels. Figure 2.14 shows the integrated workspace with several of these horizontal panels docked. (Doesn't leave much room for the Document window!)

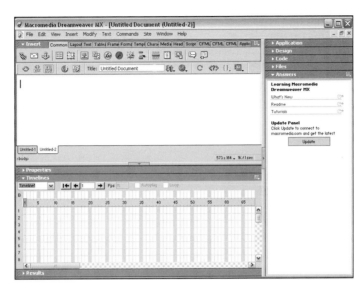

Figure 2.14   The integrated workspace showing various horizontal panels docked.

The Document Window

The *Document window* is where most of the action takes place in Dreamweaver. The Document window holds the current document that you're working on. When you open or create a new document, Dreamweaver shows it in a new Document window. If you have multiple documents open, you'll have multiple Document windows. You make your page edits here; you view your results here. Though some aspects of the Document window differ depending on the workspace you're using, every Document window includes a set of standard interface elements and a standard set of things that can be done with them.

Document Toolbar

The Document toolbar shows an icon view of frequently accessed options related to working with the Document window. As Figure 2.15 indicates, all of the buttons here relate to commands that also can be accessed from the menus—but it's handier just clicking on them here! The Document toolbar can be toggled on and off by choosing View > Toolbars > Document.

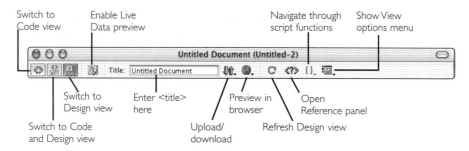

Switch to Code view

Enable Live Data preview

Navigate through script functions

Show View options menu

Switch to Design view

Enter <title> here

Preview in browser

Open Reference panel

Switch to Code and Design view

Upload/ download

Refresh Design view

Figure 2.15   The Document toolbar shown here as part of an undocked Document window.

Document Views

You can write code in a few different ways: You can choose to write the code manually; you can choose not to deal with the code at all; or you can watch Dreamweaver write the code as you work in the Design window. These options are set by the three Document window views. Each view is activated by one of the buttons in the Document toolbar.

Design View

Design view enables you to see the page approximately as it will look in the browser (see Figure 2.16). The code is completely hidden from view. While in Design view, you can see the code a couple of other ways. One of those is the *Code inspector*, another panel that shows just the source code. The other is the *Tag Inspector*, which lists all the tags on the page and defines their structure. To activate Design view, click the Design View button in the Document toolbar.

Figure 2.16   The Document window showing a page in Design view.

Code View

Code view shows only the raw HTML code (see Figure 2.17). When you open a new HTML document in Code view, you will see the basic framework of HTML code. Code view enables you to work as if you were working in a basic text editor. This view is for users who are very familiar with HTML and prefer to write the code directly. Some features and functions, such as adding behaviors, layers, and Layout mode, will not be available in Code view. To activate Code view, click the Code view button in the Document toolbar.

Figure 2.17   The Document window showing a page in Code view.

Code and Design View

Code and Design view splits the Document window horizontally so that you can see the Design view and the Code view at the same time. Many people find this view to be the most convenient because it enables them to see exactly where they are in the code as they are designing. This view proves convenient when dealing with complex coding tasks such as selecting a particular row or column in an embedded table (see Figure 2.18).

Figure 2.18   The Document window showing a page in Code and Design view.

Note that, even though both views are visible, one or the other will always have focus. (That is, Dreamweaver will consider it the active view.) To give a particular portion of the Document window focus, click in that half of the window, or use Ctrl+` (Windows) or Cmd+` (Mac) to toggle focus between the two windows.

Note

Keep in mind that many of Dreamweaver's menus and panels are context-dependent. Different options will appear, or different commands will be grayed out, depending on what view is active. This is true when working in Code view or Design view. For instance, additional options are available in the Insert bar when working in Code view because those options are useful only when working on source code.

Live Data View

If you use Dreamweaver to create data-driven web sites, Design view normally displays your pages with placeholders marking where the server will eventually insert information from a database. For instance, an online catalog page viewed in Dreamweaver will display placeholders for each catalog item's names, prices, and descriptions. Engaging Live Data view will make Dreamweaver replace these placeholders with actual information from a database, giving you a much better preview of what your page will eventually look like online (see Figure 2.19).

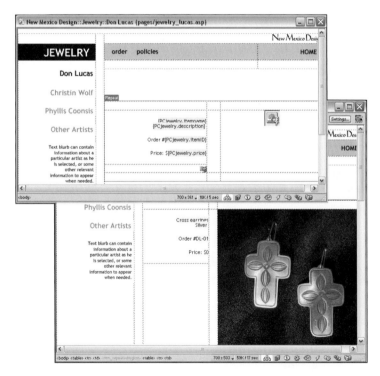

Figure 2.19 A dynamic document viewed with Live Data off (top) and on (bottom).

The Status Bar

Located at the bottom of the Document window (or directly below a docked Document window), the status bar provides a lot of information about your page and allows you to access your code and panels with a quick click (see Figure 2.20).

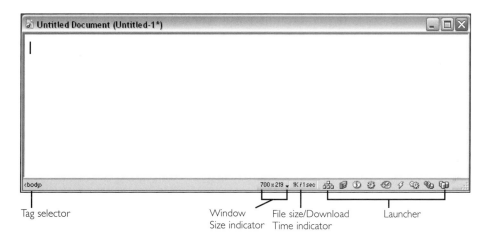

Figure 2.20   The status bar shown here at the bottom of an undocked Document window.

Window Size

The Window Size indicator tells you, in pixels, the current width and height of the "live" area of the Document Window. (The live area is the part of the window where there's actually content, as opposed to toolbars and status bars and other so-called "chrome" elements.) This can be important information if you're trying to design your pages to fit within common browser window sizes (and who isn't?).

The Window Size indicator only reports the size of the Design view portion of the window. If the Document window is displaying Code view, the Window Size indicator disappears. If the Document window is displaying Code and Design view, the indicator shows the size of the Design view portion of the window.

If you're working in the integrated workspace (Windows only), and have your Document window docked (maximized), the Window Size indicator shows the size of the visible portion of the window (for example, from the bottom edge of the Insert bar to the bottom of the Document window, and from the left edge of the application window to the vertical divider that begins the panel dock). Figure 2.21 shows this happening.

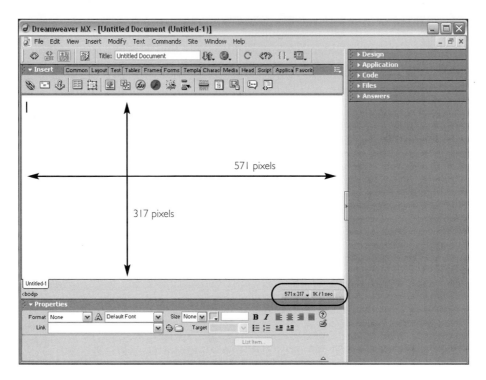

Figure 2.21   Determining the window size for a docked Document window in the integrated workspace (Windows).

The Window Size indicator also includes a pop-up menu that quickly resizes the Document window to any of several default sizes that match the window sizes of browsers at common monitor resolutions. Choose from this pop-up menu to quickly check how your page contents will fit into some common window sizes. You're not limited to the default window sizes Dreamweaver has provided, either. If, for instance, you're designing for an intranet and you know that your target audience will all have their browser windows set to 600×300, you can add that set of dimensions to the pop-up menu. Just do this:

1. From the Window Size indicator pop-up menu, choose Edit Sizes. This opens the Status Bar category of the Dreamweaver Preferences dialog box (see Figure 2.22).

2. In the Preferences dialog box, edit the list of window sizes as you like.

    - To change any of the existing sizes, just select one of the dimensions shown and enter a new number.

    - To add a new size, click in the area below the existing entries to activate it, and type in a new dimension. Your new entry can have width, height, or both.

3. When you're done, click OK to close the Preferences dialog box. From now on, your new entry appears in the Window Size indicator pop-up menu.

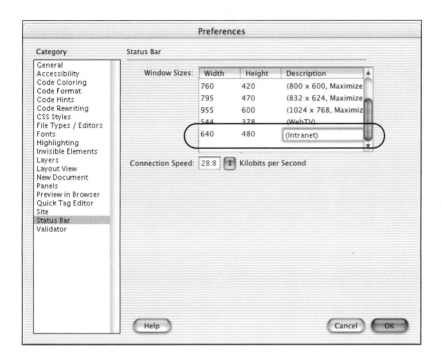

Figure 2.22   Adding a default window size to the Window Size indicator pop-up menu.

Document Size/Download Time Indicator

The Document Size/Download Time indicator displays two related pieces of information: the file size for the current document and all of its embedded media, and the estimated time that this material will take to download. Unless you have a corner on the market of extremely patient visitors, this is crucial information to have at your fingertips as you're creating your pages. The file size indicator (on the left) calculates the size of your current HTML file itself as well as the sizes of any images, Flash movies, or other files that will need to download before your page can display in a browser, rounded off to the nearest kilobyte (K). The estimated download time calculates how long that much content will take to download over a specific connection speed, rounded to the nearest second. For instance, if your page consists of a 1K HTML document and a 27K image, at a connection speed of 28.8 it will take approximately 1 second to download. The display for this setup would look like this: 27K/1 sec.

The default connection speed for calculating download time is 28.8 kbps, or kilobits per second (the speed of a fairly old modem, or a new modem at peak traffic times). You can change this speed to suit whatever connection speeds you think your target audience will have. For instance, if you're producing an online film festival for high-end users who are all going to have some sort of broadband access, you'll want to set your connection speed at several hundred kbps. To adjust the connection speed, do this:

1. Choose Edit > Preferences and go to the Status Bar category.

Tip

If you're in a hurry, you can get quickly to the right set of preferences by clicking the Window Size indicator to access its pop-up menu and choosing Edit Sizes to open the Preferences dialog box. This takes you directly to the Status Bar preferences.

2. In the Connection Speed text input field, enter whatever value you think represents an average download speed for your target audience.

3. When you're done, click OK to close the dialog box. The status bar will now display its download time based on document size and this new connection speed.

Note

What are some standard speeds? Telephone modems can connect at up to 56K (kbps). ISDN connections can range from 56–112K. Cable and DSL connections range from 112K–1M (a thousand kilobits per second). Don't forget that when determining your ideal connection speed, individual connections can be much slower than the average.

The Launcher

The *Launcher* is a set of buttons that let you quickly open and close various Dreamweaver panels (or expand and contract them, if they're docked). Clicking the icon for a panel in the Launcher has the same effect as going to the Window menu and choosing the panel's name. If the panel is closed, clicking the icon opens (expands) it; if the panel is open (expanded), clicking the Launcher icon closes (contracts) it.

By default, the Launcher is not showing in the Document window status bar. To enable the Launcher, and to determine which panels will be represented in it, do this:

1. Choose Edit > Preferences and go to the Panels category (see Figure 2.23).

Figure 2.23   Enabling and configuring the Launcher.

2. Enable the Launcher by selecting the Show Icons in Panels and Launcher option. The list of panels at the bottom of the dialog box show which panels will be represented in the Launcher, and in which order.

   - To remove a panel from the list, select it and click the minus (–) button.
   - To add a panel to the list, click the plus (+) button and choose an item from the pop-up list that appears. (Only items not already in the list will be accessible from this menu.)
   - To rearrange the order of items in the list, use the up/down triangle buttons.

The Site Panel

Just as the Document window is the center of the document-editing universe, the Site panel is the main interface for site building. The Site panel is an odd duck in the Dreamweaver interface, not quite a panel but not quite any other kind of window.

Note

The Site panel is discussed more in depth in Chapter 22, "Local Site Management," and Chapter 23, "Site Publishing and Maintenance."

In the integrated workspace, the Site panel is docked in the Files panel group and behaves as a docked panel (see Figure 2.24). In other workspaces, it is a fully independent floating window, similar to the Document window (see Figure 2.25).

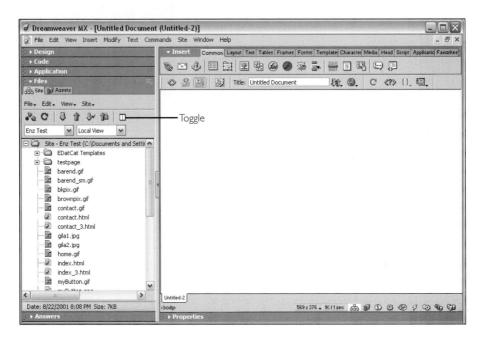

Figure 2.24   The Site panel as it appears in the integrated workspace (Windows).

Figure 2.25   The Site panel as a free-standing window.

In all workspaces, the Site panel includes a Site toolbar along its top, containing tools for performing common site-related tasks.

The fully expanded Site panel has two side-by-side panes that can hold a variety of content. In its contracted form, it shows only the right-side pane. When it's being used as a free-standing window, use the little triangle button in the lower-left corner to expand/contract it. When it's being used as part of the integrated workspace, the Site panel appears in the panel dock in its contracted form, with an expand/contract icon in its upper-right corner.

Getting Help

There are many places to get help if you are having difficulties with your pages or Dreamweaver itself. Between the Dreamweaver Help, the Reference panel, the Answers panel, and the Dreamweaver Support Center at the Macromedia web site, the answer is most likely within reach. This section explains your Help options.

Contextual Assistance: the Reference Panel

Do you have piles of reference books surrounding you as you work? If so, the Reference panel is ready to be your best friend (see Figure 2.26). This panel contains the complete text from several web reference guides, including O'Reilly's *HTML Reference*, *CSS Reference*, *JavaScript Reference*, and *Sitespring Project Site Tag Reference*, *Wrox ASP 3.0 Reference*, *JSP Reference*; *Macromedia CFML Reference*, and the *UsableNet Accessibility Reference*.

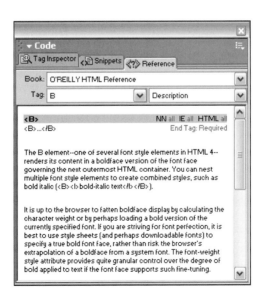

Figure 2.26   The Reference panel, showing contextual help for HTML.

You can use the Reference panel on its own to look up information or use it in tandem with the Document window to get contextual help information. To look up contextual help on whatever tag or script you're currently working on, do this:

1. Click inside the element you want to reference.

2. In the Document toolbar, click the question mark icon.

3. The Reference panel will open, showing a description and sample syntax for the selected item.

Searchable, Indexed Assistance: Online Help

Dreamweaver MX has *Dreamweaver Help* that covers the basic usage of every element of the program. Dreamweaver Help is a valuable resource for any questions concerning the properties of Dreamweaver.

To access Dreamweaver Help, choose Help > Using Dreamweaver. This launches your operating system's Help application with Dreamweaver Help showing. Figures 2.27 and 2.28 show Dreamweaver Help for Windows and Macintosh.

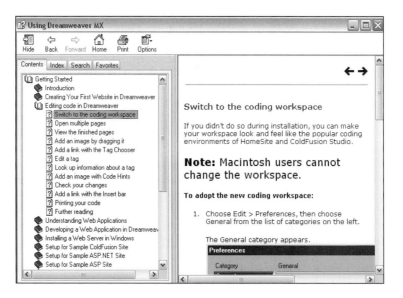

Figure 2.27   The Dreamweaver/Windows Help.

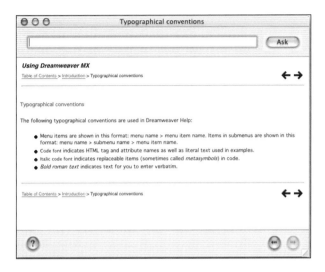

Figure 2.28   The Dreamweaver/Mac Help.

Note

If you are upgrading from previous versions of Dreamweaver, you'll notice that the Dreamweaver Help no longer uses HTML and the default browser to display Dreamweaver Help. This has advantages and disadvantages. The OS help applications offer more built-in functionality but might be less familiar to you than navigating a browser interface and are missing some lovely browser features. The Mac OS Dreamweaver Help, for instance, comes complete with teeny tiny text and pages that can't be printed.

Community Assistance: the Answers Panel

New to Dreamweaver MX, the Answers panel (see Figure 2.29) contains all sorts of tips, tutorials, tech notes, and other help for using Dreamweaver. If you're connected to the Internet as you work, this panel connects you directly to the Dreamweaver Support Center so you get the latest and greatest information at your fingertips.

Figure 2.29 The Answers panel, a new dynamic Dreamweaver Help connected to the Macromedia web site.

To access the Answers panel, choose Window > Answers (or expand the Answers panel group, if it's showing in your panel window).

To choose whether Answers panel information displays in a Dreamweaver Help window or in your browser, choose Settings from the panel's topics menu and choose the appropriate radio button.

To get information from the Answers panel, choose a main topic from the topics pop-up menu (Get Started, Extending, and so on). The panel will then display the latest information available on this topic from the Dreamweaver Support Center. Click on a topic to learn all about it!

Note

To use the Answers panel properly, you must have an open Internet connection.

Summary

Dreamweaver has an intuitive, highly customizable interface that puts almost every object and function within easy reach. Most options can be reached with one or two clicks. There is almost always more than one way to insert an object or change a property within the Dreamweaver interface. Spend some time getting used to the interface and try the different ways of performing common tasks. The more familiar you are with the interface and the options available to you, the better you can take full advantage of Dreamweaver functionality.

Chapter 3

Creating and Working with Documents

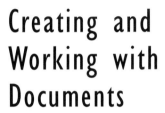

This chapter covers that most basic of tasks—creating a new document, setting it up, and turning it into a web page. Unless you're a complete Dreamweaver newbie, you've probably done this before. However, even old-time Dreamweaver users might have some culture shock dealing with the new document-making opportunities in Dreamweaver MX.

Because the whole process of document creation is the foundation of everything else the program does, this is the foundation chapter for much that follows. If you're new to Dreamweaver, you'll find some basic concepts and skills to get your started in this chapter. This chapter also discusses some important foundation tools that more experienced Dreamweaver users might just want to know more about, such as the new Edit Tag command and Tag Inspector, the new options for creating documents, as well as new options for document validation and accessibility.

Creating New Documents

Dreamweaver isn't just for HTML anymore, although that still might be the main kind of page with which many users will want to work. With Dreamweaver MX, however, just about any kind of text-based web document can be created, edited, and sometimes even graphically rendered in Design view. This includes not only HTML, but also all the various live data document types, such as ASP, CFM, PHP, JSP; support document types, such as CSS and JS; and that's not to mention the alphabet soup of document types such as XML, XHTML, WML, and so on.

Because of these choices, creating a new document might still be one of the most basic things you can do in Dreamweaver—but it's no longer the simplest. This section covers the New Document dialog box, which enables you to create documents from scratch as well as perform various techniques to bring documents and data into Dreamweaver from other sources.

Note

You also can create new documents through the Site panel, but the options differ slightly. See Chapter 22, "Local Site Management," for more on this.

New Document Dialog Box

 When you choose File > New or press Ctrl/Cmd+N to create a new document, by default the New Document dialog box appears (see Figure 3.1). This dialog box presents you with a wealth of options for creating almost any kind of web document.

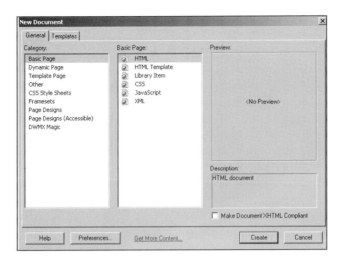

Figure 3.1   The New Document dialog box.

Types of Document to Create

Most of the dialog box is taken up by the many options for creating different document types. The leftmost column of choices represents the categories of document types: Basic, Dynamic, Template, and so forth. Many of these types are beyond the scope of this chapter and are referenced later in this book. Table 3.1 lists the categories along with some of their entries and a brief description of each. To create a standard, plain-vanilla HTML page, use the Basic > HTML option. Select the Basic category from the left column, and HTML from the next column.

Because you have such an overwhelming number of choices to sift through, the dialog box includes a description area in its lower-right corner to help you out. Select any file type from the second column and read a quick description of what it's for before you choose to create that kind of document. For some choices, you also can see a preview in the upper-right corner.

Note that although Dreamweaver can create any of the document kinds listed here, not all of them display in Design view. Only the file types intended for creating viewable web pages will show a usable preview in Design view. Other file types, such as JS, CSS, TXT, and so on, must be viewed and edited in Dreamweaver Code view.

Table 3.1   Document Types Available in the New Document Dialog Box

Category	Description
Basic	These are the most commonly used document types for web sites that don't involve server-side scripting and live data. They include HTML and XML for creating viewable web pages, and other file types that will hold supporting information for web pages (for instance, JS for JavaScript and CSS for style sheet information). In addition, with library items and templates, you can create special documents for use with Dreamweaver sites. (See Chapter 25, "Templates and Libraries," for more on Dreamweaver library items and templates.)
Dynamic	These file types create web pages that will use server-side scripting to connect with databases and provide live data web sites. The entries in this category represent all the live data technologies Dreamweaver supports: ASP, ASP.NET, ColdFusion, PHP, and JSP. (See Chapter 26, "Introduction to Dynamic Dreamweaver," for more on live data sites.)
Templates	The entries in this category enable you to create Dreamweaver templates (predefined documents with special Dreamweaver coding for design team productivity) using a variety of web languages, including good old HTML and various languages related to live data sites.
Other	This catchall category enables you to create just about any kind of text-based document you can imagine—including TXT files.
CSS Style Sheets	Cascading Style Sheets (CSS) enable web authors to store page-formatting information outside the web pages themselves, in external CSS documents that can be referenced by many pages in a web site. This category contains a whole selection of predefined CSS documents. (See Chapter 13, "Using Cascading Style Sheets," to learn all about CSS.)
Framesets	Framesets are collections of individual documents that will be displayed together in one browser window. This category contains a selection of predefined framesets—including all documents needed to create a frame-based web page. When you choose from this category, you're creating several new documents at once! (To learn what frames are and how to work with them, see Chapter 12, "Designing Frame-Based Pages.")
Page Designs and Page Designs (Accessible)	These categories contain predefined "stationery" web pages—HTML pages with basic layout setup and placeholder elements ready for you to customize. The accessible designs have been specially created to be accessible to visitors with disabilities. (See the section on "Making Your Pages Accessible" at the end of this chapter for more on this.)

Stationery

As Table 3.1 shows, Dreamweaver ships with a variety of predefined page layouts that are yours for the customizing. They're in the Page Designs and Page Designs (Accessible) categories. Dreamweaver also comes with predefined CSS documents, ready to be applied to your documents to quickly add text and layout formatting.

To create a web page based on one of the stationery HTML pages, select an entry from either of the Page Designs categories and click OK. Dreamweaver will create a new document with the placeholder content and formatting in place (such as the one shown in Figure 3.2). Save this document as part of your web site and customize its content to create your own new web page quickly.

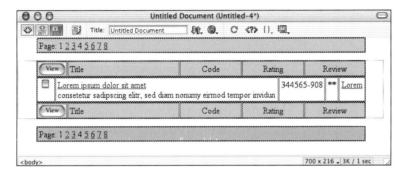

Figure 3.2   A new document based on the data: Comparative Grid stationery.

Creating a CSS document based on the choices in this dialog box won't give you a page that can be viewed in a browser—CSS files are meant as supporting files for HTML and other viewable documents. To create a CSS style sheet from one of the stationery choices listed here, select an entry from the CSS category and click OK. Dreamweaver will create a CSS file (it won't display in Design view) that contains a list of styles for formatting HTML pages. Save this document in your web site with the .css file extension. To make use of your new CSS document, you must link one or more HTML pages to it. (See Chapter 13 for instructions on doing this.)

Note

It's general usage to refer to files that create documents that browsers can display—files that hold web pages, in other words—as HTML files. This is true even though many viewable document types, such as ASP, don't have the .html or .htm filename extension. Throughout this book, when you read about creating and working with HTML files, know that this generic term includes documents with .shtm, .shtml, .asp, .cfm, .jsp, .php, and possibly other file extensions. As long as the document uses HTML coding to create a page that the browser can display, it can be generically described as an HTML document.

XHTML Compliance

As long as you're choosing one of the file types that creates a viewable "HTML page," the dialog box offers you the choice of making your new document XHTML compliant or not. XHTML is the newest flavor of HTML, intended to eventually replace HTML.

XHTML is based on XML. It has some very slight syntactical differences from HTML and is stricter in its rules than HTML. The browsers of the future will require XHTML to create *valid* documents. If you tell Dreamweaver to make your new document XHTML compliant, it will create slightly different syntax as it writes code for you. (XHTML is too big a topic to be covered fully here. Read Chapter 32, "Technical Issues," for a discussion of XML, HTML, and XHMTL and how they all relate.)

Note

If you're creating web pages that just need to work properly in the popular browsers— Netscape Navigator, Internet Explorer, Opera, and a few others—you don't need to worry about XHTML compliance quite yet. All that the standard browsers require is HTML.

New Document Preferences

By default, when you choose File > New, Dreamweaver presents you with the New Document dialog box, with HTML as the default file type and XHTML compliance turned off. To change these and a few other defaults, click the Preferences button at the bottom of the New Document dialog box. This opens the Preferences > New Document dialog box (see Figure 3.3). Note that this is the standard Dreamweaver Preferences dialog box. You also can access this same dialog box by choosing Edit > Preferences and choosing the New Document category from the list on the left side of the dialog box.

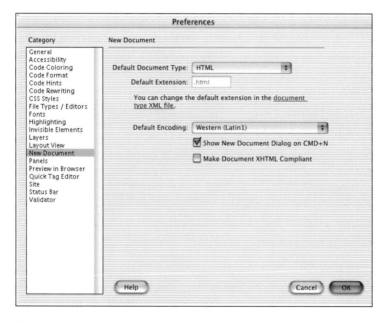

Figure 3.3 New Document Preferences.

Note

While you're in the Preferences dialog box, note that you also can use the categories list at the left to go to General preferences. In the General preferences screen, the very first option enables you to stop Dreamweaver from automatically opening a new document whenever the program launches. Just enable the Show Site panel Only on Startup option, and those automatically created new documents are a thing of the past.

Note

If you like, you also can change the default file extension that your default file type comes with—for HTML files, you can change from .html to .htm, for instance. This is a little bit more involved, however. From the New Document Preferences dialog box, click the link to the `document type XML file` (shown in Figure 3.3). This opens Dreamweaver Help at the "Document Type Definition File" section that provides instruction on modifying the Dreamweaver document type configuration information. (Of course, you can always override the default file extension when you save your files, just by typing in your own extension.)

Workflow in Dreamweaver

You've created your new Dreamweaver document, or you've opened an existing document. You're ready to start working. The more you understand (and agree with) how Dreamweaver expects you to work, the easier time you'll have. This section covers the basic page-building workflow in Dreamweaver. If you're brand new to the program— even if you've coded web pages or used other web editors before—this will give you a handle on working in this environment.

Working with Design

You like a graphic user interface. You like to see the pages you're building, as you build them. You like to drag and drop things, resize and reposition with a click of the mouse. You're ready to work with Dreamweaver design tools.

Inserting Objects and Setting Properties

The three central windows for the visual designer in Dreamweaver are the Document window (showing Design view), the Insert bar, and the Property inspector (see Figure 3.4). The main working procedure that you're expected to follow is this: Use the Insert bar to insert a page element (table, image, form element, and so on); the element shows up in the Document window; select the element, and its properties will show up and be available for editing in the Property inspector. The items in the Insert bar are also present in the Insert menu, if you would rather choose from a menu than from the panel.

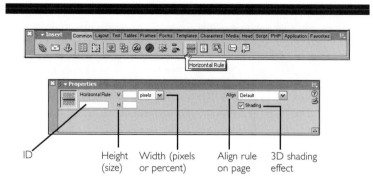

Figure 3.4   Using the Document window, Insert bar, and Property inspector to insert and format a horizontal rule.

Although exceptions apply, you can insert most Dreamweaver objects in several ways:

- In the Document window, click to put the insertion point where you want the object to appear; then click the object in the Insert bar.

- In the Document window, click to put the insertion point where you want the object to appear; then choose the object to insert from the Insert menu.

- Drag and drop from the Insert bar to the Document window. Dreamweaver will insert the object as close to where you drop as is feasible.

Many objects bring up dialog boxes when you insert them, to establish basic properties. After an object has been inserted, selecting it causes the Property inspector to display the properties that can be set for that object.

Note

If you're new to web design, one feature of properties might be strange to you. Unlike, say, a word processing program, in which every property must have a value (have you ever tried to assign *no* text size in Microsoft Word?), many properties of HTML objects are optional. If a property isn't assigned, the browser determines what its value will be. To assign browser defaults when formatting a Dreamweaver object, leave the appropriate text input field in the Property inspector or dialog box empty; or choose Default or None from a pop-up menu. Never choose 0 as an alternative for not setting a property. Zero is a value, and it might not be the browser's default value for your property.

Choosing Colors

One of the properties that can be set for many kinds of objects—as well as for the page itself—is color. Whenever you have the option to color text, tables, page backgrounds, or other elements, you get to use the Dreamweaver color palette. It's a lovely, compact, and powerful little interface, and you'll use it throughout this book.

In a dialog box, panel, or the Property inspector, the color palette is accessibly by clicking the color box that typically has a text field next to it (see Figure 3.5). If the element currently has no color set for it, the chip will be gray, so you might not recognize it as a color-choosing tool. But it is!

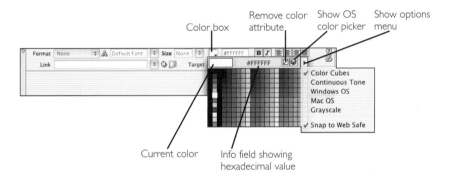

Figure 3.5   The color box, color palette, and color picker.

To Choose a Color Without Using the Color Picker

When you see the color box and its associated input field, just type the name or hexadecimal number for the color in the input field. The color box will change to display the color you've chosen.

To Choose a Color Using the Color Palette

When you see the color box, click in it. This brings up the default color palette, showing 216 web-safe color swatches (see Figure 3.5). If you pass your cursor over the color swatches, the hexadecimal code for each one will show in the text field at the top of the color palette. (Those six-digit hexadecimal codes are browser-speak for specifying colors.) Click a color swatch to choose its color.

To Make the Color Palette Display a Different Set of Color Swatches

Click the color box to open the color palette. In the palette, click the triangle in the upper-right corner—this gives you access to the color picker (see Figure 3.5). Shown here are the five different sets of color swatches you can choose to display in the color palette. They are as follows:

- **Color cubes (the default palette).** It displays the 216 web-safe colors according to their hexadecimal value.

- **Continuous Tone color palette.** This palette displays the 216 web-safe colors according to their hue (color). Many designers find this a more intuitive arrangement for finding the color they want.

- **Windows OS.** This palette displays the 256 standard Windows OS colors.

- **Mac OS.** This palette displays the 256 standard Mac OS colors.

- **Grayscale.** This displays 128 different shades of gray—good if you're designing for folks with grayscale monitors.

The final option in the color picker menu, Snap to Web Safe, guarantees that no matter what color you choose, Dreamweaver will substitute the nearest web-safe color.

Note

What are web-safe colors? The short answer is, they're colors that display without dithering on any Windows or Mac computer, even if that computer is set to 8-bit color mode (only displaying 256 colors). For a longer answer, see Chapter 8, "Design Issues."

To Sample a Color from Another Program or Web Page

What if you see a color you love and want to use that color in your web page, but you don't know what the color's hexadecimal code or name is? Are you stuck? No! With the color picker, you can sample any color from anywhere on your computer screen and Dreamweaver will determine its hexadecimal code and use it in your document.

To choose a color by sampling, follow these steps:

1. Click the color box to access the color palette, as you normally would to choose a color.

2. The cursor changes to an eyedropper when you do this. Instead of clicking one of the color swatches in the palette, move the cursor away from the palette, over some other area of your screen. Note that back in the color palette, every color you pass the cursor over is registering in the top area (see Figure 3.6).

Figure 3.6   Sampling to choose a color for a Dreamweaver page element.

3. When you are over a color you want to sample, click. That color is now chosen!

Note that when you choose by sampling, you might be sampling colors that aren't web-safe. If staying web-safe is important to you, use the color picker to enable Snap to Web Safe before sampling. After you've done that, for every color you sample Dreamweaver will choose the nearest web-safe color.

To Access the Full Spectrum of Colors

Color swatches are nice. Sampling is great. Sometimes, however, you just want to choose exactly the color you want from the full spectrum. Whether you're on Windows or Mac, you can access your operating system's color-picking tools through the Dreamweaver color palette. To do so, follow these steps:

1. Click the color box to access the color palette, as you normally would to choose a color.

2. When the color palette appears, click the tiny color-wheel button (System color picker button) in the upper-right corner.

    On Windows, this opens the Windows color picker; on Mac, it opens the Apple color picker.

3. Choose your color using your system's interface, and click OK to close the Windows or Apple color picker. The color you've chosen is now in your Dreamweaver document. (If you used the Snap to Web Safe option described earlier, Dreamweaver will substitute the nearest web-safe color for whatever you chose.)

Removing a Color Attribute

If a page element has a color assigned to it (because you picked one or because Dreamweaver gave it one by default), you can remove the color by doing one of the following:

- In the text input field that shows your color's hexadecimal number or name, select the text and delete it, leaving the field blank.
- Click the color box and, in the color palette, click the square with a red diagonal line through it (in the upper-right corner of the palette, called the default color button).

Either of these restores the element's default color by removing its color attribute.

Setting Page Properties

Some of the most basic properties you can set in a Dreamweaver document are the properties for the page itself. These include page margins, default colors for background, text, links, and the page title. In Dreamweaver, they can all be set using the Page Properties dialog box, which is accessed by choosing Modify > Page Properties (see Figure 3.7). The following sections discuss the page properties you can set.

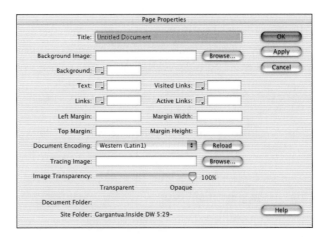

Figure 3.7   The Page Properties dialog box, good for setting basic page characteristics.

Page Title

This isn't the same as your document's filename! The page title appears in the browser window's title bar when visitors are browsing your page. It also appears in the Bookmarks or Favorites menu when a visitor bookmarks your page. In addition, search engines use it when they're searching for and displaying information about your page. By default, every Dreamweaver document has a title of "Untitled Document"—not something you want your adoring public to see atop your pages, so always remember to set the page title. In addition to the Page Properties dialog box, you also can set the title in the Document toolbar (see Figure 3.8).

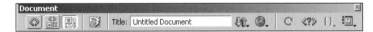

Figure 3.8   Setting the page title in the Document toolbar.

Color Scheme

Using the color boxes in the Page Properties dialog box, you can set the page background color as well as the default colors for text and links. When you set these colors here, Dreamweaver adds them as attributes to your document's <body> tag. Note that these are optional attributes for the <body> tag. If you don't assign default colors, the browser determines them. The default text color for browsers is black; the default link color is blue. The default page background color is white except in older versions of Netscape, in which case it's gray.

Note

Link color determines the color of all text links that haven't been visited yet. Visited Link color determines the color of links that have been recently visited. Active Link color determines the color of links while the user is clicking them and waiting for the browser to take him to his destination page.

Tip

If you don't trust your ability to choose well-coordinated, web-safe color schemes for your pages, or if you're just in a hurry and still want a nice-looking, colorful page, try Commands > Set Color Scheme. This command opens a dialog box that enables you to choose from dozens of predefined color schemes. Choose a color scheme and click OK; Dreamweaver will assign values to your page background, text, and various link states in one fell swoop. Web notables Lynda Weinmann and Bruce Heavin have created color schemes for you.

Background Image

Instead of—or as well as (and note that it is always best to assign a color if assigning an image in case the user has images disabled in his browser or the image is a bad link)—assigning a background color for your page, you can choose any GIF or JPEG image to display behind your page elements. Any image that doesn't fill the entire width and height of the browser window will tile to fill the window. (For more on background images, see Chapter 5, "Working with Images.")

Page Margins

Margin Settings define the margin for the upper-left corner of the browser. By default, most browsers give all pages a margin of several pixels, so no page content smashes up against the left or top edges. To override this default in Internet Explorer, set the Left and Top attributes; to override the default in Netscape, set the Width and Height attributes. (To cover both browsers, set all four.) If all four attributes are set to 0, the page contents will be allowed to touch the left and top edges of the browser window. (Note that not all version-3 browsers understand these attributes.)

Quick Start for Defining Dreamweaver Sites

If you're brand new to Dreamweaver, or even brand new to web authoring, you probably want to get right into creating pages. That's why you're here, right? To make web pages. Throughout the book, however, the exercises will ask you to define a site before proceeding with the fun stuff. A web site is a collection of pages. Dreamweaver likes to know, before it starts working for you, what web site your pages will belong to. Although you can skip defining a site—even when working with the exercises here—if you do so, you're missing out on a lot of little things Dreamweaver can do for you. And you might end up creating some Dreamweaver errors, because the program expects every web page to have a home.

What Dreamweaver needs to know, before you begin working on a project, is two things: what you would like to call your site, and what folder on your computer will store all the files that belong to that site. After you've defined those two items, all you have to do is continue saving your pages into that folder and all will be well.

To define a site in Dreamweaver, follow these steps:

1. Choose Site > New Site.

2. In the dialog box that appears, there are two modes of working—Basic and Advanced. Oddly enough, it's easier to work quickly in Advanced mode. Click the Advanced tab to bring it to the front.

3. In the first input field, enter a name for your site. (It can be anything from My Site to Howard's Very Excellent Web Pages! to whatever you like.)

4. For the second input field, click the browse button (the folder icon next to the text input field) to show Dreamweaver the folder on your hard drive that will hold your site's files. The official name for this is the local root folder.

5. That's it! Click OK to close the dialog box and create your site.

You can have as many sites as you want in Dreamweaver. From now on, you can use the Site pop-up menu in the Site panel to switch between them.

To learn all about defining sites, see Chapter 22.

Exercise 3.1   Creating a Simple Dreamweaver Document

In this exercise, you use the New Document dialog box to create a new HTML document. Then you use Design view and several objects to start adding content to your page.

For most of the exercises in this book, you are asked to define a Dreamweaver site before proceeding with the exercise. In fact, if you go through the book chapter by chapter, you'll end up with a site for almost every chapter. And this chapter is no different! If you're new to Dreamweaver and want to get up and running as quickly as possible, read the "Quick Start for Defining Dreamweaver Sites" sidebar. Then come back here.

Before you start the exercise, copy the **chapter_03** folder from the CD to your hard drive. Define a Dreamweaver site called **Chapter 3**, with the **chapter_03** folder as your local root folder.

1. To start, create a new document. Choose File > New. When the New Document dialog box appears, choose to create a Basic HTML page. Select the Make Document XHTML Compliant option and click OK. When the new document opens, make sure you're looking at it in Design view. You should see a blank, white Document window. If you check under the View menu, the View > Design command should have a checkmark next to it.

2. The first thing you'll do is save your new document. Strange as it might seem to be saving empty documents, in Dreamweaver even an empty document is rarely completely empty (there's HTML code back there somewhere); and saving early and often is always a good idea. Choose File > Save, and in the dialog box that appears, name your file **basicpage.html** and save it in the **chapter_03** folder you copied from the CD.

3. Notice that even though you've saved the document, the title bar of your Document window still says "Untitled Document." That's because you haven't given it a page title. In the Document toolbar, change the page title to **A Basic Web Page**.

4. Now change the page's basic colors to something more interesting than black on white. Choose Modify > Page Properties. When the dialog box appears, find the color box that represents background color.

   Click the color box to open the color palette. From the swatches in the palette, choose whichever color you want.

   Repeat the procedure to assign a different text color than black. Your color boxes should now show the new colors you've chosen, although your document doesn't yet.

   To see how your page will look with its new background, click Apply. (Because there's no text on the page, you can't test that color yet.) If you like your background color, click OK. If not, choose another background color and then click OK to close the Page Properties dialog box.

5. The simplest thing to add to a web page is type. Click in the Document window and type **Welcome to My Web Page**. It will show up in the text color you specified in Page Properties. Leave the insertion point inside the words you just typed. In the Property inspector, from the Format pop-up menu (in the upper-left corner), choose Heading 1. Your typing is now a big, bold heading.

6. Now you'll see how Dreamweaver objects work by adding a horizontal rule after your title. Click at the end of your heading, so that the insertion point appears after the last letter. Go to the Insert bar and make sure the Common tab is in front. Look through the objects in the bar until you find the horizontal rule object. (Let the cursor hover over each icon in turn and their tooltips will tell you who they are.) When you find the Horizontal Rule, click its icon.

7. A horizontal rule appears in your document, right after your heading. The Property inspector now shows you various horizontal rule attributes (see Figure 3.9). If you click outside the rule to deselect it, you can see it better, but its properties disappear from the Property inspector.

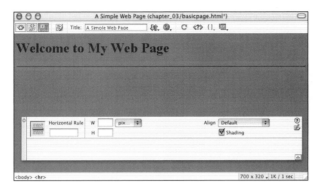

Figure 3.9   The **basicpage.html** document with heading and horizontal rule in place, and the Horizontal Rule Property inspector showing.

8. To see how default properties work, select the horizontal rule in your document again. Look at the Property inspector, and you'll see that there is a Width and Height field, but both are blank. That means the browser determines how wide and how tall the rule is. Because browsers automatically format rules to be about 2 pixels high and 100% of the window width, Dreamweaver displays the rule that same way in Design view.

In the Property inspector, enter a width of **500** and a height of **6**. Deselect the Shading option. To see your rule better, click in the Document window outside the rule to deselect it. Now that looks a lot different!

This exercise showed you the basic procedure for working with objects in Design view. Now you'll start thinking about code.

Working with Code

Whether you think of yourself as a mean, lean coding machine, or whether you love working in the visual design environment and couldn't care less about code, you can't be really efficient as a web designer without at least being aware of the HTML code that sits behind your pages. One of Dreamweaver's strengths is how close it keeps you to the code at all times, whether or not you know it. Dreamweaver even provides a variety of tools for watching your code, and maybe tweaking it or even editing it extensively, without leaving the cuddly world of Design view.

What the Code Looks Like

HTML pages are built from a hierarchical series of elements (tags). Each page is surrounded by a pair of `<html></html>` tags identifying it to the browser as a page in Hypertext Markup Language. Within that main element, the structure of a basic HTML page looks like this:

```
<html>
<head>
<title>My Document</title>
</head>
<body>
<h1>This is the visible part of my page.</h1>
</body>
</html>
```

The `<h1>` tag, which displays a big bold headline on the page, is nested within the `<body>` tags, which hold all the page content that display in the browser. The page also needs its `<head>` tag, which contains organizational and other nondisplaying information, such as page title and URL encoding. No matter how complex your web pages get, most of them will be built on this simple framework. The more tables and images and paragraphs of text you have, the more full of tags the `<body>` will be. The more scripts and search engine data and linked style sheets you have happening behind the scenes of your page, the more tags will be nested inside the `<head>`. Often, with complex pages, half the battle of dealing with the code is ferreting out these structural relationships in the lines and lines of code.

The Tag Inspector/Tree View

If you like working in Design view, presumably you're a visual sort of person. You might have trouble grasping the code structure of an HTML document just by looking at Code view, because the structure doesn't look clear. You're going to love the Tag Inspector and its tree display (see Figure 3.10). To access the Tag Inspector, go to Window > Tag Inspector or expand the Code panel group. Whenever you have a document open, the top half of this panel shows you your document's code structure represented like an expandable tree or outline structure. The page contents are not shown—only the structure of tags. Nested tags are shown nested inside each other, with indentation helping make the nesting clear. Expand/collapse buttons enable you to hide or show as many levels of the outline structure as you want, to make the document structure visually clear.

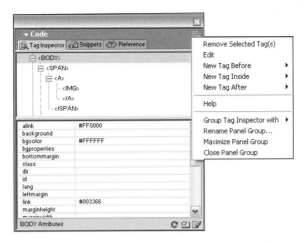

Figure 3.10   The Tag Inspector showing the tree display at the top of the panel and the attribute editor at the bottom.

In addition to the visual aid of the tree view, the Tag Inspector enables you to work on your code without having to actually edit code. After you've selected a tag in the tree view, the bottom half of the Tag Inspector panel enables you to view and edit all of that tag's attributes (see Figure 3.10). If you truly love working this way, you can even add and remove page elements by adding and removing their tags. Just click the triangle in the panel's upper-right corner to access the pop-up options menu (see Figure 3.10), and you can add a New Tag Before, New Tag After, and more.

The Tag Selector

If HTML pages are built from a hierarchical series of tags, any time you're working in an HTML document, you're tinkering around somewhere within the hierarchy. It's the job of the tag selector, part of the status bar at the bottom of the Document window, to always show you where you are in the hierarchy—what tags you're within, and how those tags fit into the structure of the whole document (see Figure 3.11). You can use the tag selector to give yourself a mental picture of "how deep you're buried" in the hierarchy of nested tags. You also can use it to select page elements. If your tag selector looked like the one in Figure 3.11, for instance, you could click the <h1> element shown in the selector and it would immediately select your entire heading—the <h1> tags and everything in between them. Although this might seem simple now, when you start working on complex pages with lots of nested elements, the tag selector can be your ticket to sanity. It enables you to select just exactly what you want to select, quickly and easily.

Figure 3.11   The tag selector showing that the user is working on a heading that exists within a pair of <h1> tags, which are in between the two <body> tags.

The Tag Chooser and the Edit Tag Command

MX   One of the criticisms that are often raised against web editing software—especially WYSIWYG web editors—is that they actually squelch the web author's creativity by providing only a small set of HTML tags and attributes with which to design. HTML is a wide, rich language, full of little-known goodies and sneaky possibilities for optimizing your pages. There are so many wonderful bits of HTML, in fact, that it's impossible to cram them all into one simple GUI without overwhelming the interface—and the user.

The last thing Macromedia wants is for you to feel limited! If the Property inspector gave you the choice of setting every possible option for every page element, however, it would be a huge, unwieldy inspector.

The Macromedia solution is to put the most commonly used page elements in the Insert bar, and the most commonly assigned properties in the Property inspector. And for those times when you might want to go outside the envelope, they've provided the Tag Chooser and the Edit Tag command.

Adding Attributes with the Edit Tag Command

You've got a table in your document and you know there's more to formatting a table than the options that appear in the Property inspector. In the Document window (in Design view), select your table and do one of the following:

- Choose Modify > Edit Tag.
- Right-click (Ctrl-click) the table and, from the contextual menu, choose Edit Tag.

Any of these will open the Edit Tag dialog box (see Figure 3.12). Within the various parts of this dialog box, you can find all the attributes for this tag that exist in the Dreamweaver database, along with an indication of which browsers support each attribute and even handy pop-up menus, color boxes, and other interface elements to make choosing values for each attribute nice and easy.

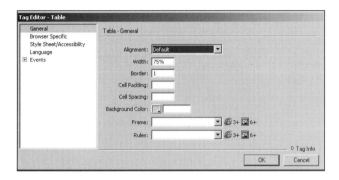

Figure 3.12   The Edit Tag dialog box.

Tip

To examine and alter the Dreamweaver database of tags and attributes, use the Tag Library editor. See Chapter 33, "Writing Code in Dreamweaver," for detailed instructions on working with this new feature.

Choosing Tags

Hmm, you want to add a caption to your table, and you think you remember reading about a `<caption>` tag somewhere. But you don't remember exactly what it was called, or what attributes you could assign it. Follow these steps:

1. In the Document window, click to put the insertion point where you want the new tag to be added.

2. From the Common tab of the Insert bar, choose the Tag Chooser object (see Figure 3.13); or choose Insert > Tag. This opens the Tag Chooser dialog box, which contains information about all the tags Dreamweaver has in its database—even the most obscure ones.

Figure 3.13   The Tag Chooser object in the Insert bar.

3. In the Tag Chooser dialog box, navigate through the categories of tags until you find the one that you want to insert (see Figure 3.14). Select that tag in the dialog box and click Insert.

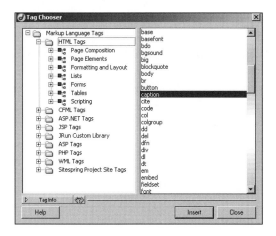

Figure 3.14   Using the Tag Chooser dialog box to insert a new page element.

4. The Edit Tag dialog box opens, showing you all the possible attributes that can go with this tag. (Read all about it in the preceding section.) Choose whichever attributes you want to assign to your new tag.

5. When you're done, click OK to close the Edit Tag dialog box. Then click Close to close the Tag Chooser dialog box.

Tip

If you click Insert in the Tag Chooser dialog box again after you've finished in the Edit Tag dialog box and closed it, you'll insert your tag twice. Don't do that!

The Quick Tag Editor

Every Dreamweaver page element (image, table, heading, and so on) is really just a chunk of HTML code. The Quick Tag Editor gives you a way to see and edit the code for a selected page element without having to leave Design view or even look at the rest of the code in your document. If you just want to do a little bit of coding, or if you are in a hurry and don't want to leave Design view just to tweak a little code, the Quick Tag Editor is for you.

Accessing the Quick Tag Editor

To access the Quick Tag Editor, and edit whatever item you currently have selected in the Document window, do one of the following:

- In the Property inspector, click the Quick Tag Editor icon (see Figure 3.15).
- Choose Modify > Quick Tag Editor.
- Press Ctrl+T (Windows) or Cmd+T (Mac).

This opens the Quick Tag Editor, a little pop-up coding window.

Figure 3.15   Property inspector showing the Quick Tag Editor icon.

Quick Tag Modes

Depending on which tag you have selected, and what you want to do with it, the Quick Tag Editor will launch in one of three modes (see Figure 3.16):

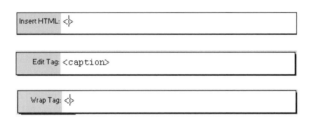

Figure 3.16   The Quick Tag Editor in each of its three modes.

- Edit Tag mode shows you the code for the tag that represents the selected page element. Use the keyboard to navigate around in here and edit the code. This mode appears if the page element you have selected is created from one main HTML tag (such as an image or a table).

- Wrap Tag mode enables you to type in a new tag that will then be inserted as an opening and closing tag pair wrapped around the current selection. This mode appears if your selection consists of text without a text, or multiple tags.

- Insert HTML enables you to insert a brand-new bit of code that you type in to the Quick Tag editing window. This mode appears if you don't have anything selected (if the Document window shows only a flashing insertion point instead of a selected chunk of text).

When the Quick Tag Editor is open, and if it opened in the wrong mode, press Ctrl/Cmd+T again and again to make it toggle through its three modes. Keep pressing the shortcut key until the mode you want pops up.

If you're not comfortable working with code, you probably won't feel too much at home in the Quick Tag Editor. If you do like a little bit of HTML with your web designing experience, however, it provides a great, quick access to the coding world.

Working with Code and Design

Chapter 2, "Setting Up the Dreamweaver Workspace," discussed the three ways to view any document: Code view, Design view, and Code and Design view. If you like working with the Dreamweaver visual interface, but still want to keep your eye on your code, Code and Design view can be your best friend (see Figure 3.17). Both views are visible in the Document window, and you're free to edit either code or design just by clicking in the relevant portion of the window.

Figure 3.17   Working in Code and Design view.

Working in the Code and Design view, when you select anything in one view it's also selected in the other view. If you're new to HTML coding, this can be a great way to get used to which HTML elements create the different page elements.

When you edit anything in the Design portion of the split window, the HTML in the Code portion of the window automatically updates.

When you edit code in the Code portion of the window, the Design view will not update automatically. That's because Dreamweaver waits for you to finish entering your code before it tries to display it visually. To see your code changes happen in Design view, either click inside the Design portion of the window, click the Refresh button in the Property inspector, or press F5.

If your code editing results in invalid code, you'll see the problematic part of the code highlighted in the Design view portion of the window.

Exercise 3.2   Working with a Simple Document in Code and Design Views

In this exercise, you build on the basic page your created in the preceding exercise, adding a few more elements and checking the document structure in various coding views.

If you haven't done so yet, copy the **chapter_03** folder on the CD to your hard drive. Define a site called **Chapter 3**, with this folder as the local root folder.

1. Start by opening **basicpage.html**, if it isn't already open.

2. Your simple document consists of several HTML tags, including <h1> for the heading you created and <hr> for the horizontal rule. The tag selector can help you see and work with these tags.

   Click inside the heading you created and examine the tag selector. It will tell you that your cursor is inside the <body> tag, and within that tag it is inside the <h1> tag. (This is an accurate description of your document's body structure—the <h1> tag is nested inside the <body> tag.)

   To see how the tag selector can help you select things, click the <h1> button in the tag selector. Your entire heading is selected! Now click the <body> button in the tag selector. Your heading and your horizontal rule are selected! Selecting the <body> tag selects all the visible content on your page.

3. Now take a look at your document's structure as it appears in the Tag Inspector. Choose Window > Tag Inspector, or expand the Code panel group from the docked interface so that the Tag Inspector shows. Stretch the Tag Inspector panel out to be as tall as you need so that you can see it decently.

   The top half of the panel looks something like a very complex outline, with lots of topics and subtopics. To clean the display up, click the expand/collapse triangles to contract the display until you're only seeing the <html>, <head>, and <body> tags. See how they're nested? Now expand the <body> tag's triangle so that you see your page contents. There's an <h1> tag and, below it, the <hr> tag.

   Still in the Tag Inspector, select the <hr> tag. Then take a look at the bottom half of the inspector, and you'll see all the possible attributes for this tag (many more than show in the Property inspector). Width, Height, and Noshade are filled in. You can change these values here, if you like.

4. Finally, let's see the code itself. From the Document window toolbar, click the Code and Design view button. Your Document window splits into two sections, with code on top and design on bottom. In the Design view portion of the window, drag across your heading text to select it. See how, in the Code view portion, the <h1> code for the heading scrolls into position and is now selected?

Now in the Code portion of the window, deselect the heading and select only a word or two from the heading. See how, in the Design view portion, part of the heading is selected? It's easy to keep track of what code creates what design elements when you work in this split-window view.

In the Design portion of the window, change one or two of the words in your heading. Change it to **Welcome to Fred's Web Site**, or something like that. Notice how, as you type, the Code view display shows your typing.

Now, in the Code view portion of the window, find the code for your horizontal rule. (Hint: It starts with <hr.) Find the width attribute and change its value to 50. Change the size attribute's value to 50 as well. (This changes the height.) What's happening in Design view? Nothing! That's because Dreamweaver doesn't know whether you have finished typing yet. Click anywhere in Design view, or click the Refresh button in the Property inspector, and your changes will take effect.

Doing and Undoing

Everybody makes mistakes. It's the job of good software to give you a break when you do. In Dreamweaver, if you do something you wish you hadn't done, you can take yourself back and forward in time using the Undo and Redo commands or using the graphic interface of the History panel.

The Undo and Redo Commands

Whatever you did last, you can usually undo it by choosing Edit > Undo. In fact, when you go to the Edit menu, the Undo command even tells you exactly what it's going to undo. It will say Undo Typing, Undo Backspace, Undo Insert Table, or whatever it was you last did. And then, after you've undone yourself, if you decide you really didn't want to undo, you can undo the undo by choosing Edit > Redo Typing, or Redo Backspace, or whatever it is you really wanted to do. Dreamweaver will enable you to undo/redo as many steps as it can remember, limited by how much memory your computer has available and how many steps you want it to remember. (See the following section for more on limiting steps remembered.)

Tip

When you get into more complex multidocument tasks in Dreamweaver, such as working with linked style sheets or JavaScript files, you'll find out that the Undo command doesn't always work the way you expect it to. If, as Dreamweaver is editing your currently open document, it also needs to edit a linked file that isn't currently open, that linked file will be edited and immediately saved and closed. No amount of undoing will be able to fix any mistakes you made in that linked document. You'll have to fix your mistakes without Undo.

The Revert Command

A very drastic way to undo all sorts of actions is to choose File > Revert. This removes all changes you made to the document since the last time you saved it. The command isn't available if you haven't yet saved. After you've reverted, you cannot undo the revert. Reverting is the same as closing the document or quitting Dreamweaver without saving.

The History Panel

If you prefer your undoing and redoing to take place in a more visual interface, you can use the History panel, accessed by choosing Window > Others > History (see Figure 3.18). The History panel represents every step you take in your document-creation process as an entry in its list. If you like, you can use it just as a visual indicator of where you've been and what you've been doing lately. The last line in the list, and the location of the triangular slider button at the left, indicates the very last thing you did.

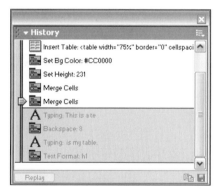

Figure 3.18   The History panel, a visual interface for undoing and redoing.

To undo with the History panel, drag the triangular slider up to a previous step in the list. When you do this, all steps lower than the slider turn gray, indicating that they're undone. In the Document window, the steps have been undone and you're looking at an earlier stage of your document brought back to life.

To redo with the History panel, drag the triangular slider back down the list. The grayed-out steps will turn solid again, and your document reconstructs itself to where it was before you undid. Note that after you've undone any steps by dragging the slider to a previous step, if you perform any other edits in your document you destroy your ability to redo. The grayed-out steps in the panel disappear forever.

The History panel and the Undo command use the same reserve of Dreamweaver memory to recall earlier document stages. Like the Undo command, the History panel will remember as many steps as it can, up to the number of steps specified in your preferences. To see or change the maximum number of actions that will be remembered, choose Edit > Preferences > General, and set the Maximum History Steps. The default is to remember the last 50 steps.

Why would you want to limit the number of steps remembered? The more there is to remember, the more work Dreamweaver has to do. If the program is spending too many of its resources remembering steps, it might become sluggish in dealing with other memory-intensive tasks, such as refreshing the list of files in a site and performing other complex code-crunching activities. If you're ever desperately short of memory and want to speed up Dreamweaver as much as possible, you can clear its entire memory of steps by accessing the History panel's pop-up options menu and choosing Clear History. This frees up some computer memory that you might need for an immediate task.

Note

The History panel isn't just for undoing and redoing. You also can use it to save and replay actions, and even to remember actions as commands. For a full discussion of this aspect of working with History, see Chapter 34, "Customizing Dreamweaver."

Importing Pages from Other Sources

You can use Dreamweaver to edit any HTML page, whether it was created in Dreamweaver or somewhere else. There is no such thing as a "Dreamweaver file." It does not create a proprietary file format like Flash does. A Flash FLA file can be opened only with Flash. You can open up pretty much any type of web file within Dreamweaver and edit it. This includes HTML web pages, JavaScript files, and even regular text files.

Converting a FrontPage Site

Microsoft FrontPage is another WYSIWYG HTML editor. It contains many of the same functions as Dreamweaver, including some automated features specific to Microsoft FrontPage Server Extensions (which are located at your server and are proprietary to FrontPage). However, it still does not write the most efficient code, and many people are converting from FrontPage to Dreamweaver. Although by default Dreamweaver can edit any HTML page, available extensions can help you with the conversion process.

Note

Extensions are additions to Dreamweaver that are written by developers to enhance and extend the inherent functionality of the program. Extensions are discussed in more detail in Chapter 35, "Working with Extensions." These extensions are available at the Macromedia Exchange for Dreamweaver and help you strip out FrontPage-specific code. They also enable you to connect to a FrontPage server.

Working with GoLive

If you open a page in Dreamweaver that was created in Adobe GoLive, you might see a lot of proprietary code, especially if the pages were created using GoLive's Layout Grid feature for automatic table generation. The Clean Up HTML command in Dreamweaver will go a long way toward getting rid of this extra source code. Choose Commands > Clean Up HTML to access this Dreamweaver function.

Copy and Paste Code

You can copy code and text into Dreamweaver from any source. You can copy text from a word processor and paste it into the Design window. Dreamweaver will write the code for it automatically, but you will lose all textual formatting except for paragraphs. You also can paste pure HTML code straight into the Code view.

Dreamweaver MX brings back the Copy as HTML and Paste as HTML features. These enable you to copy and paste from the Design window and bring the HTML along with it. Generally, if you copy text from the Design window and paste it into, for instance, Notepad, only the text will copy over. If you select something in the Design window, choose Edit > Copy as HTML, and then paste into Notepad, you will get all the source code that goes along with it. To learn more about using text, refer to Chapter 4, "Working with Text."

Note

For specific information on using Microsoft Word and Dreamweaver together, see Chapter 4.

Importing Tabular Data

Dreamweaver can import tabular data and automatically create a formatted table with this data. For this feature to work, the file must be in a *delimited* format, meaning that it needs to be saved in a format that retains only the data. Dreamweaver will then parse (sort) this data into a discernable format. Generally, spreadsheet programs have an option to Save As in a variety of formats. These might be tab-delimited text or a comma-separated value (CSV). Dreamweaver can parse delimited files by the following:

- Tabs
- Commas
- Colon
- Semicolon
- Other (When Other is chosen, you are given a field into which you put the delimiting value.)

In a CSV file, for instance, only the cell data is saved. A comma separates the cell data for a row, and a new row is denoted by a carriage return. Any other media or formatting is lost in this conversion. Therefore, when you take this CSV file and bring it into Dreamweaver, it will know to make a cell for each value between a comma; when it gets to a return or new line, it will start a new row in the table.

Exercise 3.3   Importing a CSV File into Dreamweaver

In this exercise, you import a CSV file into Dreamweaver.

If you haven't done so yet, copy the **chapter_03** folder on the CD to your hard drive. Define a site called **Chapter 03**, with this folder as the local root folder.

1. Open a new HTML file in Dreamweaver (File > New). Save it as **element_table.htm**.
2. Choose File > Import > Import Tabular Data. The Import Tabular Data dialog box will display.
3. For the Data File field, click the Browse button and find the **element_table.csv** file that is in the site root folder. Select it, and then click Open. Notice that the Delimiter field should have automatically changed from Tab to Comma.
4. Select the table settings:
   - Table Width = Fit to data
   - Cell Padding = 2
   - Cell Spacing = 2
   - Format Top Row = No formatting
   - Border = 2
5. Choose OK. Dreamweaver will parse the data file and make a table of all the elements. Figure 3.19 shows the completed table.

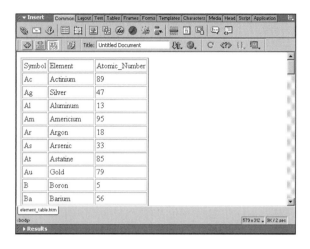

Figure 3.19   The completed table.

6. Save the file as **element_table_done.htm**, and then close it.

Note

Many spreadsheet programs today have an option to Save As HTML (or as Web Page). This is another way to place data into Dreamweaver. If you use the Import Tabular Data option, Dreamweaver will be able to make the HTML table, and it will almost always be better coded.

Dealing with Browsers

If you're designing web pages, the browser is the center of your universe. What browsers are your visitors using? How do your pages display in the different browsers? How can you make sure your target audience is seeing your pages at their best, despite browser differences? Dreamweaver offers a variety of tools to deal with these fickle mistresses of cyberspace.

Setting Up the Browser Preview

Design view is for designing; it's meant only as an approximate rendering of what your page will look like when it's online. How do you tell how your page will look in a browser? You look at it in a browser! Unlike other web editors, such as FrontPage or GoLive, Dreamweaver has no internal previewing window. Instead, Dreamweaver has tools for quickly launching your computer's browsers to do your previewing there.

Defining Browsers

Before you can use Dreamweaver to help you preview in your browser, you need to tell
Dreamweaver which browsers are available on your system and where they're stored. You
can define as many browsers as you want (as long as they're installed on your system).
You also can designate one browser as your primary browser and one as your secondary
browser. (The primary and secondary browsers are easier to launch than the others.) For
each browser on your system, follow these steps:

1. Choose Edit > Preferences and go to the Preview in Browser category (see
   Figure 3.20).

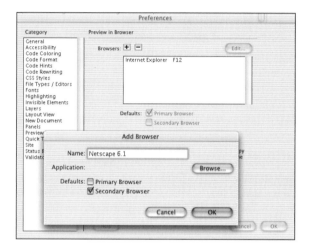

Figure 3.20   Setting up a list of browsers to preview in.

2. The list in the center of the dialog box will show you whether any browsers have
   already been specified.

3. To add a new browser, click the plus (+) button. In the dialog box that appears,
   navigate to one of your browsers and click OK. (You're on your own finding
   where the browsers are on your computer; Dreamweaver has no feature for
   automatically searching your hard drive for browsers.)

4. Back in the Preferences dialog box, select whether you want the new browser to
   be your primary or secondary browser.

5. Repeat steps 2–4 for as many browsers as you want to add to the list here.

Previewing in a Browser

After you have added your installed browsers to Dreamweaver's browser list, you can quickly see how any of your documents will look in those browsers by opening the document and doing one of the following:

- For your primary browser, press F12.

- For your secondary browser, press Ctrl/Cmd+F12.

- For any browser in your list, go to File > Preview in Browser and choose your browser from the submenu; or use the Preview/Debug in Browser menu in the Document window toolbar (see Figure 3.21).

Figure 3.21 The Document window with the Preview/Debug in Browser menu showing.

As soon as you do this, Dreamweaver launches the specified browser and opens your document in it. It doesn't even matter whether you've saved your document first.

Working with Temporary Files

By default, when you Preview in Browser, Dreamweaver doesn't open your HTML file in the browser. Instead, it creates a temporary file (with a name such as **TMPdcrhgv23u0.htm**), identical in every way to your file, and opens that in the browser. Why does this happen? It's meant to be a good thing, enabling you to Preview in Browser without having saved your document first. If you preview frequently (a good thing), it can be a hassle having to save every time—although saving frequently is a good thing, too.

Be aware, however, that these temporary files can generate their own minor problems. For one thing, these temporary files end up on your hard drive. They're not doing any harm, but they're a bit of extra clutter; and if you don't know what they are, you might wonder what gremlins are creating them. Dreamweaver is supposed to delete all temporary files when it shuts down, but it doesn't always do this. You might even end up with some **TMPdcrhgv23u0.htm** files uploaded to your web server.

A more confusing side effect to using temporary files, however, is how the browser preview and browser refresh works. Imagine this: You're working on a document and you Preview in Browser and see that the document needs some tweaking. So, you minimize or hide the browser window and return to Dreamweaver, where you make your changes. Then you return to the browser window and click the Refresh button to update the view. But your page doesn't change! Are you in the cyber-Bermuda triangle? No! When you modified your document, Dreamweaver didn't modify the temporary file. Dreamweaver expects you to generate a new temporary file by choosing File > Preview in Browser (F12) again. Every time you want to see another preview in the browser, choose the command again. Don't just leave the original temporary file open and press Refresh.

MX If you don't like working with temporary files, Dreamweaver MX also can Preview in Browser without them, by opening your original HTML file in the browser. To set this up, choose Edit > Preferences > Preview in Browser, and deselect the Preview Using Temporary File option (see Figure 3.22). The upside to this is you don't end up with extra **TMPdcrhgv23u0.htm** files on your computer, and you can use the browser's Refresh button to update your preview. The potential downside is that you will have to remember to save before every preview, and you won't be able to preview unsaved documents.

Checking Target Browsers

If you've worked at all with the Edit Tag command, you've seen how Dreamweaver can tell you which tag attributes are going to work with which browsers (refer back to the discussion about Figure 3.12). The information that shows up in the Edit Tag dialog box is part of the Dreamweaver database of tags and attributes. Any time you want to check the code in a document against the database, use the Check Target Browsers command, as follows:

1. Open a document that you want to check. (The document must have been saved at least once before you can use this command.)

Note
While the current chapter is focusing on documents, you also can check target browsers across an entire site. Do it by activating the Site panel before choosing the command.

2. Choose File > Check Page > Check Target Browsers.

3. A dialog box will appear listing all the browsers represented in the Dreamweaver database. From this list, select the browser you want to check against. Note that you can select only one browser. If you select multiple browsers from the list, the last one in the list is considered the target.

4. Click Check to close the dialog box and perform the check. After a few moments, the Results window opens with the Target Browser Check tab in front. It shows the results of your check. Any nonsupported tag or attribute shows up in the window as a problem.

Checking Page Validity

MX

Validation is an important concept in the web development world. Validation is the process of checking the code of an HTML, XML, or XHTML document to make sure it is properly coded (correct syntax and no nonstandard tags or attributes) before it has to be displayed in a browser. Part of the reason today's browsers are so large and unwieldy is that they are programmed to deal with all sorts of invalid code, even to guess how a page should be presented if the syntax or elements are incorrect. In an ideal browsing world, each page's code would be checked for validity—validated—before the browser tried to display it; invalid pages would not display at all. The browsers could be lean and mean because they would be able to predict that only correctly coded pages would ever come their way.

If you're just getting started in web design, or if you're a professional on tight deadlines, you can put off worrying about validation for now. None of the major browsers requires it—yet. But eventually, they will.

Validating Document Markup

Dreamweaver MX now offers a validation service for all HTML documents. To check the validity of a document, follow these steps:

1. Open the document you want to validate.

2. Choose File > Check Page > Validate Markup; or, if the Results window is open, from the panel option's pop-up menu, choose Validate Current Document.

3. After a moment or two, the Results window will open, showing the Validation tab, with your document's report card showing.

You also can validate all the documents in a site by going to the Results window's panel options pop-up menu and choosing Validate Entire Site. You can validate some of the documents in a site by selecting those files in the Site panel and choosing Validate Selected Files in Site from the Results window's panel options pop-up menu.

Determining Validation Settings

Validation involves checking your document(s) against a standard; and there are all sorts of standards out there, from HTML 2.0 to XHTML strict and beyond. To see what standard Dreamweaver is using to validate your documents, and to change the standards as needed, choose Edit > Preferences > Validator or, in the Results window, access the panel options pop-up menu and choose Settings. Both of these commands open the Preferences > Validator dialog box (see Figure 3.22).

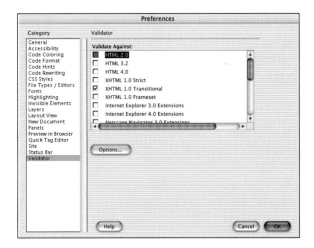

Figure 3.22   The Preferences dialog box showing the validation settings.

Making Your Pages Accessible

Your pages preview beautifully in the major browsers. They pass the proper validation tests, so you know you're being a good coding citizen. But are they accessible? Accessible web pages are designed to be usable by people with visual, auditory, or motor disabilities. This includes people using screen readers and other special software and hardware to browse the Internet. For the World Wide Web to be truly universal, it needs to be accessible. And if you're designing government-related web sites, accessibility is more than a good idea; it's the law. Section 508 of the Federal Rehabilitation Act states that any web site for use by government employees, or for the purpose of disseminating government information, must comply in some very specific ways with the Americans with Disabilities Act.

What Makes a Web Page Accessible?

You can make your web pages accessible in a variety of ways, including the following:

- Add alt labels to all images so that screen readers and other people without access to the images can still understand the intended meaning of the images.

- Use logical markup to structure your pages, rather than presentation markup. Use <em> and <strong> rather than <b> and <i>, for instance.

- Take advantage of the extra attributes—such as D-Links and LongDesc for URLs and images, for instance.

- If your page includes form elements or navigation controls that need to be clicked, provide keyboard shortcuts and Tab indexes where possible so that those with motor impairment can still navigate through your content.

Dreamweaver Accessibility Options

 To help you create accessible web pages without compromising your efficiency, Dreamweaver MX gives you quick access to each of your page element's accessibility attributes. To enable accessibility attributes, choose Edit > Preferences and, in the dialog box, go to the Accessibility category (see Figure 3.23). The list of options represents different page elements that have special accessibility attributes in HTML. For each item you select, every time you click an object to insert that object, its dialog box will include those special attributes. Figure 3.24 shows the Insert Table dialog box with and without accessibility attributes enabled.

 Note

The Accessibility Options for Tables dialog box appears only if accessibility is enabled and displays only after you click OK in the Table dialog box.

Figure 3.23   The Preferences dialog box showing the Accessibility settings.

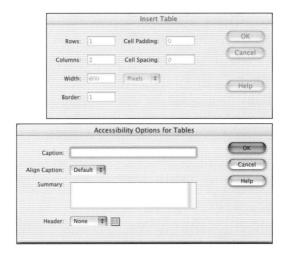

Figure 3.24   The Insert Table dialog box without and with accessibility attributes.

Summary

This chapter covered a lot of ground. For Dreamweaver newcomers, you got your feet wet in the world of HTML code and in the Dreamweaver coding and designing interface. Other Dreamweaver users, you might have discovered some basic tools you didn't know about or might have been introduced to some of the new features available in Dreamweaver MX. The next several chapters cover the various aspects of working with documents in more detail—text, images, links, and head content. After that, basic training is over, and it's off to the world of web design and beyond.

Chapter 4

Working with Text

HTML text is the staple food of the World Wide Web—a fast-loading, flexible, and easily editable component that arguably has the potential to communicate more and better than anything else on the web.

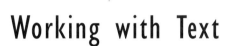

With the rise of graphics and multimedia, text has begun to see some neglect, as designers spend more and more time and effort trying to dazzle viewers. Most web users are looking for information, however, and for that, well formatted and styled text is hard to beat. With the rise of Cascading Style Sheets (CSS), the possibilities for styling text are constantly pushing the old limits, and the opportunities for artistry in typography are as exciting as in the world of graphics.

Knowing how to add text to an HTML document and how to format it properly is essential to the craft of web page design.

HTML and CSS

Although HTML provides the `<font>` with which to style text, the use of this tag is now discouraged by the World Wide Web Consortium (W3C). Cascading Style Sheets (CSS) not only provide much more flexibility, but also adheres a lot more closely to the original concept of HTML as a structural markup language.

HTML Beginnings as a Structural Markup Language

The original concept for HTML was that of a language used to mark up text to describe the different structural elements of a document. HTML tags (see table 4.1) identified which portion of a document was a heading, which portions were paragraphs, which portion was part of a list, and which words needed to be emphasized. The browsers were designed to interpret these structural elements in such a way that the text onscreen made sense to the reader (see Figure 4.1). Not every browser displayed text the same; one might show text marked "emphasize" in italics and another boldfaced, but either way the text was emphasized. The goal was readable documents that would display with structural definition across a variety of platforms (see Figure 4.2).

Table 4.1   Common Structural HTML Tags

HTML Tag	Encloses What Kind of Text
`<p></p>`	Paragraph
`<h1></h1>`	Top-level heading
`<h2></h2>`	Second-level heading
`<h3></h3>`	Third-level heading
`<em></em>`	Emphasized
`<strong></strong>`	Strongly emphasized
`<ul></ul>`	Unordered list
`<ol></ol>`	Ordered list
`<li></li>`	List item
`<blockquote></blockquote>`	Quoted text

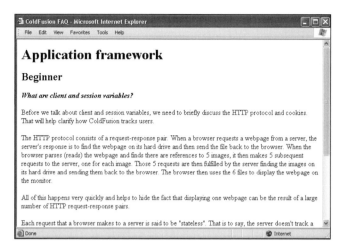

Figure 4.1   Text styled only with structural markup is plain, but readable.

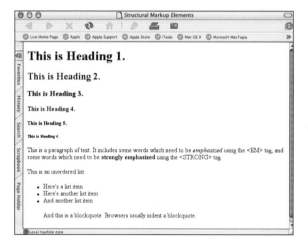

Figure 4.2   Basic structural markup tags as they display in a browser window.

Increasing Use of Presentational Markup

With the advent of graphical browsers and the rapid expansion of the web came the demand from HTML authors for new tags that would specify presentational effects rather than just structure. Designers were no longer satisfied to specify that a word needed to be emphasized somehow; they wanted to be able to specify exactly *how* the word would be emphasized (by bolding, for instance). In response to this pressure, *physical* elements such as `<b>` and `<i>` began to enter the language. Soon a structural language was evolving into a presentational one, and the `<font>` tag for styling text came into wide usage.

Note

Logical elements, such as <em>, indicate the meaning or role of certain text; the browser in some way should emphasize text marked <em>, but the markup doesn't dictate exactly how. *Physical elements*, such as <b>, do just the opposite: They specify how the text should be styled (in this case, in boldface), but indicate nothing about the part the text plays in the document's structure.

What's Wrong with Presentational Markup?

Web site designers were happy to have some control over presentation, but as they stopped using structural formatting, it was no longer possible to deduce the structure of the information from the source. This has a number of negative repercussions, including the following:

- The code produced doesn't convey anything about the meaning of the text being presented. Structurally, these pages are just strings of letters. A speech-synthesis browser, for example, will read text marked with <h1> tags as a main heading; it will read text marked to be rendered in large type and bold just like any other text.

- Unstructured markup is much more difficult to maintain. Text marked up logically according to the meaning of the content results in clean code that makes sense.

- Unstructured pages are very difficult to index. If page headings and section headings are clearly marked, search engines can use them to enable the user to perform targeted searches for relevant information. (See Chapter 7, "Utilizing Head Content," for a full discussion of search engines and indexing.)

This Is a Job for CSS

The W3C quickly recognized that the nature of HTML was being changed by the increasing use of presentational markup and that a solution was needed. As a direct response, work began on Cascading Style Sheets, and in 1996, CSS was made a full W3C Recommendation.

CSS is designed to allow the web designer a lot of control over how his pages display, while retaining the basic essence of HTML as a structural language. It allows for much more complex and varied presentation of text than HTML ever could, permitting styling such as the creation of borders, determining the amount of space around elements, variations on capitalization, decoration (such as underlining), letter spacing, and many other possibilities (see Figure 4.3).

Figure 4.3   CSS allows for much more advanced typography than the styling possible with presentational HTML based on the `<font>` tag.

Almost as exciting is the lightening of the web developer's workload brought about by the use of linked style sheets, where a single change to a style declaration can affect specifically targeted text sitewide.

CSS is clearly the direction of things to come for web designers, and should be part of the tool kit of any serious web designer. The Cascading Style Sheets specification is covered thoroughly in Chapter 13, "Using Cascading Style Sheets."

Note

With the proliferation of new and alternative web browsing devices such as cellular phones, handhelds, personal digital assistants, and web TV, logical document structuring might well become critical. In conjunction with CSS, this approach allows for very different presentations as determined by the device being used to view the page—exactly as in the original concept for HTML.

The *<font>* Tag as an Alternative

However, you also can style text by using the `<font>` tag. Although this is not ideal for the reasons previously discussed, and because it is deprecated (discouraged) by the W3C, if you need to style your text quickly and choose to postpone learning CSS, Dreamweaver offers formatting tools for this purpose, and this chapter explains how to use them.

Typing, Copying/Pasting, and Importing Text into Dreamweaver

Before text can be formatted and styled, it needs to find its way into a document in the first place. There are several ways this usually happens:

- Text is typed directly into the document in Design view in Dreamweaver.
- Text is copied and pasted from an outside source into the document.
- Text is imported from a program such as Microsoft Word.

Typing Text Directly into a Dreamweaver Document

Text can be typed into any HTML document in the Dreamweaver Document window in Design view in much the same way as with a word processor. However, Dreamweaver enables you to format text only in ways that HTML allows; for instance, HTML does not allow tabs, and so none are available in Dreamweaver.

One difference between Dreamweaver and a typical word processor often confuses those just starting out, and that is the difference between a *paragraph break* and *a line break*. The following sections explain this.

Ending a Paragraph and Beginning a New Paragraph

In Dreamweaver, pressing Enter ends the current paragraph and begins a new paragraph; in the source code, both paragraphs are formatted with `<p></p>` tags. In the Dreamweaver Document window, the break between paragraphs displays as a double space; most browsers display paragraphs like this as well.

Ending a Line of Text and Beginning a New Line of Text

Pressing Shift+Enter ends the current line and begins a new line; in the source code, a `<br>` tag is entered. In the Dreamweaver Document window as well as in the browsers, the text just begins at the far left on a new line.

Tip

You can spell-check your text inside Dreamweaver. To access the spell checker, pull down Text > Check Spelling from the main menu, or use the keyboard shortcut Shift+F7.

Your typed-in text naturally will need some formatting; this can be done either with CSS (see Chapter 13) or with the `<font>` tag, explained later in this chapter.

Copying/Pasting Text from Another Program

If you want to paste text into Dreamweaver after copying it to the Clipboard from another program, you have two choices, which you can see by pulling down the Dreamweaver Edit menu. One is called Paste; the other is called Paste HTML. Although the reasoning for the names of these two options is slightly obscure, the difference between them is clear.

Paste inserts your Clipboard contents into your document, retaining the line breaks and, in some cases, the formatting (such as bold letters).

However, retaining line breaks from the original document is usually not a good idea. Ideally, text should "flow" inside its container on an HTML page, with line breaks being determined on-the-fly by the browser; having predetermined line breaks, or *hard returns*, will usually cause some undesired results.

However, the Paste option might be appropriate for situations in which you want the speed and convenience of dropping formatted text onto a Dreamweaver HTML document.

With Paste HTML, all line breaks are removed, leaving you with one long string of unbroken, unformatted text, retaining only the single-space breaks between words (see Figure 4.4).

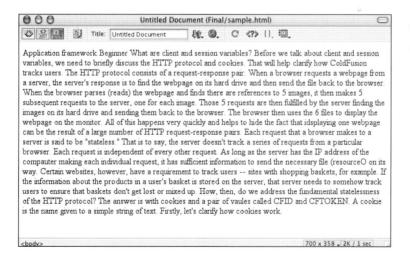

Figure 4.4   Using the Paste HTML option removes all line breaks from a document copied from a browser or word processor window.

The main advantage of using the Paste HTML option is that, with all formatting removed, you can format your text exactly the way you choose. If the document is not a large or complex one, this is probably the best option.

The real use for Paste HTML, though, is for use with actual HTML code. So, for example, if you copy the contents of a web page, then paste into the Dreamweaver Design window, you will get text with line breaks and some simple formatting. If you view the source of that same web page, copy from the browser, then paste HTML within Code view, you get the entire page with all formatting.

Exercise 4.1   Copying/Pasting Text from Microsoft Word

This exercise requires Microsoft Word. Here you'll copy text from a Word document and paste it into a Dreamweaver document, using first the Paste feature, then the Paste HTML feature. This will clarify the difference between the two features.

Before you start, copy the **chapter_04** folder on the CD to your hard drive. Define a site called Chapter 4, with this folder as the local root folder.

1. Within your local **chapter_04** folder, find and open the file **nc_facts.doc** in Microsoft Word.

2. Choose Site > Site Files View > New File to open a new Dreamweaver document. Name the document **nc_facts.html**.

3. In the open Word document, choose Edit > Select All, and then Edit > Copy.

4. Back in your new blank Dreamweaver document, place the cursor on the page and choose Edit > Paste. The text will be pasted into your HTML document. As you can see, most of the formatting from the Word document has been lost, but some paragraphs and line breaks have been retained. What was a bulleted list in Word is now a kind of jury-rigged list in Dreamweaver using a special character for a bullet. Switch into Code view to take a look at the source code; you can see that a somewhat random mix of <p> and <br> tags have been used to format the text. This illustrates why it is usually preferable to use the other Dreamweaver option, Paste HTML, and do the formatting yourself, as you'll see in just a moment.

5. At the bottom of the Dreamweaver Document window, in the Quick Tag Selector, click the <body> tag and press Delete on your keyboard. This will delete all the content you just added.

6. The copied text from the Word document is still in your Clipboard. Now choose Edit > Paste HTML. Your text will be pasted in again, but this time without the sketchy formatting.

7. Save your Dreamweaver document; you'll return to it in Exercise 4.2.

Importing Text from Microsoft Word

You can copy and paste text from a Microsoft Word document as described in the preceding section. However, you might come across a Microsoft Word document that has
elaborate formatting (such as charts and lists), which could mean hours of HTML coding for you. Instead of pasting the text and laboriously formatting it yourself, you can
utilize some special features in both Word and Dreamweaver to save yourself time and
produce a serviceable HTML document. First, use the Save as Web Page command in
Microsoft Word (called Save as HTML in some versions of Word) and open the resulting HTML file in Dreamweaver.

Tip

You can open Word HTML inside Dreamweaver with the File > Open menu option.

Freshly imported into Dreamweaver, the code of a Word HTML document is full of
extraneous markup. Take a close look at the code that appears at the top of Figure 4.5.

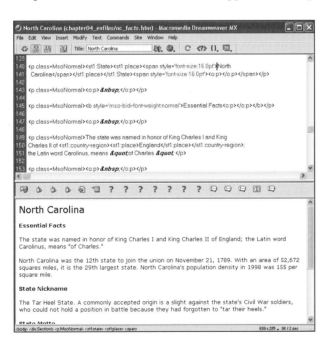

Figure 4.5   Microsoft Word HTML shown in Design and Code view.

The problem with using the Save as Web Page command in Microsoft Word is that Microsoft Word HTML is actually a mix of HTML and XML code. It also includes an abundance of CSS styles and countless <meta> tags, which significantly worsen the situation. The code in the upper window of Figure 4.4 is a far cry from the plain HTML you would write if coding by hand.

A Microsoft Word HTML file like the one in Figure 4.4 will usually look presentable in most web browsers, especially Microsoft Internet Explorer. As you've seen, however, the automatic conversion to HTML results in bloated and unwieldy code that is far from ideal simply due to its sheer size; it is also almost impossible to edit. If you have no need to edit the page in Dreamweaver or any other HTML editor, using the document as Microsoft Word produces it is an option.

If you want to be able to edit the Microsoft Word HTML file, however, you should use the Dreamweaver Clean Up Word HTML command first to remove extraneous code. Your cleaned-up document will be much closer to standard HTML, and it will be both easier and safer to make changes to it.

To use the Clean Up Word HTML command, open your Word HTML file inside Dreamweaver, and select Commands > Clean Up Word HTML.

Figure 4.6 shows the resulting window. The checked boxes inside this box indicate the Dreamweaver defaults.

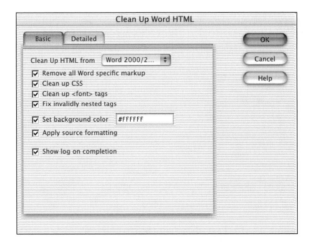

Figure 4.6   The Clean Up Word HTML dialog box.

Inside this box you'll find two tabs, Basic and Detailed. Click OK to simply accept the defaults and convert the HTML, or choose from among the Basic or Detailed options. For more information about the options under the Basic tab, take a look at Table 4.2.

Table 4.2   Clean Up Word HTML, Basic Options

Option	Description
Remove All Word Specific Markup	Removes all XML from HTML tags and other formatting specific to Microsoft Word.
Clean Up CSS	Removes tags that refer to CSS, including inline CSS styles (as long as the parent style shares the same style properties). It also removes style attributes beginning with mso, and non-CSS-style descriptions. This is beneficial because Microsoft Word HTML relies heavily on CSS styles for formatting, most of them being document-level styles that increase page-loading time in the web browser.
Clean Up <font> Tags	Removes the <font> HTML tags and converts the default body text to size 2.
Fix Invalidly Nested Tags	Removes invalid <font> tags. Invalid <font> tags are those found in spotswhere the <font> tag shouldn't be, according to the W3C. Specifically, these are the <font> tags outside the paragraph and heading (block-level) tags.
Set Background Color	To use a hexadecimal value to set the background color of your document, enter it into the Text field box. Without a set background color, the document will have a gray background. By default, the background color is white, or #FFFFFF.
Apply Source Formatting	Applies the source formatting options that you specified in your **sourceformat.txt** file. This file is located in your **Configuration** folder. (See Chapter 34, "Customizing Dreamweaver," for more about setting your preferences.)
Show Log on Completion	Check this box to see a log listing what changes have been made.

You can use the options in the Detailed tab to make even more changes to the conversion.

After you make your selections, click OK. Dreamweaver processes the file and a cleaned-up version of the page appears in the Document window.

Tip

If you find that your HTML code contains unwanted tags even after you clean up, try looking at your HTML Format preferences (from the main menu, choose Edit > Preferences and then choose Code Format) to make sure you have them set the way you want. Alternatively, you can run an advanced Find/Replace query to get rid of even more tags, or run the general Clean Up HTML command. See Chapter 33, "Writing Code in Dreamweaver," for a full discussion of code rewriting, code formatting, and using Find/Replace for code cleanup.

Formatting Text with the Property Inspector

MX

When working in Design view in Dreamweaver, and when portions of text are selected, the Property inspector can be used to format and style it in a number of ways. New in Dreamweaver MX is the ability to apply CSS classes to your text using the Property inspector; this is covered in Chapter 13. Here, however, we will be looking at the non-CSS text-formatting capabilities in Dreamweaver.

The Dreamweaver MX Text Property inspector has two modes that can be toggled: HTML Mode and CSS Mode. The options available to you from the Property inspector depend upon which mode you're working in. To apply HTML formatting, as we will be doing in the rest of this chapter, you want to be in HTML mode (see Figure 4.7).

Figure 4.7   The Toggle CSS/HTML Mode button.

Note

Throughout this chapter, it is assumed that you are working in Dreamweaver Standard view, not in Layout view.

Note

Remember that text in the Dreamweaver Document window must be selected to apply any formatting with the Property inspector (see Figure 4.8).

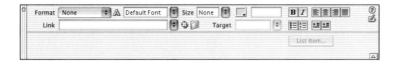

Figure 4.8   Text-formatting options of the Property inspector.

Paragraphs, Headings, and Preformatted Text

The drop-down list in the upper-left corner of the Property inspector enables you to style selected text as a paragraph, as any one of the six heading sizes, or as preformatted text. You've already read about paragraphs and headings earlier in this chapter; they are essential structural page elements.

The Preformatted Text option is used when the exact formatting of certain text must be preserved, including its spacing, returns, and tabs. Because HTML default behavior is to ignore this type of spacing, Preformatted Text is provided to enable you to retain them; the text won't reflow when the browser is resized, as with ordinary HTML text. Two instances in which preformatted text might be used are when formatting poetry or source code on an HTML page. Browsers generally render preformatted text in a mono-spaced font such as Courier.

Choosing Fonts

The next option to the right on the Property inspector is an unlabelled drop-down list that enables you to choose a font face (or *typeface*) for your text.

Tip

You also can access most of the formatting options for selected text available in the Property inspector by pulling down the Text menu.

Choosing a font for your text is simple: Just select the text, and in the drop-down list, click your choice. However, some explanation of why Dreamweaver offers these lists of fonts is called for.

It's important to understand how browsers work with regard to fonts. The crucial thing to remember is that the end user will see only fonts that he has installed on his local hard drive. If you specify a font that a particular user doesn't have installed, your text will display in his browser's default font, usually Times New Roman.

Because most web designers want to have as much control as possible over the font that displays on a web page they've created, the `<font>` tag's `face` attribute is usually written so that it includes a list of fonts, beginning with the designer's first choice, including several more choices, and finishing with a generic font category. This way, if the designer's first choice isn't available, hopefully the second or third choice is. If none of the specific font face choices are available on the user's computer, at least some font from the generic font family will be used.

On Windows, the most commonly installed fonts are Times New Roman, Arial, Courier New, Verdana, Georgia, Trebuchet MS, and MS Comic Sans. On a Mac, the most commonly installed fonts are Times, Helvetica, Courier, Verdana, Georgia, Trebuchet MS, and MS Comic Sans.

The Dreamweaver Property inspector offers you the following font-face combinations:

- Arial, Helvetica, sans serif
- Times New Roman, Times, serif
- Courier New, Courier, mono
- Georgia, Times New Roman, Times, serif
- Verdana, Arial, Helvetica, sans serif

Although this might seem at first glance to be a rather limited selection, these combinations have been chosen carefully to present a first choice for both Windows and Mac platforms and a generic font family. By using one of these combinations, you can be confident that your text will display in the font you've chosen, or at the very least, a similar font.

Tip

Verdana (sans serif) and Georgia (serif) are both good choices for body text on web sites. A type designer named Matthew Carter, who was hired by Microsoft to create two very readable screen-based families, developed them especially for screen reading.

Adding and Removing Fonts and Font Combinations

You can add or edit this list of font combinations. On the Property inspector, at the bottom of the drop-down list of font combinations, you'll see the Edit Font List option. Click that to open the Edit Font List dialog box (see Figure 4.9).

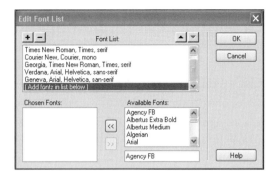

Figure 4.9   The Edit Font List dialog box.

The Available Fonts listing shows the fonts installed on *your* computer's hard drive; this is the list from which you can choose. To add a new combination, first be sure that Add Fonts in List Below is selected in the Font List at the top of the dialog box. You can then add a new font by selecting one from the Available Fonts list and then clicking the button with the double left-pointing arrows. Add as many as you want to your new combination. Always finish a font combination with a generic font family; these can be found at the very end of the Available Fonts list. When your combination list is complete, click the plus (+) button at the top of the dialog box; your new combination will now be available in the Property inspector. You can remove a font combination completely by selecting it and clicking the minus (–) button at the top of the dialog box.

Editing existing font combinations is easy; just select the font combination and use the double arrows to add or subtract fonts from the combination.

When you're finished, click OK to close the Edit Font List dialog box.

Note

Text must be selected to apply any <font> tag styles with the Property inspector. There is no way to set a default font face, size, and/or color for an entire site or even an entire page using this method. However, a pagewide or sitewide style can be easily specified with Cascading Style Sheets; this is one of the primary strengths of CSS.

Setting Font Sizes

To the right of the font face drop-down list is a drop-down menu of font sizes. You can use the Property inspector to specify *relative* sizes (which are preceded by a plus or minus sign) or *absolute* sizes (plain numbers) for your fonts. What's the difference?

Relative font size values define the font size relative to the primary font size of a document. In most browsers, this default font size is 3. So, if you specify a font size of –1, the result will be the same as an absolute font size of 2.

Using absolute fonts enables you to override the font preferences selected in your user's browser, giving you more control over the way your pages look. If you specify a font size of 5, for instance, the font appears in your user's browser as size 5, regardless of the browser's default font size. Be aware, however, that some newer browsers are allowing the user to override even absolute font settings. It is best to never base a page design on the assumption that your text will render in precisely the way you specify.

When working using the Property inspector to format text with the <font> tag, you might become frustrated at the limited number of available font sizes. If so, it is time to learn how to use CSS.

Tip

If you have trouble applying font faces, it could be that you have inadvertently doubled your <font> tags by applying them too many times. Use the Clean Up HTML command (default settings) from the Commands menu to remove extra tags.

Text Colors

Colored text can increase the visual impact of your web pages. For instance, you might want to put your body copy in a color that contrasts against your heads and subheads. You also might want to use other techniques—for example, make colorful headlines, subtle footnotes, or white text that pops out against a black background. Although it's not always easy to make design choices about text color, Dreamweaver helps you to implement those choices after you make them.

In the Property inspector, click the text color box. From the color palette that pops up, you can select your text color.

In the Property inspector, click the text color box. This accesses the standard Dreamweaver color palette, from which you can select your text color. (See "Working with the Color Picker" in Chapter 2, "Setting Up the Dreamweaver Workspace," for a discussion of how to use the color palette. If you want to learn more details about web color, see Chapter 8, "Design Issues.")

Bold and Italic

You can use the Property inspector to style your type as bold or italic, using the buttons marked B and I (see Figure 4.7). This will add `<b>` and `<i>` tags to your formatted text:

```
<font face="Arial">This is your <b><i>chance</b></i>!</font>
```

When text formatted as bold or italic is selected, the corresponding button will appear pressed down; the button can be used to toggle bold or italic formatting on and off.

 New in Dreamweaver MX is the option to set a preference (Edit > Preferences > General) that will make using the B button insert a pair of `<strong>` tags and the I button insert a pair of `<em>` tags. Because `<strong>` and `<em>` are structural tags—specifying the role of the text they are applied to—rather than presentational tags, which specify only the how the text should be presented, their use is preferred by many web developers.

Alignment

The Property inspector offers four tools for aligning your text left, right, center, or fully justified (see Figure 4.8). The text-alignment tools are to the far right, on the top row, next to the question mark icon.

To align text to the right, left, or center, select it and then click the icon of the alignment type you want to use. To remove alignments, select the type again and click the button off.

Tip

When text is contained within a table cell, it can be aligned left, right, or center by setting the table cell alignment. Select the table cell using the tag selector (at the bottom of the Dreamweaver Document window) and from the drop-down Horizontal list, choose Left, Right, or Center.

Tip

Don't confuse *text alignment* with *image alignment*. When an image is selected, the Property inspector will display a drop-down list of image alignment choices; these affect the placement of the image in relationship to the text around it. Text alignment works very much the way it does in a word processor, and affects only the text itself.

Making Lists

Numbered and bulleted lists have been around since the beginning of HTML.

The two icons on the Property inspector used to make lists are located below the bold and italic icons (see Figure 4.7). To create a list, click the list button (either bulleted or numbered) on the Property inspector, and then type your first list item. When you've finished typing the item, press Enter; the cursor will move to the next line, and a new list item will be created.

Another way to create a list is to type the list items one by one, separating them by pressing Enter at the end of each line. Then, select the whole list and click the desired list button on the Property inspector. Note that if your list items are separated with simple line breaks (using the <br> tag), the list function considers everything on your list to be one single item, and only one bullet point appears, adjacent to the topmost list item.

To make a nested list, or a list inside a list, separate the nested list items with hard returns, select them, and press the Indent button on the Property inspector.

To remove numbered or bulleted list formatting, select the list item or items and click the Bulleted List or Numbered List icon.

The List Item button, below the two list icons, can be clicked when the cursor is within an existing list, and enables you to edit a number of list-formatting options.

Indenting Text

Sometimes you want to indent text without adding bullets or list numbers. You can do so by using the Indent and Outdent icons on the Property inspector. See Figure 4.7.

Select the text you want to indent and click the Indent icon. This moves your text inward, indenting from both the left and right margins. You can click the icon again to move the text in even more. However, it's important to remember that when using these indent icons you are actually inserting <blockquote> tags into your code, and when you click the icon several times, you're inserting several pairs of tags. The <blockquote> tag pair is intended to display quoted blocks of text; using multiple nested pairs of these tags is not good HTML.

The best way to indent text is with CSS (covered in Chapter 13). The indent icons provide a workaround, which can suffice in a pinch.

To remove indents, select the text and click the Outdent icon. This moves the text back to the left side of your document.

Exercise 4.2   Formatting Text with the Property Inspector

This exercise is divided into two parts. In this first part, you learn how to mark up the document structure.

If you haven't done so yet, copy the **chapter_04** folder on the CD to your hard drive. Define a site called Chapter 4, with this folder as the local root folder.

1. Open the file **nc_facts.html** that you created in Exercise 4.1.

2. In the Dreamweaver Document window, place the cursor after the words `North Carolina` and press Enter.

3. Select the words `North Carolina`. In the Property inspector, from the Format drop-down list, click H1 to wrap this text in `<h1>` tags and make it a top-level heading (see Figure 4.10).

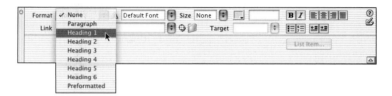

Figure 4.10   Formatting paragraphs and headings with the Property inspector.

4. Now place the cursor after the words `Essential Facts` and press Enter. Select `Essential Facts`, and in the Format drop-down list, click H3 to style this text as a subheading. (You're skipping H2 and going straight to H3 for this next level of subheadings simply because H2 is usually rendered rather large in browsers.)

5. Place the cursor after the words `per square mile` and press Enter. Notice that Paragraph appears in the Format drop-down list; this block of text is now formatted as a simple paragraph.

Note

> In Dreamweaver MX, there is now a preference which will cause it to revert automatically to paragraph formatting after creating a heading and pressing Enter. This is usually more convenient than having the ensuing line made into a heading as well. To be sure this preference is chosen, go to Edit > Preferences > General and check Switch to Plain Paragraph After Heading.

6. Place the cursor after `State Nickname` and press Enter. Select `State Nickname` and use the Property inspector's Format drop-down list to style it as another H3 heading.

7. Place the cursor after the words `tar their heels` and press Enter.

8. Select the words `The Tar Heel State` and from the menus, choose Text > Style > Strong.

9. With the cursor after `State Motto`, press Enter.

10. Select `State Motto` and again, in the Property inspector, choose H3.

11. With the cursor after the words `rather than to seem`, press Enter. Select the complete quotation—`"To be, rather than to seem"`—and in the Property inspector, on the right side, press the button with the right arrow to wrap this text with `<blockquote>` tags.

12. Place the cursor after `Largest Cities` and press Enter. Select `Largest Cities` and style it as another H3 heading.

13. One at a time, place the cursor after each of the numbers in the last paragraph and press Enter. Then, select all four city names and population count numbers. In the Property inspector, on the right side, click the button that shows bulleted text to format this as an unordered list.

14. Save your work, and if you want to, view the document in your favorite browser by pressing F12 (see Figure 4.11). This is very basic structural formatting; in the next part of this exercise, you try some more advanced text formatting using the Property inspector.

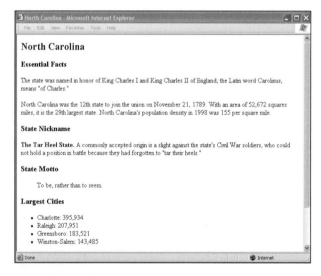

Figure 4.11   Fully formatted page from the first part of Exercise 4.2 as it appears in Internet Explorer.

In the second part of this exercise, you'll add some presentational styling to the document using the Property inspector.

1. With the document from the first part of this exercise, **nc_facts.html**, still open, select the words `North Carolina`. In the Property inspector, from the Fonts drop-down list, choose the combination beginning with Courier New. Then click the color box and choose a nice Carolina blue, such as #3399FF, for this main heading.

2. Select all the text from just below `North Carolina` to the end of the document, and choose the font combination that begins with Verdana.

3. Select each of the H3 subheadings, one by one, and to each one do the following: Using the color palette, make them green (your choice of shades), and then make each italic by clicking the I button.

4. Select the paragraphs of body text under each heading, one by one, and from the Font Size drop-down list, choose 2.

5. Save your document and press F12 to view it in your default browser (see Figure 4.12).

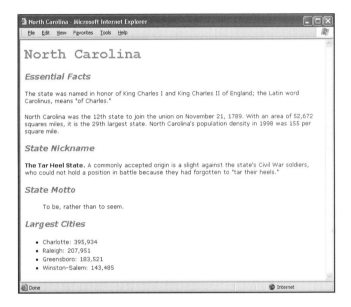

Figure 4.12   Fully formatted page from the second part of Exercise 4.2 as it appears in Internet Explorer.

Text Formatting with the Dreamweaver HTML Styles Feature

If you are working with a large amount of text, it pays to explore options for automating the process.

The following section takes you through the ins and outs of a non-CSS, Dreamweaver-specific way to add automation to your text formatting: HTML Styles.

The Dreamweaver HTML Styles feature works in this way: A user-determined set of specific HTML tags is saved within Dreamweaver and then can be applied to selected text using the HTML Styles panel. This method enables you to quickly re-apply a set of HTML tags anywhere in your site.

It's important to understand, however, that HTML Styles uses no CSS whatsoever, but uses presentational HTML formatting, usually based heavily on the `<font>` tag. As discussed earlier, this type of formatting is not ideal; and in fact, in the HTML 4.0 specification released by the W3C in early 1998, the use of HTML formatting tags is deprecated. However, because it is available to you in Dreamweaver, it is explained here.

In some ways, this feature mimics CSS. However, it is important to be aware of one major difference: If an HTML style is changed or edited, only *future* uses of that HTML style will reflect the changes; past instances of that HTML style will not be updated to reflect those changes. In contrast, CSS styles in a linked style sheet, when updated, instantly update instances of that style sitewide.

Dreamweaver HTML Styles are created by first formatting some text with the Property inspector, then saving this combination as an HTML Style in the HTML Styles panel. Figure 4.13 shows the HTML Styles panel.

Figure 4.13   The HTML Styles panel.

To access the HTML Styles panel, choose Window > HTML Styles.

Create a New HTML Style Based on Existing Text

You can create a new HTML Style from scratch, or based on formatting you have already applied to existing text. To create a new HTML Style based on existing text, follow these steps:

1. If you have some already formatted text you want to use as the basis of the HTML style, select it.

2. Select text that has the HTML formatting you want to use as the basis of your new HTML Style. (You'll need some existing formatted text to create an HTML Style.) In the HTML Styles panel, click the new style icon (the plus [+] button) in the lower-right corner.

3. In the Define HTML Style dialog box, name the style. If you had formatted text selected before you started, its formatting will appear in the dialog box. If not, choose the formatting you want here. You also can adjust the formatting if you like.

4. Determine whether you want to apply the HTML Style to selected text or to entire paragraphs. A *paragraph style* is applied to the entire paragraph in which the insertion point is located, whether or not the text is selected. Determine whether you want the HTML Style applied in addition to, or instead of, any existing formatting, either HTML or in-line CSS.

5. Make selections from the Font Attributes or Paragraph Attributes fields as desired, to alter or add to the style already present in the selection.

6. Click OK to close the dialog box and create the style.

Create a New HTML Style from Scratch

In the HTML Styles panel, click the New Style icon, and proceed in the same manner as when creating a new HTML Style based on existing text, as discussed in the preceding section.

Apply an HTML Style to Text

To apply a paragraph style, place the cursor within the paragraph. To apply a selection style, select the text. Then, follow these steps:

1. In the HTML Styles panel, select the desired style.

2. Apply the style one of two ways, depending on whether the Apply check box at the bottom of the panel is selected:

   - With Apply checked (selected), just click the style once.
   - With Apply unchecked (deselected), click the style and then click Apply.

Edit an HTML Style

To edit an existing HTML Style, follow these steps:

1. In the HTML Styles panel, deselect the Apply check box to turn off the Auto Apply option. (If the Auto Apply option is not turned off, selecting a style will automatically apply that style to text in your document.)

2. In the HTML Styles panel, select a style, and then click the triangle in the upper-right corner of the panel to display the drop-down context menu. Choose Edit. Or, you can double-click the style name.

3. In the Define HTML Style dialog box, edit the style as desired. When you're finished, click OK.

Delete an HTML Style

To remove an HTML Style, follow these steps:

1. In the HTML Styles panel, deselect the Apply check box to turn off the Auto Apply option.

2. Select an HTML Style. Click the Delete Style (trash can) icon in the lower-right corner of the panel.

Note

When using HTML Styles, it is important to understand the difference between a paragraph style and a selection style.

A paragraph style, indicated on the HTML Styles palette with a paragraph symbol, applies that style to the entire paragraph, no matter whether any text is selected. In other words, if your cursor is blinking inside a paragraph, and you click a paragraph style in the HTML Styles palette, the style will be applied.

A selection style can be applied only if text is selected. A selection style is indicated in the HTML Styles palette by a lowercase a with a line beneath it (<u>a</u>).

Special Characters

When working with text, you will no doubt encounter a need for special characters such as accented letters, copyright symbols, or the angle brackets used to enclose HTML elements. To use such characters in an HTML document, they must be represented in the HTML by special codes that take the form &*code*, in which *code* is a word or numeric code indicating the actual character you need to display onscreen.

There are hundreds of special characters; this discussion focuses on the set provided by Dreamweaver.

How to Use Special Characters

To add a special character to your document in Dreamweaver, follow these steps:

1. On the Insert bar, choose the Characters tab (see Figure 4.14).

2. The Insert bar then offers you a series of icons that represent some of the most commonly used special characters. Click the character you want to use and it will appear in your text. If you switch to HTML Code view, you can see the code as it appears in the text.

An alternative method is to choose Insert > Special Characters from the Dreamweaver main menu.

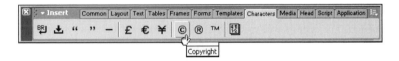

Figure 4.14   Inserting special characters with the Insert bar.

If the special character you need is not listed, click the Insert Other Character icon, also located in the Insert bar, adjacent to the TM icon (see Figure 4.14). You also can use the Insert pull-down menu from the main menu bar and select Special Characters > Other.

This option results in a new window from which you can choose a special character (see Figure 4.15). When you click a character icon, it will appear in the text field box at the top of the window. You also can type your own special character code into the box.

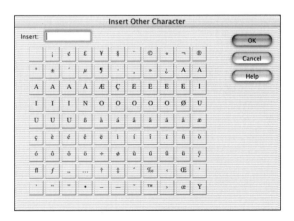

Figure 4.15   The Insert Other Character dialog box.

Tip

You might find yourself using a special character frequently that isn't included with the set provided in the Insert bar. Adding a special character to the Insert bar is not difficult and is covered in Chapter 36, "Creating Extensions."

Using Images as Text

HTML text is one of the "lightest" components of any web site; a page can contain more than 5,000 words and still "weigh" only 40 KB. Text also flows easily with differences in the size of the browser window, and can be edited very quickly. Because of these major advantages of text over images, it is almost always best to use straight HTML text whenever possible, instead of using images containing text.

Exceptions apply, however. As discussed earlier in this chapter, HTML text can display only in a font face installed on the user's computer; this greatly limits the designer's options with regard to typefaces. This is usually acceptable for body text, where fancier typefaces are usually a detriment anyway. For titles and headings, however, it is sometimes desirable to use an unusual typeface. GIF and JPEG images and Flash text enable you to achieve this, and merit a mention here.

Using Images for Titles

With a graphics program such as Fireworks, it is a fairly simple matter to create an image containing text in any font face installed on your computer. Of course, almost limitless choices of size and color are available, as well as special effects such as drop shadows and bevels. This type of graphic can usually be saved as a GIF file with a fairly small file size, and can easily be added to a Dreamweaver document using the Image object found on the Common tab of the Insert bar.

Flash Text

The Dreamweaver Flash Text object enables you create and insert a Flash movie that contains text only. This enables you to create a small, vector-graphic movie with the designer fonts and the text of your choice (see Figure 4.16).

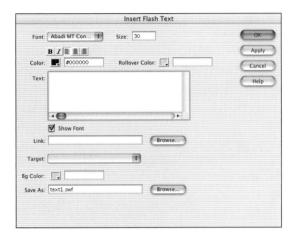

Figure 4.16   The Insert Flash Text dialog box.

In addition to their small file size, a major advantage of using the Flash Text object over a GIF or JPEG image is that the Flash Text object enables you to provide a mouseover effect without using multiple images, as is necessary with ordinary graphic rollovers.

A potential disadvantage to using Flash for titles and other text is that visitors must have the Flash Player plugin installed in their browser to see it.

For a full discussion of Flash text, see Chapter 20, "Building Web Pages with Flash." For a discussion of plugin issues, see Chapter 19, "Plugins, ActiveX, and Java."

Working with Dynamic Text Elements

Dynamic text elements are the contents of database fields, placed in your page as text. Prices, names of things, and descriptions are all good candidates to be inserted as text elements. Depending on how much text the database field contains, the dynamic element can be as short as a few letters or words, or as long as several paragraphs. Dynamic text elements all appear as placeholders in Design view:

```
(Recordset1.category)
```

Or in Code view:

```
<%=(Recordset1.Fields.Item("category").Value)%>
```

Remember, the placeholder is not an indication of how much room the actual text will take up.

continues ▶

Inserting Dynamic Text

The simplest way to insert dynamic text into a document is to drag a recordset field from the Bindings panel into the Document window, wherever you want your text to appear (see Figure 4.17). After the text is in place, the Server Behaviors panel will show that a new Dynamic Element behavior has been added to the document.

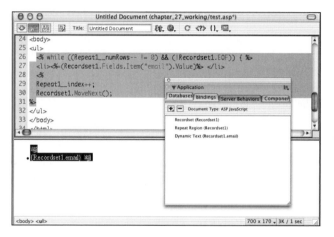

Figure 4.17   Dynamic text, formatted as a list item and set to be a repeating region.

Formatting Dynamic Text

Any formatting you would normally apply to text, you can apply to the place-holder for dynamic text. Just select it and use the Property inspector or CSS panel as you normally would. If you look at your page in Code view, you'll see that the formatting code is wrapped around the placeholder code—like this:

```
<h1><%=(Recordset1.Fields.Item("category").Value)%></h1>
```

Applying Prefab Formatting

You can tell Dreamweaver to build certain formatting instructions into the page code—things like adding dollar signs or other currency symbols to numbers, displaying numbers with only a set number of decimal points, applying capitalization to text, and so forth. Do this:

1. Insert some dynamic text.

2. In the Server Behaviors panel, find the behavior that corresponds to the text you want to format.

Tip

When you select a placeholder in Design view, the behavior responsible for creating that item should highlight in the Server Behaviors panel.

3. Double-click the server behavior to edit it.

4. In the dialog box that appears, choose your desired formatting from the pop-up Format list. When you're done, click OK.

Interspersing Dynamic Text with Regular Text

You can mix and match dynamic text placeholders and actual text any way you like. Two placeholders can be placed in subsequent paragraphs, or separated only by a space, or right next to each other—whatever you need.

This code:

```
The lovely <%=(Recordset1.Fields.Item("category").Value)%> in our
jewelry collection are from known artists. The current page shows
<%=(Recordset1.Fields.Item("artistname").Value)%>'s most prized
works.
```

Will generate HTML like this:

```
The lovely bracelets in our jewelry collection are from known
artists. The current page shows Duncan Smith's most prized works.
```

Using Text Chunks as Repeated Regions

Any chunk of HTML code—including individual words, lines, and list items—can be turned into repeating regions that will display multiple records from a database. To turn a piece of text into a repeating region, simply select it and, from the Server Behaviors panel, choose Repeat Region.

Warning

Make sure you have selected carefully, so you're repeating exactly the code you want—this might mean working in Code and Design view so you can see the HTML source as you work. To repeat a list item, for instance, you want to make sure the opening and closing <li> tags are both selected, but not the <ul> or <ol> tags around them.

Summary

Text is a critical aspect of any good web site, and Dreamweaver provides many excellent tools for incorporating and manipulating text. This chapter discussed the various ways to bring text into a Dreamweaver document, the difference between structural and presentational markup, the importance of Cascading Style Sheets, and the features Dreamweaver offers to make styling text with presentational HTML markup easy.

Chapter 5

Working with Images

Graphic images provide much of the artistry and visual appeal of the web. Used with care and imagination, images can add sparkle and charm; used without discretion, they can slow download times to a crawl and cause more annoyance than enjoyment. Understanding graphics and being able to manipulate them on web pages is critical to a web designer's success.

This chapter examines web image formats, and discusses how to insert graphics into a web document and set their attributes using Dreamweaver. You will learn about the use of the Dreamweaver Assets panel, and then delve into some special uses for images: background images, sliced images, image maps, and single-pixel GIFs. This chapter ends by showing you how to easily create a web photo album with Dreamweaver.

Images and the Web

Images destined for use on the web need to be planned and handled much differently than print-media graphics, and a grounding in the basics of these distinctions is important for the web developer.

Supported File Formats

Web browsers currently support two types of graphic file formats, GIF and JPEG, with a third, PNG, beginning to gain support. Although all three graphic types are compressed, they each compress the graphic data differently.

GIF

The most commonly used kind of image on the web is the *GIF* (Graphics Interchange Format), which has a file extension of .gif. There are two basic types of GIFs: GIF87 and GIF889a. For the purposes of this book, only the more modern 89a form is discussed. The GIF format is 8-bit, allowing only 256 colors per image. GIF compression is based on compressing contiguous pixels of the same color.

GIFs compress data by restricting the number of colors used in the image to 256 or less. Therefore, GIFs are best suited for line art and other illustrations with limited color palettes and areas of solid color. These graphics can be converted into GIF format without loss of image quality, and the resulting file size is almost always smaller than the same image would be in JPEG format (see Figure 5.1).

Figure 5.1   The GIF format is ideal for illustrations consisting mostly of areas of solid color.

GIFs are not usually a good choice for photographs or photographic-style imagery, which are best handled with the JPEG format discussed in the next section.

GIF images have several useful features, including the following:

- **Transparency.** One color of a GIF can be set to be transparent so that the background of the page in which it appears shows through. This makes a variety of interesting effects possible (see Figure 5.2).

Figure 5.2   Transparency allows graphics to look as if they are other than rectangular in shape.

Tip

When a GIF with a transparent background is planned for use on a page with a colored background (blue, for example), you need to take special measures because of the way anti-aliasing affects the edges between an image and its background color.

It's best to proceed this way: Within the graphics program, change the background of the image to the exact color of the page where it will be used. This causes the pixels of color that smooth the transition from the edge of the graphic to the background to blend with the blue. Then make the blue background transparent.

- **Interlacing.** This feature allows an image to load in a Venetian-blind fashion rather than in the typical manner, from top to bottom, one line at a time. Interlacing enables a user to get an idea of what a graphic looks like before the entire file has loaded.

- **Animation.** Animation, which is supported by the GIF89a format, allows a single GIF to contain a series of GIF images. These individual GIF images serve as the individual frames of the animated GIF. These animations can be built so that one image displays after another, like a paper flipbook. It also allows timing and looping information to be added. GIF animations are popular on the web, although the designer must be careful not to allow them to become too large in file size, or to annoy the visitor with jerky or repetitive motion.

Note

GIF images use the LZW (Lempel-Ziv-Welch) compression scheme (patent held by Unisys). There has been concern that payment would be required for the use of this proprietary scheme, but this concern has not been substantiated. Still, in part due to this potential problem, the PNG format described later in this chapter is being positioned to take the place of the GIF format.

JPEG

The second most common web image format is *JPEG*, an acronym for Joint Photographic Experts Group, which was the name of the committee that wrote the standard. JPEGs usually have a file extension of .jpg or .jpeg, and are a format designed for compressing photographic images that might contain thousands, or even millions, of colors and shades of gray. JPEGs store high-quality photographic images in significantly smaller files than GIFs, reducing download time over the Internet.

Unlike GIFs, JPEGs are not well suited to illustrations or text. When illustrations are saved in JPEG format, they might acquire extraneous information, sometimes in the form of unsightly dots known as *artifacts* (see Figure 5.3). However, JPEGs are ideal for photographs or photographic-type images. However, JPEGs are idea for photographs or photographic-type images.

Figure 5.3   When illustrations are saved in JPEG format, they can acquire unsightly dots known as *artifacts*.

JPEGs do not support transparency or animation; for these effects, GIFs must be used. JPEG images do allow a kind of interlacing in a format known as the *progressive JPEG*. Progressive JPEGs fade onto the screen from a low to a high resolution, starting out fuzzy and becoming more and more clear. Like interlaced GIFs, progressive JPEGs tend to be a little larger in file size than their nonprogressive equivalents.

PNG

PNG stands for Portable Network Graphics. The PNG format has comparable features to the GIF89a, and a few more. PNGs feature greater color depth support, color and gamma correction, and 8-bit transparency (useful for anti-aliased edges, translucent drop shadows, and so on). Especially notable is the fact that the compression algorithm for PNG is not proprietary, which makes PNG likely to take the place of GIF. No 4.x-generation browser supports PNG well enough to rely on it, so web developers would be wise to avoid this format until the browser support improves.

Images and Bandwidth Considerations

Bandwidth is the amount of data that can be transmitted across a link on the Internet in a certain length of time, often measured in bits per second (bps), kilobits per second (Kbps), or megabits per second (Mbps). Although high-speed connections are becoming steadily more common with the increasing availability of Cable Internet and DSL (Digital Subscriber Line) service, many web users still depend on slow dial-up connections. Frustration over slow-loading web pages is almost universal. A web site developer who keeps this in mind and makes every effort to produce fast-loading pages will find that his creations are much more popular than sites with a longer load time.

Graphics are the primary culprit in this problem, and so the web designer's effort to provide quick-loading pages needs to focus on reducing the total file size of graphics on each page. Because graphics can deliver such a powerful visual impact, it's easy to get carried away with using them, but some restraint is definitely in order.

Some basic strategies for reducing a page's total file size include the following:

- Eliminate all unnecessary images.
- Reduce the number of colors in GIF images. Reducing the bit depth of a GIF from 8 bits (256 colors) to 5 bits (32 colors) can significantly reduce the file's byte count.
- Use the right kind of compression format for each image. GIFs are almost always better for illustrations and JPEGs for photographs.
- When using JPEGs, increase the degree of compression as far as possible while not sacrificing too much image quality.

Images and Accessibility Issues

Web site developers need to be aware that the target audience for most web sites includes those people with visual impairments. Currently, the web's most serious accessibility problems are related to blind- and sight-impaired users, simply because most web pages are so visual.

A number of considerations must be remembered when building handicapped-accessible web sites; a good resource for learning more can be found at http://www.cast.org/bobby, a web site maintained by the Center for Applied Special

Technology (CAST). This site provides information, links, and a free service to help web page authors identify and repair significant barriers to access by individuals with disabilities.

The use of images is one of the areas in which web designers stray the furthest from providing accessible web pages, and so this usage deserves a special mention. The following list enumerates some of the most important considerations with regard to web graphics and accessibility:

- Images should always include `alt` attributes. This code provides an alternative way to "display" your images to people who can't see them. Ideally, an `alt` attribute verbalizes the meaning or role of the image, describing what the image is intended to communicate and what will happen if it is clicked. `alt` text should be brief and to the point, and can be added to an image tag in Dreamweaver easily using the Property inspector.

- Text colors and backgrounds can contribute to legibility, or can make reading your text almost impossible. Be sure that your color combinations have enough contrast and that they aren't unreadable for red-green colorblind users. Busy background patterns are often annoying to normally sighted visitors and can cause your page to be useless to a partially sighted user.

- Image maps should use `alt` attributes for each area's link option.

 Dreamweaver MX offers some helpful new options for making sure that web pages are as handicapped-accessible as possible. One of these is a user preference which, when turned on, causes Dreamweaver to prompt you to include certain attributes when you are inserting an image. This preference can be turned on by choosing Edit > Preferences > Accessibility, and checking Show Attributes When Inserting Images.

When this preference is set, and you use Dreamweaver's Insert bar or Insert > Image menu command and select an image to insert, the Image Tag Accessibility Attributes dialog box opens, as shown in Figure 5.4.

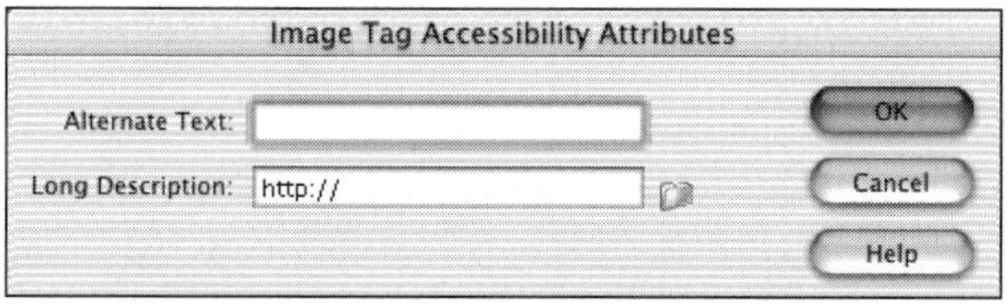

Figure 5.4 The Image Tag Accessibility Attributes dialog box.

Here you can specify an `alt` attribute for the image as well as a `longdesc` attribute. The `longdesc` attribute's value can be any URL; its purpose is to further describe and identify the image verbally.

Note

Using Dreamweaver's Site Reports, you can check to be sure you have included `alt` attributes in all your `<img>` tags. To run the report, choose Site > Reports. From the drop-down menu at the top of the Reports dialog box, choose which documents you wish to check. Check the box Missing ALT Text, and click Run. Dreamweaver will run the check and display its findings in the Results panel.

Note

Search engines are essentially like blind users; many of the techniques you employ to accommodate the visually impaired also make it possible for search engine spiders to navigate your site and index your content without being able to "see" the images. See Chapter 7, "Utilizing Head Content," for more on maximizing your pages' searchability.

Designing with Images

Certain essentials with regard to the use of images usually become part of the Dreamweaver web developer's skill set; this section presents some of the ABCs of the effective use of web graphics.

Good Basic Practices

Care in the naming of image files and in organization of image files in your directory structure are good habits worth learning.

File Naming

Much of what enables a beginner to become an intermediate designer, and an intermediate an expert, is the simple ability and willingness to be careful and fastidious in the organizational chores involved in building a web site. The naming of image files is one of these prosaic but crucial practices.

The following are the most important "do's and don'ts" of file naming:

- *Do* make your filenames meaningful. Filenames do not need to be limited to eight characters, and it is often wiser to use complete words than abbreviations, which can be misspelled.

- *Do* use underscores to aid readability. You'll stay more organized with names such as **headshot_fred.jpg** than with **phtofrd.jpg**.

- *Do not* use special characters other than the underscore or hyphen in file names.
- *Do not* use spaces in file names.

Folder Organization

Also critical to a web developer's work is the arrangement of site files in a folder hierarchy that makes sense. It is recommended that, even for the very simplest of sites, a separate folder below the site root be created to hold all the site's image files.

Many developers follow this practice on site after site, even naming the folder the same way every time (often "images" is used) and never have to think twice about where in the site structure a GIF or JPEG is located.

Inserting an Image

You can insert an image in a Dreamweaver document in several ways. With the document insertion point where you want the image to appear, do one of the following:

- On the Insert bar, from the Common tab, click the insert image icon (it looks like a picture of a tiny tree).
- From the main menu, choose Insert > Image.
- Press Ctrl+Alt+I (Windows) or Cmd+Option+I (Mac).

Another way to insert an image is to drag the Insert Image icon from the Insert bar to the point in the document where you want the image to be inserted.

All these methods result in the Select Image Source dialog box being opened (see Figure 5.5).

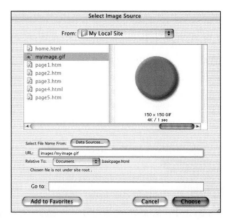

Figure 5.5   The Select Image Source dialog box.

The Select Image Source dialog box enables you to choose an image file from any location on your local system. Browse to the desired image file, and select it. When you have set all necessary options, click OK.

At the bottom of the dialog box is an option that deserves special mention, the Relative To field. When you insert an image into your document, Dreamweaver adds HTML code to the page, which specifies the path to the image; this path gives the browser directions as to how to find the image so that it can be displayed. For files within the site, these directions can be given in two ways: relative to the site's root directory or relative to the document. A *relative to site root path* describes where the file is located in relation to the directory that contains all the site's files, as set in your Dreamweaver Site Definition. An IMG tag with a site-root-relative path looks like this:

```
<img src="/images/clock.jpg">
```

A *relative to document path* describes where the file is located in relation to the HTML file where the image is being added. An `<img>` tag with a document-relative path looks like this:

```
<img src="images/clock.jpg">
```

This setting in Dreamweaver is "sticky"—it will remain on one setting until and unless it is changed. Unless there is a compelling reason to do otherwise, when working in Dreamweaver, it's best to stick with document-relative paths for images, and for all other internal links. See Chapter 6, "Links and Navigation," for more about document-relative, site-root relative, and absolute URLs.

Note

Absolute paths provide the complete URL of the linked document, including the protocol to use (usually `http://` for web pages). For example, `http://www.macromedia.com/support/dreamweaver/contents.html` is an absolute path. You must use an absolute path to link to a document on another server that is not part of your site.

Setting Image Properties

When you insert an image into your document while working in Design view, the image will appear in the Document window, and it will be selected. While the image is selected, take a look at the Property inspector, which provides the opportunity to set a number of different attributes for the image (see Figure 5.6).

Figure 5.6   When an image is selected, the Property inspector allows a number of properties to be set.

Exercise 5.1   Inserting an Image with Wrapped Text

In this exercise, you'll insert an image into a web page and allow text to flow (or *wrap*) around it.

Before you start, copy the **chapter_05** folder on the CD to your hard drive. Define a site called Chapter 5, with this folder as the local root folder.

1. From the **chapter_05** folder on your hard drive, open the file **insert_image**. You'll see that the file displays some strange-looking Latin "filler text."

2. Place the cursor at the beginning of the first paragraph and, on the Common tab of the Insert bar, click the Image icon.

3. In the Select Image Source dialog box, browse to the **images** folder (within the local **chapter_05** folder) and select **zoli.gif**. At the bottom of the dialog box, be sure that the Relative To option is set to Document and click OK. You'll see that the image has been inserted into your document (see Figure 5.7).

Figure 5.7   When an image is first inserted, the default alignment property causes it to sit on its own line.

4. With the image still selected, notice the W and H fields in the Property inspector. Dreamweaver has entered the exact width and height of the image in pixels as attributes of the `<img>` tag. It is best to leave these fields exactly as they are, and to always make any changes to an image's dimensions in a graphics program.

5. With the image still selected, on the Property inspector, from the Align drop-down list, choose Left. The text will flow around the image and continue on below it (see Figure 5.8).

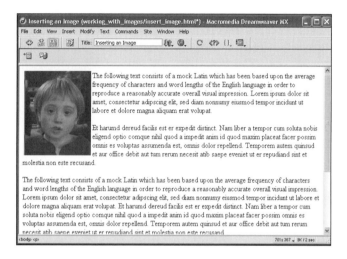

Figure 5.8   When an image is aligned left, it will sit on the left side of the browser window or containing element, and text will flow around it on its right side.

6. With the image still selected, now try setting Align to Right.

7. Return the image to left-aligned, and note that the text comes very close to the edge of the image, both at the graphic's right side, and possibly above and/or below the image, depending on the size of your Dreamweaver Document window and the way the text flows. To give the image more space, select it, and in the Vspace field enter **5**; in the Hspace field, enter **10**. Notice how this gives the image white space of 5 pixels on both the top and bottom and 10 pixels on both the right and left.

8. Select the image again, and in the Property inspector, in the ALT field, type a text string to serve as an alternate to the actual graphic. This is important for those who are browsing the web with images turned off or who are visually impaired. You might use Close-Up Photo of Little Boy.

9. Save your document and choose File > Preview in Browser (or press F12) to view it in a browser. Note what happens when the cursor lingers over the image for a few seconds.

Tip

The various versions of Netscape Navigator 4 are infamous for their problematic renderings of HTML pages. One such "bug" sometimes occurs when images are right- or left-aligned and text needs to flow around them. In certain circumstances, Netscape 4 allows the text to accommodate the image, but the text will not return to flowing across the full screen (or container) after it gets past the bottom edge of the image. A workaround for this problem is to use double line-break tags (

) to separate paragraphs.

Positioning Images Using Tables

Using tables to position page elements is covered in detail in Chapter 10, "Using Dreamweaver's Page Layout Aids." This section briefly touches on the usefulness of tables for aligning images on an HTML page. The following exercise provides a good example of an application of this technique.

Exercise 5.2   Positioning Images Using Tables

In this exercise, you'll arrange several images on a page, using HTML tables to position them.

If you haven't done so yet, copy the **chapter_05** folder on the CD to your hard drive. Define a site called Chapter 5, with this folder as the local root folder.

1. Open a new blank document and name it **acme_widgets.html**.

2. Pull down the Modify menu and choose Page Properties. In each of the fields Left Margin, Top Margin, Margin Width, and Margin Height, place a **0**. This tells the browser not to maintain the usual default margins on the top and left side.

3. In the Common tab of the Insert bar, click the Insert Table icon (it looks like a little gray 3×2 table). In the Insert Table dialog box that opens, specify these attributes:

   - Rows: 1
   - Columns: 2
   - Width: 100%
   - Border: 0
   - Cell Padding: 0
   - Cell Spacing: 0

4. Click OK to insert the table into the document (see Figure 5.9).

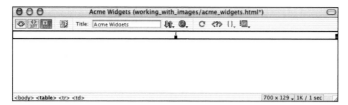

Figure 5.9   A table as it looks upon first being inserted in the Dreamweaver Document window.

5. The table has two columns, each consisting of one cell. Place the insertion point in the left cell. Click the Insert Image icon, browse to the **images** folder (within the **chapter_05** folder), choose **header_left.gif**, and click OK. Relative To should have remained set to Document and should not need to be reset (see Figure 5.10).

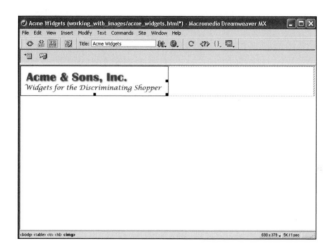

Figure 5.10   The exercise page with just the left graphic inserted.

6. Place the cursor just to the right of the image you've inserted and press Tab; this moves the insertion point into the right table cell, which can be hard to do otherwise. Now click the Insert Image icon again, browse to **header_right.gif**, and insert it (see Figure 5.11).

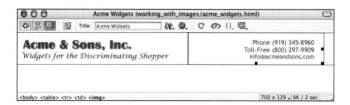

Figure 5.11   The second image won't sit on the far right where it belongs until the table cell alignment is set.

7. The goal is to force the second image to the right side of the browser window. To accomplish this, put the insertion point anywhere in the right cell. In the tag selector at the bottom left of the Document window, click the rightmost `<td>` tag to select the table cell in which you've just inserted the second graphic image. In the Property inspector, in the Horz drop-down list, choose Right. This aligns all the content in that table cell to the right.

8. Save your document and press F12 to view it in your primary browser. Try resizing your browser window—drag the edges to make it narrower and then wider. Because of the way it has been made in two parts and inserted into a 100%-width table, the header you've created stretches and shrinks to accommodate the size of the browser window (see Figure 5.12).

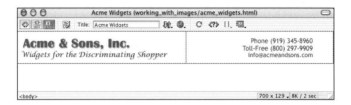

Figure 5.12   Exercise 5.2 as it should look when completed.

Note

Setting an image's alignment, as you did in the first exercise in this chapter, tells the browser where to put the image in relation to the text around it. Setting a table cell's alignment tells the browser where to align any content contained within the table cell. Because no text is involved in this second exercise, using table cell alignment was used, although setting the image alignment would have the same effect.

Tip

The tag selector is one of the easiest ways to select an HTML element. The tag selector shows the tags that contain the current selection or insertion point. The tags display from left to right in order of the outermost tag to the innermost tag. Selecting a tag in the tag selector activates the appropriate Property inspector for that element.

Linking Images

Images can be used as hyperlinks, and images are frequently used as graphic buttons. Making a single image into a link is quite simple with Dreamweaver. Just follow these steps:

1. Select the image.

2. Toward the middle of the Property inspector, click the yellow browse-for-file button next to the empty Link field and choose the file you want to link to.

Alternatively, just type the URL into the Link field (see Figure 5.13).

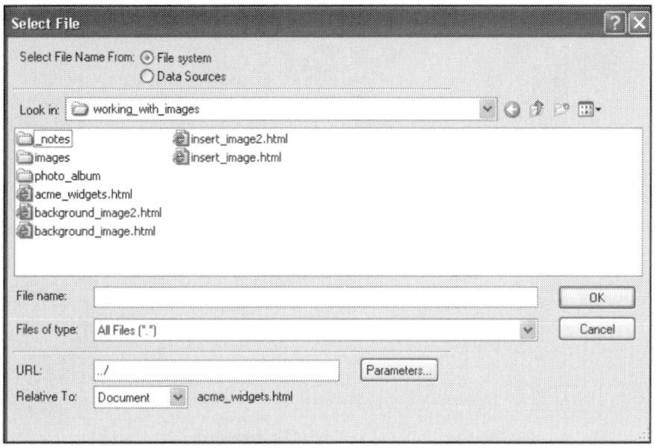

Figure 5.13   The Select File dialog box.

Adding a link to an image encloses the <img> tag in <a> tags, as in this example:

```
<a href="acme_widgets.html"><img src="images/zoli.jpg" width="150"
height="184" border="0"></a>
```

Normally, a browser will display a hyperlinked image by putting a border around the image in the same color as a colored text link. This was useful in the early days of the web to indicate that an image was a link. Many web developers feel this visual cue is not necessary any longer because there are other signs that an image is a link (primarily, the "little hand" mouse-pointer). To remove this border, just select the image, and enter **0** in the Border field in the Property inspector.

The possibilities for using images as links go much further. Image maps are discussed briefly later in this chapter, and are covered more thoroughly in Chapter 6. You also read about rollover buttons in Chapter 6 as well as in Chapter 16, "Getting Interactive with Behaviors."

Using the Dreamweaver Assets Panel with Images

The Dreamweaver Assets panel provides a useful way to organize and reuse elements within a particular site, and is covered in Chapter 22, "Local Site Management."

One of the nine asset categories is Images. When working on an active document within a given site, the Assets panel will display a complete list of all GIF, JPEG, and PNG files used in the site (see Figure 5.14).

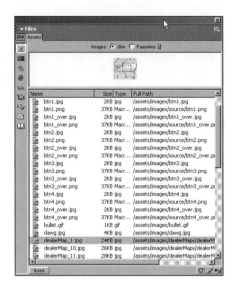

Figure 5.14   When the Images category is selected, the Assets panel will display a list of all image files used in the site.

As with the other types of elements included in the Assets panel, images can be previewed, inserted directly into a document, opened in an external editor, or copied to another site.

Note

You must define a site before you can use the Assets panel; see Chapter 22.

Tip

When a site has a large number of images, certain images that will be used repeatedly can be added to the Assets panel's Favorites list. Images included in the Favorites list are easier to locate and can be managed in several ways that ordinary assets can't.

Interview: Marion Kaltenschnee

Business Name: Kaltenschnee Webdesign

URL: www.kaltenschnee.de

How did you get started in Web design? What has your learning process been like? What kind of work are you currently doing?

I bought my first computer in 1986. My computer's OS was on a DD floppy disk (the very same floppy disk that also held my entire thesis of 150 pages). That's not how I got into web design, but that's how I got into working with computers. My friends considered this a cold and calculating act. However, I was sick of writing papers on my electric typewriter. Wasting paper and time typing stuff over and over again and yet never being able to deliver a beautiful clean copy.

Ever since then, I worked with computers. Over the years, I worked with scheduling programs, graphic programs, databases, charting programs…yet…nothing fulfilled me. Then, I read about HTML and coded a page with horizontal rules and <h1> headers in Notepad. I was hooked. I was also five months pregnant and had to move across Canada. Couldn't find a job. So I learned HTML. Recently, I started learning ColdFusion.

Everything I know, I learned by trial and error, which took a long time. In retrospect, it would have been more efficient to take courses or to start reading books much earlier, but in a way, this was a long intensive road of discovery that helped me ripen as a web designer. I am doing freelance work for small businesses.

What hardware and software do you use in your work?

Single-sided ideology is not my thing. I prefer Macs, yet own a PC. For software, I use Macromedia Dreamweaver, Fireworks, and Flash, the Corel Suite and Corel Knock-out. For dynamic sites, I use Homesite. When I grow up, I shall upgrade to UltraDev. For dynamic sites, I found myself using a pencil…Is that considered hardware or software? The lead was a 1B.

Tell us a little about the ways you normally work with web graphics.

- Photos. Scanned-in material usually needs some work to better harmonize with the color scheme and style of the web site. Brightness, contrast, intensity, hue, and saturation to say the least. Sometimes, photos need to be retouched heavily: get the photographer's knee out of the picture; cover up those pimples; touch up that fold line from the company's brochure.

- Anything to make the graphic material supplied by the customer more aesthetic. There's a lot of trial and error involved, but you develop an eye what to try.

- Vector graphics. Sometimes, it is more useful to redraw a company logo with a Bezier tool than to scan it in, for example, when working with Flash. Some scanned-in logos can be vectorized using tools like Corel Trace. The result is a smaller, cleaner file that you can manipulate to your heart's content.

When you have had the opportunity to be a little more creative with images, what have you tried? What would you like to experiment with?

It is fun to scan real-life stuff. You can scan in just about anything that is flat or flatten-able. I've scanned in medieval parchment, roses, lavender, peacock feathers, hair, fur, silk, lips, gift wrap, and leaves.

I use bits and pieces of this stuff for lots of things—for example, to make my own patterns or textures for Fireworks.

I'd like to make collages. rich in color, luminescent. And I'd like to learn more about making realistic-looking objects *a la* Japi Honoo.

What trends on the web and in the web designer's work do you see as important?

- **CSS.** Learning all about it is a win-win situation.
- **Flash.** In my opinion, it is overused by people who don't know how to use it but customers want it.
- **XML/XHTML.**

What advice would you give to someone just starting out in Web design?

- Keep your daytime job (at first).
- Be tolerant and generous. Helping others helps you learn and makes the world a better place.
- Don't forget there's a whole wide natural world out there.

Special Uses for Images

Going beyond simple inline images opens the door to techniques that allow for a great deal more variety and complexity; this section reviews some of the most popular and more advanced web graphic techniques.

Background Images

Since the early days of the web, images have been used as page backgrounds, with results ranging from subtle and artistic to garish and distracting. Used with discretion, background images can add distinctive visual effects to a web page.

HTML provides the ability to associate an image with the background of a document by using the BACKGROUND attribute of the <body> tag:

```
<body background="bluegreen.gif">
```

This attribute will cause a browser to load the file **bluegreen.gif** and then "tile" it in the document background, repeating it in both the horizontal and vertical directions to fill the entire document (see Figure 5.15).

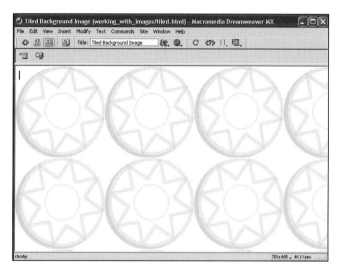

Figure 5.15   A tiled background.

Cascading Style Sheets also enable you to specify an image as a background, but allow a whole lot more flexibility and control, enabling you to create varied and interesting effects.

Refer to Chapter 13, "Using Cascading Style Sheets," for a fuller explanation of the process of writing style sheets with Dreamweaver. This chapter just goes over some of the effects possible with CSS background images.

The examples use a document-wide (internal) style sheet, but the style declarations discussed also can be included in a linked (external) style sheet. It is important to note as well that not every CSS property is supported by every browser. This chapter sticks mostly to widely supported styles, but testing in all the target browsers is always necessary.

Tip

With CSS, a background image can be applied to any element, whether block-level or inline, including paragraphs, headings, anchors, tables, table cells, and so on.

Tip

A background image can be applied to an HTML element either by redefining the element, or by applying a custom class to a particular instance of the element on the page.

The possibilities for background images with CSS are almost limitless. Table 5.1 shows some of the potential options.

Table 5.1   CSS Background Image Properties

CSS Property	Use
background-image	For specifying an image file URL to be used as a background image.
background-repeat	For determining whether an image is to be repeated horizontally, vertically, in both directions, or not at all.
background-position	For specifying where the image should be positioned in relation to the element to which it is applied.
background-attachment	For declaring a background image as fixed with respect to the viewing area, and thus unchanged by the effects of scrolling.

Exercise 5.3 walks you through experimenting with some CSS background image possibilities.

Exercise 5.3   Using Background Images

In this exercise, you'll explore some of the different ways that CSS can be used to position background images.

If you haven't done so yet, copy the **chapter_05** folder on the CD to your hard drive. Define a site called Chapter 5, with this folder as the local root folder.

1. Open the document **background_image.html**.

2. Open the CSS Styles panel by clicking its icon on the Mini-Launcher at the bottom of the Document window, or by pulling down the Window menu and choosing CSS Styles.

3. Click the New CSS Style icon at the bottom of the CSS Styles panel, as shown in Figure 5.16.

Figure 5.16   Click the New CSS Style icon to open the New CSS Style dialog box, as shown in Figure 5.17.

Figure 5.17   The New CSS Style dialog box.

4. Next to Type, select Redefine HTML Tag. From the drop-down list next to Tag, select Body. Next to Define In, select This Document Only. You've just told Dreamweaver that you want to redefine the <body> tag in a document-wide style sheet.

5. Click OK. This opens the CSS Style Definition for Body dialog box. On the left side of this box, you'll see a list of categories; choose Background (see Figure 5.18).

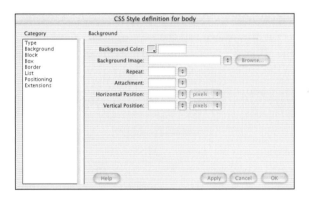

Figure 5.18   The CSS Style Definition for Body dialog box.

6. Click the Browse button next to the Background Image field and browse to the **chapter_05/images** folder, and choose **star_small.gif**. Click OK, and in the next box, click Done.

7. In the Dreamweaver Document window, the image appears as a background to the page, and is tiled in both directions to fill the viewing area. Although the Dreamweaver Document window displays many CSS styles, it doesn't display all of them, and it's important to preview CSS-styled pages with actual browsers. Use F12 and Control+F12 (Windows) or Cmd+F12 (Mac) to view this page in your default preview browsers for the remainder of this exercise (see Figure 5.19). (Default browsers for previewing in Dreamweaver are set up in Edit > Preferences > Preview in Browser.) It's best to close the browser window used to preview after each use.

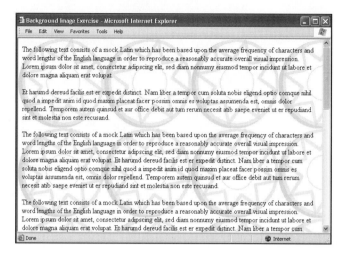

Figure 5.19   The exercise document at Step 8, shown in the browser window.

8. Now return to the Document window, and in the CSS Styles panel, select the radio button for Edit Styles. The left-hand pane of the panel should now list Body. Double-click the word Body, and choose the Background category.

9. From the Repeat drop-down list, choose no-repeat. Click OK and Done, and preview in the actual browser again. You'll see that the star image now appears only once, in the upper-left corner (see Figure 5.20).

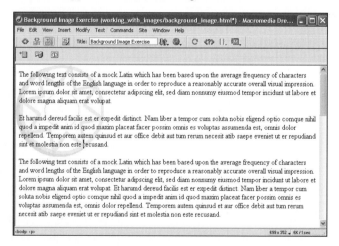

Figure 5.20   The no-repeat value for the property background-repeat keeps the image from tiling.

10. Repeat step 9. This time, choose Center as the horizontal position and Center as the Vertical position. Click OK and Done. Preview with the browser (see Figure 5.21). Here, the image is centered vertically and horizontally in the <body> of the document. Remember, it is important to preview your document in an actual browser, because Dreamweaver's Document window provides only an approximation of the actual result in a browser, and does not support all CSS styles.

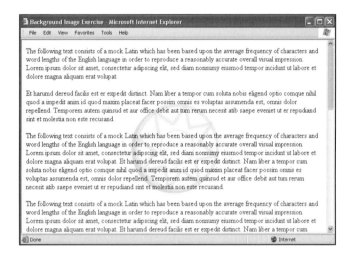

Figure 5.21   The background-position property enables you to specify the location of the image within the element.

11. Repeat step 9. Now choose Attachment: Fixed, click OK and Done, and preview with the browser. Use the right scrollbar, and notice the fixed position of the background image. Note that this property is *not* supported by Netscape 4 series browsers.

12. Once more, repeat step 9. This time, choose Repeat: repeat-Y. Click OK and Done and preview with the actual browser. You'll see that the image repeats along the horizontal axis of the page (see Figure 5.22).

13. Try using an image of your own, perhaps a much larger or much smaller one (images with subtle color and low contrast are best for backgrounds) and experiment with the different options. Remember that a background image can be applied to elements other than the <body> tag as well; you might try adding a table and applying a background to one of its cells. The possibilities can be very stimulating to the designer's creative abilities!

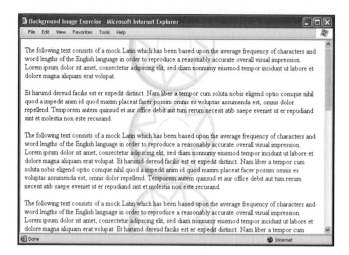

Figure 5.22   The `repeat-Y` value for the `background-repeat` property causes the image to tile along the horizontal axis only.

Sliced Images

Many of the best web sites make use of image slices and tables. An *image slice* is a portion of a larger image, like a puzzle piece, except that image slices are always rectangular. When image slices are arranged in the same table, and the Cell Spacing and Cell Padding are set to O, the layout design is seamless and no one can tell that you are actually using a set of chopped-up images.

Note

Tables without set dimensions behave like "shrink wrap," closing in tightly around whatever they contain.

Fireworks includes a variety of tools for making image slices and for exporting the slices as a table you can view in Dreamweaver.

After you have sliced your image, you can name and export each slice individually and build the table in Dreamweaver on your own. You can also save the HTML for the table directly from Fireworks.

When your images are sliced and placed seamlessly into a table, select a specific slice and use the Link field on the Property inspector to link it to another file. You also can give each slice its own name and `alt` attribute in the Property inspector. In addition, you can link certain parts of image slices using an image map.

Image Maps

An *image map* is HTML code that designates areas of a graphic image as *hotspots*. Hotspots can have hyperlinks so, in the browser, when a user clicks a hotspot, an action occurs, such as a new page being loaded.

Image maps can be very useful; Chapter 6 covers them in detail.

Single-Pixel GIFs

A *single-pixel GIF* is just what it sounds like: a GIF image consisting of only a single pixel, and usually made transparent. These little units are popular with web designers because they easily solve some common layout problems and contribute to some interesting design possibilities. Two of these uses are described here.

A *single-pixel GIF* can easily be created in any graphics program; just open a new document with the dimensions 1×1 and save (or export) it as a transparent GIF.

Note

Single-pixel GIFs are often referred to as *spacer GIFs* or *shims*.

Single-Pixel GIFs as Spacers

Web browsers will interpret the size of a graphic from the `width` and `height` attributes of the `<img>` tag, and so it is possible to stretch the size of an image. As discussed earlier, it's usually not a good idea to change the `width` and `height` attributes to resize an image in the browser, but the single-pixel GIF is the one exception to this rule. Strategically placed in a page layout, and sized with the desired `width` and `height`, a spacer GIF can help to arrange page elements in the desired positions, while contributing almost nothing to page weight and remaining invisible.

Tip

Single-pixel gifs are tiny, and hard to see in Design view! When inserting a single-pixel GIF, be sure to adjust its height and width before deselecting it—after you've deselected it, it's very hard to find and select it again. If you do lose a single-pixel GIF, select the items around it and go to Code view. somewhere in the selected code, you'll find the `<img>` tag. Change the width and height there.

Single-Pixel GIFs as Rules

An interesting technique involving single-pixel GIFs allows the creation of horizontal or vertical *rules*. Rules are straight lines for separation of page content, or just for decoration. HTML provides a horizontal rule tag, and these beveled gray lines have been seen on the web since its first days; but with tables and GIF spacers, many special effects can be created that are impossible with the <hr> tag.

The technique is based on tables. In its simplest form, a table is created whose only purpose is to create a rule (or perhaps several rules parallel to one another). A transparent single-pixel GIF is inserted into the empty table cell just to prop it open, and the background color of the cell is set to the desired color for the rule. The table is then set to the desired width. When percentage-based tables are used, lines can be built to stretch and shrink to fit the user's browser window size.

Because tables without set dimensions act like shrink wrap, the table cell holding the GIF will close in around it, allowing only a thin line of the cell's background color to show.

In this way, some distinctive visual effects can be created with almost no graphics, and with the ability to flow with a "liquid" page layout.

You also can create vertical rules, although, because of the nature of tables and vertical dimensions, they depend on being placed in one column of a table where an adjacent column holds content that will serve to prop open the cell.

Working with Dynamic Images

Generally, images and other media files are not stored in databases. Rather, the database stores a file name or URL that points to the image. The dynamically generated web page can then contain an <img> tag that uses a database field in the src attribute. Like this:

```
<img src="<%=(Recordset1.Fields.Item("filename").Value)%>">
```

Assuming that the database contains a record with the filename field set to "necklace.gif", the above references would generate code like this:

```
<img src="necklace.gif">
```

To insert a dynamic image (simplest method):

1. In the Insert bar, click the Image object, as you would for any image (see Figure 5.23).

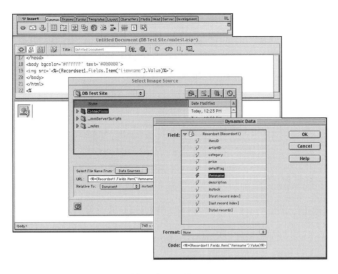

Figure 5.23   Inserting an image with a dynamic source.

2. When the Insert Image dialog box appears, select Data Source instead of
   File System.

3. A list of available fields in the current document's recordset(s) will appear.
   Choose one of these fields and click OK. The image is inserted in the
   document with a placeholder (lightning bolt) icon.

Look in the Server Behaviors panel and you'll see that a new Dynamic Attribute
behavior has been added to the page. The dynamic attribute is your image's `src`.

Assigning Width and Height

Note that, when you insert a dynamic image, Dreamweaver doesn't give it a width
or height. That's because, since the image `src` information has not yet been determined, Dreamweaver doesn't know its dimensions. If you know for certain that all
images referred to in your database will have the same dimensions, and you know
what those dimensions are, you can add the width and height yourself, by entering
them in the image Property inspector. If you're not sure of the dimensions, or if
your images' dimensions might vary, leave these attributes unassigned.

Working with Partial URLs

The database field used to generate the `src` does not have to contain the entire
absolute or relative path to the image. If, for instance, your images will be in an

continues ▶

images subfolder, and the database field called on includes only the filename, you can create the rest of the path as you're placing the dynamic image. In the Insert Image dialog box, after you've chosen the database field to use as the `src`, type the rest of the path information into the URL field, like this (added code is in bold):

```
images/<%=(Recordset1.Fields.Item("filename").Value)%>
```

If you name your images carefully, you can even do away with the `filename` database field entirely. Say your database has a field called `itemname`. You can tweak the code that appears in the URL field when you insert the dynamic image, to look like this (added code in bold):

```
images/<%=(Recordset1.Fields.Item("itemname").Value)%>.gif"
```

Assuming the `itemname` field for one of your collected records contains `necklace`, the generated HTML will look like this:

```
<img src="images/necklace.gif">
```

Making Other Image Properties Dynamic

Any property of an image can be filled in with the value from a database field, assuming the field contains meaningful information relevant to that property. (It's pointless setting the width or height to get their values from a field that might not always contain numbers, for instance.) Other properties you might want to set dynamically include `alt`, `id`, and `lowsrc`. To make other properties of an image dynamic, use the Tag Inspector (see Figure 5.24), like this:

Figure 5.24   Using the Tag Inspector to assign dynamic image properties.

1. Insert the image as described in the previous section.

2. With the image selected, open the Tag Inspector. Make sure the `<img>` tag for the image is highlighted. All properties of the tag will show in the inspector.

3. From the list of properties, find `alt`, `lowsrc`, or whatever property you want to change. Click in the value area next to that property.

4. For some properties, a lightning bolt icon will appear. Click the icon to open a dialog box showing the currently available database fields. Choose one, and that field's value will be assigned to that property.

4. For other properties, a browse/folder icon will appear. Click the folder icon to open a dialog box for choosing a source file. In this dialog box, choose Data Source instead of File System, and a list of database fields will appear. Choose one.

Editing Images: Working with External Editors

Whether you use Macromedia Fireworks or another image editing program, Dreamweaver enables you to specify your choice of external programs so that they can be easily accessed when it is time to work on the graphics needed for a web site.

Using Fireworks with Dreamweaver

Dreamweaver and Fireworks are designed to be used together; and it is easy to work on files interchangeably between the two. Designed to allow a streamlined workflow for editing, optimizing, and placing web graphics in HTML pages, these two programs are an ideal combination for building professional web sites. This subject is covered in detail in the Appendix A, "Using Dreamweaver and Fireworks Together."

Using Other Graphics Programs with Dreamweaver

Dreamweaver MX provides preferences for automatically launching specific applications to edit specific file types. If desired, graphics programs such as Adobe Photoshop, Adobe Illustrator, CorelDRAW, or Paint Shop Pro can be specified as the external editor for images in Dreamweaver. Here's how:

1. In Dreamweaver, choose Edit > Preferences and select File Types/Editors (see Figure 5.25).

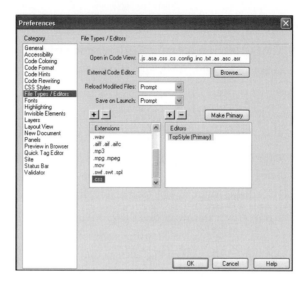

Figure 5.25   The File Types/Editors pane of the Preferences dialog box.

2. In the Extensions list, select a web file extension (.gif, .jpg, or .png).

3. In the Editors list, select the application desired and click Make Primary. If the application doesn't appear in the list, click the plus (+) button just above the Editors field, browse to the application, and double-click it. If the Editors list has more than one application in it, select your chosen application and click Make Primary.

4. Repeat as necessary to set your graphics program as the editor for other web graphics file formats.

With your chosen graphics program set up as the primary editor for a file type, double-clicking a file of that type in the Site panel will open that application.

Summary

Web graphics can do great things for a web page when they're understood and used properly. This chapter covered the basics of the use of images on the web, looking at some of the simple and fancier ways to incorporate them. In upcoming discussions of tables, layers, and frames, you will learn more about the numerous possibilities for arranging images, along with text, on web sites.

Chapter 6

Links and Navigation

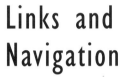

The advent of electronic hyperlinked documents might bring about changes to the way human beings communicate that are almost as profound as the invention of the printing press. The humble hyperlink, enabling the visitor to jump from one document to another or a place within a document, is the foundation for a system of organizing written information that is profoundly different from any other.

It's important to have the skills to place links in a web document and to build navigation bars, image maps, and menus. Even more important, however, is to have an understanding of the way visitors read and navigate web sites and the web at large. Visitors access content on the web for information and to accomplish tasks, and often are surprisingly disinterested in a web site's clever features, especially if those features impede the visitor's quest. A truly effective web site must be built around a well-conceived system of links that enable visitors to find the information they need quickly and easily.

How Links Work in the Browser

Dreamweaver makes it very easy to add links, and even more complex linking systems, to documents; but it's still very important for a web developer to understand what is going on "under the hood" with hyperlinks.

The <a> Tag: Syntax and Usage

Hyperlinks are defined in HTML using the anchor element, <a>. For the purposes of linking, the <a> element requires only one attribute: HREF, for *hypertext reference*. The HREF attribute is set to the URL of the target resource. The text or image enclosed by the <a> tags becomes a spot that, when clicked with the cursor, activates the link. Here is an example of the HTML code for a simple hyperlink:

```
<a HREF="http://www.nytimes.com">Read the New York Times on the web</a>
```

When a web browser is displaying the HTML page containing this code, the text that has been marked as *hot* (a clickable link) is marked in some way so that it is clearly distinguishable from ordinary text. In most browsers, hypertext is rendered underlined and with a bright blue color; after being visited, the same link usually is rendered in purple (see Figure 6.1). An image with a hyperlink might be displayed with a border in the same link color, although designers frequently set an image border to not display at all. The cursor usually changes to show that it is hovering over a link, and information on the link might show in the browser window's status bar.

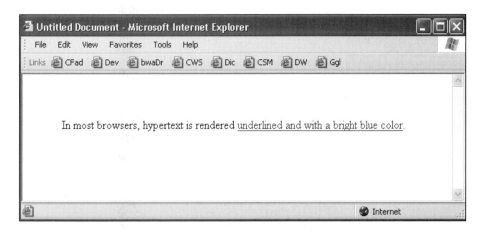

Figure 6.1   By default, link text is usually displayed by browsers underlined and colored blue.

Although underlined blue text (and images with blue borders) represented hyperlinks for many years, conventions have been changing gradually but steadily. The appearance of links is discussed in more detail a little later in this section.

Absolute Versus Relative Paths

A *URL*, or web address, is essentially a pointer to a given document or object located on the Internet, and this pointer is given as a path describing how to get to the document; however, several distinct types of paths exist.

An analogy to a real-world situation might help explain the differences. Imagine that you're a college basketball fan and want to go and see the UNC Tar Heels play tonight at the Dean Dome in Chapel Hill, North Carolina, where you've just relocated. So you send emails to three different friends, asking for directions, hoping that at least one will reply in time for you to get to the game.

To your surprise, all three friends reply right away, and interestingly, they give you three slightly different sets of directions.

Friend number one (who is a little eccentric) gives you directions similar to an *absolute path*. He says, "On planet Earth, in the United States of America, in North Carolina, in the town of Chapel Hill, on Manning Drive, you'll find the Dean Dome."

Friend number two has been to visit you and knows exactly where you live, and so gives you directions very much like a *document-relative path*: "Pull out of your driveway and make a right on Weaver Dairy Road, and then make another right onto Erwin. At the stoplight, go right onto 15-501; take it all the way to Manning Drive. Make a right on Manning, and the Dean Dome will be on your left."

Your third friend doesn't know where you live, and so gives you directions from a common point you both know, and her directions are somewhat like a *site-relative path*. She writes: "From Franklin Street downtown, go south into Carrboro. Make a left on Greensboro, and take it all the way down to 15-501. Get on 15-501 going north, and make a left onto Manning Drive, where you'll find the Dean Dome."

Table 6.1 shows a link to the same document written in three different forms.

Table 6.1   A Link to the Same Document Shown as Each of the Three Types of URL Paths

URL Path Type	Link
Absolute	`http://www.acmewidgets.com/retail/products.html`
Document-Relative	`../products.html`
Root-Relative	`/retail/products.html`

Absolute URLs

An *absolute URL* is one that spells out the complete information about the document's location on the Internet and how it is to be retrieved, including its protocol, host, directory, and filename. An absolute URL looks like the following:

`http://www.carolinawebsolutions.com/portfolio.html`

When creating links, you can use an absolute URL even for documents that are part of the local web site, and the requested document will be retrieved. However, using absolute paths forces the visitor through the front door of the web site after clicking each link. To compare with the directions analogy, taking literally the directions provided by your first friend, you would have to first consider where Earth is, then where the United States is, and where North Carolina is, before you could even start navigating your way around Chapel Hill. Using absolute URLs for local documents significantly increases the burden on the server and the time it takes to load the page, and so relative paths are preferable in this situation.

Tip

When creating HTML documents to be sent as email, it is necessary to use absolute URLs for all image references and hyperlinks. The email program on the individual's local computer will display the HTML file that comprises the email message, and the image files will be called from their location on a remote server and displayed along with the email message. Similarly, any hyperlinks must be absolute URLs because they refer to files residing on remote servers. (See Chapter 7, "Utilizing Head Content," for a discussion of using <base> to help specify links in HTML email.)

Relative Paths

A *relative path* is a shortened form, in which various parts of the address—the protocol, site address, and directory—might be inferred from other information available. There are two types of relative URLs, discussed in the following sections.

Document-Relative Paths

A *document-relative path* provides the path from the document where the link is being written to the destination document. Document-relative links must be used between documents located in the same site root. If the two documents are in the same directory, the path can be as simple as this:

```
portfolio.html
```

A link to a file in a directory below (within) the current directory would look like this:

```
webdesign/portfolio.html
```

A link to a file in a directory above (containing) the current directory would take this form:

```
../portfolio.html
```

And a link to a file two directories above the current directory would be written this way:

```
../../portfolio.html
```

Note

If you want to preview your pages locally inside a browser and without a web server, you must use document-relative paths. Why? Because web browsers cannot understand what local root folder you are using, so the only paths that can be followed are relative to the document currently being viewed.

Root-Relative URLs

If you are working on a large web site that uses several servers, or your web server hosts several different web sites, you might want to use *root-relative paths*. You also would use them if you plan on moving files around within your site quite a bit.

Whereas a document-relative path establishes the relationship between two files, a *root-relative path* establishes the relationship between a file and the root of the site. Continuing the analogy used earlier, it is like establishing the relationship between a defined point (downtown Franklin Street) and the destination (the Dean Dome). In that set of directions, nothing was said about where you live. Therefore, if you wanted to email directions to a friend who lives on the other side of town, you would choose this set of directions, rather than the ones that explain how to proceed from your own driveway. In the same way, files within a site using all root-relative paths can be moved within the site without changing the paths contained within the files, because the paths are described in a way that doesn't even take into consideration the location of the current document.

So, if you have your company newsletter online, and move the monthly articles to a directory called Archive when the new issue goes online, root-relative links will save you the time it would take to change links to reflect the new path structure.

An absolute URL has some of these same advantages, because it doesn't depend on the location of the current document to describe its path either. As discussed earlier, however, there are good reasons not to use absolute paths except when required.

Root-relative links always have a slash in front of the path name, as follows:

```
/poetry/bookshelf.html
```

In this example, the path leads to the **bookshelf.html** file, located in the **poetry** subfolder of the site's root folder. Once again, root-relative links are defined by your web server, not by the web browser. Therefore, if you open a page from your hard drive that uses root-relative links, the links will not work.

Note

Be warned that not all web servers are configured to handle root-relative paths correctly. Check with your server administrator before employing this kind of link in your site.

Targeting Links

By default, a link will open in the current browser window. HTML enables you to specify that a link be opened in a new browser window, or on a frame-based site, in a particular frame. This is written using the `target` attribute of the anchor tag, `<a>`, like this:

```
<a href="http://www.macromedia.com" target="_new">Click here!</a>
```

For more information on using this attribute in frame-based sites, see Chapter 12, "Designing Frame-Based Pages."

How Links Appear

To the person who visits a web site, the appearance of links is of great importance. Whether they are text or image, links need to convey their "linkiness." In other words, the visitor needs to be able to recognize links without any effort or thought. Various web design techniques generally are employed to ensure this.

Conventions

Link appearance conventions are used widely on the web, and it is often best to use them. Designers are often tempted to be artistic and even mysterious in their use of links, and although this might greatly impress other web designers, it generally only annoys users.

Conventions do shift gradually, however, and it isn't necessary to restrict oneself to a rigid set of link styles.

For the first few years that the web existed, text links were almost universally displayed by browsers underlined and in a blue color that changed to a purple for visited links. Images were shown with a one-pixel border in the same link colors. Graphics used as links were commonly three-dimensional, mimicking real-life buttons (see Figure 6.2). However, there has been a gradual shift, and to the extent that designers have shifted more or less en masse to new conventions, those conventions have been accepted by the great majority of visitors.

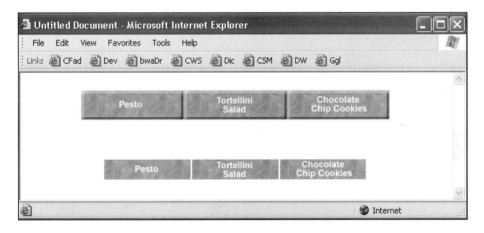

Figure 6.2   Three-dimensional navigation buttons were once ubiquitous but have given way to other two-dimensional button styles.

For example, text links are often shown as some other contrasting color than blue and removing the underlines has become quite common. (See Chapter 13, "Using Cascading Style Sheets," to learn how to accomplish this with Dreamweaver.) In addition, the CSS pseudoclass a:hover has enabled designers to produce a "rollover" effect with plain-text links, so that the link color changes when the visitor passes the cursor over it—at least in some browsers.

Image links are often two-dimensional and don't necessarily resemble buttons; their "link-iness" is usually communicated primarily by their placement on the page and labeling.

These variations on the display of links pose no problem to most users *if they are implemented with care.* Links should look the same, or close to it, throughout a site; buttons shouldn't be three-dimensional on one page and flat on another. And sites should always be tested on real users, even if only informally. Few things are as eye opening to a web designer as to watch an ordinary person using her web site; much can be learned from these sessions.

The cursor itself communicates "linkiness" in that, in nearly all browsers, it changes shape, usually to a little pointing hand icon, when the user rolls his mouse over a link. Although this can be altered with CSS, be warned that a differently reacting cursor is usually at best a distraction, and at worst, an impediment to the use of a web site.

Navigation Bars

Some very common conventions have developed around the placement and general appearance of *navigation bars.* A navigation bar is just a part of a page where a collection of links is presented, usually in a vertical or horizontal pattern. Although links in a navigation bar might not display overt signs of "linkiness," such as underlined text, rollovers, or 3D buttons, the very commonness of their layout arrangement, combined with clear labeling, is often enough to signal their purpose (see Figure 6.3).

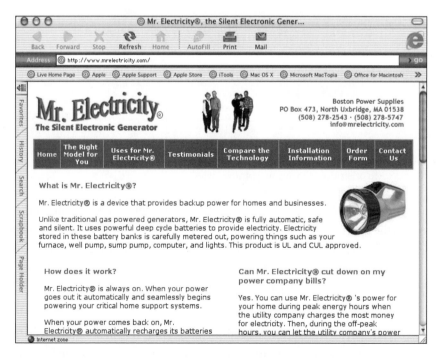

Figure 6.3   One example of frequently used types of navigation bars.

Links and Rollovers

As discussed earlier, a convention has evolved for *rollovers*—link text that changes color when the cursor passes over it. This convention also extends to image rollovers. Using JavaScript, one image can be swapped for another when the visitor mouses over it, giving the appearance of the image changing. Common implementations for image rollovers are buttons that appear to light up when the cursor is moved over them.

The important principle here is that users have come to be accustomed to hyperlinks, whether text or images, responding to the cursor hovering over them. If you have the chance to observe users interacting naturally with a web page, you'll notice that most will move the cursor around the page, looking for the signals that certain spots on the page are links; the designer's job is to make this process so easy for the user that he never even has to think about it.

Basic Link Creation in Dreamweaver

Creating links is one of the common tasks that Dreamweaver makes very simple. When the principles of URL paths, as discussed earlier, are understood, adding hyperlinks within Dreamweaver is very straightforward.

Once again, the hard-working Property inspector panel is the tool used to create links. Anytime an image or text element is selected in Design view, the Property inspector includes a set of link fields and controls for specifying link information (see Figure 6.4).

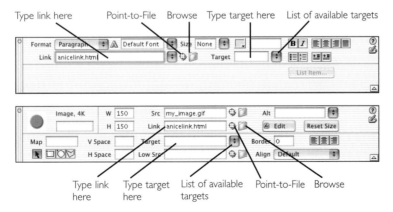

Figure 6.4   The Text Property inspector (top) and Image Property inspector, both showing their link controls.

Assigning Absolute Links

Because you can't browse to the file indicated by an absolute URL, and you can't point to it, all absolute links must be typed into the Link field of the Property inspector. Be sure to type the complete link, including the protocol (usually `http://` for links to other HTML pages). Be aware that Dreamweaver will not display images in Design view if they are referenced with an absolute path, unless that absolute path refers to the image's location on the local computer.

Assigning Relative Links

Relative links can be assigned to any image or text element by selecting the element, then either typing the relative URL in the Link input field, or using the Browse or Point-to-File icons. Using either of these methods will cause Dreamweaver to construct a document-relative or root-relative path to the specified location.

Note

If you do not save your file before inserting an image or creating a link, Dreamweaver does not understand where this HTML document is located. Therefore, you will get a message reminding you to save the file. Until you save the file, Dreamweaver creates a link specific to your workstation. This link will not work after you upload your document, so get into the habit of saving your new documents into the proper directory as soon as you create them.

Browsing for Links

Browsing is probably the most common way to assign a relative link. To assign a link by browsing to it, do this:

1. Select the text or image that will become the linked element.

2. In the Property inspector, click the Browse button next to the Link field.

3. In the dialog box that appears, browse to the desired file.

4. At the bottom of the dialog box, choose whether to create a document-relative or root-relative link. The correct URL will appear in the dialog box.

5. Click OK to create the link.

Using Point-to-File

Depending on how much you like dragging things around, as opposed to choosing from dialog boxes, you might prefer to assign your links by pointing to them. Any file whose entry you can see in the Site panel's Site Files or Site Map pane, you can point to; pointing to the file links to it. To assign a link using Point-to-File, do this:

1. Select the text or image that will become the linked element.

2. Make sure your Site panel is open and at least partially visible on your screen. The particular file you're pointing to doesn't have to be visible.

3. In the Property inspector, find the Point-to-File icon (see Figure 6.5). Drag from that icon to the Site panel, which will come to the front if it's partially hidden by another window. Keep dragging over the site map, list of site files, or even the computer icon that allows you to explore your computer's file system. Don't let go until the cursor is on top of your destination file, and that file is highlighted.

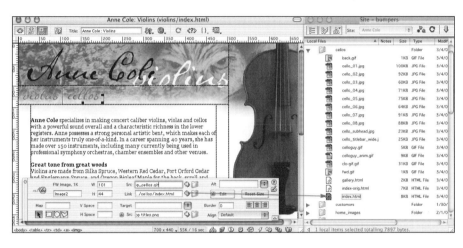

Figure 6.5   Creating a relative link using Point-to-File.

4. Let go! A relative link to that file has been created in your document.

Document-Relative and Root-Relative Links in Dreamweaver

Every time you browse to create a relative link, Dreamweaver gives you the option of creating that links as document-relative or root-relative. Note that this setting is sticky—if you change it, it will stay that way until you change it again. This is not retroactive (it does not change links that are already set relative using another method).

When you create a relative link using Point-to-File, you aren't given the option of choosing what kind of relative link to create. Instead, whatever default you established the last time you browsed to a relative URL will be used. To change the default, assign at least one link using Browse, choosing the desired kind of link in the Select File dialog box.

Also, as mentioned earlier, root-relative links can't be previewed locally in your browser. Within Dreamweaver, if you preview a page containing root-relative links, Dreamweaver will temporarily convert those URLs into document-relative paths. When you click a link in the previewed page, it will work, but any paths on subsequent pages will not work locally because they are site-root relative. For this reason, you will be able to preview only one page at a time.

Exercise 6.1   Creating Text and Image Links

In this exercise, you'll practice creating both text links and image links.

1. If you haven't yet, copy the **chapter_06** folder from the companion CD onto your hard drive, and define a Dreamweaver site named chapter_06 with the folder **chapter_06** as its root directory.

2. From the **chapter_06** folder, open the document **pattys_recipes.html** (see Figure 6.6). You'll link this document to three others, providing both button image links and text links.

Figure 6.6   The file **pattys_recipes.html** ready to have links inserted.

3. First, the text links. At the bottom of the page, select the text Pesto. In the Property inspector, click the Browse button. In the Select File dialog box that appears, link to **pesto.html**, in the **chapter_06** folder. For the type of link, choose document-relative.

4. Repeat step 3 to create a link using the words Tortellini Salad to the file **tortellini.html**, also in the **chapter_06** folder.

5. To create a link to the Chocolate Chip Cookies recipe page, you'll use the Point-to-File icon. You'll need to see and access the Document window, the Property inspector, and the Site panel all at once; depending on which Dreamweaver workspace you're using, this might involve some rearranging of windows. Select the words Chocolate Chip Cookies, and in the Property inspector, click the Point-to-File icon, just to the left of the Browse icon (see Figure 6.4). Drag the icon to the Site panel and drop it on top of the file **chocolate_chip.html**.

6. Save your file. Now you'll make the buttons into links. Select the Pesto button, and just as before, look for the Browse icon in the Property inspector. Just as before, link to the file **pesto.html**.

7. In the same way, link the next two buttons to the appropriate files.

8. Save your document, preview in your favorite browser, and test your links.

Changing Default Link Colors

As discussed earlier, by default, text links display with each browser's chosen style, usually underlined and blue (purple for visited links). In HTML, the default color for links can be changed in two ways: by adding attributes to the <body> tag, or by using CSS. The former method is deprecated (discouraged) in the HTML 4 specification, in favor of the latter.

In Dreamweaver, to change default link colors by adding attributes to the <body> tag, choose Modify > Page Properties, which will open the Page Properties dialog box. The dialog box that appears allows you to set an alternative color for regular text, links, active (in the process of being clicked on) links, and visited links .

To change default link colors in Dreamweaver by using CSS, see Chapter 13.

Dynamic Links

All or part of a URL can be stored in a database field and put into your page as dynamic content. If the URL is inserted as the `href` attribute of an `<a>` tag, it will create a dynamic link, like this:

```
<a href=<%=(Recordset1.Fields.Item("page").Value)%>>Click here</a>
```

To insert a URL as a dynamic link:

1. Begin as if you were assigning a normal link, by selecting the text or image you want the `<a>` tag to surround (see Figure 6.7).

2. In the Property inspector, find the Link field. Click the Browse icon.

3. In the dialog box that appears, choose Data Source instead of File System. A list of available database fields from the document's recordset(s) will appear.

4. Choose the desired field.

5. If the database contains complete URLs in one of its fields, go to the next step. If the database contains pieces of information that you want to use in a larger URL, edit the entry by adding any extra URL elements needed, like this (added code is in bold):

http://www.domain.com/`<%=(Recordset1.Fields.Item("page").Value)%>`

---

continues ▶

Figure 6.7   Assigning a dynamic source to a URL and adding a parameter.

6. If the contents of the requested field contains unacceptable characters for a URL—such as spaces or ampersands—use the Format pop-up menu, and choose URL Encoding.

Passing Parameters in URLs

Any time you browse to choose a link using the Select File dialog box, you have the opportunity of passing one or more parameters as part of the link's URL. Information passed as a parameter is coded as a name/value pair appended to the end of the URL, separated from it by a question mark (?). Typical parameters might be username = fred, category = rings, color = green, and so forth. Added to a URL, these parameters would look like this:

```
mypage.html?username=fred&category=rings&color=green
```

(This is the same kind of URL that occurs when you submit a form using the GET method.)

When working with live data pages, the page you're linking to can use passed parameters to construct its recordset. This is the core of how dynamic search pages work.

To add a parameter to a URL:

1. Create a link, as described above (see Figure 6.7). The link doesn't have to be generated from dynamic information.

2. In the Select File or Dynamic Source dialog box, click the Parameters button.

3. In the Parameters dialog box that opens, enter a name for the parameter (any name will do, as long as it's something you'll remember). Choose a dynamic value for the parameter value.

To retrieve information from a passed parameter:

1. Open a page that has been linked to using a passed parameter.

2. In the Bindings panel, click the plus (+) button and add a new recordset.

3. In the Recordset dialog box, choose URL Parameter from the Filter pop-up menu (see Figure 6.8). Specify the name of the parameter that will be passed and the value it should be compared to.

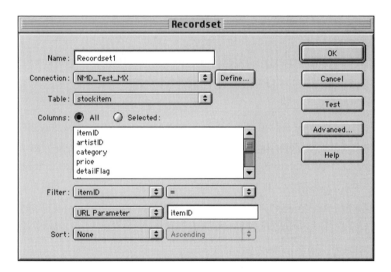

Figure 6.8   Collecting a recordset based on a passed URL parameter.

Email Links

Email links are coded a little bit differently than links to files, because they use a different protocol: mailto. When an email link in a browser window is clicked, the email program that the user has specified in his browser preferences will open. If the user hasn't specified an email program for the browser to call, he will receive an error message instead. The code for an email link looks like this:

```
<a HREF="mailto:fredsmith@somebigcompany.com">Email Fred Smith now!</a>
```

Note that email links are considered to be absolute URLs (in other words, they must always have a protocol).

Email Links with the Property Inspector

The simplest way to make an email link in Dreamweaver is by using the Property inspector, following these steps:

1. Select the text or image you want to use for the email link.

2. Click your cursor in the Link field of the Property inspector and type in the `mailto:` code as shown here:

   mailto:youraddress@domainname.com

   Note that there is *not* a space after the colon.

Email Links with the Email Link Object

If you prefer not having to remember and type the `mailto:` protocol every time you enter an email link, Dreamweaver also provides an Email Link object. To use it, follow these steps:

1. In the Document window, click your cursor at the spot where you want to insert an email link. To create an email link from an image, for instance, click the image to select it. To create an email link from text, either enter the text and select it, or position the cursor where you want the text to go.

2. Choose Insert > Email Link from the Dreamweaver main menu. Or click the Email Link object from the Common tab of the Insert bar (see Figure 6.9).

3. The Insert Email Link window will appear (see Figure 6.9). Type or edit the link text, if necessary. In the Email field, type the email address to which you want mail to be sent.

4. Click OK. Your email link is inserted!

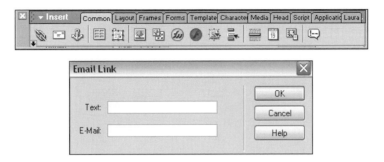

Figure 6.9   The Email Link object and its dialog box.

> **Tip**
>
> Whether you prefer using the Property inspector or Email Link object, pick one method and stick to it. Otherwise, you might get confused and end up accidentally adding the `mailto:` protocol when you shouldn't (when using the object) or omitting it when you should (when using the Property inspector), and creating a nonfunctional link.

Named Anchors

Don't you appreciate it when you visit a web site where the designers have taken the time to make links that allow you to navigate within a long page, so that you don't have to scroll up and down to find what you're looking for? When you make a link to a specific place in a document—rather than just linking to the document itself—you are creating what's called a *named anchor link*.

Creating Named Anchors

To create a named anchor in Dreamweaver:

1. In the Document window, in Design view, place the insertion point where you would like the named anchor.

2. Do one of the following:

   - Choose Insert > Named Anchor.

   - Press Control+Alt+A (Windows) or Cmd+Option+A (Macintosh).

   - Select the Common tab of the Insert bar and click the Named Anchor object (see Figure 6.10).

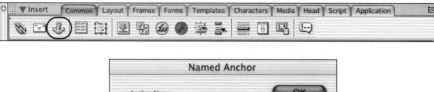

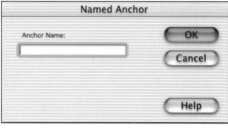

Figure 6.10   The Named Anchor object and its dialog box.

3. This opens the Named Anchor dialog box. In the Anchor Name field, type a name for the anchor (see Figure 6.10).

4. If you have invisible elements set to show, the anchor marker will appear at the insertion point. If you don't see the anchor marker, choose View > Visual Aids > Invisible Elements. Figure 6.11 shows the inserted anchor.

Note

The little gold anchor icon might look as if it's scooting the page contents around it out of position. This is an illusion of Dreamweaver Design view. In the browser, the icon will be invisible and won't take up any space.

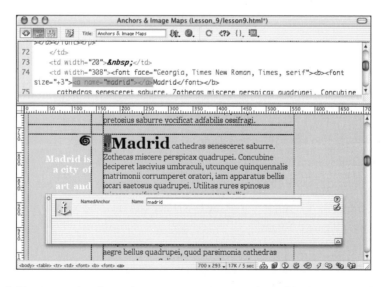

Figure 6.11   A named anchor as it appears in Design view if invisible elements are showing.

Linking to Named Anchors

The HTML code for linking to a named anchor is to call it by name. To link to an anchor named outerspace, located within the current document, the code would be:

```
<a href="#outerspace">Click to read about outerspace!</a>
```

This means, "within the current page (#), go to the anchor named outerspace." To link to the same anchor but from another document, the code would be:

```
<a href="myfile.html#outerspace">Click to read about outerspace!</a>
```

This means, "within the document **myfile.html**, go to the anchor named outerspace."

Dreamweaver gives you several options for creating these links.

Link by Entering the Anchor Name

Select the text or image from which you wish to create the link. In the Property inspector, type a number sign (#), followed by the named anchor's name into the Link field. If the anchor is named outerspace, type **#outerspace** into the box.

To link to a named anchor in a different file, type the file name (and path, if appropriate) followed by the number sign and anchor name: **myfile.html#outerspace**.

Link Using Point-to-File

The Point-to-File icon also can be used for linking to named anchors. Select the text or image to be made into a link and click the Point-to-File icon and drag it to the anchor marker on the page (see Figure 6.12). If the named anchor is in a separate document, open that document and drag from the Point-to-File icon to the anchor within it.

Figure 6.12 Using Point-to-File to link to an anchor.

Exercise 6.2   Creating Named Anchor Links

In this exercise, you'll create a system of links between a list of page contents at the top of a document and the actual contents further down the page.

1. If you haven't yet, copy the folder **chapter_06** from the companion CD to your hard drive, and define a Dreamweaver site named chapter_06 with the folder **chapter_06** as its root directory.

2. Open the file **lyrics.html**. The file contains song names at the top of the page that need to be linked to the appropriate spot inside the text of the page. Because the first song at the top of the page will be visible anyway, and therefore doesn't need a link, start with the second song, "The Ballad of Vicki Smith."

   Scroll down the page until you reach the lyrics to the song "The Ballad of Vicki Smith." Place the cursor just before the song title, and choose Insert > Named Anchor.

3. In the Insert Named Anchor dialog box, type a name for the anchor. The name should not include spaces or special characters, and because they are case-sensitive, it is recommended that you use only lowercase letters—in this case, `theballad`. Click OK.

   Your anchor marker should then appear. If you don't see the anchor marker, choose View > Visual Aids > Invisible Elements.

   Now that you have made the anchor, you need to link to it. Back at the top of the page, select the song title "The Ballad of Vicki Smith."

Note

When naming your anchors, be careful not to use any spaces or special characters in the name. Also remember that these names are case-sensitive. Finally, make sure you are not putting the anchor itself inside a layer, because this will fail in Netscape 4.

   In the Property inspector, enter **#theballad** into the Link field. Don't forget to put the pound sign in front of all your anchor links. If you forget the pound sign, the anchor won't work.

4. Save and preview your page to ensure that the link works. If the link doesn't work, check first to make sure that you have spelled it correctly in the link box.

5. To practice making anchors, create anchored links to all the songs in the file **lyrics.html**, choosing your own anchor names. Preview in a browser as you go, to be sure that you've done them correctly.

Image Maps

An *image map* is a graphic image that has been given numerous hotspots, which function as links. Coordinates that form rectangles, circles, or polygons within the image determine the hotspots. Figure 6.13 shows a typical example of an image map at work.

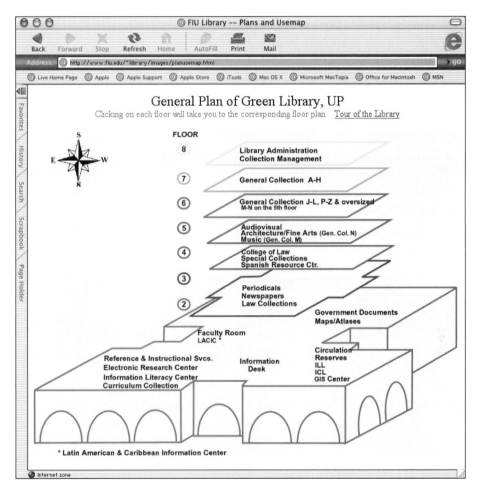

Figure 6.13   The Green Library site uses a map of the library for navigation

There are two types of image map: *server-side image maps* and *client-side image maps*. With server-side image maps, the coordinate information is stored on the server, which can slow down the loading of the linked pages considerably. Client-side image maps can contain all the mapping information in the same HTML file that contains the image. Client-side image maps are preferable for several reasons, including the following:

- There is no need for a server to be visited to determine the destination, so links are resolved more quickly.

- The user can be shown the destination URL when he mouses over a hotspot.

- Image maps can be tested locally.

Working with Image Maps in Dreamweaver

Dreamweaver has tools for creating, configuring, and editing image maps and their hotspots, without having to worry about the code behind them. The Dreamweaver hotspot tools create client-side image maps.

Creating an Image Map

To create an image map in Dreamweaver, follow these steps:

1. In the Document window in Design view, select the image.

2. In the Property inspector, type a unique name for the image map.

3. Define the image map hotspots by using one or more of the Hotspot tools (see Figure 6.14).

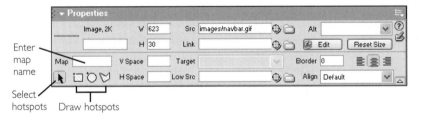

Figure 6.14   The Image Property inspector showing Dreamweaver's Hotspot tools.

- To use the rectangle or circle tool, click the relevant icon and drag the pointer over the image in the Document window to create a rectangular or circular hotspot.

- To use the polygon tool, click its icon, and in Document window, click once over the image for each corner point of the desired polygon-shaped hotspot, and then click the arrow tool to close the shape.

Tip

It's crucial to officially finish drawing the polygon hotspot by clicking the arrow tool (in the Property inspector). If you don't do this, every mouse click you make inside the image will continue adding corners to your polygon. If this happens to you, click the arrow tool to leave polygon-drawing mode, select the tangled-up hotspot you've created, and delete it.

The code that Dreamweaver creates for an image map consists of a <map> tag that defines the hotspots and appears below all other <body> content:

```
<map name="travelmap">
    <area shape="rect" coords="163,18,250,90" href="page1.html">
    <area shape="rect" coords="56,175,154,244" href="page2.html">
    <area shape="rect" coords="365,19,485,95" href="page3.html">
</map>
```

And a link to the map code in the image's <img> tag:

```
<img src="planets.gif" width="576" height="360" border="0" usemap="#travelmap">
```

Working with Hotspots

After you create a hotspot in Dreamweaver, you can set its properties using the Hotspot Property inspector (see Figure 6.15). The inspector's Link, Target, and Alt fields function exactly the same as those you fill in when you create a simple image hyperlink and can be completed in the same way.

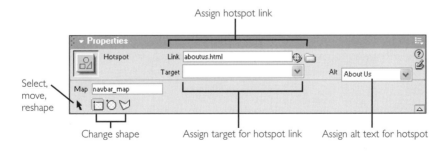

Figure 6.15   The Hotspot Property inspector.

To edit the hotspot after you've created it, use the arrow key (found in the Hotspot Property inspector). Click in the hotspot's central area to select it. Drag to move it. To reshape it, click-and-drag on any of the selection points that appear around the selected hotspot's edge (see Figure 6.16).

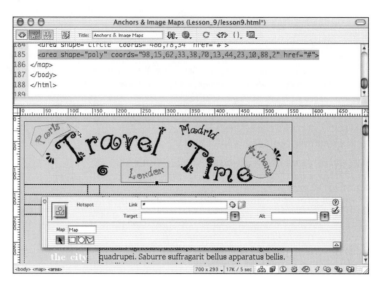

Figure 6.16   Using the arrow tool to reshape a hotspot.

Strategies for Working with Image Maps

Image maps enable the designer to create navigational controls that are more complex and varied than what is possible with text or grouped single images, including using rectangular, circular, and polygonal shapes for hotspots. Keep in mind a few special considerations when using image maps.

Image Maps and Accessibility

HTML, and Dreamweaver, offer various options to make your image maps more accessible to visitors who might not be able to view the images involved.

Alt Text

Just as with any images used on the web, it is important that the individual hotspots on image maps be labeled with `alt` (alternate text) attributes, so that users browsing with speech browsers, or with images turned off, can read a text label specifying to what destination each hotspot leads. Most browsers support hotspot `alt` attributes, displaying them as tool tips when the user mouses over the hotspot. The URL destination also is usually shown in the browser's status bar at the bottom of the browser window.

However, it is a good practice to provide secondary text link navigation mirroring the choices offered by the image map. This makes the site accessible for nongraphical browsers and offers an option for users on slow connections who might not want to wait for the image map to download completely (see Figure 6.17).

In Dreamweaver's Preferences (choose Edit > Preferences in the Accessibility category, you can select an option (check Show Attributes When Inserting Images) that will cause Dreamweaver to prompt you to add attributes to your image map code to make it accessible.

Figure 6.17   An image map with secondary text navigation.

Focus and Tab Order

Most browsers normally display image maps so that, when clicking a hotspot, a dotted-line border is shown around the hotspot area. Also, even before clicking a hotspot, a user can use the Tab key to move through the hotspots and hyperlinks in succession. These *focus lines* exist mainly for accessibility; many web surfers, especially the visually impaired, but also those who surf with keyboards, rely on these kinds of features as good navigational tools.

However, designers are often unhappy with what they call "those ugly dotted lines" and prefer to remove them. Project Seven Development has an extension called IE Link Scrubber, which removes those focus lines. Project Seven also recently released another version, Scrubber 2, which, for accessibility purposes, removes the focus lines while still enabling the user to Tab through the links in succession; it is available from www.projectseven.com.

Making Friendly Hotspots

Because the Dreamweaver Hotspot tool makes it so easy to create image maps, you might be tempted to try unusual shapes and patterns for image maps. However, it is important to remember that a good web page is always easy for the user to understand and navigate. Hotspots should be more or less uniform in size, if not in shape, and large enough so that they can be easily found by the cursor. A hotspot should always correspond with a portion of the graphic that clearly communicates the URL destination; if words aren't used, universally understandable icons (such as a mailbox for an email link) should be employed. Also, be aware that irregular hotspots require a fair amount of code and can quickly add to the page's overall weight.

Limitations of Image Maps

To a large extent, the use of image maps is being replaced by sliced images. Especially when large graphics are used for image maps, download time can be significant; with sliced images, slices download successively, so that some usable content appears much sooner. Image maps also are limited in that they don't allow the *text slices* that are possible with sliced images. For more about sliced images, see Chapter 5, "Working with Images."

Image rollovers are possible with image maps, but can be done much more simply and with fewer bandwidth issues by using sliced images.

Exercise 6.3   Creating an Image Map in Dreamweaver

In this exercise, you create a simple image map using Dreamweaver.

1. If you haven't yet, copy the **chapter_06** folder from the companion CD to your hard drive, and define a Dreamweaver site named chapter_06 with the folder **chapter_06** as its root directory.

2. Open the file **image_map.html**. Click once on the green navigation bar image to select it. In the Property inspector, on the bottom left, click the blue square icon near the word Map.

3. Now hover the cursor over the navbar image; you'll notice that the cursor has turned into a crosshair. Click and drag to form a rectangle around the word Home. The rectangle should show as a shaded turquoise-blue region; if it does not, go to View > Visual Aids and be sure that Image Maps is checked. If you make a mistake, just be sure that the blue hotspot is selected and press the Delete button on your keyboard.

4. When you've drawn a hotspot you're satisfied with, leave it selected, and use the Property inspector to link it to the file **home.html**. For alternate text, enter **Go to Home Page** in the Alt field (see Figure 6.18), being sure to click anywhere in the Document window to activate the PI change.

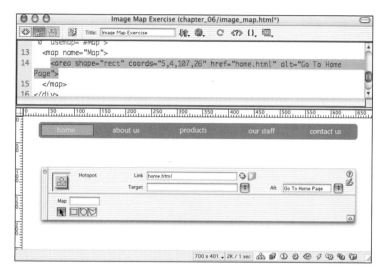

Figure 6.18   The Property inspector for **image_map.html** with the link and `alt` information filled in.

Note

An image map needs a `name` attribute. You can assign it one of your own choosing using the Property inspector; if you don't, Dreamweaver will name it Map. This is perfectly adequate; but you might find a more descriptive name helpful, especially if you have more than one image map on a page.

5. Create hotspots linking the other words on the navbar image to the corresponding pages in the **chapter_06** folder; each link on the navbar has an HTML document with the corresponding name (such as **about_us.html**). Save and preview in a browser.

Importing Image Maps

Image maps don't have to be built within Dreamweaver; graphics programs such as Fireworks and ImageReady can produce the HTML for image maps, which can then be imported into Dreamweaver by opening the document that contains them in Dreamweaver, by copying and pasting the relevant code into a Dreamweaver document, or (for image maps generated using Fireworks) by using the Fireworks HTML object.

Note

For more on Fireworks/Dreamweaver integration, see Appendix A, "Using Dreamweaver and Fireworks Together."

Jump Menus

A *jump menu* is a form `<select>` item which displays as a drop-down (or pop-up) list of options; clicking an option is the equivalent of clicking any other kind of link. (For more about form objects, see Chapter 11, "Working with Forms.") A jump menu can provide links to local or remote documents, email links, or links to any other type of file that can be linked to within HTML (see Figure 6.19).

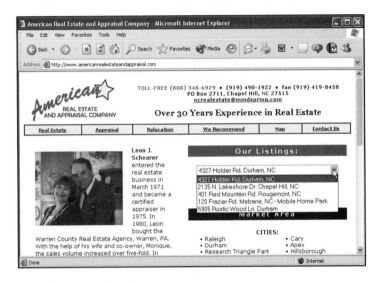

Figure 6.19   A jump menu in action.

A jump menu often includes a menu selection prompt, such as Country or Choose One, which displays at the top of the list. Clicking a list option will activate the link.

There are specific applications where jump menus are best used. Generally, when saving space is important, when the user does not need to see all the menu options at once, or when there are a great deal of menu items, a jump menu is appropriate.

Creating a Jump Menu in Dreamweaver

Dreamweaver makes creating jump menus simple. Just follow these steps:

1. Open your document in Design view, and position the cursor where you want the jump menu to appear.

2. Do one of the following:

   - In the Insert bar, bring the Form tab to the front, and click the Jump Menu object (see Figure 6.20).

   - Choose Insert > Form Objects > Jump Menu.

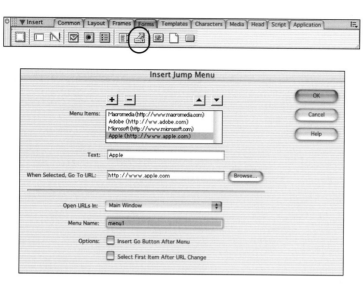

Figure 6.20   The Jump Menu object and its dialog box.

3. The Insert Jump Menu dialog box opens (see Figure 6.20). Use this dialog box to specify what entries will appear in the jump menu, and what location to send the browser to, when visitors choose this option. Type the text labels desired into the Text field; click the plus (+) button to add them to the menu. Use the Browse button to choose URLs, or type them in manually. You also can use this dialog box to set your Jump Menu's options, such as whether to include a Go button. (See the following sections for more on this.)

Jump Menu Code

The code for a jump menu consists of a `<form>` and enclosed `<select>` tag, and JavaScript—in the guise of the jump menu or Jump Menu Go behavior—to make it go. After you've inserted the jump menu, if you have invisible elements set to show in your document, you'll see the red rectangle of the form surrounding your jump menu. If you select the jump menu, you'll see the appropriate behavior in the Behaviors panel (see Figure 6.21).

Note

Even if the jump menu is not being used in an actual interactive form, some browsers require that any form item be enclosed in `<form>` tags, and so Dreamweaver inserts them automatically.

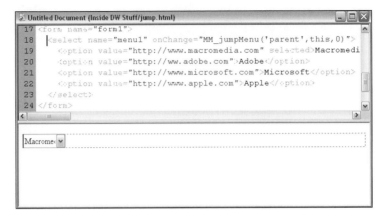

Figure 6.21   A jump menu as it appears in Design and Code views.

To Go, or Not To Go

When you create your jump menu, you have the option of building it as a pop-up menu only, or as a pop-up menu with associated Go button. A Go button is a form button labeled "Go," which will activate the jump menu when it's clicked.

Jump menus don't need Go buttons, because normally the menu activates as soon as a visitor chooses a destination from the menu. But what happens when the visitor's desired destination is already appearing in the menu—for instance, the destination might be the default menu choice (the first item in the list of specified destinations); or the visitor might have arrived at the page using the browser's Back button. For such occasions, the Go button provides a means of activating the menu without changing the selected destination.

Tip

To avoid having to use a Go menu to activate your first menu entry, don't make the first entry a destination at all. Give it a text label of "Choose one" or "Destination," and leave the value (URL) field blank.

To include a Go button when defining your jump menu, select the Insert Go Button After Menu option in the Insert Jump Menu dialog box.

Using Jump Menus with Frames and Multiple Windows

Jump menus can be used to load new pages into new windows, or into different windows of a frameset. To specify this, use the Open in Main Window option for each URL when defining the jump menu's destinations (see Figure 6.20).

If the jump menu opens its destination URL in a separate window, you're presented with another decision: After the destination has been loaded, do you want the jump menu to continue displaying the entry for the loaded destination, or do you want it to revert to displaying its default (first) entry? Probably, if you're opening the destination in a new browser window (assigning a target of _blank), you want the menu to revert; if you're opening the destination in a separate frame within the same browser window, you don't (see Figure 6.22). Whether the jump menu reverts or not is determined by the Select First Item After URL Change option, in the Insert Jump Menu dialog box.

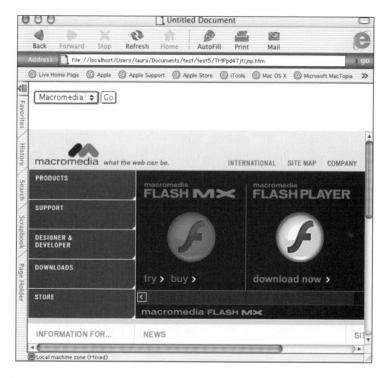

Figure 6.22   A jump menu in a frameset opening a new URL in a different frame (the jump menu is not reverting to its initial selection).

Editing a Jump Menu

After a jump menu has been created, you can edit the menu itself, and its "jumping" functionality, using the Property inspector and Behaviors panel. You also can edit, add, or remove Go buttons.

The Jump Menu Property Inspector

Select the jump menu to view the Jump Menu Property inspector (see Figure 6.23). This is actually nothing more than the List/Menu Property inspector, with jump menu entries in place. In addition to changing the jump menu from a pop-up menu to a list, if you like (so several entries appear at once), you can edit the destinations from here by clicking the List Values button. (For more on List/Menu objects, see Chapter 11.)

Figure 6.23   The List/Menu Property inspector for a jump menu.

The Jump Menu Behavior

Select a jump menu, and in the Behaviors panel you'll see that the jump menu behavior has been added to the form element using the onChange event trigger. (This means the behavior will execute any time the menu selection is changed.) Double-click that behavior, and the Jump Menu behavior dialog box will open. This dialog box is almost identical to the Insert Jump Menu dialog box—it's only missing the Menu Name and Insert Go Button options, which can only be defined when the jump menu is created.

Playing with Go Buttons

If you created your jump menu with a Go button, the button will have the Jump Menu Go behavior applied, to be triggered onClick. This behavior is really nothing more than an alternate means of calling the Jump Menu function. Double-click to edit the behavior, and you'll see that the only option it allows for is which jump menu clicking the button should trigger.

If you decide you don't want a Go button after all, you can safely select and delete your Go button at any time.

If you decide, after having created your jump menu that you really do want a Go button, you can add one by doing this:

1. Insert a form button within the form that contains your jump menu. (Put the insertion point directly after the jump menu and choose Insert > Form Objects > Button.)

2. Using the Property inspector, set the button's label to "Go."

3. Select the button and, from the Behaviors panel, assign the Jump Menu Go behavior to it.

Tip

Go buttons don't have to be form buttons. Any page element that can have link applied to it—including text links and images—can be used to trigger the Jump Menu Go behavior.

Most visitors prefer jump menus that jump to their destinations as soon as they choose from the menu. If, however, you want your menu to activate *only* if visitors first make a selection and then click the Go button, do this:

1. Create the jump menu with a Go button, or use the above instructions to add a Go button later.

2. Go to Code and Design view. In the Design portion of the Document window, select the jump menu.

3. In the Code portion of the window, find and examine the code for the menu (the `<select>` item). Delete the event handler and function call, as shown here (code to be deleted shown in bold):

```
<select name="menu1" onChange="MM_jumpMenu('parent',this,0)">
```

Note that, after you've done this, Dreamweaver will not recognize the `<select>` item as a jump menu any more, so you won't be able to use the Behaviors panel to edit its behaviors.

Exercise 6.4   Creating a Jump Menu

In this exercise, you will create a jump menu that will allow visitors of a home page to jump to various pages within a web site.

1. Open your chapter_06 site in Dreamweaver, and open a new blank page. Save it as **jump_menu.html**.

2. Choose Insert > Form Object > Jump Menu. The Insert Jump Menu dialog box appears

3. Type into the Text field the text **Choose a Section**. This is not actually a menu choice, but will appear in the menu in its non-dropped-down state to prompt the user to pull-down the menu.

4. In the Menu Name field, type a short descriptive name, such as **navigation**, for the menu.

 5. Click the plus (+) button to add a menu item.

 6. In the Text field again, type **Home**. Next to the When Selected, Go to URL field, click the Browse button to choose the file named **home.html**. (You're linking to the same pages you used in the image map exercise.)

 7. Repeat steps 5 and 6 to add and link menu items About Us, Products, Our Staff, and Contact Us.

 8. Choose Main Window in the Open URLs In field. (This opens the destination URL in the same browser window that contains the jump menu.)

 9. Your jump menu doesn't require a Go button, because your first menu entry isn't a link that will ever need to be activated; and your jump menu won't need to be reset after the URL changes, because you're not working in frames or multiple windows for this exercise. Therefore, you can leave both of these options deselected.

 10. Click OK to insert the jump menu. There's your jump menu! Notice that, if you have invisible items showing, your menu appears surrounded by a dotted line (typically red, with default color settings); this indicates that the jump menu has been placed inside of a <form> tag.

 11. Save your document and preview in your browser (see Figure 6.24). Try it out and see how the navigation works.

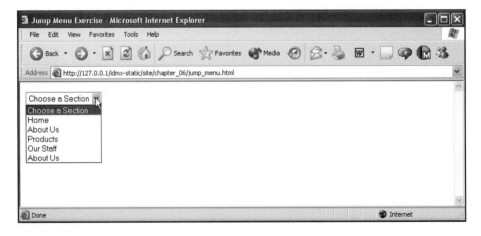

Figure 6.24   The **jump_menu.html** file with its completed jump menu in place.

12. Try fancying up your jump menu a bit by adding a Go button. In the Document window, place the insertion point immediately after the menu, and choose Insert > Form Objects > Button. In the Button Property inspector, set the Label field to "Go!". With the button selected, open the Behaviors panel (Window > Behaviors) and from the plus (+) menu choose Jump Menu Go. In the dialog box that appears, make sure your jump menu is selected as the menu to control.

13. To give your Go button something to do, you'll need to change the first edit item in your menu to an actual destination. Select the jump menu (the menu itself, not the button), and in the Behaviors panel, double-click the Jump Menu behavior to edit it. When the dialog box opens, replace your first entry with an entry labeled Macromedia, which sends users to the following URL:
http://www.macromedia.com

(You'll need to type in the URL by hand, as you can't browse to it.)

14. Now try your menu in a browser! When the page first loads, the Macromedia entry is visible in the jump menu. Because you can't choose that entry (it's already chosen), click the Go button and be whisked off to Macromedia.

Rollovers

As discussed earlier, one of the conventions that has arisen on the web, and which has come to be easily understood by users, is the concept of a navigation link changing in some way when the cursor rolls over it. This type of feature, when applied to an image, is known as a *rollover*.

A rollover actually consists of two images: the *primary image*, which displays when the page first loads; and the *secondary image*, which the browser substitutes for the primary image when the cursor moves across the primary image. The two images must be the same size. If they are not, the secondary image will be sized by the height and width attributes of the first image.

Creating a Rollover in Dreamweaver

Image rollovers can be created easily in Dreamweaver, thanks to the Rollover Image object (see Figure 6.25). The idea is, instead of inserting a regular image into a document, you insert an image that will automatically turn into another image when rolled over.

Follow these steps:

1. Open your document in Design view. In the Common tab of the Insert bar, click the Rollover Image icon, which opens the Insert Rollover Image dialog box (see Figure 6.25).

2. Type a name in the Name field. Images that will be used in a rollover must be named; if you don't name your image, Dreamweaver will assign it a default name.

3. Use the Browse button to browse for the Original image and Rollover image, or type the file name and path for each into the field.

4. Check the Preload Images box if you want this option. (See the next section, for more on preloading.)

5. Provide alternate text in the Alternate Text field. (This will become the primary image's `alt` attribute.)

6. Use the Browse button to browse to and select the URL to send the visitor to when the rollover image is clicked. If you don't want the rollover to actually send the browser anywhere—for instance, if you want the image to trigger a behavior instead of going to a URL—enter a number sign (#) in this field.

7. Click OK to insert the rollover image.

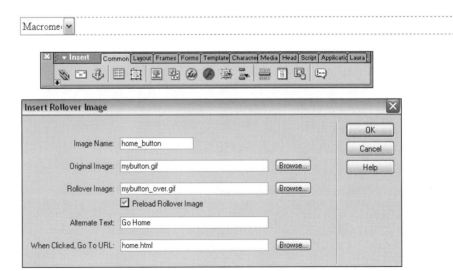

Figure 6.25   The Rollover Image object and dialog box.

Preloading and Rollovers

Normally, the browser downloads page resources—including images—the first time they appear on a page. Preloading means telling the browser to download an image into its cache before the image will actually be used, so it will be ready and waiting to display promptly when called on.

When a page includes a rollover image, the primary image is downloaded as the page downloads. The secondary image, however, is not needed until a user rolls over the primary image, and so is not downloaded until then. Depending on the user's connection speed, this can cause anything from a brief hiccup to a noticeable delay in the rollover effect happening. The user might move his mouse over an image, and then have to wait several seconds before the secondary image springs into view. Definitely not a good state of affairs.

When you choose the Preload Images option in the Rollover Image dialog box, Dreamweaver writes a JavaScript telling the browser to download the primary and secondary images when the page first loads, thus eliminating that delay. Therefore, it's a good idea to make sure this option is selected when using the Rollover Image object.

Editing Rollover Images

Using the Rollover Image object is actually a shortcut for the more complex Dreamweaver procedure of inserting an image, assigning it a link, and adding a Swap Image and Swap Image Restore behavior to it. After you have inserted a rollover image, it becomes simply an image with a link and a behavior applied (see Figure 6.26). To edit the image and its link, select it and use the Property inspector. To edit the rollover code, select the image and, in the Behaviors panel, double-click the Swap Image behavior. This will give you access to the Swap Image dialog box, from which you can change the secondary image and preloading options (among other things). To learn more about Swap Image, see Chapter 16, "Getting Interactive with Behaviors."

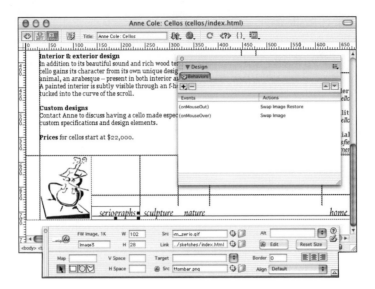

Figure 6.26   A rollover image revealing itself to be a linked image with several behaviors applied.

Exercise 6.5   Create an Image Rollover in Dreamweaver

In this exercise, you'll create a simple rollover button.

1. If you haven't yet, copy the **chapter_06** folder from the companion CD into a folder named idmx on your hard drive, and define a Dreamweaver site named chapter_06 with the folder **chapter_06** as its root directory.

2. Open a new document and name it **rollovers.html**. In the Insert bar Common tab, click the Insert Rollover Image icon. The Insert Rollover Image dialog box appears.

3. In the Image Name field, type a name for the rollover image; for this exercise, use **news_button**.

4. In the Original Image field, click Browse and select from the **chapter_06/images** directory, the image **button_news_up.gif**.

5. In the Rollover Image field, click Browse and select **button_news_over.gif**.

6. Select the Preload Images option so that the images will be preloaded in the browser's cache. This ensures that there is not a delay when the secondary image is called from the server.

7. In the When Clicked, Go to URL field, just type a number sign (#). This is a *null link*, or a link that goes nowhere but is helpful in situations like this where a link is required; it's used here for simplicity. Any link could be used.

8. Click OK to close the dialog box and insert the code. Save the document and preview in the browser.

9. To see how your rollover image is constructed, select the image. Examine the Image Property inspector and the behaviors in the Behaviors panel.

Navigation Bars

The term *navigation bar* can refer to any set of links arranged horizontally or vertically on a web page; generally they are a prominent feature of a web site and remain consistent from page to page, providing an easy way for the user to move between pages and files. A navigation bar (or *navbar*) can be made of text links, linked images, or an image map. A more elaborate type of navigation bar is often made with sets of images which change based on the actions of the user, using JavaScript. Dreamweaver provides the Navigation Bar object to make creating this kind of navbar simple.

Each button or element in a Dreamweaver navigation bar can have up to four states:

- **Up.** The image shown when the user hasn't yet interacted with the element.

- **Over.** The image shown when the pointer hovers over the Up image. The element's appearance changes to signal that it is interactive (see Figure 6.27).

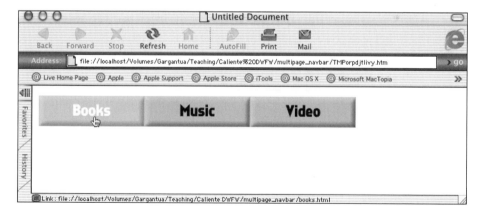

Figure 6.27   The Over image appears when the element is rolled over by the pointer.

- **Down.** When the navbar is in a frameset, this is the image that appears after the user clicks the element. When an element is clicked and a new page loads, the navigation bar, still displayed, shows the clicked element with a changed appearance to signify that it has been selected (see Figure 6.28).

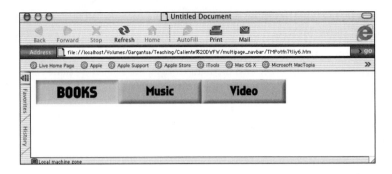

Figure 6.28   The Down image appears when the element has been selected.

- **Over While Down.** When the pointer is rolled over the Down image, this image appears.

It isn't necessary to include all four states in every navbar. Often just the Up, Over, and Down states are used.

Creating a Navigation Bar

To insert a Navigation Bar with Dreamweaver, follow these steps:

1. Either choose Insert > Interactive Images > Navigation Bar, or select the Navigation Bar object from the Common tab of the Insert bar. The Insert Navigation Bar dialog box appears (see Figure 6.29).

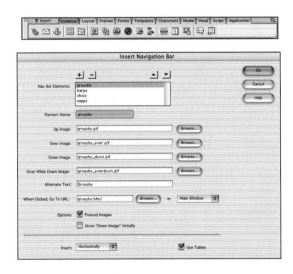

Figure 6.29   The Navigation Bar object and dialog box.

2. Each Element corresponds to a button in the navbar, and each button has up to four states. One by one, name your elements and use the plus (+) button to add them to the navbar. Use the Browse buttons to assign images for the different states.

3. Supply Alternate Text in the field by that name, and use the Browse button to specify the URL to which the user should be sent when the button is clicked in the When Clicked, Go to URL field. Choose the window or frame in which you want the URL to open in the field just to the right of the URL field.

4. Choose Preload Images if you like. (See the discussion on preloading images in the "Rollovers" section of this chapter.) Choose Show Down Image Initially if you would like that particular element to be in its Down state when the page loads. This is appropriate, for instance, on a Home Page, where you would want the Home button to indicate that you are already on the Home page.

5. At the bottom of the dialog box are two more options. Choose to insert your navigation bar horizontally or vertically, and choose whether or not you want HTML tables to be used.

6. Click OK to insert the navigation bar.

Editing a Navigation Bar

After a navigation bar has been inserted, it consists of several images, each of which has several Set Nav Bar Image behaviors applied to it. If you chose to have your navigation bar structured as a table, it will also include a `<table>` tag (see Figure 6.30).

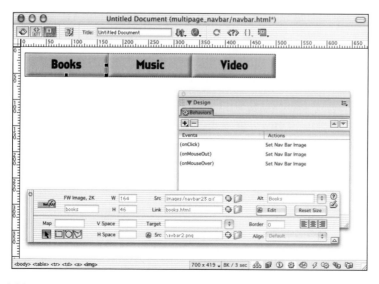

Figure 6.30   A navigation bar inserted and ready for editing.

You're free to rearrange the images in the navigation bar, adjust the properties of the table that contains them, change the URLs the images link to, and even delete some images, without disturbing the navigation bar.

To edit the entire navigation bar at once, choose Modify > Navigation Bar. This opens the Modify Navigation Bar dialog box, which is very similar to the dialog box you used to create the navigation bar.

To edit the various rollovers that make up the navigation bar, select any image in the group and, in the Behaviors panel, double-click any of the three Set Nav Bar Image behaviors. The dialog box that appears contains two tabs: The Basic tab lets you adjust the rollover settings for the currently selected image; the Advanced tab lets you set some very fancy image changes for the other images in the navigation bar, based on what's happening to the selected image. (See Figure 6.31.)

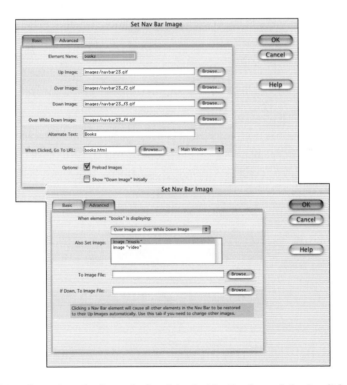

Figure 6.31   The Basic and Advanced tabs of the Set Nav Bar Image behavior dialog box.

Exercise 6.6   Creating a Navigation Bar with Dreamweaver

Dreamweaver makes building a navbar easy, but you still have to create the images needed. You'll need an image for each element (or button) in each state. In this exercise, you make a navigation bar using all 4 states for each of 4 buttons; the 16 images needed are already in your **chapter_06/images** folder. In Exercise 6.7, you'll place the same navbar on other pages so that you can see the Down and Over While Down states in action.

1. If you haven't yet, copy the **chapter_06** folder from the companion CD to your hard drive, and define a Dreamweaver site named chapter_06 with the folder **chapter_06** as its root directory.

2. Open a new blank document and name it **seasons.html**.

3. From the Dreamweaver main menu, choose Insert > Interactive Images > Navigation Bar. This opens the Insert Navigation Bar dialog box. You'll insert four buttons: Winter, Spring, Summer, and Fall. Each has four states.

4. For the first item in the navigation bar, start with the Element Name field, and type in **Winter**.

   For Up Image, click Browse and, from the **images** folder, choose **winter_up.gif**. For Over Image, click Browse and choose **winter_over.gif**. For Down Image, click Browse and choose **winter_down.gif**. For Over While Down Image, choose **winter_overdown.gif**. For When Clicked, Go to URL, click Browse and choose **winter.html**.

5. Then click the plus (+) button at the top of the dialog box to add another button.

6. Repeat step 5 to create the *Spring* button. Continue adding items and filling in fields to create the *Summer* and *Fall* buttons.

7. Select Preload Images and choose Insert Horizontally. Then click OK to insert the navbar into the document.

Tip

In the Insert Navigation Bar dialog box, you can select an element and use the up-pointing and down-pointing triangle icons near the top of the box to change the order of the elements in the navbar.

8. Save and preview in the browser (see Figure 6.32). You can see how the Over state works; however, because the pages you have linked to don't exist yet, you'll get a Page Not Found message when you click the links. Just use your browser's Back button to return to the Seasons page. In Part II, "Design with Dreamweaver," you'll create the linked pages so that you can see the Down and Over While Down states in action.

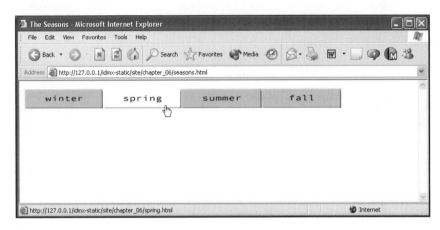

Figure 6.32   Previewing the navigation bar in **seasons.html**.

Exercise 6.7   Using a Navbar Across Multiple Pages

In this exercise, you'll place the navbar you created in Exercise 6.6 on three other pages.

1. Open **seasons.html**.

2. Choose File > Save As, and save the file with a new name, **winter.html**. Change the page title to **Winter**. Choose Modify > Navigation Bar to open the Modify Navigation Bar dialog box.

3. In Navbar Elements, select **winter**. At the bottom of the box, select Show "Down Image" Initially and click OK. Save.

4. Open **seasons.html** again and repeat steps 2 and 3, naming the new page **spring.html**, changing its title, and in the Modify Navigation Bar dialog box, select **Spring** and select Show "Down Image" Initially.

5. Open **seasons.html** again and repeat steps 2 and 3 again, creating **summer.html**.

6. Open **seasons.html** again and repeat steps 2 and 3 again, creating **fall.html**.

7. Preview **seasons.html** in the browser.

Each page should show the Over state when the pointer rolls over the image, and the page for each particular season should display the appropriate button in a darkened state. When you're on the Spring page and you roll over the darkened Spring button, you'll see the Over While Down state (see Figure 6.33).

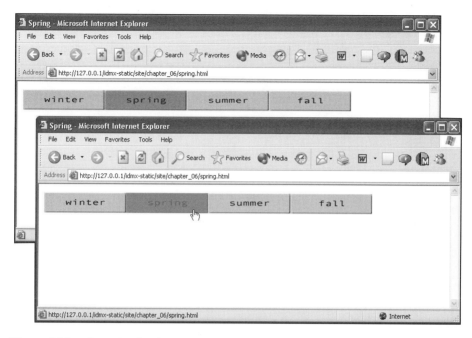

Figure 6.33   The **spring.html** page as it appears in a browser demonstrating the Down (top) and Over While Down (bottom) states of the navigation bar.

Summary

Hyperlinks are an essential and defining feature of the World Wide Web, and a skillfully designed navigational system is one of the highest priority considerations in the creation of a web site. In this chapter, you learned about linking URLs and about how links appear in the browser and what these appearances say to the user. You looked at email links and named anchors, and tried out several widely used types of navigation controls: image maps, jump menus, linked rollover images, and multistate navigation bars. A web developer familiar with these techniques has some excellent tools to choose from when planning the structure and navigation of a new web site.

Chapter 7

Utilizing Head Content

In your frenzied rush to create the best, most beautiful, knock-their-socks-off web page, don't overlook the unglamorous but entirely practical world that lives inside your document head. This chapter discusses what goes into the head. You'll also see how Dreamweaver handles head elements such as search keywords, page refreshes, and document encoding. And you'll see how you can use these and other tools to maximize your working efficiency and web presence.

How Head Content Works

A standard HTML page contains a `<head>` tag and a `<body>` tag. The body contains all the page content that will actually display in the browser window. The head contains a variety of information that won't display (at least, not directly), although it can be accessed to determine how the page will be handled. Some head content will be accessed by the browser; some will be accessed by other programs, such as server software, search engines, and validation software; some might not be accessed at all, except by humans who might view or edit the code. The W3C specifies several elements that a well-formed head section could use. Unfortunately, the browsers have not yet fully implemented them all, so we can't take full advantage of the head.

Table 7.1 lists the standard head elements, along with a brief description of each.

Table 7.1   Standard HTML *<head>* Elements

Tag	Purpose	Browser Support	Example(s)
`<title>`	Contains the page title, to be displayed in the browser window title bar and user bookmark menu. (See Chapter 3, "Creating and Working with Documents.")	Yes	`<title>Webley's Web Widgets</title>`
`<link>`	Specifies a relationship between the current document and another document. (See Chapter 13, "Using Cascading Style Sheets.")	Only for use with style sheets	`<link rel="stylesheet" href= "widgetstyles.css" type="text/css">`
`<base>`	Specifies a URL and/or target, to which all document links will be relative.	Yes	`<base href="http://www. webwidgets.com/"> <base target="_top">`
`<basefont>`	Specifies default font and/or type size settings for the current document. (See Chapter 4, "Working with Text.")	Yes (deprecated, in favor of CSS)	`<basefont face="Georgia, New York, Book Antiqua"> <basefont size="2">`

Tag	Purpose	Browser Support	Example(s)
`<meta>`	A generic tag for adding miscellaneous information to the document (for example, keywords, character encoding).	Yes	`<meta name="generator" content="BBEdit 6.1.2">` `<meta http-equiv="Content-Type" content="text/html; charset=iso-8859-1">`
`<script>`	Encloses JavaScript or other script statements for the browser to execute, or links to an external script file. (See Chapter 11, "Working with Forms.")	Yes	`<script language="JavaScript"> function helloWorld() {window.alert("Hello, world!");}</script>` `<script src="widgets.js"> </script>`
`<style>`	Encloses CSS style sheet information to affect the display of the current document. (See Chapter 13.)	Yes	`<style type="text/css">a { font-weight: bold; text-decoration: none}</style>`

Interview: Lisa Tannenbaum

Business Name: Grass Roots Consulting

URL: www.compugoddess.com

Lisa Tannenbaum

Lisa Tannenbaum is Internet Program Coordinator for the University of New Mexico's IT Training Center. She teaches all aspects of online development, focusing on online marketing and business practices. Her web site includes various tutorials and helpful links.

How important do you think search engines are in the overall marketing strategy for a web site?

They're *hugely* important. Even if you think you don't want to put a lot of energy into promoting your web site through the search engines, people *must* be able to find your site if they search for it.

An example: I had oral surgery a while ago with a doctor who had a beautiful web site and was actively using it to pre-register his patients (for example, new patients could go online to fill out their medical history, so it would be available for their first appointment). Several months later, I tried to find his web site, using a number of search engines, to no avail—I had to call his office to find the URL. As it turned out, there were no meta tags whatsoever in his pages, nor had the site ever been submitted to any of the search engines.

That's an example of the very *least* visibility a site must have on the search engines. And although some of the search engines have started to charge for submissions, a search engine presence is still one of the least expensive—and potentially most powerful—ways to market a web site.

Just think about how you use the search engines yourself: when you want to learn about something new, what do you do? Chances are that you look at the first page or two of results returned to you by a search engine, and sample some sites from that list. That's exactly the way everyone else does it, too. Why not get some of those people to your web site?

Can you share any tips or tricks for creating lists of searchable keywords?

Let's imagine you're marketing a new brand of potato chips. Here are some of the techniques you might consider using:

- Make use of all the most obvious keywords and phrases. In this example, your list might include "potato chips, snacks, chips."

- Use both plural and singular forms of keywords and phrases. Thus, you'd also add "potato chip, snack, chip" to your list.

- Add common misspellings to the list, such as "potatoe chips" and "patato chips."

- Considering using either Initial Caps or ALL CAPS in your list, for the benefit of case-sensitive search engines (AltaVista is one). A search for "potato chips" (lower case) in a case-sensitive search engine will return *all* pages with the phrase "potato chips" in them, regardless of case; while a search for "POTATO CHIPS" (all caps) will return *only* those pages where the phrase exists in all caps. That might not be a good search technique for the searcher, but that's not the point— don't you want to show up in a searcher's results, regardless?

- Be alert to the keywords/phrases that competing sites use—you might pick up some relevant words that you never would have thought of on your own.

Do you focus on a few popular search engines? If so, which ones?

I normally submit to only a few search engines. However, as pay-to-play is becoming more prevalent on the web, the no-cost choices have narrowed considerably. However, I still always submit to Lycos, HotBot, and AltaVista (at the time of this writing, all still allow free submissions, although you might have to work to find them). I also sometimes submit to Google and AskJeeves.

Open Directory (www.dmoz.org) is also free, although I wait until I have a site *full* of content before I submit to them. Actual human beings, as opposed to robots, index their pages and I basically submit to them (at the most) once a year. This is the same technique I use with Yahoo! and LookSmart (which generally are *not* free).

What head content do you typically use in your web pages? Do you stick with the basics (keywords and description), or do you take advantage of any of the other meta tags?

I just stick to keywords and description. However, I should mention that meta tags are becoming quite a bit less important in most search engines' algorithms—probably because misleading tags have duped so many robots. For example, as far as the search engine observers can tell, Google doesn't use meta tags at all, either in their algorithms or site descriptions.

The description tag is still very important, in spite of this trend, because many search engines still use it in their site descriptions, if not in the search algorithms. It's a great 25-word opportunity to get people interested enough in your web site that they click on the link.

How often do you recommend updating the keywords or other head elements, for better search engine results?

Whenever you think of a new one.

How important is it to register with the search engines?

It's absolutely essential. There's no point in having a web site if no one can get to it.

Working with Head Content in Dreamweaver

Dreamweaver provides two main interfaces for dealing with head content: the category of Head objects in the Insert bar, for adding content to the head; and the Head Content view option, along with Property inspectors for each kind of content, for examining and editing head content.

Viewing and Examining Head Content

Head content cannot be dealt with directly in Dreamweaver Design view, because the Design view only shows the content that will display in a browser (<body> content, in other words). Although you're always free to access head elements directly through Code view, the Code inspector, or Tag Inspector, Dreamweaver also provides a visual interface that shows an icon for each element present in the head (see Figure 7.1).

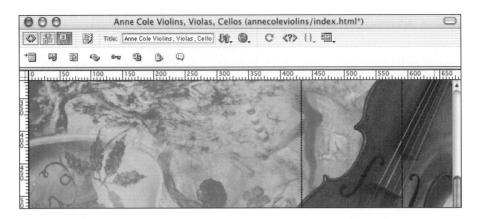

Figure 7.1   Displaying head content as icons in Design view.

View/Hide Head Content

To view/hide head content, choose View > Head Content to toggle the head content display on/off. Alternatively, use the View Options pop-up menu in the Document window's toolbar, and choose Head Content for the same result. (Note that Head Content won't show up as an option in the pop-up menu unless you're in Design view/Code and Design view.) A gray bar appears, at the top of the Design View window, showing an icon for each head element (see Figure 7.1).

Examine/Edit a Head Element

To examine/edit a head element, click its icon in the display bar, and use the Property inspector to view and change the element's attributes.

Rearrange Head Elements

In most cases, the order of elements in the head doesn't matter, because each element serves a different function, and is called on when needed regardless of position. In some situations, however—when linking multiple external style sheets to one document, for instance—the order can be very significant. In these cases, just drag and drop the icons in the gray display bar to rearrange the items in the code.

Adding Head Content

Dreamweaver inserts some head elements automatically as you create and edit pages (title, script, and style, for instance). Other commonly used head elements have corresponding objects in the Head tab of the Insert bar (see Figure 7.2). If you want to add an element that isn't in the Insert bar, you must enter it in Code view, either by typing it in yourself or using the Tag Chooser (see Figure 7.3).

> **Note**
>
> You can also increase your <head> content options by searching the Macromedia Exchange for Dreamweaver for an extension that does what you want. Alternatively, you can create your own Head object extension; read all about custom objects in Chapter 36, "Creating Extensions."

To insert a head element, click one of the Head objects in the Insert bar (see Figure 7.2)—or choose from the Insert > Head Tags submenu.

Figure 7.2   The Head tab of the Insert bar.

Figure 7.3   Using the Tag Chooser to insert head content not represented in the Insert bar.

You can insert head elements from either Design or Code view, but with a few important differences. If you're working in Design view, placement of the insertion point isn't crucial when working with head content. No matter what element in the <body> you might have selected when you insert, Dreamweaver knows to put head content in the head. If you have one of the icons in the head element display selected when you insert, Dreamweaver will place the new element immediately after the selected element. If no head elements are selected when you insert, Dreamweaver will insert the new head element at the end of all other head content.

If you're working in Code view when you insert a Head object, the code for the object will be inserted wherever the insertion point is—even if that means inserting it outside the <head> section entirely, or even inserting it within another HTML tag. (Obviously, unless you know your way around HTML tag syntax, it's safer to use Design view for adding your Head objects.)

Note

If you like working in Code and Design view, remember that either the Design or Code portion of the Document window must always have focus. If you insert Head objects while the Code portion has focus, your insertion point must be in a proper location within the <head> tags for the object to be correctly inserted.

Working with *<meta>* Tags

Meta means "about." The purpose of the <meta> tag is to store information about the current document for possible processing by browsers, servers, search engines, or even lowly humans viewing the source code. For each different kind of information you want to store, you use a different <meta> tag. HTML documents can have as many <meta> tags as needed, all stored in the head.

How *<meta>* Tags Store Information

Information is generally stored in the <meta> tag as a name/value pair, using the name and content attributes. Like this:

```
<meta name="generator" content="Dreamweaver">
```

Over time, certain name/value pairs—such as keywords, description, and refresh—have become standard in HTML use, and are collected and processed by browsers and/or search engines. However, web authors also are free to create any desired name/value pairs to store other document-related information. Many popular HTML editing programs, for instance, use a "generator" <meta> tag when generating code, to sneak some free advertising into user documents. Some web authors let potential code-borrowers know whom they're borrowing from with an "author" tag, as follows:

```
<meta name="author" content="Julius Marx">
```

The various `<meta>` tags are useful enough that Dreamweaver supplies several objects representing different kinds of meta information. The following paragraphs examine these.

The Character-Encoding *<meta>* Tag

This kind of `<meta>` tag isn't in the Insert bar. Dreamweaver inserts it automatically into every HTML document it generates. The code looks like this:

```
<meta http-equiv="Content-Type" content="text/html; charset=iso-8859-1">
```

(See the following section for more on `http-equiv`, which is used here in place of `name`.)

This standard `<meta>` tag tells the browser what character set to use in representing the text portions of the page. `ISO-8859-1` refers to Latin-1 encoding, used for most western European languages. Examples of other encodings include `ISO-8859-5` (Cyrillic) and `SHIFT_JIS` (Japanese). Unless you know what you're doing, don't mess with this tag.

<meta> Tags and the Generic Meta Object

Because, ultimately, every `<meta>` tag consists of a name and some content, the Dreamweaver generic Meta object is the perfect bare-bones tool for inserting custom meta information. Figure 7.4 shows the generic `<meta>` tag being inserted.

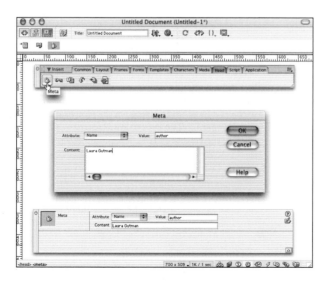

Figure 7.4   Inserting meta content with the generic meta object.

To insert a `<meta>` tag, follow these steps:

1. Click the Meta object (or choose Insert > Head Tags > Meta).

2. In the dialog box that appears, use the pop-up menu to choose either the `name` or `http-equiv` attribute to include. (The `http-equiv` attribute maps the attribute and its respective name to the HTTP response header for processing. Unless you know specifically what you want, and are sure that `http-equiv` is appropriate, use the `name` attribute.)

3. In the dialog box's Value text field, enter the value you want the `name` (or `http-equiv`) attribute to have.

4. In the dialog box's Contents text area, enter the value you want the `content` attribute to have.

Figure 7.4 shows how the dialog box insertion areas translate into the finished `<meta>` tag code. Why not use this generic object to insert all meta content? The `<meta>` tags that use standard keywords, those that a browser or other agent will be processing, also require standardized syntax for their content. Dreamweaver's specialized Meta objects take care of those syntax requirements for you. Dreamweaver does not include all the `<meta>` tags that you might want to use. Table 7.2 lists some of those `<meta>` tags not included with Dreamweaver.

Table 7.2   Some Useful `<meta>` Tags Not Included in the Dreamweaver Insert Bar

Syntax	Description/Purpose
`<meta http-equiv="expires" content="15 Apr 2001 23:59:59 GMT">`	Specifies a date after which the browser cache for the current page will expire. This guarantees that visitors' browsers won't show an out-of-date version of the page. The date and time should be formatted as of-date version of the page (as shown). The time information is optional.
`<meta http-equiv="Set-Cookie" content=cookie_name=cookie_value; expires=1 Jan 2002 23:59:59 GMT">`	Sets a cookie with whatever name and value are specified in place of `cookie_name` and `cookie_value` (for example, `favorite_color=green`). The expiration information is optional; if it's not present, the cookie expires when the browser is shut down.
`<meta http-equiv="pragma" content="no-cache">`	Prevents the browser from caching the page. Note that Internet Explorer versions 4 and later ignore this tag.
`<meta http-equiv="Content-Script-Type" content="text/language_name">`	Specifies the language to be used in all `<script>` tags within the document. The content string might read `text/javascript` or `text/vbscript`, for instance.

Meta Keywords and Descriptions

Undoubtedly the most commonly used, and most generally practical, of the <meta> tags are those that help search engines locate and retrieve information about our documents. The most common of these are the `"keywords"` and `"description"` tags:

```
<meta name="keywords" content="Marx Brothers, humor, vaudeville, movies,
Groucho, Harpo, Chico, Zeppo, Gummo"><meta name="description"
content="An unofficial look at America's kings of slapstick and wise-
cracking. With links and freebies.">
```

The `"keywords"` tag contains a comma-separated list of words that web visitors might type into a search field; these should lead them to the current document. The `"description"` tag contains a few sentences that can be used in a search results page to represent the current document. A Dreamweaver object represents each of these (see Figure 7.2). To insert either into your head section, click its object (or choose from the Insert > Head Tags submenu) and enter the appropriate information in the dialog box. Figures 7.5 and 7.6 show these tags being inserted (in Design and Code views).

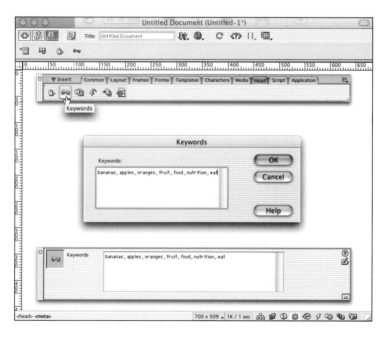

Figure 7.5 The `"keywords"` <meta> tag being inserted and later inspected using the Keywords object.

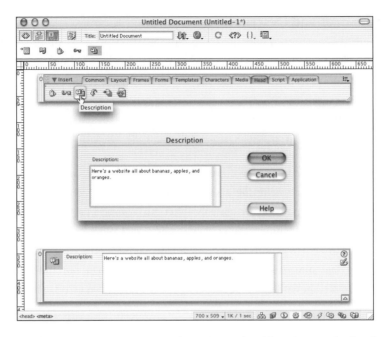

Figure 7.6   The `"description"` `<meta>` tag being inserted and later inspected using the Description object.

Maximizing Searchability

Using keywords and descriptions, and using them well, are two different things. The more you know about how search engines work, and how to take full advantage of their offerings, the better your standings in the search results will be.

Search engines work by sending out automated programs, called *robots* (or *web crawlers*, or *spiders*, or *bots*) to index web pages. Indexing consists of retrieving documents and recursively retrieving all documents referenced (that is, linked) from those documents. Robots determine which pages to start indexing by various means, including when a web page author or webmaster registers the page with the search engine. When a visitor accesses the search engine and enters one or more search words, the engine returns results based on its analysis of the documents it has retrieved. Results are based on matched keywords, but also on other factors; matched words in the description, the page title, visible document content, links, and alt text are commonly searched as well.

> **Note**
>
> There is much more to this subject than will fit in this chapter. Luckily, the web is full of wonderful resources. A great place to start is World of Design (www.globalserve.net/ ~iwb/search_engine/killer.html). This site includes articles, tutorials, and a host of useful links related to <meta> tags and search engines in general.

Here's the code for how a sample head section is set up for maximum searchability:

```
<head>
<title>The Web Widgets Construction Materials Home Page</title>
<meta name="keywords" content="web, widgets, construction materials,
building tools, web tools, snarflators, crambangers, diffusion devices,
child, children, diffuse, diffusion, .....">
<meta name="description" content="The Web Widgets Construction Materials
Company, home to a vast selection of snarflators, crambangers and other
web tools. Visit us for daily specials and our unique how-to section.">
<!--The Web Widgets Construction Materials Company, home to a vast selec-
tion of snarflators, crambangers and other web tools. Visit us for daily
specials and our unique how-to section.-->
</head>
```

What elements make this code so searchable?

- **Page title.** The information in the `<title>` tag is descriptive and readable (can be searched, and might show up on some search results pages) and uses several words present in the keywords list.

- **Keywords.** Keywords are case-sensitive and are in the plural where appropriate. (If the keyword is singular, and the user searches using a plural, no match will be found.) No words are repeated except where necessary. (Unnecessary repetitions will either be ignored or will be considered "spamming," and might get the entire site banned from the search engine.) The keywords list is approximately 900 characters long, which is the maximum length that will be accepted by some search engines (some engines accept as many as 1024).

- **Description.** The description uses words from the keywords list. It is slightly under 200 characters long, which is the maximum acceptable length for most search engines (some accept fewer). Note that if your description or keywords are too long, they won't be considered in the search; it doesn't necessarily mean the robot will reject the page.

- **Comment.** A comment is inserted, repeating the contents of the description. This is to address those few robots (most notably Excite and Magellan) that do not search `<meta>` tags.

Limiting Searchability

Wait a minute. Why would you want to stop robots from indexing your documents? Quite simply, you might have any number of reasons. Certain areas of a web site might contain private or secure data. If your site uses frames, you might not want framed pages to be indexed outside their framesets. Certain areas, such as ASP and CGI folders, might contain scripts that will run when accessed, with undesirable results. On a large site, the increased traffic of robots indexing every single page might be a drain on the web server.

You can limit robot traffic in two ways, one of which Dreamweaver can help with.

- **The robots.txt file.** This file, which resides on the server, can specify certain folders within a site that robots should not index. Using **robots.txt**, you can isolate these site areas from all robots or from specific robots. The contents of the file might look something like this:

  ```
  USER-AGENT: *
  DISALLOW: /asp/
  DISALLOW: /cgi-bin/
  DISALLOW: /private_folder/
  ```

  The disadvantage to using **robots.txt** is that each web server must have only one such file, located in a folder at the root level of the server. Customizing it is therefore the province of the server administrator, not the individual web authors.

- **The "robots" <meta> tag.** Less reliable than **robots.txt**, but more easily accessible, is adding a <meta> tag to your document with a name of "robots" and one or more of the following values, in a comma-separated list, for content: all, none, index, noindex, follow, nofollow. To explicitly allow access to all links within a page, use the following code:

  ```
  <meta name="robots" content="all, follow, index">
  ```

  To deny access to a page and its links, use this:

  ```
  <meta name="robots" content="none,noindex,nofollow">
  ```

  To allow access to the current document, but not its links, use this:

  ```
  <meta name="robots" content="index,nofollow">
  ```

Because Dreamweaver does not offer a specific Meta Robots object, use the generic Meta object to insert this tag. From the Head tab of the Insert bar, click the Meta object. Figure 7.7 shows a "robots" <meta> tag being added to a document, with typical settings in the dialog box.

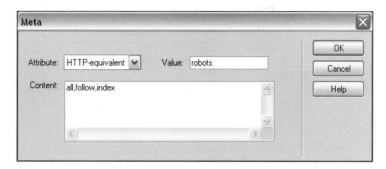

Figure 7.7   Using the generic Meta object to insert a `"robots"` `<meta>` tag into a document.

Exercise 7.1   Making a Document Searchable

In this exercise, you set up the Walt's Web Widgets home page to take maximum advantage of search engines. The files for this exercise (and the following exercises) are on the CD that accompanies this book, in the **chapter_07** folder. If you haven't done so already, copy those files to your hard drive so that you can work and save changes. Figure 7.8 shows Walt's home page.

Figure 7.8   Walt's Web Widgets home page (**main.html**) as it appears in a browser.

Walt's Web Widgets sells widgets—also known as doodads, gewgaws, thingamajigs, and whatsits. His stock consists of, among other things, bent nails, rusty screws, anonymous keys, rubber bands; you name it, Walt's has it. When people need just the perfect little piece of junk for a very particular job, Walt wants them to find him. Keep that in mind as you're filling out the keywords and description for this page.

1. From the **chapter_07** folder, open **main.html**. You will be setting up searchability for Walt's home page. In the Document window, show the head content (View > Head Content, or use the View Options icon in the toolbar). In the Insert bar, bring the Head tab to the front.

2. Start with keywords. Remember, you want to end up with 900 characters, if possible, to take full advantage of your allotted space in the search engine's index. From the Insert bar, click the Keywords icon to insert a `"keywords"` `<meta>` tag. In the dialog box, enter as many words related to widgets—and Walt's stock in general—as you can think of, separated by commas (spaces are optional). Use the following to help you get started:

```
widgets, doodads, thingies, thingy, thingummies, thingummy,
thingamajigs, thingimajigs, whatsits, geegaws, gewgaws, odds and
ends, junk, stuff, paper clips, bent screws, rusty nails, wire
pieces, rubber bands, string, washers, nuts, bolts, screws,
pushpins, tacks, thumbtacks
```

Remember to use the plural rather than the singular, and not to repeat words unnecessarily. Note that in the sample words shown here, some plurals and singulars appear (`thingies`, `thingy`). That's because the plural and singular are spelled differently; so in this case, users searching for the singular won't find it from the plural. Also note that alternative spellings (`geegaws`, `gewgaws`) are included. If you can think of a common way that people tend to misspell (or mistype) words, those variants also are good items to add to the list. That 900-character limit is higher than you might think!

Note

How fun is it to keep counting characters as you go? Not much. Unfortunately, Dreamweaver, unlike some text editors, has no tool for automatically counting words or characters. If you have a text editor that can count characters, you could use it as an external code editor (see Chapter 33, "Writing Code in Dreamweaver"). Or you could create the keyword list in a word processor that can count. Alternatively, if your JavaScripting skills are up to it, you might decide this is a dandy opportunity to create a custom Dreamweaver extension—a keyword counter! (See Chapter 36 for a full discussion of this.)

3. Check the page title. Hmm, "Welcome to Walt's" might look nice in the Bookmarks list, but it doesn't contain any real information, and—more important for the search engines—it contains no keywords. Change the page title to something more suitable (Walt's Web Widgets; Widgets, Doodads, and Thingies).

4. Add the `"description"` `<meta>` tag. From the Insert bar, click the Description object. In the dialog box, enter a 100–200-character description of Walt's. Maybe something like this:

```
Visit Walt's Web Widgets for the world's largest supply of
doodads, thingummies, and whatsits, all at unbelievable prices.
We can find hard-to-get items.
```

5. Repeat the description in a comment. No, you don't have to type it in again! Just do this:

   - From the head content display bar in the Document window, select the description icon.

   - In the Description Property inspector, select the text you entered and copy it (Ctrl/Cmd+C).

   - Go to Code view, and place the insertion point just before the closing `</head>` tag.

   - From the Common tab of the Insert bar, click the Comment object, which will insert the opening and closing comment tags. (Or you can just type `<!-- -->`.)

   - Put the insertion point between the two double dashes, and paste (Ctrl/Cmd+V).

     The new comment will appear in your head section, immediately following the description. You'll see the little comment icon in the head content display bar.

6. Finally, you will give the robots some instructions, letting them know they can search Walt's entire site. (Walt has no secrets!) In the Insert bar, click the generic meta object. Set the dialog box entries to match those shown in Figure 7.7.

Walt's Web Widgets is now ready to go public!

Meta Refresh

Another standardized and popular kind of `<meta>` tag is the `"refresh"` tag. This tag, when present, is processed by the browser, causing the page to either reload itself or load a new page after a set amount of time has elapsed. To reload the current page after 10 seconds, the syntax looks like this:

```
<meta http-equiv="refresh" content="10">
```

To load a new page after 5 seconds, the syntax looks like this:

```
<meta http-equiv="refresh" content="5;URL=pagetwo.html">
```

Refresh tags that reload the current page are often used with pages that contain dynamic data, such as breaking news, stock quotes, or the time and temperature. They're also used with web cam pages—every few seconds, the page reloads and a new web cam picture is automatically loaded into place. Refresh tags that load new pages are often used with redirection pages: Our site has moved!. They're also used with splash screens that show a brief welcome message or graphic for several seconds, and then whisk viewers away to the true home page. And they can be used in tandem with plugin media for scriptless plugin detection. (See Chapter 19, "Plugins, ActiveX, and Java," for a full discussion of this.)

Dynamic Tables

In a live data page, it's not the table itself that's dynamic, but its contents. Table rows, and even entire tables, can be used as repeating regions to display multiple records on a page (see Figure 7.9).

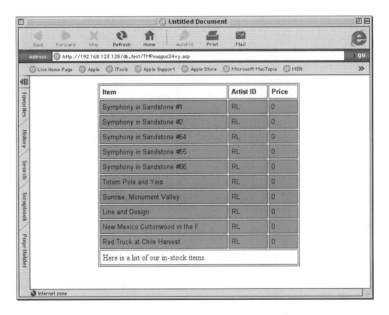

Figure 7.9   A table populated with dynamic data.

To declare a table row as a repeating region, select the entire row (use the tag selector, or drag to select all cells in the row). In the Server Behaviors panel, click the plus (+) and choose Repeat Region. Note that the repeating region doesn't need to be the only row in the table, though it can be. It also doesn't need to be the first or last row in the table.

To declare an entire table as a repeating region, select the table (it's safest to use the tag selector to do this). In the Server Behaviors panel, click the plus (+) and choose Repeat Region.

The Meta Refresh Object

In Dreamweaver, you insert refresh tags using the Refresh object, as shown in Figure 7.10. Click the object in the Insert > Head panel (or choose Insert > Head Tags > Refresh from the menus) and enter the number of seconds that should elapse before the refresh and whether to load a new page or reload the current page.

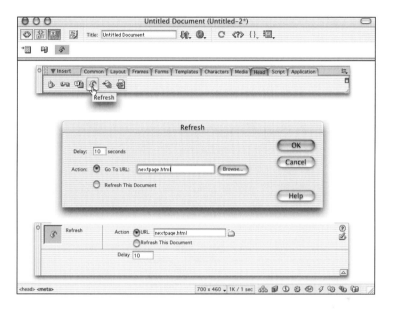

Figure 7.10   A refresh <meta> tag being inserted and later inspected, using the Refresh object.

Tips for Refreshing

Although using the tag is nice and straightforward, as with all things there are issues to consider:

- Unfortunately, refresh tags are not only used by the good guys. They also are used for much more sleazy purposes by disreputable sites (porn sites, for instance), allowing visitors to bookmark seemingly innocuous pages, such as "Aunt Bee's Quilting Zone," that are actually automatic links to "Hot Babes R Us" or "How to Construct a Nuclear Bomb." For this reason, some search engines will not index pages that contain refresh tags.

- Deciding how long to pause before refreshing (especially if the refresh will load a new page) requires some thought. How long is too long? If there is content on the current page (an animation, text to read), how long is long enough?

- If the refresh will be going to a new page, you might consider including a clickable link to that new page, so impatient users don't have to wait the required number of seconds.

Exercise 7.2   Create a Refreshing Splash Page

To get some experience with the refresh tag, you can use the Web Widgets files from the preceding exercise. In the **chapter_07** folder, along with **main.html**, is **splash.html**, shown in Figure 7.11. Open that file now. It contains an animated logo and welcome message, and Walt wants his customers to see it for a few seconds before going on to visit the rest of the site.

Figure 7.11   The Walt's Web Widgets splash page (**splash.html**), as it appears in the browser.

Note

No matter what size the browser window, the page content of **splash.html** will be vertically and horizontally centered onscreen. The effect is created by placing the content in a table with a width and height of 100%, and cell alignment of center (horizontal) and middle (vertical).

1. To begin with, add the refresh tag. In the Head tab of the Insert bar, click the Refresh icon. When the dialog box appears, choose **main.html** as the file to load. How long should you have visitors wait? Start by entering 10 seconds into the Delay field.

2. Before proceeding any further, try the page out in a browser. Choose File > Preview in Browser, then sit and wait until the refresh occurs. (If it doesn't occur, go back to Dreamweaver and double-check your steps!) Is 10 seconds too long? Try 5 seconds—or, find your own best delay time.

3. What about the viewers who don't want to wait any time at all? For them, you will add a regular link to **main.html.** You can add the link to the animated logo itself, or you can add a line of text, **click to enter**, beneath the logo. Alternatively, you can do both, just to cover all your bases. After you've done that, try it out to make sure it works before proceeding.

4. Finally, change the scenario. What if the splash page has something on it that people might want to read? A joke, an introductory sentence or two, an interesting news tidbit. Add some lines of text to the page so that it looks like the page shown in Figure 7.12.

Figure 7.12   The final Web Widgets splash page, with its added content, ready to entertain and divert visitors.

5. Now preview the page in a browser and imagine you're a first-time visitor. Maybe you want a few more seconds to read the text? Or maybe you think the delay time you've chosen still works fine. Just remember: The more there is to absorb on the page, the longer you might want to delay.

Note

Why do web sites have splash pages? First, there's a psychological reason. You're "framing the picture," mentally putting visitors in the mood for the web site to come. Obviously, this goal is more appropriate for some web sites (entertainment sites, online brochures) than others (informational sites). Second, there's a technical reason. While the viewer is seeing the splash page, you can be performing a browser check, starting the download of large graphics or media files that will be needed later, checking cookies, and so forth.

Working with Other Head Content

You'll probably spend more time using the various Dreamweaver Meta objects than either of the other Head objects, but both `<link>` and `<base>` have their uses as well.

Base Tags and the Base Object

In HTML, the purpose of the `<base>` tag is to provide an absolute URL and/or a link target that the browser will automatically use to resolve all links within the document. It sounds more complicated than it is.

Base Tags and Absolute URLs

When a browser encounters relative URLs in an HTML document, it constructs absolute addresses from them by accessing a "base" URL, usually that of the current document itself. If your web page address is `http://www.yourcompany.com/index.html`, and the page contains a link to `images/spacer.gif`, the browser combines those two addresses to construct an absolute URL for the image: `http://www.yourcompany.com/images/spacer.gif`.

If your document head uses the `<base>` tag to specify an alternate URL, like this

```
<base href="http://www.webwidgets.com/store/">
```

all relative links in the document will now be calculated relative to that address.

```
<a href="pricelist.html">Home</a>
```

resolves to

```
http://www.webwidgets.com/store/pricelist.html
```

```
<img src="../images/spacer.gif">
```

resolves to

```
http://www.webwidgets.com/images/spacer.gif
```

These addresses will be used even if the actual URL of your document is entirely different, like this:

```
http://www.homepagesRus.com/index.htm
```

When would you want to use the `<base>` tag to override your document's own URL for relative addressing? You would want to on two occasions:

- When creating mirror sites, where sets of pages on different web servers refer to a common resource pool of images or pages, `<base>` makes it possible to just port the pages to the mirror server. Using `<base>`, the relative links can be made to point to resources that are on the original server.

- When inserting HTML into email messages, all links must either be absolute or be relative to a specified `<base>`. This is because email messages have no URL for the email browser to use in constructing absolute paths. (Note that some email software, most notably Hotmail, cannot correctly construct URLs using `<base>`. It's safer, therefore, to just use absolute URLs throughout, and not specify a `<base>`.)

Base Tags and Link Targets

Targets in links determine in which browser window a linked document will appear. (See Chapter 12, "Designing Frame-Based Pages," for a full discussion of targets and target names.) Valid targets include the assigned name of any open window or frame in a frameset, or any of the generic keywords—such as `_blank` for a new window, or `_top` for the main window in a frameset. The normal link syntax looks like this:

```
<a href="widgets.html" target="_blank">
```

If, however, the document head includes a base tag that points to a target, like this

```
<base target="_blank">
```

all links in the document will be opened in that target window, exactly as if the target were specified in each individual link. A link coded as

```
<a href="widgets.html">
```

will behave as though it were coded using the full targeting syntax.

Why would you want to use the `<base>` tag to specify targets document wide, instead of specifying them individually for each link? It results in more efficient HTML, especially if your page contains many links (a resources or bibliography page, for instance). It also makes life easier because you don't have to remember to specify every single target; it also makes editing simpler, if you change your mind about where links should be targeted. Instead of changing dozens of individual links, you need change only the `<base>` tag.

Note

If you specify a target using the `<base>` tag, does that mean every single link in your document absolutely must use that target? No—you can override the `<base>` target for specific links by specifying a different target for the link itself. So if the `<head>` section specifies `<base target="content">`, but a link on the page specifies `<a href="mypage.html" target="nav">`, that particular link will open in the window named nav.

Tip

If you're a smart Dreamweaver user, of course, you could use a tag-specific Find & Replace to quickly change all those targets, instead of using the `<base>` tag. Tag-specific searches are discussed in Chapter 33.

Using the Base Tag in Dreamweaver

To insert a `<base>` tag into a Dreamweaver document, use the Base object in the Head tab of the Insert bar, as is shown in Figure 7.13. This object enables you to enter a URL and/or a target name. As with any head content, it doesn't matter where the insertion point is when the object is chosen; the `<base>` tag will automatically be inserted into the head.

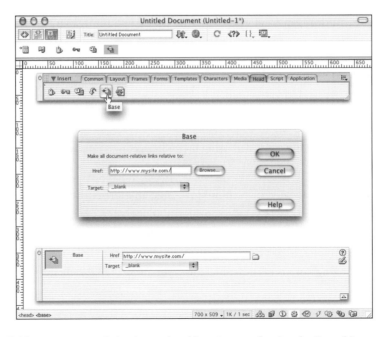

Figure 7.13   A `<base>` tag being inserted and later inspected, using the Base object.

Remember the following few tips when working with the `<base>` tag in the Dreamweaver environment:

- **Only one `<base>` tag per document.** Dreamweaver won't stop you from inserting multiple `<base>` tags in your document, but it's not legal HTML. Don't do it.

- **Remove empty `href` attributes.** If you specify a base target and no base URL, Dreamweaver will write the code for the `<base>` tag like this (problem code is highlighted):

  ```
  <base href=" " target="_blank">
  ```

  Although this is technically legal, it can cause the browser to misinterpret all the links on your page. (A link to `spacer.gif` is resolved to `http://spacer.gif`, which is a meaningless address.) Avoid the problem by going to Code view and manually deleting the empty `href` attribute.

Note

If you find yourself repeatedly using the `<base>` tag for targeting, and manually removing code, you might want to download Massimo Foti's Base Target object from the Macromedia Exchange for Dreamweaver.

- **Type in the absolute URL.** Although Dreamweaver allows you to browse to choose the base URL, doing this will create a relative address. For standard use, the `<base>` tag requires an absolute address.

  Don't forget the final slash (/). The browser will ignore any part of the URL that falls after the final slash. The following base URLs are considered equivalent:

  ```
  http://www.webwidgets.com/
  http://www.webwidgets.com/index.html
  http://www.webwidgets.com/images
  ```

- **Previewing pages with base URLs.** After you have specified an absolute base URL, you won't be able to properly preview the page (in Dreamweaver or your browser) until you've uploaded all relevant files to the server. If you really want to preview the page while you're working locally, you need to substitute the address of your local site folder. This is a URL beginning with the `file://` protocol. To access that information, open one of your site's documents in Dreamweaver and use Preview in Browser (F12) to view the page in any browser. Look at the URL in the browser's address field—the path will end in the name of the temporary file, but it should begin with the absolute URL of your local site folder. Like this (the local folder address is shown in bold):

  ```
  file:///Power%20Girl/Web%20Widgets/Local%20Site/TMP2onxb308wp.htm
  ```

Copy the relevant part of the address from the browser and paste it into your `<base>` tag. (Be sure to include the final slash!)

```
<base href=" file:///Power%20Girl/Web%20Widgets/Local%20Site/">
```

After you've done this, you can preview locally, but not by using Dreamweaver's Preview in Browser feature. You'll need to open the page manually from the browser. And of course, don't forget to restore the proper base URL before uploading the page!

- **Don't use the Site panel to move files.** After you have got a base URL in place, you're in charge of the relative links. If you rearrange your site's file structure using the Site panel's File view, Dreamweaver will try to update all relative links—don't let it! It will corrupt the links and nothing will work. To be safest, do your file rearranging outside of Dreamweaver, using your operating system's file management (Windows Explorer or Macintosh Finder).

Exercise 7.3   Add a Base Target to a Page's Links

Back to Walt's Web Widgets for this exercise. Walt has decided that he wants all the subject pages on his site to open in a new browser window, so the visitor never leaves the home page. You can accomplish this quickly by adding a `<base>` tag specifying a target of `_blank`.

1. From the **chapter_07 folder**, open **main.html**. Make sure head content is showing, and that the Insert bar is showing the Head category. It doesn't matter what in the Document window, you have selected.

2. In the Insert bar, click the Base object. When the dialog box appears, leave the URL field empty. From the pop-up target menu, choose `"_blank"`. Click OK to exit the dialog box.

3. Set the Document window to show Code and Design view. In the Head content display bar, click the Base object icon to select your newly inserted `<base>` tag. This action also should select the code for the `<base>` tag, in the Code view.

4. In Code view, delete the `href` attribute from the `<base>` tag, so the tag reads as follows:

```
<base target="_blank">
```

That's it! Preview the page in a browser and click any of the page's links. Each should open in a new window.

Link Tags and the Link Object

With the `<link>` tag, it's theoretically possible to specify all sorts of complex relation-ships between web documents. This includes specifying certain documents as next and previous in a series, linking alternative language versions of pages, page glossaries, and much more. Unfortunately, none of the major browsers support this functionality yet, although Lynx (a text-based browser) and iCab (a Macintosh browser) do to some extent. For current use, the only reliable implementation of the `<link>` tag is to link external style sheet documents. For a full discussion of this topic, see Chapter 13.

Summary

Did you ever think so much could be going on behind the scenes of a web document? The various head elements might not be visible in the browser, but they are capable of doing a lot. By taking advantage of them, you can make coding links easier (`<base>`), make your page available to search engines (`<meta>`), as well as perform all sorts of other nuts-and-bolts tasks.

Chapter 8

Design Issues

A web developer might need to have dozens of skills and areas of knowledge, but nothing is as central to web development work as the actual design and layout of pages. As the web and HTML have evolved, new technologies and techniques have emerged, therefore there are many ways to build a page. Topics covered in this part of the book (Part II, "Design with Dreamweaver") include using tables for page layout and the Dreamweaver page layout aids; designing and working with forms; designing frame-based pages; and using layers for page layout.

This chapter discusses some general issues of page design, including usability, navigation, methods of page layout, page composition issues, and use of color.

Usability

Web sites are for users. Whether strictly informational or interactive, whether commercial or non-profit, a site's entire purpose and reason for existing is to enable the end user to get his information, do what he needs to do, and leave. If his experience has been good, he may well return; if it has been frustrating or fruitless, the site will probably never see him again.

There is a strong tendency for web developers to lose this perspective. Many who work in this field are artistic; many love technology for its own sake. And although artwork can be delightful, and technical wizardry fascinating, most users are not using the web in hopes of being impressed by prowess in these areas.

Criteria for a Positive User Experience

Jakob Nielsen, a widely respected authority on web usability, suggests in his book *Designing Web Usability (Published by New Riders)* that there are four main areas of focus with regard to providing a positive user experience; these criteria can be described using the acronym HOME:

- High-quality content
- Often updated
- Minimal download time
- Ease of use

There is no simple method for designing a web site with all of these criteria given high priority. Instead, the web developer should think in these terms as he makes each decision, large or small, in the design of both the site structure as a whole and the individual pages.

Informal User Testing

Testing web sites, even very informally, can be extremely informative and valuable to the designer. Take every opportunity possible to just watch someone use your web site. Resist the urge to give any instructions or information about the site, but allow your tester to explore it on her own, or possibly look for a piece of information to accomplish something, while you look on. Because we as designers know how to find something, watching someone else attempt to find something can be an eye-opening experience with the potential to encourage a rethink about the way web sites are built.

Download Time and Ease of Use

Nielsen's first two criteria, with regard to content, are beyond the scope of this chapter. "Minimal download time" is an unquestioned essential and is by far the most violated of all basic web design principles. Keeping download time at its lowest is a challenge that arises in almost every aspect of site and page design and is discussed throughout this book.

His last criterion, "ease of use," covers a broad range of theory and practice. Essentially, the user should never need an explanation as to how your web site works; navigation and all other interactive functions should be entirely intuitive. The designer's job is to think the way a multitude of users are most likely to think, and to create a site that makes accomplishing tasks as smooth and easy as possible. Ease of use is a concept that has numerous concrete applications and should never be far from the designer's mind when creating any aspect of a web site's user interface. The remainder of this chapter touches on this subject in various ways.

Navigation and Site Structure Design

By its very nature, the web demands its own very distinctive theory, protocols, and techniques with regard to navigation.

Although print media has always had navigational systems and its own traditions—tables of contents, indexes, and even the Dewey Decimal System, for instance—most of these systems have been fully developed for centuries. Because books have been used for hundred of years, and the methods for assisting the user to find information in books have developed slowly over vast periods of time, consideration of navigation was just not the urgent priority it has become on the web.

The sheer size of the web with its billions of documents, the very newness of it as a medium, and the emphasis on efficiency and speed of the typical web user all produce a demand for easily navigated web sites.

Without a good navigational system, a web site is an almost useless, unordered collection of documents; with a good navigational system, a web site's value vastly increases.

Site Structure

A web site's navigational system is connected directly to the site's actual structure—what information is placed on what pages, and how the pages are linked. In its best and purest form, *navigation* is a visual representation of the user's current location and options for movement in relation to the site's information structure.

Even the best visual representation is not much use, if it represents an information structure that is difficult to understand and use. Therefore, good site navigation must always begin with careful planning.

Information Architecture Planning

For even the smallest web site, planning the information structure should precede any graphic design or page layout work. Careful consideration at this point in the process can pay off many times over later in the site production process; no amount of attractive visuals or cutting-edge techniques can compensate for a chaotic site structure.

A web developer in the role of site structure designer needs to find out the full scope of information and services the site needs to provide, and aim for the ideal organization of categories and subcategories. This type of planning can often benefit from flowchart-type diagramming, whether using special software for this purpose, handfuls of sticky notes, or even pencil and paper (see Figure 8.1).

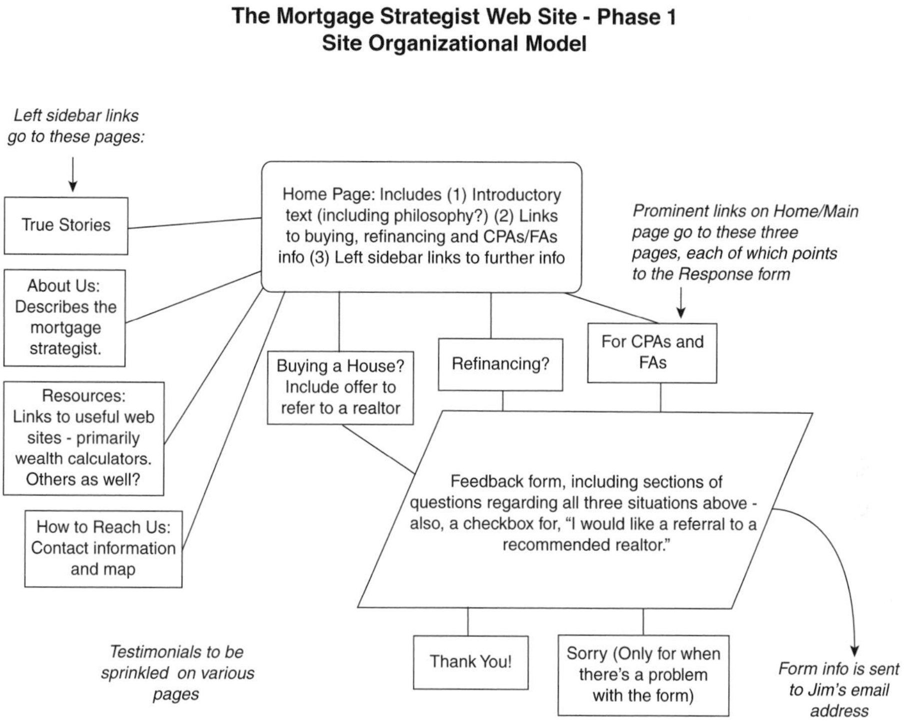

The Mortgage Strategist Web Site - Phase 1
Site Organizational Model

Left sidebar links
go to these pages:

True Stories

About Us:
Describes the
mortgage
strategist.

Resources:
Links to useful web
sites - primarily
wealth calculators.
Others as well?

How to Reach Us:
Contact information
and map

Home Page: Includes (1) Introductory
text (including philosophy?) (2) Links
to buying, refinancing and CPAs/FAs
info (3) Left sidebar links to further info

Prominent links on Home/Main
page go to these three
pages, each of which points
to the Response form

Buying a House?
Include offer to
refer to a realtor

Refinancing?

For CPAs and
FAs

Feedback form, including sections of
questions regarding all three situations above -
also, a checkbox for, "I would like a referral to a
recommended realtor."

Testimonials to be
sprinkled on various
pages

Thank You!

Sorry (Only for when
there's a problem
with the form)

Form info is sent
to Jim's email
address

Figure 8.1   Careful site structure planning is essential.

User-Centered Versus Company-Centered Information Structure

As previously said, every aspect of web site development needs to be considered primarily from the point of view of the user. The goal is always to provide a positive user experience. It is crucial for the web developer to remember that his own perspective, and that of his colleagues, can differ significantly from that of a typical web user.

During the process of information structure design, however, the client himself often can benefit from some consciousness-raising as well. In particular, an all-too-common pitfall can be the tendency for the representatives of a company to want to structure a site according to the company's own departmental organization, or at least according to its own ways of thinking about itself. As any marketing expert can attest, however, the end user/customer usually has a very different way of thinking about a company's products and services; it is critical to a site's success that its information be ordered in a way that makes sense first and foremost to the user.

Principles of Good Navigation Systems

Anyone who has used the web can confirm that countless types of navigation systems exist; the designer has an almost limitless range of choices. However, the web designer whose goal is to produce a site that users love to use will follow certain basic principles:

- Navigation should be based on a carefully planned site information structure.

- The user should always know what site he is on—a logo or other identifier should appear on every page, ideally in the same location.

- Navigation *controls*—the text or graphic links—should be obvious on the page and clear as to their function.

- The user should always know where he is in relation to other areas of the local site, a clear communication that "you are here." This should include his specific location in the site hierarchy; for instance, if he is two levels away from the site's start page, this should be clear (see Figure 8.2).

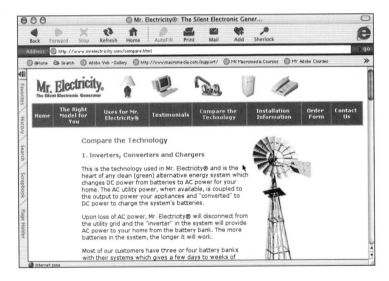

Figure 8.2   A navigation system should always show the user "you are here."

- Each page's navigation links should make clear where the user can go from where he currently is.

- Ideally, even on a very large site, the visitor should be able to reach the destination of his choice within two or three clicks.

- When graphic elements are used for links, secondary text navigation should be provided somewhere on the page for the non-graphical-browser user.

Note

The function and appearance of individual links is discussed in more detail in Chapter 6, "Links and Navigation."

Web developers sometimes tend to fall prey to the notion that users are weary of the "same old thing" with regard to navigation systems. However, one only needs to talk to a small cross-section of actual web users to confirm that just the opposite is true. Typical users (web designers excepted) simply do not go to the web hoping to find pages whose navigation systems are flashy, mysterious, or cutting-edge; just the opposite is true. In the vast majority of situations, users go to the Internet to get information and accomplish tasks. An ideal navigation system, from the user's point of view, is almost transparent, a humble servant: there exactly when he needs it, but never drawing attention to itself.

Methods of Page Layout

When graphical browsers first appeared, they didn't offer any page layout control. Text could be placed into paragraphs, headings, lists, and a few other formatting features, and images could be set to appear inline. But regardless, all elements started at the upper-left corner of the browser and proceeded left-to-right in lines down the page; there was no other way to arrange page elements (see Figure 8.3). Web site designers, accustomed to the measure of freedom and control over layout possible in print media, created a demand for page layout features that was soon met, initially by tables.

Figure 8.3   Before the advent of tables, HTML offered very little in the way of page layout aids.

Since that time, both the HTML specification and the support of major browsers for complex features has grown and developed significantly. Nowadays, the web designer can choose from a number of different ways to place images, text, and other elements on a web page, and design possibilities are almost limitless.

As of yet, however, no one content layout method gives the perfect combination of browser compatibility and flexibility. The various methods each have strengths and weaknesses. Some designers choose one method of page layout and use it almost exclusively, but the strongest approach is to become familiar with each tool and use it in the situations for which it is best suited.

Some web developers even use several of these layout tools on a single page to very good effect, but the ability to do this well is based on a thorough knowledge and lots of experience.

Tables

Basic table formatting was among the early additions to the original web browsers, and all major browsers have supported at least the simplest table tags since version 1.1 of Netscape. Although originally intended for laying out rows and columns of data, tables were soon being used for a very different purpose: to place elements more precisely within a page (see Figure 8.4).

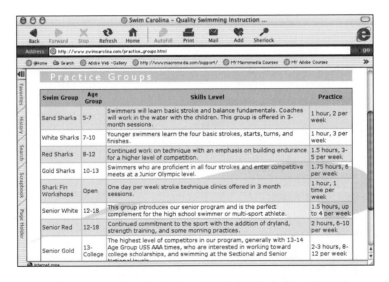

Figure 8.4   Tables were originally intended specifically for displaying tabular data.

As of this writing, tables still represent a viable and useful page layout option, compatible with even very old browsers. But they are definitely not a quick-and-easy solution: To use tables well, you must be willing to spend time learning to understand their many quirks and limitations.

Dreamweaver provides a complete set of table-building features that make building this type of page extremely quick and convenient. Designing with tables is covered in detail in Chapter 9, "Building Tables."

Frames

Frames are sometimes treated as a newcomer to the scene, when in fact both major browsers have supported them for several years, since Netscape 2 and Internet Explorer 3. They are included in the HTML 4.0 specification.

The use of frames enables you to specify rectangular areas of a browser window into which new, smaller pages of content can be loaded and reloaded, independently of each other. The most common use of this involves placing elements such as navigation bars and headers into frames, with page content appearing in a separate frame; the content frame can then be reloaded without disrupting the other frames. In this way, static elements need to be loaded only one time and stay in view as you navigate through various content pages (see Figure 8.5).

Frames allow a kind of flexibility that is hard to duplicate with any other method of page layout. However, some drawbacks are worth mentioning:

- Users often find frame sites confusing to navigate.
- Individual frames cannot be bookmarked.
- If not handled carefully, frame sites can be difficult for search engines to index.

Still, the designer who understands frames and uses them carefully can produce some striking and useful designs. Designing with frames is covered in detail in Chapter 11, "Working with Forms."

Tip

Framesets are the HTML documents that describe how individual *frames* (also HTML documents) are to display in the browser.

Layers

First, it's important to clarify some concepts and terminology with regard to the word *layers*.

- Netscape introduced the `<layer>` element starting with Netscape 4. This is a Netscape-specific tag that has never become part of the HTML specification; its use is discouraged and later versions of Netscape have discontinued support of the tag. None of the discussions here or in Chapter 14, "Using Layers for Page Layout," refer to the use of this proprietary element.

- The term *layer* does not appear in any HTML or CSS specification.

- Dreamweaver offers a tool/concept referred to as layers that is completely unrelated to the Netscape tag described in this list. Dreamweaver layers are actually `<div>` elements positioned with inline CSS.

- Dreamweaver layers are distant relatives of the CSS technique referred to as CSS-P or CSS Positioning. Both use `<div>` tags to define rectangular elements, and both use CSS declarations to specify the properties of these `<div>` elements. However, CSS-P takes the concept further (as discussed later in this chapter).

Dreamweaver Layers

Dreamweaver layers are supported only by version 4 and above browsers; older browsers will either present an error message or display the page with missing or misarranged elements. However, Dreamweaver layers are integral to DHTML (see Chapter 17, "Controlling Layers with JavaScript," and Chapter 18, "Animating Layers").

Dreamweaver layers can be an extremely useful tool when used properly. However, inexperienced users, wishing that page elements could simply be "dragged and dropped" onto a web page the way they can in print layout applications, sometimes turn to them as a convenient shortcut; this is not a good use for layers. Their drawbacks and quirks make them a poor substitute for either tables-based layouts or CSS-P.

Tip

Layers should not be used as an easy shortcut to page layout. A rule of thumb when choosing between tables and Dreamweaver layers is this: If the design can be accomplished using tables, they are a much better choice, in that they are much more widely supported by the browsers. Layers should be used only if and when your design involves DHTML or timeline animation, or for other reasons that can be accomplished only with layers.

Tip

For a detailed treatment of Dreamweaver layers, see Chapter 14.

CSS Positioning

CSS Positioning, or *CSS-P*, is part of the CSS 2 Specification, which is a full recommendation of the W3C. As of this writing, the major browser vendors have failed to implement significant portions of the CSS 2 specification, but positioning is fairly well supported.

Important points to remember about CSS-P include the following:

- Provides a way to achieve the functionality of the proprietary `<layer>` element with the `<div>` tag and style sheets.

- Allows the *separation of structure and presentation*, which is central to the theory upon which HTML is built (see Figure 8.5).

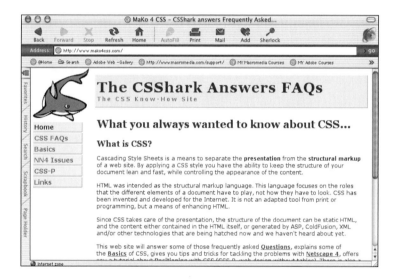

Figure 8.5   A fast-loading, "liquid," handicapped-accessible CSS-P page.

- Can be used to build page layouts that are easily manipulated and updated from a single linked style sheet

- Can be used to build flexible, "liquid" page layouts

- Lends itself very well to creating handicapped-accessible pages

- Avoids the page-loading delays associated with table-based layouts

- Although supported partially by Internet Explorer 4.x and later, and Netscape 4.x and later, should be tested thoroughly on numerous browsers and platforms.

See Chapter 14 for further discussion of CSS-P.

Interview: Corey Eiges

Business Name: **10 Digit Tender, Inc.**

URL: `http://YouNeedaWebstore.com`

How did you get started in web design? What has your learning process been like? What kind of work are you currently doing?

I began web design when I took over an unfinished site for the company for which I was working at the time. I wound up scrapping it and starting all over, using Dreamweaver and learning as I went.

My learning process has been mostly by designing and reverse engineering, as opposed to by books or classes. I learned what works and what doesn't by personal experience, playing with code, and examining the works of others I have found through the Macromedia Dreamweaver and UltraDev newsgroups.

Currently I am creating e-commerce and database sites, as well as standard "brochure-ware" sites.

What hardware and software do you use in your work?

I work on a Windows 2000 Pro laptop networked to a Windows 98 desktop with cable modem Internet access for both, and use an Olympus digital camera, a Visioneer scanner, and an Epson color printer. My software includes Dreamweaver 4 and UltraDev 4 for web design (I keep both on the system), Fireworks 4 with a BladePro plugin for graphics, eyedropper for color matching, SnagIt32 for screen captures and some image editing, CuteFTP for file transfers, and of course my own handcoded software (registry utilities) for disaster prevention and recovery.

What are some characteristics of web pages that you consider to be well-designed?

For me, navigation is what it's all about. When I first started out as a newbie, I used "mystery meat" navigation, which looks cool but is user-unfriendly. I no longer do that. A site rarely has what I want on its home page, so where do I go from there? If I have to look for more than a few seconds to figure out how to get to what I need, then that site begins to irritate me. We have become a world that requires instant gratification, and a designer should take that into consideration.

A well-designed site has something that has a degree of familiarity to it. Even on sites with outlandish color schemes or graphics, if there is a sense of order or balance to it, I might consider it well-designed. Or if the site is, visually-speaking, as dull as dishwater, yet has that sense of familiarity that invites me back, that too might qualify as well-designed. That sense of familiarity includes the navigation structure, but really it is much more. Whether the layout or the lines or amount of white space, or even the size and placement of the logo, something on the page has to say, "Stay awhile. You have friends here."

Do you primarily use tables, frames, layers, CSS Positioning, or some combination? Which direction do you plan to move in?

I use a combination of these, with frames and CSS Positioning being used less than layers and tables. Although some people have a predisposition to avoid frames, I don't. Sometimes they are the best solution for a project. Nevertheless, I primarily use layers and tables, and almost always tables within layers.

I plan to use CSS Positioning a bit more, but I might wait to see what sort of improved integration with CSS Dreamweaver will provide in future releases.

What trends on the web and in the web designer's work do you see as important?

Netscape dying an ignominious death, falling off the edge of the Earth, is the most important Web trend for which I look. My productivity would zoom if I didn't have to deal with Netscape-related issues.

Beyond that, the rush to standardization, although important, really won't affect me personally in the near term. I enjoy using CSS and as far as this web designer is concerned, that is the trend that's most important.

What advice would you give to someone just starting out in web design?

Don't be afraid to get your hands dirty with code. You can create decent-looking sites using a tool such as Dreamweaver, but unless you look under the hood of the car, (look at the code), you will have learned little. The sense of accomplishment you will have after receiving your "aha!" epiphany will be far greater than the satisfaction of making a handsome and functional web site.

Page Composition Issues

The basic unit of a web site is the HTML document—the page; a user is generally looking at a single page at a time. Although the structure of a site and its navigation system are very important to the user experience, the layout of the individual pages also is crucial. You have already read about the techniques by which pages are composed—using tables, frames, layers, or CSS positioning; this section discusses a few of the pertinent issues and considerations in page composition design.

The Use of Screen Real Estate

The web designer's canvas is the browser window's *viewport*, the rectangular area available for displaying web content. This canvas, sometimes described as *screen real estate*, is valuable space. You have this finite number of pixels to present your message, and it is wise to carefully consider and plan how to use each part of it.

Always remember these few basics concerning the use of screen real estate:

- Because of the way HTML documents load in the browser window, the top and the left portions of the document are the first to come in view; this renders the top and left areas more important than farther to the right or farther down on the page.

- The portion of a document that fits into the user's browser window upon loading is far more valuable than any portion he has to scroll to see. Users generally will scroll vertically, although sometimes grudgingly; after all, web pages are scroll-like documents and are expected to reach beyond the bottom of the browser window. However, user testing has shown that users strongly dislike scrolling horizontally. Don't ask your users to scroll horizontally

Tip

A cardinal rule of page layout: Don't ask the user to scroll horizontally. An exception is sometimes made for the very lowest resolution settings, such as 640×480, which are becoming quite uncommon, and whose users are accustomed to horizontal scrolling.

- Users come to your web site for content, and the majority of a page's available space should be filled with relevant, useful content.

- Repeating content such as headers, navigation bars, and footers is important to the cohesiveness of a site, but it shouldn't take up a large percentage of each page. Also these elements should load in exactly the same location on each page, so that the user doesn't have a visually jarring sensation when moving from page to page.

Page Width, Resolution, and Window Size

The web was designed as a platform-independent medium; ideally, web pages should be viewable in some acceptable form using any type of device, from giant monitors to handheld devices. At the very least, designers must be sure that pages display properly at all the most common resolution settings for desktop and laptop computer monitors.

New web designers often ask how to design their pages "so that they will look good on any size monitor"; this represents some errors in thinking. The size of the monitor is not the issue; what matters are the resolution setting and the browser window size.

A user with a 21-inch monitor set at an 800×600 pixel resolution will see your web page looking the same as a user with a 15-inch monitor set at 800×600, assuming that both have the browser window maximized. The lucky user with the 21-inch monitor will just see it a lot larger; he won't see any more content.

So it isn't of any use to talk about the size of the monitor. However, an issue beyond the resolution setting also needs to be considered: the size of the browser window itself. A browser window can be resized by the user to any dimensions he desires, of course, by dragging the edges of the window with his cursor. Although some users keep the browser window maximized, many do not (see Figure 8.6). Especially with larger monitors with higher resolution settings, it just isn't necessary to run programs maximized; the desktop space that isn't being used for the browser can be used for other purposes. Suppose, for example, that a user has his monitor resolution set to 1024×768 pixels, but his browser window resized to about 800 pixels wide and 600 pixels in height; he will see your web page the same way as the two previously mentioned users.

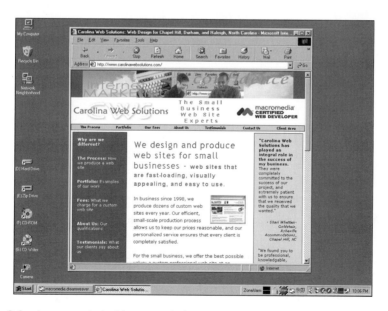

Figure 8.6 A non-maximized browser window.

As of this writing, the majority of Internet users are using an 800×600–pixel resolution setting. A much smaller but fast-growing group uses 1024×768 pixels. A very small and fast-shrinking group has the monitor set to 640×480 pixels. The users with the higher resolution settings do not always maximize the browser window, and so need to be considered along with the group with the lower resolution settings.

Another important factor in this discussion is that pages can be designed so that they are *liquid* or *flexible* and accommodate themselves to the size of the user's browser window viewport, as opposed to *fixed-width* pages (see Figure 8.7). This is the ideal solution, and a way to achieve it is discussed in Chapter 9. Even when designing flexible pages, however, in most cases a design will look better at one size than another, and the designer needs to decide for whom to optimize the design. Therefore, assuming that the designer wants to please the largest number of users, while not ignoring any, the issue of how many are browsing at what window size is still very relevant.

Figure 8.7   A flexible-width page accommodates itself to almost any browser window size.

One last consideration is the fact that browser windows contain *chrome*—the toolbars, status bars, gray edges, and scrollbars, which take up screen pixels. So even those with the browser window set to 800 pixels wide do not have the full 800 pixels for viewing your web page (see Figure 8.8).

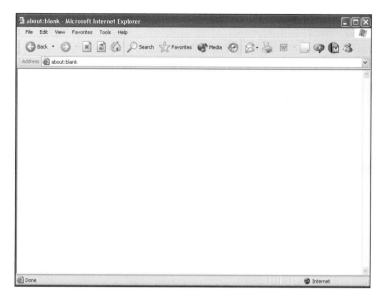

Figure 8.8 Browser window chrome.

At the time of this writing, the best suggestion is to design pages to be flexible, and that pages fit without scrolling into a browser width of less than 800 pixels. To allow for the browser chrome, use about 760 pixels. Pages should look good at about 1024 pixels wide as well, this being the second-most-common window size, and one that is growing rapidly. And pages should look good, or at least respectable, at 640 pixels wide. The most relevant content should be placed at the top and left of the page, and if some scrolling is required, it's probably acceptable to 640×480 resolution users.

Use of Fonts

New web designers often ask, "How can I control the way the fonts on my page will display for the user, so that he can't resize them and break my design?" The only way to do this is by turning the text into graphics. Even when text size is specified by CSS in pixels, the user can override the setting in some browsers. This is a difficult reality that designers need to be aware of; page designs must be built so that they still display well when the text size is altered. However, there's a good reason for the browsers giving the user this capability: those with visual impairments need to be able to choose a text size that works for them.

Use of Images

As powerful as images can be as a page layout tool, some restraint is advised in their use for several reasons:

- Every image used adds to page download time; large images can add significantly.
- Pages based on images are more difficult to make accessible to the less-common *user agents* (devices used to view the web) such as speech browsers and handheld devices.
- Heavy use of images makes building flexible pages much more difficult.

Heavy use of images makes accommodating user changes in text size (see the last item in the preceding list) much more difficult.

White Space

White space is a term used in the print media industry for empty space on a page; note that white space can be of any color. Far from being wasted space, white space serves important purposes. One use for white space is just separating page elements. However, a more important use is related to the way people see and read; white space provides a much-needed "rest" from the visual busy-ness of most pages. Good use of white space can make a page much more pleasant to look at and easier to read (see Figure 8.9).

Figure 8.9 Good use of white space.

Use of Color

The use of color can make or break a web site. A consistent and well thought out color scheme sets the mood, establishes visual cohesiveness, and draws the user's eye as needed. Bad color choices—too many colors, inconsistent use of colors, colors with too much or not enough contrast—make the site look amateurish and hurts its usability. From a practical standpoint, web designers also have to decide whether to limit their choices to web-safe colors.

Working with the Color Wheel

The color wheel, like that shown in Figure 8.10 and in the **chapter_08** folder on the accompanying CD, is an important design tool when choosing a color scheme. Relationships between colors become apparent when viewed in this structure. And choosing a good color scheme is all about determining relationships.

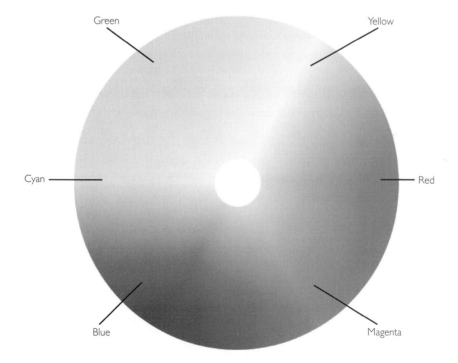

Figure 8.10   The color wheel with major colors marked.

Hue, Saturation, Brightness

These are the principal characteristics of any color. *Hue* is the perceived color—red, purple, green, and gold. *Saturation* refers to the intensity of the color—a bright fire-engine red as opposed to a dusky rose color, for instance. Adding gray desaturates colors. *Brightness* refers to the amount of black added—fire-engine red compared to a deep, heavy maroon. When mixing colors for a color scheme, you usually want to choose colors that contrast in more than just hue.

Warm Versus Cool Colors

The basic mood of a site can be determined by whether it primarily uses warm or cool colors. Warm colors are the colors of fire—oranges, golds, reds, and yellows. Warm colors can be inviting and cozy, or assertive and in-your-face, demanding attention. Cool colors are the colors of water and air—blues, greens, and turquoises. Cool colors can be restful and recessive, or even aloof, crisp, distant.

Complementary Colors

When two colors have hues that lie opposite one another on the color wheel, they are said to be *complementary*, and have a very strong visual impact together. Two complementary colors of equal brightness and saturation, placed up against each other, will be very jarring. They might even appear to "dance" where they meet. Two colors with complementary hues, but differing brightness and saturation values, will look as if they were made for one another. A bright, sharp turquoise and deep, dark maroon; a deep, rich blue and pale, muted gold; these are the start of a wonderful color scheme.

One popular method of using complementary colors to create a color scheme is to choose several variations of color from a particular area of the color wheel—differing shades of gold and brown, for instance; and offset them with one choice from the opposite side of the wheel, like a bright sky blue.

Note

Dreamweaver offers two tools to help set up and implement a cohesive color scheme. Choose Commands > Set Color Scheme to apply one of dozens of pre-defined color schemes to your page. If you don't trust your ability to choose color wisely, this can be an inspiring place to start learning. After you've chosen your site's color scheme, the Assets panel can help you keep track of your colors, through its color category. See Chapter 22, "Local Site Management," for a full discussion of the Assets panel.

Colors on the Web

In the print world, designers are limited by the colors their available inks can reproduce. Web designers aren't limited by ink, but have to consider other limiting factors when choosing colors.

Web-Safe Colors

A *web-safe color* is one that appears without dithering in Netscape Navigator and Microsoft Internet Explorer on both Windows and Macintosh systems running in 256-color mode; 216 colors are commonly considered to be web-safe. *Dithering* is a pattern like a tiny checkerboard made up of a combination of two colors in an attempt to approximate a third color, which the system is incapable of displaying.

On newer monitors using 24-bit True Color, colors other than the web-safe colors don't present a problem; these systems can display more than 16 million colors accurately. As more and more of these monitors come into use, and the old machines running 256 colors are retired, ignoring the web-safe palette is becoming a viable option. Many designers opt to use custom non-web-safe colors, deciding that possible display problems for a small percentage of users is an acceptable risk for the benefit of being able to choose from a rainbow of colors. However, the jury is definitely still out; many designers think that it is important to restrict themselves to the 216 web-safe colors.

> **Note**
>
> As you're using the Dreamweaver color picker, be aware that the color cubes and Continuous Tone color palettes offer web-safe colors. The Windows OS, Mac OS, and Grayscale palettes are not web-safe. If you are using one of these, and then choose Snap to Web-Safe, the selected color will be replaced with the closest web-safe color. (See Chapter 2, "Setting Up the Dreamweaver Workspace," for more on the color picker.)

Gamma and Calibration Differences

Because most computer monitors are not calibrated to display color accurately, there is no guarantee that your colors will look exactly the same on any two computers. PCs tend to display colors darker and more saturated than Macs, for instance; this is especially noticeable in the very dark shades. In addition to this, color shifts occur in monitors as they warm up in the morning, as they age, and even as they reflect light from a window or overhead light.

How worried should you be about variation? Your colors are not going to be hijacked—red will still be red; green will still be green. They might just be different shades of red or green. The colors at most risk of really hurting your design as they change are those on the cusp between warm and cool. A nice, warm gold can shift into a sickly greenish gold very easily.

Summary

It takes study and practice to learn how to plan and build attractive, useful web pages. In this chapter, you learned the basics of web page design: how to think in terms of the user experience, how to structure a site that is easily navigable, the pros and cons of the different page layout methods, and how to arrange a page that will look good on numerous different user agents. This chapter finished with a look at the skillful use of color on the web. The remainder of this part of the book examines the major page layout tools in depth.

Chapter 9

Building Tables

When web designers dream, they imagine themselves placing page elements wherever they please on an HTML page, and their layout being displayed with pixel-perfection in every browser on the market.

In the morning light, however, reality hits home: Although there are a number ways to position page elements, none is simple, and none is even close to browser-foolproof. This chapter covers the original purpose of tables and their use as layout tools, the basics of table code, how to insert a table with Dreamweaver, how to modify and format a table with Dreamweaver, and some different approaches to using tables for page layout.

HTML Tables: Only for Tabular Data?

Tables were originally conceived as containers for "tabular data"—pieces of information that are best arranged in rows and columns, as in a spreadsheet. They are ideal for it, and are still widely used this way, as shown in Figure 9.1.

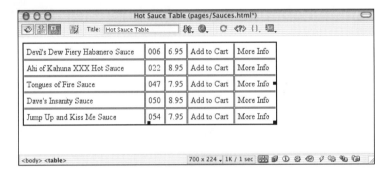

Figure 9.1   Data arranged in rows and columns with an HTML table.

Very soon after the advent of HTML tables, however, web designers began using them as a tool for arranging and separating elements on a page; the rows and columns designed for lining up pieces of data are very useful for placing an image here and a block of text there. Positioning of page elements is now possible using Cascading Style Sheets (CSS), and this method will eventually supercede positioning with tables as the browsers offer better support for CSS. But for the time being, tables are the main tool designers use to create page layouts.

How Table Code Works

Dreamweaver makes using HTML tables easy, and this chapter focuses on building tables with Dreamweaver. However, an understanding of the way table code works is useful. Sooner or later, you will probably find it necessary to edit your table code directly, and familiarity with the HTML tags that make up a table will make that much easier. As emphasized throughout this book, the Dreamweaver user who can use its visual design tools, as well as be aware of the underlying code, is in a position to create truly professional web sites.

Simple Tables

A table places information inside *cells* by dividing a rectangle into rows and columns. HTML represents a basic table using three elements. A table, defined by its surrounding `<table></table>` tags, contains one or more rows, `<tr> </tr>`. Each row, in turn, contains one or more *table data* cells, `<td></td>`. A very basic table would be built with code like this:

```
<table border="1">
  <tr>
    <td>Chapel Hill</td>
    <td>Durham</td>
  </tr>
  <tr>
    <td>Raleigh</td>
    <td>Cary</td>
  </tr>
  <tr>
    <td>Hillsborough</td>
    <td>Apex</td>
  </tr>
</table>
```

This code is rendered in Internet Explorer 5.5 as shown in Figure 9.2. To create more complex structures, table cells can be made to span several rows or columns by using `rowspan` and `colspan` attributes. The table shown in Figure 9.1 uses a `colspan` attribute to create its top row, where one large cell spans the entire table.

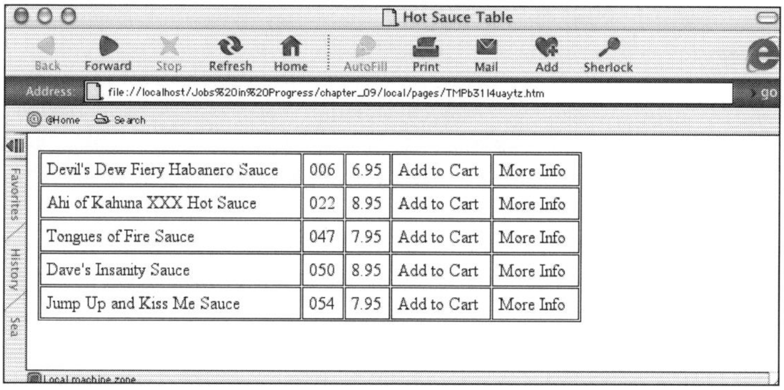

Figure 9.2 A browser rendering of a very basic table.

Other Table Elements

In addition to these commonly used table elements, various other tags can be placed within a table. Most of them extend the table's accessibility—describing and structuring the table's content areas logically for interpretation by a wide variety of devices, including nongraphical browsers. Table 9.1 lists several of these elements. The `<table>` tag itself can also use the `summary` attribute to present a longer text summation of the table's contents.

Table 9.1   HTML 4 Table Elements

Tag	Purpose
`<th>`	An alternative to `<td>`, used to create header cells. (Most browsers display content in these cells as bold and centered.)
`<caption>`	Brief descriptive text about the table. Most browsers display this above or below the table.
`<thead>` *	Specifies a table header.
`<tfoot>` *	Specifies a table footer.
`<tbody>` *	Specifies a table body.
`<colgroup>` *	Defines a group of one or more columns.
`<col>` *	Indicates an individual column within a `<colgroup>`.

* Indicates items that are part of the HTML 4 standard.

Working with Tables in Dreamweaver

Because tables are a ubiquitous part of web development, Dreamweaver offers several methods to create and work with them. The best method for most web designers is to work in Design view, using the Table object, Property inspector, and the various commands in the Modify > Table submenu.

Note

This chapter focuses on using Dreamweaver in Design view. Layout view is covered in Chapter 10, "Using Dreamweaver's Page Layout Aids." The new Dreamweaver Table objects for working in Code view are covered in Chapter 32, "Technical Issues."

Creating Tables

To create a table in Design view, position the insertion point where you want the table inserted, and do one of the following:

- From the Common tab in the Insert bar, click the Table object (Figure 9.3).

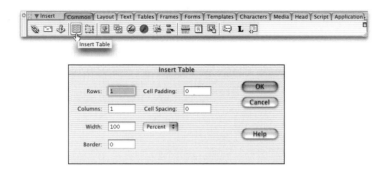

Figure 9.3   The Table object and Insert Table dialog box.

- Go to Insert > Table.
- Use the shortcut key, Ctrl+Alt+T (Windows), or Cmd+Opt+T (Mac).

The Insert Table dialog box will appear (see Figure 9.3), giving you a chance to set some of your table's basic properties. After the table is inserted, you can use the Table Property inspector to change these and other properties (see Figure 9.4). You can also set the properties of individual cells by using the table cell Property inspector (see Figure 9.5). Note that table cell properties will only show if the inspector is in its expanded state.

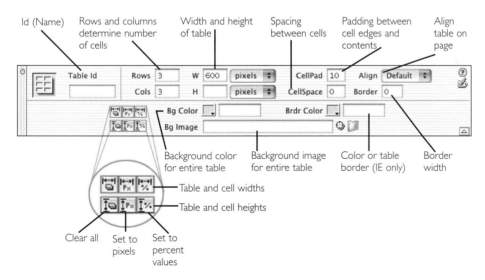

Figure 9.4   The Table Property inspector.

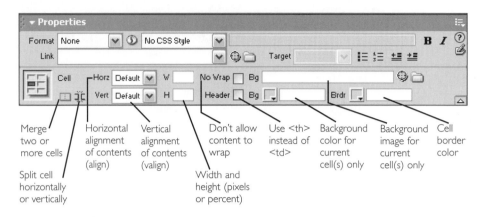

Merge two or more cells

Split cell horizontally or vertically

Horizontal alignment of contents (align)

Vertical alignment of contents (valign)

Width and height (pixels or percent)

Don't allow content to wrap

Use <th> instead of <td>

Background color for current cell(s) only

Background image for current cell(s) only

Cell border color

Figure 9.5   The expanded Property inspector showing table cell properties.

> **Note**
>
> MX   Are your tables accessible? To enable accessibility options for tables, go to Edit > Preferences, and choose the Accessibility category, then select the Tables check box. After you've created the table, if you're working in Code view you can access lists of accessibility attributes with the Modify > Edit Tag command and with code hints. See Chapter 2, "Setting Up the Dreamweaver Workspace," for a full discussion of accessibility in Dreamweaver. See Chapter 33, "Writing Code in Dreamweaver," for more on working with Dreamweaver code tools.

> **Note**
>
> After the table is inserted, if you look at it in Code view, you'll see that each cell contains a nonbreaking space ( ). This is present because most browsers won't correctly display completely empty table cells—and Dreamweaver assumes you want your cells to display. As soon as you enter content into a cell, Dreamweaver will remove the nonbreaking space.

Selecting Tables and Table Parts

One of the trickiest aspects of working with tables is selecting the portion of the table you want to work with.

Selecting the Entire Table

The Property inspector will only show table formatting options if the entire table—the <table></table> tag pair and all they contain—is selected. You can select the entire table from within the Document window, by clicking on the outermost edge of the table.

But this requires really good hand-eye coordination, and you might accidentally move the mouse and adjust the table's dimensions as you're doing it.

A better way to select an entire table is to use the tag selector. Place the cursor anywhere within the table, and in the tag selector at the bottom of the Document window, click the <table> tag. The table will display with a black line around it in the Document window, and can then be modified. Figure 9.6 shows the tag selector being used with table code.

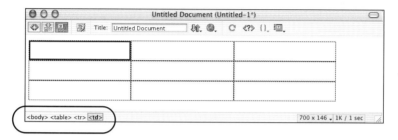

Figure 9.6   The tag selector showing a selected table cell.

Selecting Rows and Cells

Selecting the individual parts of a table is easier than selecting the whole.

To access an individual cell's properties, just click the cursor inside the cell. The bottom half of the Property inspector will show the table cell attributes for the cell you're in.

To select multiple, contiguous cells, do one of the following:

- Starting with the cursor inside one of the cells, drag across as many cells as you want to select. (Just don't accidentally start with your cursor on the border between two cells, or you'll resize them!)
- Click inside one cell. Then hold down the Shift key and click inside other cells to select them. If the cells you click in aren't next to each other, all intervening cells will also be selected. Shift-clicking again in a selected cell will deselect it.

If you select an entire row of cells using one of these methods, you have effectively selected the <tr> tag. Any formatting options you choose will be added to the <tr> tag, not to the individual <td> tags. You can accomplish the same thing by clicking inside a cell, and then using the tag selector to select the <tr> tag.

To select multiple cells that aren't contiguous, start by clicking inside one cell. Then hold down Ctrl/Cmd and click inside other cells to select them. Ctrl/Cmd-clicking inside a selected cell will deselect it.

Selecting Outside the Table

Especially if your table is large, selecting outside it can be the hardest thing of all! To position your cursor outside a table, select the table and press the right- or left-arrow key on your keyboard. The cursor will appear as a flashing line, the same height as the table it is adjacent to, even if the table is very long.

Working with Table Contents

In an effort to make tables as user-friendly as possible, Dreamweaver has adapted various features you might be familiar with from working with tables in word processing and spreadsheet programs.

Using Tab to Navigate

With the cursor inside a table cell, pressing the Tab key will move the cursor into the next table cell, moving in a left-to-right direction across each row, and a top-to-bottom direction through the rows. It can be difficult to place the cursor into some very small table cells, and this technique can be useful.

Pressing the Tab key when you're in the very last cell of the table (bottom right) will add a new row to the bottom of the table. A few things to note about this feature:

- The new row will take on various characteristics of the row above it. Background colors, horizontal and vertical alignment, colspan values, widths, and heights will all be copied down to the newly added row.

- If you have set a height for your table, the new row will need to fit into that height. If your cells don't have heights assigned, they'll all shrink to make room for the new row. If your cells do have heights, the combined cell heights might be larger than the table height, which will make your table unstable in the browser.

Using the Arrow Keys to Navigate

You can also use the up, down, left, and right arrow keys to navigate through your table's contents and cells, though this works a little differently than using tab. The arrow keys will first of all move you within the cell's contents—if your cell contains three lines of text, for instance, pressing the down arrow will move the cursor from one line of text to another. But when the cursor reaches the end of the cell's contents, pressing the arrow key again will move to the next cell up, down, left, or right.

Tip

Sometimes when a cell contains an image or other media element, it can be difficult to select the cell and not its contents, especially if the cell is no larger than the item it contains. One way out of this problem is to select the content item, then use the tag selector to select the parent `<td>` tag. Another way is to select the content item, then click the left or right arrow key once (this puts the cursor after the contents but still inside the cell).

Deferred Table Update

Have you ever noticed that, when you have edited a table or its contents, the Design view display doesn't always update immediately? Usually, this happens when you have deleted table contents or changed a dimension value, and the table doesn't resize itself right away. This isn't a bug; it's a feature called *deferred update*. Dreamweaver can work faster if it doesn't need to worry about recalculating table dimensions, and redrawing the Document window, every time you edit your table.

Because of deferred updating, you need to refresh the Document window's display before the view will update. Clicking outside of the table will usually redraw the table; however, sometimes it is also necessary to click the tag for each table that has been affected in the tag selector. With a little practice, this will become second nature.

If deferred updating is a nuisance you'd rather not deal with, you can turn it off. Go to Edit > Preferences, and choose the General category. Find the check box for Faster Table Editing, and deselect it (see Figure 9.7).

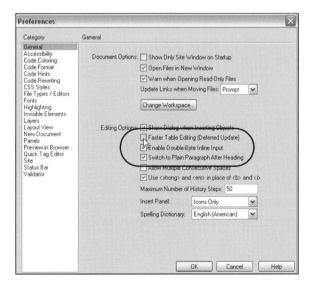

Figure 9.7   De-activating the deferred table update in Preferences.

Modifying Table Structure

How big is your table? How many cells does it contain? Do you want cells to span multiple rows or columns? All these structural aspects can be adjusted by manipulating the table in Design view, using the Property inspector, and using the Modify > Table submenu commands.

Tip

Inspect your table structure! If you want to keep on top of your table's code structure, but find looking at Code view overwhelming, check out the new Tag Inspector, as shown in Figure 9.8. The top portion of this panel shows your table's code as an expandable outline that clarifies the structure visually. The bottom portion lists all the attributes that can be applied to the various table elements. Read all about the Tag Inspector in Chapter 33.

Adding and Removing Rows and Columns

After the table is created, you can change the number of cells it contains by changing its rows and columns. You can do this in any of the following ways:

Figure 9.8   The Tag Inspector diagramming the structure of a simple table and listing possible attributes for the table elements.

- Select the table, and change the numbers in the Rows and Columns fields in the Property inspector. Note that, if you add rows here, they'll be added to the bottom of the table; if you add columns, they'll be added to the right. Similarly, if you remove rows or columns by entering smaller numbers in the Property inspector fields, they'll be deleted from the bottom and right of the table (contents and all).

- To delete a row or column, drag across all its cells to select them (as described in the previous section), and press the Delete or Backspace key.

- You can also delete a row or column by clicking to put the insertion point inside a cell in that row or column and go to Modify > Table > Delete Row or Modify > Table > Delete Column.

- To add a single row or column, click to put the insertion point inside the table and go to Modify > Table > Insert Row or Modify > Table > Insert Column. A new row will be added immediately above the row containing the insertion point; a new column will be added immediately to the left of the insertion point.

- For ultimate control and flexibility, click to put the insertion point inside the table and go to Modify > Table > Insert Rows or Columns. This command opens a dialog box that lets you specify exactly how many rows or columns to add, and where they should be added in relation to the insertion point.

Tip

All of the commands in the Modify > Table submenu are also available in the contextual menu that appears if you right-click (Windows) or Ctrl-click (Mac) inside a table.

Setting Dimensions

As noted above, neither a table nor its cells needs any dimensions. Tables without dimensions will shrink to fit their content. You can change a table's dimensions using the following methods.

Setting Width and Height with the Property Inspector

You can resize a table or its cells by changing the width and height values in the relevant Property inspector (refer to Figure 9.5). To set the table to a percent-based width or height, use the percent/pixels pop-up menu. To set a cell to a percent-based dimension, type a percent sign after the number in the width or height field. To remove a dimension attribute, delete the contents of the relevant field.

Note

The `height` attribute of the `<table>` tag is not part of the HTML specification. Although some browsers might attempt to honor a value set for the `height` attribute, it is better left unused so that the browser can calculate table height based on the contents.

The Property inspector is an invaluable ally in sizing your table. But you must be careful when using it, because you can turn your dimensions into a mathematical mess that won't display reliably across browsers. All table cells in a row, for instance, logically must have no height value or the same height value. A table with two columns shouldn't have both columns set to 25% wide. A table set to 200 pixels wide shouldn't contain one column set to 150 pixels and another column set to 100 pixels. Dreamweaver will allow you to create all of these mathematical impossibilities, if you enter your values through the Property inspector. But your table will not behave properly in the browser, if you do.

Tip

Usually, an empty width or height field in the Property inspector indicates that the property has not been assigned. If multiple table cells are selected, however, an empty field could indicate that different cells have different dimensions. To make sure a particular cell has no width or height, select that cell only and then examine the Property inspector.

Resizing in the Document Window

You can also resize a table and its components in the Document window by dragging the outer or inner edges. This seems like an intuitive way to proceed. Rest assured that Dreamweaver won't create any mathematical anomalies if you resize this way; but it's very difficult to get accurate results by drag-resizing. Also note that when you resize this way, Dreamweaver might add more dimensions than you want. You might have wanted to add width or height to the cells but not the table, for instance; or only to certain cells; or only to the table itself. When you drag-resize, you have to carefully check the resulting code to see if Dreamweaver gave you only the dimensions you asked for.

Setting All Widths and Heights at One Time

The table Property inspector includes four buttons for setting all the dimensions of a table at once (see Figure 9.4). As their names indicate (Convert Table Widths to Pixels, Convert Table Widths to Percents, and so forth), these buttons allow you to set width and height attributes for all cells within the table to pixels or percent. They can be real time-savers, if you really do want to add dimensions to everything in your table at the same time. But you will probably discover that, as you're working on real jobs, you generally don't want all those dimensions set at once.

Clearing Widths and Heights

A handier set of buttons in the table Property inspector is the Clear Row Heights and Clear Column Widths buttons (see Figure 9.4). Because it's so easy to accidentally set dimensions where you don't want them (usually by drag-resizing), these buttons can quickly get you back to nice, clean table code.

Merging and Splitting Cells

If you're used to working with spreadsheets and word processing tables, the concept of merging and splitting cells is probably as familiar as an old shoe. But there is no merging or splitting in HTML. Instead, Dreamweaver hides some very complex table restructuring behind a lovely, familiar merging-and-splitting interface.

To merge two or more table cells, select the cells and either click the Split icon in the Property inspector, or go to Modify > Table > Merge Cells. What's happening to the HTML when you do this? Dreamweaver adds a `colspan` or `rowspan` attribute to the upper-leftmost cell selected, and removes all other cells, after moving their contents to the remaining cell.

To split a table cell, click to put the insertion point inside the cell and either click the Merge icon in the Property inspector, or go to Modify > Table > Split Cell. A dialog box will appear, asking you exactly how you want to split the cell. What's happening to the HTML here? Dreamweaver performs some fairly extensive restructuring of the table, adding rows or columns as necessary, and adding rowspan or colspan attributes where needed.

Tip

Splitting table cells to fix structural problems can often leave you with a table that just won't behave the way you want it to. A better practice is to create the table with the proper number of rows and columns to begin with, and use nested tables as needed to create `rowspan` and `colspan` cells.

Formatting Tables

Borders, background colors, and other formatting properties can make tables look just how you want them—even if you want the table to look like nothing at all. Before you go overboard with the fancy formatting, however, be aware that not all formatting properties are supported—or interpreted the same way—by all browsers. The following sections discuss some of the most common table formatting, and how Dreamweaver can help you apply it.

Borders, Cell Spacing, and Cell Padding

These three formatting options have to do with what happens between the cells, and how the table's contents are spaced. They're all properties of the table itself, and so are set from the table Property inspector (refer back to Figure 9.6).

Border width, set in pixels, determines the thickness of the outline around the table and between the cells. To create a borderless table, set the border width to **0**. Border color can also be set, but only IE will use this attribute. All table borders in Netscape appear gray.

Tip

Many designers prefer a thinner table border than is possible with the `border` attribute. You can achieve this with a simple inline CSS declaration such as
`<TABLE style="border: 1px solid black;">`.

Cell padding is space added between cells. Cell spacing is empty gutter space around the inner edge of each cell, where no cell contents are allowed to go. Remember, leaving either of these two fields in the Property inspector blank is not the same as setting their values to **0**. If the fields are left blank, and the attributes therefore not defined, most browsers will default to cell padding and cell spacing of 2 pixels. Remember also, when setting these, that their values will affect the overall table width.

Background Colors and Images

The entire table can have a background color; individual cells can also be assigned colors. Cell colors will override the table color. Note that, in Netscape, cell color does not include the cell padding area, though table color does. In IE, cell color and table color extend across the padding between cells.

The entire table, or individual cells, can also be assigned a background image. This image will tile, just like the background image for a page (see Figure 9.9).

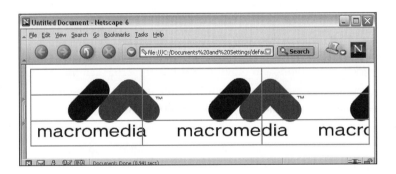

Figure 9.9   A table background image tiling across multiple cells.

Note

If there's a chance that visitors will be using Netscape 4.x to view your page, be aware that this browser version (on any platform) will tile the image separately within each table cell rather than across the entire table.

Cell Alignment

Each cell in a table can have its own `align` and `valign` properties, which determine how the content sits within that cell, horizontally, and vertically. If these attributes are not specified, most browsers will align `<td>` contents vertically centered and to the left, and `<th>` contents vertically and horizontally centered.

Using cell alignment is not the only way to horizontally center contents within a cell. If your content is a text element, or is contained within a text element, the alignment attribute can be applied either to the cell or to the text's formatting tag:

```
<td align="center">Hello, world</td>
```

```
<td><p align="center">Hello, world</p></td>
```

There is no equivalent alternative for vertically aligning content, however. To float cell contents to the top of a cell, use the Property inspector to assign `valign`, like this:

```
<td valign="top">Hello, world</td>
```

Exercise 9.1   Creating a Table Calendar

In this exercise, you'll create a monthly calendar, using a table to provide the row and column structure. Figure 9.10 shows the finished calendar layout you're aiming for.

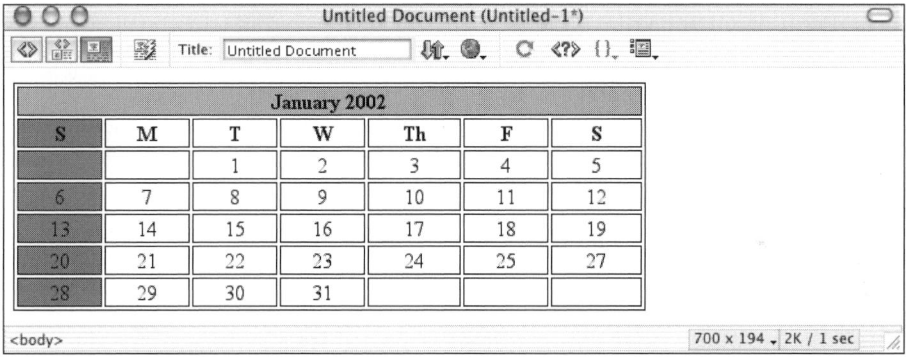

Figure 9.10   A calendar created and formatted using an HTML table.

If you haven't done so yet, copy the files from the **chapter_09** folder on the CD to your hard drive. Define a site called Chapter 9, with this folder as the local root folder.

1. Create a new HTML document, and save it in the **chapter_09** folder as **calendar.html**.

2. Before creating your table, you need to determine what its structure will be. By examining Figure 9.10, you see that you need seven rows and seven columns, with the top row consisting of one large, merged cell.

3. From the Insert bar, bring the Common tab to the front and click the Table object. When the Insert Table dialog box appears, fill it in to look like the one shown in Figure 9.11, and click OK.

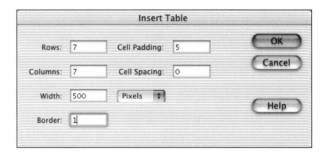

Figure 9.11   The Insert Table dialog box ready to create a calendar table.

4. To create the top row, you'll need to merge all the cells in that row. Drag across the entire row to select it; then click the Merge Cells button in the Property inspector (refer back to Figure 9.5).

5. Enter the calendar data in your table. This will give you a good opportunity to practice moving from cell to cell (using Tab or the arrow keys).

6. For each cell, you want its contents centered vertically and horizontally within the cell. This is done with cell alignment, and can be done for all cells at once by selecting them all and then using the Property inspector. To select all the cells in the table, start with the cursor in the upper-left corner of the table, and drag down to the lower right. After you've done this, in the Property inspector set the Horizontal and Vertical fields to Center and Middle, respectively.

7. Format the text in the cells however you like. As in the previous step, you can format all the text in multiple cells at the same time, by selecting the cells and using the Property inspector or CSS panel.

8. To make your table's colors match that shown in Figure 9.10, you'll need to change the table's border color to black, and the background color for various cells to whatever coordinating colors you like. (Refer back to Figures 9.4 and 9.5 to find the border and cell coloring fields in the Property inspector.)

9. Preview your table in Internet Explorer, and in Netscape (if you have access to both browsers). The border will display differently in the two browsers, as shown in Figure 9.12.

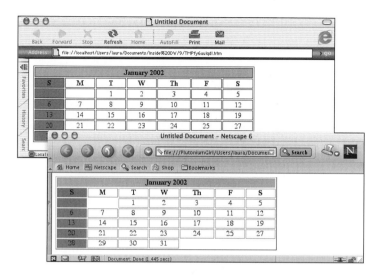

Figure 9.12   The completed **calendar.html** displaying in two different browsers.

One disaster that might strike you is cells that don't display properly (see the Netscape display in Figure 9.12). This happens because browsers won't display empty cells; and although Dreamweaver starts out by inserting a non-breaking space in all empty cells, you might have inadvertently deleted these while tabbing around in your cells. If you have this problem, back in Dreamweaver enter a non-breaking space into the offending cells (Insert > Special Characters > Non-Breaking Space).

Tables and Page Layout: If You Can't Beat 'Em, Join 'Em

If browsers all implemented tables properly, knowing how to use the tags and attributes discussed so far would be enough. You would just place the tables as you pleased on your pages, setting `width` and `height`, `colspan` and `rowspan`, and feel assured that your designs would display correctly in the currently used browsers.

However, there's no reason for despair. You're going to learn a different approach to building pages with tables, one based on the way tables actually work. Tables do behave in predictable ways (a fact often not learned until after much trial and error). If these tendencies are understood, and the designer is willing to accommodate himself to them, smoothly working table pages are quite possible.

Some Do's and Don'ts of Real-World, Table-Based Page Design

These principles apply to all table-based designs, but are especially important when building "liquid" (as opposed to fixed-width) designs:

- *Don't* drag table borders in the Dreamweaver Document window. When you do this, Dreamweaver inserts dimensions into each <td> tag. The problem with this is that table cell dimensions cannot be counted on to hold the dimension of the cell at the specified size when rendered in the browser.

- *Don't* set the width and height attributes of table rows or cells to specify these dimensions. As explained in the preceding point, this does not work consistently and will most likely cause table problems.

- Don't rely on splitting or merging table cells. Some browsers have a difficult time rendering table code containing these attributes, and with a little planning, the same effect can be produced in other ways.

- Do set the width of the table itself, either in pixels or percentages, depending on your design goals (see the section "Fixed Versus Liquid, and How They Work," later in this chapter).

- Do think of tables as "shrink wrap"—as an elastic-like container that will be sized by its contents.

- Do use rigid objects such as graphic images and nested tables when you need a table cell to shrink no further than a certain minimum size.

- Do use stacked tables—tables placed vertically one after another on the page—when possible, as opposed to very large or nested tables. Nested tables take longer for browsers to render, and complex nested tables can cause problems. Nested tables can and should be used when necessary, but some restraint is advised.

- *Do* use nested tables, but only when necessary.

- *Do* use 1×1 pixel transparent GIFs, sized as necessary using the width and height attributes of the <img> tag, as shims to prop open table cells as necessary; but use as few as possible.

Creating Fixed-Width Layouts

Table-based pages can be built so that their layout remains at a fixed pixel width regardless of the user's monitor resolution and browser window size; or they can be built so that the width of the layout expands and contracts to take up a certain percentage of the browser window width. Each approach has its advantages and disadvantages.

Fixed Versus Liquid, and How They Work

Layouts built using fixed-width tables are easier to construct, and it's easier for the designer to predict how the layout will appear to all of its visitors. But by choosing a fixed-width layout, you are essentially guessing how wide the visitor's window will be; if you guess wrong, your layout will either display with its right edge cut off, or with vast expanses of empty page surrounding it. Figure 9.13 shows examples of fixed-width layouts at work.

Figure 9.13   A fixed page layout seen at different browser window widths.

Layouts built using liquid tables (Also referred to as flexible tables, stretching tables or expanding and contracting tables), on the other hand, will adjust themselves to the browser window width, so they fit perfectly no matter what the size. But to achieve this effect, some part of the layout must be able to stretch and squash without ruining the design. Not all layouts are suited to this kind of treatment. Liquid layouts are also more difficult to construct. Figure 9.14 shows examples of Liquid layouts at work.

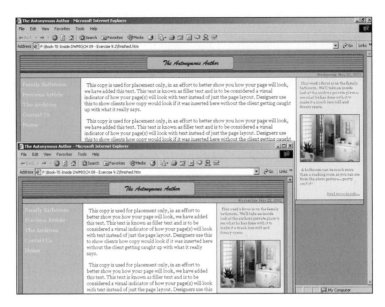

Figure 9.14   A liquid layout seen at different browser window widths.

Constructing Liquid Layouts

There is nothing magical about making a liquid table—it's just a matter of knowing the right steps, applying those steps and doing a little planning up front prior to developing the liquid layout.

The whole table can be liquid, or only a single column, or several columns. You'll learn how to make a three-column table with the middle column being liquid in Exercise 9.2. One thing to note is that a row cannot be liquid in vertical height programmatically, that is, controlled by content and content alone.

The planning consists of using pad and pencil (yes, even in this day and age) and working through which segments of the table should be fixed and which should be liquid. After you have that decided and figured out, you'll need to use Dreamweaver to convert your sketch to a working liquid table.

There are several methods used to create a liquid design with tables, but there is really only one cross-platform and cross-browser method. We'll work through it in Exercise 9.2.

Exercise 9.2 Building a Liquid Page with Tables

In this exercise, you build a simple page that flows with the browser size starting at 740 pixels wide. The page consists of a header, a navigation bar, the content area (the liquid part), and a sidebar. Liquid pages can be much more complex or simpler than this, but after you use and become comfortable with the technique you can go about experimenting with your own pages.

Figure 9.15 shows the finished exercise page, displayed in a browser window at about 800×600 pixels.

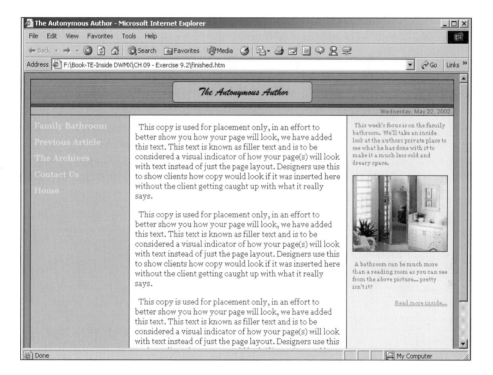

Figure 9.15 The finished liquid page.

1. If you haven't yet, copy the folder **chapter_09** from the companion CD to your hard drive, and define a Dreamweaver site named **chapter_09** with the folder **chapter_09** as its root directory.

2. Open **start.htm** and immediately save it as **index.htm**. You're starting with this page because we have already done some basic groundwork for you by linking an external style sheet and setting the body margins.

3. Insert a table. Using the Insert Table dialog, give your table 1 row and 1 column, set the cell spacing, cell padding and border to **0** and set the width to **100%** (and be sure to select percent from the drop down). Open the Property inspector (with the table still selected) and type in **#000000** in the Bg Color field. (This is in preparation for giving the inner table structure a black border effect).

4. Position your cursor inside this new table and insert another table, this time using 5 rows, 3 columns, and cell padding of 5. Set cellpadding to **5** so that we can still select the proper cell later in the project. At the end of the project we will be changing this value to 0 so that the table collapses properly. Set cell spacing to **1**, give it a **100%** width and a border of **0**.

5. Next, we want to merge some cells in the table rows to make a single cell in the rows for other content.

   Select the top row by positioning your cursor in the top-left cell, click and hold the left mouse button, and drag across the top-right row, and then merge the 3 cells using the Modify > Table > Merge cells menu item. Repeat for row 2, 3 and 5.

6. Position your cursor in row 1; using the Property inspector, use the Browse button beside the Bg field and navigate to **hd_bg.gif** in the **image** folder. Change the Horz field from Default to Center. Using Insert > Image, insert **logo.gif** in this cell. It should be center-aligned at this point, with the background showing in the entire table cell.

Tip

The TR and TD Property inspectors look identical, so as a safety precaution, use the tag selector to select the TD when your cursor is positioned inside the desired cell. This will ensure that property changes affect the TD and not the TR.

This also sets the cell background to match up with the provided logo and inserts the provided logo in the top most cell. The cell height is controlled by the content; in this case, the content is a specifically sized image.

7. Position your cursor in table row 2. In the Property inspector, change the Bg Color to **#990000** and using the Insert > Image menu item, navigate to **spacer.gif**. Using the Image Property inspector, change its height to **4** and the width to **100** pixels.

8. Place your cursor in the third row, and using Modify > CSS Styles, select date. The date class will apply to the TD tag of the cell because it is currently empty. The cell should now be a powder blue color. Using the Insert bar Common tab, click the Date button to insert the date with the following dialog properties: Day format should be Thursday, leave the Date and Time Format at their defaults, and place a check in Update automatically on save. Click the OK button and a semi-dynamic date is inserted on the page.

This completes the header section of the liquid table (see Figure 9.16). Next we will be dealing with the footer content.

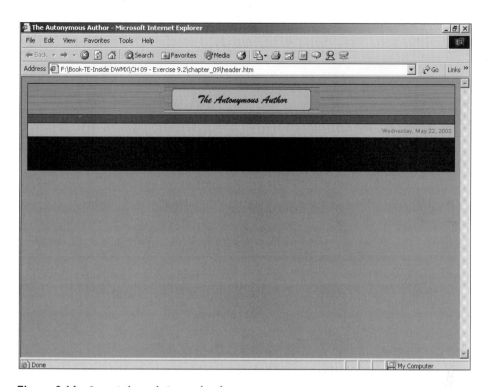

Figure 9.16   Steps 1 through 8 completed.

9. Position your cursor in Row 5 (the last row), using Text > CSS Styles, select copy from the list. Your background should be the same powder blue as the date row and the cursor should be flashing in the center of this cell. Now type in **Copyright 2002**, Your Name (Replace Your Name with your actual name or company name if you like. You could also replace the word Copyright with the Copyright symbol located in the Insert Bar, Characters tab). Save the page and preview it in Netscape and IE.

That's all there is for the footer of this liquid table (see Figure 9.17). Next we will be dealing with the sidebar.

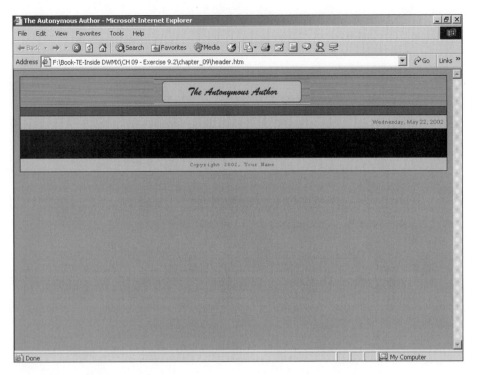

Figure 9.17   Step 9 completed.

10. In row 4, position your cursor in the right most cell. Using Text > CSS Styles, select sidebar from the list. The cell should change to a pale orange color. Change the Vert field of the Property inspector from Default to Top.

11. Type the following in this cell: **{spacebar}This week's focus is on the family bathroom. We'll take an inside look at the author's private place to see what he has done with it to make it a much less cold and dreary space.** Select this text, using the Property inspector change the format to Paragraph. Press the right arrow key so that the paragraph is no longer selected and press the Enter key. Notice that the cell expansion is controlled by the content? We'll take care of that in a bit so don't worry about it right now.

12. Using the Insert > Image menu item, navigate to and select **image.jpg**, then click the OK button. Press the right arrow key again to deselect the image and press the Enter key.

13. Type in the following text at the current cursor position: **{spacebar}A bathroom can be much more than a reading room as you can see from the above picture... pretty isn't it?** And press the Enter key

14. Type the following text at the current cursor position: **Read more inside....** Use the Text > Align > Right menu item and using the Property inspector, type in **javascript:;** in the Link field. Save the page and preview it in Netscape and IE.

This completes the sidebar content (see Figure 9.18). Click inside the row 4 left-most cell, and we will work on the navigation bar next.

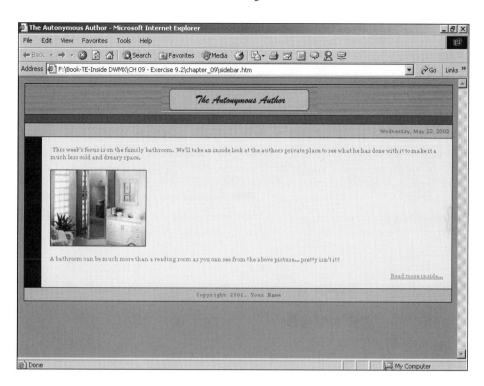

Figure 9.18 Steps 10 through 14 completed

15. Using the Property inspector, change the Vert from Default to **Top** and change the Bg Color to **#99CCCC**. This sets our navigation bar background color and ensures that our menu system is always at the top of the cell. Now, select Insert > Table and in the Insert Table Dialog, specify **5** Rows, **1** Column, **0** for Cell spacing, Cell padding and Border. Change width to **75** Pixels. Previously we used percent, but for this table we want it to always be displayed at 175 pixels. Click OK to insert the table inside its container cell.

16. Place your cursor in the top most cell of this new table and insert a spacer image 100 pixels wide and 5 pixels high. There are two functions to this spacer image: The first is to provide a spacer from the top of the outer table cell, the second and most important is to force the table to 175 pixels wide. Why you might ask? Even though the table is specified at 175 pixels it theoretically should stay that way, but the browsers do not necessarily implement it correctly, and this is a safety feature to ensure that the table doesn't collapse at all, regardless of cell contents.

17. In each subsequent cell of this single column table, type in sequence: **Family Bathroom**, **Previous Article**, **The Archives**, **Contact Us**, and **Home**. In each row, starting with the first, change the Format to Paragraph, type in **javascript:;** in the link field and apply the Menu class to the <P> tag all using the Property inspector.

Tip

To use CSS in the Property inspector, click on the A icon beside the Format field of the Property inspector.

Warning

Order and applying is important. Set the Format to Paragraph, then Apply the menu class from the CSS dropdown in the Property Inspector, then type in **javascript:;** in the Link field. Failure to follow this order will result in the menu class being applied to the <TD> tag instead of the <P> tag, which in turn will cause rendering issues in the menu system.

After you have performed this step with each navigation bar item, the navigation system is completed and we will move on to the liquid section of this table (see Figure 9.19). Save the page and preview it in Netscape and IE.

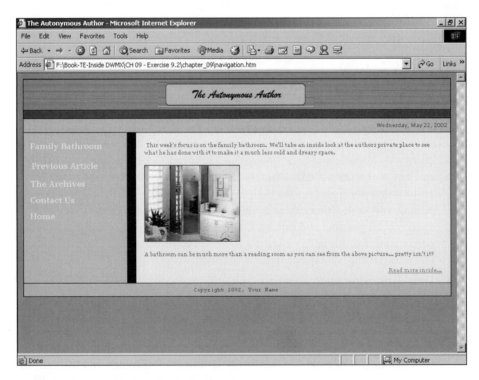

Figure 9.19   Steps 15 through 17 completed.

18. Position your cursor in Row 4, center column; it should be the only black background column remaining on the page. Using the Property inspector, change the Vert field to Top, the width to **100%** (don't forget to type in the % symbol) and change the Class to Content. Now, also change the Format field to Paragraph. Why this order here? We don't want the Content CSS Class being applied to each Paragraph tag but rather the cell as a whole; so we apply the css with no format selected, which applies the CSS Class to the TD instead.

The cell should have adopted a white background and the cursor should be positioned in the top-left corner of the cell.

19. Using your favorite Filler Text extension (there are several on the Macromedia Exchange for Dreamweaver) add some content to this cell. If you don't have a Filler Text extension, you can use the following text: **This copy is used for placement only. In an effort to better show you how your page will look, we have added this text. This text is known as filler text and is to be considered a visual indicator of how your page(s) will look with text instead of just the page layout. Designers use this to show clients how copy would look if it were inserted here without the client getting caught up with what it really says.** Press the Enter key, copy the text you've just typed, and paste it to add it again (repeating this twice to get three paragraphs in the cell).

Save the page and preview it in Netscape and IE. Resize the browser window to cause page changes widthwise in your browser, and notice that the middle cell (known as content) resizes itself to allow for scaling in the browser. Notice how small the cell gets when the browser is down to about 640×480—ugh—what do we do about that? Remember what we did with the navigation table when we inserted that spacer image—ahh ha! You got it, we do that here too in the next step.

20. We have to decide what minimum browser resolution we want to support without having horizontal scrollbars. For the purpose of this exercise, we are going to choose 800×600. The typical viewable area of our desired resolution is about 740 pixels wide. So now we need pencil and paper again or a calculator.

> 740 pixels wide minimum
> −175 pixels that we set the navigation nar
> −170 pixels for the sidebar image
> =395 pixels left for the content cell

> Making allowances for cell spacing and cell padding, and some padding and margins allowed for in the external CSS file. We'll be using 320 as the spacer image width.

21. Now that we have our size requirement, where do we apply it? In the content cell (the white one at Row 4, center column), position your cursor at the very beginning of the first paragraph. Insert a spacer image, setting the width to **320** and the height to **1**. Press the right arrow key, and add a line break (Shift+Enter) after the image.

22. Save the page and preview it in Netscape and IE. The browsers should go slightly below 800×600 size with no horizontal scrollbar and expand up to any resolution with only the center column changing it's width in the browser.

23. There is one thing left to do. Remember that in step 4, we changed the cell padding to 5. Now we want to change it back to **0** so that the image in the header looks proper. So position your cursor in the liquid cell (Row 4, middle cell) and using the tag selector, select the closest Table tag. After you select this, the Property inspector should populate with the current values. Change cell padding from 5 to **0**. Save the page and preview it in Netscape and IE (see Figure 9.20).

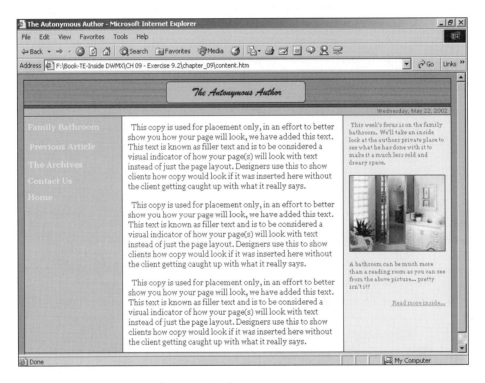

Figure 9.20   Steps 18 through 23 completed.

Question: What if you don't want an image in the sidebar? How do you hold that cell open to the desired width?

Answer: You would basically repeat the procedure for step 21, except instead of performing it in the middle cell, you would do it for the right most cell on Row 4; and the image width would be whatever you desired, but make sure that you compensate in the center cell for your minimum width requirements.

Sliced-Image Tables

The "shrink wrap" nature of tables is perfect for putting together sliced images. A table without cell padding or cell spacing, and without `width` or `height` attributes, will naturally close in around images placed within its cells. The image slices are held together tightly by this "elastic" tendency of HTML tables, so that the visual effect in the browser is such that the image appears completely seamless.

An image is sliced for one or more of these purposes:

- To allow the image to load in pieces, instead of forcing the visitor to wait while the complete image loads
- To allow the separate slices to be used as links
- To allow the separate slices to be used for rollovers or disjoint rollovers
- So that portions of a large image can include nongraphic text (a "text slice" in Fireworks terms)

Macromedia Fireworks includes a variety of tools for making image slices and for exporting the slices as a table that can be opened and edited with Dreamweaver. Figure 9.21 shows a Fireworks-built sliced image table in Dreamweaver.

Note

For more on working with Fireworks and Dreamweaver together, see Appendix A.

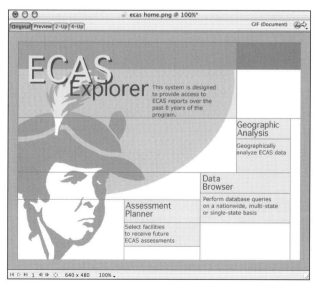

Figure 9.21   A sliced-image table created in Fireworks and being edited in Dreamweaver.

Summary

HTML tables have provided web designers with a workable, cross-browser way to lay out page elements for years. Although positioning with CSS is the W3C recommendation and the direction of things to come, as of this writing, tables are still one of the most reliable page layout techniques.

In this chapter, you looked at the HTML code that makes up tables, learned how to insert and format a table with the Dreamweaver Table Property inspector, went over some do's and don'ts of table layout, learned to build a flexible page with tables, and looked at the usefulness of tables in building sliced-image pages.

Chapter 10

Using Dreamweaver's Page Layout Aids

Like ice cream, web designers come in all flavors. Some love their code and want nothing more than to be close to it. They can appreciate a visual design interface like Dreamweaver's because of the amount of time it saves, but feel compelled to keep an eagle eye on the Code view, monitoring every tag Dreamweaver writes. Others are happy to allow Dreamweaver to translate for them, instructing it to place this or that element on the page and trusting that the software will take care of things behind the scenes. The preceding chapter discussed using tables for page layout, and how to make the code work for you in designing. This chapter looks at the various options you have to let Dreamweaver do the table coding for you, including Layout view and the Convert Layers to Table command. It also covers rulers, grids, and tracing images—viewing aids that can help you create layouts in Design view regardless of how you approach your page layout tables.

Viewing Aids

Graphic designers are used to having certain tools at their disposal when they build their layouts. Rulers, guides, tracing images—most print-based page layout environments have at least some of these features. For those of you who sorely miss having such helpers as you work, Dreamweaver offers rulers, the grid, and tracing images. (Sorry, no ruler guides!)

Rulers

Dreamweaver rulers work similarly to rulers in most graphics programs. They display across the top and down the left side of the Document window; they can be set to display various measurement systems; they can be turned off and on; and they indicate the current cursor position with a dotted line. Figure 10.1 shows the rulers in action.

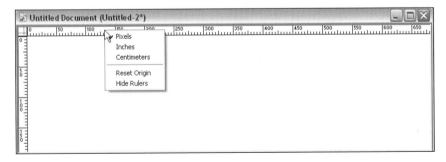

Figure 10.1   Dreamweaver rulers and their options.

To configure and show or hide the rulers, use commands in the View > Rulers submenu:

- **Showing and hiding.** The View > Rulers > Show command acts like a toggle, turning the rulers on and off. You can also use the Rulers toggle command in the View Options menu, in the Document toolbar, or right-click (Mac users Ctrl-click) on the ruler itself to access its contextual menu.

- **Choosing a unit of measurement.** From the View > Rulers submenu, choose pixels, inches, or centimeters. You can also right-click (Ctrl-click) on the ruler in the Document window, to access its contextual menu. Pixels (the default) is definitely the most useful choice.

- **Changing and resetting the origin point.** The origin is the zero-point, the location on the page where the horizontal and vertical ruler read 0. By default, this is the upper-left corner of the page. To change the origin point, position the cursor over the little square where the left and top rulers meet (see Figure 10.1), and drag out into the document area. To reset the origin back to the top-left corner, choose View > Rulers > Reset Origin, or right-click (Ctrl-click) on the ruler itself to access its contextual menu.

Grid

Dreamweaver might not have moveable rulers you can pull out from the rulers, but it does have a grid. The grid overlays the Design view display with horizontal and vertical rules at fixed intervals, and can be a helpful design aid if your layout is built on those fixed intervals (a column every 100 pixels, for instance). Figure 10.2 shows the grid being used in a document.

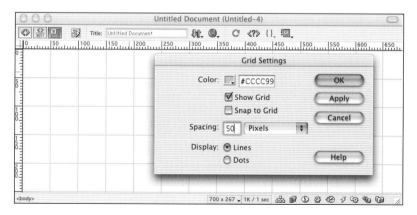

Figure 10.2   The Dreamweaver grid set to its default of 50×50 pixels.

To configure and show or hide the grid, use commands in the View > Grid submenu:

- **Showing and hiding.** The View > Grid > Show Grid command acts like a toggle, turning the grid on and off. You also can use the Grid toggle command in the View Options menu, in the Document toolbar.

- **Choosing grid size and appearance.** The grid can be set to display rules at any fixed interval from 1 pixel on up, and measured in pixels, inches, or centimeters. It can display as solid lines or rows of dots, in any color you choose. To alter these settings, choose View > Grid > Grid Settings. (Okay, a 1-pixel grid is not very useful—but it's nice to know it's possible!)

Note

The grid starts measuring in the upper-left corner of the document, not necessarily at the zero point but where the page content starts. If you haven't specified page margins for your document (using Modify > Page Properties), the grid will start about 8 pixels in from the top-left corner.

- **Snapping to the grid.** When creating layouts using Layout View or Layers, or when dragging to resize tables, a snap-to feature can be helpful for accuracy. Toggle snapping on and off by choosing View > Grid > Snap to Grid.

If you want, you can have your layout tables and cells automatically snap to the grid. The snapping behavior can be controlled by changing the grid settings.

To show the grid, choose View > Grid > Show Grid, or select Grid from the Options drop-down menu on the toolbar.

Tracing Images

If you're the kind of designer who creates your layouts first by sketching them with pencil and paper, or building prototypes in a graphics program, and then recreating the effect in Dreamweaver, you might find the Dreamweaver tracing image feature a great help. A tracing image is any GIF, JPEG, or PNG file that you choose, that will appear as a ghosted-back image in Design view—as if you were viewing it through tracing paper. The idea is, you place your layout sketch "behind" your Dreamweaver design and use it as a guide to construct the tables or layers that will create your HTML layout. When you're done, you remove the tracing image, and all is well with the world. Tracing images are configured and set using the commands in the View > Tracing Image submenu, or the Modify > Page Properties dialog box. Figure 10.3 shows a tracing image being used.

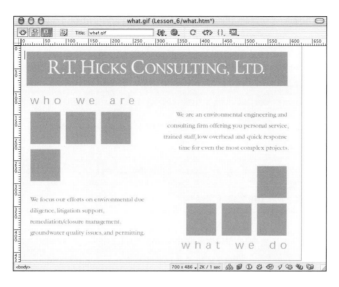

Figure 10.3   A Dreamweaver document with tracing image in place.

Setting a Tracing Image

To put a tracing image "behind" your Dreamweaver Design view, do this:

1. Create the GIF, JPEG, or PNG file any way you like—by scanning a sketch, saving a Fireworks or Photoshop file, taking a screenshot of a desired layout, and so on.

2. In Dreamweaver, open your document and go to Modify > Page Properties (see Figure 10.4).

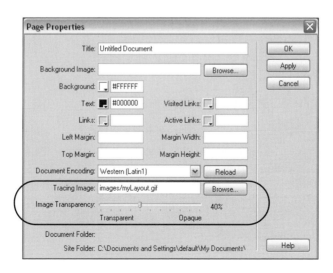

Figure 10.4   Using Modify > Page Properties to set the tracing image.

3. From the Page Properties dialog box, find the tracing image options and click the Choose button. Browse to select your tracing image file.

4. Still in the Page Properties dialog box, set the image opacity slider to around 30–50% (to create the faded-back, tracing paper effect). Click Apply to see how your tracing image looks, and adjust the opacity more until you like the effect.

5. Click OK to close the Page Properties dialog box. There you go!

Tip

You can also use View > Tracing Image > Load to choose a tracing image, but you can't assign it an opacity value using that method.

To see how Dreamweaver creates the tracing image, go to Code view and examine the code for your <body> tag. You'll see several nonstandard attributes assigned (shown in bold):

```
<body bgcolor="#FFFFFF" text="#000000" tracingsrc="images/myLayout.gif"
tracingopacity="40">
```

The browser won't recognize these attributes, and so will ignore them. If you Preview in Browser with a tracing image in position, it won't show. But it will show in Dreamweaver Design view.

Note

If your page has a background image assigned, either as part of the <body> tag or in a Cascading Style Sheet, the tracing image won't be visible—it's hidden behind the other image. To see the tracing image, you'll have to temporarily remove your background image.

Adjusting Tracing Image Position

Your tracing image might not be positioned exactly where you need it—by default, it appears slightly offset from the top and left of the Document window.

To adjust the tracing image position manually, do this:

1. Go to View > Tracing Image > Adjust Position. A dialog box will appear, displaying the current x (horizontal) and y (vertical) coordinates of the image, and allowing you to change these.

2. You can change the image's position either by entering new values in these fields, or by using your arrow keys to nudge the image one pixel at a time in any direction.

3. When you're done, click OK!

To adjust the tracing position to match a certain page element (such as a graphic, table or layer), do this:

1. Select the element you want to align the image with.

2. Go to View > Tracing Image > Align with Selection.

After you've done your repositioning, check your code, and you'll see that more attributes have been added to the <body> tag (shown in bold):

```
<body bgcolor="#FFFFFF" text="#000000"

tracingsrc="images/myLayout.gif" tracingopacity="40"

tracingx="-5" tracingy="150">
```

Tip

Don't use the tracing image to get pixel-perfect layouts in place—use it to get the overall positioning down, and then remove it. HTML layouts can't always perfectly match layouts created in graphics programs.

Removing a Tracing Image

Eventually, the tracing image will start getting in your way, and you'll want to remove it—either temporarily, by hiding it, or permanently, by removing its code from the <body> tag.

To temporarily hide the tracing image, go to View > Tracing Image > Show, to toggle the command off; or go to Modify > Page Properties, and set the opacity slider to 0%.

To remove the tracing image permanently, go to Modify > Page Properties, and delete it from the Tracing Image input field; or go to Code view and remove the tracing image attributes.

Layout View

Dreamweaver Design view includes two separate modes of working: Standard view and Layout view. *Layout view* is an alternate way of viewing and working with documents containing table-based layouts, where the tables and cells appear more like rectangular boxes full of content than like HTML tables—something like the text boxes and picture boxes that print designers are familiar with from QuarkXPress and InDesign. To create the layout, draw some boxes. To adjust the layout after it's been created, adjust the size and shape of your boxes. Meanwhile, behind the scenes, Dreamweaver is creating and adjusting the HTML table code for you.

Note

Unfortunately, the Layout View feature has a *bug* (a flaw in the way the software functions), which was present in Dreamweaver 4 and was not fixed in Dreamweaver MX. When Dreamweaver writes table code from the design you create in Layout View, it often includes *empty table cells*, which look like this:

`<td></td>`

Empty table cells produce serious display problems in some browsers, and might cause your page to look very different than you expect or intend. Netscape 4 browsers, in particular, don't display empty table cells well.

For this reason, we recommend that Layout View be used only when absolutely necessary, and when it is used, that the empty table cells be filled with either a *non-breaking space character* (` `) or a single-pixel GIF spacer. This can be done by using Dreamweaver's Find and Replace feature, or simply by reviewing the page code and adding the non-breaking spaces or GIFs manually.

There's another problem with the code written by Dreamweaver when pages are designed in Layout View; it often specifies table heights and widths in pixels. As of this writing, the commonly used browsers do not all display table and cell heights and widths as specified in pixels.

If you do use Layout View, these height and width attributes should be removed. See the discussion on "Formatting Layout Tables," later in this chapter for more on removing height values.

About Layout Cells and Layout Tables

Layout view enables you to add *layout cells* and *layout tables* to your page, to facilitate placing page elements where you want them. When you draw a layout table, Dreamweaver creates an HTML table. When you draw a layout cell inside a layout table, Dreamweaver creates a cell (`<td>` tag) inside the table. Just as a table cell can't exist outside a table, a layout cell must always be contained by a layout table. (If you create a layout cell without first creating a layout table, Dreamweaver will automatically create a layout table for you.)

A page could consist of a single layout table with several layout cells. However, just as you might use multiple HTML tables in one page, you might want to use multiple layout tables. Using multiple tables isolates sections of your layout so that one section isn't affected by another; within the same table, the size of a cell often affects the other cells in its row and column.

Just like regular HTML tables, layout tables also can be nested.

Switching Between Layout and Standard View

Layout view and Standard view are two different viewing modes within Design view. Normally, when you're in Design view, you're in Standard view.

Note

Just because you're working in Layout view doesn't mean you can't keep an eye on your code. While you're in Layout view you can still switch between Design view and Code view, or even work in Code and Design view.

Accessing Layout View

To switch into Layout view, first be sure you are in Design View by choosing View > Design, and then do one of the following:

- Choose View > Table View > Layout View (Ctrl+F6).
- Click the Layout view button in the Layout tab of the Insert bar (see Figure 10.5).

After you're in Layout view, any tables your document already contains will now display as layout tables. If your document is empty, you can use the objects in the Layout tab of the Insert bar to build your page layout.

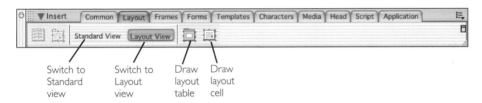

Figure 10.5   Switching views using the Insert bar.

Accessing Standard View

After you're in Layout view, to switch back into Standard view, go to the Layout tab of the Insert bar and click the Standard View button (see Figure 10.9). All layout tables are now displayed as standard HTML tables, and can be edited using the methods covered in the preceding chapter.

Note

You can go back and forth between Layout and Standard view as often as you like, in building your pages. You can even start with a page created entirely in Standard view, using the standard HTML table-creation tools, switch to Layout view, and start editing the table as a Layout table.

Creating Tables and Cells in Layout View

Working in Layout view, you can draw both layout cells and layout tables.

Note

Layout view is a Dreamweaver-specific tool. Although you're creating HTML tables in Layout view, many of the terms and concepts used don't exist in HTML, but only in the Dreamweaver software.

Drawing Layout Tables

Use the Draw Layout Table button to draw a table on an empty area of the page, or inside another layout table. To draw a layout table, follow these steps:

1. Make sure that you are in Layout view, and then, in the Layout category of the Insert bar, click the Draw Layout Table button (see Figure 10.5). The cursor will change to a crosshair (+).

2. Place the cursor at the point on the page where you want one corner of a layout table and click and drag to draw the table—as if you were drawing a rectangle in a graphics program. Note that if you want the table to be the only table on the page, or the first of several tables, you must draw it so that its upper-left corner is at the upper-left corner of the page.

Note

If you draw a layout table in the middle of an empty document, Dreamweaver will create it as a table nested inside a larger table. If this happens and you don't want it to, Edit > Undo and draw again, being careful to begin or end in the upper-left corner.

3. On your page, the new table will appear outlined in green (see Figure 10.6). At its top is the Column Header area, which displays the column's width in pixels. In this case, the table consists of only one column, so this width will also be the table's width. (See below for more on setting up flexible, percent-based, layout tables.)

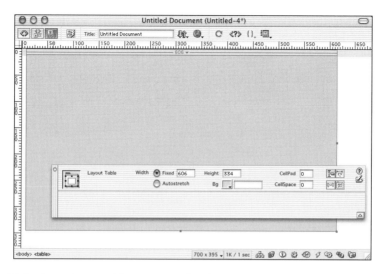

Figure 10.6   A new layout table, set to a pixel width of 606.

Layout tables can be placed in empty page areas, nested within existing tables, or drawn around existing cells and tables. Like all HTML tables, they cannot overlap each other.

Note

To draw a number of layout tables without clicking the Layout Table button each time, hold down Control (Windows) or Command (Mac). This technique also applies to drawing a number of layout cells.

Drawing Layout Cells

To draw a layout cell, follow these steps:

1. Be sure you're in Layout view. In the Layout tab of the Insert bar, click the Draw Layout Cell button (see Figure 10.5). This causes the cursor to change to a plus sign (+) or *crosshair* (+) in preparation for drawing a cell.

Note

Layout cells can only exist within a layout table. If you draw a layout cell outside the boundaries of a layout table, or without drawing a layout table first, Dreamweaver will create the layout table for you.

2. Place the cursor within a layout table, at the point where you want to position one corner of your layout cell, and drag to create the cell. To draw more than one cell, you must click the Draw Layout Cell button again for each new cell.

3. The cell will display in the Dreamweaver Document window with a blue outline (see Figure 10.7). Because cells must exist within a row and column grid, the layout table containing your cell might show additional subdivisions—these are other cells in the HTML table that are being created as you work. The layout table's Column Header now shows the widths for all columns.

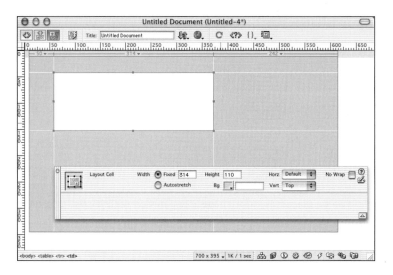

Figure 10.7   A layout cell inside a layout table.

Cells must stay within a row-and-column grid, but can span several rows or several columns. They cannot overlap, however. Dreamweaver helps you stay within this structure by snapping new cells to existing cells, or to the side of the page, if you draw them within 8 pixels. To temporarily stop snapping of cells, hold down Alt (Windows) or Option (Mac) while drawing the cell.

Cells in the same column can be different widths; cells in the same row can be different heights. Dreamweaver will create additional cells in the HTML table it's building, to create the layout that you specify.

Dreamweaver will draw whatever additional cells are needed to maintain the layout you specify; these cells will be displayed with a gray background.

Creating Nested Layout Tables

Just like HTML tables, layout tables can be placed within existing layout tables; this is referred to as *nesting* tables. Nested layout tables can only be drawn in the portions of a parent table that don't already contain layout cells (in other words, only in the gray portions of the parent table).

To draw a layout table nested inside another layout table, follow these steps:

1. Draw the parent layout table.

2. Click the Draw Layout Table icon in the Insert bar.

3. Position the cursor within the parent table, as though you were going to draw a new layout cell, and drag to create the table. Dreamweaver will create a cell within the layout table, and draw your new, nested table within that cell (see Figure 10.8).

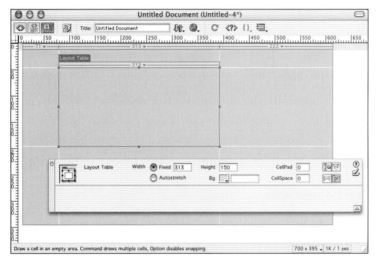

Figure 10.8   Creating a nested table by drawing a layout table within an existing layout table.

Note

As noted earlier, if you draw a layout table in an empty document, but don't position it in the upper-left corner, Dreamweaver will automatically create it as a table nested inside another layout table.

As you can see from Figure 10.8, nested layout tables display with a Layout Table tab, in addition to a Column Width header. The header displays only if the nested table is selected; the tab always displays. This is your visual indication that the element is in fact a nested table, and not just another table cell. You can also click on the tab to select the nested table.

Manipulating Table Structure in Layout View

A major attraction of Layout view is that, after you've created your page layout in this way, you can adjust it much more intuitively than you can when working with HTML tables in Standard view. In addition to special Property inspectors for layout tables and cells, you can interactively resize and reposition your layout directly in the Document window.

Interactive Adjustments: Selecting, Moving, Resizing

Layout cells and nested layout tables can be moved and resized interactively, without referring to code or Property inspectors, by click-and-drag methods in the Document window.

Selecting (Tables and Cells)

To select a layout table, click its Column Width header or Layout Table tab (if it has one), or click anywhere inside the table and use the tag selector as you would in Standard view. A selected layout table displays with a green outline and selection handles (see Figure 10.6).

To select a layout cell, click its edge or click anywhere inside the cell and use the tag selector. You also can Control-click (Windows) or Command-click (Mac) anywhere in the cell to select it. A selected layout cell displays with a blue outline and selection handles (see Figure 10.7).

Resizing (Tables and Cells)

To resize a layout table or cell select it, and use the selection handles to drag the edges. Note that resizing a nested layout table will resize the table itself and the cell of the parent table that contains it. When resizing a layout table, remember the following:

- Cells and nested tables will automatically snap to existing cells when within 8 pixels of an existing cell.
- A layout table cannot be resized so that it would be smaller than the cells it contains.
- A layout cell cannot be resized beyond the borders of its containing table.
- No overlapping is allowed.
- A layout cell is always at least as large as the content it contains.

Moving (Nested Tables and Cells)

You cannot move a layout table that isn't nested inside another table. To move a nested layout table or a layout cell, click-and-drag or use the arrow keys to move it 1 pixel at a time. Hold down Shift while using the arrow keys, to move 10 pixels at a time.

Using the Property Inspector

Layout tables and cells each have their own Property inspector, allowing you to set all the standard table and cell properties—just like in Standard view.

Formatting Layout Tables

When you select a layout table, the Layout Table Property inspector appears (see Figure 10.9). Some properties, such as width and height, cell padding and spacing, and background color, are the same as those you would find in the Property inspector for a standard table. But there are some differences, and items of special note. In particular:

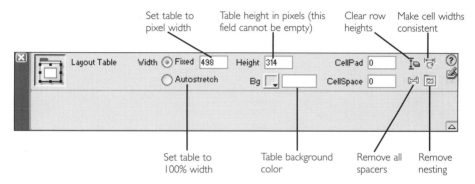

Figure 10.9   The Layout Table Property inspector.

- Instead of choosing pixels or percent for width, layout tables allow you to choose between a fixed pixel-width and autostretch. For more information on autostretch, see the section on "Creating Flexible Layouts" later in this chapter.

- The Property inspector specifies a table height attribute, measured in pixels. You can change this attribute, here or by resizing the table in the Document window; but you can't remove the attribute completely. Layout tables must have a height attribute.

- Layout tables can be assigned background colors, but not background images using the Property inspector.

- Because most designers prefer to use gutter cells in their tables, rather than assigning cell padding or spacing, the cell padding and spacing attributes are set to 0 by default. (A gutter cell is an empty cell placed between two neighboring cells to separate their contents. The advantage of a gutter cell over cell padding or spacing is that it only adds space to one particular area of a table; cell padding and spacing will add space equally between all cells.)

- The Clear Row Heights button removes all cell height attributes. If the table does not yet contain any elements, this will cause it to collapse; it is best used after all content has been added. Because not all browsers support the height attribute for table code, doing this will produce more stable code for your layout. You also can clear cell heights by accessing one of the drop-down menus in the table's Column Header area, and choose Clear Cell Heights (see Figure 10.10). Note that clearing row heights will reduce your layout table's height, but won't clear its height attribute.

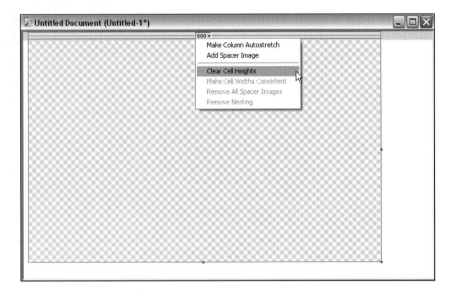

Figure 10.10   The Layout Table Column Header menu.

- The Make Widths Consistent button resets the HTML width attributes of each cell to match its content. If you are using a fixed-width table, set this attribute after you've added your content, to ensure stable code.

- Remove Nesting will convert a nested layout table to cells within the parent table. The nested table will disappear, and its cells and their contents will become part of the parent table.

- Remove All Spacer Images does just that. For more information on spacer images in layout tables, see the section "Using Spacer Images in Autostretch Tables" later in this chapter.

Formatting Layout Cells

To edit the properties of a layout cell, select it and the Layout Cell Property inspector will appear (see Figure 10.11). As with layout tables, the properties that appear are generally the same as those you can set for table cells in Standard view. A few items of special note:

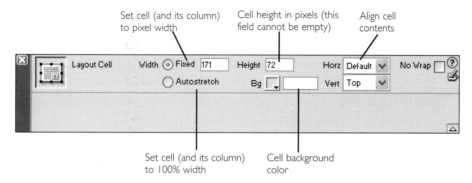

Figure 10.11   The Layout Cell Property inspector.

- Like layout tables, layout cells can be set to a fixed (pixel) width or to autostretch. See the section "Creating Flexible Layouts" later in this chapter, for more on this.

- Like layout tables, layout cells can be assigned background colors but not background images using the Property inspector.

- To set the horizontal or vertical alignment for the cell contents, use the drop-down menus labeled Horz and Vert. Because most designers prefer their layout content to be aligned to the tops of cells, the default vertical alignment is top.

- Though you can set cell heights here, as mentioned above doing so will produce nonstandard and possibly unstable code.

Adding Content

Text, images, and other media can be added to layout cells just as you would add content to a regular HTML table in Standard view. However, the only place content can be inserted is in a layout cell, so the necessary cells must be drawn first. Just click in the cell where you want to insert content and type or insert the element. A few tips about layout cells and content:

- When Dreamweaver creates layout cells, it automatically assigns them a vertical alignment of top. Any content you enter will float to the top of the cell.

- Just like a normal HTML table cell, a layout cell will expand as needed to hold its content. As a cell expands, surrounding cells also might be affected, and the column the cell is in will expand.

- As you created your layout cells, Dreamweaver might have subdivided the layout table to create other cells, to maintain the grid structure of the table. Those cells appear in the Document window as grayed-out areas marked by outlines. You can't enter content into one of those "placeholder" cells—to add content, you must use the Layout Cell tool to draw a cell in that space.

- Because you're in Layout view, you can't create a table using the standard Table object. If you want to insert a regular table (for displaying tabular data) into your layout table, you'll have to go to Standard view to do it.

Exercise 10.1   Creating a Page Layout Using Layout View

In this exercise, you use Layout view to build a simple page design based on a fixed-width layout table. Along the way, you'll get a chance to see some of the strengths and limitations of Layout view, and how you can work with it to get the results you want. You'll also experiment with grids as a visual aid in page setup. Figure 10.12 shows the finished layout you'll be creating.

Figure 10.12   The desired layout for **bumpers.html**.

If you haven't yet, copy the folder **chapter_10** from the companion CD into a folder named **idmx** on your hard drive and define a Dreamweaver site named **chapter_10** with the folder **chapter_10** as its root directory.

1. You'll be creating the layout page from scratch, so start by choosing File > New to create a new blank HTML page. Save it in the **chapter_10** folder as **bumpers.html.**

2. To help you draw accurately, you'll use the grid. Go to View > Grid > Show Grid, to turn the grid on. The default grid setting is too large for the requirements of your layout, so adjust it. Go to View > Grid > Grid Settings, and in the dialog box that appears, enter a grid size of 20 pixels. Finally, so the grid can be of maximum help as you draw, go to View > Grid > Snap to Grid.

3. Your desired layout is 640 pixels wide. To help you gauge widths as you're drawing tables and cells, go to View > Rulers > Show. Make sure the rulers are set to measure pixels, by checking that View > Rulers > Pixels is the selected option.

   Finally, if you want ruler measurements and grid measurements to match each other, you must set the origin point of the rulers to the upper-left corner of the grid. Position the cursor over the zero-point corner of the rulers, and drag down and right until the zero-point crosshair lines up with the top left edge of the grid (see Figure 10.13).

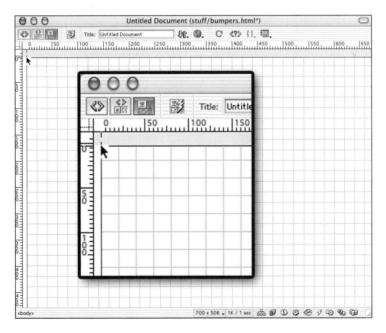

Figure 10.13   Resetting the rulers' zero-point to match the grid.

4. Now switch to Layout view by going to the Insert bar and bringing the Layers tab to the front. Click the Layout View button (refer back to Figure 10.5) to switch to Layout view.

5. Now you're ready to draw. In the Insert bar, select the Draw Layout Table button, and draw a table that starts in the page's upper-left corner and is 640 pixels wide and a few hundred pixels tall. (You'll be removing the height values later, so they're not crucial for now.) The grid snap feature should help you get your measurements accurate.

    If you draw your table and it isn't 640 pixels wide, you can adjust its width by dragging its edge or by selecting it and using the Layout Table Property inspector to manually enter a width of 640. Figure 10.14 shows how your document should look, with grid, rulers, and layout table in place.

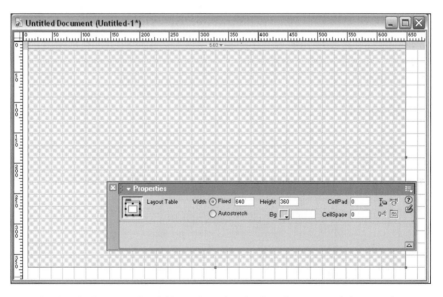

Figure 10.14 The **bumpers.html** file, with grid and rulers showing, and the main layout table in position.

6. Using the Draw Layout Cell tool, create four cells: one for the banner across the top, and three for the main columns. Make your left-hand and right-hand columns 100 pixels wide each. Leave a 20-pixel gutter between those columns and the center column. Again, the grid snap should help you draw accurately. If necessary, select the cells after drawing and use the Property inspector to correct their widths. Figure 10.15 shows how your layout table should look at this point.

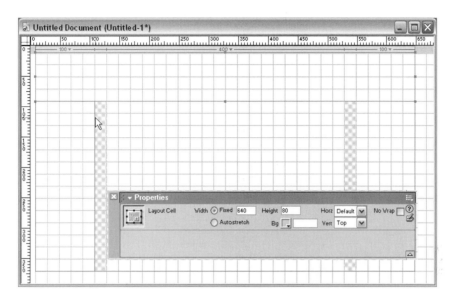

Figure 10.15   The **bumpers.html file** with layout cells in place.

7. You've just created an HTML table, disguised as a layout table. To test this out, go to the Insert bar and click the Standard View button. Your table is revealed! Check it out in Code view; examine it with the Property inspector. It's just a regular table—but you created it in a special way.

   When you're done examining the table, go to the Layout tab of the Insert bar and click the Layout View button, to return to Layout view.

8. It's time to add some content. For the banner, click inside the top layout cell and insert the **banner.gif** image from the **chapter_10/images** folder. (You can drag-and-drop the image from the Site window or Assets panel, or use the Image object to insert it.)

   Depending on how tall you made your layout cell, the image might be too tall for it, and might stretch it out. This won't be a problem for you, because you're going to remove cell heights later—so don't worry about it now.

   By default, the image aligns to the upper left of the layout cell. You want the image centered in the cell, and you want the cell background color to match the image. To accomplish this, select the layout cell (using any of the methods outlined earlier), and use the Property inspector to change the horizontal alignment to center and the background color to a purple that matches the image. (Hint: Sample the image color to create the color.) When you're done, the top portion of your page should look just like the finished layout in Figure 10.12.

9. The center column of your layout is for the page's main text. If you've installed one of Macromedia's filler text extensions (as described in Chapter 4, "Working with Text"), use it to fill this area with text. If you haven't, open **filler_text.html**,

in the **chapter_10** folder, and copy and paste the text from that file to your layout cell. Add a header, if you like, so the page looks more like the finished layout.

10. The left-hand column is for the five navigation buttons. There are various ways you could structure this stack of buttons, including just inserting them as a series of images. For this exercise, you'll put them in separate table cells—which means you need a nested table to sit in that left-hand column.

    If you try to draw a layout table inside the layout cell, you'll discover that Dreamweaver doesn't allow that. So, select and delete the left layout cell. In its place, draw an identically sized layout table. After you've drawn the table, draw five layout cells in it, each 60 pixels tall and as wide as the table. Figure 10.16 shows what your layout should look like at this point.

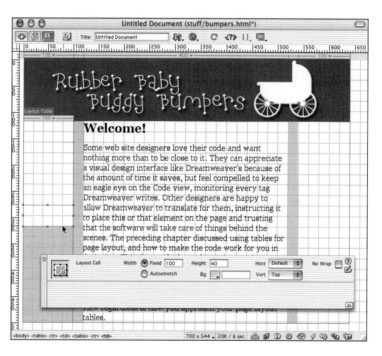

Figure 10.16   The **bumpers.html** page with nested layout table in place.

11. Create your page's navigation bar by inserting one button image in each of the new layout cells. (The button images are all in the **chapter_10/images** folder, called **button1.gif—button5.gif**.)

    Hmm. If you're looking carefully, you might notice a problem in your table structure at this point. The Column Header for the nested table, and for the left-most column of the parent table, both show two width figures. This is because the images are all 103 pixels wide, and the table and column are set to 100 pixels wide (see Figure 10.17).

Figure 10.17   Double values in the column headers indicate that the left-most column is set too narrow for its contents.

To fix this problem, use the drop-down menu for each column with a double value, and choose Make Cell Widths Consistent. Problem solved! But this indicates that the grid has outlived its usefulness, so turn it off by choosing View > Grid > Show Grid, to toggle the command off.

Note

If your column is narrower than the image, most browsers will ignore the specified column width and display the column wide enough to accommodate the image. If your column is wider than the image, and you are counting on the column maintaining that width, you will probably have a problem when the page displays in the browser; the column will shrink to the size of its widest rigid object, the image.

12. To match the finished layout, your left and right layout cells need colored backgrounds—a light purple or light blue, or any color you think looks good.

    Colorizing the right cell is easy—select the cell and use the Property inspector to assign a background color.

    Colorizing the left cell is not so easy, because it has a nested table in it. You don't want to colorize the background of the nested table because that won't guarantee that the color extends the full length of the layout. You want to colorize the cell containing the table. But if you remember, when you created this nested table, Dreamweaver created an automatic cell to hold it. And you can't use Layout view to set the properties of cells created automatically.

    You're stumped, unless you remember that you can always return to Standard View if you need to, and then come back to Layout view. Do that now—in the Layout tab of the Insert bar, click the Standard View button. After you're in

Standard view, use the tag selector to select the table cell behind the nested table, and use the Property inspector to colorize its background (see Figure 10.18). When you've made your change, return to Layout view.

Figure 10.18   Switching to Standard view to add a background color to a hidden table cell.

13. To make your code more stable and compliant, it's time to get rid of all height values. Start with the nested table: Select it, and from the drop-down menu in its Column Header, choose Clear Cell Heights (refer back to Figure 10.10, if necessary). That shrinks up your navigation bar pretty severely! Next, select the parent table and repeat the process.

14. To make the navigation bar look a little nicer, you don't want the buttons all smashed together. For each button image, use the Property inspector to add a vspace and hspace of **10** pixels. That will force the table, and its enclosing cell, to expand. If you end up with double values in the Column Headers because of this, make your cell widths consistent as you did before.

15. How does your design look? If you haven't done so yet, Preview in Browser to check it out.

    One last touch: For any visitor with a large monitor, your fixed layout hugs the left edge of the browser window. This is a fixed-width layout, but you can make it look nicer in large windows by centering the layout (that's what Figure 10.12

shows). Normally, you would do this by giving the main table an alignment of center. But if you select your layout table and check the Property inspector, you'll see that there is no option for table alignment. Once more, go back to Standard view; select the table, and use the Property inspector to add the center alignment; then return to Layout view. Your page is complete!

Creating Flexible Layouts

Dreamweaver Layout view provides tools for creating "flexible" pages. (See Chapter 8, "Design Issues," for a complete discussion of flexible versus fixed-width pages. Chapter 9, "Building Tables," discusses how percent-based tables are used to create flexible layouts.) In Layout view, the Dreamweaver-specific term *autostretch* is used to describe a layout table or column that is set to a percentage width so that it expands to fill all available space.

Autostretch Tables and How They Work

When you first create a layout table, it has a fixed width. You turn it into an autostretch table by assigning either the table itself, or one of its columns, to have an autostretch width instead of a fixed width. When you do this, Dreamweaver assigns the table and one of its columns a width of 100%. All other columns in the table retain their fixed widths. An autostretch layout table must have one column, and one column only, designated as autostretch. A few tips on autostretching:

- Layout tables set to autostretch are always assigned a width of 100%. If you want a flexible layout table set to, say, 90%, you'll have to leave Layout view and change the width using Code view or the Table Property inspector.

- Autostretch tables do not always display correctly in Dreamweaver. They might look as though they stretch too far, beyond the boundaries of your Document window. This is a quirk of Design view, rather than a problem with the table. Previewing the page in a browser will show that the table does in fact correctly size itself to the window. (Remember, the goal isn't to create pages that display nicely in Dreamweaver, but pages that display nicely in the browser.)

Using Spacer Images in Autostretch Tables

The preceding chapter discussed some of the benefits of using *spacer images* to stabilize tables. A spacer image is usually a 1×1–pixel transparent GIF inserted into a table cell and given a width attribute in pixels; this "props open" the column containing that cell, preventing it from shrinking any smaller than the dimensions of the spacer. Spacer images are especially important to the workings of Dreamweaver autostretch tables.

As mentioned in the preceding section, autostretch tables include one column set to 100%. That percentage means, "this column should take up 100% of the available space in the browser window." The available space is all space not being taken up by other columns. If you define a column as autostretch, and other columns in the table don't have some sort of content in them propping them open, the stretching column will shrink them down to nothing, regardless of what their fixed pixel widths are. If your table's fixed columns contain content, such as images, this will keep them from shrinking. But in case they don't, this is the time to use a spacer image.

Automatically Adding Spacers (Before Generating Autostretch Tables)

You can tell Dreamweaver that, whenever you define an autostretch table, it should automatically add spacers to the fixed-width columns. Dreamweaver will even create the transparent GIF image for you, if you like. Do it like this:

1. Go to Edit > Preferences, and choose the Layout category (see Figure 10.19). (For Mac users of OS X, choose Dreamweaver, Preferences.)

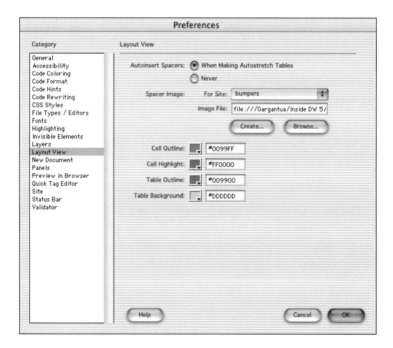

Figure 10.19   The Dreamweaver Layout View preferences, including options for automatically generating spacer images.

2. From the options shown, choose to autoinsert spacers when making autostretch tables.

3. If your site already includes a transparent GIF that you could use as a spacer image, click the Browse button to select it. Otherwise, click the Create button and show Dreamweaver where to store your spacer image and what to call it. The default name is **spacer.gif**. Dreamweaver will remember this choice for all documents in the current site.

> **Note**
>
> The Layout View Preferences include options for customizing the colors used in layout tables and cells, as well. If you don't find the default colors to your liking, experiment with these settings until you create something you like better.

After doing this, the next time you turn one of your layout tables into an autostretch table, Dreamweaver will add a 1-pixel high row to the bottom of the table, with a spacer image in each fixed-width cell. If your table has two columns, the first set to 100 pixels wide and the second set to autostretch, the following code will be added to the bottom of your table:

```
<tr>
    <td height="1"><img src="images/spacer.gif" alt="" width="100"
height="1"></td>
    <td></td>
</tr>
```

In web geek circles, this is known as a *control row*. Many hand-coders manually add them to the bottoms of their tables to solidify flexible tables.

Manually Adding Spacers (After Generating Autostretch Tables)

You also can add a spacer image to any column at any time by going to the Column Header drop-down menu and selecting Add Spacer Image. This will add a control row, if one doesn't already exist, and will add a spacer image to the relevant cell. Note, however, that the width of the spacer image will be based on the current width of the column—if you have already run into the column-squishing problem described earlier in this section, that might not be the width you want.

Removing Spacers

After Dreamweaver inserts spacer images, you are free to remove some or all of them, but be warned that this might generate some unexpected and undesired results. To remove a spacer image from a particular column, go to the relevant Column Header drop-down menu and select Remove Spacer Image. To remove all spacer images from a table, select Remove All Spacer Images from the column header menu, or select the layout table and click the Remove All Spacers button in the Layout Table Property inspector.

Setting a Table to Autostretch

One way to create a flexible layout is to select the layout table and use the Property inspector to set its width to autostretch (see Figure 10.9). If you do this, the table will be given a 100% width, and all the cells in its rightmost column will also be assigned a width of 100%. All other cells will retain their fixed pixel width. This is a good solution if, for instance, your layout consists of a left-hand navigation column (which shouldn't stretch) and right-hand content column (which should).

Note

Whether you set the table or a column to autostretch, Dreamweaver might ask if you want to use a spacer image to create your flexible table. If you choose not to, you'll get a warning about possible instability in your table.

Setting a Column to Autostretch

If you don't want your right-hand column to be the flexible column, instead of setting the layout table to autostretch, you will need to select a particular column and specify it as having an autostretch width. When you do this, the table will automatically be set to autostretch as well. You can set a column to autostretch in one of two ways:

- Select a cell in the desired column and, in the Property inspector, set the width attribute to autostretch.

- Go to the layout table's Column Header area, and from the drop-down menu, select Make Column Autostretch (see Figure 10.20).

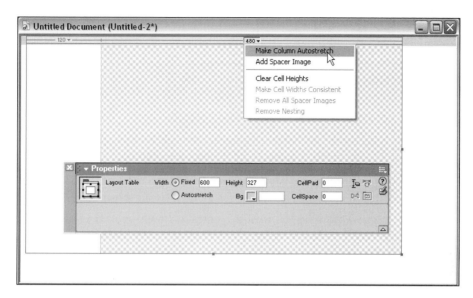

Figure 10.20   Using the Column Header menu to make a column autostretch.

Note

Occasionally, a page with table cells set to 100% width won't browse properly—the offending column will cause it to stretch beyond the edges of the window. If this happens to you, go back to Standard view and remove the width from all cells previously set to 100% wide. Leave the table width at 100%.

Setting Columns or Tables Back to Fixed Width

After a table has been set to autostretch, you can set it back to fixed width by doing one of the following:

- Select the autostretch table, or one of the cells in the autostretch column, and in the Property inspector select the fixed width option.

- In the table's Column Header, go to the drop-down menu for the autostretch column and select Make Column Fixed Width.

Doing either of these will automatically set the width of the table, and the column, to a pixel value that matches their current width. In some cases, you might see two numbers in the column header menu. One is the actual width of the column, and the other is the width that currently appears in the HTML code. This can happen in situations such as one in which a width was specified, and then content was subsequently added which exceeded that specified width. It is best to have column widths reflect the width of their content. To make this adjustment automatically, go to the Column header drop-down menu and select Make Cell Widths Consistent.

Exercise 10.2   Creating a Flexible Layout in Layout View

In this exercise, you'll use the autostretch feature to refine the **bumpers.html** file you created in Exercise 10.1, so that it stretches to fill the browser window.

1. Open **bumpers.html** and save it as **bumpers2.html**. Go to Layout view, if you're not there already. It should contain the fixed-width layout shown in Figure 10.12.

2. To make this layout flexible, you want the center column to autostretch, and the left and right columns to remain fixed. To make this happen, from the Column Header drop-down menu of the main table, choose Autostretch (see Figure 10.21).

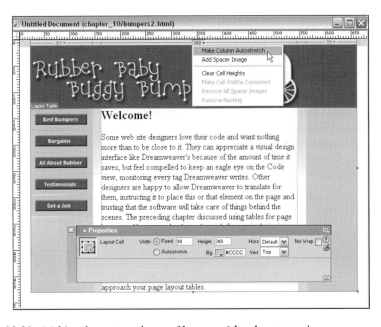

Figure 10.21   Making the center column of **bumpers2.html** autostretch.

Note

For purposes of this exercise, if Dreamweaver asks if you want to insert a spacer image, choose not to. Normally, you'll probably want to say yes to this option.

Does something horrible happen? If you haven't told Dreamweaver to use spacer images for autostretch, you'll probably see something like the disaster shown in Figure 10.22. That's not good! Go to Edit > Undo, to get your fixed-width table back.

Figure 10.22   What happens when autostretch is applied, and there's no content to stabilize the rest of the table.

3. To fix this problem, go to Edit > Preferences, and choose the Layout View category. (For Mac OS X users, choose Dreamweaver > Preferences.) From the options there, choose to Autoinsert Spacers When Making Autostretch Tables for the current site. Click the Create button to make Dreamweaver create a single-pixel GIF for you. When the dialog box appears, browse to the **chapter_10/images** folder to store your spacer image. When you're done, click OK to leave Preferences.

4. Now, try again to set your center column to autostretch. The result looks much better! If it still looks a little odd in Dreamweaver, Preview in Browser. Your layout should be up against the outer edges of the browser window. The center column should stretch, and the two outer columns remain fixed.

   There is a chance the browser won't cooperate with you, and your table will stretch beyond the browser window width. If this happens, come back to Dreamweaver, go to Standard view, and select all the cells in the autostretch column. Their width will be set to 100%. Remove the width attribute entirely. The page might now look a little strange in Dreamweaver (see Figure 10.23), but it will browse just fine.

Figure 10.23   Removing the 100% `width` attribute from the autostretch cells (in Standard view) and the resulting shift in Dreamweaver Design view.

Back in Dreamweaver, go to Standard view or Code view and investigate the structure of your table. The table itself, and the middle cell are both set to 100% width.

5. But what if you want your layout to stretch not to the very edges of the browser window, but just close to it? This is done by setting the table width to 90%—but you can't do this in Layout view. Go to Standard view, select your table, and use the Property inspector to set its width to **90%**. Then Preview in Browser again, and see how the layout behaves when you stretch and squash the window.

Note

Chapter 9 has an exercise in building a more complex flexible-tables layout.

The Convert Layers to Table Command

Another Dreamweaver layout aid that can help you create tables without coding tables is the Convert Layers to Table command. This command is provided as an aid to those who like designing pages using layers, with all the advantages of drag-and-drop and pixel-specific positioning; but who do not want their finished layouts to remain in layers, perhaps because they are concerned about inconsistent browser support of layer-based layouts. (See the next chapter for more on using layers for page layout.) Using this command, you can create your layout using layers, and convert the layers to a table-based layout when everything is set to your liking.

Note

The Convert Layers to Tables command has a *bug* (a flaw in the way the software performs) of which you should be aware. It is very similar to the problem with Layout View discussed earlier in this chapter. Convert Layers to Tables often creates empty table cells; this code will cause your pages to display poorly in some browsers. For this reason, it is recommend that if you use the Convert Layers to Tables command, be sure to place either non-breaking space characters or spacer GIFs in these empty table cells. This can be done manually in Code view, or by using Find and Replace.

Note

Convert Tables to Layers is intended to be used in conjunction with Convert Layers to Tables, so that a layout can be converted back to layers for future modifications.

The Basics of Converting Layers to Table

Essentially, this is a simple command, though it does require some care in setting up your layer-based layout before it will work properly. It requires setting up your layers a certain way, doing some planning as you build, and making some strategic decisions as you apply the command.

Note

Creating layer-based layouts, and using Convert Layers to Table, can only be done from Standard Design view, not from Layout view.

Prepare Your Layers

Layers that overlap each other cannot be converted to a table. If you're thinking ahead, before you create your layer-based layout you'll open the Layers panel (Window > Other > Layers, which opens the Advanced Layout panel group) and select the Do Not Allow Overlaps option (see Figure 10.24). This option won't affect any overlapping layers you might already have created, but it will stop you creating any new overlaps.

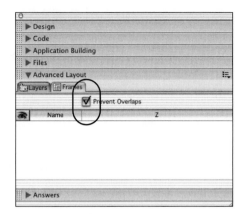

Figure 10.24   Disabling layer overlaps in the Layers panel preparatory to using the Convert Layers to Table command.

If you've already created your layers without this safeguard enabled, and still want to use the command, use your eyeballs and your judgment to try to eliminate all overlaps. (If you miss any, Dreamweaver will tell you about it when you try to convert!)

Choose and Configure the Command

When you're ready to convert, go to Modify > Convert > Layers to Table. The dialog box that appears (shown in Figure 10.25) gives you various options for determining how the conversion will take place, and what kind of table code it will create. The Layout Tools options are not crucial to a good result; they simply offer some automatic choices like opening the Layers panel. The Table options are crucial, as they determine how the table code will be generated. They're discussed in the following sections.

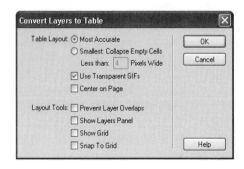

Figure 10.25   The Convert Layers to Table dialog box.

Table Complexity: Most Accurate Versus Smallest

You must tell Dreamweaver to create the most accurate table it possibly can, or the most efficient table. When you choose most accurate, Dreamweaver will attempt to create a pixel-perfect reproduction of your layer structure in the table. This often means many small (sometimes very small!) table cells, a real mess for you to edit and for the browser to display. When you choose smallest, Dreamweaver will automatically collapse any table cells within the size limit you specify, to create simpler table code; but your layout might shift slightly from its layer-based positioning.

Table Stability: Use Transparent GIFs

As discussed in the preceding chapter, and in the section on "Layout View" earlier in this chapter, transparent single-pixel spacer images help to solidify table structure. If this option is selected, Dreamweaver will automatically include a control row of transparent pixels in the table code. (See the discussion on using spacer images in Layout view, earlier in this chapter, for more on control rows.)

Table Alignment: Center Table

This option applies the `align="center"` attribute to the table, so it floats in the middle of the page.

Working Smart with Convert Layers to Table

There are limits to what kind of page structure you can create with this command. Because Dreamweaver layers have fixed pixel widths, you can't use them to create flexible layouts. Because the command converts all layers in a document into one big table, you can't use it to create multi-table layouts, or layouts with nested tables.

But just because the command is limited doesn't mean you can't use it wisely, within its limitations. If you're careful and smart, you can use Convert Layers to Table to create workable pages, fairly quickly and very intuitively.

Tidy Layers Make a Tidy Table

If you understand what makes a good table, you'll know how to arrange your layers to create the same effect. Tables exist as row and column grids—respect this. Align layers carefully; match their dimensions where appropriate, so they form the simplest grid structure you can get them in. Don't create two layers where one will do.

To help accomplish simple table structure, choose the Smallest option in the Convert Layers to Table dialog box, allowing Dreamweaver to combine small cells into larger ones.

Know When to Use Other Tools

Just because your table started out life as a series of layers, doesn't mean you can't use the standard table-editing tools to clean it up or extend it. To make a flexible layout, convert your fixed layout to a table and then add percent-based widths as necessary to the table and its columns. To make a layout that uses multiple tables (nested or otherwise), use layers to build the layout for one table in one document, and convert to table; then use layers to build the layout for the second table in another document, and convert to table; then copy and paste to combine your tables.

Never Say Die!

And if at first you don't succeed, try again! If your conversion creates an unlovely table structure, Edit > Undo, tweak your layers to be tidier, and run the command again. You also can use the Modify > Convert > Table to Layers command to get your layers back—though doing so might not reproduce exactly the structure of layers you started with.

Note

In particular, if you convert Layers to Table and then reverse the process to converting Tables to Layers, you might end up with a whole row of skinny little layers at the bottom of your layout. These layers have been created from the table's control row—they contain that row's spacer images. You can safely delete these layers before continuing. The next time you convert Layers to Table, Dreamweaver will create another control row.

Exercise 10.3   Building a Page Layout Using a Tracing Image and the Convert Layers to Table Command

In this exercise, you'll create a layout by starting from a tracing image, creating a layer-based layout to re-create the design of the tracing image, and convert the whole thing to a table. You'll experiment with different conversion settings, and examine the resulting code to see how it's been created, how it can be improved on, and how it might have been done differently by constructing the table manually.

All files for this exercise are in the **chapter_10** folder from the CD. If you haven't done so already, copy the folder to your hard drive and use it to create a Dreamweaver site called **chapter_10**.

1. For this exercise, you'll build a different version of the Rubber Baby Buggy Bumpers home page used for previous exercises in this chapter (see Figure 10.26). Start by creating a new HTML file and saving it in the **chapter_10** folder as **bumpers3.html**.

Figure 10.26   The desired layout for the **bumpers3.html** page.

2. The new layout for the Bumpers home page was created in Adobe Illustrator, captured as a screenshot and saved as **bumperLayout.gif**. To load this image as a tracing image, go to Modify > Page Properties.

In the portion of the dialog box regarding tracing images, click the Choose button and browse to **bumperLayout.gif** (it's in the **chapter_10/images** folder). After the image is in place, click the Apply button to see it in your document. You don't want to use it at 100% opacity, because it will be hard to tell which parts of your layout are tracing image and which parts are real layout elements—so set the opacity slider to around 40%. Click Apply, if you want to see if 40% is a good setting for you, and adjust it if needed.

Before leaving the Page Properties dialog box, set the document's page margins to **0**. When your dialog box looks like the one in Figure 10.27, click OK to close the dialog box.

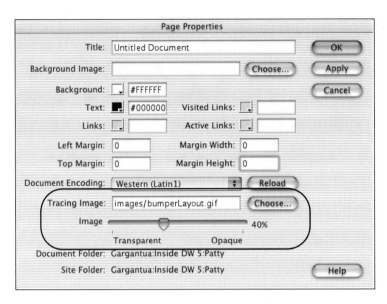

Figure 10.27   The Page Properties dialog box for **bumpers3.html** establishing the
tracing image.

3. The positioning of the tracing image could be improved. To match the finished
layout shown in Figure 10.26, you want the banner flush against the top and left
edges of the page. So your tracing image should be aligned that way, to help you
work.

Go to View > Tracing Image > Adjust Position. When the dialog box opens, use
your arrow keys to nudge the tracing image until it's in position. Figure 10.28
shows the Document window with tracing image, ready for use.

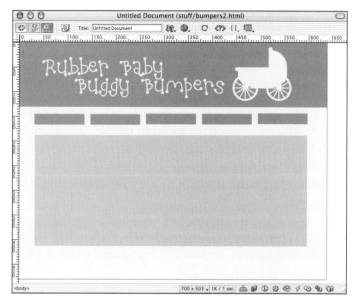

Figure 10.28   The **bumpers3.html** page with tracing image in place.

4. Now it's time to start creating layers. To keep yourself from accidentally overlapping them, open the Layers panel and select Prevent Overlaps (Window > Other > Layers, or expand the Advanced Layout panel group).

From the Common tab of the Insert bar, select the Draw Layer object and start drawing layers. You want one layer for the banner, one for each button, and one for the text block (see Figure 10.29).

Figure 10.29   The layers for the **bumpers3.html** layout in position aligned with the tracing image.

5. Using the images in the **chapter_10/images** folder, and the text in the **chapter_10/filler_text.html** file, fill your layers with content. Everything should be looking close to the tracing image by now, except the main banner. The layer containing it needs a background color matching the color of the image; and the image needs to be centered in the layer. To accomplish the first task, select the layer and use the color picker in the Layer Property inspector to sample the image's color. The second task can't be accomplished using the Property inspector—there are no alignment controls for layers listed there. But don't worry about it—you'll be able to set the alignment after you've converted to a table.

   Preview your page in a browser. As long as you're not using a version 3 browser, which doesn't support layers, you'll see your layout, looking almost perfect. The tracing image won't show.

6. Back in Dreamweaver, remove the tracing image—it has served its purpose. Go to Modify > Page Properties, find the tracing image input field, and select and delete the contents. When you close the dialog box and return to Design view, your tracing image will be gone.

7. It's time to convert your layout—and for a bit of experimenting with settings. Choose Modify > Convert Layers to Table. In the dialog box that appears, select Most Accurate, and Use Transparent GIFs. You can deselect all the Layout Tools options. When you're all set, click OK.

Note

If you have overlapping layers, you'll get an error message when you try to convert. Check your layout carefully, looking for and adjusting all possible culprits, and try again.

How does your page look? Unless you were very precise in aligning layers, your table is probably pretty complex and ugly, like that shown in Figure 10.30. That's not an optimal result!

Figure 10.30   The results of using the most accurate setting, converting **bumpers2.html** from layers to a table.

8. Try again. Go to Edit > Undo, to get your layers back. Then choose Modify > Convert Layers to Table again. This time, change the settings to Smallest, collapsing all cells smaller than 6 pixels. Click OK, and check your table. That's much better! (See Figure 10.31).

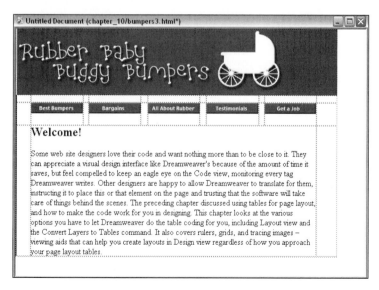

Figure 10.31   A much more compact table created from more efficient settings in Convert Layers to Table.

9. Now that the layout is in a table, you can fix the banner alignment problem. Select the cell containing the banner and use the Table Property inspector to set the `align` attribute to **center** and `valign` to **middle**.

   Preview your page in a browser, to check it out. Now it looks like the desired layout you wanted to create.

10. If you examine your table in Dreamweaver, you might see all sorts of ways in which it could be structured more efficiently than it is. Looking at the example in Figure 10.31, the center text column is slightly off-center; several rows have heights assigned, which isn't quite kosher; and you might think of various alternatives to having so many columns separating all the buttons (maybe a nested table, or multiple stacked tables creating the page). But it's not bad.

11. Now, for the ultimate challenge—can you make this layout flexible? A good flexible structure for this table would be if the banner cell stretched from side to side, and the empty columns at left and right stretched equally, so the fixed width content and button areas in the middle remain centered no matter what. While Dreamweaver couldn't create the table this way, using Convert Layers to Table, you can now tweak it.

    First, select the table itself and assign it a width of **100%**.

    Next, drag to select all the cells in the leftmost column, and use the Property inspector to assign a width of **50%** (see Figure 10.32).

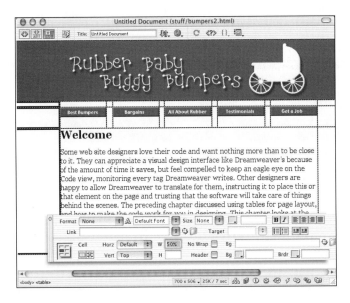

Figure 10.32   Assigning a width of **50%** to one column of **bumpers2.html**, part of turning it into a flexible table.

Repeat the process for the rightmost column.

The table might look a little strange in Dreamweaver, stretching slightly beyond the edges of the Document window. Preview in the Browser, to see your final flexible layout (see Figure 10.33).

Figure 10.33   The final, flexible version of **bumpers2.html** as seen in the browser.

Summary

This chapter covered some of the more obviously graphic-designer-friendly tools and techniques for working in Dreamweaver that really maximize the possibilities of Design view. Rulers, grids, and tracing images are great tools for getting more visual feedback from Design view and the Document window. Layout view and the Convert Layers to Table command allow you to quickly, intuitively translate your layout ideas into HTML structures. As you saw from the exercises, both of these latter tools have their limitations—this is true with any design tool that does things automatically for you. As always with web design, the more you know about HTML, and the more you keep one eye on the code as you work, the better off you'll be. But used wisely, and if they fit your working style, they can be valuable additions to your web development toolbox.

Chapter 11

Working with Forms

When a web site and its visitors can respond to one another, its usefulness increases greatly, both to the user and the site owner; this is often referred to as *interactivity*.

Forms are one of the primary tools that enable the web user to talk to the site's administrators.

A form allows you, the developer, to ask structured questions of the visitor, enabling you to elicit desired information. With a form, you can just ask for the visitor's name and email address; you also can have visitors take a survey, sign a guest book, provide feedback on your site, or even make a purchase. Forms are standard tools for the web designer.

Topics covered in this chapter include how forms work in the web environment, the basic HTML for building forms, how to create forms with Dreamweaver, how to use behaviors with forms, the secrets of building attractive, user-friendly forms, and some special additions and enhancements for forms.

Along the way you'll have the opportunity to work through a series of exercises that show you how to build a simple mail form, add more complex features to it, format it with CSS, and get it ready to be processed by a server-side script.

How Forms Work in the Browser

The HTML code you create in Dreamweaver (or any other web-authoring program) is only part of what is required for a form to do its job. Forms require a *script* (a set of instructions, generally a text file, that is executed within an application) in order for the information input to the form to be processed.

Form-Processing Scripts

The most common way to process form data is a Common Gateway Interface (CGI) script. CGI scripts are typically written in Perl or another programming language, possibly C++, Java, VBScript, or JavaScript.

Forms also can be processed by server-side technologies such as ASP, ASP.NET, ColdFusion, PHP, or JSP, which function essentially in the same way as CGI scripts. In conjunction with these technologies, forms are commonly used to collect information to be added to databases. (See Chapter 26, "Introduction to Dynamic Dreamweaver.")

Before creating interactive forms, check with the administrator of the server where you plan to host the web site and find out what type of scripting technology is supported. Perl CGI scripts are very commonly supported, and some host companies will even provide these scripts already set up for use on their servers.

The specifics of setting up scripts are beyond the scope of this book; but at the end of the chapter, you'll find some web resources that will point you in the right direction.

HTML Forms

The HTML code for form creation is not very complex. Even if you manage to do much of your web page building with Dreamweaver without looking at the source code, it's particularly helpful in the case of forms to at least be somewhat familiar with the tags and attributes involved. When it comes time to troubleshoot a form that doesn't work as it should, a careful look at the HTML might reveal the error.

Tip

As you build the forms in the exercises in this chapter, and as you build your own forms, you either should work in Code and Design view so that you can see the HTML source code as well as Design view, or you should switch back and forth frequently from Design view to Code view and keep an eye on the code Dreamweaver writes for you.

The <form> tag

Forms begin and end with the <form>...</form> tag pair. Between these tags will usually be some normal HTML markup for formatting purposes, and *form controls*—the text fields, check boxes, and other elements used to gather information. Dreamweaver refers to these elements as *form objects*.

Note

In some situations, a form might not require the <form>...</form> tag pair, such as a client-side-only form, which doesn't involve sending information to a server at all. Some browsers, however, particularly Netscape up to and including version 4.7, will not display form elements outside of a <form> block, so it's best to include it.

The <form> tag has seven possible attributes, as shown in Table 11.1.

Table 11.1   Attributes of the *<form>* Tag

Attribute	Function of Attribute
name	Assigns an identifier to the entire form element. This value is particularly useful when using scripts that reference the form or its controls.
action	Specifies the URL to be accessed when the form is being submitted. The URL might be to a CGI program, or to an HTML page that contains server-side scripts.

continues ▶

Table 11.1   Continued

Attribute	Function of Attribute
method	Forms might be submitted by two possible HTTP methods: GET and POST. This attribute specifies whether the form data is sent to the server appended to the ACTION attribute URL (GET) or as a transaction message body (POST).
target	Allows a window or frame destination other than the current one to be specified as the location to load the HTML page that has been designated to be returned by the server after the form data is processed.
enctype	Sets a MIME type for the data being submitted to the server. For typical form submissions sent by the POST method, the default MIME type is the correct one.
accept	Enables you to specify one or more MIME types for permissible files to be uploaded to the server when using INPUT elements of the type FILE. Provides client-side validation of a file type.
accept-charset	Advises the server about which character sets it must receive from a client form.

Here is an example of an opening <form> tag using hypothetical attribute values, to demonstrate the syntax:

```
<form name="order_form" method="get"
action="http://www.mydomain.com/cgi/FormMail.pl">
```

Tip

When naming forms and form elements, keep a few things in mind. First, don't use spaces or special characters. Second, it is a good idea to use names that clearly identify the form or element's role. Third, develop your own *naming conventions*, and be consistent. Either don't use capitals at all, or use them in a consistent way; either don't abbreviate English words at all, or abbreviate in a consistent way; either use underscores between words, or run the words together. This helps you to remember the names you create and avoid typos. Finally, be aware that scripting languages have certain *reserved words* that have special meaning and can cause problems. The word *date* is a common example. You might want to research which reserved words exist in the scripting language you're using, especially if you run into problems that seem to have no other explanation.

The <input> tag

In between the <form>...</form> tags, a form will have <input> tags with various attributes. It also might have <select>, <option>, and <textarea> tags.

The <input> element provides an object that can collect user data, such as a text field, a check box, a radio button, a list, or menu; a Submit button also is written using the <input> tag.

The <input> element accepts numerous attributes; the type attribute of the <input> tag determines the kind of control that appears on the page. The type attribute can have a number of different values, including checkbox, radio, text, submit, and reset. The <textarea> element produces a multiple-line text box area. <select>, along with <option>, produce drop-down menus and list boxes. Each of these kinds of form objects is shown in Figure 11.1.

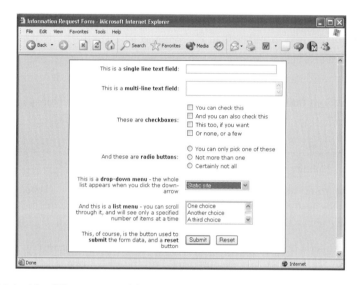

Figure 11.1   The different types of form objects shown in a browser window.

Creating Forms in Dreamweaver

Dreamweaver makes building HTML forms very easy. All common form tags can be added using the Forms tab of the Insert bar. The same objects also are available by choosing Insert > Form as well as Insert > Form Objects from the main menu. Figure 11.2 shows the different buttons available from the Forms tab of the Insert bar.

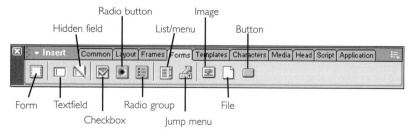

Figure 11.2   The Forms tab of the Insert bar.

The basic steps involved in building an HTML form with Dreamweaver are as follows:

1. Add a `<form>`...`</form>` tag pair, and set its attributes using the Property inspector. The placement of the form tag will be displayed in the Dreamweaver Design window as a red dashed line.

2. Between the `<form>` tags, if desired, add a table to give your form elements a neat layout.

3. Add elements one by one, using the Property inspector to set their attributes. You'll usually need to add ordinary HTML text labels to the form objects; in other words, if a text field is designed for the user to type in his name, you'll want to place the word Name next to the form field to identify its intended purpose.

4. Add a Submit button, and once again, use the Property inspector to set its attributes.

Exercise 11.1   Building a Simple HTML Form

In this exercise, you build a simple HTML form that includes several `<input>`. As you go through the steps, feel free to experiment with the different tags and attributes. See what results you have in the Document window, and in Code view as well.

If you do experiment, however, it's probably best to return each object to the values specified in the exercise, because later exercises build on this one. In Exercise 11.2, you'll add several more form elements to this page, producing a longer and more complex form.

Before you start, copy the **chapter_11** folder on the CD to your hard drive. Define a site called Chapter 11, with this folder as the local root folder.

1. From the **chapter_11** folder, open the file **form.html**.

2. Place the cursor after (below) the box with the heading and text. In the Insert bar, bring the Forms tab to the front. Click the Form Object icon. You should see a red dotted line forming a narrow rectangle just below the text box. If you don't see this red dotted line, choose View > Visual Aids > Invisible Elements. This represents the `<form>` block in your document; all form elements need to be placed within this red dotted line (see Figure 11.3). For now, you won't set any attributes to the `<form>` tag.

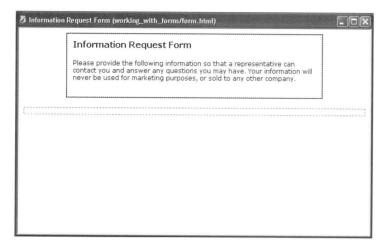

Figure 11.3   The Exercise document with the `<form>` block shown by a red dotted line.

3. Now place an HTML table within the `<form>` block; this table will enable you to align the form elements nicely. Place the cursor inside the `<form>` block and choose Insert > Table from the main menu. In the Insert Table dialog box, give your table 7 rows, 2 columns, a width of 70 percent, a border of 0, cell padding of 5, and cell spacing of 0. Click OK to insert the table in the document; while it is still selected, in the Property inspector, choose Align > Center. In the upper-left table cell, type **Name**.

4. Place the cursor in the upper-right table cell; you can use the Tab key to step from cell to cell within a table in the Dreamweaver Document window, left to right, top to bottom. Click the Text Field button in the Insert bar.

5. Notice that a text field has been inserted. As with many elements in Dreamweaver, while it's still selected, the Property inspector displays a number of options and attributes associated with the element. On the left side of the Property inspector is a field displaying the words textfield; here you can specify a name for the text field. Name it **visitor_name**.

6. Give the text field a Char Width (character width) of 30; this adds an attribute `size="30` to the `<input>` tag. Leave the other fields in the Property inspector at their default settings. Your form should look like Figure 11.4.

Figure 11.4   The exercise with one text field and its label.

7. The label Name is a long way from the field it identifies. To fix this, place the cursor in the table cell with the word Name. In the tag selector, at the bottom of the Document window, select the rightmost <td> tag. In the Property inspector, set Horz (horizontal cell alignment) to Right. The text Name should now be placed on the right side of the cell, as shown in Figure 11.5.

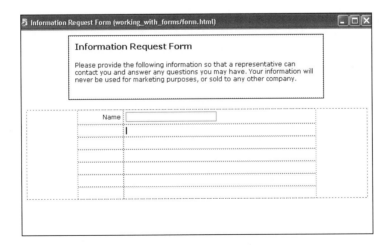

Figure 11.5   Aligning the text label within its cell.

8. All of your form labels will be in cells in the table's left column, and you'll want them all right aligned. This can be done in one operation. It requires selecting multiple table cells, as follows: Place the cursor in the left cell of the second row.

Click, and holding the mouse button down, drag downward across all seven left-hand cells. Each cell will "light up" with a black border as you select it. With all seven cells selected, in the Property inspector, choose Horz > Right.

9. In the second row, type **Email Address** into the left cell, and in the cell on the right, add another text field. Give it the same attributes as the Name text field but a unique name: **email**. The form object's name goes in the field on the far left in the Property inspector.

10. In the third row, left cell, type the text **Please send me information on these services**. In the right cell, you will add a number of check boxes.

11. To add the first check box, place the cursor in the right cell of the third row and click the Checkbox button. A check box will appear. With it still selected, in the Property inspector, fill in its name in the field on the far left; use **web_design_info**.

12. The text you type into the Check Value field will be the text that will be sent with the user's form data if the user checks this check box. While the check box is still selected, fill in the Check Value field with the word **yes**. In this case, if the user checks this box, the data sent will indicate that the check box web_design_info has a value of yes.

13. In the Document window, directly to the right of the check box, type **Web Design**.

14. After the words Web Design, press Shift+Enter to create a line break, and add another text box. Give this one the name **web_hosting_info** and the value **yes**. In the Document window, add the label **Web Hosting** to the right of the second check box. Your document should now look like Figure 11.6.

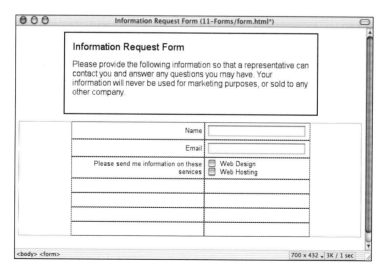

Figure 11.6   The exercise with check boxes added.

15. In the fourth table row, you'll add radio buttons to get the answer to a yes-or-no question. In the left cell, type the text **I have an existing web site**. With the cursor in the right cell, click the Radio Button button on the Insert bar.

16. With the radio button still selected, in the Property inspector give the radio button the name **have_web_site** and the Check Value **yes**.

17. Press Shift+Enter to add a line break, and add another radio button. Give it the same name as the preceding radio button; a radio button group must all have the same name. Give it the Check Value no.

18. In the Document window, next to the first radio button, type **Yes**; next to the second radio button, type **No**. Your page in the Document window should now look like Figure 11.7.

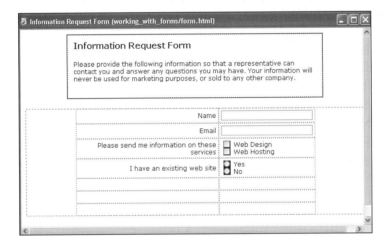

Figure 11.7   The exercise page with radio buttons added.

This completes Part I. You have left empty table rows for the elements you'll add in Exercise 11.2. Save your document and view it in a browser.

Note

MX   New to Dreamweaver MX is the Radio Group object in the Forms tab of the Insert bar. Clicking the Radio Group button opens the Radio Group dialog box, where you can specify all the radio buttons in a group at once, giving them the required common name. Using this function allows you to add both the values and the HTML labels for each radio button, and to choose whether or not to separate the buttons with an HTML table, or simply with line breaks.

Exercise 11.2   Scrolling Lists, Drop-Down Menus, and a Submit Button

If you haven't done so yet, copy the **chapter_11** folder on the CD to your hard drive. Define a site called Chapter 11, with this folder as the local root folder.

1. Now you add a menu. Open your document from Exercise 11.1, **form.html**. Place the cursor in the fifth row, left cell, and type **Select the type of web site you are considering**. Place the cursor in the right cell and click the List/Menu button on the Insert bar.

> **Note**
>
> Form lists and form menus are different; read about their best uses in Table 11.2. In Dreamweaver, however, you insert them using the same button and use the same Property inspector to set their attributes and properties.

2. With the List/Menu object selected in the Document window, in the Property inspector, leave the default setting of Type - Menu, and name this menu **type_of_site**.

3. Click the List Values button to open the List Values dialog box, as shown in Figure 11.8.

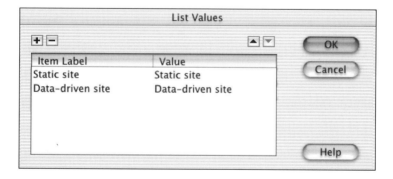

Figure 11.8   The List Values dialog box.

4. Click the plus (+) button and just beneath Item Label, type the words you want to appear in the form menu. Start with **Static site** for this item. Beneath Value, type the value you want to be submitted with the form data. Usually this will be the same as the Item Label, but in some situations they could differ. Here, for Value, type **Static site** again.

5. Add a second menu item with both the Label and Value **Data-driven site**.

6. If you like, use your imagination and add several more menu items. With a menu, the user will be able to choose only one item; you'll want to keep that in mind when building real-world menus; but here, add several more items so that you can see how a menu object looks and behaves. Click OK to close the dialog box and enter the menu in your document.

7. Save the document and view it in the browser. It should look like Figure 11.9.

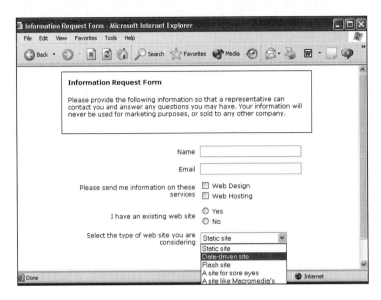

Figure 11.9   The exercise page with a menu object added.

8. Next add a list object. In the sixth row, left column, type the text **Select some basic features you might want to include**. Place the cursor in the right cell and click the List/Menu button on the Insert bar again. With the object still selected, in the Property inspector, select Type > List. Name it **features**, and give it a height of 3. This setting determines the number of list items that will be visible without scrolling.

9. Check Allow Multiple Selections, and then click the List Values button as you did with the menu object. In the List Values dialog box, add a number of list items, giving each the same Value as the Item Label. Start with **Company logo**, **Descriptive text**, **Feedback form**, and **Guestbook**; and, if you like, use your imagination and add a few more. Save your document and view in the browser. It should look like Figure 11.10.

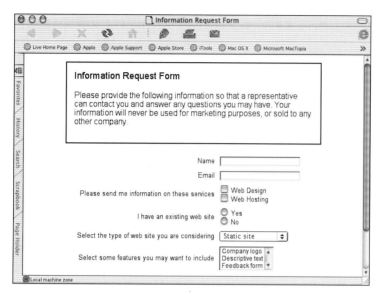

Figure 11.10   The exercise page in the browser at Step 9.

Tip

When adding multiple list items in the List Values dialog box, you can use the Tab key to go from an Item Label field to its Value field and then on to the next Item Label field.

10. Add the Submit button. Place the cursor in the left cell of the seventh row and click the Button button. With the object still selected, in the Property inspector, choose the options you need. For example purposes, the default name Submit and default label Submit are adequate, but try experimenting with the Label; you might use **Submit your request now** or the like.

11. For the Action, in this case, choose Submit. Reset would be chosen if you wanted to supply the user with the option to wipe his form clean and start over. You would choose None if you are using a script that provides a different action when the button is clicked.

12. Save the document and view it in a browser. It should look like Figure 11.11.

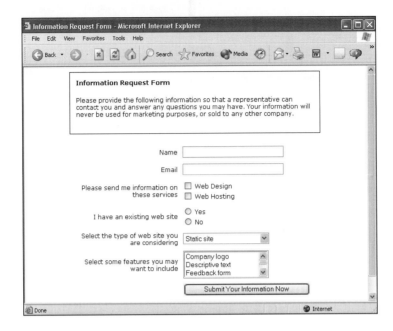

Figure 11.11   The finished exercise page.

Note

Form buttons can be used for functions other than submitting a form, such as resetting the form to its defaults (so that a user can undo mistakes and start over) or calculating an order based on data submitted.

Tip

You can make more creative Submit buttons by using the Image Field object and inserting a graphic file of your choice.

Behaviors and Forms

Dreamweaver behaviors are some of its most powerful and useful features. A behavior enables the visitor to interact with a web page to change it or to cause certain tasks to be performed, and consists of a combination of HTML and JavaScript written by Dreamweaver. Chapter 16, "Getting Interactive with Behaviors," looks at Dreamweaver behaviors in depth.

Behaviors can be attached to forms and form objects by using any of the behaviors that appear in the Behaviors panel when the form or object is selected. This chapter discusses two behaviors commonly used with forms, Validate Form and Set Text of Text Field. Note that the scripting being used here is client-side, as opposed to server-side, scripting; all the action takes place before the page is submitted to the server.

> **Tip**
>
> When applying behaviors, make sure that every form object in your document (and every other object) has a unique name. If you use the same name for two objects, behaviors might not work properly.

Validate Form

The Validate Form behavior (see Figure 11.12) checks the contents of specified text fields to ensure that the user has entered the correct type of data, or that he has at least entered some data.

You can attach this behavior in two ways:

- Attach it to the individual text fields with the onBlur event to validate the fields as the user is filling out the form.
- Attach it to the form itself with the onSubmit event to evaluate several text fields simultaneously at the point when the user clicks the Submit button.

Attaching this action to a form prevents the form from being submitted to the server if any of the specified fields contain invalid data.

Note that only text fields can be validated. The behavior can check to be sure that the field is not empty (check Required) that it is an email address (check Email), that it is a numeric value (check Number), or that it is a numeric value within a specified range (check Number between and fill in a starting and ending numeric value).

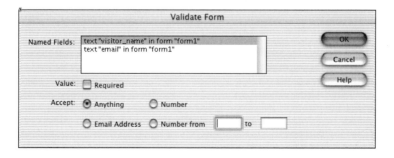

Figure 11.12 The Validate Form dialog box.

Exercise 11.3   Attaching the Validate Form Behavior to the *onSubmit* Event

In this exercise, you attach the Validate Form behavior to the onSubmit event to check the text fields in your form before submitting it to the server. This exercise builds on Exercises 11.1 and 11.2, which should be completed before you proceed with this exercise.

If you haven't done so yet, copy the **chapter_11** folder on the CD to your hard drive. Define a site called Chapter 11, with this folder as the local root folder.

1. Open your **form.html** document from Exercise 11.2. In the tag selector at the bottom of the Document window, select the <form> tag. If you don't see it there, place the cursor within the red dotted lines in the Document window and it should appear.

2. From the main menu, choose Window > Behaviors, or click the Behaviors icon on the Launcher bar, to open the Behaviors panel. Click the plus (+) button, and from the drop-down menu, choose Validate Form, which opens the Validate Form dialog box (refer to Figure 11.12).

3. Select the text field you named visitor_name. Select Required so that the field has to contain some data. From the Accept options, select Anything.

4. Then select the text field you named email. Again, select Required. This time, however, from the Accept options, select Email address. This will require that this field at least contain an at sign (@) to be accepted.

5. Click OK to insert the behavior. Note that if you would like to edit any aspect of this behavior, you can select the <form> tag, and in the Behaviors panel, double-click the Validate Form action where it appears in the panel's main window to reopen the Validate Form dialog box.

6. Save the document and preview it in a browser. You can test the form to some extent without having it actually connected to a script; when you press Submit, the browser will return an error message, because you haven't specified a place to submit the data. Before you receive that error message, however, you can observe the Validate Form behavior in action. Try submitting the form without filling in a name; you should get an error message in the form of a small gray browser pop-up box (see Figure 11.13) Then try it with a name filled in, but with an invalid email address containing no at sign (@); you should get another error message. If you fill in these two fields with valid data and click Submit, you shouldn't get any more validation error messages, but might still receive an error message indicating that the form doesn't have a correct action specified. Don't worry about this; until the form is hooked to a script or application, it can't actually be used to submit data.

Figure 11.13   A browser's form validation error message.

Set Text of Text Field

The Set Text of Text Field behavior replaces the content of a specified text field with the content you specify.

Any valid JavaScript function call, property, global variable, or other expression can be embedded in the text. A JavaScript expression must be placed inside braces ({}).

Exercise 11.4   Applying the Set Text of Text Field Behavior to a Single Text Field

In this exercise, you apply the Set Text of Text Field behavior to a single text field. This exercise can be done independently of the others in this chapter.

If you haven't done so yet, copy the **chapter_11** folder on the CD to your hard drive. Define a site called Chapter 11, with this folder as the local root folder.

   1. From the **chapter_11** folder, open the file **set_text.html**. You have a head start on this page: a form with a single form field, a text field named page_url. Select the text field and open the Behaviors panel. Click the plus (+) button and, from the drop-down menu, choose Set Text > Set Text of Text Field. This opens the Set Text of Text Field dialog box (see Figure 11.14).

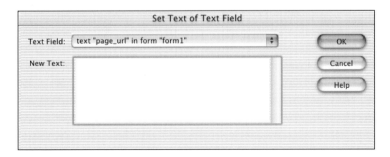

Figure 11.14   The Set Text of Text Field dialog box.

2. Notice that the text field, page_url, displays in the field at the top of the box. If other text fields were present on the page, you would need to choose a particular text field to which to apply the behavior. In the New Text box below, type the text you want to appear in the text field. For this example, use the following:

```
This page's URL is {window.location}
```

3. Click OK. With the form field selected, check the Behaviors panel to see that the behavior you've just added is displayed in the main panel window. By default, its action should be set to the onBlur event; this means that the behavior's action will be triggered when the focus is put on the text field, and then removed from it.

4. Save the document and test it in a browser. Click in the form field and then somewhere else on the page; the form field should fill with text reading something like this:

```
This page's URL is file:///C:/idmx/chapter_11/TMPsx81staup5.htm
```

If you see something like this in the text field, you've completed the exercise correctly.

Strategies for Working with Forms

As you have seen, building a form with Dreamweaver is fairly straightforward, but creating really useful, attractive forms requires a little more thought and planning.

The User Interface

As with any aspect of a web site, the user interface is crucial, but it is especially so in the case of forms. Filling out a form is not a favorite activity for most web visitors; when forms are nice-looking and easy to understand and use, they're more easily tolerated.

Use the Right Input Type for the Job

Choosing the appropriate input type for each form element requires some analysis of the kind of information being collected; Table 11.2 describes the best uses for each.

Table 11.2   Best Uses for Form Input Types

Input Type	Best Suited For
Text field	A single word or short phrase response, such as a name or street address.
Multiple-line text fields	A response that might require a full sentence, several sentences, or even several paragraphs.
Password field	Inputting passwords; the browser displays the input as asterisks or bullets to preserve privacy.
File field	Enabling the user to type, or to browse for, a file to upload.

Input Type	Best Suited For
Hidden field	Gathering or sending information along with the form data without displaying it to the user.
Check boxes	A group of yes-or-no options, when more than one can be chosen.
Radio buttons	A group of yes-or-no options, when only one can be chosen.
Scrolling list	When there are many choices and limited space; when more than one option needs to be able to be chosen; when you want to display x number of options on the page before the user clicks or scrolls.
Drop-down menu	When space is very limited; when only one option can be chosen; when it's acceptable to have only one option display by default.

Labeling and Positioning

Even seemingly small factors can make a big difference in the usability of a form. Form controls should be labeled unambiguously; try putting yourself in the position of the end user, and see whether your labels are clear and make sense. If you want the user to type her full name, for example, you're better off using the label Full Name than Name, because many forms ask for the last name and first name separately.

Submit buttons and other form buttons, such as Reset, should also have labels whose meaning is obvious. Submit Now or Send Your Information Now can be good choices, especially when your users might be inexperienced with the web in general; that kind of language helps make clear what will happen when the button is clicked.

The positioning of form controls in relationship with their labels is also important. Take a critical look at any form you're creating to see whether it's entirely clear which label goes with which input item. Don't give the user anything to figure out; everything should be as plain and intuitive as possible.

Text Fields and Netscape 4

If you preview the form you built in Exercises 11.1 and 11.2 in Internet Explorer, the text fields should look about the same as they do in the Dreamweaver Document window. You specified that they should have a size of 30, and the form field IE displays looks as if it is approximately the same width as 30 text characters in the font size you've declared for the page. (The font face and size for the page is set with a document-side style sheet; you can see it in the page's source code in the document <head>.)

If you have a copy of Netscape 4 (any version), and preview the form page with it, you'll see that the form's text fields appear much longer. This is because Netscape 4.x calculates the width of a form field a different way than IE does. Netscape 4.x takes the specification of 30 characters and uses the widest possible character in the default monospace font as the unit of measurement, as shown in Figure 11.15.

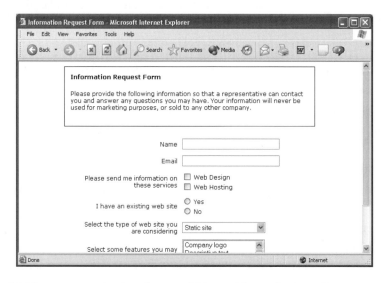

Figure 11.15   Netscape 4 (top) renders text fields much longer horizontally.

In the case of this form, the longer form fields don't present a serious problem. If you need a 100-character text field, however, Netscape 4 will display it much wider than a typical browser window width. This problem is inconvenient at best, and serious at worst.

It can be solved with CSS by creating a custom class and applying it to the form fields. The custom class should declare the font to be a monospace font of about 11 or 12 pixels, and is applied directly to the `<input>` tag. Refer to Chapter 13, "Using Cascading Style Sheets," for an in-depth treatment of CSS.

Form Layout

Forms present their own unique layout challenges, and HTML tables are still the most widely used tools for making form elements behave on the page. By placing form controls and their text labels in separate table cells, they can be made to line up neatly and vertically. In Exercise 11.1, you used a table to align form elements and text for a readable form with a good appearance.

A background color applied to certain table cells can make form fields stand out more to the eye, and just provide some interest and variety. Table borders, applied with the `border` attribute to the `<table>` tag, add borders to all cells as well, and can create order in more complex forms. Cell padding can be used to space form elements ideally.

In Exercise 11.5, you experiment on the form you built in Exercises 11.1, 11.2, and 11.3, adding some table formatting.

Exercise 11.5   Using Table Formatting to Make Attractive, Readable Forms

If you haven't done so yet, copy the **chapter_11** folder on the CD to your hard drive. Define a site called Chapter 11, with this folder as the local root folder.

1. Open the file **form.html** you built in Exercise 11.1.
2. Select the table that holds the form elements, and in the Property inspector, in the Bg Color field, type **#DFDFDF**. Press Enter. Save and view the document in a browser. You might want to try some other colors; click the color chip in the Bg Color field and use the color picker to experiment.
3. Select the table again, and in the Property inspector, in the Border field, enter the number **1**, and press Enter. When no color is specified, most browsers render a table border as gray and 3D. Select the table again, and this time apply a border color. Preview the document. Try out various border colors and background colors in combination, or you might prefer to leave out the border entirely for this simple form.

4. Select the table again, and use the Cell Padding field in the Property inspector to adjust the number of pixels between the content and the border in each cell. You gave your table 5 pixels of cell padding in Exercise 11.1; you might prefer more or less.

5. For a pencil-thin border around only the table itself, try adding an inline CSS declaration to the table tag. First, set the table's border attribute to 0. Select the table and press Ctrl+T to open the Quick Tag Editor. The Quick Tag Editor has three modes: Edit Tag, Wrap Tag, and Insert HTML; pressing Ctrl+T cycles through these three modes. Press Ctrl+T once or twice more until you see Edit Tag. The tag should look something like this, although your experimentation might have changed some of the values:

```
<table WIDTH="70%" CELLSPACING="0" CELLPADDING="5" ALIGN="CENTER"
BGCOLOR="#DFDFDF">
```

Place your cursor just before the closing bracket, and type in the following CSS code:

```
STYLE="border: 1px solid #000000">
```

Press Enter to close the Quick Tag Editor and add the code you've just typed.

6. Save the document and preview it again. In Internet Explorer 4.0 or later, you should see a nice thin black border around the table (see Figure 11.16; unfortunately, Netscape 4 versions and earlier don't support this CSS style).

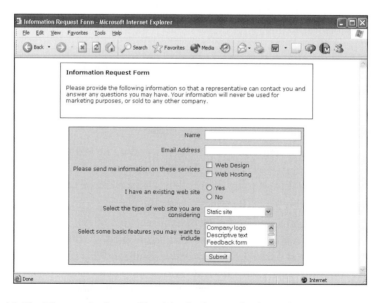

Figure 11.16   The exercise form table with a background color and a thin CSS border.

7. Continue to experiment with various table attributes and settings until you're satisfied with the look of your form.

Dynamic Data and Forms

dynamic data bits

Forms are used heavily in dynamic sites for collecting information. Search pages, login pages, information update pages—all use forms to collect user input and either query or edit the data source.

If you only need the form to collect information, you don't need your form elements to be dynamic. But if you also want the form to present information from the data source—a pop-up menu of choices based on database contents, for instance, or a personal data page that users can check and update—you need to use dynamic data to determine the contents and status of the form elements.

Dynamic List/Menu

The trick to creating a concise pop-up menu or list with dynamic entries is to eliminate all duplicates from the data source. (Even if your database includes 300 necklaces in its stock table, you probably only want the "Necklaces" entry to appear once in the list.) To create a dynamic list/menu with no duplication:

1. When collecting the Recordset for the document, after you have chosen which fields to collect, go to the Advanced tab of the dialog box. Edit the SQL query to add a GROUP BY clause, grouping by the field that you plan to use in the dynamic list/menu. Note that, if there is an ORDER BY clause, it must remain at the end of the query.

2. Add a regular form Menu object and click the Dynamic button in the List/Menu Property inspector.

3. In the dialog box that appears, choose each list item's name and value from Recordset fields.

Dynamic Check Box

A dynamic check box will appear selected or not, depending on a field value in the recordset. To create a dynamic check box:

1. Insert a regular check box into your form (Insert > Form Objects > Checkbox). Using the Property inspector, give the check box a name you'll remember.

2. In the Server Behaviors panel, click the plus (+) button and choose Dynamic Form Elements > Dynamic Checkbox.

3. In the dialog box that appears, choose your check box's name. Then specify which Recordset field should be examined, and enter a value that field must be equal to for the check box to appear as checked. The dialog box only allows for comparisons based on equality (no less than, more than, and so on).

Dynamic Radio Button

A dynamic group of radio buttons will have one of their members selected, depending on a field value in the Recordset. To create a dynamic radio group:

1. Insert a group of radio buttons, as you normally would (Insert > Form Objects > Radio Button or Insert > Form Objects > Radio Group). Use the Property inspector to give the group a name, and each button a unique value.

2. In the Server Behaviors panel, click the plus (+) button and choose Dynamic Form Elements > Dynamic Radio Group.

3. In the dialog box that appears, choose your radio group's name. Then specify a Recordset field each button in the group should be compared to, to determine if it will be selected in the form.

Dynamic Text Field

Dynamic text fields will appear in the form filled with text from a specified Recordset field. To create a dynamic text field:

1. Insert a text field, as you normally would (Insert > Form Objects > Text Field). Use the Property inspector to give the text field a name you'll remember.

2. In the Server Behaviors panel, click the plus (+) button and choose Dynamic Form Elements > Dynamic Text Field.

3. In the dialog box that appears, choose your text field's name. Then specify the Recordset field whose value should appear in the text field.

Taking Forms Further

Forms can be both made more accessible and dressed up visually with some of the newer features discussed in this section. Most of what is presented here will require some hand coding. Again, even the beginner—especially the beginner—should venture into Code view, get accustomed to the look and syntax of HTML code, and try some hand coding.

Making Forms Accessible

HTML 4.0 introduced some new elements and attributes that provide improved support for accessibility in forms, although they are not fully implemented by all browsers as of this writing. These include the `<label>` element and the `accesskey` and `tabindex` attributes. Dreamweaver MX makes it easy to include these accessibility attributes in forms (and in other page elements, as well) with its new Accessibility preferences.

The *<label>* Element

Most form `<input>` elements are given text labels that are associated visually with form control in the browser's display, but these labels are not actually part of the element's tag. The `<label>` element makes it possible to logically (rather than just visually) associate the labels with the controls they describe. This is particularly useful to speech-based browsers, which can then clearly connect the two.

The `<label>` element can be applied in two ways. In the first method, the form control tag is enclosed by the opening and closing `<label>` tags:

```
<label>Phone Number:
<input TYPE="text" NAME="PhoneNumber" >
</label>
```

However, this first method sometimes can't be used, because a form label and the control it describes are often contained within two separate table cells.

When the label and its control are in different table cells, the second method can be used: the `id` attribute of the control element is assigned to the `for` attribute of the `label` element:

```
<table>
    <tr>
        <td>
        <label for="PhoneNumber" >Phone Number: </label>
        </td>
        <td>
        <input type="text" ID="PhoneNumber">
        </td>
    </tr>
</table>
```

The *accesskey* Attribute

The `accesskey` attribute defines a keyboard shortcut, or *accelerator key*, which activates an element's form control. Depending upon the operating system and browser, a modifier key such as Control, Alt, or Command might need to be pressed with the access key to activate the link. `accesskey` does not work in Internet Explorer for the Macintosh.

`accesskey` can be used as an attribute for `<label>`, `<input>`, `<button>`, or `<legend>`. When it is used with `<label>`, it is the form control associated with the `<label>` element, which is focused, not the label.

A common convention used in a Windows GUI is to highlight the letter that will activate the field. The HTML 4.0 specification states that browsers should provide their own type of highlighting for an access key, but the browsers are not yet consistent in implementing this. You might want to dictate this highlighting yourself by underlining the letter using HTML, as in:

```
<label ACCESSKEY="p"><u>P</u>hone Number:
<input TYPE="text">
</label>
```

The tabindex Attribute

A form field must be *focused* for data to be entered into it; in other words, keystrokes or mouse clicks need to be directed to that particular control. If the user clicks in the field, that field gets the focus. The user also can use his Tab key to proceed from one focusable element to another on the page.

The <input> types—button, check box, file, password, radio, reset, submit, and text—are all focusable elements. The <input> tag will accept the attribute tabindex with a numeric value, enabling you to specify the tabbing order in a document. (Unfortunately, Netscape 4 browsers do not support this attribute.)

Tip

tabindex will accept a numeric value between 1 and 37,767.

Focus starts with the element with the lowest tabindex value and proceeds in sequential order to the element with the highest value, ignoring the element's physical location on the page or location in the source code.

The code would look something like this:

```
<input type="text" tabindex="3">
```

The attributes discussed above, and all other attributes associated with a form element, can be edited using Dreamweaver MX's Edit Tag feature. Select the form element and either right-click and choose Edit Tag, or choose Modify > Edit Tag. This opens the tag editor dialog box, as shown in Figure 11.17.

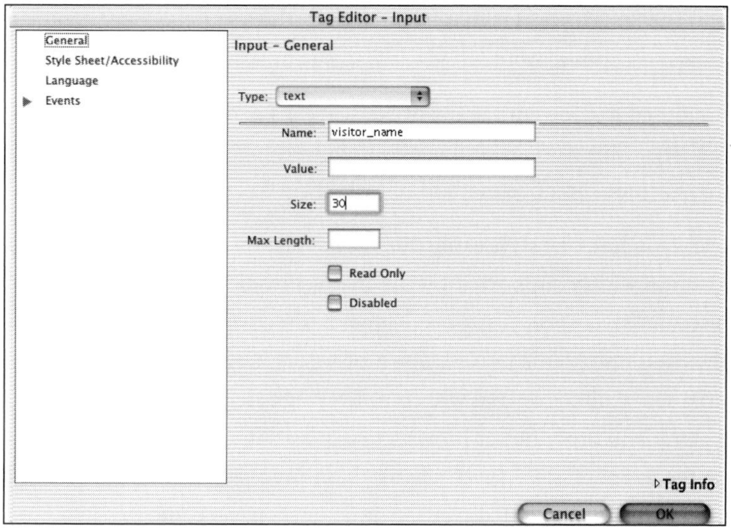

Figure 11.17   The tag editor dialog box.

Four categories of attributes are listed in the dialog box's left-hand column. Clicking a category provides you with a list of possible attributes for the element, allowing you to fill in values for any you choose.

Dreamweaver's Page Accessibility Features

If you choose, you can set your preferences so that Dreamweaver MX will remind you whenever a form element for which accessibility options are available is added to the document. Before the element is inserted, the Accessibility Attributes dialog box opens, allowing you to set the <label> element, the accesskey attribute, and the tabindex attribute.

To turn on this feature, choose Edit > Preferences > Accessibility and check Form Objects.

Using CSS with Forms

Form fields can be dressed up and made more interesting by use of CSS. As of this writing, mainstream browsers don't support CSS styles applied to check boxes, radio buttons, lists, or menus. But text fields, both single- and multiple line, can be given background colors and borders, at least in recent versions of Internet Explorer.

However, Netscape 4.xx browsers can be a challenge to support. The problem is not just that Netscape 4 browsers fail to support these properties; in fact, in some cases they do display them. The real concern is that in some cases the text fields can become nonfunctional, no longer accepting input. Obviously, this is unacceptable.

A workaround used to cope with many of Netscape 4's deficiencies is to use two separate linked style sheets. This workaround is often referred to as "The @Import Trick" due to its use of the @import directive method of style sheet linking.

With this trick, you link one style using the <link> tag; this is a *master style sheet*, including styles that are widely supported by the major browsers, including Netscape 4. You then link a second style sheet using the @import directive; the second style sheet holds the styles that cause problems in Netscape 4 browsers. Conveniently, Netscape 4 doesn't support the @import directive, and will completely ignore its existence in the document. Internet Explorer and other newer browsers, such as Netscape 6, will see and implement the styles in the @import style sheet, giving them precedence over those in the <link> style sheet, because the @import directive comes later in the code.

The code for linking these two style sheets looks like this:

```
<link rel="stylesheet" href="master.css" type="text/css">
<style type="text/css">@import url(newbrowsers-only.css);
</style>
```

Interview: Adrian Senior

Business Name: Webade

URL: http://www.webade.co.uk

How did you get started in web design? What has your learning process been like? What kind of work are you currently doing?

I originally became interested in web design out of curiosity, really. I finally got myself connected and I just wondered, "How do they make those things?" I tend to be a curious person by nature; I have this need to know how things work and that set me off on searches for HTML tutorials. The interest grew from there really; I started with all the tutorials I could find on the web and used Notepad to write them with. Later I came across a demo of HoTMetaL in a magazine; this was my first introduction to WYSIWYG code editors. The program also contained a CSS (Cascading Style Sheet) interface, which was again something completely new to me at that time.

Looking back I'm pleased I had the benefit of not discovering WYSIWYGs straight away. The hand coding gave me a good grounding in what actually goes on behind the scenes.

I believe this is a great advantage while designing, as it enables the designer to move back and forth between the design interface and the Code view as necessary. Although the WYSIWYG interface simplifies and speeds up much of the design process, it is often necessary to delve into Code view to make minor corrections or adjustments, so a working knowledge of the required languages is a big advantage.

At this moment in time, much of my work requires database integration; as most of my work is done on Windows servers, the database integration is done with ASP technology; however, there are, of course, other methods you could use. I find data-driven sites are becoming more and more popular; they provide a more interactive experience for the user and allow the web site's content to be manipulated by the client. This allows the site to be truly instant in reflecting the client's business progression; they can just log on to the administration interface we provide for them from anywhere they have an Internet connection. The client is then able to make changes to the information stored in the database; these changes are then reflected immediately on the web site, which dramatically reduces the time required to update the site.

What hardware and software do you use in your work?

I have only ever bought one factory-produced PC and that was the first one I owned. Since moving into web development, I have preferred to build my own machines to the specifications I require. Being an eternal fiddler, I tend to change the hardware on a fairly regular basis with a major overhaul of the machine about every 18 months or so. The last configuration change was a major rebuild to the following specifications:

Processor: AMD Thunderbird 1.2

RAM: 1024MB RAM

Hard drive: 40GB 7200rpm

Operating System: Windows 2000 Pro

Monitor: Dual-monitor setup

Win on CD CDRW

48× CD-ROM

The dual monitors are an important part of the setup for me. I find the ability to work with multiple open programs a great advantage. Much of the software I work with uses the floating panel–type of setup; the second monitor is home for these panels, which keeps my work area tidy and uncluttered.

The software I use has changed a fair bit over the years, although I feel happy with what I have at my disposal now. Dreamweaver UltraDev is, I suppose, what you would call my core development tool. It is central to everything I do, the hub that everything else revolves around. For image manipulation, I use Fireworks and Freehand as my main tools, although I always have Adobe Photoshop and Corel Photopaint on hand. Each of these programs provides facilities that I find indispensable. Images often find they make the full trip from Fireworks to Photopaint to Photoshop and back to Fireworks. I just like the way each individual piece of software performs certain tasks, so I use whichever one I think is best for the job at hand. TopStyle is a must-have program. If you're using CSS, and you should be, this has to be number one for creating your style sheets. I couldn't do without it; it just makes it so much easier to manage a site's appearance. Flash is a tool I also find myself using more. When used properly, it can provide a nice addition to any web site.

In working with forms, what techniques are standard for you?

Forms are the web site's heartbeat. They are the means by which we provide interactive communication with the users of our sites, and are, I believe, often underdeveloped. Forms no longer have to be sets of boring white boxes; the power of CSS gives enables us to design forms that blend well with the design of our sites. I use forms for simple communication and data collection from users and also for inserting, updating, and deleting information in databases; this allows easy and quick updates of the web site.

The problem with many of the options available to us is the need to support the Netscape 4 browser. This browser is more than 4 years old and therefore cannot cope with many of the changes that have been implemented in that time; however, it still accounts for somewhere in the region of 10 percent of all Internet users, far too great a number of potential clients to ignore. The poor level of support that Netscape 4 offers on today's Internet does, however, provide us with a workaround that enables us to design forms and our sites in general in such a way that more compliant browsers can render our design as we want.

The workaround involves using two Cascading Style Sheets; this gives us the freedom to design for Netscape 4 without compromising our designs for the more sophisticated browsers.

Other points to take into consideration when designing your forms are the text content and defining its appearance. Both the major browsers render form content differently. So to gain a good standard of equality in your forms appearance on a cross-browser basis, it is advisable to set the text to a monospace font such as Courier or Courier New and to define a specific size for the font. You also have the option to color it to suit your design.

Another aspect I like to include is the personalization and content building that can be built in to a form by requesting form elements from the previous page. Using this method, it is possible to build multipart forms over a series of pages. This provides the user with the option to view previous sections of the form as dynamic data on each page as they complete a more complex form, and we also can provide the ability to return to an earlier form section to correct or change details if necessary. On a similar note, you can request the contents of, say, the first and last names of a person from a completed form and display them dynamically on a thank you page; it's quick and easy to do and provides a personal touch for the user.

When you have had the opportunity to be a little more creative with forms, what have you tried? What would you like to experiment with?

With the release of Netscape 6, and the hopefully in the not too distant future with the release of Mozilla, new support for CSS is going to be available. Although at this moment in time, it is Netscape/Mozilla proprietary, hopefully it will make it through into CSS3. Using the proprietary Mozilla CSS attributes, it makes it possible to apply a radius to your page elements such as form elements and even tables can be manipulated to carry a curved border around their boundaries. I would think it would be some way off before the majority of our viewers can see these effects, but they are available to be used now and experimentation with them is fun and a good learning process.

The following sample code gives form input elements fully rounded ends; you can reduce the radius to give only the corners of the elements a small radius, in effect gently rounding off the sharp edges.

```
input{
-moz-border-radius: 15px;
background-color : #eaf9ff;
border : 1px solid #000000;
font-family : "Courier New", Courier, monospace;
font-size : 12px;
padding-left : 7px;
padding-right : 7px;
}
```

As Cascading Style Sheets standards develop, I'm sure we will see the introduction of many new features, features that will provide greater functionality and allow greater freedom of design for the developer.

Although Microsoft and Netscape might make proprietary CSS available to their own browsers, such as the coloring of scrollbars in IE and the radius options among others in Mozilla and Netscape 6. I don't think that's really a problem so long as one doesn't interfere with the other. What we don't need is conflicts of the type we have now with Netscape 4.x.

What trends on the web and in the web designer's work do you see as important?

In a word, standards. With the introduction of XHTML and the improving support for Cascading Style Sheets, I think the Internet is heading in that direction.

The most important aspect of web design, I think, is the planning stage. Getting it right from the outset will save so much time further down the road. From the beginning of any new site I have to develop, I am looking carefully at the maintenance aspect. This area of our work can be so time consuming and fraught with difficulty, especially when returning to the site after a long period of inactivity.

Cascading Style Sheets are possibly the web developer's greatest asset. The ability to update a site's appearance across hundreds of pages utilizing linked styles is really quite remarkable; a simple change of font or color can be completed in seconds.

Dreamweaver itself includes similar features. The utilization of templates in the development of your site and the use of library items both go a long way to simplifying the maintenance of a web site. We can make a single change in a template or a library item and sit back as Dreamweaver propagates those changes through all the child elements.

What advice would you give to someone just starting out in web design?

The best advice I think I could offer to people starting out in web design is don't rely 100 percent on the WYSIWYG view. Buy a good HTML book and learn the code. The benefits of being able to delve into the source and debug are immense—if you know what you are looking for, you will save hours of frustration. The best resource for how to design a site is often right in front of you, on the Internet itself. Just download pages and interrogate the code in Dreamweaver. I'm not saying you should reproduce what other authors have done, but look at how they have achieved what you like and learn from them.

Server-Side Scripts for Processing Forms

As discussed earlier in this chapter, forms consist of two components; the purpose here has been to show you how to build an HTML form. A server-side script of some kind is necessary for form data to be processed, but the use and development of these applications is beyond the scope of this chapter.

Note

For more information on using ASP, ASP.NET, ColdFusion, PHP, or JSP with forms, see Chapters 27 through 31.

Many host servers support Perl CGI scripts, and these scripts are easily available, often for free, and can be used to process forms. One well-known script of this type is FormMail, written by programmer Matt Wright. FormMail, when installed and connected with an HTML form, processes the form data and emails the contents to one or more recipients. This script is free, and an excellent tutorial explaining how to install and configure it is available at `http://www.appbuild.com/formmail_help.html`.

Appendix B, "Online Resources for Dreamweaver Web Developers," includes the URLs of other web sites with information, instructions, and tutorials on installing CGI scripts.

Summary

In this chapter, you learned how forms work to capture data on the web and process it. You also learned the basics of the HTML code used to build forms, and found out how to use Dreamweaver to quickly add forms and form elements to an HTML document. Using behaviors with forms was discussed; you found out how to use the Validate Form behavior and the Set Text of Text Field behavior. You worked through some issues involving the usability and the appearance of forms, and finished with a look at some of the newer form attributes and CSS styling possibilities.

Connecting an HTML form to the application needed to process is obviously crucial; you're encouraged to see this book's chapters on using server-side languages (Chapters 27 through 31) and to look into using the many available Perl CGI scripts and the wealth of information on CGI on the web.

Chapter 12

Designing Frame-Based Pages

Frames—the very mention of the word can cause ordinarily well-behaved web developers to lose their composure. Because they have both very useful applications and potentially significant disadvantages, frame-based sites have both strong proponents and vocal opponents. And this is not only in the world of web designers; users often have something to say about frame sites. It sometimes seems as if no one is neutral on the subject.

This chapter addresses the issues that make frames controversial as a web design tool and explains ways to avoid problems and pitfalls. Topics covered in this chapter also include when to use frames and when to avoid them, the HTML code behind frame sites, using Dreamweaver MX to build frame sites, setting frameset and frame attributes, linking and targeting in frame sites, and providing `<noframe>` content.

Frame Basics

When you view a frame-based page in the browser, what you're really seeing is several HTML documents at once, loaded into the individual *frames* of a *frameset*. Figure 12.1 shows a frame-based page as it appears in the browser along with a peek at its actual frameset structure.

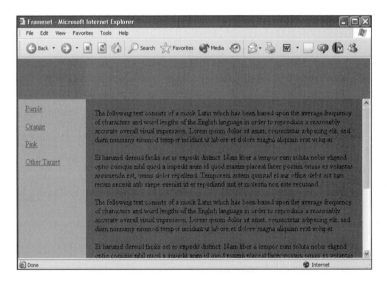

Figure 12.1   A basic frame page.

Frames provide the web developer with a page design tool very different from any other. With frames, rectangular areas of a page can be specified as distinct "windows" into which content can be loaded and reloaded, independent of the rest of the page.

A typical application for frames is a page in which a *header* along the top of the page, sporting the company logo, tagline, and contact information, remains static in one frame, a navigation bar which runs down the left side of the page remains static in another frame, and the remaining rectangular space is a frame into which various content can be loaded by clicking the navbar links.

Why Use Frames?

Before deciding to build a web site using frames, it's wise to think through the needs and goals of the site and its individual pages. Even though much of what can be accomplished with frames can also be done in other ways, frames have several distinct advantages to recommend them, and can be ideal for certain situations. So what are the pros of frame-based sites?

Unchanging Content

First, frames enable you to keep certain content onscreen while other content changes. On most web sites, it is desirable that certain elements be present on all (or many) pages. These elements usually fall into two categories:

- **Visuals**, such as a company logo or other graphics important for consistency and branding.
- **Controls**, such as navigation links or buttons.

In either case, nonframe sites just repeat this content on numerous pages, which can work well; after the first page has loaded, the repeating graphics are cached on the user's hard drive and will load quickly on the next page on which they appear, and text content usually doesn't create loading-time issues. However, placing the unchanging content in frames adds a special advantage: There is literally no loading time and none of the "page jump" that sometimes is seen even with well-designed nonframe sites. The unchanging content in a frame remains completely steady as the user clicks through changing content in another frame; it's an appealing effect.

Internally Scrolling Content

Frame pages also allow certain areas to be scrolled while others remain unmoved. Again this can be an appealing and even striking effect, particularly when frame borders are removed and the scrolling content disappears seamlessly behind the unchanging frame content above it.

An Unchanging Bottom Element

Frames are commonly used to "float" unchanging content at the top and left edges of the browser viewport, but there is another application of this capability that is even harder to produce in any other way: floating content at the bottom of the browser window. With frames, this can be accomplished so that the viewer sees the bottom-frame content at the very bottom of his browser window regardless of the way the window is sized. Creating an effect like this with tables, layers, or CSS positioning is tricky and inconsistently implemented in the browsers at best, but it's simple using frames.

Complex Nested Frame Layouts

Frames also open up possibilities for complex layouts that can stimulate the creative energies of the web designer to new heights. Because framesets can be nested within frames, the possibilities are limited only by the designer's willingness to keep track of the rapidly multiplying files, targets, and links.

Options for Printing and Saving

Portions of a frameset page can be printed and saved for offline viewing separately. In all major browsers, right-clicking in a particular frame will bring up a menu which will allow you to choose from a number of options, including Add to Favorites, View Source, and Print in recent versions of Internet Explorer, as shown in Figure 12.2.

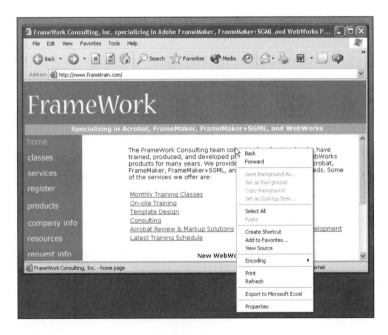

Figure 12.2   Right-clicking within a frameset in Internet Explorer 6 displays a menu of options.

Hiding Internal Page References

Sometimes a web developer prefers that internal page references not be obvious to the user. With frames, the page can be set up so that the browser's address field always shows the frameset URL. The technique involves using a two-frame frameset with one frame at 100 percent and the other frame at 0 percent.

Simulating Scripting Effects

In the hands of sneaky designers, frames can be used to create a variety of effects that otherwise would require complex or impossible scripting. They're manipulated much more easily than layers—often with no scripting required at all—and can be used to pass information from page to page without server-side scripting or cookies. Instead of using complex and unreliable DHTML to dynamically load or control Plugin media, for instance, a frameset document can include navigation controls in one frame that load and unload pages in another frame, mimicking the effect of loading and unloading different movies or soundtracks. (See Chapter 19, "Plugins, ActiveX, and Java," for more on scripting and media elements. For an example of using frames to load and unload media, check out the **frameset.html** file in the **chapter_19** folder of the CD.)

Why Not Use Frames?

As discussed already, frames are controversial, and there are some good reasons why many designers and many users dislike them. Instead of rejecting them outright, however, you should become educated as to the facts about the downside of frames. If you understand the both the pros and cons, you can make an informed choice as to whether a particular site might best use frames or avoid them.

Usability Problems

All web developers have to stop every now and then and remind themselves of their highest priority in planning a site: How easy it is for the visitor to use? There are exceptions in which the purpose is to dazzle the user with artistry and technical wizardry, but majority of web surfers just want to accomplish something while visiting your site—get information, sign up for something, or purchase something, for example. They want to do it without a lot of effort or thought, and they should be able to. After all, if magazines required explanations to be used, how many people would curl up with one?

More Complex Authoring

Frameset pages actually consist of more than one HTML document, as you'll see later in this chapter when you look at the code used to create frame pages. Even a very simple frame page, consisting of a frameset document with two frames, each displaying as its source a separate HTML document, amounts to three files. As more frames are added, the complexity increases. To change the content of frames with links, the developer needs to keep track of which frame is which, the frame names, and the filenames of the documents to be loaded in them, and provide the proper link URLs and link targets. This requires some extra effort at file organization, and some careful coding.

Search Engine Issues

Frames can prevent some search engine spiders from indexing your site, and thus limit your site's capability to rank well in the search engines. However, you can minimize the negative aspects of frames with regard to search engine positioning by making sure you add `<meta>` tags, `<title>` information, and `<noframes>` content to your frames. (For more on maximizing your site for search engines, see Chapter 7, "Utilizing Head Content.")

Older Browser Issues

One frequently voiced objection to frame sites is that some browsers don't support frames. This is virtually a nonissue, however. Frames and framesets are supported by all browsers since Netscape 2.0 and Internet Explorer 3.0; the percentage of users of browsers prior to these is a fraction of a percent and shrinking daily, as the last remaining users of these very old browsers upgrade their browser or retire the old computers running them.

Design Challenges

Because of their divide-and-conquer nature, frames lend themselves to dividing and subdividing the available screen real estate, and some frames will require scrollbars to ensure that all viewers can see them. Therefore, screen real estate can be used up very quickly, with large proportions going to scrollbars, unless some restraint and finesse is exercised in the design of frame pages.

Interview: Murray Summers

Business Name: Great-Web-Sights, Inc.

URL: www.great-web-sights.com

How did you get started in Web design? What has your learning process been like? What kind of work are you currently doing?

I am a freelance web developer. My first serious attempt at building a site came as a result of a friend who had some Photoshop layout pages and wanted to "make them work on the web." I had built one site a year or so earlier (using HoTMetaL) and thought it would be fun to try again with something more challenging. The rest is history. I quickly moved from FrontPage to Dreamweaver and have been busy ever since. The most important learning tool for me during the past three years has been the Macromedia NNTP forums, and plenty of experimentation, of course!

What hardware and software do you use in your work?

I am working in DW4/UD4/FW4 exclusively. In addition, I find Homesite5 and TopStyle Pro to be indispensable tools. I am ambidextrous in the sense that I have both a Mac and a PC in my workspace, although I prefer to use the PC as my development environment. My development PC is a Dell Dimension 933 with W2Kpro and 256MB RAM. I have Photoshop on the Mac and I use it from time to time for compatibility reasons (I collaborate with several Mac people), but I am finding that Fireworks is becoming my principal graphics editor more and more.

Why do you use framesets and frames? What are they most useful for in your design work? What creative ways have you used them?

I use frames when I need them for a specific purpose. Some examples of those specific purposes include the following:

- Centering content in any browser configuration without resorting to complex JavaScript solutions to deal with layers and other page content

- Holding content that always floats at the bottom of the browser viewport

- "Cloaking" internal page references so that the browser's address field always shows the frameset URL (by using a two-frame frameset with one frame at 100 percent and the other frame at 0 percent)

- Keeping a complex navigational scheme onscreen throughout the site while content changes

- Keeping company "branding" with logos onscreen (as above)

What is most crucial for a designer to know regarding the use of frames? Are there any misconceptions about frames you would like to correct?

The misconception I'd like to clear up is that frames are "evil." I have seen this often expressed on the Dreamweaver forum, and it just tells me that the poster doesn't understand frames. They are quite useful. In fact, you are probably not aware how many framed pages you visit because many people understand how to use them "transparently."

The most important thing to know about frames is what their limitations are. I believe that these limitations can be summarized by saying that framed pages can produce unexpected (and sometimes puzzling) behavior when they are bookmarked or printed, and when the browser's "back" option is used. Knowing these before being surprised can help the developer anticipate problems.

What trends on the web and in the web designer's work do you see as important?

I think that browser support for CSS positioning is the most important current trend for web development. Every web developer must understand the concept of using CSS for his pages to be successful over the long term.

What advice would you give to someone just starting out in web design?

I would counsel them to learn HTML well—the sooner the better. Without a good understanding of the structure and utility of the underlying code, a web developer will never be able to debug their pages and accommodate different browsers.

HTML Coding for Frames

Using Dreamweaver, you can build frame sites without coming anywhere near the source code, if you like—Dreamweaver's excellent visual page-creation tools make this possible. However, it is strongly recommended that you gain at least a basic familiarly with the underlying code for frames. There will inevitably come a time when you can't make some aspect of your page work the way you want, and being able to examine the HTML code and edit it can save you a lot of grief.

The tags and attributes described in this section are the ones that Dreamweaver will write for you as you use its point-and-click interface. If you make their acquaintance now, you'll feel that much more secure as you later use Dreamweaver to build your frames and framesets and set their attributes.

A web page divided into frames involves three new HTML tags:

- `<frameset>` defines where the separate frames will appear on the page and how they will share the space, and specifies some of their characteristics.

- `<frame>` defines how a single frame will look and what content it will display. Usually, a frame's content is another distinct HTML document.

- `<noframes>` enables you to display some content for users whose browsers do not support frames.

The page that holds the `<frameset>` and `<frame>` elements and defines how the frames are arranged is often referred to as the *frameset document*. Pointing a browser at the frameset document will first load that, and then the HTML pages that the code specifies should populate each frame.

The code for a basic frameset document written by Dreamweaver MX looks like this. (All attributes have been left out to just show the way the `<frameset>`, `<frame>`, and `<noframes>` tags are used.)

```
<html>
<head>
<title>Untitled Document</title>
</head>
<frameset>
  <frame>
  <frame>
</frameset>
<noframes>
  <body>
  </body>
</noframes>
</html>
```

The following sections look at each of these three elements in turn.

<frameset>

The `<frameset>` element specifies how the browser window should be divided up into frames. It encloses the `<frame>` tags, and supports the attributes `cols` and `rows`.

`cols` defines the number and widths of columns that will be used to divide the frameset's *parent element*. The syntax is as follows:

```
<frameset cols="100, 530">
```

The columns are read by the browser from left to right. The comma-separated values can be any one of the following:

- An absolute value in pixels, as in the preceding line of code
- Relative widths, as the columns compare to one another; this is shown in this way: `cols="1*, 3*, 2*"`. This would produce a frameset in which the column widths were in the ratio of 1:3:2.
- A percentage of the width of the parent frameset, written like this: `cols="20%, 80%"`

Columns widths also can be given the value *, which means that the column will take up whatever width is not used up by the other columns.

Columns can be set to a combination of these values.

`rows` defines the number and heights of the rows that will be used to divide the frameset's parent element horizontally. The syntax is as follows:

```
<frameset cols="100, 530" rows="80%, 20%">
```

The values for `rows` can be drawn from the same options as the values for `cols`, and produce comparable results, although with horizontal rows of various heights rather than vertical columns.

By declaring values for both `cols` and `rows` in your frameset, such as in the following code, you can create a grid of frames.

```
<frameset cols="150, *" rows="10%, 80%, 10%">
```

By adding `<frame>` tags, you can specify the content that will be used as the source of each frame. The complete `<frameset>` tag pair might look like this:

```
<frameset cols="150, *" rows="10%, 80%, 10%">
<frame src="doc1.html">
<frame src="doc2.html">
<frame src="doc3.html">
<frame src="doc4.html">
<frame src="doc5.html">
<frame src="doc6.html">
</frameset>
```

The resulting page would look something like Figure 12.3.

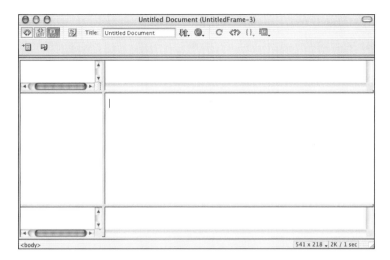

Figure 12.3   A frameset with two columns and three rows.

The frameset is populated by the source documents listed in the `<frame>` tags starting at the top left and moving left to right until a row is finished, and then proceeding to the next row down and moving through the frames left to right.

Although interesting layouts can be produced this way, at times you will definitely need to break out of the "checkerboard" grid pattern. To do this, you can use *nested framesets*.

Like tables, framesets can be nested within framesets. The nested frameset takes the place of a frame, and has its own `cols` and `rows` and other attributes, just like any other frameset. Here's an example:

```
<frameset rows="10%, 80%, 10%">
    <frame src="doc1.html">
     <frameset cols="200, 200, *>
          <frame src="doc2.html">
          <frame src="doc3.html">
          <frame src="doc4.html">
     </frameset>
    <frame src="doc5.html">
</frameset>
```

This code would produce a page like Figure 12.4.

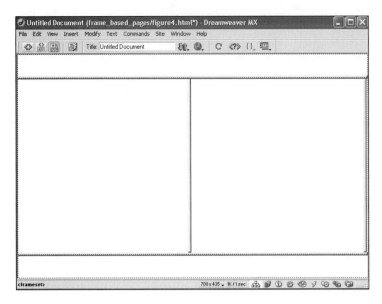

Figure 12.4   A frameset with a nested frameset.

Framesets can be nested within each other to many levels, although the complexity of such arrangements can soon become impractical.

<frameset> accepts several other attributes, as shown in Table 12.1.

Table 12.1   Other Common *<frameset>* Attributes

Attribute Browser Support	What It Does	Syntax, Values
name	IE4+, NN4+ Enables you to give an identifying name to your frameset, allowing it to be referenced via script. name="value"	Values: One or more alphanumeric characters
framespacing	IE3+ Determines the space in pixels between frames in a frameset. framespacing="value"	Values: Any integer
frameborder	IE3+, NN3+ Specifies whether a 3D border displays between the frames. frameborder="value"	Values: 1 (borders shown) 0 (borders not shown) yes (same as 1) no (same as 0)
bordercolor	Specifies the main color of the 3D frame border. bordercolor="value"	Values: A color name or hexadecimal value
border	IE4+, NN3+ Like framespacing, determines a value for the width of a frameset border. border="value"	Values: Any integer

<frame>

The `<frame>` element specifies how one of the rectangles in a frameset grid will look. It supports the attributes shown in Table 12.2.

Table 12.2   Common Attributes of the *<frame>* Tag

Attribute	What It Does	Syntax, Values
frameborder	Determines whether specific frame's borders are shown. Values: 1 (show borders) 0 (don't show borders) yes (same as 1) no (same as 0)	frameborder="value"
marginwidth	Specifies frame's left and right internal margins. marginwidth="value"	Values: Any integer
marginheight	Specifies frame's top and bottom internal margins. marginheight="value"	Values: Any integer
noresize	Turns off users' ability to drag and resize frame borders. Just "noresize"	
scrolling	Determines whether a frame will contain scrollbars. scrolling="value"	Values: yes (frame must have scrollbars) no (frame must never have scrollbars) auto (frame must have scrollbars only when necessary)
src	Tells the browser which source file a frame will contain. src="value"	Values: Relative or absolute URLs
name	An identifying name for the frame. name="value"	Values: one or more alphanumeric characters

<noframes>

The `<noframes>` element enables you to supply content that will be viewed by users whose browsers do not support frames. It can be placed at the end of a frameset and contain an alternate message to those users.

Note

As discussed earlier, the percentage of users with browsers that don't support frames is tiny—much less than 1 percent—and shrinking rapidly. However, `<noframes>` content is important for non-graphical browsers. Also, search engines will index `<noframes>` content, which can be valuable for positioning in search engine results.

Building Framesets in Dreamweaver

Dreamweaver offers several ways to do the initial building of frame pages. After you've designed your frameset by whatever method, frameset and frame attributes can be set or changed as necessary.

Regardless of which method you use to build a frame layout, you need to be sure to cover the following steps, not necessarily in this order:

- Create the frameset and frames.
- Save every file used in the frameset. Remember that each frame and frameset is an independent HTML document and must be saved. Using meaningful names for your documents will help avoid confusion.
- Set the properties for each frameset and each frame, including a name for each frame.
- Where links are included, be sure that they include targets so that the browser knows in which frame to load the content.

Creating a Frameset Manually

As you may already know, Dreamweaver has a number of visual aids that can either be turned on or off, depending on whether they're helpful to you in your design process. One of these is frame borders. Most people find it much easier to work with frames with this aid turned on. You can make frame borders visible by choosing View > Visual Aids > Frame Borders from the main menu.

Note that turning on frame borders has no effect on the actual border attributes that you set for your framesets or frames; regardless of these attributes, when the frame borders visual aid is turned on, you will see frame borders in Dreamweaver's Document window.

To create a frameset manually, select Modify > Frameset > Split Frame Left, Right, Up, or Down. This will insert a simple two-frame frameset.

To create more frames, drag one of the frame borders into the Document window to split the area horizontally or vertically. Dragging the borders from one of the corners divides the document into four frames.

To split an inner frame, use Alt-drag (Windows) or Option-drag (Macintosh).

To delete a frame, drag its border off the page or to the border of its parent frame.

Using Frame Objects to Create a Frameset

Dreamweaver includes a set of predefined framesets that enable you to create a frameset very quickly. To create a frameset in this way, follow these steps:

1. Start with an open, saved document. This document will become the source for one of the frames in the frameset you're building. Place the insertion point in the document.

2. From the Frames category of the Insert bar, select a predefined frameset. The Frames category provides a visual representation of each of the predefined framesets available (see Figure 12.5). Clicking the icon, or clicking and dragging it to the Document window, will insert the frameset. The frames icons each have a blue portion. This blue portion indicates into which frame the existing page will load.

Figure 12.5   The Frames tab of the Insert bar.

A predefined frameset also can be inserted by choosing Insert > Frames > Left, Right, Top, Bottom, Left and Top, Left Top, Top Left, or Split from the main menu. A nested frameset can be created by placing the insertion point within an existing frame and inserting another complete frameset from the Insert bar.

> **Note**
>
> Some of Dreamweaver's predefined Frame objects use nested frames to achieve their layout.

> **Tip**
>
> A free third-party extension, More Framesets by Mark Erickson, is available at the Macromedia Exchange for Dreamweaver at www.macromedia.com/exchange/dreamweaver/.

Using the New Document Dialog Box to Create a Frameset

A third way to create a frameset is by using the Dreamweaver New Document dialog box. To use this method, follow these steps:

1. With the document open, choose File > New and select the General tab. From the Category list, select Framesets.

2. From the framesets list, choose a type of frameset. A preview and description will appear in the right-hand pane.

3. Click Create to insert the frameset.

Saving Frame and Frameset Files

When you use Dreamweaver to create frame pages, each new frame and frameset document is given a temporary file name, such as **untitledframeset-1.htm**. You must save the frameset document and its associated frame documents before you can preview the pages in a browser. Dreamweaver offers several save options to help you be sure that all necessary documents are saved; you can save a frameset document or a frame document individually, or you can save all open frame files and the frameset page.

When you select one of the save options from the File menu, the Save As dialog box opens ready to save a document with the temporary name it has been given. It's up to you, however, to provide filenames that have meaning for you; taking care with naming will make working with frames much less bewildering. If you find it difficult to tell which frame file is being saved, look at the frame selection lines in the Document window—this identifies the current document (frame) being saved, as shown in Figure 12.6.

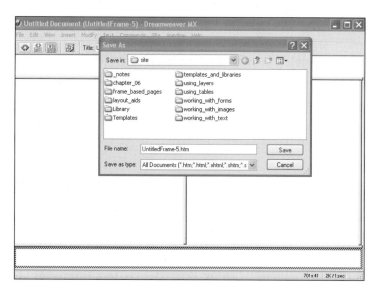

Figure 12.6   Saving framesets and frame documents.

To save a frameset file, select the frameset in the Document window or in the Frames panel, and choose File > Save Frameset.

To save a document that is inside a frame, click in the frame in the Document window to select it, and then choose File > Save Frame or File > Save Frame As. Selecting frames and framesets is covered below in "Working with Selections in Framesets."

To save all files in a frameset in addition to the frameset itself, choose File > Save All.

Tip

You can tell if you've got the frameset selected, because the File menu now says Save Frameset, instead of Save Frame. Also, the tag selector will include the `<frameset>` and/or `<frame>` tags.

Exercise 12.1   Building a Frameset

In this exercise, you build a simple frameset and frames from scratch. The documents you will use, with their solid-color backgrounds, are designed to clarify the way frames and framesets work.

Before you start, copy the **chapter_12** folder on the CD to your hard drive. Define a site called Chapter 12, with this folder as the local root folder.

Note

As always, feel free to experiment on your own as you proceed through the exercise; this is often one of the best ways to learn. However, the subsequent exercises in this chapter build on this one, so when you're finished with experimenting, you might want to return the document to the design specified in this exercise. The History panel is an excellent tool for experimenting and backtracking; see Chapter 3, "Creating and Working with Documents," for more on the History panel.

1. With the Site panel open and the site **chapter_12** displayed, from the Site panel's menu, choose New > New File. When **untitled.htm** appears in the Site panel, name the file **red.htm**. Open the document and give it the page title **Red**.

2. Choose Modify > Page Properties and click the Background color square. Choose a nice shade of red and click OK.

3. Now you're going to tell Dreamweaver that you want to create a frameset with one frame displaying the document **red.html**. First choose View > Visual Aids > Frame Borders so that frame borders are visible in the Document window. Remember, this is only as visual aid for the design process and has no bearing on whether you give your frames borders that can be seen in the browser. Frame borders in the Document window are seen as thick gray 3D lines.

4. With the cursor, click and drag the top frame border a little way down into the page's body area. Similarly, click and drag the left border a little way to the right into the body area. Your document should look something like Figure 12.7.

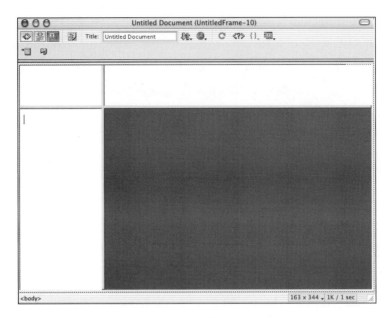

Figure 12.7   The exercise document with a two-column, two-row frameset.

5. You now have a document defining a frameset and four frames, each frame hav-
    ing a separate HTML document as a source file. The documents all need to be
    saved. Go to File > Save All. This option cycles through each of the files you've
    created, enabling you to name them, or to retain the temporary name that
    Dreamweaver has given them—catchy names such as **Untitledframeset-01.htm**.
    Rename the files as follows: **frameset.htm**, **blue.htm**, **green.htm**, **gold.htm**. The
    fourth frame is the document you started with, **red.htm**. Close the frameset.

6. Now give each of the frame source documents a background color. Open the
    Dreamweaver Site panel and double-click the file **blue.htm** to open it. Choose
    Modify > Page Properties, click the Background color chip, and pick a nice blue;
    click OK. Give the page the title **Blue** by typing it into the Title field just about
    the Document window. Save and close the file. In the Site panel, double-click
    gold.htm and give it a gold-colored background and title **Gold**; save and close it.
    Open **green.htm**, give it a green background and title **Green**, save, and close.
    Open **frameset.htm** again; it should look something like Figure 12.8 in the
    Dreamweaver Document window, with each of the four frames a different color.

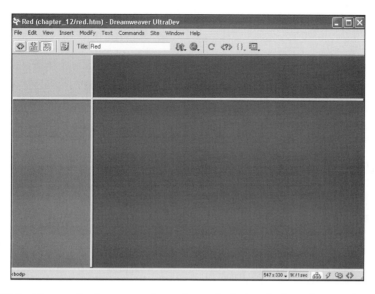

Figure 12.8 The exercise document after saving and coloring the framed source documents.

7. Spend some time familiarizing yourself with the way Dreamweaver displays a frameset and frame documents in its Document window. Notice that if you click in an individual frame, you'll see its filename in the Document window's top blue bar, and its title in the Title field. If you switch to Code view, you'll see the source code for the html file that loads into that frame only. Note, however, that clicking a frame in this way does not actually *select* that frame. To select a frame, Alt-click it (Windows) or Option+Shift-click (Macintosh), or choose it in the Frames panel. You'll see that it is selected by a dotted line around its perimeter, and by the fact that the Property inspector changes to the Frame Property inspector.

8. Clicking a frame border in the Document window will display the frameset's filename in the top blue bar and its title in the Title field. (You probably haven't titled the frameset document, but you can do that now; title it **Frameset**.) With the frameset document active in the Document window, switching to Code view will display the source code for the frameset document.

9. Choose File > Save All; this is a good habit to develop when working with frames, because it's easy to neglect saving one of the many files involved. You will also have to save files before previewing them in the browser. Preview the frameset document in a browser; it should look very much like it appeared in the Document window. In the exercises that follow in this chapter, you'll add some formatting and content to these documents.

Note

Why do you need to save frames before previewing, when you don't need to save regular nonframed documents? Browsers can only preview saved files. When you preview a regular document, Dreamweaver creates and saves a temporary file to launch in the browser so that you don't have to save your document. But frameset documents contain links to other documents (those that show in the frames). If those other documents haven't been saved, the browser won't be able to load them in the frameset—and there won't be any value in previewing.

Working with Frames

After your frame layout is created, you'll undoubtedly need to manipulate the frameset and frames in various ways in order to achieve the design you envision.

The Dreamweaver Frames Interface

The Dreamweaver interface allows easy manipulation of the placement, size, and attributes of frames and framesets, using the Frames Panel, the Property inspector, and the tag selector.

Using the Frames Panel

To open the Frames panel, either choose Window > Others > Frames, or press Shift+F2 (Windows) or Command+F10 (Macintosh); see Figure 12.9. The Frames panel is part of the Advanced Layout panel group. After you've chosen the panel the first time, if you're using the docked panel interface, the Advanced Layout group remains visible, able to be expanded or contracted as needed.

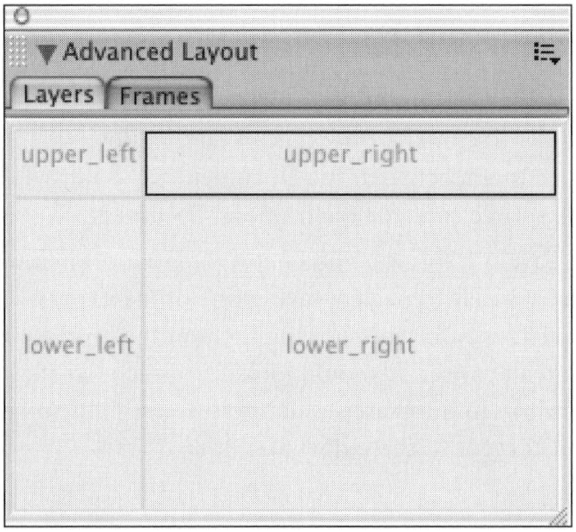

Figure 12.9   The Frames panel.

The Frames panel provides a visual representation of the currently active frameset and can make working with frames in the Document window much easier. Frames and framesets can be clicked in the Frames panel to select them in the Document window. The Frames panel also shows the hierarchy of the frameset structure in a way that might not be as easy to see in the Document window. In the Frames panel, each frameset is surrounded by a thick three-dimensional border; frames are surrounded by a thin gray line, and each frame is identified by a frame name.

Using the Property Inspectors

As with many other elements in Dreamweaver, a specific Property inspector appears when a frame is selected; another Property inspector appears when a frameset is selected, as shown in Figure 12.10. (If you don't see the Property inspector, choose Window > Property inspector, or Ctrl+F3/Opt+F3.)

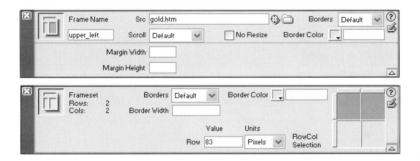

Figure 12.10   The Frameset Property inspector and the Frames Property inspector.

The Property inspectors for frames and for framesets enable you to view, set, and edit many of the attributes that HTML allows for frames and framesets. You'll learn about setting these attributes in detail in the section "Setting Frame Attributes" later in the chapter.

Using the Tag Selector

The tag selector, located along the bottom edge of the Document window, is an important visual aid and tool when working with frames. One of the trickiest aspects of working with frames in Dreamweaver is determining which file is currently active (one of the frames? the frameset?), and which tag is currently selected (<frame> or <frameset>). As Figure 12.11 shows, the tag selector is a lifesaver for working with the abundance of tags and documents.

Note
See Chapter 2, "Setting Up the Dreamweaver Workspace," for more about the tag selector.

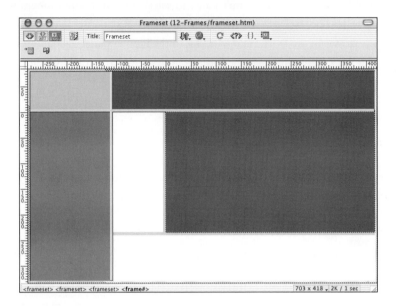

Figure 12.11   The tag selector showing a selected frame in a frameset.

Working with Selections in Framesets

To work with frames, you'll want to get comfortable with selecting frames and frame-sets, because this is necessary to edit their properties. You can select items from within the Document window itself, or you can use the Frames panel.

Selecting Frames

To select a frame in the Document window, Alt-click (Windows) or Option+Shift-click (Mac) inside the frame.

To select a frame using the Frames panel, click anywhere within the part of the diagram that represents the frame.

Selecting the Frameset

To select a frameset in the Document window, click any frame border. If View > Visual Aids > Frame Borders is turned off, you will not be able to click a frame border to select a frameset.

To select a frameset using the Frames panel, click the black border around the edge of the panel.

Determining the Current Selection

In the Document window, when a frame is selected, it has a dotted-line border. When a frameset is selected, all the frames that it contains have a dotted-line border (see Figure 12.12).

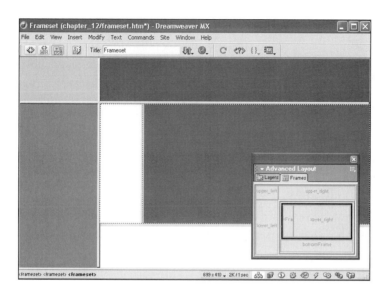

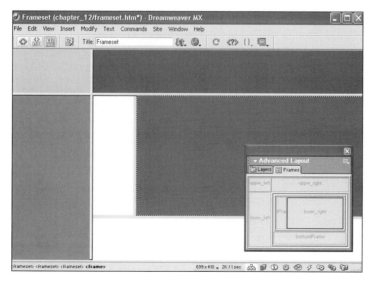

Figure 12.12   A frameset (top) and a frame selected in the Document window.

When you select a frame, you're working with the frameset itself, not with the document that the frame contains. To select the document, click in the Document window, and check the tag selector for the <body> tag.

Resizing Frames

Frames can be resized by just dragging their borders; this can be a good technique to use to "rough out" the basic size of your rows and columns. However, you'll probably want to use the Property inspector to be sure that columns and rows are allocated space according to your plan for the page layout. As discussed earlier in this chapter, both columns and rows can be given absolute, percentage, or relative sizes, and how you use these values will determine how the page looks at different window sizes. You'll learn about this in more depth in the upcoming section "Setting Attributes."

Setting Attributes

After you have created and saved your frameset and frames (and nested framesets and frames, possibly) you can set a number of their *attributes* (this term is used interchangeably with the Dreamweaver term *properties* here) using the Dreamweaver Property inspector. In this discussion of the HTML code involved with frame sites, earlier, in Tables 12.1 and 12.2, you read about the commonly used attributes for both framesets and frames; most of these can be set using the Property inspector. Any attributes not available through the Property inspector, of course, can be set by editing the source code directly, or by using the tag editor.

Frameset attributes and frame attributes work together using the *cascade principle*: Setting a frame property overrides any setting for that property in a frameset. If you set border attributes in a frame, for instance, and these attributes are different from the border attributes set for the frameset itself, the border attributes of the frame will take precedence.

Setting Frameset Attributes

When you manually create a frameset in Dreamweaver, no attributes are added to the code except for a src attribute for each <frame> element. All other common attributes can be added using the Property inspector.

When you use Dreamweaver predefined framesets, the following default property values are automatically applied: no borders, no scrollbars, and no resizing of frames in the browser. These properties can be easily changed, and others set, using the Property inspector.

To view frameset properties, be sure that the Property inspector is open, and, select the frameset, using the Document window or the Frames panel.

- In the Document window, click a border between two frames. The frameset will be selected, which is indicated by a dotted line around all frames.

- In the Frames panel, click the border that surrounds the frames.

Notice that a specialized Frameset Property inspector now displays, as shown in Figure 12.13, allowing you to view and edit the frameset's properties.

Figure 12.13   The Frameset Property inspector.

Frameset Borders

The Borders drop-down list enables you to make one of three choices:

- **Yes**. Borders will display around the frames in this frameset in the browser.

- **No**. Borders will not display around the frames in this frameset in the browser.

- **Default**. The user's browser will determine whether borders will display.

Frameset Border Width

In the Border Width field, you can type a number to specify the width of the borders in the frameset.

To create a set of borderless frames that will work in all current major browsers, you need to explicitly set `frameborder` to `"no"` and border to `"0"`.

Frameset Border Color

In the Border Color field, use the color picker to select a color for the border, or type the hexadecimal value.

Frameset Column Sizes and Row Sizes

In the Frameset Property inspector on the far right is a small visual representation of the frameset, the RowCol Selection box. Along the left and top sides of the box are tabs; clicking these tabs selects the corresponding row or column. With a row or column selected, you can use the Value and Units fields to set the size of each column. As discussed earlier in the section "HTML Coding for Frames," using the different unit types—absolute (pixels), percentage, and relative—will have different effects in the browser, and combining them will have yet more complex effects.

Frame borders can be dragged in the Document window to set approximate row and column sizes, and the Property inspector then used to make slight numeric corrections and to adjust the type of unit of measurement used. Table 12.3 explains the columns and row sizing units and their effects in the browser.

Note

One of the common mistakes made in coding frameset pages is not assigning absolute and relative sizes carefully, causing frames to display unpredictably in browsers. (If your frames are set to `cols="100,600"`, the page will only display correctly if visitors have their browser windows at exactly 700 pixels wide.) Dreamweaver generally does a very good job of making sure this doesn't happen – but it's still a good idea to keep an eye on things yourself. Especially after you've been dragging frames to resize them, use the Frameset inspector to make sure you know how your frames will behave in the browser.

Table 12.3   Frameset Row and Column Size Units

Unit	Effect
Pixels	Sets the size of the selected column or row at an absolute value; its size will not change regardless of the browser window size, and a column or row with this type of unit will be allocated its share of space before a column or row with a percentage or relative value.
Percent	Specifies that the current frame should make up the determined percentage of space available in its frameset. Columns or rows set with percent units are allocated space after those with units set in pixels, but before those set to Relative.
Relative	Determines that the column or row be allocated whatever space is left over after pixel-unit and percent-unit columns or rows have been allocated their space.

Giving a Title and a Name to a Frameset Document

A *frameset document* is an HTML document, and it can be given a `<title>` in the same way as any other HTML document. In Dreamweaver this is done by selecting the frameset and going to Modify > Page Properties or using the Document toolbar to assign a title.

The `name` attribute of the `<frameset>` tag is completely different from the `<title>` tag of the frameset document. A `name` attribute is set when the frameset needs to be referenced by a script. The Property inspector doesn't allow this attribute to be set, but it can be added manually to the source code. With the frameset selected, press Ctrl+Tab to access Code view. Locate the `<frameset>` tag and add the `name` attribute with this syntax:

```
<frameset name="myframesetname">
```

The ID attribute is also used to reference a frameset from a script, and can be added using the tag editor.

Tip

To view the source code for a frameset document in Dreamweaver, be sure that View > Visual Aids > Frame Borders is selected, click any frame border in the Document window, and press Ctrl/Cmd+Tab to view the frameset document in Code view. When in Code view, you can edit attributes by typing, or by using Edit Tag or the Tag Chooser object.

Setting Frame Attributes

To view frame properties, be sure that the Property inspector is open, and select the frame. The Frame property inspector will appear, as shown in Figure 12.14.

Figure 12.14   The Frame Property inspector.

Frame Names

Entering a one-word name in the Name Frame field of the Property inspector adds a `name` attribute to the `<frame>` tag.

Frame names are important; they are used as targets for hyperlinks, to instruct the browser as to *where*—into what frame—a document should be loaded. They also can be used by scripts to reference the frame. A frame name should not include any spaces or special characters; underscores are the only character allowed. Be careful not to use *reserved words* such as `top` or `blank`; it's safest to choose distinctive, unusual words. The name is what appears in the Frames panel. Dreamweaver frame objects are created automatically with names, but these names can be changed to whatever you choose.

Frame Source

The attribute `src` determines the source document for the frame (the document that will show in that frame). In the Src field, enter a filename and path, or click the folder icon to browse to and select a file. A file also can be opened in a frame by placing the cursor in the frame in the Document window and choosing File > Open in Frame.

Frame Scroll

The Scroll field enables you to determine whether scrollbars appear when there is not enough room to display the content of the current frame. You have three choices: Yes, No, or Auto. Yes will cause scrollbars to appear whether they're needed or not. No will prevent scrollbars from appearing whether they are needed or not. Auto will cause them to appear only when needed. Most browsers default to Auto. Frames without borders can't be resized regardless of how this property is set.

Frame Noresize

When checked, this option prevents users from dragging the frame borders when the site is accessed in a browser.

Frame Borders

This field enables you to set the border properties of the frame; whatever options you choose will appear for the current frame, overriding the frameset border properties. The options are Yes, No, and Default. If you don't choose an option, Dreamweaver defaults to No. If you choose Default, the browser's default display will apply, and most browsers default to Yes.

Note

If a frame is surrounded by frames whose borders are set to Yes, it will appear to have borders even if none are specified. If a frameset has borders specified, this will also give the frames it contains the appearance of having borders.

Frame Border Colors

In the field Border Color, you can set a border color that will apply to all the borders adjacent to the current frame. This setting overrides the border color of the frameset.

Margin Width and Margin Height

Margin width sets the width of the frame's left and right margins (the space between the content and the frame border).

Margin height sets the height in pixels of the top and bottom margins (as with margin width, the space between the content and the frame borders).

Exercise 12.2   Setting Frameset and Frame Attributes

In this exercise, you'll add some attributes to your frameset and frames. This exercise builds on Exercise 12.1. If you haven't completed Exercise 12.1, a completed version of the exercise files is available on the CD in **chapter_12/exercise_1_completed/**. If you haven't done so yet, copy the **chapter_12** folder on the CD to your hard drive. Define a site called Chapter 12, with this folder as the local root folder.

1. Open the file **frameset.htm** from the **chapter_12** folder. First, you'll set some frameset properties. To set frameset properties, the frameset needs to be selected in the Document window; do this by clicking on any frame border. The frameset is selected when you see dotted lines surrounding all the frames, and when you see the Frameset Property inspector displayed.

2. You are going to make a borderless frameset page, so from the Borders drop-down list, choose No. Choose File > Save All and preview the frameset document with a browser. Depending on which browser you're using, you might still see frame borders, despite setting the frameset border property to No. Browsers as recent as Internet Explorer 5.5, Internet Explorer 6.0, Netscape 4.7, and Netscape 6.2 will still display frame borders, given this code. The workaround for this is to be sure to set the Border Width property to 0 as well. Change this setting, then choose File > Save All again and preview the frameset document. In the browser, you should now see a borderless frame page, as in Figure 12.15. (In the Dreamweaver Document window, you'll still see frame borders, because you have the visual aid frame borders turned on. This is unrelated to the actual frame borders.)

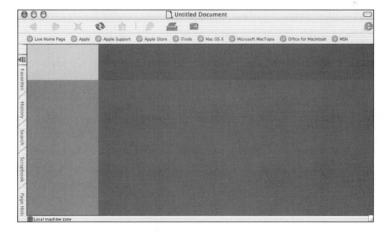

Figure 12.15   The exercise document as borderless frameset.

3. Back in the Document window, select the frameset again. Now set the size of the columns and rows. On the right side of the Property inspector, in the little diagram of your frameset, click the tab at the top of the left column, and in the Column Value field just to the left, specify a width of 150, and a Column Units of pixels. Click the tab at the top of the right column and specify a Column Units of Relative. (Dreamweaver fills in a 1, but Relative has no actual numeric value.) This configuration will fix the left column at 150 pixels wide, but allow the right column to fill whatever space remains of the browser window viewport. Choose File > Save All. Only **frameset.htm** has been modified, but it's best to get into the habit of saving all documents when working with framesets.

4. Now, in the Property inspector, select the top row by clicking its tab along the left edge of the frameset diagram. Set its height to 20 percent by setting the Row Value to 20 and the Row Units to Percent. Click the bottom row's tab and set its height to 80 percent. This will create rows which both adjust to the available browser window size, each taking up its allotted percentage of vertical space. Save all frames again. The frameset should still look much as it did before, depending on how you originally sized the rows and columns when you dragged them into place, and depending on what size you keep your Dreamweaver Document window.

Note

The window size drop-down menu at the bottom of the Document window is useful for sizing your Dreamweaver window in such a way that it best represents the average browser window size you want to accommodate with your design. When working with frames, however, you have to take special care when using it. If a frame is selected and you resize the window, Dreamweaver will attempt to resize the frame itself to the size you specify. Instead, you want to select the frameset and resize the window; this will let Dreamweaver know that it is the frameset document that you want resized.

5. Now set some frame attributes, starting with the upper-left frame. If you just click in that frame, you'll see that the Property inspector doesn't change at all; this is because just clicking in the frame doesn't select it. To select it, you must Alt-click (Option+Shift-click the Mac) or click on the frame in the Frames panel. Select the upper-left frame (see Figure 12.16).

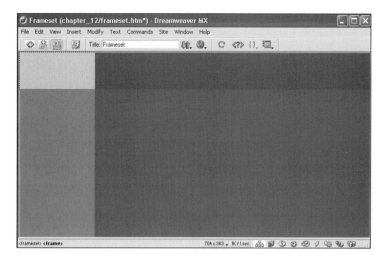

Figure 12.16   Selecting the upper-left frame.

6. If you were planning to reference this frame with a script, it would need a name, so give it one for practice. You will also need to name a frame in order to target it with a link. In the Name field, type **top_left**. Then check the Noresize box; suppose, for example, that you don't want the user to resize your frames. You also wouldn't want scrollbars in that frame, and won't need them, so set the Scroll field to No.

7. Moving on, select the upper-right frame. In this frame, you want no resizing, so check that box again. You also want to be sure you don't see any scrollbars, and you know that none will be called for, so you set scrollbars to No. Name this frame **upper_right**.

8. Now select the lower-left frame. Set the Noresize and Scroll options the same as the two upper-row frames. For this frame, you also need margins. Set Margin Height to 10 and Margin Width to 15. Now type a sentence or two into that frame so that you can see the margins you've created. Name this frame **lower_left**.

9. Finally, select the lower-right frame, the largest one. Again set Noresize, but this time you might need scrollbars. You're going to fill this frame with content, and because a lot of it will be text, depending on the user's browser window size, they might need scrollbars to see it all. If the scrollbars aren't necessary to a given user in a given configuration, however, you would much rather not look at them in your pretty design. So set Scroll to Auto, which will do exactly what you want in each situation.

10. Name this frame **main_content_frame**.

11. With the lower-right frame still selected, set some margins. Make both Margin Width and Margin Height 20. Now add some content to that frame's source document. If you haven't yet acquired an extension such as Filler Text Fever, Latin Text, or Corporate Mumbo Jumbo from the Macromedia Exchange for Dreamweaver (www.macromedia.com/exchange/dreamweaver/), you really should. Either use your filler text extension to pour a couple of paragraphs of text into that frame, or find some text to copy and paste there; the point is to fill the frame with content past the overflowing point. Depending on the shades of background color you used, the text color might not be easily readable, but don't worry about that for right now.

12. Save all frames, and preview your work in a browser; it should look something like Figure 12.17.

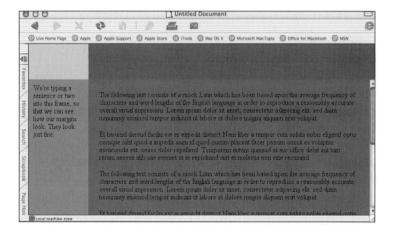

Figure 12.17   The Exercise 12.2 frameset document as it should look now.

13. Still previewing the document in the browser, try resizing the browser window. Note the way the columns and rows behave at different window sizes. Also note that the large main frame has scrollbars only when needed, and that you cannot drag and change the frame borders. You're done for now; in Exercise 12.3, you'll add some navigation links and new source documents to your little frame-based site.

Linking and Targeting

Creating links on a frame site distinctly differs from on nonframe sites. On a frame site, if a link is to be opened within one of the frames of the current frameset, the link needs to include a *target*, an attribute instructing the browser *where* to open the new document.

A link also can target other locations in which a document can be opened; these are explained in this section.

To create a link that targets a frame, follow these steps:

1. Select the text or object that is to serve as the link anchor.

2. Create a link. Next to the Link field in the Property inspector is the Target drop-down list. From that list, choose the location where you want the linked document to appear. Table 12.4 shows the choices that should appear.

Table 12.4   Link Target Options

Target	Causes Linked Document to Open In
Frame name: If you've named your individual frames, their names should appear in the Target drop-down list.	The frame whose name is specified
_blank	A new browser window
_parent	The parent frameset of the link, occupying the whole browser window
_self	The current frame, replacing the content in that frame
_top	The outermost frameset of the current document, replacing all frames

If no target is chosen, the link will open in the current frame.

Exercise 12.3   Adding Targeted Links to a Frameset

In this exercise, you'll make links in your frameset to display various documents in the main content frame. This exercise builds on Exercises 12.1 and 12.2. A completed set of Exercise 12.2 files is available on the CD in the folder **chapter_12/exercise_2_completed/**; you can build on them for this exercise, if you like. If you haven't done so yet, copy the **chapter_12** folder on the CD to your hard drive. Define a site called Chapter 12, with this folder as the local root folder.

1. For this exercise, you need more source documents than your current Red, Blue, Gold, and Green documents. In the Site panel, select the **chapter_12** folder that contains **frameset.htm** and choose File > New File. Name the new file **purple.htm** and open it. Give it a purple background color, title it **Purple** in the Title field, and pour or type some filler text onto the page, at least a paragraph or two. Save the file and close it.

2. Create another new file, name it **orange.htm**, give it an orange background and the title of **Orange** in the Title field. Place some filler text on the page, and then save and close it. Create another file, name it **pink.htm**, give it a pink background and the title **Pink** in the Title field. Place some filler text on the page, and then save it and close it.

3. Now open the frameset document you built in Exercises 12.1 and 12.2, **frameset.htm**. Delete the couple of sentences you placed in the lower-left frame; you need that space for your navigation links. In that lower-left frame, type the word **Purple**. Press the Spacebar and type **Orange**. Press the Spacebar again and type **Pink**.

4. Select the word Purple. In the Property inspector, click the browse-for-file icon (the yellow file folder) and browse to the file you just created, **purple.htm**. Either double-click it or select it, and then click OK. With the text Purple still selected, in the Property inspector, specify a target in the Target drop-down list. You should see the four standard options, _blank, _parent, _self, and _top, and also the name of your lower-right frame, main_content_frame—choose it.

5. Next select the text Orange, and follow the same steps outlined in step 4 to link it to the file **orange.htm** and tell the browser to open it in the lower-right frame. Save all frames.

6. Finally, select the text Pink, and repeat the same steps you did for Purple and Orange. Save all frames.

7. Preview in a browser. (Be *sure* that you have saved all frames by choosing File > Save All.) Click each of your links—they should swap the source file for the frame named main_content_frame, the lower-right frame. The frameset page should look like Figure 12.18.

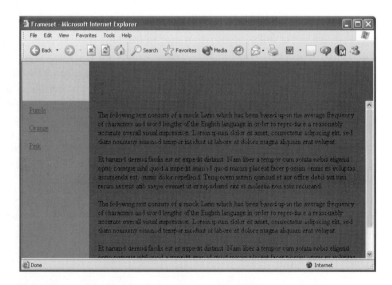

Figure 12.18   The exercise document with left-hand navigation links.

8. Add one more to your navigation link list by typing **Other Target**. Select it, link it to the **purple.htm** document, but this time, choose _blank for a target. Save all frames and preview; clicking that link should open the Purple page in a completely new browser window. Go back, select the link Other Target again, and change the target to _parent. Save all frames and preview; this time, the current window will be replaced with the Purple document, with no frameset involved.

9. Try the target _self; the new file will replace the current frame. Finally, try _top; in this configuration, it will have the same effect as _parent, filling the browser window.

Working with *<noframes>*

If the user who accesses your frameset document is using an extremely outdated browser—a version of Netscape *previous* to Netscape 2.0, or a version of Internet Explorer *previous* to IE 3.0—he won't be able to view your framed content. The <noframes> element is provided for the purpose of displaying content for these users

<noframes> also can be used to one's advantage in search engine positioning, and this tactic is worth considering when a frame site needs to be positioned competitively.

Ideally, you might want to include all of the content included in the frames portion of your web site in the <noframes> section in some form. You can link to a full set of non-frame HTML pages containing all of the site's content, if you choose.

The <noframes> tag pair contains a <body> tag pair; the source code structure looks something like this:

```
<noframes>
<body>
This is the no-frames content.
</body>
</noframes>
```

To define <noframes> content with Dreamweaver, follow these steps:

1. Choose Modify > Frameset > Edit NoFrames Content. This causes the Document window to be cleared; the words NoFrames Content appear at the top of the document body area.

2. In the Document window, type or insert any content you like, just as you would with any other HTML page.

3. To return to the normal view of the frameset document, uncheck Modify > Frameset > Edit NoFrames Content.

Tip

If you switch back and forth between Code and Design views, the position of the cursor within the document code will determine whether Design view shows you your standard or <noframes> content. If you're working in Code and Design view, selecting code in one section or another will automatically switch the display in the Design view portion of the window.

Exercise 12.4   Adding *<noframes>* Content

This exercise builds on Exercises 12.1, 12.2, and 12.3. A set of completed Exercise 3 files is available on the CD in the folder **chapter_12/exercise_3_completed/**; these documents can be copied to your **chapter_12** folder and used as the basis for Exercise 12.4.

If you haven't done so yet, copy the **chapter_12** folder on the CD to your hard drive. Define a site called Chapter 12, with this folder as the local root folder.

1. Open the document **frameset.htm,** created in the preceding three exercises.
2. From the main menu, select Modify > Frameset > Edit NoFrames Content. The Document window should be replaced by a gray window with the words NoFrames Content at the top.
3. Type a message, such as **Here is my <noframes> content.** Add any formatting you like.
4. Uncheck Modify > Frameset > Edit NoFrames Content.
5. Save all frames. If you can upload your frame pages to a server on the Internet, perhaps to a temporary subdirectory of a site to which you have FTP access, you can use the Browser Emulator at www.dejavu.org/ to see how your noframes content looks to someone with a really ancient browser such as Netscape Navigator 1.0. Only the noframes content should show.

Summary

This chapter discussed the pros and cons of using frames, and familiarized you with the HTML code that makes up frameset documents and the file structure of frame sites.

With Dreamweaver opened, you discovered how its frame-building tools can make putting together a frameset simple. This chapter covered the different attributes that you can set for framesets and frames and showed you how to set many of them easily with the Dreamweaver Property inspector.

This chapter also addressed how to sort out some of the complexities of linking from a frameset to a frame and discussed some other link targeting options available. Finally, this chapter discussed adding content to a frameset document that will display when a user with a very old browser accesses the page.

The exercises in this chapter walked you through building a frameset and frames, setting their attributes, and adding targeted links and noframes content. However, you should experiment and play with frames within Dreamweaver to discover more of the inherent possibilities.

Chapter 13

Using Cascading Style Sheets

Cascading Style Sheets (CSS) offers a way to extend the formatting capabilities of your web page beyond the limitations of HTML. CSS enables you to define and change the look of your web site quickly and easily.

This chapter discusses CSS: what it is, why it is, and how to use it.

What Are Cascading Style Sheets?

A *Cascading Style Sheet* at its most basic is a set of instructions that define how an HTML document is going to display. The great thing about CSS is that it can be defined in an external file, or sheet. This external sheet is first read by the browser, then applies the rules to the specified content on the page. In this way, the style and formatting of the page are separate from the content. This is an important concept in designing web pages. It also gives you a powerful and detailed way to update your entire web site.

You can create a style sheet that defines your text as Arial, 12 point, red, bold, and left-justified with a blue background. Attach your sheet to all the pages on your site, and all your text will appear that way. If you have a change of heart, you can change that one style sheet and make the text Times, 28 point, green, italics, and right-justified. Save that new sheet, and the entire web site is automatically updated.

CSS also enables you to do things that HTML just can't do. You can set a layer on your page to be scrollable. This way you can have a window in the middle of your page with scrollable content. You can define different colors for every facet of a table border. You can set custom graphics for bullets and you can remove the underline from hyperlinks.

Note

While browser support is getting better with every release, some browsers do not display all CSS elements, nor do they display some elements in the same way. It is always a good idea to test your page in multiple browsers. One important idea of CSS is that if the style is not supported in the browser, the information will still be there—it will just not show the offending styles.

IE 5 and above and Netscape 6 do a fine job of displaying most CSS elements. Netscape 4 has some limitations.

CSS gives you unprecedented control over your page. The W3C is now recommending the use of CSS for page formatting. It has even deprecated the <font> tag in deference to CSS. It would do you well to explore the possibilities of CSS in your web design.

A note about semantics:

- A *style* is generally defined as a set of parameters for a tag or a class.
- A *sheet* is the file that contains the styles. A sheet can contain many styles.

Format of a CSS Style

The format of a style sheet has a few basic parameters and can be further subdivided depending on the complexity of the sheet.

CSS Selectors

The easiest of the styles to understand is the CSS selector. A *selector* is any HTML element or tag. To affect the appearance of the tag you apply a set of rules, that set of rules defines how the tag should display in the browser.

The basic format of a selector style is as such:

```
selector {property:value}
```

The `selector` is the tag being changed. The `property` is the name of the property being set. The `value` is the value of the property being set.

A basic CSS example is this:

```
p {color: green}
```

This sets any text within the `<p></p>` tags to green for any page that uses this style.

You also can group several settings into one style:

```
p
{
color: green;
text-align: right
}
```

This will set the green text to the right of the page.

Note that CSS is frequently written in separate lines for clarity, but can be combined on one line if you prefer.

If you want to assign multiple tags the same style, you can list them in the selector:

```
p,div,H2
{
color: green;
text-align: right
}
```

Notice that a comma separates each tag, a full colon separates the property from the value and semicolons separate properties (with the far right semicolon being optional—in the example above, it is not present).

Contextual Selectors

Contextual selectors are another way of applying styles to specific tags. This is a bit more specialized, because a selector works by only being applied when a certain condition or set of tags are present.

For instance, you can create a CSS selector that you only want to be applied to table headings that are boldfaced. So you would set up a selector that looks for a tag combination of B TH (bold, table heading) and would then apply the style. Table headings that are not bold would be left alone by this style.

Classes

You can have more than one set of styles for a tag. The most flexible method of defining more than one set of styles is to specify classes. A *class* is a set of style rules that can be applied to any element, unlike a redefined HTML tag, which is *automatically* applied to all specified elements. Define a custom class, and it will then show up in the list on the Apply Styles tab. You then highlight an element on the page and specify which class you want to use in your tag:

```
.red {color: red}
h2.green {color: green}
```

When you want to specify a particular class in a tag, it would look like this:

```
<H2 class="green">This is Green text</H2>
```

This tells the tag to use the green class. As this is applied directly to this tag, it will influence this tag only. <h3 class="green">This is not green text</h3> would not be affected because the .green class is directly associated with the <h2> tag.

You can use the red class with any tag and it would apply because it is not assigned to a specific tag, so the following would actually display properly:

```
<h2 class="red">This is Red Text</h2>
<h3 class="red">This is Red Text</h3>
```

Pseudo-Classes

The most common usage of *pseudo-classes* is to display links in different states, those states being Link, Visited, Hover and Active. These are preset definitions for link styles. It differentiates between Links, Active (links that are being clicked on), Hover (when mousing over a link), and Visited (links that have already been visited). You can use selectors to define a style for each of these states. (This is what is used to remove the underline from links.) These four selector styles are available in the Name drop-down field when you select Use CSS Selector. Order of their use in the CSS file is important: It must be Link, Visited, Hover, Active, or their functionality will not work as desired. An example could be:

```
a:link{text-decoration:underline}
a:visited{text-decoration:overline}
a:hover{text-decoration:none}
a:active{text-decoration:none;cursor:wait}
```

Psuedo-classes work with IE 4+, Netscape 6+ but not with Netscape 4.x, so if you are experiencing problems with Netscape 4, wonder no more.

Styles, Style Sheets, and Where They're Kept

Styles can exist in a document as individual styles placed inline with the document, or they can be grouped together in collections called *style sheets*. A style sheet can be internal or external, depending on where it is stored relative to the document that it's formatting. The following sections discuss the relative advantages and disadvantages of inline styles, internal style sheets, and external style sheets.

Inline Styles

Inline styles are those defined directly within the tag on the page. The CSS is written right into the tag as an attribute. Although this style will take precedence over all other styles, they are applied only on a tag-by-tag basis. Therefore they can be edited only by directly editing the HTML page. Imagine though, having to edit a page with 50 inline CSS references on it; it would be time-consuming and also take more bandwidth to serve your page. This way of applying a style is limited and therefore should be used for changing specific tags on a case-by-case basis.

An inline style looks like this:

```
<div id="Layer1" style="position:absolute; width:200px; height:115px;
z-index:1; left: 121px; top: 103px;">
```

This is the code for a layer in Dreamweaver. A layer is really a CSS block element. The style is written into the tag because it is unique to this <DIV> tag. It clearly specifies the properties of the layer within the actual tag.

Internal Style Sheets

Internal style sheets are defined within the actual HTML page in the <head> region using the <style> block. This way, the styles are available to the whole page without being dependent on another file.

A typical internal style will look like this (see the browser rendering in Figure 13.1):

```
<head>
<style type="text/css">
body {background-color: blue}
h2 {text-align: right; color: red}
</style>
</head>
<body>

<h2>This is the red heading</h2>
```

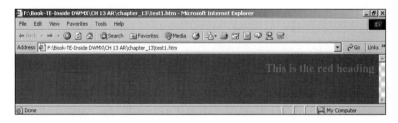

Figure 13.1   Internal Style Sheet in browser.

As you can see, the background is blue, the h2 text is red and right-aligned as we have specified using CSS.

As you can see, if you want to put the headings on the left and change the color, just edit the CSS in the head and the changes will be made automatically to all headings in the document (see Figure 13.2).

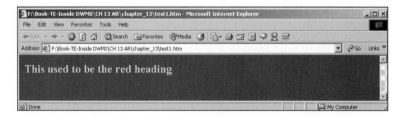

Figure 13.2   The modified Internal Style Sheet in browser.

The referenced file above appears after applying a change of Text Alignment to left and changing the text color to blue.

If multiple pages all had the same styles, however, the change to a style would have to be made to all of the pages. Again, this isn't very efficient, but it's better than using inline styles.

External Style Sheets

External style sheets enable you to take full advantage of the capabilities of CSS. External style sheets contain all the styles and definitions in an external file, usually with a .css extension. This is arguably the best way to store your styles. Using this method, the style information is completely independent of the HTML code. You can change the look and feel of your entire site just by editing this external file. The site will automatically update depending on the information in that sheet after it is uploaded to the server. After you learn all the options that CSS presents to you, you can take full advantage of this functionality.

A typical external style sheet is linked to the page by code like this:

```
<link rel="stylesheet" type="text/css"
href="mainstyles.css">
```

Where:

- `rel="stylesheet"` defines the relationship between the open page and style sheet. Style sheets can be persistent, preferred, or alternate. A persistent style sheet is always used when style sheets are enabled. A preferred style sheet is automatically applied. Giving the style sheet a title attribute in the link field specifies this. An alternate style sheet is one that can be set by the user. Used for giving users a choice of styles.

- `type="text/css"` defines the file format (MIME type) of the CSS file. This is used so that browsers can ignore CSS files that it cannot understand. `"text/css"` will almost always be used.

- `href="mainstyle.css"` is the path to the actual CSS file. It can be either relative, as in the example, or absolute.

The actual style sheet file will just have a list of selectors and classes listed, as follows:

```
p
{
color: green;
text-align: right
}

.red {color: red}
h2.green {color: green}
```

Warning

HTML tags should *never* be included in external CSS files as they can cause your CSS to not be interpreted correctly in the browser. This includes HTML comment tags:

```
<!--HTML Comment-->
```

CSS has its own type of comment tag:

```
/* CSS Comment */
```

After you link the external style sheet to your site, you just change the settings in the file and everything updates. This is the tremendous advantage of using CSS!

Cascading and Inheritance

One of the advantages of CSS styles is that they all work together if needed and can over-write each other as needed. Cascading and inheritance work together to make this cooperation happen.

Cascading refers to the use of multiple styles and sheets and the order in which they are read. The order in which the styles appear within the code determines which particular trait will display. If the external style sheet says that <h2> text should be blue, but there is an inline style on a particular <h2> tag that says the text should be yellow, the yellow will win because it is closer to the actual text code.

Inheritance means that in styles that cascade, the closer style will overwrite only those parameters that both styles share. In the preceding example, if the external style says that the <h2> tag should be right justified, the inline style will not overwrite that because it does not have a parameter that controls justification. Therefore, the <h2> tag will be yellow because of the inline style, but it will inherit the right-justification from the external style.

Creating Cascading Style Sheets in Dreamweaver

You can use Dreamweaver to create style sheets or you can use and modify existing sheets. Dreamweaver displays most CSS formatting in Design view. Probably the easiest way to work with styles in Dreamweaver is by utilizing the CSS Styles panel; you can also choose File > New, and choose to create a CSS document with your own manually entered code, if you prefer (see Figure 13.3).

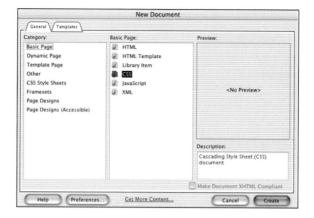

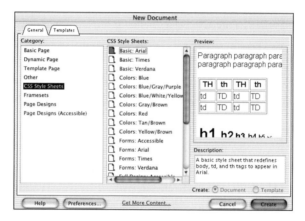

Figure 13.3   Creating a new CSS file.

You can create a new blank CSS file or use a style stationery that is available from the new document interface.

Working with the CSS Styles Panel

Styles are manipulated and controlled in the CSS Styles panel, part of the Design panel group (see Figure 13.4). You can access this panel by going to Window > CSS Styles (Shift+F11).

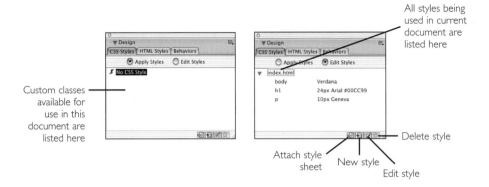

Custom classes available for use in this document are listed here

All styles being used in current document are listed here

Attach style sheet

New style

Delete style

Edit style

Figure 13.4   The CSS Styles panel showing the Style Editor and Style Applier.

MX   An update has been made to the CSS Styles panel in Dreamweaver MX; the Style Editor view has been added. This view shows the structure of all styles on the page. This view also shows both linked and internal styles, along with the list of parameters for the styles. In this view, double-click the style to bring up the editor. To apply a style in this view, right-click (Ctrl-click) and from the contextual menu choose Apply. This new view makes it much easier to see your style definitions.

MX   The Style Applier view is also new, and is found in the classic Dreamweaver panel. This panel will only show custom classes. To apply a custom class in this view, simply highlight the portion of the page and click on the style in the list. It will automatically be applied. Click on the (none) class to remove any style applied to the selection.

Creating New Styles

To create a new style, in the CSS Styles panel click the New CSS Style button (see Figure 13.4). This button is available in either the Style Applier or Style Editor views. The New CSS Style dialog box will appear (see Figure 13.5).

- **Attach Style Sheet.**   Prompts you for an existing style sheet filename; use the browse button to locate it.
- **New CSS Style.**   Brings up the New CSS Style dialog box for you to create the new style.

- **Edit Style Sheet.**   Either brings up the External Style Sheet dialog box, opens the CSS Editor dialog box, or opens the CSS Definition Editor dialog box.

Figure 13.5   The New CSS Style dialog box.

You can define a custom class or redefine a tag or redefine a selector and you can specify in the local document or have it create or update an external style sheet. If you create the external style sheet, then the program automatically adds the appropriate linking information in the <head> section of your document.

Note

It is important to keep an eye on the names of the dialog boxes when making style sheets. Some of the windows are similar, and you need to know where you are in each step.

The options here are as follows:

- **Name.** Name of the style. This is the name that shows up in the CSS Styles panel. It is a good idea to name them so that they reflect what they do. This will make keeping track of styles easy, especially if you are working with other developers. Complex sites can have quite a few styles and good naming helps you keep everything straight.

    The Name field is context-sensitive: it will have a different name depending on the type of style selected. If Redefine HTML is chosen, the field will be called Tag and the drop-down menu will list all available tags. If Use CSS Selector is chosen, the field will be called Selector. Into this field you would select the link style from the drop-down list or enter in the tag combination for the selector.

Tip

If you want to define more than one tag with the same CSS, you would enter them as follows in the Selector field:

```
td, p
```

Another example might be:

```
body, td, p
```

- **Type.** What kind of style is this going to be:
  - *Make Custom Style.* This will make a custom class that can be applied to any tag.
  - *Redefined HTML Tag.* This will create a style that will affect every instance of the selected tag.
  - *Use CSS Selector.* Creates a style for a specific combination of tags or allows you to set link styles.
- **Define In.** Determines whether this will be part of an external style sheet, or whether it will be an internal style.

  To define a style as part of an external style sheet, use the pop-up menu to either choose an existing CSS file the style should be added to, or create a new CSS document.

  To define an internal style, which will affect the current document only, choose the second option.

After you've decided what kind of style to create, click OK. The Style Definition dialog box will open (see Figure 13.7), ready for you to specify what formatting the new style should include. (See the section on style definitions for more on this.)

Note

To create a custom inline style, the code must be entered directly into the tag. With the new Tag Inspector, however, you can easily code style elements within the tags of your page.

Removing Styles

Removing a style from a page or an element is quite simple. Dreamweaver MX makes it even easier. The redesigned CSS Styles panel now shows all the styles being used. With items such as redefined HTML tags or pseudo-classes—or in other words, those style elements applied to the whole page—you need to delete the style definition from the page or the external style sheet. You can highlight the style in the CSS Styles panel and right-click (Ctrl-click) and from the contextual menu choose Delete, or you can press the Delete Style button in the lower-right corner of the CSS Styles panel (refer to Figure 13.4).

For custom classes, you can either remove the style from the specific element to which it is applied and/or you can remove the style from the style sheet.

To remove the style from the page, go to the Edit Styles panel and highlight the style. Click on the Remove CSS Style button in the lower-right corner of the panel. This works in two ways. If you remove a linked style sheet, it simply removes the link from the page; it does not affect the external file. If you remove an internal style, it deletes the style definition from the head tag, permanently removing that style.

To remove a custom class from the element itself, select the element and go to the Apply Styles panel. Click the No CSS Style button and the CSS code will be removed from the element tag.

Linking to Style Sheets

Although you can use the CSS Styles panel to create style sheets, you also can link to existing style sheets. If you are adding more pages to a web site that has a series of pre-made styles, you can easily link those pages to your new pages and apply them as you want. They will act no differently than styles created in Dreamweaver: Redefined HTML tags will automatically update and the list of custom classes should appear in the CSS Styles panel.

To link to an existing style sheet, simply click on the Attach Style Sheet button in the lower left of the CSS Styles panel (refer to Figure 13.4). You will be prompted to browse to the .css file. You also have a choice between linking and importing. Generally Link will be the best choice. The difference is slim: Link uses an href to link to the sheet, while the import uses a Style or URL link to find the file.

Tip

The Link generally is used for a style sheet that contains styles that work in Netscape 4. The Import link generally is used to hide styles that aren't Netscape 4 compliant but are compliant with other browsers and Netscape 6. The reason for this is because Netscape 4 ignores the @import directive.

Click OK to complete the linking. The redefined HTML tags and selectors will be applied automatically, and the list of the Custom Classes will be available in the Apply Styles panel.

Working with Style Definitions

The interface for specifying CSS style formatting is the Style Definitions dialog box (see Figure 13.6). This dialog box will appear as soon as you create a new style, and every time you want to edit existing styles. Its eight different windows cover different aspects of CSS control. They are described in the next few sections.

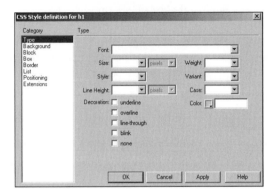

Figure 13.6   The CSS Style Definition dialog box.

Type

Table 13.1 lists the Type options available in the Type category of the CSS Style Definition dialog box (shown in Figure 13.7).

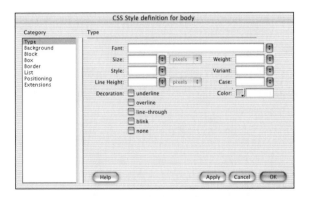

Figure 13.7   The Type Category options.

Table 13.1   CSS Options for Formatting Type, As Shown in the CSS Style Definition Dialog Box

Option	Description
Font	Selects the fonts to be used in the style. These are the same groupings that have been set in Dreamweaver. You can edit this list by clicking the down arrow and choosing Edit Font List. (See Chapter 4, "Working with Text," for a full discussion on font lists.)
Size	Enables you to specify font size. Notice that you can choose a number value or absolute size values. Absolute size values set the medium value to the default settings of the user's browser or defined styles rules and then scales from there.
Style	Sets the font to normal, italic, or oblique. The difference between italic and oblique is this: Italic is a distinct version of the font. Most fonts have an italic version. Oblique is simply the original version of the font that has been angled by the computer. In reality, there is usually no difference between the two in the browser, but there can be variances between fonts and sizes. If this distinction is critical, test both settings in the browsers.
Line Height	Defines the height of a single line of text. If you are more used to working with print projects, this is comparable to line spacing or leading. Normal line height is calculated based on type size; lines will be approximately 20% larger than the type size. Absolute line height can be assigned based on any of the measurement systems covered in the following sidebar.
Weight	Sets the boldness of the font. The number values are absolute settings, whereas the bolder and lighter are relative to the default size. (Boldness is not always rendered the same way across browsers; always preview in several different browsers if you choose any setting here other than `normal` or `bold`.)
Variant	Normal or small capital letters. Determines whether lowercase letters will be substituted with small capital letters.
Case	Sets the font to all uppercase, all lowercase, or all capitalize. Displays text as all uppercase, all lowercase, or capitalize every word.
Color	Sets the color of the font.
Decoration	Sets options for lines on the text. Use the None option for removing the underline from hyperlinks.

Dreamweaver MX now renders most CSS elements in the Design window. It is still a good idea to preview the page in multiple browsers to make sure that your pages will actually render correctly.

Defining Font Sizes

There are many different ways to define font sizes. They are generally grouped into two groups: Absolute and relative lengths. They each have their pros and cons. The sizes are:

Absolute

Absolute sizes imply that they are set in size, no matter where they are used. One centimeter is the same the world around, except on the computer screen.

- **Points (pt)**. Taken from the print industry, a point is 1/72 of an inch.
- **Picas (pc)**. A pica is another term from the typography world. A pica is 12 points. It is simply a bigger unit, like 12 inches (points) equals a foot (pica).
- **Centimeter (cm)**. A standard metric length. 2.54 cm equals 1 inch.
- **Millimeter (mm)**. A millimeter is 1/100 of a centimeter.
- **Inch**. Another standard length, equal to .394 of an centimeter. Not used too often in the web world, but another option nonetheless.

Relative

Relative lengths are bigger or smaller than some defined length. Percentage is a relative measure: Y is 10% bigger than X. X can be any size and Y will always be 10% bigger.

- **Pixels (px)**. The standard way of defining sizes on computers. Most elements on the web page are defined in pixels. A pixel is one small block of monitor space, the physical building blocks of your screen. A pixel is *defined* as a fraction of an inch on the screen. The difficulty in using pixels is that Macs and PCs have chosen different fractions for determining size. And to confuse the issue even more, the CSS spec pegs the 'reference pixel' at about 90 pixels per inch, which sadly neither operating system uses. But pixels remain the most used measuring entity around.
- **Percentage (%)**. A universal concept, a percentage value is X% bigger than a standard value. The question for development is: Bigger compared to what? It will use the default setting of the parent tag as the baseline size. For instance, if the default size of a font is 10 units, setting the font to 120% will make the font show at 12 units. Setting the percent value to 20% will show it at 2 units. Another example is tables. Set a table to be 80 percent wide and it will show as 80% of the window, because the body tag is the parent element. Set a table cell to 80% and it will take up 80% of the table, because the table tag is the parent element.
- **em**. An em is an obscure but useful value. It is defined as equal to the point size for a given font element. If a font is set as 12 pixels, then 1 em equals 12 pixels. This way, you can set a custom class to be 2em of a certain setting, say the above font. If you apply this class to a piece of text, it will be 2em big, or 24 pixels.
- **ex**. Ex is a relative setting that is based on the height of a lowercase 'x' in the chosen font. While this can be of great help when using a certain font, keep in mind that different fonts have different relative 'x' sizes. One fonts 'x' can be half the size of a capital letter and another font's 'x' can be 60-70%. This will make 'ex' render differently between fonts.

Background

The *Background category* controls how the background is rendered. Note that with CSS, you can control the background of every block element. This means that every paragraph, layer, table, or other discrete element can have its own background style. Keep this in mind as you apply background styles. Make sure that you are applying it to the correct tag. For instance, if you want to apply a background to the whole page, you must apply the style to the <body> tag.

Table 13.2 lists the Background Category options you see in Figure 13.8.

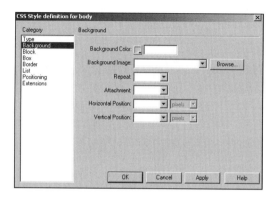

Figure 13.8   The Background Category options.

Table 13.2   Background Category Options

Option	Description
Background Color	Sets the background color of the selected element.
Background Image	This is the preferred way to set a background image because you get additional controls over it. Browse to choose the image.
Repeat	Controls whether the image repeats in the background. You can repeat, not repeat, and repeat horizontally or vertically.
Attachment	Sets whether the background image will scroll with the page or remain static in the background and allow the page to scroll over it.
Horizontal Position	Enables you to control whether the image is left, right, or centered. You also can specify a specific value for the position.
Vertical Position	Allows the same control as the horizontal position in the vertical axis.

In the Dreamweaver window, the image set here might show up in the upper-left corner of the Design window. Preview in Browser for a correct look at the page. There are browser limitations with some background images settings, especially with Netscape 4. As always, test in multiple browsers for compatibility.

Block

Block elements are discrete pieces of HTML. For instance, a paragraph is a block level element. For CSS reasoning, it is considered a block of code and when applying a custom class to a paragraph, it will only affect the code between the opening and closing paragraph tags. This way, each paragraph is treated as a separate element. Most block elements have an opening and closing tag. This is distinct from *inline elements,* which can be placed anywhere within a block element. An image is a good example of an in inline element. An image does not have a closing tag.

The block category controls how the element is presented on the page. Table 13.3 lists the Block Category options you see in Figure 13.9.

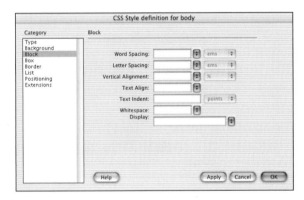

Figure 13.9   The Block Category options.

Table 13.3   Block Category Options

Option	Description
Word spacing	Enables you to define the amount of space between each word.
Letter spacing	Enables you to define the space between each letter.
Vertical Alignment	Enables you to control the vertical aspect of word spacing. You can use this to specify subscripts and superscripts.
Text Align	Enables you to set the justification settings: Left, Right Center, or Justify. Check in the browser when using Justify as browser support is inconsistent.
Text Indent	Enables you to choose an indentation value from the edge of the page.
Whitespace	'Normal' collapses multiple spaces into onespace.
	'Pre' leaves multiple spaces.
	'Nowrap' does not permit line wrapping without a break tag.
Display	Controls fundamental aspects of the block element. You can controls whether the element displays or not. You can also change aspects of the behavior of the tag itself. Test there settings as there is limited browser support.

Box

Use Box options to control element placement and spacing on the page. Every block level element, such as a paragraph, is considered an element and can be arranged using the Box settings. Note that many of these settings will show up only in the browser. Preview frequently to check your page. Table 13.4 lists the Box Category options you see in Figure 13.10.

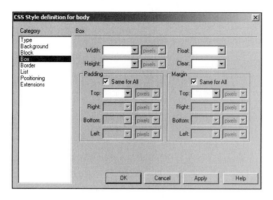

Figure 13.10   The Box Category options.

Table 13.4   Box Category Options

Option	Description
Width and Height	Sets the width and height of the element.
Float	Float is used to separate an element from the rest of the page. Other elements will flow and wrap around this element as if it were something like an image. Only with an image will this setting show up in Design view.
Clear	Clear is used to define an area that does not allow elements to overlap. A layer that appears on a side set to clear will be moved below the clear area. This will keep block level elements from occupying the same horizontal space.
Padding	Used to set the space between the contents and the border (or the margin if a border is not set). Similar to the Cell Padding setting in a table.
Margin	Defines the amount of space between the element border and the other elements.

New to Dreamweaver MX is the Same for All check box. You can now set one value and check that box for consistent values. Uncheck the box for customizing the individual values.

Border

Border options are used to set a border around the chosen element. It is this border from which the Box padding and margin are referenced. Although this is similar to a table border, you have a lot more control and choice in how it displays. Table 13.5 lists the Border Category options you see in Figure 13.11.

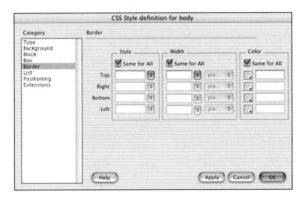

Figure 13.11   The Border Category options.

Table 13.5   Border Category Options

Option	Description
Style	Enables you to set a style of border. You can choose from Dotted, Dashed, Solid, Double, Groove, Ridge, Inset, and Outset. Browser support for these differs. Use the Same for All check box for quickly setting a consistent border. Uncheck the box to set each side individually.
Width	Set the width value for the border.
Color	Set the color for the borders.

List

This List category provides more options when making a numbered or bulleted list. You can even use a custom graphic as the bullet. Table 13.6 lists the List Category options you see in Figure 13.12.

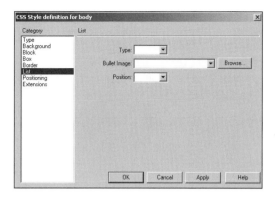

Figure 13.12   The List Category options.

Table 13.6   List Category Options

Option	Description
Type	Choose the type of bullet: Disc, Circle, Square, Decimal, Lowercase Roman Numerals, Uppercase Roman Numerals, Upper- and Lower-case Letters.
Bullet Image	You can create any kind of custom image and use that as your bullet. Press the Browse button to link the image.
Position	Use Outside to wrap an item to an indent and use Inside to wrap the item to the margin.

Positioning

This is the main interface for controlling where the page elements will appear on your page. While CSS positioning can be applied to most block level elements, they are generally used with Layers. Layers are actually `<div>` tags that contain an inline style with absolute positioning. Draw a layer on a page and check out the code created for it. Dreamweaver MX now displays positions in the Design window. For browser support issues, again, always preview in multiple browsers to confirm support.

There are a few important settings here for control over your page. Table 13.7 lists the Positioning Category options you see in Figure 13.13.

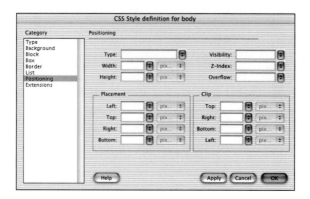

Figure 13.13   The Positioning Category options.

Table 13.7   Positioning Category Options

Option	Description
Type	Controls what kind of positioning you are using:
	Absolute. Positions the block element relative to the upper-left corner of the page.
	Relative. Position is determined relative to the spot in the document where the positioning style appears in the document.
	Static. Puts the block element in the same location in which it appears in the document.
Visibility	Controls the initial visibility of the element.
	Inherit. Gives the element the same visibility setting as the parent tag. Defaults to visible.
	Visible. Makes the element visible when loaded.
	Hidden. Makes the element invisible when the page is loaded.
Width	Defines the width of the block element.
Height	Defines the height of the block element.
Z Index	Determines the stacking order of the elements. Lower number Z indexes will appear below higher numbered elements. Used for controlling visibility. This also can be set in the Layers panel.
Overflow	This is used when the content of a layer is larger than the layer size. Setting the Overflow parameter determines what happens to that extra material
	Visible. Allows all the content of the layer to be shown simultaneously, no matter what the size setting.
	Hidden. Strictly enforces the layer's size and cuts off any content that overflows this layer size.
	Scrollbars. Adds scrollbars to the layer whether it needs them or not. Watch for browser support on this if you are displaying important content.
	Auto. Will create scrollbars only when needed.

Option	Description
Placement	Enables you to specify where the layer will display. The Top and Left settings will be dependent on the Type setting you have chosen. Right and Bottom can give you a greater level of control for layout.
Clip	Used to specify the part of the layer that is visible. This is not a required setting. It is used only if you want to hide a part of the layer without Overflow controls. Used in combination with JavaScript to create interesting effects.

Extensions

Extensions options are used for special considerations and customization. Extensions are CSS Level 2 options. CSS Level 2 is the next specification of CSS. It has advanced features that go well beyond CSS Level 1, the specification of which we have been mostly speaking. Be careful, however, because this does not yet have full browser support. Table 13.8 lists the Extensions Category options you see in Figure 13.14.

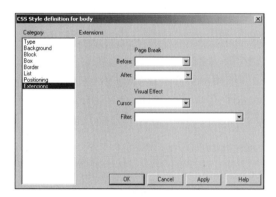

Figure 13.14   The Extensions Category options.

Table 13.8   Extensions Category Options

Option	Description
Page Breaks	Used for setting page breaks when setting up the page for printing. Use this setting for determining whether the page break comes before or after this element.
Visual Effect	Enables you to change the look of the cursor when it is over the element with this setting. Test this setting because there is limited browser support.
	Filter can enable you to set special effects to images on the page. As of this writing, they only work in IE 4.0 and above. Check out filter.htm in the **chapter_13** folder for some examples of this feature.

You can use these style settings in combination to exactly lay out your page and have complete control over the look and feel of your page. A consistent use of CSS will help you separate content from style.

Interview: Nick Bradbury

Business Name: Bradbury Software, LLC.

URL: `http://www.bradsoft.com`

How has working in Dreamweaver MX made your life easier?

I tend to work almost entirely in code view and keep everything else hidden, so the code editing improvements in DW MX have been a big hit with me. I can stay in Dreamweaver for both Code and Design views now, which makes my job simpler.

Code editing in previous versions was almost primitive, but the changes in DW MX put it on par with dedicated HTML text editors.

You do a lot of CSS work. Talk about some of the improvements for CSS in DW MX.

Well, I'm obviously thrilled to see the integration with TopStyle. Being able to use TopStyle to edit style rules and style sheets from within Dreamweaver makes it so easy to get the best of both worlds. I can rely on Dreamweaver's design tools and then quickly switch to TopStyle for more powerful CSS editing and validation.

What's your favorite new feature(s) in DW MX?

I'd have to say it's a tie between the code editing improvements and the new dockable user interface. I was never comfortable with the floating palettes found in previous releases, but the UI in DW MX feels right to me.

Do you have any recommendations for new DW MX users/Web site builders?

I always recommend designing with an eye for maintenance, which goes hand-in-hand with using CSS. Style sheets offer tremendous maintenance benefits in that they enable you to store formatting in a centralized location. If you decide to change the look of your site, you can simply change a single style sheet instead of hundreds of HTML documents.

For a nice illustration of this, stop by the TopStyle home page at `http://www.bradsoft.com/topstyle/`. We enable you to change the style sheet used by our entire site, which really shows off how separating your site's style from its content makes it easy to change your site's appearance.

But make sure to stick to the basics when it comes to CSS. It might be fun to experiment with everything CSS has to offer, but spotty browser support means that a site which looks wonderful if one browser might look like a ransom note in another.

Used correctly, CSS can save you a lot of work; used incorrectly, and you'll have a lot of maintenance problems down the road. So, if using CSS doesn't make your job simpler, then you need to simplify how you're using CSS.

Working with Redefined HTML Tags

Redefined HTML tags are used when you want every instance of a certain element to have identical properties. For instance, you can set every paragraph to automatically have blue text.

Redefined HTML tags can be internal or external, just as any other style. Linking the style sheet with a page will automatically convert the redefined tags.

Also because the style is written in the head or externally, and no class tag appears in the page, you can easily overwrite a particular instance of the tag by applying a custom class.

Keep in mind that according to the cascading principle, an internally redefined tag (one defined on the page) will take precedence over a redefinition on an external style.

Note

Because the style is written on the page itself, and because it is applied to every instance of the tag, these redefined styles do not show up in the Style Applier view of the CSS Styles panel. If you have a redefined tag on the page, double-click on the tag in the Style Editor view of the CSS Styles panel and the Style Definition dialog box will open.

Exercise 13.1   Redefining an HTML Tag in an Internal Style Sheet

This exercise demonstrates how a redefined HTML tag will be applied to every instance of that tag.

Before you start, copy the **chapter_13** folder on the CD to your hard drive. Define a site called Chapter 13, with this folder as the local root folder.

1. Open **custom_tag.htm** in the **chapter_13** folder. This page contains a section of the table that you imported in Chapter 3, "Creating and Working with Documents."

2. Open the CSS Styles panel (Window > CSS Styles).

3. Click the New Style button.

4. In the New Style dialog box, choose the following:
   - Redefine HTML Tag
   - For Tag, choose Table
   - Define In: This Document Only

5. Click OK.

6. In the Style Definition for Table, for Type, choose the following settings:
   - Font, Courier or any other font if you don't have that one
   - Size, 16 pixels
   - Color, Red

   For Background, choose the following:
   - Background Color, type in **#FFCC99**

   For Block, choose 5 pixels for Letter Spacing.

7. Click OK to close the Settings dialog box and then Done to close the Edit Style Sheet dialog box.

   Your table should now reflect the settings that you just made. It should have red letters on a gold/yellow background and the letter spacing should be set.

8. Preview in Browser (F12) to make sure that the design view and the browser match.

9. Now insert another table (Ctrl+Alt+T). Choose the default settings and click OK. Notice that the table already has the background color.

10. Type in a few letters and notice that they are set to Red.

This goes to show how redefining an HTML tag will automatically apply it to all instances of that tag on the page. Use custom classes to further customize individual instances of a redefined tag; see Figure 13.15 for a representation of the finished exercise.

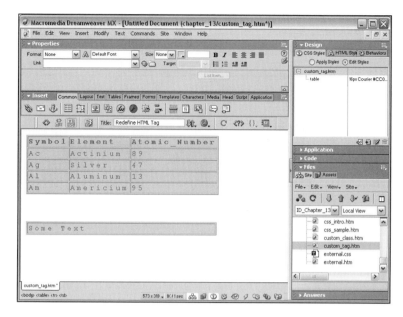

Figure 13.15   Representation of the finished exercise.

Working with Custom Classes

Custom classes are the most common way of applying a style to a page. With a custom class, you define the characteristics of the block element (the paragraph or the table) and then apply the style to that block element.

Using custom classes, you can be selective with the elements that you want to be styled, as opposed to redefining an HTML tag, which will change all instances.

To create a custom class, click the New Style button in the CSS Styles panel. For settings, choose Make Custom Style (class). Choose This Document Only for the Define In field. For Name, give it a descriptive name. Click OK to go to the Style Definition box. Set the definition parameters you wish. You can set the color and style of the font, give it a background color in the Background tag and set the letter spacing in the Block tab. Click OK when done. The custom class will now show in the Apply Styles panel.

There are five ways to apply this custom class:

- Highlight some text on your page and click on the Property inspector's, Toggle CSS/HTML Mode button (see Figures 13.16 and 13.17). Select the class name from the dropdown to the right of the button. The style will automatically be applied to that text wrapped by a <span> tag.

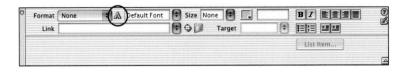

Figure 13.16   The Property inspector (HTML mode).

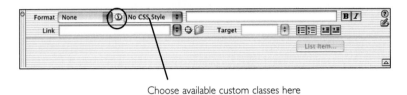

Choose available custom classes here

Figure 13.17   The Property inspector (CSS mode).

- Highlight some text on your page, and using the tag selector, select the rightmost tag. Right-click (Cmd-click) the tag, navigate to Set Class from the menu that appears, and click the class name (see Figure 13.18). The style will automatically be applied to that text parent tag. Note that this does not apply a <span> tag and affects whatever is in the selected tag.

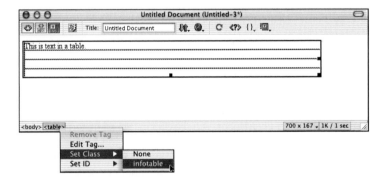

Figure 13.18   The tag selector.

- Highlight some text on your page and click the class name in the Apply Styles window (see Figure 13.19). The style will automatically be applied to that text wrapped by a <span> tag.

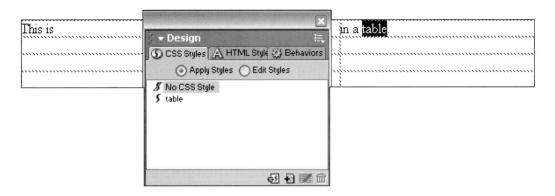

Figure 13.19   The CSS Styles Panel > Apply Style interface.

- Highlight some text on your page, right-click (Cmd-click) and choose CSS
  Styles, then select your desired style to apply (see Figure 13.20). The style will
  automatically be applied to that text wrapped by a <span> tag.

Figure 13.20   Contextual CSS Styles menu.

- Highlight some text on your page and choose Text > CSS Styles, then select your desired class to apply (see Figure 13.21). The style will automatically be applied to that text wrapped by a <span> tag.

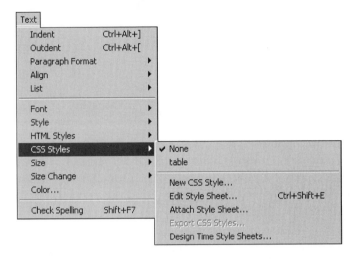

Figure 13.21   The Text > CSS Styles menu item.

Applying Custom Classes to Page Elements

After you have defined the custom styles in the Edit Styles panel, switch to the Apply Styles view. You will see a list of available custom classes that you have created.

To apply the class style to an element, select the element or text. Then click on the name of the style in the CSS Styles Panel > Apply Styles (see Figure 13.4). It will be applied automatically. Another way of applying a class is from the Property inspector. Next to the Font field in the Property inspector, is the letter 'A'. Click on that 'A' and it will switch to the CSS Styles icon. You will now have a drop-down list of available styles and a description of the selected style. (See Figures 13.16 and 13.17.)

Highlight the element and choose the class from the dropdown. It will be applied instantly. Yet another way to access the classes if from the right-click menu (see Figure 13.20). Highlight the element and right-click (Ctrl-click). From the contextual menu, choose CSS Styles, and the custom classes list will appear. Choose the style and click to apply.

Removing Styles from Page Elements

To remove a custom class from a page element, highlight the element and then in the Apply Class drop-down list, choose None. This will remove the `Class` attribute from the tag.

Exercise 13.2   Creating a Custom Class in an External Style Sheet

In this exercise, you develop a custom class and then apply to it elements of the page. This will demonstrate the difference between that and a redefined HTML tag.

If you haven't done so yet, copy the **chapter_13** folder on the CD to your hard drive. Define a site called Chapter 13, with this folder as the local root folder.

1. Open **custom_class.htm**.

2. Open the CSS Styles panel and click the New CSS Style button.

3. For Type, choose Make Custom Style. For Name, enter **tablestyle**.

4. For Define In, choose New Style Sheet File. Click OK. Because you chose to make a new style sheet file, you will be asked to save the style in a new CSS file (sheet).

This will create an external CSS style file and on it will be the table style. Remember that a CSS file can have many styles defined within it.

5. In the Save Style Sheet File As dialog box, call it **tablestyle.css** and save it in the same folder as the **custom_class.htm** file.

6. The Style Definition dialog will display. In this box, make the following settings:

Type:

- Font, Courier or anything else if you don't have that font
- Size, 18 pixels
- Weight, Bolder
- Color, **#6633cc**
- Decoration, None

Background:

- Background Color, **#CC9933** (you can just type it in the field)

Block:

- Word Spacing, 5 pixels
- Text Align, Center

Border:

- Width, Top, 4 (all in pixels)
- Width, Right, 3
- Width, Bottom, 3
- Width, Left, 3

- Style, Groove, same for all
- Colors, Top and Bottom, #CC0000; Right and Left, **#CCCC66**

Positioning:

- Type, Absolute
- Placement, Left, 300; Top, 300

Extensions:

- Cursor, Crosshair

7. Click OK to set the style. Granted, this will not be pretty, but it will give you an idea of how to use CSS to lay out your page.

8. Highlight the table in the page. You can use the tag selector in the lower-left corner of the program to select the table tag. This will highlight the entire table.

9. With the table selected, click the table style in the Style Applier view of the CSS Styles panel. The table should change color and position in the Design window. Preview in Browser to see the page in the browser.

10. Insert another table onto the page (Insert > Table). Use the default settings.

It should appear as a normal table. This is because there is no style attached to it. If you are not in Code or Code and Design view, switch to it. Notice that in the code for the first table, there is a `class="table"` attribute in the table tag. This is the code that calls the style from the external style referenced in the `<link>` tag in the head of the page. Until that attribute is there, no style is applied. Once again, this highlights the difference between a custom class and a redefined HTML tag. In the example for redefined tags, the style was instantly applied to the table when inserted on the page. See Figure 13.22.

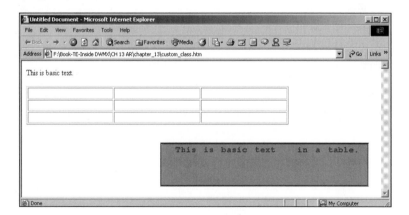

Figure 13.22   Representation of Exercise 2 completed.

Because custom classes can be used for positioning, you might end up with many custom classes. It is vital that you name them with clarity for you and other developers. You also can start to see the benefits of different types of styles and different ways of applying them. Having an understanding of how each works will enable you to use them with maximum efficiency and flexibility.

There is also a way to add a custom class to a small piece of text rather than to the entire element. If you highlight a piece of text and then apply a custom class, you will see a <span> tag that wraps the selected text. A <span> tag is used for just this reason: applying a custom class to a subset of the element. Although span tags can be good for making small tweaks to your page, you should be careful to not use too many of them. The whole idea of CSS is to have the styles globally applied. Having a large set of <span> tags to define your styles will defeat the idea of CSS. All those <span> tags will add to your file size. Use spans only when needed. Also, there is better browser support if you apply your classes to block level elements. Take advantage of the rules you have available to you.

CSS Selectors

There is one more way to make and use styles in Dreamweaver: the CSS selector.

In Dreamweaver, CSS selectors refer to two things: pseudo-classes or pseudo-elements and contextual selectors.

Pseudo-Classes

Pseudo-classes are CSS elements dependent on a certain condition to be active. Certain conditions are not dependent on the HTML code. The most popular pseudo-class has to do with links.

A link is always in an anchor tag (<a>). Although this never changes in the actual code, in reality, there are different states of linked: links that have been visited and links that have not been visited, links that the mouse is over (Hover) and links that are active.

Although the code for these is the same, you know that they have different display properties depending on whether the link in question has already been visited. Blue links have not been visited and purple links have already been visited. Therefore, this means that hyperlinks have at least two different states that are independent of the actual code. So, a pseudo-class refers to a style dependent on an external condition. CSS recognizes this and gives you a way to customize these states.

For links, four pseudo-classes apply (order is very important!):

- **Link**. The Link pseudo-class is the default color/settings of the link.
- **Visited**. The Visited pseudo-class replaces the default purple color/settings for links that have been visited already.
- **Hover**. The Hover pseudo-class is activated when you are mousing over the link. This is a very common way to indicate an active link, especially when the link is not underlined. You also can set the font size to be bigger or smaller for a better indicator.
- **Active**. The Active pseudo-class is activated when you are actually clicking the link (`onMouseDown`).

Using these pseudo-classes, you can set your links to have a custom style, including color and size. In any of these pseudo-classes, you can set the link to not be underlined, set font type, sizes, or any other CSS parameter.

Contextual Selectors

Contextual selectors are styles applied only when a defined set of conditions are met, usually a specific combination of tags. Using these rules, you can, for instance, apply a specific style to text but only if that text is bold and within a table. Text outside of the table will not be affected by the style.

The rule for the preceding example would look like this:

```
TD B {color: #6600CC}
```

This says that any text within a TD tag that is also coded within a B (bold) tag will display as #6600CC (a purple).

To create a contextual selector, click the New Style button. Choose Use CSS Selector and This Document Only. For the Selector field, type in the set of tags that will define the selector. To use the above example, type **TD B** and then click the OK button. Set a style for the selector. In this case, it will be applied to any bold text within a table cell. Click OK when done.

To use the selector, add a table to a the page and then add some text to a cell. Select the text and make it boldface (you can apply Bold in the Property inspector). The style will instantly be applied to the text accordingly.

Exercise 13.3   Adding Contextual Styles to a Linked External Style Sheet

In this exercise, you link an existing style sheet to a page. To this linked sheet, we will add a CSS Selector for use on the page.

If you haven't done so yet, copy the **chapter_13** folder on the CD to your hard drive. Define a site called Chapter 13, with this folder as the local root folder.

1. Open the **external.htm** file from the **chapter_13** folder on the companion CD.

2. Open the CSS Styles panel (Window > CSS Styles).

3. Click the Attach Style Sheet button.

4. Choose the **external.css** file from the **chapter_13** folder and click OK.

   You should now see the initial changes that the style sheet makes. It has a selector for the <h2> tag. It should now have a gray background and be aligned to the right side of the page.

   The block quote text in the table should have an olive background and a different font and size.

   The block quote text has a contextual style that applies to block quotes that are within a table cell.

5. Highlight the table. You can click the border or click inside the table and then choose table from the tag selector in the Design window's lower-left corner.

6. Within the CSS Style panel's Style Editor view, use the Apply Style drop-down menu, choose tablestyle. This should now make the background gray. Preview in Browser to see changes made to the border.

7. Select the table again.

8. In the CSS Styles panel, double-click the table.positioning class. This will apply the style to the highlighted table. The table should move so that it is halfway across the page. (I have set this style to put the table at 50 percent of the screen from the left side of the page. I also have used the CSS to change the table width from pixels to 50 percent of the page. This setting will keep the right border at a constant distance from the right side of the page.)

9. Preview in Browser. Resize the window and notice how the table size reacts. Notice that it will change size and horizontal position as you resize the Browser window. The table, on the other hand, will not change its vertical position. The distance from the top of the window has been set as a pixel value, so it will remain constant.

10. In order to add another CSS Selector, click the New CSS Style button in the CSS Styles panel.

11. Choose Use CSS Selector and for Define In:, choose external.css.

12. We are going to apply a selector to the paragraph that is within a table tag. In the Selector field, type **TD P** and then click OK. Selectors are defined as the tag in the order in which they appear in the code, separated by a space.

13. Under Type, for Font choose Verdana, Size 14. Set the Style to italic and the color to blue. (the vertical strip of color on the left of the color panel is the pure colors). Click the Apply button. The text in the table should change.

In the Block tab, set the Letter spacing to 5 pixels. Click the Apply button again and the letters should space out. Click OK to close the style.

14. Go to the table and type in more text. The style will automatically be applied to the text as you type. Type in some text outside of the table and it will not be affected by the style. (If you change the text outside of the table to a H2 tag, what happens and why?)

One other thing to notice when you apply the positioning style is that the gray background goes away. This is because tablestyle and positioning are both custom classes applied to the table tag. When you apply one to the table, the other is taken off. If you want to have all the properties on the table, add all the parameters to one custom class. See Figure 13.23.

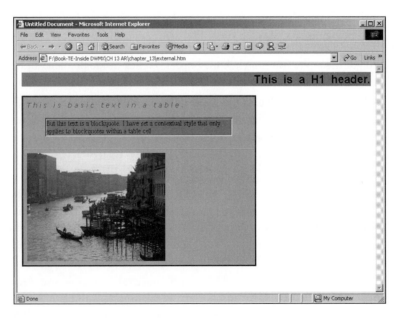

Figure 13.23   Representation of Exercise 3 completed.

Combining Style Sheets

Thanks to the properties of inheritance and cascading, you can have external sheets on one page or have an external page and an internal style on the same page. Remember that the "cascading" in CSS means that styles can be additive and the code closest to the actual element trumps higher-level style rules. Understanding the benefits and drawbacks of combining sheets will enable you to take full advantage of CSS.

External style sheets are very useful because they enable you to specify many parameters for your site in a central location, and therefore these style parameters are easily update-able. You can change the look of thousands of pages by changing one line in the style sheet. This kind of power goes both ways. You can easily change every <h2> tag in your site by updating the selector on the external style sheet. If you have a certain section where you need the <h2> tags to be different from all the rest, however, this external style will not help you. You can use the cascading principle to your advantage by combining your external style with an internal style for those specific pages. Because the internal style is closer to the actual H2 element, the external style sheet, the internal rules will be used and your section will look correct.

Of course, the drawback to this is that if your special section needs to be updated, you need to change the internal style on every page. Although Find and Replace is an option in such a case, this shows one of the difficulties of internal styles.

If you already have an externally linked style sheet, to combine these with an internal style, merely create a new style in the New CSS Style dialog box. Then choose This Document Only. Dreamweaver will place the style in the head.

You also can use multiple external style sheets on one page. When doing this, it is vital that sheets and styles have good names so that it is clear to everyone which style does what.

You might have one sheet that handles the look of the page: text colors, background images, border styles, and so on.

Your other style sheet can handle positioning elements: right- and left-justifying, place-ment and float of page elements, and other nonstyle considerations. In this way, not only is content separate from form, but now style is separate from placement. If you are deal-ing with large sites, this might be a good routine for compartmentalizing your develop-ment and making your development scheme more accessible to other developers.

What happens, however, when you have two styles that affect the same element? It depends.

It has to do with specificity and inheritance. If you have two external style sheets and both specify only the background color of an <h2> tag, which one wins? In this case, two <link> tags in the head specify the external style sheet. The style sheet listed lower in the code will win. This is because HTML pages are rendered from the top down. The browser will hit the first style sheet link and see that it needs to color it red. It does so and then continues. In the next line, it reads the CSS link and notices it needs to color the <h2> tag blue and it does so. Because cascading says that the style closest to the element wins, two styles that are equal are decided upon merely by ordering in the code.

Inheritance makes this a little more complicated. Suppose in the preceding example that the style that colors the <h2> tag red is above the blue rule. This means that the H2 will be blue. If the red H2 style specifies a font face for the <h2> tag, however, this will be incorporated on the page because it is more specific than the blue rule. In this case, therefore, you will have an <h2> tag with the chosen font and a blue background.

This exact scenario is demonstrated in **cascade_test.htm** in the **chapter_13** folder.

Exercise 13.4   Demonstrating Cascading and Inheritance

This exercise demonstrates the idea of cascading and inheritance and uses multiple external style sheets to do so.

If you haven't done so yet, copy the **chapter_13** folder on the CD to your hard drive. Define a site called Chapter 13, with this folder as the local root folder.

1. Open the **cascade_test.htm** file.
2. Go to Code and Design view (View > Code and Design).
3. Open the CSS Styles panel (Window > CSS Styles).
4. Notice in the CSS Styles panel that two external style sheets are listed: **blue.css** and **red.css**. Notice that they both have H2 selectors. **blue.css** defines only the background as blue. **red.css** defines the background as red and defines the font as Comic San Serif.

   In the code, **red.css** is listed after **blue.css**. As described earlier, this means that the red style will trump the blue style. In the Design window, you will see the Comic font on a red background.
5. In Code view, highlight the <link> line that contains the blue style.
6. Click and drag that line so that it is placed below the red <link> line.
7. Click back in the Design window to refresh the window.

   You should now see the blue background, but the Comic font stays the same.
8. In the Style Editor view of the CSS Styles panel, right-click (Ctrl-click) the H2 selector in the **blue.css** file and from the contextual menu choose Edit.

9. Go to the Block section and for Text Align choose Right. Click OK to save the new setting.

    The H2 text should jump to the right.

    You can deduce from inheritance that if you were to move the blue style link so that it was again above the red link, the H2 would be red with the Comic font; but because the alignment specified in the blue style is more specific, the text will be on the right side.

10. In the Code window, highlight the blue line and click and drag it so that it is above the red style link. You should now see right-aligned text with a red background.

Removing Style Sheets

Removing a style sheet from a page or an element is quite simple. Dreamweaver MX makes it even easier. The redesigned CSS Styles panel now shows all the styles being used. With items such as redefined HTML tags or pseudo-classes—or in other words, those style elements applied to the whole page—you need to delete the style definition from the page or the external style sheet. You can highlight the style in the CSS Styles panel and right-click (Ctrl-click) and from the contextual menu choose Delete or you can press the Delete Style button in the lower-right corner of the CSS Styles panel.

To remove a custom class from a page element, highlight the element and then in the Apply Class drop-down list, choose None. This will remove the `class` attribute from the tag.

Summary

CSS is an important aspect of web design and it will become only more important in the future. This chapter acquainted you with CSS and the basics of its structure, use, and possibilities. This chapter discussed the theory of separating content from style, cascading and inheritance, and ways to link to styles. Experiment with CSS, using the styles provided or creating styles of your own. Try using all the different parameters available to you, and then check them in both browsers to get an idea how they react.

Knowing CSS will go a long way to increasing your web design ability and creativity.

Chapter 14

Using Layers for Page Layout

What is a *layer*? If you search an HTML reference, you'll find that there is a Netscape-specific tag called <layer>, but this is not what is meant by the term in Dreamweaver or its current usage. This book uses *layer* as it is now commonly used, to refer to a specific page building block produced by Dreamweaver. A layer is a `<div>` (or occasionally a `<span>`) element, positioned with inline CSS styles.

Topics discussed in this chapter include layer basics (uses, cautions, and how they're coded), working with layers in Dreamweaver, setting layer properties, setting layer preferences, and strategies and tips for making layers work well. Last, we'll look at true *CSS Positioning*, the cutting-edge technique that is a distant relative of the layer.

Layers: The Basics

On one level, Dreamweaver layers are an attempt to give web designers the kind of control over the positioning of elements on a page as is available in print media. To some extent, layers do provide that kind of functionality. To those new to web design, layers often appear to be the web's answer to the concept of text boxes in programs such as Microsoft Publisher. A *text box* is a rectangular container that can be placed anywhere on the page to position elements exactly as desired. For reasons we'll discuss later, however, it's best not to use layers in this way.

But layers do have a lot of great uses. For example, layers are the best choice for achieving effects such as:

- Swapping images that have different dimensions
- Displaying pop-up text messages
- Moving elements around on the screen
- Building drop-down or fly-out menus
- Incorporating DHTML visual effects into your sites

If the design you have in mind can be accomplished using tables or frames, however, that is usually a better choice for cross-browser compatibility. For more about the different ways of laying out a page with Dreamweaver, see Chapter 8, "Design Issues."

Layers and CSS-P

Layers are defined and positioned with CSS, and in this respect are related to the technique known as *CSS positioning* (CSS-P). In true CSS-P, however, `<div>`s and other elements are positioned with external, linked style sheets, achieving the kind of separation of structure and presentation that is part of the essential concept for HTML. (See Chapter 4, "Working with Text," for more on this concept.) With true CSS Positioning, the idea that inspired the web begins to come into bloom. Dreamweaver layers, with their inline CSS declarations, make use of CSS but don't separate structure and presentation, and so miss the mark on one of the main purposes of CSS-P.

CSS-P is discussed later in this chapter. Although using standard Dreamweaver layers is *not* the same as using CSS-P, they *can* be an extremely powerful and useful tool—especially for animating web pages with scripting. Chapters 17, "Controlling Layers with JavaScript," and Chapter 18, "Animating Layers," handle this in detail; here you'll learn the basics of laying out page elements with layers.

You Are Now Free to Move About the Page: The Benefits of Layers

Layers enable you to create effects that are just not possible without them. Layers can be stacked one on top of another and can be positioned anywhere on the page. You can hide some layers while showing others, move a layer across the screen with a timeline, or allow images to appear and then fade. The possibilities are almost limitless, and with Dreamweaver you can achieve these effects from within its point-and-click interface.

When Worlds Collide: The Risks of Using Layers

The primary danger in using layers is the lack of browser support. Only IE 4.0 and later browsers display layers correctly. In Netscape 4 and other older browsers, a page dependent on layers might display very poorly, with elements not placed even approximately where you intended. Further, even in newer browsers, support for layers isn't consistent.

A document containing layers is only as sturdy as the browser from which it is viewed; if that browser doesn't completely understand or support the code used to create layers, much could go wrong.

It's important to decide from the outset whether the use of layers is called for in a given situation. As you proceed through this chapter, you'll come across some specific strategies and tips to help you avoid problems with layer-based pages.

How Layers Are Coded

When you insert a layer into a page, Dreamweaver MX writes HTML code for you using one of two tags: `<div>` or `<span>`. `<div>` is a block-level element, and `<span>` an inline element

By default, Dreamweaver uses the `<div>` tag to create layers; this default can be changed in your Dreamweaver preferences, as discussed later in the "Setting Layer Preferences" section.

The `<div>` tag is given several attributes that describe its position, dimensions, stacking order, and visibility.

HTML code for a single layer looks something like this:

```
<div ID="Layer1" STYLE="position:absolute; left:150px; top:80px;
width:350px; height:165px; z-index:1"></div>
```

HTML code for a layer nested within a layer looks something like the following:

```
<div ID="Layer1" STYLE="position:absolute; left:150px; top:80px;
width:350px; height:165px; z-index:1">
    <div ID="Layer2" STYLE="position:absolute; left:80px; top:50px;
width:195px; height:65px; z-index:1"></div>
    </div>
```

If you are at all familiar with CSS, you might recognize the attributes of the `<div>` tags in the preceding examples as inline CSS code.

Working with Layers in Dreamweaver

Dreamweaver makes working with layers easy, at least in the sense that its point-and-click tools enable you to add layers to your pages and set properties for them without any knowledge of the underlying code. However, be careful that this ease of use doesn't lull you into a false sense of security; the fact that Dreamweaver enables you to add an element on a page that generates code doesn't mean that this code will work in every browser and every situation. In working with layers, as with any and all web design work, it is necessary to test your pages early and often in a number of different browsers, at least in the browsers that will be used by your target audience.

Creating Layers

Dreamweaver gives you several options for creating layers. Your main choice is one of work style—would you rather draw your layers, like you would in a graphics or page layout program? Or would you rather insert your layers ready-made, without drawing?

Drawing Layers

To draw a layer, follow these steps:

1. In the Common tab of the Insert bar, click the Draw Layer button (see Figure 14.1). The cursor will turn into a crosshair, ready for drawing.

2. In the Document window, click-and-drag to draw the layer the size you choose.

3. As soon as you release the mouse button, the cursor will return to normal and you're out of the Draw Layer tool.

Figure 14.1   The Draw Layer object in the Insert bar.

Note

You must be in Standard view, not Layout view, to insert layers.

To draw multiple layers one after another, do this:

1. Click the Draw Layer button.

2. Press and hold the Ctrl key (Windows) or Cmd key (Mac).

3. Draw your first layer. When you release the mouse button, the cursor remains in its crosshair persona, and the Draw Layer tool remains active.

4. When you're finished drawing layers, release the Ctrl/Cmd key and the cursor returns to normal.

Inserting Layers

If you prefer not to draw, you can insert your layers instead. To insert a layer, do one of the following:

- Drag and drop a layer onto the Document window from the Draw Layer button on the Insert bar (Common objects tab).

- Place the insertion point on the page where you want the layer and choose Insert > Layer.

Dreamweaver will create your inserted layer with a default width and height.

Invisible Elements: Layer Markers

As soon as you've created/drawn/inserted a layer, if you have invisible elements turned on, you'll see a little gold icon appear in the upper-left corner of the Document window. For every subsequent layer you draw, another gold icon will be added. These icons are layer markers; they represent the code for each layer. Why are they here? With most page content, it's easy to tell from within Design view where the code for an item has been inserted: If the item is at the top of the page, that's because its code is at the top of the <body> section. If the item is halfway down the page, right after a big banner image, that's because the code for the item is halfway down in the <body> code, right after the <img> tag for the banner.

But because layers use absolute positioning, their placement in the Design view layout isn't necessarily anywhere near where their code has been inserted. So Dreamweaver gives you layer markers as a visual indicator of where the code is actually sitting in relation to the code for other items on the page. Figure 14.2 shows these visual aids at work. If you don't find layer markers helpful, you can hide layer markers by choosing View > Visual Aids > Invisible Elements (this command toggles invisible elements on and off).

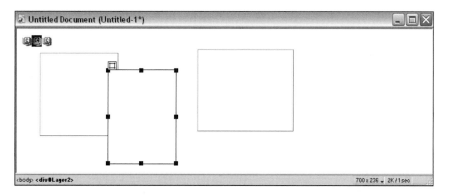

Figure 14.2   A document showing several newly created layers and their anchor point icons.

Managing Layers with the Layers Panel

The Layers panel (see Figure 14.3) helps you manage your layers. It tells at a glance how many layers your document contains, what they're names are, what their stacking order is (which is in front, which is behind), and whether they're visible or not. (Invisible layers are not too useful for creating page layout, but are a staple of DHTML scripting.) You also can use the Layers panel to select layers that might otherwise be tricky to select, either because they're invisible or because they're stacked behind some other layers.

To access the Layers panel, choose Window > Others > Layers. After the Layers panel has been opened, it appears as part of the Advanced Layout panel group, docked with your other panels.

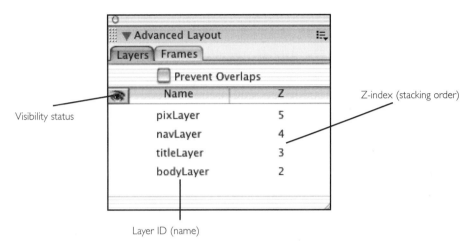

Visibility status

Z-index (stacking order)

Layer ID (name)

Figure 14.3   The Layers panel, a vital layer management tool.

The layers you've placed on the current page are shown in the panel as a list of names that reflects their stacking order (or z-index). The stacking order can be manipulated by dragging layers up and down in the list.

The left column with the eye icon at the top enables you to change the visibility of layers. See Chapter 17, "Controlling Layers with JavaScript, for more on playing with layer visibility.

You can allow or disallow overlapping layers by checking or unchecking the Prevent Overlaps box. As discussed earlier, overlapping layers are at more risk of misbehaving in browsers than layers that don't overlap. You might also want to disable overlapping if you think you might later want to turn your layers into a table for a more browser-compatible layout. (See Chapter 10, "Using Dreamweaver's Page Layout Aids," and the section on "Converting Layers to Tables" later in this chapter, for more about this.)

Designing with Layers in Design View

If you're a visual sort of person who feels quite at home creating and manipulating design elements in programs like QuarkXPress or Photoshop, you'll love how intuitive it is to create page designs using layers in Design view. The following sections discuss how to perform all the basic layer-manipulating tasks you can do in Design view, with a few tips and tricks along the way. (For more information on manipulating layers numerically, see the section "Setting Layer Properties" later in this chapter.)

Selecting Layers

There are three possible selection states for a layer, each represented in Design view by a different graphic state (see Figure 14.4):

- When the layer is selected, it will display a little white box in its upper-left corner as well as eight solid black squares around its perimeter. The white box is the selection handle. The black squares are resizing handles.

- When the insertion point is inside the layer, the layer will appear as a box with a selection handle but no resize handles. The layer appears this way just after it has been inserted, because Dreamweaver assumes you want to start putting content in the newly created layer right away.

- When the layer is not selected, it will appear as a plain beveled box, with no selection or resize handles.

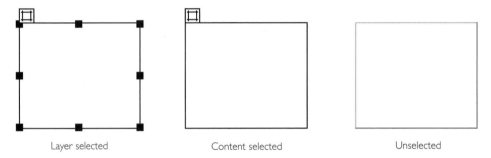

Layer selected   Content selected   Unselected

Figure 14.4   The three different appearances of a layer in the Document window.

To select a single layer, do one of the following:

- Click one of the layer's borders. (This is straightforward and obvious, but requires a bit of hand-eye coordination to click precisely on the layer border.)

- Click inside the layer so the selection handle shows in the upper-left corner, and click the handle. (This is a slower, two-step process, but requires less accurate clicking.)

- Click inside the layer and use the tag selector at the bottom of the Document window to select the `<div>` or `<span>` tag that is the layer.

- If invisible elements are showing, click the layer's layer marker.

- In the Layers panel, click the layer's name.

To select multiple layers from within the Document window, click on the borders or selection handle of the first layer you want to select, and then Shift-click anywhere within each additional layer. If invisible elements are showing, you also can Shift-click on each layer marker in turn. To select multiple layers using the Layers panel, Shift-click the names of the layers you want to select. (Discontiguous selections are allowed.) No matter which selection method you use, the last layer you select will show its resizing handles in black; other selected layers will show resizing handles in white.

Naming Layers

Each layer in a document must have a unique name. When you create a layer, Dreamweaver gives it a name based on the naming scheme Layer1, Layer2, Layer3, and so on. In the code, these names become ID attributes. (ID is a CSS selector somewhat like `class`, except that an ID selector should appear only once on an HTML document.) Layer IDs are used for CSS reference and also for any scripts that reference the layers. Layer names must be one word only, with no special characters.

While you don't *need* to change your layers' default names, it is a good idea to give your layers names that are more descriptive than Layer1 or Layer2, so you can easily identify them as you work. Even better, name them according to a naming scheme in which each layer's name tells you something about its position and/or function. For example, you might name a layer containing a navigation bar **LayerNav**, and a layer holding the page footer **LayerFooter**.

Use the Layers panel to change a layer's name. Double-click the layer in the Layers panel and type the new name into the text field area.

Inserting Content into Layers

Inserting content into a layer is simple: Just click inside the layer and insert in the usual way. Content can be inserted using the Dreamweaver Insert bar or Insert menu, dragged from the Assets panel or from elsewhere on the page, or pasted from the Clipboard.

Drag-Resizing Layers

To size a layer in the Document window, first select it so its resize handles show. Then just click-and-drag any of its resizing handles (see Figure 14.5). Use the corner handles to resize horizontally and vertically at the same time, or the non-corner handles to resize in one direction only.

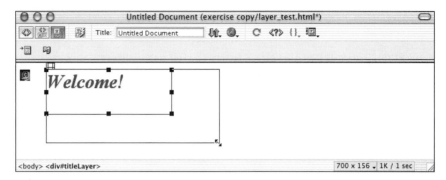

Figure 14.5   Resizing a layer by dragging.

Moving Layers Around

To change a layer's position from within the Document window, just grab it either by the selection handle or over the border, and click-and-drag. The cursor will turn into a four-headed arrow when it moves over the selection handle, or a grabber hand when it moves over the border, to indicate that clicking-and-dragging is possible.

Warning

Be careful not to grab the layer in its middle and drag. You won't be able to move the layer this way, and you might accidentally drag its contents (an image, for instance) out of the layer entirely.

To nudge a layer a pixel at a time, select it and use the arrow keys to move it. To nudge a layer ten pixels at a time, hold down Shift while using the arrow keys to move it.

Aligning Layers

Graphic designers migrating from the print world will be happy to know that Dreamweaver has a lovely feature for aligning layers. To align one or more layers with a border of another layer, do this:

1. Determine which layer you want the other layer(s) to align to (which layer will remain stationary, in other words, as the others shift to align with it).

2. All layers will be aligned to the last layer selected. So, using any of the selection techniques outlined earlier, select the layers you want to align, selecting the align-to layer last. (Its resize handles will show in black, indicating that it will remain stationary.)

3. Go to Modify > Align, and from the submenu choose one of the alignment options (Left, Right, Top, or Bottom).

Figure 14.6 shows several layers being aligned to one stationary layer.

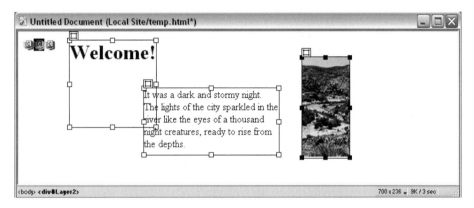

Figure 14.6   Using Modify > Align to align two layers to a third.

Matching Layer Sizes

Following the procedure for aligning layers, you also can modify layers so that their dimensions match. To do this, just select your layers, go to Modify > Align, and choose Make Same Height or Make Same Width. As with aligning, the last layer selected will determine the final height or width of all selected layers.

Nesting Layers

A *nested layer* is a layer created inside another layer. Nesting is often used to group layers. A nested layer will move along with its parent layer and can be set to inherit visibility from its parent.

To create a nested layer, use any of the following procedures:

- Place the insertion point inside an existing layer and choose Insert > Layer.
- Drag the Draw Layer button from the Insert bar and drop it into an existing layer.
- Click the Draw Layer button in the Insert bar, hold down Alt (Windows) or Option (Mac) and draw a layer inside an existing layer.

- In the Layers panel, select a layer, and then Ctrl+drag (Windows) or Cmd+drag (Mac) the layer's name onto the layer you want to be its parent.

- If invisible elements are showing, drag the child layer's layer maker inside the parent layer.

After one layer is nested inside another, the child layer (the nestee) might jump to a new location in the Document window. This is because the layer's position is now being calculated relative to the parent layer's position. This also means that from now on if you move the parent layer, its child moves with it; but if you move the child, the parent won't move.

Figure 14.7 shows how nested layers appear in the various areas of the Dreamweaver interface. In the Document window, if invisible elements are showing, the gold anchor points indicate nesting status. In the Layers panel, a nested layer is shown with its name indented under its parent layer. Click the plus/minus (+/−) button to the left of the parent layer name to show or hide its children.

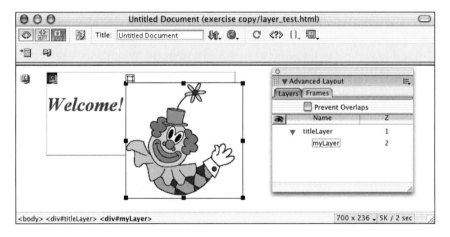

Figure 14.7   One layer nested inside another as they appear in Design view, the tag selector, and the Layers panel.

Warning

Not all browsers respect the relative positioning of parent and child. If accurate and predictable positioning of page content is important to you, test your pages thoroughly in a variety of browsers or don't use nested layers.

Deleting Layers

To delete a layer, select the layer (in the Document window or Layers panel) and press the Delete key. To quickly delete multiple layers, do one of the following:

- Shift-click to select the layers you want to delete (in the Document window or Layers panel) and then press Delete.

- Hold down the Delete key and then (in the Document window) click on each layer you want to delete in turn.

Exercise 14.1   Creating a Basic Layer Page

In this exercise, you'll build a simple page layout using layers. For the Student Ministries home page, you want to place some images on a page in such a way that some of them overlap one another and some are transparent, allowing the images beneath to show through, so you've chosen layers to achieve this result. Figure 14.8 shows the final effect you're looking for.

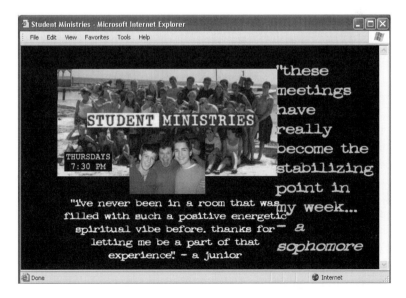

Figure 14.8   The desired layout for the Student Ministries home page.

Before you start, copy the files from the **chapter_14** folder on the CD to your hard drive. Define a site called Chapter 14, with this folder as the local root folder. All the files for this exercise are in the **chapter_14/ministries** folder.

1. Select File > New to create a new document. Save it in the **chapter_14/ministries** folder as **student_ministries.html**. To get your workspace ready for layer work, choose Window > Other > Layers (or press F2) to show the Layers panel. To achieve the desired layout, you'll need to create overlapping layers; so if Prevent Overlaps is selected in the Layers panel, deselect it.

2. You'll create your first layer by drawing it. In the Insert bar, click the Draw Layer button. The cursor changes to a crosshair, ready for drawing. In the Document window, drag to draw a layer roughly the size and shape shown in Figure 14.9. (You'll adjust the size later.)

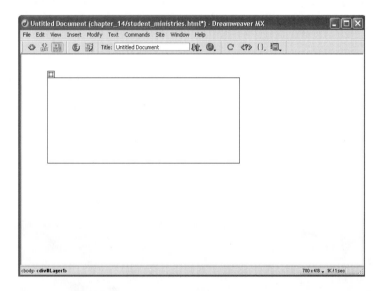

Figure 14.9   Drawing the first layer.

3. Now put some content—an image—inside the layer. Click inside the layer to give focus to its content area. Go to the Insert bar and click the Image button. When the Select File dialog box opens, browse to the file **images/student_ministries.jpg** (in the **chapter_14/ministries** folder) and insert it.

4. To create the second layer, click the Draw Layer button again and draw a layer roughly the size and shape shown in Figure 14.10. For this layer's content, insert the **images/three_guys.jpg** image.

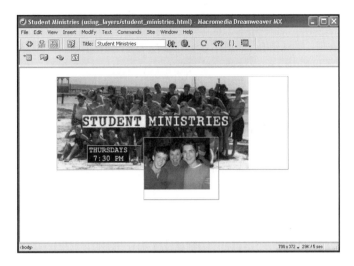

Figure 14.10   The second layer drawn in the Document window.

Note that you only need to place the layers and their graphics approximately at this point. Later you'll position them exactly the way you want them.

5. Add two more layers, inserting **images/quote1.gif** into the first and **images/quote2.gif** into the second. These images will look a little funny at this point because they're designed to sit in front of a black background. You're working on a white background for now, because layers are hard to see and select against a black background. You'll switch the background color later. Your document should now look somewhat like Figure 14.11.

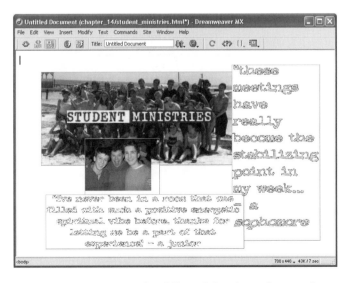

Figure 14.11   The **student_ministries.html** file with four layers drawn and content inserted.

6. Now add a nested layer. You want to place another graphic in such a way that it displays along with the Student Ministries graphic regardless of how you rearrange the layers. To do this, you'll nest a layer within the layer containing that graphic. Click the Draw Layer button on the Common tab of the Insert bar to choose the Draw Layer object. Starting from within the layer that holds the Student Ministries graphic, Alt/Opt-drag to draw a new, smaller layer. When you've done this, put the cursor inside the new layer and insert the **images/thursday.gif** graphic into it.

7. You're getting quite a collection of layers here. Before proceeding any further, take a moment to name them. In the Layers panel, select the layer that Dreamweaver has named Layer1. Double-click its name and give it a more useful name: **studentministries**. (Layer names must consist of only letters and numbers.) Rename Layer2 **threeguys**.

Can you see a naming convention developing here? Each layer is being named after the image it contains, minus the filename extension. Continuing this convention, rename the other three layers. When you're done, your Layers panel should look like the one shown in Figure 14.12.

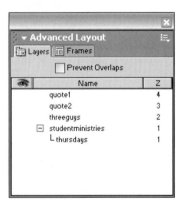

Figure 14.12   The newly named layers of **student_ministries.html** as shown in the Layers panel.

8. You've now added four layers and an image in each one, and named your layers. Save your page. It should look something like the layout shown in Figure 14.8. Note that the quote graphics will look a little odd until you set the dark background color. In Exercise 14.2, you'll edit and adjust the properties of the layers you've created.

Setting Layer Properties

When a layer is selected in the Document window, the Layer Property inspector displays, allowing you to format your layer and work with it numerically (see Figure 14.13). The following sections describe the options available in this inspector.

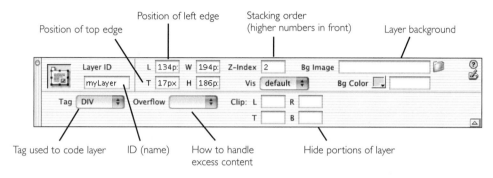

Figure 14.13   The Layer Property inspector.

Tag

The Tag field determines the HTML tag used as a basis for the layer. As mentioned earlier, Dreamweaver defaults to <div>. Either <div> or <span> will make a layer that will work in both Netscape 4+ and Internet Explorer 4+.

Layer ID

Layer ID is the identifying name for a layer. See the section on "Naming Layers," earlier in this chapter, for more on this. When you change a layer's name in the Layers panel, you're changing the Layer ID. If you assign a new Layer ID using the Property inspector, a new layer name will appear in the Layers panel.

L and T (Left and Top Coordinates)

These fields determine the left and top coordinates of the selected layer. The numbers describe the location of the top-left corner of your layer, relative to the top-left corner of the page or of the containing element.

W and H (Width and Height Coordinates)

Use these fields to set the width and height of a layer in pixels. When Dreamweaver enters width and height properties for a layer, it adds px to specify pixels; when you're typing in your own dimensions, you need to add the **px** yourself. You also can specify

pc (picas), **pt** (points), **in** (inches), **mm** (millimeters), **cm** (centimeters), or **%** (percentage of the parent element's value). The abbreviations must follow the value without a space: for example, **300px**.

Z-Index

A layer's z-index is the order in which it is stacked relative to other layers inside the same document. The layer with the highest z-index will be the topmost layer. The layer with the lowest z-index (you can even use negative numbers for z-indexing) will be the layer farthest to the back. When you rearrange layers in the Layers panel, you're adjusting the z-index of the layers. You can also change the z-index value here in the Property inspector and see the changed stacking order in the Layers panel.

Background Colors and Images

Use these fields to assign a background color (`bgcolor`) or image (`background-image`) for a layer, if desired. Any background image you assign to a layer will be tiled if the layer's dimensions are larger than the image's dimensions.

Vis (Visibility)

Use this field to specify the visibility property of the selected layer. In Dreamweaver, new layers are assigned a visibility of Default. Most browsers understand this to mean that the layer should be visible. If you want to be sure that the layer is visible in every browser, set this field to Visible. To hide a layer, set it to Hidden. This property is used most often with Show-Hide Layer behaviors. (See Chapter 17 for more about using behaviors with layers.)

Overflow

If you insert contents into a layer that are larger than the set width or height of the layer, the `overflow` attribute determines what happens to the excess. This setting becomes important because different browsers render certain contents—particularly text—in different sizes. It is possible that the page won't need an overflow property in one browser, but will need it in another. Note that the overflow attribute is completely ignored in Netscape 4.x.

When there is text in a layer, you should use an overflow setting. Although some methods of sizing text provide more control than others, methods cannot be overridden by the user's preferences in some browsers.

Overflow settings and their effects are as follows:

- **Visible.** This choice increases the layer's size as necessary so that all of its contents can be seen. The layer expands to the right and toward the bottom of the browser window. Note that this setting can cause the contents of one layer to expand over the contents of another layer.

- **Hidden.** Content that doesn't fit into the layer's set size will be hidden from view.

- **Scroll.** In browsers that support layer scrollbars, this option provides them, and they will appear even if the layer's contents are larger than the set size.

- **Auto.** Scrollbars will appear even if the layer's contents are larger than its set size (again, assuming the browser supports these scrollbars).

Figure 14.14 shows the various overflow settings at work.

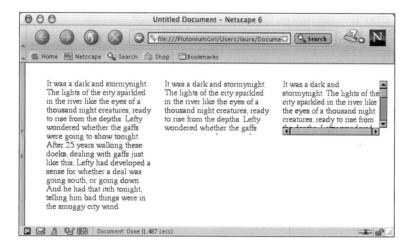

Figure 14.14   Visible, hidden, and scroll overflow attributes as seen in a browser.

Clip

If you want to show only a section of a layer's contents, and hide the rest from view, use the `clip` option. Working in pixels, clip out layer contents by specifying values that represent the amount of distance from the layer's boundaries (see Figure 14.15). Note that T (`top`) and L (`left`) values must be relative to the layer, not to the page.

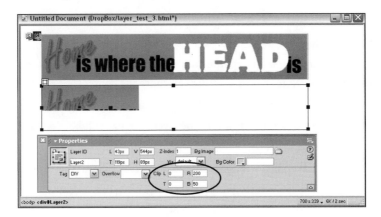

Figure 14.15   A layer without, and one with, clip parameters set.

Setting Properties for Multiple Layers

When two or more layers are selected at the same time, a modified Layer Property inspector appears, offering a subset of the usual layer properties. The upper portion of this Property inspector displays text properties (see Figure 14.16).

Figure 14.16   The Layer Property inspector with multiple layers selected.

With multiple layers selected, various properties can be set for all layers simultaneously, including position, size, and visibility. This can be a handy way to quickly align layers or make them the same size (comparable to the Modify > Align commands).

Exercise 14.2   Editing Layer Properties

Building on Exercise 14.1, here you edit and adjust properties of the layers you've added and become familiar with using the various Dreamweaver tools for working with layers.

If you haven't done so already, copy the files from the **chapter_14** folder on the CD to your hard drive. Define a site called Chapter 14, with this folder as the local root folder. All the files for this exercise are in the **chapter_14/ministries** folder.

1. Start by opening the **student_ministries.html** file to which you added layers and images in Exercise 14.1.

2. First, have a look at the page with the black background it is intended to have. To change the page background using CSS, open the CSS Styles panel and switch to Edit Styles mode by selecting its radio button. On the left side of the panel, find and double-click the word body to edit the CSS styles already applied to the <body> tag. This opens the CSS Style Definition for Body dialog box (see Figure 14.17).

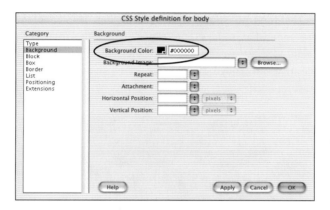

Figure 14.17   Changing the body background color using CSS.

In the dialog box, go to the Background category. In the Background Color text field, change #FFFFFF to **#000000**. Click OK to close the dialog box. Your page now shows a black background. Try selecting your layers. It is a little trickier. If you feel comfortable working with the black background, leave it. If not, just choose Edit > Undo to undo the change and return to the white background.

3. In the previous exercise, you added images to each layer, but the size of the layer doesn't reflect the size of the image, and it is best if they are set to exactly the same dimensions. First, select the **studentministries.gif** image and examine the Image Property inspector. You'll see that the image has a width of 417 and a height of 198.

The studentministries layer should have these same dimensions. Select this layer, either by clicking its name in the Layers panel or by clicking one of the layer's edges in the Document window. You can tell that the layer is selected when the Layer Property inspector appears (and not the Image Property inspector or Text Property inspector). If you're working with a white background, you can also see the eight solid black squares around the perimeter of the later.

Set the W value of the studentministries layer to **417px**, and the H value to **198px**. (Remember to add the **px** after the number, with no space in between.)

4. Repeat this process for the remaining layers. Select each image, remember or jot down its dimensions, then select the image's containing layer and assign the W and H values to those dimensions. (Remember to add the **px**.)

Tip

In the Layer Property inspector, be careful not to confuse the L and T (Left and Top) fields with the W and H (Width and Height) fields.

5. Next, arrange the layers on the page by dragging them, and arrange their stacking order as necessary using the Layers panel. If you like, you can imitate the design shown in Figure 14.18, or you can be creative and come up with your own. Remember that the whole point of using layers here is to enable you to overlap your images somewhat, so be sure to experiment with some overlapping. You'll probably want to leave your background color black from this point on to see the design the way it is intended, and you'll want to save and preview in a browser frequently.

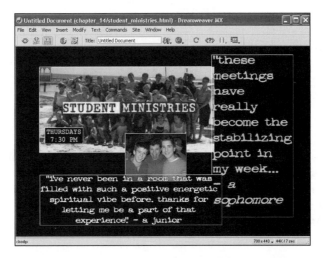

Figure 14.18   A suggested final layout for the **student_ministries.html** page.

6. Save your page and preview in a browser. Note that some older browsers might have problems displaying this page.

Layer Preferences

Layer preferences determine what default attributes Dreamweaver will assign for layers as you create them, and what kind of code gets added to your document when you use layers. If you find that the default settings aren't the settings you use most often—or if you have a specific use for layers, and you make the same type of layer over and over—you might want to set layer preferences to match your needs.

To change Layer preferences, go to Edit > Preferences and choose the Layer category (see Figure 14.19). (For Mac OS X users, choose Dreamweaver > Preferences.) The following sections describe the defaults you can change in this dialog box.

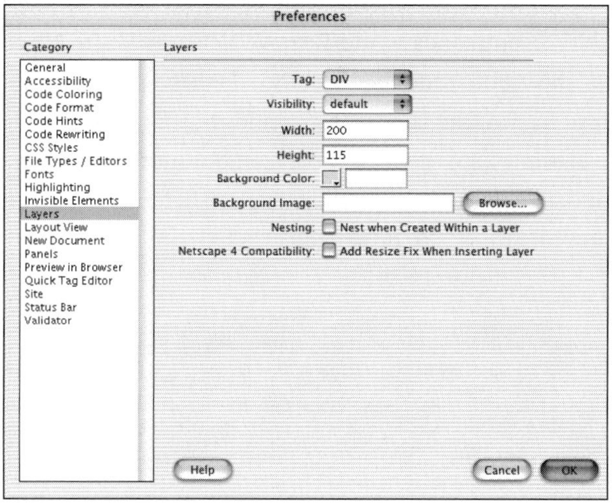

Figure 14.19   Setting layer preferences.

Default Layer Properties

When you create a layer, by drawing or inserting it, Dreamweaver determines how the layer will be coded and what attributes it will be given based on the settings found here. Changing the Tag, Visibility, Background Color, and Background Image properties changes how all new layers are created. Changing Width and Height changes what dimensions will be assigned to layers created by inserting. Any of a layer's default properties can of course be changed after its creation.

Layer Nesting

This option determines whether a layer drawn within the boundaries of an existing layer will be nested, or stacked on top of, the existing layer. Whether you choose to enable nesting here or leave it disabled, you can temporarily switch the preference as you're creating a new layer by holding down Alt (Windows) or Opt (Mac) as you draw the layer.

Netscape Compatibility

Netscape 4.x has a well-known problem maintaining the layout of layers-based pages when the browser window is resized. The workaround solution to this problem is to add JavaScript to documents containing layers, instructing the browser to reload the page every time the user resizes the window. If the Netscape compatibility option is enabled in Layer preferences, the proper JavaScript code will be added to your document automatically as soon as you draw or insert your first layer.

The code added by this preference is the same code that can be added to a document manually through the Commands > Add/Remove Netscape Resize Fix command. If you enable Netscape compatibility, and then later decide that a particular document doesn't need that JavaScript fix, you can choose Commands > Add/Remove Netscape Resize Fix to remove it (see Figure 14.20). If you disable it, and want to add the code later, choose the same command. Dreamweaver is smart enough to determine whether the JavaScript is there to be removed, or needs to be added.

Note

Why would you want to disable Netscape compatibility? If you know for certain that your page will never be viewed in Netscape 4 (for instance, if your document is destined for an intranet), you needn't clutter up your page or use up bandwidth with the extra JavaScript.

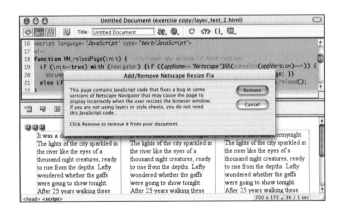

Figure 14.20   The Add/Remove Netscape Resize Fix command, a JavaScript workaround to the Netscape 4 problem with displaying layers.

Converting Layers to Tables

There are various reasons why you might start out designing a page in layers and end up needing to rebuild it using tables for layout. Perhaps you create your masterpiece and then discover the hard way that not all browsers will display your layout the way you want. Perhaps you want to create an alternate page for users with older browsers, or those with non-cooperative newer browsers. Dreamweaver offers two tools for converting a layers-based layout to a table-based layout: the Layers to Table command and the

3.0 Browser Compatible command. Whichever of these commands you use, you cannot have any overlapping layers or the command will not work. (If you really love those overlapping graphics, like in Exercise 14.2, consider substituting one large graphic constructed from overlapping pictures, or even a sliced image, instead.)

If you want to change your existing document from layers to a table, choose the Modify > Convert > Layers to Table command. This command rewrites the code of your page to replace all layer code with one large table. (See Chapter 10 for a full discussion of this command.)

If you want your existing document to remain in layers, but want to create a backward-compatible alternative for your visitors, choose File > Convert > 3.0 Browser Compatible. This command creates a duplicate of your current document with the layer code replaced by a table, but leaves the current code untouched. After you've created both versions of your page, you can give visitors the choice of which to view, or you can ferry them to the proper page based on browser kind and version by adding a Check Browser behavior to your page. (See Chapter 16, "Getting Interactive with Behaviors," for a full discussion of the Check Browser behavior.)

Taking Dreamweaver Layers Further

MX

The Dreamweaver interface for handling layer-based layouts is not limited to working with Dreamweaver-generated layers. Starting with Dreamweaver MX, any page element styled with CSS positioning will appear in Design view as a layer, with its own Layer Property inspector and taking advantage of all the techniques and commands for dragging-and-dropping, nudging, aligning, and eyeballing, that Dreamweaver's own layers have—regardless of what HTML tag is being used to create them, or even whether the positioning attributes are coded as an inline style or a custom class in an internal or external style sheet. Working with this kind of layer code is still not quite as slick and easy as just dragging and dropping layers around the page—but it's close!

Creating True CSS-P Pages with Dreamweaver MX

The general procedure for building a CSS-positioned page in Dreamweaver is this: Using the CSS Styles panel, create the class that contains the CSS-P formatting; using any of Dreamweaver's visual or coding tools, create page element(s) and use the class to style them; in Design view, using the various tools available there, refine your page design and create whatever special effects tickle your fancy.

Creating a Custom Class for CSS Positioning

A custom class for formatting CSS positioned elements is just the same as any custom CSS class (see Chapter 13, "Using Cascading Style Sheets," for more on this), except that it takes advantage of the various formatting options related to positioning block elements. To create a class that includes CSS positioning, follow these steps:

1. If you want the custom class to be stored as part of an internal style sheet, open the document you plan to format. If you want the class to be stored in an external style sheet, open and save an HTML document that you want the style sheet to link to.

2. In the CSS Styles panel, click the New CSS Style button. When the dialog box comes up, set it to Create New Custom Style, in the current document or in a new style sheet file or in an existing CSS document, if you have one you'd like to use. Figure 14.21 shows this happening.

Figure 14.21   The New CSS Style dialog box set up to create a custom class for CSS-P.

3. Click OK to close this dialog box and open the CSS Style Definition dialog box. From here, start by choosing the Positioning category. Set the Type to absolute, and set any other formatting options you like (see Figure 14.22). While you're at it, you can also choose formatting from any of the other categories in the dialog box as well. But the only crucial attribute, to make Dreamweaver treat elements with this class as layers, is the `position` attribute.

Note

While absolute positioning is the most common and well-supported CSS positioning method, it's not the only choice. *Absolute positioning* treats the layer as a free-standing entity, whose position is determined relative to the origin point of the window (or, in the case of nested layers, the origin point of the parent layer). *Static positioning* places the layer in the normal flow of page elements, as if there were no CSS positioning applied at all. *Relative positioning* begins by determining the layer's static position, but then allows left, top, right, and bottom values to be specified that will shift the element from that position. Dreamweaver-generated layers always use absolute positioning, but if you're creating your own custom CSS-P class, you can specify any of these options. As long as you specify one of them, Dreamweaver will treat the page element as a layer for purposes of editing and display.

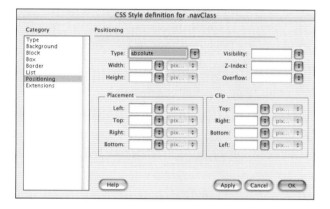

Figure 14.22   Setting positioning properties for a custom class (and for all layers that will use this class).

4. When you're finished, click OK to close the dialog box. The positioning attributes you've just added to this class are the same attributes that appear in the Layer Property inspector for Dreamweaver-generated layers—but after you've entered them in the CSS Style Definition dialog box, they become part of the class instead of part of an inline style governing only one layer.

Designing with CSS-Positioned Elements in Dreamweaver

After you've got the class defined, it's time to create the page elements that will refer to that class. If you're using an external style sheet, begin by linking each document that will use that class to the external style sheet. After you've done that, to create page elements that use that class, choose from one of the following methods.

Method #1: Using the Draw Layer Tool

Assuming that you want your class to format a layer created with `<div>` or `<span>`, you can use the Draw Layer tool, with just a little tweaking of its code. Do this:

1. Create a layer using the Draw Layer object or the Insert > Layer command.

2. With the layer selected, go to the CSS Styles panel, switch to Apply Styles mode, and click on your custom class to apply it to the layer.

3. If you look at your layer's code, you'll see something like this:

```
<div id="Layer1" style="position:absolute; left:94px; top:40px;
width:127px; height:85px; z-index:1" class="myClass"></div>
```

In Design view (and in the browser), the size and position of your layer aren't reflecting the instructions set in the class because the layer's inline style is overriding the class. To stop this from happening, you need to remove the style attribute and its values. You can do this by any of the following methods:

- In Code view or the Quick Tag Editor, select and delete the entire `style` attribute and value.

- In the Tag Inspector, select the `<div>` or `<span>` tag. Find the `style` attribute and remove it by deleting the value associated with it. (Figure 14.23 shows this happening.)

Figure 14.23   Using the Tag Inspector to remove the `style` attribute from a Dreamweaver-generated layer.

- Choose Modify > Edit Tag. In the tag editor, go to the Style Sheet/Accessibility category and remove the information from the Style input field.

As soon as you do any of these, your layer will adopt the formatting indicated in the class.

Method #2: Creating and Wrapping Content

This method assumes you already have some content you want to put in your CSS-P layer, or don't mind creating the content first. Do this:

1. In Design view, enter whatever text, image, or other content that should eventually sit inside the CSS-P layer.

2. Select the content.

3. Enter the Quick Tag Editor (Ctrl/Cmd+T, or click the Quick Tag Editor button on the Property inspector). Toggle to Wrap Tag mode.

Note

See Chapter 32, "Technical Issues," for more on using the Quick Tag Editor and setting its preferences.

4. Start typing the tag that you want to wrap your content in. If you have code hints enabled in your Quick Tag Editor preferences, Dreamweaver will help you with your typing. Include the `class` attribute, set to the name of your custom style, and the `id` attribute, set to any unique name (see Figure 14.24). When you're finished, don't type the closing tag; Quick Tag Editor will do that for you.

Figure 14.24   Using the Quick Tag Editor to wrap existing content in a CSS layer.

Method #3: Using the Tag Chooser

If you really hate typing code, here's another method that can be done entirely without it. Do this:

1. Click to place the insertion point anywhere within Design view. (It doesn't matter where your code is entered, because absolute positioning will govern the page appearance.)

2. From the Insert bar (Common tab), click the Tag Chooser button. This opens the Tag Chooser dialog box, from which you can select the tag you want to insert. To insert a `<div>`, choose Markup Languages > HTML Tags > Formatting and Layout > div.

3. Click Insert. The tag editor will open. Go to the Style Sheet/Accessibility category and enter a unique ID and the name of your class.

4. Click OK, and Close to exit all dialog boxes.

Method #4: Using Other Block Elements

When you're in charge of generating your own CSS code, you're not limited to using `<div>` and `<span>`. Any block level page element (`<p>`, `<h1>`–`<h6>`, and so on) can be used as a "layer" when it's styled with CSS positioning. To use elements other than `<div>` and `<span>` as layers, do this:

1. Create whatever content you want to go in the layer, formatted so it sits inside a `<p>`, `<h1>`, or other block level HTML element.

2. Select the block element. (Use the tag selector for safest and quickest selecting.)

3. In the CSS Styles panel, choose Apply Styles mode and click to apply the custom class you created earlier; or, if the element is a text tag, in the Property inspector choose CSS mode and use the CSS style pop-up menu to apply the custom class.

Design View and the Property Inspector for CSS-Positioned Elements

After you've followed any of the above methods to apply the custom class with its positioning attributes, a wonderful thing happens—Dreamweaver Design view displays the element as a layer, with CSS Styles positioning and formatting applied (see Figure 14.25)! Select the element, and the Layer Property inspector appears (even if the block element being styled is not `<div>` or `<span>`). And best of all, in the Property inspector, any changes made to properties that are part of the class will automatically update the class—thus updating all other documents that use this class. That's the power of CSS2 at work.

Figure 14.25   A CSS-positioned page element in Design view displaying as a layer.

Exercise 14.3   Designing a Set of Web Pages Using CSS Positioning in an External Style Sheet

This exercise gives you a chance to take some of the new Dreamweaver layer-related tools for a spin. You'll create a set of custom classes in an external style sheet, attach them to elements within several documents within a site, and use the Dreamweaver layers inter-face to quickly format the entire site by formatting one page. Along the way, you'll also get a good look at how forms separate content to make a more flexible web site.

If you haven't done so already, copy the files from the **chapter_14** folder on the CD to your hard drive. Define a site called Chapter 14, with this folder as the local root folder. The files for this exercise are all in the **chapter_14/enviro_site** folder.

  1. Begin by opening any one of the six HTML documents that comprise the Enviro "mini-site." Examine the page in Design view and Code view to see that it's built from unformatted images and text. The page isn't very pretty yet (see Figure 14.26) because there is no layout—this is just content without formatting. All the pages in this folder are built exactly the same way, with comparable content.

Figure 14.26   One of the documents in the Enviro site (**chapter_14/enviro_site**) showing
unstructured content ready for styling.

2. Your first task is to create all the CSS building blocks (such as the custom classes)
that this content requires. Don't close the document you've been examining.
Open the CSS Styles panel (Window > CSS Styles or expand the Design panel
group).

Click the New Style button to open the New CSS Style dialog box. Set your new
style to be a custom class named **.banner**, part of a new style sheet document
(see Figure 14.27). Click OK to close the dialog box. When the Save Style Sheet
File As dialog box appears, name your new style sheet **siteStyles.css**, and save it
in the **chapter_14/enviro_site** folder.

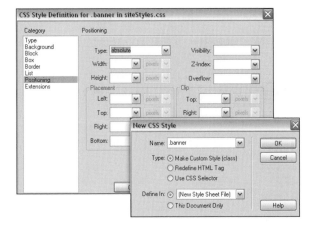

Figure 14.27   Creating the first custom class for the Enviro site, along with the external style
sheet that will contain it.

3. When you click OK to close the Save Style Sheet File As dialog box, the CSS Style Definition dialog box opens. For now, you only need to set one property. Go to the Positioning category and set the Position pop-up menu to absolute (see Figure 14.27). When you've done that, click OK to close this last dialog box.

4. Repeat the previous two steps for each class your files will need. In addition to the `.banner` class you just created, define the following classes:

> `.title`
>
> `.bodycopy`
>
> `.divider`
>
> `.handsbutton`
>
> `.dropsbutton`
>
> `.scalebutton`
>
> `.stampbutton`
>
> `.peoplebutton`
>
> `.phonebutton`

For now, don't worry about assigning any properties except positioning to these classes. Figure 14.28 shows what your CSS Styles panel should look like when you're finished.

Figure 14.28   All the custom classes needed for the Enviro site documents.

Here's where the fun starts! By applying the custom classes with their absolute positioning to your various page elements, you'll be creating Dreamweaver layers.

5. Start with the banner (the banner graphic at the top of the page). Your strategy for this element is to embed it in a `<div>` tag and apply the class to that. Do it this way (the process is shown in Figure 14.29):

Figure 14.29   Wrapping the banner image in a `<div>` tag governed by the `.banner` CSS class.

- Select the **banner.gif** graphic.
- Press Ctrl+T (Windows) or Cmd+T (Mac) to open the Quick Tag Editor. You want Wrap Tag mode to show in the editor. Keep pressing Ctrl/Cmd+T until it does.
- When your Quick Tag Editor looks like the one in Figure 14.29, type **div class="banner"**.
- Close the Quick Tag Editor by pressing Enter.

    If you look in Code view now, you should see the `<img>` tag for the banner enclosed within a pair of `<div>` tags. In Design view, the image shows with a layer.

Note

For more on the Quick Tag Editor, see Chapter 33, "Writing Code in Dreamweaver." If you don't want to use the Quick Tag Editor, you also could cut the image out of the document (Edit > Cut), create a layer (Insert > Layer), and paste the image into the new layer (Edit > Paste). If you use this method, remember that Dreamweaver adds inline style information when it creates layers. You'll have to use the Tag Inspector or some other method to remove the layer's `style` attribute, then use the CSS Styles panel to apply the .banner class.

6. Next, you'll apply the .title class to the page's main heading, this time by applying it directly to the `<h1>` tag. Click the cursor somewhere inside the heading. In the Property inspector, click the CSS button to engage CSS mode. From the pop-up list of available styles, choose heading.

Look at the interesting happenings! In Code view, the <h1> tag now has a class. In Design view, the heading looks like it's in a layer (complete with resize handles and the layer tab at the upper left). If you click on the borders or the tab of this layer, the Property inspector will show properties for a layer. If you click within the text of the heading, the Property inspector shows text controls. The tag selector shows the heading and class.

7. Repeat the procedure from the previous step to add the .bodycopy custom class to the paragraph containing the document's body copy. As you do this, the paragraph will turn into a layer and also will shift position (as absolute positioning kicks in). Use the Layer tab to move your body copy, heading, or banner layer out of the way as needed. Note that, as you do this, Layers Property inspector shows changing L and T values. But if you check your code, you'll see that no new values are being added to your code. That's because your changes are updating the custom classes in the **siteStyles.css** file, not the current HTML document.

8. Finally, each navigation image in the document must have the appropriate "button" class applied to it. Because the Image Property inspector doesn't have an option for assigning styles, use the CSS Styles panel for this. Switch the panel to Apply Styles mode, then select each image in turn, and click its matching class (for example, handsbutton applied to the hands picture). Figure 14.30 shows the page layout as it appears with everything turned into layers (but no organizing or formatting yet!).

Figure 14.30   The **acquisitions.html** page with all page elements assigned custom classes and being treated as layers.

Note

CSS elements often have ID attributes included with them. As you work, note that Dreamweaver interprets an image's name as its Layer ID (even though the attribute is name, not id). Layers created from text or other elements that have no names will not have Layer IDs unless you use the Layers Property inspector to assign them.

9. Your next step is to add formatting information to your custom classes. You do this by using the Dreamweaver layers interface and the CSS Styles panel. Start by using all the various layer tools introduced earlier in this chapter to position your page elements where you like them. Drag layers to move or resize them; use the Property inspector to change their position or size numerically; use the arrow keys to nudge them or the Modify > Align commands to align them.

You can also take this opportunity to add text formatting to the title and body-copy classes. For each of these, click the cursor inside the text element and, in the Text Property inspector, click the Style pop-up and choose Edit CSS Style (see Figure 14.31). When the CSS Style Definition dialog box opens, apply whatever formatting you choose to make your text look nice. (Just don't switch the Property inspector to HTML mode and format your text using the choices there, or you'll be adding local formatting and not updating the custom class.)

Note

As always when working with external style sheets, the Undo command might not work as you expect it to. If you change an element's formatting and that change is stored as part of the class definition (in the external file), you can't Edit > Undo because that document isn't open.

When you're done formatting, check your document in Code view. You'll see that no formatting code has been added! Other than the added class assignments, and the added <div> tag around the banner, the document code looks just the same as it did at the beginning of the exercise.

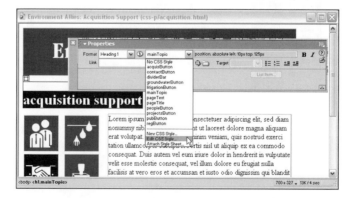

Figure 14.31   Adding text formatting to a layer by updating a custom class.

10. The true power of CSS is that classes stored in external style sheets can control many documents simultaneously. To get an idea how that works, you have six HTML files to play with in the **chapter_14/enviro_site** folder. As soon as you apply the custom classes to any of these documents, it will immediately adopt the formatting of the page you just made.

   Open one of the remaining HTML documents, and do this:

   - In the CSS Styles panel, click the Attach Style Sheet button and link to the **sitestyles.css** document. Your custom classes will now appear in the panel.

   - Repeat steps 5–8 to apply the classes to your page elements. As you work, the layout and formatting you created in the first file will magically take over your page. (The new formatting might hide some page elements under others, making them inaccessible. If this happens, Edit > Undo the last style assignment you did and apply the styles in a different order, so all elements remain accessible.)

   How industrious do you feel? To see how this technology works, it's important to get at least two pages formatted. If you want more practice, format all six documents!

11. From now on, no matter which of your formatted documents you're working on, any change in position, size, text formatting, or other layer properties will change the style sheet itself and so the layout of all documents. Try it and see how efficiently you can restructure your entire set of pages. How many different possible layouts can you create?

   In particular, try out effects like these:

   - Select the banner layer and set its width to **100%**, and L and T to **0**. Then set its background color to match the blue of the banner image. For all of your pages, the banner now bleeds off the top and sides of the page, no matter how big the browser window.

   - Though it can't be done from the Layer Property inspector, layers can also be measured based on their distance from the right or bottom edge of the browser window. Edit your various button classes by removing the L and T values and replacing them with R and B values (see Figure 14.32). R (right) measures the distance in pixels between the right edge of the layer and the right edge of the browser window; B (bottom) measures the distance between the layer's bottom and the browser window's bottom. You can set either or both of these, to hug either or both edges.

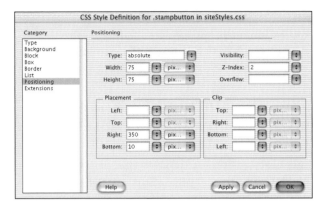

Figure 14.32   Setting the Positioning attributes for a CSS custom class, creating a layer that positions itself relative to the lower-right corner of the browser window.

- Try setting the text layer to a percent-based value less than 100%. Note that you can use percent-based settings even if the element doesn't start at L or T set to 0. A text layer with its left edge at 200px and its width set to 75% will stretch and squash while still leaving margins on either side of itself (one fixed and one slightly flexible margin).

Using variations of these settings, you can create flexible layouts in which different page elements hug different edges of the browser window. Just because you're not using tables doesn't mean you can't have liquid layouts! Figure 14.33 shows an alternate layout that uses several of these methods.

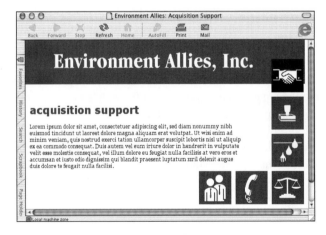

Figure 14.33   A flexible alternate layout for the **chapter_14/enviro_site** pages.

Note

If you want to investigate CSS positioning further, try these free online tutorials (highly recommended!):

MaKo's CSS Positioning Tutorial:
`www.mako4css.com/Tutorial.htm`

Denis Wilford's Flexible Page Tutorial:
`http://deniswilford.com/graphic/tut1/tut1a.html`

BrainJar's CSS Positioning Tutorial:
`www.brainjar.com/css/positioning/default.asp`

Interview: M. Kosloff

Business Name: Orion Hi-Tek

URL: **www.orion-hitek.com**

How did you get started in web design? What kind of work are you currently doing?

The employee who was supposed to do most the web design/development left the company, and we had already signed a contract for a sensitive site. With no time to waste....

My current work is building web sites mostly for businesses in CSS, CF, and ASP, and intranet development in ColdFusion.

What hardware and software do you use in your work?

Hardware: PC (Pentium II, 450, 196MB RAM, 40GB ATA100 hard drive, 16MB AGP graphics, 17-inch monitor. Laptop: Compaq Pentium III 800, 128MB RAM, 20GB, 15-inch TFT.

Software: HomeSite, TopStyle Pro, PhotoImpact, XaraX, Dreamweaver, Fireworks, ColdFusion Studio

How do you use CSS positioning in your design work? Why do you prefer it?

I use CSS-P exclusively. CSS-P is elegant and future-oriented, and it enables me to create fast sites. It's also backward-compatible, disabled-accessible, user-friendly, and easy to change and to maintain.

I like the logical approach and the clean separation of structural markup and presentation.

What are the most important things for a designer starting out learning CSS-P to know?

It helps to know about HTML tags and structure. But even more important is to get a fresh look at web sites; to get rid of the old, complicated way of thinking in "tables." Layout with CSS-P is different. Instead of trodding the worn-out ways of table layout, one should go back to the basics: Where do I want what to be, and how should it look?

What trends on the web and in the web designer's work do you see as important?

For the web, I see the following:

- Standards compliance in browsers
- More weight on usability and accessibility
- Different thinking (web is not print; give the control to the visitor)
- Diversity

For web developer, I see that database-driven, professional web sites are the future.

What advice would you give to someone just starting out in web design?

- Web is not print.
- Control is an issue, not a way to create web sites.
- Learn everything you can, and as fast as you can. The web is a very fast-paced environment. Even if you are on top of the game, the moment you stand still the web and all those emerging technologies will leave you in the dust.
- Design is a vehicle to transport a message. Creating web sites for clients is *not* a means to express your artistic capabilities. Your client's customer is the person who counts.
- Be a business person, or go looking for a partner who is.

Summary

CSS-P is the future of page layout. And the Dreamweaver interface for creating and working with "layers" provides an intuitive and visual environment for creating and working with this kind of page design. Whether you use Dreamweaver-generated layers right "out of the box," or create your own custom classes with positioning attributes, you can use Design view to arrange them and the Property inspector to set their attributes. The next two chapters cover another use for layers—probably their most popular use so far in the web community: controlling them with JavaScript to create DHTML interactivity and animation.

Chapter 15

Multimedia Issues

This section covers the tools and capabilities Dreamweaver offers the multimedia developer. Before delving into the details of how multimedia works in Dreamweaver, however, you need a good understanding of what multimedia is and how it fits into web design. This chapter discusses what multimedia is, how it exists on and off the web, and what purposes it serves (and doesn't serve) as part of an onscreen presentation.

What Is Multimedia?

As its name indicates, *multimedia* means using multiple kinds of media—text, graphics, animation, video, music, narration—to communicate. However, it's more than that; after all, going to the movies can involve multiple media, but it's not a multimedia experience. Multimedia implies interactivity as well. Audiences become users. They click things, roll over things, make choices, move things around, ask and answer questions. The focus is on the experience, and the experience is nonlinear, directed by the user.

Seen from this perspective, all web sites partake of multimedia to some extent. Even the simplest web page usually has at least a few pictures and some text; users click links to navigate through information structures. Presentation becomes nonlinear, user-directed. Normally, of course, when reference is made to multimedia, you think of something fancier than this, with more complex interactivity and a broader range of media elements. Just don't forget that it's not an either/or situation—"yes, I will use multimedia," or "no, I will not." It's a continuum, involving how complex you want your interactivity to be, and how many different media types you want to use.

Multimedia on CD-ROM

Back before there was the World Wide Web, multimedia presentations were distributed on CD-ROMs, they were presented on kiosk computers, they were even delivered on floppy disks and shared across networks. Life was a lot simpler then, because presentations existed in much more controlled environments than they do today.

Because multimedia includes interactivity, a presentation in those days had to be created in an authoring environment, using a scripting or programming language to encode its instructions; the final presentation functioned like a piece of software, interpreting the coded instructions as the user interacted with it. The authoring environments were programs such as Director and Authorware, which had the capability to collect and control various media types, and which had their own internal scripting languages (Director's Lingo, for example) to create the interactivity. These programs generated presentations as standalone applications, also called *projectors* or *players*, which were then burned onto CDs or otherwise distributed to their audiences or installed onto public kiosk computers. The user didn't need any special software to run a multimedia presentation, because the presentation itself was the software. Just pop the CD in the drive, launch the executable or application file, and you're off to the races.

Figure 15.1 shows a flowchart of the development process for creating a multimedia presentation using authoring software such as Director. Resources are collected, interactivity is programmed in, and the final presentation, in the form of a projector, is produced.

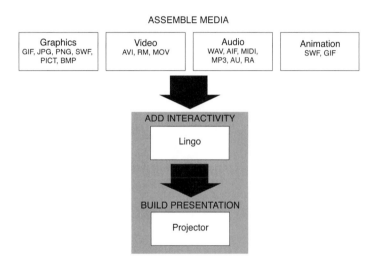

Figure 15.1   The multimedia authoring process, for CD-ROM–based presentations created with authoring software (Director, Flash, Authorware, and so on).

Multimedia and the Browser

With the advent of the web, everything changed. Instead of delivering entire miniapplications containing interactive presentations, the web relies on the user already having certain software (that is, a browser) on his computer. Web multimedia presentations consist of a collection of media files along with instructions for the browser to use in building the final, functional product.

The main problem with this scenario is that browsers were not intended for this purpose. Browsers are HTML interpreters, and HTML is a markup language, not a scripting language. Browsers can display images and text, but no other media types. Various solutions have developed to address this problem, including the following:

- **JavaScript.** Originally developed by Netscape, JavaScript is a scripting language that resides inside an HTML framework and is interpreted by the browser. The JavaScript/HTML combination is the foundation of web-user interactivity. The combination of JavaScript and CSS-P creates what is commonly referred to as *dynamic HTML*, or *DHTML*.

- **Java.** Developed by Sun Microsystems, Java is a platform-independent programming language capable of creating *applets* (applications that will run inside a browser window). In addition to providing complex interactivity, Java applets can contain media elements such as sounds and video. The combination of Java, JavaScript, and HTML was originally intended to provide a complete multimedia solution for web delivery.

- **Plugins and ActiveX controls.** Instead of working within the browser, plugins and ActiveX controls extend the functionality of the browser, allowing it to access and display media types (such as video and sound) that are otherwise beyond its reach. Plugins also can allow the browser to display presentations created in the more traditional multimedia authoring applications, such as Director, Flash, and Authorware. Because such presentations contain their own internal scripting, no JavaScript or Java components are needed to provide interactivity.

The biggest technical challenge to providing multimedia on the web is picking and choosing from among all these choices. Figure 15.2 shows a flowchart of the multimedia authoring process as it works for web multimedia. As you can see, compared to the chart in Figure 15.1 the process requires much more strategizing because each task can be accomplished in so many different ways. So, you want an interactive menu: Do you add a JavaScript to the HTML code? Build a Java applet and insert it into the page? Use Flash and let the plugin handle things? So, you want video: Do you find a Java applet to control the video? Or, if you use a plugin, which plugin do you use? QuickTime? Shockwave? RealMedia? Windows Media Player?

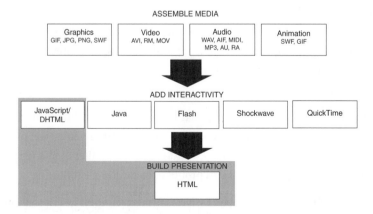

Figure 15.2   The multimedia authoring process for creating a web-based presentation that will appear in a browser. Items in the shaded area can be created in Dreamweaver.

Note that you don't have to stick entirely with one particular technology, even within the same page. Your job is to choose the best tool for each individual task. Figure 15.3 shows a web site (www.macnabdesign.com) that mixes Shockwave, animated GIFs, DHTML, and even some Java to create its various elements. The cascading menus on main pages are created from DHTML. The logo and other artwork showcase sections are Shockwave. The magnetic poetry game is a Java applet.

Figure 15.3   Several screens from the Macnab Design web site.

Designing with Multimedia

It isn't enough to know how to put multimedia elements on your web pages. You also have to know why. What are all those bells and whistles doing there, and are they worth all the fuss? You have probably visited web sites where animations, background music, or fancy bits of interactivity were detrimental to the web experience, instead of being a constructive part of it. Because of this, some pundits consider multimedia the enemy, with no useful place in good web design. This isn't true. Multimedia isn't suitable for all web sites; however, if used wisely, it enables you to take full advantage of the possibilities of web communication. Your job, as a web designer, is to be clear about what purpose multimedia is serving in your web pages, so you can determine when to use it, how to maximize it, and when to leave it out.

Use Multimedia When It's the Best Way to Present Information

Sometimes, you just need media. If the purpose of your web site is to sell music or advertise movies, obviously it's appropriate to have audio or video content (see Figure 15.4). It's also important to have enough interactivity that users can navigate through the content, can start and stop playback, and can maybe find and isolate favorite portions for playback.

Figure 15.4   Using multimedia to sell media. Customers at Amazon.com can listen to music samples before buying (www.amazon.com).

Use Multimedia to Illustrate or Demonstrate

The old writer's adage tells that it's better to show than to tell. Web authors also know that people don't like to read long chunks of text onscreen. Complex processes and structures can often be more clearly conveyed with a simple animation than with endless paragraphs, charts, or still pictures (see Figure 15.5). Virtual panoramas and 3D models can convey detailed product and location information much more quickly and efficiently than still pictures, text, or diagrams (see Figure 15.6). A narration is often less distracting as an explanatory accompaniment than yet another text block cluttering up the screen. All of this is subject to bandwidth considerations, of course. When it comes to showing, rather than telling, however, multimedia is often the most efficient means to the end.

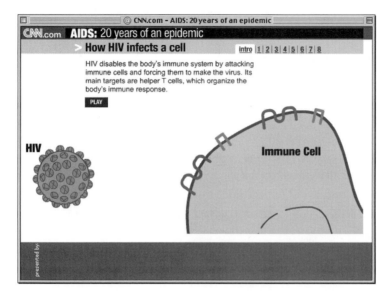

Figure 15.5   An online movie enacts the complex biochemical process behind the HIV virus (`www.cnn.com/interactive`).

Figure 15.6   Virtual reality allows potential car buyers can try out a VW beetle, inside or out (`www.vw.com/newbeetle/360cam.htm`).

Note

For more examples of multimedia in action, visit the virtual chemistry lab at Oxford University (www.chem.ox.ac.uk/vrchemistry); take an armchair tour of Japan's castles (castle.ad-g.tv/); virtually climb Denali (www.pbs.org/wgbh/nova/denali); watch an animated explanation of cloning, or a 3D virtual-reality view of the space shuttle (www.cnn.con/interactive).

Use Multimedia to Direct Attention

Things that are moving draw our eyes. Things that are making noise catch our attention. Anybody who's suffered through the annoyance of endlessly blinking, spinning, or throbbing ad banners at the tops and bottoms of commercial web pages knows this. Drawing attention doesn't have to be a bad thing, however. It's a well-established principle in graphic design that a layout should lead the reader's eye, drawing attention as needed to different elements on the page. The same is true in multimedia design. You can use movement and sound to help guide the user through a set of information the same way graphic designers use contrast, size, and placement (see Figure 15.7).

Figure 15.7   This layout is focused on the feature picture in the center, which is also animated to draw further attention (www.rollingstone.com).

Leading eyeflow can be especially useful in linear instructional presentations, such as tutorials, where it's crucial that the viewer follow the activity as it unfolds (see Figure 15.8). The animation starts when the user clicks the "show me" button, when presumably his eye is focused on the button. (To view this movie, look in the **chapter_15** folder on the CD, and browse **ShowMe.html,** which uses the embedded media file **aftershock.dcr**).

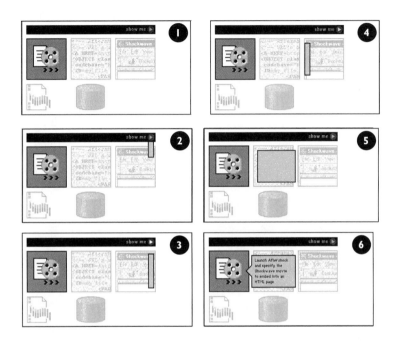

Figure 15.8   A sequence from the **aftershock.dcr** Show Me tutorial movie, part of Macromedia Director's online Help.

Use Multimedia to Engage, Entertain, and Distract

This is probably the most overused and least thought-out application of fancy stuff. However, it's still an important and valid use, in its place. The key decision you have to make before adding this kind of multimedia is, do your visitors *want* to be entertained? Give them plenty of opportunities *not* to be entertained, if they just want to head straight to the meatier parts of your web site.

Use Multimedia to Provide Feedback and Help Users Navigate Complex Information Structures

This is the lowliest, and yet probably most widely applicable, use of multimedia. Feedback tells users what to expect from a presentation. It lets them know the presentation is interacting with them. Cursor changes and rollover effects draw attention to links and let the viewers know that these are links. If a button makes a "click" sound or changes color when a user clicks it, the user knows the computer has registered that mouse click and is processing the request. (This is especially important when slow connections or overloaded servers might take several seconds to process a user request.) A cascading, expanding, or drop-down menu can provide a graphic overview of a web site's complete navigation structure in one easy-to-read information screen.

Figure 15.9 shows various examples of this use of multimedia. Pictured here, the Yale University home page fits numerous menus and submenus into one clean interface, using cascading menus (`www.yale.edu`).

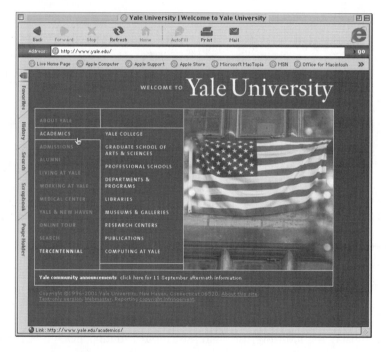

Figure 15.9   Web sites use multimedia effects to build a complex user interface (`www.yale.edu`).

The Big Picture

Before you can use multimedia wisely in a web site, you need to be clear about the purpose of the web site. Different kinds of sites, with different target audiences, call for different approaches. Following are some of the different web purposes that can benefit from rich multimedia, and suggestions on how the whole package fits together.

Entertainment

Obviously, if your web site is devoted to entertainment, if your emphasis is on providing a diverting experience, it's your job to entertain your visitors (see Figure 15.10).
Whip out that video extravaganza; get your 3D toys out there. It's show time!

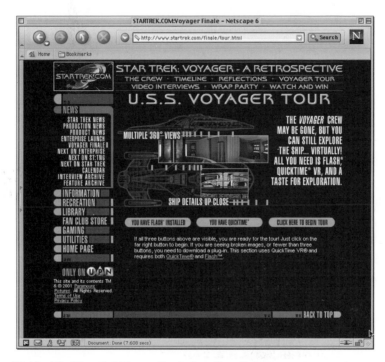

Figure 15.10   The "Star Trek Voyager" web site offers all the immersive experiences any trekkie
could want (`www.startrek.com/finale/tour.html`).

Online Brochures

Some web sites serve the function of being online brochures, whose main purpose is presenting a corporate image. For these sites, setting a certain mood and engulfing the visitor in an immersive experience can be valid goals (see Figure 15.11). The entire Tiffany's
web site is a subtle Flash presentation geared toward creating a mood of elegance, opu-
lence, and comfort (`www.tiffanys.com`). For an entirely different mood, visit the Sheer
Blonde site (`www.sheerblonde.com`), which uses animation, soundtrack, and sophisticated rollover effects for a high-energy, exciting mood.

Figure 15.11   Creating a mood through multimedia (`www.tiffany.com`).

Splash screens and opening animations can be good mood setters, which is why they're used so often. Games and activities also can be used to attract repeat visits to a web site. In Figure 15.12, sports teams can see their team jackets as they customize them, with Boathouse's Garment Generator (`www.boathouse.com/garmentgen/garment_demo.asp`).

Figure 15.12   Engaging the user, as part of the online experience (`www.boathouse.com/garmentgen/garment_demo.asp`).

Education

New information can be overwhelming. Learning new things often involves overcoming mental blocks, which is inherently stressful. Many people learn better and are less intimidated if there are friendly animations or narrations rather than dry presentation through text and still pictures. People also learn better when they're engaged, through activities, games, self-quizzes, and such (see Figure 15.13).

The History Channel UK offers an in-depth learning site for high school students, complete with activities, self-quizzes, and reference resources (www.thehistorychannel.co.uk/ historystudystop). For more multimedia learning experiences, visit MOMA's Art Safari (www.moma.org/onlineprojects/artsafari); and National Geographic's *World* magazine (www.nationalgeographic.com/world).

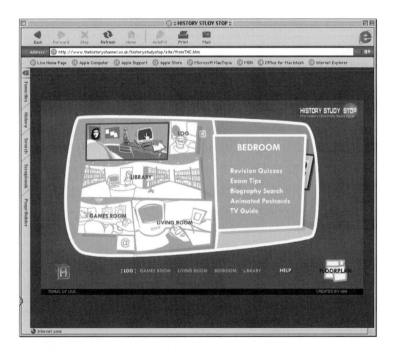

Figure 15.13   Engaging users for educational purposes (www.thehistorychannel.co.uk/ historystudyshop/site/fromTCH.htm).

Summary

Web multimedia is full of challenges, both technical and artistic. Just deciding how to get media and complex interactivity onto a web page requires strategizing and skill. Determining when and why to put multimedia elements on the page is an entirely different, no less important, challenge.

The following chapters examine the various ways to create web multimedia and how Dreamweaver can help you implement them. Chapter 16, "Getting Interactive with Behaviors," covers using Dreamweaver Behaviors to add JavaScript functionality to web pages. Chapters 17, "Controlling Layers with JavaScript," and 18, "Animating Layers," cover Dreamweaver features for implementing DHTML. Chapters 19, "Plugins, ActiveX, and Java," and 20, "Building Web Pages with Flash," discuss using Dreamweaver to work with plugins, ActiveX controls, and Java to incorporate media and interactivity into web pages.

Chapter 16

Getting Interactive with Behaviors

Behaviors are user-friendly pieces of JavaScript prebuilt by Dreamweaver that enable you to create advanced interactions within a page without actually having to script them yourself. With the many popular Dreamweaver behaviors, you can create dynamic, advanced interactive page elements such as rollover images and pop-up menus that greatly enhance your site. You can even create redirection scripts that will load alternate pages depending on the user's browser.

Topics covered in this chapter include an introduction to JavaScript fundamentals, how Dreamweaver writes JavaScript, and how to attach and work with behaviors in Dreamweaver.

Behaviors and JavaScript

Don't worry—you don't have to know how to write JavaScript to use Dreamweaver behaviors. But you'll be better able to understand, and even tweak, the code Dreamweaver writes if you're familiar with a few of the basic concepts of the language.

JavaScript and HTML

HTML was originally designed for scientists and researchers to put their documents in an electronic format that could be shared and viewed over a wide range of computers. Therefore, it is primarily designed to display static text with a simple, basic structure. The current state of the web has stretched HTML way beyond the purpose for which it was designed. The rising needs of early web developers created a demand to extend the basic functionality and interactivity of the web. JavaScript was developed and incorporated into HTML to satiate this demand.

JavaScript is a scripting language loosely based on the Java programming language. A *scripting language*, by definition, is not self-executable. This means that it is a set of instructions that are read and executed by another program, in this case the browser. This is in contrast to Java, which is a compiled language. This means that the program is compiled or packaged into a self-contained program that can be run by itself.

Because it is a scripting language, you do not need a special program with which to write the script. Scripting languages can and are written as text files. The browser reads the script and executes the functions it finds there.

Working with Events and Actions

A Dreamweaver behavior, like most JavaScript interactions, consists of an *event* and an *action*. When the user clicks on something, that's an event. That event (clicking) triggers an action such as a new window opening, a sound playing, or a picture changing.

What Are Events?

The browser is on the alert constantly watching for events. When the browser detects an event, it looks to see if there's an *event handler* that contains a series of instructions for handling that event. Those instructions are the action (a window popping open, a sound playing, and so forth.)

What Are Actions?

An action is made up of one or more scripting statements that are *do* statements, imperatives that command—do this, do that, then do the other thing! When an action might get performed more than once on a page, it's more efficient to combine all of those imperative statements into a single unit called a *function*. A function is a recipe for action. When there are functions are involved, the event handler doesn't have to say "do this, do that, do the other thing." The event handler can simply so, "go find this function and perform the actions it specifies."

How Dreamweaver Writes Behaviors

When Dreamweaver writes a behavior, the action part of the behavior is put into what is called a *function*. The event part of the behavior is added to your page as an *event handler* containing a function call (which contains all the instructions that will be executed when the event happens) that calls up that function. We say the event handler (the event part) calls that function (the action part). Calling the function makes the function execute and (*voila!*) the action happens.

For example, if someone tells you to run around the yard three times and do a cartwheel, it's comparable to a set of statements that will happen the moment the browser sees them. Just like you instantly running around, the browser performs the commands as soon as it loads the page reads this insturction.

But if someone tells you to run around the yard three times and do a cartwheel, but not until he calls your name and says *go*, that's a function. When he actually calls your name and says *Go!*, that's the function call. What do you do in response to the function call? You run around the yard three times and do a cartwheel, which is the action. When the function is called (by the function call), the browser it performs its action.

So, in terms of the code, imagine you have a simple text link in your document (like the one shown in Figure 16.1), and you add a simple behavior like the Popup Message behavior to it. Dreamweaver adds the following code to the <body> of your document (new code shown in bold):

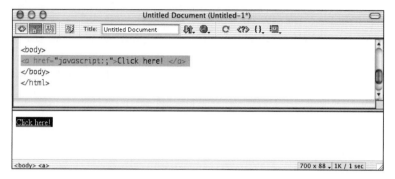

Figure 16.1   A very simple text link ready to receive a Dreamweaver behavior.

```
<a href="javascript:;" onClick="MM_popupMsg('Hello, world!')">Click here!
</a>
```

The <a> tag contains a link ("javascript:;") and an event handler (onClick=) that contains the function call (MM_popupMsg('Hello, world!')).

The actual function that is run is in the <script> tag in the head of the page. It looks like this:

```
<script language="JavaScript" type="text/JavaScript">
<!--
function MM_popupMsg(msg) { //v1.0
  alert(msg);
}
//-->
</script>
```

 Note

The linkto javascript:; is a *null link*, a link that doesn't send the browser anywhere. It's comparable to the # null link but safer to use because linking to # can cause the browser to scroll back to the top of the current document.

Other examples of actions are:

- Checking to see what browser is being used
- Changing any element (image, text) on a page
- Going to a different page

Actions are always things only the computer does (noninteractive).

Other examples of events include:

- Clicking
- Moving the mouse over something
- Loading
- Unloading
- Saving

Events are things the computer and the user do together (interactive).

Working with Behaviors in Dreamweaver

Behaviors can add functionality to your page that goes well beyond basic HTML. Some of these behaviors are popular and used quite often. Others are little things that will give your site a professional touch. Understanding events and how they influence the usability of your page is key to making your page work the way you want and the way the user expects.

In this section, we discuss how to add behaviors to page elements and how the elements that are chosen affect the behavior options.

Using the Behaviors Panel

The Behaviors panel is the one place where the behaviors can be added, subtracted, and manipulated (see Figure 16.2). To open the Behaviors panel, go to Window > Behaviors or press Shift+F3 (Windows) or Cmd+F3 (Mac).

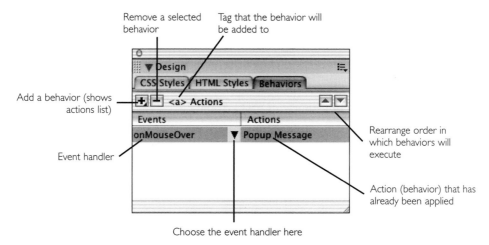

Figure 16.2   The Behaviors panel.

The plus (+) button is used to attach behaviors from a list of available behaviors for the selected element. You can attach more than one behavior to an element. The up and down arrow buttons control the order in which the behaviors are stacked. Alphabetically, events determine the order of behaviors. The up/down only changes the order of behaviors if more than one behavior uses a single event.

Attaching Behaviors to Page Elements

To attach a behavior to a page element:

1. Select the page element.

2. With the element selected, open the Behaviors panel.

3. Click the (+) button and select a behavior. Note that the element to which you are attaching the behavior will determine what behaviors are available. Also, page content will determine some of the options. The Timeline behaviors will only be active when there is a timeline animation on the page.

4. Complete the chosen behavior's dialog box and click OK. The behavior is now attached
to the page element. Notice that the behavior is listed in the panel when that element is selected.

5. Highlight the behavior in the panel, and choose the event drop-down arrow to select an appropriate event for the behavior.

As mentioned previously, you need to remember two very important points when using behaviors:

- The event options depend on the browser setting. There are events for the following:

  - 3.0 and later

  - 4.0 and later

  - IE 3 to 6 (individual browser versions)

  - Netscape 3 to 6 (individual browser versions)

The number of events available goes up as the browser version goes up. It is advisable that you choose 4.0 and above unless you know you have a targeted audience and you need the advanced functionality of a more specific setting. Click the plus (+) button and go to Show Events For (see Figure 16.3).

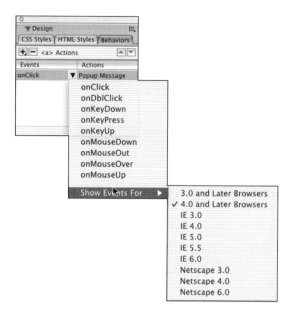

Figure 16.3   The Show Events For options.

- The behaviors and events available also depend on the element to which you are attaching the behavior. The list of behaviors available will differ significantly if you are attaching the behavior to the body of the page, an image, or a hyperlink around an image or text.

Here's a common example of how these two ideas work. You type some text in the Document window. Then looking to attach a behavior to it, you open the Behaviors panel and click the plus (+) button. You select the Popup Message behavior, type in your message, and click OK. Now back in the Behaviors panel, you see your new behavior. The event is set to onLoad. You don't want that one, so you click the arrow to select your events. There are only two: onLoad and onUnload. That doesn't seem right. You want onClick. Then you realize that it must be the browser setting. Ah! It was set to 3.0 and later. You change it to 4.0 and later and all will be well. You click the arrow to select the onClick event. However, now there are only four more and none is the one you want. You realize that they are all noninteractive events. onLoad, onFocus…something else must be wrong.

Because you are in Code and Design view, you check the code. Ah! You notice that the call to the MM_popupMsg function is set to onLoad and written to the <body> tag! You didn't apply it to a link! So you delete the behavior again, make the text into a null link, attach the behavior to the link, go to Events, and there it is: nine interactive events. You select onClick and all is well. For fun, you change the Show Events For setting to IE 5, and you now have more than 30 events from which to choose.

So keep an eye on your browser settings and the elements to which you are attaching behaviors.

Exercise 16.1   Setting the Browser Events Level

In this exercise, you learn how the browser setting influences your choices for events.

1. Open a new document (File > New > HTML) and type **behavior test** in the Design window.

2. Select the word Behavior and in the Property inspector type in **javascript:;**. That text is now a link.

3. Open the Behaviors panel.

4. Select the word Test.

5. Click the plus (+) button and select Popup Message.

6. In the dialog that opens, type in a message and click OK to close the dialog box.

7. In the Behaviors panel, click the down arrow in the Events field and notice your selections.

8. Click the plus (+) button again and go to Show Events For. If it is set for 3.0 and later, set it to 4.0 and later. If set for 4.0, set to 3.0. Notice the change in available events.

9. Highlight the linked text and apply this behavior to it. Notice the difference in event options.

10. Change the Show Events For to IE 5.0 and notice all the events that are now available.

11. Set to onClick and then Preview in Browser (F12). Click the link to activate the pop-up message.

Note

Some behaviors are content-dependent. The Drag Layer behavior will be active only if there is a layer on the page. Control Flash or Shockwave will be active only if you have a Flash or Shockwave movie on the page. The Validate Form behavior will work only if there is a form on the page.

Applying Behaviors to the <body> Tag

In some instances, you will want to attach the behavior to the body. Some behaviors are designed specifically for the <body> tag.

The following behaviors are usually attached to the <body> tag:

- Check Browser
- Check Plugin
- Preload Images

The following behaviors can be attached to the <body> tag:

- Call JavaScript
- Change Property
- Go To URL
- Open Browser Window
- Play Sound
- Popup Message
- Set Text of Status Bar

For instance, if you want a small window to pop up when people come to your site, you can set the Open Browser Window behavior to activate when the page loads (onLoad event). This way, the browser window will open without any user interaction.

To attach a behavior to the body, you must make sure that the body tag has focus or is selected. You can do this in two ways:

- Go to the tag selector at the bottom-left corner of the page and click on the body tag.
- Click on an empty part of the page, making sure that no other page element is selected. You can then add a behavior, and it will be written to the body tag.

Applying Behaviors to Images

Behaviors can be added to images. Unlike adding behaviors to plain text, which will instead look to a containing element to hold the behavior (the <a> tag usually), available behaviors can be added directly to an image. At this stage, it is important to realize that there is a difference between an image and an image that is a hyperlink. You can certainly add behaviors to images, but it might be better to make the image into a link. One benefit of attaching behaviors to links is that the cursor changes to a hand over links. This gives users a visual indication that something will happen if they click. If you add a behavior to a plain, non-linked image, the behavior will still work but the user won't know that it is a clickable item. You might also run into browser concerns as not all browsers know how to handle event handlers attached to regular images. There is better browser support for behaviors within links.

Some behavior-event combinations will add a link tag when applied. This is because the link tag is required for that particular event. You can determine these events because they are within parentheses. For example, if you attach a Popup Message behavior to a regular image, by default the (onClick) event is chosen. A check of the code will show that an <a> tag has been added and the behavior is attached to the <a> rather than the image tag, which was the element selected when you added the behavior. The following exercise will demonstrate the difference between these ideas.

Exercise 16.2   Attaching a Behavior to an Image

In this exercise, we will attach a behavior to an image. Specifically, we will attach a Popup Menu behavior to an image.

Before you start, copy the **chapter_16** folder on the CD to your hard drive. Define a site called Chapter 16, with this folder as the local root folder.

1. Open **pop_up.htm** from the **chapter_16** folder on the CD.
2. Click the image to highlight it and go to the Behaviors panel (Windows > Behaviors).
3. Click the plus (+) button and select Popup Message.
4. In the dialog box, type in **Window in Venice** and click OK.
5. In the Events field of the Behaviors panel, click the down arrow and choose onClick.

    If this is not available, click the plus (+) button and under Show Events For, choose 4.0 and later. onClick should now be available.
6. Preview in Browser (F12) and click in the image. The pop-up message should appear.

Keep this Dreamweaver window open because you will go back to it in the next section.

Now what's wrong with this picture? The behavior works fine, but your users will have no visual indication that clicking this image will actually do anything! They need some visual clue that this is an interactive element (perhaps the cursor changing as if it were a link, for instance).

You might have noticed that there are many events available for your behaviors. Some of them seem redundant, such as onClick and (onClick). These are quite different in the code that is generated and how the browser reacts to it.

Those events without parentheses will be added directly to the selected element. While this might work fine in some browsers, there will be no visual indication that the item is clickable, as it is not a link.

Events within parentheses will wrap the selected element within an <a> tag. This will do two things:

- Change the cursor into a hand so that users know that it is clickable.
- There is better support for behaviors added to the <a> tag.

We will now change the file we just created so that it is wrapped within the <a> tag.

1. Back in the page you just built, click the image and remove the behavior.
2. Click in the image to highlight it.
3. Go to the Behaviors panel and apply the Popup Message behavior.
4. For an event, choose (onClick) (the one within parentheses).
5. Preview in Browser (F12). Notice that now, when you mouse over the image, the cursor changes to a hand, indicating that the image is clickable. Go to the code and notice that Dreamweaver has automatically added an <A> tag to the image.

This defines, again, the difference and importance of knowing where in the code the behavior is attached and how this affects the functionality of your page.

Just for fun, go back to the behavior and change the Show Events For to IE 5 and look at the sheer number of events available to you.

Behaviors and Dynamic Data

Behaviors use client-side scripting; live data pages use server-side scripting. But you can use dynamic data sources in your behaviors. The application server will use the server-side scripting to construct the JavaScript code that goes into the behavior; the browser will then execute the behavior.

How you integrate dynamic sources into your behaviors is up to your own imagination. Any behavior that causes a file to open will let you choose a data source for the file's URL. This includes Open Browser Window, Go To URL, Show/Hide Pop-up Menu, and even Jump Menus. Behaviors that show images, such as Swap Image, will let you supply a dynamic src for the image chosen. Behaviors that show text messages, such as Popup Message, Set Text of Layer, and Set Text of Status Bar, can

continues ▶

be configured to show dynamic text elements instead of static text. The following section shows how you can be sneaky, if needed, to get your dynamic behavior assembled.

Popup Message Behavior

You cannot assign a dynamic text source to this behavior as you're creating it, but you can be sneaky and add dynamic text after the fact. Do this:

1. Apply the Popup Message behavior as normal, entering some brief temporary text to be displayed in the message.

2. Go to Code view or Code and Design view, and find the code for the behavior's function call.

3. Select and delete the temporary text you entered when you created the behavior.

4. From the Bindings panel, choose a Recordset field, and drag it into the Code window, exactly where you deleted the temporary text (see Figure 16.4).

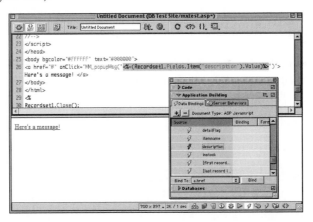

Figure 16.4   Sneaking a dynamic text element into the function call for the Popup Message behavior.

Jump Menu

A *dynamic jump menu* is simply a cross between a standard jump menu and a dynamic list/menu form item. Create it like this:

1. Create a jump menu as you normally would (Insert > Form Objects > Jump Menu), but in the dialog box that appears, assign it no entries.

2. In the Server Behaviors panel, click the plus (+) and choose Dynamic Elements > List/Menu. When the dialog box appears, choose your jump menu as the list/menu to affect.

3. Assign each menu entry a name and value from your recordset. Remember that the value must come from a field that creates a valid URL.

Some Useful Behaviors

This section discusses some of the popular behaviors that come with Dreamweaver. Keep in mind that some of the element-specific behaviors are covered in other chapters. For instance, the behavior that deals with Form Validation is covered in Chapter 11, "Working with Forms."

Some behaviors, such as the Popup Message and the Open Browser Window, have already been discussed in examples throughout the book.

Pop-Up Menu

Dreamweaver can now create its own pop-up menus. This functionality was originally available in Macromedia Fireworks 4. Because it was the first implementation of this feature, it had some limitations, such as menu placement. Dreamweaver MX solves this issue, and an improved interface has been added.

To use this behavior, you need to attach it to an image or a hyperlink. Insert an image on your page. Select the image and then open your Behaviors panel. Select Show Pop Up Menu. Then follow these steps:

1. On the opening screen, enter the name of the menu item. This is the text that will appear on the button. Then assign the text a link by browsing to another page or entering in an absolute URL. You can set the target here if you are using Frames.

2. Click the plus (+) button to add this menu item. Click the Indent Item button if you want to create a submenu off the next higher menu item. Items will continue to be indented until you click the Outdent Item button. Use the up and down arrow buttons to arrange the order in which the menu items will appear.

3. When you have completed adding your menu items, go to the Appearance tab. Here you will determine the look of your menus.

4. Select whether this will be a vertical or horizontal menu. The Preview area will give you an approximate look of the menu. Choose the font name, size, and style of the menu text. Choose a justification setting. Choose the text and cell colors for the Up and Over states.

5. When set there, go to the Advanced tab. Here you can specify specific settings of your menu. As there are really tables, you can set cell width and height, padding and spacing, and delay time. You can also specify borders and specific colors of the borders. (These settings might be browser-dependent.)

6. Now go to the Position tab. This tab lets you specify the position of the pop-up menus relative to the image to which they are attached. If you wish, you can specify any pixel number for the X and Y values.

7. Click OK and your pop-up menu will be built. It will not show up in the Design window, so Preview in Browser to see it in action!

Exercise 16.3   Building a Pop-Up Menu

In this exercise, we will create a pop-up menu using Dreamweaver's built in behavior. This is a very popular way to quickly build an advanced navigation system.

If you haven't done so yet, copy the **chapter_16** folder on the CD to your hard drive. Define a site called Chapter 16, with this folder as the local root folder.

1. Open a new HTML document and save it as **pop_up.htm**.

2. Insert the **navigation.gif** image (from the **chapter_16** folder on the CD) onto the page. Make sure that it is selected on the page.

3. In the Behaviors panel, click the plus (+) button and select Show Pop Up Menu. The wizard shown in Figure 16.5 will display.

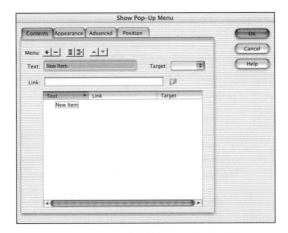

Figure 16.5   The Show Pop-Up Menu dialog box.

4. In the contents panel, type in **Macromedia** in the Text field. In the Link field, type in `http://www.macromedia.com`.

5. Click the plus (+) button. Type in **Dreamweaver**. In the Link Field, type in `http://www.macromedia.com`.

6. Click the plus (+) button again and type in **Page 3**. In the Link field, click the Browse folder and browse to **swap_image.htm** in the **chapter_16** folder.

7. Click on the Indent Item button. This will indent Page 3 relative to "Dreamweaver". This will create another level of pop-up menu.

8. Click on the Appearance tab. This panel is where you determine the look of the menu.

9. You can choose between Vertical Menu and Horizontal Menu. Look at both options but choose Vertical Menu. Leave the rest of the default options.

10. Go to the Advanced tab. Leave the defaults here, but notice that these options are equivalent to table settings. Dreamweaver is actually creating tables to make these menus.

11. Go to the Position tab. This menu allows you to set the position of the menu relative to the image to which this behavior is attached. This is a nice improvement from the Fireworks 4 implementation of this feature!

12. Click on the leftmost button. This will make the menu appear from the lower-right corner of the image.

    The Hide Menu on onMouseOut Event option should be checked. This will make the menu disappear when you move off it, and will add a Hide Pop Up Menu behavior to your Behaviors list. This behavior is only used in conjunction with a pop-up menu and should only be added with this check box.

13. Click OK to create the menu. It will not be functional in the Design window.

14. Press F12 to Preview in Browser and test your menu!

Open Browser Window

You can use this behavior to open a new window of the browser. This differs from setting the target to _blank (see Chapter 12, "Designing Frame-Based Pages") because with this behavior, you can define the size of the window, you can give a name to the window, and you can dictate the appearance of the window, such as what menu bars it gets, whether it gets a status bar, and so on. Setting the target does not produce this kind of control.

To use the Open Browser Window behavior, do this:

1. Create two files: One will be the main page that contains the behavior that opens the new window; the other document will appear in the new window.

2. With the main page open, select whatever page element you want to trigger the behavior.

3. In the Behaviors panel, click + and choose Open Browser Window.

4. In the dialog box that appears, enter the specifics for the new window. This includes the URL of the second page you constructed in Step 1, and various options for the window.

5. Name your new browser window.

To test, Preview in Browser and click in the link.

Exercise 16.4   Using the Open Browser Window Behavior

The Open Browser Window behavior (see Figure 16.6) is used quite a bit in web design. It can be used for special messages that need to get attention. It can be used if you have a large page that shouldn't have to be reloaded every time the user goes away from it. For example, if you have a page with lots of image thumbnails, you can use this behavior to open a new window with the full-size image. Then the user would not have to reload the thumbnail page when they want to see a different photo.

Figure 16.6   Open Browser Window options.

In this exercise, we will use the Open Browser Window behavior. With this behavior, you can set the size of the window and control what options it gets, such as scrollbars and a status bar.

If you haven't done so yet, copy the **chapter_16** folder on the CD to your hard drive. Define a site called Chapter 16, with this folder as the local root folder.

1. Open a new document and save it in the **chapter_16** folder. Type **My Link**, and type **javascript:;** in the Link field of the Property inspector.

2. Highlight this link text and then click the + sign button in the Behaviors panel and select Open Browser Window. The Open Browser Window dialog box is shown in Figure 16.6.

3. Enter these settings:
   - URL to Display: Click the Browse button and select the **browser_window.htm** file from the local root folder or any other page you want.
   - Window Width: 300
   - Window Height: 200
   - Attributes:
     - Select Scrollbars as Needed
     - Status Bar
     - Resize Handles
   - Window Name: New

4. Click OK to finish the behavior.

5. Preview in Browser and click the link. The new window should open with the attributes you assigned.

There are limitations to this behavior. You cannot define where on the screen it will open. You cannot tell it to open behind the main window. You can set these and other properties by customizing the JavaScript, but this must be done manually in the code. As mentioned earlier, that requires a rather strong understanding of JavaScript. Note that there is a "Close Window" function in the included Snippets panel in Dreamweaver MX. This can be added to the page that is being opened in the new window.

Extensions that offer other options are available for opening a browser window. Check out the table at the end of this chapter for examples. Extensions are discussed in Chapter 35, "Working with Extensions."

Setting the Text of the Status Bar

This behavior sets the text in the status bar at the bottom of the browser window. This behavior gives your page that little touch that would appear to be difficult but is made easy with Dreamweaver MX.

To use this behavior, open a page and click the plus (+) button on the Behaviors panel. Choose Set Text > Set Text of Status Bar. In the dialog box that opens, type in some text. Click OK.

Since we didn't select anything, it will be added to the body tag with an onLoad event. This means that it will show as soon as the page loads. Preview the page, and the text you typed should show up in the status bar. Keep in mind that the status bar is an option in most browsers, so do not put critical information in this behavior. It's more of a nice detail.

<u>Exercise 16.5   Using the Set Text of Status Bar Behavior</u>

This behavior adds a little professional touch to your web page.

1. In an open document, type **Status Bar**.

2. Select this text and make a null link. (Type **javascript:;** in the Link field.)

3. Go to the Behaviors panel, and click the plus (+) button. Go to Set Text > Set Text for Status Bar.

4. In the dialog box, type in **This behavior is easy!!** and click OK.

5. In the Behaviors panel, make sure the event is set for onMouseOver. If this option is not available, check your Show Events For setting and make sure it is set for 4.0 and later.

6. Preview in Browser. Roll the cursor over the link and notice that in the lower left of the browser, your text now appears. After you mouse over that link, the text is there to stay until you leave the page or the user activates another instance of this behavior.

7. Let's smooth out the functionality of this behavior. Back in the Dreamweaver window, highlight the text link. The applied behavior will show in the Behaviors panel.

8. Click the plus (+) button and select the Set Text of Status Bar again. This time, leave the field blank and click OK.

9. Back in the panel, change the event to onMouseOut.

10. Preview in IE.

Notice that now when you move the mouse off the link, the text disappears. Although this is a cleaner design, you should certainly use this functionality however you need.

Performing a Browser Check

You can set up your site to show different content depending on the browser the user is using. Although this might increase the number of pages in your site, you can be assured that they will be viewed as you designed them without browser-incompatibility concerns.

This might be required only if you have a lot of DHTML, with animated layers and other elements that might be prone to cross-browser issues. This behavior uses JavaScript to determine the browse name and version and then automatically links to the determined path.

To use this behavior, you are deciding a few things. The behavior decides among IE, Netscape, and others. For testing this behavior, you will need at least three browsers installed. Also, you will need to make pages that let you know that it is working. For instance, you will need to make a page that says `This is Netscape` or `This is IE` and `this is the other page`.

There are also a couple ways to set this up. Since the behavior is going to happen as the page is loading, you can set up an empty page that contains only the behavior. It will then direct you to the correct page. Or, for those browsers that don't support JavaScript or for those that have disabled it, put the behavior on the initial page. This page should have content for those users. Others will be directed accordingly.

You have three choices for redirection:

- Stay On This Page
- URL
- Alt URL

Using these combinations, you can set up your redirection. You also have browser versions to consider. By default, they are set to 4.0. So the behavior is asking, "What browser is it?" but also "What version?". So those with version 3 browsers can be sent somewhere else.

For this example, we will set up the behavior so that the other browser will stay on the same page, and IE and Netscape users will be redirected. Again, you will need at least three different browsers installed to really see this. For this requirement, you can have a combination like Netscape 3 and 6, and IE 4 or above.

1. With the initial or JavaScript-free page open, click on the plus (+) button of the Behaviors panel. Choose Check Browser.

2. For URL, browse to the page you have created for Netscape 4 and above users. For Alt URL, choose the page you created for IE 4 and over users. All others are going to stay on this page.

   For Netscape 4.0 or later, choose Go to URL. For Otherwise, choose Stay on This Page.

   For Internet Explorer 4.0 and later, choose Go To Alt URL and for Otherwise, choose Stay on This Page.

   For Other browsers, choose Stay on This Page.

3. Save and Preview in the various browsers to confirm that everything is working as planned.

4. The accompanying CD contains an example page set up to detect the browser version and then redirect accordingly. Go to the **chapter_16/samples** folder and open **browser_check.htm** directly in the browser. It should show text according to the browser type.

Open this file in Dreamweaver and notice how the behavior is set up. Also notice that it is in the <body> tag. This means it will be executed when the page loads. The redirect to the alternate pages will take a fraction of a second. Or as discussed earlier, apply the behavior to the initial page that has content for non-JavaScript enabled browsers and then set the "stay on this page" options for those that do not get redirected.

You can use the browser version number to further refine the behavior. You can have extended functionality in pages designed for IE 5.0 and higher. If someone comes in with IE 4.0, you can send her to less-complicated pages. This might be useful if you are using other behaviors that use 5.0 events. You can redesign these behaviors to work with 4.0 events for these viewers.

Keep in mind that this behavior is not foolproof. As with every stage of development, make sure to test all your functionality as you go.

Swapping Images

One of the more popular behaviors used on many sites is the capability to change or swap images depending on user interaction. Dreamweaver has a built-in way to make a *rollover image,* as it's often called. This is when one image is swapped with another image when you roll over it. You can use behaviors to extend this functionality, creating advanced rollovers.

Basic rollovers can be created quickly in Dreamweaver, using the Image Rollover object (see Chapter 6, "Links and Navigation," for more on this.) In this section, you will learn how to make more complex rollovers.

Actually, two behaviors are used when making a rollover image:

- Swap Image
- Swap Image Restore

These are two separate behaviors that enable you to control exactly when you want things to appear and change. This is the same idea as in the status bar text example: one behavior to show it, and another to make it disappear. By default, when you add the Swap Image behavior, the Restore Images onMouseOut option is checked, and this option writes the Swap Image Restore behavior.

To make a simple rollover, click Insert > Interactive Images > Rollover Image. You will be presented with the Insert Rollover Image dialog box (see Figure 16.7).

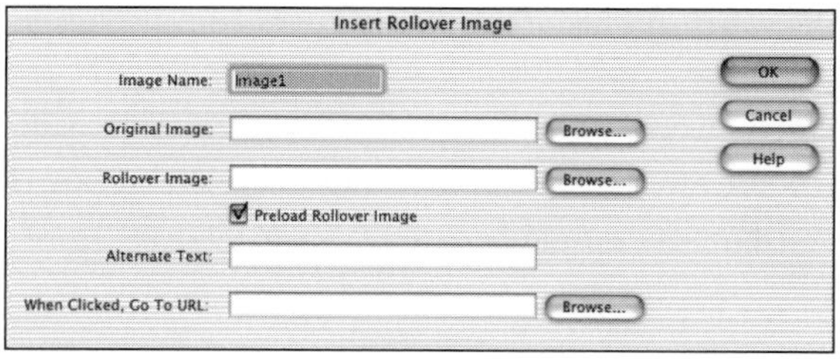

Figure 16.7   The Insert Rollover Image dialog box.

For Original Image, browse to the image that you want to initially show.

For Rollover Image, browse to the image you want to show on the event. You can give the image Alternate text if you wish. This is for those who cannot view images. It also shows up when you pause your mouse over the image.

If you want this rollover image to be a link, go to When Clicked, Go to URL field and browse to the desired file. Click OK.

A rollover image is really a Swap Image behavior with a Swap Image Restore behavior. If you click on the image, you can see these in the Behaviors panel. By default, the event is set to onMouseOver.

Preview in Browser to see this in action. Simply roll your mouse over the image and it will swap.

Disjointed Image Swaps

These behaviors can be combined in many ways, and more than one behavior can be added to any image for more complex interaction.

Using combinations of these behaviors, you can have an image on one side of the page swap an image on the other side of the page. This is called a *disjointed rollover.*

Multiple-Image Swaps

An image can be set to swap itself and other images on the page with one event. This is called a *multiple-image swap.* Exercise 16.6 demonstrates a multiple-image swap.

To make a multiple-image swap:

1. Insert two images onto the page. Save it. For this behavior, it is important to name them. For each image, type in a name in the top-left field of the Property inspector.

2. Click on the first image and then go to the Behaviors panel. Click the plus (+) button and choose Swap Image. In the Swap Image dialog box (see Figure 16.8), your two named images should be listed.

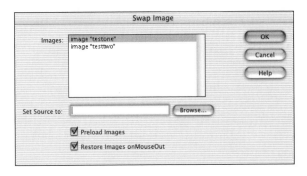

Figure 16.8   The Swap Image dialog box.

3. Make sure the first image is selected, and in the Set Source To: field, browse to the image you want to be the rollover image. Leave the two boxes checked at the bottom. Now, click the second image. In the Set Source To: field, browse to the image that you want the second image to swap with.

4. Click OK to close the dialog box. The critical idea for this is that we just set two different images to swap when you roll over the *first* image, because we applied the behavior to that first image.

5. Preview in Browser. Roll over the first image. Both images should swap. Now roll over the second image. Nothing happens because there is no behavior *applied* to that image. The behavior is applied to the first image but controls the second. That is the essence of a multiple-image swap (also called a *disjointed rollover*).

Exercise 16.6   Creating a Rollover Image

In this exercise, you first make a rollover image the easy way and see how it was created. Then you add complexity to it.

If you haven't done so yet, copy the **chapter_16** folder on the CD to your hard drive. Define a site called Chapter 16, with this folder as the local root folder.

1. In a new document, go to Insert > Interactive Images > Rollover Image. The Insert Rollover Image dialog box will display (refer to Figure 16.7).

2. In Image Name, give it a name that describes the content. Here, call it **Pisa**.

3. For Original Image, browse to the **chapter_16/samples/images** folder on the accompanying CD. Choose **pisa1.jpg**.

4. For Rollover Image, choose **pisa2.jpg**.

5. Leave Preload Rollover Image checked. Leave the Go to URL field empty. You can use it to navigate to another page, but for the example purposes here, you can leave it empty.

6. Click OK to close the dialog box.

7. Preview in Browser and roll your mouse over the image. It should immediately swap to the second image. Mouse off of it and it will revert to the first image.

   Now go back to Dreamweaver and see what it built for you.

8. Open the Behaviors panel. In the Design view, click the image.

   Notice that the list contains two behaviors. Click in an empty part of the Design window or click the body tag in the tag selector. Notice that the Preload Images behavior is listed. You added this via the check box in the initial dialog box. If you didn't have this behavior, the image would not be downloaded until you moused over the image. This would introduce a lag time into the swap. This behavior brings down the image as the rest of the page loads, and it is then ready for the swap.

9. Click again on the image. Double-click the Swap Image behavior in the panel. It will open the dialog box shown in Figure 16.8.

Note

The Swap Image Restore behavior can be used only in conjunction with the Swap Image behavior. There are no settings for it other than setting the event, which is onMouseOut by default.

10. Now add complexity to this image behavior. Put the cursor on the page and then select Insert > Image and choose **gcanal1.jpg**. This image is found in **chapter_16/samples/images** on the CD.

    In the Name field next to the thumbnail in the Property inspector, type in **canal**.

    It is important to name the images because Dreamweaver uses this to keep track of the behaviors. Also, only named elements can be changed with JavaScript.

    Now you are going to use the Pisa image to change the canal image. This means that when you roll over the Pisa image, you expect the canal image to change.

11. Click the Pisa image. Double-click the existing Swap Image behavior. You can use this one instance of the behavior to control many images at once.

12. Choose the canal image. For Set Source To, click the Browse button and choose **gcanal2.jpg** from the **chapter_16/samples/images** folder.

Now both images in the list should have a source file.

13. Click OK to close the dialog box, and then Preview in Browser.

Roll over the Pisa image and both images should change. Mouse out and they both switch back.

Roll over the canal image and nothing happens. There is no behavior attached to it.

14. Now give this one more level of complexity. In Dreamweaver, click the canal image. In the Behaviors panel, click the plus (+) button and add a Swap Image behavior.

15. In the dialog box, select canal in the list and for source select **gcanal2.jpg**. Click OK to set the behavior.

Now you expect that rolling over the canal image will cause a swap to occur.

To view the final result, open **swap_image.htm** in the **chapter_16** folder.

16. Preview in Browser.

Rolling over the Pisa image will still cause both images to swap. Rolling over the canal image will cause only the canal image to swap.

Working Sneakily with Behaviors

Borrowing function calls and moving functions to shared files are two really cool and sneaky techniques to learn with behaviors.

"Borrowing" Function Calls

After you understand how functions and function calls work in Dreamweaver behaviors, you can extend your use of behaviors by "borrowing" their function calls to put in unusual places, essentially allowing you to attach behaviors to elements not normally allowed by the Dreamweaver interface. For instance, you can call behaviors from within media elements, like Flash or QuickTime movies. You can even call behaviors from within other behaviors.

It works like this:

1. Start by creating a temporary text link (something you'll delete when you're done). Somewhere in the document, type a word or two of text, and link it to # (a null link).

2. With the new text link selected, open the Behaviors panel and apply the behavior whose function call you want to borrow. (Maybe you want to call the Popup Message behavior from within a Flash Button, for instance. You would start by applying that behavior to your temporary text link.) Configure the behavior as desired. Test it out in a browser to make sure it does what you need it to do.

3. In Code view, find the code for your text link (see Figure 16.9). It will include the function call from the behavior, like this (function call is shown in bold):

```
<a href="#" onMouseOver="MM_popupMsg('Hello, world!')">click me</a>
```

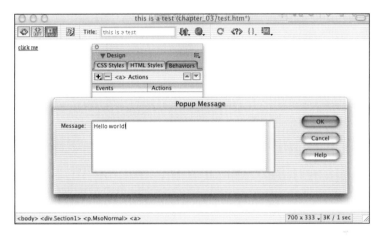

Figure 16.9   Creating a function call by applying a behavior to a temporary text link.

Select and copy the function call code—all the code between the double quotes, starting after onMouseOver= (just like the bold code shown here). Don't include the quotes themselves, though!

4. You are now free to attach this function call to any other behavior or page element. To add the function call to Flash Button or Text, for instance, double-click the Flash object to open its editing window. In the Link field, type the word **javascript** followed by a colon, then paste your function call (see Figure 16.10). For the Popup Message behavior, the call should be javascript: MM_popupMsg('Hello, world!').

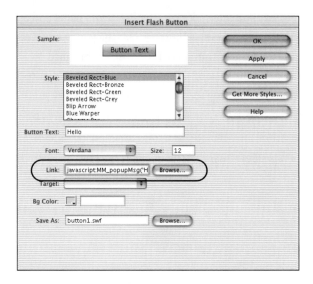

Figure 16.10   Adding the borrowed function call to a Flash object.

5. Delete the temporary text link. Be careful here, however! If you just select the link in Design view and delete, Dreamweaver will remove the function as well as the function call. So instead, go to Code view and delete the item from there. (After you've deleted the link, look through the document <head> to make sure the main function is still present.)

Note

See Chapter 17, "Controlling Layers with JavaScript," for examples of using this technique to call behaviors from other behaviors. See Chapter 19, "Plugins, ActiveX, and Java," and Chapter 20, "Building Web Pages with Flash," for examples of using the technique with media elements.

Moving Functions to Shared Files

Experienced scripters know that any code that will be used repeatedly should be accessed from a single, shared resource for greatest efficiency. This makes the code easier to read and edit, and also—especially if the code is extensive—trims download time and browser overhead. When dealing with JavaScript in HTML documents, this often means moving the functions to a linked JS file that can be shared between HTML documents.

Any time you use a Dreamweaver behavior repeatedly across a site, you have an opportunity to streamline your code by moving the function code to a shared file. Dreamweaver will even help you. You must cut and paste the function code to a new

JS file, and create a link between the two documents. You can then easily share that JS file between documents, and Dreamweaver will recognize its presence.

To move one or more function calls to a shared JS file:

1. Open an HTML file that contains one or more applied behaviors that you know you'll be re-using in other documents.

2. In Code view, scroll to the <head> section of the document and find the <script> tag containing your behaviors' functions.

3. Select everything between the opening and closing <script> tags (but not the tags themselves), and select Edit > Cut. (See Figure 16.11.)

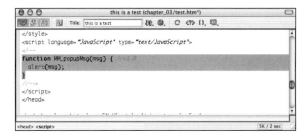

Figure 16.11   Removing a behavior's function from the document <head>.

4. Go to File > New to access the new document dialog box. Here, choose the Basic category of files, and choose to create a new JavaScript file.

5. When the new file opens, place the insertion point in a new paragraph after the opening comments and Edit > Paste. (See Figure 16.12.)

Figure 16.12   Adding the behavior function to a new shared JS file.

6. Save the file, with the .js extension, into your site. (After you've created this shared file, you can simply add other behavior functions to it later; you don't have to create a new JS file every time. Each site you work on can have its own shared JS file.)

7. Close the JS file, and return to your HTML document.

Your behaviors are now broken, until you link your HTML document with the new shared JS file. To link the shared file, do this:

1. Go to View > Head Content, so the Document window shows the little gray strip of icons that represent your document head.

2. Find and select the script icon. (This should select the now-empty `<script>` tag from which you removed the functions.)

3. In the Property inspector, find the Src field. Click its Browse button, and browse to the shared JS file. (See Figure 16.13).

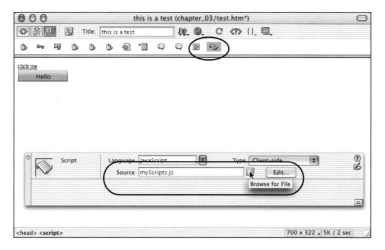

Figure 16.13   Changing a `<script>` tag to contain a link to a shared JS file.

4. After you've done this, save your document and Preview in Browser. If you did everything correctly, the behavior should still work.

The major benefit of creating JS files is that you can reuse them in other HTML documents. To reuse a shared behavior:

1. Open another document in which you want to use the same behavior. Don't apply the behavior yet!

2. Go to View > Head Content.

3. Open the Assets panel, and choose to view Scripts. Your shared JS file will appear there.

4. Drag the shared file from the Assets panel to the head content bar in your
    Document window. If you examine your code after having done this, you'll see
    that a link to the shared file has been added. (See Figure 16.14.)

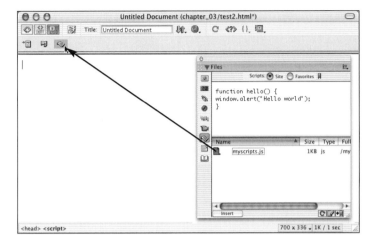

Figure 16.14   Using the Assets panel to link a new HTML document to the shared JS file.

5. Now you can apply any behavior that uses the functions in the shared JS file.
    Dreamweaver will know not to add the functions to your document, because
    they're already present in the shared file.

Note

If you love the idea of sharing functions, but want some help with it, try Paul Boon's
"Create and Hot Swap JS Files From Script Tags" extension, available from the
Macromedia Exchange.

Summary

Behaviors go a long way to giving your web page advanced functionality and that professional flair. They enable you to go well beyond the limitations of basic HTML.

Other behaviors are available, and these are discussed throughout the book in chapters
relevant to their specific functionality. You also can download and install any other functions in Dreamweaver that will go beyond the set included here. You can find these at the
Macromedia Exchange for Dreamweaver. The Macromedia Exchange for Dreamweaver
is discussed in Chapter 35.

In the next chapter, you will learn about even more behaviors and how they relate to
using layers in your page design.

Chapter 17

Controlling Layers with JavaScript

So far in this book, you have learned
what CSS is and how it can be used as a
sophisticated page layout tool. The next
two chapters cover the dynamic aspect of
DHTML—how to use JavaScript to control

CSS page content. The current chapter examines the various Dreamweaver behaviors for controlling layers, including determining visibility, changing layer content, and setting other properties; the next chapter will focus on performing these activities over time—or in other words, animating your layer control.

Dynamic HTML: Layers and Scripting in the Browser

DHTML is a series of overlapping technologies for creating *dynamic web pages*—pages capable of responding in complex ways to user interactions—without using server-side processing, plugins, or other helper applications. CSS and JavaScript are the key players in DHTML, along with various proprietary technologies such as Netscape's JSS (JavaScript style sheets) and Microsoft's ActiveX filters.

Note

For more about CSS and Layers, see Chapter 14, "Using Layers for Page Layout."

About the DOM

The heart of live data page control is the DOM. The *DOM*, or Document Object Model, is a hierarchical description of the structure of objects in an HTML page. In scripting terms, an *object* is an element that can be accessed and altered by scripting commands. The browser window is an object, for instance; with scripting, you can determine what size it is, and what location (URL) it's currently displaying, and you can even tell it to change its location to a new URL. The document currently being displayed in the window is an object, and so is a form sitting in the document, and each input field inside the form. A JavaScript statement like

```
window.document.theForm.textField1.value="Hello world"
```

enables you to climb up the document "tree" to talk to a text field inside a form, inside the document that is currently inside the browser window, and finally to change that text field's value. By accessing that value, you have just navigated the DOM.

Like everything else about computers, the DOM develops and has versions. Basic form access, like that shown here, is part of the Level 0 DOM. The more total page access used for Dynamic HTML requires the more developed Level 1 DOM. Only browsers 4.0 and above can understand the Level 1 DOM; therefore, only those browsers can handle DHTML.

DOM Incompatibility

The DOM is important to you because all DOMs are not the same. The single biggest problem facing most DHTML developers is that the Netscape DOM—the hierarchy you must use to access page elements in that browser—is very different from the Internet Explorer DOM. The IE DOM is more sophisticated and more in line with the official Level 1 DOM standards set by the W3C. Though the Netscape 6 DOM is closer to the standard than the Netscape 4 DOM, it's still not the same as the IE DOM. This means that, even if you consider only these two major browsers, you have three different DOMs to deal with.

In general, DHTML authors have a choice of the following:

- Pick one browser to design for, and ignore the rest.
- Try to be as inclusive as possible by using only features that work everywhere.
- Try to be reasonably inclusive but also use new features, by putting two or more sets of code in each page, each directed at a different browser.

Dreamweaver's DHTML Authoring Strategy

One of the reasons Dreamweaver is popular as a DHTML authoring tool is that it shields designers from most of these compatibility problems. By default, it writes its layer code using the cross-browser `<div>` tag. All of its layer-related behaviors are written with the proper JavaScript to work as well as possible in both major browsers. DHTML features that are purely browser- or platform-specific (such as the IE/Windows filters and page transitions) are either not included or not emphasized in the interface.

You can never be completely shielded, however. Certain items will display differently across browsers—and across platforms in different browsers. Certain behaviors will behave differently in different browsers—or they won't behave at all, despite Dreamweaver's robust coding. This chapter focuses on how to use Dreamweaver tools for dynamically controlling layers. Be aware, as you go through it, that not everything you do will work equally well in all browser/platform situations.

Controlling Layer Visibility

One of the simplest, and most reliable, layer properties you can control with scripting is visibility. By dynamically hiding and showing layers, you can create pages that store much more information than is visible at any given time. The designer's buzzword for this is *nested content*. Nested content can include contextual information popping up where needed, drop-down navigation menus, and different sets of body content that display as users click navigation controls. The possibilities are limited only by the designer's imagination and ingenuity.

You control layer visibility in Dreamweaver with the Show-Hide Layers behavior. As Figure 17.1 shows, it's simple and straightforward to use.

Note

Visibility control as scripted by Dreamweaver is supported by Netscape Navigator 4 and 6, IE 4-6, and Opera 5–6 across platforms.

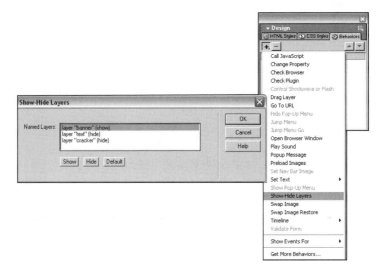

Figure 17.1   The interface for Show-Hide Layers behavior.

The Basics of Showing and Hiding Layers

As with any behavior, start by creating the layer to show or hide, and selecting the object that will trigger the visibility change. Showing and hiding can be triggered by rollovers, mouse clicks, form data changes, or even pages loading. Then follow these steps:

1. In the Behaviors panel, choose the Show-Hide Layers behavior.

2. In the dialog box that appears, select a layer from the list.

3. Choose the visibility state you want it to have.

4. Repeat steps 2 and 3 for any other layers you want to change with this instance of the behavior.

Note that you can change the visibility of as many layers as you like, in this one dialog box, with just one instance of the Show-Hide behavior. If you have three alternate content layers, for instance, one instance of Show-Hide will show one content layer and hide the other two. (That's the scenario being illustrated in Figure 17.1.) Here are a few other tips.

Setting Visibility Versus Changing Visibility

It's important not to confuse the use of JavaScript to change a layer's visibility with the use of HTML to assign the layer's initial visibility. You assign the latter through the Property inspector or Layers panel (see Figure 17.2). If you want your layer to be invisible from the moment the page starts loading, set its visibility to be hidden here. Only if you want your layer's visibility to change based on user interaction or browser activity do you need to use the Show-Hide Layers behavior.

Note

What's the difference between setting the property initially and using the behavior to set it onLoad? Behaviors that execute onLoad will execute only after the page has finished loading. You can, for instance, create a loading screen by making a layer containing the word Loading, and setting it to start out visible, but become hidden onLoad.

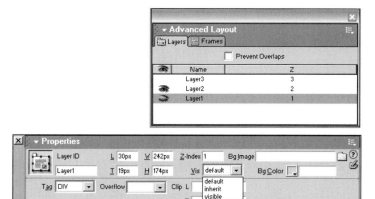

Figure 17.2   Setting layer visibility in the Property inspector or Layers panel.

Showing, Hiding, and Default

When you choose the Show-Hide behavior, you have three visibility choices. Show and Hide are self-explanatory. Default sets the visibility state to inherit. (See Chapter 14 for a full discussion of inherited visibility.)

Choosing Not to Show or Hide a Particular Layer

What if you're in the Show-Hide dialog box, and you've selected a particular layer and set it to show or hide, and then you realize you had the wrong layer chosen? You don't have to cancel the whole operation. Just choose the same option for the same layer again to toggle it off. If you've set the layer "Fred" to "show" by mistake, for instance, just leave Fred selected and click the Show button again.

Working with Invisible Layers

After you start working with this behavior, you are likely to run into the following situation. You've created a layer that will start out invisible, until the user clicks a button or mouses over something that makes it show. How do you continue working with the layer in Design view, now that it's invisible? One solution is to leave it visible until you've finished editing the page. The very last thing you'll do before saving, closing, and uploading the file is use the Property Inspector or Layers panel to set the layer's visibility to Hidden.

For any of you who have less-than-perfect memories, however, this is a dangerous idea, because it's easy to forget that last step when you're facing down a deadline and have a million things to do. Instead, use the Layers panel to select your hidden layer. Clicking a layer's name in the panel will select it, and as soon as it's selected, it will become visible and will stay visible as long as you're editing its contents. As soon as you deselect it, however, it will disappear again. Making the layer temporarily visible in this way doesn't change the HTML code at all (that is, the code still defines the layer as being invisible), so there's no danger of it getting uploaded and displayed on the web improperly (see Figure 17.3).

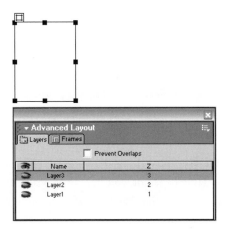

Figure 17.3   Selecting an invisible layer in the Layers panel to make it temporarily visible in Design view.

Exercise 17.1   Creating a Drop-Down or Cascading Menu

In this exercise, you'll create one of the most popular hidden-layer effects, a graphic menu bar with menus that appear when the mouse rolls over topics on the menu bar. This sort of menu is called a *drop-down menu* when the menu bar is placed horizontally across the top of a page (like the menu bars in standard applications), and a *cascading menu* when the menu bar is vertical and the menus appear to the side. All files for the exercise are located on the CD in the **chapter_17/menus** folder.

If you haven't done so already, copy the **chapter_17** folder to your hard drive and define a site with that folder as the local root folder.

1. Start by opening **dropdown.html** and examining its contents and structure. This file contains four layers—one for the menu bar and three for the menus that will appear from it. The three menu layers are nested within the main menu bar layer, so the whole menu system can be repositioned by moving only the main layer. Preview the file in a browser and you'll see that the first of the menus already contains rollovers for each entry (see Figure 17.4).

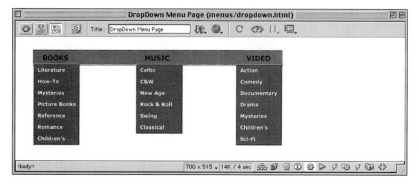

Figure 17.4   The **dropdown.html** file, before any Show-Hide Layer behaviors have been applied.

2. When working in depth with layers, an important habit to get into, is giving them names you'll recognize when you see them in a dialog box or inspector. Before proceeding with the scripting in this exercise, take a moment to rename the layers. Name them "main," "books," "music," and "video."

3. The three books, music, and video layers should initially be invisible. Using the "eyeball" column in the Layers panel, make the books, music, and video layers invisible by clicking until the closed eye icon shows (see Figure 17.5).

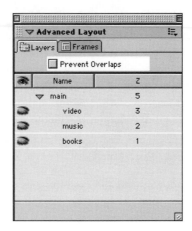

Figure 17.5   The Layers panel for **dropdown.html**, with layers renamed and "eyeballs" closed, signifying that the layers are hidden.

4. You want each menu to appear when the user mouses over the appropriate title in the menu bar. This means attaching the Show-Hide behavior to the three main graphics in the menu bar. Start with the BOOKS image.

   • Select the image.

   • Open the Behaviors panel, and choose Show-Hide Layers from the actions list.

   • In the dialog box that appears, from the list of layers, find "books" and set it to "show" (see Figure 17.6).

   • When you're done, click OK to close the dialog box.

Figure 17.6   The Show-Hide Layers dialog box, showing the "books" layer.

After you've applied the behavior, check the Behaviors panel to make sure the (onMouseOver) event trigger is chosen. (Remember to use the event trigger that appears in parentheses, to ensure maximum cross-browser compatibility. For more on this, see Chapter 16, "Getting Interactive with Behaviors.")

Preview in Browser to make sure the behavior is working. Then repeat the above procedure for each of the other two menu topics.

5. After you've applied all three behaviors, the menus should appear on cue—but they never disappear. The mechanics of making that happen aren't difficult—it's just a matter of applying another Show-Hide behavior. But what event should trigger the behavior? That's a matter of strategy.

One strategy is to make each menu button (BOOKS, MUSIC, VIDEO) trigger its own menu to show and the other menus to hide. To accomplish that, select one of the menu title graphics—BOOKS, for instance—and, in the Behaviors panel, double-click its Show-Hide behavior to edit it. For the BOOKS graphic, the books layer should already be set to show. Select the music layer and set it to hide; then set the video layer to hide also. Using this one behavior, you've now created a script that shows one menu and hides the other two (see Figure 17.7).

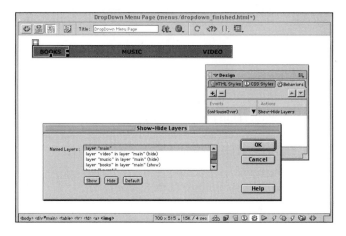

Figure 17.7   The Show-Hide Layers dialog box for the BOOKS menu title, set to show the books layer and hide the other two menu layers.

Repeat this process for each of the three title graphics. Rolling over any menu title should show that title's menu and hide the other two menus.

When you're finished, check out the result in the browser. Assuming that your users will check out each of your menus and then choose a destination from one of them, your menu system should work perfectly. There's one niggling interface flaw remaining, however. What if your visitors check out all the different menus, and then decide not to choose a destination from any one of them? After the menus have started showing, there's no way to get all three of them to hide. Again, this is a matter of strategy. What event can be used to trigger all menus hiding?

A sneaky solution is to put another layer behind all of the menu layers, fill that layer with an invisible image, and set that image to trigger all menus hiding when it is rolled over. Figure 17.8 shows this happening.

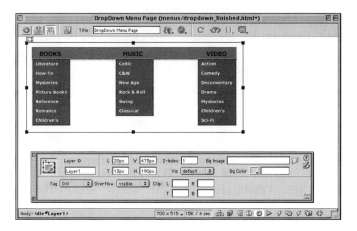

Figure 17.8   Adding a large layer behind the menus, to be used in triggering all menus to hide.

7. Start by drawing a new layer. Make it large enough to cover the entire area of your menu bar and menus. While you're at it, jot down its width and height from the Property Inspector. (Don't nest the background layer in with the main layer, or the effect won't work.) Because it will sit behind the other layers, as a kind of invisible background for them, name it **menubg**.

   Arrange the new **menubg** layer behind all the other layers by going to the Layers panel and dragging it to the bottom of the list of layers.

   With the cursor inside this new layer, use the Image object from the Insert bar to insert **trpix.gif**. This transparent, single-pixel GIF image is located in the **chapter_17/menus/images** folder with the rest of the image files for this exercise. Set the width and height of the image to match the dimensions of your layer.

8. With this large transparent image selected, go to the Behaviors panel and add another Show-Hide Layers behavior. Set this behavior to hide all three menu layers. Set the triggering event to onMouseOver or (onMouseOver).

   When you're finished, preview the page in a browser. When a menu is showing, moving the mouse away from the menu should hide all menus.

   What's happening here? When the mouse rolls over the transparent image, all menus will hide. But when the mouse is over another image, in another layer, which is in front of the transparent image, its event handler is disabled. So, effectively, you've created a trigger that will hide all menus only when the mouse is in the vicinity of the menu system but not actually over any menus or the menu bar.

   Should you use onMouseOver or (onMouseOver) as the trigger for the transparent image? As was discussed in Chapter 16, any time an <img> tag is selected, you have a choice of event triggers with or without parentheses. Choosing a trigger with parentheses will add the behavior's function call to an <a> tag surrounding the image (and will even create the <a> tag, if necessary). Choosing a trigger with no parentheses will add the function to the <img> tag itself. Since Netscape 4.x does not support event handlers for <img> tags, it's safer to use the triggers in parentheses. But adding an <a> tag also causes the cursor to change to a pointing finger. This is the user's cue that a link is present. In the case of your menu system, users are going to be confused if, any time the mouse gets anywhere near the hidden menus, the cursor changes to indicate a link. That's bad interface design.

For this exercise, try the menu system out both ways—with onMouseOver and (onMouseOver). See what the difference means to you. Figure 17.9 shows what the user will see if you choose the safer (onMouseOver) event handler.

Note

To access the nonparenthetical onMouseOver trigger, set the event handlers pop-up menu to show events for IE 4.0.

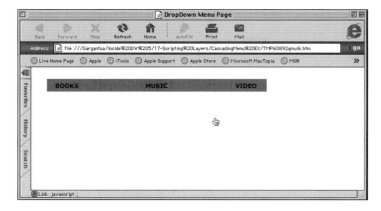

Figure 17.9   The pointing finger cursor appearing over empty space, if an <a> tag is added to the transparent image behind the menus.

9. Optional challenge: Can you see how the menu system you've just created could function as a vertical menu bar with cascading menus, without any change in scripting? The only changes required are layout changes—altering the table structure of the main layer, the relative positions of the various menu layers, and the dimensions of the invisible image and layer in the background. See if you can create a sideways cascading menu from this file. If you get stuck, check out **cascading_finished.html**, in the **chapter_17/menus** folder for a completed example. Figure 17.10 shows a cascading menu system in action.

Figure 17.10   The dropdown menu system, redesigned as a cascading menu.

Working Smart with the Show-Hide Behavior

The actual mechanics of applying this behavior are not complicated. However, working with invisible page elements brings up a host of questions that you'll undoubtedly stumble across when you least expect them. Here are a few points to consider.

Downloading and Invisible Layers

Any content within an invisible layer is still considered part of your page. It will download when the page downloads. This has all sorts of ramifications. If your page contains many layers that are initially invisible, and if those layers have substantial content in them, your page will take a while to download even though it looks like a simple, fairly empty page. If a user clicks a button that makes a layer visible, and that layer's contents haven't finished downloading yet, he'll experience a delay. After the page has finished downloading, however, layers that become visible will display immediately. In essence, you've preloaded the contents of those layers.

Triggering JavaScript Actions Within Invisible Layers

Because layers can contain just about anything, your layers might include buttons or text links that have their own behaviors attached to them. Be aware that triggers won't work if a layer is invisible. If you have a rollover set to open a new window when the mouse moves over it, and that rollover is hidden in an invisible layer, no visitor is going to accidentally trigger the new window opening by moving his mouse over that hidden item.

Media Objects in Invisible Layers

Embedded video, audio, Flash movies, and other media objects can be placed in layers (see Chapter 19, "Plugins, ActiveX, and Java," for more on this); but this limits the functionality of the layers. Depending on the browser, the platform, and the media plugin involved, the layer might not become properly invisible, or it might not be possible to change layer visibility with scripting. If you want to use media objects in conjunction with DHTML effects like this, test your pages carefully in all target browsers.

Controlling Layer Contents

An alternative approach to putting nested content on pages is to change the contents of a single layer, instead of hiding and showing multiple layers. In Dreamweaver, you do this with the Set Text of Layer behavior.

> **Note**
>
> As coded by Dreamweaver, the Set Text of Layer behavior works in IE 4+, Netscape 4.x, and Netscape 6.x. It will not work in Opera 5-6.

The Basics of Setting Layer Text

The Set Layer Text behavior is tucked away in the Set Text submenu of the Behaviors panel's Actions pop-up menu. Choosing it brings up a dialog box in which you can choose any of your document's layers and enter any text you want to appear in that layer (see Figure 17.11). Whatever you enter here will replace the existing layer contents—regardless of the contents. You can even change the contents of the layer containing the object the behavior is attached to. If you leave the dialog box's input area empty, the contents of the specified layer will be deleted.

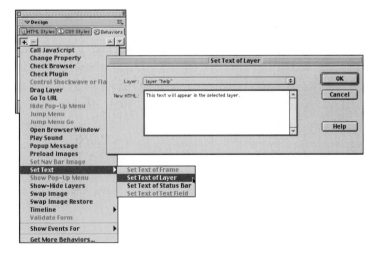

Figure 17.11   The Set Text of Layer behavior in the Behaviors panel Action list, and the dialog box it calls up.

Working Smart with Set Text of Layer

What can you do to really take advantage of this behavior?

Setting More Than Text

Despite its name, Set Text of Layer is not limited to text effects. You can use it to put almost any content into a layer, by entering HTML code rather than straight text into the input field of the dialog box. Code such as

```
<h1>Welcome!</h1>
<p>Are you ready for the <b>big</b> moment?</p>
```

will display a formatted text message in the specified layer. Tables and images, links, and forms can all be written into layers using this behavior. A more accurate description for the behavior might be "Set HTML Content of Layer."

Here are a few tips to consider when using Set Text of Layer.

Watch Those Quotes

Whatever text or HTML you enter in the dialog box will be inserted into the behavior's function call, like this:

```
onClick="MM_setTextOfLayer('Layer1','','Hello World')"
```

If you have set your Code Rewriting Preferences to URL-encode special characters and attribute values, any HTML source code you enter will be inserted into your page code looking like this:

```
onClick="MM_setTextOfLayer('help','','%3Cimg src=%22duck.gif%22
width=%2250%22 height=%2250%22%3E')"
```

While this code will work perfectly fine in a browser, it isn't too readable if you later want to hand-edit your HTML. You can avoid this mess by going to Edit > Preferences > Code Rewriting (Mac OS X: Dreamweaver > Preferences > Code Rewriting) and disabling both Special Characters options—the Encode Special Characters in URLs and Encode <, >, &, and " in Attribute Values Using & options. With these options deselected, Dreamweaver will escape all quotes with \ and leave all other characters alone. If you do this, however, you must only include single quotes in your HTML code. This code, for instance, will break the behavior:

```
<img src="duck.gif" width="50" height="50">
```

But this code will work fine:

```
<img src='duck.gif' width='50' height='50'>
```

It will be inserted into your page code as the following function call:

```
onClick="MM_setTextOfLayer('violin','','<img src=\'duck.gif\'
width=\'50\' height=\'50\'>')"
```

For a full discussion of functions and function calls in Dreamweaver behaviors, see Chapter 16. For more on the Code Rewriting preferences, see Chapter 33, "Writing Code in Dreamweaver."

Avoid Hand Coding

If you want to insert HTML formatting using Set Text of Layer, but don't want to type all that code yourself, work smart with Dreamweaver. Create the desired display in Design view, either in the same file you're working on or in a temporary file; then go to Code view and copy the code from there. Open the Set Text of Layer dialog box, click in the input area, and paste. Remember, though, that Dreamweaver always encloses tag attributes in double quotes. So if you have disabled the Special Characters options as described earlier, you'll have to replace all double quotes with single quotes, either by hand or using the Find & Replace command, before the behavior will work.

Don't Include Media Objects

Browsers won't display embedded media properly when the `<embed>` code appears as part of this command. Media objects and layers often don't mix well.

Exercise 17.2   Setting Layer Text to Display Context-Sensitive Information

This exercise builds an interactive illustration that puts different data in an information layer depending on what part of the illustration the mouse rolls over. All the files for the exercise can be found in the **chapter_17/violin** folder on the CD.

1. Open and examine **violin_write.html**. This file, pictured in Figure 17.12, presents the user with a picture of a violin. Image map hotspots will be used to trigger a behavior that puts different information in the help layer as the user's mouse rolls over those parts of the illustration. If you browse this file, you'll see that some of the hotspots already trigger basic text-only information to appear. You'll be adding the same behavior to the remaining hotspots and then dressing up the way the contextual information displays. (To see the final presentation in action, browse **violin_write_finished.html**.)

Figure 17.12   The **violin_write.html** presentation as it should appear in the browser when complete.

2. Select the hotspot at the top of the violin picture. Open the Behaviors panel and choose Set Text of Layer from the Actions list. In the dialog box, choose the help layer from the pop-up menu, and type the word **Scroll** in the input field. After you have finished, make sure the event triggering the action is onMouseOver. Figure 17.13 shows the dialog box with information entered.

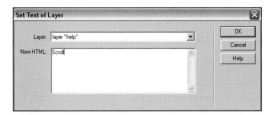

Figure 17.13   The Set Text of Layer dialog box, set to enter a simple text message in the help layer.

You also need to blank out the help layer when the mouse rolls off of the violin scroll. With the same hotspot selected, add another instance of the Set Text of Layer behavior. Choose the help layer from the pop-up menu again, but this time leave the input field blank (enter no text). When you're done, change the trigger event to onMouseOut.

Repeat the procedure for the hotspot directly below this one, configuring it to show the word **Neck** onMouseOver. Make sure you preview in the browser, to make sure you've coded the effect properly, before proceeding to the next step.

3. Now make the Scroll and Neck messages a bit fancier. Select the top hotspot, and double-click its `onMouseOver` behavior to edit the text that will appear. Replace the original message with this code:

```
<h1>Scroll</h1>
<p>Scrolls are curly and brown, and have wooden pegs sticking
out of both sides.</p>
```

Close the dialog box and Preview in Browser. Rolling over the violin scroll should now display information like that shown in Figure 17.14.

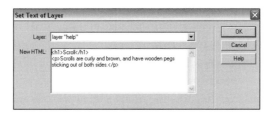

Figure 17.14   The Set Text of Layer behavior used to display HTML-formatted text.

4. After you've verified that your behavior is working, check your code to see how the HTML was inserted into the function call. (You can do this quickly by going to Code and Design view and selecting the hotspot in the Design View portion of the Document window.) Depending on how your URL encoding preferences are set, you might see a mess like this:

```
<area
onMouseOver="MM_setTextOfLayer('violin','','%3Ch1%3EScroll%3C/h1%3E%0D%
3Cp%3E Scrolls are curly and brown, and have wooden pegs sticking out
of both sides.%3C/p%3E')" shape="rect" coords="65,3,145,89" href="#">
```

To clean up this code, go to Edit > Preferences (Mac OS X: Dreamweaver > Preferences), and choose the Code Rewriting category. Deselect both Special Characters options. After this is done, return to the Behaviors Panel and double-click the scroll hotspot's Set Text of Layer behavior to open its dialog box. You don't need to change anything in the dialog box; just click OK. Check your code again, and you should see a more readable function call than before:

```
<area
onMouseOver="MM_setTextOfLayer('violin','','<h1>Scroll</h1><p>
Scrolls are curly and brown, and have wooden pegs sticking out of
both sides.</p>')" shape="rect" coords="65,3,145,89" href="#">
```

5. For the Neck hotspot, use Dreamweaver to help write the formatted code. Create a new Dreamweaver file, and save it in the **chapter_17/violin** folder as **temp.html.**

In **temp.html**, type the following text:

```
Neck
Violin necks are long and skinny, and since they're made of wood
they're not much good for swallowing.
```

Now use the Property Inspector to format the first line as <h1> and the rest as <p>.

Go to Code view, select all the HTML code for the formatted text, and copy it. (If you copy directly from Design view, you'll get only the text, not the formatting code.)

Back in **violin_write.html**, select the Neck hotspot and open its Set Text of Layer behavior for editing. Delete the contents of the input field and paste in the HTML code from the temporary file. Preview in Browser again; rolling over the Scroll and Neck hotspots should display similarly formatted text in the help layer. If you changed your Code Rewriting preferences in the previous step, your page's source code should contain a nice, readable (non-encoded) chunk of HTML in the Neck hotspot's function call.

6. To make things even fancier, replace the <h1> title with a GIF image, again using the **temp.html** file as a handy code-creating workshop.

Open **temp.html** (or bring it to the front) and go to Code and Design view. In the Design portion of the Document window, delete the heading, and in its place insert the image **scroll.gif**. Figure 17.15 shows how the revised scroll message should appear in the temp file.

Figure 17.15   Creating a fancier chunk of display information in **temp.html**.

If you have disabled URL encoding in your preferences, you'll need to replace all double quotes with single quotes. To do this, go to Edit > Find and Replace. Set your search parameters to Current Document and Source Code. Search for double quotes (") and replace with single quotes ('). Since this is only a temp file, go ahead and click the Replace All button to perform the search quickly.

When this is complete, activate the Code view portion of the Document window, and select and copy all the code for the image and text. Then go back to **violin_write.html**, open the Scroll hotspot's behavior for editing, and replace its contents with the new code.

7. Preview your violin page in the browser. If you entered your code correctly, you should see a result like that shown in Figure 17.12. If your browser preview doesn't work properly, double-check the code for your page. The scroll hotspot's event handler should contain escaped single quotes.

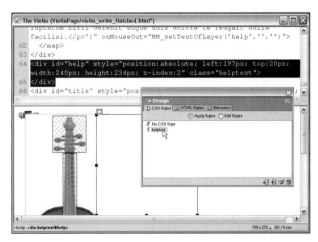

Note

Let Dreamweaver's color coding work for you. If your pasted code contains incorrect quote marks, the improperly terminated string literals will turn blue. If the quote marks are correct, the entire function call (everything after `onMouseOver=`) will be pink.

8. If you want to complete the violin-browsing experience and get some practice with this behavior, repeat the previous steps to dress up the rest of the violin hotspots. All the required GIF images are in the **chapter_17/violin** folder.

Using CSS Layer Styles to Format Text

A lovely, efficient way to put nicely formatted text into a layer without having to enter and reenter the HTML formatting for each new set of text is to assign a custom CSS class to the layer itself. It works this way (see Figure 17.16):

1. Create the layer you're going to be targeting with the behavior.

2. Using the CSS Styles panel, create a new custom class. Include any text formatting, positioning, or layer formatting you like in this style.

3. In Design view, select the layer and apply the style to it.

After this is done, whenever you Set Text of Layer, you need to enter only the text itself. All formatting will be supplied.

Figure 17.16   Setting up and applying a CSS class to control the formatting of a layer that will have its content set dynamically.

Set Text of Layer or Show-Hide Layers?

Repeatedly setting the text of a single layer can create a similar effect to starting with a stack of hidden layers and showing them one at a time. Why choose one method over another?

- **Loading and preloading.** If all of the document's content is present when the page initially loads (as it is when using Show-Hide Layers), it will all display immediately when called on. Depending on your project, you might decide that this is a good thing, or not. If you know ahead of time that users are probably going to access all the content, you'll want to download it as soon as possible—so use Show-Hide Layers. If you think users will probably want to access only one or two layers' worth of contents, you might not want to make them wait for the other layers' content to download—so use Set Text of Layer.

- **Simple text changes.** If your content all consists of similarly formatted text, it will probably be more efficient to create and edit content using Set Text of Layer. You can use a CSS style applied to the layer to control formatting, and need only enter unformatted text in the behavior's dialog box.

- **Different content, identical layers.** If your content will all appear in the same position on the page, it's easier to format, resize, and position one layer than several. Use Set Text of Layer.

- **Browser compatibility.** Setting layer text as it is scripted in the Dreamweaver behavior is supported by all current versions of Netscape and IE, but not by Opera. If this extra browser support is important to you, stick with Show-Hide Layers.

Dragging and Dropping Layers

It's easy in Dreamweaver's Design view to move layers around on the page, but after the page is created and published on the web, everything is cemented in place. Or is it? With the Drag Layer behavior, you tell layers to track the coordinates of the user's mouse. You can use this scripting to create repositionable navigation menus and pop-up windows, drag-and-drop games, shopping carts, and even slider controls.

Note

Note that the Drag Layer behavior as implemented in Dreamweaver will not work in Netscape 6 or in Opera.

The Basics of Dragging and Dropping

Applying the Drag Layer behavior is not as straightforward as applying the other layer behaviors, because it must be triggered when the page loads, not when the user presses the mouse down on a layer. What you're doing is declaring a given layer to be "draggable"—after that, it's up to the user to drag it around or not. To set up a draggable layer, follow these steps:

1. Open or create a document that has at least one layer in it.

2. Deselect all page content, or use the tag selector to select the <body> tag.

3. Open the Behaviors panel and choose the Drag Layer behavior from the Actions list. In the dialog box that appears, use the pop-up menu to select the layer that you want to be draggable. Configure any other settings as desired, or leave the default settings in place.

4. Make sure the event triggering the action is onLoad.

That's it! For the life of this document, the layer is draggable. Figure 17.17 shows the Drag Layer behavior dialog box, with its various options diagrammed.

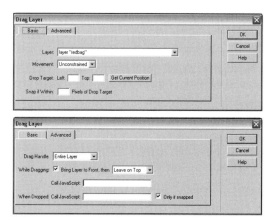

Figure 17.17   The Drag Layer behavior dialog box in Basic and Advanced mode.

Draggability Options

You can customize a layer's draggability in various ways. You can control which portion of it is draggable, where and how far it can be dragged, what happens to its z-index (position in the stacking order) as it is dragging, and what should happen when the user drops it. Some of these options can be tricky to use, but they are responsible for the power of the behavior.

Constraining the Drag Area

If you apply no constraints, the user is free to drag the layer anywhere within the browser window. Depending on why you've made the layer draggable in the first place, you might want to limit users to dragging only within a certain area. If you're creating a game, for instance, you might want the draggable game pieces to stay within the defined game boundaries.

Assigning a constraint area is easy: Just select the Constraint option from the Movement menu in the Basic tab of the Drag Layer dialog box.

The tricky part is determining what constraint values to specify in the four text fields. These fields all ask the same question: Starting from its current position, how many pixels up/down/left/right should the layer be allowed to move? Depending on what kind of constraint you're trying to create, figuring these values out can be simple or it can require some tinkering and thought.

If you love solving engineering problems and are good at diagramming and math, you probably don't need any help with this. For everybody else, here's a simple strategy:

1. Grab a pencil and paper, and in Dreamweaver open the History panel.

2. Select the layer you want to constraint, and write down its starting L (left) and T (top) position.

3. Drag the layer to the topmost, leftmost position you want it to go. Note the new T (top) position, and subtract it from the starting T value. That's your "up" value. Note the new L (left) position, and subtract it from the starting L value. That's you're "left" value.

4. Drag the layer to the bottommost, rightmost position you want it to go. Note the new T position, and subtract the original T value from it. That's your "down" value. Note the new L position, and subtract the original L value. That's your "right" value.

If you're not sure which value to subtract from which, just remember that all constraint numbers must be positive integers, or 0. (A value of 0 means the layer isn't allowed to move in that direction.) Subtract the smaller from the larger. Figure 17.18 shows a form you might find handy for your note taking.

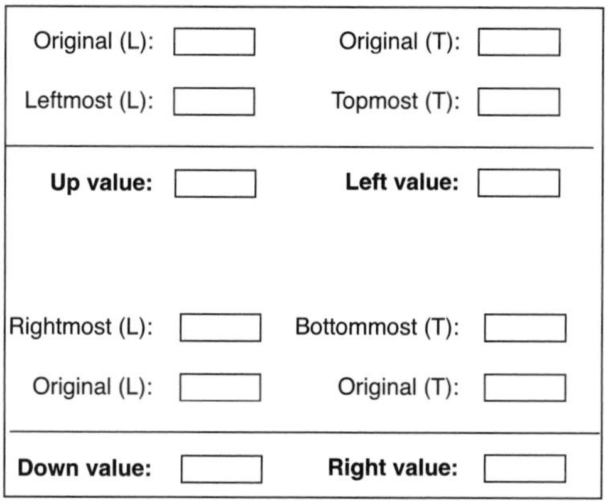

Figure 17.18   A form for determining constraint values in the Drag Layer dialog box.

Assigning a Drop Target (And Snapping to It)

A *drop target* is the location where you want the user to drop the layer. If you're creating a game, such as a matching game, this would be the location of the correct answer. If you're creating a shopping cart interface, this would be the cart graphic that tells you the user wants to buy an item. This option is specified in the Basic tab of the Drag Layer dialog box.

You specify the drop target as Left and Top coordinates, which represent where the upper-left corner of the layer should be when it's dropped. Because it's almost impossible for a user to drop a layer on exactly those coordinates (not one pixel right or left, up or down), you enable snapping and assign a "snap-to" distance, also measured in pixels. If the user drops the layer within that many pixels of the target, the layer snaps into place and is officially on target.

How do you figure out what values to use for the drop target? The dialog box gives you a helpful Get Current Position button—click the button and the current coordinates of the draggable layer will be entered. This is useful, however, only if the layer is currently sitting at its target location. Therefore, one way to approach the problem is to close the dialog box, move the layer to its desired destination, return to the dialog box, and click the button. Then close the dialog box again and move the layer back to its starting position.

Another way to handle this situation is to move the layer to the drop target destination, write down the coordinates, and then choose Edit > Undo or use the History panel to put the layer back where it started. Then go to the dialog box and type in the values you wrote down. (The second method has the advantage of putting your layer back in exactly the same position where it started.)

Specifying a Drag Handle

Do you want the user to be able to click anywhere on the layer to start dragging it, or can he drag only from a particular location (like a handle)? If your layer contains a puzzle piece or shopping item, for instance, you probably want the entire layer to be draggable. If it's an interface item, however, like a mini-window or Popup Message, you'll probably want users to drag it only by its title bar (just like a real computer window).

Choose the Area Within Layer option from the Drag Handle menu in the Advanced tab of the Drag Layer dialog box. Text fields will appear, asking you to specify the drag handle's left edge, top edge, width, and height. The left and top measurements are relative to left and top of the draggable layer. To use a temporary layer to determine the appropriate values for a drag handle, follow these steps (demonstrated in Figure 17.19):

1. Draw a temporary layer to use as a proxy for the drag handle. Resize and position this layer to where you want the handle to be.

2. Jot down the new layer's W, H, L, and T values from the Property inspector.

3. Select the draggable layer, and jot down its L and T values. The temporary layer's W and H values will become the drag handle's W and H.

4. Subtract the draggable layer's L and T values from the temporary layer's L and T values, to get the drag handle's L and T values.

5. When you're done, delete the temporary layer.

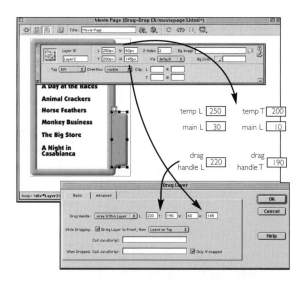

Figure 17.19   Using a temporary layer to determine measurements for a drag handle.

Note

If you repeatedly find yourself scratching your head over pixel coordinates and measurements, try using an onscreen pixel ruler utility. You can find plenty of them available at shareware sites such as www.download.com.

Changing the Z-Index

The *z-index* determines which layers are on top of which other layers. While a layer is being dragged, it should probably be on top—dragging a layer that goes behind other layers is a weird experience. When the layer is dropped, you might want it to stay on top, or you might want it to return to its normal position in the stacking order. Use the Advanced tab of the dialog box to specify how the z-index is treated.

Exercise 17.3   Creating a Draggable Shopping Cart Interface

In this exercise, you use the Drag Layer behavior to create a graphic shopping experience where visitors can drag shopping bags into a cart. All the files for this exercise can be found on the CD in the **chapter_17/shoppingcart** folder.

1. Start by opening **shopping.html** and examining its contents (see Figure 17.20). All the page elements are in place, and the layers have been given descriptive names. None of the scripting has been added.

Figure 17.20   The **shopping.html** file, ready for adding behaviors.

2. You want all three shopping bag layers to be draggable, so you need three instances of the Drag Layer behavior, each triggered when the page loads. Deselect all page content, or use the tag selector to select <body>. Then open the Behaviors panel and create a Drag Layer behavior for each shopping bag. Preview in the browser to make sure the bags are indeed draggable.

3. For your first refinement, limit the draggable area for the shopping bags. You don't want users dragging and dropping bags on top of the title bar or shopping instructions, so define an official "shopping area" from the bottom of the title bar to the bottom of the shopping cart, and from the left edge of the price fields to the right edge of the shopping cart.

Before plunging back into the dialog boxes, you need to calculate the Up, Down, Left, and Right constraint values for each bag. Using the method outlined earlier (or any other method you like better), determine the values for each bag. Then configure each Drag Layer behavior instance with the correct numbers. Figure 17.21 shows the editing dialog box for the red bag layer, with appropriate values entered.

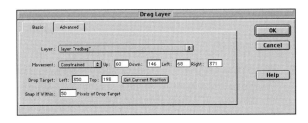

Figure 17.21   The Drag Layer dialog box for the redbag layer, showing its correct constraint values.

4. Now set drop targets for all three bags.

Move all three bags to where you think their final destination should be in the cart (see Figure 17.22). For all three, jot down their L and T values. Then use Edit > Undo or the History panel to put the bags back to their original positions, and enter each bag's values in the appropriate Drag Layer dialog box. For each bag, enter a snap-to distance of 100 pixels.

Figure 17.22   The desired location of all three shopping bags, after they're dropped in the cart.

5. You want each bag to come to the front as you're dragging it. When the bags are dropped, however, you need to reset the z-index so that they end up sitting inside the cart rather than on top of it. Open up each Drag Layer behavior and bring the Advanced tab to the front. Make sure that Bring to Front is selected and choose Restore z-index from the pop-up menu.

6. Try it out! In browsers that support the Drag Layer behavior, you should be able to drop items in the shopping cart or leave them lying around the window—but not outside your official shopping rectangle.

Triggering Actions with Drag and Drop

Being able to drag items around onscreen might be fun, but it can really be useful when you use it to trigger other actions. If the layer is a slider, if it's a game, or if it's a shopping cart, you might need to know three things:

- That an object is currently being dragged
- That an object has been dropped
- That an object has been dropped on target

Calling JavaScripts from the Drag Layer Behavior

In Dreamweaver, you use the Call JavaScript options in the Drag Layer dialog box's Advanced tab to trigger other actions based on the user's dragging and dropping. As you can see from the dialog box, the behavior can be configured to trigger a script as soon as the user starts dragging, when the user drops the layer, or only when the user drops the layer on target. Any JavaScript statement(s) entered into the appropriate input field will execute when the specified condition is met. In the dialog box shown in Figure 17.23, for instance, dropping the layer on target will pop open an alert window with a short message.

Note

Another handy one-liner to use with **Drag Layer** is `location='anypage.html'`, which will cause the browser to go to the specified relative or absolute address as soon as an item is dropped on a target.

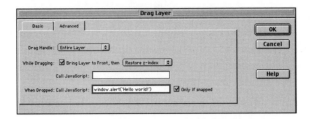

Figure 17.23   The Drag Layer dialog box, configured to open an alert window with the "Hello world" message if the layer is dropped on target.

Using Drag Layer to Trigger Another Behavior

If you want the Drag Layer behavior to trigger scripts longer than a line or two, you don't want to enter the entire script in those tiny little input fields. It's better to create a JavaScript function in the document `<head>` and enter the function call here. On the other hand, wouldn't it be nice if you could just trigger another Dreamweaver behavior from here, instead of having to manually code scripts? The previous chapter presented a sneaky technique for using behaviors in unusual places by inserting a behavior into a document and then "borrowing" the function call portion of the behavior (see the section on "Working Sneaky with Behaviors" in Chapter 16). In working with the Drag Layer behavior, this means placing the function call from another behavior into one of the Call JavaScript fields, in the Drag Layer dialog box. Figure 17.24 shows this happening.

Figure 17.24   Borrowing the function call from the Popup Message behavior to use in the Drag Layer dialog box—the Popup Message behavior will be executed when the dragged layer is dropped.

Exercise 17.4   Responding to Items Dropped in a Shopping Cart

In this exercise, you'll add more functionality to the draggable shopping cart developed in the preceding exercise. If the user drops a shopping bag in the cart, you'll trigger another script that responds in various ways.

1. If you completed the preceding exercise and are happy with your results, open the **shopping.html** page you created. If you would rather start fresh, open **shopping_finished.html** from the **chapter_17/shoppingcart** folder on the CD. Whichever file you open, save it as **buying.html**.

2. In the Behaviors panel, open any of the Drag Layer behavior instances to open its editing window and bring the Advanced tab to the front. In the When Dropped: Call JavaScript text field, type the following code:

```
window.alert('You bought me!')
```

This nice simple statement will make a Popup Message appear. So that the message appears only if the bag is in the cart, select the Only If Snapped option.

Try the new improved shopping cart out in your browser. Dragging the bag to the cart should call up a pop-up window like the one shown in Figure 17.25.

Figure 17.25   Dragging a shopping bag to the cart, and the resulting alert window.

3. Now get your shopping cart to do something fancier, by inserting a function call for a Dreamweaver behavior. You'll make your document's three price layers invisible to start out with and then have each one become visible as its matching bag is dropped in the cart.

To set up the effect, make each of the price layers (redprice, greenprice, blueprice) invisible, by closing its eye in the Layers panel.

4. Following the steps outlined earlier, you'll start by adding a fake text link. Create a new, small layer somewhere on your page. Type the words **buy me!**, or some other simple word or phrase, into the layer, and use the Link field in the Property inspector to link the text to "#". Figure 17.26 shows this happening.

Figure 17.26   Creating a simple text link as a temporary holder for a function call.

5. With the text link selected, use the Behaviors panel to add a Show-Hide Layers behavior. In the behavior dialog box, configure it to show the redprice layer.

   Before proceeding, test this behavior in the browser to make sure it's working properly.

6. Now copy the function call. Select the text link and go to Code view or Code and Design view. The code for the text—including its <a> tag, event handler, and function call—should be selected and therefore easy to locate. Deselect the code, and select only the function call. Your code and selection should look like this (selected code is shown here in bold):

```
<div id="Layer1" style="position:absolute; left:263px; top:116px;
width:138px; height:61px; z-index:7"><a href="#"
onClick="MM_showHideLayers('redprice','','show')">buy me! </a></div>
```

   Copy the selected code and go back to Design view.

7. Now paste the function call into the Drag Layer behavior. In the Behaviors panel, find the Drag Layer instance that controls the red shopping bag, and open its dialog box. In the Advanced tab, if there's any code written in the When Dropped field, delete it. Then paste the function call into that input field. Your dialog box should now look like the one shown in Figure 17.27.

Figure 17.27   The Drag Layer dialog box showing the pasted function call from the Show-Hide Layers behavior.

Try the result in your browser! If it doesn't work, check the pasted function call and make sure you pasted exactly the code shown in Figure 17.29 (that is, everything after the onClick event handler and between the double quotes).

8. Finally, delete the layer containing the text link, because you don't need it anymore. Select the layer in Design view, and then go to Code view. Make sure you have everything including the <div> tags selected, and delete. Then scroll up to the top of the page to make sure the MM_showHideLayers() function is still present. After you've done this, check the page in a browser again to make sure the behavior still works.

Note

When in Code view, to quickly determine what JavaScript functions are present in a document, go to the toolbar and click the {} icon to get a pop-up list of functions. See Chapter 33 for a full discussion of navigating in Code view.

9. You still need to add the same behavior to the other two shopping bags. Although you could go through the entire process again (yuck) for each bag, with a tiny bit of hand coding you can accomplish your task quickly and easily.

   The function call for Show-Hide Layers should still be on the Clipboard from your preceding copy-paste action. In the Behaviors panel, open up another of the Drag Layer instances. In the dialog box, note which shopping bag this instance is controlling (green or blue). Then bring the Advanced tab forward, click in the When Dropped text field, and paste again. Examine the pasted code. Find the reference to redprice, and change the color name to match the color of this bag. Repeat this process for the third Drag Layer behavior instance, and all three of your shopping bags should now be scripted.

Note

Aren't you glad you gave your layers easy-to-remember names like redprice, greenprice, and blueprice? This is a good example of the importance of good naming conventions as you work.

10. One more revision. What if, after putting an item in the shopping cart, the user decides not to buy that item? When a bag is dragged out of the cart, you want the relevant price layer to hide. You can accomplish this task as well, within the limits of the Drag Layer behavior, by using the While Dragging: Call JavaScript setting in the behavior's dialog box. With just a little more hand coding, you can even reuse the function calls you've already added.

In the Behaviors panel, open one of the Drag Layer instances and bring the Advanced tab forward. In the second input field (the one you just filled in), drag to select the entire function call entry and copy. Paste that code into the first input field. In the first field, find the reference to show and change it to hide. Everything else remains the same. Your first code entry will read as follows:

```
MM_showHideLayers('greenprice','','hide')
```

The second entry will look like this:

```
MM_showHideLayers('greenprice','','show')
```

Repeat this process for the other two Drag Layer instances and try the finished page in the browser. As soon as you start dragging a shopping bag, the price will disappear; if you drop it in the cart, the price will reappear. (If you get stuck, **buying_finished.html** contains the completed exercise.)

Controlling Other Layer Properties

You've changed visibility, you've changed the contents, and you've dragged layers around. However, those are only a few of the layer properties you can control. Depending on which browser(s) you're scripting for, you can change background color, position, width and height, style, and clipping—you name it. The Dreamweaver general, all-purpose behavior for controlling everything not covered by other behaviors is Change Property.

Using the Change Property Behavior

This behavior isn't just for changing layer properties. It's more of a catch-all behavior for changing any property of any scriptable page element. Depending on the browser you're targeting, and the DOM it supports (see the discussion on DOMs at the beginning of this chapter), you can change properties for form elements, various kinds of layers, and even images. Figure 17.28 shows the Change Property dialog box with its various parts identified.(See Chapter 11, "Working with Forms," for a discussion of using this behavior with form elements.)

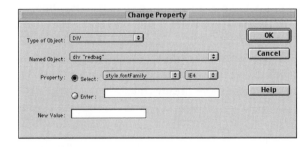

Figure 17.28   The Change Property dialog box.

To use Change Property to alter layer properties, follow these steps:

1. Set up your document with whatever layer (or form or image) elements you want to use and change.

2. Select whichever object will trigger the behavior and choose Change Property from the Behaviors panel Actions list.

3. From the first pop-up menu, choose the tag of the object you want to change (`<div>`, `<layer>`, and so on). Unless you have changed the default, a layer in Dreamweaver will be created with the `<div>` tag.

4. The second pop-up menu will now be populated with all named instances of the chosen tag that appear in your document. From this menu, choose the specific instance you want to control. (Unlike Show-Hide Layers, you can control only one object with each occurrence of this behavior.)

5. Choose a target browser from the pop-up list on the third line of the dialog box. What you choose here will determine what choices will appear in the Property pop-up list to its left.

6. Choose a property to change. If the Property list is empty, the object you have chosen is not scriptable in the DOM of the browser you have targeted. If you want to change a property that isn't on the list, but that you know is scriptable, enter it by hand in the text field below.

7. Enter a new value for the property. It's up to you to choose a value acceptable for that property. The Change Property dialog box shown in Figure 17.29 is set to change the `font-family` of all text within the `<div>` layer named caption. If the value field for this dialog box didn't contain a valid font name, the property change would have no effect.

Change Property and Browser Compatibility

Because it's a generic behavior, with a very basic purpose, Change Property does not necessarily create cross-browser scripts. After you choose a target browser in the dialog box, the script will be entered using the syntax required for that browser. If all you're doing with the behavior is scripting form fields, your script will probably work across browsers because only basic DOM access is required for this kind of page element. If you're scripting layers, your behavior will definitely be browser-specific.

Controlling Netscape Layers

As discussed in Chapter 14, Netscape 4.x functions best if its proprietary `<layer>` tag is used to create layers, even though layers created with other tags will work there. If you target Netscape 4 in the Change Property behavior and specify that you want to change `<div>` layers, no scriptable properties will show up in the dialog box. If you choose the `<layer>` tag to change, however, you'll still be allowed to choose named instances of `<div>` layers, and the property list will supply a list of Netscape-formatted properties to change. Figure 17.29 shows this strange occurrence in action. This configuration will work fine in Netscape 4 or Netscape 6.

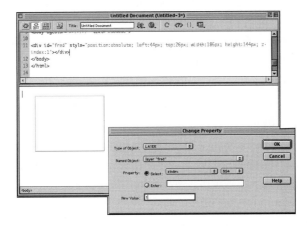

Figure 17.29   The Change Property dialog box set up to change the `z-index` property of a `<div>` layer.

Doubling Up for Multiple Browsers

For some properties, it is possible to target IE and Netscape Navigator just by attaching two instances of Change Property to the same event handler. Figure 17.30 shows two separate configurations of the behavior, each set to change the vertical position of the specified layer on the page. Both behaviors are being applied to one text link, to be activated `onClick`. This strategy won't work with all properties. If you attempt to change the layer's background color in this way, for instance, IE interprets the Netscape syntax as a command to change the page's background color.

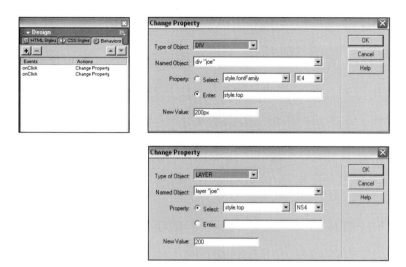

Figure 17.30   Two instances of the Change Property behavior, each set up to change the T (top) property of a layer called caption.

Summary

Dynamic HTML—the ability to use JavaScript to control page elements such as layers—is an exciting technology with much promise, although browser incompatibility issues turn it into a minefield for designers. In this chapter you have seen the primary Dreamweaver tools for helping you navigate this minefield safely. You also have seen how you can sometimes push the envelope to make the Show-Hide Layers, Set Text of Layer, Drag Layer, and Change Property behaviors work for you. The next chapter examines one more layer-handling tool in Dreamweaver: the Timelines window.

Chapter 18

Animating Layers

Probably the most glamorous and eye-catching DHTML effect is JavaScript-based animation of document contents. The concept of JavaScript animation is simple—any page element that can have its properties altered by scripting can be animated by having its properties changed repeatedly over time. The actual JavaScript code required to create animations is complex enough to deter all but the most intrepid code writers. Luckily for the rest of us, Dreamweaver provides an intuitive and efficient interface for creating JavaScript animations and writes fairly robust cross-browser code to bring animated pages to life.

This chapter covers the Dreamweaver timeline interface for JavaScript animations and discusses how to create DHTML animations. You'll learn how to animate layer and image properties, how to execute behaviors over time, and how to integrate multiple timelines in one document. In this chapter, you also come up against the limits of DHTML animation, and learn ways to implement it wisely.

How JavaScript Animation Works

Before plunging into Dreamweaver timelines, tweening, and sprites, it's important to have a basic idea of how JavaScript animation works. From the previous chapters, you know how a JavaScript statement can alter the properties of a layer or other page element in reaction to some event. You also know that different browsers require different syntax to make this happen. For Internet Explorer, the following very basic function will move the layer on the page by changing its left property:

```
function moveLayer() {
var pos1 = myLayer.style.left;
var pos2 = parseInt(pos1) + 20;
myLayer.style.left = pos2;
}
```

To animate the property change, the script must repeatedly call this function, with a time delay between each call. JavaScript's setTimeout() window method creates the time delay; by having the function recursively call itself using setTimeout(), the property will repeatedly change, creating animation, as follows:

```
function moveLayer() {
var pos1 = myLayer.style.left;
var pos2 = parseInt(pos1) + 20;
myLayer.style.left = pos2;
window.setTimeout("moveLayer()",100);
}
```

After called, this function will move the layer myLayer 20 pixels to the right every 100/1000ths of a second, or 10 times a second.

Of course, to work properly across all browsers and platforms, this simple code must become much more complex and robust. For every page element being animated at once, a setTimeout() function must be called repeatedly. The browser must recalculate position and other properties and redraw the screen 10–15 times per second. Sophisticated JavaScript animations often require long, complex code to execute. As Figure 18.1 shows, complex animations can overwhelm the browser's capabilities, causing improper display and sometimes even crashing the browser entirely. The moral of this story is, treat JavaScript animations with respect. Dreamweaver makes the entire process easy for you, but it's never easy for the browser.

Figure 18.1   When good animations go bad—an example of what can happen to the browser display when a JavaScript-based animation overwhelms it.

Note

IE/Mac is notorious for breaking under the weight of complex JavaScript layer effects, especially animations.

The Timeline Interface

Dreamweaver enables you to create and manipulate JavaScript animations within a timeline interface, using the Timelines panel (accessible from Window > Others > Timelines) and the Modify > Timeline menu for creating and manipulating timelines. Timeline interfaces are not the only way to approach computer animations, but they do provide an easy-to-grasp, visual representation of the time dimension that many developers are already familiar with from animation programs such as Director, Flash, and Fireworks.

The Timelines Panel

Figure 18.2 shows the Timelines panel and its various elements. The timeline looks something like a spreadsheet, showing units of time as columns and each animated element as a row. Note that, though the figure shows the panel in its undocked state, if you're using Dreamweaver/Windows with the integrated workspace it might initially appear docked at the bottom of the application window.

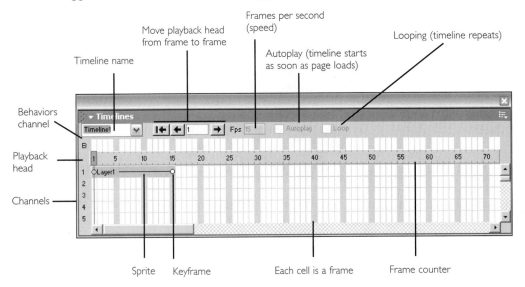

Figure 18.2   The Timelines panel with interface elements annotated.

Frames and the Playback Head

Each time unit, or column in the spreadsheet, is a *frame*. Like the frames in a movie reel, each frame represents how the stage (the HTML document) will look for that unit of time. The playback head (red vertical line) determines which frame is currently being shown. The animation effect is created by moving the playback head through the frames in sequence, at a set rate of *frames per second* (fps). For JavaScript animations, which will be played back through a web browser, the fps should be kept at 15 or lower, as this is the best speed most browsers can handle. (In contrast, film animations play at about 24 fps, and video animations at about 30 fps.)

Note

So, what happens if you set your fps higher than the browser can play back? The browser will try its best to play the animation as quickly as it can, probably not any faster than 15 fps. For very complex animations, browsers might not even be able to keep up with that speed. Complex animations lead to slow, sometimes lurching playback.

Sprites

Each page element to be animated appears in the timeline as a purple bar called a *sprite*. (That bit of terminology is borrowed from Director.) The sprite's length determines the duration of the object's animation on stage. The scripting tools in Dreamweaver enable you to animate layers and images; therefore, each sprite in a Dreamweaver timeline is a reference to one of the document's images or layers.

Keyframes and Tweened Animation

Two more concepts are borrowed from animation programs and adapted for use with JavaScript animation. In animation terminology, a *frame* is a unit of time that passes during the animation. A *keyframe* is a frame in which some element onstage changes (appears, disappears, changes its properties, and so forth). *Tweening* means creating two keyframes showing distinct property states of a page element and telling the computer to interpolate the change in property across the intervening (or in-between) frames. Circles within a sprite represent keyframes in the Dreamweaver timeline.

For Flash and Director Users

If you're used to working in true animation programs such as Flash or Director, you need to unlearn a few things. Remember, the Dreamweaver timeline interface for animation is merely a convenience to make authoring more intuitive; it does not represent how the JavaScript animation is built, the way a Flash or Director timeline would. In particular, note the following:

- The Dreamweaver JavaScript-based timeline must be explicitly started, unlike other timelines that automatically play unless told to stop.

- A sprite's length on the timeline does not indicate when it appears or disappears from the stage (that is, the document), as it does in Flash and Director. Instead, the length of the sprite indicates when the object's animation begins and ends. To create the illusion that an animated layer is appearing and disappearing, you need to alter its visibility property (as discussed later in this chapter). To create the illusion that an image is appearing or disappearing, you need to change its `src` to an invisible image (as discussed later).

- Unlike Flash or Director, no "master timeline" governs the entire document presentation. Multiple timelines can coexist, to control different page elements at different times.

- Because tweening is presented for ease of authoring only, a tweened animation does not provide the same efficiency in JavaScript that it does in Flash or Director.

> (That is, tweened animations are not necessarily less processor-intensive or more memory-efficient than frame-by-frame animations.)
>
> - Unlike Flash but like Director, if tweening is possible between two properties, it occurs automatically between keyframes. Tweening doesn't need to be turned on, and it can't be turned off. Also like Director rather than Flash, keyframes exist only within sprites. It's not possible to select an empty frame in the timeline and convert it into a keyframe.

The Timelines Menus

In addition to the interface of the Timelines panel itself, Dreamweaver offers a variety of commands for manipulating animation timelines. The main menu containing these commands is the Modify > Timeline submenu. The same commands are also available from the Timelines panel's options menu and from the timelines contextual menu, accessed by right-clicking (Windows) or Ctrl-clicking (Mac) within the Timelines panel. Throughout this chapter, instructions will refer to the Modify > Timeline submenu. If you prefer using the panel or contextual menus, feel free to choose the same commands from those locations instead of from the Modify menu.

Animating Layers

Are you ready to start some animation? Think of this next section as Animation 101.

Animating Layer Position

Most people, when they think of animation, think of things moving around on the page. Although this isn't the only kind of animation you can create, it's useful and straightforward, and serves as a good introduction to working with the timeline. Animating a layer's position involves three main steps:

1. Adding the layer to the timeline.

2. Establishing its starting position (at the first keyframe).

3. Establishing its ending position (at the second keyframe).

Adding a Layer to the Timeline

To be animated, a layer must be present on the timeline as a sprite. Create a layer, access the timeline (choose Window > Timelines), and do one of the following:

- **Drag and drop.** In the Document window, grab the layer by its edge or its tab, and drag it into the timeline. Figure 18.3 shows this happening. This doesn't disturb the position of the layer in the document, but it does create a sprite representing the layer in the timeline.

- **Using a Menu Command.** In the Document window, select the layer. Choose Modify > Timelines > Add Object to Timeline. Figure 18.4 shows this happening.

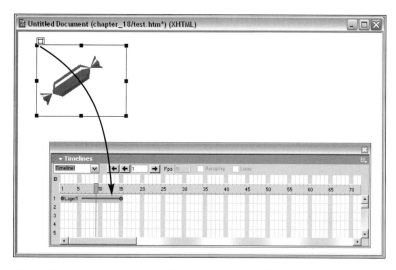

Figure 18.3   Using drag and drop to add a layer to the timeline.

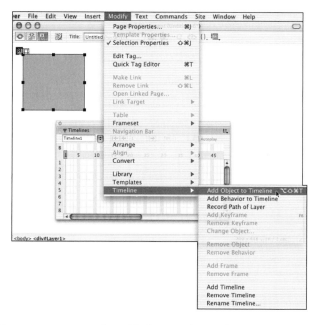

Figure 18.4   Using a menu command to add a layer to the timeline.

Creating Tweened Motion

After the layer is in the timeline, note that its sprite begins and ends with a keyframe (a tiny circle icon in the sprite). Clicking in the middle of the sprite selects the entire sprite, but clicking either keyframe selects only that keyframe. Animated motion in the Dreamweaver timeline is created by specifying a starting and ending position and letting Dreamweaver tween the intermediate positions.

- **To establish the starting position:** In the timeline, select the first keyframe of the sprite. In the Document window, drag or nudge the layer to its starting position; alternatively, in the Property inspector, change the L and T properties to reposition the layer.

- **To establish the ending position:** In the timeline, select the second keyframe of the sprite. In the Document window, drag or nudge the layer to its starting position; alternatively, in the Property inspector, change the L and T properties to reposition the layer.

That's it! If you correctly selected the individual keyframes before repositioning your layer, and you have the layer selected, you will see a thin gray line in the Document window, indicating the path the tweened motion will follow. Dreamweaver will automatically supply the tweening between the two positions.

Figure 18.5 shows a sprite correctly set up for tweening between two keyframes. The timeline shows the sprite with its two keyframes. In the Document window, the motion line indicates how the layer will animate.

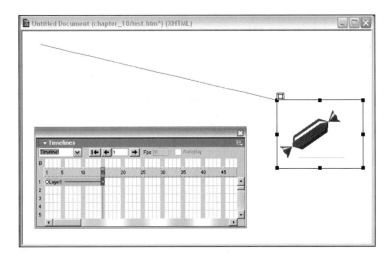

Figure 18.5 A Dreamweaver document set up for tweened layer animation.

Changing the Speed of the Animation

The number of frames involved and the frame rate, or fps, determines animation speed. The simplest way to slow down or speed up a particular animation is to alter the sprite length so that it occurs over more or fewer frames. To do this, just grab and drag the final keyframe of the sprite.

Although it is also possible to change speed by changing the frame rate, remember that the fps governs the quality of the animation as much as its speed. The lower the fps, the more jerky the animation will become. The higher the fps, the smoother the animation—but browsers cannot usually keep up with speeds higher than about 15 fps. Figure 18.6 shows different ways of changing an animation's speed.

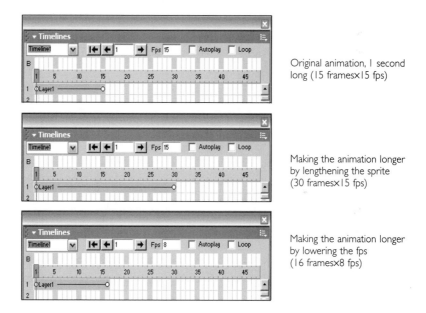

Original animation, 1 second long (15 frames×15 fps)

Making the animation longer by lengthening the sprite (30 frames×15 fps)

Making the animation longer by lowering the fps (16 frames×8 fps)

Figure 18.6   Timelines showing a tweened animation being slowed down by lengthening the sprite and by lowering the frame rate.

Creating Complex Motion Paths

Dreamweaver tweens motion in a straight line between two keyframes. Every change of direction in the motion path requires a new keyframe.

To add a keyframe to a sprite, do one of the following:

- Hold down the Ctrl key (Windows) or the Cmd key (Mac) and position the cursor over a sprite. The cursor turns into a tiny circle. Click on the sprite to add a keyframe. Figure 18.7 shows a keyframe being added to a sprite using this simple, quick method.
- Select the sprite. Move the playback head to the frame where you want the keyframe inserted. Choose Modify > Timeline > Add Keyframe.

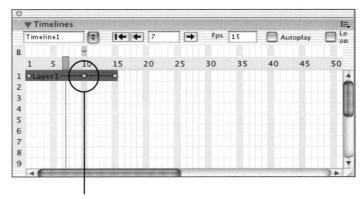

Cursor, ready to create keyframe

Figure 18.7   Ctrl/Cmd-clicking to add a keyframe to a sprite in the timeline.

To remove a keyframe from a sprite, select the keyframe to remove. Choose Modify > Timeline > Remove Keyframe.

Figure 18.8 shows an animation with a fairly complex motion path and the keyframes needed to create it. Note that after keyframes have been added within a sprite, they can be dragged back and forth to adjust the timing of the motion.

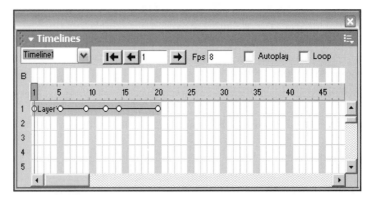

Figure 18.8   The Timelines panel, showing a complex motion tween consisting of several keyframes.

Making the Animation Play

When you add sprites and keyframes to the timeline, you're telling Dreamweaver how to write the JavaScript function that will control your animation. Like all JavaScript functions, however, the animation function has to be called before it will execute. You can choose to have the animation play as soon as the page loads. You can also choose to have the user start the animation by clicking or rolling over a button, or performing any other standard event.

To set the animation to play as soon as the page loads, in the Timelines panel select the Autoplay option (see Figure 18.2). When you do this, the Play Timeline action is being added to the document using an on onLoad event so that the timeline will start where the page loads.

To set the animation to play only when a user triggers it, perform the following steps:

1. In the Timelines panel, make sure the Autoplay option is not selected.
2. Elsewhere in your document, create an image, text link, or form element that will trigger the animation.
3. With the triggering object selected, open the Behaviors panel and choose Timeline > Play Timeline from the plus (+) list.

Starting and stopping the timeline is discussed in greater detail later in this chapter.

Looping the Animation

By default, the timeline will play through once and stop. To make an animation loop, select the Loop option in the Timelines panel. When you do this, Dreamweaver might open an alert window explaining that a new behavior is being added to the timeline. You'll also see an indicator in the B (behaviors) channel of the timeline, representing the looping behavior. (refer back to Figure 18.2). Looping and other timeline behaviors are discussed in more detail later in this chapter.

Managing Sprites

Sprites hold animation instructions in the form of keyframes. Each sprite is associated with an object (for example, a layer) that it animates. After you get used to these concepts, you can be sneaky and manage your sprites efficiently.

- **To change the object that a sprite animates:** Select the sprite and choose Modify > Timeline > Change Object. This can be especially useful if you've already created a complex motion path in a sprite and don't want to recreate it just because you've changed your mind about what layer you want to animate.

- **To duplicate a sprite:** Select the sprite and choose Edit > Copy, then Edit > Paste. The duplicated sprite will appear immediately following the original in the timeline. You can then move it to where you want it. Used in conjunction with changing a sprite's target object, this means you can create a complex motion path and then use that path animate to multiple layers in your document.

- **To remove a sprite entirely from the timeline:** Select the sprite and choose Modify > Timeline > Remove Object. Note that this doesn't delete the layer the sprite is animating. It only deletes the animation instructions.

Note

When you delete a page element that is associated with a sprite, that sprite disappears from the timeline.

Exercise 18.1   Animating a Title Banner

This exercise adds a snazzy slide-on title banner, as well as some floating balloons, to a home page. You put the title in its own layer and have it slide onto the page after the rest of the document has loaded. Then you'll animate the balloons floating from the bottom of the page to the top. Along the way, you'll experiment a little with the Timelines panel.

Before you begin, copy the files from the **chapter_18** folder on the CD to your hard drive. Define a site called Chapter 18, with this folder as the local root folder.

1. Start by opening **party_home.html** and examining its contents and structure. The page layout is created from five layers—one for the title banner, one for the text, and three more containing balloons. Access the Timelines panel and you'll see that none of these layers is set up for animation yet. Browse the page and see that all five layers just appear, in position, when the page loads.

2. Prepare the title layer for animating by dragging it into the timeline to create a sprite for it (refer back to Figure 18.3). To give yourself an idea how sprites and timeline work in Dreamweaver, try this: Move the sprite to the right so that it begins at around frame 16 (about 1 second into the animation). Then preview the page in a browser. Especially if you're used to animating in Flash or Director, you might expect that the title layer won't appear until about 1 second after the text layer. But that's not what happens. Instead, the page will load and behave exactly as it did before you created the sprite. Remember, sprites in Dreamweaver timelines control only animation timing. They don't make page items appear and disappear.

3. Animate the title layer so that it slides from bottom to top as the page loads. Do this by selecting the first keyframe of the sprite and then, in the Document window, dragging the layer down to the bottom of the page. Note the gray motion

path line that appears as you move the layer. (If that line doesn't appear, check the Timelines panel and make sure you have selected only the first keyframe of the sprite, not the entire sprite.) If you want the layer to slide straight up, tweak the layer's opening position until the gray line is perfectly vertical. Remember, you also can use the Property inspector or your arrow keys to tweak the layer into position.

Note

Here, as always when dealing with layers, it's crucial that you grab and move the layer itself and not the image inside it. Always drag layers by their edges, or by the little tab in the upper-left corner. If you drag from the center, you risk dragging the image out of the layer.

4. Trigger the animation to play automatically by selecting the Autoplay option in the Timelines panel, then preview in a browser.

5. Sliding from bottom to top isn't that exciting. A nicer effect is to slide in from "offstage"-left to its proper position. To make this happen, all that's needed is to select the first keyframe of the sprite and adjust the title layer's position. The tricky bit here is that you can't drag the layer to position it offstage. Instead, use the Property inspector to reassign the L (left) and T (top) values. The new T value for the first keyframe should match the T property from the final keyframe. (You want the layer to slide sideways only, not up and down.) For the new L value, assign a negative number that's greater than the layer's width. Figure 18.9 shows the new values being entered to create the horizontal slide effect.

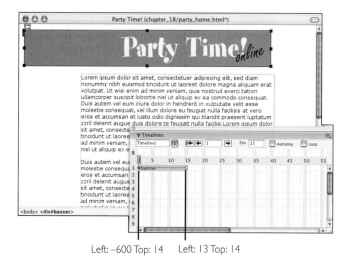

Figure 18.9   Animating the title banner so it slides in from offstage-left.

6. Animate the balloons next. Each balloon should float slowly up from the bottom of the page to end up in its position as part of the banner. Following the steps outlined already, add each balloon layer to the timeline and adjust the keyframes so that the balloons slide from below the bottom edge of the screen to the top of the screen. To make the balloons float up one at a time, stagger the sprites in the timeline. Figure 18.10 shows the final timeline to create this animation.

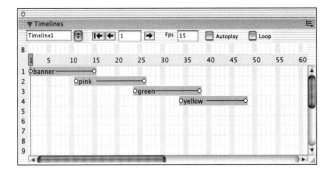

Figure 18.10   The Timelines panel for **party_home.html** file, showing sprites for the animated title banner and floating balloons.

7. Finally, how about adding a few keyframes to the balloon sprites so that they don't float straight up but waft in a slight breeze as they go? For each balloon sprite, do this:

- Lengthen the sprites to slow down the motion of the rising balloons.
- Ctrl/Cmd-click to add an extra keyframe or two in the sprite. Space the extra keyframes evenly along the duration of the sprite for a nice, smooth motion.
- Select each new keyframe, and in the Document window scoot the balloon layer to the right or left slightly. The gray motion path line should arc slightly to show the altered movement.

Figure 18.11 shows how one of your altered sprites and motion paths might look for a wafting balloon effect. (To see a completed version of the file, find **party_home.html** in the **chapter_18/completed** folder of the CD.)

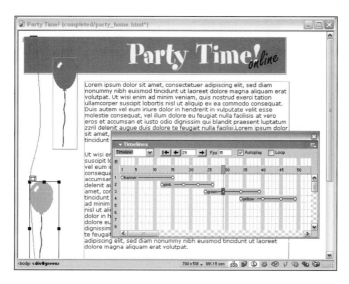

Figure 18.11   The timeline and Document window for **party_home.html**, showing extra keyframes in the balloon sprites to create more complex motion paths.

Recording Layer Animations

The more complex a motion path, the more keyframes it requires. If you want to animate a layer along a complex motion path, you might not want to add all those keyframes individually. For such occasions, you can show Dreamweaver what motion path you want to create and have the program automatically create all necessary keyframes. This is called *recording a motion path*.

Basics of Recording Motion Paths

This procedure is slightly different from the steps outlined earlier, because you don't begin by adding the layer to the timeline. Instead, begin by positioning the layer in the Document window where you want it to be at the start of the animation. Then follow these steps:

1. In the Document window, select the layer.

2. From the Timelines panel options menu, choose Record Path of Layer; or right-click (Windows) or Ctrl-click (Mac) to access the Layer contextual menu and choose Record Path.

3. In the Document window, drag the layer along the path you want it to follow in the animation. As you're dragging, you'll see the dotted gray line of the motion path appear behind you. When you're done, release the mouse button and a new sprite (with all keyframes in place) should appear in the timeline.

Figure 18.12 shows an animation path being recorded and the resulting sprite that is added to the timeline. Note how many keyframes have been added to reproduce the complex motion.

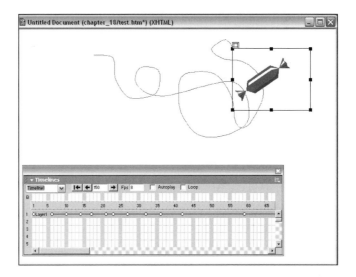

Figure 18.12   Recording a motion path, and the sprite created with this method.

Strategies for Recording Motion Paths

Although the basic steps for recording the motion path are simple, the procedure can produce unwanted or unexpected results if you aren't careful:

- **How to begin and end:** The recording doesn't begin until you start dragging the layer; after it begins, it ends when you release the layer. If you accidentally deselect the layer after you've chosen the Record Path of Layer command, your recording session has ended. Depending on when you accidentally deselected, you might end up with a truncated animation or no animation at all. If this happens, remove any incomplete sprite from the timeline (select the sprite and choose Modify > Timeline > Remove Object); then choose the Record Path of Layer command again and start the recording process over.

- **Timing is important:** After you've started dragging and Dreamweaver has started recording, the speed of your motions will be translated into the timing of the animation. Quicker movements will result in keyframes placed close together, sometimes one right after the other; slower movements will create keyframes placed further apart. Remember, you can always adjust the timing of the animation after it has been recorded by moving keyframes closer together or farther apart.

- **Drag slowly, add speed later:** The more slowly you drag when creating the motion path, the more you'll be able to control it; but you'll probably end up with an animation that's just much too slow. That's okay! After you have finished recording, you can adjust the overall speed of the animation by dragging the last keyframe of the sprite to the right (to slow things down) or left (to speed things up). Dragging the last keyframe will stretch or compress the entire sprite, without distorting the relative timing between keyframes any more than is necessary.

Tip

If you want to adjust the final keyframe in a sprite without altering any other keyframes in the sprite, Ctrl-drag (Windows) or Opt-drag (Mac) when repositioning the keyframe.

- **Reshape or reposition the motion path, if needed:** To reshape the motion path, go to the Timelines panel and select an individual keyframe; then, in the Document window, reposition the layer. To move the entire animation without reshaping the path, go to the Timelines panel and select the entire sprite by clicking between any two keyframes. Then, in the Document window, reposition the layer. The gray motion line should move without reshaping.

Exercise 18.2 Animating a Complex Motion Path

In this exercise, you create another animated title banner for a web page. Instead of having balloons floating gently (and simply!) up the page, however, this page will include a firecracker hurling in from the right, along a curly-cue flight path.

If you haven't done so already, copy the files from the **chapter_18** folder on the CD to your hard drive. Define a site called Chapter 18, with this folder as the local root folder.

1. Start by opening **party_surprise.html** and examining its contents and structure. You'll see that it's built similarly to the **party_home.html** page used in the previous exercise, with a banner layer sliding in from the left. Preview the page in a browser and you'll see that the banner animation has already been created. The little firecracker graphic has not yet been animated. You want the firecracker to fly in from "offstage"-right, doing a little loop-the-loop before landing in its position at the left side of the banner. You'll use a recorded motion path to make this happen.

2. To prepare for the animation, open the Timelines panel if it's not already open, and make sure you either have all panels docked (Windows integrated workspace only) or position all free-standing windows and panels so that you can see the upper half of your page in the Document window as well as the Timelines panel. Remember, don't add the firecracker layer to the timeline—Dreamweaver will do that for you when you record the motion path.

3. Position the cracker layer where you want it to begin its animation, as far to the right as you can see and about halfway down the page. Make the Document window as wide as you need it to be, to scoot the cracker beyond the page contents to the right.

Tip

To reposition the playback head without selecting a sprite, click in the row of frame numbers above the sprite area of the timeline.

4. In the Timelines panel, position the playback head on the frame where you want the animation to start (frame 15 is a good choice, so the cracker animation won't start until the banner animation has finished). Then access the panel menu and choose Record Path of Layer.

5. In the Document window, drag the cracker layer along a path similar to that shown in Figure 18.13, ending up in the upper-left corner of the page. For best control, drag slowly but evenly. Remember, timing can always be adjusted later. After you have finished, release the mouse; recording will stop automatically.

Figure 18.13   The **party_surprise.html** page, recording the "cracker" layer's motion path.

6. Refine the animation path as needed, which might involve the following:

- If the path looks good, but the cracker ends up in the wrong position, move the entire path. In the Timelines panel, click between keyframes in the fire cracker sprite (this should select the entire sprite); then move the playback head to the final frame (so that you can see where the cracker should end up); then, in the Document window, move the cracker layer until it looks good.

- If the path looks good, but it's going too slowly, find the last keyframe in the sprite and drag it to the left to make the sprite shorter. If you compress the sprite until it consists only of keyframes, and the animation still moves too slowly, remove some of the internal keyframes (select each keyframe to be removed and choose Modify > Timeline > Remove Keyframe) so that you can compress it further.

- If the internal timing or positioning is off, select and adjust individual keyframes.

7. You'll probably want to adjust the overall timing of the page animation so that the cracker hurls into place after the banner has slid into position.

Figure 18.14 shows how the final timeline for this animation might look. To see a completed version of the file, find **party_surprise.html** in the **chapter_18/completed** folder of the CD. (Would you like the cracker to spin while it's coming in? That's a little harder to achieve. You'll tackle that later in this chapter, in Exercise 18.4.)

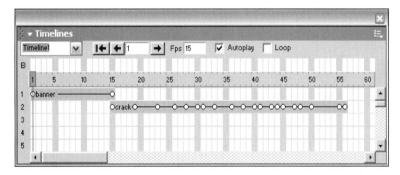

Figure 18.14   Timeline for the **party_surprise.html** page.

Animating Other Properties of Layers

When you animate a layer's position, what you're actually doing is changing its `left` and `top` properties over time. While people generally think of animation as involving motion, left and top position aren't the only layers properties that can be animated. Any property of a layer that can be controlled through scripting can, theoretically, be controlled over time to create an animation. You can use the Dreamweaver timeline interface to alter `width`, `height`, `z-index`, and `visibility`. Changes in `width` and `height` will even partake of tweening, making the layer appear to grow or shrink as the animation progresses, although these effects will work properly only in IE4+ and NN6+.

Basics of Animating Layer Properties

The procedure for altering width, height, z-index, and visibility over time is basically the same as that for altering position, as follows:

1. Start by adding the layer to the timeline, using one of the methods outlined earlier in this chapter.

2. In the Timelines panel, add any extra keyframes to the sprite, as described earlier.

3. Select a keyframe where you want the property change to occur.

4. In the Layer Property inspector, change the desired property. The width and height properties also can be changed by dragging the layer to resize it in the Document window.

Strategies for Animating Layer Properties

Be aware of the following when using the timeline to animate layer properties:

- **When changes will occur:** Changes to visibility and z-index will occur on the specified keyframe. Changes to width and height will be tweened from previous values.

- **Browser compatibility issues:** Changes to width and height will show up only in IE4+ and NN6+. Neither NN4.x nor Opera supports changing these properties.

- **Clipping values:** Although it is possible, using scripting, to alter the clipping values of a layer, the scripting created by the Dreamweaver animation timeline doesn't support animation of this property change.

Exercise 18.3   Animating a Title Banner's Dimensions and Visibility

This exercise creates a variant of the sliding banner animation created in Exercise 18.1. Instead of creating a title banner that slides on, as you did in that exercise, here you create a solid color banner that grows from nothing to full width. When the banner is at full size, the title pops into visibility on top of it, completing the effect.

If you haven't done so already, copy the files from the **chapter_18** folder on the CD to your hard drive. Define a site called Chapter 18, with this folder as the local root folder.

1. Start by opening **party_cakes.html** and examining its structure and contents. You'll see that the title banner is built from two layers—an empty banner layer with a colored background and a title layer containing a graphic with transparent background so the banner layer shows through. The candle graphic in the upper left is in its own layer, as is the page's main text block. None of these layers has been added to the timeline for animation.

2. You want the title, banner, and candle layers to be invisible when the page loads. Use the Layers panel or Property inspector to set the `visibility` property of each layer to Hidden.

3. As soon as the page loads, you want the banner layer to become visible—but only as a thin vertical strip at the left edge of the document. You then want the layer to animate to its full width, all the way across the top of the page.

4. To prepare the layer for animation, add it to the timeline as a sprite, using any of the methods outlined earlier in this chapter, and enable the timeline's Autoplay option.

To create the banner animation, give the sprite the following keyframes, with the following properties set:

- **Keyframe 1 (the first frame of the sprite).** Set the W value to 10. Leave the `visibility` at Hidden.

- **Keyframe 2 (the second frame of the sprite).** Leave the W value at 10. Set the `visibility` to Visible.

- **Keyframe 3 (the last frame of the sprite).** Set the W value to 600. Set the `visibility` to Visible.

Figure 18.15 shows the proper structure for the sprite. With this setup, the sprite should become visible at its second frame and then tween its width from 10 to 600 pixels. Before proceeding to the next step, make sure this animation effect is working properly. (Remember, the effect will show up only in IE4+ and NN6+.)

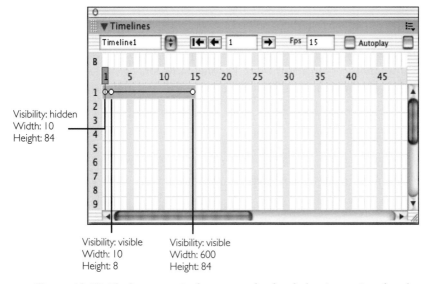

Visibility: hidden
Width: 10
Height: 84

Visibility: visible
Width: 10
Height: 8

Visibility: visible
Width: 600
Height: 84

Figure 18.15 The banner sprite for **party_cakes.html**, showing settings for a layer that will start out skinny and invisible and end up full-width and visible.

5. After the banner has grown into position, the title should pop into visibility. To accomplish this, add the title layer to the timeline as a sprite. As is shown in Figure 18.16, the new sprite can begin and end with the banner sprite. Set the following keyframes and properties for the title layer:

- **Keyframe 1 (the first frame of the sprite).** Make sure the visibility is set to Hidden.

- **Keyframe 2 (the last frame of the sprite).** Set the visibility to Visible.

6. The candles should appear after the title has appeared. To create this animation effect, add the candles layer to the timeline. Set its sprite to end a few frames after the title layer ends. Set its keyframes and properties to match those of the title layer (Hidden and then Visible). Figure 18.16 shows this sprite in place.

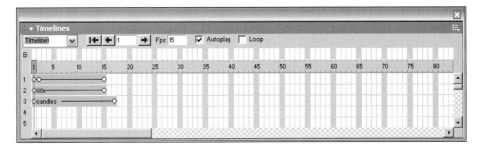

Figure 18.16   Creating the title and candles sprites for **party_cakes.html**.

That's it! Preview your page in a browser to make sure it animates correctly, with everything growing or popping into position at the desired time. (To see a completed version of the file, find **party_cakes.html** in the **chapter_18/completed** folder of the CD.) Don't forget, this effect will not work in all browsers. For alternative strategies that are more browser-compatible, see the section on "Animating Behaviors" later in this chapter.

Animating Images

In addition to animating layer properties, you can use the Dreamweaver timeline interface to animate the src property of images. Any named image, whether or not it is in a layer, can be used for animation.

Basics of Animating an Image's *src* Property

The basic procedure for animating images is the same as that for animating layer properties, as follows:

1. Select the image to be animated and add it to the timeline using one of the methods outlined earlier (drag it into the Timelines panel, select Modify > Timeline > Add to Timeline, and so on). The image will be represented on the timeline as a sprite.

2. Add as many keyframes as desired to the sprite, by Ctrl/Cmd-clicking or using one of the other methods outlined earlier.

3. Select the keyframe where you want the image src to change.

4. In the Property inspector, choose a new src for the image.

Figure 18.17 shows the proper setup for animating an image using this method.

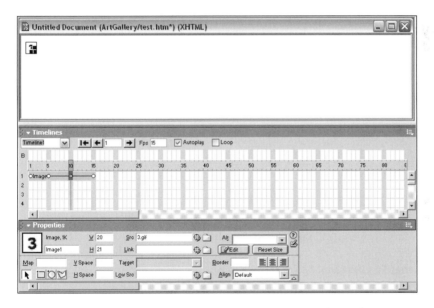

Figure 18.17   Animating an image's src property over time, using the timeline.

Strategies for Animating Images

Here are a few items to be aware of when using the timeline to animate images:

- **Name your images:** Only named images can be animated. Before attempting to animate an image, select it and use the Property inspector to give it a name. As with all names intended for use by scripts, the name must be one word only and contain no special characters.

- **Layers aren't necessary:** Images do not need to be placed in layers to have their src properties animated. (See the sample in Figure 18.17.)

- **Only the source file can be animated:** The src property is the only property of an image that can be animated in this way. To create the illusion of a picture growing, shrinking, or rotating, you'll have to animate between several separate source files, each with the same dimensions but containing different versions of the picture. To animate an image's position on the page, place the image inside a layer and animate the layer (like you have been doing in the exercises).

Note

If all you need is a simple automatic slide show effect—separate images replacing each other in sequence—an animated GIF is a much simpler solution than JavaScript animation, but it does limit you to using GIF images. If you want to create a slide show comprised of JPG images, use the Dreamweaver timeline as described here.

Exercise 18.4   Animating Images in an Animated Title Banner

This exercise builds on the animation created in Exercise 18.2. For that animation, you made a firecracker loop across the page to land on top of the title banner. Now you will spiff up that animation so that the firecracker looks like it's spinning as it flies and explodes on impact.

If you haven't done so already, copy the files from the **chapter_18** folder on the CD to your hard drive. Define a site called Chapter 18, with this folder as the local root folder.

1. Start by opening the **party_surprise.html** file you created in Exercise 18.2. If you didn't finish that exercise, find and open **party_surprise.html** in the **chapter_18/completed** folder.

2. Although you could create multiple, rotating versions of the cracker picture and use them to build an animated "spin" effect, it's simpler to use an animated GIF that shows a spinning cracker. This much animation can be done without using the timeline at all. In the Document window, select the crackerpic image and change its src to **cracker_spin.gif**. (You can browse to this file; it's in the **chapter_18** folder.)

3. To create the "exploding-on-impact" effect, use timeline animation. Add the crackerpic image to the timeline using one of the methods outlined earlier. Note that although the cracker layer has already been added to the timeline, the image itself must be added separately. Figure 18.18 shows this happening.

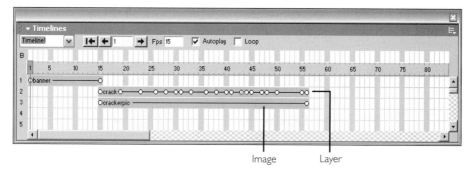

Image   Layer

Figure 18.18   The timeline of **party_surprise.html**, showing the crackerpic image and the layer containing as separate sprites in the timeline.

4. Make the image sprite begin and end at the same time as the cracker layer sprite. (This isn't necessary, but will help you synchronize the timing between layer movement and image properties.)

5. In the timeline, select the final keyframe of the crackerpic sprite and change the src property for the image to **cracker_open.gif**. (This file also is in the **chapter_18** folder.)

Try out your animation! If all went as planned, the cracker should spin (slowly) as it flies into position and then change to a static "burst" image when it lands on the banner. To see a completed version of the file, find **party_surprise_2.html** in the **chapter_18/completed** folder of the CD.

Timelines and Behaviors

In addition to straightforward animation effects, timelines can be combined with behaviors to create complex interactive animations. Timeline frames can contain behaviors that will be triggered when the playback head reaches them. And timelines can be started, stopped, and have their looping controlled interactively through Timeline behaviors triggered by user events (such as onMouseOver or onClick) or window events (such as onLoad).

Animating Behaviors

Just as you can use the timeline to change image and layer properties at specified times, you can set any Dreamweaver behavior to execute at a certain time by attaching it to the timeline. (Flash users: This is similar to using frame actions, except that no keyframes need be set.) Referring back to Figure 18.2, note the channel labeled B. This is the behavior channel. Any Dreamweaver behavior can be attached to any frame in this channel, and will execute when the playback head passes that frame.

Adding a Behavior to a Timeline

The procedure for attaching a Dreamweaver behavior to a timeline frame is basically the same as the procedure for adding a behavior to any page element. Follow these steps, as illustrated in Figure 18.19:

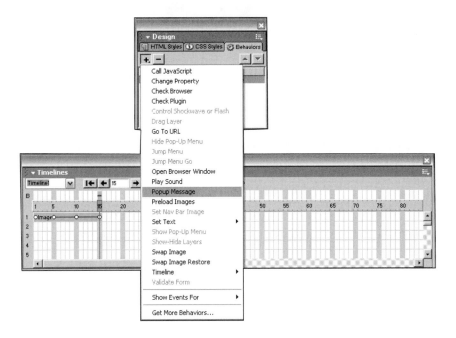

Figure 18.19   Adding a behavior to a frame in a timeline.

1. Open any document that contains a timeline. Open the Timelines panel and the Behaviors panel, and either dock them (Windows only) or arrange them so that you have a clear view of both.

2. In the Timelines panel, click in any frame in the B (behaviors) channel to select it. The frame will highlight to show that it is selected.

3. From the plus (+) menu, choose any behavior. Enter data into the behavior's dialog box and click OK, as you normally would when attaching a behavior to an image, text link, or other page element.

4. After you have finished, examine the Timelines panel. In the B channel for your chosen frame, an icon appears indicating that a behavior has been added (see Figure 18.19).

Editing Timeline Behaviors

After you've created the timeline behavior, you can change its parameters any time, the same as you would with any behavior. Follow these steps, as shown in Figure 18.20:

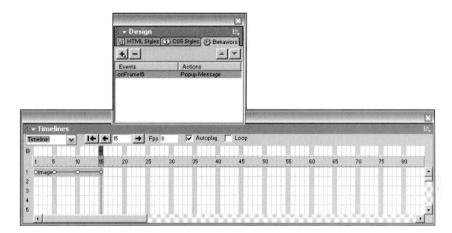

Figure 18.20   Editing behaviors that have been attached to timeline frames.

1. In the Timelines panel, select any B channel frame that shows a behavior icon.

2. The Behaviors panel will now show all behaviors attached to that frame, using the onFrame*N* event handler. (Note that this is not a real JavaScript event handler; Dreamweaver shows it this way only to help the authoring process.)

3. In the Behaviors panel, double-click the behavior to change its parameters; or select the behavior and click the minus sign (–) button to remove it entirely.

Exercise 18.5   Adding a Behavior to an Animation Timeline

Any behavior can be added to a timeline, as long as it's appropriate for your page. For this exercise, you create another animated opening banner similar to the one created in Exercise 18.4. For this exercise, however, instead of changing layer visibility, you'll use the Show/Hide Layers behavior to reveal the banner. The advantage of using this method over the method in the previous exercise is that this animation will work in all 4+ browsers.

If you haven't done so already, copy the files from the **chapter_18** folder on the CD to your hard drive. Define a site called Chapter 18, with this folder as the local root folder.

1. Open the **party_activities.html** file and examine its structure and contents. The sliding banner animation has already been added to the timeline. The streamers should be invisible until the main banner has slid into place, which means that your job for this exercise is to hide and then show the streamers layer, using a timeline behavior.

2. Using the Layers panel or Property inspector, set the streamers layer's visibility to Hidden. (Because the layer should start out hidden, you don't need a behavior to hide it—it's more efficient to establish visibility as an HTML attribute than to create it with scripting.)

3. Open the Timelines and Behaviors panels, if they're not already open.

4. In the Timelines panel, go to the B (Behaviors) channel and select a frame a few frames after the banner has finished sliding on.

5. In the Behaviors panel, from the plus (+) menu choose Show-Hide Layers. Set the behavior to show the streamers layer. Figure 18.21 shows this behavior being applied.

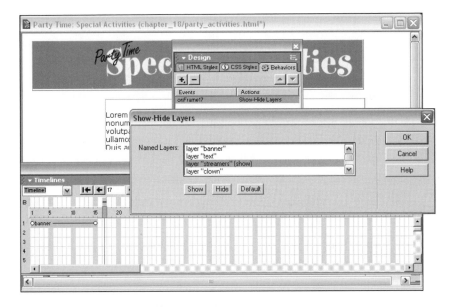

Figure 18.21   Adding a Show-Hide Layers behavior to the timeline of **party_activities.html**.

6. Try the new animation in various browsers. It should animate properly in all browsers that support layers, including NN4+ and Opera 5.

7. To adjust the timing of the animation, try moving the behavior to a different frame in the B channel. To do this, just select the behavior's frame and drag left or right to a new frame.

To see a completed version of the file, find **party_activities.html** in the **chapter_18/completed** folder.

Controlling Timeline Playback with Timeline Behaviors

As described earlier in this chapter, timeline animations are built from JavaScript functions, and like all JavaScript functions they must be triggered by some event before they will play. When you enable Autoplay in the Timelines panel, you're creating code that will trigger the animation to play onLoad, which means as soon as the page loads. But that's not the only event you can use. You can use any of the standard event triggers—onMouseOver, onClick, and so on—to tell your timeline to start, stop, or go to a specific frame based on browser or user action. Timeline playback is controlled by the Play Timeline, Stop Timeline and Go to Timeline Frame behaviors, all located in the Behavior panel's actions menu under the Timelines submenu (see Figure 18.22).

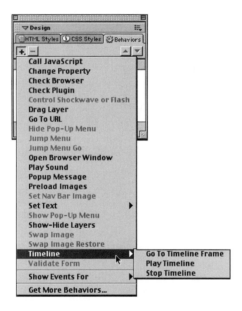

Figure 18.22   The Behaviors panel, showing the Timeline submenu of behaviors.

The Play Timeline Behavior

The Play Timeline behavior starts a timeline playing from its current frame. When you choose Autoplay from the Timelines panel, this behavior is automatically added to the <body> tag of your document, to be triggered onLoad. But you don't have to start your animations onLoad. If you disable Autoplay so your animation doesn't start onLoad, you can place a "Start" button, or image, or text link, in your document and use the Behaviors panel to assign the Play Timeline behavior to that element, to be triggered onClick, or onMouseOver, or on any event those items will support.

The Stop Timeline Behavior

As its name indicates, the Stop Timeline behavior stops playback of a timeline (or all timelines) at the current frame. The browser will remember this current frame as long as the page is loaded in memory. If a timeline is stopped and then told to play again, it will begin playing from the current frame.

Note

Don't get tangled up in your stopping and starting! If a timeline that has not been set to loop stops at its final frame, and then another event triggers the timeline to play, the timeline will attempt to play starting from that final frame. But since there is no looping, and this is the end of the animation, there are no frames left to play! It will seem as though the behavior is broken, because no animation will happen.

The Go To Timeline Frame Behavior

The Go To Timeline Frame behavior sends a timeline's playback head to a specified destination frame. What the playback head does when it gets to that frame depends on whether Autoplay, Looping, or the other Timeline behaviors are also controlling this timeline. Possible results include:

- If the timeline is stopped when the Go To Timeline Frame behavior is triggered (for example, if Autoplay is not enabled and no other triggers have called Play Timeline), the playback head will move to the destination frame and stop.

- If the timeline is already playing when Go To Timeline Frame is triggered (for example, if Play Timeline has been executed and Stop Timeline has not), the playback head will move to the destination frame and continue playing.

- If the playback head is not moving because it has reached the animation's final frame and looping is not enabled, the timeline is officially still playing. When Go To Timeline Frame is triggered, the playback head will move to the destination frame and continue playing.

Controlling Timeline Looping.

Looping occurs when the Go To Timeline Frame behavior is triggered from within the timeline itself (from a frame in the Behaviors channel) and is configured to send the playback head to a frame before the frame containing the behavior. When the playback head reaches the frame containing the behavior, it will automatically be bounced back to the destination frame. Because behaviors attached to timeline frames will only be triggered if the timeline is playing, and because a playing timeline will always continue playing after going to the destination frame, the playback head will continue playing after it reaches the destination frame. Because the destination frame is earlier in the timeline than the frame calling the Go To Timeline behavior, the playback head will eventually again run into the behavior, and will again be bounced back to the destination frame. In other words, it will loop.

You can add looping to a timeline in one of two ways:

- by selecting the Timelines panel's Loop option.
- By selecting a frame in the timeline's B channel and using the Behaviors panel to attach the Go To Timeline Frame behavior to that frame.

In fact, when you select the Loop option in the Timelines panel, Dreamweaver adds a Go To Timeline Frame behavior to the frame following your animation's final frame, set to loop back to frame 1 (see Figure 18.23). No matter which of these two methods you use to create your timeline looping (manually setting up the behavior or using the Timelines panel's Loop option), after it's in place it's a regular Go To Timeline Frame behavior. To edit it, select the B channel frame that contains it and, in the Behaviors panel, double-click on its name to open the Go To Timeline Frame dialog box.

A few notes about configuring looping using Go To Timeline Frame:

- There's no reason you need to loop all the way back to frame 1. You just need to loop back to a previous frame in the animation. (If you send the playback head forward in the animation, that's not looping!)
- If you leave the Loop input field empty, the animation will loop forever. If you fill in a numeric value, it will loop only that number of times.

Note

By definition, a looping behavior must be triggered from within the timeline that's being looped. Even though you can attach the Go To Timeline Frame behavior to any page element, if you try to enter a value into the loop field as you're configuring that behavior, you'll get an error message.

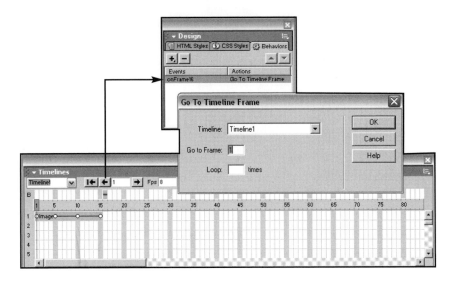

Figure 18.23   Editing a timeline's looping.

Working with Multiple Timelines

If you think having one timeline is fun, guess what? You can have more than one! Each timeline in a Dreamweaver document controls one animation. For more complex documents, you might want to include several animations, each triggered by a different event. To support this, Dreamweaver allows multiple timelines to be defined for each document. You might, for instance, want one animation to play when the page loads, and another to play when the user rolls over or clicks a button. You might even want one animation for each of several navigation buttons. Each timeline operates independently of the others. Two or more timelines can even be used to control the same page element (layer or image) but be triggered by different events.

Adding a Second Timeline to a Document

Every Dreamweaver document starts out with one timeline—Timeline1—already set up in the Timelines panel. That's why, if you only need one timeline for a document, you don't have to create one before dragging sprites to the Timelines panel. To add more timelines, follow these steps (see Figure 18.24):

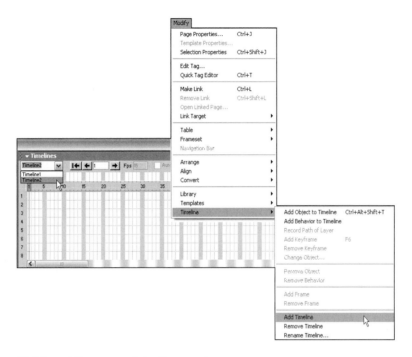

Figure 18.24   Adding a second timeline to a document.

1. Open the Timelines panel, if it's not already open, and choose Modify > Timeline > Add Timeline. A new, empty timeline will appear in the Timelines panel, with the default name Timeline2.

2. (optional) Repeat this procedure to create additional timelines. Each new timeline will be added with incremental names (Timeline3, Timeline4, and so on).

Managing Multiple Timelines

Extra timelines require extra management tools. You can rename them, copy and paste animations between them, and (of course) delete them.

- **To switch between timelines:** Use the pop-up menu in the Timelines panel's upper-left corner to edit and view different timelines.

- **To rename any of your timelines:** Choose it as the active timeline and either enter a new name in the Timelines panel's Name field or choose Modify > Timeline > Rename Timeline.

If you rename a timeline after having created behaviors that refer to it (Play Timeline, Stop Timeline, Go To Timeline Frame), you'll need to amend those behaviors to refer to the new name. For each behavior, open it from the Behaviors panel and select a new target timeline. (You might have to wade through a few error messages as you do this, as Dreamweaver lets you know that the original timeline name no longer exists.) Note that this only applies to behaviors you've created yourself. Autoplay and Loop, if enabled in the Timelines panel, will update automatically to reflect the new name.

- **To move or duplicate sprites between timelines:** Select the sprite you want to move or duplicate and choose Edit > Copy. Switch to the timeline you want the sprite copied to, and choose Edit > Paste. If you are moving instead of duplicating, return to the original timeline and delete the original sprite (select the sprite and choose Modify > Timeline > Remove Object).

- **To remove a timeline:** Make it the active timeline and choose Modify > Timeline > Remove Timeline. Note that this doesn't delete any objects from your document! It only removes all animation instructions contained in the timeline.

Exercise 18.6   Adding Multiple Timelines to a Document

This exercise builds on the PartyTime Activities page you started in the preceding exercise. In addition to the animated banner you have already added to the page, you want each of the other illustrations (clown, game pieces, party favor) to be hidden offstage-left until the user interacts with the related text link. To do this, you need three additional timelines—one to be triggered by each text link. All exercise files can be found in the **chapter_18** folder on the CD. If you haven't yet completed Exercise 18.5, find and open the **party_activities.html** file in the **chapter_18/completed** folder.

1. Open **party_activities.html** and examine its contents. The text portion contains three links—Clowns, Games & Toys, and Party Favors. Each of those links matches one of the pictures (each in its own layer) at the left of the page. The goal is to position each layer offstage-left and have it slide into view when the user clicks, or rolls over, the appropriate text link.

2. Start with the clown. To create a new timeline for the clown, open the Timelines panel; from the panel menu, choose Add Timeline. When the new timeline appears, change its name to **clowntime**.

3. Drag the clown layer onto the timeline. The clown should start offstage-left and then slide into partial view, pause for a moment, and then slide back offstage. To create this effect, you need a total of four keyframes (see Figure 18.25). Tweak the timing and positioning until you like it.

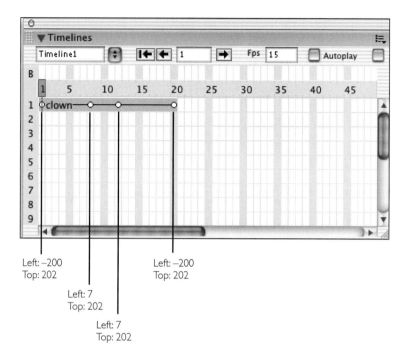

Left: −200
Top: 202

Left: −200
Top: 202

Left: 7
Top: 202

Left: 7
Top: 202

Figure 18.25   Adding the clown layer to the clowntime timeline. Each keyframe contains a different left (L) value for the layer.

4. This animation will be triggered when the user rolls over the Clowns text link in the main text layer. First, make sure the Timelines panel does *not* have Autoplay enabled for this timeline. Then select the text link. In the Behaviors panel, click the plus (+) button and choose Timeline > Play Timeline (see Figure 18.26). In the dialog box that appears, choose Clowntime from the Timelines pop-up menu. After you have finished, change the default event in the Behaviors panel from onClick to onMouseOver.

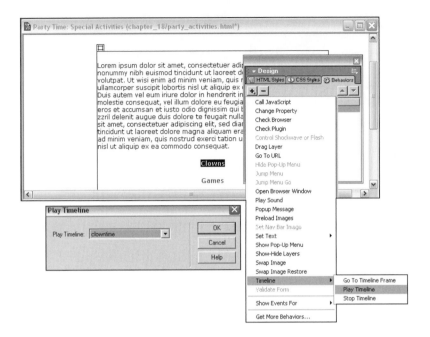

Figure 18.26   Attaching the Play Timeline behavior to the Clowns text link.

5. Try your animation in the browser! Mousing over the text link should result in the clown peeking out and then retreating. There's still one problem, however. The effect works only once. The second time the user mouses over the text link, nothing happens. This is because the clown's timeline has already finished playing, and is not set to loop.

To solve this problem, add two behaviors to the timeline. First select the Loop option, to add a Go To Timeline Frame behavior to the end of the animation. Then set the timeline to stop on the frame immediately preceding the loop. Do this by selecting the B channel frame immediately preceding the frame containing the looping behavior. In the Behaviors panel, click the plus (+) button and choose Timeline > Stop Timeline. In the dialog box that appears, choose to stop the clowntime timeline. What's going to happen here? The first time the animation is triggered, it will stop at your stop action frame. The next time it's triggered, it will continue playing from that frame—which will take it to the frame containing the loop command, which will send it back to the beginning. Figure 18.27 shows the correct setup to stop the timeline.

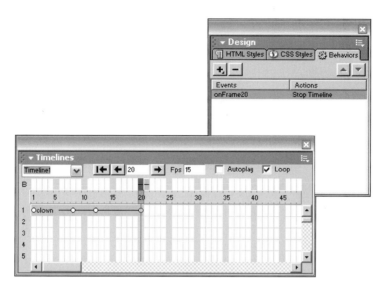

Figure 18.27   The clowntime timeline, revised to stop and loop so it can be triggered
repeatedly.

Optional: If you're up for a challenge, set up the other two illustrations on this page to
animate when the user interacts with the associated links. You can set them up to match
the clown animation (slide out onMouseOver, slide away onMouseOut), or create your
own different animation. To see a completed version of the file, find **party_
activities_2.html** in the **chapter_18/completed** folder of the CD.

Note

Note for Flash/Director users: Because there are no frame labels in the Dreamweaver
JavaScript-based timeline interface, the Go To Timeline Frame behavior must always refer
to frame numbers.

Summary

In this chapter, you have seen how the Dreamweaver timeline interface makes it possible
to create robust, cross-browser-compatible JavaScript animations efficiently. The timeline interface is, of course, only a convenience for authoring purposes. JavaScript animations will never display as smoothly, or achieve the complexity, available using dedicated
animation formats such as Flash, Director, or QuickTime. But thanks to Dreamweaver,
you can integrate animation effects seamlessly into your web pages, and your visitors
won't need plugins to take advantage of them.

Chapter 19

Plugins, ActiveX, and Java

Chapters 17 and 18 showed how DHTML

can be used to add complex interactivity

and visual effects to web pages—subject

only to the limitations of the browser itself.

In this and the next chapter, you'll see how

you can add different kinds of media and interactivity by extending the browser's capabilities. This chapter discusses how plugins, ActiveX controls, and Java can enable you to go beyond the browser, and how Dreamweaver helps you work with all of those so-called "rich media" technologies. In particular, this chapter covers Shockwave, QuickTime, RealMedia, and Windows Media. Because of the extensive integration of Dreamweaver with Flash, Chapter 20, "Building Web Pages with Flash," covers that topic.

Extending the Browser with Plugins and ActiveX

The most common way to extend browser functionality and create media-rich pages is through plugin content. Creating web pages that rely on this kind of browser extension can be a frustrating experience—even in Dreamweaver!—unless you understand the limitations of the technology underneath it and how to use that technology intelligently.

How Plugin Media Works in the Browser

Browsers are essentially HTML decoders. Their job is to translate the markup instructions in an HTML file into a visible, functional screenful of information. By adding JavaScript to your HTML, you can add a certain amount of interactivity to web pages. By themselves, however, browsers cannot handle the rich variety of media you might want your pages to contain. They cannot display video, they cannot manipulate and present sound, and they cannot present PDF content. Because of browser differences, it's also difficult to reliably create complex interactive content that will work across browsers and across platforms, solely through JavaScript and HTML.

Lucky for us, browsers are extensible: They call on external entities to do what they alone cannot do. In fact, they do this frequently as you surf the web, whether you're aware of it or not.

MIME Types, Plugins, and Helper Applications

Every time a browser encounters a file, it must determine what kind of file it is and what should be done with it. Browsers do this by examining the file's *MIME type.* The MIME (Multipurpose Internet Mail Extension) type is part of the information the web server usually sends along with the file when a web page is downloaded to a user's computer. The MIME type includes a description of the file's category, and helps the browser determine what should be done with it.

As a backup, in case the web server does not send the MIME information with the downloaded file, the browser also examines the suffix, or filename extension, of all downloaded files. Some standard MIME types, along with their associated filename extensions, are shown in Table 19.1.

Table 19.1   Common MIME Types and Associated Filename Extensions

MIME Type	Filename Extensions
image/gif	.gif
image/jpeg	.jpg, .jpeg
audio/wav	.wav
audio/aif	.aif, .aiff
audio/x-midi	.mid, .midi
video/mov	.mov
video/avi	.avi
application/zip	.zip
application/x-macbinary	.bin
application/pdf	.pdf
application/x-shockwave-flash	.swf
application/vnd.rn-realmedia	.rm

If the MIME type or filename extension indicates that the file is something the browser can't deal with, it calls on outside help. This help is either a helper application or a plugin.

A *helper application* is a program that can deal with the file type in question. A helper application can be any program on your computer. Any time the browser comes across a file with an extension of .doc or a MIME type of application/doc, for instance, it will probably attempt to find and launch Microsoft Word or an equivalent word processor that has been defined as the helper application for that kind of file. Any of these programs also can be launched independently of the browser.

A *plugin*, like a helper application, has functionality the browser doesn't, but it is not a standalone application. Plugins cannot launch and run on their own. Instead, they add functionality to the browser. Plugins must reside in the **Plugins** folder, inside the browser's own application folder. The Flash, QuickTime, and Shockwave plugins, as well as the Flash and Shockwave ActiveX controls, are examples of this kind of help. When the browser comes across a file with an extension of **.swf** or a MIME type of application/x-shockwave-flash, it will probably look for and attempt to launch the Flash Player plugin.

Configuration and Customization

You might be wondering why the browser will *probably* respond in a certain way to a certain MIME type? Because each browser must be configured to interpret certain MIME types in certain ways; and any two browsers—even if they're the same version of the same browser, on the same platform—might be configured differently. Browsers are already configured when you install them; depending on where you got the browser (promotional or application CD, computer manufacturer install, download from Microsoft or Netscape, and so forth), it might be configured differently from other copies of the same browser obtained from somewhere else. And of course, individual browser users also can customize the configuration if they like.

Potential Configuration Problems

Web authors can't control how browsers will handle given file types; they can only try to predict how their target audience will have their browsers configured, and set pages up to deal gracefully with failure in this regard. (Authoring strategies are discussed later in this chapter.) The most common configuration problems are:

- **Unavailable plugins or helpers.** Just because a plugin or helper application is called for in the configuration setup doesn't mean it's available on the user's computer. This is the most common problem plaguing web designers who want a variety of plugin-based media on their pages.

- **Unknown MIME types.** If a file is downloaded that the browser does not recognize, either by MIME type or filename extension, the user will be asked what to do with the file.

- **Unexpected or inappropriate disposition.** The helper or action specified in the default configuration might not be the one that is expected; it might not even be the best choice, given the particular setup of a user's computer system.

Netscape Plugins Versus ActiveX Objects

Years ago, to enable web authors to put media content on HTML pages, Netscape developed the capability to add plugins to itself; to support plugin-based media content, Netscape created its own, nonstandard HTML tag—<embed>. Although the <embed> tag was never made part of the W3 Consortium's official HTML specification, it was a big hit with users. Internet Explorer adopted the <embed> tag and the plugin system, and for several years it was the standard method used to insert media into web pages.

Meanwhile, Microsoft was developing its own set of technologies to allow applications of all kinds to share information and work together. Object Linking and Embedding (OLE) and the Component Object Model (COM) eventually developed into ActiveX technology. For web use, Microsoft built into its browser the capability to understand miniprograms called *ActiveX controls*, which could control and share information with ActiveX objects placed on a web page using the <object> tag. ActiveX controls can be written to work with various applications, including Internet Explorer. Microsoft's scripting language, VBScript, can be used to communicate between the ActiveX control and the browser, much as JavaScript (which was developed by Netscape) communicates between plugins and the browser.

As a result, there are two ways to insert media content into browsers: as plugin objects using <embed>, or as ActiveX objects using <object>. And there are two sets of browser technology available for interpreting that content: Netscape-style plugins and ActiveX controls. Only IE supports ActiveX; and, because ActiveX is so tied in with Microsoft's other technologies, it works only on the Windows platform. Until recently, both Netscape and IE supported Netscape-style plugins; but starting with versions 5.52-SP2, IE/Win no longer supports plugins, only ActiveX controls (though it does still support the <embed> tag for ActiveX content). Older versions of IE/Win, and all versions of IE/Mac, while they do theoretically support plugins, don't offer very good support. In Netscape, you can communicate with plugin content using JavaScript; Internet Explorer does not allow JavaScript access to plugin objects or ActiveX objects; VBScript can be used to communicate with ActiveX objects, but not with plugin objects. And because Internet Explorer/Macintosh does not support ActiveX, this severely limits what you can do to control cross-browser, cross-platform media content.

Note

It's confusing but important to remember that, although IE/Windows no longer supports Netscape-style plugins, it does support the <embed> tag. When the browser sees an <embed> tag, it first looks for an ActiveX control to handle the content. If there is no ActiveX control, older versions of the browser will look for a plugin; the newest versions will not.

As a web author, you tread daily through this minefield. Dreamweaver helps by offering support for both technologies and by taking care of as many details as it can to make your pages accessible to all.

Note

According to the World Wide Web Consortium's official HTML specification, the `<object>` tag is to be used for placing all media elements the browser can't normally display (including Java applets) on web pages. In practice, however, browser support for this tag is not widespread beyond Internet Explorer's ActiveX technology.

Netscape Plugins (The <embed> Tag)

In Dreamweaver, to insert media content using the `<embed>` tag, use the Plugin object, found in the Media category of the Insert bar. This generic object can be used with a variety of plugin and MIME types. Figure 19.1 shows the object as it appears in the Insert bar, and the Property inspector that goes with it.

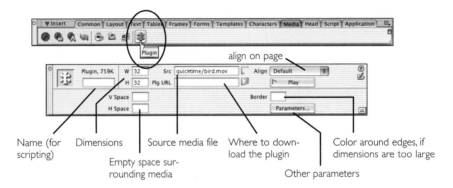

Figure 19.1   The Plugin object, and its associated Property inspector.

The Property inspector for elements created with this object includes the following generic parameters, which can be used with any media content:

- **src.** The URL of the source file for the content. Required.

- **pluginspace (Plg URL).** The URL of a site where the required plugin can be downloaded. If a value is entered in this parameter, and the user's browser does not have the appropriate plugin to handle the source file, the broken plugin icon will link to this URL. Optional, but recommended.

- **name.** As with any HTML element, media content must be named if it will be referred to by scripts. Optional.

- **width and height.** Specifies the dimensions the content will take up on the page. These values default to 32×32 pixels, because Dreamweaver cannot determine the dimensions of plugin content. Required by most plugins.

- **vspace and hspace.** Adds white space around the content. Optional.
- **align.** Determines how the content will align with text when it is placed inline on a page. Optional.
- **border.** Adds a border around the content area. Optional.

Accessing Plugin Specific Parameters

Because the Plugin object's Property inspector must work for any type of embedded plugin content, it includes only generic attributes. Most plugins will accept more attributes than this. To add plugin specific attributes, click the Parameters button in the Property inspector, which accesses a special Parameters dialog box (see Figure 19.2). For each parameter added in this way, you must know the parameter's name and what values it will accept.

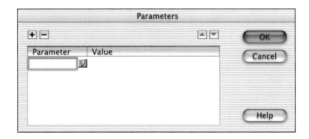

Figure 19.2   The Parameters dialog box for adding attributes not available in the Plugin or ActiveX object Property inspector.

Playing Embedded Content

Dreamweaver won't automatically display embedded media content in the Document window; instead, it shows a generic placeholder. Click the Play button in the Property inspector to see and hear the media. As long as you have the relevant plugin installed in any browser on your system, Dreamweaver will be able to preview the media. (See the sidebar on "How Dreamweaver Plays Media Content.")

How Dreamweaver Plays Media Content

Dreamweaver uses Netscape plugins to play embedded media. Every time you click the Play button to preview a media element, Dreamweaver looks for the required plugin, first in its own **Configuration/Plugins** folder, and then in the **Plugins** folders of all installed browsers. If it finds the plugin, the media will play. If not, the media won't play.

Dreamweaver/Windows users take note, however! Dreamweaver uses plugins—not ActiveX controls—to preview media content. If the only browser installed on your system is Internet Explorer, or if your other browser(s) have no plugins installed, you will not be able to preview embedded media from within Dreamweaver unless you do one of two things:

- Install Netscape or Opera (or any other plugin-using browser), and configure that browser with the required plugins.

- Obtain a copy of the required plugin—from another computer, or from the company that has created the plugin—and copy its class file (such as ShockwavePlugin.class) to your **Dreamweaver/Configuration/Plugins** folder.

This isn't an issue for Dreamweaver/Mac users, because all Macintosh browsers use Netscape plugins.

If the particular content you are working with has no related plugin—only an ActiveX Control—you won't be able to preview it in Dreamweaver no matter what you do. Windows users, preview in the browser; Mac users, you can't preview at all.

ActiveX Objects (The <object> Tag)

In Dreamweaver, to insert ActiveX content using the <object> tag, use the ActiveX object, found in the Media category of the Insert bar. Figure 19.3 shows the object as it appears in the panel, and the Property inspector that goes with it. Like the Plugin object, this is a generic object that can be used with a variety of ActiveX controls.

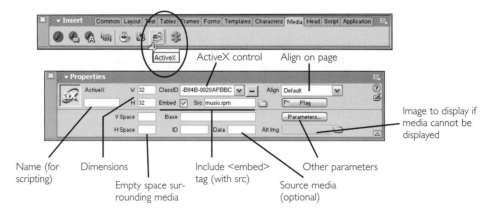

Figure 19.3   The Insert ActiveX object, and its associated Property inspector.

In addition to the parameters listed for plugin objects, the Property inspector for ActiveX objects includes the following:

- **classid (Class ID).** The name of the ActiveX control to be used to handle the content. The Shockwave, Flash, and RealMedia controls appear on the pop-up list; names of any other controls must be typed in. After a control name has been manually entered, it will appear in the pop-up list until removed (by clicking the minus (−) button next to the pop-up list).

- **id.** Used to refer to the object in scripting. Optional.

- **codebase (Base).** The URL of a site where the required control can be downloaded. If a value is entered in this parameter, and the user's browser does not have the appropriate ActiveX control to handle the source file, the control will be automatically downloaded if possible. Optional, but recommended.

- **data.** The URL of the source file for the content. This parameter is not required by many ActiveX controls (including Flash, Shockwave, and RealPlayer). Some controls, such as RealPlayer, require a src parameter instead. But as the Property inspector doesn't offer this as an option (except as part of the <embed> tag, discussed in the next section), src must be added using the generic Parameters dialog box.

Note

Coding note: If you examine your code after inserting an ActiveX object, you'll see that the <object> tag doesn't follow the standard HTML syntax of <tag attribute="value">. Instead, each attribute generates a nested tag with the syntax <param name="attribute" value="value">. For your web authoring purposes, the effect is the same as if these were standard attributes.

In addition to the previous options, which are added as parameters to the <object> tag, the following will create tags nested within the main <object> tag, both to be used as alternate content:

- **Alt image.** Specifying an image file here adds an <img> tag within the <object> tag. If the required ActiveX control is not available in a particular browser, the image specified here will display in the browser instead.

- **Embed.** If enabled, this adds an <embed> tag inside the <object> tag, to support Netscape on all platforms and Internet Explorer on non-Windows platforms. The src parameter listed in the Property inspector is used with this tag (not with the <object> tag).

Playing ActiveX Content

Click the Play button in the Property inspector to see and hear the media (see Figure 19.3). As long as you have the relevant plugin (not ActiveX control!) installed in any browser on your system, Dreamweaver will be able to preview the media. (For more on this, see the sidebar on "How Dreamweaver Plays Media Content.")

> **Note**
>
> Almost any media element can be accessed without using either <embed> or <object>, by linking directly to it. To create a link to a media file, just set up a text or image link on a page; then, in the Property inspector's Link field, browse to the media file. This is a fairly crude way to get media on your web site, however, because it gives no control over parameters or scripting.

Working with Specific Plugins

To use plugin media content effectively on your web pages, you need to familiarize yourself with the various plugins and ActiveX controls, and how each works—in the browser, and in Dreamweaver.

Shockwave

Shockwave is a plugin and related file format that allows content developed with Macromedia Director to be viewed in the browser. Director has long been industry-standard software for developing interactive CD-ROMs. Director movies can contain sound, video, and animation. Director's internal scripting language, Lingo, can create sophisticated interactivity. The current version of Director (8.5) includes support for 3D content, including extensive scripting of 3D worlds. Using Director Multiuser Server software, Director movies can even be used for multiplayer games, chat rooms, and other web application tasks. Director content is sprite-based, for efficient memory use, and makes use of client-side streaming for efficient web delivery. Director is also extensible through dozens of third-party Xtras, allowing Director content to include database connectivity, PDFs, and sophisticated printing functionality.

For CD-ROM use, Director movies are saved as standalone applications called *projectors.* For web use, movies are saved in a special "shocked" format, with the .dcr filename extension and application/x-director MIME type. To view this content, users must have the Shockwave plugin from www.macromedia.com.

> **Note**
>
> To learn more about Shockwave, visit www.macromedia.com/shockzone.

Shockwave Issues

Shockwave is a cross-browser and cross-platform plugin. It is available as a Netscape plugin and an ActiveX control. Many corporate web sites use Shockwave content to provide fun, illustrative, or heavily interactive content to entice users. According to Macromedia, 167 million users worldwide have the Shockwave plugin installed.

Inserting a Shockwave Object

In Dreamweaver, inserting Shockwave content is done with the Shockwave object (shown in Figure 19.4). This object is located in the Media category of the Insert bar. The object inserts Shockwave content using the `<object>` tag, with an included `<embed>` tag.

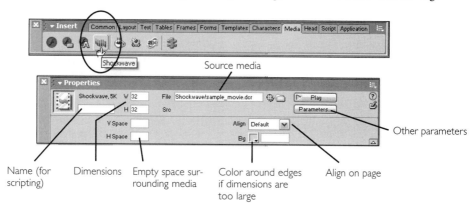

Figure 19.4   The Shockwave object and its associated Property inspector.

> **Tip**
>
> If you have a site defined, you can also use the Assets panel to organize, preview and insert your Shockwave movies. Just click the Shockwave icon in the panel to view your movies. (See Chapter 22, "Local Site Management," for more on the Assets panel.

The Property inspector for Shockwave content is fairly sparse, because several basic parameters—such as `pluginspage` and `codebase`—are set automatically by Dreamweaver. Note that `width` and `height` are not set automatically; Dreamweaver sets these to a default of 32×32 pixels, regardless of the movie's dimensions. You must find the correct movie dimensions in Director itself, or by using trial and error in the browser. If the `width` and `height` parameters in the Property inspector are set smaller than the original movie size, the movie will be cropped; if the dimensions are set larger than the original size, empty space will be added around the edges of the movie.

Passing Parameters to Shockwave

As Table 19.2 shows, it's possible to pass all sorts of information to a Shockwave movie in the form of parameters entered in the <object> and <embed> tags, as long as the movie knows what to do with the information it's receiving. These parameters include basics such as autostart and loop, as well as a whole series of parameters that Director authors can tie into the movie's Lingo scripting. Inside Director, these parameters are accessed through the externalParamValue(), externalParamNumber(), and externalParamName() functions. The parameter defined in Dreamweaver must have exactly the same name as the parameter called in the Lingo code.

Table 19.2   Parameters a Shockwave Movie Will Accept, with a Description of Each and Suggested Values Where Applicable

Parameter Name	Value	Description
name	One-word name	Required by the <embed> tag if the movie is to referred to by scripting.
id	One-word name	Required by the <object> tag if the movie is to be referred to by scripting.
width	Number of pixels	The horizontal space the movie will be allotted on the page. Dreamweaver cannot determine this automatically. If the width assigned is different from the movie's width, the movie will be cropped or surrounded by empty space.
height	Number of pixels	The vertical space the movie will be allotted on the page. Dreamweaver cannot determine this automatically. If the height assigned is different from the movie's height, the movie will be cropped or surrounded by empty space.
align	(Choose from the pop-up menu)	Determines how the browser will align the movie when text or other page elements are placed next to it (in the same table cell or paragraph, for instance).
bgcolor	(Choose from the color picker or enter a 6-digit hexadecimal number)	If the width and height values assigned are larger than the movie's dimensions, this is the color that will fill up the rest of the allotted space.

Parameter Name	Value	Description
vspace	Number of pixels	Adds empty white space above and below the movie. Specify a number of pixels.
hspace	Number of pixels	Adds empty white space to the right and left of the movie. Specify a number of pixels.
autostart	true or false	Whether the movie will start playing as soon as it loads.
loop	true or false	Whether the movie will repeat indefinitely, or play only once. This only has effect if the movie's own internal scripting doesn't have its own looping or stopping controls.
sound, progress, swLiveConnect, swRemote, swStretchStyle, swStretchHAlign, swStretchVAlign, swAudio, swBanner, swBackColor, swForeColor, swColor, swFrame, swList, swName, swPassword, swPreloadTime, swSound, swText, swURL, swVolume, swPreLoadTime, sw1, sw2, sw3, sw4, sw5, sw6, sw7, sw8, sw9	Can take any value	These parameters can be used to pass any values to a Shockwave movie. The movie's internal scripting must specifically call the parameter for it to take effect. It's up to the author whether swSound, for instance, passes any information about sound to the movie, or whether it passes completely unrelated information. Internet Explorer requires that passed parameters to Shockwave use these names and these names only. (In Netscape, any parameter name can be used, as long as the Director movie's internal scripting calls on that parameter.)

To access and assign other parameters for the Shockwave movie, click the generic Parameters button to open the parameters dialog box. From here, click the plus (+) button to get a list of potential parameters that can be set. (Figure 19.5 shows this happening.)

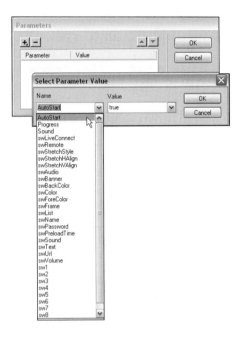

Figure 19.5   The Parameters dialog box for assigning Shockwave-specific parameters.

Exercise 19.1   Inserting a Shockwave Movie

In this exercise, you'll place a Shockwave movie on an HTML page and test its basic properties. Before you begin, copy the **chapter_19** folder from the companion CD to your hard drive and define a Dreamweaver site named **chapter_19** with this folder as its root directory. The current exercise uses files in the **chapter_19/shockwave** folder.

1. Open **shockwave_sampler.html**. This is a formatted but otherwise empty document, ready to receive media content.

2. Using the Shockwave object, place **welcome.dcr** onto the page.

3. Resize the movie to its correct dimensions, 640×340.

4. Click the Play button in the Property inspector to play the movie; then click the button again to stop the movie, so you can continue working on it.

Note

Windows users: Because IE uses ActiveX Controls instead of plugins, and Dreamweaver uses plugins to preview media content, Dreamweaver might not be able to play your plugin content if you only have IE installed. To solve this problem, install Netscape or install the respondent plugin from the plugin website and copy the dll file to your **Macromedia/Dreamweaver MX/Configuration/Plugins** folder. Alternatively, you can press the F12 button to preview the page in IE using the ActiveX control.

5. Experiment with resizing the movie and playing it. Set the movie's dimensions to smaller than they should be; then play the movie. Set the dimensions to larger than they should be; then play the movie. You'll see how the movie is either cropped or surrounded by empty white space, but its contents are never resized.

6. Examine the code. You'll see that the `<object>` tag has been used to place the movie, with an `<embed>` tag included.

7. This isn't just an ordinary Shockwave movie. This movie is programmed to expect a parameter called sw1 that specifies the name of a person to be welcomed. All you have to do in Dreamweaver is set that parameter and you can personalize the movie.

   With the movie selected, click the Parameters button to access the Parameters dialog box. When the dialog box appears, click the plus (+) button to access the pop-up list of parameters, and choose sw1.

8. For the value of the parameter, enter your name. Click OK to apply the SWI parameter, and click OK agian to close the Parameters dialog box.

9. Try the movie out in a browser. Does the name you entered come up in the welcome banner? It should. (If it doesn't, double-check that you used the sw1 parameter in your code.) What's the benefit of this? Imagine how easy it can be to quickly customize Shockwave presentations on a web site, without having to generate new Shockwave movies. Movies can be multipurposed so that the same movie, downloaded once, can serve in several places on the web site.

QuickTime

Don't be fooled. Just because QuickTime is made by Apple doesn't mean it's only for Macs. QuickTime is a cross-platform, system-level extension and browser plugin that provides synchronized media and interactivity similar to that found in Shockwave and Flash. QuickTime movies are made of synchronized tracks—video tracks, sound tracks, music tracks, sprite tracks (for interactive and animated elements), 3D tracks (for 3D modeling), VR (virtual reality) tracks, text tracks, even Flash tracks, each of which can contain an entire Flash movie, interactivity and all. QuickTime 4+ movies automatically use client-side streaming (called *FastStart*). When used with special QuickTime server software, they also can use true server-side streaming. QuickTime movie files use the **.mov** filename extension.

All professional-level audio, video, and animation software is capable of creating QuickTime content. QuickTime authoring programs include Electrifier Pro (Mac only), LiveStage (Mac/PC) and Adobe GoLive (Mac/PC), which includes a pretty nifty little QuickTime authoring miniprogram inside the web editor. Limited authoring capabilities are also built in to Apple's QuickTime Pro utility. Flash also can export interactive presentations as QuickTime movies. Various free utilities for working with QuickTime are available at `http://developer.apple.com/quicktime/quicktimeintro/tools/`.

Note

To learn more about QuickTime, visit www.apple.com/quicktime. For more on the new QuickTime ActiveX control, visit www.apple.com/quicktime/download/qtcheck and www.apple.com/quicktime/products/tutorials/activex.html.

QuickTime Issues

The QuickTime plugin has long been considered a staple of web multimedia, ubiquitous and reliable on both Windows and Mac platforms, in both major browsers. According to a recent Apple announcement, 100 million copies of the QuickTime player and browser plugin have been distributed and installed worldwide. QuickTime has long been available as a plugin; recently, in response to Microsoft's decision not to support plugins for IE/Windows, Apple has released QuickTime as an ActiveX control as well.

Inserting a QuickTime Object

In Dreamweaver, you can insert QuickTime content using the Plugin or ActiveX object. For best compatibility with the newest versions of Internet Explorer, it's best to use ActiveX—though, at the time of this writing, the QuickTime plugin is more responsive than its (brand-new) ActiveX cousin. Whichever method you use, the Property inspector will be generic, with no QuickTime-specific options. As with Shockwave, width and height are always set to a default value of 32×32 pixels. If the dimensions are set smaller than the original movie size, the movie will be cropped; if the dimensions are set larger than the original size, empty space will be added around the edges of the movie.

Passing Parameters to QuickTime

QuickTime movies accept a wide variety of parameters. As with other media types, use the Parameters dialog box, accessible by clicking the Property inspector's Parameters button, to assign these attributes. Table 19.3 shows a list of some useful parameters that QuickTime movies can accept. (This list is not exhaustive.)

Table 19.3 Some Useful Parameters That Can Be Used with QuickTime Content

Parameter	Value	Description
autostart	true or false	Whether the movie will start playing as soon as it loads.
loop	true or false	Whether the movie will repeat indefinitely, or play only once.

controller	true, false, qtvr	Whether a controller bar will appear at the bottom of the movie, and what kind of controller bar it will be. Use the qtvr controller for QuickTime virtual reality movies. (If the controller is visible, set the height parameter to the movie's height plus 16 pixels. Otherwise, the controller will be cropped.)
scale	Aspect, ToFit, or a number	This determines whether the movie will appear at its original size, or enlarged or reduced. ToFit will scale the movie to match the width and height parameters; Aspect will do the same, but without distorting its aspect ratio. A scale value of larger than 1 will enlarge the movie; smaller than 1 will reduce the size.
bgcolor	Color	If the width and height values assigned are larger than the movie's dimensions, this color will fill up the rest of the allotted space.
volume	0-100	Determines the volume of any audio in the movie.
kioskmode	true or false	If true, doesn't allow the user to save a copy of the movie.
starttime	Time, using format 00:00:00:00	Determines at what point in the movie it should start playing.
endtime	(Same as above)	Determines at what point in the movie it should stop playing.
href	Absolute or relative URL	If this parameter is present, clicking anywhere on the movie will launch the specified URL.
qtnext*n*	Absolute or relative URL	Specifies a movie to play after the current movie is finished. The name of the parameter must end in an integer (represented by *n* in the column to the left). Like this: qtnext1, qtnext2, and so forth. Multiple qtnext parameters can be used to play a series of movies.
target	myself or the name of a window or frame	If you're loading a new QT movie with the href or qtnext*n*, use myself to load it into the same place as the original.

Exercise 19.2   Adding a QuickTime Movie to a Document, and Setting its Parameters

In this exercise, you'll insert a QuickTime movie into a page using `<object>`, and experiment to see how you can customize it with parameters. All files for this exercise can be found in the **chapter_19/quicktime** folder.

1. Open **quicktime_parameters.html**.

2. Insert a generic ActiveX object. In the Property inspector, set the basic `<object>` parameters as follows:

   `classid` (Class ID) = clsid:02BF25D5-8C17-4B23-BC80-D34888ABDDC6B

   `width` = 250

   `height` = 345

   `codebase` (Base) = `http://www.apple.com/qtactivex/qtplugin.cab`

   (The true height of the movie is 329 pixels, but you're adding 16 pixels for the controller bar that will appear at the bottom of the movie onscreen.)

Note

The first time you place a QuickTime movie in a document using the ActiveX object, you'll have to type in the `classid` yourself, as it doesn't appear in the ClassID pop-up menu. You only have to do it once, though. After that, Dreamweaver will remember what you typed, and you can simply choose it from the pop-up menu.

3. Still in the Property inspector, select the `<embed>` option, and set its `src` to **bird.mov**. (This is the first time you've specified which movie you intend to play.)

4. Click the Parameters button to access the Parameters dialog box. Experiment with the different parameters listed in Table 19.3 to see how they work. In particular, try setting the following:

   - `controller = false`   Preview the movie and you'll see that, without the controller bar, there's no way to start or stop the movie. (You'll also have an extra 16 pixels in the movie's height setting.)

   - `loop = true`

   - `autoplay = false`   You'll certainly need the controller back on for this one. Otherwise, there's no way to start the movie playing!

   - `scale = ToFit`   After you've set this parameter, change the movie's width and height so it's really short and squatty. You'll see how the movie resizes to fill the space, even if it means distorting the picture.

   - `scale = Aspect` and `bgcolor = #FF0000`   Leave the movie short and squatty, and preview again. The movie won't be distorted anymore, and you'll see the red background color filling in part of your page.

   - `href = http://www.newriders.com`   After this parameter has been set, clicking the movie in the browser should connect you to the New Riders home page.

   - `href = flowers.mov` and `target = myself`   As long as the **flowers.mov** file from the CD-ROM is in the same folder as **bird.mov**, clicking the movie should replace the first movie with the new movie. (Also see what happens if you remove the `target` attribute.)

- pluginspage = http://www.apple.com/quicktime/download. As discussed above, this is an important parameter for users relying on plugins and not ActiveX controls. Within the ActiveX Property inspector, it must be set using the Parameters dialog box.

Figure 19.6 shows the Parameters dialog box with some of these values in place. For each attribute set, preview in a browser to see the effect on the movie presentation.

Figure 19.6   The generic Parameters dialog box showing various optional QT parameters, as used in **quicktime_sampler.html**.

5. After you've set several parameters, examine your code. You'll see that Dreamweaver has added each of the parameters to both the <object> and the <embed> tag, using the syntax appropriate to each.

Dreamweaver has even added the pluginspage attribute to both tags, though it is only meaningful for the <embed> tag. If you like your code mean and lean, you can delete the <object> pluginspage parameter tag—but it isn't hurting anything by being there, and if you delete it, Dreamweaver won't recognize this parameter or show it in the Parameters dialog box.

RealMedia

RealNetworks has long been at the forefront of server-based streaming media delivery for the web. The various components of its RealSystem—RealAudio, RealVideo, RealPix, RealText, RealFlash—enable web authors to place a variety of streaming media content on web pages. Different RealMedia elements can even be combined into multimedia presentations using an offshoot of XML called *SMIL* (Synchronized Media Integration Language). Table 19.4 shows the various RealSystem MIME types and their associated filename extensions.

Table 19.4 Commonly Used MIME Types and Filename Extensions for RealSystem Media Files

Description	MIME Type	Filename Extensions
RealAudio	audio/x-realaudio	.ra
RealAudio	audio/vnd.rn-realaudio	.ra

continues ▶

Table 19.4 Continued

Description	MIME Type	Filename Extensions
RealVideo	video/vnd.rn-realvideo	.rv
RealPix	image/vnd.rn-realpix	.rp
RealText	text/vnd.rn-realtext	.rt
RealG2 with Flash	image/vnd.rn-realflash	.rf
SMIL document	application/smil	.smi, .smil
Ram	audio/x-pn-realaudio	.ram
Embedded Ram	audio/x-pn-realduio-plugin	.rpm

RealAudio and RealVideo files can be created in many professional video and audio programs. RealPix files (which present and coordinate series of still images) can be created using any text editor; the images themselves are standard JPEG, GIF, or PNG files that have been prepared for streaming delivery with JPEGTRAN, a free utility available from RealNetworks. RealText files (used for displaying and animating text) and SMIL files also can be created in any text editor. RealNetworks also has a variety of content-creation software available—RealProducer, RealPresenter, RealSlideShow. Some of these programs even come in free, basic versions; and many are available cross-platform.

Note

To learn more about RealMedia, visit the RealNetworks web site at
`www.realnetworks.com`.

Note

SMIL is not part of the RealSystem technology; it's just a markup language, derived from XML. SMIL files also can be read by the QuickTime player and browser plugin, and by Windows Media Player. To learn more about SMIL, visit the W3C web site at `www.w3.org/AudioVideo/`. For a full discussion of XML, see Chapter 32, "Technical Issues."

RealMedia Issues

The RealSystem technologies are compatible across platforms and browsers. Although it is fairly common for RealMedia clips to open in RealPlayer, it is also possible to embed them in web pages. A RealG2 plugin and a RealG2 ActiveX control are both available, for best results in both browsers. According to RealNetworks, more than 170 million users worldwide have RealPlayer and its associated browser utilities installed.

To take advantage of streaming delivery, the RealMedia content must reside on a web server with RealServer software. Browsers use the RealPlayer application and the RealG2 plugin and ActiveX control to handle these media types.

Because of how RealMedia files are set up to work on the server, they require a special metafile called a *RAM file* (filename extension **.ram** or **.rpm**) to work properly. For delivery from a standard web server, the RAM file must be a text file containing the absolute path name of the RealMedia content. For delivery from a RealServer, RAM files can be dynamically generated by the RAMGEN utility; links to RealMedia files housed on RealServers with RAMGEN must use a special addressing scheme that includes a ramgen parameter.

Note

Why use metafiles? This enables server-side streaming to work. The browser downloads the tiny metafile, which in turn activates the media files on the server and starts their delivery. Because of this, the media itself needn't be downloaded.

Inserting RealSystems Media Objects

In Dreamweaver, you can insert any RealMedia content using either the generic Plugin or ActiveX object, though the latter method is best for cross-browser compatibility. The steps for insertion are as follows:

1. Create the media to insert. (See Table 19.4 for acceptable RealMedia file formats.)

2. Unless the media will be streamed from a RealServer, create the RAM file. (See the next section for more on this.)

3. In Dreamweaver, use the Plugin or ActiveX object to embed the RAM file in your document. (If you use the ActiveX object, be sure to choose the RealMedia classid from the Property inspector.)

Passing Parameters to RealMedia

RealMedia presentations accept a variety of parameters, controlling how the media will behave and appear in a web page (see Table 19.5). In particular, the many possibilities for the controls attribute provide a great deal of choice over the control interface itself (see Table 19.6). Because different control setups are different sizes, use the recommended width and height values shown here for each setting.

Table 19.5   Parameters Accepted by RealPlayer, the RealG2 Plugin, and ActiveX Control

Parameter	Value	Default	Description
src	URL	[required parameter]	Specifies a source clip. (Note that, in Dreamweaver, this required parameter must be entered via the generic Parameters dialog box.)
width	Number	[required parameter]	Sets the window or control width, in percent or pixels.
height	Number	[required parameter]	Sets the window or control height, in percent or pixels.
maintain aspect	true or false		Preserves the image's aspect ratio if the width and height don't match the original size.
autostart	true or false	False	Determines whether the clip starts playing as soon as the page loads.
background-color	Color or RGB hex value		Sets the background color for the name or clip.
loop	true or false		Determines whether the clip loops indefinitely, or plays only once.
numloop	Number		Loops the clip a given number of times.
center	true or false		Centers the clip in the window.
console	Name, _master, or _unique		Links multiple controls.
controls	Control name (See the Table 19.6 for a list of possible values.)	All	Adds RealPlayer controls to the Web page.
nojava	true or false	False	Prevents the Java virtual machine from starting as the movie loads. (Java is only needed if JavaScript will be used to control the clip.)
region	SMIL region		Ties a clip to an existing SMIL region.
shuffle	true or false	False	Randomizes playback.
nolabels	true or false	False	Suppresses presentation information.
nologo	true or false	False	Suppresses the RealLogo.

Table 19.6   Possible Values for the *controls* Parameter, for RealSystem Media Clips

Value	Suggested size	Description
all, or default	375×100	Displays all controls
imagewindow	176×132 or more	Displays the image window, for video and animation
controlpanel	350×36	Play, pause, stop, fast forward and rewind, position slider, volume slider, mute button
playbutton	44×26	Play/pause button
playonlybutton	26×26	Play button
pausebutton	26×26	Pause button
stopbutton	26×26	Stop button
FFCtrl	26×26	Fast forward control
RWCtrl	26×26	Rewind control
MuteCtrl	26×26	Mute button
MuteVolume	26×88	Mute button and volume slider
VolumeSlider	26×65	Volume slider
PositionSlider	120×26	Clip position slider
TACCtrl	370×32	Clip info field
HomeCtrl	45×25	The Real logo
InfoVolumePanel	325×55	Presentation information, along with volume slider and mute button
InfoPanel	300×55	Presentation information panel
StatusBar	300×50	Status panel (shows informational messages), plus network congestion LED and position field
StatusField	200×30	Status panel only
PositionField	90×30	Clips current place in the presentation timeline, and total clip length

Exercise 19.3   Inserting a RealAudio Sound Using *<embed>*

When working with RealMedia, procedures vary slightly depending on whether you're accessing the media file locally (that is, from your computer, for development purposes), from a regular web server, or from a RealServer for streaming access.

For this exercise, you develop your web page assuming that the RealAudio clip will be housed locally. Then you adjust the code for upload and delivery on a standard web server. Finally, you'll see how to adjust for upload onto a RealServer. All files used here can be found on the CD, in the **chapter_19** folder. Copy that folder to your hard drive, if you haven't done so already. The files for this exercise are in the **chapter_19/realmedia** folder.

1. The audio file being used in the exercise is **handel.rm**. If you have RealPlayer on your system, you can launch the sound file directly in that program to test it out. (Double-clicking the file from the Finder or Explorer should launch RealPlayer.)

2. All RealMedia files need a RAM file for proper delivery in the browser. Because you're starting out by accessing the file locally, you need to create a RAM file that points to where the audio file is locally stored. You can create the RAM file in any text editor, or in Dreamweaver Code view.

3. In Dreamweaver or your text editor, create a new file to serve as the RAM file. (To create a completely empty file in Dreamweaver, go to File > New and, from the New Document dialog box, choose Script Files/Text File.) Save it in the **chapter_19/realmedia** folder as **handel.rpm** (note the filename extension).

Note

Use RAM files with the **.rpm** extension to play media in the browser window. Use the **.ram** extension to play media in the RealPlayer window.

4. In this file, enter the protocol **file://**, followed by the absolute or relative URL of the **handel.rm** audio file. The code in the RAM file should look like this:

```
file://handel.rm
```

When you're done, save the file and close it.

5. Now it's time to set up the HTML page that will contain the audio clip. From your exercise files, open **realaudio_sampler.html**.

6. Insert an ActiveX object into the document. For the `classid` parameter, choose the RealG2 ActiveX control from the pop-up menu. For `codebase`, enter `http://www.realnetworks.com`. Set the width and height to 350×100. (These values represent the dimensions of the default RealG2 sound control panel, which visitors can use to access your audio clip.)

Use the Parameters button and generic Parameters dialog box to add a `src` parameter to the `<object>` tag with a value of `handel.rpm` (the RAM file).

For cross-browser compatibility, make sure Include Embed is selected and the `src` parameter to choose the file to insert (**handel.rpm**).

Note

Why specify the src twice? The src field listed in the Property inspector adds a `src` parameter to the `<embed>` tag. But the `<object>` tag also needs a `src` specified. But as there is no place in the Property inspector to add this parameter, it must be added using the generic Parameters dialog box.

Note

RealPlayer should come up as an option in the ClassID pop-up menu. If it's not on that list, you'll have to type it in manually. The listing should look like this:

```
clsid:CFCDAA03-8BE4-11cf-B84B-0020AFBBCCFA
```

7. Try the page out in a browser! Assuming you've got RealPlayer and its plugins, your browser page should look like the one shown in Figure 19.7. Because you didn't set an `autostart` parameter, and this parameter defaults to false for this plugin, you'll have to click the Play button in the control panel to get the music to play.

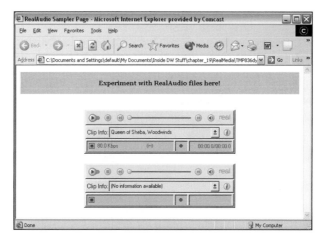

Figure 19.7   The **realaudio_sampler.html** file as it appears in the browser, with the default control panel showing at its recommended size.

8. After the page has been developed, and you're ready to share it with the world, it's time to prepare the file for upload to a web server.

9. To prepare for upload to a standard (nonstreaming) server, open the RAM file in your text editor or Dreamweaver Code view. Instead of the file protocol and relative URL, type in an absolute web address, such as the following:

```
http://www.webdomain.com/media/handel.rm
```

If you want to try this out, you can enter a real address here, and upload the HTML file, RAM file, and music file onto a web server and try to access it.

To prepare for upload to a RealServer, the process differs slightly. Again, if you don't actually have access to a RealServer account, you won't be able to test this out. But here's the procedure:

1. Forget the RAM file; it's no longer necessary.

2. Open the HTML file and select the plugin content placeholder, to access the Property inspector. For the `src` parameter, you need to enter an address something like this:

```
http://realserver.company.com:8080/ramgen/media/handel.rm?embed
```

You can discuss the details of exactly how this URL should appear with your RealServer administrator.

Note

If you're going to be working a lot with RealMedia, you might want to extend your copy of Dreamweaver by installing the RealG2 custom objects, available free from the Macromedia Exchange.

Windows Media

Windows Media is the Microsoft answer to QuickTime and RealMedia. It's a comprehensive platform for delivering audiovisual media, including streaming delivery and the capability to combine different media types in complex presentations. As a Microsoft product, Windows Media is closely integrated with both the Windows operating system and Internet Explorer, and only reaches its full potential in this all-Microsoft environment. Table 19.7 lists the major Windows Media filename extensions. Note that, in addition to its own proprietary formats, WMP/Windows also supports a number of generic audio and video file formats.

Table 19.7   File Formats for Use with Windows Media Player

Description	Filename Extensions	Platform
Windows Media (audio)	.wma	Windows, Mac
Windows Media (video)	.wmv	Windows, Mac
Windows Media metafile (for use with audio files)	.wax	Windows, Mac
Windows Media metafile (for use with video files)	.wvx	Windows, Mac
Windows Media metafile (old)	.asf	Windows, Mac
Windows audio	.wav	Windows
Windows video	.avi	Windows
MP3 audio	.mp3	Windows
MPEG video	.mpg	Windows
Windows still image	.bmp	Windows

Microsoft offers a number of free software utilities for creating and working with Windows Media, including the Windows Media Encoder and Windows Media Resource Kit. (All are available for Windows only.) PowerPoint 2002 presentations also can be exported to a format readable by the Windows Media Player.

Note

To learn more about Windows Media, visit `www.microsoft.com/windows/windowsmedia`.

Windows Media Issues

Windows Media Player is shipped as part of the Windows operating system, giving it a very wide user base. The player exists as an ActiveX control, with a powerful set of parameters and scripting controls available to it—but only for those browsing with IE/Windows. The player is available as a (much less powerful) plugin, for Netscape and Macintosh users. But its true glory is in its close relationship with Internet Explorer and the Windows operating system.

Like RealMedia, Windows Media can be streamed from special servers, or played without server-side streaming from standard web servers. Also like RealMedia, Windows Media utilizes metafiles containing pointers to media files. It's the metafile, and not the media file itself, that gets embedded into the web page. Windows Media metafiles are written in an XML-derived markup language, and have the **.wvx** (video) or **.wax** (audio) filename extension. The file must contain an absolute or relative path name to the media file. The syntax looks like this:

```
<ASX version="3.0">
  <entry>
    <ref href="http://www.mydomain.com/mediafiles/myAudio.wma"/>
  </entry>
</ASX>
```

Inserting Windows Media Objects

Because the Windows Media Player is an ActiveX control, you insert Windows Media content with the Dreamweaver ActiveX object. The steps are as follows:

1. Create the media content. (See Table 19.7 for a list of supported file formats.)

2. Create the metafile, using the preceding syntax.

3. With the Dreamweaver ActiveX object, embed the metafile in the document. Because the `classid` for Windows Media is not in the Dreamweaver pop-up list, in the Property inspector, you have to enter the following ClassID manually:

   `6BF52A52-394A-11d3-B153-00C04F79FAA6`

(You should only have to do this the first time you embed Windows Media content—after that, the information will be part of the pop-up list.)

Passing Parameters to Windows Media Objects

Table 19.8 lists the parameters accepted by the Windows Media ActiveX control. With these parameters, you can determine how your media object will look and behave on the web page. Most must be added using the Dreamweaver generic Parameters dialog box.

Table 19.8   Some Useful Parameters Accepted by Windows Media Player 7. (This List Is Not Exhaustive.)

Parameter Name	Value	Description
url	URL	For proper streaming, specify the path-name of the metafile, not the media itself. (Dreamweaver note: If you check the Include Embed option in the Property inspector, and specify a **src** for that tag, this parameter will be entered automatically for you. If not, you must enter it manually, using the generic parameters dialog box.)
width	Number of pixels	The horizontal space the media and its controller will be allotted on the page.
height	Number of pixels	The vertical space the media and its controller will be allotted on the page. (The controller itself is 40 pixels high; the information bar above that is 20 pixels high. Values are calculated from bottom to top, so assign a height of **40** to present only a controller bar.)
uimode	Full, mini, or none	How the controller bar appears. (To create invisible media, choose **none** and set the width and height to **0**.)
autoStart	true or false	Whether the media will begin playing automatically as soon as the page loads.
playCount	Number of loops	How many times the media will play (for example, looping).
currentPosition	Number of seconds	Where in the media's timeline it begins to play, measured in seconds from the beginning.
currentMarker	Marker number	Where in the media's timeline it begins to play, based on markers inserted into the media. (Use the Windows Media ASF Indexer utility to embed markers.)
volume	0 to 100	How loud audio content will play.
balance	-100 to 100	Whether audio content will play from the left speaker (-100), the right speaker (100) or some combination of both. A value of 0 plays from both speakers equally.
mute	true or false	Whether audio content will play or be muted.

Exercise 19.4   Inserting Windows Media Objects

In this exercise, you'll insert two Windows Media files into an HTML page—one containing audio and video, and one containing only audio. All exercise files are in the **chapter_19/windowsmedia** folder.

1. As you did with RealMedia, you start by locating the media and creating metafiles that point to it. The audio file is called **jazz.wma**. The video file is **aspirations.wmv**.

2. You can create the metafiles in a text editor, or in Dreamweaver Code view. (If you want to work in Dreamweaver, see the previous Note, in the RealMedia section, on changing the program preferences to recognize new filename extensions. The extensions you'll need to add are **.wax** and **.wvx**.) For the audio file, create a text file and save it as **jazz.wax**. Enter the following code:

```
<ASX version="3.0">
  <entry>
    <ref href="jazz.wma"/>
  </entry>
</ASX>
```

For the video file, create another text file and save it as **aspirations.wvx**. Enter the following code:

```
<ASX version="3.0">
  <entry>
    <ref href="aspirations.wmv"/>
  </entry>
</ASX>
```

Note that for the preceding code to work properly, the metafiles and the media files must be stored in the same folder. If you have them stored differently, you'll have to adjust the relative URL accordingly. (Note also that unlike RealMedia RAM files, there's no `file://` protocol at the beginning of the path name.)

3. Now you can insert the metafiles into your document. From your exercise files, open **windowsmedia_sampler.html**.

4. Using the ActiveX object, insert a new media element onto the page. In the Property inspector, set the width and height to 320×240. Set the `classid` as follows:

```
6BF52A52-394A-11d3-B153-00C04F79FAA6
```

Make sure the Include Embed option is selected, and set the `src` to **jazz.wax**. When this is done, you can try out your file in the browser. The audio track should play and the Windows Media controller should appear (see Figure 19.8).

Figure 19.8   The **windowsmedia_sampler.html** exercise file with audio file in place, as it appears in the browser.

5. Now you add the video. Back in Dreamweaver, with the same exercise file open, add a paragraph break after the first media object and insert another ActiveX object. Set the width and height to 320×240. Turn on Include Embed and set the src to **aspirations.wvx**.

   Later in this chapter, you will learn about passing parameters to Windows Media and revisit this cacophonous document.

6. If you try your file out in the browser now, you're in for an overwhelming experience as both files start to play at once. Using the Property inspector's Parameters button and generic Parameters dialog box, assign each media element an autoStart parameter set to **false**.

7. Now you adjust how the controls look. This is done with the uimode parameter and the width and height.

   - **For the video file.** The video doesn't quite fit in the 320×240 box you created for it. Set the height to 300 pixels—that adds 40 pixels for the controller, and 20 pixels for the information bar. Now when you play the file in a browser, the movie should fit nicely into its box.

   - **For the audio file.** You want your sound to show on the page only as a simple controller, taking up a minimum of space. To start, add a uimode parameter set to mini. This simplifies the control but doesn't remove the swirling picture above it. To get rid of this, change the height to **40**—because the height is calculated from the bottom of the box, this value will truncate the display at the top edge of the controller. Figure 19.9 shows this.

Figure 19.9   The **windowsmedia_sampler.html** file, as it appears in the browser when all
parameters have been set.

8. Now make the sound loop. To set looping, decide how many times you want the
   sound to play and set the `playCount` parameter to that number. (You'll have
   noticed that there is no `looping` parameter.) You might have to change the
   `autoStart=false` parameter to **autostart=true**, before the looping will work.

9. Experiment with the other parameters as you like, to see what each can do. As
   you're experimenting, don't forget to browse in Netscape as well as Internet
   Explorer (to see how your media fares). If you have access to different computers
   and platforms, try the files on those systems as well.

Adding Sound to Web Pages

Adding sound to a web page can be one of the most challenging, and confusing, of
media-related tasks. It's not that hard to get browsers to make sounds—just about any
computer with a sound card in it will have some sort of sound-capable plugin for the
browser. What's hard is deciding how best to get predictable, desirable results out of your
sounds.

Targeted Versus Untargeted Media Placement

You can choose from a number of sound file formats when adding sound to a web page, each with its own strengths and weaknesses. A number of plugin/ActiveX technologies are also available to handle sounds. Some formats, such as RM files for RealAudio, are proprietary—only one plugin can handle them. Others, such as AIF and WAV, are supported by a variety of plugins. The first choice you'll have to make when determining how to add sound to a page is whether to target a specific plugin and risk losing audience members by using a proprietary format or to avoid targeting but give up predictability by using a more generic format.

Table 19.9 shows the main sound file formats currently in use on the web, along with their supporting plugins. Each different plugin presents the user with a different control panel for handling sounds; each accepts different parameters.

Table 19.9   Specifications of the Major Sound File Formats Available for Web Use

Filename Extension	Description
.wav	The native format for Windows audio files. Understood widely, offers fairly good compression-to-sound quality.
.aif	The native format for Macintosh audio files. Understood widely, offers fairly good compression-to-sound quality.
.mp3	The latest and greatest file format, not supported by many older plugins but quickly becoming a standard. Offers very good compression-to-sound quality.
.au	The native format for Unix audio files. Understood widely (and the only format available for use in Java), but offering poor compression-to-sound quality.
.mid, .midi	File format for synthesized (i.e., computer-generated, instead of digitally recorded) sounds. Understood widely, and offers extremely small file sizes. Files contain instructions for playing sounds, which are then implemented by software-based musical instruments within the computer itself.

Working with Untargeted Media

For maximum audience coverage, most web authors don't target specific plugins when adding sound to a page. What are the ramifications of this?

ActiveX or Plugin?

When you place media with the ActiveX object, you must specify a `classid` (and thus a target ActiveX control). If you want your sound to be untargeted—to play in whatever plugin or helper application is available on each user's browser—you need to use the

Plugin object. (Remember, the Plugin object inserts content using the `<embed>` tag, and IE/Windows still recognizes this tag, as long as the user has an ActiveX control of some kind to play the sound.)

Dealing with Controllers

The *controller* is the visual representation of an embedded sound clip in a web page. It lets the visitor know that a music clip or other sound is present, and lets him control its playing. When you design a page with embedded sound, therefore, you need to leave room for this element in the page layout. But how can you do this wisely, when you don't know which plugin will be handling the sound, and so don't know what size the controller will be? Any page that includes an untargeted sound must be able to accommodate any of them. Follow these two rules:

- **Think big.** As a general rule, it's better to allow too much space rather than not enough. Small controls, such as the QuickTime controller, can easily float in a large space; but large controls, such as the WinAmp control panel, don't fare too well when squeezed into a small space. Good default width and height settings are 144×60. These are the dimensions for the Netscape LiveAudio plugin and are large enough to accommodate other controls fairly comfortably.

- **Use background color.** Most plugins will accept some sort of parameter specifying a background color. This is the color that will appear surrounding the controller (if it's placed in a too large space). Use this parameter to ensure that any extra space matches the background color of the surrounding page or page elements, so it doesn't look so obviously like a small fish in a large pond.

Overloading the Parameters

Different plugins accept different parameters. You therefore need to be smart about assigning your parameters. You need to know which parameters are more widely supported than others. You also can double up on, or "overload," the parameters—setting multiple parameters to handle the same sound attribute, to make sure you're covering all of your bases. Table 19.10 lists various useful sound-related parameters, along with strategies for their use in multiple plugin situations.

Table 19.10   Some Standard Parameters for Controlling Audio Files

Parameter Name	Value	Description
src	URL	Name of the sound file to play.
width	Number of pixels	The horizontal space the media controller will be allotted on the page. (Controllers will be resized, if possible, to fit the specified width.)
height	Number of pixels	The vertical space the media controller will be allotted on the page. (Controllers will be resized, if possible, to fit the specified width.)
bgcolor	Color	If the width and height values assigned are larger than the controller's dimensions, this color that will fill up the rest of the allotted space.
hidden	true or false	Whether the controller should be visible on the page. (Warning: Some browsers won't play a hidden sound.)
autostart, autoplay	true or false	Whether the audio will begin playing automatically as soon as the page loads. Some plugins require autostart, some require autoplay. Use both to be safe.
loop	true or false	Whether the audio will play once, or loop indefinitely. (Some, but not all, plugins will accept a numeric value here.)
volume	0 to 100	How loud the audio will play. Not all plug-ins recognize this value.

Exercise 19.5   Creating a Sound Sampler Page

In this exercise, you add several sound files, in various formats, to a web page, to get some practice working with nontargeted sounds. To get maximum benefit from the exercise, after you have finished creating the sampler file, try viewing it from as many different computers, and browsers, as you can. All files for the exercise can be found in the **chapter_19/audio** folder.

1. To begin the exercise, open **sound_sampler.html**. This file contains a page layout ready to hold different sounds and their controllers.

2. With the file open, use the Dreamweaver generic Plugin object to insert a sound clip into each of the slots in the layout. (Figure 19.10 shows the page layout with audio objects in place—the controllers shown are QuickTime, RealMedia, and Windows Media Player.) Use the sound files in the folder provided with the exercise files. Try one each of the various different file formats, to see how browsers handle the file types. Use the small slots in the layout to notate which file types are being placed so that you can better analyze the results later.

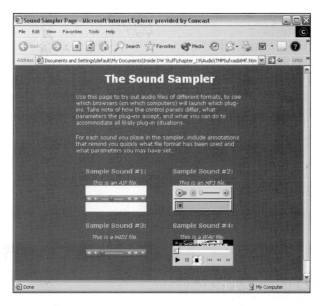

Figure 19.10   The **sound_sampler.html** page layout, with audio objects and descriptive text in place.

3. For each sound clip placed, set whatever parameters you like. (Use Table 19.10 as a guide.) In Figure 19.10, note that one of the two samples showing the QuickTime controller has been assigned a bgcolor matching the page background; doesn't that look nicer than that ugly white box in the other sample?

4. After you have constructed your sampler file, try it out in the browser. Better yet, try it out in multiple browsers. If you have access to different computers, and different operating systems, try it out there as well. Pay attention to all the different results you get. Try to tweak the parameters to get the best results you can, in all the different plugin/browser/platform situations. When you're done, you can save the file as a reference for future sound use.

Scripting Plugin Media

Sometimes it's not enough to put media on your pages. Sometimes you want your media to be controllable. You want it to interact with other page elements; you want to replace the standard controller bars and other visual elements with your own tasteful buttons and bows. In other words, you want to script it. Can you script media elements? Yes—and no. Most plugins accept a variety of commands. Dreamweaver even has a few built-in behaviors to help you implement those commands. However, they might not always work the way you want them to.

How Media Scripting Works—And Why It Doesn't Always Work

To understand how scripting of media elements works—and doesn't work—in browsers, you need to revisit the browser wars. As you learned in Chapter 16, "Getting Interactive with Behaviors," JavaScript is the main language used for client-side scripting in the browser. But JavaScript, like the `<embed>` tag, was originally created by Netscape for use with that browser. In Netscape, it's possible to use JavaScript to pass commands to any plugin media element that has been inserted using the `<embed>` tag.

Microsoft not only has its own browser and its own plugin technology (ActiveX), it also has its own scripting languages, VBScript and JScript. Media placed on a page using the `<object>` tag, and controlled by an ActiveX control, can receive commands using these languages—but not JavaScript.

To further complicate matters, Internet Explorer does not allow any scripting control of standard plugin content placed using `<embed>`. What does this mean?

- **Internet Explorer.** It's impossible to send any scripting commands to media such as QuickTime that has no ActiveX control.

- **Internet Explorer/Mac.** It's impossible to send scripting commands to any plugin media, because ActiveX and its related technologies don't function outside the Windows operating system.

- **Netscape.** It's impossible to take advantage of the powerful scripting possibilities offered by many ActiveX controls.

The good news is you're not going crazy when you notice that your media scripting works only in some of the browsers, some of the time. The bad news is there's not much to be done about it. If your web pages are aimed at a target audience using one browser or one platform, your media-controlling horizons are broader than if you're trying to target the general populace in all its diversity.

Controlling Specific Plugins

Each plugin or ActiveX control offers its own set of scripting commands it can accept (to control its media). Sometimes, as with JavaScripting for QuickTime or JScript controls for Windows Media, these commands are extensive and powerful. For more information on this, check the web sites listed earlier for each technology.

Controlling Audio: The Play Sound Behavior

The Dreamweaver Play Sound behavior is an excellent example of the perils and pitfalls of scripted media control. It seems simple—create a button or text link, apply the behavior, choose a sound file to play, and whenever the user clicks the button the sound should play. The only problem is, because of the problems outlined earlier, it works in some browsers and in others it doesn't.

Strategies for Controlling Media

If you can't rely on scripting to control media elements, what else can you do? Here are a few suggestions.

Put the Scripting in the Media Itself

If you really want reliable, controllable media, the simplest answer is to avoid browser scripting entirely. Flash, Shockwave, QuickTime movies, RealPlayer SMIL files—all of these offer internal scripting. If you want buttons that make "click" sounds when you click them, make them in Flash. (See the next chapter for more on this!) If you want music with a cool-looking control panel, put the sound and the controls into a Flash, Shockwave, QuickTime, or RealPlayer movie and insert the whole thing into your web page. If you want controllable video files, build the controls into a QuickTime file or put the QuickTime video into Shockwave.

The **chapter_19/scripted_media** folder contains several sample files that use their own internal scripting to create interactivity: **flash_sound.swf**, a Flash-based sound control panel; **qt_sound.mov**, a QuickTime sound control panel; and **click_button.swf**, a Flash button complete with sound effects. Check these files out and see how they work in a web page. (Inserting Flash media is covered in full in the next chapter.)

Be Sneaky with Frames

Start thinking outside the box—or inside the frame, anyway. If you're willing to use frames in your web site, you can do some lovely things to integrate media files into pages without running into any scripting nightmares. It works like this: Suppose you want to put a variety of music samples on a web page, controllable from a custom interface you've created (say, in Fireworks). You know you can't reliably use JavaScript to control sounds on a page. But you also know that an autoplaying, looping sound will play only as long as the file containing it is loaded in the browser window. What if you control the sound by loading and unloading different pages? Look in the **chapter_19/media_frames** folder for **sound_frameset.html**, and check it out. You'll see that, by embedding each sound in a separate HTML document, and using targeted links in the frameset to call different documents, the sounds can be started and stopped interactively, with no scripting at all. (And see Chapter 12, "Designing Frame-Based Pages," for a full discussion of working with frames in Dreamweaver.)

Plugin Detection

So, you've decided to use content that requires one or more plugins or ActiveX controls on your web site. What do you want to do about those potential site visitors who won't have the proper browser setup?

Strategic Decisions

Do you want to provide alternative content? Creating non-media-intensive versions of everything you do is time-consuming and makes site maintenance twice as much work. But do you want to leave a portion of your potential audience high and dry, without anything to look at?

If you do provide alternative content, how do you want to direct visitors to it? Your basic choice is between being visible and being invisible about redirecting users.

Visible redirection means starting your site with a page that asks users, "Do you have the such-and-such plugin?" Clicking a "yes" answer will send the user to the media-intensive pages. Clicking "no" will send him to the alternative pages. In case users aren't sure whether they have the plugin, it's a good idea to put some sample plugin content on the page for them to see. "If you can see the above animation/video/hear the music, you have the plugin." You also can provide a link to where users can download the required plugin, if you like. Visible redirection annoys some users, who say they don't like the extra step between them and the web site; but it is pretty foolproof, and easy to set up.

Invisible redirection means detecting plugins behind the scenes and automatically sending the user to one set of pages or another without him realizing it's even happening. This is an attractive option because it streamlines your web site from the visitor's point of view; but it can be tricky to set up, and a lot of things can go wrong with it.

Scripted Detection with the Check Plugin Behavior

The standard method for invisible plugin detection is to use a JavaScript that executes when the page loads. That's what the Dreamweaver Check Plugin behavior does.

Using the Check Plugin Behavior

There are two ways to use this behavior:

- The behavior can be put in the page that contains the media content. If the plugin is found, the browser stays on the page; if not, the browser is sent to an alternative page.

- The behavior can be put on an empty, dummy page. In this case, if the plugin is found, the browser is sent to the page containing the media; if not, the browser is sent to the alternative page.

The second scenario is more efficient for downloading because it doesn't make visitors without the plugin wait for a complex page full of media to start loading before they're sent to another page. The first scenario is easier to set up and maintain because there's one less HTML file to keep track of.

To use the Check Plugin behavior, follow these steps:

1. Start by creating all the files you'll need. You'll need at least the file containing the media and a page of alternative content. You also might want to create a blank, dummy page that will eventually contain only the behavior and nothing else.

2. Open the file you want to insert the behavior into. This might be the media page or it might be the dummy page.

3. In the tag selector, click the <body> tag. The behavior needs to be called from this tag.

4. In the Behaviors Inspector, choose Check Plugin from the Actions list. The dialog box that comes up will look like the one shown in Figure 19.11.

Figure 19.11   The Check Plugin behavior dialog box, with sample entries in place.

5. From the pop-up menu in the dialog box, choose the appropriate plugin for which you want to test. The most commonly used plugins are available; if a plugin isn't listed, you must type its name in yourself.

6. In the other fields of the dialog box, enter the names of the files you created earlier. If you're adding the behavior to the page containing the media, leave out the optional "if found" destination file. If you're adding the behavior to a dummy page, enter the media page as the "if found" destination. Enter the name of the alternative content page as the "if not found" destination.

7. Important! Make sure the option to Go to First Page if Detection Is Impossible is selected. Internet Explorer/Mac does not allow JavaScript plugin detection. If this option is *not* selected, users with that browser will always be sent to the alternative content, even if they have the plugin (obviously a very distressing experience).

Limitations of Scripted Detection

If it involves scripting, there's something that can go wrong with it. As noted earlier, some browsers don't allow scripted detection. Also if you're using the Check Plugin behavior for your scripting, it's important to keep in mind that this script checks only for the presence of a plugin, not the version. What if your QuickTime content requires QuickTime 5, but the user only has QuickTime 3? The Check Plugin behavior will direct your users to the QuickTime version of your web page, but they won't be able to access the content. Those users are high and dry.

Extending the Browser with Java

If you're tired of playing the plugin game, there's another, totally different way to extend the browser's capabilities: Java.

What Is Java?

Java is a platform-independent, object-oriented programming language created by Sun Microsystems. (Despite the similarity in names, Java is not related to JavaScript.) Java can create fully functional, freestanding applications. It also can create mini-applications, called *applets* that run inside a web browser. Because Java is a complete programming language, similar to C or C++, Java applets can be as powerful and diverse as you like. Java applets are commonly used for everything from online games to animation and special effects to visitor counters, clocks, calculators, and navigation tools.

How Java Works

To understand what makes Java so well suited to web use, you need to know how it differs from other programming languages.

Computers don't directly "understand" C++ or Java or any other so-called high-level programming language. Instead, computers understand a numeric language called *machine code*. After a program is written in a high-level language, it must be compiled, or translated, into machine language. Machine language is platform-specific; this is why your copy of Dreamweaver will run only on a PC or only on a Mac. Programs must be compiled for a certain type of computer, and then they will run only on that type of computer.

Java is different. Java is compiled to run on a pretend computer called a *virtual machine*. The virtual machine is actually itself a program, which is compiled to run on a specific platform. On Windows computers, the virtual machine is Microsoft VM; on Macs, it's Mac OS Run-Time for Java (MRJ). When a Java application or applet is run on a virtual machine, the virtual machine translates the code into platform-specific machine code. Thus the Java applet itself is platform-independent.

Note

To learn more about Java, visit Sun's web site at http://java.sun.com. To learn more about implementations of the Java virtual machine, visit Microsoft at www.microsoft.com/java and Apple at www.apple.com/java.

Java Issues

The good news is, Java applets are not only platform-independent, they're browser-independent as well. As soon as a browser encounters an applet on a web page, it launches the virtual machine and steps out of the way. You don't have any plugins to worry about. The only things needed to run a Java applet are a virtual machine (which most computers already have installed) and a Java-enabled browser (which almost all browsers are).

The bad news is, nothing is perfect. Some virtual machines are slower and buggier than others; it takes time to launch the virtual machine, which can seem like excessive download time to a frustrated user; and, because the virtual machine is running through the browser, complex applets that require lots of processing power can (and do!) crash browsers.

Java also can create security problems. Some so-called hostile applets are actually designed to behave like viruses; others can cause damage to a system accidentally. It's the job of the virtual machine to protect the computer system from these dangers, but virtual machines themselves can never be completely hackproof. Consequently, many institutions that deal in sensitive information will set their firewalls not to accept any Java, and individuals might choose to disable Java in their browser preferences.

Java and Media

Java applets can contain images and sounds, which will then display in the browser without the need for additional plugins or system components. All images must be GIF or JPEG. All sounds must be AU files. Java cannot handle video; however, it can create animations or "fake video" from a series of still images. Java animations are not as smooth and do not run as quickly as those created in Flash, Shockwave, or QuickTime.

Working with Applets

Working with applets is not like working with Shockwave or QuickTime movies, or any other kind of web media, because applets are not structured like those elements. Your first encounter with an applet will probably involve the words "what are all these bits and pieces, and where's the applet?"

Class Files

A basic compiled Java applet is a file with the filename extension **.class**—not **.java**, which is used for uncompiled source code.

However, an applet often consists of more than just one file. A complex applet might have several class files, of which only one is the applet itself. The others are supporting players that the applet will call on as it works. With some applets, naming conventions make it clear which is the main file—if the program is called Tabulator and there's a class file called **tabulator.class**, for instance. With other applets, however, it can be a challenge knowing which class file to actually embed in the web page. (The best applets usually have documentation that spells this out for you.)

Media Files

If an applet uses any media files—images, sounds, movies, and so on—these also will be in separate files, sometimes in separate folders. You must keep the internal folder structure of the applet the way the applet author intended, or the applet won't be able to find its media files.

Archive Files

You might come across a Java applet that has been packaged up into one or more archive files. These files will have filename extension of **.jar**, **.zip**, and **.cab**. With an applet like this, you'll have to refer to the archive file(s) and the main class file in your HTML code. Refer to the applet's documentation to find the name of the class file (because it's inside the archive, and you can't get in there).

Obtaining Java Applets

Most Java applets are written by Java programmers. There isn't one standard authoring environment for creating them. This is why every applet is so different from every other applet.

If you want to use Java on your web site, you can program it yourself, hire someone else to program it, or use one of the many prewritten applets available on the web and elsewhere. Sun's own applet resource page (`http://java.sun.com/applets`), which has links to other major resource sites as well as a selection of applets to download, is a good place to start looking. Some applets are free, some are shareware, and some are commercial. Some are also better documented than others and allow more customization. Some work better than others do.

Working with Applets in Dreamweaver

Dreamweaver provides several features for working with Java applets, including the Applet object and the Applet Property inspector. You can use these tools to insert an applet into an existing page, or to examine and alter the sample HTML code that usually comes with commercially available Java applets.

Inserting an Applet

In Dreamweaver, use the Applet object, found in the Special Objects panel, to place Java applets on a page. The actual process is simple. Click the Applet object. In the dialog box that follows, browse to the appropriate `class` file and click OK. There! You have an applet. If you look at your code, you'll see that the applet has been inserted using the `<applet>` tag.

Figure 19.12 shows the Applet object as well as the Property inspector for a Java applet. Because every applet is different, this is another generic inspector, with a Parameters button for adding applet-specific parameters. Aside from the standard parameters (`width`, `height`, `vspace`, `hspace`, `align`, `alt`, and `name`), the only two settings available are Code and Base. Code adds a `class` parameter, and should be set to the name of the class file. Base adds the `base` parameter, and should be set to the name of the folder, if any, that contains the Java applet files. (It's customary to store an applet in its own folder so that all the files that comprise it can easily be kept together.) As with plugin media, additional parameters used by specific applets are added with the generic Parameters button.

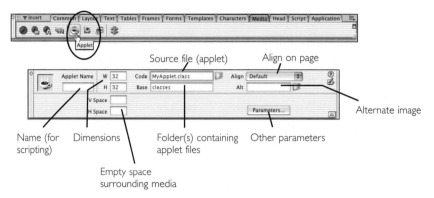

Figure 19.12   The Applet object and the Property inspector for a Java applet.

Exercise 19.6   Inserting a Java Applet

In this exercise, you insert an applet that puts a continually changing series of quotes on the web page. (This applet is one of several freebies offered at the Sun Java site, `http://java.sun.com/openstudio/guide.html`. To see it in action on a web page, look on the CD-ROM in **chapter_19/java** for **quote_finished.html**. Figure 19.13 shows a static screenshot from this file.)

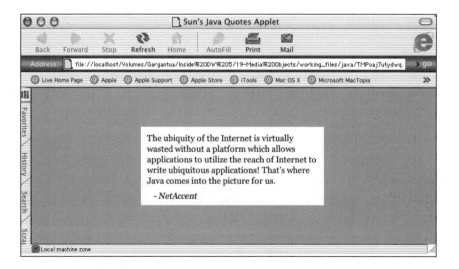

Figure 19.13   Sun's Java Quotes applet as it appears in a web page.

According to the documentation, the applet takes several parameters. Table 19.11 lists them. Some of these parameters might be optional, others might be required; the documentation doesn't specify. You'll use them all.

Table 19.11   Parameters for the Sun Quotes Java Applet Along with
Descriptions and Suggested Values

Name	Value
bgcolor	The background color of the applet in RGB hexadecimal.
bheight	The border height, in pixels.
bwidth	The border width, in pixels.
delay	The delay between frames, in milliseconds.
fontname	The name of the font to be used for the applet.
fontsize	The size of the font, in points.
link	A URL to load if the applet is clicked.
random	True or false, determining whether the quotes should appear randomly or in a set order.
number	The number of quotes.
quoteN (N is an integer)	This parameter must appear once for each quote to be included, based on the number of quotes specified above. The first quote will be quote0, the second quote will be quote1, and so on.
	For each occurrence of the parameter, the value must be a vb] delimited string where the first item is the quote, the second item is the author, the third item is the RGB hexadecimal text color, the fourth item is the RGB hexadecimal background color and the last item is the length of time in seconds to dis play the quote.
space	The distance in pixels between the quote and the author name.

1. To start out, find and examine the **Quote** folder, which contains this applet. You'll see several class files. Can you tell by their names which one is the applet?

2. In **chapter_19/java**, open **java_quotes.html**.

   Using the Insert Applet object, insert the applet. The main `class` file you should insert (you might have figured this out already) is **JavaQuote.class**. The `codebase` option should say `quote/classes/`.

Note

Java is case-sensitive! Make sure all references to files, folders, parameters, and values are in their correct case, or your Java applets won't work.

3. Next, set the `width` and `height` for the applet to occupy in your layout. For this applet, there is no required size—the dimensions just determine how much space the quotes will be allotted on the page. If you want your page to match the examples shown here, set your width and height to 300×125.

4. Referring to the Parameters list in Table 19.11, and using the generic Parameters dialog box, set the parameters for the applet. Experiment until you get results you like.

   (You might find it difficult to see what you're doing when you try to enter the quote parameter, because most quotes are fairly long and the dialog box won't show them in their entirety. If you like, you can type each quote first in a text editor, such as Notepad or Simple Text, and then paste it into the parameter's value field. You also can work directly in Dreamweaver Code view, of course, if you feel comfortable there.)

   When you're done, your Parameters dialog box will look something like the one shown in Figure 19.14.

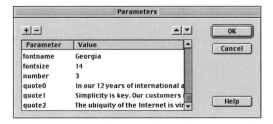

Figure 19.14   The Parameters dialog box, showing entered parameters and values for the Sun Quote Java applet. (Only the last few parameters are visible.)

5. Try it out in a browser! If everything got entered correctly, your virtual machine should load and show you an ever-changing set of quotes.

Working with Java Archives

With more complex applets, including those that have been packaged in JAR, CAB, and/or ZIP archives, it's often easier and better not to use the Insert Applet object. Instead, because almost all applets come with sample HTML code showing how they should be inserted on a page, just copy and paste that code into your file, or use the sample page as the basis to create your own file. If you do this, you need to make sure your HTML file is in the same place relative to the applet as the sample source—if the sample file sits in the same folder as the applet, for instance, place your HTML file in the same folder as the applet.

After you've done your copying and pasting, of course, if you view the page in the Dreamweaver visual editor, you'll be able to select the applet and check the Property inspector, just as if you had inserted the applet yourself.

Summary

In this chapter, you got a taste of the major technologies available for adding media content to the web. Are these the only technologies? No! The web is worldwide and full of variety. This chapter didn't discuss Beatnik, an alternative plugin for handling sound. You didn't learn about QuickTime's virtual-reality capabilities through QTVR, or the AVI or MPEG file video formats. As you read this, more media technologies are no doubt being thought up and implemented. If you want a different media experience for your web visitors, it's up to you to do the research; then use Dreamweaver tools, as you've been doing, to put it all together.

Chapter 20

Building Web Pages with Flash

In today's world of plugin media, Flash rules. You can integrate Flash into HTML pages in so many ways, and Dreamweaver offers so many tools for helping you do it, that this next chapter focuses solely on working with this one kind of plugin media content. The discussion covers the specifics of working with the Flash plugin, and special Dreamweaver features for coordinating Flash and HTML content.

What Is Flash?

Flash content is plugin-based media, following all the rules and restrictions of QuickTime, Shockwave, and the other media covered in the preceding chapter. The file format for online Flash movies is SWF (pronounced "swiff"). Most Flash media is created in the Macromedia Flash authoring program—though, since Macromedia opened up the format to other developers, more and more content is being developed in other programs as well. Viewing SWF movies requires the Flash Player, which is available as a plugin and an ActiveX control. Macromedia estimates that 96 percent of the web-browsing public has some version of the Flash Player installed. Internet Explorer 6 for Windows comes with the ActiveX control preinstalled.

Advantages of Using Flash in Web Sites

Why is Flash so popular? Apart from being the right format in the right place at the right time (and well-promoted, as well), Flash content offers a variety of benefits perfectly suited to web developers interested in multimedia content.

Vector-Based Graphics

Probably the number one reason for the immense popularity of SWFs on the Internet is their small file sizes. *Vector graphics* create substantially smaller files than pixel-based graphics, such as GIFs and JPEGs, and the SWF format is currently the only way to put vector images on web pages and guarantee that most people will be able to see them. This opens the doors to full-screen, high-quality images and lengthy animations that won't choke low-bandwidth connections.

Pixels Versus Vectors

There are two main ways that computers create, manipulate, and store graphics: as pixels, and as vectors.

A *pixel* is a little square of color. Pixel-based graphics are built from a grid of pixels, like a tile floor where each tile is a different color. Pixels can be any size, but each pixel must be a solid color, and the pixels must exist in a grid. The computer stores the image information as a grid map, indicating how many pixels are in each row and column, and what color each one is. The more pixels there are, the larger the file will be.

A *vector* is a mathematical formula that describes a shape (a line, a curve, a closed geo-metrical shape, for example). Vector-based graphics are built from shapes, each of which is essentially an open or closed vector curve that functions as an independent object in the picture. Each vector shape must be a solid color, but it can be any shape and any size; an image can contain any number of vectors. The computer stores the image infor-mation as a series of mathematical statements, each representing a vector. The more shapes there are, and the more complex they are, the larger the file will be.

One of the many differences between pixel-based and vector-based graphics is that vec-tors take up much less storage space than pixels, so vector files are much, much smaller than their pixelated counterparts. Vector images can also be resized on the fly without losing image quality or increasing file size; pixel images cannot.

Unfortunately, in our present state of computer technology, computers cannot display vector graphics; they can only display pixels. Any vector-based image must be translated into its pixel equivalent before it can appear onscreen—some sort of graphics software is required to do this. Because computer displays are associated with pixels, the Internet and web browsers were developed with the ability to view pixel-based images, such as GIF and JPEG files. But because vector images are so much more efficient for download-ing, they are more suited to web display.

Unlike pixel graphics, vector graphics also are scalable, enabling designers to resize items on-the-fly in the HTML editor, create images that scale to match browser window size (without losing quality), and even enable web visitors to zoom in on images without los-ing detail, as in zoomable online street maps. The Flash Player takes advantage of this scalability, enabling users to zoom in on any Flash page content through a contextual menu. Figure 20.1 shows this happening.

Note

Finding and exploiting a widely supported vector graphics format has been something of a holy grail for web multimedia developers. At the moment, Flash is the clear leader in this race. Another developing format, the SVG (Scalable Vector Graphics) markup lan-guage, is poised to give Flash some competition in this area. See Chapter 32, "Technical Issues," for more on SVG.

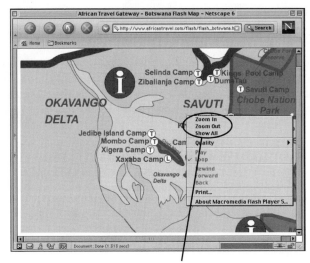

Zoom in on your Flash content

Figure 20.1   Using the Flash Player's contextual menu to zoom in on an online map created in Flash.

Client-Side Streaming

In addition to their naturally small file sizes, Flash movies partake of client-side streaming delivery. (See Chapter 19, "Plugins, ActiveX, and Java," for more on streaming.) This makes it possible, without any special server software, to create lengthy Flash animations that play as they download.

Animation

From its humble beginnings as FutureSplash Animator, Flash has developed into a powerhouse animation tool, used for everything from spinning corporate logos to full-length animated cartoons. The SWF format supports processor-efficient tweened animation, morphing, and other sophisticated effects. Several 3D animation programs (Swift3D, Amorphium Pro, and Strata3D) now offer the ability to export 3D Flash animations.

Interactivity

Each new version of Flash, and the Flash Player, supports more and more complex scripting and data-processing power through ActionScript, Flash's internal scripting language. ActionScript now looks and works much like JavaScript. Flash movies can send form data, using GET or POST, and can therefore be used in dynamic web sites with CGI and other server-side scripting.

Sound

Flash movies can contain sounds, optimized using MP3 compression for high-quality playback with minimal file size (see Chapter 19 for a discussion of sound formats and putting sound on web pages).

Disadvantages of Using Flash

Probably the single biggest complaint about Flash from web pundits is that it's used badly in web sites. But that's more a problem with Flash designers than with Flash itself. There's no inherent reason why Flash-based web sites cannot be as well-integrated, efficient, and effective as HTML sites. Flash does bring with it some technical problems, however.

The Plugin Problem

Anytime there's plugin media, there's a chance that some visitors might not have the plugin. There's also the problem of plugin versions. Although 96 percent of the browsers out there might have the Flash Player installed, not all of them have the most recent version (6). If you're in charge of creating the Flash content for your web site, you have to ask yourself whether you need to use the latest and greatest Flash technology available, or whether it's safer to scale yourself back and only create content that earlier versions of the plugin can access.

Ease of Updating

For web pages that change frequently, HTML is quicker to update than Flash, because you don't have to generate and upload an entirely new SWF file for every minor text change. Savvy Flash authors know how to make updating as easy as possible, and Dreamweaver's new Flash integration features help as well. But updating regular HTML pages is still more efficient.

Accessibility

Flash movies aren't accessible to users with text-based browsers, or browsers for the visually impaired. Flash movies aren't wide open to search engines. If there's internal navigation within a Flash movie, users can't bookmark specific sections of the movie or even use the browser's Back and Forward buttons to get around.

Note

Though Flash accessibility is still limited compared to HTML, Flash MX and the corresponding Flash Player 6 do offer improvements in this area over previous versions.

Dynamic Data

Flash-based web pages can send and receive form data and interact with CGI and application servers. Through the Flash Generator application server, they're even capable of generating data-driven graphics at runtime, such as animated 3D bar charts that reflect current sales trends. However, you might not have access to technical staff that can accomplish this integration; knowledge of integrating server-based data and HTML is much more common.

Flash's Role in a Web Strategy

Flash content can be integrated into a web site in a variety of ways, just as it can be used for a variety of purposes. At the simplest level of involvement, small Flash animations can be used rather than animated GIFs to liven up pages. Many web sites open with a splash page containing a Flash animation that then segues to a standard HTML home page interface. Some sites present a full-screen Flash movie as the home page, moving on to standard HTML content on other site pages. Others put Flash content in page headers or footers, leaving the central content area in HTML. Although it's not done often, it's possible to create an entire site from full-screen Flash movies, so that the HTML serves only as a framework for holding the movies. (Figure 20.2 shows this strategy in action.)

Figure 20.2   The Tiffany's web site presents its entire interface in Flash, though an HTML-only version is also available.

Note

It's important to remember that even a full-screen Flash movie exists as an object embedded in a web page, surrounded by an HTML framework. Although it's possible to link directly to a SWF file, so that the Flash movie plays without an HTML framework, this limits the control you can have over the movie within the browser. You cannot assign parameters to it, or control it through scripting. Normally, even completely Flash-ified web sites are written as a series of Flash movies inside separate HTML documents.

Working with Flash in Dreamweaver

Dreamweaver makes the process of putting Flash movies into web pages easy—although the more you know about how Flash operates, the more you'll be able to take advantage of it.

Inserting Flash into a Document

To insert a SWF movie into an HTML document in Dreamweaver, use the Insert Flash object, found in the Media tab of the Insert bar (see Figure 20.3). Like the Shockwave object, this object inserts the Flash content using the `<object>` tag with an included `<embed>` tag. This combination targets the Flash ActiveX control where it's available and the Flash plugin where it's not. The code for the inserted object looks like this:

```
<object classid="clsid:D27CDB6E-AE6D-11cf-96B8-444553540000"
codebase="http://download.macromedia.com/pub/shockwave/cabs/flash/swflas
h.cab#version=5,0,0,0" width="365" height="250" title="myflashmovie"
accesskey="a" tabindex="3">
  <param name="movie" value="myflashmovie.swf">
  <param name="quality" value="high">
  <embed src="myflashmovie.swf" quality="high"
pluginspage="http://www.macromedia.com/shockwave/download/index.cgi?P1_P
rod_Version=ShockwaveFlash" type="application/x-shockwave-flash"
width="365" height="250">
  </embed>
</object>
```

The Flash object

Figure 20.3   The Flash object as it appears in the Media tab of the Insert bar.

Tip

Don't confuse the regular Flash object with the Flash Text or Flash Button objects. Use the Flash object to insert Flash movies that already exist; use the others to create new, simple Flash movies for navigation or titling purposes.

Examining this code, note that the `codebase` and `pluginspage` parameters are both used, to allow visitors without the Flash Player installed to download it. If you have enabled Flash accessibility options in the Accessibility Preferences, your code might also include `title`, `accesskey`, and `tabindex` attributes. (For more on Dreamweaver's new accessibility options, see Chapter 3, "Creating and Working with Documents.")

Using Flash Assets

You can also add Flash movies to your documents from the Assets panel. In the panel, click the Flash icon to see a list of all SWF movies in your site. Flash movies can be added to Favorites and partake of all other asset-related benefits. When a Flash movie is selected in the Assets list, the panel display includes a Play button for previewing the animation (see Figure 20.4). For a complete discussion of using assets, see Chapter 22, "Local Site Management."

Note

Flash assets won't be available to you if you haven't defined a site.

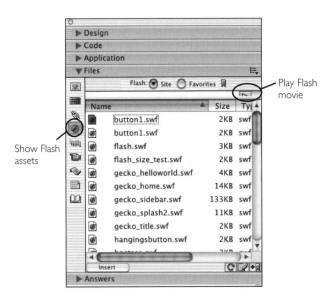

Figure 20.4   Viewing a Flash movie in the Assets panel.

Playing the Movie

Like other media elements, the Flash movie appears in your document as a gray box. To see the movie play, click the Play button in the Property inspector (see Figure 20.6). While the movie is playing, you can continue editing other content on the page, and even change some of its properties. To access other properties, or to resize the movie by dragging it in the Document window, copy it, or move it, you'll need to click the Stop button.

Cloaking Flash Media for Site Synchronization

MX The new Dreamweaver cloaked media feature can be a big help in managing sites where a lot of Flash files are used. It used to be that if you kept your original Flash authoring files (FLAs) in your local root folder, you had to work around them when synchronizing local and remote folders. With Dreamweaver MX, you can specify that all files with the .fla extension be excluded from consideration when running the Select Newer Local, Select Newer Remote, and Synchronize commands.

To cloak all FLAs in your site, access the Site Definition dialog box by choosing Site > Edit Sites, and in the dialog box that appears choosing a site and clicking the Edit button. In the Site Definition dialog box, choose the Cloaking category (see Figure 20.5). Enable cloaking, and enable cloaking by file type. Then make sure the **.fla** file extension is in the list of file types to be excluded. From now on, all FLAs within your local root folder will appear with a red line through them, and will be excluded from synchronization. (For more on cloaked media, see Chapter 22, "Local Site Management.")

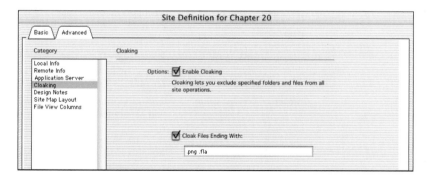

Figure 20.5   Enabling cloaking in the Site Definition dialog box, so exclude FLAs from site synchronization.

Setting Flash Parameters

Figure 20.6 shows the Flash Property inspector, with typical and default settings in place. Flash movies accept a variety of parameters, some common to all media types and some unique to Flash. Most can be added using the Property Inspector; some are set automatically by Dreamweaver, and don't appear anywhere in the inspector. Some must be added using the generic Parameters dialog box. Table 20.1 lists parameters for the Flash plugin and ActiveX player, noting which parameters must be added manually.

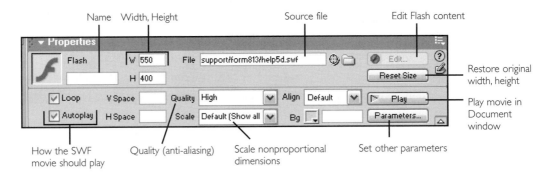

Figure 20.6   The Flash Property inspector.

Table 20.1   Specifications of the Parameters Accepted by the Flash Player Plugin and ActiveX Control

Parameter Name	Value	Description
name	Any one-word name	Required by the <embed> tag if the movie is to referred to by scripting.
ID	Any one-word name	Required by the <object> tag if the movie is to be referred to by scripting.
width	Integer or Percent value	The horizontal space the movie will be allotted on the page. If the width assigned is different from the movie's width, the movie will be resized (see "scale parameter").
height	Integer or Percent value	The vertical space the movie will be allotted on the page. If the height assigned is different from the movie's height, the movie will be resized (see "scale parameter").
align	Baseline, top, middle, bottom, texttop, absmiddle, absbottom, left, right	Determines how the browser will align the movie when text or other page elements are placed next to it (in the same table cell or paragraph, for instance).

Parameter Name	Value	Description
`bgcolor`	Choose from the palette or enter a 6-digit hexadecimal number.	If the width and height values assigned are larger than the movie's dimensions, the color that will fill up the rest of the allotted space.
`vspace`	Integer (pixels)	Adds empty white space above and below the movie. Specify a number of pixels.
`hspace`	Integer (pixels)	Adds empty white space to the right and left of the movie. Specify a number of pixels.
`autoplay`	`true` or `false`	Whether the movie will start playing as soon as it loads.
`loop`	`true` or `false`	Whether the movie will repeat indefinitely, or play only once. This only has effect if the movie's own internal scripting doesn't have its own looping or stopping controls.
`quality`	`low`, `medium`, `high`, `best`, `autolow`, `autohigh`	Determines whether Flash Player will anti-alias the movie as it plays. (Quality doesn't change the file size, but can affect playback speed for processor-intensive animations.) See Table 20.2 for details.
`scale`	`show all`, `noborder`, `exactfit`	Determines how the movie's contents will be resized, if the `width` and `height` parameters are used to resize the movie object nonproportionally. Defaults to show all. See Table 20.3 for details.
* `salign`	`left`, `center`, `right`, `top`, `middle`, `bottom`	If the movie object has been scaled nonproportionally, this attribute determines how the movie's contents align within the object shape. See Table 20.4 for details.
* `menu`	`true`, `false`	Determines whether right-clicking (Windows) or Ctrl-clicking (Mac) on the Flash movie in the browser will cause a contextual menu to appear. Defaults to true.

continues ▶

Table 20.1   Continued

Parameter Name	Value	Description
* devicefont (Windows only)	true, false	Determines if an anti-aliased system font replaces text when specified fonts are not available. (Note: Normal, static text is automatically embedded in Flash movies; this setting refers to dynamic text and input fields only.) Defaults to false.
* wmode (IE/Windows only)	Opaque, window, transparent	Determines whether the background of the Flash movie is opaque or transparent, sitting in front or in back of other layered page elements. See Table 20.5 for details.
** pluginspage	http://www.macromedia.com/shockwave/download/index.cgi?P1_Prod_Version=ShockwaveFlash	Used by the <embed> tag. Allows users without the plugin to link directly to Macromedia's plugin download site.
** codebase (part of <object> tag, not a standard <param>)	http://download.macromedia.com/pub/shockwave/cabs/flash/swflash.cab#version=5,0,0,0	Used by the <object> tag. Allows IE/Windows users without the ActiveX control to automatically retrieve the control from Macromedia.

* Indicates parameters that must be set using the generic Parameters dialog box.

** Indicates parameters that Dreamweaver handles automatically.

Because Flash is not quite like any other plugin media, the meaning and potential uses of some of these items are not immediately obvious.

Width and Height

Flash movies can be resized numerically by entering values in the Width and Height fields of the Property inspector, or interactively by dragging the selection handles in the Document window.

Tip

Movies can only be drag-resized when they're not playing. To resize a movie while it's playing, enter new values in the Property inspector's Width and Height fields.

Scalability is one of the most liberating aspects of designing with Flash. Unlike its handling of other plugin media, Dreamweaver is capable of determining the original dimensions of a Flash movie, and can reset its size if the current width and height don't represent its true dimensions. Also, unlike other plugin media, altering a Flash movie's width and height attributes will actually scale the movie, not simply adjust its cropping. Flash movies can even safely be set to percent-based dimensions, much like tables, so that they resize as the browser window resizes. To set a Flash movie to percent-based dimensions, type a number followed by the percent symbol into the Width or Height field (see Figure 20.7).

Figure 20.7   Setting a Flash movie's dimensions to percent-based numbers.

Note

Although any graphics created within Flash are vector-based and therefore scalable, Flash movies also can contain imported pixel images. Any pixel image inside a Flash movie has the same limitations as a pixel image outside Flash: Its presence will dramatically increase the movie's file size; and if the movie is scaled, it will lose image quality.

Quality

Vector graphics such as those in Flash movies do not define pixels, but they must still be rendered by something that only understands pixels: the computer monitor. When the screen displays objects, it displays them with either aliased (jagged) or anti-aliased (smooth) edges. When the Flash Player plays a movie, each frame must be redrawn with either aliased or anti-aliased edges. How the player handles this is determined by the quality parameter. Table 20.2 lists possible values the parameter can take.

Movies playing at low quality will have jagged edges, but will play quickly. Movies set to high quality will have to be translated, frame-by-frame, into anti-aliased graphics, and so will have smooth edges but might not play at full speed on all computers. The other quality settings are all variations on this basic setup.

Table 20.2   Options for Setting the *quality* Attribute for Flash Movies

Option	Description	Example
Low	No anti-aliasing (fastest playback).	
* Medium	Some anti-aliasing on vector graphics; none on internal bitmaps.	
High	Smooth anti-aliasing on vector graphics; internal bitmaps are anti-aliased, unless they're animated.	
* Best	Anti-aliasing on vector and bitmap graphics, including animated bitmaps.	
Autolow	Starts in low quality mode, then switches to high quality if the user's computer is fast enough.	
Autohigh	Starts in high quality, then switches to low if the user's computer cannot keep up.	

* Not available in the pop-up menu—must be typed into the input field.

The "auto" settings (Autolow and Autohigh) are the most flexible for dealing with a wide variety of computer speeds. Each tells the Flash Player to start out at a particular quality level and adjust the level as needed, depending on whether a particular user's computer can anti-alias and keep up with the frame rate. Of these two, Autolow will always play the first second or two of a Flash animation with jagged, aliased graphics, even on the fastest computer. Autohigh starts out with anti-aliasing turned on, so users with faster computers never have to see jagged graphics. If your Flash animation is at all complex, or if it includes a soundtrack, this is the best choice.

Note

The quality setting does not affect the Flash movie itself, and therefore has no effect on file size or download time. Its only purpose is to instruct the Flash Player how to display the movie.

Scale

Because Flash graphics are scalable, and because you can set them to percent-based sizes that will change with browser window sizes, you need to determine what will happen when the movie's onscreen dimensions aren't the same proportions as the movie's true dimensions. Table 20.3 shows the details of this parameter, its possible values, and the effect of those values on the movie's appearance. If you examine the samples shown there, you'll see why Default (show all) is the default setting for this parameter—it's definitely the most useful.

Table 20.3   Values for the *scale* Attribute, and Their Effects on Movie Appearance

Value	Description	Example
show all (default)	The movie contents are scaled proportionally, based on the smaller dimension (width or height) so that no contents are cropped away. Adding background color makes up extra space in the movie object along the larger dimension.	
noborders	The movie contents are scaled proportionally, based on the larger dimension (width or height), causing contents to be cropped along the smaller dimension.	
exactfit	The movie contents are scaled non-proportionally, to match the movie object's scaling.	

Note

Some designers, in trying to create truly full-screen Flash, mistakenly think that the noborders scale setting will eliminate any page borders around the movie. As you can see from the samples shown in Table 20.3, this isn't the case. To make a Flash movie hug the browser window edges when setting dimensions to 100%×100%, use Modify > Page Properties and set the page margins to 0.

Scale Align (salign)

Don't confuse salign with the more standard align attribute. The purpose of salign is to work with the scale attribute, to determine how a proportionally scaled movie will fill a nonproportional box. Table 20.4 shows the settings for this attribute, and the effect of those values on movie appearance. Note that there are no values for centering horizontally or vertically; these are the default values, and needn't be specified at all.

Table 20.4   Values for the salign Attribute, and their Effects on Movie Appearance

Value	Description	Example
L	When used with default scaling (show all), aligns the movie at the left (L) edge of any extra horizontal space. When used with scale=noborders, shows the left side of the movie if horizontal cropping must occur.	

continues ▶

Table 20.4   Continued

Value	Description	Example
R	When used with default scaling (show all), aligns the movie at the right (R) edge of any extra space. When used with scale=noborders, shows the right side of the movie if horizontal cropping must occur.	
T	When used with default scaling (show all), aligns the movie at the top (T) edge of any extra vertical space. When used with scale=noborders, shows the top part of the movie if vertical cropping must occur.	
B	When used with default scaling (show all), aligns the movie at the bottom (B) edge of any extra vertical space. When used with scale=noborders, shows the bottom part of the movie if vertical cropping must occur.	
(multiple values)	To assign both horizontal and vertical salign parameters, enter both relevant letters as the parameter's value (LB, LT, RB, or RT). The resulting code will look like: salign="LT", and so forth.	

The salign parameter does not appear anywhere in the Flash Property inspector. To set this parameter, click the Parameters button in the inspector to access the generic Parameters dialog box. (See Chapter 19, and refer to Figure 19.7, for a full discussion and example of working with generic Parameter settings.)

Window Mode (wmode)

Window mode is an attribute of the Flash ActiveX control only, so it only takes effect in IE/Windows. Within that environment, however, the wmode parameter allows you to control whether the Flash movie's background is transparent and how Flash movies interact with other page elements when DHTML layers are used. Table 20.5 details the various options for this attribute, and shows the effects of each.

Table 20.5   Values for the *wmode* Attribute, For Use by the Flash Player ActiveX Control

Value	Description	Example
opaque (default)	The background is opaque, using the Flash movie's internally specified background color; other layers can appear in front of the Flash movie.	It was a dark and stormy night.
window	The background is opaque; all other layers appear behind the Flash movie.	It was a dark and stormy night.
transparent	The background is transparent; other layers can appear in front of the Flash movie, or show through from behind it.	was a dark stormy

If you are accessing your Flash content through the plugin, rather than the ActiveX control, Flash movies will always have opaque backgrounds, and any layer with Flash content will always show in front of all other layers.

Exercise 20.1   Inserting a Flash Banner

The exercises in this chapter give you a chance to practice working with Flash content in Dreamweaver; they also provide a chance to examine the various different ways Flash can be integrated into a site. In this first exercise, you start with a page that has an animated GIF banner and replace it with a SWF banner; and you examine the pros and cons of each choice. You can find all the required files for this and the other exercises in this chapter on the accompanying CD in the **chapter_20** folder. Before proceeding with the exercise, copy that folder to your hard drive, and create a new site with that as your local root folder.

1. To start, from the exercise files on the CD find and open **gecko_gifbanner.html**. This sample home page includes an animated title banner, made from an animated GIF. Preview the page in your browser to see how the animation works. (Figure 20.8 shows the page.) The animation is set to play only once; if you blink, you miss it!

2. Go to File > Save As, and save a copy of the file as **gecko_swfbanner.html**. (You will be comparing the animated GIF with a SWF banner, so you don't want to change the original page.) Select the GIF banner and delete it.

3. Use the Flash object to insert **gecko_banner.swf** into the banner spot. Dreamweaver will size the banner automatically and set other defaults. Are there any defaults that you need to change to make the new banner behave just like the old one? (*Hint*: How many times does the lizard run across the page?) Remember, you can preview the animation without previewing the entire page in a browser, by clicking the Play button in the Flash Property inspector.

Figure 20.8   The **gecko_gifbanner.html** page as viewed in a browser.

4. Open the original file (**gecko_gifbanner.html**) and compare it to the new version. You should notice right away how much smaller the file size is for the SWF animation—GIF animations are made of pixels, and therefore aren't suited to large graphics. One difference you won't see unless you upload both pages to a web server and view them live is that the timing of the SWF will be better than that of the GIF. This is because the first time any animated GIF plays through, the frames display as quickly as they download, regardless of their built-in timing. It's only on the second and subsequent loops that the frame delay becomes consistent. Flash movies stream much more efficiently.

5. In **gecko_swfbanner.html**, the layout table is currently pixel-based, and therefore nonflexible. Using The Table Property inspector or Dreamweaver Layout view, change the table to a flexible table that is always 100 percent of the browser window's width. Then set the SWF banner so that it too has a width of 100 percent. Leave the `scale` attribute at the default so that extra space is added to make up for the excess width that could be added. Now you're taking advantage of Flash scalability. After you've done that, you might decide that the lizard animation looks silly in the middle of a big, wide page—so, using the generic Parameters dialog box, set the `salign` so that the image hugs the right side of the page. Figure 20.9 shows how both of these settings will look in the various parts of the Property inspector.

6. Preview your page in the browser to see how the banner looks and how the animation resizes as you resize the window.

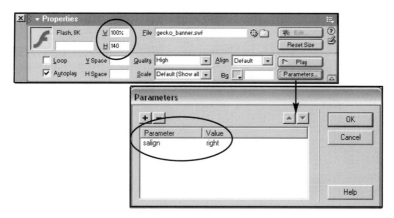

Figure 20.9   The Flash Property inspector and generic Parameters dialog box, showing the gecko banner being assigned a variable width and right-side alignment.

Optional: Have you actually done anything with the SWF banner that can't also be done with the animated GIF? Really, because you have only scaled the movie horizontally, you haven't resized the graphics—only given the browser permission to add extra space on either side if needed. The same effect could be generated using the animated GIF, by setting the table to be 100 percent wide and changing the bgcolor of the banner's table cell to match the brown of the banner. Then you could set the cell alignment to right to mimic the salign.

Exercise 20.2   Stacking Flash Content and HTML with Layers (IE/Windows Only)

In this exercise, you'll see how much fancier your page can become if you layer HTML content over a Flash movie—although this effect will only work for visitors with Internet Explorer 4+/Windows who are using the Flash Player ActiveX control.

1. This exercise creates an alternate version of the home page you saw in Exercise 20.1. Begin by opening **gecko_layers.html**. Examine the file and you'll see that the text and navigation bar are present, each in its own layer. This file includes an animated banner that extends under the page elements and becomes, in essence, an animated background.

2. You want to insert the background SWF movie on the page but not in a layer, and therefore behind all other layered content. (You could insert the SWF in its own layer, stacked behind the other two layers; but, because the movie will just be sitting in the background, this isn't necessary.) With the insertion point outside all layers, and using the Flash object, insert **gecko_bg.swf**. Leaving all the parameters at their default settings, preview the page in any browser you choose. You should get a lovely preview of the animated background, but the content layers won't show, even in IE/Windows. That's because you haven't set the wmode yet.

3. Select the background SWF and assign whatever parameters you think appropriate. In particular, use the generic Parameters dialog box to set the wmode to opaque (see Figure 20.10).

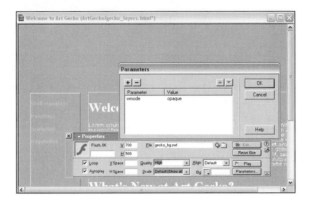

Figure 20.10   Setting the parameters for **gecko_bg.swf** in **gecko_layers.html**.

4. Change the page's bgcolor to match the background of the SWF. You want the movie to blend seamlessly with its environment, so that it looks more like a background element.

To match movie color and page color, do this:

- Select the SWF and click the Property inspector's Play button to play it (so its colors show).

- With the movie still playing, go to Modify > Page Properties. Click the Background Color button, and when the eyedropper appears, use it to sample the SWF movie's color. (Figure 20.11 shows this happening.) Voila! Seamless integration. (For more on color sampling in Dreamweaver, see "Working with the Color Picker" in Chapter 2.)

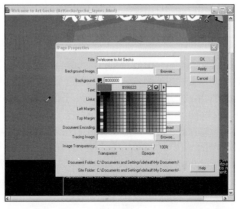

Figure 20.11   Playing a Flash movie in Dreamweaver, and sampling its color for the page background color.

Note

Do your colors match? If your monitor is set to display thousands of colors (16-bit color depth), you might notice that it's impossible to get the Flash movie color to match your page background. This is because the Flash Player renders colors slightly differently than the browser does. The difference won't show up on 8-bit monitors (displaying 256 colors) or in 24-bit monitors (millions of colors). However, any visitor who views your page on a 16-bit monitor will see the difference. It's not because you mismatched the colors, and there's nothing you can do about it.

5. Preview your layered page in various browsers. In IE/Windows, you should see a complete page as shown in Figure 20.12. In other browsers and platforms, you'll just see the background movie.

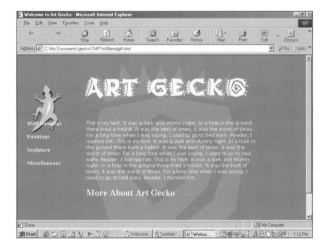

Figure 20.12   The completed **gecko_layers.html** page as it appears in IE/Windows, with text showing on top of animated background.

Editing Flash Movies from Within Dreamweaver

New to Dreamweaver MX is a closer integration with Flash, similar in some ways to the Dreamweaver/Fireworks integration. Dreamweaver users with Flash MX on their computers can automatically launch Flash to perform edits, and even generate new SWFs. Links coded into SWF movies can be viewed and changed without leaving the Dreamweaver interface.

Note

The Flash integration features will only work if you have both Dreamweaver MX and Flash MX on your computer. Earlier versions of Flash can't be used for this.

Flash Launch-and-Edit

The procedure for creating a Flash movie and incorporating it into a Dreamweaver HTML page involves creating the main Flash file (FLA), exporting a SWF, and launching Dreamweaver to build an HTML document that houses the SWF. If you're working away in Dreamweaver and discover that the Flash movie needs editing, you have to launch Flash, open the FLA, make your edits, and export a new SWF, before coming back to Dreamweaver and continuing work on your HTML pages.

> **Note**
>
> In case you want to practice using Flash integration features on the exercise files from this chapter, the **chapter_20/FlashFiles** folder contains several of the original FLAs for the ArtGecko site.

With the new launch-and-edit feature, the procedure is somewhat simpler.

1. Create the FLA in Flash MX, and export a SWF.

2. In Dreamweaver, insert the SWF into an HTML document.

3. In the Src field in the Flash Property inspector (see Figure 20.13), browse or use Point-to-File to show Dreamweaver the FLA used to create this SWF. Dreamweaver will create a Design Note storing the information.

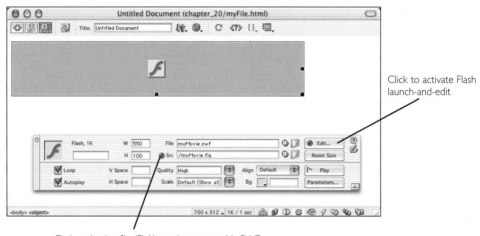

Click to activate Flash launch-and-edit

Flash authoring file (FLA) used to create this SWF (only appears if Flash MX is installed)

Figure 20.13   An embedded SWF and its Property inspector, with Flash integration features highlighted.

4. The next time you need to edit the FLA, select the SWF in your Dreamweaver document, and click the Property inspector's Edit button (see Figure 20.13). Dreamweaver will launch Flash and open the source file you specified earlier.

5. In Flash, make your changes to the FLA. When you're done, instead of re-exporting, click the Done button (see Figure 20.14) to return to Dreamweaver. Flash exports a new SWF, and Dreamweaver now displays your document with the new movie in place.

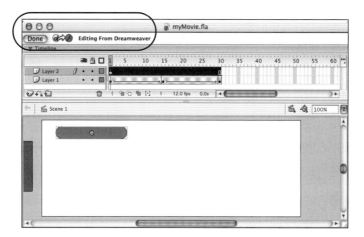

Figure 20.14   The Flash authoring file (FLA) for an embedded SWF, showing in the special launch-and-edit version of the Flash application window.

 Note

Launch-and-edit for Flash movies works the same as the launch-and-edit feature for integrating with Fireworks. For more on Fireworks integration, see Appendix A.

Updating Links in SWF Files

If your SWF file contains links (ActionScript getURL() actions), you can change these links without launching Flash at all, using the Dreamweaver site map and Change Links command. Do it this way:

1. Configure your site map preferences to show dependent files. Choose Site > Edit Sites, and in the dialog box that appears, select your site and click Edit. In the Site Definition dialog box, choose the Site Map Layout category. If you haven't done so already, use the Home Page field to define a home page for your site. (You need to do this before you can use the Site Map feature.) Select the Show Dependent Dependent Files option (see Figure 20.15).

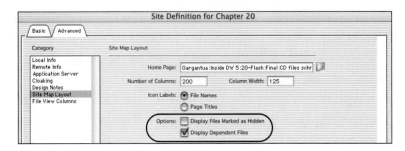

Figure 20.15   Setting site preferences so the site map displays dependent files.

2. In the Site window, click the Site Map button to show the site map. Your embedded SWF file will show as a dependent file of its parent HTML document. All links within the SWF file will also be shown as dependents (see Figure 20.16).

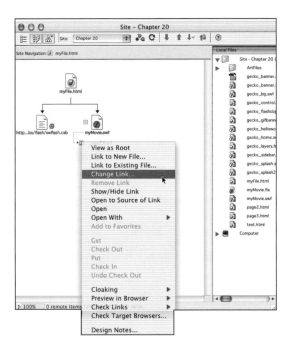

Figure 20.16   Site map showing an HTML document, the SWF embedded within it, and the link within the SWF, along with the Change Links command.

3. Right-click (Windows) or Ctrl-click (Macintosh) on the linked file you want to change to access the contextual menu (as shown in Figure 20.16), and choose Change Link. In the dialog box that appears, choose a new file that the SWF should link to.

When you do this, several things happen. Dreamweaver updates the getURL() action within the SWF. It also generates a Design Note noting that this has been done. The next time you launch the FLA in Flash, that Design Note will tell Flash that a link has been changed, and it will offer to change the link in the source file as well (see Figure 20.17). (If you don't let Flash update the link in the source file to match the link Dreamweaver altered in the SWF, the next time you export a SWF the link will revert to whatever it was before you used Dreamweaver to change it, because the SWF Dreamweaver created will be overwritten.)

Figure 20.17   Launching a FLA file after Dreamweaver has updated a link in the SWF will cause Flash to prompt you with this alert.

Note

In case you're curious about how all this inter-application communication works, you can open and examine the Design Note that makes it happen. Because Design Notes are invisible in the Site window, leave Dreamweaver and use Explorer (Windows) or the Finder (Macintosh) to examine your root folder. Design Notes are stored in that folder, within a **_notes** folder. Open that folder and you'll find a text file with the name of your SWF file followed by the .mno extension—**myFile.swf.mno**, for instance. Open that file in a text editor (or in Dreamweaver Code view) and you'll see in <infoitem> tag identifying the source FLA file, one for each original link in the SWF, and one for each changed link. Dreamweaver accesses this Design Note to populate the Flash Property inspector and to generate the Flash items in the site map; Flash accesses it to determine if any links need to be updated within the original FLA, when you open that file for editing.

Interview: Jennifer Bennett

Business Name: Grass Roots Consulting

URL: www.g-r-c.com

Jennifer Bennett has long been one of the top Macromedia authorized Director trainers in the country, and a few years ago added Flash to her curriculum. She has trained Macromedia personnel, and given workshops at the Macromedia and MacWorld Expos, as well as providing in-house training across America.

Why is Flash so popular in web sites today? Do you see that trend continuing?

Flash gives designers or developers a great way to express themselves with graphics and text as opposed to text only. Also, the interactive aspect of Flash makes web sites more interesting, whether that interactivity is used for navigation or information. For web sites used for training, Flash content provides the ability to explore the subject matter in ways that help retain the information as opposed as simply reading text. I definitely see Flash's popularity continuing. I think eventually all web sites will incorporate Flash.

Some web design experts, like Jakob Nielsen, argue that Flash is more often a detriment than an asset to a web site. Would you say this is a fair assessment? What problems do you most often see in web sites that use Flash?

Flash is still a new technology and with any new technology, people feel they *must* use it, for good or bad. This churns out a lot of bad Flash design, which reflects on the technology as a whole badly. However, even though the technology is still new, Macromedia claims that 98.6% of browsers have the Flash plugin, which is a phenomenal number. Two years ago I would have said that having Flash on a web site could be a detriment because you don't want people to have to download a new plugin just to view your site, but that really isn't the case with Flash any more. I do still see problems with Flash and accessibility for those with disabilities. It doesn't matter how beautiful your design is if someone with a visual disability can't navigate your site because of the Flash elements.

How effective is Flash at creating data-driven sites, compared to straight HTML? What are the advantages of using Flash for this, over HTML?

I love Flash interfaces for data-driven sites. Flash offers a new dimension for these sites that has not been seen before. Flash and Generator allow the data to be retrieved to be graphics, sounds, charts, and more instead of simply text.

You do a lot of training for Flash users. What would you say Flash is mostly being used for, out there in the real world? Is it being used to its full potential?

There are still only a few sites that I think are using Flash to its full potential—mostly because of the young age of the technology. However, those few sites just can't be beat. Strangely enough, I feel that Macromedia's site is not using Flash as effectively as it could. I think it's the young designers who don't know the "old school" rules of web design so they can more easily think "outside of the box" that are using Flash more effectively. They haven't heard "no, Flash can't do that," so they find a way to accomplish what they want with the application.

You really can't mention just one use of Flash out there. It's being used for Internet-based training, entertainment, navigation, disseminating information, and just about anything else you can think of.

What strategies do you recommend to web designers when dealing with plugin detection, redirection, and so forth?

Luckily, Flash can do a lot of that for you without you knowing anything. The Publish command in Flash will generate an HTML document for you that will detect whether the correct plugin is available. If the designer can take the time to fully research the Publish command, or take advantage of the Dreamweaver Check Plugin behavior, detection and redirection should not be a problem.

Working with Full-Screen Flash Pages

In a full-screen Flash page, the Flash movie is the only content on the page, and for all viewing and interactivity purposes, it becomes the page. Full-screen Flash can be used for an entire splash screen or opening animation; for individual pages, such as the home page or main section pages; or even for an entire web site.

Dreamweaver's Job: Create the HTML Framework

If the HTML document exists only as a framework to hold the Flash movie, there isn't much work to be done in Dreamweaver. Typically, your job in Dreamweaver is to do the following:

- **Set movie parameters.** The `<object>` and `<embed>` tags and their parameters govern how the browser and Flash Player will present the movie. `quality`, `scale`, `loop`, and `autoplay` must be set for the movie to play as desired. The movie can be left to its original dimensions (best if it contains photographic elements), or set to be truly full-screen by assigning width and height to 100%×100%.

- **Set page margins.** The HTML code determines where on the page the movie sits, including how closely it's allowed to snuggle up against the top and left edges of the browser window. To make the movie completely cover the browser window space, set its dimensions to 100%×100% and set the page margins to 0. (Do this in Modify > Page Properties. See Chapter 3 for more on margins.)

- **Set page background color.** It's always a good idea to match the page and movie background colors, so no slivers of a different color appear at the edges of the browser window.

- **Perform plugin and browser checks.** If the user's computer doesn't have the correct plugin, the entire full-screen movie won't play. You can use JavaScript behaviors, which execute onLoad, to make sure the movie will play and to reroute visitors who can't see the movie. (See Chapter 19 for a discussion of plugin detection in Dreamweaver.)

Flash's Job: Create Interactivity and Links

Because, after the page has been loaded, the Flash movie is the entire interface, all interactivity—including links—must be built in to the SWF. A Flash movie might just call another Flash movie to replace itself on the page, in which case the document's URL doesn't change and the visitor probably won't even be aware that there has been a change. This is done internally with Flash's loadMovieNum() ActionScript command.

The Flash movie also might link to another HTML document that contains other Flash movies. In this case, the user will see the URL change, and the browser's Back and Forward buttons can be used to navigate between movies. This is done internally with Flash's getURL() ActionScript command.

Exercise 20.3   Creating a Flash Splash Page

In this exercise, you add an opening splash page to the Art Gecko home page created in the preceding exercise. The splash page will consist only of a full-screen Flash animation with a built-in link to the home page. All exercise files can be found in the **chapter_20** folder on the CD.

1. If this were a real project and you were responsible for it, you would start by creating the Flash movie and assigning a getURL() command within the movie to make it automatically load the home page. Because this isn't a real project, **gecko_splash.swf** has already been created for you, with the link in place. Figure 20.18 shows how the link has been added. (You can test-play **gecko_splash.swf** by opening it directly from your desktop—double-clicking it should automatically launch the Flash Player.)

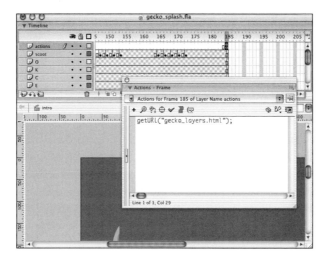

Figure 20.18   The **gecko_splash.swf** file being created in Flash. The `getURL()` action has been assigned to the final frame of the timeline, so it executes automatically as soon as the animation finishes playing.

2. To house this movie, create a new Dreamweaver document. Save it in the **ArtGecko** folder. (It must be in the same folder as the home page, because of how the relative URL has been written into the Flash movie). Call it **gecko_splash.html**.

3. Use the Flash object to insert **gecko_splash.swf**. To make the movie automatically resize with the browser window, set Width and Height to 100%×100%. In the Property inspector, make sure Autoplay is selected. Because you want the movie to play only once, you can deselect Looping; but because of the movie's internal scripting, it won't loop regardless of what setting you choose here in your HTML parameters.

4. To make the movie completely take over the page, you need to set the page's background color and margins. First, so you can sample the color, use the Property inspector's Play button to start the movie playing. Then go to Modify > Page Properties. Remove the page margins by setting Left Margin, Top Margin, Margin Width, and Margin Height all to 0. Using sampling, set the page background color to match the Flash movie (like you did in the preceding exercise) and click OK. If you check your code after having done this, your <body> tag should look like this:

   ```
   <body bgcolor="#996633" text="#000000" leftmargin="0"
   topmargin="0" marginwidth="0" marginheight="0">
   ```

5. Save your file and try it out! When the page loads, the Flash animation should take over the screen. It should play once through and then load your layered home page. (If the home page doesn't load properly, make sure the filename is still **gecko_layers.html**, and that it and the splash page are in the same folder.)

Note

The relative pathname used in the Flash movie's internal link requires that the two HTML documents be in the same folder. The **gecko_splash.swf** file does not need to be stored in that same folder. Try it and see—you can move the SWF file to a subfolder (making sure to change the reference to it in **gecko_splash.html**), and when you browse the document it will still call **gecko_layers.html**.

Exercise 20.4   Creating a Full-Screen Flash Page

In this exercise, you create an alternate home page for the Art Gecko web site, doing away with the multilayered setup from the preceding exercise by using a Flash-built version of the entire opening presentation. You'll also see how Flash's internal `loadMovie()` command can be used to navigate between SWF movies without creating new HTML documents or changing the URL in the browser window. All exercise files can be found in the **chapter_20** folder of the CD.

1. For this exercise, you need two Flash movies: a revised splash movie, and a movie containing the full-screen home page presentation. Again, in the real world you would start this project by building both the **gecko_splash2.swf** and **gecko_home.swf** files in Flash. You would assign a `loadMovie()` action to the final frame of the splash movie, to automatically load the home page movie. You can launch both files from your desktop to see what each one contains. Figure 20.19 shows the `loadMovieNum()` command begin to add to **gecko_splash2.swf**.

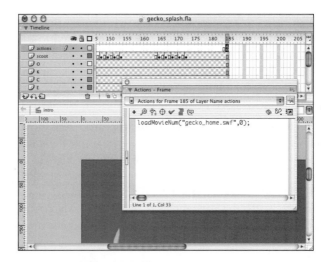

Figure 20.19   The **gecko_splash2.swf** file being created in Flash, with `loadMovieNum()` action being added.

2. You now need an HTML document to hold the Flash movies. Instead of creating a new page from scratch, open **gecko_splash.html** and save it as **gecko_fullscreen.html**.

3. This page currently contains **gecko_splash.swf.** If you delete this movie and insert the new movie, you'll have to set its parameters all over again. So, instead, use the existing movie code, but just change the src parameter to point to the new movie. Select the Flash movie, and, in the Property inspector, find the File input field and click the Browse button next to it. In the dialog box that appears, find and choose **gecko_splash2.swf.**

4. That's it! Try the movie out in a browser to see it work. Can you tell at which point the new movie is being loaded? Note that the URL shown in the browser's location bar doesn't change when the new movie loads. (This makes it impossible for users to bookmark the home page. They can bookmark only the splash page.)

Flash and JavaScript

Scripting Flash movies in the browser follows the same rules as scripting any plugin media type (see Chapter 19 for more on this). Whenever you want Flash movies to talk to the browser, or the browser to give commands to the Flash Player, you use Flash ActionScript to send JavaScript instructions, or JavaScript to send ActionScript code.

Scripting In: Using JavaScript to Control Flash

A variety of JavaScript commands exist for communicating with the Flash Player, in its plugin and its ActiveX form. Table 20.6 lists some of the most commonly used of them. As you can see from examining the figure, it's possible to send the Flash movie to a certain frame in its timeline; to start and stop playback; and even to control embedded movie clips by setting their properties and controlling their timelines. (The more you know about Flash authoring, the more useful this information will be to you.) Before relying on any of these commands, remember that although ActiveX media controls support extensive scripting for IE/Windows, no commands given to media objects will work within IE/Mac. Netscape 6 also has some difficulties passing commands to Flash movies.

Table 20.6   A Selection of JavaScript Methods Available for Controlling the Flash Player

Name	Syntax	Description
Play()	myMovie.Play()	Starts playing the specified movie.
StopPlay()	myMovie.StopPlay()	Stops playing the specified movie.
Rewind()	myMovie.Rewind()	Sends the movie to its first frame.
GotoFrame()	myMovie.GotoFrame (*frameNumber*)	Sends the movie to a specified frame number.
Zoom()	myMovie.Zoom(*percent*)	Zooms the view by a factor ( ) specified by *percent*. Numbers smaller than 100% increase the magnification.
SetZoomRect()	myMovie.SetZoomRect (*left, top, right, bottom*)	Zooms in on a rectangular area of the movie. Values are integers representing twips (1440 twips per inch; 20 twips per point).
SetVariable()	myMovie.SetVariable (*varName, value*)	Sets the value of a specified Flash variable. Both arguments are strings.
GetVariable()	var a = myMovie.GetVariable (*varName*)	Returns the value of a specified Flash variable, as a string.
TCallFrame(), TCallLabel()	myMovie.TCallFrame (*target, frameNumber*), myMovie.TCallLabel (*target, frameLabel*)	In the target timeline, executes any frame actions in the specified frame. (Similar to the Flash call() method.)
TPlay()	myMovie.TPlay(*target*)	Plays the specified movie clip.
TStopPlay()	myMovie.TStopPlay (*target*)	Stops playing the specified movie clip.
TGotoFrame(), TGotoLabel()	myMovie.TGotoFrame (*target, frameNumber*), myMovie.TGotoLabel (*target, frameLabel*)	Sends the timeline of the specified movie clip to the specified frame.
TCurrentFrame(), TCurrentlabel()	var a = myMovie. TCurrentFrame(*target*), var b = myMovie. TCurrentLabel(*target*)	Returns the number or label of the current frame, for a specified movie clip.

Not all methods work with the Flash plugin. For a complete list of supported JavaScript methods, visit www.macromedia.com/support/flash/publishexport/scriptingwithflash/scriptingwithflash_03.html.

Scripting Within Dreamweaver: The Control Shockwave or Flash Behavior
For basic Flash control using JavaScript, the Control Shockwave or Flash behavior lets you use HTML page elements to start, stop, rewind, and send movies to specific frames without writing a lick of code. (Note that the only reason to use this behavior is if you want non-Flash page elements to control the movie. Flash movies are capable of containing their own internal buttons that will start, stop, and so on. If the movie contains its own interactivity, you don't need to add any JavaScript in Dreamweaver.)

To control a Flash movie using this behavior, follow these steps:

1. Insert a Flash movie in your document.

2. Give the movie a one-word name. You can do this in the Flash Property inspector by filling in the name field in the upper-left corner (refer back to Figure 20.6).

3. Decide what sort of page element, and event, you want to trigger the action (when the user clicks a text link, when the page loads, and so forth).

4. Select the element that should trigger the action (page, text link, and so on) and use the Behaviors panel to apply the behavior. Figure 20.20 shows the behavior being chosen and the resulting dialog box with its various options.

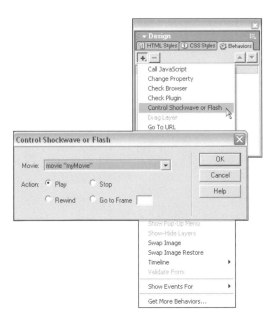

Figure 20.20   Choosing and configuring the Control Shockwave and Flash behavior.

Note

As its name implies, the Control Shockwave or Flash behavior also can be used to con-trol a Director Shockwave movie. The same procedure outlined here would apply. (See Chapter 19 for more on working with Shockwave.)

Scripting Out: Using Flash to Send JavaScript Instructions

Just as you can (theoretically, anyway) send scripting messages from the browser to the Flash Player, so you can send messages from the Flash movie to the browser. Because this is done in Flash, not in Dreamweaver, it's beyond the scope of this discussion. But it's handy knowledge to have, anyway. Just like, in the preceding exercise, you used `javascript:` in a link field to send a JavaScript command in to Flash, Flash uses the same syntax in its `getURL` link command to send commands out.

Figure 20.21 shows the Flash file **gecko_helloworld.swf** with this link in place. To see how the link works, find that file in the **chapter_20** folder, place it in an HTML docu-ment, and preview in a browser. Note that, because this is JavaScript coming out of a Flash movie instead of going in, it should work much more reliably in the different browser/platform combinations.

Figure 20.21   The **gecko_helloworld.swf** file being created in Flash.

Flash Text and Flash Buttons

You've seen how complex Flash content, including interactive movies, can be inserted into HTML pages within Dreamweaver. The Flash Button and Flash Text objects enable you to create, customize, and insert simple Flash-based page elements (buttons and text) into a web page without ever leaving Dreamweaver, and without having to own or know how to use Flash (see Figure 20.22). This opens up all sorts of new horizons for integrating different kinds of Flash content in your web sites, quickly and inexpensively.

Figure 20.22   The Flash Button and Flash Text objects, as they appear in the Common tab of the Insert bar.

How Dreamweaver Creates SWF Files

The technology that makes Dreamweaver-created SWF files possible is Macromedia Flash Generator. *Generator* is a software system for creating Flash graphics dynamically from changing information in a database, similar to the way ASP and ColdFusion create text and page layouts dynamically. To work with Generator, the Flash author creates a special *SWT* (small web template) *file*, which is essentially a SWF file with placeholders for collecting and displaying dynamic data. When the page is uploaded to a web server, then, as visitors access it, the Generator application server, which sits on the server, creates SWF files to display on the page by filling in the SWT placeholders with data from a server-side database.

Using Generator technology, Dreamweaver creates Flash Text and Flash Button objects from SWT files stored in its **Configuration** folder. Whenever you choose one of the Flash objects from the Insert bar, Dreamweaver collects information from you (text to enter, typestyle, and so on), feeds that information into placeholders in one of its SWT files, and generates a SWF file. Figure 20.23 shows an overview of the whole process.

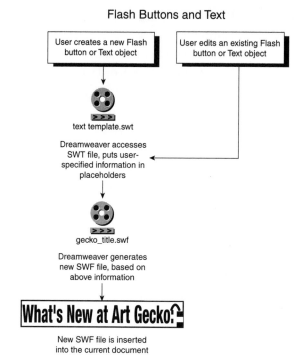

Figure 20.23   How Dreamweaver creates the SWF files for Flash Button and Text objects from SWT templates.

Creating and Inserting Flash Objects

You create Flash Buttons and Text at the same time as you insert them—by clicking the Flash Button or Flash Text object in the Insert bar. When you click the object, a dialog box displays, enabling you to customize the button or text that will be created. When you click OK to exit the dialog box, the SWF file is created and the object is inserted.

 Note

For some reason, the code Flash Text nor Flash Button is not XHTML/HTML 4.01–compliant. Not all attribute values are placed within quotes, as XML standards require. To make your code compliant, go to Code view and add quotes around all attributes for your Flash objects.

Figures 20.24 and 20.25 show the dialog boxes for the Flash Button and Flash Text objects. They give you similar choices for specifying type, color, and linkage. The Flash Button dialog box also enables you to choose a button style.

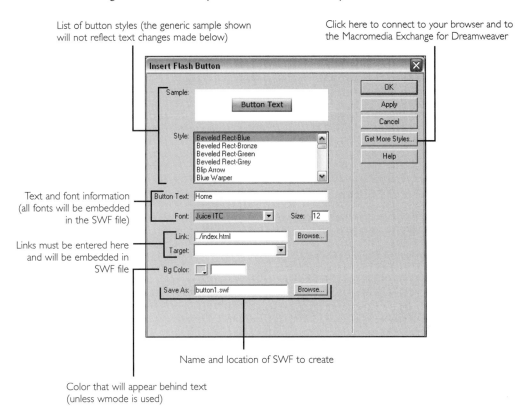

List of button styles (the generic sample shown will not reflect text changes made below)

Click here to connect to your browser and to the Macromedia Exchange for Dreamweaver

Text and font information (all fonts will be embedded in the SWF file)

Links must be entered here and will be embedded in SWF file

Name and location of SWF to create

Color that will appear behind text (unless wmode is used)

Figure 20.24   The Flash Button dialog box, which enables you to choose a button "style" or template to work from, and to customize its text and behavior.

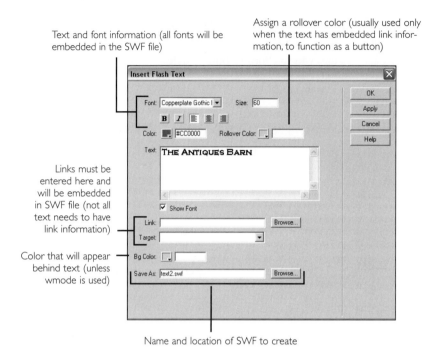

Text and font information (all fonts will be embedded in the SWF file)

Assign a rollover color (usually used only when the text has embedded link information, to function as a button)

Links must be entered here and will be embedded in SWF file (not all text needs to have link information)

Color that will appear behind text (unless wmode is used)

Name and location of SWF to create

Figure 20.25   The Flash Text dialog box, which enables you to specify text and typestyle, colors, and links for the new text.

Button Style (Flash Button Object Only)

When you insert a Flash Button, Dreamweaver creates a SWF file based on one of a dozen or more SWT templates. Each template contains the graphic elements for a different button. In this dialog box, each SWT template is shown as a separate button style. The graphic appearance of the button styles (color, shape, decorations, and so on) is not customizable because this information is built in to the SWT. Any rollover effects also are built in to the button style and can't be edited here.

To get more button styles from the Macromedia Exchange, click the Get More Styles button in the editing dialog box. This will launch your browser and connect you to the Exchange (if your computer is connected to the Internet). When at the Exchange, navigate to the Flash Media category of extensions to see currently available buttons and other Flash-related extensions. Each set of button styles is saved as a Macromedia Extension Package (MXP) file, ready for use with the Extension Manager.

Text and Typestyle (Button and Text Objects)

If you're inserting Flash Text, or if the Flash Button style you're inserting includes a text label, you can determine what text will appear and how it will be formatted. Note that, because fonts are automatically embedded in all Flash movies, you can set the typeface to any font installed in your system. This font will then become part of the SWF movie.

Link and Target Information (Button and Text Objects)

If you want your Flash objects to contain any links, you need to assign the link information in this dialog box. The link will then become part of a getURL() command in the generated SWF file. This is because, unlike images and text, media objects cannot just be wrapped in an <a> tag—so you can't use the Property inspector to assign links. (For more on links and targets, see Chapter 6, "Links and Navigation.")

Background Color (Button and Text Objects)

Like pixel images, Flash content always exists inside its own rectangle. This means that if you're creating Flash Text, or if the Flash Button style you've chosen is not square or rectangular, you'll need to assign it a background color that matches the color of whatever it will be sitting on (page, table cell, layer, and so on). The following tips apply to assigning background colors:

- Color sampling works here like it does throughout Dreamweaver. To match your web page's background color, just position the Flash object dialog box so that you can see some portion of your document behind it, and then click the color swatch; when the eyedropper cursor appears, click to sample the page or other desired background color.

- Background color is not just for Flash Text! Even for rectangular Flash Buttons, you still want to assign a background color, unless you want your button to be surrounded by a little white halo on the page.

- Although this will have an effect only when seen in IE/Windows, you can use the wmode parameter to make the background invisible. After you've exited the dialog box, select the Flash object and use the generic Parameters dialog box from the Property inspector to assign wmode=transparent.

Previewing Your Work (Button and Text Objects)

Note that the dialog box offers only limited preview capabilities as you're creating the SWF. You can preview in general what a button style will look like, but other than that, you have no visual feedback as you're working. This is because, as you're making your

choices in the dialog box, Dreamweaver has not yet created the SWF file it will be inserting, so there's nothing to preview. If you're using the dialog box to create a new Flash
object, instead of editing an existing one, you can't even use the Apply button to see your
changes in the Document window, because Dreamweaver can't apply changes to a SWF
it hasn't created yet. For this reason, creating Flash Button and Text objects usually
involves several trips to the editing dialog box.

Working with Flash Objects

After inserted, the Flash Button or Text is coded into your HTML the same way that any
SWF file would be, using `<object>` and `<embed>` tags. Just like any Flash movie, you can
assign any of the parameters listed in Table 20.1. By default, Dreamweaver assigns Flash
Text objects a scale value of `exactfit`, allowing nonproportional scaling. Unlike standard Flash movies, the movie contents are always visible in Dreamweaver Design view,
meaning you don't have to use the Property inspector's Play button to preview them.
This makes resizing more intuitive, because you don't have to stop the playback before
using the object's resize handles. Here are a few other things to consider when working
with these Flash objects.

Editing

You edit a Flash Button or Text object by going to the Property inspector and clicking the
Edit button or by double-clicking the object itself. Either method reopens the original
Flash object dialog box, ready to accept customization changes. Be aware that, because
SWF files can't be edited after creation, when you open the dialog box, make changes,
and click OK, Dreamweaver is generating a new SWF, not editing the existing one.

Undoing

Again because Dreamweaver is creating SWF files as it goes, you can't use Edit > Undo
or the History panel to undo edits made to Flash text or buttons. It makes sense when
you think about it—when you perform your edits, Dreamweaver creates an uneditable
SWF file and saves it to your hard drive. Because that file is not editable, and is already
saved, there's nothing to undo. The only way to undo changes to Flash Text and Button
objects is to reopen the editing dialog box and manually change things back to the way
they were.

Resizing

An obvious statement, but one worth repeating: Flash objects are resizable. Have a blast,
with no worries about losing image quality if you scale an object up.

Duplicating

After you've created a Flash object, you can of course duplicate it as you would any page element (copy and paste, or Option/Ctrl-drag). Be aware, however, that each duplicate is an instance of the same SWF file. To change the text, color, link information, or other embedded properties in a Flash object, you'll need to tell Dreamweaver to generate a new SWF file, instead of replacing the original. The procedure is as follows:

Tip

Every program has its own way of handling dragging to duplicate. To Ctrl-drag in Dreamweaver/Windows, click the Flash button and hold the mouse button down until the cursor changes to an arrow with a dotted square; then press Ctrl, and a plus sign (+) will appear in the square; then drag. If you don't wait for the cursor change, the duplication might not work.

1. Duplicate the Flash Button or Text object in the Document window.

2. Double-click the new object to open its editing dialog box, and make whatever changes you like.

3. Before closing the dialog box, go to the Save As Input field at the bottom of the dialog box, and enter a new filename.

4. Click OK to exit the dialog box. Dreamweaver will now generate a second SWF for you.

Exercise 20.5   Populating a Page with Flash Buttons and Text

It's time to create yet another Art Gecko home page! This time, you use **gecko_banner.swf** for the top banner, but create your own navigation sidebar from Flash Button objects. Then you'll dress up the text headings by replacing them with Flash Text.

1. From the **chapter_20** folder, open **gecko_flashobjects.html**.

2. First, replace those boring headings. Select `Welcome to Art Gecko` and delete it. With the insertion point still in position, go to the Media tab of the Insert bar and click the Flash Text object. Create a new `Welcome to Art Gecko` heading, using whatever font, size, style, and color your heart desires.

   Leave the Link field and rollover color swatch blank; you don't need your heading text to link anywhere.

   For a filename, you'll probably want to choose something more descriptive than **text1.swf**. Set the filename to **welcome.swf**.

Finally, don't forget to set the background color to match the page color, or your new heading will appear in its own little white box.

When everything is set, click OK to close the dialog box.

3. Back in Design view, resize the new Flash heading until it's just the right size and shape for you. Note that the `scale` parameter for this Flash object defaults to `exactfit`, so you can squish and stretch the type if you like. (*Warning*: Typographic purists frown on this sort of activity. Resizing type nonproportionally distorts the letter shapes and can make them ugly.)

4. To replace the `What's New at Art Gecko?` heading, start by deleting the text heading that's currently there. Then copy the Flash Text heading you created in the previous step, and paste it into position where the text heading was. Double-click the new Flash Text heading, change the wording to **What's new at Art Gecko?**, and use the Save As Input field to enter a new filename—call the new file **whatsnew.swf**.

5. Next, add your own sidebar buttons. With the insertion point in the sidebar table cell, go to the Objects panel and click the Flash Button object. Choose any button style you like, as long as it includes a text label.

For a text label, type in **Wall Hangings**. Format the type any way you please. Because you won't be able to preview the type without creating the button, you have to guess at what type size will be appropriate.

For the link, browse to **ArtFiles/art1.html**. For the filename, enter **art1_button.swf**. And don't forget to set the background color!

After you have finished, click OK to close the dialog box.

6. Back in Design view, you might discover you don't like the button's size or the size of the type you put in it. You can resize the button by dragging its selection handles. (Note that the scale parameter for this Flash object has been set to show all, so the button maintains its proportions as you scale it. You can, of course, change this to `exactfit` if you like, although you risk making the button and its label look ugly.) To resize the text label in relation to the button, you have to double-click to reenter the Flash Button dialog box and change the number in the Type Size field. Keep tweaking the button until you like how it looks on your page.

7. You have three more buttons to create. You can start by copying and pasting the Flash Button you just created three times.

To change each Flash Button's text and link information, double-click the button to open the editing dialog box; change whatever settings you need to; then, in the Save As field, enter a new filename for the new SWF file that must be generated.

Note

It's crucial, when duplicating Flash Text or Buttons, to change the filename in the Save As Input field. If you don't remember this step, you'll be changing the original SWF file you duplicated from.

8. After you have finished, your page should look something like the one shown in Figure 20.26. Preview in a browser to check it all out.

Figure 20.26   The **gecko_flashobjects.html** home page, with Flash objects in place.

Using Flash Objects to Trigger JavaScript Commands

What if you want to use your Flash Button or Text object not as a standard link, but as a link that triggers a JavaScript action? You can't just select a Flash object and assign a behavior to it, as you would with regular text or images, because in HTML the `<object>` and `<embed>` tags don't accept event handlers. (See Chapter 16 for more on this.) JavaScript links, like other links, must be embedded in the Flash file itself.

If you read the earlier section on sending JavaScript out of Flash movies, however, you already know it's possible to embed a JavaScript command in a Flash link. Therefore, just as you can add links to Flash Button and Text objects, you can add JavaScript links. You just use the `javascript:` keyword, followed by whatever command you want to execute. The Flash Button dialog box shown in Figure 20.27, for instance, will create a button that opens an alert window with the message `Hello, world!`

Figure 20.27   Creating a Flash Button object that will execute a JavaScript command when clicked.

This is fine if you like writing short little JavaScript statements by hand. To execute more complex scripts, write the code as a function in the document <head> and use the previous technique to embed the function call in the Flash object.

By following the procedure described in Chapter 17 for "hijacking" behavior function calls, you can even use the Flash object to trigger a Dreamweaver behavior, adding complex scripting functionality to your Flash object with minimal coding on your part. The steps are as follows:

1. Create a dummy text link—a temporary page element that can be discarded later.

2. Select the text link and use the Behaviors panel to apply the desired behavior, configuring the behavior as you like.

3. Switch to Code view and find the text link, along with its function call. Copy the function call (everything between the quotation marks, after the onClick event handler).

4. Create the Flash button. In the button's dialog box, in the Link field, type **javascript:**. Then paste the function call in after the colon.

5. Back in Code view, find and delete the fake text link. Check the document <head> to make sure Dreamweaver hasn't deleted the function itself.

Figure 20.28 shows a Flash Button configured to call the Open Browser Window behavior function.

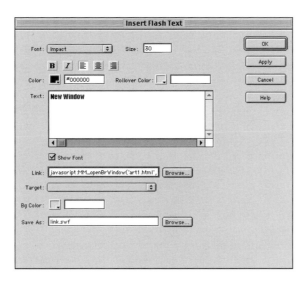

Figure 20.28   "Hijacking" a Dreamweaver behavior's function call for use in a Flash Button.

Summary

In this chapter, you got a taste of the possibilities for integrating Flash into a web site and you saw how Dreamweaver makes this task easier. Each of the different Art Gecko home pages you created represents a different approach to Flash/HTML coexistence. Each has its advantages and disadvantages. In your web design experience, you'll find that each project has its own needs and limitations, so you might use different strategies at different times. No matter what your Flash authoring strategy, though, Dreamweaver's Flash Text, Flash Buttons, and Flash integration features will make publishing and maintaining your Flash web site easier.

Chapter 21

Development Issues: Planning Your Site

Planning the presentation of your web site is one of the most important things you must do when attempting to create a high-quality site. Proper site planning will save you more time than you can imagine.

From determining your target audience, to sitting down and creating a sketch of how you want your site to look, extensive presentation planning directly correlates to successful web site development.

What Do You Want to Do?

The question isn't just about what you want to do today, but also what you want to do a month from now—maybe even a year from now. Defining what you want out of your site before you even start building it will keep your mind focused and your head clear of distractions. You have probably seen some poorly defined web sites. Many "personal" web sites (as well as many professional ones) tend to present a chaotic and cluttered message. Often these jumbled sites result from lack of proper planning.

The first thing you must decide is what you want your site to accomplish. Whether it's to provide the most up-to-date national news or to provide the latest and greatest in the world of computer video cards, your site needs purpose before structure.

When establishing your site goal(s), define them specifically, but don't inhibit your site's potential by chaining it to goals that focus on minutiae. Saying that your site will be "the biggest and best site about electronics" is not very specific. On the other hand, saying your site will "provide detailed instruction on the planting and care of the *picea pungens* (blue spruce tree)" might be a bit too specific. You must achieve a balance. An example of a balanced (and therefore better) site goal is to "provide updated news, weather, sports, dining, and other happenings of Salt Lake City, Utah." This goal targets a specific group (residents of Utah—specifically, Salt Lake City), but it still retains a broad enough scope to leave room for future possibilities (an example might be adding a tourism section later for potential visitors to the city to review places to go, sites to see, and hotels available with rates charged) in your initial design.

You might want a multitiered goal as well. Instead of attempting to realize a whole vision in one scheme, you might decide to divide it into smaller projects, each adding incrementally to the previous ones. You must consider all these factors during the planning process.

Who Is Going to Visit Your Site?

Closely related to your site goals is your target audience. These two things are even interchangeable at times. Sometimes you might identify a specific lifestyle or otherwise-defined group of people you want to attract and then figure out what you need to create for them. In every case, you must determine whom you *want* to visit your site and who *will* be visiting your site. A distinct difference exists between the two. Often you will anticipate a particular audience but end up with a completely different one. It would be extremely difficult, perhaps quixotic, to attempt to create a site for every man, woman, and child. Opinions, priorities, and lifestyles vary with characteristics such as gender, race, nationality, wealth, age, occupation, and so forth.

An understanding about who is most likely to visit your site will help you choose how to promote the site as well as decide on the type of advertising (if any) you want. Identification of your target audience also will enable you to create meta tags, which effectively drive traffic to your site. (For more information on meta tags, refer to Chapter 7, "Utilizing Head Content.") Another consideration is the flexibility of your target audience goals. It's all about demographics; choosing the right groups of people to target will maximize your effectiveness and success. This must be flexible as demographics change and so should your target audience goals. A few modifications to your goals, for instance, might double your number of visitors.

Another important factor to consider after you have determined who will come to your site is how they will get there. Whether you're creating a site for a company intranet or a financial advice site, knowing how your visitors will access your site is very important. For instance, many companies use a uniform operating system and browser. In such cases, you might decide to include browser-specific features. Maybe you're creating a web site that offers retirement real estate in Florida. Your target audience might be of the 55 to 70 age group, and you're estimating that most are not up to date on the newest hardware and software. If so, compatibility with older browser versions and slower hardware might be paramount.

Along the same lines, you might opt for a multiversion site. Although this might involve more work, it offers a few distinct advantages. Users with slower systems won't have to watch choppy Flash intros, whereas visitors with screaming systems and DSL connections can enjoy every last ounce of them. An increasing number of wireless web browsers are becoming available as well. Whether they're PDAs or cellular phones, these stripped-down versions of web browsers will certainly gain momentum in the near future. Remember to consider all the things when defining your target audience.

What Are They Going to See?

After determining the purpose of your site and the target audience, you should begin to develop possible structuring schemes for the site. At the top of the list should be considerations such as the overall design and layout, as well as the navigation you will provide that enables users to easily go from one area to the next. The following sections discuss these topics in detail.

Design and Layout

During the design and layout phase, your creative juices have to flow. You can save a lot of time in the long run by creating a very basic idea or sketch of how you want the site to look and feel. Likewise, a detailed plan now will save you a lot of time and grief later. Such a plan enables you to logically decide on content placement or where the navigation items will best be utilized. During this time, you also can view the site in your mind as a single object, not a collection of various pages. If you create the look and feel before you start adding content, you will most likely maintain consistency throughout your site. If visitors are easily confused by how your site looks, chances are good that they won't hang around long enough to see whether it has valuable content.

Navigation

The navigational method you choose to implement will be one of the most scrutinized aspects of your site. Whether vocally or subconsciously, each user will rate and remember how easy it was to go from page to page. If the interface that you provide is intuitive, simple, and well organized, you can bet that visitors will stick around a while longer, because they can actually navigate and find what it is they are there for. The alternative is that they get frustrated with obscure navigation systems, leave your site, and generally don't return.

When choosing a navigation structure for your site, remember your own casual web browsing experiences. Your own experiences will help make you aware of many important design issues. You have undoubtedly become frustrated sometimes by poorly formatted content or a hard-to-understand navigation bar. Likewise, you have most likely run across some sites that just amaze you with their simplicity and intuitiveness. In the future, make a mental (or physical) note of such sites for reference and try to determine what made them so easy to navigate. After all, what good is your content if your visitors cannot find it?

Note

Have you ever noticed that you can navigate some sites without actually considering every navigational element? Sites that accomplish this capture the largest audience. Try to make your navigation items as descriptive and inclusive as possible. If users have to figure out your navigation scheme, then it might be too complex or muddled.

Other Considerations

When designing a site, you should consider a few other things. The importance of these issues varies from site to site, but to some degree all will definitely be factors in how a site functions and appears.

The two most potentially restricting aspects of creating a web site are money and time. Money will strongly influence the type of technology used, as well as the detail and originality put into the site, and it will possibly dictate how the initial content will be presented to the end user.

Certain technologies—such as Flash animations, PHP or other database-driven applications, and custom-written Perl or CGI scripts—tend to cost your client more than basic HTML. The use of these features will add to the overhead of your client's site cost. Designers charge not just for the time used to pump out content, but also for the time it takes to create a unique and catchy design for the site. Basic designs or template-based sites obviously cost less than custom-designed ones.

Time is another important consideration—and often a constraint as well—to assess. If a company asks you to complete a site in two weeks, the length of time allowed for site design will be significantly less than if the same company could wait two months. You might opt for a prebuilt, template-based site for a temporary solution and then create an original site as a second phase. Then again, what if the budget doesn't allow for that type of double-site creation? You will find that the time frame for completion and available finances generally conflict. It's your responsibility to find the happy medium between time and budget constraints.

Note

Project Seven Development (www.projectseven.com) creates extremely effective and professional templates for Dreamweaver. They call them *design packs*. These include all source HTML, images (PNG, JPG, and GIF), CSS files, as well as detailed instructions in HTML format that are required to create small or large sites. Many times, they also include custom Extensions for Dreamweaver, made specifically to bring that design pack to life. These are especially useful for those who have limited design capability or for clients who want to save on the costs of their site.

Organizing Your Files

After all this planning, you are probably itching to start cranking out page after page of your upcoming masterpiece. That's fine; but where are you going to put these files? You have already figured out how the site should be structured visually; now it's time to think about how you should physically create the directories and files that you'll need.

When you create a site with Dreamweaver, you start by creating a local version of the site on your hard drive. In fact, this is how you should always start a site. First define the local root folder within Dreamweaver, and then create the site itself. Dreamweaver is not designed to maintain local sites that aren't on your local machine or mapped network drive, so you must have a local copy. This is called a *local site*, and it should have the exact same file and directory hierarchy as the public or remote site. Keeping them the same will make it easier for you and others to understand. In fact, doing this will prevent major problems with future site maintenance. It also will enable you to utilize some of Dreamweaver's site-management features, such as tracking links and the Synchronize command. This, of course, has been said tongue in cheek. There is not always a requirement to have the local and remote site exactly the same, and there are situations when you shouldn't have them the same. For instance, if you are a lone developer, do not upload your **_notes**, **Templates**, or **Library** folders (doing so could allow people to steal your source files if they find them), but if you are collaborating with someone in another city, then you might have to upload these referenced source files so that the job can be completed. It can be said that the **cgi-bin** folder does not need to reside on your local machine, but it is better to have duplication that can be used as a backup than not have it at all and have to start from scratch when your server or local hard drive dies.

Tip

Maintaining a copy of the live site locally not only makes it easier to work with in Dreamweaver, but also provides a level of data redundancy. If the live site should become corrupt or experience data loss for some reason, you can always just upload the local site again.

Note

You also can store your local copy on a floppy disk (if there's enough space), a Zip disk, or some other form of rewritable storage medium besides your hard drive. The only possible problem with using removable media is its tendency to become corrupted. If you insist on using this method of local site storage, it's strongly recommended that you back up your data on another medium as well.

Files

Identify the rough number and type of files that you will use in each logical section of the site. You can then begin to determine how they should be organized and separated into subdirectories for easy navigation from the back end. You want to create logical sections, which means that you want to group files together that logically belong in the same directories. Usually this will be very intuitive and shouldn't take much time.

As an example, the National Basketball Association's web site (www.nba.com) divides each team's pages into its own directory. This makes perfect sense. If you need to change information for the Indiana Pacers, you know that every file specifically relating to the team is in the **pacers** subdirectory. See Figure 21.1.

Figure 21.1   The NBA.com's Indiana Pacers web page. Notice the URL path.

While you think through this process, keep in mind that browsers keep a copy of every graphic they download. This is called the *browser cache*, and if you plan ahead, you can utilize this feature to help your pages load faster. By using the same background image source or reusing the navigation bar images as much as possible, the browser will have to download them only once. On additional page views in the same session (sometimes future sessions as well), the browser will load the cached files instead of downloading them again from your server. This typically means faster load times and less bandwidth usage on both the server and the client side, both of which are very good things.

Directories

After you have categorized the logical grouping of your files, you should think about how to further define differences. If your site is large enough, you might want to keep all your images and media files in a place separate from your HTML documents. You also might further divide your media content, such as your SWF or PDF files. Whether you need to do this depends greatly on the size of the site in question. However, doing this will enable you to quickly navigate to the correct file when creating links in your HTML. If you need to edit or replace an image, you'll know its exact location and can avoid wading through a mess of file types.

This is the basic reason computers use a hierarchy of directories to organize data. You "can group a broad subject into a directory and then make additional groupings more specific. These specific directories are children of the main directory and are called *sub-directories*. Figure 21.2 shows a potential site directory structure.

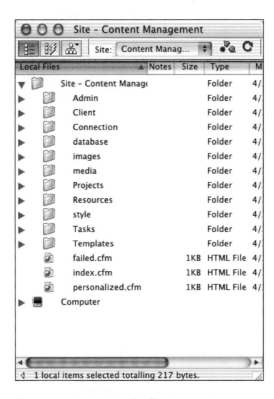

Figure 21.2   One of many ways to organize the files in your site.

Write down possible directory combinations for your project. You might think that this point seems trivial to the success of your site, but I guarantee that you will save an incredible amount of time by following this simple procedure. After you have managed your site for a while, understanding directories and hierarchies will become much more natural and intuitive. As a result, you'll greatly reduce the time needed for this portion of site development.

Before turning to how to set up your site information in Dreamweaver, it's important to emphasize one more point. If you have all the images and other media type content of your site finished before you begin writing the actual HTML, you will find that the document creation process (the process of putting your design and layout into HTML format) will flow much more smoothly. Likewise, creating a basic "shell" or blank document to act as a placeholder for the final version is advantageous. This enables you to establish any internal links at any time, without having to create a new document. When you're working as a team of designers, this might be difficult; but it is highly recommended that, when possible, you create all your images and pages before starting the HTML production.

Interview: Angela C. Buraglia

Business Name: DreamweaverFAQ.com

URL: `http://www.DreamweaverFAQ.com`

What made you decide to start web developing?

I wasn't expecting to become a web developer. It just sort of turned out that way. I was a new mom, and needed to find a way to stay at home with my baby while still earning an income. Shortly before getting pregnant, I'd started a small business selling invitations for special occasions. I was persuaded by family to take that business online. Clueless, I sought out to build my first web site.

The first few times I used Dreamweaver in September 2001, I was completely lost. With nobody to help me, I searched online. I soon found the Macromedia Dreamweaver Newsgroup and my learning process began. I read every post, even though nothing made any sense at the time. I knew I might need it later. I bought a few books and started learning new things. Then about two months later, I attended a conference in Monterey, California. I learned so much in those two days, and I met some great people. Without the support of the newsgroup community, I'd probably have given up.

I built my first web site and was hooked! I knew web development was the way to go. What I didn't realize was how hooked I would get on Dreamweaver itself. Now, I find I spend most of my working hours maintaining DreamweaverFAQ.com, writing tutorials and help files for commercial extensions, and anything else Dreamweaver related that I can.

What is your claim to fame?

I'm not famous! People probably know me best from my involvement in the Macromedia Dreamweaver newsgroup community as a Team Macromedia volunteer. From that involvement, I saw a need for a web site that covered basic and frequently asked questions on the newsgroup. I bought the DreamweaverFAQ.com domain in January 2001, with no intention of using it for at least a year, as I still very much considered myself a "newbie." (Remember, I'd only been working with Dreamweaver seriously since I returned from the conference in November.)

In late March 2001, I started posting to the newsgroup a daily list of questions, answers, and cool resources that I developed with the help of Kindler Chase. As time progressed, we saw a need to put up a web site to host an online version of the list. Kindler gave me some server space at his domain, and we hosted it there temporarily. Unfortunately, Kindler was unable to pursue the site with me as he was already committed to his love of professional cycling. Throughout May and June, I worked on planning, gathering content for, and developing the permanent site: DreamweaverFAQ.com.

Daniel Short, whom I'd met at Monterey, and I began to talk more and more, offered me free server space for the new domain. His helpfulness didn't end there; he got involved and spent countless hours helping me prepare. He built all the ASP functionality into the site including the Style Changer, Font Changer, Snippets Exchange, and all the while had enough patience to teach me along the way. I can't thank Dan enough for all he's done for me; he's like a brother to me.

On June 27, 2001 DreamweaverFAQ.com (a.k.a. DWfaq.com) was launched with three main sections: FAQs, Tutorials, and Resources. The site began with contributions of tutorials from a dozen members of the newsgroup community, each with their very own style (color scheme). Since then, many more tutorial authors [have been added], and the site itself has expanded tremendously.

Over the last year, DWfaq has become practically a full-time job for me, and I wouldn't have it any other way! So, I suppose you could call it my "claim to fame," but I couldn't have gotten there without all the help and generosity I've received over the last year.

I am confident that my involvement with DWfaq and the support of those who have helped me has led me to my most recent accomplishments as the lead technical editor for *Dreamweaver MX Bible* (Wiley Publishing), contributing author to *Dreamweaver MX Magic* (New Riders), and contributing author to *ColdFusion MX Web Application Construction Kit* (Macromedia Press).

What are your thoughts on site planning? Did you plan your site or develop it on-the-fly?

When I built DreamweaverFAQ, I spent a lot of time deciding on the structure of the site. I knew I wanted to break it down into categories and subcategories that would make complete sense to the user. I started off with a pencil and a paper and did a flow chart. I had the home page and the top level, of course. Tutorials, FAQs, Resources, and Help were my second levels. I then broke my second levels down into more specific topics. It's a very simple site structure that makes a lot of sense for users and is great when adding "breadcrumb trail" navigation.

For the most part, I always plan a site in the same way that I described. Sometimes, there is an element of "developing on-the-fly," but the core structure is always established first.

One of the most important things for me when developing a site is keeping naming conventions and folder structure intuitive and organized. If ever the site gets to be what I feel is sloppy, I take advantage of Dreamweaver's Site panel and move files and folders from there so that all links to moved files are corrected automatically for me. It saves a ton of time being organized when you're managing larger sites. I've been known to say many times, that I get annoyed browsing for files because it wastes so much time. An organized Site panel makes things just so much faster and easier.

Did you allow for expansion, or was that an afterthought?

The structure of DreamweaverFAQ is so simple that there is always room for expansion, although there are some limitations to the design. When I developed the design, I knew that there was room for a couple more categories on the navigation bar. What I didn't expect was that we'd eventually run out of room. I didn't foresee that there could be so many main categories! I planned for it to some degree, but as design limitations crept upon me, I had to re-arrange things and adapt for those limitations.

The great thing about it is, with such a solid and organized structure in place, I can easily change the layout of the site (when the time comes) without disrupting any of the functionality. Header and footer information are stored in Server-Side Includes, thus allowing me to completely change the look of the site or navigation elements by updating only two files on the server.

Would you recommend people spend time planning prior to development?

Absolutely! It will eventually come to a point where you will develop your own way of organizing a site and using the same naming conventions. For example, I always have a 1×1 transparent GIF file in my **images** folder named **shim.gif** in every site. I always name my main CSS file **master.css**.

The more you plan and organize before you begin, the better off you'll be down the road. Of course, you can plan as you go along, but there can be a danger in that if you don't plan ahead—you can run into issues that will slow production. Knowing what you need to get the job done before you begin is very important. If you like to plan as you go along, at least have a good idea of the bigger picture while doing so, [to] be able to move along smoothly.

Choosing a Web Host

The final thing you really should consider when beginning a project is how people will be able to access the site when it's done. Deciding on the best web host is never an easy thing. The following system is a solid foundation to help determine which host best fulfils your needs and budget:

1. Determine the site's requirements. (Is the site going to be built using a server-side language? Do you need database services? How many email addresses will the client require? How much space and bandwidth do you think the site will require? Will the site require immediate e-commerce or not, or possibly in the future?)

2. Find several web hosts that meet these requirements.

3. Weed out the companies that don't give extensive information in their plan details. Depending on the number of hosts at this point, you also might throw away those that just don't "feel right."

4. Visit various newsgroups and online forums. Ask people about any negative *or* positive experiences with the hosts in your list. Bad experiences help you know which hosts to eliminate. By the same token, asking (and receiving) positive responses might help you rank those that remain.

5. After narrowing the list to a few companies, try to determine which might best accommodate future needs.

The following sections discuss in detail some of the more important aspects of picking the best web host.

Determining Site Requirements

Although this might seem obvious, many people sign up with a web host, only to find out the host doesn't support everything they need. From a developer's viewpoint, sometimes some "extra" settings on the server side seem default. Remember this isn't always the case. If your site requires anything beyond basic services, be sure the host supports such requirements. Some common site requirements include the following:

- Server-side scripting languages such as PHP, ASP, ColdFusion, JSP, and so on.
- Database support including Oracle, MySQL, MS Access, MS SQL Server 2000, mSQL, and so on.
- Most e-commerce packages.
- Email—Although some clients opt to run their own email services, many will not.
- SSI (server-side includes).
- CGI/Perl access.
- Server space and bandwidth allotted.

Note

You might think some of the features in this list should be considered "basic" and included by default. Many times they are; however, some hosts will undoubtedly neglect to offer at least a few of these services.

Tip

Sometimes I don't know everything a site is going to need until I start working on it. In such cases, I find it effective to write down each requirement as I work on that part of the site. That way I'm sure to get everything I need.

Comparing Companies

After you have determined what your site needs to function properly, you can begin the relentless search for a host. Several available resources can help you with this. Search engines will return hundreds or thousands of individual companies. You also can find web sites dedicated to listing many hosting companies. One such web site is TopHosts.com (`www.tophosts.com`). They list companies located all over, including the United States, Canada, and the United Kingdom.

Sites such as TopHosts.com are good resources primarily because they provide similar information about several providers in a compact space. This enables you to easily compare pricing and features.

After you have compiled a list of companies that meet your needs, you might want to see which ones provide additional services, such as the following:

- Phone support (preferably 24 hours)
- Excellent email support

- Database access (MySQL, PostgreSQL, SQL Server 2000, mSQL, and so on)
- Domain redirects (pointing additional domains to subdirectories on the same account)
- Comprehensive online FAQs
- Easy site/user management
- Online and/or automatic billing
- Reasonable prices
- Bandwidth speed and capacity
- Reliability and uptime
- E-commerce functionality
- Domain registration
- Web-based email access
- Reseller capability

Remember that a good web host for your site probably doesn't need all of these features; most would go unused. That said, always ask for proof of a provider's uptime history. If it's relatively shaky, drop that host from consideration immediately!

Planning for the Future

A common mistake is underestimating the growth of a site. This especially holds true when databases are used to store various site and user information. Make sure the potential web hosts provide for future expandability at a reasonable cost. It is a pain in the neck to change providers after you have everything up and running. Consider the following elements and how much of each your site might require in the future:

- Monthly transfer in gigabytes (GB)
- Disk storage in megabytes (MB)
- Number and size of any databases
- Future email needs

Although this list is not exhaustive, considering these items will definitely reduce the chance that your site outgrows the web host.

Common Mistakes

By now, you have all the knowledge necessary to make an informed decision abut where your site should be hosted. As a final cautionary measure, Table 21.1 shows some possible pitfalls (and solutions) you might run across in your search. Good luck!

Table 21.1   Possible Pitfalls and Solutions When Searching for a Web Site Host

Symptom	Possible Cause	Solution
Noticeably low prices	The provider might be significantly overselling its bandwidth or have limited/cheap access to the Internet.	Check with the provider to confirm its average bandwidth utilization. Also be sure to find out what type of access the provider has outside of its network.
Vague features listing	This might point toward a provider who is actually just a "reseller" for a larger host. It also might show that its services are geared toward "basic" account types.	Email or call the provider to clarify any confusion. Also consider just dropping that host from consideration.
Lack of phone numbers	This could indicate a "half-hearted" hosting attempt, especially by a reseller. The host might just want to make a quick buck.	Look for phone numbers. Email the service department and see how quickly you get a response. Sometimes hosts might rely more heavily on email-based support to track issues. If the reply time is within a few hours, the host is probably okay.
Windows 2000 *or* UNIX/Linux (but not both)	This host might be extremely new or inexperienced in anything except the platform it provides.	On the same note, the host might intentionally specialize on one operating system for a purpose. This should not be an issue in most cases; if it is, however, drop the host.

Tip

A final word on web hosting: If (or when) you decide to change hosts, be sure to maintain the old account for four to seven days after changing the service to the new host. Some DNS servers require significant time to update. Having a four to seven day overlap will ensure uninterrupted access for everyone.

Summary

This chapter focused on three main areas of site development: presentation, organization (both on the user and server side), and finding a proper web host.

By now you should be aware of issues such as who your target (and *real*) audience is and the need to plan for various viewing methods. You also learned in this chapter about general attributes that make site navigation effective. This chapter also discussed the importance of organizing your files on the server in a logical manner. You learned in this chapter about site requirements to keep in mind while searching for a company to host your new web site. And you now know how to compare hosts and how to avoid common mistakes.

The following list summarizes the topics covered in the remaining chapters in this section:

- **Chapter 22, "Local Site Management."** This chapter discusses how to define and use your local site. File and link management are discussed as well. This chapter also discusses the Assets panel.

- **Chapter 23, "Site Publishing and Maintenance."** This chapter discusses the inner workings of remote site setup, and how to work with the remote site. You also learn how to keep your local and remote site synchronized through Dreamweaver.

- **Chapter 24, "Workplace Collaboration."** This chapter discusses some of the challenges of working as a team (and also poses possible solutions). The Check In/Out system, as well as other server-based version control systems, is covered. You also learn how to create reports in Dreamweaver that increase productivity and efficiency.

- **Chapter 25, "Templates and Libraries."** This chapter discusses how to create and manage somewhat dynamic content using Dreamweaver Templates and Library items. Server-side includes are discussed as well.

Chapter 22

Local Site Management

No web page is an island. In web development, each document you work on exists as part of a collective. In that collective might be linked pages, images, multimedia files, and other resource files. All of these parts must be tracked, uploaded, and maintained as a unit. Managing all of those files can be a daunting task. Exactly which files need to be part of the web site? How should they organized into directories and subdirectories? What colors are to be using sitewide? What about external style sheets or script documents? What if you decide, halfway through building the site, that you really should have been more consistent in naming your pages, or that you want your images in their own folder? You can't even think of uploading your site to a web server and sharing it with the world until you have these management concerns taken care of.

Luckily for those of us who are more creative than organized, Dreamweaver offers a whole set of easy-to-use, powerful tools to make local site management a breeze, from link checking to sitewide searches and diagnostic tools to keeping track of files for you. Dreamweaver will even help you visualize your site's logical structure as you build it. Is it magic? No, it's just good organization.

This chapter discusses the process of defining a local site in Dreamweaver, how to work with the Site panel, and Dreamweaver tools available for file and asset management.

How Dreamweaver Handles Local Sites

At the core of Dreamweaver site management is the concept of the local site. The *local site* is a complete version of your web site that exists on your computer. It consists of all the same documents and resources that will eventually become your published web site, in the same arrangement of files and folders. Your local site is your developmental testing ground. You store pages you are currently working on as well as any other resources in the local site. You create an organized folder structure for your elements and manage your page content from here. Local site tools built into Dreamweaver allow you to perform spell checks, find-and-replace operations, and consistency checks.

You define a local site in Dreamweaver by pointing Dreamweaver to the folder on your computer where you plan to store all of your local site files. This folder is called the *local root folder*. After you've designated a folder as the local root folder, Dreamweaver will treat any item placed within that folder as part of your site. To add a document or resource to your site, simply put it in this folder; to remove a document or resource without actually deleting it from your computer, move it out of this folder. All the while you're working on the various files in your site, Dreamweaver is watching the local root folder, keeping track of which files are being added or removed, noting whenever files or folders are renamed or rearranged, and examining the relationships between documents to make sure the site's relative links are accurate. The local root folder is integral to your Dreamweaver site-building experience.

If you've done any of the exercises in the book so far, you've already been asked to define a local site and work within a local root folder. If you tried to go through the exercise without defining a local site, you probably discovered that some of the exercise steps didn't work as expected. While it is possible to build individual documents without defining a local site, it's standard practice to always work within the framework of a local site, even for simple projects. Outside the context of a local root folder, Dreamweaver might not be able to calculate document-relative links between files.

Defining a Local Site

Creating and managing sites in Dreamweaver is done through the Edit Sites command. Setting up each site's options is done in the Site Definition dialog box.

To create a new site or change the settings of an existing site, using the Site Definition dialog box. Choose Site > Edit Sites (or, in the Site panel toolbar, choose Edit Sites from the Sites pop-up menu). This opens the Edit Sites dialog box. This dialog box is the central launching point from which you can click New to create a new site or Edit to change the settings for an existing site (see Figure 22.1).

To create a new site without going through the Edit Sites dialog box, you can also choose Site > New Site.

Figure 22.1   Managing sites through the Edit Sites dialog box.

The Site Definition dialog box offers two modes for setting up your site information: Basic mode (also known as the Site Wizard) and Advanced mode. Each of these modes lets you assign settings for the local site, the remote site, application server connectivity, and a host of other categories. The basic core of site definition is always establishing the local site. While the Basic mode offers a friendlier interface, especially handy for defining complex dynamic sites, Advanced mode gives you more control over your settings and in the long run offers more efficient access to your site's information. Fortunately, the two modes are not mutually exclusive; it's simple to toggle between them and see your site definition from both perspectives. The following sections look at setting up a local site using each mode in turn.

Defining a Site in Basic Mode (the Site Wizard)

If you're brand new to creating sites (or if you're new to creating dynamic sites that involve complex server setups), the Site Wizard eases you into the process gently by asking you a series of fairly simple questions. Answer the questions and when you're done you'll have created a site with all basic settings in place. While the Site Wizard does not allow you to set any but the basic site information, it's a good place to begin and a great learning tool.

To define a local site using the Site Wizard, start by accessing the Site Definition dialog box (as described earlier, by choosing Site > New Site or Site > Edit Site and click the New button). Bring the Basic tab to the front to access the wizard. As the interface shows (see Figure 22.2), the site information is divided into questions about Editing Files, Testing Files, and Sharing Files. The local site is defined by answering questions in the three Editing Files screens.

Figure 22.2   The Site Wizard (Basic tab of the Site Definition dialog box) ready to begin defining a local site.

- **What would you like to name your site? (Editing Files)?** This creates the name Dreamweaver will use to identify your site for its own internal purposes. Your site's name will appear in the Edit Sites dialog box and in the Site panel's Edit Sites pop-up menu. Because the name won't ever be used by the browser or web server, it can contain spaces and special characters. Choose a descriptive name that will be easy for you to recognize in a menu. When you're done, click Next to progress to the next screen.

- **Do you want to work with a server technology? (Editing Files, Part 2)?** This determines what kind of default document Dreamweaver will associate with your site (HTML, CFML, ASP, PHP, JSP). Unless you're planning to create a dynamic site that uses database connectivity, answer no to this question. When you're done, click Next to progress to the next screen.

Note

See Chapters 26 and following for instructions on setting up dynamic sites.

- **How do you want to work with your files during development? (Editing Files, Part 3)?** This determines where your local root needs to be created, and how it will be accessed. Since the whole point of a local site is that it is local, the recommended answer to this question is the default, "Edit local copies on my machine, then upload to server when ready." Don't change this option unless you really must work another way.

- **Where on your computer do you want to store your local files? (Editing Files, Part 4)?** If you're going to edit your site using files on your computer, as recommended, you must then tell Dreamweaver which folder on your computer will be the local root folder. To answer this question, click the Browse button and use the Choose Local Root Folder dialog box to select a folder. (If you haven't yet created a folder to use for this, use the New button in the dialog box to do so now.) When you've answered this question, click Next to progress to the next screen.

- **How do you connect to your remote server?** Assuming you are not working with a server technology (the question in Editing Files, Part 2 screen), the Site Wizard will skip past the Testing Files category and proceed directly to Sharing Files. You don't need to worry about sharing files until you're ready to define a remote site. Choose None from the dropdown menu and click Next to progress to the next screen

- **Summary.** The final screen that appears is the Summary. This shows you how the questions you've answered translate into settings for your new site. If you don't like any of the settings, use the Back button to change them. If you want to set further options not available in the Site Wizard, bring the Advanced tab to the front. If you're happy with your summary, click Done to close the dialog box and create your site. Dreamweaver creates the intial site cache for your new local site. What Dreamweaver is doing is looking at all the files you have in the folder you have designated as your root folder and creating an internal list of them for use later.

Defining a Site Using the Advanced Method

After you have the hang of defining sites, you'll probably find it more efficient to use the Advanced tab of the Site Definition dialog box to set up and edit your site information (see Figure 22.3). This tab allows you to set all the same basic information that the Site Wizard collects, plus many more options. The information is presented in logical categories, but without the friendly question-and-answer approach of the wizard.

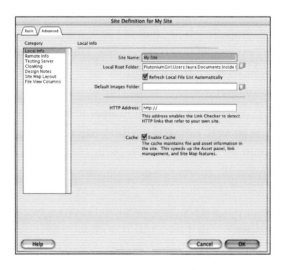

Figure 22.3   The Advanced tab of the Site Definition dialog box.

To define a local site using the Advanced method, start by accessing the Site Definition dialog box (Site > New Site or Site > Edit Sites > New) and click the Advanced tab to make it active. The site information is divided into categories covering all aspects of static and dynamic sites. To define a local site, only the information in the Local Info category (shown in Figure 22.3) need be filled in, and only two items from this category are absolutely required to define a site.

Required information in the Local Info category (this information is also collected by the Site Wizard):

- **Site Name**. This enables you to specify the name with which Dreamweaver will associate with your site. This is the same information collected in the Editing Files screen of the Site Wizard.

- **Local Root Folder**. This sets the local folder on your computer that will be used as the root for your site. Click the Browse button to select this folder. This is the same information collected in the Editing Files, Part 3 screen of the Site Wizard.

Optional information in the Local Info category (this information cannot be set in the Site Wizard) is as follows:

- **Refresh Local File List Automatically**. Selecting this option automatically refreshes the local file list every time files are copied to your local site. This is a handy feature, so it's a good idea to leave it selected. If you choose to not enable it, however, you can manually refresh the local file list in the Site panel by choosing View > Refresh (Windows), or Site > Site Files View > Refresh Local (Mac). If you have used the Site Wizard to define your site, this item defaults to true.

- **HTTP Address**. Enter the complete HTTP address your site will eventually have as its root when it is uploaded to the web server, for example `http://www.mydomain.com`. If your site uses absolute links between site documents, Dreamweaver can use this information to verify these links when you perform link checking operations. If you won't be using absolute links for internal site navigation, you can leave this field alone. (See the section on "Managing Links" later in this chapter for more information on this.) If you have used the Site Wizard to define your site, this address defaults to `http://`.

- **Enable Cache**. As discussed earlier, Dreamweaver automatically keeps track of file and asset information for your local site as you work. It does this by maintaining a *site cache*, or temporary storage area, in your computer's memory. For small to medium sites, using the cache can significantly speed up sitewide operations like Find-and-Replace, Spell Check, and link management. For very large sites, the site cache can actually slow these operations down (because there's too much information for Dreamweaver to remember). A good general strategy is to enable the cache when you first define a site, and if you later notice that sitewide operations are sluggish, try disabling it. If you have used the Site Wizard to define your site, this item defaults to true.

If you like using the Site Wizard to set up your basic site information but want to customize these optional settings, remember that you can switch back and forth between the Basic and Advanced tabs of the Site Definition dialog box as often as you like.

Importing Sites from Other Programs

Sometimes you're not creating sites from scratch. You might inherit an existing site from someone else who may or may not have worked in Dreamweaver. You might have started building the site yourself in another web authoring program or text editor. You might be asking yourself, "How do I import that Front Page or GoLive or other site into Dreamweaver?"

Because most web file formats are non-proprietary, you don't need to do anything special to "import" the standard files in those sites for use in Dreamweaver. Just use File > Open to open any HTML, ASP, JSP, CSS, or other document in Dreamweaver and start working on it. To create a Dreamweaver site based on pages built in other programs, just create a local site as described in the previous sections and put your HTML and other documents in the local root folder. Those files are now official members of your Dreamweaver site in full standing and with full rights and privileges. Their code might not be written or formatted exactly like Dreamweaver code, but that won't stop Dreamweaver from handling it. Any code that a browser can understand, Dreamweaver can understand.

Note

There is a chance your imported pages might include code that Dreamweaver can't display in Design view. This is mostly true of hand-coded pages that include extensive embedded scripting (JavaScript or server-side scripting) or CSS.

The only files you won't be able to just open and use in Dreamweaver are application-specific files like GoLive stationary files or Front Page template files. Like Dreamweaver templates and library items, those files are not intended for use by the browser, so they're not in a standardized format the Dreamweaver can process. To re-create the functionality of these pages, you'll need to build Dreamweaver equivalents.

Tip

Tip for Mac users: After you've started working on pages in Dreamweaver, you might want to change their file creators to Dreamweaver so you can open them in Dreamweaver by double-clicking on them in the Finder. Various utilities, such as File Buddy and Creator Changer, are available for this.

Managing Multiple Sites

Dreamweaver lets you create as many sites as you need. Each site has to have at least its local information specified, though it can also include remote and other information. When you choose Site > Edit Sites, the Edit Sites dialog box will list all defined sites on your computer. You can also see a list of defined sites by opening the Site window and selecting site > Open Site in the Dreamweaver 4 layout. If you are using the Dreamweaver MX layouts you can open the site panel and use the dropdown to switch between sites.

Unless you have no sites at all defined (for example, the Edit Sites dialog box shows no defined sites), there will always be a current site. The current site will show in the Site panel and its name will be checked in the Site > Open Sites submenu. To switch the current site to a different site, go to Site > Open Site and choose the desired site from the submenu, or use the Site pop-up menu in the Site panel toolbar.

To change the settings for an existing site, choose Site > Edit Sites to access the Edit Sites dialog box; then select the site you want to edit and click Edit.

To delete a site, choose Site > Edit Sites to access the Edit Sites dialog box; then select the site you want to delete and click Remove. Note that deleting a site does not delete any of the files that are part of that site from your computer, nor does it change the local root folder in any way. It only deletes the site information you specified when you created the site—including the site name and the designation of a specific folder as the local root folder.

Exercise 22.1   Defining the Grandpa's Ice Cream Web Site

In this exercise, you'll turn start with a set of files that have already been created and define a site to let you work with them using the Dreamweaver site management tools.

Before you start, copy the files from the **chapter_22** folder on the CD to your hard drive. These files will contain all the pages and resources for the Grandpa's site. But as of now, Dreamweaver doesn't know they're supposed to be thought of as a site. While you could work with the files individually in Dreamweaver, the program won't treat them as an organized site until you tell it to.

1. You'll start by setting the site up with the Site Wizard. In Dreamweaver, go to Site > New Sites to open the Site Definition dialog box. If the Basic tab isn't in front, click it to bring it to the front. (The Basic tab is the Site Wizard, remember!)

2. In the first screen, you're asked what you would like to name your site. Call your site **Grandpa's Ice Cream**. (Notice that you're allowed to use spaces and even an apostrophe in your site name. That's because it will only be used to identify the site within Dreamweaver, and special characters don't confuse Dreamweaver.) Click Next to proceed to the next screen.

3. In the next screen, you're asked if you want to use a server technology. Select the radio button next to No. Click next to proceed to the next screen.

4. In the next screen, you're asked where you want to edit your local files. Leave the default option selected (Edit Local Copies on My Machine, Then Upload to Server When Ready). Then click the Browse button to show Dreamweaver where your local files will be stored. Browse to the **chapter_22** folder you copied from the CD before you began this exercise. Click next to proceed to the next screen.

5. Now you're asked about your remote server. Since you're not ready for that yet, choose None from the pop-up menu. Click next to proceed to the next screen.

6. Dreamweaver now shows you a summary of the information you have entered (see Figure 22.4). Congratulations! You've defined a site. Click Done to close the Site Definition dialog box. You'll get an alert window telling you the site cache is about to be created. Click OK to close that. After a few seconds, your Site panel will look like the one shown in Figure 22.5. Your site is already full of files because the folder you defined as your local root folder (the **chapter_22** folder) had those files in them. It doesn't matter whether or not those files were created in Dreamweaver.

Figure 22.4   The Site Definition Summary screen for the Grandpa's Ice Cream site.

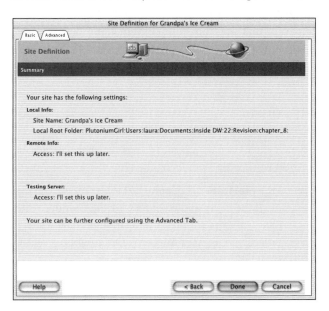

Figure 22.5   The Site panel for the Grandpa's Ice Cream site.

7. After you've defined the site, you can change any of its settings any time you like by returning to the Site Definition dialog box. To do this, choose Site > Edit Sites. When the dialog box appears, select the Grandpa's Ice Cream site and click Edit. Here you are, back in the Site Definition dialog box!

8. This time, click the Advanced tab to bring it to the front. From the categories list at the left, choose Local Info. Your local information has been gathered based on the questions you answered in the Site Wizard.

9. The Advanced tab offers you more settings than the wizard did. One new piece of information you can save is the absolute URL that Grandpa's site will have after it's up on the web server. In the HTTP Address field, type **http://www.grandpasicecream.com** (no spaces or special characters here!). The dialog box will look like the one shown in Figure 22.6.

10. Click OK to close the dialog box. If Dreamweaver needs to re-create the site cache, allow it to do so.

Figure 22.6   The Local Info screen of the Advanced Site Definition tab for the Grandpa's site.

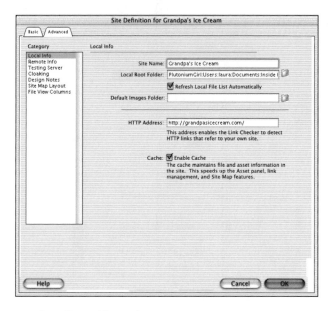

Working in the Site Panel

After you have a site defined, the Dreamweaver Site panel is your interface for performing any and all site-related tasks. It's your window on the world of your site. It's a good idea to always leave it open while you work. Use this window to see your site's files and hierarchical structure at a glance, to perform file management tasks, and more.

Managing the Site Panel

The Site panel is a complex interface, packed to the gills with information and functionality. One of the most essential basic site management skills you can develop for working in Dreamweaver is managing the Site panel itself.

The Site Panel and the Integrated Workspace (Windows)

As introduced back in Chapter 2, Dreamweaver/Windows users now have the choice of viewing the Site panel as a free-standing window floating in front of the rest of the workspace or as a docked panel. To access the Site panel, choose Window > Site, or (Windows only) expand the Files panel group. To use the Site panel as a free-standing window, undock it from its panel group by dragging the Site tab out of the panel dock. To turn it back into a docked panel, drag it back into its group. Figure 22.7 shows the window in its docked and undocked states.

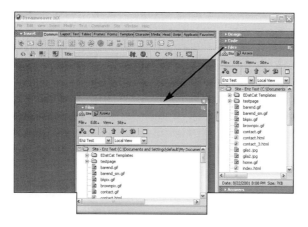

Figure 22.7   The Site panel as part of the integrated workspace (Windows only) shown being docked and undocked.

Expanding and Contracting the Site Panel

The Site panel with all of its information showing can take up a lot of screen real estate, which can be a problem unless you have a very large monitor or a dual monitor set up at your workstation. To alleviate this problem, the window can be shown in full or abbreviated form. The Expand/Collapse button, located in the Site panel toolbar (Windows) or at the bottom of the Site panel (Mac), toggles between full mode (where both left-side and right-side panes are visible) and abbreviated mode (where only the right-side pane is visible). Figure 22.8 shows both states of the window as they appear in Dreamweaver/Mac.

Figure 22.8   The expanded and contracted Site panel in Dreamweaver/Mac.

In the integrated workspace (Windows only): When it is docked in the Files panel group, the Site panel is abbreviated to show only its right-hand pane. Expanding the docked Site panel causes the window to take over the entire Dreamweaver application window (see Figure 22.9). When it is used as a free-standing window, the Site panel expands without taking over the entire application window. Note, however, that when the window is in its expanded (two-pane) state, the Site tab becomes a standard title bar. This means the window cannot be re-inserted into the dock while in expanded state.

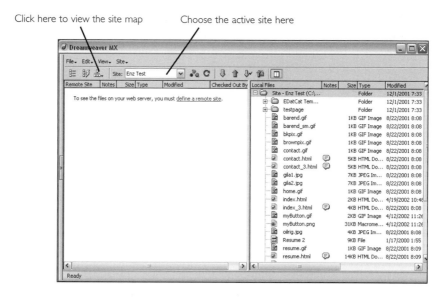

Figure 22.9 The docked Site panel as it appears when expanded.

Note

Whether used as part of the integrated workspace or in the classic interface, the Site panel for Dreamweaver/Windows contains its own menubar with File, Edit, View, and Site menus. These menus contain a variety of commands for working with files in the site (File), editing something (Edit), setting view options for the Site panel (View), and performing sitewide operations (Site). For Dreamweaver/Mac, the Site panel contains no menubar. Instead, the various site-related commands can all be found under the Site > Site Files View and Site > Site Map View submenus. Most of these commands will be grayed out unless the Site panel has focus.

Site Files View

The right-hand column of the Site panel (the only column, if the window isn't maximized) shows the Site Files list. This is a list of all the contents of your local root folder, arranged hierarchically as if you were viewing it in Windows Explorer or the Macintosh

Finder's List view. Just like the lists of files in your operating system, every folder shows with a plus/minus (+/-) sign (Windows) or triangle (Mac) to show or hide its contents. Most of the powerful file management features in Dreamweaver center around the Site Files view.

Working with the File View Columns

The Site Files list is more than just a list of names. It includes columns of information about each file: name, size, type, modified date, and more. If your Site panel is wide enough, you can learn a lot about your files by just looking at their column information. Just as you can with Windows Explorer or the Macintosh Finder List view, you can also choose to view your files organized by any column, by clicking on that column.

If the Site panel is not organized optimally for your work habits, you can change it. Dreamweaver allows you to customize how you view your Site panel by using the View > File View Columns command (Windows) or Site > Site Files View > File View Columns (Mac). When you choose this command, the Site Definition window opens with the Advanced Tab selected (see Figure 22.10) and the File View Columns category showing.

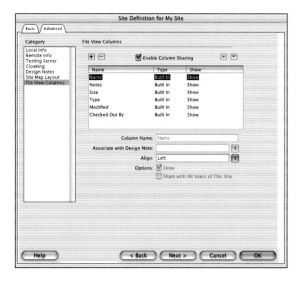

Figure 22.10   The Site Definition dialog box showing the File View Columns category.

In this window, you can see all the names of the columns visible in the Site panel, whether the columns are built-in by Macromedia or created by you. You can also see if the columns are visible or not.

If you would like to add your own custom column, click the plus (+) button. You can then name the new column, whether you want to assign a Design Note to it, how the information in the column is to be aligned, and whether the column is visible or not. (Read Chapter 24 to learn how to use file view columns with Design Notes.) When you create your own column, its type will be Personal. To delete a column you have created, click the – (Delete) button.

In order to understand where the new column you create appears in the Site panel, you will need to use your imagination. Visualize the Site panel. Recall that the first column in the window contains the names of files located in your local site. The next column holds Design Notes. The third column indicates the size of the files, and the fourth column tells you the types of files. Here, we see the names of the columns (which appear horizontally in the Site panel) vertically. Because Dreamweaver places the new column by default at the bottom of the list, which means the new column is placed on the far right of the Site panel. If you want to change the location of your new column, use the up and down arrows located in the upper-right portion of the Site Definition window. By clicking the up arrow, you are moving your column to the left in the Site panel. Click the down arrow if you want to move your column to the right of the Site panel. You can also move the built-in columns except for the Name column. That always must remain at the top of this list.

Note

You cannot delete a Dreamweaver default column. If you don't want to see it, however, you may deselect the Show option. This hides the column from your view, giving the appearance that it has been deleted.

The File Explorer

New to Dreamweaver MX, the Site Files view also includes a special icon representing your computer's file structure. Expanding this icon gives you access to a hierarchical view of all the files in your computer—just like the file lists in your operating system do. (If you have a very large hard drive or two, it might take Dreamweaver a few moments to generate the list of files when you expand the computer icon.) As you'll see later in this chapter, having access to your computer's files outside the local root folder is a blessing for quickly adding assets to your site.

Site Map View

So far, you have looked at the elements of your site as a list. This list, however, doesn't tell you how the files relate to each other. Which file is the first one viewed when someone goes to your site? How many pages link to your first page? Dreamweaver gives you an easy way to answer all these questions—Site Map View.

Designating a Home Page

Before you can use the Site Map view, you need to tell Dreamweaver what your "home" page is. This is the page that is first visible when someone goes to your site. Just because it's called the home page doesn't mean the document itself needs to be named **home.html**. In fact, the home page is typically named **index.html**. To define a home page for your site, access the Site Definition dialog box (Site > Edit Sites > Edit) and go to the Site Map Layout category (see Figure 22.11). Click the folder icon to browse for your home page or type its name in the home page field. Then click OK.

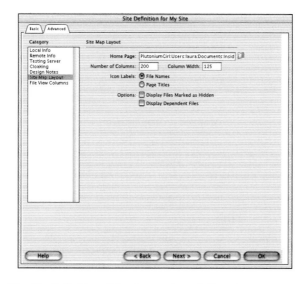

Figure 22.11   The Site Definition dialog box ready to define a home page.

Note

If you named your home page **index.html**, you don't need to specify it as the home page—like a web server, Dreamweaver assumes that any file with this name is the home page.

Viewing a Site with the Site Map

After you have selected your home page, you can view the site map. With the Site panel expanded, press the Site Map button, and from the pop-up menu choose Map Only or Map and Files. Figure 22.12 shows the Site panel displaying map only.

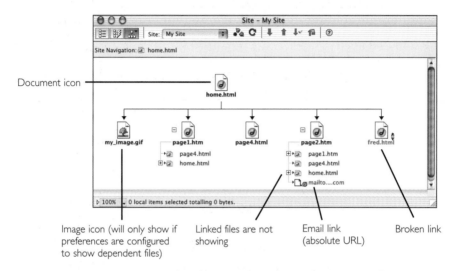

Figure 22.12   The Site panel showing the site map for a simple site.

As Figure 22.12 shows, the Site Map view displays your site as a hierarchy of linked files with the topmost file being your home page. Below the home page are files linked directly from the home page. Included as well are email links, external links, and links to any sort of media embedded in the page.

Icons, Names, and File Types

The site map uses small icons to give visual clues to a file or link's status. After you get used to the visual language being used, a glance will tell you a world of information about your site:

- **Icons.** Each kind of item in the site map has its own icon to represent it. Dreamweaver file icons with black labels represent files. A globe icon with a blue label represents absolute URLs and other special links. Broken links are represented by a broken chain icon with a red label.

- **Labels.** A file is represented with a file icon and labeled with the filename. If you'd rather label your icons with page titles than file names, go to View > Show Page Titles (Windows) or Site > Site Map View > Show Page Titles (Mac). To change them back to filenames, use the same command to toggle Show Page Titles off.

What Shows and What Doesn't

By default, dependent files (such as linked media, and linked script and CSS files) don't display in the site map. If you want to see these items, go to View > Show Dependent Files (Windows) or View > Site Map View > Show Dependent Files (Mac). To hide them again, use the same command to toggle Show Dependent Files off.

Showing the Hierarchy

If your site is complex, the site map might be difficult to read because of all the icons and links shown. But you can simplify the view by hiding and showing links.

To hide all the links coming from a particular file, click the minus (–) button next to the file icon. To show the links again, click the plus (+) button. (The button changes state depending on whether links are shown or hidden.)

To view only a portion of the site at a time (for instance, only show the Menswear section of a Clothing Catalog web site), select the file at the top of the hierarchy you want to view. (To view only the Menswear section, start by selecting the Menswear section main page.) Then choose View > View as Root (Windows) or Site > Site Map View > View as Root (Mac). The site map shifts so that the selected file appears as the new home page at the top of the hierarchy, with all of its child links showing. No other parts of the web site are visible. At the top of the site map window, a special icon shows the relationship of the current view to the home page (see Figure 22.13).

To return to viewing the entire web site, after you've switched to this temporary view, click the home page icon at the top of the site map window (see Figure 22.13).

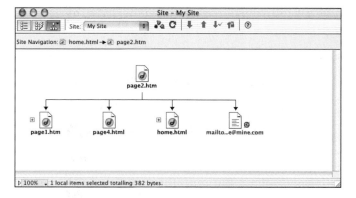

Figure 22.13   Viewing a page as the root of the hierarchy and returning to view the entire hierarchy.

Modifying the Site Map Home Page

Dreamweaver lets you change the existing home page to either an existing page or a completely new one, including non-HTML files such as an image or a SWF file. Select Site > New Home Page on Windows or Site > Site Map View > New Home Page to create a new home page document. This brings up the New Home Page dialog box. You can enter the filename and page title of your new home page here. After creating this new page, you can re-create your links using the Link to Existing File command as well as the Point-to-File icon. This process was discussed in the previous sections of this chapter.

To set an existing page as the new home page in the site map, select that file from the local Site panel (you must be in Map and Files View mode to do this). Then select Site > Set as Home Page on Windows or Site > Site Map View > Set as Home Page on the Macintosh. This re-creates the site map with the newly defined home page and its links. You can also select the file in the Site panel; bring up the context menu by right-clicking on Windows or Ctrl-clicking on the Macintosh and then choosing Set as Home Page.

Customizing Site Map Layout

To customize your current site's site map, do the following:

1. Select Site > Edit Sites. From the Define Sites dialog box, select the current site and click Edit.

2. Select the Site Map Layout section of your site definition.

From this window, you can select the number of columns and the column width for your site map display. This number specifies the number of pages to display on each row; the default is 200. You will typically not need to adjust this value because you will rarely have more than 200 pages linked to from your main page.

Next you can select whether the site map should represent documents by their filenames or their page titles. If you have been diligent in creating effective page titles, using the page titles in the Site Map view might be a good way to display your site. Displaying your site files by their page titles also gives you an idea of whether the titles are easy to understand. You might be surprised how confusing some page titles can be when you're not looking at the page itself.

Finally, you can choose options that you want to include in your site map. The first option enables you to specify whether the site map should show files marked as hidden. When this is checked, hidden files will be shown. The other option, Display Dependant Files, displays all dependant files (such as images and other files linked in the HTML) in the site map. These files are listed in the order in which they are located in the HTML code.

Creating an Image from the Site Map

How handy would it be if you could save your site map as an image that you could then email to or print out for your client? Dreamweaver makes this task incredibly easy!

To save the site map in Dreamweaver/Windows, choose File > Save Site Map. In the Save Site Map dialog box, name your image and choose the location in which to save it. In the File Type pop-up menu, choose .bmp to save the file as a bitmap or .png to save it as a PNG file. Click Save.

Note

PNG format is Macromedia Fireworks' native file format.

To save the site map in Dreamweaver/Mac, choose Site > Site Map View > Save Site Map as PICT, or Site > Site Map View > Save Site Map as JPEG. A Save As dialog box will appear. Choose a name for the file image and a location in which to save it. Click Save.

Exercise 22.2   Creating a site map for the Grandpa's Ice Cream Site

In this exercise, you'll build on the Grandpa's Ice Cream site you defined in Exercise 22.1. You'll define a home page, generate a site map, and create an image of that site map. (If you haven't yet done Exercise 22.1, go back and do that now!)

1. Before Dreamweaver can generate a site map for you, it needs to know which file in your site is the home page. The site map is built by following links from the home page. You specify a home page in the Site Definition dialog box. To access this dialog box, at the top of the Site panel click the Site pop-up window and choose Edit Sites (see Figure 22.14).

Figure 22.14   Choosing Edit Sites from the Site pop-up menu in the Site panel.

2. In the Edit sites dialog box, select Our Site and click Edit. In the Site Definition dialog box, choose the Site Map Layout category from the categories on the left (see Figure 22.15). When the category options appear, look at the input field for Home Page. The information has already been filled in! If you examine the entry in this field, you'll see that Dreamweaver recognized that your site contained a file called **index.htm**—like a web server, Dreamweaver assumes that this is your home page. Which it is! So your home page is already defined. Click OK to close the Site Definition dialog box.

Figure 22.15   Setting a home page for the Grandpa's site.

3. Now it's time to look at your site map. Expand the Site panel so both panes of it are showing.

    In the expanded Site panel, press the Site Map button. From the pop-up menu that appears, choose Map Only. There's your site map, showing links from **index.htm** to the other three pages in the site. Figure 22.16 shows this happening.

    To see your site map and your list of files at the same time, press the Site Map button (at the top left of the window) and from the pop-up menu choose Map and Files.

4. You might want to use the site map in some of your printed materials, or maybe even use it as a graphic on one of your web pages. Windows users: To save your site map as an image, go to the Site panel menu bar and choose File > Save Site Map; in the Save dialog box that appears, set the Save as Type popup menu to PNG. Navigate to you chapter_22 folder and call the file sitemap.png. Click OK to close the Save dialog box. Mac users: From the main menu bar, choose Site > Site Map View > Save Site Map > Save Map as JPEG. In sitemap.jpg. Click OK to close the Save dialog box.

5. Check your Site Files list. You'll see the new **sitemap.jpg** file in place.

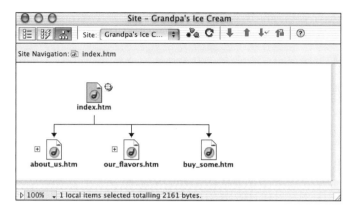

Figure 22.16   Viewing the Grandpa's site map.

File and Link Management Within a Site

The biggest ongoing chore of web site development is site management—keeping track of all the files in the site, making sure the folder structure is logical, the file names make sense, the links all work, and that everything is where you can find it quickly for editing and upload. After you've defined your Dreamweaver site, all the formidable power of its local site management tools is at your disposal. Working from your "central command window"—in other words, the Site panel—you can keep your finger on the pulse of your site and control your files like a general marshalling her troops.

Managing Files and Folders

Think of the Site panel as a substitute for Windows Explorer or the Macintosh Finder. Leave it open all the time as you work on your site. Use it to perform all basic file operations across your site. Site Files view is your key to managing the file structure of your site; Site Map view is your key to managing its links.

Opening Files

As always, there's more than one way to open files in Dreamweaver. The first and perhaps most popular method is to select File > Open from the menu. You can then use the Open dialog box to navigate to the file that you want and click Open. A faster method is through the Site panel. You can double-click a file in the Site panel (Site Files of Site Map view) and it will open. It's as simple as that! Now that you know this snazzy new way to open a document in one step, will you ever use the old way again?

Creating Files and Folders

Note

Always close all documents before performing any file management operations on them. Dreamweaver can't properly update links, change file names, and so on, if the files are open.

To create a new file or folder from Site Files view, do one of the following:

- Click on the folder that you want to contain the new item and Choose File > New File or File > New Folder (Windows), or choose Site > Site Files View > New File or Site > Site Files View > New Folder (Mac).

- Right-click (Windows) or Ctrl-click (Mac) on the folder that you want to contain the new item and, from the contextual menu, choose New File or New Folder.

A new, untitled file or folder will appear in the Site Files list. (For new files, Dreamweaver creates files of the default document type for this site.)

Duplicating Files

Sometimes you might want to save the same document as two different files. You don't have to copy and paste the HTML code into a new document and then save it. Instead, you can select File/Save As from the menu. This enables you to save a copy of the current file with a different name. Be sure to remember that after you do this, the document to which you return will be this new copy of the original document. If you want to return to the original copy, you must open it as discussed in the previous section. As with normal saving, make sure that you save the document somewhere inside the local root folder; otherwise, your links could become broken.

Copying Files from Outside Your Site

New to Dreamweaver MX, the Site Files list puts the entire file structure of your computer at your disposal. Have you ever wanted to use that particular graphic or page in a web site, and then remembered at the last minute that it's not stored in your local root folder? In the bad old days, this would have meant leaving Dreamweaver, moving or copying the needed file into the local root folder, then coming back to Dreamweaver to find it now available in the Site Files view.

In Dreamweaver MX, to copy a file from outside the local root folder, do this:

1. In the Site Files pane of the Site panel, expand the Computer icon to show the contents of your hard drive.

2. From this hierarchy of choices, find the file you want to move into the Dreamweaver site.

3. To copy the file into your site, do one of the following:

   • Drag-and-drop the file from the Computer hierarchy to the local root folder hierarchy (see Figure 22.17).

   • Select the file in the Computer hierarchy and Ctrl/Cmd-C to copy it; then select the folder within your local root folder and Ctrl/Cmd-V to paste it.

   • Select the file in the Computer hierarchy and right-click (Ctrl-click) to access its contextual menu, and choose Copy; then select the folder within your local root folder and right-click (Ctrl-click) to access its contextual menu, and choose Paste.

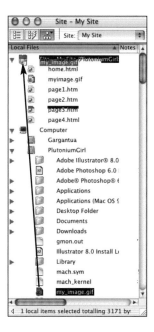

Figure 22.17   Dragging-and-dropping to copy a file into the local root folder.

Renaming and Rearranging Files and Folders

Regular humans who aren't super-organizers rarely get the best possible organization system going until they're halfway into a site development project. They might also come across the perfect naming scheme after already creating a half dozen files with useless names that must be changed. The nightmare of this scenario is that, after you've started building a web site—complete with links to graphics and links between files—any little change in the location or name of a file will mean having to update every single relative link that points to or comes from that page.

If you use the Dreamweaver Site Files view to perform any of these naming or organizing tasks, Dreamweaver will automatically update all links as needed.

To move a file or folder from one location in the file structure to another, just drag the item to its new location in the Site Files view.

To rename a file or folder, click twice on its name in Site Files view or Site Map view, or right-click (Ctrl-click) on it and choose Rename from the contextual menu; then type in a new name. Note that, if you change the filename of the home page, the site map won't be able to display properly until you refresh it by choosing Site > Recreate Site Cache.

If your change will require any links to be updated, Dreamweaver will present you with the Update Links dialog box showing you all the files that will need to be updated as a result of your action. From here, simply click Update and Dreamweaver will change all links in the listed files, so none of your links are broken.

Note

Why would you ever not want to update links? Imagine a scenario where you have two alternate home pages—maybe one for when the company is having a sale, and one for other times—with identical links coming from them but different content. You might leave both home pages in the local root folder, one called index.html and the other called index-sale.html. The next time there's a sale going on, you can easily switch home pages by renaming them index-nosale.html and index.html. When you change the name of index.html to index-nosale.html, Dreamweaver will offer to update your links for you. Don't do it! You still want all links in the site pointing to index.html. When you change the name of index-sale.html to index.html, all links in the site will now point to the alternate home page.

Managing Links

You've already seen some pretty wonderful link management, in the way Dreamweaver updates links when you update your file structure. But that's only the first step in a comprehensive link management system. By utilizing the site map, various Site menu commands, and Site Reports, you can truly be in command of your site's link structure without once moving from your command chair.

Creating Links with Point-and-Shoot

Do you like dragging-and-dropping? Is it your dream to create a sitewide navigation system quickly and easily, possible without even opening a single file? You're going to love point-and-shoot.

Point-and-Shoot from Within a File

If you have a document open and the Site panel at least partially visible on your computer screen, you can create a link from within that file to another file in your site using point-and-shoot. Do it this way:

1. Open the file that you want to contain the link. If you're using the integrated workspace, and the Site panel is docked with the rest of your panels, make sure it's expanded so you can see it. If your Site panel is free-standing, make sure you can see at least a corner of it peeking out from behind your Document window and other panels.

2. Make sure the document you're going to link to is closed. (Always do this before performing file management tasks.)

3. Select the text or image that will become the link.

4. In the Property inspector, find the Link field, but instead of clicking the Browse button or typing a name in the input field, find the Point-and-Shoot button.

5. Press down on this button and drag over to the Site panel. (If the Site panel is free-standing, just drag so you're over some portion of it and it will pop to the front so you can see the whole window.) Keep dragging until you're on top of the file to which you want to link. This file will highlight when you're in the right position.

6. Let go of the mouse button. If your hand-eye coordination was working right, your open document now contains a link to the item you pointed to. It's point-and-shoot! (See Figure 22.18.)

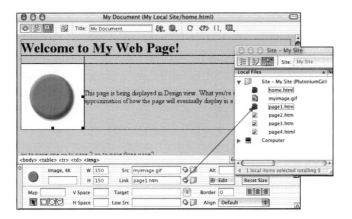

Figure 22.18   Using point-and-shoot to create a link.

Point-and-Shoot from the Site Map

If you're in a hurry to create some navigation controls in your site, and don't even want to open the files to do it, you'll love the ability to point-and-shoot from the site map. Just do this:

1. Close all documents. (Always do this before performing file management tasks.)

2. Open Site Map view in the Site panel.

3. In the site map, select the file you want to link from. A little point-and-shoot icon appears beside the file.

4. Press down on that icon and drag to the file to which you want to link. You can drag to another file in the site map or to a file in the Site Files list. When you're on top of the desired file and it highlights, let go. Your link is created! (See Figure 22.19.)

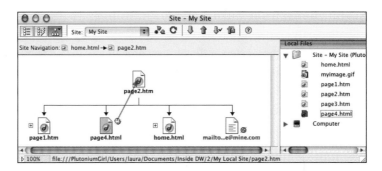

Figure 22.19   Using point-and-shoot to link two files in the site map.

The site map changes to show that a link has been added between the two files. But what kind of link is it? Open the file you linked from and scroll down to the bottom of the page. You'll see that Dreamweaver has added a text link to the other file, with its text derived from the other file's filename. If you continue adding links from this same file, Dreamweaver will eventually create a whole text-based navigation bar along the bottom of the page. It's not fancy, but it's accessible, and it works. And you didn't have to open a single file to do it. (You just opened the file to see the results.)

Creating Links with Menu Commands and the Site Map

If pointing-and-shooting isn't your cup of tea, you can still quickly add links from one file to another without opening either file by using menu commands. You must be in Site Map view to do this, but there's no dragging-and-dropping involved.

Linking to an Existing File with the Site Map View Menu

To link one file to another existing file without opening either file or using point-and-shoot, do this:

1. In Site Map view, select the file you want to link from and choose Site > Link to Existing File (Windows) or Site > Site Map View > Link to Existing File (Mac); or right-click (Ctrl-click) on the file you want to link from and, from the contextual menu, choose Link to Existing File.

2. When the Select HTML File dialog box appears, browse to the file you want your file to link to. Click Choose to close the dialog box.

That's it! Your link is in place and will show up as an additional link in the site map. To see how the link was created in the originating file, open that file and scroll to the bottom of the page. You'll see that, just as with the point-and-shoot links described above, Dreamweaver has added a text link to the other file, with its text derived from the other file's filename.

Linking to a New (Non-Existent!) File with the Site Map View Menu

This little feature is the unsung hero of Dreamweaver site management. From the site map, you can determine what files your site will need and which should be linked to which and essentially build the entire site without opening a single file. To create a new file and link to it all in one process, do this (see Figure 22.20):

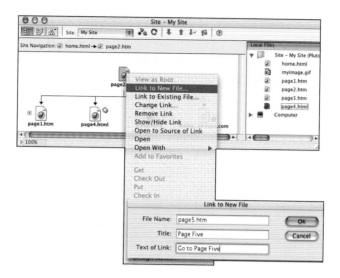

Figure 22.20   Linking to a new file in the site map.

1. In Site Map view, select the file you want to link from and choose Site > Link to New File (Windows) or Site > Site Map View > Link to New File (Mac); or right-click (Ctrl-click) on the file you want to link from and, from the contextual menu, choose Link to New File.

2. When the Link to New File dialog box appears, fill in the following information:

   - **Filename**. Dreamweaver is about to create a new file for you. What would you like it to be called?

   - **Title**. What would you like the page title (contents of the `<title>` tag) of the new file to be?

   - **Text of Link**. After the new file is created, Dreamweaver will create a text link in the original file pointing to the new file. What would you like it to say?

3. When you've got all the information entered, click OK to close the dialog box. There's your link! And there's your new file! Open the original file, and you'll see that the link has been added as a simple text link after all other page content. If you keep repeating this process, you can build an entire web site starting from one lowly home page. And all without ever leaving the Site Map view.

Changing Links

You've created your site and you've linked several pages to the **gallery.html** page. But then you have a brainstorm and decide those pages should link to the slideshow.html page instead. Are you in for an afternoon of opening files and changing link field information? No! With Dreamweaver, you can modify what links point to either individually or all at once across the site—and again, all without opening a single file.

The Change Link Command

To change all links in a site that point to one page, to make them point to another page instead, follow these steps:

1. Select the linked page that you want to modify. The linked page is the page you navigate to, not from. (In the example cited above, this would be the **gallery.html** page.)

2. Choose Site > Change Link (Windows) or Site > Site Map View > Change Link (Mac). This brings up the Select HTML File dialog box.

3. Select the new file you want your site's links to point to. (In the example above, this would be the **slideshow.html** page.) When you're done, click Select.

4. The Update Files dialog box appears, displaying a list of all the files in the site that should be updated. To change all links and close the dialog box, click Update.

The Change Links Sitewide Command

The Change Link Sitewide command operates in much the same fashion as the Change Link command, but with a few crucial differences. Like the preceding command, its purpose is to change all links within a site that point to one file so that they point to another file instead. To use this command, do the following:

1. Optional: Select the linked page that you want to modify. The linked page is the page you navigate to, not from (the **gallery.html** page, in the previous example).

2. Choose Site > Change Link Sitewide.

3. When the Change Link Sitewide dialog box appears (see Figure 22.21), enter the following information:

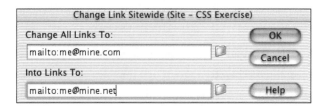

Figure 22.21   The Change Link Sitewide dialog box.

- **Change All Links To**. If you selected a file before choosing the command, this information will be filled in for you. Otherwise, enter the link here.

- **Into Links To**. Enter the new link that you want to replace the old link with (in the previous example the slideshow.html page).

4. Click OK to close the dialog box.

5. The Update Files dialog box appears, displaying a list of all the files in the site that should be updated. To change all links and close the dialog box, click Update.

How is the Change Links Sitewide command different from the Change Links command? The purpose of Change Links is to recalculate the document-relative links between two documents in your site, and that's all the command does. Change Links Sitewide is more of a straight Find and Replace command, simply replacing the href attribute for certain links from one value to another. This has the following ramifications:

- Change Links Sitewide can only be used with absolute or root-relative links, not document-relative links. If you browse to choose a link for the Change Link Sitewide dialog box, Dreamweaver will calculate that link's root-relative URL. If you type in a document-relative link, you'll get an error message. If you want to change all references to a document within your site, and you're not using root-relative paths, use Change Links.

Note

For more on root-relative versus document-relative links, see Chapter 6, "Links and Navigation."

- Change Links can only be used to change links that point to documents. Change Links Sitewide can be used to change any `href` attribute into any other `href` attribute. For instance, you can update `mailto:` links when your email address changes or change all null links from # to the safer `javascript:;` with Change Links Sitewide. Any time you're changing links that are not document-relative links within your site, use Change Links Sitewide. (For more on null links, see Chapter 16, "Getting Interactive with Behaviors.")

Checking and Repairing Links

In the next few sections, you will learn how to check all of your links with Dreamweaver. Then you'll see how to fix any errors it finds.

Checking Links

You can check links one file at a time, several files or folders at a time, or check the entire site in one massive sweep. The Dreamweaver Check Links function reports three types of possible problems:

- **Broken links**. These are files that have links located internally that don't contain the proper path for the link to work correctly. This means that Dreamweaver could not find internal links referenced on paged of your site.

- **External links**. External links are perhaps the most notorious for creating broken images and the dreaded `Error 404: File not found` message. These are files that are located outside your site (and look like `http://www.somesite.com`). External links are displayed so that you are aware of the possible problems associated with them. Note that a link on the external links list does not mean that the link is broken; it simply means that it's beyond the scope of Dreamweaver's link management system to check these links.

- **Orphaned files**. These are files that have no incoming links pointing to them. In other words, these are files in which there is no navigation to get to them. Typically these files are older versions and aren't in use anymore. However, you can't just assume that all orphaned files are not used. Be careful to make sure that orphaned files aren't necessary before deleting them.

Whether you check all of your site's files simultaneously, or only check one or two files as needed, the procedure is basically the same.

To check your site's links all at once, do this:

1. Save all open documents.

2. Choose Site > Check Links Sitewide (Ctrl/Cmd+F8); or right-click (Ctrl-click) any file or folder in the Site Files list and choose Check Links > Entire Site from the contextual menu.

To check links for only a few files in the site, do this:

1. Save and close all open documents.

2. In the Site Files list or site map, select the file(s) you want to check. Shift-click or Ctrl/Cmd-click to select multiple files.

3. Right-click (Ctrl-click) any selected file and from the contextual menu choose Check Links > Selected Files/Folders.

To check links for only one document, do this:

1. Open the document you want to check, and save it if needed.

2. Choose File > Check Page > Check Links.

Whichever method you choose, Dreamweaver checks your links and then shows you the results by opening the Results window with the Link Checker tab displayed (see Figure 22.22). Using the pop-up menu at the top of this window, you can view any of the three type of links reported (Broken Links, External Links, Orphaned Files). On the left side of the window, the file that has the problematic link is displayed. To the right is the specific link with which Dreamweaver is having a problem. The Orphaned Files section doesn't have a second column because there is no link associate with it.

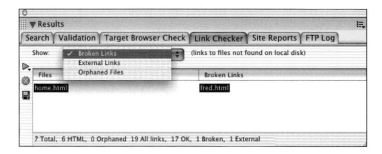

Figure 22.22   The Results window showing the results of checking links across a site.

From here you can either close the Results/Link Checker window or save the list as a tab-delimited text file. This saves all three link types as one file. You can then import the list into a page by using the File/Import/Import Tabular Data option or import the text file into a word processor to be printed out for reference.

Note

It is possible to lose track of the Report window where your Link Checker information is stored. This is because although the box appears in the Site panel initially (if you are currently viewing the Site panel), it moves to the Document window if you switch from the Site panel or even click the menu. The only way to get back to the Report window is to switch to the Document window. It might even be necessary to open a document if there isn't one currently open.

Fixing Links

Two methods exist for fixing broken and external links (if they actually need fixing). Both are accessed via the Results/Link Checker window.

The first method is to double-click the filename of the file with the broken or external link. This opens the file in a Document window and highlights the suspect link. If your Property inspector is open, the link also is highlighted in the Link or Src section of this inspector. You can then manually type the correct reference or use the folder icon or Point-to-File icon to select the correct file you want to link to.

The second method is probably quicker and easier, if you know your site well. From the Link Checker window, click once on the link in question in the right column. This makes the link manually editable (see Figure 22.23). If you're currently troubleshooting the broken links section, a folder icon appears that enables you to easily browse to the correct link. If there are other broken links with the same reference, Dreamweaver asks you if it should update them as well. Now, could that be any easier?

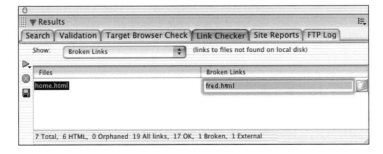

Figure 22.23   Fixing a broken link with the Results window.

Note

If you are using the file Check In/Check Out system on your site, Dreamweaver attempts to check out the file so that it can change the link. If it cannot do so, Dreamweaver displays a warning message and leaves the link as broken. For more on Check In/Check Out, read Chapter 24.

Exercise 22.3   Rearrange Files and Manage Links in the Grandpa's Site

In this exercise, you'll build on the Grandpa's Ice Cream site you created in previous exercises. (If you haven't yet done Exercise 22.1, go back and do that now!) You'll rearrange your file structure, allowing Dreamweaver to update links for you. You'll create new files and folders. And you'll see how to use the Site panel to add links, correct links, and change links.

1. Expand your Site panel so you can see the list of Site files on the right and the Site map on the left. Have you noticed that the organization of files within the Grandpa's site is not too good? This is what's called a *flat structure*—all the files are loose in the main folder. Not too easy for finding things. You want to create an images folder in the local root folder and put all of your images in there. But you don't want to break the links when you do so.

2. In the Site Files pane of the Site panel, select the folder icon that represents your local root folder (it's the one at the top of the list). Right-click (Ctrl-click) on this folder to access the contextual menu, and choose New Folder.

   A new untitled folder appears in your site list, with its name selected and ready to change. Rename the folder **images**.

3. Now it's time to move all of your image files into that folder. To make this job as easy as possible, from the column names at the top of the Site panel click the Type column. This arranges your files by type. Now all of your images (type: GIF) are displayed together in the list.

   Select the top image in the list. Then Shift-click to select the bottom image in the list. Then release the Shift key and drag the selected images into the images folder. Dreamweaver will ask if you want to update your files. Click Update. After a few seconds, your images are moved! (See Figure 22.24.)

   To test this out, double-click the **index.htm** file to open it. When the home page opens, all the images still display. Select the ice cream cone image and examine the Src field of the Image Property inspector. The src attribute is images/main1.gif, indicating that the image is in an **images** subfolder.

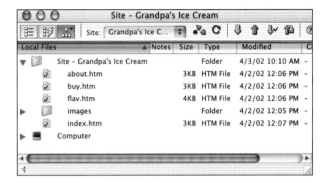

Figure 22.24   The Grandpa's site with all images moved to a special images folder.

4. Now it's time for some link management. Open **index.htm**, if it's not already open, and Preview in Browser (F12). Notice that, in the browser, you can navigate to any of the three subpages, but after you're there you can't navigate back home. A definite limitation.

Back in Dreamweaver, close all open files. (Never perform file management chores when files are open!) In the Site panel, go to the Site Map pane and select **about.htm**. Note that, when the file is selected, the point-and-shoot icon appears next to it. Press down on that icon and drag back up to **index.htm**. When you let go of the mouse (if you were on top of **index.htm** when you let go), a new link appears under **about.htm**.

Repeat this same procedure to add links from **flav.htm** and **buy.htm** back to the home page. Then add links from each of the three subpages to each other. This creates a complete site navigation system. When you're finished, your site map will look like the one shown in Figure 22.25.

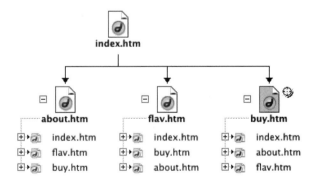

Figure 22.25   The Grandpa's site map showing links added.

You'll also notice that it looks like you suddenly have a lot of pages in your site. If you expand all the plus (+) icons to view the entire hierarchy, your site looks immense! But you still only have four files in there. This is because the site map has no way to represent reciprocal links (such as two pages that link to each other).

5. After you've done all this, open **about_us.htm** and examine the new text links that have been added at the bottom of the page. There they are—serviceable but not too pretty (see Figure 22.26). You're going to fix that up.

Figure 22.26   The automatically added links in **about_us.htm**.

Choose Edit > Find and Replace. In the dialog box that appears, set your options to match those shown in Figure 22.27. You'll be searching all the text in the current site for the word index, and replacing it with the word Home.

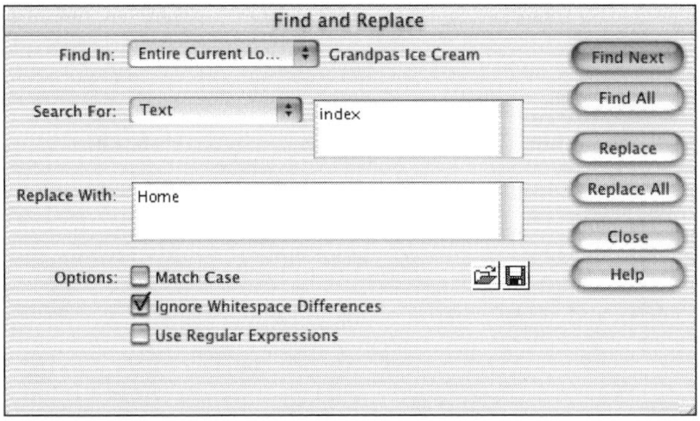

Figure 22.27   Finding and replacing the index links with Home.

Click the Replace All button. Dreamweaver will warn you that this is dangerous, because it's going to search all the files of the site and you won't be able to undo its changes. For the current exercise, be brave and allow it to do so. When you're working in the real world, you might want to be more circumspect and click the Replace button instead, to change one instance at a time. Replace All is much faster, but more dangerous.

Repeat this process three more times, changing `flav` to Our Flavors, `buysome` to Buy Some, and `aboutus` to About Us.

6. When you've finished all this finding and replacing, open one of your pages and Preview in Browser (F12). How does your navigation system look and work?

Assets Management with the Assets Panel

The Assets panel keeps track of and enables you to easily update or insert certain elements used in the site, such as images, colors, rich media files (Flash, Shockwave, and so on), and scripts. This is particularly helpful if you plan to reuse one of these items on many pages throughout your site.

To open the Assets panel, click Window > Assets, or expand the Files panel group in your panel dock and bring the Assets tab to the front (see Figure 22.28). The panel consists of two main sections: the assets list (the lower half of the panel) and the display area (the upper half). Selecting an asset in the assets list will display it in the display area. Since assets are organized by *type* rather than by the hierarchical directory structure used in the Site panel, you'll only ever be looking at one type of asset at a time. To switch between different asset types, click the buttons along the left side of the panel. Types of assets are:

- **Images**. These are image files such as GIF, JPEG, or PNG contained in your site. (For information on handling and using images, see Chapter 5, "Working with Images.") These are image files that are in your root site folder, regardless of whether they are currently linked to a document or not.

- **Colors**. These are all the colors used in your site, including background colors as well as text and link colors.

- **URLs**. These are external URLs found linked to by documents in your site. These include HTTP, HTTPS, FTP, JavaScript, local file, email, and gopher links. (See Chapter 6, "Links and Navigation," for more information on links and linking in your documents.)

- **Flash movies**. These are Flash movies found in your local root folder. Only the SWF files are listed here, not FLA source files or the SWT template files.

- **Shockwave movies**. These are Shockwave movies created with Director or Authorware found in your site.

- **QuickTime and MPEG movies**. These are movies in either Apple QuickTime (.mov or .qt files) or MPEG format.

- **Scripts**. These are JavaScript and VBScript files found in your site. Only independent script files are listed. JavaScript located in your pages is ignored.

- **Templates**. When used correctly, templates provide an easy way to build and edit similar pages quickly and easily. Before relying too heavily on template-based design, be sure to spend time learning them inside and out.

- **Library**. Libraries are similar to templates in that you only change one instance to update many. These are typically small content elements that are used on many pages throughout a site such as a company logo or a default navigation panel.

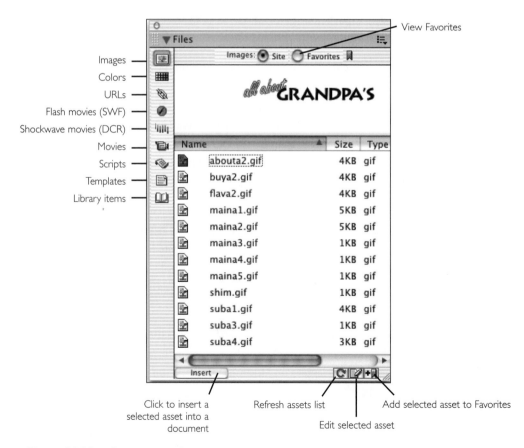

Figure 22.28   The Assets panel.

Note

To learn more about using Flash assets, see Chapter 20, "Building Web Pages with Flash." To learn about using Templates and Library items in the Assets panel, see Chapter 25, "Templates and Libraries."

Tip

The site cache determines the contents of the Assets panel. If you have recently added a media element, color, URL, or other asset to your site, yet it doesn't show up in the Assets panel, click the Refresh button at the bottom of the panel to get an updated list of assets.

Inserting Assets

Why are assets so wonderful? For one thing, the Assets panel makes it easy to find and insert images and other assets quickly into your documents as you work.

Inserting Media Elements from the Assets Panel

Images and other media elements (Flash movies, Shockwave movies, and more) are the simplest to insert from the Assets panel. It's all a matter of drag-and-drop, or select-and-click. To insert a media element into a document using drag-and-drop, do this:

1. Open the Assets panel and click the desired icon to view the type of asset you want to insert.

2. In the Document window, make sure Design view is active.

3. From the assets list, grab the item you want to insert and drag it to the desired location in your document. Note that even though you can drag-and-drop an asset anywhere within your page, its final position within the document will depend on the flow of content around it. Dragging an image into the middle of a paragraph of text will cause the text to wrap around it. Dragging it to the right side of the page will not position it on the right if the page contents are aligned left. (For ultimate positioning control, you'll have to drag items into layers. See Chapter 14 for more on this.)

To insert a media element using the Insert button, do this:

1. In the Document window, make sure Design view is active. Click to position the cursor where you want the asset to be inserted.

2. Open the Assets panel and click the desired icon to view the type of asset you want to insert.

3. In the Assets panel, select the asset you want to insert. Then click the Insert button.

Inserting URLs from the Assets Panel

Inserting URL assets is slightly trickier than inserting media elements, because the URL must be inserted as the href for a link. To insert a URL asset, follow these steps:

1. Open a document and make sure you're in Design view.

2. In the document, select the text or image that you want to link to the URL.

3. Open the Assets panel and click the URL icon to show URL assets.

4. Do one of the following:

   - Find the URL you want to apply, and drag it to the selected item in the Document window.

   - Select the URL you want to apply, and click the Apply button.

Inserting Color Assets

In one way, color assets aren't quite as useful as you might think, because they can't be inserted or applied to very many document elements. The only kind of page element that will accept application of a color asset is text, and when text is colored using this method the color is added as part of a <font> tag (which has been deprecated in favor of CSS formatting). But used in conjunction with the Dreamweaver color picker and its sampling tool, color assets can be very handy indeed.

To use a color asset to color text, do this:

1. Open a document and make sure you're in Design view.

2. In the document, select the text that you want to colorize.

3. Open the Assets panel and click the color swatch icon to show color assets.

4. Do one of the following:

   - Find the color you want to apply, and drag it on top of the selected text in the Document window.

   - Select the color you want to apply, and click the Apply button.

To use a color asset to colorize any other element in a Dreamweaver document, do this (see Figure 22.29):

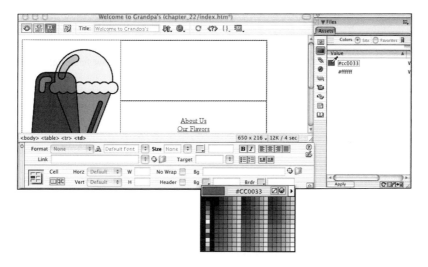

Figure 22.29   Sampling a color from the Assets panel.

1. Open the Assets panel and click the color swatch icon to show color assets.

2. Open the document you want to work on, and either select the item you want to colorize (layer, table, table cell, and so forth.) or open the dialog box from which you'll be choosing a color (Page Properties, CSS Style Definition, or another option).

3. Colors are always chosen in Dreamweaver using the color button and color picker. From whatever dialog box or Property inspector you're in, find the color button and click on it to activate the color picker.

4. Instead of choosing from the color swatches in the color picker, move the eye-dropper cursor over to the Assets panel and click on the color asset swatch you want to sample. There's your color!

Your Favorite Assets

Your site's assets list contains every single asset in the site, including colors, images, and URLs you might only use once in the entire site. Typically, as your site becomes larger, the number of assets in your site will increase as well. When you begin handling a 30-page site, you can easily have 50 or 60 different images, if not more! As you can imagine, this makes the assets list rather cumbersome and slow to navigate through.

To solve this problem, Dreamweaver has Favorite Assets. From all the assets in your site's assets list, you can choose only those that you know you'll be using over and over, and declare them to be Favorites. Favorite assets show in the Assets panel when you switch to Favorites view (see Figure 22.28). Not only is it easier to navigate a list of 10 favorites than a list of 100 site assets, but also the Favorites view can even be organized into folders for easier and more logical access. This section shows you how to organize and use Favorite-specific features.

Viewing and Working with Your Favorite Assets

All of the functionality of the Assets panel can be applied to favorite assets just as it is to site assets. To see and work only with your favorite assets, click the Favorites radio button at the top of the Assets panel.

Note

The Favorites section begins completely empty. You must build it up as you go. This can be a slow and tedious process, but it can result in large pay-offs in the end, depending on the structure of your site.

You can add a site asset to your Favorite assets by doing one of the following:

- In the Assets window, select the asset(s) that you want to add to the Favorites list then click the Add to Favorites button at the bottom right of the window. This button looks like a plus (+) symbol and a purple ribbon.

- Select the asset(s) that you want to add to the Favorites list in the Assets window. Access the context menu by clicking the right arrow button on the upper-right corner of the panel. You can also bring up this menu by right-clicking (Windows) or Ctrl-clicking (Mac) on the asset(s).

- In Design view of the Document window, select the asset(s) (or object) that you want to add. Right-click (Windows) or Ctrl-click (Mac) the object(s) to access the context menu. Select Add to [Asset Type] Favorites.

Note

Note that when adding text to your Favorites, Add to Color Favorites will appear if the text does not contain a link; otherwise, Add to URL Favorites will appear.

The Favorites list wouldn't be worth much if you couldn't change your mind and delete an item from the list. To remove an asset from your Favorites list, follow these steps:

1. Select the asset(s) that you want to remove from your Favorites list.

2. Click the Remove from Favorites button. You can also right-click (Windows) or Ctrl-click (Mac) the asset and select Remove from Favorites from the context menu that appears. Alternately, you can also select the asset in the favorites list and press the Delete key. You can remove the entire **Favorites** folder as well, which removes all the folder's contents along with it.

Assets that you remove from the Favorites list are not actually deleted from your site in any way; they're simply removed from your Favorite Assets list.

Grouping Your Favorite Assets

To reduce clutter even further, you can group your assets in folders. This enables you to keep images that are part of your main navigation in their own folder, while keeping other commonly accessed images in another.

Creating **Favorite** folders and placing assets inside them does not change the location of the actual file in the directory structure of your site. It simply offers an easy way to further organize your assets.

To create a **Favorites** folder and place assets inside it, simply do the following:

1. Access your Favorites listing.

2. Click the New Favorites Folder button located at the lower-right corner of the panel. You might also select the New Favorites folder from right-clicking (Windows) or ctrl-clicking (Mac) the asset.

3. Name the folder and drag the desired assets into the folder (see Figure 22.30).

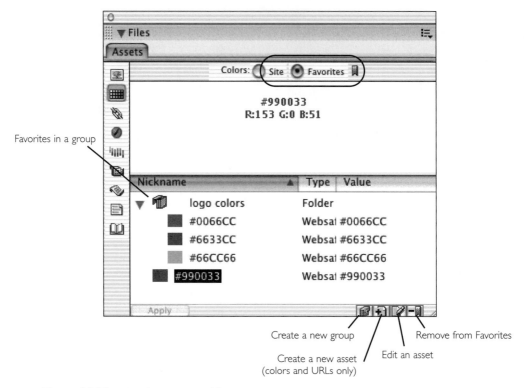

Favorites in a group

Create a new group

Create a new asset
(colors and URLs only)

Edit an asset

Remove from Favorites

Figure 22.30   Creating a group of favorite assets.

Customizing the Assets Panel

Like most things in Dreamweaver, you can customize the Assets panel in many ways. You can use the Favorite Assets feature to keep a separate list of the assets that you use most. If you have a company logo that you use on multiple pages, you can add the logo image to your Favorites listing and then don't need to wade through all the images that you use only once or twice to get to the one that you use all the time. Favorites are so handy that they've been given their own section in this book. Read "Your Favorite Assets," later in this chapter, for more information about them.

Another method is to change the listing order of the assets. By default, the assets are listed in ascending alphabetical order (from A to Z) by name or value. You can change the order of the listing by clicking the column heading with which you want to sort. This sorts the assets ascending alphabetically by that column's attribute. Clicking a column header a second time sorts the listing alphabetically still, only in descending order (from Z to A). If you sort a column of numbers, such as file size, the ordering will be sorted numerically rather than alphabetically, from smallest to largest (ascending) initially.

You can also change the width of the columns in the Assets panel, as shown in Figure 22.28. To do this, simply hold your cursor directly over the divider line that separates two columns. You will notice that the pointer changes to a double-headed arrow column. You can now click and drag the column to any width that you want. This typically holds true for most windows that use columns.

Using Assets Throughout Your Site

Dreamweaver allows you to use assets in many ways. It even allows you to copy assets and share them among various sites.

To copy an asset from one site to another, follow these steps:

1. Select the asset(s) that you want to copy to another site. You can copy entire folders of assets in your Favorites listing.
2. Click the right arrow button located in the upper-right corner of the panel.
3. Select Copy to Site from this menu. A submenu will appear with a list of the possible sites to copy the asset(s) to. Choose one of these sites listed.

The selected asset(s) is copied into the specified site and placed in folders that correspond to their locations in the current site. Any folders that don't already exist are created automatically. It's also important to note that assets copied in this fashion are automatically added to the other sites' Favorite Assets listing.

After the site on which you are working becomes rather large, you might forget where certain assets have been used. Dreamweaver will help you find them. If you would just like to find where a certain asset (or group of assets) being used in the local site, follow these steps:

1. In the Assets panel, select the asset or assets that you want to locate.
2. Right-click(Windows) or Ctrl-click (Mac) to bring up the context menu. You can also access this menu by clicking the right arrow button located in the upper-right corner of the panel.
3. Choose Locate in Site from this menu. The Site panel will appear, and the assets you searched for will be highlighted.

The Locate in Site option is not available with colors and URLs. This is because these two asset types do not have files associated with them; they are simply strings of text inside files.

Editing Your Assets

The Assets panel provides an easy way to edit assets as well. This can come in handy when you want to edit multiple pictures but don't want to wade through the complex directory structure of the Site panel.

To edit an asset through the Assets panel, do one of the following:

- Double-click the asset name. This launches the default editor (as specified in your preferences—see Chapter 34, "Customizing Dreamweaver," for more details).

- Select the asset and then click the Edit button found in the lower-right corner of the panel.

The type of asset that you want to edit dictates what happens next. With assets such as images and Flash movies, an external application is launched with the file in question open inside that program. In this case, simply edit the asset and then export it again to your local site folder, overwriting the older version.

Colors and URLs will not launch a separate application. In fact, you can edit these types of assets only if they are in your Favorites section. Editing a color brings up a swatch box, where you can choose a new color. Editing URLs brings up an Edit URL box, where you can change the URL as well as the nickname that the Assets panel uses to describe the URL. Library items and templates will be opened for editing directly in the Document window.

Note

If you are editing a color, you can get out of the color swatch box without choosing a new color by pressing the Esc key.

Note

If nothing happens after you double-click an asset to edit it or use the Edit button, be sure to check the File Types/Editors section of your preferences to see if there's an application associated with that type of file.

Creating New Assets

While you cannot create every type of asset from the Asset panel, You can create new color, URL, template, and library assets. (Image, Flash and Shockwave assets are created outside of Dreamweaver.) You must be viewing your Favorites to create new colors and URLs.

To create a new color, make sure that the Favorites listing is currently being viewed, and select the Colors section. Click the New Color button in the lower-right corner of the panel. You can also use the context menu, either by right-clicking (Windows) or Ctrl-clicking (Mac) in the list or by selecting the right arrow button in the upper-right corner of the panel, and selecting New Color. This brings up a color swatch, where you can pick out your new color (see Figure 22.31). After you have selected a color, you can give it a nickname.

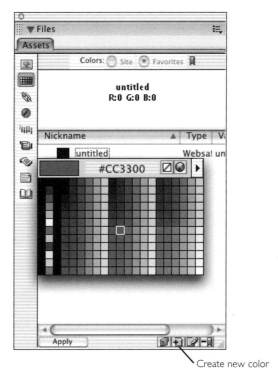

Create new color

Figure 22.31   Creating a new color asset.

To create a new URL, make sure that the Favorites listing is currently being viewed, and select the URLs section. Click the New URL button in the lower-right corner of the panel. You can also use the context menu, either by right-clicking (Windows) or Ctrl-clicking (Mac) in the list or by selecting the right arrow button in the upper-right corner of the panel, and selecting New URL. This brings up the Add URL dialog box, where you can define both the nickname and the URL path for this new asset.

Note

Notice that any colors or URLs you create in the Favorite Assets listing won't appear in the site listing until they've actually been used in the site. For a full discussion of creating templates and library items, see Chapter 25.

Summary

This chapter showed you the wide and wonderful world of Dreamweaver local site management. Before you ever even think of uploading your site to a web server for publication, all the behind-the-scenes work of file, link, and asset management has to take place. In this chapter, you learned how to use the Site panel—including the Site Files and Site Map view—to rearrange, rename, create, and delete files within a site. You learned how Dreamweaver can help you manage links across an entire site easily and painlessly. And you learned about managing media elements, colors, and URLs through the Assets panel. In the next chapter, you'll take your show on the road, by publishing your site masterpiece to a remote web server.

Chapter 23

Site Publishing and Maintenance

The preceding chapter helped you set up a

folder on your computer in which to store

all your files for your web site. After you

have the local root site folder all set up, you

will see that Dreamweaver has many tools

available to help you make sure your site stays together as well as tools that allow you to do sitewide searches and changes. However, no one but you will see the site while it lives solely on your own hard drive. You need to publish your site by putting it on a computer that anyone can access, such as a web server. This server might be for an internal intranet or for the Internet.

Where you put your site so others can see it is called the *remote site*. The remote site is generally a web server. If you are running your own server on your computer, then the remote site can be as simple as another folder on your computer. In the long run, what makes your web site a success (or failure) is what is in your remote site, because that is what the world will see. Dreamweaver has many tools to help you make your remote site up-to-date and functioning properly. Topics discussed in this chapter include how to define a remote site, including various access methods, working with your remote site, including uploading and downloading files and keeping your local and remote sites synchronized.

How Dreamweaver Works with Remote Sites

Before delving into the remote site functions and features Dreamweaver provides, you need a basic understanding of how Dreamweaver thinks about your remote sites.

As you've undoubtedly wandered about on the Internet, you're sure to have noticed that the web page addresses typically follow a basic and hopefully intuitive naming scheme. For instance, many home pages, or default documents, are called **index.htm**. If you click to view a certain company's products page, more often than not you'll be directed to the products subdirectory. Not only does this allow for better organization and maintenance, it just makes sense.

When you upload, or *put*, your web site, Dreamweaver will mirror its structure as closely as possible (always with *few* exceptions) on the remote site. If you have a file called **widgets.htm** in the products subdirectory on your local site, after the site is published you'll end up with a **widgets.htm** file in the products subdirectory on your remote site. Although this might seem rudimentary, this mirroring helps out in a few ways, including

- Assists in making updating and maintaining your site easier.
- Helps prevent broken, orphaned, or otherwise incorrect links.
- Helps prevent multiple copies of a web page or image file, conserving server space, and in some cases, the amount of bandwidth used.
- Adds to the level of professionalism your page exhibits.
- Makes it easier to understand and follow document-relative links.

In fact, to use many of the Dreamweaver remote file features, the local and remote site must mirror one another. Maintaining the file/folder structure is vital to maintaining all your links. This really isn't an issue, however, because Dreamweaver does this for you (including creating the required subdirectories) automatically with commands such as Synchronize, Get, Put, and so on. Next, you will learn how to properly configure your remote site in the Site Definition.

Defining a Remote Site in Dreamweaver

As with defining a local site, entering remote site information in Dreamweaver can be done either in Basic (Site Wizard) or Advanced mode. The latter is more efficient—a little bit scarier for web publishing newbies—than using the Site Wizard and offers more options.

To define remote information for a Dreamweaver site using Advanced mode, access the Site Definition dialog box by choosing Site > Edit Sites and, in the Edit Sites dialog box, select your site and click Edit. When the Site Definition dialog box appears, click the Advanced tab to bring it to the front. From the categories at the left, choose Remote Info (see Figure 23.1). The only option available when you first view the Remote Info section is the Access menu. What you select here will dynamically generate the remaining options. The following sections look at your choices here.

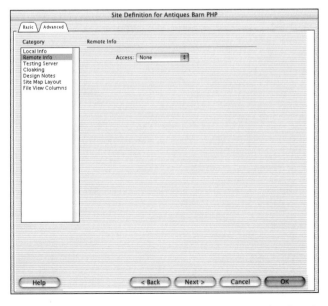

Figure 23.1   The Advanced Site Definition window with Remote Info selected.

Specifying No Connection

Choosing None as your access method offers no options and restricts you from uploading your site via Dreamweaver. You also cannot utilize some of the advanced site management features in Dreamweaver if you don't establish a remote connection.

Although having no remote access method established in the Site Definition prohibits you from using Dreamweaver to perform remote site functions (such as uploading your site), you can still do this with a third-party FTP client such as CuteFTP on Windows (`http://www.cuteftp.com/`) or Fetch on the Mac. If you're not familiar with such practices, however, it's strongly recommended you use the built-in remote site management features of Dreamweaver.

FTP

FTP stands for *File Transfer Protocol* and is easily the most widely used method for uploading web pages to a server (see Figure 23.2). You almost certainly will use this method when creating other organizations' web pages. Similar to HTTP (Hypertext Transfer Protocol, the protocol used to transfer web pages over the Internet), FTP requires a client and server application. In this instance, Dreamweaver acts as the FTP client. Software on the remote server acts as the FTP server. If you choose FTP as your access method in Dreamweaver, the Site Definition dialog box asks you for the following information (see Figure 23.2).

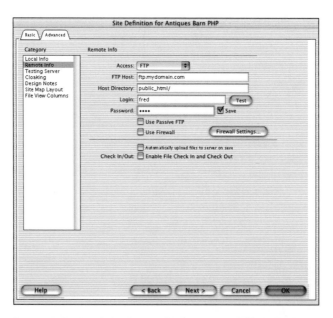

Figure 23.2   The Site Definition dialog box ready to set up an FTP connection to the remote site.

- **FTP Host**. This enables you to specify the address for the remote host of your web server. An example would be `ftp.remotehost.com` or `ftp.yourwebsite.com`. If you don't know this information, contact your network administrator or host provider (ISP).

- **Host Directory**. This specifies the directory on the server where your uploaded site will be located. A directory on the server is just like a folder on your local computer. A lot of servers have the site root set as `www`, `htdocs`, or `public_html/`. If you are unsure about the host directory, then leave it blank. This will default to the main directory of the FTP host. If there is an incorrect path in the host directory field, Dreamweaver might fail to connect even though your FTP information is correct, and you can connect with other FTP clients. If you are having trouble connecting, remove any value from the host directory field. After you can connect, then you can verify the correct folder.

- **Login**. This is the username of your account.

- **Password**. This is the password used to authenticate your account and gain access to the FTP server.

- **Use Passive FTP.** This is required by some firewalls, and enables Dreamweaver to set up the FTP session instead of having the FTP server do it. If you're unsure what this should be, leave it unchecked and ask your network administrator.

- **Use Firewall**. This dictates whether Dreamweaver should use the firewall preferences to connect to the FTP server. Ask your network administrator if you need to set these.

- **Use SSH Encrypted Secure Login**. This allows you to encrypt your login information. It does not encrypt the files that are being transferred. To enable SSH, Dreamweaver uses Putty, a free program that does the encrypting. You need to download Putty and install it before you can use the encryption.

- **Use Check In/Check Out**. This enables Dreamweaver's versioning software and is discussed in detail in Chapter 24, "Workplace Collaboration."

Note

You can set several more options for all of your sites' FTP connections by choosing Edit > Preferences > Site.

Local/Network

A local/network connection is used when the web server you will be publishing your pages on is located on the same local area network (LAN) as you are. Often this option is used when developing a company intranet site, or if you are providing the design and hosting for a site.

For this connection type, you must provide the path to the remote folder (see Figure 23.3). You can either type the information or use the browse button to locate your remote site folder.

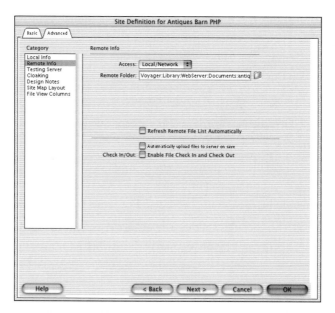

Figure 23.3   The Site Definition dialog box ready to set up a Local/Network connection to the remote site.

With this method of connection, you have the option of refreshing the remote file list automatically. If enabled, this causes Dreamweaver to refresh the file list for you (for example, reconnect to the remote folder and re-generate the list of remote files) every time files are added or deleted to the remote file. If you don't enable this option, you can still do this manually by choosing View > Refresh in the Site panel or Panel (Windows) or Site > Site Files View > Refresh (Mac).

SourceSafe Database, RDS, and WebDAV

Visual SourceSafe, RDS, and WebDAV are all *versioning systems*, meaning tools that allow multiple developers to work together and keep track of files so that developers don't overwrite each others work. Visual SourceSafe (VSS) is a Microsoft program. RDS and WebDAV are *protocols* (like FTP), meaning they are a set of rules used to communicate and track files. A protocol is a set of rules that computers agree upon to transfer files back and forth. These remote setting options are all just different ways of connecting to other computers and transferring files.

To learn more about Visual SourceSafe and WebDAV, and how they work in Dreamweaver, see Chapter 24.

Note

What about the Site Wizard? In the Site Wizard (the Basic tab of the Site Definition dialog box), remote site information is added in the Testing Files section. When you get to this screen of the Wizard, you're asked "How do you connect to your testing server?" The answer to this wizard question gives Dreamweaver the information it needs to set up your remote site. The same basic choices are available here as in the Advanced tab of the dialog box, beginning with choosing an access method.

Exercise 23.1   Setting Up Remote Information for the Grandpa's Ice Cream Site

In this exercise, you will set up the remote site information for the Grandpa's Ice Cream Site.

1. First, make sure you have your local site defined and your local root folder established. The **chapter_22** folder from the CD should be your local root folder. If you've already done the exercises in Chapter 22, "Local Site Management," you can use the same site and files for the exercises in this chapter.

   If you haven't gone through those exercises, copy the **chapter_22** folder from the CD to your hard drive. Define a site called Grandpa's Ice Cream, with the **chapter_22** folder as the local root folder.

2. Now, set up the remote folder. For this exercise, you'll assume that your workstation will double as your web server, so your remote folder will be another folder on the same computer.

Note

In the real world, if you were going to use your own computer as a web server, would you bother specifying a local and remote folder? Why not just publish the local folder and not have to worry about any remote site? Even in this unlikely circumstance, you're better off defining separate local and remote folders, because you can work on the local copies of your files while the general public is busy surfing your remote files.

3. Now that your ducks are in a row, it's time to define a site. Choose Site > Edit Sites. Select the Grandpa's Ice Cream site and click Edit.

4. This opens the Site Definition dialog box. Click on the Advanced tab to bring it to the front. From the categories at the left, choose Remote Info.

5. From the Access method pop-up menu, choose Local/Network. This adds a series of input fields to the dialog box.

6. The most important task here is to tell Dreamweaver where the remote folder is. Click the browse button and use the dialog box that appears to navigate to your **chapter_23** folder. Dreamweaver/Windows users: Be sure you're inside the **chapter_23** folder before clicking Select. Dreamweaver/Mac users: Be sure you're outside the **chapter_23** folder and have it selected in the dialog box before clicking Choose.

7. You can also set your Local/Network connection options. Enable Refresh local file list automatically. Leave the other two options unselected.

8. That's it! Figure 23.4 shows what your settings should look like. Click OK to close the Site Definition dialog box. Then Click Done to close the Edit Site dialog box.

That's all there is to it! Now you are ready to rock and roll (and publish your site as well).

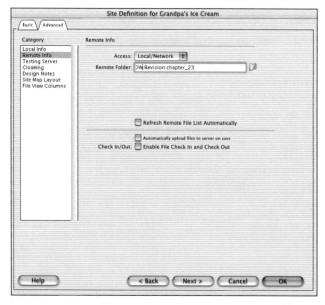

Figure 23.4   The Remote Info category of the Site Definition dialog box for the Grandpa's Ice Cream site.

Working with a Remote Site

Now that you've set up the remote site information in your Site Definition dialog box, you can interact with the remote server. This section teaches you the steps involved in basic remote site file management. More advanced discussion, such as on the Synchronization feature, appears later in this chapter. This section discusses two primary functions: connecting to and disconnecting from the remote server, and uploading and downloading files. Figure 23.5 shows the Site panel with items relevant to remote site management highlighted.

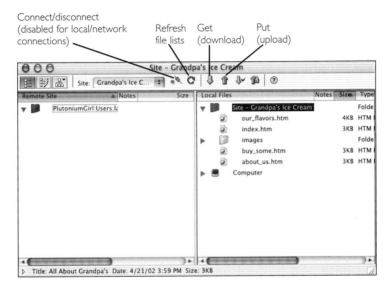

Figure 23.5   The Site panel.

Viewing Remote Information in the Site Panel

When you expand the Site panel to show both its left and right panes, you have the option of showing the site map or the Remote File list in the left-hand pane. To show the Remote File list, click the Files icon at the upper-left corner of the expanded window (see Figure 23.5).

In contrast to Dreamweaver, most FTP programs show local information on the left and remote information on the right. If you would prefer your Site panel to use this setup, choose Edit > Preferences > Site and reverse the order there.

Connecting and Disconnecting

The Connect/Disconnect button (see Figure 23.5) enables you to connect to and disconnect from a remote FTP server. This option also is available if you use a source control system such as SourceSafe or WebDAV. If you publish to a server located locally on your computer or your network, this button will be grayed out because you are automatically connected to the local server. This button will also be grayed out if you have not specified a remote FTP server in your Site Definition.

If you are using an FTP connection, you would select the Connect button to connect to the FTP server before moving your files from the local to the remote folder. When you connect, a green light appears in the lower-left portion of the Connect button icon. This lets you know that you're connected to the remote server and toggles the button's function to Disconnect. Pressing the button in this state disconnects you from the remote server.

If you experience problems connecting to your remote server (or perhaps if you just want to know what Dreamweaver is really doing when you press the Connect button), you can view the FTP log by selecting View > Site FTP Log (Windows) or Site > Site FTP Log (Mac). This provides a real-time client/server log of your FTP requests and responses. This also shows you how Dreamweaver creates directories, uploads and downloads files, and uses many other FTP commands.

Note

Macromedia maintains a TechNote that lists FTP commands and shows you how to interpret an FTP log. The address for this resource is www.macromedia.com/support/dreamweaver/ts/documents/ftp_errors.htm.

Getting and Putting

After you're connected to your remote site, it's time to either place your files there or to download files from there to work on them. When you want to upload, or place a file on the remote server, it's called *putting* because you are putting your files on the remote site. When you want to download a file from the remote server, it's called *getting* because you are getting a file from the remote folder. In Dreamweaver, you can get and put in a variety of ways:

- Select the files you want to upload or download and click the Get or Put button at the top of the Site panel (see Figure 23.5).

- Select the files to upload or download and use the menu commands: Site > Get or Site > Put.

- Select the files to upload or download and right-click (Ctrl–click) on your selected files to access Get or Put in the contextual menu.

- Select the files to upload or download and use the shortcut keys, Ctrl/Cmd+Shift+D or Ctrl/Cmd+Shift+U.

- The fun but dangerous way, drag-and-drop your files from one site of the Site panel to the other.

When you put or get, if an older version of a file exists in the target location, it will be overwritten.

When you select to either Get or Put files, the Dependent Files dialog box appears, asking whether it should include all files linked to inside the HTML documents. These files include images and other media content. Select Yes or No accordingly. You also might tell Dreamweaver whether it should ask you this in the future. If you decide to have Dreamweaver not ask you in the future, you might decide later that you would like it to. You can turn on this prompt again by going to the Site section of your Preferences and checking Prompt on Get or Put. If you decide to leave this feature hidden, you might force Dreamweaver to ask you on a one-time basis by holding Alt (Windows) or Opt (Mac), while selecting the Get or Put buttons.

Tip

If you press the Get or Put button without being connected to the remote site, Dreamweaver will connect automatically if possible.

Keeping Local and Remote Sites Synchronized

During your life as a web designer/programmer, you are sure to spend a late night or two trying to get a project done on time. It is possible that as the sun is rising and you are working away furiously that you might lose track of whether or not you have uploaded the most recent version of a document to the remote site. How can you keep track of the most recent files and whether they have been placed on the remote site? Dreamweaver offers two ways to do this: manually and automatically. The next section covers the old-fashioned manual method. Then the discussion turns to the powerful Synchronize command, which enables you to do this automatically.

Select Newer Local/Remote Files

You can use the Select Newer Local or the Select Newer Remote command to manually synchronize your sites. This function compares the modified date on the local machine for each file with the modified date on the remote server for each file.

Select Newer Local

To select the newer files on the local site, select Edit > Select Newer Local (Windows) or Site > Site Files View > Select Newer Local (Mac). After Dreamweaver has compared the modified dates on both the local and remote sites, it will highlight all the files in the local window that are more current than those on the remote site. From here, you can simply click the Put button and all the files that are more current on your local site will be uploaded to the remote site.

Select Newer Remote

If you are working as part of a team on a single site, it is possible that the remote site has a more current version of a document than you have on your local site. In this case, before you make any changes on a document you should check to see if there is a more recent version on the remote server. You can do this by selecting Edit > Select Newer Remote (Windows) or Site > Site Files View > Select Newer Remote (Mac). In this case, the files that have a more recent modification date on the remote side as compared to your local site will be highlighted. Then all you need to do to get the most recent versions is click the Get button and they will be downloaded to your local site.

Note

The first time you upload your files to the server, you might notice that your local modified dates are not accurate. With the initial upload, Dreamweaver will change the local timestamp so that it matches the server time. That way, in the future it can compare timestamps and calculate what files have been changed and should be synchronized.

If Dreamweaver is unable to determine the timestamp on the server, you'll get a warning that synchronization can't occur. You can still get and put files, but you will be unable to find the newer files, either on the local or remote site.

Because Dreamweaver highlights only files that are newer, those that are exactly the same (that is, those that have the same modification date and time) will not be selected. If your site is already synchronized, no files will be selected after running both of these commands. You might think that nothing happened, but it's just that the sites are already up-to-date.

Be aware that because Dreamweaver checks all the files of a site, the Select Newer Remote command could take a long time. This is the case if you have a slow connection to the remote server. Sometimes this might be mistaken as Dreamweaver "freezing." Please be patient, especially if you are connecting via a modem.

The Synchronize Command

To access the Synchronize command, choose Site > Synchronize. The Synchronize command provides a much better way to synchronize your files than the method of manually selecting newer files. Part of the beauty and power of this command is that you can choose to synchronize as much or as little as you want. This means that you can synchronize just one folder, just one file, or the entire site. You also can choose to remove any file on the remote site that is not located on the local site copy, or vice versa. This is not possible with the previous (manual) method.

To synchronize your site using the Synchronize command, follow these steps:

1. Unless you want to synchronize the entire site, select the files you want to synchronize.

2. Choose Site > Synchronize. The Synchronize Files dialog box displays (see Figure 23.6).

3. From the Synchronize pull-down menu, choose whether to update the entire site or just the selected files.

4. From the Direction pull-down menu, select what you want to do from these options:

   • Put only those files that are newer locally to the remote site. (You will only send files.)

   • Get only those files that are newer remotely to the local site. (You will only receive files.)

   • Synchronize both the local and the remote site with each other. (You will both send and receive files.)

Figure 23.6   The Synchronize Files dialog box.

5. If you select Get and Put Newer Files from the Direction menu, go straight to step 6. If you select one of the other two directions, you can specify one additional option. If you are putting newer files to the remote site, you can select to delete remote files not on the local drive by checking the appropriate box. If you are getting newer files from the remote site, you have the option to delete any local files that aren't on the remote site. To select the delete option, check the box on the lower left. Remember that deleting a file is final and cannot be undone. Use this option with great care.

6. Press Preview. This processes your files for synchronization and opens the Synchronize window (see Figure 23.7). This gives you a preview of what will happen when you click OK, showing how many files are to be updated, the action that will be taken on that file (get, put, or delete), and the filename.

7. By default, all check boxes are checked in the Action column of this dialog box. Deselecting a check box removes the file from being processed. This enables you to ensure that you know exactly what is happening and lets you change what Dreamweaver does, just in case you know something that it doesn't.

8. Press OK.

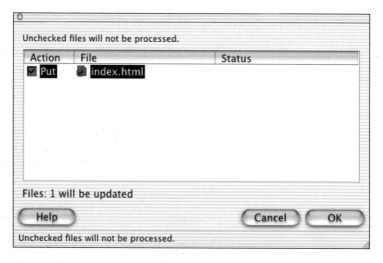

Figure 23.7   The Synchronize window showing one file needing to be uploaded.

When synchronizing with the Direction option Get Newer Files from Remote, you can delete files locally that aren't found on the remote server. When synchronizing the other way, with Get Newer Files from Local, you can delete files on the remote server that aren't found locally. Be extremely careful with both of these options, however. It is common to keep source files, such as Photoshop *.psd** files or Fireworks *.png** files in folders within your local site for convenience that shouldn't be uploaded or deleted. Similarly, you might have necessary files on the web server (the remote site) that don't have counterparts in your local site—script files or web site stats, for instance.

After you have completed the synchronization, you will be able to see the actions that Dreamweaver performed. Dreamweaver shows the progress of the synchronization and, after it's done, enables you to save a text file of the procedure for future reference.

Exercise 23.2   Working with Grandpa's Local and Remote Sites

In this exercise, you will get some practice uploading, downloading, and synchronizing between the local and remote Grandpa's Ice Cream sites. Before going through this exercise, make sure you've defined the local and remote sites as outlined in Exercise 23.1.

1. Make sure Grandpa's Ice Cream is the active site. Expand your Site panel so you can view both local and remote file lists at the same time.

2. To start with, the remote folder for Grandpa's is empty! That's the way you normally start out when you create a new web site. There's nothing on the server.

   To upload the entire site, click the folder at the top of your local Site Files list. This selects the entire site.

3. At the top of the Site panel, click Put. Dreamweaver will probably ask if you want to upload dependent files. Choose No. (Because you have all of your dependent files selected, it doesn't really matter what you choose in this dialog box.) Figure 23.8 shows the results of this.

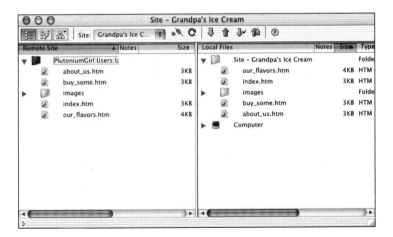

Figure 23.8   The local and remote Grandpa's sites showing mirror structures.

4. You're going to test the Dreamweaver synchronization features by altering one of the local files and seeing if Dreamweaver notices.

   From your local Site Files list, double-click **our_flavors.htm** to open it.

5. Change any of the ice cream flavors that you like. Add your favorite; subtract anything you think is disgusting. When you're finished, save and close **our_flavors.htm**.

   Repeat the process to change **buy_some.htm**. Maybe you should remove Montgomery Wards from the list of stores, because it doesn't exist anymore. Any stores you'd like to add? When you're finish, save and close.

6. Choose Edit > Select Newer Local (Windows) or Site > Site Files View > Select Newer Local (Mac). Dreamweaver thinks for a split second, then highlights **our_flavors.htm** and **buy_some.htm** in the local Site Files list. Remember, the goal is to make the remote site a mirror of the local site. That's what synchronizing is all about.

7. Those are your two updated files. Now that they're selected, click the Put button to put them. (There's no need to upload dependent files.)

8. That was handy! Now, though, you'll try something a bit fancier. In the local Site Files list, right-click (Ctrl-click) on the local root folder and from the contextual menu choose New Folder. When the new folder appears, name it **pages**.

   Still in the local Site Files list, move **buy_some.htm**, **our_flavors.htm**, and **about_us.htm** into the **pages** folder. (You're tidying up your site organization.) When Dreamweaver asks if you want to update your links, click Update.

9. Now try synchronizing again. Choose Edit > Select Newer Local (Windows) or Site > Site Files View > Select Newer Local (Mac). When Dreamweaver makes its selection, click the Put button to upload all selected files.

   How do your remote and local sites look (see Figure 23.9)? Are they still mirroring each other? No! Dreamweaver added a new **pages** folder and filled it with pages—but it didn't remove the old HTML files. Why not? Because it doesn't realize that you haven't created any new files, you've just rearranged existing files.

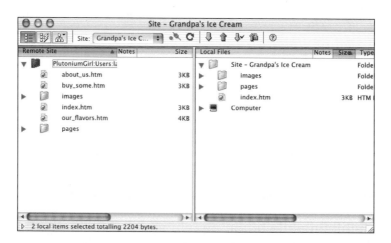

Figure 23.9   The Grandpa's site after manual synchronization, not quite perfectly aligned anymore.

This is a good example of what happens quite frequently when dealing with local and remote sites. Slowly, over the course of editing and rearranging your files, old files start collecting on the web server, not doing any harm but taking up vital storage space. Manual synchronization doesn't get rid of them.

10. Time to synchronize the automatic way! Choose Site > Synchronize. When the dialog box appears, choose to synchronize the entire local site, putting newer local files to remote. And enable the Delete Remote Files Not on Local Drive option. (This is the Clean-up command.)

11. When you've set your options, click the Preview button. Dreamweaver now compares the modified dates of the local site and remote site and lists the items that are newer on the local site in the Synchronize window (Figure 23.7). Notice that from this list you can choose whether or not you want to upload, or put, each item individually. This is an important safeguard, giving you every chance not to delete needed files from the server. For this exercise, don't deselect any files.

12. Click Update. Now the list shows you that the extra files have been deleted and the synchronization is complete (see Figure 23.10).

13. Click OK. Your synchronization is done!

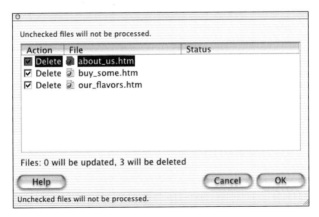

Figure 23.10   The Synchronize window showing the extra files that must be deleted.

Cloaking

MX

Because it is so common to keep assets in your local site folder that you never want to upload to your remote site, Macromedia has incorporated a cloaking function into Dreamweaver MX. *Site cloaking* allows you to exclude folders or file types in a site from certain site operations, such as Get or Put. Note that you can cloak file types, such as PNGs but not individual files. The items you choose to cloak are site specific meaning that each site on which you work can cloak different folders or file types. You can cloak folders or file types on either the local or remote site.

When a folder is cloaked, it will be excluded from the following operations:

- Put/Get

- Check In/Check Out

- Undo checkout

- Reports

- Select newer local/Select newer remote

- Check links sitewide/Change links sitewide

- Synchronize

- Search/Replace sitewide

- Asset panel contents

- Template updating/Library updating

Enabling Cloaking

The ability to use the cloaking feature is enabled by default. If you want to turn it off temporarily or permanently, you have that option. If you disable cloaking, all cloaked files will be uncloaked. If, later, you choose to use cloaking again, previously cloaked files become cloaked. To disable cloaking, choose Site > Cloaking > Enable/Disable Cloaking in Current Site (see Figure 23.11).

Figure 23.11   Enabling cloaking in the Preferences dialog box.

Specifying a Cloaked Folder

To cloak a folder, simply select the folder you want to cloak then choose Site > Cloaking > Cloak. You will see a red line through the folder icon in the Site panel (see Figure 23.12).

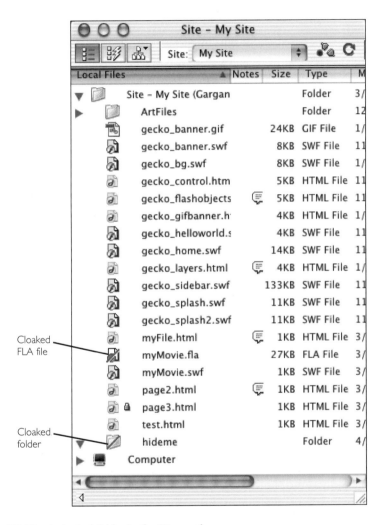

Figure 23.12   A cloaked folder in the Site panel.

Cloaking Specific File Types

Cloaking specific file types is a little different. If you want to cloak a file type, you need to use the Advanced Site Definition options. Do it this way:

1. Select Site > Cloaking > Settings. This opens the Site Definition dialog box's Cloaking category.

2. Enable cloaking based on file type by clicking the Cloak Files Ending With check box. You can see that by default Dreamweaver is offering to cloak PNG and FLA files. (These are the authoring files for Fireworks and Flash.)

3. Specify the types of files to cloak by typing the three letter extension belonging to the file type you wish to cloak. Separate the entries with a space. If you don't want to cloak PNG or FLA files, just delete those entries.

4. When you're finished, click OK to close the Site Definition dialog box. Dreamweaver brings up an Alert dialog box indicating that the cache will be re-created. Click OK to close this window.

From now on, all files belonging to the type you designated show up in the Site panel with a red line through them.

To uncloak a specific file type, open the Site Definition window, go to the Cloaking category, and uncheck the Cloak Files box.

If you want to uncloak all cloaked files—regardless of whether they were cloaked by file type or by location—choose Site > Cloaking > Uncloak All. Dreamweaver makes sure you really want to perform this task by bringing up a dialog box that asks "Are You Sure You Want To Do This?". Click Yes. Now all files and folders are uncloaked, regardless of the technique used to cloak them.

Summary

In this chapter, you learned how to define a remote site. You learned how to work with your remote site, including uploading and downloading files. And finally, this chapter discussed the ways that Dreamweaver enables you to keep your local and remote sites synchronized and up-to-date (manually and automatically), and how to exclude certain files from synchronization by cloaking them. The next two chapters expand your site management horizons by looking at features aimed specifically at design teams working together on large sites.

Chapter 24

Workplace Collaboration

So far in this part of the book, your site has been discussed mainly as a single-developer project. Although a great many issues are the same regardless of the number of people involved in the development and enhancement of your site, some distinct differences exist, including some challenges. This chapter addresses those differences. If you are always the sole developer of your sites, most of this information isn't going to apply to you. However, some of it might prove beneficial or interesting, so you should at least skim each area briefly. Topics discussed in this chapter include the challenges you face when working in a collaborative environment, how to utilize Design Notes to make managing your workflow easier, including customizing file view columns, implementing and using the built-in version control system in Dreamweaver, implementing and using other version control systems (such as WebDAV and Visual SourceSafe), and creating and using reports about project workflow.

Challenges of Working in a Design Team

Often, designing, creating, and implementing a web site by yourself is a daunting and challenging task. Throw in a group of people who are trying to accomplish the same tasks simultaneously, and you introduce a whole slew of additional possible problems and issues. Most of these issues can be categorized in one of two areas: technical or interpersonal.

Technical

Technical challenges are issues related to software (Dreamweaver or your web server software) and hardware (computers) that present themselves when trying to move from a single-user development arena to a multiuser situation. For web development, common technical issues include the following:

- Making sure all developers edit the newest revisions and that their changes are immediately available for other team members to view/edit

- Making sure some form of version control—either through the Dreamweaver Check In and Check Out or another method—will prohibit developers from editing the same file simultaneously

- Providing a central repository that is accessible by the entire team (including any telecommuters) where development files can be stored

Interpersonal

Interpersonal challenges are issues related to communication within the team. Functioning as part of a team involves more than just working on computers and going in and out of the same door. People must work together. Communication is essential because misperceived instructions and ignorance of current information will cause disastrous delays and expense.

For web development, common interpersonal issues include the following:

- Making sure all developers are suited to functioning in a team environment, which is different from being a "star" designer off on one's own

- Making sure all developers communicate regularly, and understand each other's communications

- Making sure all developers edit the newest revisions and that their changes are immediately available for other team members to view/edit

Using Design Notes for Improved Workflow

The idea behind Dreamweaver Design Notes is simple: a *Design Note* is a piece of information about a document, that follows that document wherever it goes (from your office computer to all the other computers in the office, and even to the web server itself if necessary), and that can be accessed at any time by any design team member. Therefore, Design Notes enable you to leave notes associated with specific files for yourself and your coworkers. This means that you can track changes to documents, map their progress and history, or update and change a document's completion status. Though this chapter focuses on using Design Notes to save information such as file status for HTML documents, they can potentially store any type of information that you can think of, and can be attached to any kind of file.

Note

Design Notes as they pertain to image editing are discussed in Chapter 5, "Working with Images." Customizing your file view columns using Design Notes is covered in Chapter 22, "Local Site Management."

How Design Notes Work

Have you ever noticed that, after you've created a Dreamweaver site and worked on several files in it, your computer suddenly shows a new folder called **_notes** inside the local root folder? That folder doesn't show up when you view your files using the Site Files pane of the Site panel; but when you leave Dreamweaver and return to Windows Explorer or the Macintosh Finder, there it is.

The **_notes** folder is the repository for all of your site's Design Notes. Open this folder, and you'll see a selection of files, all named after various files from your site, but with the **.mno** extension added (see Figure 24.1). These are your Design Notes files. Open one of the files, either in your favorite text editor or in Dreamweaver Code view, and you'll see a chunk of XML code that looks something like this:

```
<?xml version="1.0" encoding="iso-8859-1" ?>
<info>
    <infoitem key="status" value="draft" />
    <infoitem key="author" value="Julius Marx" />
</info>
```

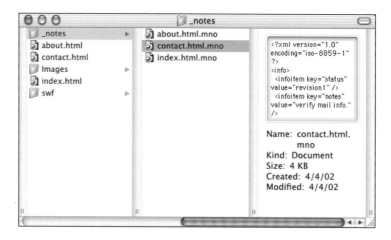

Figure 24.1   Design Notes as they appear in the local root folder structure.

Each piece of information about the parent file is stored as an `<infoitem/>` tag containing a key/value pair (status/draft, for instance). The first time a document needs a piece of information about itself to be stored, Dreamweaver creates the MNO file. After that, every new piece of information that needs to be stored will add another `<infoitem/>` tag. Dreamweaver, Fireworks, and Flash can all access and read the same Design Notes, which is what makes the tight integration between the programs possible. And when the site files are moved from one computer to another, the Design Notes are moved as well, so various team members can all access the same pieces of information and coordinate their work.

Enabling Design Notes for a Site

Before you begin using Design Notes, you need to set up basic Design Notes capability in your site. To enable Design Notes, follow these steps:

1. Access the Site Definition dialog box by choosing Site > Edit Sites, selecting your site in the Define Sites dialog box, and clicking Edit.

2. In the Site Definition dialog box, choose the Design Notes category (see Figure 24.2).

3. Make sure that the Maintain Design Notes option is selected. This is the very basic item that you must have checked to use any type of Design Notes capability on the site.

4. If you're using Design Notes as a communication aid in a collaborative work environment, select Upload Design Notes for Sharing. With this feature enabled, every time you upload a document to the Remote site, the file's associated Design Note is uploaded with it. This allows all team members who share work on a document to view the status of a document or image quickly and easily, and send notes regarding work to be done on the document.

   If you're only using Design Notes for your own benefit, in a single-user environment, leave this option deselected to speed up file transfer between Local and Remote sites.

Figure 24.2   The Design Notes category of the Site Definition dialog box.

Working with Design Notes

After you've enabled Design Notes, you (and your coworkers) can view, create, edit, and delete notes as you need them, to store any document-related information you like.

Accessing Notes

The main interface for working with Design Notes is the Design Notes dialog box (see Figures 24.3 and 24.4). To access this dialog box, do one of the following:

- Open the file whose Design Note you want to work with, and Go to File > Design Notes.

- In the Site Files pane of the Site panel, right-click (Windows) or Ctrl-click (Mac) on the file whose Design Note you want to work with, and from the contextual menu that appears, select Design Notes.

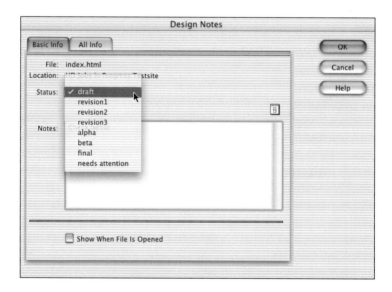

Figure 24.3   The Design Notes dialog box, Basic Info tab.

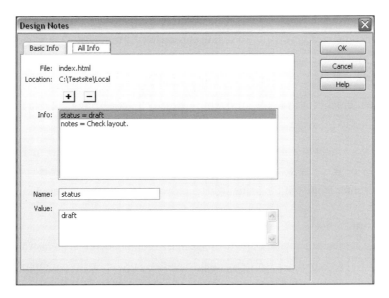

Figure 24.4   The Design Notes dialog box, All Info tab.

The Basic tab contains a nice, friendly interface for assigning document status and jotting down comments to share with coworkers (or reminders to yourself). The All Info tab displays all Design Notes for the current document, including status, comments, and any other Design Notes (including those added automatically by Dreamweaver, Fireworks, or Flash for working with the document). For most day-to-day collaborative tasks, the Basic Info tab will probably be enough; the All Info tab is for those who are serious about taking Design Notes to the max.

Note

If the file Check In and Check Out system is in use, you need to check out a file before accessing its associated Design Note.

Creating, Editing, and Deleting Notes

After you've accessed the Design Notes interface, you can create notes, edit them, and remove them using the Basic Info and All Info tabs of the dialog box. The Basic Info tab provides a nice, friendly interface for commonly used items of information; but the All Info tab gives you a better sense of how Design Notes work, by presenting its information as name/value pairs.

Setting Document Status

Labeling documents according to their current status (draft, revision1, and so on) is an important tool in a collaborative workflow. Setting the status Design Note for a document is quick and easy, but also offers powerful options.

To set the document status to one of the pre-defined choices, bring the Basic Info tab of the dialog box to the front, and choose from the Status pop-up menu.

To set the document status to a value not on the list of choices (Beta 1, Beta 2, for instance), bring the All Info tab to the front. Click the plus (+) to add a new note. In the Name field, enter **status**; in the Value field, enter your custom value (**beta 1**).

Adding Comments

Any miscellaneous notes you want to make regarding a document—instructions on what needs to be revised, peer review, whatever—can be saved by typing into the comment field in the Basic Info tab. To put a date stamp on the note, click the date icon above the note field. After you've filled in a note, bring the All Info tab to the front will reveal that the note is actually saved as a name/value pair Design Note, just like status.

Adding Other Information

Any name/value pair can be saved as a comment, by using the All Info tab of the Design Notes dialog box. For collaborative workflow, for instance, you might want to track authorship of documents, due dates, or task hours. To add any of these pieces of information, bring the All Info tab to the front, click the plus (+) button to add a new pair, and enter a name and value.

Tip

Design Notes are great for job tracking, because documents can be organized and searched according to the name portion of the name/value pair. If you want to use custom Design Notes for this purpose, however, make sure you are consistent and predictable in naming your name/value pairs. It's no good trying to track authorship of documents across a site, for instance, if some documents have a Design Note named author and others have a Design Note named writer.

Viewing Design Notes in the Site panel

You can see at a glance which files in your site have Design Notes by examining the Site Files list. Any file with at least one Design Note will display an icon in the Notes column. If your Site panel doesn't display the Notes column, either because the column doesn't fit in the window pane or because the column is not enabled, you can change the File View Columns settings in your Site Definition dialog box so that it does show (see Figure 24.5).

Note

For more on File View Columns in the Site panel, see Chapter 22.

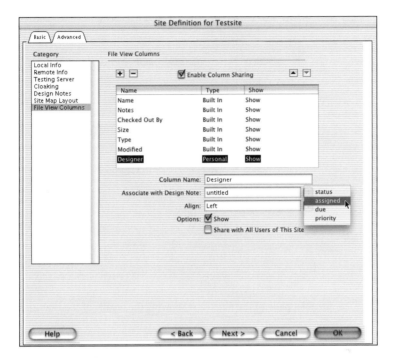

Figure 24.5   The File View Columns category of the Site Definition dialog box showing rearranged columns and a new Design Note column being added.

You can also customize the File View Columns in the Site panel to show the value of a particular Design Note. To do this, follow these steps:

1. Open the Site Definition dialog box for the site, and go to the File View Columns category (see Figure 24.5).

2. Click the plus (+) button to add a column. Your new column will appear at the bottom of the list of columns.

3. In the Column Name input field, enter the name that you want to appear the top of the column.

4. In the Associate with Design Note input field, type the name of the Design Note whose value you want to appear in the column (or choose from the pop-up menu of names).

5. Use the up/down buttons at the top of the dialog box to rearrange the order of columns, if you like. Figure 24.6 shows the resulting changes to the Site panel.

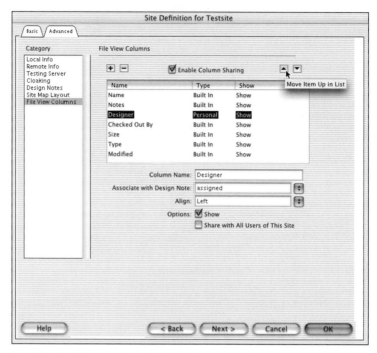

Figure 24.6   The Site Files pane of the Site panel showing the results of the changes made.

Exercise 24.1   Creating a Status Design Note, and Viewing It in the Site Panel

In this exercise, you'll create status Design Notes for several files within the Grandpa's Ice Cream site. You'll set different status values, and examine how Dreamweaver is implementing the Design Note. And you'll customize the Site panel to display your Design Note for easy tracking.

Before you start, copy the files from the **chapter_22** folder on the CD to your hard drive.

1. The site you'll be working with is Grandpa's Ice Cream. The files for this site are all in the **chapter_22/local** folder. Define a site called Grandpa's Ice Cream, with **chapter_22/local** as the local root folder and **chapter_22/remote** as the remote folder. (See Chapter 22 and 23, if needed, for more about defining local and remote sites.)

2. With your Site panel set to view Site Files, examine the file structure of the Grandpa's site. You'll see several HTML files and their supporting images.

3. Start by assigning a draft status to **index.htm**. Open the file, and go to File > Design Notes.

   In the Design Notes dialog box that appears, from the Status pop-up menu choose draft.

   To see that Dreamweaver is interpreting this note as a name/value pair, bring the All Info tab of the dialog box to the front. Dreamweaver has generated a name/value pair consisting of status/draft.

   When you're done, click OK to close the dialog box.

4. To see how the Design Note has been saved as a Design Note file, use Windows Explorer or your operating system's file browser to examine the files in the local site's folders. You'll see a **_notes** folder, which will now contain a file called **index.html.mno**. Open that file (it will open in Code view) and examine the XML code within. When you're done, close the file.

5. Repeating the above procedure twice more, assign draft status to **buy_some.htm** and **about_us.htm**.

6. For the remaining file—**our_flavors.htm**—Grandpa wants you to assign a new status called approved. This requires a slightly different procedure.

   As before, open the file and go to File > Design Notes to access the dialog box. But instead of choosing from the Status pop-up menu (which doesn't contain the word approved), bring the All Info tab to the front.

   Click the plus (+) button to add a new Design Note. In the Name input field, type **status**. In the Value field, type **approved**.

7. Now you want the Site panel to show you which site files have been assigned which status. You'll do that by creating a custom column for the Site Files pane. Start by opening the Site Definition dialog box for the Grandpa's site, and going to the File View Columns category.

8. To add a new column, click the plus (+) button. This activates the input fields at the bottom of the column information area.

   In the Column Name field, enter **Status**.

   For the Associate with Design Name field, choose status from the pop-up menu (or type it into the field).

   Finally, use the up and down arrows at the top of the dialog box to rearrange your columns so the new Status column is located below the Name column.

   When you're done, click OK to close the dialog box.

   Check out your Site panel! Figure 24.7 shows how your view of Grandpa's site should now look.

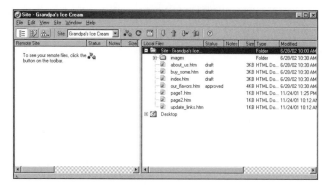

Figure 24.7   The Site Files view for Grandpa's web site, after assigning status Design Notes and adding them to the File View Columns.

Version Control

Imagine that you come to work bright and early and decide to redesign your company website's homepage. Two hours later, the fellow down the hall comes to work and—without talking to you—he also decides to redesign the home page. You finish first and upload your redesigned homepage to the web server and go to lunch. Later that day he finishes and uploads his redesigned home page to the web server. Your home page is now gone. This is what can happen without version control.

Server-Based Version Control

Dreamweaver 4 added support for source and version control systems such as Microsoft Visual SourceSafe (VSS) and WebDAV-enabled software—two large, complex pieces of administrative software that are installed on web servers to control workflow. These applications act like librarians sitting on the server. Any time a team member wants to work on a particular file, she must "check it out" from the server, like checking a book out from the library. After a book is checked out, it still exists on the server, but no other team members are allowed to access it until the original member has checked it back in. Just like a human librarian would, the server software keeps track of who has checked files out and when, so team members and managers can watch the workflow progress by monitoring which files are being accessed.

> **Note**
>
> A few basic differences between VSS and WebDAV could be important when deciding on the right solution for you. VSS is distributed by Microsoft and, as such, is a for-sale solution. It also maintains a database of file information and status for its control mechanism. WebDAV, on the other hand, is a freely distributed "open-standard" that runs on top of an existing web server.

If your web server uses either of these technologies, you can take advantage of their version control features while working in Dreamweaver by using special protocols to connect to the remote server, as defined in the Remote Info section of the Site Definition dialog box.

Visual SourceSafe Integration

Currently, only Windows computers are able to connect to a VSS server-side database. Windows users, you need to obtain and install the Microsoft Visual SourceSafe 6.0 client software on your computer before you can configure Dreamweaver to work with VSS.

Note

Currently, there is no way for Macintosh users to connect to a VSS database. MetroWerks used to make a client that was used to connect Macintoshes to VSS, but they have discontinued that product. Current owners of MetroWerks VSS client should be able to connect with Dreamweaver MX. find out the latest on this, visit www.macromedia.com/support/dreamweaver/ts/documents/vss_on_mac.htm.

To set up Visual SourceSafe for your site, follow these steps (see Figure 24.8):

Figure 24.8   Using the Site Definition dialog box to set up Visual SourceSafe integration.

1. Open the Site Definition dialog box for the site, and go to the Remote Info category.

2. From the Access pop-up menu, choose SourceSafe Database. This is the method Dreamweaver will use to connect to the remote server.

3. The dialog box will change to present VSS options. Click the Settings button, which appears next to the Access menu. The Open SourceSafe Database dialog box displays. Enter the settings as follows:

   - For the Database Path, browse to or enter the path of the SourceSafe database that you want to use. This will be a **srcsafe.ini** file and will be used to initialize SourceSafe.

   - For the Project, enter the SourceSafe project that you want to use as the root of the remote site. Note that this field must contain a $/, but anything else is optional.

   - Enter your username and password into the remaining fields. You can choose to save your password or require it to be entered each time you connect to the database.

   - When you're done, select OK to close the Settings dialog box.

Note

If you're unsure of any of these settings, contact your system or network administrator for assistance, or consult the Microsoft Visual SourceSafe documentation.

4. Back in the Site Definition dialog box, choose the Check Out Files When Opening option in the check box if you want Dreamweaver to check out the files from the SourceSafe database when double-clicking them in the Site panel.

5. Click OK to save these changes and close the dialog box.

You now can connect and disconnect from the SourceSafe database and use normal Dreamweaver file control commands such as Get, Put, Check In, Check Out, and Refresh.

WebDAV Integration

Short for *World Wide Web Distributed Authoring and Versioning*, WebDAV is a protocol rather than an application. It defines additional HTTP methods and headers, and is an extension to the HTTP/1.1 protocol. WebDAV can be integrated into HTTP servers such as Apache and Microsoft's Internet Information Server (IIS). Unlike VSS integration, to connect to a WebDAV server you don't need any special client software on your computer.

Note

For more information on HTTP servers—how they work and what they do—see Chapter 26, "Introduction to Dynamic Dreamweaver."

To set up WebDAV integration for your site, follow these steps (see Figure 24.9):

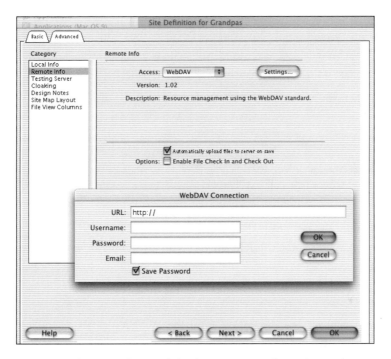

Figure 24.9   Using the Site Definition dialog box to set up WebDAV integration.

1. Open the Site Definition dialog box for the site, and go to the Remote Info category.

2. From the Access pop-up menu, choose WebDAV. This is the method Dreamweaver will use to connect to the remote server.

3. The dialog box will change to present WebDAV options. Click the Settings button, which appears next to the Access menu. The WebDAV Connection dialog box displays. Enter the settings as follows:

   - For the URL, enter the full URL of the site to which you want to connect. This includes the protocol used (`http://`) as well as the directory, if not just the domain root. *Important tip*: HTTP requests are usually routed by the server to port 80. If you want to use a port other than 80 to connect to

the WebDAV server (recommended), you just append :PortNumber to the
end of the URL—for example, http://webdav.org:81 as opposed to
http://webdav.org.

- Enter your username and password into their respective fields. You can
  choose to save your password or require it to be entered each time you connect to the database.

- Enter a valid email address in the Email textbox. This is used on the
  WebDAV-enabled server to identify who is using a particular file and it offers
  contact information accessible via the Site panel.

- When you're done, select OK to close the Settings dialog box.

Note

If you're unsure of any of these settings, contact your system or network administrator
for assistance. You can also consult the WebDAV documentation or go to
www.webdav.org for help (and you'll probably need it).

4. Back in the Site Definition dialog box, choose the Check Out Files When
   Opening option in the check box if you want Dreamweaver to check out the files
   from the SourceSafe database when double-clicking them in the Site panel.

5. Click OK to save these changes and close the dialog box.

You now can connect and disconnect from the WebDAV database and use normal
Dreamweaver file control commands such as Get, Put, Check In, Check Out, and
Refresh.

Version Control Using Check In/Check Out

Unless you're working in a large corporation, you probably won't need the power of VSS
or WebDAV. No matter where you're working, your design team might not have any say
in the software configuration of the company web server. But you might still benefit
from some sort of version control system.

The Dreamweaver Check In/Check Out feature provides a good, inexpensive alternative
to server-based version control, along the same lines as that found in VSS and WebDAV,
but without any server-based components. Similar to those other solutions, when using
Check In/Check Out Dreamweaver acts as a librarian, keeping track of who has accessed
what files, and never allowing the same file to be accessed by two different team members at the same time.

Because Dreamweaver doesn't reside on the web server, like VSS and WebDAV do, it approaches this librarianship differently. When Check In/Check Out is enabled on the team members' computers, each member's Dreamweaver program will treat the files on the remote server as a repository, like a library. To open files and edit them, users must "check the files out" from the server. When a user does this, Dreamweaver creates an invisible file on the server, stored in the same directory as the file being checked out, named with that file's name followed by the extension .lck. If someone has checked out the file **about.htm**, for example, Dreamweaver would create a file called **about.htm.lck**. This "lock" file indicates that the file in question is currently checked out, and should not be edited. When another user tries to open the same file using Dreamweaver, that user's program will try to check the file out, will find the LCK file on the server, and will inform the user that the file is checked out already. When the original user is done editing the file, he checks it back in, and the LCK file is deleted from the server. Other copies of Dreamweaver will now allow recognize the file as available.

Note

Though the LCK files will not show within the Dreamweaver interface, you can view them by accessing the remote site with another FTP program or Telnet window. Or, if the remote site is located on a Windows or Macintosh computer, and if you have local network access to that computer, you can view them by setting your system preferences to show hidden files.

Note that, because the site documents on the web server have not actually been made read-only—just marked with LCK files that only Dreamweaver recognizes—only Dreamweaver will consider the files locked. Other programs, such as other FTP programs and web editors, will be able to open and edit the files. This means that Check In/Check Out is not a secure system. It presumes that all team members will play fair, and not try to access locked files while no one else is looking.

When a user checks a file back in, Dreamweaver makes the local version read-only. This prohibits team members from making changes to a file without "permission" to edit it.

Configuring the Check Out/Check In System

The Check In/Check Out system cannot be used until you have established remote site information in your Site Definition. This is because when you check out a file, you are doing so from the remote site (which everyone on the project has access to). Setting up your remote site is discussed in the section "Defining a Remote Site" in Chapter 23, "Site Publishing and Maintenance."

To set up your file Check In/Check Out options, follow these steps:

1. Access the Site Definition dialog box by choosing Site > Edit Sites, selecting the site that you want to modify, and clicking Edit.

2. In the Site Definition dialog box, go to the Remote Info category. Either FTP or local/network should be the access method used to enable file Check In/Check Out on your site.

3. Select Enable File Check In and Check Out. When you do this, additional entry boxes will appear (see Figure 24.10). Fill them out as follows:

   - **Check Out Files When Opening.** Selecting this option automatically checks out files whenever you open them by double-clicking them in the local Site Files list. If you open a file by choosing File > Open, you are prompted to check out the file or open it as read-only, even if this option is selected.

   - **Check Out Name.** The name that will be displayed in the Site panel next to any file you have checked out. This should be either your name, if you access files from only one computer, or perhaps a location, such as John-Home or John-Office. This will help you and others know who has checked out the file and where that person might be.

   - **Email Address**. Enter your email address into this area. This causes your check out name to become a blue hyperlink in the Site panel. Other team members can then click this link to email you regarding the file. When they do so, their default email application will open with your email address in the To field and the file in question, as well as the site that the file is from, in the Subject line. It is highly suggested that you utilize this feature of the Check In/Check Out system.

4. After you have selected your options, click OK.

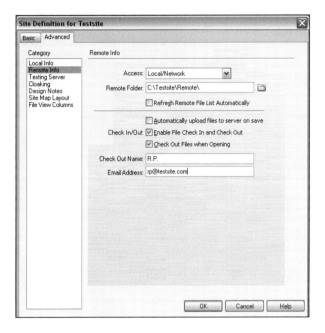

Figure 24.10   Configuring the Check In/Check Out feature in the Site Definition dialog box.

Check In/Check Out in the Site panel

After you've enabled Check In/Check Out, various features of the Site panel become available, and the Remote and Local Site Files lists will display information indicating their status (see Figure 24.11).

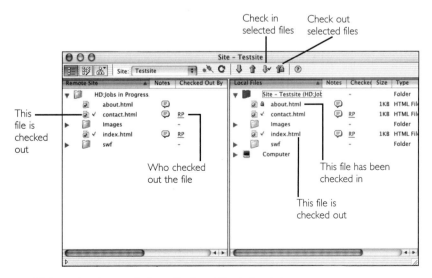

Figure 24.11   The Site panel when Check In/Check Out is in use.

Checking Files In and Out

You can use either the Site panel or the Document window to check files in and out (see Figure 24.12). Additionally, if you are editing a document and decide to discard the changes you've made, you can effectively "undo" the Check Out function.

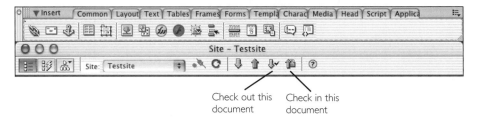

Check out this document   Check in this document

Figure 24.12   Document and Site panel toolbars for working with Check In/Check Out.

To check files in and out using the Site panel, do one of the following:

- Select the file (or files) in the Local Site files pane of the window, go to the Site panel toolbar, and click the Check In or Check Out button.
- Select the file(s) in the Local Site files list, and choose Site > Check In or Site > Check Out.
- Right-click (Windows) or Ctrl-click (Mac) on the file in the files list to access the contextual menu, and choose Check In or Check Out.

To check files in from within the Document window, do one of the following:

- With a checked-out document open, go to the Document Toolbar and click on the File Management icon. From the File Management menu, choose Check In.
- With a checked-out document open, go to Site > Check In.

After you've checked in an open document, it will remain open and editable, but the File > Save command behaves like File > Save As, because the original file is now read-only.

Tips for Working with Check In/Check Out

As with any powerful organizational tool, Dreamweaver Check In/Check Out offers various handy options you can take advantage of, and a few pitfalls you can stumble into.

"Undoing" File Checkout

To "undo" a file checkout, select the file(s) that you want to discard any changes to, and select Site > Undo Check Out from the menu. This differs from just checking the file back in because the version of the file returned to the server is exactly the same as the one you originally checked out. You also can right-click the file(s) in the Site panel and select Undo Check Out from the context menu that appears. Choosing this action closes the files, discarding any changes made, and reverts to the version that existed before you checked out the file. It also sets your local copy to read-only and allows other teammates to check out the file.

If you check in the currently active document this way, it will be saved (according to your preferences—see Chapter 34, "Customizing Dreamweaver") and then checked in to the remote server. If you check out a currently active document this way, the copy on the remote server overwrites it, and any changes you had made that don't exist in the remote version are lost.

Remembering to Check In

Checking in files is something that many Dreamweaver users have a hard time remembering to do. They tend to just use the Put command instead. Although this will still update the remote copy of the file, it will *not* check in the file and remove the checked-out status. You might forget to do so as well and get the occasional email from coworkers wondering what's taking you so long with a file that you were finished with two days ago.

Unlocking Checked-In Files

After you've checked a file in, you no longer have access to it for editing, because it has been set to read-only at the system level. But occasionally, you might need to edit these locked files. Your coworker might have checked the file out and gone on vacation, taking his computer with him. Or your company might have decided not to use Check In/Check Out, and so you have disabled it on your computer (by deselecting it in the Site Definition dialog box).

Note

Checked-in files can also be unlocked outside of Dreamweaver, by right-clicking the file in Windows Explorer and choosing Properties from the contextual menu; or selecting the file in the Macintosh Finder and choosing File > Get Info. In Windows, turn off the read-only option. In Macintosh, deselect the Lock option.

To unlock a checked-in file, do one of the following:

- In the Site panel, select the file and choose Site > Unlock.

- In the Site panel, right-click (Windows) or Ctrl-click (Mac) the file to access the contextual menu, and choose Unlock.

- If Check In/Check Out has been disabled, select the file in the Site panel and choose File > Open, or double-click the file to open it. Dreamweaver will prompt you to choose between viewing the file as read-only or making it writeable (unlocking it).

When To Use Check In/Check Out

So when is the Check In/Check Out feature ideally used? It is most often utilized in a workgroup environment where multiple people are working as a team on a particular site and plan to work on the same specific files or documents. It should (or could, at least) be used anytime there is more than one computer accessing the files and changing them. This could even be a small office/home office (SOHO) environment in which you are the only person changing the site but may do so from more than one workstation. It is also conceivable that you might take some work on the road with you via a notebook computer and want to make sure that you or someone else doesn't inadvertently modify files from your work or home workstation.

Note

If you need to take work on the road, be sure to check out any files that you might need to edit while you're away. You will probably not have access to the remote server while you're gone, and so won't be able to access your files to check them out. This is especially true when the remote site is located on a LAN server. In the worst-case scenario, you can make the files editable (Dreamweaver gives this option when you try to edit them) and use a different FTP client to check them in.

Exercise 24.2   Checking Files In and Out

In this exercise, you'll work some more with the Grandpa's web site (created in the previous exercise). You'll enable Check In/Check Out and experiment with checking files in and out.

If you haven't done so already, copy the files from the **chapter_22** folder on the CD to your hard drive. Define a site called Grandpa's Ice Cream, with **chapter_22/local** as the local root folder and **chapter_22/remote** as the remote folder. (See Chapter 22 and 23, if needed, for more about defining local and remote sites.)

1. To enable Check In/Check Out for the site, access the Site Definition dialog box and go to the Remote Info category.

   Select the Enable Check In/Check Out option.

   Select the Check Out When Opening option.

   For your Check Out Name, enter your name. (It's a matter of strategy whether your team will want complete first and last names, or short usernames that will be easy to read in the Site panel.)

For your Email, enter an email address.

When you're done, click OK to close the dialog box.

2. Checking in and out involves working between the local and remote site, so expand the Site panel to show both sets of site files (as shown in Figure 24.11).

3. Files must be checked in before they can be checked out. Select all files in the Local Site Files list and click the Check In button in the Site panel toolbar (as shown in Figure 24.11).

   Note how all files in the Local site now have padlock icons next to their names. These files are now locked.

4. Check out **index.htm** by selecting it in the Remote site and clicking the Check Out button in the Site panel toolbar. (If you get a dialog box asking if you want to include dependent files, say no.)

   Now that file appears in the Remote site and in the Local site with a green check-mark by its name. That file has been checked out by you. (To all other design team members who access the Remote site, the file will appear with a red check-mark.)

   Your name will also appear in the Remote site file list, in the Checked Out By column. Adjust the size of the Site panel and its panes, if necessary, until you can see this column.

   If you entered an email address when you enabled Check In/Check Out, your name will appear as a link (blue and underlined). Click on it, and your default email program will launch, ready to send a message regarding the checked-out file.

5. Now, from your Local site files, try opening **our_flavors.htm** just by double-clicking on it. Because, when you enabled Check In/Check Out, you selected the Check Out File When Opening option, the file will open. But if you look at your Site panel, the file appears with its little green checkmarks in place, indicating that it has been checked out.

6. Close any files that are open. It's time to check in! In the Local site, select **index.htm** (it should still be checked out from earlier in the exercise) and click the Check In button on the Site panel toolbar. Its green checkmarks disappear, and a padlock appears in the Local site file. That file is checked in.

7. Now see what happens if you put a file without checking it in. Select **our_flavors.htm** and click the Put button, instead of the Check In button, in the Site panel toolbar. The green checkmarks are still there—the file has been uploaded to the Remote site but not checked in.

8. Finally, see what happens when you disable the feature. Access the Site Definition dialog box for the Grandpa's site, and go to the Remote Info category. Deselect the Enable Check In/Check Out option. Click OK to close the dialog box.

9. Examine your Site panel. All padlocks are still in place! Try to open one of the HTML files in the Local site. Dreamweaver knows Check In/Check Out is disabled, so you won't be prompted to check the file out; but since the file is locked, you will need to unlock it before you can edit it.

To unlock all the files in the site with one action, select all files in the Local site and choose Site > Unlock. All padlocks disappear. Elvis has left the building.

Creating Project Workflow Reports

You learned in Chapter 23 that using reports is an easy and powerful way to gather information about a site and project workflow statistics. You also learned about running HTML reports in the "HTML Reports" section of Chapter 22.

Workflow reports in Dreamweaver include information about file Check In/Check Out, as well as Design Notes properties. In this chapter, you will look at each workflow report in greater detail.

Before getting started, however, be aware that workflow reports require a remote connection to be set up in your Site Definition, and you must have the ability to connect to the remote site. If you are unsure whether you have done this, refer back to the section on "Defining a Remote Site" in Chapter 23.

Design Notes Reports

Running a Design Notes report enables you to view Design Note names and values, and search for files within a folder or site that have certain values assigned to certain Design Notes. You can run a general search to see *every* Design Notes attribute, or you can narrow the search to a particular Design Note or multiple notes. As with all the other reports, you can search a single document, an entire site, a specific folder, or the currently selected files (files selected in the local site).

To run a Design Notes report, follow these steps:

1. Choose Site > Reports, to open the Reports dialog box (see Figure 24.13).

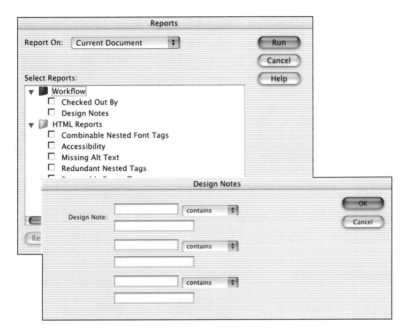

Figure 24.13   The interface for setting up a Design Notes report.

2. In the dialog box, choose the scope of your search from the Report On pop-up menu (current document, entire local site, folder, selected files in site).

3. In the Select Reports section, make sure the Workflow Reports category is expanded, and select the Design Notes option.

4. The Report Settings button will become active. Click it to open the Design Notes dialog box (see Figure 24.13).

5. In this second dialog box, enter from one to three Design Note name/value pairs to search for, along with the search criteria to use (contains, does not contain, is, is not, matches regex). The report being set up in Figure 24.13 will search for documents in a site whose status includes the word revision and whose author is Fred Smith. If your team has been using the default status choices, this will find all documents authored by Fred Smith whose status is Revision1, Revision2, or Revision3.

Note

The matches regex search option allows you to perform searches based on regular expressions. For a full discussion of regular expressions, see Chapter 33, "Writing Code in Dreamweaver."

6. When you've entered your settings, click OK to close the Design Notes settings dialog box, and click Run. The dialog box will close, and Dreamweaver will perform the requested search and generate the report. The results will appear in the Results window (see Figure 24.14).

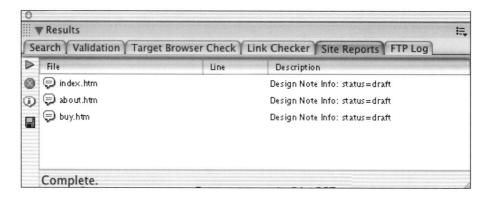

Figure 24.14   The Results window showing the results of a Design Note workflow report.

The following exercise shows you how to run a Design Notes report.

Exercise 24.3   Design Notes Reports

In this exercise, you'll work some more with the Design Notes you created earlier for Grandpa's web site, generating a workflow report on document status. (Before you can proceed with this exercise, you need to complete Exercise 24.1 so you'll have the proper Design Notes to work with.)

1. Grandpa wants a report showing how many web files are at draft status—and it's your job to provide it. With Grandpa's site as the active site, access the Reports dialog box by choosing Site > Reports.

2. From the Report On pop-up menu, choose Entire Current Local Site. Grandpa wants to know it all.

3. From the Select Reports area, select Design Notes.

4. Click the Report Settings button located in the lower-left part of the Reports window.

5. When the Design Notes settings dialog box appears, set your report criteria to match those shown in Figure 24.15. When you're done, click OK to close the Design Notes settings dialog box.

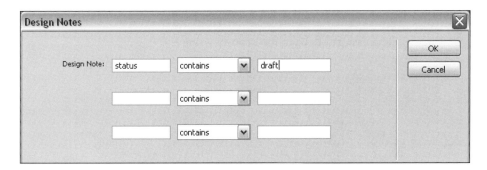

Figure 24.15   Report settings for the Grandpa's Ice Cream Design Notes report.

6. Click Run to generate the report. Dreamweaver runs the report and opens a
Results box listing all files with the draft status (see Figure 24.16).

Note

For more on saving and printing reports, see the section on "HTML Reports" in
Chapter 22.

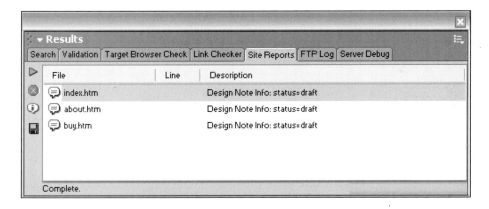

Figure 24.16   Grandpa's report results are ready to be viewed, saved, or printed.

Checked-Out Files Reports

Running a report on checked-out files enables you to see who has checked out any file.
You can run a general search to see *everyone* who has checked out files, or you can narrow the search to the files checked out by a particular individual. As with all the other
reports, you can search a single document, an entire site, a specific folder, or the
currently selected files (files selected in the local site).

To run a Checked-out Files report, follow these steps:

1. Choose Site > Reports, to open the Reports dialog box (see Figure 24.17).

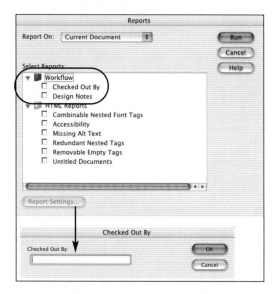

Figure 24.17   The interface for setting up a Checked-out Files report.

2. In the dialog box, choose the scope of your search from the Report On pop-up menu (current document, entire local site, folder, selected files in site).

3. In the Select Reports section, make sure the Workflow Reports category is expanded, and select the Checked Out By option.

4. The Report Settings button will become active. Click it to open the Checked Out By dialog box (see Figure 24.18).

5. What you do in this second dialog box depends on what sort of report you want to create.

   To generate a list of all checked-out files, no matter who checked them out, leave the text field blank.

   To generate a list of files checked out by a particular team member, enter the Check Out Name of the person you wish to find (such as the name that person entered in the Site Definition dialog box, when enabling Check In/Check Out). This search is case-sensitive, but you do not need to enter the entire string. If you are searching for files checked out by a team member named Jeffrey Stewart, for example, you can just enter Jeff, Jeffrey, or Stewart. Be sure to remember that if you're searching for Jeff, multiple individuals might appear—Jeffrey Stewart as well as Jeff Daniels and Ann Jeffrey, for instance.

6. When you've entered your settings, click OK to close the Checked Out By settings dialog box, and click Run. The dialog box will close, and Dreamweaver will perform the requested search and generate the report. The results will appear in the Results window (see Figure 24.18).

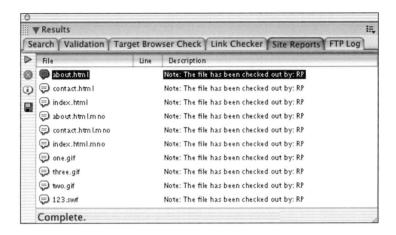

Figure 24.18   The Results window showing the results of a Checked Out By workflow report.

Tip

The Reports dialog box and Results box tend to like the Document window more than the Site panel. If you ever lose track of them, either switch to an open document or open one to see whether you can find them there.

Summary

This chapter discussed all the features in Dreamweaver for improving workflow in a collaborative environment. It is important to keep both technical and interpersonal requirements and considerations in mind when you're in an environment with multiple developers since failing to do so will only lead to disaster. These are features used in multideveloper design environments and, for the most part, have nothing to do with problems or issues you'll run into when developing by yourself. This chapter has informed you of such issues and helped you implement protocols for prevention and avoidance should you be in environments where they might occur.

Chapter 25

Templates and Libraries

Almost every web site has some repeated content. Whether it is a header with the company logo and tagline, a navigation bar, a footer with more essential information, or other features, it's very common to use the exact same content on more than one page.

Repeated content is important to usability. When the pages of a web site have as very similar appearance, the user feels secure about his location; he knows he's still somewhere on the Acme Widgets Company site because the Acme Widgets logo is still in the upper-left corner. He also is comforted greatly by the fact that the same navigation he used to browse from the Home page to the Products page also is present on the Products page.

Web designers, therefore, are frequently called on to create a number of pages that look very much alike in certain ways. Designers also find themselves in the position of inserting similar content on many different pages, even if it doesn't necessarily make up part of the page's basic structure. A real estate site with many pages of listings, for instance, might have a `Take a 360-degree tour of this home!` link that is formatted nicely in a bright-yellow box. Dreamweaver templates and library items are the ideal tool for this need. Although quite different in function, templates and library items can both be thought of as site-wide content tools: features that enable you to create, propagate, and update certain content over numerous web pages with ease.

This chapter covers what a Dreamweaver template is, what a Dreamweaver library item is, how templates and library items work, how to create templates and library items, how to build pages based on a template, how to insert content in a page using a library item, how to update a page by updating its template or library items, how to attach and detach templates, and how to work with templates and libraries involving JavaScript behaviors.

Dreamweaver MX provides some exciting new tools that make templates even more powerful and flexible than in previous versions.

Templates and library items can seem confusing at first, but with a little familiarity and practice, you'll find that they operate in a very logical way and are actually very easy to use. In fact, it's the theory behind them that takes a little time to understand; using them is usually fast and easy, and can save huge amounts of time.

Dreamweaver Site-Wide Content Tools

Dreamweaver offers two different types of tools for managing site-wide content: templates and library items (sometimes also called *libraries*). A basic understanding of how these two features work makes it much easier to decide which to use in a particular situation and how to avoid problems.

What Are Templates and Library Items?

Templates and library items have some similarities and some distinguishing features. This section defines them and then moves on to discussing how they function within Dreamweaver.

A Dreamweaver template fits within the ordinary definition of the word *template* in that it is a page that serves as a pattern for others like itself. Even those who don't use Dreamweaver templates might create a template page and just resave it with a new name for each page of that type needed. However, Dreamweaver templates take the concept further, adding a measure of power and ease: The pages made from a template can be updated automatically, all at once, just by updating the template itself.

Therefore, a Dreamweaver template is an HTML page, but a special type of HTML page. Special code inserted by Dreamweaver makes it possible for the template and its *child pages* (the HTML pages made from the *parent* template) to be connected in such a way that an update to the template updates all child pages.

Dreamweaver library items are similar to templates. The main distinction between the two is in the fact that Dreamweaver templates are complete HTML pages, whereas library items are special sections of code. A second important difference is the capability of templates to have *editable regions* and *noneditable regions*, whereas the entire library item is editable.

As just described, library items consist of sections of code. However, they differ in several important ways from Dreamweaver Snippets. First, library items are available only to one particular site as defined in Dreamweaver (although they can be transferred from one to another), whereas Snippets are universally available. Library items, after inserted in a page, can be instantly updated when the parent library item is updated. Snippets are just code.

How Site-Wide Content Works

When you save a template or a library item, Dreamweaver does three things:

1. It inserts code into the template page or the library item in the form of HTML comments. As you probably know, HTML comments are code that is not displayed by any web browser, but serves some other purpose.

2. It saves a template as a file with the extension .dwt and a library item as a file (not a page, but a file nonetheless) with the extension .lbi.

3. Dreamweaver saves the template or library item into a specific folder underneath your site root folder. Templates are saved in a folder named **Templates**, and library items in a folder named Library; Dreamweaver creates the folders. It is crucial to the operation of both of these features that the files are left in the folders where Dreamweaver places them, and that the folder names not be changed.

These special characteristics given by Dreamweaver to the files allow the program to keep track of the template or library item and of all the pages that are made from it, and to update the pages made from the template or library item when the original is updated.

Templates, Library Items, and the Web Server

When you edit a template or library item, and Dreamweaver updates a number of HTML documents automatically, everything takes place on your local hard drive. The actual HTML in the child pages has been changed. The resulting changed pages need to be uploaded to the server for the changes to be reflected on the remote site. However, templates and library items themselves never need to be uploaded to the server. All of their work takes place locally.

Working with Templates

If you plan to have many similar pages on a web site, and you want to maintain a consistent look and feel from page to page, templates can prove extremely useful. When you create a template, you specify which page elements will be editable; all other page elements are noneditable, or locked.

After a template has been created, *child* pages can be made from it. In the child pages, the editable regions can be altered in any way you choose, whereas the noneditable regions are unchangeable.

When a change is needed to the noneditable areas of the pages based on a template, the change can be made just once, to the template itself; you can then instruct Dreamweaver to propagate the change to the child pages. The editable regions, however, always remain independent, just like normal HTML documents.

Note

Throughout this chapter, the term *template file* or just *template* refers to the original DWT document. *Template-based page* or *child page* refers to documents made from, and attached to, a template file. Taking care to be aware of which type of document is being discussed will make understanding templates a lot easier.

The Templates Category of the Assets Panel

Templates don't have their own panel, but are managed through the Templates category of the Assets panel (part of the Files panel group), as shown in Figure 25.1. To open it, choose Window > Assets from the main menu, and then, on the left, click the Templates icon to open that category of the Assets panel.

Figure 25.1   The Templates category of the Assets panel.

Creating Templates

The first step in building a template-based web site is to create a template upon which to base multiple pages. You can create a Dreamweaver template from a new blank page or from an existing HTML document.

To create a new, blank template, follow these steps:

1. Choose Window > Templates to open the Assets panel and display the Templates category.

2. Click the New Template button at the bottom of the Assets panel. A new template, untitled, is added to the list of templates in the panel.

3. With the template still selected, enter a name for the template. Template names should follow the same restrictions as other filenames used on the web: No spaces, no special characters, and all lowercase is recommended.

4. Double-click the new template name to open the blank file. Proceed to build your page and to create editable regions, as described later in the section "Setting Editable Regions."

To save an existing document as a template, follow these steps:

1. Open the document.
2. Choose File > Save as Template.
3. In the Save as Template dialog box, select the site and enter a name for the template in the Save As box. This name will be used as the template's filename, so observe the normal restrictions for filenames. Dreamweaver will add the .dwt file extension in the **Templates** folder.
4. A template file contains no editable regions until you create them. Set some regions as editable by following the instructions in the section "Setting Editable Regions."

To edit a template file, follow these steps:

1. Choose Window > Assets. The Assets panel will appear, open to the Templates category, with all the available templates listed. The top pane will display a preview of the template that is selected.
2. Double-click the name of the template to open it in the Document window. Edit the template as desired. You can edit noneditable regions—keep in mind that they are noneditable in child pages, not in the original template—and your changes will be propagated to all the child pages based on the template. You can edit editable regions of a template, but there's no good reason to, because the content of editable regions of a template file don't propagate to the child pages.
3. Save the edited template by choosing File > Save.

When you attempt to save and close a template file that doesn't contain editable regions, you will be warned that your template contains no editable regions. You can save and close a template without including any editable regions, but it is virtually useless, because pages based on it will all be identical and cannot be edited. It is best to create editable regions at this point.

Note

Dreamweaver templates *must* be left in the **Templates** folder where Dreamweaver puts them, and the **Templates** folder must be left within your local site root directory. If the Templates directory or template files are moved, they will not function properly.

Setting Editable Regions

When a page is made from a template, certain parts of it cannot be edited, and certain parts can. When you create the template itself, you make these determinations. Until you specify that one or more areas of the page will be editable, all regions are locked (noneditable).

Although you are editing the template file itself, you can make changes to both editable and locked regions, but the changes you make to editable regions will affect only the template file. Generally, there is no reason to place any content at all in the editable regions of a template.

In a page based on the template, you can make changes only to the editable regions.

To specify a part of a template page as an editable region, follow these steps:

1. Open the template file by double-clicking its name in the Templates category of the Assets panel.

2. Select the text or content you want to make an editable region.

> **Tip**
>
> One of the easiest ways to select the elements you want to make into editable regions is to use the tag selector at the bottom of the Document window. The tag selector will display different tags based on where the insertion point is in the Document window; to find the tag you want, place the insertion point within or near the element in the Document window, and then try selecting tags in the tag selector until you see by the highlighting in the Document window that you've found the correct one.

3. Choose Insert > Template Objects > Editable Region.

4. In the New Editable Region dialog box, enter a unique name for the region (see Figure 25.2). Avoid spaces and special characters in template names; the underscore character and hyphen are acceptable. Click OK.

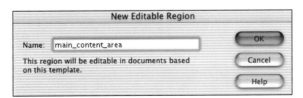

Figure 25.2   The New Editable Region dialog box.

In the Document window in Design view, the editable region is enclosed in a highlighted rectangular outline in the template, with a tab at the upper left displaying the region's name. The color used for highlighting might be changed in your Dreamweaver preferences (see "Setting Template Preferences" later in this chapter).

In a page made from a template, the editable region also will be outlined and highlighted and show the upper-left name tab. But unlike template files, pages made from templates also have some added visual cues in the Document window in Design view. The entire page is surrounded by a different-colored outline, with a tab at the upper *right* giving the name of the template on which the document is based. Figures 25.3 and 25.4 show a template file and a page made from a template in the Document window.

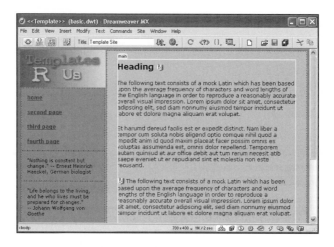

Figure 25.3   A template and a template child page, with highlighting.

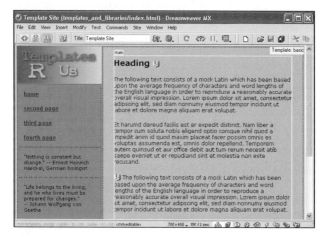

Figure 25.4   Highlighting in template pages and in documents made from templates.

Table 25.1 gives some guidelines as to which HTML elements can and which cannot be made an editable region.

Table 25.1   Elements That Can and Cannot Be Made Editable Regions

Element	Whether Can Be Made Editable Region
An entire table	Can be made an editable region.
A single table cell	Can be made an editable region.
Contents of a cell	Can be made an editable region, but this is exactly the same as making the containing table cell an editable region.
Multiple table cells	Cannot be made an editable region.
A single layer	Can be made an editable region; its position will be editable.
A layer's contents	Can be made an editable region; the layer's position cannot be changed, but its contents can.
A document's title	By default an editable region.
The <head> region	Locked by default. However, there is a workaround for this; see "How CSS Affects Template-Based Pages" later in this chapter.
An empty editable region	Can be created by inserting and naming a new editable region at the insertion point, with nothing selected.

Removing Editable Regions

To remove an editable region—in other words, to convert the region back to a locked regions—select it and choose Modify > Templates > Remove Template Markup. An editable region can be selected by clicking its tag in the tag selector at the bottom of the Document window.

Note

A region can be converted from editable to noneditable only in the template file itself. In a page made from a template, an editable region can't be made locked.

How Links Work in Templates

Always use the folder icon to browse for the desired link, or the Point-to-File icon, when you add links to a template file. When you browse or point to a file to specify a link, Dreamweaver is able to handle the coding so that even document-relative links work properly in the pages made from a template, regardless of their location in the folder structure. An exception to this rule is in the case of external links, where a complete path can be typed into the link field.

Template files are saved in a folder named **Templates**, which Dreamweaver creates directly under your site root directory. When you allow Dreamweaver to write the code for the links you place in a template file, it knows to make the links with the path relative to the file in the **Templates** folder. When you make child pages from the template, and save those files to a location within your local site, Dreamweaver knows to adjust the link so that its path is relative to the child page.

To summarize, don't type links into templates, or the links in the pages made from the template might not be correct, especially if you're using document-relative links. For more on document-relative, site-root-relative, and absolute paths, see Chapter 6, "Links and Navigation."

Tip

To find an editable region and select it, choose Modify > Templates and choose the name of the region from the list at the bottom of that submenu.

Other Types of Template Regions

In addition to editable regions, Dreamweaver MX allows the creation of three other types of template regions.

Editable Tag Attributes in Templates

This feature makes it possible to make certain attributes of a tag editable, without making the tag itself editable. For example, a page design might include a box that needs to have background colors that differ from page to page, although the text content within needs to remain unchanged. The background color attribute of the table can be made editable; in the template-based page, that background color can be changed, although the table itself is not editable.

An element can have multiple editable tag attributes. To make an attribute editable, it needs to be present in the tag. A default value can be set for each editable attribute.

To define an editable tag attribute, first select the object with the attribute. Then choose Modify > Templates > Make Attribute Editable. This opens the Editable Tag Attributes dialog box (see Figure 25.5).

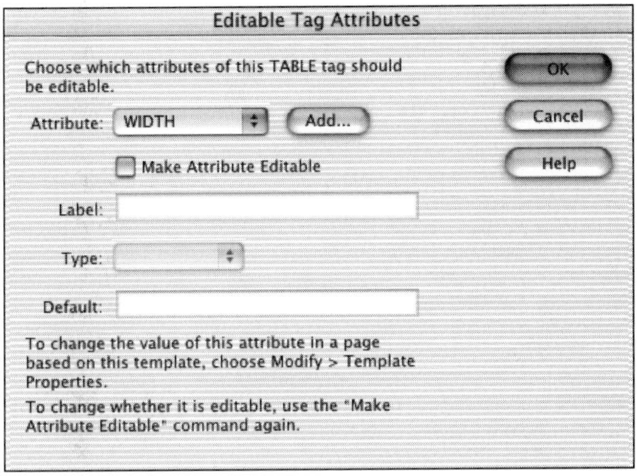

Figure 25.5   The Editable Tag Attributes dialog box.

The Attribute drop-down list will display attributes that already are defined for the selected object. Check to see if the attribute you wish to make editable appears there. If so, click it to select it. If your desired attribute is not in evidence in the drop-down list, click the Add button, and then enter the name of the attribute. Then, click OK. Check the Make Attribute Editable checkbox. Then, fill in the remaining three fields. In the Label field, type a unique name to help you later identify the attribute; it is a good idea to include an indication of both the tag and the attribute in the label (for example, CellBgColor). In Type, specify whether the attribute value is a text string (such as in ALIGN="center"), a URL, a color, true/false, or a number. Finally, for Default, specify the value you want the attribute to have by default, until and unless it is edited in the template's child page.

While the dialog box is open, you can set other attributes of the same tag as editable, following the previous steps and clicking OK when you're finished.

On a child page made from a template containing editable tag attributes, these attributes are edited using the menu command Modify > Template Properties. This opens the Template Properties dialog box (see Figure 25.6).

The editable tag attributes present in the document should be listed at the top by name. To change an attribute, select it, fill in the new value in the field below, and click OK.

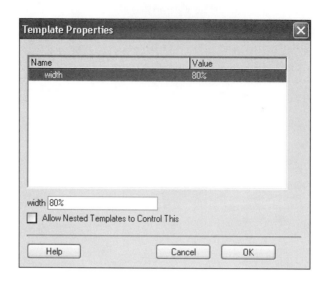

Figure 25.6   The Template Properties dialog box.

Note

To avoid confusion, note that two separate menu items are associated with templates. Most commands used for creating and modifying templates are found by choosing Modify > Templates. Others are found under Modify > Template Properties.

A tag with an attribute marked as editable can be relocked if desired; this change is made in the template document, after which the template's child pages must be updated. To do this, with the template document open, choose Modify > Templates > Make Attribute Editable. Select the attribute from the drop-down menu, deselect the Make Attribute Editable check box, and click OK. When you save the template, you will be prompted to update pages based on the template. To do so, click Update, and then in the resulting dialog box, click OK.

Optional Content Regions in Templates

When an optional content region is placed in a template, its child pages display that region—or don't display it—based on conditions set by the template author. Specific values can be set for a template parameter, or a conditional statement can be defined.

To insert an optional content region, follow these steps:

1. Select the element you want to set as an optional content region.

2. On the Insert bar, choose the Templates category and click the Optional Region button.

3. The New Optional Region dialog box opens (see Figure 25.7); enter the desired settings. Use the Basic tab to name a new optional content region and to set whether the optional content displays by default. On the Advanced tab, you can link the region you are creating to an already existing optional content region, or to create a template expression.

4. Click OK.

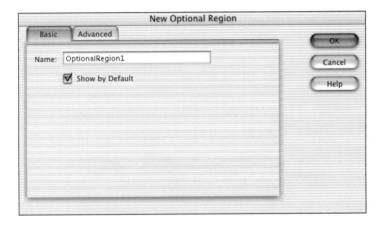

Figure 25.7   The New Optional Region dialog box.

Template parameters and conditional expressions can be created in the Advanced tab of the New Optional Region dialog box, or directly in Code view. Those parameters that you create using the dialog box can be accessed and edited in the template-based document by using the Template Properties dialog box; choose Modify > Template Properties. Parameters and expressions entered in Code view must be edited in the template-based document's code.

Repeating Content in Templates

By making a page element (such as a table row) a repeating content region, you enable that element to be repeated in the child pages, while still maintaining a locked containing element, such as the table holding the rows.

Typically, repeating content is used with tables, but other elements can be defined as repeating content regions as well.

A repeating content region is not automatically an editable region unless specifically defined as such; you must also create an editable region for the element. In nearly all cases, repeating content needs to be contained within an editable region.

Note

A repeating content region is a Dreamweaver template function and is not the equivalent of a *repeat region* produced by server-side code. The two are used together.

To make an element in a template a repeating content region, follow these steps:

1. Select the desired element.

2. Do one of the following:

    - Choose Insert > Template Objects > Repeating Region.

    - Right-click (Windows) or Control-click (Macintosh) the selected content, and from the context menu, choose New Repeating Content.

3. In the Templates category of the Insert bar, click Insert Repeating Content. The Repeating Content dialog box opens (see Figure 25.8).

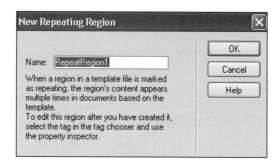

Figure 25.8   The Repeating Content dialog box.

4. Give the new repeating region a unique name, avoiding single or double quotation marks (' "), angle brackets (< >), and ampersands (&). Click OK. The repeating region is entered into the document.

To add, delete, or change the order of a repeating content region, place the insertion point within the region and choose Modify > Templates > Repeating Entries. Select from the options in the menu to insert a new repeating entry, delete an entry, or move the selected entry to another position in relation to the other entries.

Nested Templates

Perhaps the most exciting new template feature in Dreamweaver MX is the capability to create nested templates. With this tool, it is possible to build a site with several levels of templates, so that different site subsections have a design common to just the subsection, but all pages share an overall design.

Nested templates operate according to the inheritance principle, in the sense that a template nested within a parent template will inherit all of its parent's locked regions, but only the portion of its parent's editable regions specified. Typically, each level of nesting restricts more and more page areas, with the most deeply nested templates having the most limited amount of editable area.

This feature is perfect for the typical hierarchical site structure in which all pages share certain elements and subsections share a subset of page elements. Templates can be nested to as many levels as necessary.

To create a nested template, follow these steps:

1. In the Templates category of the Assets panel, select the template file you want to use as the base, or first-level, template. Right-click its name and choose New from Template. This creates a document based on the template.

2. Choose File > Save as Template, and name your new second-level template.

3. Within an editable region (or regions) of the new template, select an element (or elements) to become editable regions in the second-level template, and make it an editable region. (To learn how to do this, see "Setting Editable Regions" earlier in this chapter.)

4. Save the new second-level template.

Pages produced from the first-level template will have a certain set of editable regions. Pages produced from the second-level template will have only the editable regions specified when it was saved.

A nested template, after it has been given editable regions distinct from its parent, no longer has the editable regions its parent has, unless they are specifically made editable. On the other hand, a nested template will have all the locked regions its parent has. Changes to the locked regions of a parent template will be inherited by its nested templates, and by all pages created from the parent and the nested template. Nested templates will not inherit changes to the editable regions of a parent template, or by any pages made from either template; this is the normal behavior of any Dreamweaver template.

Creating Pages Based on Templates

You can create a page based on a particular template in two ways: using a template as the starting point for a brand-new document or applying a template to an existing document. Either way, the result is a page based on a template.

Creating a new page from a template is the simpler process of the two. Applying a template to an existing page requires that the existing page's content be matched with editable regions in the template, which can be tricky.

Creating a New Page from a Template

To build a new document based on a template, do one of the following:

- In the Assets panel, choose the Templates category. Highlight the name of the desired template, right-click, and choose New from Template.
- From the main menu, choose File > New. In the New Document dialog box, choose the Templates tab. From the left Category pane, choose the name of the Dreamweaver site containing the desired template. From the middle pane, choose and double-click the name of the template.

The new template-based page is created; save it with a unique document name with the appropriate file extension (**.htm**, **.html**, and so on).

You may then make any changes you like to the editable regions of the child page. The noneditable regions cannot be edited unless you detach the page from the template; see the section "Detaching Pages from Templates" for instructions.

Applying a Template to an Existing Page

When you apply a template to an existing page, the page becomes a copy of the template file, with the existing page's content placed within a single editable region that you specify.

Behaviors and other scripts in the existing document's <head> will remain after you apply a template to it. Other <head> items, however, such as <meta> tags, are discarded.

To apply a template to a document that has already been created, first open the document. Then, with the Templates category of the Assets panel displayed, select the name of the template and click Apply.

Applying a Template to an Existing Template-Based Page

A template also can be applied to an existing template-based page. When you do this, Dreamweaver turns the document into a copy of the new template and places the content from the existing document's editable regions into corresponding editable regions in the new template wherever possible. Dreamweaver does this by matching the names of the editable regions in the document to the names of the editable regions in the new template. Where there isn't a match, Dreamweaver asks you where you want to place the orphaned content.

Exercise 25.1   Creating a Template and Template-Based Pages

In this exercise, you build a Dreamweaver template and then create pages based on it. Before you start, copy the **chapter_25** folder on the CD to your hard drive. Define a site called Chapter 25, with this folder as the local root folder.

1. From the **chapter_25** folder, open the file **starter.html**. Assume for this example that this is a page you've just finished designing for your new Templates R Us web site. You like the look of it, and you want all the pages in the site to have the same page structure, left-hand navigation, and logo; you just want the large right-hand section to be different on each page. Choose File > Save as Template. The Save as Template dialog box will open (see Figure 25.9). Be sure that the correct site is showing in the field at the top, and in the bottommost field type the name **basic** for the template. Click Save.

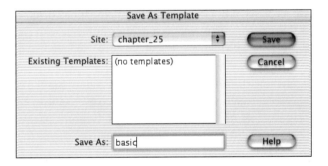

Figure 25.9   The Save as Template dialog box.

   The page **starter.html** will be replaced in the Document window by the template you've just created, **basic.dwt**.

2. Now create an editable region. The only part of the document you plan to change from page to page is the right-hand content area, which consists of a two-row, two-cell table. The top cell, which now contains several paragraphs of filler text, is the element you want to make into an editable region. Click

anywhere in the filler text on the page, and in the tag selector at the bottom left of the Document window, click the `<td>` tag that appears furthest to the right. If you've selected the right one, you'll see the rectangle around the filler text highlighted with a bold dotted line. Choose Insert > Template Objects > Editable Region, which opens the New Editable Region dialog box (see Figure 25.10).

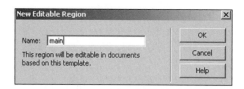

Figure 25.10   The New Editable Region dialog box.

3. In the New Editable Region dialog box, type a name for the editable region, **main**, and click OK.

4. Now choose File > Save. You now have a Dreamweaver template, ready for action. Next you'll make three new pages based on this template.

5. In the Templates category of the Assets panel, select **basic.dwt**. Right-click (Ctrl-click on the Mac) it and choose New from Template. (This command can be chosen regardless of which page is open in the Document window; the template need not be open.)

6. A new page opens, looking exactly like the template page. Dreamweaver gives it a name, such as Untitled-3, until you name it. Choose File > Save, which opens the familiar Save As dialog box. Give the page the name **index.html**, and save it in the **chapter_25** directory. This will be your site's home page. If you have View > Visual Aids > Invisible Elements selected, the page will look like Figure 25.11.

7. Try clicking anywhere in the left-hand column of the page; Dreamweaver won't let you edit anything there, because it is a locked region. But the right-hand content area behaves normally. Change the heading to **Welcome to Templates R Us** (or something else that makes it clear that this is the home page). Edit some of the text in such a way that you can identify it as having changed. Save the document.

8. Repeat steps 5, 6, and 7. This time, give the document the filename **second.html** and give it a heading that includes the word *second* (**Here Is My Second Page**, or something equally clever.) Save.

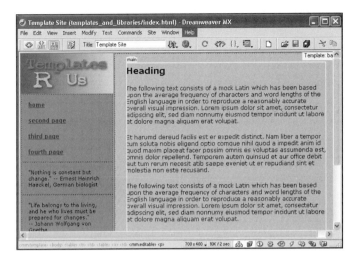

Figure 25.11   The template-based document with Invisible Elements selected.

9. Repeat steps 5, 6, and 7 again. This time, give the page the filename **third.html**
   and change the heading to something witty with the word *third* in it. Save.
   Repeat steps 5, 6, and 7 again, naming the file **fourth.html** and giving it a heading identifying it in some way as *fourth.*

You now have a template and four pages attached to the template. (The file **starter.html**
was just a prototype; it won't be part of the actual site.) In Exercise 25.2, you will edit the
template and update the pages automatically.

Editing and Updating Templates and Their Child Pages

After pages have been made from a template, you can go back and edit the template in
such a way that the changes you make are also made to all the pages attached to that template. This is the strength of templates, and the whole reason for using them.

Keep in mind that, although you can edit both editable and noneditable regions of a
template file, only the changes to the noneditable regions will be made to the child pages.

To edit or update (these terms are used interchangeably here) a template, open the template file by double-clicking its name in the Assets panel or its filename in the **Templates**
folder in the Site panel. Make whatever edits you choose to the editable regions of the
template. When you're done, choose File > Save. This will open the Update Template
Files dialog box (see Figure 25.12).

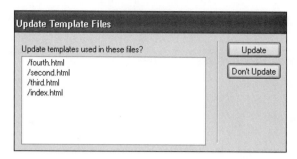

Figure 25.12   The Update Template Files dialog box.

The dialog box lists the pages attached to the template and gives you the options Update or Don't Update. Choosing Update makes the changes you have made to the template file to all of the template file's child pages, and displays the Update Pages dialog box. There you can examine a log showing which pages have been updated (see Figure 25.13).

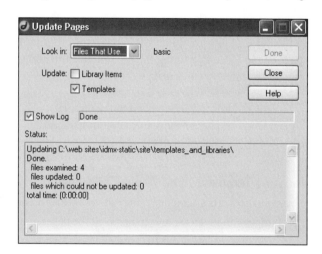

Figure 25.13   The Update Pages dialog box.

Clicking Close completes the process.

Exercise 25.2   Updating Multiple Pages by Updating a Template

In this exercise, you edit the template and update the pages automatically. This exercise builds on Exercise 25.1. If you haven't done so yet, copy the **chapter_25** folder on the CD to your hard drive. Define a site called Chapter 25, with this folder as the local root folder.

1. Open the template **basic.dwt** you built in Exercise 25.1 by double-clicking its name in the Template pane of the Assets panel, or by double-clicking its filename in the Site panel. (Remember, it will be in the **Templates** folder.)

2. Now that you have several other pages in your little site, you'll want the navigation links on the left to work. Thanks to your template, you need to make the links only once. Select the text home, and, in the Property inspector, click the browse folder icon. Remember, always browse to links (or use the Point-to-File icon) when working with a template so that Dreamweaver can insert the correct link in the child pages. Browse to the file **index.html** and choose it.

3. Choose each of the navigation text labels in the left column in turn (second page, third page, fourth page) and browse to and choose the corresponding page in your site.

4. Choose File > Save. The Update Template Files dialog box will open.

5. Underneath the question "Update Templates Used in These Files?" is a list of the pages that will be updated. Click Update. Dreamweaver will do your work for you, and the Update Pages dialog box will open, showing you exactly which files have been examined and which have been updated. Closing this window finishes the update process.

6. Open **index.html**. Its left navigation links should reflect the changes you just made to the template. Preview **index.html** in your browser so that you can use the links to page through the site, and see that all of your pages now have the new navigation links.

In Exercise 25.3, you'll add a library item to the site.

Using Dreamweaver 4 Templates with Dreamweaver MX

Dreamweaver MX uses a template syntax that differs from that of Dreamweaver 4. But working with templates made with Dreamweaver 4 in Dreamweaver MX presents no problem

You can even retain the ability of a Dreamweaver 4 template to be usable in both versions of Dreamweaver. A template created in Dreamweaver 4 can be opened and edited with Dreamweaver MX and the template syntax will not be automatically changed, unless new template regions are added from within Dreamweaver MX. After new template regions are added with Dreamweaver MX, however, the template will no longer be useable in Dreamweaver 4.

Detaching Pages from Templates

A page can be detached from its template. When detached, any portion of the page can be edited freely. However, it will no longer be updated when the template is updated.

After the page has been detached, the template has no more connection with it; it is on its own. Its template-specific comments are removed from the code, and it has no more noneditable areas; it becomes an ordinary HTML, containing all the content from its previous noneditable and editable regions.

Detaching a page from a template is usually not a good idea, because all the advantages of using a template are lost. A better system is to plan the site so that it isn't necessary to detach pages from the template. The judicious use of editable and noneditable regions in the original template can help greatly with this, as can using nested templates and including library items in templates.

The Source Code in Templates and Template Files

If you examine the source code used in templates and the pages that use them, you'll see the Dreamweaver-specific comments that Dreamweaver uses to make them work.

Pages made from templates begin with a comment like this one:

```
<!-- #InstanceBegin template="/Templates/my_template.dwt"
codeOutsideHTMLIsLocked="false" -->
```

This comment allows Dreamweaver to recognize that the page is attached to the template **my_template.dwt**, which it will look for in the **Templates** folder in the site root directory.

In pages made from templates, and in the templates themselves, editable regions are marked with comments that identify their editable status as well as the name given to the region. In the following code example, a table cell has been made an editable region:

```
<td> <!-- #InstanceBeginEditable name="EditRegion1" -->
     <p>
        Here's some text in my editable region.
</p>

<!-- #InstanceEndEditable -->
```

Note

Every template-made document has an editable region for the page title, named doctitle.

Setting Template Preferences

In your Dreamweaver preferences, you can specify color preferences for the highlighting that marks editable and locked regions of a template.

To view highlight colors in the Document window, be sure to choose View > Visual Aids > Invisible Elements.

To change highlight colors, follow these steps:

1. Choose Edit > Preferences. Select the Highlighting category (see Figure 25.14).

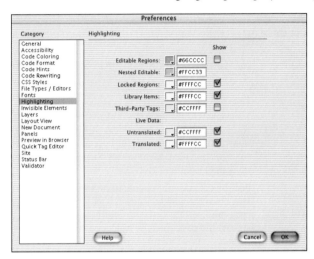

Figure 25.14   The Highlighting category of the Preferences dialog box.

2. The first two boxes affect template highlighting. Click in the Editable Regions color box and select a color using the color picker, or enter a hexadecimal number in the text box. Click the Locked Regions color box, and choose the color you want to be used for highlighting locked regions.

3. Check the Show option, assuming that you want the enable the display of these colors in the Document window.

Tip

When you save a template, Dreamweaver automatically checks the template syntax. If the syntax is badly formed, an error message dialog box appears, describing the error and referring to the specific line in the code where the error exists.

You can use the Check Template Syntax command to check the template syntax at other times as well. If you made edits to the template parameters in Code view, it is a good idea to use this command to check that the code follows correct syntax.

To run the Check Template Syntax command, choose Modify > Templates > Check Template Syntax.

Working with Library Items

Library items can be a real time-saver; it is well worth your while to get to know them. Whereas templates are complete HTML pages, library items are chunks of code; although both enable you to update many pages instantly, library items are used in a very different way than templates.

What Is a Library Item?

A *library item* is a section of code that you plan to not only reuse, but also update. Users often confuse library items, assets, snippets, and server-side includes; Table 25.2 compares and contrasts them.

Table 25.2   Library Items, Assets, Snippets, and SSIs Compared and Contrasted

Item	Description
Library items	Sections of code; when the original library item file, which resides in a folder in your local site, is updated, Dreamweaver automatically updates all pages containing it. The pages must then be uploaded to the server. Site-specific, although they can be copied to other sites.
Snippets	Sections of code independent of any particular Dreamweaver site, always available. They can feature opening and closing code, and so can "wrap" a selection. When a snippet is added to a page, the page must be uploaded to be viewable from the remote server. The major difference between Snippets and Library items is that a change to a Snippet does not affect the pages into which it has been inserted in any way, whereas a change to a Library item updates every instance of that Library item on every page where it has been inserted.
SSIs	Sections of code in a file that resides on the server. A tag in an HTML document calls the SSI, which is then "included" in the page at the point where the tag is. The SSI file can be edited and uploaded; whether it is included in one page or 1,000 pages, it will appear in all of them immediately without the pages being re-uploaded.
Assets	Single elements used in a particular site, including images, colors, URLs, Flash movies, Shockwave movies, MPEG and QuickTime movies, scripts, templates, and library items. They can be dropped easily into any page of the site with which they are associated.

Library items should be used when the element will need to be inserted in multiple pages and later updated.

A good use for a library item is the *footer* that many designers include on a web page. The footer might include the company's contact information and a copyright notice; when the email address needs to be changed, or the year of copyright updated, it's easy to update many pages automatically.

Dreamweaver keeps track of library items in much the same way it does with templates, by inserting special comments into the page. The library item itself is made into a file with the extension **.lbi** and stored in a folder that Dreamweaver creates under the site root, named **Library**. Again, as with templates, each Dreamweaver site has its own **Library** folder and library items. They aren't accessible to other sites, but they can be copied from one site to another using the Assets panel's Copy to Site command. When an element such as an image is used within a Library item, and the Library item is copied to another site, the image needs to be copied to the new site as well.

Creating Library Items

To create a library item, follow these steps:

1. Select the part or parts of the document you want to save as a library item; use the tag selector to be sure you have the exact elements you want included.

2. Do one of the following:

   - Choose Modify > Library > Add Object to Library (see Figure 25.15).

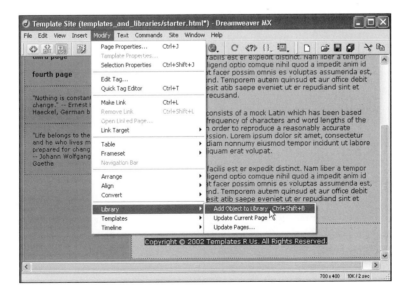

Figure 25.15   Creating a library item.

- Click the New Library Item button at the bottom of the Library category of the Assets panel.

- Drag the selection onto the Library category of the Assets panel.

3. Type a name for the new library item.

Using Library Items

When it's time to add a Library item to your document, the first step is to place the insertion point at the spot in the document where you would like the Library item to go. Then, open the Assets panel, and display the Library category. Select the name of the item you wish to insert, and click the Insert button.

Library items have some limitations and idiosyncrasies, including the following:

- When a library item refers to linked elements, such as images, the library item stores only a reference to the item; for the library item to work, the linked item must continue to reside at the location in the file hierarchy where it was when the library item was created. If the linked item needs to be moved, the Dreamweaver Site panel should be used. Dreamweaver will then update the link within the Library item to reflect the new location.

- Library items can contain behaviors, but special requirements apply when a behavior is edited within a library item.

- Library items can be made from a section of a page that is linked to a Cascading Style Sheet, but the style sheet link is not copied along with the library item. If the same style sheet is applied to the pages into which the library item is inserted, however, the CSS will affect the code in the library item just as if it were not a library item.

Tip

By default, library items in the Document window are highlighted yellow. To see high-lighting, choose View > Visual Aids > Invisible Elements.

To change the color Dreamweaver uses to highlight library items, choose Edit > Preferences and select the Highlighting category. Click the library item's color box and use the color picker to choose a color (or type in a hexadecimal). Select Show, assuming that you want the highlight color to display in the Document window.

Exercise 25.3   Creating and Using a Library Item

This exercise builds on Exercises 25.1 and 25.2. In this exercise, you create a library item made up of some text that will be used as a page footer and add it to the template file. If you haven't done so yet, copy the **chapter_25** folder on the CD to your hard drive. Define a site called Chapter 25, with this folder as the local root folder.

1. Open the original file **starter.html** from Exercises 25.1 and 25.2. Although this library item could be created in the template itself, library items are often created on ordinary non-template pages, and the process is clearer using an ordinary page. First create a place for your page footer. Below the cell that holds the filler text is a second table row containing a single cell; place the cursor inside that table cell.

2. In that cell, type the following:

   Copyright © 2002 Templates R Us. All Rights Reserved.

   To insert the © symbol, choose Insert > Special Characters > Copyright.

3. Select the text you just typed, and in the Property inspector, from the Format drop-down menu, choose Paragraph. With the text still selected, choose Modify > Library > Add Object to Library. The Assets panel will open with the Library category displayed; an icon representing your new library item will be listed, named Untitled. Type a name, **footer**, for your library item and click anywhere outside of the library item Name field.

4. Now open the template file **basic.dwt**. Again, place the cursor in the table row/cell below the one that holds the filler text.

5. Open the Assets panel to the Library category, and drag and drop the library item footer to the cursor location in the lower row/cell. Click once anywhere in the page to refresh it. The library item will appear; if you have View > Visual Aids > Invisible Elements selected, it will be highlighted in yellow.

6. Save the template file. Dreamweaver will take you through the Update Template Files and Update Pages dialog boxes; click Update and Close, respectively. The three pages attached to this template will be updated.

7. Now open **index.html**. The footer should appear in it as well. Note that it is in a noneditable area. The footer cannot be accidentally removed from the template; but if it needs to be edited, it can be, as you'll see in Exercise 25.4. Figure 25.16 shows how **index.html** should look.

8. Preview **index.html** in your browser and try the other links on the site; the footer should display on all four pages.

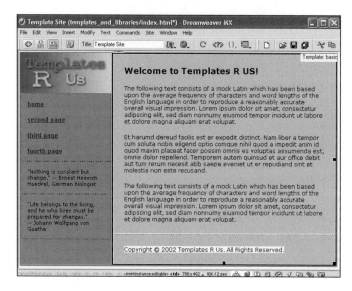

Figure 25.16   The exercise document **index.html** after Exercise 25.3.

Editing and Updating Library Items

Library items can be opened individually and their code edited and resaved. In the Libraries category of the Assets panel, double-click the name of the library item; it will open in a Document window with a gray background (see Figure 25.17). It is not an HTML page, but consists only of the page elements you chose when you created it. It can be edited in much the same way as a normal Dreamweaver document.

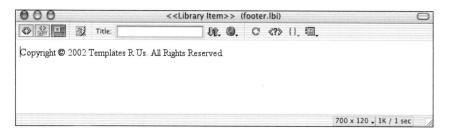

Figure 25.17   A library item open for editing.

When you save your changes, the Update Library Items dialog box appears (see Figure 25.18), showing you which pages contain the library item and giving you the options Update or Don't Update. If you choose Update, the Update Pages dialog box appears (see Figure 25.19), and the changes are made; the dialog box can be closed.

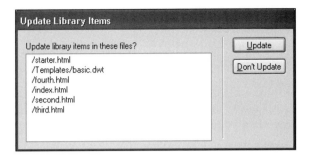

Figure 25.18   The Update Library Items dialog box.

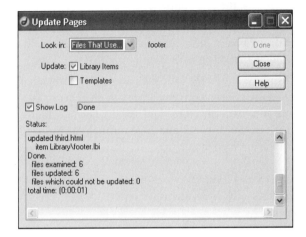

Figure 25.19   The Update Pages dialog box.

If you choose Don't Update, no documents will be changed until you use Modify > Library > Update Current Page or Update Pages.

Note

Some Dreamweaver features—the CSS panel, Timelines panel, and Behaviors panel—are grayed-out and unavailable when you are editing a library item; this is because library items are limited to <body> elements. Timeline and CSS code is part of the <head>, and behaviors insert code into the <head> as well as into the <body>. See "Using CSS with Templates and Library Items" later in this chapter for more on this. The Page Properties dialog box is also unavailable, because these tags are inserted into the <head> and library items don't include a <head>.

Exercise 25.4   Updating a Library Item

This exercise builds on the previous three exercises. In this exercise, you edit the library item you added in Exercise 25.3 and update all four pages of the site. If you haven't done so yet, copy the **chapter_25** folder on the CD to your hard drive. Define a site called Chapter 25, with this folder as the local root folder.

1. Open the Assets panel to the Library category and double-click the footer library item. It will open in a Document window (refer back to Figure 25.17).

2. You've decided that the footer really should be centered in its table cell, and bolded and italicized, while you're at it. Select the text, and in the Property inspector click the Center Text button on the upper right. Then click the Bold button, and then click the Italic button.

3. Choose File > Save. You'll be taken through the Update Library Items and Update Pages dialog boxes; click Update and Done, respectively. Close the Document window that displays the library item.

4. Open **index.html**. (If any of the four site pages or the template file were open when you edited the library item, you'll need to save them now. If they are closed, they are automatically edited and saved.) The new footer should display. Preview the page in your browser and page through the links; all four pages should display the updated footer.

Here ends this chapter's exercises. Use these files as a starting point for some experimentation with templates and library items.

Making Library Items Editable in a Document

A library item in a document is not editable. You can break the link between the library item in the document and its original, and the library item in the document will be editable; but after this has been done, it can no longer be updated automatically when the original is updated.

To make a library item editable, just select it in the Document window and click Detach from Original in the Property inspector. The selected instance of the library item is no longer highlighted, and can now be edited.

Deleting Library Items

To delete the original of a library item, select its name in the Assets panel and then click the tiny garbage can icon at the bottom right. You also can right-click the item's name and choose Delete.

The Source Code in Library Items

When you insert a library item into a document, Dreamweaver inserts special comments that allow the program to keep track of the instance of the library item and update it when the time comes. A library item wrapped in its Dreamweaver comments looks something like this:

```
<!-- #BeginLibraryItem "/Library/my_library_item.lbi" -->This is my
library item.<!-- #EndLibraryItem -->
```

Interview: Becky Tench

Business Name: <bt> design

URL: www.beckytench.com

How did you get started in web design? What has your learning process been like? What kind of work are you currently doing?

I began designing web sites as a hobby when I was a freshman in college. I "taught" others how to do their own sites through a very basic knowledge of HTML and <gasp>Netscape Composer!</gasp>. When I discovered I could major in it, well, let's just say I didn't think twice. I took classes and workshops, but I really learned what I know through getting instruction/information from online tutorials and the Dreamweaver newsgroup and then applying that to real-world clients. Right now I am a web designer for the training/e-learning company, Productivity Point.

What hardware and software do you use in your work?

I struggled over the decision of whether to go Mac or PC for quite a while. But, ultimately money constraints and familiarity won out and I went PC. I am a mix of Macromedia and Adobe products, being more comfortable with Photoshop/Illustrator for graphics design and adamant about using Dreamweaver for my web development. I also use Visual SourceSafe for Check In/Out and version control, and that integrates nicely with Dreamweaver.

How do you use templates and/or library items in your web development work?

My web designs depend greatly on templates and includes. I think that the fewer sources/versions of information you can have, the better!

Basically, I start out with templates. I only make what absolutely has to be editable, editable. Then I make the uneditable regions includes. This way I am able to edit the template if need be, but that should be a very rare occurrence. I don't like checking out hundreds of files for one change, and uploading them up to the server, and so on. It's a waste of time!

The uneditable regions are made into includes so that I can edit one file, upload it, and the change is made!

Consider this example of when your site has a footer and it's on every single page of the site. If you make the footer an uneditable part of your template but insert it as an include in that template, you can then update that one file, upload it, and your footer is changed on every page. You don't need to update the template, you don't need to check out any extra files, or upload anything unnecessarily. It's a nice mix and enables you to have flexibility in your site without a lot of hours of repetitive work or waiting while files are checked out and uploaded.

What are the most important things for the new designer to know when using templates and library items?

Think ahead and be smart about things. Don't be generous about making things editable; you will just waste your time. If in doubt, make it uneditable and go back to correct it if necessary. Learn about the value of includes so that you can avoid unnecessary updating time and make sure you use root relative or absolute links in your includes!

What trends on the web and in the web designer's work do you see as important?

Browser compatibility and standards are important to me. It takes 30 minutes to make something work in Internet Explorer, but hours to make it work across browsers/platforms.

Dynamic sites (database-driven) are very important and I think something that we'll all have to delve into sooner than later, if you haven't already. They add so much to a site and don't bog you down with the mindless and repetitive updating.

CSS and its expanding capabilities and consistency cross browser interests me a lot. I think that a mix of style sheets and CSS positioning web sites could really change the way the web/browsers work.

What advice would you give to someone just starting out in web design?

Designing web sites is not rocket science, but it can't be done without effort and hard work. You have to love it in order to be happy doing it full time because it can really be a frustrating thing sometimes. However, if you want to, you can learn something new every single day. It's creative and technical and constantly changing. If it's something you want to do, then go out there, be proactive, and *learn.* Take tutorials, read the Macromedia Dreamweaver newsgroup often, and don't be afraid to mess up or scream loudly if necessary.

Strategies for Working with Templates and Library Items

This section covers some techniques and tips to make templates and library items really work for you.

Using CSS with Templates and Library Items

Cascading Style Sheets can work very well with Dreamweaver sites that use templates and library items, after you understand a few basic principles.

Placing CSS Code in the Template File Itself

Style sheets can be linked to a template file, and every child page will have that style sheet linked to it. This is a good technique; every page will already be linked to the same style sheet, and yet the style sheet can be changed and still affect the page.

However, adding document-wide styles to a template file requires that the code be modified, as explained later in this section. (For more about CSS itself, see Chapter 13, "Using Cascading Style Sheets.")

Inline CSS styles can be placed in the noneditable regions of a template file, and the code will be propagated to the template's child pages, just like any other code.

To add document-wide styles to a template file, the code must be altered, as follows:

1. Open the template file and view the source code.

   The <head> section will contain the following code:

   ```
   <!--#BeginEditable "doctitle"-->
   <title>Untitled Document</title>
   <!--#EndEditable-->
   ```

   This code allows the title of each document based on a template to be editable.

2. To add new document-wide style tags, enter the following code so that it follows right after the closing title tag, `</title>`:

```
<style></style>
```

This section of code should now look like this:

```
<!--#BeginEditable "doctitle"-->
<title>Untitled Document</title>
<style></style>
<!--#EndEditable-->
```

If the template file already contains document-level CSS styles, you will need to move the entire `<style></style>` code block so that it resides just after the `</title>` tag.

After an editable `<style>` tag has been placed in the template file, document-level CSS styles can be added to individual template-based pages.

Placing CSS Code in the Library Item File Itself

As with template files, CSS code actually placed within a library item will be copied along with the library item, and will be inserted into a new page when the library item is inserted. In the case of library items, there is never a `<head>` region, and so only inline styles could be involved. However, linked style sheets and document-level CSS styles might affect the display of library items, just as they affect the display of any other HTML code; remember, as far as the browser is concerned, the code in a library item is just code and nothing more. The fact that it is a library item matters only to Dreamweaver and to you.

Saving Page Content as a Library Item When a Linked CSS Has Been Applied to the Page

When you select some page content and save it as a library item, and the page contains linked or document-wide CSS styles, Dreamweaver will warn you that the CSS styles are not being copied along with the library item code. In this situation, the simplest recourse is to be sure that the pages into which the library item will be inserted have the same linked style sheets or document-wide styles applied to them. In this way, the library item will appear on each new page exactly the way it did on the original page.

Linking a Style Sheet to a Page Based on a Template

Despite the document's `<head>` being a locked region other than the `<title>`, as you have seen, Dreamweaver does allow a style sheet to be linked to a page based on a template, in the usual way.

How CSS Affects Template-Based Pages

When a template-based page has a linked style sheet, or has document-level style declarations, these styles will affect the display of the page just as if it were not a template page. In other words, the browser doesn't know that the page is based on a Dreamweaver template. It sees the Dreamweaver comments and ignores them, and interprets and displays the HTML tags just as it always would.

Therefore, regardless of whether the code is within a locked region or an editable region, CSS styles, which under any other circumstances would affect the display of the page, will still affect it.

When a linked style sheet is edited, a new style sheet is added, or a document-level style declaration is changed, the regions that would normally be affected will display the changes. If either a locked region or an editable region includes the following code

```
<h3>This is a heading.</h3>
```

And the linked style sheet contains a redefinition of the <h3> tag, such as

```
h3 { font-size: 16px; }
```

And the style declaration is altered, changing <h3> headings to a size of 20px, the heading within the locked regions in the template-based pages will reflect this change when viewed with a browser.

How CSS Affects Library Items on the Page

As with template-based pages, a browser has no interest in the fact that certain code on a page is a Dreamweaver library item. The comments that define the library item, which are so crucial to Dreamweaver, are ignored by the browser. Therefore, when a linked style sheet or a documentwide style would normally affect the code that makes up a library item, it will behave exactly the same as if it were not a library item.

Using Templates and Library Items Together

Templates and library items can be used together to good advantage. Combining them provides flexibility that would not otherwise be possible.

Here are some options for combining the two:

- When creating a template file (or when editing one), a library item can be added to a locked region. This opens up possibilities for editing content within a locked region in pages based on the template; despite the region being locked, an update to the library item changes the locked region.

- A library item can be created and inserted into the editable region of template-based pages. This can enable you to include updateable, repeating content in template-based pages that can be manipulated independently of the template.

Using Behaviors and CSS in Templates

Thanks to a special editable region within the `<head>` region of Dreamweaver MX templates and template-based documents, behaviors can now be added to both. However, behaviors cannot be applied to a portion of the document that is locked, although locked regions can change as a result of applying behaviors.

You also can add CSS style sheets to both templates and template-based documents. A library item can include a behavior, but it requires some special handling. When you create a library item out of page content that includes a Dreamweaver behavior, Dreamweaver copies the element and its event handler (the attribute that specifies which event triggers the action—such as `onClick` or `onLoad`—and which action to call when the event occurs) to the LBI file. Dreamweaver doesn't copy the associated JavaScript functions themselves into the library item, but when the library item is inserted into a document, Dreamweaver automatically inserts the needed JavaScript functions into the `<head>` of the document.

Because library items don't have a `<head>`, the Behaviors panel is unavailable when editing a library item. To edit a behavior that is part of a library item, a special workaround is needed. The library item is inserted into a document, detached from the original library item, edited, and saved. The old library item is then replaced with the new library item by deleting the old item and saving the new item with the exact same name.

Summary

This chapter covered two Dreamweaver features, templates and library items, similar in their use as a tool for creating and editing content that occurs across an entire site, or at least across many pages. You learned how Dreamweaver keeps track of template pages and pages containing library items, and how to use each of these features. This chapter also covered how to use CSS with templates and library items and how to use templates and library items in tandem. The discussion in this chapter also included a workaround for the problem of the locked `<head>` region in templates.

Chapter 26

Introduction to Dynamic Dreamweaver

Once upon a time, there was Dreamweaver and there was Dreamweaver UltraDev. If you've spent years happily using Dreamweaver to generate web sites that haven't required database connectivity,

UltraDev was probably out there on the fringes of your consciousness, something you'd heard about but weren't quite sure what it was or how it related to the Dreamweaver you knew and loved. Dreamweaver UltraDev was regular Dreamweaver plus an additional set of tools, commands, and site options for connecting to databases and working with ASP, ColdFusion and other server technologies.

With Dreamweaver MX, UltraDev functionality has been folded into the main Dreamweaver program. Now, everybody has access to all the server-side tools, all the time. For those of you who haven't worked with UltraDev, that means a new category of Application objects in the Insert bar; several new panels, including the Database Explorer, Bindings and Server Behaviors; an extra category of Application Server choices in the Site Definition dialog box; and various odd little lightning-bolt icons throughout the interface (lightning = dynamic!).

Can you ignore all of this new functionality, and just continue using Dreamweaver as you always have, to create static HTML pages? Sure. But you might decide that now is the time to cross that new frontier, and learn what all the excitement's about with data-driven web sites.

This section of the book is for you if you're venturing into dynamic web development for the first time. This introductory chapter will start with an overview of what dynamic sites are, how they work, and what the various terms and technologies mean. Then we'll cover how to set up your workstation for dynamic development, and how Dreamweaver MX fits into the picture. Each of the remaining chapters in the section covers a particular server-side technology—ASP, ASP.NET, ColdFusion, PHP and JSP—with exercises for defining a site, connecting to a database, and building several simple kinds of pages.

How Should You Use This Part of the Book?

Probably the most overwhelming aspect of getting into dynamic web development is that all of the really hard work, and big decisions, must be done up front. Choosing a server technology, setting up a development workstation, installing and connecting to a database—all must be done before you start building pages and "getting your feet wet."

If you're new to this whole field, start by reading the first section of this chapter, "Dynamic Web Sites and How They Work," to get an idea how all the pieces—databases, web servers, application servers, drivers—fit together. For each different server technology, examine the list of server and database requirements to see what kind of setup it will require.

Based on what you've read, decide what server technology you want to start learning. In the "Setting Up Your Workstation" portion of this chapter, determine whether you want to develop your sites locally (on your own computer) or remotely (by connecting to another computer). Determine what HTTP server and DBMS you'll need. Work your way through the sections that are relevant to you, setting up your workstation as you go.

Finish the chapter by reading the section on "Dynamic Development Tools in Dreamweaver MX." As you read, take a few minutes to go through the Dreamweaver MX interface, identifying the various dynamic development tools.

When you're all done with this chapter, turn to the specific chapter that covers the server technology you've chosen (Chapter 27, "Building a Basic ASP Site," for ASP, Chapter 28, "Building a Basic ASP.NET Site," for ASP.NET, and so on), and work through the exercises there. If you have some time on your hands, and you're not sure which technology to try, go through them all. You'll see that Dreamweaver tries to make the development process as similar as possible across technologies.

After you've done all that, you're up and running. Work on your own projects. Set new challenges for yourself. Go back through the other sections of this book, looking for the Dynamic Data sidebars—they'll help you work with the dynamic aspects of all Dreamweaver tools. Your web sites will never be the same!

Dynamic Web Sites and How They Work

More and more as the web develops, increasingly complex data processing needs require more than just static, or hard-coded, pages. You want your visitors to be able to ask questions, place orders, get results immediately. You need absolutely current information posted at all times, without having behind-the-scenes humans constantly updating and uploading pages. In other words, you need web pages that can be generated and updated automatically, calling information as needed from a central source such as a database, and updating that source as visitors buy things, add their names to lists, and sign in and out. You need data-driven web sites.

Dynamic Versus Static Web Pages

A *static web page* is one that's completely created in advance, with all text and images in place, and housed on a web server to await a visitor coming to look at it. A *dynamic web page*, by contrast, contains placeholders for content that will be inserted by the server at the moment a visitor requests the page—at "runtime"—along with instructions to the server on how to construct the completed page. A look at how web pages are processed between the server and the browser will show you how this works.

How Static Web Pages Are Processed

Figure 26.1 shows the typical set of events in the life of a static web page. The page exists on the server. When a visitor clicks a link or types a URL in the address field, the browser sends a "request" in the form of the desired URL to the web server. The server software then finds the page and "responds" by sending it back to the browser. This is called the *request-and-response model.* The request is an HTTP request, using the http:// protocol to begin the URL; the web server software is also called the *HTTP server.*

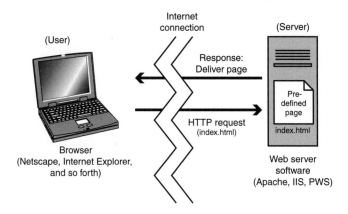

Figure 26.1   The standard request-and-response process for static web pages.

How Dynamic Web Pages Are Processed

Dynamic data can enter into this equation in three main ways:

- Server-side includes (SSIs)
- CGI scripts
- Database connectivity using application servers

Although the purpose of this section is to show you the third method, all three are covered here so that you can see how they relate.

Server-Side Includes (SSI)

The simplest kind of dynamic content—and the easiest to understand—is the server-side include, or SSI. An SSI is a placeholder that sits in an HTML document, containing instructions to the server to replace it with some dynamically generated data. The data inserted can be anything from a chunk of pre-defined code to the current date or time to information collected from processing a script or querying a database. The code for an SSI might look like any of the following:

```
<!--#include virtual="mydata.html" -->

<!--#echo var="DATE_LOCAL" -->

<!--#exec cgi="/cgi-bin/sample_script.pl" -->
```

The HTML document containing an SSI is saved with a special filename extension—typically **.shtm** or **.shtml**. —to alert the server that SSIs are present.

Figure 26.2 shows the web page request-and-response process for an HTML page using SSIs. When the server receives a request for an SHTML document, it responds by finding any embedded SSIs in the page, executing their instructions, and inserting the resulting data in the document, which it then passes to the browser. Usually this involves substituting some real data (such as the date or time, or the even the contents of another file stored on the server) in place of the SSI placeholder code.

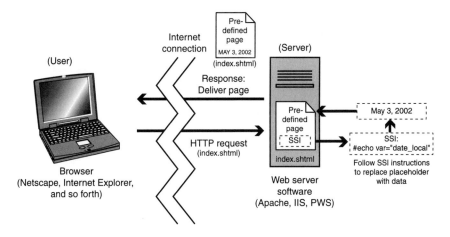

Figure 26.2 The request-and-response process for web pages that use SSIs.

CGI-Scripted Documents

A more truly dynamic web page can be created using CGI scripting to process browser requests and respond by saving user input, delivering web pages with filled-in placeholder content, and even building pages at runtime from collections of code snippets. Within the Dreamweaver model of web page construction, CGI is usually only used for processing simple form input. Chapter 11, "Working with Forms," briefly discusses CGI scripting.

For this discussion, you need to know only that CGI scripts (usually written in Perl) are stored in a special folder on the web server generally called **cgi-bin**. When a user fills out a form, the form action might contain the URL of a CGI script, like this (URL is in bold):

```
<form name="theForm" action="http://www.domain.com/cgi-bin/myscript.cgi"
method="post">
```

Clicking the form's submit button will cause the browser to request the specified script, passing it the form variables as part of the URL or as an attached posting. Figure 26.3 diagrams the request-and-response process that ensues. The web server knows, because of the extension of the file that is called (**.cgi** or **.pl**, depending on how the server software is set up), that the requested page should not just be downloaded back to the browser. Instead, it finds the script and executes it.

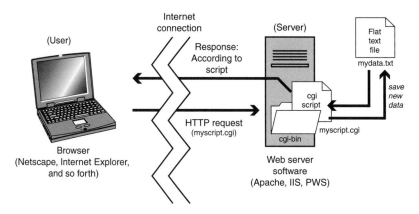

Figure 26.3   The request-and-response process for web pages that access CGI scripts.

The script can do any number of things at this point:

- It can email user input to a designated address, or save the information into a text file.

- It can tell the server to respond by delivering a particular HTML page (like the Your Order Has Been Processed pages you get when shopping online).

- It can insert text or images (that is, dynamic content) into the HTML page before telling the browser to deliver it.

- It can even collect individual code snippets and assemble an HTML page on-the-fly, and then tell the server to deliver it.

Although this method is not as powerful or efficient for large-scale projects as using databases and application servers, it definitely creates dynamic, data-driven web pages. Figure 26.4 shows a web site built using a CGI script to read and write stored information and dynamically constructs pages.

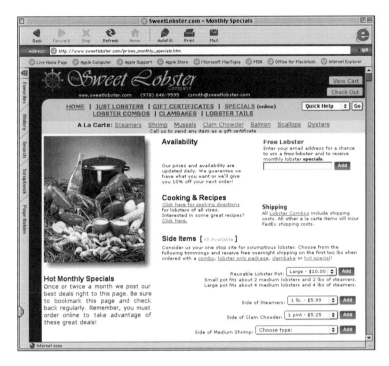

Figure 26.4   The Sweet Lobster web site (www.SweetLobster.com) uses a CGI-based shopping cart to generate its pages, calling data from flat text files stored on the server.

Application Servers and Database Connectivity

The third and most powerful way to create dynamic web pages—what this section of the book is all about—is using databases to provide content, and special software modules called *application servers* to construct pages at runtime. Figure 26.5 diagrams the basic response-and-request process for this kind of dynamic content. Figure 26.6 shows a database-built web site in action.

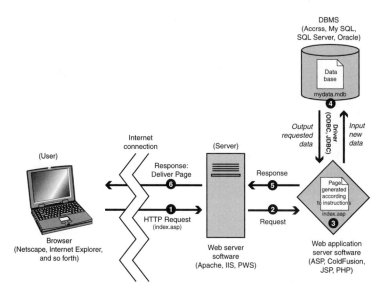

Figure 26.5   The request-and-response process for web pages built using an application server and database connectivity.

Figure 26.6   The Philadelphia Inquirer web site (`http://www.philly.com/mld/inquirer`) was built and is maintained using a JSP-based application server with database connectivity.

The general procedure is as follows:

1. The browser sends an HTTP request consisting of the URL for a document with a filename extension such as **.asp**, **.cfm**, **.php**, or **.jsp**.

2. The web server software recognizes the extension and finds the requested page and activates the application server. This might be the Active Server controls built into Microsoft web servers, ColdFusion Server, Tomcat Java server, or the PHP module.

3. The application server reads the document and either executes any scripts or interprets any custom tags it finds. These scripts and tags usually contain requests for some database information (place the contents of the Product Name database field from the Widget International database here, for instance) or instructions to change the database information (add John Smith to the Username database field in the Books Online database, for instance).

4. The application server sends these requests and instructions—collectively called *queries*—to a database management system such as Access or MySQL, which finds the appropriate database and performs the requested actions. If any information was requested, it's sent back to the application server.

5. The application server then constructs an HTML-formatted page, containing the requested information formatted according to the instructions in the originally requested document and sends the whole lot back to the web server.

6. The web server returns this page to the browser.

That's how the process works. Now it's time to take a look at whom all the players are, and how they all need to fit together.

The Elements of Dynamic Web Pages

Obviously, setting up a database-driven web site involves a lot of variables and requires learning all sorts of new names and technologies. What HTTP server software will you be working with? What application server should you choose? What database management system do you need, and how much do you need to know about databases? The following sections examine the pieces of the puzzle one at a time.

The Server OS and HTTP Server Software

The web server itself is a computer, using some version of Windows, UNIX/Linux, or Mac OS as its operating system, running special web software for processing HTTP requests. The term *web server* in a discussion of dynamic sites that usually refers not to the computer itself but to the server software. This software is also called the *HTTP server*, to distinguish it from the application server (discussed in the section on "The Application Server," later in the chapter). The most common server software is described in the following sections.

Apache

Created and maintained by the Apache Software Foundation, Apache is the most popular server software today, installed on more than 50 percent of web servers worldwide. Apache is open-source software, and is therefore either free or very cheap to obtain; it's stable and powerful; and it runs on just about any operating system.

Internet Information Server

Microsoft's Internet Information Server (IIS) software is second only to Apache in popularity. It's powerful and flexible, although as a Microsoft product it will run only on servers using the Windows operating system (NT, 2000, or XP).

Personal Web Server

Microsoft's Personal Web Server (PWS) is a scaled-down version of IIS, originally built to provide Windows 95/98 computers with limited web publishing capabilities.

The Database

The heart of the data-driven web site is, of course, the database. For the system to work, there must be a database, and it must reside on the web server (or on a computer accessible to the web server). To create the database and work with it offline, you must have access to a piece of software called a *database management system* (DBMS). To make the database part of an online system, a DBMS must reside on the server.

Note

To keep things simple, this discussion focuses on all the components for server-side data processing stored on one server computer. In fact, multiple networked computers might be involved. This won't change how the system works, however.

To author database-driven web pages online, you don't need to be a database expert. However, you do need to know at least how they store data, how to ask them questions and give them commands, and how to use drivers to communicate with them.

Hierarchical Data Storage

Databases store information in tables, as a series of fields (columns) and records (rows). Figure 26.7 shows a simple table structure at work. Adding a new customer to the database would add a new record, or row. Adding a new field, or column, would mean storing one more piece of information about each customer. This table structure is called *hierarchical data storage.*

Customer Information

Fields

ID*	First Name	Last Name	Address	City	State	Zip
01	Moe	Howard	132 Park Ave.	Anaheim	CA	97125
02	Larry	Howard	456 Mulberry Drive	Culver City	CA	98140
03	Curly Joe	Howard	789 Elm St.	Pasadena	CA	95001

Primary key field (unique for each record)

Figure 26.7   Data stored in a hierarchical, or table, structure.

Relational Databases

Hierarchical information storage is fine as far as it goes, but it doesn't go far enough to handle complex information. The more sophisticated databases—the ones generally used with data-driven web sites—are *relational databases,* run by relational database management systems (RDBMSs). Relational databases offer features such as:

- **Multiple tables.** A relational database that stores information in a series of tables, related by common key fields. Figure 26.8 shows the same information table shown in the previous figure, but with a second and third table added to store different kinds of data.

- **Primary and foreign keys.** Keys create the relationships between the tables. Each table must contain one field designated as the *primary key field*, which contains a unique entry for each record. That enables you to call up a specific record by searching for the value in this field. Each table relates to the other tables by having its primary key present in the other table as a foreign key. As the dotted lines in Figure 26.8 show, the Customer ID and Product No. primary keys become foreign keys in the Order table, establishing the relationships between the tables.

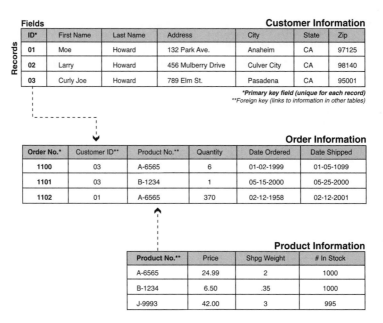

Figure 26.8   Three related tables storing customer, order, and product data.

Queries and SQL Statements

A database is useful only if you can find, update, and analyze information in it. You do this by using the database management system to query the database. How many people have ordered product J-9995 since January of last year? Is that more, or less, people than ordered the item the preceding year? What is the most expensive item ordered since March? When is the last time Moe Howard ordered anything? Sort the customer database by name, or by zip code, or by state. Raise all prices in the product database by 5 percent. The standard language used for querying databases is Structured Query Language (SQL). Hence database queries also are called *SQL statements*.

> **Note**
>
> How do you pronounce SQL? Some database pros say "sequel." Others say it like they're spelling it, "ess-cue-ell." Take your pick. The first way is less of a tongue-twister.

Drivers (ODBC and JDBC)

Application servers communicate with database management systems through *drivers*—pieces of software that define how to move information in and out of databases. The most common driver formats are the Microsoft Open Database Connectivity (ODBC) and the Sun Microsystems Java Database Connectivity (JDBC). A database management system that can connect using one of these formats is said to be ODBC-compliant or JDBC-compliant.

Standard DBMS Programs

To function as part of an online system, a database management system should be a relational database; must be able to run in whatever operating system is required by the server; must understand SQL statements; and must be compliant with ODBC, JDBC, or some other standard driver format. Common database management systems for online use are:

Microsoft Access, the most popular database program for general business use, is often used for small to mid-size online databases. Access isn't the most powerful DBMS around, however; its main limitation for online use is that it cannot accept large numbers of users trying to access it simultaneously. It is reasonably priced, however, and easily available as part of Microsoft Office. As a Microsoft product, it will run only on Windows operating systems, which means it cannot be used on UNIX, Linux, or Mac servers.

SQL Server is the big brother to Access, intended for large-scale sites with huge amounts of data and a significant number of simultaneous hits. This powerful program is expensive, and learning it is not for the faint of heart. Like Access, it runs on Windows only.

MySQL, a DBMS with its roots in UNIX, is a good alternative to Access if you are on a tight budget or not working on Windows. It doesn't have the same multiple-access limitations as Access, and is famous for its speed and stability and for being able to handle large amounts of data. But it is missing some of Access' advanced features, such as stored procedures. In its basic form, MySQL uses a command-line interface, so it might seem intimidating at first. However, several free GUI MySQL interfaces are available. Its learning curve is surprisingly gentle compared to Access. Depending on how you're using it, it's either free or cheap, and will run on Windows, UNIX, Linux, or Mac OS X.

PostgreSQL, sort of a big brother to MySQL, is the most advanced open-source DBMS available. It runs in UNIX-based environments, including Linux and now Mac OS X. For the non-Microsoft crowd, it's a good alternative to SQL Server.

Oracle, from Oracle Enterprises, is the most powerful database management system available. It's also not a program for small businesses or anyone on a tight budget. It's very expensive, and comes with a steep learning curve and very expensive authorized training. Oracle runs on Linux, UNIX, and Windows operating systems.

Note

For more information on Access and SQL Server, visit www.microsoft.com. To learn about (and to download) MySQL and PostgreSQL, visit www.mysql.com and www.postgresql.org. To learn about Oracle, visit www.oracle.com.

The Application Server (Middleware)

Databases, and database management systems, are a big topic—but they're only half the story. The application server software functions as *middleware*, allowing communication between the browser and the DBMS. Choosing an application server is like getting married. You (and your client, and your company) are going to be up close and personal with this software on a daily basis, for a long time. You'll use the application server language to write your pages. You'll be limited by its limitations, and empowered by its strengths.

ASP

ASP is the acronym for the most popular application server today, Microsoft Active Server Pages. ASP is not an independent program or software module, like other application servers are. Rather, it's a functionality built into the Microsoft web server software (IIS and PWS). The language is script-based, using VBScript or JavaScript to formulate database queries and construct pages based on the results. A typical ASP statement looks like this:

```
<%
document.write("This is an ASP page.");
%>
```

Because it's part of the main Microsoft server technology, ASP operates only on servers running the Windows operating system. Chili!Soft offers a version of ASP for UNIX-based servers.

To perform the ASP exercises in this book, you'll need a Windows computer with either IIS or PWS installed and either Microsoft Access or MySQL for your database.

ASP.NET

According to Microsoft, the .NET framework, which includes ASP.NET, is the new face of dynamic web development. Programs and scripts can be written in several languages, including Managed C++, C#, JScript and Visual Basic, and can be executed server-side or client-side. Live data pages can also be programmed to tie in with Microsoft's COM technology. ASP.NET offers many of the advantages of using Java/JSP (see the upcoming section on JSP), but strictly within the Microsoft fold. ASP.NET runs only on IIS web servers, and of course only on servers running the Windows OS.

To perform the ASP.NET exercises in this book, you'll need a Windows computer with either IIS or PWS installed, and either Microsoft Access or MySQL for your database. You'll also need the .NET framework (covered in Chapter 28).

ColdFusion

Macromedia's ColdFusion has become a very popular alternative to ASP, largely because it uses a tag-based, rather than script-based, means of communicating with the DBMS. The core of ColdFusion functionality is ColdFusion Markup Language (CFML). Page elements can also be built using the CFScript scripting language. A typical CFML statement looks like this:

```
#myVar#
<cfset name="myVar" value="Welcome to ColdFusion!">
```

The application server portion of ColdFusion is called *ColdFusion Server*. It operates on servers running Windows, Linux, HP-UX, or Solaris, and must be purchased separately from any web server software. Because it is only available through commercial licenses, ColdFusion might not be the most immediately attractive choice for small businesses; but the speed of page construction possible using CFML makes the long-term development costs very reasonable.

To perform the ColdFusion exercises in this book, you'll need a Windows computer with either IIS, PWS, or Apache installed, or a Mac running OS X with Apache installed, and either Microsoft Access or MySQL for your database. You'll also need the ColdFusion server (covered in Chapter 29, "Building a Basic ColdFusion Site").

PHP

PHP (the recursive acronym for PHP: Hypertext Preprocessor) is a popular open-source alternative to commercial systems. Like ASP, its commands are script-based. Standard PHP code might look like this:

```
<?php
echo "This is a PHP page.";
?>
```

PHP is available freely or cheaply, depending on its intended use. It has a large friendly user community supporting it, but no commercial guarantees behind it. PHP will work with Apache and Microsoft IIS web servers, and on UNIX, Windows, or Mac OS X operating systems. Unlike the other server technologies, PHP is database-specific. Not all installations of PHP will work with all DBMSs. Dreamweaver MX supports PHP for use with MySQL.

To perform the PHP exercises in this book, you'll need a Windows computer with either IIS, PWS, or Apache installed, or a Mac running OS X with Apache installed, and MySQL for your database. You'll also need the PHP application server module (covered in Chapter 30, "Building a Basic PHP Site").

JSP

JSP, or JavaServer Pages, is (as its name implies) a Java-based alternative to both ASP and ColdFusion. The application server is in the form of an applet—called a *container*—that resides on the server. Popular JSP containers include several commercial entries, such as Macromedia's JRun and IBM's WebSphere, as well as the popular open-source Tomcat. A typical JSP statement looks like this:

```
<%
out.print("This is a JSP page.");
%>
```

Because Java is by nature platform-independent (see Chapter 19, "Plugins, ActiveX, and Java," for more about Java), it will run on any computer that has Java virtual machine software. Because it's open-source, it's free, but can require more patience and skill to set up than prepackaged commercial software. Because JSP pages put all the considerable power of Java at the developer's fingertips, this is one of the more powerful application server technologies.

To perform the JSP exercises in this book, you'll need a Windows computer or a Mac running OS X. You'll also need the Tomcat HTTP and application server (covered in Chapter 31, "Building a Basic JSP Site").

 Note

To learn more about Microsoft ASP and ASP.NET, visit `http://msdn.microsoft.com/netframework`. To learn more about ColdFusion, visit `http://www.macromedia.com/software/coldfusion`. To learn more about JSP, visit `http://java.sun.com/products/jsp`. To learn more about PHP, visit `http://www.php.net`.

Getting Started with Dynamic Development

After you understand the basic concepts and terminology of dynamic development, the next step is to choose whatever HTTP server/application server/database management system combo you want to work with and set up your workstation accordingly. You can set up your development environment in one of two ways:

- In a "live" or "online" setup, all of the specialized software—web server, app server, DBMS, driver—is housed on a remote computer that you have FTP access to. This remote computer might even be the web server hosting your site. Developing live might seem easier to you, because it means you don't have to install any new software on your computer. But it's a cumbersome way to proceed. All of your configuration requests must go through the server administrator, which can slow you down; and you run the risk of actual web visitors trying to view pages that you are currently developing.

- In an "offline" setup, you put all software elements on your computer—including HTTP server software, DBMS, everything—and temporarily act as hosting server and developer. When your site is fully developed, you move the relevant database files, drivers, and pages to the actual web server. This is how most developers work when they can. It's how we'll be proceeding in this book. An extra benefit of developing offline is that you get a free education about how server software works.

Based on which application server technology you want to set up for, what operating system you're using on your computer, and whether or not you want to work locally, follow the instructions in the different sections below. The instructions are divided into setting up a Windows computer for local development, setting up a Mac for local development, and setting up for remote development.

Setting Up Your Workstation for Development (Windows)

If you're using Dreamweaver MX on a Windows computer, you have many options for offline development. The most popular web servers, application servers, and databases will all run on Windows.

Note

Note for Windows users: If you're planning to create ASP or ASP.NET pages, you need to install IIS or PWS as your HTTP server. If you're planning to work with ColdFusion or PHP, you can install IIS, PWS, or Apache. If you're setting up to work with JSP, you don't need to set up an HTTP server—the Tomcat application server doubles as an HTTP server.

The HTTP Server: Internet Information Services (IIS)

If you're running Windows NT, 2000, or XP, the simplest and best HTTP server to install for development is IIS. The IIS software is on your Windows Install CD.

Windows XP, Windows 2000 (IIS 5)

To install IIS 5 into Windows XP or 2000, follow these steps:

1. Insert the Windows Install CD.

2. The CD should autolaunch. If it doesn't, go to Start > Settings > Control Panel > Add/Remove Software.

3. In the window that appears, click Install Optional Windows Components.

4. From the list of optional items, find and select IIS.

5. Follow the instructions as they appear.

Windows NT (IIS 4)

To install IIS 4 into Windows NT, follow these steps:

1. Install Windows NT 4.0 Service Pack 3 (if you haven't already).

2. Install Internet Explorer 4.01 Service Pack 2 (if you haven't already).

3. Install Windows NT 4.0 Option Pack (this installs IIS 4.0).

4. Re-apply the latest Windows NT 4.0 service pack (the Option Pack overwrites some DLLs; this restores them).

Note

It's entirely acceptable to install web server software on a computer that isn't going to be used solely as a web server. You probably don't want to be doing development work on a computer while that computer is open to the public for web browsing. But simply putting server software on the computer doesn't make that computer a dedicated server.

Install PWS into Windows 98

Note that PWS is not as powerful or problem-free as IIS. If you're running Windows 98, however, it's as close to IIS as you can get.

1. Insert the Windows 98 Install CD.

2. Go to Start > Run.

3. In the command line window, type:

   ```
   x:\add-ons\pws\setup.exe
   ```

   In place of x, enter the letter of your CD drive.

4. Click OK.

5. Follow the instructions as they appear.

Using IIS and PWS

Both IIS and PWS install as services, meaning they will start up automatically when the computer boots. To access and configure IIS, go to Start > Control Panel > (Administrative Tools) > IIS. To configure PWS, go to Start > Programs > Accessories > Internet Tools > Personal Web Sharing.

- **Root directory:** Each HTTP server designates a root directory for web pages that will be accessed and browsed using HTTP requests. For IIS and PWS, this folder is

  `c:\Inetpub\wwwroot`

  Any web document stored in this directory, or in any of its subdirectories, is "visible" to the web server for purposes of HTTP requests.

- **Browsing served pages:** A browser passes an HTTP request to the server software by specifying the HTTP protocol followed by your computer's IP address or computer name, or the generic IP address (`127.0.0.1`) or name (`localhost`) that computers use to refer to themselves. Any web document placed in the root directory can be requested:

  ```
  http://127.0.0.1/myFiles/index.html
  http://localhost/myFiles/index.html
  http://192.123.128.128/myFiles/index.html
  http://LauraComputer/myFiles/index.html
  ```

  All these addresses will find a page called **index.html**, stored in

  `c:\Inetpub\wwwroot\myFiles.`

Note

To get help using IIS, launch your browser and type **http://localhost/iishelp** in the URL field.

Note that, though the effect might be similar looking, sending an HTTP request for a web page by entering **http://127.0.0.1/index.html** in the browser's URL field is not the same as browsing the same page by double-clicking on it in Explorer or by entering **c:\Inetpub\wwwroot\index.html** in the browser's URL field. Only the former method invokes the IIS or PWS server.

- **Virtual directories:** You can also create browseable web folders on your computer by declaring them as *virtual directories* within wwwroot. To do this:

  1. In Windows Explorer, right-click on the folder you want to share.

  2. From the contextual menu, choose Properties.

3. Bring the Web Sharing tab to the front.

4. Select Share This Item.

5. The Edit Alias dialog box appears. Here you can set the following options:

- **Alias**. This is an alternate name used for web access to your folder. Unless you're very familiar with web sharing and HTTP access, it's safest to leave the alias name and the folder name the same.

- **Access Privileges**. You'll be uploading files to this folder, so you want to choose both the Read and Write access privileges. Leave the other privileges and settings at their defaults.

A folder called **OtherFiles**, for instance, and stored on the D drive, can be declared a virtual directory with an alias name of OtherFiles. After this has been done, a request for `http://127.0.0.1/OtherFiles/page.html` will find the file **page.html** stored within this folder. Figure 26.9 shows a virtual directory being created.

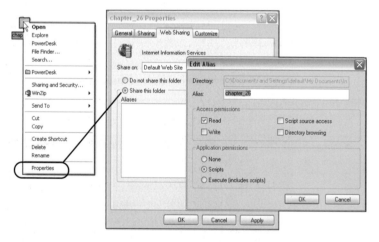

Figure 26.9   Creating a virtual directory for IIS or PWS by turning a folder's web sharing on.

 Note

For Windows 2000/XP, you can find your computer's name by right-clicking on the My Computer icon and choosing Properties from the contextual menu. You can find your computer's IP address by going to Start > Settings > Control Panel > Network Connections. Double-click on the Local Area Connection icon and bring the Support tab to the front. If your computer has been assigned a dynamic IP, this number might change from time to time.

The HTTP Server: Apache

If you're running on Windows, IIS and PWS are definitely your easiest choices. But they're not your only choices. Especially if you're working with PHP or JSP, preparatory to uploading to a UNIX server, you might want to more closely duplicate your eventual online environment by using Apache as your HTTP server. Apache is free, and should run on most Windows computers.

Install Apache for Windows

To install Apache for Windows, follow these steps:

1. Download Apache for Windows from `http://www.apache.org/dist/httpd/binaries/win32/`. From the available file listings, find the version marked "current release". The file should be an EXE with a filename something like **apache_1.3.23-win32-x86-no_src.exe**. The version number might have incremented by the time you read this, but make sure you get the win32 version, with no source, and the file extension .exe.

2. Quit any other server software (such as IIS or PWS) currently running on your system. You can do this by going to Start > Settings > Control Panel > (Administrative Tools) > Services. Find the server software in the list, select it and click the Stop link.

3. Launch the Apache EXE file, and follow the installation instructions as they appear. Unless you're planning to run only Apache server software, and want it running all the time, don't choose to install it as a service. (This allows you to explicitly stop and start Apache as needed.)

Using Apache for Windows

If you didn't install Apache as a service, start it by going to Start > Programs > Apache HTTP Server > Start Apache in Console. This launches a command line window. As long as the window stays open, the server is running. To stop the server, close the console window.

Apache's root folder for serving web documents is

`c:\Program Files\Apache Group\Apache\htdocs\`

Any web document stored in this directory, or in any of its subdirectories, is "visible" to Apache for purposes of HTTP requests.

Send all HTTP requests to Apache by specifying the HTTP protocol followed by your computer's IP address or computer name, or the generic IP address (`127.0.0.1`) or name (`localhost`) that computers use to refer to themselves. (To test Apache out, start it up and point your browser to `http://localhost/`. You should get the default Apache home page, as seen in Figure 26.10.)

Note

You can't have two servers responding to `http://localhost` or `http://127.0.0.1` requests at the same time. This means you can't have both IIS and Apache running on your computer at the same time unless each of them is being accessed through a different port. If you want to learn more about setting port values, consult your IIS or Apache documentation. For purposes of getting yourself up and running as quickly as possible, it's easier to just remember to always stop one server before starting the other.

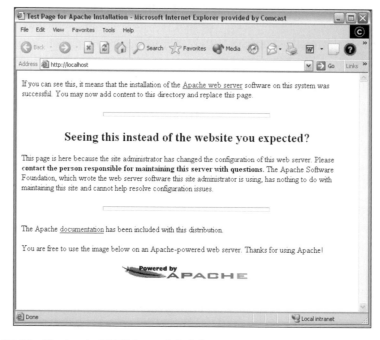

Figure 26.10   The Apache HTTP Server default home page served from your local computer.

The Application Server

What application server, if any, you need to install depends on your choice of server technology. For ASP, you don't need to install anything other than IIS or PWS. For other servers, see the individual chapters following this one.

The DBMS (Database Software)

You can't serve pages built from databases unless you have the proper database management software (DBMS) on your computer. The easiest database software to develop with is probably Microsoft Access. But remember, eventually your dynamic site must be moved from your development computer to the web host for public consumption. If your dynamic web site will eventually be housed on a UNIX server, for instance, you'll probably want to do your development in a UNIX-friendly DBMS, like MySQL.

Microsoft Access is available by itself or as part of Microsoft Office Professional.

To learn how to obtain, install, and configure MySQL for Windows, see Appendix C, "Introduction to MySQL."

Note

Remember, for PHP development with Dreamweaver, you must use MySQL.

The DSN (Driver)

After you've created your database, you must create a driver that allows the application server to talk to it. Each database you want a web site to connect to must have a driver of its very own. Your various projects employ 10 Access databases? You'll need 10 Access drivers. Each individual driver is called a *data source name (DSN)*. To create a DSN for a database do the following:

1. If you're working on Windows XP, go to Start > Settings > Control Panel > Administrative Tools > Data Sources (ODBC). If you're working on any other version of Windows, go to Start > Settings > Control Panel > Data Sources (ODBC).

2. In the dialog box that appears, bring the System DSN tab to the front. This creates a DSN that anyone on the system can use to access the database. (Other choices are User DSN and File DSN.)

3. Click the Add button.

4. A new window will appear with a list of available drivers for different DBMs. Select the driver you need. If you're using Microsoft Access, choose Microsoft Access Driver (*.mdb). If you're using MySQL, and have installed the MyODBC driver, choose the MySQL driver (see Figures 26.11 and 26.12).

Note

If you're using MySQL as your DBMS, you need to use the MyODBC driver to create your DSNs. See Appendix C for full coverage of obtaining and setting up MyODBC.

5. Depending on the kind of driver you chose, different windows will appear, requiring different information.

To set up a Microsoft Access driver (see Figure 26.11):

1. Enter a name for the driver. It can be any one-word name with no special characters, and should be something you'll easily associate with the database the driver is for.

2. Click the Select button and browse to the Access database this driver is for.

This is all the information you need to supply. Click OK to close the dialog box, and then OK again to close the ODBC control panel.

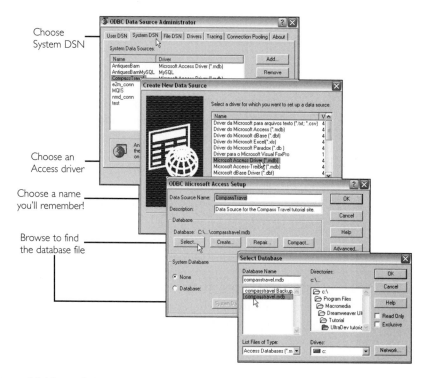

Figure 26.11   Defining a DSN for an Access database.

To set up a MySQL driver (see Figure 26.12):

1. Enter a name for the driver. It can be any one-word name with no special characters, and should be something you'll easily associate with the database the driver is for.

2. Enter the name of the database the driver is for. (You don't have to browse to the database because all MySQL databases are stored in one central location on your computer—the **mysql/data** folder.)

3. Enter the username and password (if any) that are associated with this database. If there is no required name or password, you can leave these fields blank.

This is all the information you need to supply. Click OK to close the dialog box, and then OK again to close the ODBC control panel.

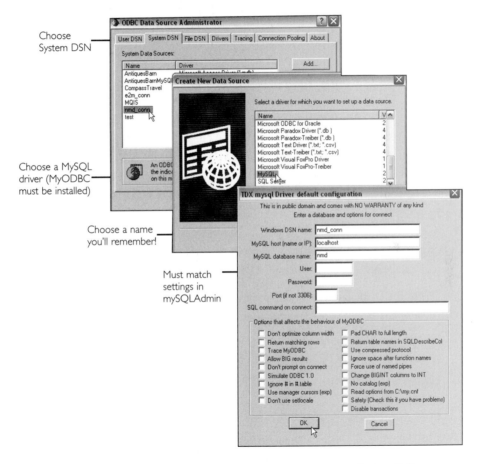

Figure 26.12   Defining a DSN for a MySQL database (MyODBC must be installed).

Setting Up Your Workstation for Development (Mac)

Life is tough for Mac users; and setting up to develop dynamic web sites on a Mac is especially tough. There are fewer server software options, fewer driver options, and fewer databases available.

If you're still working on OS 9, you cannot use your computer as a local development workstation for dynamic sites in Dreamweaver. Your only choice is to connect to a remote server running Windows, UNIX or Mac OS X, for your development. (See the section on "Setting Up For Development on a Remote Computer," later in this chapter, for more on this.)

If you're using OS X, you have access too much of the UNIX-based database and web server software—though you still must connect to a remote computer for work that requires IIS, ASP, or Access.

The HTTP Server: Apache (OS X)

The Apache HTTP server comes pre-installed with OS X. If you're running OS X, you have Apache. Be aware, however, that earlier releases of the OS X software included a "broken" version of Apache. To ensure that you have a functional version of Apache, make sure you have upgraded your system to 10.1.2 or higher. This will install Apache 1.3.22.

Starting and Stopping Apache

Though Apache is installed, by default it isn't enabled. To start the server, do this:

1. From the Dock, launch System Preferences. When the System Preferences window opens, click the Sharing preferences icon.

2. In the Web Sharing section, click the Start button to start web sharing (see Figure 26.13). Note that you need to be logged in as an administrator to do this.

3. When the window message indicates that web sharing is on, quit System Preferences.

After you have enabled web sharing, it will stay enabled even after the computer is shut down and restarted. To stop web sharing (for instance, to stop Apache), repeat the above procedure. A Stop button will replace the Start button if the server is currently running.

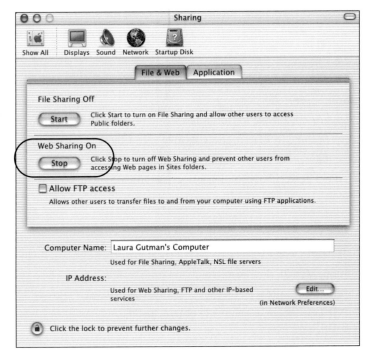

Figure 26.13   Starting web sharing in OS X launches Apache.

Using Apache

Apache designates a root directory for web pages that will be accessed and browsed using HTTP requests. The default directory is

`(your hard drive)/Library/WebServer/Documents/`

Any web document stored in this directory, or in any of its subdirectories, is "visible" to Apache for purposes of HTTP requests. The URL for the shared directory consists of the HTTP protocol followed by your computer's IP address, or the generic IP address (`127.0.0.1`) or name (`localhost`) that computers use to refer to themselves. (See Figure 26.14.)

Figure 26.14   Browsing a user-defined web page in OS X with Apache.

Note

In Mac OS X, the computer's IP address is shown in the Sharing preferences window (see Figure 26.13).

The Application Server (OS X)

You can set up your OS X Mac for local development using PHP or JSP. Both of these application servers come in Mac-friendly flavors. (See Chapters 30 and 31 for more on setting up these items.) For ASP or ASP.NET development, you'll need to connect your Mac to a Windows server. For ColdFusion development, you'll need to connect to a UNIX or Windows server with ColdFusion Server installed.

The DBMS and Driver

Access and SQL Server won't run on OS X, but there are other options. If you're looking for a free solution, MySQL and PostgreSQL are both available free. For a spiffier commercial solution, check out MacSQL at `www.rtlabs.com/macsql`. Figure 26.15 shows the free OS X MySQL at work. To learn how to obtain, install, and configure MySQL for Mac OS X, see Appendix C.

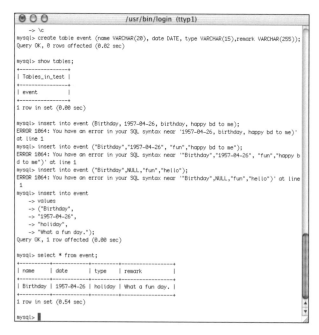

Figure 26.15 MySQL running in Mac OS X's Terminal utility.

Setting Up for Development on a Remote Computer

If you can't or don't want to set up your own computer as a development workstation, you can still create and preview dynamic Dreamweaver sites by connecting to a remote computer. The remote computer can be your web site's host, or any other computer you have network or FTP access to—as long as it has HTTP server and application server software, a DBMS, and drivers. To set up for remote development, you'll need the following.

The Remote Computer's HTTP Address (URL)

Even if you're connected to the remote computer over a local network, you must know its URL to send HTTP requests to it so you can preview your data. If your remote computer is your web host, use your site's domain name. If the remote computer is simply another computer you're networked to, you'll have to get its IP address.

To learn the IP address of a Windows computer, launch the Command Prompt or DOS Prompt. At the prompt, type ipconfig and press Return. A whole set of numbers will appear, including the IP address.

To learn the IP address of a Mac running OS X, launch the System Preferences (its icon is in the Dock) and view Sharing preferences. The IP address is at the bottom of the window.

Read/Write Access to the Shared Web Folder

If the remote computer you're using for development is your web host, you already have FTP access to your published files. If you have local network access to the remote computer (for example, if you can connect to it from your computer without using FTP), you need to make sure you have read/write access to the folder where your files will be stored.

For Mac users: If you're connected to a Windows computer as your remote host, you'll need to establish FTP access to that computer even if you are connected over a local network, unless you have Mac/Windows sharing software such as PCMacLan or Dave installed. The remote computer must have FTP access enabled for the folder that will store your web files, and you must know the FTP address to access those files.

Correct Setup on the Remote Computer

The remote computer might be your web hosting company's web server, or it might be a computer under the administration of someone else in your office, or it might be all yours. Someone—maybe you—needs to create the setup spelled out in the previous sections of this chapter: the HTTP server, the application server, the DBMS, and the driver must all be present on that computer.

Dynamic Development Tools in Dreamweaver MX

Dreamweaver provides a full range of features to help you set up, program, and preview your dynamic web sites. The general procedure for working with live data pages in Dreamweaver is as follows:

1. As part of defining a site, set up application server information (see Figure 26.16). The most important item of information here is the URL to be used when Dreamweaver sends HTTP requests for live data previewing. If you're developing locally, the URL should refer to `http://localhost` or `http://127.0.0.1`. If you're developing on a remote computer (whether or not you have local network access to it), the URL must be an absolute reference beginning with `http://`, such as that computer's IP address or your site's domain name.

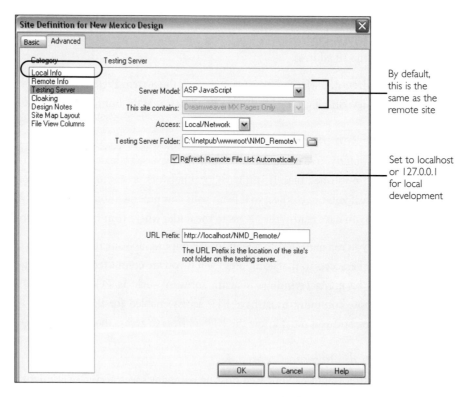

Figure 26.16 The Define Site dialog box showing the Testing Server category.

2. As part of creating a new document, choose whether it will be a static or live data page, and what server technology and language the page will use (see Figure 26.17). Your choice here will determine what kind of server-side code Dreamweaver inserts into your document, and what objects and other choices you have available to you in the MX interface as you work on the document.

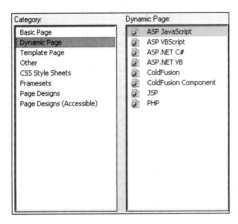

Figure 26.17   The list of file types in the New Document dialog box, showing the different server models and languages.

Note

If you're upgrading from UltraDev 4, you might have noted that you no longer have to specify a server technology while defining a site. The server language can now be set separately for each document in a site, allowing you to mix server technologies and languages within a site.

3. Use the Databases panel to set up a connection to an online database, and to explore that database (see Figure 26.18). Clicking the plus (+) button in this panel lets you choose a predefined DSN or (if you're developing locally on Windows) open the ODBC Data Sources window and define one on-the-fly.

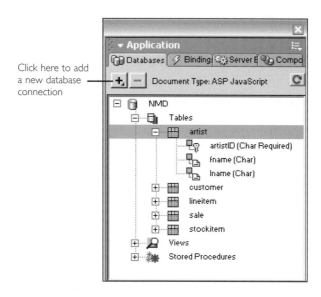

Click here to add
a new database
connection

Figure 26.18   The Databases panel showing an exploratory view of a connected database.

4. Use the Bindings panel to create SQL statements that will collect recordsets from the database to use in the page (see Figure 26.19). The SQL query can pull selected columns and selected records from a connected database, as well as sorting and grouping the information as needed. Only data from collected recordsets can be displayed in a live data page.

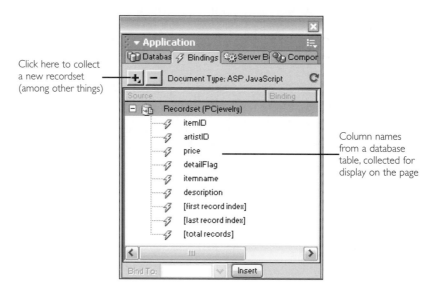

Click here to collect
a new recordset
(among other things)

Column names
from a database
table, collected for
display on the page

Figure 26.19   The Bindings panel showing a selection of records collected from a connected database.

5. Use Server Behaviors, Application objects, and dynamic input fields located throughout the Dreamweaver toolset to insert dynamic content from the record-set into the page, and control its appearance there (see Figure 26.20). As you can see, after the database connection is established and the recordset is collected, Dreamweaver gives you plenty of different ways to put the dynamic information on a page.

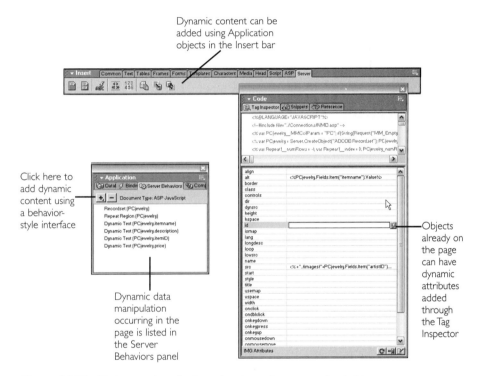

Figure 26.20   Various options for inserting dynamic content placeholders.

6. Use the Live Data View and Preview in Browser function to view the page with data from the database in place (see Figure 26.21). In Design view, each dynamic element displays as a placeholder—good for working, but not for checking what your page will really look like when it's live. The Live Data button in the Document window lets you see real data elements in place while still working, though not all dynamic effects properly display here. To see a complete preview of the constructed page, use the standard Preview in Browser command (F12).

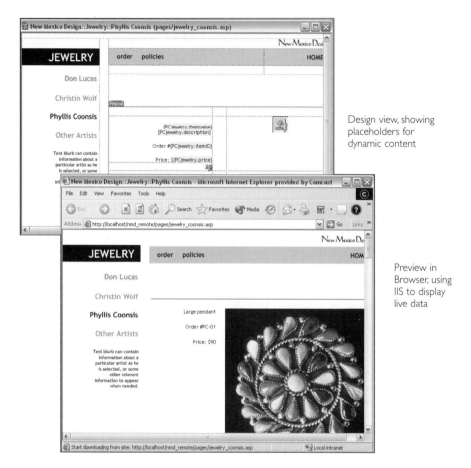

Design view, showing placeholders for dynamic content

Preview in Browser, using IIS to display live data

Figure 26.21   Viewing Live Data in Dreamweaver and in the browser.

Summary

Do data-driven web sites sound exciting? Do they sound daunting? Are you ready to try them out? Each of the remaining chapters in this section focuses on getting up and running with a different application server. Chapters 27 and 28 introduce ASP and its powerful new cousin, ASP.NET. Chapter 29 helps you get started with ColdFusion. Chapter 30 gets you going with PHP. And Chapter 31 tackles JSP. In the course of each chapter, you'll learn how to configure and set up a site; how to link to a database; how to use data bindings, server behaviors, and live objects to create a page; and how to preview your results with the browser and with Live Preview.

Chapter 27

Building a Basic ASP Site

One of the friendliest and easiest to set up of all the server technologies, Active Server Pages (ASP) can be a good place to start learning to build dynamic sites; it also can be a cost-effective and simple solution for commercial jobs, as long as your company has access to Windows-based computers for your web hosting. This chapter takes you through the steps of setting up your workstation to work with ASP, creating an ASP site in Dreamweaver, and creating a basic live data page. Along the way, you'll get used to examining ASP code and learn how this script-based language constructs HTML documents for browser display.

Setting Up Your Workstation to Work with ASP

Setting up can be the hardest (and scariest) part of creating a dynamic site. Before you can start creating pages, you need to set up a web server and an application server; set up your database, and database management system; create a database driver; and set up a folder where your web pages can officially be "served" by the web server. The following sections take you through that process for ASP.

Setting Up the Web Server and Application Server

ASP works with the IIS (Internet Information Services) and PWS (Personal Web Server) web servers, on Windows computers. The good news is, if you followed the instructions in the preceding chapter, and either installed or are connected to a computer running IIS or PWS, you're all set for ASP! Unlike other application server technologies, ASP functionality does not need to be installed separately from the web server—it's already built in. (Of course the bad news is, if you're not using one of these servers, you can't use ASP.)

Setting Up the Database

The computer housing your web server must have a database management system (DBMS) installed on it. For development purposes, most web authors use Microsoft Access with ASP; if you prefer, you can use MySQL instead. (See Appendix C, "Introduction to MySQL," for detailed instructions on setting up MySQL for use with the exercises in this book.)

After you have the database in place, you also need to create a driver that connects to it.

The Antiques Database

The exercises in this chapter use the **antiques.mdb** database. It's available on the CD as an Access or MySQL database.

If you're using Access as your DBMS, open the **databases** folder on the CD and copy the **antiques_access** folder to the computer where your web server is installed. The folder can be stored anywhere you like.

If you're using MySQL as your DBMS, open the **databases** folder on the CD and copy the **antiques_mysql** folder to the computer where your web server is installed. The folder must be stored in the **mysql/data** directory. (See Appendix C for more detailed instructions on installing the antiques database for use with MySQL.)

The Driver

The driver allows the application server to communicate with the database. It can be set up only after you have properly copied the database to your host computer. Follow the instructions in the preceding chapter to set up your driver. Figure 27.1 shows a driver being created for the Access version of the antiques database.

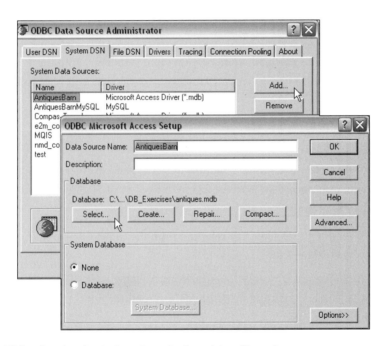

Figure 27.1 Creating the AntiquesBarn database driver (Access).

Setting Up Your Local and Remote Folders

Dreamweaver dynamic sites must have local and remote folders, just like any Dreamweaver site. If you have your web server installed on the same computer you're developing on, both folders will be on the same computer.

To set up your local root folder, copy the **chapter_27** folder from the CD onto your computer. Its exact location doesn't matter for the exercises.

Your remote folder will be called **antiques_asp** and must be located on the same computer running the IIS/PWS server and must be recognized by IIS/PWS as a shared directory for web serving. To accomplish this, do the following:

1. Somewhere on the computer where the IIS/PWS server is located, create a folder called **antiques_asp**.

2. In Windows Explorer, right-click on the **antiques_asp** folder, and from the contextual menu choose Properties.

3. Bring the Web Sharing tab to the front and select Share This Item.

4. When the Edit Alias dialog box appears, leave the alias name at the default (antiques_asp) and set the access permissions to Read/Write, and the application permissions to Scripts.

If you're working on a Mac and are networking to a Windows computer for your ASP development, you'll also have to set up FTP sharing for the remote folder. To accomplish this, do the following:

1. On the computer where the IIS/PWS server is located, go to Start > Control Panel > (Administrative Tools) > IIS or Start > Control Panel > PWS.

2. When the server management window opens, expand the hierarchical list on the left until it shows the local computer's Web Sites and FTP Sites options.

3. Expand the **FTP Sites** folder to show the Default FTP Site.

4. Right-click on the Default FTP Site, and from the contextual menu choose New > Virtual Directory.

5. Follow the Virtual Directory Creation Wizard, giving your FTP site an alias of antiques_asp and selecting the **antiques_asp remote** folder created earlier as the folder to share.

Setting Up an ASP Site in Dreamweaver

After you've got your workstation files set up, it's time to tuck into Dreamweaver. The first step here is to define a site, complete with local, remote, and application server information. Dreamweaver needs to know where your local and remote folders are. It also needs to know what kind of dynamic site you'll be creating (ASP); and, because ASP pages can be written using either JavaScript or VBScript, it needs to know which of those to use. Finally, it needs to know how to communicate with your web server.

The main difference between using Dreamweaver for static and for dynamic sites is how it previews your pages. In a static site, when you choose Preview in Browser (F12), Dreamweaver launches the browser and passes it the local address of the current page:

```
C:\Client Files\Web\My Local Site\index.html
```

or

```
file:///Client Files/Web/My Local Site/index.html
```

In a dynamic site, it's not enough just to view the pages in a browser. Dreamweaver has to activate the web server, passing it an HTTP request so that it processes the files. This requires an address like this:

```
http://localhost/mysite/index.html
```

or

```
http://192.128.164.123/mysite/index.html
```

That's why, when you define a dynamic site, you must go through the additional steps of making sure Dreamweaver can connect with your server and "serve" your pages.

Exercise 27.1   Setting Up the Antiques Barn Site

In this exercise, you define a dynamic ASP site in Dreamweaver using the Site Definition dialog box. Make sure you've set up your workstation before going through the exercise.

1. In Dreamweaver, go to Site > New Site. In the Site Definition dialog box that appears, click the Advanced tab to bring it to the front.

   What about the wizard? In this exercise, you're using the Advanced tab of the Site Definition dialog box. The information is more compactly presented using this method, easier to see and troubleshoot. After you have the site defined and work-ing, check out where Dreamweaver has stored your site information in the Basic and Advanced tabs, to see how the two methods of site definition compare.

2. From the Categories list, choose Local Info. Local site information for a dynamic site is no different from any site information. Name your site **Antiques Barn ASP**. For the local root folder, browse to the **chapter_27** folder you copied from the CD.

3. From the Categories list, choose Remote Info. You'll enter different information here depending on how you set up your workstation (as discussed earlier in this chapter).

   If you're working on the same computer that's running your web server, set your access method to Local/Network and browse to the shared remote **antiques_asp** folder you defined earlier (see Figure 27.2).

Figure 27.2   The Remote Info setup for the Antiques Barn site, if your Dreamweaver site and your web server are on the same computer.

If you're connecting to a different computer for your web server, choose FTP access. Enter the IP address of the other computer and username password, if needed (see Figure 27.3). Refer back to the discussion on IP addresses in the preceding chapter, if necessary.

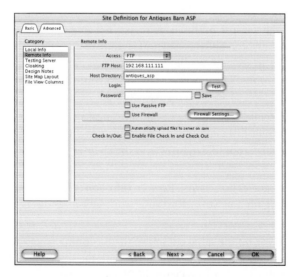

Figure 27.3   The Remote Info setup for the Antiques Barn site, if your web server software is on a different computer than your Dreamweaver site.

Note

Use FTP access even if your two computers are networked directly.

4. From the Categories list, choose Testing Server. For server model and language, choose ASP JavaScript. If the access information hasn't been filled in for you, choose the same Local/Network or FTP access information you chose in the preceding screen (see Figure 27.4 or Figure 27.5).

JavaScript or VBScript? ASP works equally well with either language. Which one you choose depends on which language you're more comfortable with. JavaScript has been chosen for these exercises, on the assumption that you're probably used to looking at the JavaScript code used for regular (client-side) behaviors in Dreamweaver. If you prefer to work in VBScript, choose that in the dialog box. You'll then have to open all ASP files in the **AntiquesBarn** folder and change the opening line of each file to read `<%@language="vbscript"%>`.

If you're using FTP access, you also have to enter the name of the FTP shared folder you or your network administrator created on the other computer. After you have done this, click the Test button to see whether you entered your settings correctly. (If you cannot connect successfully, double-check everything—IP address, folder name, username, and password.)

Figure 27.4   The Testing Server setup for the Antiques Barn site for a single workstation.

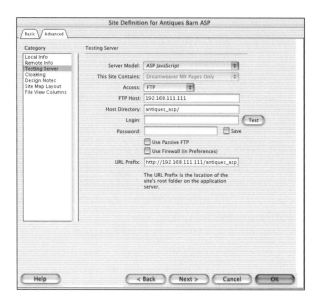

Figure 27.5   The Testing Server setup for the Antiques Barn site for a computer networked to a web server.

Also in this screen, examine the URL Prefix field. Dreamweaver should have filled in this information based on your previous entries. If you're working on one computer, the address will include the `localhost` or `127.0.0.1` IP address. If you're working on two connected computers, the address will include the host computer's actual IP address. This is the URL information Dreamweaver will use every time you preview your pages in the browser. It must be correct!

> **Note**
>
> If you defined your shared directory as a virtual directory in IIS or PWS, you might have chosen a different name for the actual folder and for the folder-as-virtual-directory. You must refer to the correct name! Pay attention to the way the addresses are constructed in the input fields. If the address starts with `file://` or `C:\\`, you must use the actual folder name. If the address starts with `http://`, you must use the virtual directory name. (For the examples here, the same name was used in both places—definitely easier to keep track of.)

When you think all the site information is correct, click OK to close the dialog box. It's time to test things out.

5. From your local root folder, open **index.html** and Preview in Browser (F12). You're probably in for a nasty surprise. Either the page will display with broken images or you'll get a File Not Found error. Why is this happening?

When you're working on a dynamic site, Dreamweaver uses the remote folder to generate its previews. (As explained earlier, this has to happen so that the page can be served rather than merely viewed.) Currently, your remote folder contains nothing! You must get in the habit of uploading files to the remote folder before previewing.

In the Site panel, select all the files in your site, and click the Put button to upload them all. Then try previewing again. If you entered the correct information in your Site Definition dialog box, you will be able to preview the page. The browser's Address field will show the `http://` address of the home page, not its file location on your computer. (If you can't preview, keep double-checking those site settings until you can. You cannot keep working in Dreamweaver until you get this part right.)

Setting Up a Database Connection

In ASP terms, the database connection is a script that calls on the driver to talk to the database. Dreamweaver creates this script for you and stores it in a special connections file when you choose data source name (DSN) from the Databases panel. Because this information gets stored in a special file that can be accessed by any ASP page in your site, you have to define the connection only once for the entire site.

Exercise 27.2   Creating a Database Connection

In this exercise, you create the connection script that will allow your pages to communicate with the antiques database. You must already have installed your database and created a driver for it (as outlined in the preceding section) before continuing with this exercise.

1. Because Dreamweaver has to know what kind of connection to create, you must have a dynamic document open before you can create the connection. From your local site, open **catalog.asp**.

2. From the Application panel group, open the Databases panel. If you have **catalog.asp** open, the panel will have a plus (+) button at the top. Click it and, from the pop-up menu, choose data source name (DSN). Figure 27.6 shows this happening.

Figure 27.6   Choosing a DSN from the Databases panel.

3. The Data Source Name dialog box will appear. For your connection's name, enter **antiques_conn**. (The connection name will be used in the connection script. It can be any one-word name with no special characters, but it's common practice to include *con* or *conn* in the name.)

4. If your server is on your working computer, the radio buttons at the bottom of the dialog box should be set to Using Local DSN, and there will be a pop-up list of drivers. Choose AntiquesBarn from the list. (Clicking the Define button will open the ODBC control panel.) If your server is on another computer, the radio buttons should be set to Using DSN on Testing Server, and the dialog box will include a DSN button. Click that button to get a list of DSNs and choose AntiquesBarn from that list. Figure 27.7 shows both of these possibilities.

 Tip

Occasionally, Mac users will not be able to get a pop-up list of drivers. If this happens to you, carefully type in the name of the driver in the DSN input field. As long as the name is exactly correct, and you have set up a successful link to the host computer in the Site Definition dialog box, this will work.

5. If you specified a name and password when you defined the driver, enter them here. Otherwise, you can leave these fields blank.

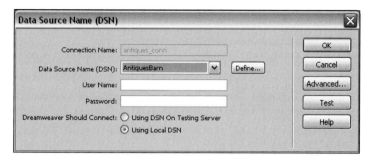

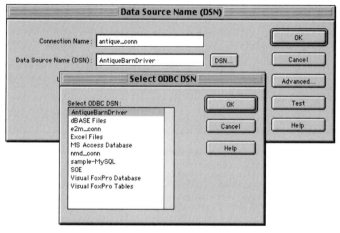

Figure 27.7 Defining the antiques_conn DSN on a computer housing a web server
(Windows) and on a computer networked to a server (Mac).

6. Before leaving the Data Source Name dialog box, click the Test button. If
Dreamweaver can find the driver, you'll get a Connection Successful message.
The most common reasons for failing the test are incorrect names and
passwords, and incorrectly named DSNs. (If you chose the name from a pop-up
menu, this won't be an issue.) After you've passed the test, click OK to close the
dialog box.

7. The Databases panel will now contain an icon representing your connection.
(Congratulations!) You can now use this panel to explore your database. Expand
the connection icon to see Tables, Views, and Stored Procedures. The antiques
database contains only tables. Expand the Tables icon all the way to see that the
database contains two tables—stockitems and customers—and to see what
columns (information fields) each table contains. You cannot see the records stored
in the database from here, but you can examine its structure (see Figure 27.8).

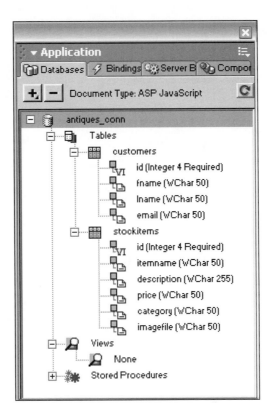

Figure 27.8   The Databases panel showing the structure of the antiques database.

8. In the Site panel, examine your local root folder. You'll see a new **connections** folder. Inside that folder is the **antique_conn.asp** file. That file contains your connection script. Open that file and examine it in Code view. You'll see the following connection script:

```
<%
// FileName="Connection_odbc_conn_dsn.htm"
// Type="ADO"
// DesigntimeType="ADO"
// HTTP="false"
// Catalog=""
// Schema=""
var MM_antique_conn_STRING = "dsn=AntiqueBarn;"
%>
```

You don't need to know what everything in there means. However, one important piece of syntax that you should get familiar with is the <%...%> tags. All ASP code in an HTML document is contained within these tags. Whatever code is inside the tags must be valid JavaScript (or VBScript, if that's the language you chose when setting up). When the application server processes this page, it looks for these tags and executes all code inside them. All other code on the page is assumed to be regular HTML or client-side scripting and is just passed back to the browser.

Displaying Dynamic Data

Probably the most basic task you'll want your ASP pages to perform is to display information from a database. This involves creating a framework of static page elements (banner, navigation controls, a table for layout, and so forth) and adding dynamic text and pictures—like a catalog page in a commerce site shows pictures and descriptions of items for sale.

Displaying dynamic data involves several tasks. First, you must query the database to collect the information you want to display (which records, which fields, in what order, and so on). This collected information is called a *recordset*. Then you create a *dynamic element* for every field you want to display. (A *field* is a column in one of the database tables, remember.) Then, unless you want your page to display only information from the first record it finds, you must create special code that steps through all the collected records and displays them one after the other. In Dreamweaver language, this is called creating a *repeating region*, and it can be refined through various *recordset navigation* controls.

Collecting a Recordset

In Dreamweaver, you collect a recordset with the Bindings panel, in the Application panel group. To collect the recordset, follow these steps:

1. Open the Bindings panel, click the plus (+) button and choose Recordset (Query).

2. In the Recordset dialog box that opens, choose whatever database elements (usually table columns, which translate into record fields) you want.

Note

When you choose items in the Recordset dialog box, you're actually telling Dreamweaver how to write a SQL query for you. To see the actual SQL syntax, click the Advanced button and examine the SQL input field. (Click the Simple button to get back to the standard dialog box.) See the preceding chapter for an brief overview of SQL.

3. After you've collected the recordset, the collected columns will appear in the Bindings panel. Because Dreamweaver has to write an ASP script to collect the recordset, technically speaking the collection action is a behavior. It will appear in the Server Behaviors panel (in the Applications panel group).

You also can create a recordset by going to Insert > Application panel, and choosing the Recordset object. Doing this is exactly the same as using the Bindings panel. Think of it as a shortcut.

Exercise 27.3   Collecting Data for the Antiques Barn Catalog Page

In this exercise, you add dynamic elements to the **catalog.asp** page, which already has its static layout elements in place. This page is meant to display all the items for sale at the Antiques Barn, so you'll collect information from the stockitems table of the antiques database. You'll display a picture, name, description, and price for each item (see Figure 27.9).

Figure 27.9   The Antiques Barn catalog page being served with one record displaying.

1. Begin by opening **catalog.asp**. Examine the layout structure in Design view, and you'll see that the middle row of the main layout table is ready and waiting for a picture in one column and various text items in another.

2. First, you have to query the database to collect some data to play with. From the Application panel group, open the Bindings panel. Click the plus (+) button and, from the menu, choose Recordset (Query). The Recordset dialog box appears.

3. You can give your recordset a custom name or accept the default name. (For the examples shown here, the default name is used.) If your DSN connection (**antiques_conn**) doesn't automatically appear in the Connections field, choose it from the pop-up menu. That will populate the rest of the dialog box with information from the antiques database.

4. You want information from the stockitems table, so choose it from the Tables pop-up menu. You don't need to collect all the columns (fields). For columns to choose, select the Selected radio button. Then Ctrl/Cmd-click to choose item-name, description, price, and imagefile. Choose to sort the information based on itemname, ascending (from *A–Z*). Figure 27.10 shows the completed dialog box and resulting Bindings panel.

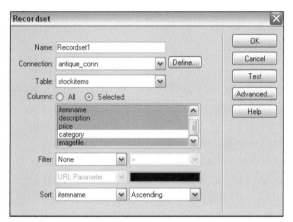
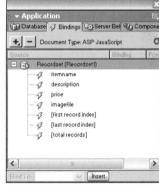

Figure 27.10   Collecting the recordset for the Antiques Barn catalog page and the resulting Bindings panel.

Tip
From within the Recordset dialog box, click the Test button to see what information your recordset will collect. This is a handy way to make sure you've collected the proper set of data, before you get too far into the process of making the page.

5. Click OK to close the dialog box. The Bindings entry is made and the appropriate code is placed in your code.

Inserting Dynamic Elements

Data from the database can be inserted anywhere in your document. Names, prices, and descriptions can become dynamic text elements—you can even format them using all the standard HTML and CSS text options. Database fields also can be used behind the scenes, to help construct the HTML code of your page. Therefore, although most databases cannot contain images or other media elements, a field might contain a filename that can be used in the src parameter for an <img>. This is how you insert dynamic images into your pages. (For details on creating dynamic text, see the dynamic data sidebar in Chapter 4, "Working with Text." For more on dynamic images, see the sidebar in Chapter 5, "Working with Images.")

Most databases used for dynamic sites cannot contain actual media, such as images or sound files. They can contain only text.

Exercise 27.4   Displaying Dynamic Data in the Antiques Barn Catalog Page

In this exercise, you use the recordset you collected in the preceding exercise to create dynamic text and image elements for **catalog.asp**. You also familiarize yourself with the Live Data previewing options in Dreamweaver.

1. Open **catalog.asp**, if it's not already open. In the Applications panel group, open the Bindings panel and expand the view of your recordset so that you can see the individual fields you have collected.

2. It's easiest to start with the dynamic text elements. As you can see from Figure 27.9, the rightmost column of the layout table should contain the item name, description, and price, each in its own paragraph.

   Inserting a dynamic text element can be done in various ways. By far the simplest is just dragging the desired field from the Bindings panel to the proper place in the Document window. Try that method for the first text element—drag the itemname field into the layout table (see Figure 27.11).

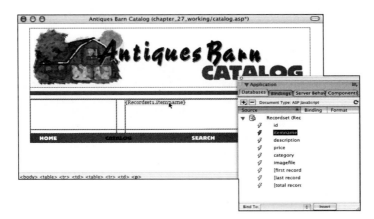

Figure 27.11   Inserting a dynamic text element by dragging a field name from the Bindings panel.

When in the document, the dynamic element becomes a text placeholder. In Design view, it looks like {Recordset1.ItemName}. Switch to Code and Design view, and you'll see that the ASP code looks like this:

```
<%=(Recordset1.Fields.Item("itemname").Value)%>
```

You should already recognize the ASP tag structure. The `<%=` tag means "insert the following value here." The code in parentheses refers to the itemname column. When the server sees that code, it will substitute whatever text is in that field for the current record.

3. As far as Dreamweaver is concerned, this item is a stand-in for real text. To demonstrate that, stay in Code and Design view but use Design view to select the new placeholder. From the Property inspector, apply paragraph formatting (choose Paragraph from the Format pop-up menu). Note that, in the code, the placeholder is now surrounded by `<p>` tags:

```
<p><%=(Recordset1.Fields.Item("itemname").Value)%></p>
```

From the Design panel group, open the CSS panel. With the placeholder text still selected, choose the `itemname` style class. Then display changes to accept the new formatting, and your code changes to the following:

```
<p class="itemname">
<%=(Recordset1.Fields.Item("itemname").Value)%>
</p>
```

The placeholder is being treated as though it were real text.

4. Use the same method to insert the description and price into the layout, each in its own paragraph in the table cell. For the price, apply the `price` CSS class.

5. When you insert dynamic text, you're actually creating an ASP behavior (a script that tells the server to insert certain text). In the Applications panel group, open the Server Behaviors panel, and you'll see one behavior for every dynamic text element you've added, plus a behavior for collecting the recordset (see Figure 27.12). Just like regular behaviors, you can double-click a server-side behavior in the panel to view its properties and edit it.

Figure 27.12 Dynamic text elements in **catalog.asp** and the server behaviors used to insert them.

You can use the Server Behaviors panel to apply special formatting to dynamic text elements—things such as changing capitalization and decimal point display. For the Antiques Barn catalog page, you probably want the item price to display a little nicer, with a dollar sign and some decimal values.

In the Server Behaviors panel, double-click the entry for the price to open it for editing. In the dialog box that appears, use the Formatting pop-up menu to choose Currency-Default (see Figure 27.13). Click OK to close the dialog box.

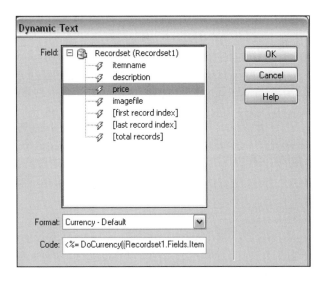

Figure 27.13 Adding scripted formatting to a dynamic text element.

Tip

To delete any dynamic element in a document, it's safest to delete the server behavior that created the element, instead of just selecting its placeholder in Design view and deleting. (Dreamweaver will warn you if you try to delete an element the wrong way.)

6. Each catalog entry must also show a picture of the item. A look at the structure of your database (in the Databases panel) will show you that the stockitems table has a field called imagefile. These can be used as the `src` attribute of an `<img>` tag to create dynamic images.

   To insert the dynamic image, start by placing your cursor in the page at the location you want to add the image and insert the image as you normally would. (Use the Image object from the Insert > Common panel.) When the Insert Image dialog box appears, however, choose the Data Source option (see Figure 27.14). The list of image files is replaced with a list of fields from your recordset. Choose imagefile and click OK.

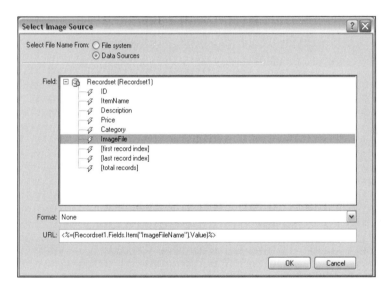

Figure 27.14   Inserting a dynamic image by specifying Data Source, rather than File System, for the `src` attribute.

Design view now shows the image as a cute little image placeholder icon (with a lightning bolt for dynamic data). If you check your code, you'll see another ASP `<%=` tag stuck right in the middle of the `<img>` tag:

```
<img src="<%=(Recordset1.Fields.Item("imagefile").Value)%>">
```

Note that no width or height has been entered. That's because Dreamweaver can't determine the dimensions from this data—because no actual image has been put here yet.

Previewing with Live Data

You're tired of placeholders! You want to see this page in action. After you've completely set up your site definition, Dreamweaver can send an HTTP request to your server and show you your page, with "live" data in place. As discussed earlier, the live preview originates from the shared remote folder you set up as an IIS/PWS directory. Therefore all image files must have been uploaded to the remote site before the preview will work properly. After you've done that, you can preview data in two ways:

- **Live Data view.** In the Document toolbar, click the Live Data button to switch from viewing placeholders to viewing actual data (see Figure 27.15).

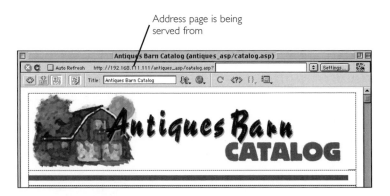

Figure 27.15   Live Data view in action.

- **Preview in Browser.** Choosing this command, when you're in a dynamic site, will activate the server and "serve" your page in your primary, secondary, or another browser.

Exercise 27.5   Previewing and Troubleshooting Live Data in the Antiques Barn Catalog Page

In this exercise, you try some different previewing methods (if you haven't already experimented), and use them to troubleshoot your code.

1. With **catalog.asp** open, click the Live Data view button. It might take a moment, but real data should pop into your Document window.

 Note

> Sometimes Dreamweaver holds the database connection open, which doesn't allow the Live Data view or previewing dynamic pages to function properly. If Live Data view doesn't engage properly, try saving the page and closing Dreamweaver. Next, open your browser and type `http://localhost/yoursitename/catalog.asp` and see if it displays. If you still get an error, your site probably isn't configured and you'll need to revisit the previous exercise and the preceding chapter to troubleshoot.

You'll immediately notice that there's a problem; your lovely dynamic image isn't displaying properly (see Figure 27.16). You might have guessed why but in case you haven't, it's time to visit the browser.

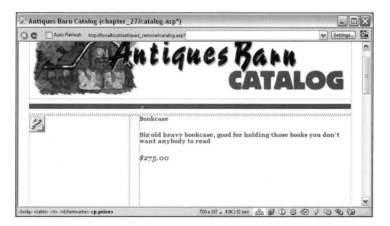

Figure 27.16   Live Data preview of **catalog.asp**, but there's a problem with the dynamic image.

2. Turn off Live Data view by clicking the Live Data button to toggle it off.

3. Preview your page in the browser (F12). You'll undoubtedly see the same problem: a missing image. Here in the browser, however, you have some troubleshooting tools at your disposal. If you're in Internet Explorer, go to View > Source. If you're in Netscape, go to View > Page Source.

   Examine the code here. You might notice that it looks different from the code you viewed in Dreamweaver. There are no ASP <%...%> tags. That's because the server has executed the script within those tags and used it to construct plain old HTML. The HTML code that was constructed to display your table row looks like this (dynamically generated code shown in bold):

   ```
   <tr valign="top">
   <td><img src="bookcase.jpg"></td>
   <td> </td>
   <td>
   <p class="itemname">Bookcase</p>
   <p>Big old heavy bookcase, good for holding those books you don't
   want anybody to read. </p>
   <p class="price">$275.00</p>
   </td>
   </tr>
   ```

   There's your dynamic text! And there's your problem, in the <img> tag. If you examine your site's file structure, you'll see that all images have been stored in an images folder, so the correct relative URL to the clock image is **images/bookcase.jpg**. However, the database entry doesn't include that extra folder name. No wonder the browser cannot find the image!

4. You could, of course, fix every single database entry to include a folder name. However, it's much easier to tweak your ASP code, just a little, to do the job for you. When you get used to the way the server just adds the placeholders right into the main code, it'll be easy.

   Back in Dreamweaver, select the dynamic image placeholder. Then open the Server Behaviors panel. The behavior that is creating your image will be highlighted. Double-click to open the editing dialog box. Because you know you have to add the folder name to the entry, manually fix the URL entry so that it looks like this (new code in bold):

   ```
   <img src="images/<%=(Recordset1.Fields.Item("imagefile").Value)%>">
   ```

5. After you've done this, try previewing your page in a browser again (F12). The image should show up! (If it doesn't, select View > Source to check your constructed code; and back in Dreamweaver, check Code view to make sure your <img> tag looks exactly like the one shown here.)

The only drawback to manually adding relative path information to your dynamic image source is that you have to know what the relative URL to your images should look like. You can't just browse to an image and let Dreamweaver do the thinking for you!

Displaying Multiple Records with Repeated Regions

A repeated region is any chunk of page code that you want to repeat for as many records as you want to show. A repeated region can be a line of text, an item in a list, a table row, or even an entire table. To create a repeated region, follow these steps:

1. Select the part of your page that you want to repeat.

2. In the Server Behaviors panel, click the plus (+) button and choose Repeat Region; or choose the Repeated Region object from the Insert > Application bar (see Figure 27.17). A dialog box will appear, asking which recordset you want to display and how many records you want to show. (Only choose to display all records if you know for sure your database won't have too many records to fit on a decent-sized web page.)

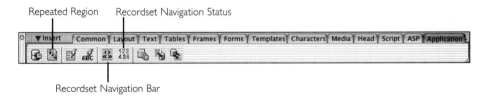

Figure 27. 17   The Repeated Region, Record Navigation Set, and Record Navigation Status objects.

Navigating Through Multipage Displays

If you've set up the repeating region not to display all records simultaneously, you need to give your visitors a way to view the first group of records, the next group after that, and so on. Dreamweaver offers two tools to help with this: Record Navigation Bar and Record Navigation Status. Both are technically server behaviors, but also are easily accessible as objects from the Insert > Application bar (see Figure 27.17).

The Record Navigation Bar object (or server behavior) determines whether there are more records in the recordset than are displayed on the current page; and if so, displays previous page, next page, first page, and last page navigation controls. All the hard work is done for you. All you have to do is insert the object (or server behavior), and Dreamweaver creates the links and adds the scripting to display different records on your page.

The Record Navigation Status object (or server behavior) determines how many total records are in the recordset, and which are currently displaying on the page, and adds a text message to the page—Records 1 to 10 of 56. Again, all you have to do is insert the object; Dreamweaver takes care of the rest.

Exercise 27.6   Displaying Multiple Records in the Antiques Barn Catalog Page

In this exercise, you build the catalog page further by displaying multiple records. You also add navigation controls that enable visitors to move between records easily.

1. Open **catalog.asp**, if it isn't already open.

2. You want the table row containing your dynamic elements to repeat. Select that row. (Drag across the cells, or click inside a cell and use the tag selector to select the `<tr>`. It's important to make sure you get exactly the right table parts selected!)

3. From the Insert > Application panel, choose the Repeat Region object. The Repeat Region dialog box will appear, asking you which recordset to base the repeats on (you have only one recordset, so there's nothing to choose here) and how many records to show. Set the number of displayed records to 5 and click OK (see Figure 27.18). Note how the Design view display has changed to indicate the repeated region.

Figure 27.18   Inserting a repeated region that will display five records at a time.

4. Preview your work in the browser (F12). There are the first five records of your recordset!

Tip

If there's anything wrong with your ASP code, you'll get a Page Cannot Be Displayed message from the server. Read through the text of this message and you'll find some very specific information on what's wrong with the page, including what line of code contains the error. Occasionally, even Dreamweaver-generated code generates errors. Examining these errors and troubleshooting them is a great way to increase your knowledge of ASP!

5. This is great as far as it goes, but the visitor can never go beyond those first five records. You need some navigation controls. Back in Dreamweaver, the new elements should be added below the repeated elements but above the bottom navigation bar.

You need to add a new table row for the controls. Be careful here! If you place the insertion point in the table row that contains the dynamic elements, and insert a new row below it, Dreamweaver will assume that you want the new row to be part of the repeated region. Instead, you must position the cursor in the empty table row directly above the navigation bar and insert a row above. You'll have to be sneaky doing this, because that "empty" row is actually filled with transparent GIF images. Select one of the images. Then use the tag selector to choose the parent <td> tag. Then go to Modify > Table > Insert Row. (Unless you're very accurate with your mouse clicks, it's easier to choose the menu from the menu bar than to right-click to access the contextual menu.)

You want the new navigation elements to stretch all the way across the layout, so select all three cells in the new row and merge them (Modify > Table > Merge Cells).

6. With the insertion point in the new merged row, choose the Recordset Navigation Bar from the Insert > Application bar. In the dialog box that appears, choose to use text navigation elements and click OK. Figure 27.19 shows the resulting insertion.

Figure 27. 19   The Recordset Navigation Bar being inserted in the Antiques Barn catalog page.

7. Preview your page in the browser again (F12), and you'll see the navigation controls at work. You can click to move forward and back through pages of displayed records. Also note that the controls appear only if there are records to view—you cannot go to previous or first, if you're at the first page already, for instance (see Figure 27.20).

Oops! If you inserted your new table row inside the repeating region, you'll get navigation controls after every single record. There is no easy fix for this, unless you're willing to tinker around in the code. The quickest solution is to Edit > Undo, or use the History panel, backing up to before you inserted the new table row. . .and start again.

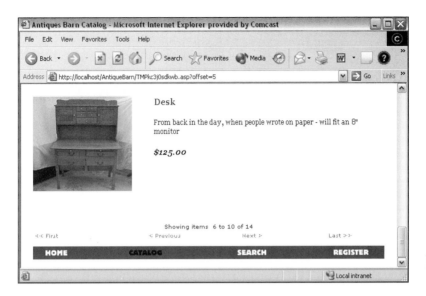

Figure 27.20   The Antiques Barn catalog page with all recordset navigation elements in place.

8. The newly inserted elements are just dynamic text links in a table. Feel free to format them as you like—you can even change the text, so long as you don't change the link information. To match the formatting in Figure 27.20, set the table width to 640 and apply the nav CSS class to each text element.

9. Finally, you can make your catalog page complete by letting visitors know where they are in the recordset ("Records 1 to 5 of 10"). For the Antiques Barn page, you'll add that information directly above the recordset navigation controls.

   Start by adding a new row at the top of the nested table that contains the record-set navigation (see Figure 27.21). As long as you're working with this table, you're well outside the repeated region, so you don't have to worry about that.

10. Merge the cells of the new row so that it stretches across the entire table. Then, with the insertion point inside the new row, choose the Recordset Navigation Status object from the Insert > Application bar. There's your new dynamic text (see Figure 27.21). Preview in the browser to see it in action (F12).

    As with any dynamic text element, you can format the status line as you like. You also can change any of the static text, as long as you don't disturb the placeholder text. (In Figure 27.20, for instance, the word *records* has been changed to *items*.)

    Congratulations! The Antiques Barn catalog page is now complete. You've built your first ASP document.

Figure 27.21   Inserting a Recordset Navigation Status object.

Summary

In this chapter, you learned the basics of setting up an ASP site in Dreamweaver and creating a page that displays dynamic elements. This is only a taste of what you can do with ASP. Instead of displaying all stock items, you could tie the catalog into a search page so that visitors can choose what category of antiques to display. You could link small thumbnail images to separate pages containing detailed information about each item. You could have visitors sign in, so that when they revisit the site their favorite antiques will show at the top of the list. Dreamweaver provides objects and server behaviors for all this functionality and more.

Chapter 28

Building a Basic
ASP.NET Site

ASP.NET is a new web language that fits
into Microsoft's .NET framework. Built on
the ASP language, it defines a new way of
interacting on the web. It enhances the

client/server relationship, making it possible to simply build more powerful web applications. With great features such as web services, you can easily pull onto your page a wide range of functionality, from stock quotes to the position of the planets to an English-to-Pig Latin conversion feature, with just a few lines of code.

This chapter covers how to set up your computer to create ASP.NET pages. As with all of these dynamic chapters so far, you need to have programs installed for this to work correctly.

Setting Up a Workstation for ASP.NET

Before you can make .NET pages, your computer must meet the following basic requirements.

- Because .NET is a Microsoft product, it works only with the IIS server on Windows. The framework will be installed to its own directory, but you will still use the web root of IIS to serve your pages.

- If you don't have it already, you will need the Microsoft Data Access Components 2.6 or above installed. (Latest version as of this writing is 2.7; available at www.microsoft.com/mdac.) *MDAC* is a collection of files that enables ASP.NET to work together with your server and datasources. These include components for ODBC, OLE DB, and ADO technologies.

- You need to install the .NET Framework or have access to a machine that has it installed. This is the program that actually runs the .NET part of the code. It is available as a download from Microsoft. Be warned: It is 131MB! (http://www.microsoft.com/net/)

When you install the .NET Framework, the installer indicates whether you are missing needed components, such as IIS or MDAC components.

The .NET Framework install is quite painless. There is really nothing to configure after you install it. You don't even need to restart! After you have the .NET Framework installed, and you have IIS running, you are ready to build pages. (If you have installed the Apache server on your machine, make sure that it is turned off for this chapter. You generally want only one server running at a time.)

Setting Up an ASP.NET Site in Dreamweaver

First you need to set up a local site for using ASP.NET. This section covers the steps required to set up a Dreamweaver site in preparation for creating .NET pages.

This discussion explains how to set up a DataSet, which is .NET-ese for a Recordset, and then how to use this DataSet to display the live data.

Setting Up a Local Site

A *DSN* is a data source name. It basically is a setting made on your computer that points to the database and specifies a driver to use to communicate with that database. This way, Dreamweaver can simply use the DSN name to reference the database. The DSN will then use the database specified within itself. With this setup, you can establish a DSN on your local machine to build and test the site. When you are ready to upload your site to the server, you simply have to have a DSN on the server with the same name that points to your database on the server. Then everything will work as planned. If you are using an ISP, setting up a DSN on the server is usually a simple request. Most good ISPs have a webform for requesting a DSN.

To create a DSN, follow these steps:

1. Go to the Control Panel (Start > Settings > Control Panel (these instructions differ between operating systems). Open the Administrative Tools and then open Data Sources (ODBC).

   You should see something like what appears in Figure 28.1.

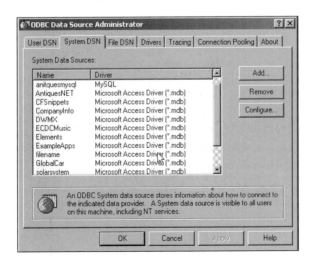

Figure 28.1 The ODBC Data Source Administrator.

2. Go to the System DSN tab. Unless you have a good reason, stick with System DSNs.

3. Click the Add button. You will be presented with a list of available database drivers. For the Access database included with the book, choose Microsoft Access Driver (*.mdb). Click the Finish button.

4. In the dialog box that opens, you'll find the Data Source Name field. This is the name of the connection and is the name that you will be choosing when selecting a DSN in Dreamweaver. Be sure to name it well. For our purposes, a name like **antiques** will work fine. For a description, you can say something like **This is the Antiques database for the Inside Dreamweaver book**.

5. In the Database section, press the Select button. This is where you actually specify the database.

6. In the next dialog box, browse to the **antiques.mdb** database that you copied to your hard drive. The database will show up in the window on the left when you are in a folder that contains an Access database.

7. Click OK when you are done. Click OK again to close the next dialog and then once more to close the Database Administrator. You have successfully created a new DSN. Now this database will be available for use in Dreamweaver.

Note

For real web applications, it is not a good idea to put the database in the web root. Those who go looking can find it and download it. It's a good idea to put it outside the web root. Most ISPs specify a specific folder for databases. For ease of database management, I create a folder like **c:\databases** and put all my databases in there. This way, I always know where they are, and it is easier to create connections.

Exercise 28.1   Setting Up the Antiques Barn Site

Now you need to create a new site for your .NET pages. In this exercise, you set up a .NET site for Antiques Barn.

Create a new local root folder in your hard drive. Copy the **chapter_28** folder from the CD into this folder. If you haven't already, copy the **antiques.mdb** database from the **databases/Access** folder on the CD and place it in your local root folder.

If you do not have one already, create a DSN to the Antiques database. (See Chapter 26, "Introduction to Dynamic Dreamweaver," for more information on DSNs.)

1. Go to Site > New Site.

2. Under Local Info, name the new site **ASP.NET**.

3. For local root folder, browse to the **chapter_28** folder you copied earlier.

4. Go to Remote Info.

5. For Access, choose Local/Network.

6. For remote folder, browse to the root of your web server. For IIS it is **c:\inetpub\wwwroot\.**

7. Go to the Application Server page.

8. For Server Model, choose ASP.NET VB.

9. For Access, choose Local/Remote. Choose the server root (same folder as in step 6) for the remote folder if it is not chosen already.

10. For URL Prefix, type `http://localhost` unless you have customized your server configuration.

11. Click OK, and Dreamweaver will build the site.

Your ASP.NET site should now be properly configured.

Setting Up a DataSet

As with all dynamic sites, you need to establish a connection to the database and create a Recordset for the page. The same is true for .NET pages, only here they are referred to as *DataSets*.

Because of the specifics of the .NET language, DataSet setup requires a slightly different process than other Recordsets require.

To set up a DataSet, follow these steps:

1. Open a new page. Go to File > New Live Data Page > ASP.NET VB.

2. Go to the Bindings panel.

3. Click the plus (+) button and choose DataSet (Query)

4. Click the Define button next to the Connection field. Click New and OLE DB Connection to create your new connection.

5. In the OLE DB Connection window, choose the Build button.

6. Go to the Provider tab. Choose the Microsoft Jet 4.0 OLE DB Provider. Click the Next button.

7. For field number 1, browse to the **antiques.mdb** database that you have copied to the hard drive. Click the Test Connection button. It should give you a success message. Click the OK button to close the dialog box.

8. Name the connection **con_Antiques** in the Name field. Click OK to complete the connection.

9. In the Tables field, select a table and then click OK to close the Dataset dialog box.

Exercise 28.2   Creating a DataSet for ASP.NET

In this exercise, you will make a DataSet from the Antiques database so that you can create the catalog page. The process differs slightly from other server models. This is due to the specifics of the .NET language.

1. In the ASP.NET site created earlier, create a new page. Choose File > New > Live Data Page > ASP.NET VB. Save the page.

2. Open the Application panel set and go to Databases. If you have set up your site correctly, the Antiques database should be listed. If it is, you can browse through the database to see the structure and data. If not, complete the unchecked requirements.

3. Click on the plus (+) button and choose OLE DB Connection.

4. In the OLE DB Connection dialog box, enter **Antiques** as the name for the database connection. Then click the Build button. The Data Link Properties dialog box will open to the Connection tab (see Figure 28.2). This dialog box enables you to establish a DSN connection for the page. The Use Data Source Name radio button should be checked. If the dialog box doesn't look like Figure 28.2, switch to the Provider tab and choose Microsoft OLE DB Provider for ODBC Data Sources. Switch back to the Connection tab and all should be well

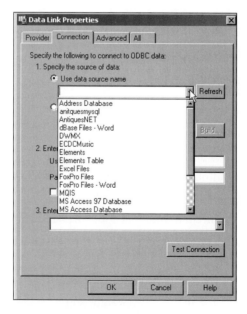

Figure 28.2   The Data Link Properties dialog box.

5. Click the drop-down menu arrow on the Use Data Source Name field to view a list of all the DSNs on your machine. The Antiques DSN that you created earlier should be on that list. Choose it and click the Test button to test the connection.

If it works, click OK to close the dialog box. If not, repeat the previous steps to set up the connection.

6. Click OK to close the OLE DB Connection dialog box.

You have now created a database connection. Now you will make the actual DataSet.

7. Go to the Bindings tab in the Application Building panel. Click the plus (+) button and choose DataSet (Query).

8. In the DataSet dialog box (see Figure 28.3), enter **Catalog** in the Name field.

9. For Connection, click the drop-down arrow and choose Antiques, the connection you just made. The Table field will now list the tables of the Antiques database.

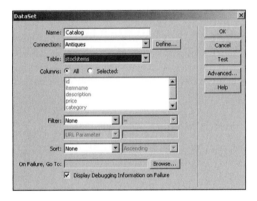

Figure 28.3   The DataSet dialog box.

10. Choose stockitems from the Table field. The rest of the settings are okay as defaults, so click OK.

The DataSet is created. Click the small plus (+) button next to the Dataset name in the Bindings panel to show a list of all the data fields (columns) You should see id, itemname, description, price, category and imagefile.

Displaying Dynamic Data Using ASP.NET

Now that you have a DataSet made, you can use it to create ASP.NET objects. An easy first step is to create a *DataGrid*, which is a table that ASP.NET creates from the DataSet. This is equivalent to a dynamic table in other server models.

To create a DataGrid, use the DataSet you just created and follow these steps:

1. Go to the Server Behavior tab. Click the plus (+) button and choose DataGrid.

2. In the DataGrid dialog box, choose the Catalog DataSet that you just created for the DataSet field.

3. Choose the All Records radio button. Click OK.

Before you can preview live data, some files need to be transferred to the server. This can be done from the Bindings panel. There is a note under the steps to deploy these files. Click on that, and the dialog box that appears will prompt you to copy the files to the server. Make sure it is pointing to the web root for this site definition (in this case c:\inetpub\wwwroot) and then click the Deploy button. This can also be accessed through the Site Menu at the top of the page (not in the Site panel). Click Site > Deploy Supporting Files. This action will copy over files that are required for live data to work.

In the Design window, you will see a table (grid) that represents the rows and columns of your data. To see the actual table, click the Live Data button or Preview in Browser.

The .NET Framework makes creating these kinds of common dynamic features quite easy. Now you can make ASP.NET work within your catalog pages.

Exercise 28.3   Creating a Catalog Page in ASP.NET

In this exercise, you use the .NET data to create the Catalog page for the Antiques site. You will use Dreamweaver behaviors to organize this into a properly formatted table.

1. In the ASP.NET site that you created earlier, open the **catalog.aspx** file. You will add the database information to create the catalog into this file.

2. Create a DataSet identical to the one created earlier. You want to use the Antiques database (Access) and create a DataSet for the stockitems table. Choose All columns. Click OK to finish the DataSet.

   Now, the live data is going to go in the middle cells of the table.

3. Put your cursor in the leftmost cell. Click the Insert Image button on the Common tab of the Insert bar.

4. At the top of the dialog box, you have the option to Select File Name From. Choose Data Sources.

5. From the DataSet, choose ImageFileName and click OK.

6. Put your cursor in the rightmost cell.

7. Go to the Bindings panel. Click and drag the ItemName record to the rightmost cell (see Figure 28.4).

Figure 28.4   Drag the record to the table.

8. Click in the cell to deselect the record. Press Enter to go to the next line.

9. Drag and drop the Description record to the rightmost cell. Click in the cell to deselect and press Enter.

10. Enter $ at the start of the line. Click and drag the price record next to the dollar sign.

11. Click on the Live Data button.

   You should see one record. But where is the image? It's not showing. This is because the database has only the image name, not the image path. If the images were in the same folder as the ASPX page, it would show properly. However, you have stored the images in a subfolder. You need to tweak the code to reflect the proper path. To do this, click off the Live Data button and highlight the image field.

12. Go to View > Code and Design to show the code and design.

   The highlighted image field code should look like this:

   ```
   <img src="<%# antiques.FieldValue("ImageFileName", Container) %>"
   width="92" height="36">
   ```

   You might recognize the standard image tag. You need to add **images/** to the front of the name in the src field.

   This code goes between the opening quotation mark (") of the src field and the first left-angle bracket (<).

   Your final code should look like this:

   ```
   <img src="images/<%# antiques.FieldValue("ImageFileName",
   Container) %>" width="92" height="36">
   ```

13. Now save the file and preview using the Live Data button. You should see the image in the table.

At this stage, only one record will show: a rather thin catalog. You must apply a behavior so that all the records show. This is a server behavior called a *Repeating Region.* As its name hints, this will loop through the selected code, inserting all the records of the database, or as many as you choose.

14. Make sure that your cursor is in the row containing the datafields. In the tag selector in the lower-left corner of Dreamweaver, select the `<tr>` tag.

15. With this row selected, go to the Server Behaviors panel. Click the plus (+) button. Choose Repeat Region.

16. In the Repeat Region dialog box, choose the All Records radio button (see Figure 28.5). Click OK.

    The table row should now be bounded by a gray box that specifies an Item Template, which is .NET for a repeat region.

Figure 28.5   The Repeat Region dialog box.

17. Click the Live Data button to see your table with the real information.

Adding Records to the Database

Using dynamic data, it is easy to create large, complex pages quickly. All you have to do is add another record to the database and your page will automatically reflect that.

Exercise 28.4   Inserting a New Record into the Database

In this exercise, you use a regular HTML form to insert a new customer record into the database and then send it to a Thank You page.

1. Open the **register.aspx** file from the .NET site.

2. Create a new DataSet for this page. Click the plus (+) button in the Data Bindings tab. Choose DataSet.

3. You have yet to create a connection for this page. Click the Define button. Choose New and then OLE DB Connection.

4. Click the Build button of the OLE DB Connection dialog box.

5. In field number 1, click the drop-down arrow and choose the Antiques DSN you created earlier. Click OK.

6. Click OK and then click Done to return to the DataSet dialog box.

7. For Connection, choose the connection you just made. For Table, choose customers. Click OK.

8. Now you are ready to apply the insert code. Highlight the Submit button on the Register form. You apply the server behavior to the button.

9. In the Server Behaviors tab, click the plus (+) button. Go to Insert Record. The Insert Record dialog box displays (see Figure 28.6). Dreamweaver makes it easy with easy-to-use dialog boxes such as this.

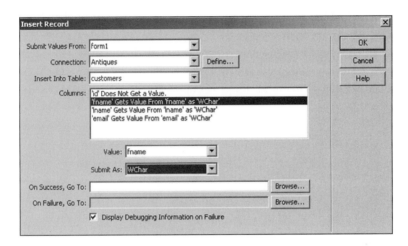

Figure 28.6   The Insert Record dialog box.

10. For Connection, choose the connection you just created. For Insert Into Table, choose MailingListTable.

11. In the Column field, click the FirstName line. The Value drop-down lists the fields of the form. Click the Value drop-down list and choose frame.

12. Click the LastName line in the Columns field. For Value, choose lname.

13. Repeat the steps for the email value.

14. For On Success, Go To, browse to the **thankyou.html** page. Click OK. That's it.

15. Now that you are going to link to the **thankyou.html** page, you need to make sure it is available on the server. Highlight **thankyou.html** in the Site panel and click the Upload button to copy it to the server. Now that server behavior will be able to find it after it inserts the record!

16. Preview in Browser and fill in the form and submit it. It should navigate to the Thank You page.

17. To check that the record was added, open the database and check the table. Better yet, use your newfound skills to create a DataGrid of the mailing list table and check for the new record there.

Summary

ASP.NET is an initiative from Microsoft that works quite differently than other server models. Some of the vocabulary is a bit different than with other languages, and .NET can do a lot more than is shown here. There are many .NET-specific sites that will detail the specific new ideas of .NET. With practice, you can learn just how much .NET and Dreamweaver MX can do to quickly build web applications with little to no hand coding.

Chapter 29

Building a Basic ColdFusion Site

ColdFusion has been the center of quite a buzz in the web development community in recent years, and for good reason. It was the very first application server; its invention created the category. Designed specifically for building web applications, it is both extremely powerful and surprisingly easy to learn and use.

With Dreamweaver MX, developing ColdFusion applications just became a whole lot easier. For the web designer just venturing into data-driven web sites, Dreamweaver makes building ColdFusion applications possible without ever writing a line of code, and the more experienced developer will be pleased by the quality of code Dreamweaver produces.

Just what is ColdFusion? The term refers to two technologies that work together:

- The ColdFusion Application Server, a piece of software that typically is installed on the same computer as the web (or HTTP) server
- The ColdFusion Markup Language (CFML), modeled after HTML.

This chapter explains how to set up a workstation for ColdFusion application development, how to set up a ColdFusion site in Dreamweaver MX, display dynamic data using ColdFusion, and how to create interactive pages using ColdFusion and the ColdFusion Markup Language (CFML).

Before building web sites that make use of application servers, such as ColdFusion, it's best to get a basic understanding of the technologies necessary and how they all fit together. Unless you are already very familiar with data-driven web applications, be sure to read Chapter 26, "Introduction to Dynamic Dreamweaver" before diving in here.

Setting Up Your Workstation to Work With ColdFusion

The process of building ColdFusion web applications demands that you have the ability to test your applications locally. You will need a setup on the computer where Dreamweaver is installed that enables ColdFusion to process pages and to communicate with a database. Both a web server and ColdFusion Server, two distinct pieces of software, are needed. You'll also need a database management system (DBMS). For Mac users: As of this writing, ColdFusion Server will not run on Mac, so you'll need to set up for remote development.

Setting Up the Web Server (HTTP Server)

First, you will either need a web server running locally or a connection to a remote computer running web server software. Any of the three servers outlined in Chapter 26 will work for ColdFusion development: Internet Information Server (IIS), Personal Web Server (PWS), or Apache. See Chapter 26 for details on obtaining, installing, and configuring these web servers.

Setting Up the Application Server (ColdFusion Server)

Next, you need to install ColdFusion Server. Fortunately, this is usually a simple process. A copy of the trial version, which reverts to a permanent single-user Developer Edition after 30 days, can be found on the Dreamweaver MX CD (Windows version only); alternatively, you can download it from `www.macromedia.com`. ColdFusion Server will run on Windows, Linux, and various other versions of UNIX. As of this writing, it is not available for Mac OS X.

During the installation process, you will be asked to indicate what web server you want ColdFusion Server to work with; ColdFusion Server will then be set up to receive requests from whatever web server you specify. You'll also be asked to specify a username and password for use with ColdFusion Server. Remember this information! You'll be asked for it when working in Dreamweaver.

Mac users will need to install ColdFusion Server on a remote computer. See the section in Chapter 26, "Setting up for Development on a Remote Computer" for more on this.

Setting Up the Database

To build sites that interact with a database, you'll need a database management system running on your local system. The most popular for small to medium-sized online databases is Microsoft Access; MySQL is also common. (See Chapter 26 for more details on DBMSs, and Appendix C, "Instruction to MySQL," for information about obtaining and installing MySQL.) Whichever you choose, it will need to be present on the remote server where you eventually publish your finished web site on the Internet. In addition to the DBMS, you'll need the database itself and a driver that allows the ColdFusion Server to connect to it.

The Antiques Database

Two databases are available for the exercises in this chapter, one for Access and one for MySQL. If you're using Access, you'll use the database file **antiques.mdb**; open the **databases/antiques_access** folder on the CD and copy **antiques.mdb** to any location on your hard drive. If you're using MySQL as your DBMS, open the **databases/antiques_mysql** folder on the CD and copy the **antiques** folder to the computer where your web server is installed. The folder must be stored in the **mysql/data** directory.

The Driver

The driver allows the application server to communicate with the database. It can be set up only after you have properly copied the database to your host computer. Follow the instructions in the preceding chapter to set up your driver.

Once you have established your ODBC driver, you need take another step to let the ColdFusion MX server know how to communicate with the data

- Open the ColdFusion Administrator by choosing Start > Macromedia ColdFusion MX > Administrator.

- Enter the password you established when you instaled ColdFusion MX.

- In the Administrator, click the Data Sources link on the left side of the page

- In the Data Sources page, type **AntiquesBarn** in the Data Source name field. For the Driver, choose Microsoft Access and click Add.

- In the Data Source Definition box, click the Browse Server button next to the Database field. Browse to the antiques.mdb data base you copied from the CD.

- Leave all the other fields blank and click Submit. You should now see your new ColdFusion MX data source in the list and the Status indicator should display "OK".

- Logout of the Administrator and close the browser.

Setting Up Your Local and Remote Folders

Dreamweaver dynamic sites must have local and remote folders, just like any Dreamweaver site. If you have your web server installed on the same computer you're developing on, both folders will be on the same computer.

To set up your local root folder, copy the **chapter_29** folder from the CD onto your computer. Its exact location doesn't matter for the exercises.

Your remote folder must be located on the same computer running the server, in a location that the server recognizes as a shared directory for web serving. Depending on which web server you will be working with, do one of the following:

- If your web server is IIS or PWS, create a folder called **antiquesbarn** and store it on the same computer that is running IIS/PWS, within the **c:/inetpub/wwwroot** directory.

- If your web server is Apache, create a folder called **antiquesbarn** and store it on the same computer that is running Apache, stored within the **c:\Program Files\Apache Group\Apache\htdocs** directory.

Setting Up a ColdFusion Site in Dreamweaver

The first step in using Dreamweaver to work with ColdFusion is defining a site that will use your web server and ColdFusion server to process its pages. The main difference between using Dreamweaver for static and for dynamic sites is how it previews your pages. In a static site, when you choose Preview in Browser (F12), Dreamweaver launches the browser and passes it the local address of the current page:

```
c:\Client Files\Web\My Local Site\index.html
```

or

```
file:///Client Files/Web/My Local Site/index.html
```

In a dynamic site, it's not enough just to view the pages in a browser. Dreamweaver has to activate the web server, passing it an HTTP request so that it processes the files. This requires an address like this:

```
http://localhost/mysite/index.html
```

or

```
http://192.128.164.123/mysite/index.html
```

That's why, when you define a dynamic site, you must go through the additional steps of making sure Dreamweaver can connect with your server and "serve" your pages.

Exercise 29.1   Setting Up the Antiques Barn Web Site

In this exercise, you define a dynamic ColdFusion site in Dreamweaver using the Site Definition dialog box. Make sure you've set up your workstation before going through the exercise.

1. In Dreamweaver, go to Site > New Site. In the Site Definition dialog box that appears, click the Advanced tab to bring it to the front.

   What about the wizard? In this exercise, you're using the Advanced tab of the Site Definition dialog box. The information is more compactly presented using this method, easier to see and troubleshoot. After you have the site defined and working, check out where Dreamweaver has stored your site information in the Basic and Advanced tabs, to see how the two methods of site definition compare.

2. From the Categories list, choose Local Info. Local site information for a dynamic site is no different from any site information. Name your site **Antiques Barn CFM**. For the local root folder, browse to the **chapter_29** folder you copied from the CD (see Figure 29.1).

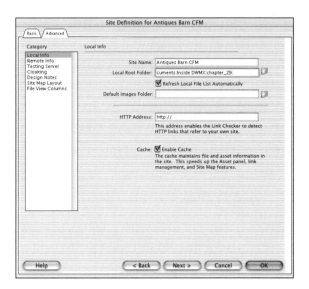

Figure 29.1   Local Info settings for the Antiques Barn exercise site.

3. From the Categories list, choose Remote Info. You'll enter different information here depending on how you set up your workstation (as discussed earlier in this chapter).

If you're working on the same computer that's running your web server, set your access method to Local/Network and browse to the shared remote **antiques_cfm** folder you defined earlier (see Figure 29.2).

Figure 29.2   The Remote Info setup for the Antiques Barn CFM site, if your Dreamweaver site and your web server are on the same computer.

If you're connecting to a different computer for your web server, choose FTP access. Enter the IP address of the other computer and username password, if needed (see Figure 29.3). Refer back to the discussion on IP addresses in the preceding chapter, if necessary.

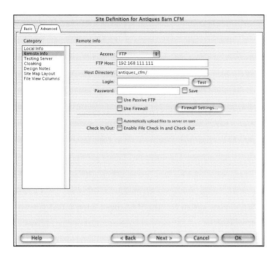

Figure 29.3   The Remote Info setup for the Antiques Barn site, if your web server software is on a different computer than your Dreamweaver site.

Note

Use FTP access even if your two computers are networked directly.

4. From the Categories list, choose Testing Server. From the This Site Contains pop-up menu, choose Dreamweaver MX pages only. If the access information hasn't been filled in for you, choose the same Local/Network or FTP access information you chose in the preceding screen (see Figure 29.4 or Figure 29.5).

   If you're using FTP access, you also have to enter the name of the FTP shared folder you or your network administrator created on the other computer. After you have done this, click the Test button to see whether you entered your settings correctly. (If you cannot connect successfully, double-check everything—IP address, folder name, username, and password.)

   Also in this screen, examine the URL Prefix field. Dreamweaver should have filled in this information based on your previous entries. If you're working on one computer, the address will include the `localhost` or `127.0.0.1` IP address. If you're working on two connected computers, the address will include the host computer's actual IP address. This is the URL information Dreamweaver will use every time you preview your pages in the browser. It must be correct!

   When you think all the site information is correct, click OK to close the dialog box. It's time to test things out.

Figure 29.4   The Testing Server setup for the Antiques Barn CFM site for a single workstation.

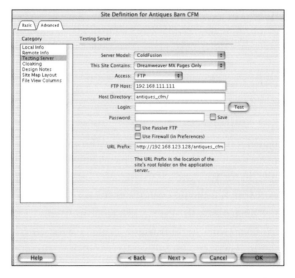

Figure 29.5   The Testing Server setup for the Antiques Barn CFM site for a computer networked to a web server.

5. From your local root folder, open **index.html** and Preview in Browser (F12). You're probably in for a nasty surprise. Either the page will display with broken images or you'll get a File Not Found error. Why is this happening?

When you're working on a dynamic site, Dreamweaver uses the remote folder to generate its previews. (As explained earlier, this has to happen so that the page can be served rather than merely viewed.) Currently, your remote folder contains nothing! You must get in the habit of uploading files to the remote folder before previewing.

In the Site panel, select all the files in your site, and click the Put button to upload them all. Then try previewing again. If you entered the correct information in your Site Definition dialog box, you will be able to preview the page. The browser's Address field will show the `http://` address of the home page, not its file location on your computer. (If you can't preview, keep double-checking those site settings until you can. You cannot keep working in Dreamweaver until you get this part right.)

Setting Up a Database Connection

In ColdFusion terms, the database connection is a script that calls on the driver to talk to the database. Dreamweaver creates this script for you and stores it in a special connections file when you choose data source name (DSN) from the Databases panel. Because this information gets stored in a special file that can be accessed by any page in your site, you have to define the connection only once for the entire site.

Exercise 29.2   Creating a Database Connection

In this exercise, you create the connection script that will allow your pages to communicate with the antiques database. You must already have installed your database and created a driver for it (as outlined in the preceding section) before continuing with this exercise.

1. Because Dreamweaver has to know what kind of connection to create, you must have a dynamic document open before you can create the connection. From your local site, open **catalog.cfm**.

2. From the Application panel group, open the Databases panel. The panel will display help information letting you know what needs to happen before you can set up your connection. If you have **catalog.cfm** open, the display will indicate that your next step is to establish your RDS login to the ColdFusion Server (see Figure 29.6).

   Click the RDS login link and the Login dialog box appears. Enter the password you established when you installed ColdFusion Server and click OK.

Figure 29.6   The Databases panel ready to log on to the ColdFusion Server.

3. As soon as you click OK, Dreamweaver connects to the server and collects a list of available data sources. The AntiquesBarn driver you defined earlier will appear in this list, along with several other drivers (see Figurw 29.7).

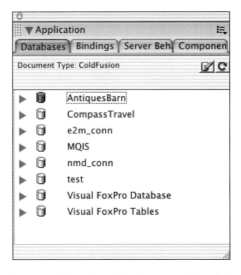

Figure 29.7   The Databases panel showing all databases available to the ColdFusion Server.

4. That's it! You're done. Congratulations! You can now use this panel to explore your database. Expand the AntiquesBarn connection icon to see Tables, Views, and Stored Procedures. The antiques database contains only tables. Expand the Tables icon all the way to see that the database contains two tables—stockitems and customers—and to see what columns (information fields) each table contains. You cannot see the records stored in the database from here, but you can examine its structure (see Figure 29.8).

Note

What happened here? If you're used to working with ASP or other server technologies, you might be wondering where Dreamweaver has put your connection information. When working with ColdFusion, there is no need for specific connection scripts stored inside your site, because the ColdFusion Server keeps track of all this information. As long as you're logged in to the server, all DSNs that the server can see are available to you.

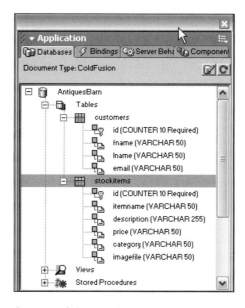

Figure 29.8 The Databases panel showing the structure of the antiques database.

Displaying Dynamic Data Using ColdFusion

You're now fully set up to build the Antiques Barn web site! In Exercise 29.3, you begin building pages that interact with the database using ColdFusion.

Probably the most basic task you'll want your ColdFusion pages to perform is to display information from a database. This involves creating a framework of static page elements (banner, navigation controls, a table for layout, and so forth) and adding ColdFusion code that draws data from the database and places it on the page.

Displaying dynamic data involves several tasks. First, you must query the database to collect the information you want to display (which records, which fields, in what order, and so on). This collected information is called a *recordset*. Then you create a *dynamic element* for every field you want to display. (A *field* is a column in one of the database tables, remember.) Then, unless you want your page to display only information from the first record it finds, you must create special code that steps through all the collected records and displays them one after the other. In Dreamweaver language, this is called creating a *repeated region*.

Creating a Recordset

In Dreamweaver, you create a recordset with the Bindings panel, in the Application panel group. To create the recordset, follow these steps:

1. Open the Bindings panel, click the plus (+) button, and choose Recordset (Query).

2. In the Recordset dialog box that opens, choose whatever database elements (usually table columns, which translate into record fields) you want.

Note

When you choose items in the Recordset dialog box, you're actually telling Dreamweaver how to write a SQL query for you. To see the actual SQL syntax, click the Advanced button and examine the SQL input field. (Click the Simple button to get back to the standard dialog box.) See the preceding chapter for more on SQL.

3. After you have defined the recordset, the collected columns will appear in the Bindings panel. Because Dreamweaver has to write a script to collect the record-set, technically speaking the collection action is a behavior. It will appear in the Server Behaviors panel (in the Application panel group).

You also can create a recordset by going to the Application tab of the Insert bar and choosing the Recordset object. Doing this is exactly the same as using the Bindings panel. Think of it as a shortcut.

Exercise 29.3   Collecting Data for the Antiques Barn Catalog Page

In this exercise, you add dynamic elements to the **catalog.asp** page, which already has its static layout elements in place. This page is meant to display all the items for sale at the Antiques Barn, so you'll collect information from the stockitems table of the antiques database. You'll display a picture, name, description, and price for each item (see Figure 29.9).

1. Begin by opening **catalog.cfm**. Examine the layout structure in Design view, and you'll see that the middle row of the main layout table is ready and waiting for a picture in one column and various text items in another.

2. First, you have to query the database to collect some data to play with. From the Application panel group, open the Bindings panel. Click the plus (+) button and, from the menu, choose Recordset (Query). The Recordset dialog box appears.

Figure 29.9 The Antiques Barn catalog page being served with one record displaying.

3. You can give your recordset a custom name or accept the default name. (For the examples shown here, the default name is used.) If the AntiquesBarn doesn't automatically appear in the Connections field, choose it from the pop-up menu. That will populate the rest of the dialog box with information from the antiques database.

4. You want information from the stockitems table, so choose it from the Tables pop-up menu. You don't need to collect all the columns (fields). For columns to choose, select the Selected radio button. Then Ctrl/Cmd-click to choose item-name, description, price, and imagefile. Choose to sort the information based on itemname, ascending (from *A–Z*) and click OK. Figure 29.10 shows the completed dialog box and resulting Bindings panel.

Tip

From within the Recordset dialog box, click the Test button to see what information your recordset will collect. This is a handy way to make sure you've collected the proper set of data, before you get too far in the process of making the page.

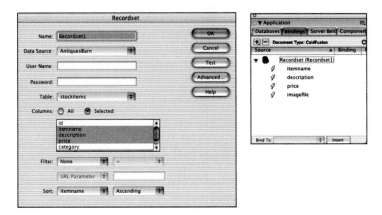

Figure 29.10   Collecting the recordset for the Antiques Barn catalog page and the resulting Bindings panel.

Inserting Dynamic Elements

Data from the database can be inserted anywhere in your document. Names, prices, and descriptions can become dynamic text elements—you can even format them using all the standard HTML and CSS text options. Database fields also can be used behind the scenes, to help construct the HTML code of your page. Therefore, although most databases cannot contain images or other media elements, a field might contain a filename that can be used in the src parameter for an <img>. This is how you insert dynamic images into your pages. (For details on creating dynamic text, see the dynamic data sidebar in Chapter 4, "Working with Text." For more on dynamic images, see the sidebar in Chapter 5, "Working with Images.")

Most databases used for dynamic sites cannot contain actual media, such as images or sound files. They can contain only text.

Exercise 29.4   Displaying Dynamic Data in the Antiques Barn Catalog Page

In this exercise, you use the recordset you collected in the preceding exercise to create dynamic text and image elements for **catalog.cfm**. You also familiarize yourself with the Live Data previewing options in Dreamweaver.

   1. Open **catalog.cfm**, if it's not already open. In the Applications panel group, open the Bindings panel and expand the view of your recordset so that you can see the individual fields you have collected.

2. It's easiest to start with the dynamic text elements. As you can see from Figure 29.9, the rightmost column of the layout table should contain the item name, description, and price, each in its own paragraph.

Inserting a dynamic text element can be done in various ways. By far the simplest is just dragging the desired field from the Bindings panel to the proper place in the Document window. Try that method for the first text element—drag the itemname field into the layout table (see Figure 29.11).

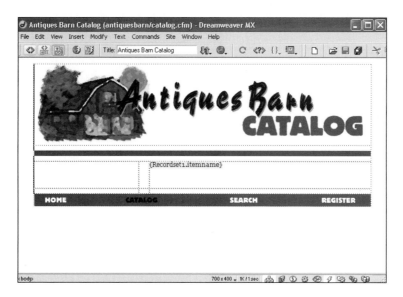

Figure 29.11   Inserting a dynamic text element by dragging a field name from the Bindings panel.

When in the document, the dynamic element becomes a text placeholder. In Design view, it looks like {Recordset1.ItemName}. Switch to Code and Design view, and you'll see that the ColdFusion code looks like this:

```
<cfoutput>#Recordset1.itemname#</cfoutput>
```

You should already recognize the CFM tag structure. The <cfoutput> tag means "insert the following value here." The code within the tag pair refers to the information in the database's itemname column. When the server sees that code, it will substitute whatever text is in that field for the current record.

3. As far as Dreamweaver is concerned, this item is a stand-in for real text. To demonstrate that, stay in Code and Design view but use Design view to select the new placeholder. From the Property Inspector, apply paragraph formatting (choose Paragraph from the Format pop-up menu). Note that, in the code, `<p>` tags now surround the placeholder:

```
<p><cfoutput>#Recordset1.itemname#</cfoutput></p>
```

From the Design panel group, open the CSS panel. With the placeholder text still selected, choose the `itemname` style class. Then display changes to accept the new formatting, and your code changes to the following:

```
<p class="itemname">
<cfoutput>#Recordset1.itemname#</cfoutput>
</p>
```

The placeholder is being treated as though it were real text.

4. Use the same method to insert the description and price into the layout, each in its own paragraph in the table cell. For the price, apply the `price` CSS class.

5. When you insert dynamic text, you're actually creating a ColdFusion behavior (a script that tells the server to insert certain text). In the Applications panel group, open the Server Behaviors panel, and you'll see one behavior for every dynamic text element you've added, plus a behavior for collecting the recordset (see Figure 29.12). Just like regular behaviors, you can double-click a server-side behavior in the panel to view its properties and edit it.

Figure 29.12   Dynamic text elements in **catalog.cfm** and the server behaviors used to insert them.

You can use the Server Behaviors panel to apply special formatting to dynamic text elements—things such as changing capitalization and decimal point display. For the Antiques Barn catalog page, you probably want the item price to display a little nicer, with a dollar sign and some decimal values.

In the Server Behaviors panel, double-click the entry for the price to open it for editing. In the dialog box that appears, use the Formatting pop-up menu to choose Currency – Dollar Format (see Figure 29.13). Click OK to close the dialog box.

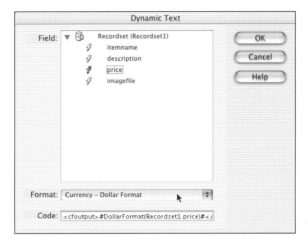

Figure 29.13   Adding scripted formatting to a dynamic text element.

Tip

To delete any dynamic element in a document, it's safest to delete the server behavior that created the element, instead of just selecting its placeholder in Design view and deleting. (Dreamweaver will warn you if you try to delete an element the wrong way.)

6. Each catalog entry must also show a picture of the item. A look at the structure of your database (in the Databases panel) will show you that the stockitems table has a field called imagefile. These can be used as the `src` attribute of an `<img>` tag to create dynamic images.

To insert the dynamic image, start by placing your cursor in the page where you want the image to be located and then insert the image as you normally would. (Use the Image object from the Insert > Common panel.) When the Insert Image dialog box appears, however, choose the Data Sources option (see Figure 29.14). The list of image files is replaced with a list of fields from your recordset. Choose imagefile and click OK.

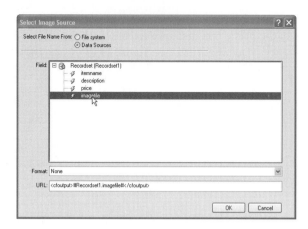

Figure 29.14   Inserting a dynamic image by specifying Data Sources, rather than File System, for the src attribute.

Design view now shows the image as a cute little image placeholder icon (with a lightning bolt for dynamic data). If you check your code, you'll see another <cfoutput> tag stuck right in the middle of the <img> tag:

```
<img src="<cfoutput>#Recordset1.imagefile#</cfoutput>">
```

Note that no width or height has been entered. That's because Dreamweaver can't determine the dimensions from this data—because no actual image has been put here yet.

Previewing with Live Data

You're tired of placeholders! You want to see this page in action. After you've completely set up your site definition, Dreamweaver can send an HTTP request to your server and show you your page, with "live" data in place. As discussed earlier, the live preview originates from the shared remote folder you set up as an IIS/PWS directory. Therefore all image files must have been uploaded to the remote site before the preview will work properly. After you've done that, you can preview data in two ways:

- **Live Data view.** In the Document toolbar, click the Live Data button to switch from viewing placeholders to viewing actual data.

- **Preview in Browser.** Choosing this command, when you're in a dynamic site, will activate the server and "serve" your page in your primary, secondary, or another browser.

Exercise 29.5   Previewing and Troubleshooting Live Data in the Antiques Barn Catalog Page

In this exercise, you try some different previewing methods (if you haven't already experimented), and use them to troubleshoot your code.

   1. With **catalog.cfm** open, click the Live Data view button. It might take a moment, but real data should pop into your Document window.

> **Note**
> If Live Data view doesn't engage properly, it means there's a problem with your site definition. If this happens to you, go back to the previous exercises and the preceding chapter if necessary, and troubleshoot.

You'll immediately notice that there's a problem; your lovely dynamic image isn't displaying properly (see Figure 29.15). You might have guessed why but in case you haven't, it's time to visit the browser.

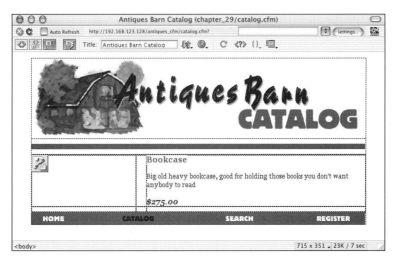

Figure 29.15   Live Data preview of **catalog.cfm**, but there's a problem with the dynamic image.

   2. Turn off Live Data view by clicking the Live Data button to toggle it off.

   3. Preview your page in the browser (F12). You'll undoubtedly see the same problem: a missing image. Here in the browser, however, you have some troubleshooting tools at your disposal. If you're in Internet Explorer, go to View > Source. If you're in Netscape, go to View > Page Source.

Examine the code here. You might notice that it looks different from the code you viewed in Dreamweaver. There are no <cfoutput> tags. That's because the server has executed the script within those tags and used it to construct plain old HTML. The HTML code that was constructed to display your table row looks like this (dynamically generated code shown in bold):

```
<tr valign="top">
<td><img src="bookcase.jpg"></td>
<td> </td>
<td>
<p class="itemname">Bookcase</p>
<p>Big old heavy bookcase, good for holding those books you don't
want anybody to read.</p>
<p class="price">$275.00</p>
</td>
</tr>
```

There's your dynamic text! And there's your problem, in the <img> tag. If you examine your site's file structure, you'll see that all images have been stored in an images folder, so the correct relative URL to the clock image is **images/ bookcase.jpg**. However, the database entry doesn't include that extra folder name. No wonder the browser cannot find the image!

4. You could, of course, fix every single database entry to include a folder name. However, it's much easier to tweak your ColdFusion code, just a little, to do the job for you. When you get used to the way the server just adds the placeholders right into the main code, it'll be easy.

    Back in Dreamweaver, select the dynamic image placeholder. Then open the Server Behaviors panel. The behavior that is creating your image will be highlighted. Double-click to open the editing dialog box. Because you know you have to add the folder name to the entry, manually fix the URL entry so that it looks like this (new code in bold):

    ```
    <img src="images/<cfoutput>#Recordset1.imagefile#</cfoutput>">
    ```

5. After you've done this, try previewing your page in a browser again (F12). The image should show up! (If it doesn't, select View > Source to check your constructed code; and back in Dreamweaver, check Code view to make sure your <img> tag looks exactly like the one shown here.)

    The only drawback to manually adding relative path information to your dynamic image source is that you have to know what the relative URL to your images should look like. You can't just browse to an image and let Dreamweaver do the thinking for you!

Displaying Multiple Records with Repeated Regions

A repeated region is any chunk of page code that you want to repeat for as many records as you want to show. A repeated region can be a line of text, an item in a list, a table row, or even an entire table. To create a repeated region, follow these steps:

1. Select the part of your page that you want to repeat.

2. In the Server Behaviors panel, click the plus (+) button and choose Repeat Region; or choose the Repeated Region object from the Insert > Application bar (see Figure 29.16). A dialog box appears, asking which recordset you want to display and how many records you want to show. (Only choose to display all records if you know for sure your database won't have too many records to fit on a decent-sized web page.)

Figure 29.16   The Repeated Region, Record Navigation Set, and Record Navigation Status objects.

Navigating Through Multipage Displays

If you've set up the repeating region not to display all records simultaneously, you need to give your visitors a way to view the first group of records, the next group after that, and so on. Dreamweaver offers two tools to help with this: Record Navigation Bar and Record Navigation Status. Both are technically server behaviors, but also are easily accessible as objects from the Insert > Application bar (see Figure 29.16).

The Record Navigation Bar object (or server behavior) determines whether there are more records in the recordset than are displayed on the current page; and if so, displays previous page, next page, first page, and last page navigation controls. All the hard work is done for you. All you have to do is insert the object (or server behavior), and Dreamweaver creates the links and adds the scripting to display different records on your page.

The Record Navigation Status object (or server behavior) determines how many total records are in the recordset, and which are currently displaying on the page, and adds a text message to the page—Records 1 to 10 of 56. Again, all you have to do is insert the object; Dreamweaver takes care of the rest.

Exercise 29.6   Displaying Multiple Records in the Antiques Barn Catalog Page

In this exercise, you build the catalog page further by displaying multiple records. You also add navigation controls that enable visitors to move between records easily.

1. Open **catalog.cfm**, if it isn't already open.

2. You want the table row containing your dynamic elements to repeat. Select that row. (Drag across the cells, or click inside a cell and use the tag selector to select the `<tr>`. It's important to make sure you get exactly the right table parts selected!)

3. From the Insert > Application panel, choose the Repeat Region object. The Repeated Region dialog box will appear, asking you which recordset to base the repeats on (you have only one recordset, so there's nothing to choose here) and how many records to show. Set the number of displayed records to 5 and click OK (see Figure 29.17). Note how the Design view display has changed to indicate the repeated region.

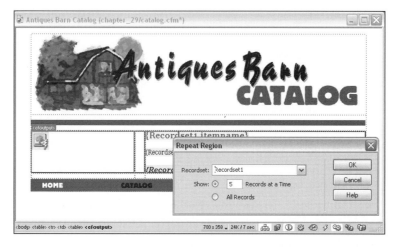

Figure 29.17   Inserting a repeated region that will display five records at a time.

4. Preview your work in the browser (F12). There are the first five records of your recordset!

Tip

If there's anything wrong with your ColdFusion code, you'll get a Page Cannot Be Displayed message from the server. Read through the text of this message and you'll find some very specific information on what's wrong with the page, including what line of code contains the error. Occasionally, even Dreamweaver-generated code generates errors. Examining these errors and troubleshooting them is a great way to increase your knowledge of ColdFusion!

5. This is great as far as it goes, but the visitor can never go beyond those first five records. You need some navigation controls. Back in Dreamweaver, the new elements should be added below the repeated elements but above the bottom navigation bar.

   You need to add a new table row for the controls. Be careful here! If you place the insertion point in the table row that contains the dynamic elements, and insert a new row below it, Dreamweaver will assume that you want the new row to be part of the repeated region. Instead, you must position the cursor in the empty table row directly above the navigation bar and insert a row above. You'll have to be sneaky doing this, because that "empty" row is actually filled with transparent GIF images. Select one of the images. Then use the tag selector to choose the parent <td> tag. Then go to Modify > Table > Insert Row. (Unless you're very accurate with your mouse clicks, it's easier to choose the menu from the menu bar than to right-click to access the contextual menu.)

   You want the new navigation elements to stretch all the way across the layout, so select all three cells in the new row and merge them (Modify > Table > Merge Cells).

6. With the insertion point in the new merged row, choose the Recordset Navigation Bar from the Insert > Application bar. In the dialog box that appears, choose to use text navigation elements and click OK. Figure 29.18 shows the resulting insertion.

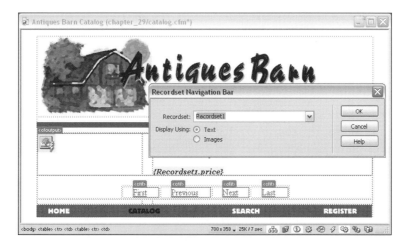

Figure 29.18   The Recordset Navigation Bar being inserted in the Antiques Barn catalog page.

7. Preview your page in the browser again (F12), and you'll see the navigation controls at work. You can click to move forward and back through pages of displayed records. Also note that the controls appear only if there are records to view—you cannot go to previous or first, if you're at the first page already, for instance (see Figure 29.19).

Oops! If you inserted your new table row inside the repeating region, you'll get navigation controls after every single record. There is no easy fix for this, unless you're willing to tinker around in the code. The quickest solution is to Edit > Undo, or use the History panel, backing up to before you inserted the new table row. . .and start again.

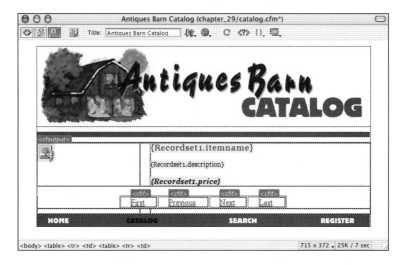

Figure 29.19   The Antiques Barn catalog page with all recordset navigation elements in place.

8. The newly inserted elements are just dynamic text links in a table. Feel free to format them as you like—you can even change the text, so long as you don't change the link information. To match the formatting in Figure 29.19, set the table width to 640 and apply the nav CSS class to each text element.

9. Finally, you can make your catalog page complete by letting visitors know where they are in the recordset ("Records 1 to 5 of 10"). For the Antiques Barn page, you'll add that information directly above the recordset navigation controls.

Start by adding a new row at the top of the nested table that contains the recordset navigation (see Figure 29.20). As long as you're working with this table, you're well outside the repeated region, so you don't have to worry about that.

Figure 29.20   Inserting a Recordset Navigation Status object.

10. Merge the cells of the new row so that it stretches across the entire table. Then, with the insertion point inside the new row, choose the Recordset Navigation Status object from the Insert > Application bar. There's your new dynamic text (see Figure 29.20). Preview in the browser to see it in action (F12).

As with any dynamic text element, you can format the status line as you like. You also can change any of the static text, as long as you don't disturb the placeholder text.

Congratulations! The Antiques Barn catalog page is now complete. You've built your first ColdFusion document.

Summary

In this chapter, you learned the basics of setting up a ColdFusion site in Dreamweaver and creating a page that displays dynamic elements. This is only a taste of what you can do with ColdFusion. Instead of displaying all stock items, you could tie the catalog into a search page so that visitors can choose what category of antiques to display. You could link small thumbnail images to separate pages containing detailed information about each item. You could have visitors sign in, so that when they revisit the site their favorite antiques will show at the top of the list. Dreamweaver provides objects and server behaviors for all this functionality, and more.

Chapter 30

Building a Basic PHP Site

PHP, the recursive acronym for PHP: Hypertext Preprocessor, is a great dynamic language. It's powerful enough for most needs, it's easy to figure out, and it's free! In addition, its clear and concise code makes it easy to understand and accounts for the rapid increase in its use by web developers. Together with MySQL (also free), PHP is giving many web designers a cheap and easy way to get dynamic.

This chapter, in conjunction with Chapter 26, "Introduction to Dynamic Dreamweaver," explains the requirements for getting your computer set up for PHP and MySQL. (Appendix B, "Online Resources for Dreamweaver Web Developers," has more information about setting up MySQL.) After everything has been installed and is running correctly, you can perform a couple of exercises related to the catalog being used to demonstrate dynamic sites.

Note

MX   PHP support is brand new to Dreamweaver MX! If you're upgrading from UltraDev, this is a welcome addition to the family.

Setting Up Your Workstation to Work with PHP

To use PHP with Dreamweaver MX, you must download and install a few things. Before you can start creating pages, you need to set up a web server and an application server; set up your database, and database management system; create a database driver; and set up a folder where your web pages can officially be "served" by the web server. The following sections take you through that process for PHP.

Setting Up the HTTP (Web) Server

PHP works with any of the three HTTP servers covered in Chapter 26: Internet Information Services (IIS), Personal Web Server (PWS), and Apache. It also works on Windows, UNIX, and Mac OS X.

If you're developing on a Windows computer, it's easiest to set up IIS or PWS, but you can set up Apache if you prefer. (See the section in Chapter 26 called "Setting Up for Development on a Remote Computer" for information on installing these servers.)

If you're working on Mac OS X, Apache is already installed on your computer, so this step is taken care of for you.

Setting Up the Application Server

The PHP application server module functions as an add-on to the web server. Before you can begin developing with PHP, you'll need to download, install, and configure PHP on your computer. Luckily, PHP is free and easy to obtain on the Internet.

Downloading and Installing PHP (Windows)

PHP for Windows works with IIS, PWS, or Apache. To set it up, just follow these instructions.

1. Point your browser to `www.php.net/downloads.php`. From the Windows Binaries section of the page, download the PHP 4.1.2 installer.

Note

PHP is always improving. If there's a newer version available by the time you read this, download that instead.

2. The downloaded file is a Windows installation file (EXE). Double-click on this file to install it, and follow the instructions as they appear.

3. Choose the standard installation and install to the default folder (**c:\PHP**).

4. For SMTP server, type **localhost** and enter **me@localhost.com** for an email address. These won't be needed for the purposes of this exercise.

5. For server type, select the web server that you are currently running. You might need to double-check what version of IIS you're running.

6. When you're asked what script mappings to choose, select WWW Service Master properties and click.

That's it! PHP is now installed.

Enabling PHP (Mac OS X)

As long as you're running version 10.1 (or higher) of the new Mac OS, the world of PHP is your oyster. Not only does the Mac OS (10.1 and above) ship with Apache, it also ships with a limited version of PHP that includes MySQL support. To get yourself up and running, all you have to do is enable it. Just follow these steps:

1. Launch the Terminal application (find it in the Applications > Utilities folder).

2. Navigate to the folder where the configuration will take place by typing this in the Terminal window:

```
cd /etc/httpd
```

Press Enter or Return to officially enter this instruction into the Terminal application. (Always end lines of Terminal code by pressing Enter or Return.)

3. Now type the following:

```
sudo apxs -e -a -n php4 libexec/httpd/libphp4.so
```

Press Enter or Return to finish this line. You'll be asked for your password. Type in the administrator's password that you use any time you make changes to your Mac system. Press Enter or Return again.

4. Finally, type the following (no typos!):

```
sudo perl -p -i.bak -e 's%#(AddType \S+-php[ -])%$1%i' httpd.conf
```

When you're sure the code is correct, press Enter or Return.

5. The computer will take a few moments to process this information. When the % prompt re-appears, you're all configured. All you need to do is restart Apache by typing this:

```
sudo apachectl graceful
```

Congratulations! Aside from a little typing frenzy, that wasn't hard at all. (Figure 30.1 shows the entire Terminal session happening.)

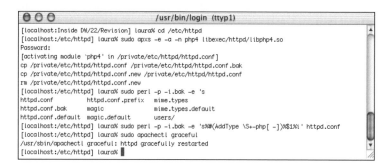

Figure 30.1   Using the Terminal window to enable PHP in Mac OS X.

Testing Your PHP Installation (Windows and Mac OS X)

To make sure PHP is indeed functioning on your computer, create a test file. Do this:

1. Open a text editor (or Dreamweaver in Code view) and create a new file.

2. Save your new file as **test.php** and place it in the default location where your web server stores served pages: For Windows, place the file in **c:\inetpub\wwwroot** for IIS/PWS, or **c:\Program Files\Apache Group\Apache\htdocs** for Apache. For Mac OS X, place the file in **/Library/Webserver/Documents**.

3. Enter the following content:

```
<html>
<head>
<title>PHP Test</title>
</head>
```

```
<body>
<?php
  phpinfo()
?>
</body>
</html>
```

4. Launch your browser and enter your page's URL in the address field:
   http://localhost/test.php. If the resulting page looks like the one in Figure
   30.2, PHP is ready for action! (If you don't get this result, make sure you've coded
   and saved your test file correctly before troubleshooting the PHP installation.)

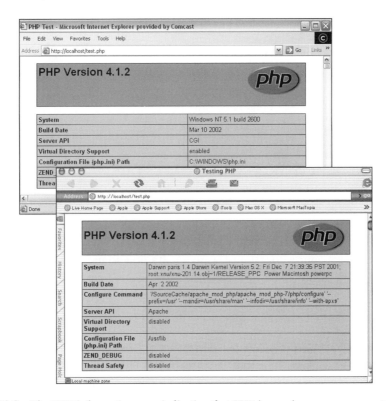

Figure 30.2   The PHP information page indicating that PHP is running on your computer.

Setting Up the Database

To work with PHP in Dreamweaver, you must also use the MySQL DBMS. (Unlike other
application servers, PHP coding is different for different DBMSs. Though it is possible
to use PHP with other systems, such as PostgreSQL, Dreamweaver only supports
PHP/MySQL coding.) Before you can proceed with the exercises here, you must install

and configure MySQL; add the antiques database to your MySQL installation; and—if you're working on Windows—install the MyODBC driver. See Appendix B for detailed instructions on all of these tasks.

Setting Up Your Local and Remote Folders

Dreamweaver dynamic sites must have local and remote folders, just like any Dreamweaver site. If you have your web server installed on the same computer you're developing on, both folders will be on the same computer.

To set up your local root folder, copy the **chapter_30** folder from the CD onto your computer. Its exact location doesn't matter for the exercises.

To set up your remote folder, create a new folder called **antiques_php** and store it where your web server can serve it. (Put it in the same folder where you put your **test.php** file earlier in the chapter.) This folder remains empty for now.

Note

If you're using IIS or PWS, you can also follow the instructions in Chapter 26 to set a virtual directory by enabling web sharing for a folder. If you do this, your remote folder can be stored anywhere on the computer housing the web server.

Setting Up a PHP Site in Dreamweaver

After you've got your workstation files set up, it's time to tuck into Dreamweaver. The first step here is to define a site, complete with local, remote, and application server information. Dreamweaver needs to know where your local and remote folders are. It also needs to know what kind of dynamic site you'll be creating (PHP).

The main difference between using Dreamweaver for static and for dynamic sites is how it previews your pages. In a static site, when you choose Preview in Browser (F12), Dreamweaver launches the browser and passes it the local address of the current page:

```
C:\Client Files\Web\My Local Site\index.html
```

or

```
file:///Client Files/Web/My Local Site/index.html
```

In a dynamic site, it's not enough just to view the pages in a browser. Dreamweaver has to activate the web server, passing it an HTTP request so that it processes the files. This requires an address like this:

`http://localhost/mysite/index.html`

or

`http://192.128.164.123/mysite/index.html`

That's why, when you define a dynamic site, you must go through the additional steps of making sure Dreamweaver can connect with your server and "serve" your pages.

Exercise 30.1   Setting Up the Antiques Barn Site (PHP)

In this exercise, you define a dynamic PHP site in Dreamweaver, using the Site Definition dialog box. Make sure you've set up your workstation before going through the exercise.

1. In Dreamweaver, go to Site > New Site. In the Site Definition dialog box that appears, click the Advanced tab to bring it to the front.

   What about the wizard? In this exercise, you're using the Advanced tab of the Site Definition dialog box. The information is more compactly presented using this method, easier to see and troubleshoot. After you have the site defined and working, check out where Dreamweaver has stored your site information in the Basic and Advanced tabs, to see how the two methods of site definition compare.

2. From the Categories list, choose Local Info. Local site information for a dynamic site is no different from any site information. Name your site **Antiques Barn PHP**. For the local root folder, browse to the **chapter_30** folder you copied earlier from the CD.

3. From the Categories list, choose Remote Info. You'll enter different information here depending on how you set up your workstation (as discussed earlier in this chapter).

   If you're working on the same computer that's running your web server, set your access method to Local/Network and browse to the shared remote **antiques_php** folder you defined earlier (see Figure 30.3).

Figure 30.3   The Remote Info setup for the Antiques Barn site, if your Dreamweaver
site and your web server are on the same computer.

If you're connecting to a different computer for your web server, choose FTP
access. Enter the IP address of the other computer, the directory (**antiques_php**),
and username password if needed (see Figure 30.4). Refer back to the discussion
on IP addresses in the preceding chapter, if necessary.

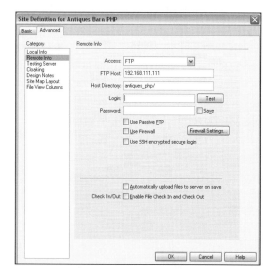

Figure 30.4   The Remote Info setup for the Antiques Barn site, if your web server
software is on a different computer than your Dreamweaver site.

Note

Use FTP access even if your two computers are networked directly.

4. From the Categories list, choose Testing Server. For server model and language, choose PHP MySQL. If the access information hasn't been filled in for you, choose the same Local/Network or FTP access information you chose in the preceding screen (see Figure 30.5 or Figure 30.6).

    If you're using FTP access, you also have to enter the name of the FTP shared folder you or your network administrator created on the other computer. After you have done this, click the Test button to see whether you entered your settings correctly. (If you cannot connect successfully, double-check everything— IP address, folder name, username, and password.)

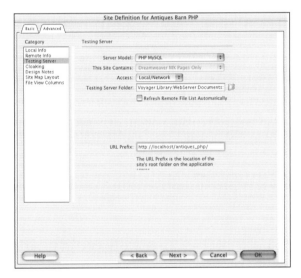

Figure 30.5   The Testing Server setup for the Antiques Barn site for a single workstation.

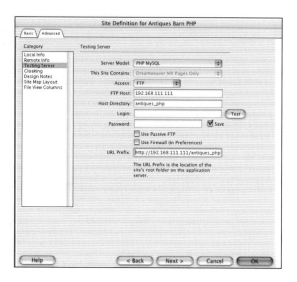

Figure 30.6 The Testing Server setup for the Antiques Barn site for a computer networked to a web server.

Also in this screen, examine the URL Prefix field. Dreamweaver should have filled in this information based on your previous entries. It needs to have the host name or IP address of your server plus the folder name of your remote folder, like this:

```
http://localhost/antiques_php
```

or

```
http://192.123.111.111/antiques_php
```

When you think all the site information is correct, click OK to close the dialog box. It's time to test things out.

5. From your local root folder, open **index.html** and Preview in Browser (F12). You're probably in for a nasty surprise. Either the page will display with broken images or you'll get a File Not Found error. Why is this happening?

When you're working on a dynamic site, Dreamweaver uses the remote folder to generate its previews. (As explained earlier, this has to happen so that the page can be served rather than merely viewed.) Currently, your remote folder contains nothing! You must get in the habit of uploading files to the remote folder before previewing.

In the Site panel, select all the files in your site and click the Put button to upload them all. Then try previewing again. If you entered the correct information in your Site Definition dialog box, you will be able to preview the page. The browser's Address field will show the `http://` address of the home page, not its file location on your computer. (If you can't preview, keep double-checking those site settings until you can. You cannot keep working in Dreamweaver until you get this part right.)

Setting Up a Database Connection

In PHP terms, the database connection is a script that calls on the driver to talk to the database. Dreamweaver creates this script for you and stores it in a special connections file when you choose data source name (DSN) from the Databases panel. Because this information gets stored in a special file that can be accessed by any PHP page in your site, you have to define the connection only once for the entire site.

Exercise 30.2   Creating a Database Connection

In this exercise, you create the connection script that will allow your pages to communicate with the antiques database. You must already have installed your database and created a driver for it (as outlined in the preceding section) before continuing with this exercise.

1. Because Dreamweaver has to know what kind of connection to create, you must have a dynamic document open before you can create the connection. From your local site, open **catalog.php**.

2. From the Application panel group, open the Databases panel. If you have **catalog.php** open, the panel will have a plus (+) button at the top. Click it and, from the pop-up menu, choose MySQL connection. Figure 30.7 shows this happening.

Figure 30.7   Choosing a MySQL connection from the Databases panel.

Note

Is you're used to using Dreamweaver with ASP or any other server technology, you might be wondering how you can make a connection before you've defined a database driver. For this kind of page, you don't need one!

3. The MySQL Connection dialog box appears (see Figure 30.8). Several pieces of information are required to fill in this dialog box. For your connection's name, enter **antiques_conn**. (The connection name will be used in the connection script. It can be any one-word name with no special characters, but it's common practice to include *con* or *conn* in the name to denote a connection.)

4. The MySQL server is the name or IP address of the computer housing the MySQL DBMS. If you're set up for local development (with the server and MySQL on your working computer), enter localhost in this field. If you're working on a remote computer, enter the IP address of the computer where MySQL and your web server reside.

5. Depending on how you set up your MySQL database, you might not think you have a username, but you do. If you can start up the MySQL client program without specifying a username, then your username is the username that you use to log onto your computer. If you don't need a password to start MySQL, leave the password field blank. You can't leave the username field blank.

6. The database field should contain the name of the database you want to connect to—in this case, antiques. You can type the name in the input field, but it's a good idea to avoid typos and test your connection by clicking the Choose button. When you do this, if you've entered the above information correctly a dialog box will appear listing all the MySQL databases on the specified host (for example, localhost or the IP address you entered). If some of your information is wrong, or if your MySQL server program isn't currently running, you'll get an error message.

7. Finally, before you leave the dialog box, click Test. If your username or password is incorrect, you'll get a permissions error. If everything is working properly, you'll get a successful connection message.

8. When you have made a successful test, click OK to close the dialog box.

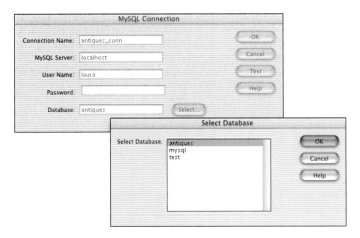

Figure 30.8   Defining the antiques_conn database connection.

9. The Databases panel will now contain an icon representing your connection. Congratulations, You can now use this panel to explore your database. Expand the connection icon to see Tables, Views, and Stored Procedures. The antiques database contains only tables. Expand the Tables icon all the way to see that the database contains two tables—stockitems and customers—and to see what columns (information fields) each table contains. You cannot see the records stored in the database from here, but you can examine its structure (see Figure 30.9).

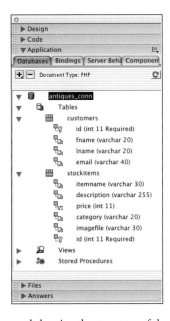

Figure 30.9   The Databases panel showing the structure of the antiques database.

10. In the Site panel, examine your local root folder. You'll see a new **connections** folder. Inside that folder is the **antique_conn.php** file. That file contains your connection script. Open that file and examine it in Code view. You'll see the following connection script:

```php
<?php
# FileName="Connection_antiques_conn.htm"
# Type="MYSQL"
# HTTP="true"
$hostname_nr = "localhost";
$database_nr = "ANTIQUES";
$username_nr = "don";
$password_nr = "maxx";
$nr = mysql_pconnect($hostname_nr, $username_nr, $password_nr) or
die(mysql_error());
?>
```

You don't need to know what everything in there means. However, one important piece of syntax that you should get familiar with is the `<?php...?>` tags. All PHP code in an HTML document is contained within these tags. When the PHP module processes this page, it looks for these tags and executes all code inside them. All other code on the page is assumed to be regular HTML or client-side scripting and is just passed back to the browser.

Displaying Dynamic Data

Probably the most basic task you'll want your PHP pages to perform is to display information from a database. This involves creating a framework of static page elements (banner, navigation controls, a table for layout, and so forth) and adding dynamic text and pictures—like a catalog page in a commerce site shows pictures and descriptions of items for sale.

Displaying dynamic data involves several tasks. First, you must query the database to collect the information you want to display (which records, which fields, in what order, and so on). This collected information is called a *recordset*. Then you create a *dynamic element* for every field you want to display. (A *field* is a column in one of the database tables, remember.) Then, unless you want your page to display only information from the first record it finds, you must create special code that steps through all the collected records and displays them one after the other. In Dreamweaver language, this is called creating a *repeating region*, and it can be refined through various *recordset navigation* controls.

Collecting a Recordset

In Dreamweaver, you collect a recordset with the Bindings panel, in the Application panel group. To collect the recordset, follow these steps:

1. Open the panel, click the plus (+) and choose Recordset (Query).

2. In the Recordset dialog box that opens, choose whatever database elements (usually table columns, which translate into record fields) you want.

Note

When you choose items in the Recordset dialog box, you're actually telling Dreamweaver how to write a SQL query for you. To see the actual SQL syntax, click the Advanced button and examine the SQL input field. (Click the Simple button to get back to the standard dialog box.) See the preceding chapter for a brief overview of SQL.

3. After you've collected the recordset, the collected columns will appear in the Bindings panel. Because Dreamweaver has to write a PHP script to collect the recordset, technically speaking the collection action is a behavior. It will appear in the Server Behaviors panel (in the Applications panel group).

You also can create a recordset by going to Insert > Application panel, and choosing the Recordset object. Doing this is exactly the same as using the Bindings panel. Think of it as a shortcut.

Exercise 30.3   Collecting Data for the Antiques Barn Catalog Page

In this exercise, you add dynamic elements to the **catalog.php** page, which already has its static layout elements in place. This page is meant to display all the items for sale at the Antiques Barn, so you'll collect information from the stockitems table of the antiques database. You'll display a picture, name, description, and price for each item (see Figure 30.10).

Figure 30.10   The Antiques Barn catalog page being served with one record displaying.

1. Begin by opening **catalog.php**. Examine the layout structure in Design view and you'll see that the middle row of the main layout table is ready and waiting for a picture in one column, and various text items in another.

2. First, you have to query the database to collect some data to play with. From the Application panel group, open the Bindings panel. Click the plus (+) and, from the menu, choose Recordset (Query). The Recordset dialog box appears.

3. You can give your recordset a custom name or accept the default name. (For the examples shown here, the default name is used.) If your DSN connection (**antiques_conn**) doesn't automatically appear in the Connections field, choose it from the pop-up menu. That will populate the rest of the dialog box with information from the antiques database.

4. You want information from the stockitems table, so choose it from the Tables pop-up menu. You don't need to collect all the columns (fields). For columns to choose, select the Selected radio button. Then Ctrl/Cmd-click to choose Itemname, Description, Price, and Imagefile. Choose to sort the information based on Itemname, Ascending (from *A–Z*) and click OK. Figure 30.11 shows the completed dialog box and resulting Bindings panel.

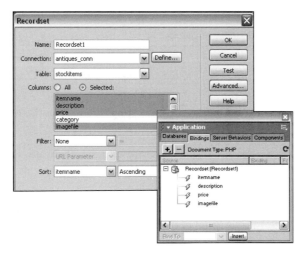

Figure 30.11   Collecting the recordset for the Antiques Barn catalog page and the resulting Bindings panel.

Tip

From within the Recordset dialog box, click the Test button to see what information your recordset will collect. This is a handy way to make sure you've collected the proper set of data, before you get too far into the process of making the page.

5. Click OK to close the dialog box. The Bindings entry is made and the appropriate code is placed on your page.

Inserting Dynamic Elements

Data from the database can be inserted anywhere in your document. Names, prices, and descriptions can become dynamic text elements—you can even format them using all the standard HTML and CSS text options. Database fields also can be used behind the scenes, to help construct the HTML code of your page. Therefore, although most databases cannot contain images or other media elements, a field might contain a filename that can be used in the src parameter for an <img>. This is how you insert dynamic images into your pages. (For details on creating dynamic text, see the dynamic data sidebar in Chapter 4, "Working with Text." For more on dynamic images, see the sidebar in Chapter 5, "Working with Images.")

Most databases used for dynamic sites cannot contain actual media, such as images or sound files. They can contain only text.

Exercise 30.4   Displaying Dynamic Data in the Antiques Barn Catalog Page

In this exercise, you use the recordset you collected in the preceding exercise to create dynamic text and image elements for **catalog.php**. You also familiarize yourself with the Live Data previewing options in Dreamweaver.

1. Open **catalog.php**, if it's not already open. In the Applications panel group, open the Bindings panel, and expand the view of your recordset so that you can see the individual fields you have collected.

2. It's easiest to start with the dynamic text elements. As you can see from Figure 30.9, the rightmost column of the layout table should contain the item name, description, and price, each in its own paragraph.

   Inserting a dynamic text element can be done in various ways. By far the simplest is just dragging the desired field from the Bindings panel to the proper place in the Document window. Try that method for the first text element—drag the itemname field into the layout table (see Figure 30.12).

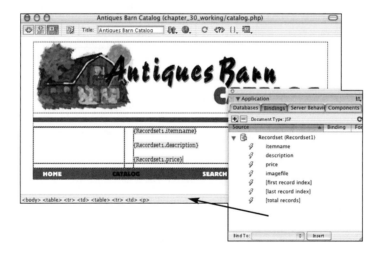

Figure 30.12   Inserting a dynamic text element by dragging a field name from the Bindings panel.

When in the document, the dynamic element becomes a text placeholder. In Design view, it looks like {Recordset1.ItemName}. Switch to Code and Design view and you'll see that the PHP code looks like this:

```
<?php echo $row_Recordset1['itemname']; ?>
```

You should already recognize the PHP tag structure. The `<?php echo` opening means "insert the following value here." The code in parentheses refers to the itemname column. When the server sees that code, it will substitute whatever text is in that field for the current record.

3. As far as Dreamweaver is concerned, this item is a stand-in for real text. To demonstrate that, stay in Code and Design view but use Design view to select the new placeholder. From the Property inspector, apply paragraph formatting (choose Paragraph from the Format pop-up menu). Note that, in the code, `<p>` tags now surround the placeholder:

```
<p><?php echo $row_Recordset1['itemname']; ?></p>
```

From the Design panel group, open the CSS panel. With the placeholder text still selected, choose the **itemname** style class. The display changes to accept the new formatting, and your code changes to the following:

```
<p class="itemname">
<?php echo $row_Recordset1['itemname']; ?>
</p>
```

The placeholder is being treated as though it were real text.

4. Use the same method to insert the description and price into the layout, each in its own paragraph in the table cell. For the price, apply the **price** CSS class.

5. To dress up the price a little bit, type a **$** before its recordset. Figure 30.13 shows this happening.

Tip

When you insert dynamic text, you're actually creating a PHP behavior (a script that tells the server to insert certain text). In the Applications panel group, open the Server Behaviors panel, and you'll see one behavior for every dynamic text element you've added, plus a behavior for collecting the recordset. Just like regular behaviors, you can double-click a server-side behavior in the panel to view its properties and edit it.

To delete any dynamic element in a document, it's safest to delete the server behavior that created the element, instead of just selecting its placeholder in Design view and deleting. (Dreamweaver will warn you if you try to delete an element the wrong way.)

Figure 30.13   Adding manual text to a dynamic text element.

6. Each catalog entry must also show a picture of the item. A look at the structure of your database (in the Databases panel) will show you that the stockitems table has a field called imagefile. These can be used as the `src` attribute of an `<img>` tag to create dynamic images.

To insert the dynamic image, start by inserting an image as you normally would. (Use the Image object from the Insert > Common panel.) When the Insert Image dialog box appears, however, choose the Data Sources option (see Figure 30.14). The list of image files is replaced with a list of fields from your recordset. Choose **imagefile** and click OK.

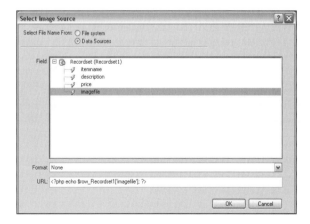

Figure 30.14   Inserting a dynamic image by specifying Data Sources, rather than File System, for the `src` attribute.

Design view now shows the image as a cute little image placeholder icon (with a lightning bolt for dynamic data). If you check your code, you'll see another example of `<?php echo` stuck right in the middle of the `<img>` tag:

```
<img src="<?php echo $row_Recordset1['imagefile']; ?>">
```

Note that no width or height has been entered. That's because Dreamweaver can't determine the dimensions from this data—because no actual image has been put here yet.

Previewing with Live Data

You're tired of placeholders! You want to see this page in action. After you've completely set up your site definition, Dreamweaver can send an HTTP request to your server and show you your page, with "live" data in place. As discussed earlier, the live preview originates from the shared remote folder you set up as an IIS/PWS directory. Therefore all image files must have been uploaded to the remote site before the preview will work properly. After you've done that, you can preview data in two ways:

- **Live Data view.** In the Document toolbar, click the Live Data button to switch from viewing placeholders to viewing actual data.

- **Preview in Browser.** Choosing this command, when you're in a dynamic site, will activate the server and "serve" your page in your primary, secondary, or other browser.

Exercise 30.5   Previewing and Troubleshooting Live Data in the Antiques Barn Catalog Page

In this exercise, you try some different previewing methods (if you haven't already experimented!), and use them to troubleshoot your code.

  1. With **catalog.php** open, click the Live Data view button. It might take a moment, but real data should pop into your Document window.

Note

If Live Data view doesn't engage properly, it means there's a problem with your site definition. If this happens to you, go back to the previous exercises, and the preceding chapter if necessary, and troubleshoot.

You'll immediately notice that there's a problem; your lovely dynamic image isn't displaying properly (see Figure 30.15). You might have guessed why, but in case you haven't, it's time to visit the browser.

Address page is being
served from

Figure 30.15   Live Data preview of **catalog.php**, but there's a problem with the
dynamic image.

2. Turn off Live Data view by clicking the Live Data button to toggle it off.

3. Preview your page in the browser (F12). You'll undoubtedly see the same problem: a missing image. Here in the browser, however, you have some troubleshooting tools at your disposal. If you're in Internet Explorer, go to View > Source. If you're in Netscape, go to View > Page Source.

Examine the code here. You might notice that it looks different from the code you viewed in Dreamweaver. There are no PHP <%...%> tags. That's because the server has executed the script within those tags and used it to construct plain old HTML. The HTML code that was constructed to display your table row looks like this (dynamically generated code shown in bold):

```
<tr valign="top">
<td><img src="bookcase.jpg"></td>
<td> </td>
<td>
<p class="itemname">Bookcase</p>
<p>Big old heavy bookcase, good for holding those books you don't
want anybody to read.</p>
<p class="price">$275.00</p>
</td>
</tr>
```

There's your dynamic text! And there's your problem, in the <img> tag. If you examine your site's file structure, you'll see that all images have been stored in an images folder, so the correct relative URL to the clock image is **images/book-case.jpg**. However, the database entry doesn't include that extra folder name. No wonder the browser cannot find the image!

4. You could, of course, fix every single database entry to include a folder name. However, it's much easier to tweak your PHP code, just a little, to do the job for you. When you get used to the way the server just adds the placeholders right into the main code, it'll be easy.

Back in Dreamweaver, select the dynamic image placeholder. Then open the Server Behaviors panel. The behavior that is creating your image will be highlighted. Double-click to open the editing dialog box. Because you know you have to add the folder name to the entry, manually fix the URL entry so that it looks like this (new code in bold):

```
<img src="images/<?php echo $row_Recordset1['imagefile']; ?>">
```

5. After you've done this, try previewing your page in a browser again (F12). The image should show up (see Figure 30.16)! (If it doesn't, select View > Source to check your constructed code; and, back in Dreamweaver, check Code view to make sure your <img> tag looks exactly like the one shown here.)

The only drawback to manually adding relative path information to your dynamic image source is that you have to know what the relative URL to your images should look like. You can't just browse to an image and let Dreamweaver do the thinking for you!

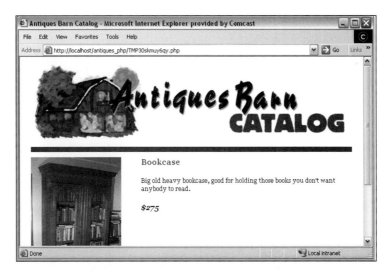

Figure 30.16   The Antiques Barn catalog page with dynamic image and text in place.

Displaying Multiple Records with Repeated Regions

A repeated region is any chunk of page code that you want to repeat for as many records as you want to show. A repeated region can be a line of text, an item in a list, a table row, or even an entire table. To create a repeated region, follow these steps:

1. Select the part of your page that you want to repeat.

2. In the Server Behaviors panel, click the plus (+) and choose Repeat Region; or choose the Repeated Region object from the Insert > Application bar (see Figure 30.17). A dialog box will appear, asking which recordset you want to display and how many records you want to show. (Only choose to display all records if you know for sure your database won't have too many records to fit on a decent-sized web page.)

Figure 30.17   The Repeated Region, Recordset Navigation bar, and Recordset Navigation Status objects.

Navigating Through Multipage Displays

If you've set up the repeating region not to display all records simultaneously, you need to give your visitors a way to view the first group of records, the next group after that, and so on. Dreamweaver offers two tools to help with this: Record Navigation Bar and Record Navigation Status. Both are technically server behaviors, but also are easily accessible as objects from the Insert > Application bar (see Figure 30.17).

The Record Navigation Bar object (or server behavior) determines whether there are more records in the recordset than are displayed on the current page; and if so, displays previous page, next page, first page, and last page navigation controls. All the hard work is done for you. All you have to do is insert the object (or server behavior), and Dreamweaver creates the links and adds the scripting to display different records on your page.

The Record Navigation Status object (or server behavior) determines how many total records are in the recordset, and which are currently displaying on the page, and adds a text message to the page—Records 1 to 10 of 56. Again, all you have to do is insert the object; Dreamweaver takes care of the rest.

Exercise 30.6   Displaying Multiple Records in the Antiques Barn Catalog Page

In this exercise, you build the catalog page further by displaying multiple records. You also add navigation controls that enable visitors to move between records easily.

1. Open **catalog.php**, if it isn't already open.

2. You want the table row containing your dynamic elements to repeat. Select that row. (Drag across the cells, or click inside a cell and use the tag selector to select the <tr>. It's important to make sure you get exactly the right table parts selected!)

3. From the Insert > Application bar, choose the Repeated Region object. The Repeated Region dialog box will appear, asking you which recordset to base the repeats on (you have only one recordset, so there's nothing to choose here) and how many records to show. Set the number of displayed records to 5 and click OK (see Figure 30.18). Note how the Design view display has changed to indicate the repeated region.

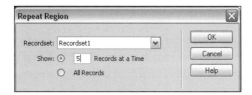

Figure 30.18   Inserting a repeating region that will display five records at a time.

4. Preview your work in the browser (F12). There are the first five records of your recordset!

Tip

If there's anything wrong with your PHP code, you'll get a Page Cannot Be Displayed message from the server. Read through the text of this message and you'll find some very specific information on what's wrong with the page, including what line of code contains the error. Occasionally, even Dreamweaver-generated code generates errors. Examining these errors and troubleshooting them is a great way to increase your knowledge of PHP!

5. This is great as far as it goes, but the visitor can never go beyond those first five records. You need some navigation controls. Back in Dreamweaver, the new elements should be added below the repeated elements but above the bottom navigation bar.

   You need to add a new table row for the controls. Be careful here! If you place the insertion point in the table row that contains the dynamic elements, and insert a new row below it, Dreamweaver will assume that you want the new row to be part of the repeated region. Instead, you must position the cursor in the empty table row directly above the navigation bar and insert a row above. You'll have to be sneaky doing this, because that "empty" row is actually filled with transparent GIF images. Select one of the images. Then use the tag selector to choose the parent <td> tag. Then go to Modify > Table > Insert Row. (Unless you're very accurate with your mouse clicks, it's easier to choose the menu from the menu bar than to right-click to access the Contextual menu.)

   You want the new navigation elements to stretch all the way across the layout, so select all three cells in the new row and merge them (Modify > Table > Merge Cells).

6. With the insertion point in the new merged row, choose the Recordset Navigation Bar from the Insert > Application bar. In the dialog box that appears, choose to use text navigation elements and click OK. Figure 30.19 shows the resulting insertion.

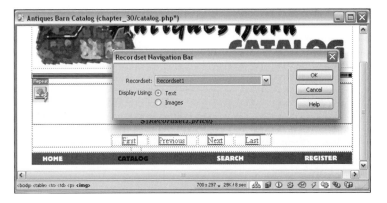

Figure 30.19   The Recordset Navigation Bar being inserted in the Antiques Barn catalog page.

7. Preview your page in the browser again (F12), and you'll see the navigation controls at work. You can click to move forward and back through pages of displayed records. Also note that the controls appear only if there are records to view—you cannot go to previous or first if you're at the first page already, for instance (see Figure 30.20).

Oops! If you inserted your new table row inside the repeating region, you'll get navigation controls after every single record. There is no easy fix for this, unless you're willing to tinker around in the code. The quickest solution is to Edit > Undo, or use the History panel, backing up to before you inserted the new table row…and start again.

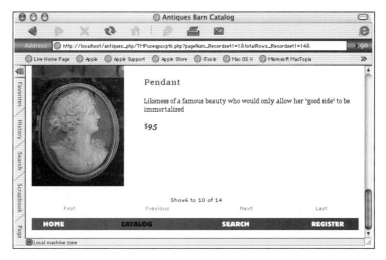

Figure 30.20   The Antiques Barn catalog page with all recordset navigation elements in place.

8. The newly inserted elements are just dynamic text links in a table. Feel free to format them as you like—you can even change the text, so long as you don't change the link information. To match the formatting in Figure 30.20, set the table width to 640 and apply the nav CSS class to each text element.

9. Finally, you can make your catalog page complete by letting visitors know where they are in the recordset ("Records 1 to 5 of 10"). For the Antiques Barn page, you'll add that information directly above the recordset navigation controls.

    Start by adding a new row at the top of the nested table that contains the record-set navigation (see Figure 30.21). As long as you're working with this table, you're well outside the repeated region, so you don't have to worry about that.

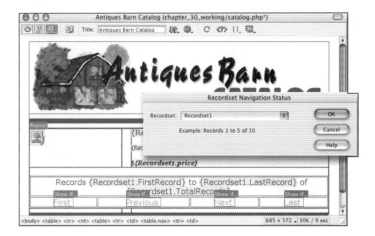

Figure 30.21   Inserting a Recordset Navigation Status object.

10. Merge the cells of the new row so that it stretches across the entire table. Then, with the insertion point inside the new row, choose the Recordset Navigation Status object from the Insert > Application bar. There's your new dynamic text (see Figure 30.21). Preview in the browser to see it in action (F12).

As with any dynamic text element, you can format the status line as you like. You also can change any of the static text, as long as you don't disturb the placeholder text. (In Figure 30.20, for instance, the word *records* has been changed to *items*.)

Congratulations! The Antiques Barn catalog page is now complete. You've built your first PHP document.

Summary

PHP is one of the easiest dynamic languages to learn and decipher. It uses a small amount of concise code to enable powerful functionality. The code is logical and easy to understand if you give it a lookover. It also, along with MySQL, gives a simple, stable and free dynamic environment in which to develop your web applications, on either Windows or Mac.

Chapter 31

Building a Basic JSP Site

Of all the server technologies, JSP is probably the most intimidating for newcomers to this arena. If you're just starting out, you might want to get your feet wet with ASP, ColdFusion, or PHP first. JSP has a lot to offer developers, but it's mostly of interest to those already working with Java. If you're reading this chapter, you're probably either working in an environment where Java is already being used for web development, or you want to learn Java. JSP has some exciting development options, such as JavaBeans and custom tag libraries—and Dreamweaver has tools for working with all of them. This chapter will take you through the steps of setting up your workstation for Java application serving, defining a JSP site within Dreamweaver, and using the Dreamweaver tools to create a basic live data page. This chapter also touches on using JavaBean collections and custom tags.

Setting Up Your Workstation to Work with JSP

As explained in Chapter 26, "Introduction to Dynamic Dreamweaver," preparing your workstation to work with any data-driven server technology involves setting up the web server and application server; making sure your DBMS and database are in place; installing any necessary drivers for the database; and making sure everything works. When working with JSP, there is also the extra step of creating a web application. The following sections walk you through obtaining and setting up the Apache Tomcat server and setting up a database and driver for Access or MySQL. Because the Tomcat server is Java, and will function on Windows and Mac OS X, instructions cover both platforms.

Note

Mac users: If you're using OS X, for the first time in Dreamweaver history you have the option of doing all development on your computer, without having to create an FTP connection to an external server. Be warned, however: All the OS X advanced web-serving capabilities are based on UNIX, and are not for the timid. If you have the option to connect to an external server, this is still probably the easiest solution for you. (See Chapter 26 for instructions on connecting to a remote server for Dreamweaver dynamic sites.)

Setting Up the Web Server/Application Server

Like the other server-side technologies, JSP requires an application server to process live data pages and construct HTML for browser display. Because JSP uses Java, the application is Java-based; in Java-speak, it's called a *servlet container*. A variety of servlet containers are available, including the following:

- **Apache Tomcat.** This open-source server is part of the same development project that creates the Apache HTTP server (see Chapter 27, "Building a Basic ASP Site"). Tomcat is free; recent releases have been proven to be stable and fast. It will run on any platform that fully supports Java, including Windows, UNIX, and now Mac OS X. Tomcat can be used in conjunction with an HTTP server, or it can be used in standalone mode, instead of an HTTP server.

- **Macromedia JRun.** This commercial server is widely popular as a robust and powerful JSP server. Although it is not free, a special free development version is available from Macromedia and is included on the Dreamweaver MX installation CD. JRun is for Windows only.

- **IBM WebSphere.** Another popular commercial server, WebSphere also is available in a free development version. WebSphere is for Windows only.

Note

A servlet is an application that is executed by the server at runtime. (It's comparable in many ways to an applet, which is run by the browser at runtime.) The servlet's function is to construct the HTML code for the browser to display. When you create a JSP document, the application server uses the Java code embedded in that document to construct a servlet. Then the servlet is executed, which creates the final page.

For the exercises in this chapter, Tomcat standalone server is used. Tomcat installation and setup is covered in the following sections, separated by OS where Windows and Mac instructions substantially differ.

Note

Why use Tomcat for development? Besides being cross-platform, Tomcat is the simplest of the servlet containers to set up. Its no-frills approach doesn't give you one more piece of complex software to deal with, or one more GUI to master. Using Tomcat makes it much easier to see what's going on under the hood of your Java web applications.

Setting Up Tomcat (Windows)

Tomcat installation for Windows is very easy, because the open source developers have provided a slick little GUI for its working. However, Tomcat requires that a Java runtime environment be set up—which means installing the Java SDK before you can install Tomcat.

Download and Install J2 SDK

Your first stop, in setting up for JSP on Windows, is to download and install the Java 2 Software Development Kit (J2SDK). This software package includes the J2SE runtime environment (the virtual machine that allows Java programs to run), along with various utilities and database drivers for programming in Java.

To download the J2SE, go to `http://java.sun.com/j2se/1.4/download.html`, or go to the Java main web page (`http://java.sun.com`) and follow the links to J2SE. From the download page, select the Windows version of the SDK.

Note

As with all web technology, the Java platform is constantly evolving. By the time you read this, newer versions of the Java runtime environment might be available. Download the latest stable release that includes the SDK (software development kit).

The downloaded file is an EXE. After the download has finished, double-click this file to launch the installer and follow the instructions to complete the installation. Accept the default install location (at the root of your c: drive) and options. When you're done, the newly installed SDK will be located on your hard drive at **c:\j2sdk1.4.0.**

Note

You must install the J2SDK whether you plan to use Tomcat or one of the other Java application servers. None of the servers can operate without the Java runtime environment.

Download and Install Tomcat

Now that Java is in place on your computer, it's time to install Tomcat. To do so, follow these steps:

1. To download Tomcat, go to `http://jakarta.apache.org/builds/jakarta-tomcat-4.0/release/v4.0.3/bin/`. From the list of Tomcat versions, select and download **jakarta-tomcat-4.0.3.exe.**

2. After the download has finished, double-click the EXE file to launch the installer and follow the instructions that appear. If you are using one of these operating systems, choose to install the WIN NT/2K/XP option. When the installation finishes, go to the Start menu and choose Programs > Apache Tomcat. There's your installed program (see Figure 31.1).

Figure 31.1   Apache Tomcat available under the Start menu (Windows).

Start and Stop Tomcat

The Tomcat server doesn't start automatically at boot-up time, the way IIS does. To start Tomcat, go to Start > Programs > Apache Tomcat > Start Tomcat. This opens Tomcat in a new command-line window. You can minimize this window, but leave it open as long as you want the server to run (see Figure 31.2).

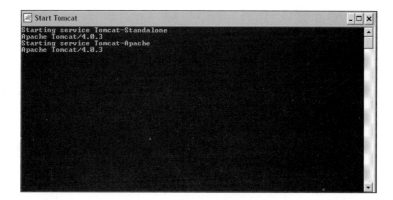

Figure 31.2   The Tomcat window showing that the server is up and running (Windows).

Tomcat will stop automatically when the computer shuts down. If you want to shut it down before then, go to Start > Programs > Apache Tomcat > Stop Tomcat. A stop message will appear in the Tomcat command-line window, and the window will close.

Tip

If you plan to be working extensively with Tomcat, place shortcuts for Start Tomcat and Stop Tomcat on your desktop, or in your taskbar, for easy access. You also can add it to your Windows Start Group if you want it to launch automatically whenever you start your computer.

Setting Up Tomcat (Mac OS X)

Tomcat installation for OS X is a fairly simple process, but it does involve a trip to the Terminal window and some work with the command-line interface. One of the nice features of OS X is that it comes with the Java runtime environment already installed and active—so, unlike Windows users, you won't have to worry about that preliminary step.

Before You Begin

You will need to know a few items of information about your system before you can install Tomcat.

- **What is your username?** Your username is the name you chose for yourself when you first set up your computer. It's the same name used for your **Home** folder. To find your username, launch System Preferences from the Dock, and view the Users preferences. Select your account from the list, choose Edit User, and look at the name in the Short Name field. (It's the short name you'll be using as you install Tomcat.)

- **What is your password?** You gave yourself a password when you set up your computer. You need to know it anytime you install software. (If you have forgotten your password, the Password tab in the Users panel will include the hint that you defined when you set up your computer.)

- **Where is Home?** This is the folder that appears when you click the home icon in the Finder window toolbar. It's named the same as your username (for instance, Fred). On your hard drive, it's located in the **Users** folder. In UNIX-speak, its address is **/users/fred**.

For purposes of the examples in this chapter, the username will be fred. Whenever you see Fred or fred in an example, substitute your username.

Download and Install Tomcat

To download and install Tomcat, follow these steps:

1. To download Tomcat, go to `http://jakarta.apache.org/builds/` `jakarta-tomcat-4.0/release/v4.0.3/bin/`. From the list of Tomcat versions, select and download **jakarta-tomcat-4.0.3.tar.gz**.

2. Put the downloaded file in your **Home** folder. (This is the folder that appears when you click the home icon on Finder window toolbars. It should have your username. Its address on your system is **/users/fred**, or ~/.)

3. Everything else in the installation process occurs in the command-line interface of the Terminal window. To prepare for that, find and launch the Terminal. (It's in **applications/utilities/terminal**.)

Tip

If StuffIt uncompressed the archive automatically as part of your downloading process, you can move the uncompressed folder into your **Home** folder and skip step 4 of this procedure.

4. The installation file you downloaded is a **tar.gz** file, which is a UNIX-style archive. To install it, you need to unpack the **tar.gz** file.

    Start by navigating to your home directory, by typing this:

    ```
    cd /users/fred
    ```

    or

    ```
    cd ~/
    ```

    To end the command line, press Enter or Return. (Do this every time you type a line in the Terminal. It tells the computer to execute the command you just gave it.)

    Unpack the archive by typing this (no typos!):

    ```
    tar -xzvf jakarta-tomcat-4.0.3.tar.gz
    ```

Figure 31.3 shows what these code entries look like in the Terminal window.

Figure 31.3   Unpacking the Tomcat archive in the Terminal window (Mac)— my username has been substituted for Fred's.

After a few moments, the Terminal window will again display the % prompt, which means it's ready to accept more commands.

5. To see the results of your unpacking outside the Terminal window, you can hide it and use the Finder to look in your **Home** folder. Figure 31.4 shows the new file structure.

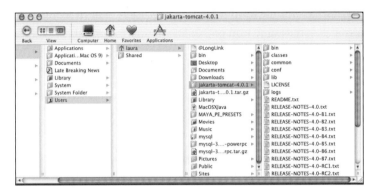

Figure 31.4   The Tomcat files installed into the **Home** folder—my username has been substituted for Fred's.

Create Scripts to Start and Stop Tomcat

Tomcat is now installed, but it isn't running—and, unlike regular programs, you can't just double-click anything to launch it. Tomcat must be launched from the Terminal window. Because you'll need to launch it every time you want to work on a JSP site, you'll create start and stop scripts. You'll also create a special folder, called **bin**, in your **Home** folder to hold those scripts. Again, it's all done in the Terminal.

1. To start, create and open the **bin** folder by going to the Terminal Window and typing the following:

```
cd ~/
mkdir bin
cd bin
```

(You just used the Terminal to navigate to the **Home** folder, make the **bin** folder, and navigate to the **bin** folder.)

2. Create a new script (text) file. Although you can do this with BBEdit or another text editor (even Dreamweaver), it's much safer to do it within the Terminal window, using a command-line text editor. And you can do it with one line of code. To create a new file in the **bin** folder and open it in the pico text editor, just type:

```
pico start_tomcat
```

3. What you're doing when you type this line is telling pico to create a file called **start_tomcat**. As soon as you press Return/Enter, the Pico screen appears (see Figure 31.5) ready to put some code in that new file.

Type the following contents (like using a word processor, but without the mouse; use arrow keys to get around, if necessary):

```
#! /bin/sh
export CATALINA_HOME=/users/fred/jakarta-tomcat-4.0.3
export JAVA_HOME=/usr
$CATALINA_HOME/bin/startup.sh
```

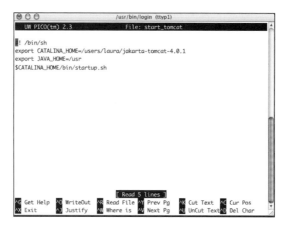

Figure 31.5   The Terminal window showing the pico text editor with the startup script text entered (Mac).

(The first line tells the OS that this is a certain kind of script file. The second line creates a variable called CATALINA_HOME—the OS will look for this variable, with this exact name, to point to your Tomcat files. The third line creates a variable called JAVA_HOME, which points to the location of the Java tools on your computer. The final line tells the OS to run the **startup.sh** script, located in the **Tomcat** folder.)

4. Save and exit pico with a series of Command key shortcuts:

- Ctrl+O (for "output to disk")

- Enter (to confirm that you're saving the **start_tomcat** file)

- Ctrl+X (for "exit")

The % prompt will reappear, indicating that you're not in pico anymore.

5. Repeat the preceding process to create the shutdown script.

    Start by typing:

    ```
    pico stop_tomcat
    ```

    In the pico editing window, type the following:

    ```
    #! /bin/sh
    export JAVA_HOME=/usr
    export CATALINA_HOME=/users/fred/jakarta-tomcat-4.0.3
    $CATALINA_HOME/bin/shutdown.sh
    ```

6. Save and quit—Ctrl+O, Enter, Ctrl+X.

7. To see your new files, type the following:

    ```
    ls -l
    ```

    This will give you a directory of the **bin** folder.

8. Currently, your scripts are text files that can only be read, not programs or scripts that can be executed. Change your files to executable by typing this:

    ```
    chmod ug+x start_tomcat stop_tomcat
    ```

9. Put your scripts to work! Start Tomcat, by typing the following:

    ```
    ~/bin/start_tomcat
    ```

If everything has been set up properly, you'll see the Tomcat startup screen (see Figure 31.6).

10. Then stop Tomcat by typing the following:

    ```
    ~/bin/stop_tomcat
    ```

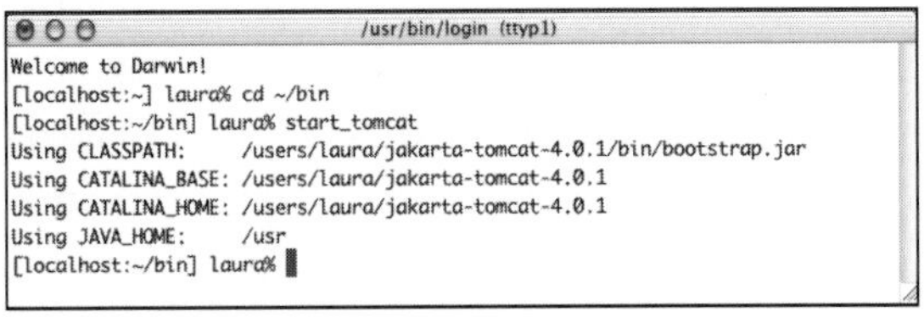

Figure 31.6   Starting up Tomcat from the Terminal window (Mac).

What can go wrong? Lots of things! If you script contains any typos, it will generate an error. If you created your script files in a regular text editor (such as BBEdit), instead of in pico, there might be bad invisible characters in there. You'll get a `Script Not Found` message. If this happens, start over at step 1 of this section and repeat the script process.

(After you've created the **start_tomcat** and **stop_tomcat** files, the next time you navigate the Terminal window to ~**/bin** and type **pico start_tomcat** or **pico stop_tomcat**, the files you created will open for editing.) You can't continue until you can successfully launch Tomcat.

Take Tomcat for a Test Drive

After you've got Tomcat up and running, it's time to test it out. Start Tomcat up, following the instructions for your operating system. Then open a browser and type the following into the URL field:

`http://localhost:8080/`

If everything is configured correctly, the Tomcat home page will display (see figure 31.7). If you completed the previous sections without error, there really isn't anything else that is likely to go wrong.

Figure 31.7   The Tomcat home page appearing at `http://localhost:8080`.

Note

> What's the :8080 for? You might not know it, but your computer has various ports through which data can be served. By default, Tomcat uses port 8080. When a port is being used, the URL always specifies the port number as part of the computer name, separated from the main name by a colon (:). If you have another server installed and running on your computer—for instance, IIS for Windows or Apache for Mac—by adding the 8080 port information, you're telling the browser to serve the page using Tomcat rather than that other server. This is how Tomcat and those other servers can coexist, running at the same time on the same system.

Setting Up the Web Application

In plain English, a *web application* is an interactive web site built with JSP, ColdFusion, or any other server technology. Within the context of JSP, however, web applications are much more formal structures. For purposes of JSP, a web application is a folder, stored where the Java server can find it, where you put pages you want to be served. That folder includes a specific structure of subdirectories that contain any special-purpose files the server might need—such as drivers, JavaBeans, and custom JSP tag libraries. Figure 31.8 shows the folder structure of a typical web application.

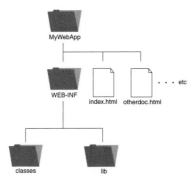

Figure 31.8   The directory structure of a web application folder.

When you install Tomcat, its internal folder structure includes a web applications folder, where all application folders must be stored. In the basic install, several applications are already defined, including the main application, called ROOT, where the Tomcat home page is located.

Figure 31.9 shows the **Tomcat** folder structure, as it appears on Mac and Windows.

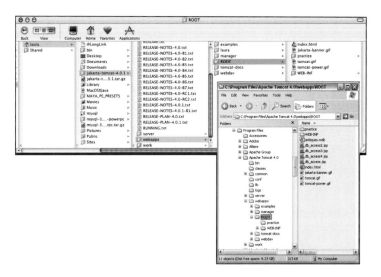

Figure 31.9   The Tomcat directory structure showing various web applications, including ROOT.

To set up a site in Dreamweaver, of course, you must define local and remote folders. To work on JSP sites in Dreamweaver, your remote folder should be a web application folder within the Tomcat directory structure. So creating a web application is a necessary pre-step to defining your Dreamweaver site.

Creating a Web Application in Tomcat

Creating a web application within Tomcat requires two steps: Create the web application folder, and add an entry to the **server.xml** file so that Tomcat will interpret the folder as a web application. To create the antiques web application for the exercises in this chapter, perform the following steps:

1. Create a folder in Tomcat's **webapps** folder. Name it **antiques**. This folder will contain your application, which will be built from any HTML, JSP, or other documents you create.

2. Within the **antiques** folder, create another folder called **WEB-INF**. This folder will eventually contain any Java files Tomcat must use to process your web application.

Note

Java is case-sensitive! For all folder and filenames, make sure your capitalization matches the capitalization shown here. Windows users will notice that your OS changes the "WEB-INF" folder name to lowercase. Don't worry about this so long as you originally typed it in uppercase.

3. Within the **WEB-INF** folder, create two more folders called **classes** and **lib**. The **classes** folder will eventually contain any Java class files that your site will use; the **lib** folder will contain any Java archive (JAR) files.

4. Next, you'll configure the **server.xml** file so that it recognizes your folder as an official web application. In the **Tomcat** folder, open the **conf** folder and find **server.xml.** Open this file in a text editor (or in Dreamweaver Code view).

There's a lot of information in there! Don't worry, you can ignore most of it. Scroll through the file until you find the <context> tags. Each <context> tag represents a web application. You're going to add a new context.

Find the <context> tag for the examples web application, and insert a few blank lines in front of it. Enter the following code:

```
<Context path="/antiques" docBase="antiques" debug="0"
reloadable="true">
      <Logger className="org.apache.catalina.logger.FileLogger"
             prefix="localhost antiques_log." suffix=".txt"
             timestamp="true"/>
   </Context>
```

After you've double-checked your typing, save and close the file.

Note

Confused by all this XML and Java? There's a wealth of information out there to learn more. The FAQ at JGuru (http://www.jguru.com/faq) is a good place to start.

5. Finally, because Tomcat reads only the **server.xml** file at startup, you must restart the Tomcat server so that it recognizes your web application.

   - On Windows, use go to Start > Programs > Apache Tomcat > Stop Tomcat, and Start > Programs > Apache Tomcat > Start Tomcat.

   - On Mac OS X, go to the Terminal window and type the following:

     ```
     ~/bin/stop_tomcat
     ~/bin/start_tomcat
     ```

(Make sure you wait for the % prompt to appear before typing each new line.)

Setting Up the Local Folder

After you've set up the web application, you have created your remote folder for Dreamweaver to use.

For your local root folder, copy the **chapter_31** folder from the CD onto your computer. Its exact location doesn't matter for the exercises.

Setting Up the Database

The computer housing your web server must have a database management system (DBMS) installed on it. For development purposes, you can use Microsoft Access or MySQL with JSP. After you have the database in place, you also need to create a driver that connects to it.

Note

For instructions on setting up MySQL for Windows and OS X, see Appendix C, "Introduction to MySQL."

The Antiques Database

The exercises in this chapter use the **antiques.mdb** database. It's available on the CD as an Access or MySQL database.

If you're using Access as your DBMS, open the **databases** folder on the CD, and copy the **antiques_access** folder to the computer where your web server is installed. You can store the folder anywhere you like. (It's not part of your site, so it doesn't need to be stored in the site folder. All that matters is that Tomcat can find it; and that gets taken care of when you define the driver.)

If you're using MySQL as your DBMS, see Appendix C for instructions on adding the **antiques** database to the MySQL server.

The Driver

The driver allows the application server to communicate with the database. It can be set up only after you've properly copied the database to your host computer. Java servers, such as Tomcat, require JDBC (Java Database Connectivity) drivers. Depending on your OS, database, and the level of effort you want to put in, you have your choice of using a JDBC-ODBC bridge driver or a standard JDBC driver.

JDBC-ODBC Bridge Driver (for Access or MySQL on Windows)

If your Tomcat server is on Windows, you'll have an easy time setting up the JDBC-ODBC bridge driver. As its name indicates, this driver acts like a translator, or bridge, between the Java server and the standard Windows ODBC driver. It's not the most elegant solution, from a programming standpoint, because it adds a whole extra layer of translation—rather like flying from Florida to New York via Spokane. However, it's very easy to set up. To set up the bridge driver, follow these steps:

1. Create a DSN for your database, using the ODBC Control Panel. (See Chapter 26 for instructions on setting up a DSN.) Figure 31.10 shows a driver being created for the Access version of the **antiques** database.

Note

One special rule when creating DSNs for JSP: Don't include the word `driver` in your driver name. This will cause problems.

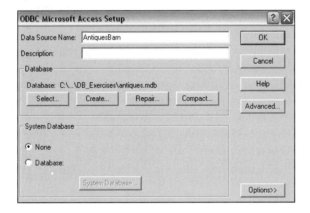

Figure 31.10   Creating the AntiquesBarn database DSN (Windows, Access).

2. That's it! Usually the second step is to install the JDBC-ODBC bridge driver, to allow the DSN to communicate with the Java server. However, this driver was installed along with your Java 2 SDK—so you're all done! (If you're wondering where the bridge driver is, you can find it at **J2sdk1.4.0\jre\bin\JdbcOdbc.dll.**)

JDBC Driver (for MySQL on Windows or Mac)

If you're using MySQL as your DBMS you also have the option of using the open-source **mm.mysql** JDBC driver. Use this driver if your application server is not on Windows (for instance, if you're developing on Mac OS X or if you're connected to a remote server running UNIX), or if you're using MySQL on Windows and don't want to use the bridge driver. Although this is a straightforward, elegant solution from a programming point of view, it's more complex to set up than the preceding option.

1. Begin by downloading the driver by following the links from `http://mmmysql.sourceforge.net/`. As of this writing, the download file for the current release is **mm.mysql-2.0.11-you-must-unjar-me.jar**.

2. The file is a Java archive (JAR). As you can tell from its name, you need to unjar it. Although you can do this using the Command Prompt or Terminal window, the easiest solution is to use an archiving utility. Both WinZip (Windows) and StuffIt Expander (Mac) can unpack a JAR archive.

3. When unpacked, the archive contains a folder of support information, including a subfolder called **mm.mysql.2.0.11**, in which you will find another JAR file called **mm.mysql-2.0.11-bin.jar**. This file is the driver.

4. Put a copy of this file in the **Tomcat** folder, in your **antiques/WEB-INF/lib** folder. The driver is an archive your web application will use and must be stored here for Tomcat to access (see Figure 31.11).

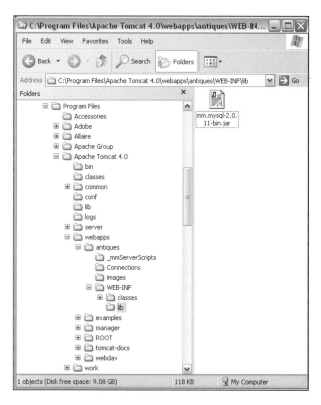

Figure 31.11   The **mm.mysql** driver in position for use with the antiques web application.

Setting Up a JSP Site in Dreamweaver

After you've got your workstation files set up, it's time to tuck into Dreamweaver. The first step here is to define a site, complete with local, remote, and application server information. Dreamweaver needs to know where your local and remote folders are. It also needs to know what kind of dynamic site you'll be creating (JSP).

The main difference between using Dreamweaver for static and for dynamic sites is how it previews your pages. In a static site, when you choose Preview in Browser (F12), Dreamweaver launches the browser and passes it the local address of the current page:

```
C:\Client Files\Web\My Local Site\index.html
```

or

```
file:///Client Files/Web/My Local Site/index.html
```

In a dynamic site, it's not enough just to view the pages in a browser. Dreamweaver has to activate the web server, passing it an HTTP request so that it processes the files. This requires an address like this:

```
http://localhost:8080/mysite/index.html
```

or

```
http://192.128.164.123:8080/mysite/index.html
```

That's why, when you define a dynamic site, you must go through the additional steps of making sure Dreamweaver can connect with your server and "serve" your pages.

Exercise 31.1   Setting Up the Antiques Barn Site (JSP)

In this exercise, you define a dynamic JSP site in Dreamweaver, using the Site Definition dialog box. Make sure you've set up your workstation before going through the exercise.

1. In Dreamweaver, go to Site > New Site. In the Site Definition dialog box that appears, click the Advanced tab to bring it to the front.

2. From the categories, choose Local Info. Local site information for a dynamic site is no different from that for any site. Name your site **Antiques Barn JSP**. For the local root folder, browse to the **chapter_31** folder you copied from the CD.

3. From the categories list, choose Remote Info. You'll enter different information here depending on how you set up your workstation (see the earlier discussion in this chapter).

If you're working on the same computer that's running your web server, choose Local/Network access and browse to the shared remote **antiques_jsp** folder you defined earlier (see Figure 31.12).

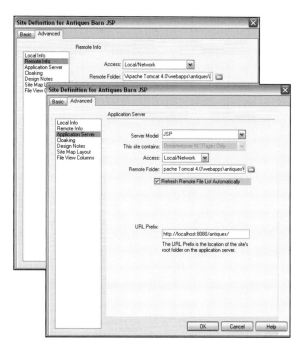

Figure 31.12   The Remote Info and Testing Server setup for the Antiques Barn site, if your Dreamweaver site and your web server are on the same computer.

If you're connecting to a different computer for your web server, choose Local/Network access if you have a direct network connection; otherwise, use FTP access. Enter the IP address of the other computer, the name of the shared folder (FTP directory) being used for FTP on that computer, and username and password if needed (see Figure 31.13). To check your FTP connection settings, click the Test button.

Figure 31.13   The Remote Info and Testing Server setup for the Antiques Barn site, if your web server software is on a different computer than what your Dreamweaver site is on.

Refer back to the discussion on IP addresses in Chapter 26, if necessary.

Note

Mac users connecting to a Windows computer: You must use FTP access unless you have a Mac/Windows sharing utility like PCMacLan or Dave.

4. From the categories list, choose Testing Server. For server model and language, choose JSP. For access information, you must establish an FTP connection to the remote computer, even if your computers have a direct network connection. If you chose FTP access for the Remote Info section in the previous step, enter the same information here. If you entered Local/Network access in the previous step, you'll need to find the IP address and FTP directory of the remote computer to enter here, as well as the username and password if those are required (see Figure 31.13).

    After you've done this, click the Test button to see whether you entered your settings correctly. (If you can't connect successfully, double-check everything—IP address, folder name, username, and password.)

    Also in this screen, examine the URL Prefix field. Dreamweaver should have filled in this information based on your previous entries, but you might need to add the port information (**:8080**). If you're working on one computer, the address should be `localhost:8080/antiques_jsp/` or `127.0.0.1:8080/antiques_jsp/`. If you're working on two connected computers, the address will be the same as this, but using the host computer's IP address. This is the URL information Dreamweaver will use every time you preview your pages in the browser. It must be correct!

When you think all the site information is correct, click OK to close the dialog box. It's time to test things out.

5. From your local root folder, open **index.html**, and Preview in Browser (F12). You're probably in for a nasty surprise. Either the page will display with broken images, or you'll get a `File Not Found` error. Why is this happening?

When you're working on a dynamic site, Dreamweaver uses the remote folder to generate its previews. (As explained earlier, this has to happen, so that the page can be served, instead of merely being viewed.) Currently, there's nothing in your remote folder! You must get in the habit of uploading files to the remote folder before previewing.

Note

Actually, it's a simplification to say that Dreamweaver uses the remote folder to generate its previews. Dreamweaver uses the files in the application server to generate previews. For the exercises in this book, however, the remote folder and the application server folder are the same folder. As you get more advanced in your work with live data sites, this might not always be the case.

In the Site panel, select all the files in your site and click the Put button to upload them all. Then try previewing again. If you entered the correct information in your Site Definition dialog box, you will be able to preview the page. The browser's address field will show the `http://` address of the home page, not its file location on your computer. (If you can't preview, keep double-checking those site settings until you can. You can't keep working in Dreamweaver until you get this part right.)

Advanced JSP Features in Dreamweaver

dynamic
data bits

In addition to the dynamic objects and behaviors covered here, Dreamweaver also supports two powerful JSP tools: JavaBeans and custom tag libraries. Unless you're already fairly knowledgeable in Java and JSP, you probably won't be using these features—but it's good to know what they are.

A *JavaBean* is a Java class file that the JSP document can call on and execute to help create the final dynamic HTML page. (You can think of a class file as a very small application, or a module that might go into creating a Java application.) You also can insert same kind of code that goes into a JavaBean directly into the JSP page, between <%...%> tags. Because it's placed in a separate bean file, however, it can be called on by many different documents, which is efficient for updating. Also, because the code is not contained in the main document, it makes that document's code easier to read. Dreamweaver cannot create JavaBeans for you; if you have them already created, however, you can use the Components panel to call on them from your JSP pages.

continues ▶

A *custom tag library* is a set of HTML-like tags that accomplish JSP tags. The tags are defined in external documents that explain what Java function should occur whenever the tag is used in a JSP document. If you have custom JSP tags defined, your page can be built from easy-to-read chunks such as `<jsp:myTag>...</jsp:myTag>`, instead of the complex scripting code enclosed in the `<%...%>` tags. The Dreamweaver Tag Library Editor enables you to import the documents where JSP tags are defined and then use those tags in your JSP pages.

Both JavaBeans and custom tag libraries enable web developers to separate the scripting from the main JSP document, making it easier for development teams to split into programming and design groups.

Interview: Harlow Pinson

Business Name: Indepth Learning

URL: www.indepthl.com

Harlow Pinson is founder of Indepth Learning, a company that provides web and multimedia publishing, hosting, and development services. Their current work focuses on providing large-scale and dynamic web-content management systems for state government and small business. He teaches Dreamweaver and UltraDev privately and at the University of New Mexico.

Your specialty is back-end web development. Do you design the front-ends, as well, or do you collaborate on your projects?

Yes, I do design front-ends, but prefer to collaborate. I work with folks who are talented graphic artists and site designers, and let them do what they do best. My talent is programming and web server administration. This exchange of complementary skills can be very productive. There is so much to know, and it is important to recognize your own talents and limits. I know when to call for help and where to find it.

I do generally insist that people I collaborate with follow a formal development process, which is proven successful for developing dynamic data-driven web sites. The process is this:

- Understand the problem. (This is the hard part.)
- Build a text-only prototype.
- Critique the prototype.
- Refine the prototype.
- Add graphics without changing the interface.

This process seems to make sense to those coming from a functional design background. Generally what I am asked to do is not art, and I have the best collaborative relationship with front-end designers who are comfortable with such an iterative design process. I also am convinced this makes for the best large web sites.

You've worked with all the major application servers. In your opinion, what differentiates JSP as a platform? Why would someone choose that? What are its limitations?

Well, not *all* of them!

I guess I take a practical approach to answering this question. I'm not going to get into the religious merits of using Java over *xyz* technology. Java is a powerful platform, and you can probably do what you need to with it.

Until recently, cost was a big reason for not choosing JSP. An enterprise implementation of the IBM WebSphere or JRun application server was prohibitively expensive and the open-source alternatives were not completely stable, at least in the Microsoft Windows environment where I mainly work. The newest stable version of the Apache/Jakarta Tomcat JSP server changes this. The venerable open-source movement has brought us another great free equivalent to the commercial products. Now a kid can set up a web site and Java application server on her Pentium 133 and DSL connection.

One practical reason for choosing JSP and Java is that there are not that many Java programmers around. There is lots of work out there, especially at the government and corporate levels. Java is an established technology and you are securing yourself a career, for at least the next few years, by learning it. If you are a fair-to-excellent Java programmer, and can cooperate in a team environment, you will probably get very good paying work. This is unlike the web design market, which seems crowded.

A limitation is that Java is not so easy to learn, comparatively speaking, for a person with a design and not a programming background. If you find JavaScript to be too challenging, Java development is probably not for you. If you come from the multimedia world of visual development tools like I do (Authorware and Director), you might find Java to be both very limiting and very powerful and exciting at the same time.

The best introduction that I know of to the JSP platform and Java is called *JSP, Servlets, and MySQL*, by David Harms (ISBN 0764547879).

In your opinion, what are the advantages and disadvantages of using Dreamweaver/
UltraDev as a development tool for working with data-driven web sites?

I think the best reason to use Dreamweaver is as a tool to learn how to program the core technologies it supports—SQL, ColdFusion, JavaServer Pages, Active Server Pages, and now PHP. Use it as a learning tool, but expect at some point to outgrow it.

You can perform tasks such as creating a database interface, quite quickly. An example of a simple database interface would be web pages that enable you to view, edit, add, and delete database records. Dreamweaver enables you to become productive quickly without knowing relatively much about web database programming.

To get started, however, you still have to know a lot! You have to know about operating systems, web servers, security, databases, and ODBC connectivity. That's quite a bit of background knowledge, and I typically take two days to cover this background in the classes that I teach. Some people get hung up here and never get to the point where they can actually get Dreamweaver's dynamic features to work.

A big disadvantage of using Dreamweaver for database development is that it encourages a black-box mentality in developers. As Phillip Greenspun says, "There is no magic programming bullet" (`www.arsdigita.com/books/panda/databases-intro`). When your Dreamweaver-generated code breaks, which it will, you have to be willing to roll up your sleeves and understand what it is that the program is doing behind the scenes.

Some are willing to do this and some are not. Those who are will be successful at web back-end development. Others will get frustrated, because the Java code that Dreamweaver writes is not exactly simple nor is it easy to understand. Many users also have experienced this with the provided JavaScript behaviors; when they break or do not do what you want, they are often a challenge to fix or modify. Dreamweaver-generated server-side scripting magnifies this problem immensely.

Another critique is that Dreamweaver does not, for the most part, separate presentation, logic, and content. The designer and programmer will still tangle their feet, especially when neither has a good idea of how the other works. Likewise, Dreamweaver encourages spaghetti coding, the bane of programmers since the 1960s, and does not take true advantage of the object-design capabilities inherent to the Java platform. True Enterprise JSP encourages separation of content, presentation, and logic. You can certainly get UltraDev to do this sort of thing with some modification.

Are you a Java programmer? Is it possible to do serious work with JSP, without knowing Java?

No, I would not consider myself a Java programmer. Out of necessity, I use the programming environment driven by any particularly project, and sometimes that is Java. Rarely do I have the luxury to choose. Given that, I can write Java if I need to, and know when and where to get help. Dreamweaver has made the transition to Java on any particular day much easier for me.

Dreamweaver certainly makes the database interface development process much easier, but keep in mind that I can also make a big mess if I rely on the code that the program produces. That code may or may not be optimal and appropriate for the problem at hand. Integration with other ways of doing things can be difficult.

Serious work? No, I would probably not bring Dreamweaver into a multideveloper production environment. If I were a single-person shop, however, and had to personally fulfill a number of developer roles, I would use it extensively. That's often the case with my own company, and I definitely use the tool enough to justify its cost.

How closely involved are you with the server setup for the web sites you develop? Would you say that's typical for a web developer using database connectivity?

I think it essential for someone doing web database work to understand how the industry standard operating systems (Windows, UNIX), web servers (IIS, Apache), and databases (MySQL, Microsoft Access) work, and how to operate them. Otherwise, when things go wrong you are in deep and expensive trouble.

Typically a web database developer wears many hats: systems administrator, web server administrator, database administrator and designer, programmer, and interface designer. In my career I have attempted to learn enough about each of these areas to function in that role. In my classes at the University of New Mexico, we spend a lot of time learning about these roles, simply because the typical student has not been exposed to them, and they are part of the everyday life of a dynamic web site developer.

Other than Dreamweaver, what development tools do you use?

My programming language of choice is Python (www.python.org) and application server environment is Zope (www.zope.org)

Why? These are the closest to a cross-platform, object-oriented language and application server that I've seen, despite Java's claims—and they are both free. Of course, you spend time learning these, and time is money.

To clarify that: I don't need any special brand of (Sun, IBM, Microsoft, and so on) Java virtual machine to get things to work. I just use the Python interpreter that works well on Linux, Windows, Mac OS, AIX; whatever! This is just like what Perl (www.perl.org) has been doing for years, with little marketing hype like Java had. Syntactically, Python is a clean language and much easier to learn than is Java. And, unlike with Perl, I can understand what I've written six months later.

My favorite application server platform is the free and open-source Zope. It is a true object-oriented web application environment, and the first that I've used that enables you to cleanly separate presentation, logic, and content. What this means is that the programmer and the graphic designers inhabit separate spaces, and don't clobber each other. Macromedia Spectra is a similar platform, based on ColdFusion, but the price tag is much higher. Certainly Zope has rough edges, and it is such a paradigm shift that it's hard to find designers, who are used to things such as file systems, who are willing to try to understand it. It requires a very different way of thinking: the web as a group of interrelated and callable objects and services. It's kind of like moving from BASIC to modular C++ in terms of how you think and work.

What advice would you give to a web designer just getting into working with datadriven web sites?

Dreamweaver is a great place to start a career in dynamic web site publishing, especially if you have no or little programming background. Use it to experiment and learn. Dreamweaver does the programming for you, and you can examine what is produces and use it as a model.

Also use it to perform the repetitive chores of simple web database interface design. It can save you time, at an understandable cost of optimization and flexibility.

Have a thorough understanding of the web editor of your choice; know a basic image editor such as Photoshop; play with a database such as Microsoft Access or MySQL; and install an inexpensive server class operating system and web server such as Linux and Apache yourself. Read all that you can online and in books, lurk in newsgroups, and hang out with people who are doing this kind of work.

Finally, like my music teacher always said, "Get back to the woodshed and practice." This, of course, takes a large investment of your own time, but like most investments, pays off handsomely in the end.

Setting Up a Database Connection

In JSP terms, the database connection is a script that calls on the driver to talk to the database. Dreamweaver creates this script for you, and stores it in a special connections file, when you choose data source name (DSN) from the Databases panel. Because this information gets stored in a special file that can be accessed by any JSP page in your site, you have to define the connection only once for the entire site. (And if you update the information later—for instance, when moving the site to a different server—you have to update it only once.)

Exercise 31.2a   Creating a Database Connection (JDBC-ODBC Bridge Driver)

In this exercise, you create the connection script that will allow your pages to communicate with the antiques database. You must already have installed your database and created a driver for it (as outlined in the preceding section) before continuing with this exercise. Only do this exercise if you want to use the JDBC-ODBC bridge driver for your database. If you want to use the **mm.mysql** JDBC driver, do exercise 31.2b instead.

1. Because Dreamweaver has to know what kind of connection to create, you must have a dynamic document open before you can create the connection. From your local site, open **catalog.jsp**.

    Take a look at the page in Code view, and you'll see that so far it contains only standard HTML code.

2. From the Application panel group, open the Databases panel. If you have **catalog.jsp** open, the panel will have a plus (+) button at the top. Click the plus (+) button and, from the pop-up menu, choose Sun JDBC-ODBC Driver (ODBC Database). Figure 31.14 shows this happening.

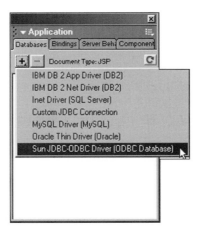

Figure 31.14   Choosing a JDBC-ODBC bridge driver for a database that already has a DSN.

3. The JDBC-ODBC Driver dialog box will appear. For your connection's name, enter **antiques_conn**. (The connection name will be used in the connection script. It's common practice to include *con* or *conn* in the name.)

4. The driver field should already be filled in as `sun.jdbc.odbc.JdbcOdbcDriver`. The URL is partially filled in, with placeholder text for the name of the DSN.

```
Jdbc:odbc:[odbc dsn]
```

To complete this entry, replace the placeholder text (and the brackets) with the name of your DSN (whatever name you gave the DSN in the ODBC Drivers Control Panel), like this (new code in bold):

```
Jdbc:odbc:AntiquesBarn
```

What you're doing here is creating a bridge driver that points to the existing ODBC driver (the DSN).

Figure 31.15 shows this happening.

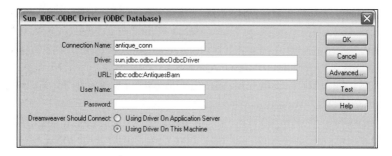

Figure 31.15   Completing the JDBC-ODBC Driver dialog box by entering the DSN that already exists for the antiques database.

5. If you specified a name and password when you defined the driver, enter them here. Otherwise, you can leave these fields blank.

6. To make sure Dreamweaver can connect to the driver, select the radio button for Using Driver on This Machine.

7. Before leaving the Data Source Name dialog box, click the Test button. If Dreamweaver can find the driver, you'll get a `Connection Successful` message. The most common reasons for failing the test are incorrect names and passwords, and incorrectly entered DSNs. After you've passed the test, click OK to close the dialog box.

8. The Databases panel will now contain an icon representing your connection. (Congratulations!) You can now use this panel to explore your database. Expand the connection icon to see Tables, Views, and Stored Procedures. The antiques database contains only tables. Expand the Tables icon all the way to see that the database contains two tables—stockitems and customers—and to see what columns (information fields) each table contains. You can't see the records stored in the database from here, but you can examine its structure (see Figure 31.16).

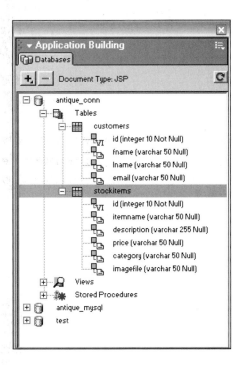

Figure 31.16   The Databases panel showing the structure of the antiques database.

9. In the Site panel, examine your local root folder. You'll see a new **Connections** folder. Inside that folder is the **antique_conn.jsp** file. That file contains your connection script. Each file in your site that needs to access the database will link to it. Open **antique_conn.jsp** and examine it in Code view, and you'll see the connection script:

```
<%
// FileName="sun_jdbc_odbc_conn.htm"
// Type="JDBC"  ""
// DesigntimeType="JDBC"
// HTTP="false"
// Catalog=""
// Schema=""
String MM_antique_conn_DRIVER = "sun.jdbc.odbc.JdbcOdbcDriver";
String MM_antique_conn_USERNAME = "";
String MM_antique_conn_PASSWORD = "";
String MM_antique_conn_STRING = "jdbc:odbc:AntiquesBarn";
%>
```

You don't need to know what everything in this code means. However, one important piece of syntax that you should get familiar with is the <%...%> tags. All JSP code is contained within these tags. Whatever code is inside the tags must be valid Java. When the application server processes this page, it looks for these tags and executes all code inside them. All other code on the page is assumed to be regular HTML or client-side scripting, and is just passed back to the browser.

Exercise 31.2b   Creating a Database Connection (**mm.mysql** JDBC Driver)

In this exercise, you create the connection script that will allow your pages to communicate with the antiques database. You must already have installed your database before continuing with this exercise. Only do this exercise if you are using the MySQL version of the antiques database and want to use the **mm.mysql** JDBC bridge driver. If you want to use the ODBC-JDBC bridge driver, or if you're using the Access database, complete Exercise 31.2a instead.

 1. Because Dreamweaver has to know what kind of connection to create, you must have a dynamic document open before you can create the connection. From your local site, open **catalog.jsp**.

 Take a look at the page in Code view, and you'll see that so far it contains only standard HTML code.

 2. From the Application panel group, open the Databases panel. If you have **catalog.jsp** open, the panel will have a plus (+) button at the top. Click the plus (+) button and, from the pop-up menu, choose MySQL Driver (MySQL).

 Figure 31.17 shows this happening.

Figure 31.17   Choosing the **mm.mysql** JDBC driver for use with a MySQL database.

3. The MySQL Driver dialog box will appear. For your connection's name, enter
   antiques_conn. (The connection name will be used in the connection script. It's
   common practice to include *con* or *conn* in the name.)

4. The Driver field should already be filled in as org.gjt.mm.mysql.Driver. The
   URL is partially filled in, with placeholder text for the name of the DSN.

   ```
   jdbc:mysql://[hostname]/[database name]
   ```

   To complete this entry, replace the [hostname] placeholder text with localhost
   and the [database name] placeholder with the name of your database. Like this
   (new code in bold):

   ```
   jdbc:mysql://localhost/antiques
   ```

   What you're doing here is telling the driver (which is a generic driver that can
   point to any database) where your particular database is—on the same computer
   where the driver is stored, in the MySQL installation, called antiques.

   Figure 31.18 shows this happening.

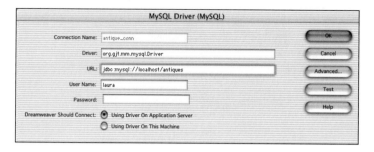

Figure 31.18   Completing the MySQL JDBC Driver dialog box by entering the location of the antiques database.

5. If you set up your MySQL database following the instructions in Appendix C, you can leave the Username and Password fields blank. (Those instructions gave any user on localhost permission to access the antiques database.)

6. From the radio buttons at the bottom of the dialog box, choose Using Driver on Application Server.

Note

Why must you use the driver on the application server? If you followed the instructions earlier in this chapter, you installed the **mm.mysql** driver inside the **Tomcat** folder, in your web application folder. Even if the **Tomcat** folder is on your working computer, technically it is the application server.

7. Before leaving the dialog box, click the Test button. If Dreamweaver can find the driver, you'll get a `Connection Successful` message. The most common reasons for failing the test are incorrect names and passwords, and incorrectly referenced databases and host names. After you've passed the test, click OK to close the dialog box.

Note

Mac OS X users take special note here: Because of how UNIX permissions work, permission errors are the most common problems in establishing your database connection. If you get an error when you test your connection, try entering your Mac OS username in the dialog box's Username field, and even your password, if needed.

8. The Databases panel will now contain an icon representing your connection. (Congratulations!) You can now use this panel to explore your database. Expand the connection icon to see Tables, Views, and Stored Procedures. The antiques database contains only tables. Expand the Tables icon all the way to see that the database contains two tables—stockitems and customers—and to see what columns (information fields) each table contains. You can't see the records stored in the database from here, but you can examine its structure (see Figure 31.19).

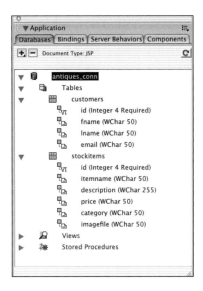

Figure 31.19   The Databases panel showing the structure of the antiques database.

9. In the Site panel, examine your local root folder. You'll see a new **Connections** folder. Inside that folder is the **antique_conn.jsp** file. That file contains your connection script. Each file in your site that needs to access the database will link to it. Open **antique_conn.jsp** and examine it in Code view, and you'll see the connection script:

```
<%
// FileName="mysql_jdbc_conn.htm"
// Type="JDBC"  ""
// DesigntimeType="JDBC"
// HTTP="true"
// Catalog=""
// Schema=""
String MM_antique_conn_DRIVER = "org.gjt.mm.mysql.Driver";
String MM_antique_conn_USERNAME = "laura";
String MM_antique_conn_PASSWORD = "";
String MM_antique_conn_STRING = "jdbc:mysql://localhost/antiques";
%>
```

You don't need to know what everything in this code means. However, one important piece of syntax that you should get familiar with is the <%...%> tags. All JSP code is contained within these tags. Whatever code is inside the tags must be valid Java. When the application server processes this page, it looks for these tags and executes all code inside them. All other code on the page is assumed to be regular HTML or client-side scripting, and is just passed back to the browser.

Note

Why put the connection in its own file? If you ever change your driver's name, type, or location, Dreamweaver needs to change only this one file, and the updated driver information will automatically be passed along to all documents in the site.

Displaying Dynamic Data

Probably the most basic task you'll want your JSP pages to perform is to display information from a database. This involves creating a framework of static page elements (banner, navigation controls, a table for layout, and so forth) and adding dynamic text and pictures—like a catalog page in a commerce site shows pictures and descriptions of items for sale.

Displaying dynamic data involves several tasks. First, you must query the database to collect the information you want to display (which records, which fields, in what order, and so on). This collected information is called a *recordset*. Then you create a *dynamic element* for every field you want to display. (A field is a column in one of the database tables, remember.) Then, unless you want your page to display only information from the first record it finds, you must create special code that steps through all the collected records and displays them one after the other. In Dreamweaver language, this is called creating a *repeating region*, and it can be refined through various *recordset navigation* controls.

Collecting a Recordset

In Dreamweaver, you collect a recordset with the Bindings panel, in the Application panel group. To collect the recordset, follow these steps:

1. Open the Bindings panel, click the plus (+) button and choose Recordset (Query).

2. In the Recordset dialog box that opens, choose whatever database elements (usually table columns, which translate into record fields) you want.

> **Note**
>
> When you choose items in the Recordset dialog box, you're actually telling Dreamweaver how to write a SQL query for you. To see the actual SQL syntax, click the Advanced button and examine the SQL input field. (Click the Simple button to get back to the standard dialog box.) See the preceding chapter for more on SQL.

3. After you've collected the recordset, the collected columns will appear in the Bindings panel. Because Dreamweaver has to write a JSP script to collect the recordset, technically speaking the collection action is a behavior. It will appear in the Server Behaviors panel (in the Application panel group).

You also can create a recordset by going to the Application tab of the Insert bar and choosing the Recordset object. Doing this is exactly the same as using the Bindings panel. Think of it as a shortcut.

Exercise 31.3   Collecting Data for the Antiques Barn Catalog Page

In this exercise, you add dynamic elements to the **catalog.jsp** page, which already has its static layout elements in place. This page is meant to display all the items for sale at the Antiques Barn, so you'll collect information from the stockitems table of the antiques database. You'll display a picture, name, description and price for each item (see Figure 31.20).

Figure 31.20   The Antiques Barn catalog page being served with one record displaying.

1. Begin by opening **catalog.jsp**. Examine the layout structure in Design view, and you'll see that the middle row of the main layout table is ready and waiting for a picture in one column, and various text items in another.

2. First, you have to query the database to collect some data to play with. From the Application panel group, open the Bindings panel. Click the plus (+) button and, from the menu, choose Recordset (Query). The Recordset dialog box appears.

3. You can give your recordset a custom name, or accept the default name. (For the examples shown here, the default name will be used.) If your DSN connection (antiques_conn) doesn't automatically appear in the Connections field, choose it from the pop-up menu. That will populate the rest of the dialog box with information from the antiques database.

4. You want information from the stockitems table, so choose it from the Tables pop-up list. You don't need to collect all the columns (fields). For columns to choose, select the Selected radio button. Then Ctrl/Cmd-click to choose itemname, description, price, and imagefile. Choose to sort the information based on itemname, ascending (from *A–Z*).

Figure 31.21 shows the completed dialog box, and resulting Bindings panel.

Tip

From within the Recordset dialog box, click the Test button to see what information your recordset will collect. This is a handy way to make sure you've collected the proper set of data, before you get too far into the process of making the page.

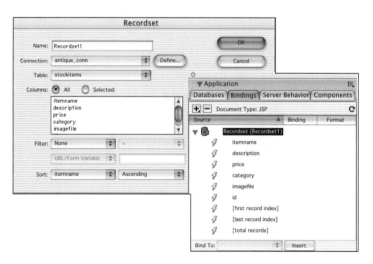

Figure 31.21   Collecting the recordset for the Antiques Barn catalog page, and the resulting Bindings panel.

5. Click OK to close the dialog box. The Bindings entry is made and the appropriate code added to your page.

Inserting Dynamic Elements

Data from the database can be inserted anywhere in your document. Names, prices, and descriptions can become dynamic text elements—you can even format them using all the standard HTML and CSS text options. You also can use database fields behind the scenes to help construct the HTML code of your page. Therefore, although most databases can't contain images or other media elements, a field might contain a filename that can be used in the `src` parameter for an `<img>`. This is how you insert dynamic images into your pages. (For details on creating dynamic text, see the dynamic data sidebar in Chapter 4, "Working with Text." For more on dynamic images, see the sidebar in Chapter 5, "Working with Images.")

Note

Most databases used for dynamic sites can't contain actual media, such as images or sound files. They can contain only text.

Exercise 31.4   Displaying Dynamic Data in the Antiques Barn Catalog Page

In this exercise, you use the recordset you collected in the preceding exercise to create dynamic text and image elements for **catalog.jsp**. You also familiarize yourself with the Live Data previewing options in Dreamweaver.

1. Open **catalog.jsp**, if it's not already open. In the Application panel group, open the Bindings panel and expand the view of your recordset so that you can see the individual fields you have collected.

2. It's easiest to start with the dynamic text elements. As you can see from Figure 31.20, the rightmost column of the layout table should contain the item name, description, and price, each in its own paragraph.

   Inserting a dynamic text element can be done in various ways. By far the simplest is just dragging the desired field from the Bindings panel to the proper place in the Document window. Try that method for the first text element—drag the itemname field into the layout table (see Figure 31.22).

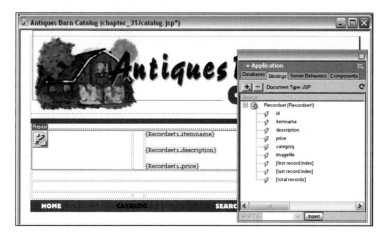

Figure 31.22   Inserting a dynamic text element by dragging a field name from the Bindings panel.

After in the document, the dynamic element becomes a text placeholder. In Design view, it looks like {Recordset1.itemname}. Switch to Code and Design view, and you'll see that the JSP code looks like this:

```
<%=(((Recordset1_data = Recordset1.getObject("itemname"))==null ||
Recordset1.wasNull())?"":Recordset1_data)%>
```

You should already recognize the JSP tag structure. The <%= tag means "insert the following value here." The code in parentheses refers to the itemname column. When the server sees that code, it will substitute whatever text is in that field for the current record.

3. As far as Dreamweaver is concerned, this item is a stand-in for real text. To demonstrate that, stay in Code and Design view but use Design view to select the new placeholder. From the Property inspector, apply paragraph formatting (choose Paragraph from the Format pop-up menu). Note that, in the code, the placeholder is now surrounded by <p> tags (shown in bold):

```
<p><%=(((Recordset1_data = Recordset1.getObject("itemname"))==null
|| Recordset1.wasNull())?"":Recordset1_data)%></p>
```

From the Design panel group, open the CSS panel. With the placeholder text still selected, choose the itemname style class. The display changes to accept the new formatting, and your code changes to the following:

```
<p class="itemname">
<%=(((Recordset1_data = Recordset1.getObject("itemname"))==null ||
Recordset1.wasNull())?"":Recordset1_data)%>
</p>
```

The placeholder is being treated as though it were real text.

Use the same method to insert the description and price into the layout, each in its own paragraph in the table cell. For the price, apply the price CSS class.

4. When you insert dynamic text, you're actually creating a JSP server-side behavior (a script that tells the server to insert certain text). In the Application panel group, open the Server Behaviors panel, and you'll see one behavior for every dynamic text element you've added plus a behavior for collecting the recordset (see Figure 31.23).

Just like regular behaviors, you can double-click a server-side behavior in the panel to view its properties and edit it.

Figure 31.23   Dynamic text elements in **catalog.jsp**, and the server behaviors used to insert them.

You can use the Server Behaviors panel to apply special formatting to dynamic text elements—things such as changing capitalization and decimal-point display. For the Antiques Barn catalog page, you probably want the item price to display a little nicer, with a dollar sign and some decimal values.

In the Server Behaviors panel, double-click the entry for the price, to open it for editing. In the dialog box that appears, use the Formatting pop-up menu to choose Currency – Default (see Figure 31.24).

Click OK to close the dialog box.

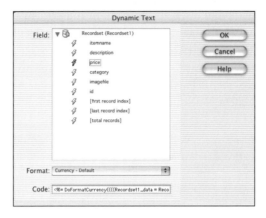

Figure 31.24 Adding scripted formatting to a dynamic text element.

> **Tip**
>
> To delete any dynamic element in a document, it's safest to delete the server behavior that created the element, instead of just selecting its placeholder in Design view and deleting. (Dreamweaver will warn you if you try to delete an element the wrong way.)

5. Each catalog entry also must show a picture of the item. A look at the structure of your database (in the Databases panel) will show you that the stockitems table has a field called imagefile. These can be used as the src attribute of an <img> tag, to create dynamic images.

   To insert the dynamic image, start by placing your cursor in the page at the location you want to add the image and insert the image as you normally would (use the Image object from the Common tab of the Insert bar). When the Insert Image dialog box appears, however, choose the Data Source option (see Figure 31.25). The list of image files is replaced with a list of fields from your recordset. Choose imagefile, and click OK.

Figure 31.25 Inserting a dynamic image by specifying Data Source, rather than File System, for the src attribute.

Design view now shows the image as a cute little image placeholder icon (with a lightning bolt for dynamic data). If you check your code, you'll see another JSP <%= tag stuck right in the middle of the <img> tag (non-JSP code shown in bold):

```
<img src="<%=(((Recordset1_data =
Recordset1.getObject("imagefile"))==null ||
Recordset1.wasNull())?"":Recordset1_data)%>">
```

Note that no width or height has been entered. That's because Dreamweaver cannot determine the dimensions from this data—because no actual image has been put here yet.

Previewing with Live Data

You're tired of placeholders! You want to see this page in action. After you've completely set up your site definition, Dreamweaver can send an HTTP request to your server and show you your page, with "live" data in place. As discussed earlier, the live preview originates from the remote folder you set up as your web application folder. So all image files must have been uploaded to the remote site before the preview will work properly. After you've done that, there are two ways to preview data:

- **Live Data view.** In the Document toolbar, click the Live Data button to switch from viewing placeholders to viewing actual data (see Figure 31.26).

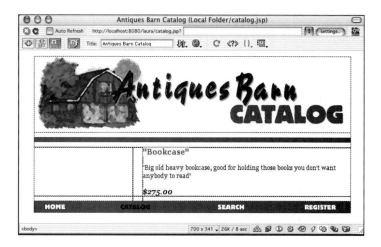

Figure 31.26   Live Data view of **catalog.jsp**.

- **Preview in Browser.** Choosing this command, when you're in a dynamic site, will activate the server and "serve" your page in your primary, secondary, or other browser.

Exercise 31.5   Previewing and Troubleshooting Live Data in the Antiques Barn Catalog Page

In this exercise, you try some different previewing methods (if you haven't already experimented!), and use them to troubleshoot your code.

1. Before trying to preview, make sure you've uploaded all your site's files to the remote server—including the **Connection** folder that was created in Exercise 31.2.

2. With **catalog.jsp** open, click the Live Data view button. It might take a moment, but real data should pop into your Document window.

Note

Sometimes Dreamweaver holds the database connection open, which doesn't allow the Live Data view or previewing dynamic pages to function properly. If Live Data view doesn't engage properly, try saving the page and closing Dreamweaver. Next, open your browser and type `http://localhost/yoursitename/catalog.asp` and see if it displays. If you still get and error, your site probably isn't cnfigured properly and you'll need to revisit the previous exercises and Chapter 26 to troubleshoot.

You'll immediately notice that there's a problem—your lovely dynamic image isn't displaying properly (see Figure 31.27).

You might have guessed why, but in case you haven't, it's time to visit the browser.

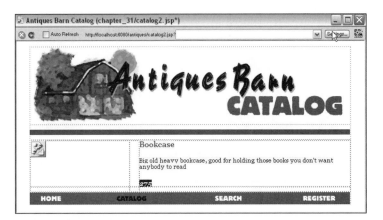

Figure 31.27   Live Data preview of **catalog.jsp**—but there's a problem with the dynamic image.

3. Click the Live Data icon to toggle Live Data view off.

4. Preview your page in the browser (F12). You'll undoubtedly see the same problem—a missing image. Here in the browser, however, you have some troubleshooting tools at your disposal. If you're in Internet Explorer, go to View > Source. If you're in Netscape, go to View > Page Source.

Examine the code here—you might notice that it looks different from the code you viewed in Dreamweaver. There are no JSP <%...%> tags. That's because the server has executed the script within those tags and used it to construct plain old HTML. The HTML code that was constructed to display your table row looks like this (dynamically generated code shown in bold):

```
<tr valign="top">
<td><img src="bookcase.jpg"></td>
<td> </td>
<td>
<p class="itemname">Bookcase</p>
<p> Big old heavy bookcase, good for holding those books you don't
want anybody to read. </p>
<p class="price">$65.00</p>
</td>
</tr>
```

There's your dynamic text! And there's your problem, in the <img> tag. If you examine your site's file structure, you'll see that all images have been stored in an images folder, so the correct relative URL to the clock image is **images/ bookcase.jpg**. However, the database entry doesn't include that extra folder name. No wonder the browser cannot find the image!

5. You could, of course, fix every single database entry to include a folder name. However, it's much easier to tweak your JSP code, just a little, to do the job for you. When you get used to the way the server just adds the placeholders right into the main code, it'll be easy.

   Back in Dreamweaver, select the dynamic image placeholder. Then open the Server Behaviors panel. The behavior that is creating your image will be highlighted. Double-click to open the editing dialog box. Because you know you have to add the folder name to the entry, manually fix the URL entry so that it looks like this (new code in bold):

```
<img src="images/<%=(((Recordset1_data =
Recordset1.getObject("imagefile"))==null ||
Recordset1.wasNull())?"":Recordset1_data)%>">
```

6. After you've done this, try previewing your page in a browser again. The image should show up! (If it doesn't, View > Source to check your constructed code; and, back in Dreamweaver, check Code view to make sure your <img> tag looks exactly like the one shown here.)

Note

The only drawback to manually adding relative path information to your dynamic image source is that you have to know what the relative URL to your images should look like. You can't just browse to an image and let Dreamweaver do the thinking for you!

Displaying Multiple Records with Repeated Regions

A repeated region is any chunk of page code that you want to repeat for as many records as you want to show. A repeated region can be a line of text, an item in a list, a table row, or even an entire table. To create a repeated region, follow these steps:

1. Select the part of your page that you want to repeat.

2. In the Server Behaviors panel, click the plus (+) button and choose Repeat Region; or choose the Repeat Region object from the Insert > Application bar (see Figure 31.28).

    A dialog box will appear, asking which recordset you want to display and how many records you want to show. (Only choose to display all records if you know for sure your database won't have too many records to fit on a decent-sized web page.)

Figure 31.28   The Repeated Region, Recordset Navigation Bar, and Recordset Navigation Status objects.

Navigating Through Multiple-Page Displays

If you've set up the repeating region not to display all records at once, you need to give your visitors a way to view the first group of records, the next group after that, and so on. Dreamweaver offers two tools to help with this: Record Navigation Bar and Record Navigation Status. Both are technically server behaviors, but also are easily accessible as objects from the Applications tab of the Insert bar (see Figure 31.28).

The Record Navigation Bar object (or server behavior) determines whether the recordset contains more records than are displayed on the current page; and if so, displays previous page, next page, first page, and last page navigation controls. All the hard work is done for you. All you have to do is insert the object (or server behavior), and Dreamweaver creates the links and adds the scripting to display different records on your page.

The Record Navigation Status object (or server behavior) determines how many total records are in the recordset, and which are currently displaying on the page, and adds a text message to the page—Records 1 to 10 of 56. Again, all you have to do is insert the object, and Dreamweaver takes care of the rest.

Exercise 31.6   Displaying Multiple Records in the Antiques Barn Catalog Page

In this exercise, you build the catalog page further by displaying multiple records. You also add navigation controls so that visitors can move between records easily.

1. Open **catalog.jsp**, if it isn't already open.

2. You want the table row containing your dynamic elements to repeat. Select that row. (Drag across the cells, or click inside a cell and use the tag selector to select the <tr> tag. It's important to make sure you get exactly the right table parts selected!)

3. From the Application tab of the Insert bar, choose the Repeated Region object. The Repeat Region dialog box will appear, asking you which recordset to base the repeats on (you have only one recordset, so there's nothing to choose here) and how many records to show. Set the number of displayed records to **5** and click OK (see Figure 31.29).

   Note how the Design view display has changed to indicate the repeated region.

Figure 31.29   Inserting a repeating region that will display five records at a time.

4. Preview your work in the browser. There are the first five records of your recordset!

5. This is great as far as it goes, but the visitor can never go beyond those first five records. You need some navigation controls. Back in Dreamweaver, the new elements should be added below the repeated elements but above the bottom navigation bar.

   You need to add a new table row for the controls. Be careful here! If you place the insertion point in the table row that contains the dynamic elements, and insert a new row below it, Dreamweaver will assume that you want the new row to be part of the repeated region. Instead, you must position the cursor in the empty table row directly above the navigation bar and insert a row above. You'll have to be sneaky doing this, because that "empty" row is actually filled with transparent GIF images. Select one of the images. Then use the tag selector to choose the parent <td> tag. Then go to Modify > Table > Insert Row. (Unless you're very accurate with your mouse-clicks, it's easier to choose the menu from the menu bar than to right-click to access the contextual menu.)

You want the new navigation elements to stretch all the way across the layout, so select all three cells in the new row and merge them (Modify > Table > Merge Cells).

6. With the insertion point in the new merged row, choose the Recordset Navigation Bar from the Insert > Application bar. In the dialog box that appears, choose to use image navigation elements and click OK. The resulting insertion is shown in Figure 31.30.

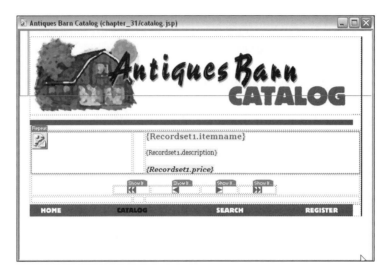

Figure 31.30   The Recordset Navigation Bar being inserted in the Antiques Barn catalog page.

7. Preview your page in the browser again, and you'll see the navigation controls at work. You can click to move forward and back through pages of displayed records. Also note that the controls appear only if there are records to view— you can't go to previous or first if you're at the first page already, for instance (see Figure 31.31).

Note

Oops! If you inserted your new table row inside the repeating region, you'll get navigation controls after every single record. There is no easy fix for this, unless you're willing to tinker around in the code. The quickest solution is to Edit > Undo, or use the History panel, backing up to before you inserted the new table row—and start again.

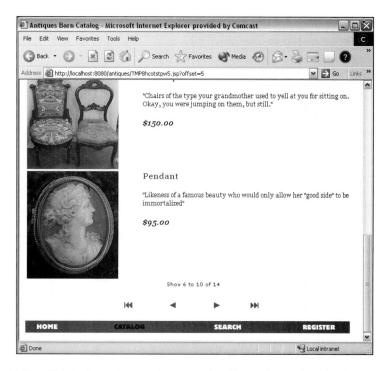

Figure 31.31 The Antiques Barn catalog page with all recordset navigation elements in place.

8. The newly inserted elements are consistent with linked images within a nested table. If you examine your Site panel, you'll see that the image files **first.gif**, **last.gif**, **next.gif**, and **previous.gif** have been added to the root level of your site. You can move these image files to your **images** folder, if you like—but be sure to let Dreamweaver update all links when you do this (see Figure 31.32)!

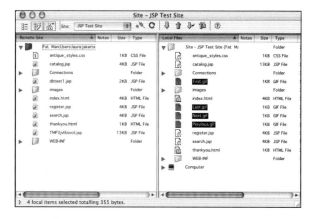

Figure 31.32 The images for the Recordset Navigation control moved to the site's **images** folder.

9. Finally, you can make your catalog page complete by letting visitors know where they are in the recordset ("Records 1 to 5 of 10"). For the Antiques Barn page, you'll add that information directly above the recordset navigation controls.

    Start by adding a new row at the top of the nested table that contains the record-set navigation. As long as you're working with this table, you're well outside the repeated region, so you don't have to worry about that.

10. Merge the cells of the new row so that it stretches across the entire table. Then, with the insertion point inside the new row, choose the Recordset Navigation Status object from the Application tab of the Insert bar. There's your new dynamic text (see Figure 31.33).

11. Preview in the browser, to see it in action.

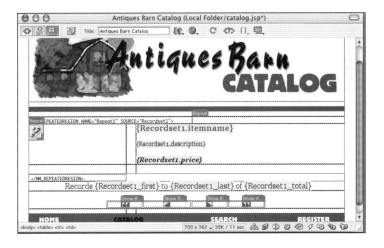

Figure 31.33 The Recordset Navigation Status object inserted.

As with any dynamic text element, you can format the status line as you like. You also can change any of the static text, so long as you don't disturb the placeholder text. (In Figure 31.31, for instance, the word *records* has been changed to *show*.)

Congratulations! The Antiques Barn catalog page is now complete. You've built your first JSP web application document.

Summary

In this chapter, you learned the basics of setting up a JSP site in Dreamweaver and creating a page that displays dynamic elements. Although you can't experience the full power of JSP without learning some Java programming, Dreamweaver provides even Java newbies the necessary tools to build a basic JSP site.

Chapter 32

Technical Issues

So far in this book, the focus has been on Dreamweaver as a visually based HTML editor that gives you easy access to the code behind it all. However, this last section examines Dreamweaver another way: as a program for working with code that includes a sophisticated previewing system for how that code will eventually display in a browser. If that sounds strange to you, remember that one of the reasons for the massive popularity of Dreamweaver in the web-authoring community is that it really can be used either way. The coding geeks and artists might not agree on *how* to use Dreamweaver, but most of them agree that it's *good* to use Dreamweaver.

This introduction to the code-centric part of the book takes a look at the web from a coding point of view. What's out there, beyond HTML and JavaScript, and how do those languages fit into the grand scheme of things?

Markup Languages

Markup languages are used to describe the structure of web documents. The most ubiquitous markup language, of course, is HTML—but it's not the only one.

SGML and the Basic Structure of Markup

HTML, XML, XHTML, WML—all the "ML" acronyms—are markup languages, as are SVG, SMIL, and various others. No matter what their other differences are, all these languages share a common syntax you should already find familiar:

```
<tag attribute="value">content goes here</tag>
```

This universal reliance on tags marked by <> isn't a coincidence. All the markup languages are based on the same meta-language, Standard Generalized Markup Language (SGML). SGML is a set of rules for creating other languages. The goal is to create a set of tags that enable authors to describe a document's structure so that computers, printers, and other devices can logically interpret the document's contents. The major syntactical rules include the following:

- Opening and closing pairs of tags, marked by <> and </>, bracket content. Tags can be nested inside other tags, creating hierarchical "tree" structures that can be used to represent hierarchical data structures:

```
<parent>
    <child>content</child>
</parent>
```

- Attributes, in the form of name/value pairs (`name="value"`), add specific characteristics to different occurrences of tags.

Although the tag and attribute names differ for different languages, all markup languages based on SGML use this same structure.

HTML, XML, and Other Languages

There's a wide world out there beyond HTML, although the whole party really started with HTML. Understanding where everybody came from, and why they developed, is an important part of expanding your web-authoring horizons.

HTML: Markup or Formatting Language?

Tim Berniers-Lee developed HTML in 1991 as a markup language to enable scientists to share technical papers across computer networks. It was simple enough that even "amateurs" could quickly master it. As the Internet developed, however, the needs of the commercial world changed HTML from its original intent. Instead of using HTML to represent document structure, with logical tags, such as <h1>, <h2>, <address>, and <strong>, authors started focusing on using HTML to create pages that would visually display a certain way in browsers, using tags such as <font>, <b>, and <i>.

CSS and the W3C

As discussed in Chapter 4, "Working with Text" and in Chapter 13, "Using Cascading Style Sheets," Cascading Style Sheets were introduced to help web authors separate structural and presentation information—document structure is described with the HTML tags, with CSS style sheets used to interpret the tags for display and printing. The World Wide Web Consortium (W3C) created CSS for just this reason: to bring HTML back to its roots as a true markup language. CSS itself isn't a markup language. It's intended to work with markup languages, to help specify how they will be interpreted under different conditions.

Note

To learn more about the W3C, and read the official specs on HTML, CSS, and other web technologies, visit www.w3.org.

XML: Another Language for Creating Languages

Have you heard of XML? Of course you have. Web pundits have been talking about XML—which will one day come to save the world from the vagaries of browsers and the intransigence of HTML—for several years. But what *is* XML?

XML Is a Set of Syntax Rules

The W3C created the eXtensible Markup Language (XML) as a set of structural rules, based on SGML, for creating other markup languages. XML syntax is basically like HTML syntax, but stricter. Be aware of the following major restrictions:

- The entire document must be enclosed in a tag pair—like `<html></html>` or `<xml></xml>`, for instance. This enclosing set of tags is called the *root element*.

- No empty *elements* (or tags) are allowed. This means tags must either occur in an opening and closing pair—`<tag></tag>`—or must be self-closing—`<tag />`.

- All tag and attribute names, and all attribute values, must be lowercase—`<tag>`.

- Attribute values must be in quotation marks—`<tag author="fred">`.

- All attributes must be in the form `name="value"`. (In HTML, by contrast, attributes without values, such as `<td nowrap>`, are allowed.)

XML Has No Specific Tag Names

The purpose of XML is to allow for extensibility and interpretation. Specific elements can be added as needed. The author of an XML-based phone book, for instance, would probably want to create elements like this:

```
<listing type="residential">
    <name>John Smith</name>
    <phone>555-1234</phone>
    <address>123 Main Street</address>
    <pubtype privacy="noaddress" />
</listing>
```

XML Itself Provides No Formatting Information

What would the preceding phone book entry look like? That depends entirely on what piece of software is interpreting the code, and what instructions that software has been given for how `<listing>`, `<name>`, and the other elements should be treated. XML works nicely with CSS or with XSL (eXtensible Style Language) so that an individual XML document with a linked style sheet can create a complete, formatted presentation in a browser.

XML Documents Must Be Valid and Well-Formed

Validation is the core of XML. Instead of leaving a browser or other application to figure out syntactical irregularities and unfamiliar tags and attributes, XML requires that the parser be able to validate the document—determine whether it is proper XML—and then parse (interpret) it accordingly. How important is this? Consider that one reason today's browsers are so bloated and unwieldy is that they devote many resources to guessing how to display badly formatted HTML documents. A well-formed document obeys all the syntax rules previously listed. A valid document uses only legal page elements (tags and attributes). To facilitate validation, all documents must begin with a

DTD, or *Document Type Definition*, that describes what flavor of XML is being used in the document and what rules should be applied when parsing the code. (See the discussion in Chapter 3, "Creating and Working with Documents," for more on DTDs.)

XML Isn't Just for Browsing

The process of interpreting an XML document is called *parsing*. Any software that performs this interpretation is an *XML parser*. In order to handle XML documents, web browsers might have XML parsers operating underneath them.

But even though web authors tend to focus on browsers and how pages will display there, XML is used for many different purposes besides web browsing. Each purpose requires some parsing software. More and more commercial programs, for instance—including Dreamweaver—are putting their configuration information into XML documents, and incorporating XML parsing capabilities into the core programs to translate this information into interface elements and other program features.

A good example of XML in action is Dreamweaver's own menu interface. The exact content, structure, and behavior of Dreamweaver menus are determined by the file **menus.xml**, in the application's **Configuration** folder. The elements in this document are all aimed at constructing menus, as follows:

```
<menubar>
    <menu name="File">
        <menuitem name="New" etc />
        <menuitem name="Open... " etc />
        etc.
    </menu>
    etc.
</menubar>
```

In this case the core Dreamweaver program provides the instructions for how that element structure should be implemented. Whenever the program sees <menu>, it adds a menu to a menu bar; each <menuitem> adds an item to the menu, with its text as specified in the name attribute; and so on. Listing 32.1 shows a segment of code from the **menus.xml** file. Figure 32.1 shows how those lines are implemented in the Dreamweaver interface.

Listing 32.1   A Sample Section from Dreamweaver's Own Configuration File menus.xml

```
<menu name="_Text" id="DWMenu_Text">
<menuitem name="_Indent" key="Cmd+Opt+]" domRequired="false"
enabled="dw.getFocus() == 'textView' || dw.getFocus(true) == 'html' ||
dw.getFocus() == 'document' && dw.getDocumentDOM().getFocus() == 'body'"
```

continues ▶

Listing 32.1   Continued

```
command="if (dw.getFocus(true) == 'document')
{dw.getDocumentDOM().indent()} else
{dw.getDocumentDOM().source.indentTextView()}" id="DWMenu_Text_Indent"
/>
<menuitem name="_Outdent" key="Cmd+Opt+[" domRequired="false"
enabled="dw.getFocus() == 'textView' || dw.getFocus(true) == 'html' ||
dw.getFocus() == 'document' && dw.getDocumentDOM().getFocus() == 'body'"
command="if (dw.getFocus(true) == 'document') {dw.getDocumentDOM().out-
dent()} else {dw.getDocumentDOM().source.outdentTextView()}"
id="DWMenu_Text_Outdent" />
<menu name="Paragraph _Format" id="DWMenu_Text_Format">
<menuitem name="_None" key="Cmd+0" file="Menus/MM/Text_Format.htm" argu-
ments="'None'" id="DWMenu_Text_Format_DefaultText" />
<menuitem name="_Paragraph" key="Cmd+Shift+P"
file="Menus/MM/Text_Format.htm"  arguments="'P'"
id="DWMenu_Text_Format_P" />
<menuitem name="Heading _1" key="Cmd+1" file="Menus/MM/Text_Format.htm"
arguments="'H1'" id="DWMenu_Text_Format_H1" />
<menuitem name="Heading _2" key="Cmd+2" file="Menus/MM/Text_Format.htm"
arguments="'H2'" id="DWMenu_Text_Format_H2" />
<menuitem name="Heading _3" key="Cmd+3" file="Menus/MM/Text_Format.htm"
arguments="'H3'" id="DWMenu_Text_Format_H3" />
<menuitem name="Heading _4" key="Cmd+4" file="Menus/MM/Text_Format.htm"
arguments="'H4'" id="DWMenu_Text_Format_H4" />
<menuitem name="Heading _5" key="Cmd+5" file="Menus/MM/Text_Format.htm"
arguments="'H5'" id="DWMenu_Text_Format_H5" />
<menuitem name="Heading _6" key="Cmd+6" file="Menus/MM/Text_Format.htm"
arguments="'H6'" id="DWMenu_Text_Format_H6" />
<menuitem name="P_reformatted Text" file="Menus/MM/Text_Format.htm"
arguments="'PRE'" id="DWMenu_Text_Format_PRE" />
</menu>
<menu name="_Align" id="DWMenu_Text_Alignment">
<menuitem name="_Left" key="Cmd+Opt+Shift+L" enabled="dw.getFocus() ==
'document' && dw.getDocumentDOM().getFocus() == 'body'"
command="dw.getDocumentDOM().setTextAlignment('left')"
checked="dw.getDocumentDOM() != null &&
dw.getDocumentDOM().getTextAlignment() == 'left'"
id="DWMenu_Text_Alignment_Left" />
<menuitem name="_Center" key="Cmd+Opt+Shift+C" enabled="dw.getFocus() ==
'document' && dw.getDocumentDOM().getFocus() == 'body'"
command="dw.getDocumentDOM().setTextAlignment('center')"
checked="dw.getDocumentDOM() != null &&
dw.getDocumentDOM().getTextAlignment() == 'center'"
id="DWMenu_Text_Alignment_Center" />
<menuitem name="_Right" key="Cmd+Opt+Shift+R" enabled="dw.getFocus() ==
'document' && dw.getDocumentDOM().getFocus() == 'body'"
command="dw.getDocumentDOM().setTextAlignment('right')"
checked="dw.getDocumentDOM() != null &&
dw.getDocumentDOM().getTextAlignment() == 'right'"
id="DWMenu_Text_Alignment_Right" />
<menuitem name="_Justify" key="Cmd+Opt+Shift+J" enabled="dw.getFocus()
== 'document' && dw.getDocumentDOM().getFocus() == 'body'"
```

```
command="dw.getDocumentDOM().setTextAlignment('justify')"
checked="dw.getDocumentDOM() != null &&
dw.getDocumentDOM().getTextAlignment() == 'justify'"
id="DWMenu_Text_Alignment_Justify" />
</menu>
```

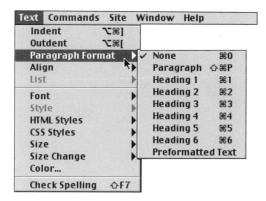

Figure 32.1 How the code in Listing 32.1 translates into Dreamweaver menu elements.

 Note

Easily configurable menus are part of Dreamweaver's "eXtensible" structure. See Chapter 34, "Customizing Dreamweaver," for an explanation of how Dreamweaver configuration and extensibility works.

XML-Based Languages

Creating an XML-based language basically means creating a set of custom tags and always using the same instructions for interpreting them. If a software company creates the language, the instructions will be built into the software itself. If the language is an official W3C standard, the official interpretation is part of the language's specification. Some of the XML-based languages you're likely to run into as a web author are discussed in these following sections.

Simultaneous Media Integration Language (SMIL)

SMIL is a set of tags and attributes for the purpose of creating multimedia documents. A unique aspect of SMIL is that, unlike other markup, it includes a time element. Custom tags and attributes cover such things as setting page layout, inserting audio or video files, determining when media elements will start and stop playing, whether two media elements play simultaneously or in sequence, and so on. Listing 32.2 shows the code for a simple SMIL presentation.

Listing 32.2   Code for a Simple SMIL Document

```
<smil>
    <head>
        <layout>
            <root-layout width="256" height="256" background-
color="black" />
                <region id="pix" left="0" top="0" width="256"
height="256" />
        </layout>
    </head>
    <body>
        <seq>
            <img src="Hello.gif" alt="Hello!" region="pix"
begin="1.00s" dur="16.00s" />
            <img scr="Goodbye.gif" alt="Goodbye!" region="pix"
dur="16.00x" />
        </seq>
    </body>
</smil>
```

Of the major browsers, only Internet Explorer 5.5 and above currently offers SMIL support, although both the RealPlayer and QuickTime Player plugins can use it. (See Chapter 19, "Plugins, ActiveX, and Java," for more about this.)

Note

As anyone who's struggled with Netscape and Internet Explorer's contradictory interpretations of HTML and CSS knows, a W3C standardized language is standardized only if the different applications that implement it agree to abide by the standards. There's nothing to force RealPlayer or QuickTime Player to both interpret the tags of SMIL in the official way. There's not even any law against them re-interpreting the tags and then still calling what they're doing SMIL. To learn more about the official SMIL specification, visit www.w3.org/AudioVideo.

Scalable Vector Graphics (SVG)

Another official W3C specification, SVG is a language for describing the structure of a document with vector-graphic content. Custom tags describe such structural features as shape, color, size, animation, and so forth. Currently in its infancy, SVG will ultimately enable web authors to create web pages that display vector text, graphics, and animation without the need for plugins or ActiveX objects. Listing 32.3 shows a very simple SVG document.

Listing 32.3   Code for a Simple SVG Document

```
<?xml version="1.0" encoding="iso-8859-1"?>
<!DOCTYPE svg PUBLIC "-//W3C//DTD SVG 20000303 Stylable//EN"
"http://www.w3.org.TR/2000/03/WD-SVG-2000303/DTD/svg-2000303-
stylable.dtd">
<svg width="450px" height="450px" viewBox="0 0 450 450"
xmlns:xlink="http://www.w3.org/2000/xlink/namesapce/"
xmlns:a="http://www.adobe.com/sbg10-extensions">
<rect style="fill:#FFFFFF;stroke:none;" width="450" height="450"></rect>
<!--rotating square-->
<g id="rotating_square">
<defs>
<g id="square_styled">
<rect id="square_styled" width="225" height="225"></rect>
</g>
</defs>
<g id="rotation" transform="translate(255 255)">
<use xlink:href="#square" x="-113" y="-113">
<animateTransform attributeName="transform" type="rotate" values="0;360"
dur="8s" repeatDur="indefinite" />
</use>
</g>
</g>
</svg>
```

Of the major browsers, only Netscape 6 has limited SVG support built in. To give SVG a test drive in a less limited environment, download the free Adobe SVG Viewer from `www.adobe.com/svg/viewer/install/main.html` (available for all platforms).

Note

Eventually, you'll be able to create SVG files from any major graphics application. As of this writing, Adobe Illustrator allows saving as SVG. To learn more about the official SVG specification, visit `www.w3.org/Graphics/SVG/Overview.htm8`.

Wireless Markup Language (WML)

Developed by the leading makers of PDAs, WML allows web pages to display on hand-held computers. Although it's not an official W3C standard language, WML has developed informally as a de facto standard for the handheld computer industry. As more people begin using PDAs for instant on-the-road web access, WML and WAP (Wireless Application Protocol) will become more important tools for all web authors. Various WAP emulation programs are available, enabling you to preview WML documents on desktop computers. Listing 32.4 shows the code for a sample WML page. Figure 32.2 shows how it will display in a WAP emulator.

Listing 32.4   Code for a Simple WML Document

```
<?xml version="1.0"?>
<!DOCTYPE wml PUBLIC "-//WAPFORUM//DTD WML 1.1//EN"
"http:www.wapforum.org/DTD/wml_1.1.xml">
<wml>
    <card id="main" title="My WAP.com">
        <do type="accept" label="Next">
            <go href="#wel"/>
        </do>
        <p>Please enter your name:
            <input type="text" name="user"/>
        </p>
    </card>
    <card id="wel" title="Welcome">
        <do type="prev" label="Back">
            <prev/>
        </do>
        <p>
            Welcome, $(user). Click Back to go to previous page.
        </p>
    </card>
</wml>
```

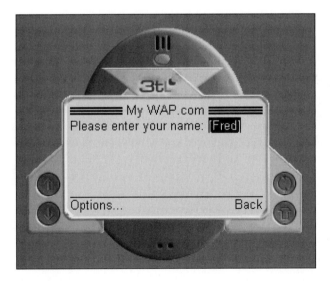

Figure 32.2   How the sample WML document shown in Listing 32.4 looks in a WAP
emulation program.

Note

There are all sorts of WAP emulators out there, including M3Gate (www.m3gate.com),
Deck-It Emulator (www.pyweb.com/tools/), and WinWap (www.winwap.org).

XHTML: The Next Step for HTML

It's the next great thing. It's here now. XHTML is the W3C's officially sanctioned successor to HTML. XHTML is basically HTML 4.01, rewritten as an XML-based language. The goal of XHTML is to promote "device-independent web authoring" for all web pages. The code for an HTML document and its XHTML counterpart might look almost identical, but the XHTML document can be repurposed for use by other software than browsers, in other devices than typical desktop computers. What's the difference? For strict XHTML compliance, the following rules apply:

- **DTDs are required.** An XHTML document must begin with a DTD statement, telling the browser or other application exactly what language is being used, and thus how to parse it.

- **XHTML documents must be well-formed and valid.** An XHTML document must follow the rules for XML syntax, as specified in the previous section, and can use only the legitimate tags and attributes that are part of XHTML. This means that no deprecated elements—such as <font>—are allowed.

- **No internal or inline CSS.** As discussed earlier in the section on XML, the goal is to separate structure and presentation formatting. That means the CSS information must be in a linked document.

- **No internal scripting.** For similar reasons, all JavaScript, VBScript, or other scripting statements must be in linked documents, not coded into the XHTML document itself.

To ease web authors into the rigors of XML, the W3C has also released an official specification for transitional XHTML, which has many of the same rules as strict XHTML but isn't so strict in enforcing them. (For more on Dreamweaver MX and XHTML, see Chapter 3.)

Note

There is a way around these last two prohibitions, by putting the CSS or scripting code inside CDATA declarations so that the XML parser will ignore them. It's a flawed workaround, however.

XHTML is the way of the future. Because it's extensible, special "dialects" can be written to meet specific needs. XHTML Basic, for instance, is the W3C's officially recommended language for PDAs, pagers, phones, and any other processor-limited Internet access device—replacing WML, which is a proprietary technology. XFORMS—a still-developing standard—allows for flexible, device-independent coding of forms.

Scripting Languages

Web scripting languages can be divided into those processed by the web server (server-side) and those downloaded to the user's computer and processed by the browser (client-side). The major server-side languages have already been covered in Chapter 26, "Introduction to Dynamic Dreamweaver," and its following chapters. This section looks at how client-side scripting works in Dreamweaver.

Client-side scripts can be embedded in the HTML document itself or saved in separate files and linked to the main document. In either case, they must download to the user's computer so the browser (client) can interpret and execute them. An embedded script can be placed inside the HTML using the <script> tag or can be quoted directly inside an event handler, using the name of the scripting language followed by a script statement. (See Chapter 11, "Working with Forms," for more on embedded JavaScript and using event handlers.)

Listing 32.5 shows various ways scripts can be embedded or linked within HTML. The most popular client-side scripting languages are JavaScript and Microsoft's JScript and VBScript.

Listing 32.5   Sample HTML Document Showing Several Ways Script Statements Can Be Embedded or Linked (Script-Related Code Shown in Bold)

```
<html>
<head>
<title>My Document</title>
<!--the following line links to an external script file, which contains
functions that can be called from this file-->
<script src="../MyScripts/external.js"></script>
<script type="text/jscript">
function testCommand() {
print("This script is written as a function, which can be called from
anywhere in the body, using an event handler. This function is called
from the <body> tag, using the onLoad event handler.");
}
</script>
</head>
<body onLoad="testCommand()">
<h1>Welcome to my Home Page!</h1>
<p>This document shows various ways client-side scripts can be inserted
into or linked to an HTML document. In XHTML, only linked scripts are
valid.</p>
<script language="JavaScript">
window.alert("This script is embedded in the body.");
</script>
<hr>
```

```
<p><a href="javascript:window.alert('This script is written directly in
the document code, using the javascript keyword.')">Click here to
execute an inline script statement.</a></p>
<p><a href="#" onClick="extFunction()">Click here</a> to execute a
function from the linked file "external.js"</p>
</body>
</html>
```

JavaScript

The most common client-side scripting language, JavaScript was originally developed by Netscape but has been adopted by other browsers. Dreamweaver behaviors are written in JavaScript. Note that JavaScript has no relationship to the Java programming language.

JScript

Very similar in syntax to JavaScript, JScript is a Microsoft scripting language for use in browsers and any other applications using Microsoft ActiveX or object linking and embedding (OLE) technologies. Among browsers, JScript works with Internet Explorer/Windows only.

VBScript

Microsoft's VBScript is a "lite" version of their Visual Basic programming language. As with JScript, it is closely tied to various Microsoft technologies, such as ActiveX, and works only with Internet Explorer/Windows.

Summary

The chapters in this section cover Dreamweaver from a coder's perspective, both inside and out. In Chapter 33, "Writing Code in Dreamweaver," you learn how you can use Dreamweaver to write the various kinds of scripting and markup language discussed in this chapter and what tools Dreamweaver provides to make that job easier. The remaining chapters cover how to work with Dreamweaver as code. Chapter 34 discusses how Dreamweaver itself is configured using JavaScript, HTML, and XML. Chapter 35, "Working with Extensions," explores the world of Dreamweaver extensions—chunks of script and markup that add to the program's functionality and enable you to affect its interface. Finally, in Chapter 36, "Creating Extensions," you learn how to write your own custom objects and commands, using either Dreamweaver or an external code editor. Affix your pocket protectors, put on your propeller-hats, and read on.

Chapter 33

Writing Code in Dreamweaver

Dreamweaver is a lot of things to a lot of people, but at heart it's a code-editing tool. This chapter examines the various code-writing features that make it a favorite program among the hand-coding and scripting crowd. This chapter reviews the Dreamweaver built-in text editor and covers how to make the most of it; how to facilitate working with Dreamweaver and external text editors, such as HomeSite and BBEdit; and how you can use Dreamweaver with more than just HTML, embracing various markup and scripting languages such as XML and JavaScript.

Using Dreamweaver as a Text Editor

The power of Dreamweaver has always been its close integration between visual and text-based editing. The program's built-in text editor, accessible through the Document window's Code view or the separate Code inspector panel, offers many features generally found only in dedicated text-editing programs. These include line numbers, word wrap control, syntax-based color coding, complex text searches utilizing regular expressions—and, new to Dreamweaver MX, several features adopted from HomeSite, such as code hints and tag completion. In addition, because the Dreamweaver text editor also is responsible for writing the code created when you work in Design view, it includes built-in source formatting and error-correction functions.

Accessing the Text Editor

You can access the Dreamweaver text editor from the main Document window by choosing Code view or Code and Design view. (For a full discussion of the Document window, see Chapter 2, "Setting Up the Dreamweaver Workspace.") Alternatively, you can open the text editor in its own tabbed panel window by accessing the Code inspector (go to Window > Others > Code inspector). All text-editing features work the same in both Code view and the Code inspector. If you're short on screen space, you'll probably want to use Code view (or Code and Design view) in the Document window. If you have a dual monitor setup at your workstation, you may prefer to display the Document window, set to Design view, on one monitor and the Code inspector, along with any other open panels, on the other monitor. Figure 33.1 shows Code view and the Code inspector, side-by-side for comparison.

Figure 33.1 The Dreamweaver built-in text editor as it appears in Code view in the main Document window (left) and in the separate Code inspector tabbed panel (right).

Code View Options

Options for setting up the text editor's workspace can be found in the Code View Options submenu (accessible from the View menu or from the Document window toolbar), and in the Preferences dialog box (Edit > Preferences). Figure 33.2 shows the Code View Options submenu for Code view. Note that choices made in the View > Code View Options submenu (left) will affect only the Document window's Code view, not the Code inspector.

Figure 33.2 The Code View Options submenu accessible from the toolbar in either the Code window or from the Document window's View menu.

Setting Text Size and Font

By default, all text in the code editor is displayed in 10-point Courier New (Windows) or 10-point Monaco (Macintosh). Because this text is used only for displaying code in Dreamweaver, you can change the size/font to anything that suits you without affecting your files at all.

Like some, you might prefer your code in the "large-print" format for easy onscreen reading without squinting. Or you might prefer to look at fonts other than Courier or Monaco. One bit of advice, however: Certain text-editing tasks, such as counting characters, are much easier to perform on monospaced fonts (such as Courier and Monaco) than on proportionally spaced fonts. One nice alternative you might have installed on your system is Microsoft's Andale Mono.

To change the text size or font of the code display, in the Preferences dialog box select the Fonts category (see Figure 33.3). Changes made here will affect both Code view and the Code inspector.

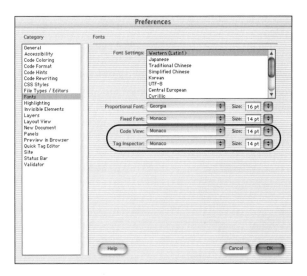

Figure 33.3   Setting the text size and font in the Preferences dialog box, Fonts/Encoding category.

Syntax Coloring

One of the most useful visual aids in text processing is syntax-based color coding. By setting certain code elements to certain colors, you can tell at a glance how a document is structured. Dreamweaver goes a step further than coloring, allowing you to set other styling attributes like bold, italic, and underlining to differentiate different syntax elements. You also can specify different formatting options for different document types (HTML, PHP, JS, and so forth).

To turn syntax coloring (and styling) on or off, go to the Code View Options menu (accessible in the toolbar or under the View menu) and select or deselect Syntax Coloring. Note that the Reference panel's context-based features will work only if syntax coloring is on. (See Chapter 3, "Creating and Working with Documents," for a full discussion of the Reference panel.) Also, keep in mind that the Code View Options menu command is only accessible when you are in the Code and Design view or in Code view.

To customize which elements are assigned which color and styling, open the Preferences dialog box and select the Code Coloring category (see Figure 33.4). Choose the document type whose styling you want to change, and click the Edit Coloring Scheme button. In the new dialog box that opens, choose any element from the list in the upper left; choose color and styling options from the options in the upper right; and check to see how your changes will look, in the preview area at the bottom of the panel (see Figure 33.4).

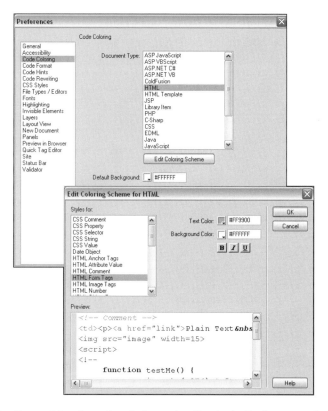

Figure 33.4   Customizing the code coloring and styling in the Preferences > Code Coloring dialog box and Edit Coloring Scheme dialog box.

Line Numbers

Line numbers are handy for finding exactly where something is happening in the code. They're mostly useful for web pages that involve scripting, as an aid to debugging (see "Scripting in Dreamweaver," later in this chapter, for more on this). Dreamweaver reports and invalid code warnings also use line numbers for identification.

To show or hide line numbers, go to the Code View Options menu (accessible in the toolbar or under the View menu) and select or deselect Line Numbers.

Word Wrap (Soft Wrapping)

Wrapping means sending text to a new line. In text processing terms, *soft wrapping* is something the text editor does on-the-fly to make the text fit in the window. The Dreamweaver code editor enables you to view your code with or without soft wrapping. Viewing code that has no wrapping often involves a lot of sideways scrolling to read long lines. Not being able to see an entire line at a time can make it more difficult to understand what's happening in the code. On the other hand, code displayed without wrapping more accurately conveys the overall structure of a document. Figure 33.5 shows the differences between code with and without soft wrapping.

Figure 33.5   HTML code fragment shown with (top) and without (bottom) soft wrapping.

To turn soft-wrapping on or off, go to the Code View Options menu and select or deselect Word Wrap. Note that if you work with line numbers showing, soft-wrap will not affect the numbering of lines, because the wrapping is a temporary visual convenience only. If you save a file created with soft wrapping on, and open it in another editor, no soft wraps will have been saved as part of the file.

Auto-Indenting

Indenting lines of code to indicate nested elements is another way to make the code more easily readable. Lines are indented by adding tabs or spaces. When you manually enter code into the Dreamweaver text editor, you indent your lines as you see fit. As you're typing, the Dreamweaver Auto-Indent feature automatically indents each new line to match the indent of the previous line. This is a handy timesaver if you're coding nested tags, where each tag's indent is based on the indent of previous tag.

To automatically indent each new line based on current indents, go to the Code View Options menu and select Auto-Indent.

Code Formatting Options

Although the Dreamweaver built-in code editor is in many ways comparable to other text-editing software, in one way it is unique. When you author in Design view, Dreamweaver is writing—and formatting—the source code for you. When you author in Code view, you are in charge of formatting your own source code. When (the most common scenario) you move freely between Code and Design view, or are using Code and Design view, you may write code that Dreamweaver will later edit and reformat. This is called *applying source formatting*. It's rather like having Mom looking over your shoulder as you work, tidying up after you, making sure you've indented properly, wrapped your text nicely, and so forth.

Dreamweaver will never rewrite your code—but will reformat it, if you allow. Dreamweaver automatically applies source formatting to a page element whenever that item is edited from within Design view. You can force the program to apply source formatting to an entire document by going to Commands > Apply Source Formatting.

Like Mom, this source formatting may be intrusive or helpful, depending on your point of view. You can turn the different aspects of source formatting on or off, and you can customize what kind of formatting is applied. Most of this customizing can be done in the Preferences dialog box, under the Code Format category (see Figure 33.6).

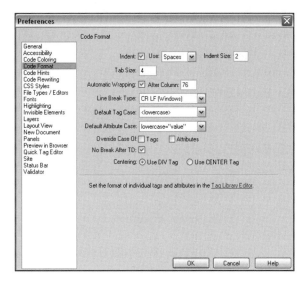

Figure 33.6   The Preferences dialog box showing the Code Format category.

Automatic Text Wrap (Hard Wrapping)

Hard wraps are returns coded into the text, using a carriage return (CR), line feed (LF), or both. As you're coding, every time you press the Return key you're hard wrapping. Just as you might use soft wrapping to make your code more readable, some web authors like to insert manual (hard) returns into the code to force line breaks for easier readability. When Dreamweaver is writing code (that is, when you're working in Design view), it will by default add hard wraps to avoid long lines of code. When you type your own code, you control the hard wraps by deciding when to type a Return. Even though you entered the code yourself, however, as soon as you edit it in Design view, or choose Commands > Apply Source Formatting, Dreamweaver will take over and add its own hard wraps wherever it finds excessively long lines.

> **Note**
>
> Hard wrap or soft wrap? If you rely on soft wrapping to display more readable code, switching between wrapped and unwrapped views is as simple as turning Word Wrap on and off. If you rely on hard wrapping, your code's line breaks are fixed unless you manually remove them. In addition, although hard wraps will not affect how a document will display on the web, CRs and LFs are characters and take up file space. Long documents can, therefore, take slightly longer to download if their coding contains many hard wraps.

To control automatic hard wrapping, open the Preferences > Code Format dialog box (see Figure 33.6). If the Automatic Wrapping option is disabled, no hard wraps will be added within a tag or text element, no matter how long the line becomes. If the option is enabled, you can specify how many characters Dreamweaver should allow in a line before it adds a hard wrap. Note that if you work with line numbers showing, hard wrapping will affect the line numbers because it is adding lines to the code. If you save a file created with hard wrapping on, and open it in another editor, the hard wraps will still be there. They are part of the file.

To determine how hard wraps are encoded, open the Preferences > Code Format dialog box and choose one of the Line Break options from the pop-up menu. This is important because different operating systems expect hard returns to be coded differently. Obviously, you want the web server where your pages will reside to recognize your hard wraps for what they are. If you will be uploading your pages using FTP set to ASCII Transfer mode, Dreamweaver takes care of this for you, coding each return character as needed based on the OS of the server. If you will be uploading your HTML documents using FTP set to Binary mode, you must set the correct return character yourself, before uploading.

Indenting

Do you like your code indented? How large an indent do you prefer? Do you want your indents made from tab or space characters? The controls in the Preferences > Code Format dialog box determine how and when Dreamweaver will indent your code during source formatting, as follows:

- **Indent or don't indent.** To turn indenting off completely, so all new lines are flush left, deselect the Use option. Selecting the Use option will enable all other choices controlling indentation.

- **Tabs/spaces.** You can specify whether indents should be created from tab characters or multiple spaces. Generally, spaces are preferable unless you plan to import your text to a word processing program for eventual printing.

- **Indent size.** Determines how many spaces or tabs each indent will be.

- **Tab size.** Determines, in characters, how big each tab will be. (If you tell Dreamweaver to calculate your indents in tabs, and set the indent size to 2 and the tab size to 3, each indent will be 6 characters wide.)

Case Control

Standard HTML browsers aren't case-sensitive when interpreting HTML. But any browser or other device that uses XML or XHTML validation is case-sensitive. In addition, many web authors prefer their code to be written consistently in one case (upper or lower).

To specify a case for code that Dreamweaver writes, in the Preferences > Code Format dialog box set the Default Tag Case and Default Attribute Case (refer back to Figure 33.6).

To have Dreamweaver change the case of existing code during source formatting, choose one or both of the Override Case Of options.

Code Rewriting

Dreamweaver promises never ever, ever to rewrite your code. However, it will warn you about, and optionally try to fix, invalid code. Invalid code consists mainly of incorrectly nested or closed tags, such as the following:

```
<b><i>This is bad nesting! </b></i>

<h1>I have too many tags!</h1></h1>

<h6>I'm missing something...
```

How Error Checking Works

To display or hide warnings for invalid code, go to the View > Code View Options menu and select or deselect Highlight Invalid HTML. (Note that this option governs only the various Code views. Dreamweaver always highlights invalid HTML in Design view.)

To allow Dreamweaver to fix invalid code, open the Preferences > Code Rewriting dialog box and set options as desired there (see Figure 33.7).

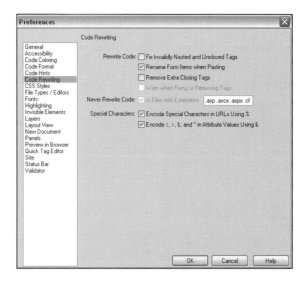

Figure 33.7   The Preferences > Code Rewriting dialog box.

To exclude file types from error checking, go to the Preferences > Code Rewriting dialog box and add the file extension to the Never Rewrite Code options list. Each new file extension must be separated from others in the list by spaces on either side.

Strategies for Using Error Checking

Dreamweaver performs its error checking, and optional error fixing, whenever a document is opened. If you have set your preferences to Warn When Fixing or Removing Tags, at this point Dreamweaver will open an alert window specifying any invalid code found and how it has been fixed. If you haven't turned the warning feature on, you won't even be aware that code is being rewritten.

Why would you want to turn warnings on? Although fixing invalid code is, in theory, a good thing, Dreamweaver isn't always perfect in determining what the desired valid code should look like. For instance, here's a segment of code with a missing </h1> tag:

```
<html>
<head>
<title>My Page</title>
</head>
<body bgcolor="#FFFFFF" text="#000000">
<h1>My Home Page
<p>Welcome to my wonderful website.</p>
</body>
</html>
```

Where should the closing tag be inserted? Directly in front of the <p> tag, probably. Here's where Dreamweaver inserts it:

```
<html>
<head>
<title>My Page</title>
</head>
<body bgcolor="#FFFFFF" text="#000000">
<h1>My Home Page
<p>Welcome to my wonderful website.</p>
</h1></body>
</html>
```

This is definitely an occasion when author intervention is needed to correct the Dreamweaver error correction. Figure 33.8 shows the warning message that will appear when Dreamweaver opens a document containing this code.

Note that the Dreamweaver alert window doesn't give you the opportunity to cancel the code rewriting. If you don't like any of the changes that have been made to your code, you can isolate them (by turning on line numbering in the code editor and using the line references from the alert message) and fix them; or you can just close the document without saving and all changes will be ignored. From there, either open the document in another text editor or open the Preferences > Code Rewriting dialog box and temporarily disable the rewriting features.

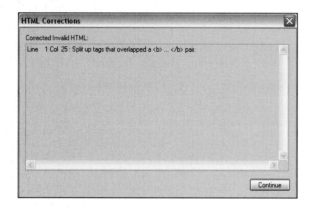

Figure 33.8   The Dreamweaver alert window listing invalid code that has been fixed in a document.

Code Writing and Editing

In addition to helping you format your code for readability and display, the Dreamweaver text editor offers a variety of tools to make working with the code easier.

Editing Commands and Shortcuts

If you like working with code, presumably you like typing. A few commands under the Edit menu, each with its own keyboard shortcut, can keep you typing instead of reaching for the mouse while you work. Table 33.1 shows these commands.

Table 33.1   Code-Editing Commands

Command	Keystroke		Description
	Windows	*Macintosh*	
Select parent tag	Ctrl+Shift+<	Cmd+Shift+<	Select any tag completely nesting the current selection.
Select child	Ctrl+Shift+>	Cmd+Shift+>	Select the first tag nested within the currently selected tag.
Indent code	Ctrl+]	Cmd+]	Increase the indent level of a selected line by one.
Outset code	Ctrl+[	Cmd+[	Reduce the indent level of a selected line by one.

MX

Code Hints and Auto Tag Completion

If you like working with code, but don't think doing all that typing is very efficient, Dreamweaver offers a variety of time- and keystroke-saving tools, including the brand-new Code Hints and Auto Tag Completion features.

Auto Tag Completion engages every time you type the opening tag of a pair, causing Dreamweaver to automatically type the closing tag, leaving the insertion point between the two tags. Type **<p>** and get </p>, and your cursor is correctly positioned to type the text you want between the two tags (see Figure 33.9). If you've ever forgotten to type that closing tag, then wondered why your page wouldn't preview properly, this is the feature for you!

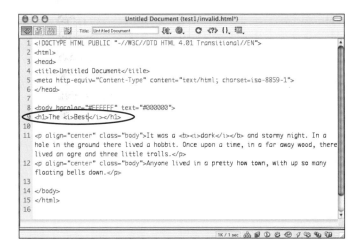

Figure 33.9   Auto Tag Completion at work creating an italic section of a page heading.

Code Hints is a more wide-ranging and configurable feature. It engages every time you type the opening characters of a tag, offering drop-down menus of possible tags, attributes, and even attribute values (see Figure 33.10). The hints aren't just for reference, either. You can navigate through and choose from any menu without moving your hands from the keyboard, for maximum efficiency. The main techniques for navigating the hint menus are as follows:

- By default, the first item in the hint menu is selected. To move down or up in the list, use the arrow keys on your keyboard.

- Menus containing lists of text items are arranged alphabetically. To jump to a particular place in the list, type the first letter of the item you want to select. Keep typing more letters to get closer to your desired selection.

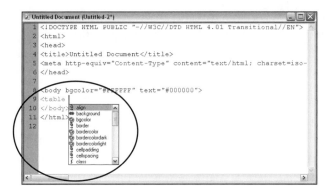

Figure 33.10   Code Hints at work presenting a menu of possible attributes for the `<table>` tag.

- Depending on the values expected for an attribute, different hint menus will appear. If the expected value is a color, the color palette will appear (use the arrow keys to navigate through the swatches). If the expected value is a relative file path, a menu containing only a browse option will appear (press Return/Enter to open a browse dialog box). If the expected value is unspecified text or a number, no code hint will appear. Figure 33.11 shows the color palette code hint menu.

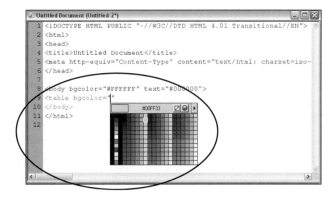

Figure 33.11   Using Code Hints to choose a color value for the `bgcolor` attribute.

- To choose a selected item, and have Dreamweaver enter it in your code for you, hit Return or Enter. The item will be inserted, and your insertion point positioned to continue typing.

To configure Auto Tag Completion and Code Hints, open the Preferences > Code Hints dialog box (see Figure 33.12). From here, you can enable or disable either feature. You also can configure the following aspects of Code Hints:

- The *Delay* slider determines how quickly after you type the menus of code hints will appear. With a delay of 0, each hint menu will appear immediately. With a longer delay, the menus won't appear unless you stop typing for the specified number of seconds. If you don't like those hint menus popping up all over the place, but still want to take advantage of them the next time you get stuck or feel lazy, set the delay to a few seconds, and see how you like it.

- The list of *Menus* determines which code hint menus will appear. Do you want Dreamweaver to finish typing tag names for you, or just to suggest attributes? Do you want suggestions for each attribute's value, where appropriate? (To edit the contents of the hint menus, you can click the link to the Tag Library Editor. Read all about this wonderful new MX feature later in this chapter.)

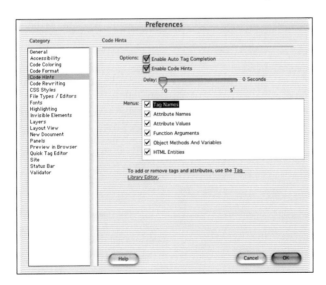

Figure 33.12   The Preferences dialog box showing the Code Hints category, which governs Code Hints and Auto Tag Completion.

Inserting Objects in Code View

Even though you're working in Code view, don't forget that you can use the Insert bar (and its partner, the Insert menu) while in Code view. In fact, new to Dreamweaver MX are a variety of objects and tabs in the Insert bar that especially appropriate to working in Code view. Though all of these objects are also available from within Design view, choosing them either inserts code that doesn't show up in Design view or switches the focus to Code view for further editing. Table 33.2 lists these items and their functionality.

Table 33.2   Useful Objects for Working in Code View

Tab	Object	Description/Result of Insertion
Common	Tag Chooser	Opens the Tag Chooser dialog box, from which any tag in the Tag Library can be inserted into the document. Switches focus to Code view.
Text	Font tag editor	Opens the Font tag editor dialog box for inserting and configuring the `<font>` tag. Inserts a tag pair around the current selection.
	`<b>`, `<i>`, `<strong>`, `<em>`	Various objects for inserting character formatting (bold, italic, strong, emphasis). Inserts a tag pair around the current selection.
	`<p>`, `<blockquote>`, `<pre>`	Objects for inserting block-level formatting (paragraph, block quote, pre-formatted text). Inserts a tag pair around the current selection.
	`<h1>`, `<h2>`, `<h3>`	Objects for inserting the most commonly used heading levels. Inserts a tag pair around the current selection.
	`<ul>`, `<ol>`, `<li>`	Objects for inserting lists (unordered list, ordered list, list item). Inserts a tag pair around the current selection.
	`<dl>`, `<dt>`, `<dd>`	Objects for inserting definitions (definition list, definition term, definition description). Inserts a tag pair around the current selection.
	`<abbr>`, `<acronym>`	Objects for inserting abbreviations and acronyms. Inserts a tag pair around the current selection.
Tables	Table	The standard Table object, found also in the Common tab. Same as using Common Table object, inserts table code framework.
	`<table>`, `<tr>`, `<th>`, `<td>`, `<cap>`	Objects for inserting specific tag pairs that go into the construction of a table. Switches focus to Code view, inserts a tag pair wrapping current selection. Each object by itself inserts an incomplete piece of table code.

Tab	Object	Description/Result of Insertion
Forms	Label	Inserts the `<label></label>` tag pair around the current selection.
	Fieldset	Inserts the `<fieldset><legend>...</legend></fieldset>` nested tag set around the current selection.
Media	`<param>`	Inserts a generic parameters tag, suitable for use with the `<object>` or `<applet>` tag, with this syntax: `<param name="name" value="value">`. Switches focus to Code view.
Script	`<noscript>`	Opens the tag editor dialog box for the `<noscript>` tag. Switches focus to Code view.

These various Code view objects imply a different working strategy than the editing commands and code hints described above. While it is possible to assign shortcut keys to objects, for the most part, inserting objects means using the mouse to choose from the Insert bar or menu. The other tools described in this section are aimed mainly at keeping your fingers on the keyboard away from the mouse. If you like working with dialog boxes and mouse clicks, even while you're working in Code view, don't forget that you can access the tag editor from within Code view by putting the cursor within a tag and choosing Modify > Edit Tag. (See Chapter 3 for a full discussion of the tag editor.)

If you like using objects, but would still rather type than use the mouse, you can use shortcuts and keyboard navigation techniques to get back to the keyboard. Do it like this:

- Use the Edit > Keyboard Shortcuts command to assign shortcuts to any commonly used items in the Insert menu. (See Chapter 34, "Customizing Dreamweaver," for a full discussion of customizing keyboard shortcuts.)

- Use keyboard commands (Tab, arrow, Return) to navigate through any dialog boxes.

- Use the pre-assigned Ctrl/Cmd+F5 keyboard shortcut to access the tag editor dialog box as needed.

This level of keyboard access is part of Macromedia's commitment to accessibility in the Dreamweaver MX interface. For more on accessibility issues relevant to the end-user and web design, see Chapter 3.

Code Snippets

Snippets, a new feature in Dreamweaver MX, allow you to save frequently needed chunks of code and insert them into a document with a few mouse clicks. Snippets can be used to store anything from comments to formatting wrapped around a selection to entire tables and page layouts.

Using the Snippets Panel

Snippets are created, organized, and inserted using the Snippets panel, which is part of the Code panel group. Access this panel by going to Window > Snippets, or by expanding the docked panel interface to view the Code panels and bringing the Snippets tab to the front. Figure 33.13 shows the Snippets panel in all its glory. Dreamweaver ships with a wide selection of snippets ready for you to use.

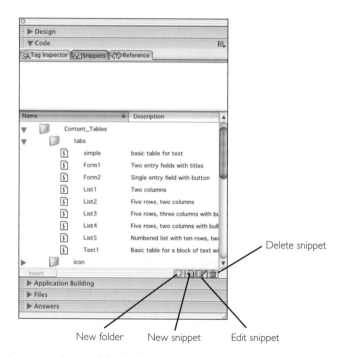

Figure 33.13   The Snippets panel, part of the Code panel group.

Inserting Snippets

You can insert a snippet into a document by drag-and-drop or by selecting the snippet and clicking the Insert button at the bottom of the panel. You will, however, want to investigate what code the snippet contains and how it will be inserted, before trying to use it.

Inserting in Code Versus Design View

Because a snippet can contain any portion of code, including incomplete tags and tags that must be nested inside other tags, not all snippets can be inserted everywhere. Some snippets can be inserted into Design view; others may require that you be in Code view before inserting. Some can be inserted as nested content inside tables, or other tags; others may not. The Meta > No-Cache snippet, for instance, can only be inserted while Code view is active; if Code view is active, it will insert at the current insertion point, wherever that is—regardless of whether the insertion point is in the `<head>` or the `<body>` section, or even in the middle of another tag. Obviously, you need to know where `<meta>` tags can and cannot go, before using this snippet.

Inserting Block Versus Wrapped Snippets

Most snippets insert a single block of code—a table, a set of form elements, a `<meta>` tag. Some snippets insert two blocks of code, wrapped around whatever you currently have selected when you insert them. The various Comments snippets, for instance, can be used to "comment out" any selected page element by wrapping it in `<!-- -->` comment tags. If you have nothing selected when you insert a comment snippet, Dreamweaver will insert an empty pair of comment tags into your document.

Editing Snippets

Snippets are easy to edit. In the Snippets panel, either select a snippet and click the Edit button, or double-click the snippet itself, to open the Snippet dialog box (shown in Figure 33.14). You can change any snippet's name, description, type (block or wrapped), as well as editing the code the snippet will insert. You can also determine how the snippet will be previewed within the Snippets panel.

Warning

There's nothing stopping you from entering invalid code into a snippet. If you break one of the Dreamweaver default snippets by fiddling with its code, the only way to restore the undamaged snippet is by re-installing Dreamweaver or tinkering around inside the Dreamweaver **Configuration** folder (another inherently dangerous activity).

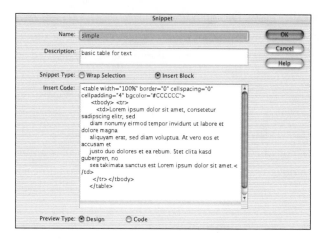

Figure 33.14   The Snippet dialog box, for creating and editing snippets.

Snippet Housekeeping

Snippets are organized in folders, some of which are nested inside other folders. You can rearrange this hierarchy as you like by dragging and dropping snippets and folders. You can rename snippets by editing them. You can rename folders by double-clicking them. You can even delete snippets or folders by selecting them and clicking the trash icon at the bottom of the panel (see Figure 33.13).

Creating Your Own Snippets

The best feature of snippets is that you can easily create your own snippets, and even your own folders to store them in.

To create a new snippet folder, do this:

1. If you want your folder to appear at the root level of the Snippets panel, start by deselecting any other folders in the Snippets panel. If you want your folder to be nested inside an existing folder, select that folder.

2. Click the Folder icon at the bottom of the panel (see Figure 33.13). Your new folder will appear.

3. Name your folder! It's ready for action.

To create a new snippet, do this:

1. Optional: If you already have the chunk of code that the snippet should contain, open the document containing that code and select it in Code view.

2. In the Snippets panel, select the folder that you want to contain the new snippet.

3. Click the new Snippet icon at the bottom of the panel (see Figure 33.13). This will create a new, untitled snippet and will automatically open the Snippet dialog box. If you had code selected, it will appear in the Content field—otherwise, type it in now. (You can't create an empty snippet!)

4. If you're creating a wrapped snippet (a snippet that inserts code before and after any selection), make sure the proper portions of code are in the Before and After fields.

5. Fill in all the other options of the dialog box, and click OK. Your snippet will now appear in the Snippets panel and will behave just like any other snippet. You can insert it, edit it, delete it, move it around—whatever you like.

Exercise 33.1   Creating a Simple Page Layout Using Code Tools Only

In this exercise, you'll create a fairly simple document using only the coding tools in Dreamweaver. While you're at it, you'll customize your working environment for working efficiently with code—and you'll see how Code view and its tools can help you learn more about HTML, even if you've always designed more visually in the past.

1. Create a new document. Save it as **generic_order.html**. To take full advantage of Code view for coding and Design view for previewing, do one of the following (depending on your available screen real estate): In the Document window, go to Split Code and Design view; or set the Document window to Design view and open the Code inspector. Either way, you want to see your design happening as you code it.

   Before starting work, you'll set some preferences. In the Code View Options menu, turn off Word Wrap. Turn on Line Numbering, Highlight Invalid HTML, Syntax Coloring, and Auto-Indent. In the Preferences dialog box, go to the Fonts category and choose whatever font and size you would like for viewing your code. Finally, make sure code hints and auto tag completion are enabled (Preferences > Code Hints).

   Figure 33.15 shows the document layout you're trying to create, as it will appear in Design view. This will require you to create a form containing a table with three rows and two columns, with the cells in the bottom row set to span two columns. Working on the code only, but using Design view for a preview, you'll create this.

Figure 33.15   The desired layout for **generic_order.html**, as it will look in Design view.

2. With Code view active, start by entering a pair of form tags in the body of the document. Type **<form>** and Dreamweaver will insert the closing tag for you. So now you have a pair of tags, with the cursor in between them, ready to continue.

3. Now you'll start building the table that goes in the form, using the various objects in the Tables tab of the Insert bar.

   From the Insert bar, select the Tables Tab and click the tabl button. Now your code should look like this, with the cursor right in the middle:

   ```
   <form><table></table></form>
   ```

   From the Insert bar, click the <tr> object. That adds a row within your table. Press Return to create a new line between the <tr></tr> tags. You'll do the rest using hand coding and hints.

4. Start creating the <td> tag, by typing **<td** followed by a space. As soon as you type a space following the tag name, the Code Hints menu will appear, showing a list of attributes for this tag. Using the down arrow key on your keyboard, select the align attribute and press Return/Enter.

   Now a Code Hints menu appears, listing the possible values for the attribute. Use the arrow keys to select right, and press Return/Enter. Your code should now look like this:

   ```
   <form><table><tr>
   <td align="right"
   </tr></table></form>
   ```

   Continue typing and choosing from hints until your code looks like this:

   ```
   <form><table><tr>
   <td align="right" valign="baseline" nowrap>Lorem ipsum:</td>
   </tr></table></form>
   ```

5. Continue the above process, using the Table objects, hand coding and hints, until your code contains all of the following elements (don't worry about where the line breaks occur, for now—just get the tags and attributes in place):

   ```
   <form>
   <table>
   <tr>
   <td align="right" valign="baseline" nowrap>Lorem ipsum:</td>
   <td align="left" valign="baseline"><input type="text"
   name="text"></td>
   ```

```
</tr>
<tr>
<td></td>
<td align="left" valign="baseline" nowrap>
<input type="checkbox" name="check"></td>
</tr>
<tr>
<td align="right" colspan="2"><input type="submit" value="Submit"></td>
</tr>
</table>
</form>
```

6. When you've got your code completed, the line breaks and indents probably make it a little bit hard to read. Go to Commands > Apply Source Formatting. Everything is now lined up and arranged, in readable format! (See Figure 33.16.) Save your file, and pat yourself on the back.

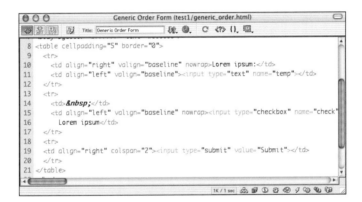

Figure 33.16   Final form code for **generic_order.html** with source formatting applied.

Exercise 33.2   Creating and Inserting Snippets

In this exercise, you'll turn elements of the **generic_order.html** document into snippets, so you can easily use them to construct other documents.

1. Open the **generic_order.html** file you created in the previous exercise. Work in Code and Design view, or in Design view with the Code inspector visible, so you can see code and design at once.

2. Open the Snippets panel (expand the Code panel group, or go to Window > Snippets). You want to create a new folder to hold your practice snippets. Select the **Content_Tables** folder, and click the New Folder icon at the bottom of the panel. Name your new folder **Practice** (see Figure 33.17).

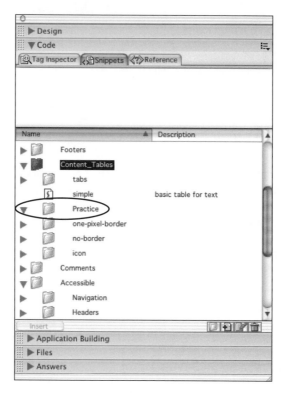

Figure 33.17   Creating a **Practice** snippets folder, in the Snippets panel.

3. You're going to create a snippet for each type of table row in the layout, complete with its form element contents. If you create a lot of similar form layouts, this can be a terrific time-saver.

   First, you'll create a snippet from the row containing your right-aligned label and left-aligned text field. In Design view, using the tag selector, or in Code View, select the code for the top row of the table:

   ```
   <tr>
   <td align="right" valign="baseline" nowrap>Lorem ipsum:</td>
   <td align="left" valign="baseline"><input type="text" name="text"></td>
   </tr>
   ```

   With that code selected, go to the Snippets panel and select the **Practice** folder. Then click the New Snippet icon at the bottom of the panel (see Figure 33.18).

Figure 33.18   Creating a new snippet from selected code.

The Snippets dialog opens. Your code should already be in place. (If it's not, you'll have to type it in by hand.) Set the dialog box options to match those shown in Figure 33.19. This will create a block type snippet called TextFieldRow. When you're done, click OK. There's your snippet in the **Practice** folder!

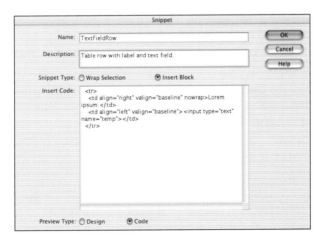

Figure 33.19   The Edit Snippet dialog box for the new TextFieldRow snippet.

4. Repeat the above process to make snippets for the row containing the checkbox and the row containing the submit button. Call them **CheckboxRow** and **SubmitRow**.

5. The final snippet you'll make contains the `<form>` and `<table>` tags that should enclose the other tags. Because this is a simple snippet, you can create it entirely in the Edit Snippets dialog box.

With no code selected, create a new snippet. Set the options to match those shown in Figure 33.20. This will create a wrapped snippet called FormTable, which will contain selected text in a `<form>` and `<table>` tag.

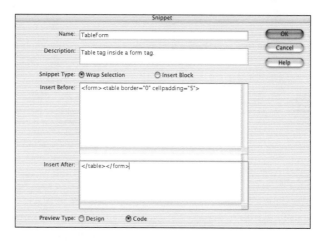

Figure 33.20   The Edit Snippet dialog box for the FormTable snippet.

6. It's time to try those snippets out! Create a new HTML document, and have your snippets panel open and ready. You'll start by inserting the various cell snippets. Then you'll wrap the whole lot in the TableForm snippet.

To start, go to Design view in the new Document. Select the TextFieldRow snippet, and click the Insert button in the Snippets panel. Nothing happens! That's because Dreamweaver won't let you insert incomplete code into Design view, and a `<td>` tag on its own is definitely incomplete code.

Now go to Code view, and put the insertion point between the `<body></body>` tags. Select the LabelCell snippet, and click Insert. There's your code!

The goal of this part of the exercise is to use snippets to create a slightly fancier version of the **generic_order.html** form. Examine the layout shown in Figure 33.21. Can insert snippets to create that layout? Start by inserting the row snippets, in order. Then select all the code for all table rows, and insert the FormTable snippet.

Figure 33.21   A more complex layout assembled from the snippets created from **generic_order.html**.

Linking to External Text Editors

So, you like working with code, and you like Dreamweaver, but you prefer your favorite text editor to the Dreamweaver Code view. You can set up a link between Dreamweaver and your external text editor and have the best of both worlds. For both Windows and Macintosh, you have the choice of standard integration with any text editor you choose, or the special options of an integrated HTML editor (HomeSite+ for Windows, or BBEdit for Mac OS 9/X).

Setting Up an External Text Editor (Non-Integrated)

The procedure for linking to and working with an external text editor other than HomeSite or BBEdit is simple and is basically the same across platforms.

To set up integration with an external editor, follow these steps:

1. In the Preferences dialog box, access the File Types/Editors category (see Figure 33.22).

2. (Mac only) Find and deselect the Enable BBEdit Integration option.

3. Browse to select the text editor of your choice.

   The Reload Modified Files option determines what will happen when you have edited a document in an external editor and are then returning to Dreamweaver. For more seamless integration, choose Always Reload; the changes will be incorporated automatically. For more control over possible discrepancies that might occur between programs, choose Prompt; Dreamweaver will warn you that changes have been made.

   The Save on Launch option determines whether Dreamweaver will save a document before launching an external text editor. Again, for more seamless integration, choose Always. If you want to be given the chance to review document changes before saving, choose Prompt.

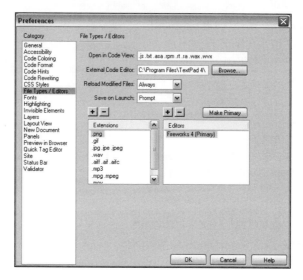

Figure 33.22   The Preferences > File Types/Editors dialog box showing options for enabling an external text editor.

Your chosen editor will appear in the Edit menu, as part of the Edit with *application* menu command (see Figure 33.23). Choose this option to open your current document in the new editor.

Figure 33.23   The Edit menu ready for integration with the TextPad text editor.

Text Editors, Beyond HomeSite and BBEdit

Many people already have a favorite text editor. No matter what your platform, if you're in the market for a newer, better, more intuitive editor, you have all sorts of choices from freeware to commercial.

Windows

If you're using Dreamweaver/Windows, you're probably using HomeSite+, because it comes bundled with Dreamweaver MX. But plenty of other choices exist, if you prefer. Some web authors like the no-frills familiarity of Notepad. Others prefer more powerful shareware alternatives like UltraText, TextPad, or CuteHTML. A search through www.download.com will present a dozen more alternatives.

Macintosh

BBEdit is definitely the king of Mac text editors, but if you're not ready to pay for this commercial software, you still have several good choices. BBEdit Lite, the freeware little brother to BBEdit, is a great alternative for OS 9 users. Pepper, the popular UNIX-based text editor, is now available as shareware for OS X. And, of course, there's always SimpleText for the true minimalists among us.

Integrating HomeSite+ and Dreamweaver (Windows)

As its name indicates, Macromedia's HomeSite+ for Dreamweaver MX integrates easily and tightly with Dreamweaver.

To set up HomeSite integration in Dreamweaver, follow the steps outlined earlier for linking to an external editor.

You also can set up Dreamweaver integration in HomeSite. By default, HomeSite should have integration enabled. In HomeSite, go to Options > Settings and choose the Dreamweaver category to check this and to configure how HomeSite will treat modified files' other options.

To edit a Dreamweaver document in HomeSite, open a document in Dreamweaver and go to Edit > Edit with HomeSite. That program will launch, if it's not already running, and your document will open for editing.

To edit a HomeSite document in Dreamweaver, open a document in HomeSite and on the Editing toolbar click the Dreamweaver icon (see Figure 33.24).

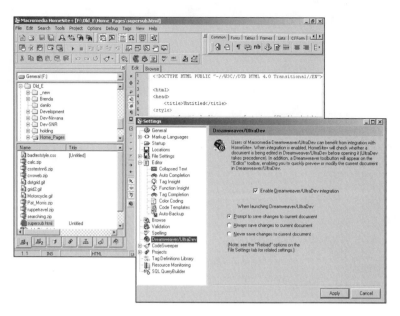

Figure 33.24   The HomeSite interface with Dreamweaver integration features highlighted.

If you have enabled both programs to automatically reload modified files and save before launching, and if you have a large monitor or dual-monitor setup at your workstation, you can leave the same document open in both programs and work back and forth fairly seamlessly, almost like working with the Code inspector.

Integrating BBEdit and Dreamweaver (Macintosh)

Dreamweaver/Mac includes very tight integration with BBEdit, unlike anything available for any other editor on either platform. If both of these applications are present on your system, integration between the two is automatically enabled; no setup is necessary.

To edit a Dreamweaver document in BBEdit, open a document in Dreamweaver, and go to Edit > Edit with BBEdit. That program will launch, if it's not already running, and come to the front, and your document will open for editing.

To edit a BBEdit document in Dreamweaver, open a document in BBEdit, and go to Markup > HTML Tools Palette to open the palette. From the palette, find and click the Dreamweaver button (see Figure 33.25).

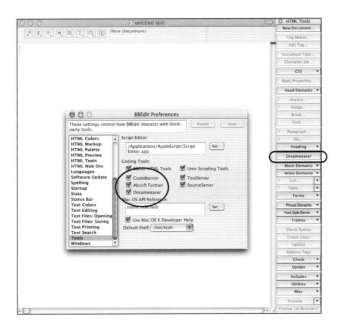

Figure 33.25   The BBEdit interface with Dreamweaver integration features highlighted.

Any code you have selected in Dreamweaver will be selected in BBEdit, and vice versa. Any changes made on a document in one program will be immediately visible in the other, as soon as that program is activated. If you have a large monitor or dual-monitor setup at your workstation, you can leave the same document open in both programs, and work back and forth seamlessly, almost like working with the Code inspector.

Tag Libraries and the Tag Library Editor

Tag libraries are at the heart of Dreamweaver functionality. A *tag library* is a database of information about a set of tags—HTML tags, ASP tags, ColdFusion tags, and so on. In that database is the information that Dreamweaver uses to perform most of its tag-related tasks, from populating code hint menus, to applying source formatting, to generating the information presented in the Tag Chooser and Edit tag editor boxes.

The Tag Library Editor is your window to the tag libraries, and your tool for editing and adding to the information stored there. Has the latest version of Internet Explorer started supporting a tag or attribute that Dreamweaver doesn't know about? Add it to the library! Do you just hate the way Dreamweaver indents table code, or where it inserts line breaks between tabs? Change the library! And it's all done with the Tag Library Editor.

Using the Tag Library Editor Dialog Box

Before you can start tinkering with tag libraries, you need to know what information and options are available to you through the Tag Library Editor dialog box. To open the Tag Library Editor, choose Edit > Tag Libraries. As Figures 33.26 and 33.27 show, the interface contains a wealth of nested information.

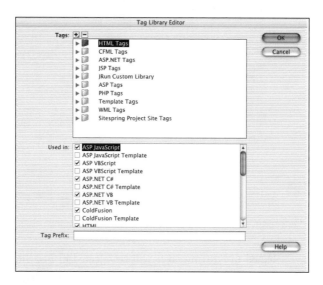

Figure 33.26   The Tag Library Editor dialog box showing all the tag libraries in the Dreamweaver database.

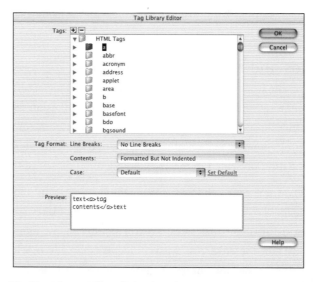

Figure 33.27   The Tag Library Editor dialog box showing settings for individual tags within a library.

The Tags List

The upper half of the dialog box is taken up by the tags list, an expandable tree structure showing all tag libraries, the tags they contain, and the attributes of those tags. The tag libraries (see Figure 33.26) are shown in the order in which Dreamweaver searches them for tag information. In other words, when Dreamweaver is determining how to handle a certain tag, only if that tag does not exist in the HTML library does Dreamweaver search for it in the ColdFusion and other libraries. Within each library (see Figure 33.27), the individual tags and attributes are listed in alphabetical order.

Tag Library Options

If you have a tag library selected in the tags list, the bottom half of the dialog box displays a list of document types that might contain tags in that library (see Figure 33.26). This doesn't mean that Dreamweaver will only allow certain tags in certain document types—but it does mean that tags in a certain library will only be meaningful to Dreamweaver within those document types. For instance, within a JavaScript document, HTML tags like <a> or <table> are meaningless. Dreamweaver won't provide code hints or other code editing help to those tags in that context.

Tag Options

When a tag is selected in the tags list, the bottom half of the dialog box displays Tag Format options for that tag (see Figure 33.27). These options include:

- **Line Breaks.** Should Dreamweaver insert a hard return in the code before and/or after the tag, or between a tag pair and its nested contents? The options in this pop-up menu determine that.

- **Contents.** Should any contents nested within a tag pair be indented beyond the tag's indentation, and should the contents be formatted? Choose from this menu to determine that.

- **Case.** Should the tag be uppercase, lowercase, or mixed case? Or should it follow an application-wide default? (Click the Default link to establish the default case for all tags.)

The Preview area, at the bottom of the dialog box, shows the results of whatever formatting options have been chosen for the current tag.

Attribute Options

When a tag attribute is selected in the tags list, the bottom half of the dialog box displays formatting options for that attribute (see Figure 33.28). These options include:

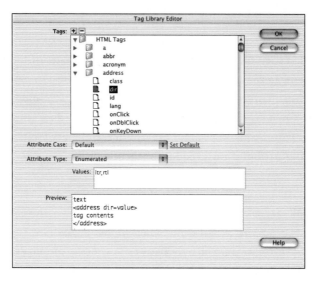

Figure 33.28   The Tag Library Editor dialog box showing settings for an individual tag attribute.

- **Attribute Case.** As with tags, case can be set to upper case, lower case, or mixed case for each individual attribute, or the attribute can use an application-wide default for all attributes. (Click the Default link to establish the default case.)

- **Attribute Type.** The option selected from this pop-up menu determines what kind of help will be available to users—in the form of code hints and Tag Inspector options, for instance—when working with this attribute. If Dreamweaver is expecting a text value, for instance, no code hint will be given; if a color value is expected, the color palette will appear; if an enumerated value is expected, a list of possible choices will appear in the Code Hint menu. Table 33.3 lists the attribute types, and their results for how the attribute will be treated in the Dreamweaver interface.

Table 33.3   Possible Attribute Types for Entries in a Tag Library

Attribute Type	Description	Code Hints
Text	Any text can be entered	(none)
Enumerated	Select values only are acceptable	Menu populated with comma-separated list entered in the Attribute Value field
Color	Color name or hexadecimal color value	Color palette
Directory	Absolute URL for a directory	Menu of protocols: ftp://, http://, and so forth

Attribute Type	Description	Code Hints
File Name	Absolute URL for a file	Menu of protocols: ftp://, http://, and so forth
File Path	Absolute URL for a file	Menu of protocols: ftp://, http://, and so forth
Flag	No value at all; the mere presence of the attribute is the flag (for example, the nowrap attribute for table cells)	(none)
Font	One or more fonts	Menu of defined font lists
Relative Path	Relative URL	Browse option
Style	CSS or other style name	(none)

- **Attribute Value**. If the attribute type is set to Enumerated, this input area should hold a comma-delimited list of possible values. These will become the entries in the Code Hint menu.

Editing Tag Library Entries

As you have probably figured out by now, you can change any setting for any library, tag, or attribute, simply by selecting the desired item in the tags list and changing the settings that appear. A few tips on making changes:

- You can't do too much serious damage to Dreamweaver, just by changing the line break or capitalization settings for tags; but you can make features like code hints unusable for certain attributes if you aren't careful with your settings. Proceed with caution.

- Don't override the default case of tags and attributes unless you have good reason to. The application-wide default becomes meaningless when most of the elements involved override it.

- Try your changes out, to see how you like them! After you've changed a formatting option, try creating and editing some samples of the changed tags in Code view. How do the code hints work? What happens when you apply source formatting? If you don't like it, go back to the Tag Library Editor and change things back.

Note

Tag Library information is stored in the Dreamweaver application folder, in various files within the **Configuration/Tag Libraries** folder. To make absolutely sure you don't do any lasting damage to your copy of Dreamweaver, take a moment to make a backup copy of the **Tag Libraries** folder before doing any serious tinkering. That way, if disaster strikes and you make a change that impairs your Dreamweaver, you can simple delete the damaged **Tag Library** folder and replace it with your backup copy.

Adding (and Removing) Entries

Adding and removing attributes, tags, and even entire libraries is a little bit more complex (and can be a lot more dangerous!) than editing existing entries. But it's also where the true customizable power of Dreamweaver tag libraries comes to your aid. All adding and removing can be done with the plus (+) and minus (–) buttons at the top of the Tag Library Editor dialog box.

Adding a Tag Library

To create a new, empty tag library, do this:

1. Click the plus (+) button at the top of the tags list, and choose New Tag Library from the pop-up menu.

2. In the dialog box that appears, give your new library a name. (This name is for your benefit only, so be descriptive and concise.)

3. Click OK to close the dialog box, and you'll see your new library at the bottom of the tags list. (New libraries are like the new kids at school—they have to go to the end of the line.)

4. With your new library selected in the tags list, select what document types should support the tags in this library.

Your new library is ready to rock and roll! The next step is to add tags to the library, so it will have some functionality.

Adding a Tag

To add a new tag to a library, do this:

1. Click the plus (+) button at the top of the tags list, and choose New Tags from the pop-up menu.

2. The New Tags dialog box will appear (see Figure 33.29). Specify what library the tag should be added to, and enter the tag's name. (The name is what will appear between the opening and closing < > symbols—don't include the symbols themselves.)

Figure 33.29   The New Tags dialog box, part of the Tag Library Editor.

3. If the tag will consist of an opening and closing pair, select the Have Matching End Tags option. If the tag will be a single tag only (like <img> or <hr>), deselect this option.

4. When you're finished, click OK. Check out the tags list—your tag will appear as an entry in the library you specified. Select the tag in the list, and edit its formatting options as desired.

After you've done this, you can try it out! Open a document of a type that will support the library containing your tag, go to Code view, and type the first few characters of your new tag. If you have code hints enabled, a hint menu should appear, with your tag as one of the entries.

Adding an Attribute

To add a new attribute to a tag, do this:

1. Click the plus (+) button at the top of the tags list, and choose New Attributes from the pop-up menu.

2. The New Attributes dialog box will appear (see Figure 33.30). Specify the library and tag the new attribute will belong to, and enter the attribute's name.

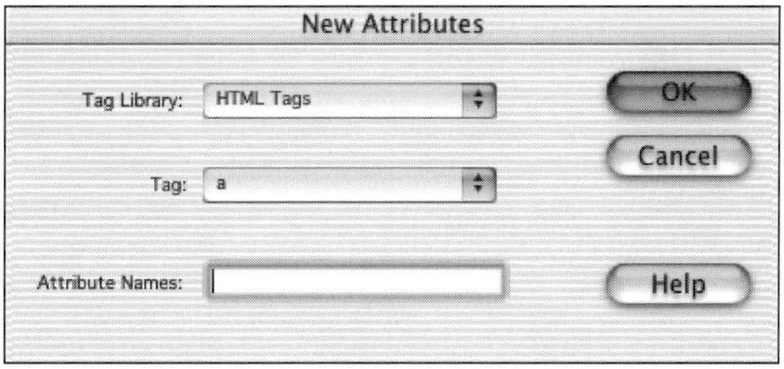

Figure 33.30   The New Attributes dialog box, part of the Tag Library Editor.

3. When you're finished, click OK. Check out the tags list—your attribute will appear as an entry for the tag you specified. Select the attribute in the list, and edit its formatting options as desired.

Exercise 33.3   Adding a Custom Tag Library and Elements

You want to get some practice working with tag library elements, but you probably don't want to risk upsetting the program's built-in functionality. So, in this exercise, you'll create a new tag library, populate it with a new tag, and assign various attributes to that tag. When you're finished, you'll remove the whole lot.

1. Start by choosing Edit > Edit Tag Libraries, to open the Tag Library Editor.

2. In the tags list, contract all categories so you're seeing a list of libraries like that shown in Figure 33.26.

3. Create the new library by clicking the plus (+) button and choosing New Library from the pop-up menu. Call the library Practice Tags.

4. In the tags list, select the Practice Tags library and make sure HTML documents are selected as one of the document types where these tags may be found (see Figure 33.31).

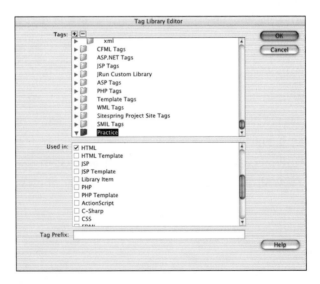

Figure 33.31   The Practice Tags library set up so its tags will be recognized when found in HTML documents.

5. Next, the Practice Tags library needs a tag of its very own. With Practice Tags selected in the tags list, click the plus (+) button and choose New Tags from the pop-up menu. In the dialog box that appears, make sure the tag will be added to the Practice Tags library. Call the tag grin. This imaginary tag has no closing tag, so deselect the Have Matching End Tags option (see Figure 33.32). Click OK to close the New Tags dialog box.

Figure 33.32   Adding the <grin> tag to the Practice Tags library.

6. Back in the Tag Library Editor, select <grin> in the tags list, and set its options. Choose whatever formatting options you like—use the Preview area to see how your choices will affect the code structure (see Figure 33.32).

7. Try out your new tag! Click OK to close the Tag Library Editor, and open a new HTML document. Make sure code hints are enabled (Edit > Preferences > Code Hints).

   Go to Code view, and in between the <body> </body> tags, type <g. Pause a moment before continuing. The code hint menu appears, taking you right to your new tag! Press Enter/Return, to insert the rest of the tag: <**grin**>. Congratulations!

8. Now, add a few attributes to your tag. Go to Edit > Edit Tag Libraries, to open the Tag Library Editor. From the tags list, find and select your <grin> tag. Click the plus (+) button and choose New Attributes from the pop-up menu.

9. In the New Attributes dialog box, make sure your Practice Tags library and <grin> tag are selected. Call your attribute **kind**. Click OK, and go back to the Tag Library Editor.

10. In the editor, select the new kind attribute. Set its Attribute Type to Enumerated, and enter a comma-separated list of possible grins in the Attribute Value field (**sly, sneaky, crooked...**). Figure 33.33 shows this happening.

Tip

When defining an enumerated list in the Tag Library Editor, be sure not to put any spaces between your commas or the list won't work.

Figure 33.33   Adding the **kind** attribute to the <grin> tag.

11. Set whatever other attribute formatting you like, and click OK to close the Tag Library Editor. Try your attribute out! In your open document, still in Code view, try entering a new <grin> tag. This time, type this much: **<grin**.

Pause for a moment. A code hint menu showing your grin types appears! Choose one, and let Dreamweaver finish coding your <grin> tag for you. Figure 33.34 shows this happening.

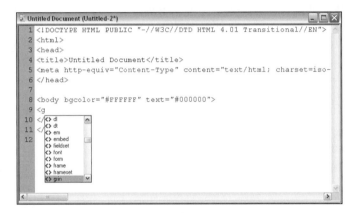

Figure 33.34   The <grin> tag in action, in Code.

12. Now, see how the new tag behaves in the Tag Inspector. Open the Tag Inspector (Window > Tag Inspector, or expand the Code panel group).

In the tree structure view at the top of the panel, find your grin tag and select it. Now look at the attribute list, in the lower half of the panel. There's your kind attribute and its value! Select the value—note that the inspector shows a pop-up triangle icon, indicating that there's a pop-up list of values for that attribute. If you click on the icon, you'll be presented with your list of attributes (see Figure 33.34).

Advanced Search and Replace

Although the Dreamweaver Find and Replace command doesn't necessarily have to be used in Code view, sophisticated searching is a feature usually associated with code editing. Back in Chapter 3, you learned the basics of using Find and Replace for HTML tags and text elements, within single documents or across folders or entire sites. In this chapter, you'll see how you can limit page text searches to text only within specific HTML tags, perform advanced searches for HTML tags and attributes using a simple pop-up menu interface, use regular expressions to construct complex search and replace patterns, and even save complex search criteria for future reuse.

Advanced Text Searches

With a basic text search, Dreamweaver enables you to search the text elements in an HTML document (that is, the text that is actually visible on the page, distinguished from HTML tags). With advanced text searching, you can limit the search to only those text elements within, or outside of, specific tags. You can specify that the text element be within one tag or multiple tags; you can even require that the enclosing tags have certain attributes. The Advanced Text search option is available through the Search and Replace window. With the window open, from the Search For pop-up menu, select Text (Advanced).

Advanced text searches are useful any time you're working with complex documents and want to refine your searches as much as possible, the advanced text search is a great aid. Maybe you want to change all instances of Minnesota to MN, except not in titles, for instance. Do a search for the state name but only when it's not in an <h1> or other title tag. Especially if you're doing sitewide changes, this sort of refinement can make it possible to complete a Replace All search in five minutes, rather than an item-by-item Replace search that might take an hour.

Figure 33.35 shows the Find and Replace dialog box set up to perform a complex advanced text search. Table 33.4 explains the various search criteria available in the pop-up menus. Use the plus (+) and minus (−) buttons to add or remove search criteria.

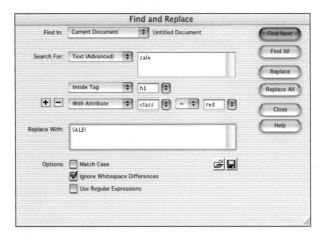

Figure 33.35   The Find and Replace dialog box set up to perform an advanced text search.

Table 33.4   Criteria for Advanced Text and Specific Tag Searches

Criterion	Description
Inside tag Not inside tag	Limit the search to text elements contained (or not contained) within a certain pair of tags. Note that only tags that occur in pairs, such as <p>...</p>, will produce valid search results.
With attribute Without attribute	Limit the search to tags that have (or don't have) a certain attribute set to a certain value; to search based only on the presence or absence of the attribute, regardless of value, leave the Value field blank.
Containing Not containing	Limit the search to tags that contain (or don't contain) a specified nested tag or text element.

Specific Tag Searches

This type of search enables you to find and modify the attributes of different HTML tags, as well as add, change, and even remove specific tags. This is powerful code-editing functionality, although not something you normally associate with searching and replacing.

After you've tried it a few times, you'll be amazed at how handy this kind of search is. What if you use the company logo throughout your site and then discover you forgot to give it an alt label? A sitewide search for every <img> tag with the attribute src="logo.gif", setting the alt attribute to "Your Logo", will fix the problem in no time flat. Or maybe you need to find all 100-percent width tables across an entire site and change them to 90-percent width; one easy search will do it.

Figure 33.36 shows the Find and Replace dialog box set up to perform a specific tag search with several criteria. Note that instead of replacing you can choose an action to perform on any found tags. The (slightly less than intuitive) procedure for this type of search is to click the Find button to search for instances of the specified tag, and then click the Replace button to perform the specified action on any found tags. Table 33.5 explains the choices available in the Action pop-up menu.

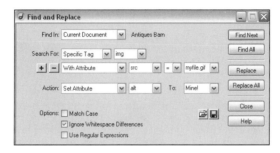

Figure 33.36   The Find and Replace dialog box set up to perform a specific tag search.

Table 33.5   Actions for Specific Tag Searches

Action	Description
Replace tag and contents	Completely replaces opening and closing tags and any nested tags or other contents with specified text. To remove the tag and its contents entirely, leave the specified text field blank.
Replace contents only	Replaces everything within the opening and closing tags with specified text, but leaves the tags in place. To remove the contents, leave the specified text field blank.
Strip tag	Removes opening and closing tags, but leaves any contents in place. Note that this action will not be executed if it would result in invalid code (such as stripping a single <td> from within a table while leaving the table contents in place).
Change tag	Replaces the opening and closing tags with another specified pair of opening and closing tags, leaving any contents intact. Note that if an unclosed or self-closing tag (such as <img> or <img/>) is specified as the replacement for a tag pair (such as <p></p>), all contents of the original tag pair will be lost.
Set attribute	Sets a specified attribute of the tag to a specified value.
Remove attribute	Removes a specified attribute of the tag.
Add before start tag	Adds specified text immediately before the opening tag.
Add after end tag	Adds specified text immediately following the closing tag.
Add after start tag	Adds specified text immediately following the opening tag. This can be used to add a new row to the top of certain tables, for instance.
Add before end tag	Adds specified text immediately preceding the closing tag. This can be used to add a new row to the end of certain tables, for instance.

Using Regular Expressions

Regular expressions aren't a kind of search, and they aren't unique to Dreamweaver. Regular expressions offer a powerful way to search code for patterns rather than specific character-by-character matches. If you're searching for all the phone numbers in a group of web pages, but you don't want to search for each phone number individually, for instance, you can use a regular expression to search for a pattern of numbers, dashes, and parentheses that all the phone numbers follow. Regular expressions are a part of Perl, JavaScript, and other scripting and programming languages. They can be remarkable simple or very sophisticated and complex, depending on what you're trying to accomplish.

If you are technically minded, be aware that the Dreamweaver searching capabilities are built from JavaScript. Therefore, all the features of regular expressions supported by JavaScript will work in defining criteria for the Find and Replace command.

Writing Regular Expressions

A *regular expression* is a description of a text string that contains certain characters in certain positions or patterns. The simplest regular expressions just consist of the letters or numbers you want to search for, and they find only instances of those specific characters. For instance, the following three search strings are all regular expressions that will find exactly the text strings specified, wherever they occur in a document:

```
Fred Flintstone
```

```
87125
```

```
laura@rocketlaura.com
```

However, regular expressions also can include various "metacharacters," which are used to describe and count characters in a document. Tables 33.6 and 33.7 list the most commonly used metacharacters. Built from metacharacters shown there, a search for phone numbers might be encoded into a regular expression like one of these, for instance:

```
(\d\d\d) \d\d\d-\d\d\d\d
(*\d{3})*[\s-]\d{3}-\d{4}
```

The second of these is fancier but more flexible, finding any of these phone numbers:

```
(800) 123-4567
(800)123-4567
800 123-4567
800-123-4567
```

Table 33.6   Regular Expression Metacharacters (Character-Matching)

Expression	Kind of Character to Match	Example
\d	Numeral (0–9)	\d matches the *2*s in R2D2, but nothing in Skywalker.
\D	Not a numeral	\D matches any character in Skywalker and the *R* and *D* in R2D2.
\w	Any alphanumeric character, including underscore	\w matches every character except the spaces and period in "R2D2 ran down the road."
\W	Not any alphanumeric character, or underscore	\W matches only the spaces and the period in "R2D2 ran down the road."
.	Any character except newline rain or region.	r.n matches ran and run, but not
[xyz]	Any character in the brackets (specify a range of characters with a hyphen)	[a-f] is equivalent to [abcdef], and either will match the *f* and *a* in favor, and the *e*, *a*, and *f* in leaf.
[^xyz]	Any character not in the brackets (specify a range of characters with a hyphen)	[l-p] is equivalent to [lmnop], and either will match any character in Chewbacca but none in moon or pool.
\b	Word boundary	\bh matches hello but not bother.
\B	Not a word boundary	\h matches "bother" but not "hello"
\s	Single white space character (space, tab, form feed, line feed)	\sone matches *one* in "is he the one?" but nothing in "someone's there!"
\S	Single nonwhite space	\Sone matches *one* in "someone's there!" but nothing in "is he the one?"
^	The beginning of a string or line	^ a matches the *a* in "all for one," but nothing in "one for all."
$	The end of a string or other selection	s$ matches the second *s* in biscuits, but not the first.
\t	Tab	
\f	Form feed	
\r	Carriage return	
\n	Line feed	
\x	The literal value of *x* (used to search for occurrences of special characters that would otherwise be interpreted as metacharacters)	hi. matches hit, hid, and so forth; hi\. matches hi.

Table 33.7   Regular Expression Metacharacters (Character-Counting)

Expression	How Many Characters	Examples
*	The preceding character, zero or more times	om* matches *om* in mom, *omm* in mommy, and *o* in son.
+	The preceding character, one or more times	om+ matches *om* in mom, *omm* in mommy, but nothing in son.
?	The preceding character, zero or one time	so?e?n matches *son* in Anderson, *sn* in snack, but nothing in soon.
{n}	The preceding character, exactly *n* times	c{2} matches *cc* in Chewbacca but nothing in charcoal.
{n.}	The preceding character, *n* or more times	6{1.} matches the *6*s in 976 and 97662, but not in 666.
{n,m}	The preceding character, at least *n*, at most *m* times	F{1,3} matches the *F*s in #F204CA and #FFCCCC, but nothing in #FFFFFF.

To learn more about regular expressions, check out *Mastering Regular Expressions* (published by O'Reilly). Many JavaScript and Perl books also have in-depth discussions of this topic.

Finding and Replacing with Regular Expressions

To use regular expressions in Dreamweaver, just enable the Use Regular Expressions option in the Find and Replace dialog box and enter characters and metacharacters in any of the dialog box's Find text fields. (It makes no sense to use regular expressions as replacement strings.)

Figure 33.37 shows examples of three search types using regular expressions. The top example shows a basic Text search that finds variant spellings of *labeled* and makes them consistent. The center example shows an Advanced Text search that finds all occurrences of the word *and* in headers only (h? will return h1, h2, h3, and so on) and replaces them with &. The bottom example shows a Specific Tag search that finds all tables with percent-based widths (\d*% finds numbers with any number of digits that end in a percent sign) and removes the width attribute.

The Use Regular Expressions and Ignore White Space options can't both be enabled at the same time, because white space cannot be ignored within regular expressions.

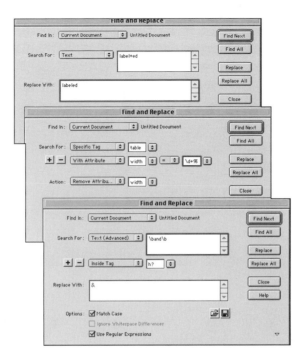

Figure 33.37   Find and Replace dialog boxes showing different search types utilizing regular expressions: basic Text search (top), Advanced Text search (middle), Specific Tag search (bottom).

The most powerful feature of the Dreamweaver Find and Replace command is its capability to save search criteria for later reuse. Any setup you create in the Find and Replace dialog box can be saved. This feature really makes it worthwhile spending time and thought to create flexible, complex searches. A good set of search criteria is like your very own utility program, ready to run on any document with a few mouse clicks.

After you've filled in all the Find and Replace options as desired, you can save any set of criteria by clicking the Save button (the one with the disk icon). You'll be presented with a standard Save dialog box. Choose a location and choose a name. After you have finished, your criteria will be saved to a file with the **.dwr** extension. Figure 33.38 shows this happening.

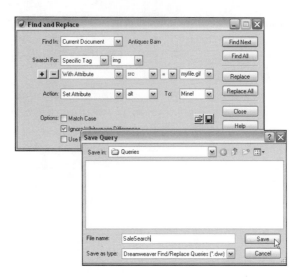

Figure 33.38   Saving the settings from a Find and Replace dialog box.

To load a saved criteria file, open the Find and Replace dialog box and click the Load Query button (the one with the file icon). A dialog box will appear asking you what file to load. Choose your DWR file and open it. The Find and Replace interface will be set to your saved settings.

You also can modify the saved criteria file. After all, DWR files are just XML files storing the various search parameters as attributes of custom tags. If you love working with code, you can always open the DWR file in a text editor (Dreamweaver, even!) and modify the criteria there. The code for the search shown in Figure 33.37, for instance, looks like this:

```
<?xml version="1.0"?>
<dwquery>
    <queryparams matchcase="false" ignorewhitespace="false"
useregexp="true"/>
        <find>
        <qtag qname="table">
            <qattribute qname="width" qcompare="=" qvalue="\d*%"></qat-
tribute>
        </qtag>
        </find>
    <replace action="removeAttribute" param1="width" param2=""/>
</dwquery>
```

Exercise 33.4   Finding and Replacing for Maximum Efficiency

In this exercise, you use various kinds of searches to efficiently edit a document that would otherwise be a nightmare of boring, repetitive tasks.

I. From the **chapter_33** folder on the CD, find and open **states.html** and examine its contents (see Figure 33.39). You can see that it consists of two types of tables: a layout table for the overall page structure, and lots of colored data tables. Your job is to make sweeping changes to those data tables.

Figure 33.39   The **states.html** file with multicolored data tables.

2. First, you want to add a row of header cells to each data table (with the headings State, Capital, and Pop.). You can do this with a Specific Tag search; but what tag do you search for? You can't search for all `<table>` tags, or the layout table will be included. You can't search by background color, because each table's color is different. If you look at the code for this document, however, you'll see that each data table has a class of `state` assigned to it. You can search by class. For each data table, you want to add a `<tr>` with specific contents. Therefore, when you find each appropriate `<table>` tag, you'll add the following code after the start tag:

```
<tr><th bgcolor="#FFFF00" align="left">State</th><th
bgcolor="#FFFF00" align="left">Capital</th><th bgcolor="#FFFF00"
align="left">Pop.</th></tr>
```

Open the Find and Replace dialog box, and set it up as shown in Figure 33.40.

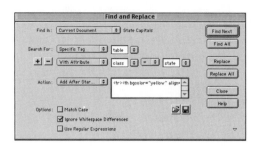

Figure 33.40   The Find and Replace dialog box, ready to add a header row to each data table in **states.html**.

3. You've seen how a class assignment can help identify items for mass changes. You can use custom classes along with CSS to more easily format your table cells. Open the CSS Inspector and you'll see that two custom classes have been defined for this document: `statetitle` and `statedata`. You want to apply those to the cells of your data tables. Can you see how a Specific Tag search can help with this? The `statetitle` class is easy; it should be assigned to all `<th>` tags. The `statedata` class is harder; you need to find some combination of characteristics that is unique for all data cells. For this document, examination of the code shows that the data cells have no attributes at all, whereas the layout cells have either height, width, or both. Figure 33.41 shows the Find and Replace dialog boxes to perform the searches required here. Perform those searches and examine your code to make sure you get the results you wanted.

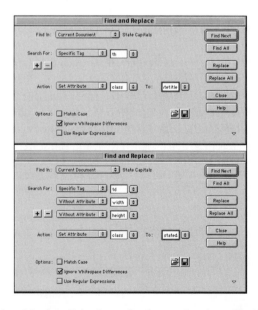

Figure 33.41   Find and Replace dialog boxes for the searches that will add `statetitle` and `statedata` classes to the data tables.

Here's an extra: Now that you have a class providing color for the `<th>` tags, you don't need the `bgcolor` attribute in those tags. Can you use a Specific Tag search to remove that attribute?

4. One of our headers has the text `Pop.`, but you've changed your mind and want it to say Population. This might be a simple Text search, but what if some text somewhere else in the document says Pop.? You want an Advanced Text search that finds only this text when it's in a `statetitle` `<th>` tag. Can you perform this search? The setup for this one isn't shown here.

5. The boss says he wants the cells with population numbers in them to have a white background so that they stand out. You need to do a tag search for all `<td>` tags with a class of `statedata`, but only those that contain numbers. Time for a regular expression! Can you think this one through? Figure 33.42 shows a setup that will work.

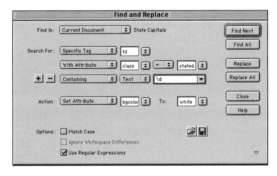

Figure 33.42   Find and Replace dialog box to search for all `<td>` tags with a class of `statedata` and containing numbers.

6. Last big challenge: If you examine the code for the style sheet in this document's `<head>`, you'll see that all styles refer to a group of sans-serif fonts, but each font list differs slightly. You want all font lists for sans-serif fonts to be identical. You want them to read like this: Verdana, Arial, Helvetica, Geneva, Swiss, sans-serif. This requires a Source search with a regular expression; you want to replace every font list that contains the word *sans-serif* with your font list. In regular expression terms, you want to find the following:

```
font-family:[^;]*sans-serif;
```

And replace it with the following:

```
font-family: Verdana, Arial, Helvetica, Geneva, Swiss, sans-serif;
```

Can you see how the regular expression works? Try it out. Perform the search; then examine your document code to make sure the changes were made successfully. If they weren't, Edit > Undo as many times as necessary and try again.

That was a pretty handy search. Maybe it wouldn't have been so difficult making a manual code change for just this one document, but what if you want to change internal style sheets across an entire site? More than that, you might find yourself needing a similar search again in the future. Do you want to have to figure out that regular expression every time? Of course not! This is a good set of search criteria to save. Open the Find and Replace dialog box again. Your preceding settings should still be in place. Save the search criteria as **Set Sans-Serif Font List**, in whatever centralized location you like. You now have a handy tool for future use.

Editing Non-HTML Markup with Dreamweaver

The Dreamweaver code editor can be used to edit other kinds of code other than the default markup languages (HTML, XML, XHTML, ASP, CFM, and so on), although you won't be able to display those files in Design view or use the Preview in Browser feature to view them.

Macintosh users should be aware that unlike many other Mac programs, Dreamweaver/Mac uses filename extensions to determine file types. A file created in Dreamweaver may even display on your desktop with the DW icon, and the program still won't be able to open or preview it if it doesn't include the proper extension.

To enable Dreamweaver to open and edit different file types, go to Edit > Preferences and choose the File Types/Editors category. Find the Open in Code View option, and add the new file extension to the text field (see Figure 33.43). Note that each extension must be separated from others in the list by spaces on either side. Don't forget to include the period (.).

To make sure Dreamweaver doesn't rewrite the code for this file type, go to Edit > Preferences and choose the Code Rewriting category. Find the Never Rewrite Code options list and add the new extension. Each new file extension must be separated from others in the list by spaces on either side. (See the section on "Code Rewriting" for more on this.)

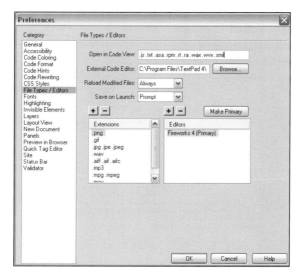

Figure 33.43   Configuring Dreamweaver to open additional file types in the Preferences > File Types/Editors category.

Writing JavaScript in Dreamweaver

In addition to other code-writing chores, Dreamweaver has several features specifically to help you hand code JavaScript.

The Reference Panel

In previous chapters, you have seen how the Reference panel can give you context-sensitive help for HTML and CSS. For scripting help, the Reference panel also provides JavaScript help. To access the JavaScript help in the Reference panel, click the <?> button on the Document toolbar and choose O'Reilly JavaScript Reference from the panel's Book pop-up menu. Figure 33.44 shows the JavaScript section of the Reference panel with all of its parts labeled for easy browsing. It's organized by object, as most JavaScript dictionaries are, so you'll need to know your object structure to take full advantage of it.

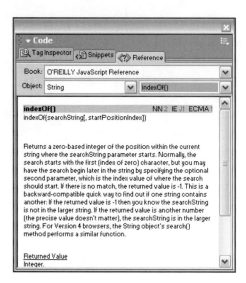

Figure 33.44   The JavaScript section of the Reference Panel, a handy source of information for scripters.

Scripting Without Using Code View

If you want to be able to add your own scripts to your page without having to navigate through one of the code editor views, you have two choices: the Call JavaScript behavior, or the Script object. The Script Property Inspector also enables you to edit existing `<script>` tags.

Call JavaScript Behavior

You apply and edit this behavior the same way you would any other item in the Behaviors panel. Instead of inserting some prewritten JavaScript action, however, the behavior adds only an event handler and whatever JavaScript statement(s) you specifically tell it to add. Any time you want to add a simple one- or two-line script statement to a page using an event handler, this is a nice, quick option. (For a full discussion on using Dreamweaver behaviors, see Chapter 16, "Getting Interactive with Behaviors.") To add the Call JavaScript behavior to a document, follow these steps:

1. Open a document and select whichever page element you want to attach the behavior to. (Be sure to select an element that can have a behavior attached to it, such as a text link, image, or image link.)

2. Open the Behaviors panel (Window > Behaviors). Double-check the panel's title bar to make sure the correct page element is selected.

3. From the plus (+) menu, choose Call JavaScript.

4. In the dialog box that appears, type in whatever JavaScript statement(s) you want to execute. (Separate multiple statements with semicolons.) After you have finished, click OK.

The `MM_CallJS()` function will be added to your document, like this:

```
function MM_callJS(jsStr) { //v2.0
  return eval(jsStr)
}
```

Your script statement will be passed as a parameter in the function call, like this:

```
<a href="#" onClick="MM_callJS('window.alert(\'Hello
world\');')">Click here!</a>
```

Figure 33.45 shows the Call JavaScript behavior being assigned.

As the preceding code shows, whatever statement you enter in this behavior will be passed as part of an event handler in double and single quotes. Always use single quotes within your script statement; otherwise the behavior will generate errors in the browser. To make sure Dreamweaver doesn't try to URL-encode your quotes (turning " into %22, for instance), go to Edit > Preferences > Code Rewriting (Mac OS X: Dreamweaver > Preferences > Code Rewriting) and disable both Special Characters options— Encode Special Characters in URLs and Encode <,>,&, and " in Attribute Values Using &. With these options deselected, Dreamweaver will escape all quotes with \ and leave all other characters alone.

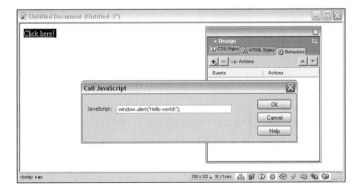

Figure 33.45   Using the Call JavaScript behavior to attach a simple script statement to a page link.

The dialog box text field has no maximum character restrictions, so you can enter as long a chunk of code as you like; although longer statements will, of course, require some scrolling to view in the text field. If you're frustrated by the viewing restrictions, you can customize the behavior to present a text area rather than a text field in its dialog box by editing the **calljavascript.htm** file (located in the Dreamweaver application folder, in **Configuration/Behaviors/Actions**). Open this file in a text editor—or in Dreamweaver itself, if you like—and change the `<input>` tag from a text field to the following:

```
<textarea name="message" cols="50" wrap="virtual" rows="5"></textarea>
```

You can set the columns and rows to any values you like. Set the wrap to `"virtual"` for best viewing in the dialog box. Obviously, don't change the name from `"message"`, or the behavior will not function properly. (For more on working with the Dreamweaver configuration files, see Chapter 33, "Writing Code in Dreamweaver.") The next time you launch Dreamweaver, the new dialog box with expanded text area should appear (see Figure 33.46).

Figure 33.46   The Call JavaScript behavior with expanded text area for better viewing.

The Script Object

The Dreamweaver Script object is a quick way to insert a complete `<script>` tag into a document without going to Code view. Scripts entered this way aren't limited to JavaScript. They can include anything a `<script>` tag normally contains, including links to separate JS files.

To insert a script block into a document using the Script object, follow these steps (see Figure 33.47):

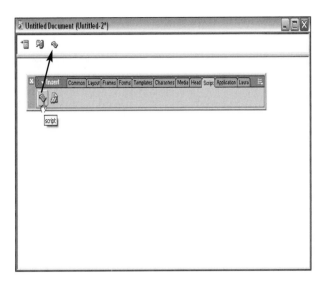

Figure 33.47   Using the Script object to insert a `<script>` tag into the document head. Note that the head content bar is visible and active.

1. Open a document.

2. To insert the script into the `<body>` section, position the insertion point where the tag should be added. To insert the script to the `<head>` section, use the View Options menu to turn Head Content on, and click in the head content bar (along the top of the Document window) to activate it.

3. In the Insert bar, choose the Script Tab. Find and click the Script object icon.

4. In the dialog box that appears, choose a scripting language. JavaScript and VBScript appear in the pop-up menu. To add version information, or to choose another language, enter the information directly into the text field.

5. Enter the complete script contents you want to enter, minus only the opening and closing `<script>` tags (and the script-hiding comment tags).

Dreamweaver will insert your script, inside `<script>` tags and with the proper language specified. It also will include comment tags to hide the script from noncompliant browsers.

To edit a script block using the Script inspector, follow these steps (see Figure 33.48):

Figure 33.48   The Property inspector for Script objects.

1. Open a document containing `<script>` tags.
2. In the View menu, be sure Visual Aids: Invisibles is enabled. Each `<script>` tag in the document should now show in Design view as a script icon.
3. Select the script icon representing the code you want to edit.
4. Use the Property inspector to change any script parameters. Click the Edit button to access and edit the code.

When you insert a Script object, you're not given the choice to add a script link. The dialog box assumes you're going to type your own script in. However, you can subvert the process (although it's easier just to use the Assets panel, as discussed later).

To insert a link to a client-side or server-side JS file, using the Script object, follow these steps:

1. Open a document and insert a Script object, as described earlier.
2. In the Script object dialog box, leave the code field blank and click OK. This inserts an empty `<script>` into your document.
3. Enable viewing of invisible items, find the script icon, and select it.
4. In the Script Object Property inspector, choose the file to which you want to attach.

Scripts in the Assets Panel

If you're working within a defined site and want to add links to JS files to your documents, the easiest way is to use the Assets panel. Every JS file within your local site folder will appear in the Scripts section of the Assets panel (see Figure 33.49). To add a script link to a document this way, follow these steps:

1. Open the document to which you want to add the link.

2. Use View > Head Content, if necessary, to show the head content bar.

3. Open the Assets panel and click the script icon to show the site's script files.

4. Find the file you want to link to and drag its icon from the Assets panel to the head content bar of your document. Figure 33.49 shows this happening.

Figure 33.49   Linking an HTML document to a JS file by dragging from the Assets panel.

JavaScript Tools in Code View

If you're editing your scripts in Code view or the Code inspector, you can take advantage of colored syntax, function navigation, auto-balancing, and various debugging tools.

Syntax Coloring for Scripts

You have already seen how syntax coloring works in Dreamweaver—how to enable it and customize text colors and styling. The Preferences > Code Coloring dialog box includes special settings for coloring text within scripts, including reserved keywords, other keywords, and strings (refer back to Figure 33.7). This coloring will apply to any code between a pair of <script> tags. It won't affect any code that is part of an event handler in the HTML, because that code is not within a <script> tag.

When working with colored script syntax, remember that if you're typing a new <script> tag into the code editor, as soon as you type the word **<script>**, the coloring for everything in the entire document from that point on will be determined by script syntax colors. This means that if you're entering a script into an already existing HTML page, the color coding for the rest of the HTML code will be overridden. This can be distracting as you work. The solution is to immediately enter both the opening and closing `<script>` tags and then come back to type in your script's code. The closing `</script>` tag tells Dreamweaver to stop applying script-based syntax coloring.

JavaScript Snippets

Snippets, discussed earlier in this chapter, can also be used to store frequently used JavaScript code fragments. In fact, Dreamweaver ships with a variety of handy JavaScript snippets that you might want to explore.

Code Navigation Menu

Whether you're working on an HTML document containing functions in its `<head>`, or a JS document, Dreamweaver enables you easily jump to different JavaScript functions with the Code Navigation menu. You can access this menu from the document or Code inspector toolbar by clicking the double curly braces icon (see Figure 33.50). The menu lists any JavaScript functions. Choosing a function will move the cursor to the first line of that function and will scroll the display if necessary to show it.

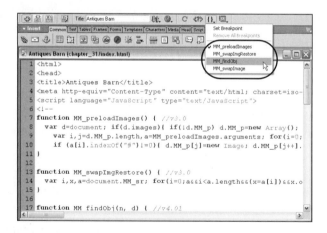

Figure 33.50   Accessing the Code Navigation menu (available only from Code view).

Auto-Balancing Braces

Losing track of opening and closing curly braces, parentheses, and quotation marks is a common problem in scripting. In Dreamweaver, you're on your own determining whether all your open quotes close properly, but the program will help you with your braces (curly braces, square brackets, parentheses). To test whether your punctuation marks are correctly paired, follow these steps:

1. In Code view or the Code inspector, select an opening brace (curly brace, square bracket, or parenthesis).

2. Go to Edit > Balance Braces. Dreamweaver will select all code between that brace and the corresponding closing brace.

If you're used to how auto-balancing is implemented in some text editors (such as BBEdit, for instance), the Dreamweaver Balance Braces command may take some getting used to. As mentioned earlier, you can't use it to balance anything but braces. Also, it works only when selecting an opening brace, not a closing brace. However, it will respond with an error beep if you have incorrectly balanced braces (for instance, more openers than closers or vice versa). For example, selecting the first opening brace in the following code will generate an error sound, because the braces don't balance:

```
function helloWorld() {
if (a==0) {
        window.alert("Hello, world");
}
```

Selecting the second opening brace, however, will not result in an error; Dreamweaver will just select the code inside the if statement braces.

Debugging Tools

Any time you get into serious script writing, you're going to be doing some debugging. Debugging is the process of finding (and fixing) errors in scripts. This involves checking the code for syntax errors. It also involves running the script a step at a time, while keeping track of variable values, to identify logical errors.

The Dreamweaver code editor offers the ability to set breakpoints and debug through various browsers. When you debug a document in Dreamweaver, the program adds two files to the folder containing the file: **mm_debug.js** and the Java applet **mm_nsapplet.class**. Using these two files, Dreamweaver first checks for syntax errors. Then it launches a browser and loads the Java applet, which checks for logic errors.

Breakpoints are stopping places in a script. When checking for logical errors, you tell the script to stop running periodically so that you can check the variables and determine whether everything is progressing as it should.

To set breakpoints for debugging, follow these steps (see Figure 33.51):

Figure 33.51   Setting a breakpoint in a Dreamweaver script, preparatory to debugging.

1. Open a document with one or more scripts you want to debug, and view it in Code view or the Code inspector.

2. Examine your script, deciding which variables you want to keep track of and where in the script you want to check their values. In the following code, for instance, it would be nice to know the value of this URL before performing any more actions on it:

```
function collectName() {
var thisURL=document.url;
var nameString=thisURL.substring(thisURL.indexOf("=")+1,
thisURL.length);
window.alert("Welcome, "+nameString);
}
```

3. Each breakpoint is attached to a particular line of the script. The breakpoint will stop the script before execution of the line where it's set. Determine which line you want the breakpoint attached to and position the cursor in that line.

4. From the {} menu on the toolbar, select Set Breakpoint. A large dot will appear to the left of the line you've chosen (see Figure 33.51).

5. Repeat steps 3 and 4 for every additional breakpoint you want to set. (You can stop as many times as you like, in the debugging process, and check as many variables as you need to check.)

Dreamweaver will remember your breakpoints even after you close the document. They will be forgotten (removed) when you quit Dreamweaver.

To remove a breakpoint, follow these steps:

1. Position the cursor in a line that currently has a breakpoint set for it.

2. From the {} menu, select Remove Breakpoint.

To remove all breakpoints, go to the {} menu and select Remove All Breakpoints.

As mentioned earlier, debugging launches a browser and runs a Java applet, through the browser. Debugging in Dreamweaver/Windows can be done in Internet Explorer or Netscape; debugging in Dreamweaver/Mac can only be done in Netscape.

To debug a document, follow these steps:

1. Save the document you want to debug (or Dreamweaver will ask whether you want to do so).

2. Choose File > Debug in Browser, and select your browser (see Figure 33.52).

Figure 33.52   The Preview/Debug in Browser menu for Windows (top) and Mac.

3. If your script contains any syntax errors, Dreamweaver will open an error window detailing the problem(s), and the debugging process will stop. Read the error message, and then click the Go to Line button to find the error. Figure 33.53 shows this happening.

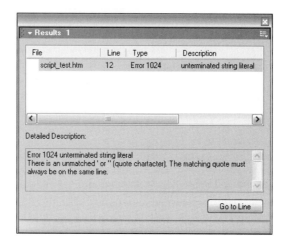

Figure 33.53   The syntax error message window showing an unterminated string literal in line 12 of the script.

4. If there are no errors, the browser will launch. A prompt window will appear, asking whether you want to start debugging. Click OK to proceed.

5. A security alert may appear, warning you that running the Java applet is a risk and asking whether you want to continue. To continue, click the Grant button. (Warning: This whole process may take a while, especially if your computer is connected to a large network.)

6. With the browser still active, the debugger window will then open (refer back to Figure 33.47). It shows the source code for your document, with breakpoints, and gives you the opportunity to set or change your breakpoints before you proceed. (It's your choice whether you want to set your breakpoints ahead of time, in Dreamweaver, or wait until now to do it.)

7. At this point, you need to create a list of watched variables. Do that in the bottom portion of the debugger window. Click the plus (+) button to get a variable name field to appear. Type the name of the variable you want to track here (see Figure 33.54). Repeat this process to add as many variables as you want to track.

Figure 33.54   The Dreamweaver debugging window showing a debug session in progress.

8. At the top of the debugger window, click the Run button to start debugging (see Figure 33.54). This will open your document in the browser window. If your script is set to run automatically onLoad, it also will begin running the script. If your script needs to be triggered, the browser and debugger will wait for you to trigger the script. After the script has been triggered, it will run until it reaches the first breakpoint. Then it will stop, and the debugger window will come to the front.

9. The debugger's list of *watched* variables will show the current values of all variables you specified. Check them. When you're ready to continue, click the Run button again. The browser window will come to the front again, and the script will continue running until it finishes, or until it reaches another breakpoint.

10. After you have finished all your debugging, close the debugger window and go back to Dreamweaver. If your script needs adjusting based on what you found out, make those changes and go through the whole process again!

Exercise 33.5   Inserting and Debugging a JavaScript

This exercise is more of a challenge. Can you use Dreamweaver to successfully debug a (not very complicated) JavaScript in an HTML document? Figure 33.55 shows what the final page should look like in the browser, when the script is functioning properly. The exercise file contains various scripting errors that prevent the page from displaying properly.

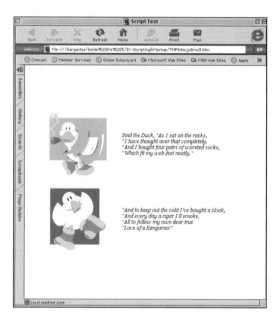

Figure 33.55   Proper browser display of **script_debug.html**.

1. From the **chapter_33** folder on the CD, find and open **script_debug.html**. Examine its contents. You can see that the entire <body> section is created from one JavaScript contained in a <script> tag. If you view the document in Design view, with invisible objects showing, you'll see a single script icon (pretty exciting, eh?).

2. To view the script from Design view, you can select the script icon and, in the Property inspector, click the Edit button. The code-viewing options are limited in the editing window, however—no colored syntax, no line numbers, and so forth—so you'll want to do your debugging and editing from Code view or the Code inspector.

3. Here's the challenge: The script contains various syntax and logical errors. Can you find them using the debugger with breakpoints? If you're an old hand at scripting, you may not need those tools, but give them a try to get used to working with them. Be sure to enable line numbers in the code editor before proceeding, for easier reference.

Summary

In this chapter, you have seen how the Dreamweaver coding environment works, and how to make the most of integrating it into your authoring workflow. You can use Dreamweaver for coding tasks from markup to scripting, and can configure it to handle whatever file types you need to edit. You can use the Document window's Code view or the separate Code inspector panel to do this. And you have a great deal of control over how the code editor formats, rewrites, and displays your code. Finally, if you don't want to use the internal code editor, you can configure Dreamweaver to link to an external text editor. If you use HomeSite (Windows) or BBEdit (Mac) for this task, special integration features are available; but you can use any text editor you choose. From a coder's point of view, who needs Design view?

Chapter 34

Customizing Dreamweaver

Right out of the box, Dreamweaver is a great program. No matter what your working style, Dreamweaver has web-authoring tools that you will love. But using the program straight out of the box is only the beginning of the story. Back in Chapter 2, "Setting Up the Dreamweaver Workspace," you learned how to set up the Dreamweaver workspace. Throughout this book, you've learned not only how to use different Dreamweaver features, but how to customize each of them with preferences. The remaining chapters will take you, a step at a time, from the friendly world of interface customization, to customizing with extensions and the **Configuration** folder, to writing your own program functionality by creating extensions.

This chapter discusses how to access and work with the interface for setting preferences, customizing panels and panel groups, modifying keyboard shortcuts, and creating simple (non-scripted) commands to automate your workflow.

Setting Preferences

Preferences give you control over many Dreamweaver options and functions. It is a good idea to go through them all so that you know which options you can set.

The simplest and most ubiquitous way to customize the interface for every task you perform in Dreamweaver is to adjust its relevant preferences. Each chapter of this book has covered a little piece of the Dreamweaver preferences interface as it discussed individual preferences relevant to the chapter topic (to learn about code preferences, read Chapter 33, "Writing Code in Dreamweaver"). This integration of preferences-related topics reflects the way the preferences interface is integrated into Dreamweaver.

All preferences are handled by the various categories of the Preferences dialog box (see Figure 34.1). By choosing Edit > Preferences, and cycling through the various categories, you can customize any of your Dreamweaver authoring tools from one central location.

But the different categories of the Preferences dialog box can also be accessed from various other places within Dreamweaver:

Note

Mac OS X users can also access Dreamweaver preferences by choosing Dreamweaver > Preferences. (This brings Dreamweaver inline with the Apple interface guidelines for setting preferences in Mac OS X.)

- In the Document window status bar, click the Window Sizes pop-up menu and choose Edit Sizes to access Status Bar Preferences.
- Choose File > Preview in Browser > Edit Browser List, or the Document toolbar's Preview/Debug in Browser > Edit Browser List to access Preview in Browser Preferences.
- From the New Document dialog box (File > New), click the Preferences button to Access New Document Preferences.

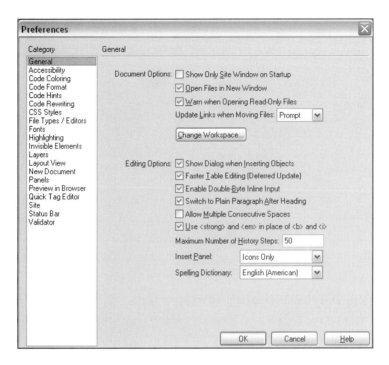

Figure 34.1   The Preferences dialog box, central interface for setting all preferences within Dreamweaver.

Table 34.1 lists the various kinds of preference stored in the Preferences dialog box, and where in this book you can read more about them.

Table 34.1   Preferences Categories and Where to Learn More About Them

Topic	Preferences Categories	Covered In
Code writing	Code-Coloring	Chapter 3,
	Code Format	Chapter 32
	Code Hints	
	Code Rewriting	
	Fonts	
	File Types/Editors	
	Validator	
	QuickTag Editor	
Text and layout	Layout View	Chapter 10,
	CSS Styles	Chapter 13,
	Layers	Chapter 14

continues ▶

Table 34.1   Continued

Topic	Preferences Categories	Covered In
Setting up the workspace	General Panels Status Bar	Chapter 2
Basic document creation and editing	General Accessibility Highlighting Fonts File Types/Editors Invisible Elements Preview in Browser New Document	Chapter 3
Working with sites	Site	Chapter 22, Chapter 23

Modifying Keyboard Shortcuts

Keyboard shortcuts are a great way to quickly access Dreamweaver functions and commands. The default Dreamweaver setup includes a keyboard shortcut for most menu commands, as well as various shortcuts for selecting, scrolling, and editing in Design or Code view. And in case your favorite command or operation doesn't have a shortcut, or in case you just don't like the shortcuts—Macromedia has chosen for you, and the shortcuts are completely customizable. You can add, subtract, and reassign shortcuts as you like. You can even create different sets of shortcuts for different purposes and switch between them at will.

The main interface for working with keyboard shortcuts is the Keyboard Shortcuts dialog box (see Figure 34.2) accessed by choosing Edit > Keyboard Shortcuts.

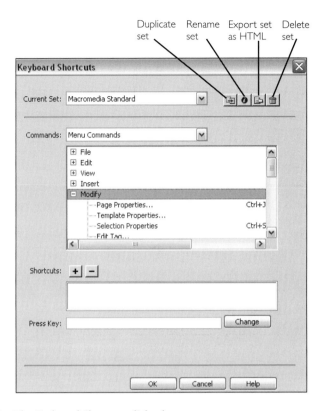

Figure 34. 2   The Keyboard Shortcuts dialog box.

Working with Shortcut Sets

Most software users like their keyboard shortcuts to be consistent across programs—especially between programs they tend to use together. Even if it doesn't interfere with your working style at all that Microsoft Word uses Ctrl/Cmd+I to italicize and Adobe Photoshop uses that same shortcut to invert colors, you might find that the discrepancy suddenly becomes a problem if you're switching frequently between those two programs throughout your work day. To help you out with this potential problem, Dreamweaver ships with four sets of keyboard shortcuts:

- **Macromedia Standard shortcuts**. The default set, for best integration with the rest of the Macromedia MX programs (Fireworks MX, Flash MX)

- **Dreamweaver 3 shortcuts**. For those upgrading users who don't want to memorize a whole new set of commands every time there's an upgrade
- **HomeSite shortcuts**. Very helpful for Windows users who switch frequently between Dreamweaver and the HomeSite+ text editor
- **BBEdit shortcuts**. Equally helpful for Mac users who switch between Dreamweaver and the BBEdit or BBEdit Lite text editors

To switch between one of these default sets, just choose its name from the Shortcut Set pop-up menu in the Keyboard Shortcuts dialog box. The new shortcut set will go into effect as soon as you click OK to close the dialog box. (There's no need to restart Dreamweaver!)

To get a nice, handy reference sheet listing all the shortcuts in a particular set, click the Export Set as HTML button. In the Save File dialog box, give your export file a name and save it anywhere you like. After the export file has been created, open it in a browser to see a nicely formatted table listing all commands and shortcuts (see Figure 34.3).

Figure 34.3   The BBEdit shortcut set exported as an HTML file and viewed in a browser.

Modifying, Adding, and Removing Shortcuts

It's quite possible that none of the default sets contains just exactly the shortcuts you need, assigned to your favorite keystrokes. Whichever of the default shortcut sets you choose to work with, you can add new shortcuts or re-assign existing shortcuts to create the perfect working environment for yourself.

Note

While you're free to change or remove any of the default shortcuts, you don't want to create a non-intuitive interface. In particular, don't customize the standard shortcuts for common functions such as cut (Ctrl/Cmd+X) and paste (Ctrl/Cmd+V) which are standard across the entire operating system.

To add a keyboard shortcut to a command or operation that doesn't currently have one assigned to it, or to change a shortcut that already exists, do this:

1. Choose Edit > Keyboard Shortcuts.

2. Select the relevant command or operation from the Commands list.

3. If you're adding a new shortcut, click the Shortcuts list plus (+) button.

4. Click in the Press Key text input field to activate it. If the shortcut already exists, it will appear as selected text in this field.

5. Press the key combination you want for your shortcut. (For Dreamweaver/Windows, letter or number combinations must include Ctrl. For Dreamweaver/Mac, they must include Cmd.) Your combination will appear in the text field as Modifier+Keystroke. If the key combination you've entered has already been assigned to another command or operation, a warning message will appear in the bottom area of the dialog box. Because the same keystroke can't activate more than one command, adding the shortcut to the currently selected command will remove it from its original place.

6. To confirm this new shortcut, click the Change button. Your shortcut will now appear in the Commands list, associated with the selected command. If you don't click Change, your change will not be recorded as part of the shortcut set.

Tip

After you've got the Press Key input field activated, Dreamweaver interprets whatever you type as an attempt to create a shortcut. If you press the wrong key combination, you can't even hit Delete to remove it, or Ctrl/Cmd+Z to undo your typing. The only way to change an incorrectly typed key combination without having to cancel your way out of the dialog box, is to deselect the command or operation by selecting another item in the Commands list, without clicking the Change button first.

Each item in the Commands list can have up to two keyboard shortcuts assigned to it.

To remove an existing shortcut, go to Edit > Keyboard Shortcuts, select the relevant command or operation from the Commands list, and click the Shortcuts minus (–) button.

Any changes you make to a shortcut set are not saved until you switch to another shortcut set (at which time you'll be given a prompt to save changes to the previous set) or click OK to close the Keyboard Shortcuts dialog box

Creating New Shortcut Sets

Instead of altering—and possibly goofing up—the default Dreamweaver shortcut sets, you can create new sets to populate with your own personalized collection of timesaving shortcuts. The buttons at the upper-right of the Keyboard Shortcuts dialog box are for creating and managing shortcut sets (see Figure 34.2).

You create a new shortcut set by duplicating an existing set and modifying it. Activate the set you want to copy and click the Duplicate Set button. When the Save as HTML dialog box appears, enter a new name for your new duplicate set and click OK to close it.

To rename an existing set, activate the set you want to rename and click the Rename Set button.

To delete an existing set, activate the target set, and click the Delete Set button.

Exercise 34.1   Creating Custom Keyboard Shortcuts

In this exercise, you'll create a copy of the Macromedia Standard shortcuts set and add a few custom shortcuts. If you like customizing shortcuts, this can be your starting point for changing as many shortcuts as you like.

1. Open the Keyboard Shortcuts dialog box (Edit > Keyboard Shortcuts).
2. For Current Set, make sure that Macromedia Standard is chosen.
3. Press the Duplicate Set button (see Figure 34.2). When the Duplicate Set dialog box appears, name your new set My Shortcuts, and then click OK to close the dialog box. Your new set will now be the current set, ready for editing.
4. Which custom shortcuts would you like to add? Chances are, if you've been working with Dreamweaver MX for even a short time, you already know which commands you frequently have to go to the menus for, or which shortcuts you never can remember because they're not intuitive for you. For this exercise, you'll add one new shortcut and modify another.
5. If you work with multiple documents open at a time, and especially if you work with frameset documents, you might get frustrated having to choose File > Save All whenever you want to save all open documents. It's time to add a keyboard

shortcut for this command! Though you can choose any shortcut you like, it's good to choose something logical that you'll remember—something involving S (for save) seems like a pretty good choice.

Start by finding and selecting this command in the Commands list. Make sure the Commands pop-up menu is set to Menu Commands; then expand the File menu category and select Save All (see Figure 34.4). You'll see that this command currently has no shortcut assigned to it.

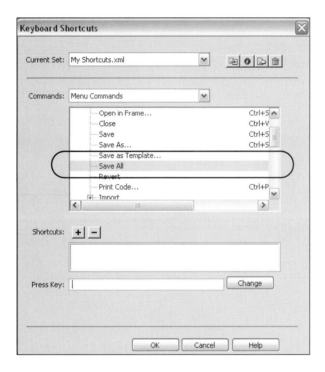

Figure 34.4   The Keyboard Shortcuts dialog box adding a new shortcut for File > Save All.

To add the new shortcut, click on the plus (+) button on the Shortcut list. Then click inside the text input field below this list.

Press the key combination Ctrl+Alt+S (Windows) or Cmd+Opt+S (Mac). This combination now appears in the text input field. But a warning message also appears, indicating that this shortcut is already assigned to the Split Cell command. At this point, if you click Change, the shortcut will be removed from Split Cell and added to Save All. But maybe you don't want this to happen! So, instead, enter the new combination Ctrl+Alt+Shift+S (Windows) or Cmd+Opt+Shift+S (Mac). The text input field shows your altered entry, with Shift added, and the warning disappears.

When you've got the right combination of keys chosen, click Change. You've added a new shortcut!

6. If you've spent years working with the Adobe graphics programs, you've probably got the Ctrl/Cmd+; command for showing and hiding rulers burned into your synapses. The Macromedia Standard shortcut for this is Ctrl+Alt+R (Cmd+Opt+R). How about changing this shortcut so you can happily move between your programs without brain-blockage?

Start by finding and selecting the Show Rulers command in the Commands list. Just like it is in the Dreamweaver menus, this command is found under View > Rulers > Show (see Figure 34.5).

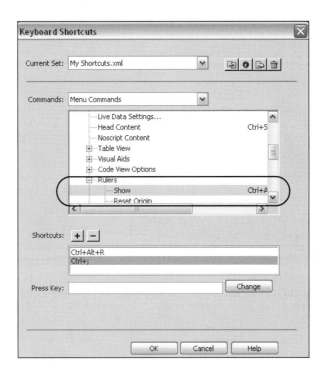

Figure 34.5   Adding a second keyboard shortcut to the Show Rulers command.

You'll see that the Ctrl+Alt+R (Cmd+Opt+R) shortcut is already assigned. Because each command can have up to two shortcuts assigned to it, you have two choices: replace the original, or add to it. For this exercise, you'll start by adding it.

In the Shortcuts menu, click the plus (+) button to add a new shortcut. Click inside the text input field to activate it. Type Ctrl+Alt+; (Windows) or Cmd+Opt+; (Mac). No warning message appears, which means no other command is currently using this shortcut.

Click Change. In the Commands list, he Show Rulers command now appears with two shortcuts defined.

If you never use other Macromedia graphics programs, you don't need both shortcuts. In the Shortcuts list, you can select the original shortcut and click the minus (–) button to remove it. If, on the other hand, you're an eclectic sort who loves working with Macromedia and Adobe programs, you'll want to leave both shortcuts enabled to suit your every working whim.

7. When you've made your changes, click OK to close the Keyboard Shortcuts dialog box. Open a document (or a frameset) and try out your new shortcuts. What other shortcuts would you like to add/modify/subtract in your custom set? Take a moment to make whatever changes you like. When you're finished, close the dialog box and check out your changes.

8. Optional: Would you like a handy record of your custom shortcut set? Choose File > Keyboard Shortcuts one more time, and in the dialog box click the Export Set as HTML button. Save your shortcut set as **My Shortcuts.html**. Open it in your favorite browser and print!

Automating Tasks with Custom Commands

If you're one of those ultra-efficient workers who likes saving steps whenever possible, you've probably already used *macros* in other programs. Macros let you record all the steps involved in performing a certain task and save them to be played back later, usually triggered by a keyboard shortcut or menu command. In Dreamweaver, instead of macros you create and deploy *custom commands*. Custom commands include temporary recorded commands, permanent commands saved using the History panel, and more complex commands that must be programmed (written as scripts). The following sections look at the first two kinds of custom commands; the more complex scripted commands are discussed in Chapter 36, "Creating Extensions."

Working with Recorded Commands (Temporary)

If you've ever performed the same tedious series of steps over and over during a work session, you'll love recorded commands. A *recorded command* is a series of steps that you tell Dreamweaver to record, and then tell it to play back as many times as you need those steps performed.

Recording a Command

To record a command, follow these steps:

1. Plan out the steps that you're going to record, and if necessary set up the conditions for the recording. (For instance, if you want to record formatting a table in a certain way, you'll need to open a document and create a table before you can start recording the formatting steps.)

2. Choose Commands > Start Recording.

3. Perform whatever steps you want to record. To format a table, for instance, you'll use the Property inspector to apply background color, cell padding or spacing, border width and color, and any other table properties. Dreamweaver can't record steps like changing the selection or changing the active document; if you perform any of those steps while recording, they'll be ignored. But you can choose from the Property inspector, enter type, and choose from the menu commands as part of your recorded steps.

4. When you're done recording, choose Commands > Stop Recording.

The command that you've recorded will stay in memory, ready to be played back, until you record over it or until you quit Dreamweaver.

Playing Back Recorded Commands

To play back a recorded command, follow these steps:

1. Set up whatever conditions need to be in place before the command can be executed. (To replay a recorded command that formats a table, for instance, you must first select a table.)

2. Choose Commands > Play Recorded Command. The individual steps that you recorded will be executed.

3. Repeat this procedure as many times as you want, to execute the command as many times as needed.

Limitations of Recorded Commands

As you can see, recorded commands are pretty wonderful. But they do have their limitations. They're meant to be quick, temporary aids in performing certain repetitive tasks. They can't do anything more complex or long-term than that, including

- Dreamweaver can only store one recorded command at a time in memory. As soon as you record a new command, whatever command was previous being remembered will be overwritten.

- Recorded commands don't include dialog boxes, and so can't be customized according to user input. Each command will always perform exactly the same set of steps, with exactly the same parameters.

- Not all actions can be recorded. If you try to record a set of steps that includes changing a selection, for instance, that step won't be recorded. When the command is played back, this might lead to undesired results.

- There is no error checking. If, for instance, you haven't made the appropriate selection before replaying a recorded command, the command simply won't work. You won't get a nice friendly alert message telling you nicely what went wrong.

Automating Tasks with the History Panel

If you like the idea of recording and replaying your actions, but want more control and flexibility, the History panel offers two alternatives to recorded commands. Its Replay Steps and Save As Commands features enable you to save and reproduce sets of consecutive or non-consecutive steps temporarily or permanently. Repeated steps are intended for use when you want to perform a set of actions and then immediately repeat those actions one or more times. Saved commands are for when you want to save your set of actions as a permanent item in the Dreamweaver interface, ready for replaying at any time in the future.

Replaying Steps (Temporary) and Saving Commands (Permanent)

The procedure for repeating steps and saving steps as commands is basically the same. Just follow these steps:

1. Plan out the steps that you want to save, and if necessary set up the conditions for them (create a table to format, for instance).

2. Open the History panel by choosing Windows > Others > History, so you'll be ready to work with it. To make sure you're starting with a clean History panel and can capture as many steps as possible, choose Clear History from the Panel Options menu.

3. Perform whatever set of actions you want to repeat. Each action will show up as a step in the History panel (see Figure 34.6). As with recorded commands, repeated or saved History steps cannot include certain kinds of actions (such as changing the selection or moving the mouse). If your actions include any of these, they'll appear in the History panel as a horizontal red line or black mouse-movement indicator line.

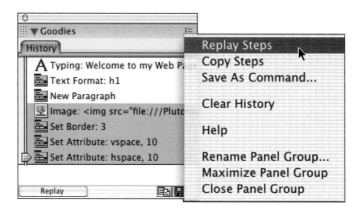

Figure 34.6   Repeating steps from the History panel.

4. When you're finished performing your procedure, and are ready to repeat it, select all the steps in the History panel that you want to repeat.

   - To select contiguous steps, Shift-click on each.

   - To select non-contiguous steps (for instance, to skip over a mouse movement), Ctrl-click (Windows) or Cmd-click (Mac) on each.

5. If you want to repeat these steps without saving them permanently, from the History panel's options menu choose Replay Steps. Each selected step will be performed again (unless it's a mouse movement or other unrepeatable action), and the History panel will show a new step called Replay Steps. Choose Replay Steps as many times as you need to; each replay will generate a new Replay Steps step in the panel.

6. If you want to save these steps as a permanent part of the Dreamweaver interface, from the History panel's options menu choose Save As Command. (If your steps include any that can't be captured, Dreamweaver will warn you of this and give you the opportunity to cancel the operation.) You'll be prompted to give your new command a name. After you've done this and clicked OK to close the dialog box, your new saved command will appear in the bottom portion of the Commands menu.

Note

For a refresher on how the History panel works, see Chapter 2.

Managing Saved Commands

After you've saved a set of History steps as a command, you can replay those steps any time by choosing your command from the Commands menu. Unlike the recorded commands described earlier, your saved command will stay saved until you get rid of it. So if you like saving commands, you'll likely end up with a variety of them. To rename or delete a saved command, choose Commands > Edit Command List (see Figure 34.7).

Figure 34.7   The Edit Command List dialog box for working with saved commands.

Exercise 34.2   Saving History Steps as a Custom Command

Are you already dreaming of all the commands you'd like to create? Before you get too excited, remember that mouse actions (such as selecting and drawing) can't be captured, so your commands can't include them. This limits the kinds of procedures that can be turned into saved commands. In this exercise, you'll try to create a command that inserts a centering table (a table with one row and one column, set to 100% width and height, with its one cell set to horizontally and vertically center any contents). Along the way, you'll see the limitations of saved commands and how to work within those limitations.

1. Start by creating a new HTML document to contain your table.

2. Open the History panel (Window > Others > History). Because you've just created this document, the panel should be empty; but if it's not, choose Clear History from the History panel options menu.

3. From the Insert bar's Common tab, click the Insert Table button to insert a table. In the Insert Table dialog box, set the options to match those shown in Figure 34.8 and click OK.

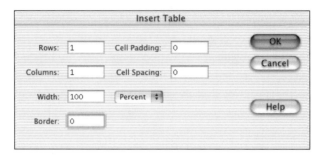

Figure 34.8   The Insert Table dialog box ready to insert a centering table.

4. One table attribute that can't be set in the dialog box is height. After the table is inserted, use the Property inspector to set the table height to **100%**. Note that your actions are appearing in the History panel as steps.

5. To make this a centering table, it must center its contents—created from cell attributes, not table attributes. To access cell properties, click inside the table. Then set the cell properties as shown in Figure 34.9). There's your centering table!

Figure 34.9   The Table Cell Property inspector set to center all cell contents.

6. Now it's time to turn those steps into a command. Examine the History panel, and you'll see that the steps for creating the table are separated from the steps for aligning contents by a black line (see Figure 34.10). That line tells you that an uncapturable mouse event occurred between those two sets of steps. (That mouse action was clicking inside the table to access cell properties.)

7. Try saving a command that uses all of these steps. In the History panel, Shift-click on each step until they're all selected. From the History panel's options menu, choose Save As Command. Dreamweaver will warn you that the command contains illegal actions that won't translate properly into a command. That's not good! Click No to close the warning dialog box.

8. Try again. This time, select only the steps for creating the table itself—up to the black line but not crossing it. Choose Save As Command from the History panel's options menu.

Figure 34.10   The History panel showing the steps involved in creating a centered table.

When the dialog box appears, name your command **Create 100% Table** and click OK.

Now select the steps for determining cell properties—those after the black line. Choose Save As Command, and name your command **Center in Table**.

9. Check the Commands menu and see your new commands in place (see Figure 34.11). You've overcome the limitations of saving commands by saving your procedure as two commands instead of one. Not a perfect solution, but still more efficient than not having a saved command at all.

Figure 34.11   The Create 100% Table and Center in Table saved commands as they appear in the Commands menu.

10. Try your command out. Create a new document. Choose Commands > 100% Table to insert the table. Then click inside the table (the mouse action that Dreamweaver couldn't record) to select its cell. Then choose Commands > Center Cell Contents. There's your command in action!

11. If you like your new commands, leave them in place. Otherwise, finish the exercise by going to Commands > Edit Command List. In the dialog box that appears, select each command in turn and click Delete. When you're finished, click Close to exit the dialog box.

Summary

Customizing Dreamweaver is a great way to maximize your working efficiency and enjoyment. Setting preferences is the first step to making Dreamweaver yours. In this chapter, you also learned all abut customizing the panel layout, modifying keyboard shortcuts, and automating tasks by creating temporary or permanent commands. All of these customizations give you a great deal of power, and they can all be handled entirely within the Dreamweaver interface. The next two chapters cover more extensive configuration changes you can make to Dreamweaver by using the Extension Manager and **Configuration** folder.

Chapter 35

Working with Extensions

Dreamweaver is unique in the world of commercial software because of the degree to which it can be tweaked, customized, and extended. Not only can you change defaults and tweak preferences, rearrange panel groups, and choose the classic or integrated workspace, but with Dreamweaver, you can actually change the program's functionality: create new panels, commands, and menu entries, and more. And it's all because of extensions.

This chapter examines how extensions work within the Dreamweaver architecture, and how you can start customizing your Dreamweaver program—without any programming knowledge required—by changing settings in Dreamweaver configuration files. The chapter also introduces the Extension Manager and the Macromedia Exchange for Dreamweaver, which you can use to download and install some of the hundreds of free and commercial extensions that have been created by other developers for your use.

How Dreamweaver Is Configured

Dreamweaver is not like other commercial software. Most programs are created in a programming language like C++, and then compiled into executable programs, meaning that you cannot delve into their structure to see how they were built or to adjust their functionality. It's become increasingly popular, over the last several years, for programs to offer plugin architecture, which allows third-party developers to create independent program modules—called plugins, or Xtras, or Xtensions, or even filters, depending on the software involved. But these modules must generally also be constructed as compiled programs built in C++ or comparable languages.

Dreamweaver, on the other hand, was built with the express idea of enabling users to modify or add to the basic core of the program. To do this, the engineers built Dreamweaver as a combination of a compiled C core, with most of the interface and many of its functions coded into external JavaScript, XML, and HTML files. These external files are called extensions. By editing these extensions, you can customize how Dreamweaver looks and works. By adding to them, you can add to Dreamweaver functionality. Though you have to know your way around JavaScript to create your own extensions, it only takes a fundamental knowledge of HTML and XML to customize an extension's interface. And the Macromedia Exchange for Dreamweaver has hundreds of extensions written by other developers, available free or commercially for download and installation.

Note

See Chapter 36, "Creating Extensions," for a discussion on how to create your own simple extensions.

Working with the Configuration Folder

The key to all these menus, commands, and functions is the *Configuration folder*. This folder, located within the Dreamweaver Application folder, contains all the extension files for the program. Examine the **Configuration** folder (see Figure 35.1), and you'll recognize many of the folders within as matching Dreamweaver elements: Objects, Behaviors, Commands, Menus, Inspectors, and so on. Within those folders are the individual files that control the appearance and functionality of the different Dreamweaver interface elements. The general breakdown of file types within the folder is as follows:

- HTML files provide the layout and interface elements for individual dialog boxes, panels, and inspectors.

- The JavaScript files—and any JavaScript code embedded within the HTML files—provide the functionality for the different extensions.

- The XML files provide the instructions Dreamweaver follows on how the different extensions should be integrated into the main program interface.

Figure 35.1 The Dreamweaver **Configuration** folder and its contents.

If you feel adventurous enough to tinker with these files, you can customize and even extend your Dreamweaver program. In this chapter, you'll get a chance to explore the HTML and XML files in the **Configuration** folder and changes you can make within them. The next chapter covers extending program functionality using JavaScript.

Warning

Important: Before making *any* changes to the **Configuration** folder, it is vital that you make a backup copy so that you may return Dreamweaver to its original state in case anything corrupts. You can store your backup wherever you want; just make sure that you copy the whole folder!

Dreamweaver Configuration in a Multi-User Environment

Beginning with Dreamweaver MX, the program is configured to support a multi-user environment. This means that, if you're working in a multi-user environment where different people can log onto your computer with different user names and passwords, each of you will have your own set of Dreamweaver Preferences, Keyboard Shortcuts, and other program settings. Generally, this is a very good thing. It keeps you and that fellow on the night shift from ruining one another's Dreamweaver experience, as you each happily customize your workspace to suit your own idiosyncratic needs. It can seem like a very bad thing, however, if you don't know it's happening and wonder why your copy of Dreamweaver has suddenly become schizophrenic, changing personalities because of the person who logged on today.

How Dreamweaver Multi-User Configuration Works

Dreamweaver creates multi-user configuration by having multiple **Configuration** folders. While most of the program's configuration tasks are carried out by the main **Configuration** folder stored within the Dreamweaver Application folder, each user also has his personal **Configuration** folder. For Dreamweaver/Windows, each user's personal configuration files are stored in:

```
c:\documents and settings\username\application data\macromedia\
dreamweaver mx\configuration\
```

For Dreamweaver/Mac OS X, they're stored in:

```
/users/username/library/application support/dreamweaver mx/
configuration
```

(For each user, substitute the correct user name for *username*.) This folder is created the first time the user launches Dreamweaver.

Examine one of these extra folders, and you'll see that it isn't a complete duplicate of the main **Configuration** folder. It contains only certain files, representing interface elements that need to be customized differently for each user. Preferences like code coloring, menus that can be customized with keyboard shortcuts, commands that can be recorded using the History panel, and even objects that save their dialog box settings from one work session to another; they are all represented in the individual user's **Configuration** folder.

Multi-User Environments and the Configuration Folder

How important is this to you? If you're just interested in being a general Dreamweaver user, all you need to know about multi-user configuration is that it's happening. If you're a tinkerer, however, working with configuration files to customize your program, you need to know which **Configuration** folder contains the files you want to work with for any given task. The general rule is this: When looking for extension files, Dreamweaver always looks in the user's **Configuration** folder first. This means that if a file exists in that folder, Dreamweaver will use it (and it won't use the duplicate file that exists in the main folder). Only if a particular extension file has no counterpart in the user's folder will Dreamweaver use the file in the main **Configuration** folder.

Are You in a Multi-User Environment?

If you're working on Windows 2000, NT, or XP, you might be working in a multi-user environment. If multiple users can log on to your computer (either because different people use the computer or because you have different user accounts for different purposes), you're in a multi-user environment. If, on the other hand, you're the only user who has access to your computer or has ever logged onto your computer, chances are you're not using multi-user capabilities and you won't have to worry about these issues. (Your c:\documents and **Settings** folder will contain folders for All Users and Default users, but no username folders will be present, and all Dreamweaver configuration files will be called from the main **Configuration** folder.)

If you're working on Mac OS X, you are in a multi-user environment even if you're the only human who ever touches or signs on to your computer. If you're working on Windows Me, or 98, or on Mac OS 9, as far as Dreamweaver is concerned you are not in a multi-user environment—even if you have multiple users logging into your system or have Multiple User Accounts enabled (Mac OS 9).

Customizing Dialog Boxes Using HTML

Most objects, commands, and behaviors that provide dialog boxes store the layout information for those dialog boxes in HTML files within the **Configuration** folder. Input fields, checkboxes, pop-up menus, and such are created from standard HTML form elements, and formatted using tables or layers. While you can't add or remove input fields without compromising functionality, you can change the dialog box layout by changing the HTML layout. Strange as it might seem, you can even use Dreamweaver itself to do this editing—though you will have to quit Dreamweaver and relaunch before your changes take effect.

Note

Dreamweaver loads HTML and JavaScript files into memory at startup, and generally doesn't access them again as it's running; this is why it's safe to work on these files while the program is running. Dreamweaver may access XML configuration files at any time, however; so it's not a good idea to work on these files from within the program itself. See Chapter 33, "Writing Code in Dreamweaver," for more information on text editors.

To customize a particular dialog box, you first need to locate its configuration file. Table 35.1 lists locations for the elements you'll be most likely to customize. Within these locations, look for an HTML file named after the object, command, or other extension that you want to customize.

For instance, say you wanted to customize the Call JavaScript dialog box. Because Call JavaScript is a behavior, you'll look in **Configuration/Behaviors/Actions**. In that folder, you'll find **Call JavaScript.js** and **Call JavaScript.htm**. The JS file contains the functionality for the behavior; the HTML file contains the dialog box layout. If you open the HTML file in Dreamweaver, you'll see the dialog box layout as a form and table (see Figure 35.2). Any changes you make to the layout here will be reflected in the dialog box. Just don't rename the form or its elements, or add or subtract any form elements, or you might break the behavior.

Note

For multi-user environments: Because the Call JavaScript dialog box does not hold any settings from session to session, it does not exist as a user-specific file in the user's **Configuration** folder. It exists only in the main **Configuration** folder.

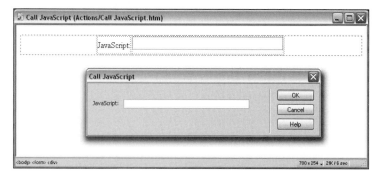

Figure 35.2   The **Call JavaScript.htm** file, as it appears in Dreamweaver Design view and in the Call JavaScript dialog box.

Table 35.1   Locations of Common Extension Types Within the Configuration Folder

Extension Type	Location
Objects (items in Insert bar and Insert menu)	Configuration/Objects (within subfolders according to category)
Behaviors	Configuration/Behaviors/Actions
Commands	Configuration/Commands Configuration/Menus/MM

Extension Type	Location
Inspectors*	Configuration/Inspectors
Panels*	Configuration/Floaters

Most panels, and many inspectors, are hard-coded into the main Dreamweaver application file, so you won't be able to customize them.

Exercise 35.1   Rearranging the Insert Table Dialog Box

In this exercise, you'll edit the HTML configuration file behind the Insert Table dialog box (Insert > Table) so that the input fields are in a different order. You'll be swapping the Cell Padding and Columns fields. This alters the tab order for users filling in this dialog box, so they'll tab from Rows to Columns to Cell Padding to Cell Spacing. Figure 35.3 shows the old and new Insert Table dialog boxes, side by side.

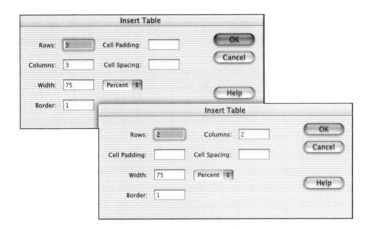

Figure 35.3   The Insert Table dialog box, in its original layout (left) and after being customized (right).

Before you begin this or any exercise in this chapter, make sure you have a backup copy of the **Configuration** folder so you can restore the default Dreamweaver configuration at any time. Open the Dreamweaver application folder and copy Configuration to some other location on your hard drive.

1. On your hard drive, locate and open the Dreamweaver **Configuration** folder (refer back to Figure 35.1 if necessary).

2. If you want to change the dialog box that belongs to the Table object, you need to determine where in the **Configuration** folder that file will be stored. Because the extension in question is an object, you'll start by looking in the Objects folder. Within that folder, the subfolders match the categories (tabs) of the Insert bar—so you'll look inside the **Objects/Common** folder. And there are the configuration files for the Table object (see Figure 35.4). **Table.gif** creates the Insert

bar icon for the object; **Table.js** contains the JavaScript code for creating and inserting the code; **Table.htm** contains the dialog box layout. That's the one you want to edit.

Figure 35.4   Configuration files for the Table object, as they appear in the **Configuration** folder.

3. Because the HTML files contain dialog box layout information, you want to edit **Table.htm**. Before you plunge into editing it, though, think twice! If you're in a multi-user environment, this might not be the copy of **Table.htm** you need to edit. If a user-specific **Configuration** folder exists, and if it has a **Table.htm** file, that's the one you'll need to edit.

- Windows users, if you have a user-specific version of the Table file, you'll find it at c:\Documents and Settings*yourname*\Application Data\Macromedia\DreamweaverMX\Configuration\Objects\Common\Table.htm (substitute your user name for *yourname*).

- Mac OS X users, if you have a user-specific version of the Table file, you'll find it at /Users/*yourname*/Library/Application Support/Macromedia/Dreamweaver MX/Configuration/Objects/Common/Table.htm (substitute your user name for *yourname*).

If you navigate to the appropriate location for your OS and there is no such file, then you're not set up for multi-user Dreamweaver use. You can safely work on the copy stored in the main Dreamweaver/**Configuration** folder.

Note

Table.htm exists in the user-specified **Configuration** folder because each time a user creates a table and uses the Insert Table dialog box, Dreamweaver remembers the settings entered (rows, columns, and so on) by rewriting **Table.htm** to include those values. All configuration files that can be rewritten like this, based on use, are considered user-specific.

4. After you've determined where your active copy of **Table.htm** is, open it in Dreamweaver. Switch to Design view, if you're not already there, and examine the layout elements. The Insert Table dialog box is constructed from a form containing a table and several form elements.

5. Using cut-and-paste or drag-and-drop (your preference!), swap the Cell Padding input field and the Rows input field. Then retype the text labels for each element to match its new placement. And finally, so that the newly placed Cell Padding label doesn't wrap in its table cell, select that cell and turn on the No Wrap option in the Property inspector. Figure 35.5 shows these changes being made.

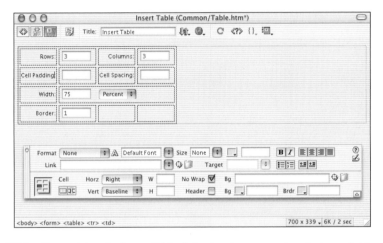

Figure 35.5   Customizing the Insert Table dialog box by rearranging the input fields and labels.

6. When you've made your changes, save the file and close it. Then quit Dreamweaver and relaunch it.

7. Now, create a new document (unless one is already open) and try inserting a table. Choose Insert > Table from the menubar, or click the Table object in the Insert bar. Your new dialog box should look just like the one shown in Figure 35.3. (If Dreamweaver gives you an error message when you try to insert a table, or if the dialog box looks wrong, you've made a mistake in your coding. Re-open **Table.htm** and try again. If the dialog box looks completely unchanged, you probably edited the wrong copy of **Table.htm**. Double-check your various **Configuration** folders to make sure you edited the correct file.)

Note

In a multi-user environment, the copy of **Table.htm** stored in the **Dreamweaver/ Configuration** folder is used as the model to create new user-specific configuration files. If you edit that file, you'll create a different table-making experience for all future Dreamweaver users who might start using your computer.

Customizing the Insert Bar with Insertbar.xml

New to Dreamweaver MX, the **Insertbar.xml** file determines what appears, and where, in the Insert bar. This XML file uses custom tags to determine the tabs (categories) that will appear in the Insert bar, what objects each tab should contain, and what order they'll appear in. While you can't add a new object without learning how to write the JavaScript that will construct the object, you can rearrange the existing objects and tabs—and even create new tabs to put existing objects in—with just a little knowledge of XML.

Insertbar.xml is located in Configuration/Objects (see Figure 35.6). To examine this file, open it in a text editor (not Dreamweaver, preferably). The structure of XML tags breaks down like this:

```
<insertbar>
    <category>
        <button />
        <button />
    <category>
    etc more categories
<insertbar>
```

Figure 35.6   The **Insertbar.xml** file as it appears within the **Configuration** folder.

The entire document is enclosed within <insertbar></insertbar> tags. Inside this *root element*, each tab of the Insert bar is represented by <category> elements (tags). Their order determines the order of tabs in the Insert bar. And within the <category> element, each object is represented by a <button/> element, whose attributes determine—among other things—which HTML file contains the object code and which GIF image should be used as the Insert bar icon. Other elements, such as <separator/> and <checkbutton/>, allow different kinds of content to be presented in the Insert bar.

Note

Because **Insertbar.xml** is an XML file, its code follows the syntax requirements of all well-formed XML documents. For a discussion of XML, see Chapter 32, "Technical Issues."

To rearrange the order that objects appear in a particular tab, open **Insertbar.xml** and rearrange the order of `<button/>` elements within the appropriate `<category>` element.

To copy an object so it appears in another tab, without being removed from the original tab that contained it, copy the object's `<button/>` element from the original location, and paste it into the new `<category>` element.

To move an object from one tab to another, cut its `<button/>` element from the original location, and paste it into the new `<category>` element.

To add a vertical separator bar between icons in the bar, add a `<separator/>` element in the appropriate location.

To create a new tab, you must do two things: First, in the **Configuration/Objects** folder, add a new folder with a unique name of your choice. Then, in **Insertbar.xml**, add a new `<category></category>` tag pair in the appropriate location (the tabs appear in the order of the `<category>` elements, remember). The `<category>` element should have the following syntax (substituting your information for the code shown in bold):

```
<category id="your_unique_ID" folder="your_folder">
</category>
```

You don't have to put anything in your new folder; but it must be present in the Configuration/Objects folder, or the tab won't show up in the interface.

Note

For multi-user environments: **Insertbar.xml** is not a user-specific file, so it will only exist in the main **Dreamweaver/Configuration** folder.

Exercise 35.2   Creating a Favorite Objects Tab in the Insert Bar

In this exercise, you'll create a new tab (category) for the Insert bar, called Favorites. To populate this tab, you'll copy references to your various favorite Dreamweaver objects from other tabs in the Insert bar. You'll also use separators to organize your favorites.

Before you begin this or any exercise in this chapter, make sure you have a backup copy of the **Configuration** folder, so you can restore the default Dreamweaver configuration at any time. Open the Dreamweaver application folder, and copy Configuration to some other location on your hard drive.

1. Before you can create a Favorites tab, you need to determine which Dreamweaver objects are your favorites. Launch Dreamweaver and browse through the Insert bar, making a note of which objects you tend to use the most. You're especially looking for objects that appear in different tabs, causing you to waste valuable work time jumping from tab to tab. (If all of your favorite objects are in the Common tab, then that's your favorite tab!)

2. Next, you need to create a Favorites folder. Using Windows Explorer or the Mac Finder, find and open the **Configuration/Objects** folder within the Dreamweaver application folder. Create a new folder. Name it **Favorites**.

3. To establish the new folder as a new tab (category), open **Insertbar.xml** in your text editor (preferably not Dreamweaver). You'll position your new tab at the end of all existing tabs—so you can find it easily—so scroll down to the last `</category>` tag , immediately preceding the closing `</insertbar>` tag. Insert the following code:

```
<category id="My_Favorites" folder="Favorites">
</category>
```

4. To populate the new category, go through your list of favorite objects. For each object, find the corresponding `<button/>` element in **Insertbar.xml**. Copy the entire `<button/>` element, and paste it in between your `<category></category>` tags. Though your objects can be in any order, you might want to place them logically—according to their original category, for instance—so your Favorites tab will be easy to read.

5. Finally, a little cosmetic smoothing out. If you have objects from several categories in your Favorites tab, you might want to separate them visually. To insert a vertical separator bar between each group of objects in your tab, insert a `<separator/>` tag in the appropriate places.

   Figure 35.7 shows a possible Favorites tab as it appears in the Insert bar. The code for this new tab would read as follows:

```
<category id="My_Favorites" folder="Favorites">

    <button id="DW_Table"
    image="Common\Table.gif"
    enabled="!_VIEW_LAYOUT"
    showIf=""
    file="Common\Table.htm"/>

    <button id="DW_Image"
    image="Common\Image.gif"
    enabled=""
    showIf=""
    file="Common\Image.htm"/>

    <button id="DW_Frames_Left"
    image="Frames\Left.gif"
```

```
      enabled=""
      showIf=""
      file="Frames\Left.htm"/>

      <button id="DW_Head_Keywords"
      image="Head\Keywords.gif"
      enabled=""
      showIf=""
      file="Head\Keywords.htm"/>

      <button id="DW_Head_Description"
      image="Head\Description.gif"
      enabled=""
      showIf=""
      file="Head\Description.htm"/>
  </category>
```

Figure 35.7   The Insert bar showing its new custom Favorites tab with objects.

Tip

Is your Insert bar getting a little bit crowded with all those tabs in there? If there are particular categories of objects that you never use, you can ease the squeeze by removing their <category> elements from **Insertbar.xml** to remove their tabs from the Insert bar. (You'll still be able to insert the objects by using the Insert menu, so you haven't lost those objects forever.) If you do this, though, be sure you have backed up your **Configuration** folder—or at least the **Insertbar.xml** file, because there's no getting it back otherwise!

Customizing Dreamweaver Menus with menus.xml

Every command that appears in the Dreamweaver menu system—which includes the application menus, contextual menus, and others—is determined by the menu configuration file, **menus.xml**. This file governs what menus appear in the menubars, what commands appear in each menu, and what action Dreamweaver should take when that command is chosen. (The action is usually to open and execute a configuration file, such as Objects/Common/Table.htm.)

Menus.xml is located in the Configuration/Menus folder. Like **Insertbar.xml**, it is a well-formed XML document. It contains a <menubar> tag pair as its root element, with various other elements (tags and tag pairs) nested within it. The main element structure is as follows:

```
<menubar>
    <menu>
        <menuitem/>
        <menuitem/>
    </menu>
    etc more menus
</menubar>
```

Note

The Configuration/Menus folder also contains **menus.bak**, a backup file for **menus.xml**. If you accidentally trash your only copy of **menus.xml**, you can duplicate **menus.bak**, change its extension to .xml, and resurrect your Dreamweaver menu system. (This doesn't mean you shouldn't back up your **Configuration** folder! If you rely on the BAK file for your backup, and it becomes corrupted, you'll need to reinstall Dreamweaver to get your menus back in working order.)

Each tag has a set of attributes that govern how each menu and command will appear, and what will happen when it is launched. Figure 35.8 shows a section of **menus.xml** and how it translates into a menu in Dreamweaver.

Figure 35.8   A section of **menus.xml** and the Dreamweaver menu it creates.

While you can't add an entirely new menu item, and give it functionality without scripting, you can still customize your menu system by tweaking the XML. You can move menu items, add separators between items, and even copy menu items so they appear in multiple places—once in a regular menu and once in a contextual menu, for instance. One caveat related to duplicating menu items, however: Each item in **menus.xml** has an id attribute, which must be unique. If you duplicate an item, you must change the duplicate's id so it is different than that of the original item.

Exercise 35.3   Adding a Command to a Contextual Menu

In this exercise, you'll climb around inside **menus.xml** and copy the Check Spelling command from its location at the bottom of the application menubar's Text menu to another location at the bottom of the contextual menu for text items.

Before you begin this or any exercise in this chapter, make sure you have a backup copy of the **Configuration** folder, so you can restore the default Dreamweaver configuration at any time.

1. To start, quit Dreamweaver (if it's running) and open menus.xml in your text editor. Note that this is a big file, and it's easy to get lost in here! To help you out, if your text editor supports line numbers and word wrap control, turn on line numbering and turn off word wrap (called soft wrap in some programs). This will make navigating and seeing the structure of the XML tags easier.

2. The hardest part of this whole procedure is finding your way around **menus.xml**. You're looking for the Check Spelling menuitem, which is at the bottom of the Text menu. You can try performing a search for "spelling," or you can use your line numbers to navigate to line 2485. (Depending on what third-party extensions you might have installed in your copy of Dreamweaver, your Check Spelling menuitem might not be exactly at line 2485, but it should be close.)

3. Select the entire Check Spelling menuitem, and Edit > Copy. Your selected code should look like this:

```
<menuitem name="Check Spelling" key="Shift+F7"
enabled="dw.getDocumentDOM() != null &&
dw.getDocumentDOM().getParseMode() == 'html' && (dw.getFocus() ==
'textView' || dw.getFocus(true) == 'html' || dw.getFocus() ==
'document' && dw.getDocumentDOM().getFocus() == 'body')"
command="if (dw.getDocumentDOM().getView() == 'code')
{dw.getDocumentDOM().setView('split')}dw.setFocus('document');
dw.getDocumentDOM().checkSpelling()" id="DWMenu_Text_CheckSpelling"
/>
```

(What's all that code for? The Check Spelling command doesn't call on an extension file; instead, all the code for the spell check is contained in the menu entry itself.)

4. Now you have to find the Text contextual menu. This is a little bit trickier because there's no unusual word like spelling to search for. But if you examine a few of the contextual menu entries (they start around line 76), you'll see that

each contextual menubar entry ends with `Context">`. Perform a search using that, and you'll find each contextual menubar. You'll find the Text contextual menu at around line 631. After you've found that, you can search for `</menubar>`, because the next occurrence of that tag will be the end of this menubar. The last menuitem entry should be Page Properties, at around line 769.

5. You want to create a new line after the Page Properties entry. To create a separator line, so your new entry sits by itself at the bottom of the menu, type the following into the new line:

   `<separator/>`

   Then create another new line and Edit > Paste to insert the Check Spelling menuitem.

6. Finally, you need to find the new menuitem's `id` attribute and change it slightly so it's unique. Find the end of that very long `<menuitem/>` tag, and change the `id` to the following (new code is in bold):

   `DWMenu_Text_CheckSpelling_`**`Context`**

   Just to make sure your new `id` is unique, perform a search of **menus.xml** for this name. You should find just one occurrence of it—the one you just added.

7. Launch Dreamweaver and try out your new menu! Type some text into a document, select the text, and right-click (Windows) or Ctrl-click (Mac). The contextual menu that appears will look like the one shown in Figure 35.9.

Figure 35.9   The Text contextual menu with separator and Check Spelling command added.

Installing and Using Extensions

If you want to move beyond customizing Dreamweaver into actually extending its functionality, you're ready for some new extensions. If you want to take advantage of the programming prowess of others, without having to write extensions yourself, you're ready for the Macromedia Exchange for Dreamweaver and the Extension Manager.

The Macromedia Exchange for Dreamweaver

The Macromedia Exchange for Dreamweaver is a huge storehouse of extensions that Macromedia has collected and put on the web for all to use. Although Macromedia has written some of these extensions, the majority was written by independent developers who created the extensions to help themselves and have agreed to share them with the Dreamweaver community. These extensions have been packaged in a common format (MXP) and put on the Exchange for all to use. Most are free, though a few are commercially produced and might have a small cost.

Note

The Exchange is not the only place to find extensions. Many extension-writing Dreamweaver developers have extensions and have placed them and others on various web sites. See Appendix B, "Online Resources for Dreamweaver Web Developers," for listings of some popular developer web sites.

Access the Macromedia Exchange for Dreamweaver by pointing your browser to www.macromedia.com/exchange/dreamweaver (see Figure 35.10). Hundreds of different extensions are available for adding all sorts of functionality to Dreamweaver—everything from enabling site searches to installing lists of country codes to adding new Flash button styles. All extensions have been tested by Macromedia to assure that they'll install and function correctly; those with Macromedia approval have been tested more rigorously, and meet Macromedia UI guidelines so they'll blend smoothly with the Dreamweaver interface. You can browse extensions by category or search by title or author. To actually download extensions, you'll need to sign up for a free Macromedia Exchange account.

Figure 35.10   The Macromedia Exchange for Dreamweaver, home to hundreds of (mostly) free extensions.

You can also access the Exchange from within Dreamweaver, by choosing any of the Get More commands, such as Insert > Get More Objects, Commands > Get More Commands, or the Get More Behaviors command at the bottom of the Behaviors panel's Actions pop-up menu. Choosing any of these commands will launch your browser and take you to the Exchange home page.

To download an extension from the Exchange, find the extension you want and follow the links to its download page; then choose the Windows or Mac version, and download. Extensions are usually very small files (most are under 100K) and therefore download quickly even on slow connections. The downloaded file will be a special installer file with the .mxp extension (Macromedia eXtension Package), which can be installed into Dreamweaver using the Extension Manager utility.

The Extension Manager

The *Extension Manager* (EM) is a utility program used to install and manage your downloaded extensions (see Figure 35.11). You can launch the Extension Manager from within Dreamweaver by choosing Commands > Manage Extensions or Help > Manage Extensions. You can also launch it from your desktop through Start > Programs > Macromedia > Macromedia Extensions Manager (Windows) or by finding and launching it from within the Macromedia Extension Manager folder (Mac). From your desktop, you can also double-click on any MXP file to automatically launch the Extension Manager.

Figure 35.11   The Extension Manager interface showing several Dreamweaver extensions already installed.

Note

The Extension Manager isn't just for Dreamweaver. It also installs and manages Flash and Fireworks extensions.

To install an extension using the Extension Manager, either double-click on the MXP file on your desktop, which will launch the EM and start the installation process, or launch the EM separately, and choose File > Install Extension. Installation generally doesn't take long. During the installation process, extension files are added to the appropriate places in the **Configuration** folder and any relevant XML files (like **Insertbar.mxl** or **menus.xml**) have new information added to them. Some extensions require that Dreamweaver be restarted before they'll appear in the interface; the EM will alert you if this is the case.

After the extension is installed, you can read all about it in the EM interface (see Figure 35.11). You can temporarily deactivate the extension by deselecting it in the extensions list. Or you can permanently delete it by selecting it and choosing File > Remove Extension.

Note

In addition to installing extensions, the Extension Manager can be used to package extensions into MXP files, and even to submit them to the Macromedia Exchange for Dreamweaver. See Chapter 36 for more on using the EM in this way.

Exercise 35.3   Downloading and Installing the Zero Page Borders Extension

In this exercise, we will download and install Andrew Wooldridge's Zero Page Borders extension, a simple but handy command that quickly sets your document's margins to 0 as if you had set all relevant values in the Modify > Page Properties dialog box.

1. From within Dreamweaver, choose Commands > Get More Commands. This will launch your browser and take you to the Macromedia Exchange for Dreamweaver.

2. If you haven't already created a Macromedia user account, take a moment to do so now. It's as simple as entering a user ID and password (see Figure 35.10).

3. Because you know the extension you want, you can search for it. In the Exchange's search field, type Wooldridge, and click Search.

4. After a moment, a list of Andrew Wooldridge's extensions will come up. Find Zero Page Borders and click on it. From here, you'll be taken to the downloads page. Choose the appropriate download format (Windows or Mac) and download.

5. You've downloaded the file! Find it on your hard drive—it's an MXP file called **Zero Page Borders.mxp**—and double-click it to launch the Extension Manager. You'll be prompted to agree to the Macromedia license for extensions (click Agree to continue), and then you'll get a message telling you the extension was successfully installed. Congratulations!

6. Examine the EM interface to learn more about this extension (see Figure 35.12). You'll see that it's a command, accessed through the Commands menu, and that it sets the page borders to zero. What could be simpler?

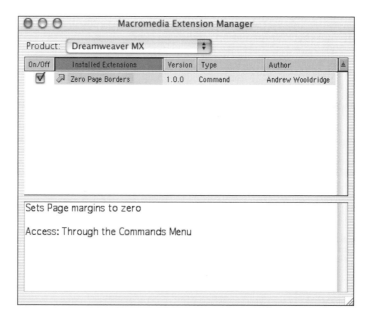

Figure 35.12   The Zero Page Borders extension as it appears in the Extension Manager.

7. If you had Dreamweaver running when you installed this extension, you didn't get prompted to quit and relaunch. That means the extension should work right away. If you don't have Dreamweaver running, launch it now.

8. In Dreamweaver, create a new document, unless one is already open. Type a few words on the page so you can see the default page margins in action (about 8 pixels worth of space on top and left). Go to the Commands menu—there's your new command! Choose Commands > Zero Page Borders. You'll get a prompt telling you the command has executed, and your margins are moved (see Figure 35.13)!

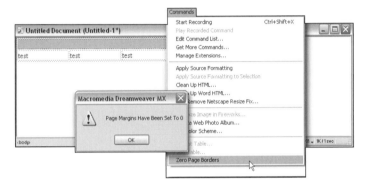

Figure 35.13   The Zero Page Borders command in action.

Summary

The extensible architecture behind Dreamweaver makes it unique in the commercial software world. Thanks to the **Configuration** folder, with its HTML, XML, and JS files, almost all aspects of the program's interface and functionality can be customized and added to relatively easily. If you enjoy tinkering with HTML and XML, the nonscripted files of the **Configuration** folder allow you to customize menus, dialogs, and even some panels. If you love souping up your program with extra functionality, but don't want to become a programming geek to do it, the Macromedia Exchange for Dreamweaver and Extension Manager open up a world of extensions that are easily installed and immediately useful. For those of you who do want to dip your toes a little deeper into the pool, keep reading: The next chapter introduces you to the wonderful world of scripting, packaging, and sharing your own extensions with the Dreamweaver community.

Chapter 36

Creating Extensions

You learned in the preceding chapter how to take advantage of Dreamweaver extensions written by other people. For ultimate power in Dreamweaver, it's also possible to write your own. This chapter discusses how

Dreamweaver uses JavaScript, HTML, and XML to create extensions, and how you can create two of the most popular and accessible types of extensions—objects and commands.

Before Getting Started

Although writing Dreamweaver extensions isn't just for propeller-heads, it isn't for sissies, either. To work with object and command files, you need to be fairly comfortable reading and writing HTML code; and you need some understanding of JavaScript. In particular, you should be familiar with the basic language structure, syntax requirements and concepts of JavaScript (expressions, variables, functions, and so on), and how to use JavaScript to process data collected by HTML forms.

Note

If you're a JavaScript newbie, or your skills are rusty, you might want to have a JavaScript reference available as you work. The handiest reference is the JavaScript section in the Dreamweaver Reference panel (see Chapter 33, "Writing Code in Dreamweaver"). If you want more in-depth information, the O'Reilly series books on JavaScript (*JavaScript in a Nutshell*, *JavaScript Pocket Reference*) are a valuable resource.

Writing extensions is also an inherently dangerous occupation. Because you are messing around in the guts of Dreamweaver, you can very easily break the program. In Chapter 35, "Working with Extensions," you learned about the **Configuration** folder and its role in Dreamweaver functionality. Writing extensions involves altering the **Configuration** folder. Always make a backup of this folder before you begin exploring and tinkering. If disaster strikes and Dreamweaver stops functioning properly, just quit Dreamweaver, trash the corrupted **Configuration** folder, and replace it with your backup. The next time you launch the program, all should be well.

You'll also need a text editor to create all the code involved in extending Dreamweaver. Odd as it might sound, many extending tasks can be done using Dreamweaver itself as the text editor. It's not recommended, though. Editing some configuration files, like **menus.xml** or **insertbar.xml**, while Dreamweaver is running can cause problems. You can also get very confused trying to create code in Dreamweaver. You might, however, want to use Dreamweaver Design view to help you design the interfaces for your extensions.

The Dreamweaver API

Dreamweaver extensions are constructed following the Dreamweaver application programming interface (API), which consists of all the procedures, file construction specifications, custom functions and formatting instructions that determine how and when commands will be processed and dialog boxes will appear, and so on. Learning how to write your own extensions means getting familiar with the API. The official "dictionary" that explains and documents the API is Macromedia's *Extending Dreamweaver* manual. This manual comes in PDF format on the Dreamweaver application CD-ROM; you also can download the PDF from the Macromedia web site (`www.macromedia.com/support/dreamweaver/`).

How Extensions Are Constructed

Each extension (object, behavior, command, inspector, floating panel, report, translator, and so on) consists of one or more files in the **Configuration** folder. The file types are as follows:

- **HTML file.** Each extension begins with an HTML file. For every command, every object, every behavior, there is one HTML file that *is* the extension. Form elements, placed in the body, become the user interface for the extension.

Note

Every time there's a rule, there's an exception. While most extensions exist in HTML and JS files, it is possible to create simple extensions that exist solely as command lines built into **menus.xml**. How that works is beyond the scope of this chapter.

- **JS file.** Each extension gains its functionality through JavaScript. The script functions can be placed in the head of the main HTML file, or (more frequently) are found in JS files linked to the HTML file. Complex extensions might link to several JS files.

- **GIF files.** Icons, buttons, and any other graphic elements that appear in the user interface are created from GIF images, which are also stored in the **Configuration** folder.

In addition to these files, each extension might have an entry in one of the XML files, such as **menus.xml** or **insertbar.xml** that Dreamweaver uses to populate many of its interface elements.

How Extensions Are Processed

For each extension type, the Dreamweaver API has a procedure that determines how the extension's JavaScript instructions will be processed. This procedure often involves custom JavaScript functions that Dreamweaver executes automatically at certain times (on startup, when the user clicks something, and so on).

How Extensions Talk to Dreamweaver

How does an extension tell Dreamweaver to open a new document, insert or edit document contents, or whatever else you want it to do? The API includes a variety of predefined JavaScript objects, each of which contains various methods (functions) that you use to communicate with different parts of the program. The main objects are as follows:

- **The Dreamweaver (`dw`) object.** This object contains dozens of methods to control application-wide behavior. Some sample methods are `dw.openDocument()`, `dw.browseForFileURL()`, `dw.openWithExternalEditor()`, `dw.undo()`. This object also contains child objects representing different parts of the application, each of which has its own set of methods—for instance, `dw.cssStylePalette.editSelectedStyle()`, `dw.historyPalette.startRecording()`, `dw.timelineInspector.setCurrentFrame()`.

- **The Document (`dom`) object.** This object contains hundreds of methods, controlling all aspects of document editing. Document object methods and properties can be used to manipulate the selection (`dom.getSelectedNode()`, `dom.setSelection()`); can change any document property (`dom.body.bgcolor="000000"`); and can access and edit any item in a document (`dom.deleteTableRow()`).

- **The Site object.** This object contains methods for working with sites and the Site panel. Site methods enable you to get and put files (`site.get()`, `site.put()`); perform sitewide file-management chores (`site.findLinkSource()`, `site.locateInSite()`); and work with the Site panel itself (`site.editColumns()`, `site.setFocus()`).

In addition to these main objects, other custom JavaScript objects give access to specific areas of Dreamweaver, such as working with web servers (the `MMHttp` object), working with Flash and Fireworks (`SWFFile`, `FWLaunch`), Design Notes (`MMNotes`), and so on. All of these objects, methods, and properties are detailed in the *Extending Dreamweaver* manual, mentioned earlier.

Creating Object Extensions

The simplest kind of Dreamweaver extension to understand and create is the object. An *object*, in terms of the Dreamweaver API, is an HTML file that contains, or uses JavaScript to construct, a string of HTML code to insert into the user's document. The user clicks an icon in the Insert bar, or selects an item from the Insert menu, and the specified code is inserted into the current document, usually at the insertion point.

Objects in the Configuration Folder

As you learned in the preceding chapter, object files are stored in subfolders of the **Configuration/Objects** folder that correspond to object categories in the Insert bar. Most objects consist of from one to three files, all with the same name but different extensions. These files are as follows:

- **An HTML file (table.htm, for instance).** This is the object file itself. The file that contains or returns the code to be inserted. This is the only file that *must* be present to constitute an object.

- **A JavaScript file (table.js, for instance).** This file contains JavaScript instructions for constructing the code to be inserted, in the form of one or more JavaScript functions, and is called on from the HTML file. This file is optional: It is entirely legal to contain the JavaScript functions in the head section of the object file instead of saving it to an external file. As experienced scripters know, it can be easier to keep track of and update JavaScripts if the code is in a separate file—but it isn't necessary.

- **An image file (table.gif, for instance).** This file contains an 18×18 pixel image that Dreamweaver uses to represent the object in the Insert bar. This file is also optional: If there is no image file, Dreamweaver will supply a generic image icon to represent the object in the panel.

Figure 36.1 shows some typical sets of object files.

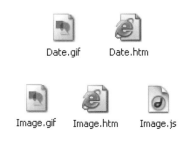

Date.gif   Date.htm

Image.gif   Image.htm   Image.js

Figure 36.1   Files for the Date object (two files only) and the Image object (three files), both found in the **Configuration/Objects/Common** folder.

Objects in the Insert Bar: insertbar.xml

 Dreamweaver MX relies heavily on XML files to help construct a unified interface from its many files and extensions. The **insertbar.xml** file, stored in the **Configuration/Objects** folder, contains a series of nested XML tags that govern what objects appear where in the Insert bar. Examine this file in a text editor and you'll see that each object category is created from <category></category> tags. Within a category, each object's presence in the panel is determined by a <button/> tag. The button tag includes attributes specifying what files the object will call on, when it will appear in the panel, and what its unique identifier is. The Common category, Date object looks like this:

```
<category id="DW_Insertbar_Common" folder="Common">
...
<button id="DW_Date"
        image="Common\Date.gif"
        enabled="true"
        showIf=""
        file="Common\Date.htm"/>
...
</category>
```

The API for Objects

Some objects, such as the Table object, use dialog boxes to collect user information; others, such as the HR object, don't. The overall structure and procedure for both is the same.

Object File Structure

Figure 36.2 shows the HTML file for a simple object that doesn't call a dialog box. Note that the body section is empty. Also note that the objectTag() function is not called anywhere in the file. Dreamweaver will call the function automatically. Figure 36.3 shows the file for the same object, with a dialog box. The body contains a form, which will become the contents of the dialog box. Note that the form does not include a submit button. Dreamweaver will supply this.

```
<html>
<head>
<title>My Simple Object</title>
<script language="JavaScript">
function objectTag() {
return "This is my object.";
}
</script>
</head>
<body>
</body>
</html>
```

Figure 36.2 The HTML file for a simple object that does not call a dialog box.

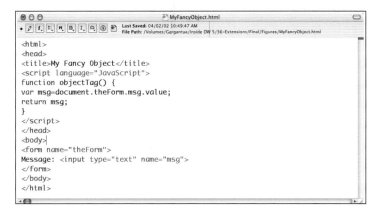

Figure 36.3   The HTML file for an object that does call a dialog box.

Both files contain the following key elements:

- **Filename.** This becomes the Insert menu entry for the object.
- **Page title.** This becomes the tooltip that pops up to identify the object in the Insert bar.
- **objectTag() function.** This JavaScript function is the most important element of the object file. The function returns the exact code you want the object to insert into your document, enclosed in quotes. The objectTag() function is part of the Dreamweaver API, so it doesn't need to be defined. It also doesn't need to be called; Dreamweaver calls it automatically when the object is chosen.
- **HTML form (optional).** This becomes the dialog box for collecting user input and customizing the code. Dreamweaver supplies the OK and Cancel buttons automatically.
- **displayHelp() function (optional).** If there is a dialog box, and this function is defined, Dreamweaver will add a Help button to the dialog box. When the user clicks that button, the function will be executed.

In the example shown in Figure 36.2, the code returned by the objectTag() function is a simple level 1 heading. Everything between the quotation marks, in the return statement, will become part of the user's document. In the example shown in Figure 36.3, form input is collected and used to construct the return statement.

The Procedure for Objects

The API procedure for processing objects determines how and when Dreamweaver uses the file elements previously discussed. The procedure is as follows:

1. At startup, Dreamweaver reads the **insertbar.xml** file, and populates the Insert bar using its entries. It also populates the Insert menu, using the filename as the menu entry.

2. When the user mouses over the object in the panel, Dreamweaver uses the `<title>` from the object file to create the tooltip that will appear.

3. When the user clicks an object, Dreamweaver reads the object file. If the file includes body content, Dreamweaver displays a dialog box containing the content, supplying OK and Cancel buttons automatically. If the file contains a `displayHelp()` function, a Help button also will appear.

4. The final step in the API process is calling the `objectTag()` function. If there is a dialog box, the function is called when the user clicks OK. If there is no dialog box, the function is called as soon as the user clicks the object icon in the Insert bar. Whatever string of text is returned by the `objectTag()` function is inserted into the user's document, usually at the insertion point. (An exception to this is when the `return` string contains head content, such as a `<meta>`, `<base>`, or `<link>` tag. In this situation, even if the insertion point is in the body, Dreamweaver will insert the code into the head.)

Pretty simple, eh? To create an object extension, all you have to do is decide what code you want inserted and create a file that matches the structure shown in Figures 36.2 and 36.3. Then create an entry for the object in **insertbar.xml**, to make it part of the Dreamweaver interface.

Note

Not all objects are created equal! Some items lurking in the Insert bar—especially those representing server-side code for live data pages—are very complex commands in object-disguise. They're way beyond the scope of this chapter.

Exercise 36.1   Setting Up Shop

In this exercise, you'll get your working space in order and learn some of the basic extension-developing features available in Dreamweaver. You will create a custom folder within the **Objects** folder to store your exercise objects, and add data to **insertbar.xml** so your custom folder becomes a custom Insert bar category.

1. To begin with, make sure Dreamweaver isn't running. You are doing this to experiment with how and when Dreamweaver loads extensions.

2. If you haven't done so already, make a backup copy of the **Configuration** folder, in case disaster strikes and you break something while tinkering with it.

3. Find and open the **Configuration/Objects** folder on your hard drive. Create a new folder inside this folder. Name it **Development**. It's a good strategy, when you're developing new objects, to put them in a special folder called **Custom** or **Development**, at least until you're sure they're running properly.

Note

Never store your object files loose in the **Configuration/Objects** folder, or Dreamweaver won't recognize them. Objects must be placed within an existing or new subdirectory within that folder.

4. In a text editor, open the **Configuration/Objects/insertbar.xml** file. Scroll to the end of the entries. Immediately above the closing `</insertbar>` tag, add the following code:

```
<category id="DW_Insertbar_ Development" folder="Development">
</category>
```

This will create a Development object category in the Insert bar, matching your **Development** folder.

5. Save and close **insertbar.xml**.

6. Launch Dreamweaver. At startup, the program checks the **Configuration** folder and loads all extensions inside.

7. Check the Insert bar for a new category called Development. Because you added the code at the end of **insertbar.xml**, it should appear as the rightmost tab of the Insert bar (see Figure 36.4). Of course, if you choose that category, it'll be empty. You'll address that next.

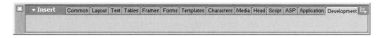

Figure 36.4   The new Development objects category in the Insert bar.

Exercise 36.2   Making a Simple Object

The simplest objects are those that don't call up a dialog box for user input, and therefore always return the same code. The simple object that you will create in this exercise is a copyright statement—just the sort of thing you might want to put at the bottom of all your web pages.

To create this object, use the text editor of your choice. Save all exercise files in the **Development** folder you created in the preceding exercise.

1. The first step when creating any object is to decide exactly what code you want the object to insert. In this case, you want a one-line piece of text, formatted however you like, utilizing the special HTML entity for ©. (See Chapter 4, "Working with Text," for more on creating HTML entities, such as the copyright symbol.) Figure 36.5 shows the copyright statement with formatting applied.

Figure 36.5   Formatting the Tom Thumb copyright statement for inclusion in an object file.

Tip

Use Design view to create and format the copyright statement; then go to Code view and the code will be there, written for you.

2. Next, create the basic object file, with all structural elements in place. Open your text editor and enter the basic required code for an object without dialog box. You can leave out the details specific to this object, for now. Your code framework should look like this (elements that you will be replacing later with custom text appear in bold):

```
<html>
<head>
<title>Title Goes Here</title>
<script language="JavaScript">
function objectTag() {
return 'inserted code goes here';
}
</script>
</head>
<body>
</body>
</html>
```

3. Enter a page title into the code. This will become the tooltip that shows in the Insert bar. A logical title for the current file might therefore be Tom Thumb Copyright Info. The top portion of your code should now look like this (new code is in bold):

```
<html>
<head>
<title>Tom Thumb Copyright Info</title>
```

4. Insert the desired line of code as the `return` statement of the `objectTag()` function. If you have the line of code already typed into your computer, you can just copy and paste it in; otherwise, type it in manually now.

   Note that the entire `return` statement has to be in quotation marks. They can be single or double quotes; just make sure they're in balanced pairs.

   Your code should now look like this (new code is in bold):

```
<html>
<head>
<title>Tom Tumb Copyright Info</title>
<script language="JavaScript">
function objectTag() {
return '<font face="Verdana, Arial, Helvetica, sans-serif"
➡size="2">&copy; Tom Thumb, 2001</font>';
}
</script>
</head>
<body>
</body>
</html>
```

Note

As with any JavaScript `return` statement, no hard returns can occur within the statement. Make sure your code is written out in one long line, or it won't work!

5. Save your file in the **Development** folder. Call it **Tom Thumb Copyright.htm**. The filename will become the menu command that appears in the Insert menu; so it's good practice to name it something descriptive. Capitalization and spacing also will carry through to the menu entry. (The extension can be **.htm** or **.html**—Dreamweaver accepts either.)

Tip

You can get more control over how the object name appears in the Insert menu by editing **Configuration/Menus/menus.xml**.

6. To make the new object appear in the interface, you'll need to add a `<button/>` tag to **insertbar.xml**. Quit Dreamweaver, if it's running, and open **insertbar.xml** in your text editor. Find the Development category tag you added earlier, and add the following code (new code is in bold):

```
<category id="DW_Insertbar_Development"folder="Development">
    <button id="DW_Development_TomThumbCopyright"
     image=""
     enabled="true"
     showIf=""
    file="Development\TomThumbCopyright.htm"/>
</category>
```

7. Test your object! Launch Dreamweaver and create a new document, if there isn't one already open.

8. Check the Development category of the Insert bar; the new object should be there, represented by its name rather than by an icon. Position the cursor over the name and the tooltip should appear (see Figure 36.6).

9. While you're at it, check the Insert menu. Your new object will appear at the bottom of the menu, identified by its file name.

Figure 36.6   The new custom object, with tooltip.

Note

Don't waste your time making custom icon files for objects while they're still in the development phase. Wait until the object is all polished and perfectly functioning; then dress it up with a custom icon. (Exercise 36.5 shows how to make an icon file.)

10. Make sure you're in Design view and click the object. The desired code should be inserted into the document at the current cursor position. Congratulations! You've made your very first object.

Troubleshooting

What If It Doesn't Work?

If your object doesn't show up in the Insert bar at all, you either saved it in the wrong place, didn't append the **.html** extension to the filename, or you might have a syntax error in the **insertbar.xml** file.

If your object shows up, but something is wrong with the code, you'll probably get an error message when Dreamweaver tries to execute the objectTag() function. Dreamweaver error messages are fairly specific in what went wrong and what needs fixing. Examine the message and fix your code accordingly.

Exercise 36.3   Creating an Object with a Dialog Box

Your simple object is fine as far as it goes, but it's not a very flexible or useful object because it always returns the same code, no matter what. What if you want to assign a copyright to someone besides good old Tom Thumb? A fully functional object would bring up a dialog box that would ask for user input, and would enter that information into the code. That's the object you will build in this exercise.

1. Open **Tom Thumb Copyright.htm** (from the preceding exercise) and save it as **Copyright Statement.htm** in the **Development** folder. Why reinvent the wheel? You can just build on your previous success by adding a dialog box and tweaking the `objectTag()` function's `return` statement to collect user input.

2. Change the `<title>` of the new object file to **Copyright Statement**.

3. Decide what pieces of the code you want to replace with user input. Check Figure 36.5 as a reminder of what the end product should look like. For this object, you want to ask the user for a copyright name (rather than Tom Thumb) and a copyright year. (If your JavaScript skills are up to it, you could have Dreamweaver automatically calculate the year; for this exercise, just ask the user to insert it.)

4. Create an HTML form that will serve as a dialog box to collect this information. To be functional, your form needs two text fields: one to collect the name and another to collect the year. So the simplest form you could possibly come up with might look something like the one shown in Figure 36.7.

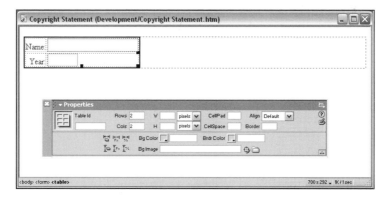

Figure 36.7   The form for the Copyright Statement object dialog box as it appears in Dreamweaver Design view.

Note

If you want to improve your skills creating user-friendly forms, pay attention to all the user interface elements in Dreamweaver. The dialog boxes, inspectors, and panels are beautiful examples of clean, transparent interface design; and they're constructed almost entirely from standard form elements.

5. Open **Copyright Statement.htm** and build the form in the body section of that file. If you like coding forms by hand, go to it. If you would rather use a visual editor, open the file in Dreamweaver and use Design view to build it, as is shown in Figure 36.7.

Note

If you're building your form in the Dreamweaver visual editor, method and action properties will be automatically added to the <form> tag. Your form doesn't need either of those because the form isn't going to be processed in the standard way. You can safely remove these properties from your code. Dreamweaver also will add background and text color properties to the <body> tag; you should remove these and let the software's UI controls determine the appropriate color scheme for the dialog box.

Your form code should look like this:

```
<form name="theForm">
<table>
   <tr valign="baseline">
          <td align="right" nowrap>Name:</td>
          <td align="left">
                 <input type="text" name="name" size="30">
          </td>
   </tr>
   <tr valign="baseline">
          <td align="right" nowrap>Year:</td>
          <td align="left">
                 <input type="text" name="year" size="10">
          </td>
   </tr>
</table>
</form>
```

Note that neither the table nor the text has any formatting in them. Dreamweaver will supply the formatting when it processes the extension. If you enter your own formatting, your dialog box won't meet Macromedia user interface guidelines, and might not look good on all computers. So don't do it!

6. Okay, your form is pretty; to make it functional, you need to rewrite the return statement of the objectTag() to include the collected user input. If you're an old coding hand, this will be a piece of cake. If you're a novice at JavaScript, the trickiest bit is balancing the opening and closing quotes, so you don't end up with any unterminated string literals. Your objectTag() function should now look like this (new code in bold):

```
function objectTag() {
return '<font face="Verdana, Arial, Helvetica, sans-serif"
➥size="2">&copy;
'+document.theForm.name.value+','+document.theForm.year.value+'
➥</font>';
}
```

Note

If you think the `return` statement is too unwieldy to read easily, you could collect the form input into variables and use those to construct the final statement.

7. Quit Dreamweaver, if it's running. To add the new object to your Insert bar, open **insertbar.xml** and add the following code to your Development category tag:

```
<button id="DW_Development_CopyrightStatement"
  image=" "
  enabled="true"
  showIf=""
  file="Development\CopyrightStatement.htm"/>
```

8. Launch Dreamweaver, and create a new document to try out your new object. You should get a lovely dialog box that looks like the one shown in Figure 36.8.

Note

As with all objects, you'll get a different experience inserting into Code view than you will in Design view. If you're in Code view (or in Code and Design view, with the code portion of the Document window active), be careful to position the cursor in between the <body></body> tags, and not in the middle of any existing tag code, before inserting.

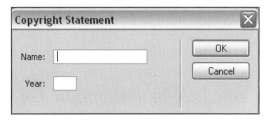

Figure 36.8   Dialog box for the Copyright Statement object.

9. When you fill in your information and click OK, a customized copyright statement line should appear in your document.

Troubleshooting

What If It Doesn't Work?

As with the earlier exercise, if there's a problem with your code, Dreamweaver should give you a helpful error message. Read the error message, try to guess what it means, and then go back to your code and look for problems. Compare your code to the code listed in this exercise to see what might be wrong.

The most common things that go wrong in this kind of object file are incorrect reference to form elements and mismatched single and double quotes in the `return` statement.

Exercise 36.4   Refining Your Object

This exercise shows that, although the only required JavaScript function for an object is the `objectTag()` function, you can add other optional functions. In fact, you can define any function you want to in the head section of the object file. Additional, locally defined functions can be explicitly called from any part of the interface, including the `<body>` (`onLoad`) or any of the form elements (`onClick`, `onBlur`, and so on).

The local function you'll add in this exercise addresses a minor annoyance you might have noticed in your object's dialog box. When the dialog box appears, the insertion point might not be in the correct position for you to immediately start entering data. Not a life-threatening problem, but less than slick.

1. Open the **Copyright Statement.htm** file in your text editor. Because this is not major surgery, you will work on the same object you created in the preceding exercise, instead of creating a new object.

2. Add an initializing function to the document head. Somewhere inside the `<script>` tags in the document's head section, add the following code:

```
function initializeUI(){
document.theForm.name.focus();
document.theForm.name.select();
}
```

What does this function do? The first line officially gives focus to whatever form element is named within it—in this case, the `name` field (your first text field). The second line selects the text (if any) in whatever form element is named within it—again, in this case, the `name` field.

Note

This function is used in many of the objects that ship with Dreamweaver. (Macromedia does not prohibit borrowing pieces of code.) Because the function is not part of the API, there's nothing magic about its name. If you would rather name it something different, feel free to do so.

3. To call the function, add the following code to the `<body>` tag of the object file:

```
<body onLoad="initializeUI()">
```

Because this function is not part of the Dreamweaver official object-handling procedure, it must be specifically called.

4. Try it out! Save and close the object file. Quit and relaunch Dreamweaver, and choose the object from the Insert bar. The insertion point will be primed and ready to enter data into the Name field of the dialog box.

Exercise 36.5   Adding an Object Icon

Professional-looking objects have their own icons. When the development phase of your object is finished, the final touch is to make an icon file to represent it in the Objects panel.

The requirements for an icon file are as follows:

- The file must be a GIF image file, preferably no larger than 18×18 pixels. (Larger images will work, but they'll be squashed into an 18×18 pixel space in the panel.)
- The file should have exactly the same name as the object file it goes with, but with the **.gif** extension. For this exercise, therefore, name the image **Copyright Statement.gif**.
- The file should be stored in the same folder as the object file it goes with. For this exercise, the icon file must be stored in the **Development** folder.
- The icon must be called on in **insertbar.xml**, by adding the image attribute to the `<button>` tag.

Icon files can have any colors you like, and the icon can look like anything you can imagine. You'll quickly discover, however, that designing icons that clearly communicate what they represent, when there are only 324 pixels to play with, is a real art.

1. Create, adapt, or borrow an 18×18 pixel GIF file containing an icon. If you have access to a good graphics program (such as Macromedia Fireworks), and want to create your own icon, do it. Otherwise, use the **Copyright Statement.gif** file in the **chapter_36** folder on the CD. (The image in this file is just a big fat © symbol, which is not hard to create.)

2. Put the icon file in the **Development** folder. The icon has to be stored in the same folder as the object file, remember.

3. Quit Dreamweaver. Then open **insertbar.xml** in your text editor and add the following code to your `<button/>` entry (new code is in bold):

```
<button id="DW_Development_CopyrightStatement"
 image="Development\CopyrightStatement.gif"
 enabled="true"
 showIf=""
 file="Development\CopyrightStatement.htm" />
```

4. Launch Dreamweaver, create a new document if needed to activate the Insert bar, and take a look at your icon! Figure 36.9 shows the **Development** folder, with a cool custom icon in place.

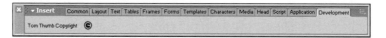

Figure 36.9   The Copyright Statement object as it appears in the Insert bar with its new custom icon in place.

Making the Most of Objects

Congratulations! You now know the foundation skills for making Dreamweaver objects. How can you make objects work for you? As you have seen, any piece of HTML code that you repeatedly use in web pages is a candidate for an object. The best object candidates, however, are pieces of code that you need to customize and then insert—changing the name and email address, specifying a certain URL to link to, and so forth.

Any time you find yourself going through the same steps over and over as you add content to web pages, ask yourself the following:

- Is the code I'm inserting similar enough each time that I could create an object from it?

- Are there differences in the code each time, or is it exactly the same code? (If the code is exactly the same each time, requiring no customization, it might be more efficient to use a recorded command or snippet.)

- How many more times do I think I'm likely to need to insert this code? Will my need continue after today? After the current assignment? Indefinitely? Creating an object is a time-consuming solution (not smart for a need that is only very temporary).

- Do I have some extra time right now to devote to making this object? (Never try a new, challenging solution when your deadline is 45 minutes away.)

Depending on your answers, you'll know whether it's time to crack open Dreamweaver and fit a new custom object inside.

Creating Command Extensions

Commands are those extensions that appear as entries in the Commands menu. (Actually, if you manipulate the **menus.xml** file as discussed in the Chapter 34, "Customizing Dreamweaver," you can make commands appear in any menu. But they appear in the Commands menu by default.) They are the most versatile and powerful of the extension types, enabling you to perform almost any edits on a document or site. Their API requirements are simple; yet, because they are so flexible, they are not easy to master. This section covers what's involved in creating simple (and also not-so-simple) Dreamweaver commands.

Commands in the Configuration Folder

Like all extensions, commands are made from HTML and JavaScript. Each command consists of an HTML file (the command file itself) and optional, associated JS files and/or graphics. Command files are stored in the **Configuration/Commands** folder. By default, all files in this folder will appear in the Commands menu.

Note

If you have ever recorded commands, or saved history steps as commands, you've created simple command files! Look in the **Configuration/Commands** folder and you'll find an HTML file for every saved command. The filename will be the name you gave the command when you saved it.

The API for Commands

Like objects, commands can exist with or without dialog boxes. They can be simple or complex. A number of API-defined functions can be part of the command file, but the file also can be very simple, with no special functions. The API procedure will be simple or complex, based on the file structure. (Note also that these are flexible extensions!)

Command File Structure

There are no required API functions for commands, although a variety of optional functions exist. Figure 36.10 shows a very basic command file, with only required elements in place. Note that the body section is empty. Note also that there are no API functions, and the main function is called onLoad.

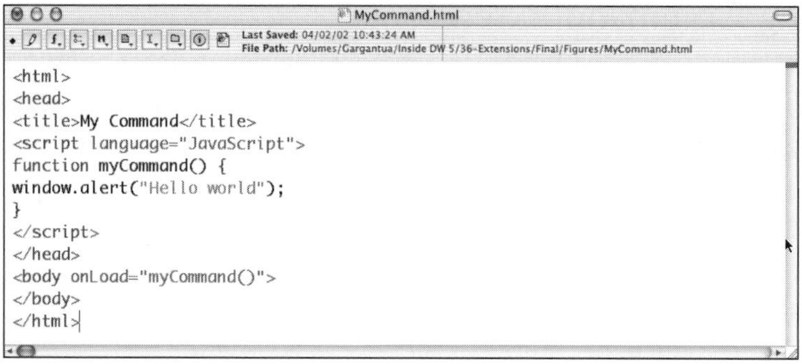

Figure 36.10   The HTML file for a simple command that does not call a dialog box.

This kind of file has the following elements:

- **Filename.** The filename, minus its extension, will become the menu entry. Command filenames can include spaces, and capitalization is respected.

- **Main function.** This is the function that makes the command do whatever you want it to do. It's a locally defined function, not part of the API, which means it must be called explicitly. If the command has no dialog box, the function should be called in the `<body>` tag, using the `onLoad` event handler. If the command has a dialog box, the function should be called as part of the `commandButtons()` function (described in the following list).

Believe it or not, that's all that's absolutely required of a command file without dialog box.

If the command includes a dialog box, a few more API elements are required. Figure 36.11 shows a sample command file with dialog box, again containing only the necessary elements. Note that the form does not include a submit button. The main command is now called from the `commandButtons()` function, not from the `<body>` tag.

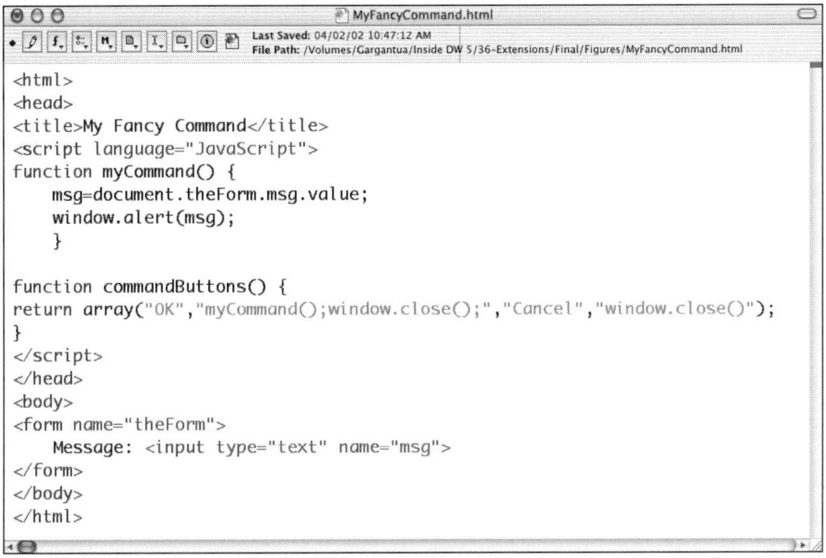

```
                          MyFancyCommand.html
  Last Saved: 04/02/02 10:47:12 AM
  File Path: /Volumes/Gargantua/Inside DW 5/36-Extensions/Final/Figures/MyFancyCommand.html

<html>
<head>
<title>My Fancy Command</title>
<script language="JavaScript">
function myCommand() {
    msg=document.theForm.msg.value;
    window.alert(msg);
    }

function commandButtons() {
return array("OK","myCommand();window.close();","Cancel","window.close()");
}
</script>
</head>
<body>
<form name="theForm">
    Message: <input type="text" name="msg">
</form>
</body>
</html>
```

Figure 36.11   The HTML file for a command that calls a dialog box.

The required elements for a command that calls up a dialog box are as follows:

- **Page title.** The title is required if the command includes a dialog box, and will become the title of the command's dialog box, if there is one. If there isn't a dialog box, the title is not required.

- **HTML form.** As with all extensions, this will create the user interface (in this case, the dialog box). Note that, as with objects, the form does not include a submit button. Unlike objects, however, command dialog boxes are not automatically supplied with buttons; instead, command buttons must be defined and given functionality using the commandButtons() function.

- **commandButtons() function.** If there is a dialog box, this function creates the buttons that will appear. If this function doesn't exist, the user will have no way to activate or close the dialog box! The commandButtons() function must return an array consisting of the name of each button, followed by the code to be executed when the button is clicked. Note that because the main command function must be called here, it should no longer be called using the <body> tag's onLoad handler.

In addition to these required elements, several optional API functions can be included. The most useful of these is canAcceptCommand(). This function determines whether the command should appear grayed out (that is, disabled) in the menu. A command that operates on the contents of a document, for instance, shouldn't be accessible if there is no document open. If the function returns true, the command will be accessible; if it returns false, the command will be grayed out. The API includes a whole slew of enablers (functions that determine whether something is possible) to help with this.

The Procedure for Commands

The API procedure for processing commands determines how and when Dreamweaver uses the file elements discussed in the preceding section. The procedure is as follows:

1. When the user clicks the Commands menu, Dreamweaver looks through all files that should appear in the Command menu, checking each for the `canAcceptCommand()` function. If it's present, and returns false, that command will be grayed out in the menu. If it's not present, or returns true, the command will be available.

2. When the user chooses a command from the menu, if there is no form, Dreamweaver executes whatever function is defined in the `<body>` tag's `onLoad` handler, and the procedure is complete.

3. If the command file does include a form, Dreamweaver calls the `commandButtons()` function to determine what buttons to add to the form. It then calls any function called `onLoad` (such as an `initializeUI()` function). It then presents the dialog box, displaying the `<title>` in the dialog box's title bar.

4. When the user clicks any of the buttons in the dialog box, Dreamweaver executes the code attached to that button by the `commandButtons()` function. Typically, an OK button calls the main function and closes the window; an Apply button calls the main function but doesn't close the window; a Cancel button just closes the window. Note that the dialog box will not close until one of the buttons uses the `window.close()` statement.

So far, it all sounds pretty simple. The complex aspect of commands is that you usually want them to act on documents. And acting on documents means dealing with the Dreamweaver DOM.

The Dreamweaver DOM

If you've worked in depth with JavaScript before—especially if you've created DHTML effects using JavaScript—you're already familiar with the concept of the document object model (DOM). The *DOM* is the hierarchical, or tree, structure of objects (tags, pieces of text, and so on) that makes up an HTML document. To gain access to any part of the document, you must navigate up and down the hierarchy, or climb up and down the tree.

Note

If you've ever torn your hair out struggling with the conflicting DOMs of Internet Explorer and Netscape, working with Dreamweaver commands will be a welcome relief, because there's only the Dreamweaver DOM to worry about.

Understanding Objects (Nodes)

An *object* is any page element that you can control by scripting. They have properties that you can access and change, and methods that represent things you can do with them. Objects are also called *nodes*.

Parents, Children, and Siblings

Just as an HTML document is constructed from tags nested inside each other, and text blocks nested inside tags, so objects, or nodes, can have parents, children, and siblings. In the following example, for instance, The `<ul>` object is the parent node of the three `<li>` objects, which are siblings of each other:

```
<ul>
        <li>Moe</li>
        <li>Larry</li>
        <li>Curly</li>
</ul>
```

The text block Moe is the only child node of the first `<li>` object. And so on. Figure 36.12 shows a typical document diagrammed as a tree of objects.

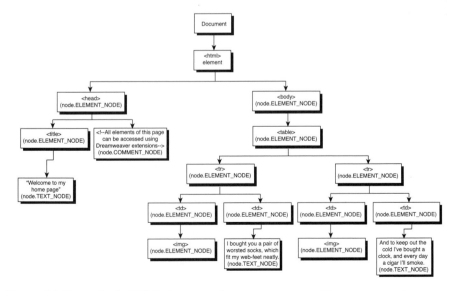

Figure 36.12   A simple HTML document shown as it appears in Dreamweaver and as a diagrammed document tree.

Node Types

There are four kinds of objects, or nodes, in a document:

- **The document node type**. The document itself, as an entity.

- **The element node type**. All HTML tags belong to this type.

- **The text node type**. Each block of text is an object of this type.

- **The comment node type**. HTML comments.

In the preceding example, the Moe object is of the text node type; its parent <li> object is of the element node type. Different node types have different properties and methods. Tables 36.1 through 36.4 list the properties and methods of the different node types, as they exist in the Dreamweaver DOM.

Table 36.1   DOCUMENT_NODE Objects

Property/Method	Return Value—(r) Indicates Read-Only
nodeType	9 (r)
parentNode	Null (r)
parentWindow	Object representing the document's parent window (r)
childNodes	NodeList containing all children (r)
documentElement	The <html> tag element (r)
body	The <body> tag element
URL	The absolute address of the document (or an empty string, if the document hasn't been saved)
getElementsByTagName (tagName)	NodeList containing all instances of the given tag
hasChildNodes()	true

Table 36.2   ELEMENT_NODE Objects

Property/Method	Return Value—(r) Indicates Read-Only
nodeType	1 (r)
parentNode	The parent tag (r)
childNodes	NodeList containing all immediate children (r)
tagName	HTML name for the tag (TABLE, A, IMG, and so on) (r)
attrName	String containing the value of the specified tag attribute
innerHTML	HTML code contained within the opening and closing tags of the element
outerHTML	HTML code contained within the tag, and the opening and closing tags
getAttributes(*attrName*)	Value of the attrName attribute

Property/Method	Return Value—(r) Indicates Read-Only
setAttribute (attrName, attrValue)	—
removeAttribute (attrName)	—
getElementsByTagName	NodeList of children of the current element that are (*tagName*)tagName elements
hasChildNodes()	true/false

Table 36.3   COMMENT_NODE Objects

Property/Method	Return Value—(r) Indicates Read-Only
nodeType	8 (r)
parentNode	Parent tag (r)
childNodes	Empty NodeList (r)
data	String of text between the opening and closing comment tags
hasChildNodes()	false

Table 36.4   TEXT_NODE Objects

Property/Method	Return Value—(r) Indicates Read-Only
nodeType	3 (r)
parentNode	Parent tag (r)
childNodes	Empty NodeList (r)
data	String of text that comprises the current object
hasChildNodes()	false

Gaining Access to the DOM

In addition to all the standard JavaScript means for accessing and controlling DOM objects, the Dreamweaver API includes the document, or dom, object and its methods. These are the primary methods you use to edit documents using Dreamweaver extensions. Before you can use any of these methods on a document, however, you have to officially gain access to the document's structure by using the dw.getDocumentDOM() function. Table 36.5 lists the specifications of this function. This function enables you to gain scripting access to the contents of user documents.

Table 36.5   Specifications for *dw.getDocumentDOM()*

Syntax	`dw.getDocumentDOM()`
Description	This function creates a DOM object, giving access to the contents of a document's object structure.

Arguments	No arguments are required. If no arguments are present, the currently active document will be used as the source of the DOM object. Optional arguments:
	`document`
	`parent`
	`parent.frames[number]`
	`parent.frames['framename']`
	A URL. (URLs must be absolute or relative to the extension file.)

Returns	The document object at the top of the DOM hierarchy (`DOCUMENT_NODE` type).

You access the current user document's DOM by assigning it to a variable, like this:

```
var theDOM=dw.getDocumentDOM();
```

After you have done this, you have access to an object of the first node type previously listed. You are officially climbing the document tree. You can now use the methods and properties of the various nodes to navigate through the document and edit it, as in these examples:

```
//change the background color to black
var theDOM=dw.getDocumentDOM();
var theBody=theDOM.body;
theBody.bgcolor="#000000";

//determine what kind of object the current selection is
var theDOM=dw.getDocumentDOM();
var theSel=theDOM.getSelectedNode();
if (theSel.nodeType=="1") {
    window.alert(theSel.tagName);
    } else if (theSel.nodeType=="3") {
    window.alert(theSel.data);
    }
```

The subject of DOM access is much bigger than this chapter covers, and it takes practice to master. But the rewards are great. After you know how to navigate a document, you can use your command or other extension to tell Dreamweaver to do almost anything to a user document. (Such power!)

Note

For more information on working with the DOM, and scripting extensions in general, read *Dreamweaver MX Extensions*, published by New Riders; or *Building Dreamweaver 4 and UltraDev 4 Extensions*, published by Osborne.

Exercise 36.6   Making a Simple Command

In this exercise, you will create a command that finds all the images in an open document and assigns them a border width of 2. You won't need a dialog box, so this will be a simple file to create. You will, however, get some practice accessing the DOM.

1. In your text editor, create a new HTML file. Save it in the **Configuration/Commands** folder as **Set Image Border.htm**. Enter the basic code framework for a command with no dialog box. You will leave the details blank for now, like this (placeholder code in bold):

```
<html>
<head>
<title>Set Image Border</title>
<script language="JavaScript">
function setImageBorder() {
//command code will go here
}
</script>
</head>
<body onLoad="setImageBorder()">
</body>
</html>
```

   In this example, you have set the <title>, although it won't be called on. You have also created a local function, setImageBorder(), and called it onLoad. That's all the framework you need.

2. The only remaining step is to fill in the main function code. Before tackling accessing the DOM, plan out the required functionality for setImageBorder(). Using the dw.getDocumentDOM() function, and the node methods and properties listed in Tables 36.1 through 36.4, you can determine that your function needs to do the following new code in bold:

```
function setImageBorder() {
//get document access
//get image access (collect images as an array)
//set the border property of each array item
}
```

Note

Plotting out the main steps of a function, as comments inside the function, can help whittle major scripting tasks into manageable chunks.

3. You'll start by getting document access (new code in bold):

```
function setImageBorder() {
//get document access
var theDOM=dw.getDocumentDOM();
//get image access (collect images as an array)
//set the border property of each array item
}
```

4. Next, you'll climb up the tree to get the images. Table 36.1 shows that the document node type object has a property called body, which gives you access to the <body> tag. Because the images are all in the body, you'll start with that. Then, because the <body> tag is of the element node type, you'll use its getElementsByTagName() method to collect all the body's <img> tags into an array. Like this:

```
function setImageBorder() {
//get document access
var theDOM=dw.getDocumentDOM();
//get image access (collect images as an array)
var theBody=theDOM.body;
var theImages=theBody.getElementsByTagName("IMG");
//set the border property of each array item
}
```

5. You have now collected the images into an array of objects of the element node type. As Figure 36.13 shows, any attribute of a tag can be accessed as an object property. So you can step through the image array, setting the border property to 2, as follows (new code in bold):

```
function setImageBorder() {
//get document access
var theDOM=dw.getDocumentDOM();
//get image access (collect images as an array)
var theBody=theDOM.body;
var theImages=theBody.getElementsByTagName("IMG");
//set the border property of each array item
for (var a=0;a<theImages.length;a++) {
  theImages[a].border="2";
  }
}
```

6. That's all there is to it! Save your document and close it. If Dreamweaver is running, quit. Then launch Dreamweaver and open a document that has several images in it.

Troubleshooting

What If It Doesn't Work?

If your command file contains a syntax error, Dreamweaver will give you a handy error message as soon as you try to choose it. Read the error message, go back to your file, and find the error.

If your object doesn't cause any errors, but doesn't change any images, there's a logic error. Probably you didn't accurately access the DOM. The `getElementsByTagName()` function requires that all parameters be specified in uppercase, so make sure your code refers to `IMG`, not `img`, or it won't work. Make sure all of your variable names match up, as you proceed into the document tree. Match your code against the code shown here, and keep tinkering until it works.

Exercise 36.7   Creating a Command with a Dialog Box

The command so far is handy—if users want a 2-pixel border around their images. How about letting the user specify how wide the border should be? (The ability to set the border to 0 might come in handy, if you ever inherit someone else's HTML pages from a web editor that doesn't set that feature automatically.) You'll now add a dialog box to the command created in the preceding exercise, asking for a width.

1. In your text editor, open the **Set Image Border.htm** command file and save it as **Set Image Border 2.htm**.

2. Create a simple form in the body section of the file. As always, you can code the form by hand or open the file in Dreamweaver and create the form in Design view. Figure 36.13 shows how the form might look when complete.

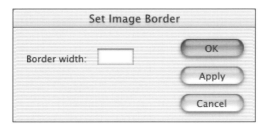

Figure 36.13   The form for the Set Image Border dialog box as seen in Dreamweaver Code and Design views.

Wherever you create the form, remember to name it—in the examples here, the form is named `theForm`, and the name of the text box is `width`.

3. Because there's now a form, you need to add the `commandButtons()` function. You will want an OK button that calls the main function and closes the window; an Apply button that calls the main function but doesn't close the window; and a Cancel button that just closes the main window. The code will look like this:

```
function commandButtons() {
return new Array("OK","setImageBorder(); window.close();","Apply",
➥"setImageBorder()", "Cancel","window.close()");
}
```

After you've done this, be sure to remove the function call from the `<body>` tag. You don't want the main function to execute as soon as the dialog box opens!

4. Finally, you need to adjust the main function so that it includes the form input collected in the dialog box. Rewrite the statement inside the `for` loop like this new code in bold:

```
for (var a=0;a<theImages.length;a++) {
   theImages[a].border=document.theForm.width.value;
   }
```

5. Try it out! Your dialog box should look like the one shown in Figure 36.14. Make sure the commands get executed properly and that all three command buttons behave as they're supposed to.

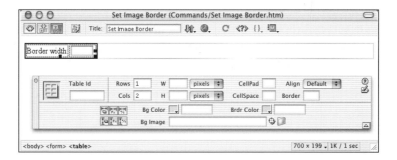

Figure 36.14   Dialog box for the Set Image Borders command.

Exercise 36.8   Refining Your Command

You can improve the functionality of this little command in all sorts of ways. Maybe you just want to set the border for images with, or without links? Maybe you want to enable the user to choose which images get borders? Maybe you want to give the user the opportunity to remove the `border` attribute completely? With DOM access, all is possible. (To work with linked images, just determine which `<img>` tags have an `<a>` tag as their parent node.) For now, however, add the `canAcceptCommand()` function. If the current document doesn't have any images, it makes no sense for the command to be available. So you'll return true if there are images, and false if there aren't.

1. In your text editor, open the **Set Image Borders 2.htm** command file. Add the framework for the new function, along with an indication of what you want it to do:

```
function canAcceptCommand() {
//access the document
//if there is no document, return false
//access the body
//access the images, collected as an array
//if the array is empty, return false
//otherwise, return true
}
```

2. As you might have noticed, the first several steps are the same as those in your main function. You can just copy and paste that code into this function, and then tack on a conditional, like this:

```
function canAcceptCommand() {
//access the document
var theDOM=dw.getDocumentDOM();
//if there is no document, return false
if (!theDOM) return false;
//access the body
var theBody=theDOM.body;
//access the images, collected as an array
var theImages=theBody.getElementsByTagName("IMG");
//if the array is empty, return false
if (theImages.length=="0") return false;
//otherwise, return true
else return true;
}
```

3. Try your command now, to see how it works. First, try it on a document with images, then one without.

Making the Most of Commands

Are you already full of ideas for your next command? If so, there's no stopping you. If not, you might just need to broaden your horizons a little bit. Try these inspiration generators:

- Whenever you're working in Dreamweaver, keep a notebook handy. If you find yourself repeating the same manual procedure over and over, wasting time performing tedious tasks, try to imagine what kind of command could be written, to help you out. Jot that inspiration down.

- Take a spin through the *Extending Dreamweaver* manual, especially the list of API methods that takes up the last half of the book. Just seeing all the different things you can tell Dreamweaver to do is likely to get your imagination moving.

- Unless you enjoy coding for its own sake, don't spend hours and hours writing a command before you check out the Exchange. You might come across an already completed one that does just exactly what you need.

The more you work with the DOM, the easier it will be. Pretty soon, you'll be wanting to create custom property inspectors, floating panels, reports, translators, and more.

Packaging Your Extensions

The Extension Manager has become the standard method for installing and sharing extensions. Although you could share your extensions by just giving away the raw files, along with instructions on where to put them, it's much safer, and user-friendlier, to provide an installation package, or MXP file for use with the Extension Manager.

Lucky for us, the Extension Manager not only installs extensions, it also packages them up neatly into special installation files. The process is even relatively painless. Just follow these steps:

1. Put all the required files (help files, HTML files, JS files, GIF icons) in one folder, outside the **Configuration** folder.

2. Create an installation file. This is an XML document with the filename **extension.mxi**, which contains all the instructions needed for installation: where the files should be stored, what versions of Dreamweaver and what platforms the extension requires, author's name, type of extension, and description. The formatting required is very exact. The best approach for beginners is to start from the Samples included with the Extension Manager. These files include a blank file (**blank.mxi**) to use as a template and a sample file (**sample.mxi**) filled in with information for a simple command.

3. Launch the Extension Manager, and go to File > Package Extension.

Figure 36.15 shows a sample folder containing all the proper files to package the **Copyright Statement** file.

Figure 36.15   The assembled elements of the Copyright Statement object all ready for packaging.

Exercise 36.9   Packaging an Extension

This last exercise will take you through the steps to create an MXP file from this extension.

1. Start by copying all needed files into one folder. Somewhere on your hard drive, outside the **Configuration** folder, create a new folder. Name it whatever you like and will remember. (Something like Copyright Statement Files, maybe?)

   Find the files that make up the object, and copy them there. This will include **Copyright Statement.htm** and **Copyright Statement.gif**.

2. On your hard drive, find the Extension Manager application folder. Inside that folder, find the **Dreamweaver/Samples** folder. Inside there, you'll see **blank.mxi**. (Figure 36.16 shows where to find these items.) Duplicate that file in your **Collection** folder, and call it **C_Statement.mxi**. (Naming conventions apply here—no spaces or special characters, no long names.)

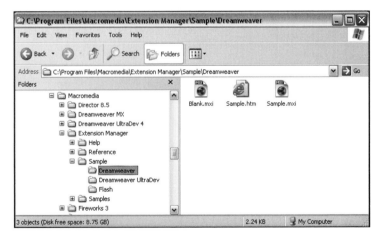

Figure 36.16   The Extension Manager application folder structure showing **sample.mxi** and **blank.mxi**.

After you've made the duplicate file, open it in your text editor.

Note

You can download a PDF file containing detailed instructions for creating installation files from the Macromedia web site. Go to the Macromedia Exchange for Dreamweaver page (`www.macromedia.com/exchange/dreamweaver`), and click the Site Help topic Macromedia Approved Extensions.

3. Fill in the blanks with the information for your object.

The blank file has all the framework you need. By examining the sample file, you can get an idea how it should be formatted. For your extension, fill in the blanks until your code looks like that shown in Listing 36.1. Information that has been added to the framework from **blank.mxi** is in bold. Pay special attention to the following when filling in the code:

Listing 36.1   The Complete Code for C_Statement.mxi

```
<macromedia-extension
      name="Copyright Statement"
      version="1.0.0"
      type="object">

      <!-- List the required/compatible products -->
      <products>
            <product name="Dreamweaver" version="3" primary="true" />
      </products>

      <!-- Describe the author -->
      <author name="Tom Thumb" />

      <!-- Describe the extension -->
      <description>
      <![CDATA[
       Inserts a formatted copyright statement, with user input for name and
year.
      ]]>
      </description>

      <!-- Describe where the extension shows in the UI of the product -->
      <ui-access>
      <![CDATA[
      Access this extension via the ThumbThings tab in the Insert bar.
      ]]>
      </ui-access>

      <!-- Describe the files that comprise the extension -->
      <files>
            <file source="Copyright Statement.gif"
destination="$dreamweaver/configuration/Objects/ThumbThings/Copyright
Statement.gif" />
```

```
<file source="Copyright Statement.htm"
destination="$dreamweaver/configuration/Objects/Thumbthings/Copyright
Statement.htm" />

        </files>

        <!-- Describe the changes to the configuration -->
        <configuration-changes>
            <insertbar-changes>
                <insertbar-insert insertAfter="DW_Insertbar_Server">
                    <category folder="ThumbThings"
id="DW_Insertbar_ThumbThings">
                        <button enabled=""
file="ThumbThings\Copyright Statement.htm" id="DW_ThumbThings_Copyright"
image="ThumbThings\Copyright Statement.gif" showIf="" />
                    </category>
                </insertbar-insert>
            </insertbar-changes>
        </configuration-changes>
```

```
</macromedia-extension>
```

- **For the author name.** Enter your name. (You've already entered Tom Thumb, Big-Time Genius—there's no law against being fanciful.)

- **For the filenames.** Enter the relative path from the MXI file you're creating to the copies of the extension files you've saved for packaging. If all these files are in the same folder, you can just enter the filename.

- **For the destination.** Enter the complete path from the Dreamweaver application folder root, as shown. If you want your extension to create any new folders in existing folders, enter them as part of the path. (You have entered ThumbThings to create a new folder within the **Objects** folder.)

- **For the version number.** Your extension, like any other piece of software, gets its own version number. Start with 1.0, and increment the number if you later revise the extension.

4. Finally, you package everything together with the Extension Manager. Launch the Extension Manager, and go to File > Package Extension. For the name of your extension, choose something descriptive that obeys the standard naming conventions (no empty spaces, no more than 20 characters, no special characters). It's good practice to use the same name you used for the MXI file, just to keep your own file organization tidy. Make sure you leave the **.mxp** extension in place.

When you're asked to choose a file, choose **C_Statement.mxi**.

If there aren't any problems, the Extension Manager will generate an extension file in the same folder as the MXI file. If there are problems, you'll get an error report. Most often, these are problems with the MXI file. Back to your text editor, fix the reported errors, and try again. Figure 36.17 shows how this process will look in the Extension Manager.

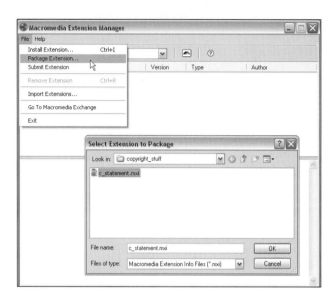

Figure 36.17   The steps through the packaging process as they appear in the Extension Manager.

7. Now use the Extension Manager to install the new extension. Start by quitting Dreamweaver, if it's running. Open the **Configuration/Objects** folder and remove the development version. Then open **insertbar.xml** and delete the code that created your Development category. Finally, install the MXP file, using the Extension Manager. (See Chapter 35 for a full discussion on using the Extension Manager to install MXP files.) If everything's hunky dory, you should get an alert message telling you the extension was installed successfully.

Your custom extension also should now appear in the Extension Manager window (see Figure 36.18).

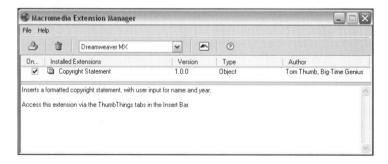

Figure 36.18   The Extension Manager window showing the installed Copyright Statement object.

6. Finish up by launching Dreamweaver and checking that everything installed correctly.

Submitting Your Extension to the Macromedia Exchange

The ultimate in sharing is submitting your extension file to the Macromedia Exchange. After you have the MXP file, the procedure is simple: Go to the Macromedia Exchange web site and click the Submit button at the top of the page. Then follow the instructions to submit (see Figure 36.19).

Figure 36.19   The Macromedia Exchange home page with Submit button.

After you have submitted an extension, Macromedia engineers will run it through a series of tests. One of three things will happen:

- If it fails, it gets returned to you with comments.

- If it passes the basic tests, it gets put on the web site with Basic Approval.

- If it also passes the more comprehensive tests, it becomes a Macromedia Approved Extension.

To learn more about the testing process and how to get your extensions accepted and approved, visit the Dreamweaver web site, and click any one of the Site Help FAQ topics. This will take you to an extensive categorized list of questions and answers.

Summary

You already know Dreamweaver is a terrific web-editing environment. This chapter has showed you how you can make it into a perfectly personalized web editor for your workflow needs. As much as you have seen, however, you've only touched the surface of all that is possible with extensions. Check out the *Extending Dreamweaver* manual. Visit the Exchange web site and read the various support files there. If you're really serious, you can join the Extensibility Newsgroup (go to `www.macromedia.com/support/dreamweaver/extend/form/`). Dust off your JavaScript books. And start rewriting history.

Appendix A

Using Dreamweaver and Fireworks Together

Macromedia Fireworks is a graphics application designed specifically for the web developer. It works beautifully side-by-side with Dreamweaver. The two programs share many of the same file edits and provide ways to establish a streamlined workflow for editing, optimizing, and inserting image files in HTML pages.

This appendix takes a quick look at some of the ways you can use the two programs together.

Placing Fireworks Files in Dreamweaver Documents

You can insert Fireworks files into Dreamweaver documents in several ways:

- Insert a single image file using Dreamweaver normal image-insertion methods; see Chapter 5, "Working with Images," for details.

- Insert Fireworks-generated HTML code, including associated images, slices, and JavaScript, into an HTML document using the Menu command Insert > Interactive Images > Fireworks HTML or the Fireworks HTML object in the Insert > Common bar (see Figure A.1).

Figure A.1   The Fireworks HTML object in the Insert bar.

- Copy and paste Fireworks HTML into Dreamweaver. In Fireworks, choose Edit > Copy HTML Code and follow the wizard; then in Dreamweaver, place the cursor at the desired insertion point and choose Edit > Paste. Alternatively, in Fireworks, choose File > Export, and in the Export dialog box specify the desired Dreamweaver site folder as the destination, choose Save As HTML and Images, choose Copy to Clipboard, and click Save. In Dreamweaver, place the cursor at the desired insertion point and choose Edit > Paste.

- Export a Fireworks file as a library item. In Fireworks, choose File > Export. When the Export dialog box opens, choose Dreamweaver Library. Name the file, specify a destination folder named **Library** located at the root level of the Dreamweaver local root folder, and click Save. (See Chapter 25, "Templates and Libraries," for a discussion of Dreamweaver library items.)

Launching Fireworks from Within Dreamweaver

Fireworks can be launched from within Dreamweaver; but to use this feature, Fireworks must be designated as the primary external editor in Dreamweaver for the common graphics file types.

To do this, choose Edit > Preferences and go to the File Types/Editors category. One at a time, select the file extensions **.gif**, **.jpg**, and **.png** from the list, and from the Editors list, select Fireworks (Primary) and click Make Primary (see Figure A.2).

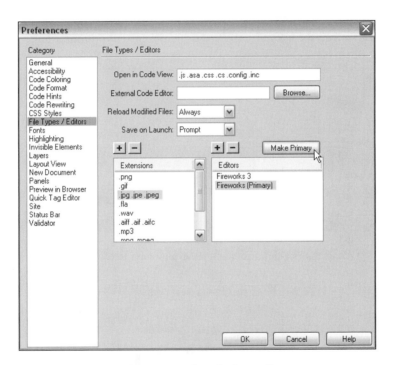

Figure A.2   Making Fireworks the primary editor for image files.

You can edit both individual Fireworks images and Fireworks tables by launching Fireworks from within Dreamweaver. This is called *launch and edit*. Dreamweaver uses Design Notes to make this integration possible, creating and maintaining a **_notes** folder containing a Design Note (MNO) file for each Fireworks object placed in a Dreamweaver document. Successful integration requires that neither the **_notes** folder nor its contents be moved or deleted. If anything happens to the **_notes** folder, Dreamweaver won't be able to find the PNG source file that corresponds to the element. (See Chapter 24, "Workplace Collaboration," for a full discussion of Design Notes.)

Note

Fireworks tables are used to construct sliced images. Each Fireworks table consists of the individual GIF or JPEG image files that make up the sliced image and the HTML table code used to assemble the slices into one big graphic. See Chapter 8, "Design Issues," for more on sliced image tables.

To launch and edit a single image, select the image in the Document window, and in the Property inspector click Edit (see Figure A.3). If necessary, specify the image source file (the Fireworks PNG that was originally used to generate it); this will open the file in Fireworks in Editing from Dreamweaver mode (see Figure A.4). Edit the image and click Done in the toolbar; the image is exported using the current optimization settings.

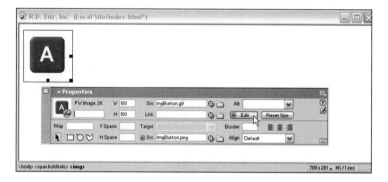

Figure A.3   Launching Fireworks from within Dreamweaver to edit a single image.

Figure A.4   Opening a Fireworks image in Editing from Dreamweaver mode.

To launch and edit a Fireworks table placed in Dreamweaver, select the table in the Document window and in the Property inspector click Edit. If necessary, specify the table's PNG source file. Dreamweaver launches Fireworks and displays the source PNG file for the table. Edit the source file and click Done; this exports the HTML and image slice files using the current optimization settings and updates the table in Dreamweaver. It also resaves the source PNG file.

Optimizing Fireworks Images or Animations in Dreamweaver

When it is necessary to make quick export changes, such as changing the compression (quality) of a JPEG, changing the file type, or even the size and area of the exported image or animation, you can launch Fireworks from within Dreamweaver and quickly make these changes.

To do this, select the desired image in the Document window and choose Commands > Optimize Image in Fireworks (see Figure A.5). If prompted, determine whether to launch a source PNG file. Make the desired edits in the Export Preview dialog box, using the Options, File, or Animation tabs as necessary. When finished, click Update; this exports the image or animation using the new optimization settings and saves the PNG source file, if one was used. If the file type was changed (for instance, from GIF to JPEG), the Dreamweaver link checker will prompt you to update references to the image filename.

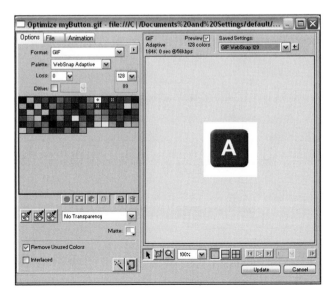

Figure A.5   Using the Optimize Image in Fireworks command.

Placeholders

You can insert a placeholder image in a Dreamweaver document, and then launch Fireworks to create the actual graphic image.

This feature requires that you have Dreamweaver MX and Fireworks MX both installed. In the Dreamweaver Document window, insert an image placeholder (Insert > Image Placeholder), using the dialog box that appears to set the placeholder's dimensions. When you're ready to replace the placeholder with an actual image, select the image placeholder object, and in the Property inspector click Create (see Figure A.6). This launches Fireworks in Editing from Dreamweaver mode and creates a new blank image document with its canvas size automatically determined by the dimensions of the place-holder image.

In Fireworks, design the image, then click Done. You are prompted to save the file as a PNG file (source document), and to export the file in a web-ready format such as a GIF or JPEG. When you have completed the saving process, the new image automatically replaces the placeholder in the original Dreamweaver document.

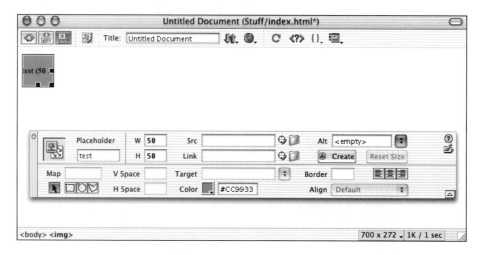

Figure A.6   Launching Fireworks to replace a placeholder image with an actual image.

Appendix B

Online Resources
for Dreamweaver
Web Developers

The Internet offers a wealth of resources
for learning to use Dreamweaver as well as
for the study of web design and development in general.

The Macromedia Online Forums

The Macromedia Dreamweaver newsgroup is probably the single most useful online resource for Dreamweaver web developers. It is a user-to-user forum, frequented by Dreamweaver users of all skill levels from every part of the world. Although a small number of Macromedia tech support staff participate, the great majority of assistance is provided by other users and by a core of volunteers known as "Team Macromedia" organized by the company.

The forum receives hundreds of posts per day, with questions and answers covering a broad range of topics. Beginners are welcome, but are encouraged to spend some time on the newsgroup before posting and to read the official Frequently Asked Questions and Etiquette Guidelines that are posted daily. Dreamweaver is the topic, but questions regarding any aspect of web development are usually answered cheerfully.

The Dreamweaver forum is an NNTP newsgroup, accessible through any standard newsreader, such as Outlook Express or Netscape. You can access this newsgroup at `news://forums.macromedia.com/macromedia.dreamweaver`.

Resources on the Web

The web provides a large number of free, easily accessible informational sites for Dreamweaver users and web developers in general. The following list is organized by topic.

Basics

The following sites offer resources related to using Dreamweaver and other general web development topics:

- Macromedia Dreamweaver Support Center
  `www.macromedia.com/support/dreamweaver`

- Macromedia Dreamweaver TechNotes
  `www.macromedia.com/support/dreamweaver/technotes.html`

- Angela Buraglia's DreamweaverFAQ.com
  `www.dwfaq.com`

- Craig Fosters's Macromedia Dreamweaver Newsgroup FAQ
  `www.cauzway.net/dreamweaver`

- DWZone

  `www.dwzone.net`

- Patty Ayers's The Patty Site

  `www.thepattysite.com`

Browsers

The following sites offer information and resources related to browsers, including older versions of Netscape and Internet Explorer, and emulators for more unusual browsers, such as WebTV:

- Browser archive

  `browsers.evolt.org`

- Browser emulator

  `www.dejavu.org`

- WebTV Viewer

  `developer.msntv.com/Tools/WebTVVwr.asp`

- Browsersizer

  `www.applythis.com/browsersizer`

- Windowing Bookmarklets

  `www.bookmarklets.com/tools/windowing/indexE.phtml`

CGI

The following sites offer resources related to server-side CGI scripting, including tutorials and information and downloadable scripts:

- How to Install a CGI Script

  `spider-food.net/install-a-cgi-script.html`

- CGI Tutorials

  `cgidir.com/Tutorials`

- HotScripts.com

  `www.hotscripts.com`

- CGI Resources.com

  `cgi.resourceindex.com`

- Perlmasters

  `www.perlmasters.com`

- BigNoseBird.Com

  `bignosebird.com/cgi.shtml`

- Matt's Script Archive

  `worldwidemart.com/scripts`

- Tutorial on Matt's FormMail

  `www.appbuild.com/formmail_help.html`

- The PERL Archive

  `www.perlarchive.com`

- scriptsearch.com

  `www.scriptsearch.com`

Color

The following sites offer information and tools related to the web and color:

- Color Resources for Web Developers

  `www.factxpress.com/webmaster/color31.html`

- Webmasters' Color Laboratory

  `www.visibone.com/colorlab`

- Digital Studios' Color Schemer

  `www.godigitalstudios.com/www/color`

- Color Schemer Software

  `www.colorschemer.com`

- The Browser-Safe Color Palette

  `www.lynda.com/hex.html`

- Death of the Web-Safe Color Palette?

  `hotwired.lycos.com/webmonkey/00/37/index2a.html`

CSS

The following sites offer a wealth of information, tools, and coding help related to Cascading Style Sheets:

- World Wide Web Consortium (W3C)

  `www.w3.org/Style/CSS`

- Master Compatibility Chart

  `www.webreview.com/style/css1/charts/mastergrid.shtml`

- A CSS Reference Guide

  `www.webreview.com/style/`

- Using Cascading Style Sheets

  `www.macromedia.com/support/dreamweaver/layout/css`

- MaKo's CSS Know-How Site

  `www.mako4css.com`

- Selectoracle: English translations of CSS2 and CSS3 Selectors

  `gallery.theopalgroup.com/selectoracle`

- CSS References

  `www.meyerweb.com/eric/css/references/`

- TopStyle Pro 2.5

  `www.bradsoft.com/topstyle`

- The Web Design Group—CSS Reference

  `www.htmlhelp.com/reference/css`

- W3C CSS Validator

  `jigsaw.w3.org/css-validator`

Extensions

The following sites offer a variety of Dreamweaver extensions for download, and information about extensions:

- The Macromedia Exchange for Dreamweaver

  `www.macromedia.com/exchange/dreamweaver`

- David Miles's Extensions

  `www.z3roadster.net/dreamweaver/`

- Deva

  `www.devahelp.com`

- Dreamweaver Supply Bin

  `home.att.net/%7EJCB.BEI/Dreamweaver/`

- Dru's Dreamweaver Fever

  `www.dreamweaverfever.com`

- DWzone

  `www.dwzone.net`

- Hal Pawluk's Extensions

  `www.pawluk.com/public`

- Massimo's Corner

  `www.massimocorner.com`

- Paul Davis's Kaosweaver

  `www.kaosweaver.com/Extensions`

- Pretty Lady II by Brad Halstead with the works of Eddie Traversa and Robert J. Sherman

  `www.prettylady2.net`

- Project VII

  `www.projectseven.com/extensions`

- Rabi's Extensions

  `www.dreamweaver-extensions.com`

- Spider Food

  `spider-food.net/dreamweaver-extensions.html`

- WebAssist.com

  `www.webassist.com/Products/Products.asp`

- Yaromat

  `www.yaromat.com/dw`

JavaScript

The following sites offer JavaScript help, reference materials, and sample code, to help you get started as a web scripter:

- Client-Side JavaScript Reference

  `docs.iplanet.com/docs/manuals/js/client/`
  `jsref/contents.htm`

- DHTML Shock

  `www.dhtmlshock.com`

- Dynamic Drive

  `www.dynamicdrive.com`

- The JavaScript Source

  `javascript.internet.com`

- mickweb

  `www.mickweb.com/javascript`

Search Engine Placement

The following sites offer information and services related to publicizing your web site using search engines:

- J.K. Bowman's Spider Food
  www.spider-food.net

- Search Engine World
  searchengineworld.com

- Link Popularity
  www.linkpopularity.com

- Search Engine Watch
  www.searchenginewatch.com

Utilities

The following sites offer a variety of utilities and services to make your web work more fun and efficient:

- Registry Utilities for Dreamweaver and UltraDev
  youneedawebstore.com/resources.htm

- Top Style Pro
  www.bradsoft.com/topstyle

- How to Create Favicons
  www.favicon.com

- Atomz Search Engine
  www.atomz.com

Statistics

The following sites provide great information on your potential web audience, including who's browsing, what browsers and plugins they're using, what kind of computers they're browsing on, and more:

- Global Statistics from thecounter.com
  www.thecounter.com/stats

- BrowserWatch
  browserwatch.internet.com

- WebTrends
  www.webtrends.com

Section 508 Compliance

The following sites offer information and site-checking services for any developer interested in creating accessible web sites—especially those concerned with ADA and Section 508 compliance:

- UsableNet

  `www.usablenet.com`

- 508 Universe

  `159.142.162.122/508`

A p p e n d i x   C

Introduction to MySQL

If you're using Microsoft Access for your

dynamic data development, your setup is

easy. If you can't or don't want to use

Access, your most accessible alternative is

MySQL. MySQL is free, and has all sorts of

other features in its favor—but you need to know how to get it, set it up, and at least get around in it before you can plunge into development. This appendix takes you through the basics, for Windows and Mac OS X, to get you up and running as quickly as possible.

What Is MySQL?

As explained in Chapter 26, "Introduction to Dynamic Dreamweaver," MySQL is a free, easily available database management system (DBMS) available for Windows and various flavors of UNIX (including Mac OS X). It's a great development tool, and is used for online database systems all over the world. In addition to its cost benefits, it's fast, stable, and can handle huge amounts of data and heavy traffic (lots of people accessing it at once).

Note

MySQL might be free for most uses, but it is not an open-source product.

MySQL uses the client/server model. Before beginning work with MySQL, you must know what that means. MySQL consists of several independent programs:

- **Server.** The server program (called *mysqld*, or the mysql daemon, in UNIX-speak) controls everything—which users are allowed to use the program, how online access is handled, and so forth. The server must always be running before the system will function.

- **Client.** The client program (called mysql) enables users—such as you—to create and edit databases. This program must be running before you can work with a database; but it needn't be running while you access the database from Dreamweaver or a browser.

- **Admin.** Various utility programs are part of the MySQL package. The one you'll use most often (maybe the only one you'll use) is the admin program (mysqladmin).

Setting Up MySQL (Windows)

You can approaching MySQL for Windows in a variety of ways. All of them involve spending a little bit of time in the Console window (MS-DOS window, on Windows 98). These instructions minimize that, and you should find this a pretty smooth setup.

Downloading

MySQL for Windows is available from the MySQL web site (www.mysql.com). At the time of this writing, current downloads are available at http://www.mysql.com/downloads/mysql-3.23.html. On this page, scroll down until you find the Windows download section. Download the Zip installation file.

Note

As always with software, MySQL is evolving. By the time you read this, the current version might have changed from 3.23. Download the latest stable release.

Installing

To install MySQL, follow these steps:

1. After downloading, use WinZip or another unzipping utility to unpack the archive.

2. From the archived files, find and launch **setup.exe**. Follow the setup instructions as they appear. For best results, accept the default install location (at the root of the C: drive). After you have finished, you'll have a new **mysql** folder on your C: drive.

Configuring and Setting Up

To use MySQL, and in particular to use it with the exercises in this book, you'll need to configure it and set up the Antiques database. This section also covers how to start and stop the MySQL program every time you want to work with it.

1. MySQL stores its databases in a folder called **data**. If you look within that folder (**c:\mysql\data**), you'll see that it contains several folders—each of those represents one database. To copy the Antiques database to your computer, you'll need to store its folder in this location.

    a. On the CD, find the **databases** folder. Open that folder, and the **antiques_mysql** folder within it. Inside there is another folder called **antiques**.

    b. Copy that entire folder to the **c:\mysql\data** folder. Don't rename it or disturb any of its contents.

2. Now you need to launch the server portion of MySQL. If the server portion isn't running, you cannot work with MySQL or any of its databases. Doing this is

easy because the server is accessed by a nice, friendly utility called *WinMySQLAdmin* (see Figure C.1). (This is a GUI for the mysqladmin and other utility programs discussed in the previous section.). To launch the server, follow these steps:

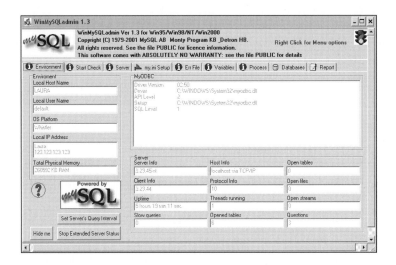

Figure C.1   The WinMySQLAdmin interface (Windows).

a. Browse or explore to **c:\mysql\bin\WinMySQLAdmin.exe**, and launch it. The WinMySQLAdmin interface window that opens look like that shown in Figure C.1.

b. Bring the Databases tab to the front.

c. The upper-left pane lists existing databases. (The **mysql** database contains all the administrative information for the system, like such as who the users are and so forth. The test database is empty; it's just a test.)

d. Right-click in this pane, and from the contextual menu, choose Refresh Databases. If you have copied the **antiques** folder to the data folder, it will now appear in your list of databases.

c. If you like, you can explore the other panes of this window, to see what tables and columns are contained in this database. You cannot edit the database from here, however.

Tip

The Databases pane of WinMySQLAdmin contains the name and IP address of your computer. You'll need that IP address in a few minutes. Jot it down somewhere while you're here, so that you don't have to look it up later.

3. WinMySQLAdmin needs to be running in the background before you can use or access any of the MySQL databases. Therefore, you don't want to quit the program. But, you can hide it. If you're in the Environment Tab, just click the Hide Me button in the lower-left corner of the window. Or right-click anywhere in the window and, from the contextual menu that pops up, choose Hide Me. The program window disappears, and a little stoplight icon appears in your system tray on the task bar. The stoplight shows a green light, which means the MySQL server is running (see Figure C.2).

Note

Don't try to hide WinMySQLAdmin by clicking the close box in the upper-right corner of the interface. This stops the MySQL daemon and MySQL will not be active!

Figure C.2   The WinMySQLAdmin system tray icon, indicating that the MySQL server is running (Windows).

Any time you want to access WinMySQLAdmin again, click the stoplight icon, and choose Show Me.

To exit the MySQL server, when you have finished working just show the MySQLAdmin window and close it (click in the close box) instead of hiding it. The program doesn't take up much memory, however; if you want, you can leave it running all the time. If you shut down your computer with the stoplight still showing in the system tray, the next time you boot up, MySQL server will launch automatically, and the stoplight will reappear.

4. Now you need to launch the MySQL client program (the one that you actually manipulate database information with). This is done through the Command Prompt window (called the MS-DOS prompt, on Windows 98). To open this, go to Start > Programs > Accessories > Command Prompt (or MS-DOS Prompt).

5. This is a command-line interface, so there's no mousing around it. You'll launch the MySQL client program by typing the full path to the program file. Type this:

```
c:\mysql\bin\mysql
```

End the line by pressing Enter or Return. (Always do this in the command-line interface.) As long as you have started up the server already, the prompt will change to `mysql>`. You'll also be presented with some welcome information. You're now in the MySQL client program (see Figure C.3).

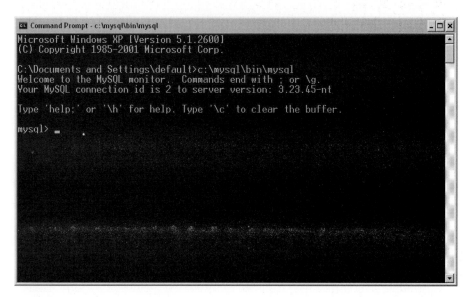

Figure C.3   Launching the MySQL client program in the Command Prompt window (Windows).

6. Now you need to tell the server who will be using your databases, and how much access they should have. With the `mysql>` prompt still showing, type this:

```
GRANT all privileges on antiques.* to ""@localhost;
```

(End the line by pressing Enter/Return.) If you get an error message, check your typing and try again until it works.

Next, check your notes and find the IP address for your computer. (Remember, this was displayed in the WinMySQLAdmin window.) Type this, substituting your IP address for the numbers shown here:

```
GRANT all privileges on antiques.* to ""@192.123.123.123;
```

You've just given anybody on your computer permission to access the Antiques database. You did it in two different ways, because different application servers sometimes require different access methods.

Note

You'll need to add permissions like this for every new database you create. MySQL itself might let you access its items without setting permissions, but some of the application servers you work with will require username and password information before you can work with MySQL online. If you want to just grant permissions once and for all, instead of specifying **antiques.***, specify *.*—note that this is a security risk if your computer is on a network or if you're connected to the Internet (especially if you have an always-on connection such as a cable modem or DSL, and aren't behind a firewall). Enterprising hackers have access to even the administrative tables of your MySQL installation.

7. After you have finished working in the MySQL client program, you can quit by just typing the following:

```
quit;
```

The program will tell you goodbye, and the `mysql>` prompt will disappear. Note that this quits only the client program, not the server; and that's the way you want it. The server must be up and running as you work on your Dreamweaver files.

> **Note**
>
> If you ever try to launch the client program using the command in step 4, and get an error message that the socket is not available, that means the server program is not running. Use WinMySQLAdmin to launch it.

Setting Up MySQL (Mac OS X)

MySQL for Mac OS X is basically MySQL for UNIX. It's not for the timid. Setting it up involves using the Terminal window for command-line input, and probably learning more about system security than you ever wanted to know. The process is not as simple as it is on Windows. If you're willing to give it a try, however, the instructions here were created to make the installation as painless and friendly as possible.

Before You Begin

You'll need to know a few pieces of information about your particular system before you can proceed. Take a moment to find these things, and jot them down for easy reference:

- **What is your user name?** Your user name is the name you chose for yourself when you first set up your computer. It's the same name used for your **Home** folder. To find your user name, launch System Preferences from the Dock, and view the Users preferences. Select your account from the list, and choose Edit. Your user name is the "short name" that appears in this dialog box (see Figure C.4). For purposes of the examples in this appendix, the user name will be fred. Whenever you see Fred or fred in an example, substitute your user name.

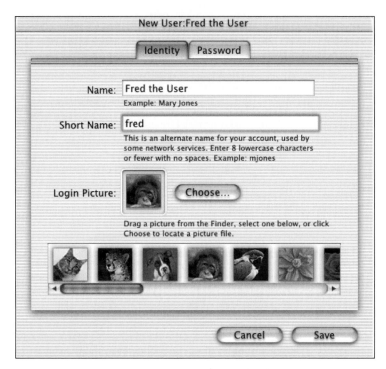

Figure C.4   Finding your short user name in the System Preferences (Mac).

- **Where is your Home folder?** This is the folder that appears when you click the home icon in the Finder window toolbar. It's named the same as your user name (for instance, fred). On your hard drive, it's located in the **Users** folder. In UNIX-speak, its address is **/users/fred**.

- **What is your computer's IP address?** The IP address is your official address in the world. You'll need to reference it at various times. To find your IP address, launch System Preferences from the Dock and view the Internet preferences. The IP address will be listed there. Write it down!

- **What, and where, is the Terminal?** The Terminal is a utility program on your computer. It is command-line interface for working with all UNIX-style programs and functions on Mac OS X. Most of your MySQL activities will be done through the Terminal. You can find the Terminal in Applications/Utilities, on your hard drive. Figure C.5 shows the Terminal window, ready for action.

Note

If you're not willing to use the Terminal, you should set up your Dreamweaver workstation to network to a Windows computer or a computer at your ISP. See Chapter 26 for instructions on "Setting Up for Development on a Remote Computer."

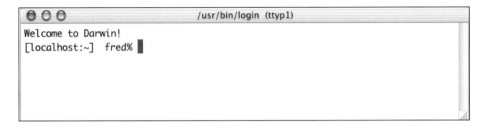

Figure C.5   The Terminal window, showing the % prompt (Mac).

Downloading

MySQL for Mac OS X is available from the MySQL web site (www.mysql.com). At the time of this writing, current downloads are available at `http://www.mysql.com/downloads/mysql-3.23.html`. On this page, scroll down until you find the Mac OS X download section. Don't download the version for OS X Server; you want the version called *MacOS X 10.1.1 (Darwin 5.1.x) (PowerPC)*.

Note

As always with software, MySQL is evolving. By the time you read this, the current version might have changed from 3.23 10.1.1. Download the latest stable release. If you download a later version of MySQL than the one used here, every time you see instructions that involve typing the full name and version of the program, substitute your version number.

The downloaded file has the extension **.tar.gz**; this means it's a UNIX archive file, similar to a Zip or StuffIt archive. Depending on your browser configuration, StuffIt Expander might have automatically uncompressed the archive for you into a folder called **mysql-3.23.47-apple-darwin5.1-powerpc**. If this didn't happen, find StuffIt or StuffIt Expander and drag the archive on top of it to uncompress.

After you have the uncompressed folder, rename it **mysql** and move it to your **Home** folder (see Figure C.6).

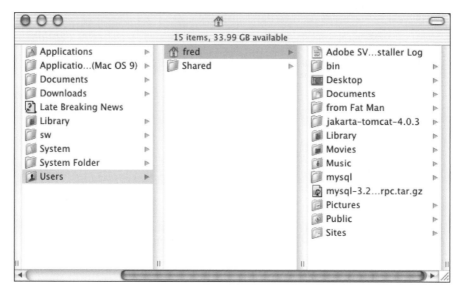

Figure C.6   The **mysql** folder in Fred's **Home** folder (Mac).

Installing

You're probably not used to installing UNIX applications. Guess what? You've done the first part of the installation already, just by uncompressing the archive and moving it to the folder where you want it to live. All that's left is to run the install script.

Find and launch the Terminal. (It's in Applications > Utilities > Terminal.) In the Terminal window, type this (substituting your user name for Fred's):

```
cd /users/fred/mysql
./scripts/mysql_install_db
```

Wait for the % prompt to reappear. Your MySQL database manager has been installed!

Note

Any UNIX gurus out there will recognize that this is a non-standard install method. It was developed to be user-friendly above all, for non-UNIX gurus. It will work fine, as long as you're not using your computer in a multi-user environment (that is, as long as you're the only person using your computer).

Configuring and Setting Up

To use MySQL, and in particular to use it with the exercises in this book, you'll need to configure it and set up the Antiques database. This section also covers how to start and stop the MySQL program every time you want to work with it.

1. Copying files can be done in the Terminal window—but one of the benefits of installing MySQL in your **Home** folder is that you can access this folder from the Finder (as you saw earlier). Leaving the Terminal window open (you can hide it, or minimize it down into the Dock), use the Finder to browse through your **Home** folder. Inside the **mysql** folder, there's a **data** folder. That's where you need to put the folder containing the various files of the Antiques database. Figure C.7 shows this happening.

   a. On the CD, find the **databases** folder. Open that folder and the **antiques_mysql** folder within it. Inside there is another folder called **antiques**.

   b. Copy that entire folder to the **mysql/data** folder in your **Home** folder. Don't rename it or disturb any of its contents.

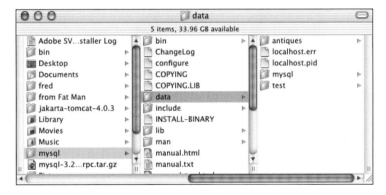

Figure C.7   Putting the antiques folder into MySQL's data folder (Mac).

2. Go back to the Terminal. To launch the server, type this in the Terminal window:

   ```
   ~/users/fred/mysql/bin/safe_mysqld --user=fred &
   ```

   (Remember to substitute your name for Fred's!) To test that the server launched, type this:

   ```
   ~/users/fred/mysql/bin/mysqladmin ping
   ```

   If the server is running, you'll get a response message that says `mysqld is alive`. If it's not running, you'll get an error message. You'll need to troubleshoot this (try re-typing the preceding command) and get the server to launch before you can continue.

3. Now you need to launch the MySQL client program (the one that you actually manipulate database information with). Type this:

   ```
   ~/users/fred/mysql/bin/mysql --user=root
   ```

The prompt will change from the % prompt to simply mysql> . That's how you know you're in the program.

4. Now you need to tell the server who will be using your databases, and how much access they should have. With the mysql> prompt still showing, type this:

```
GRANT all privileges on antiques.* to ""@localhost;
```

Note

Permissions will be a big factor in whether you succeed or fail at installing and working with MySQL on Mac OS X. In UNIX, everybody is locked out of everything unless you specifically start unlocking things for certain people. If you don't unlock things correctly, Dreamweaver and the browser won't be able to access your data and you won't be able to continue.

By launching the mysql client program with the special --user=root addition to your code, you're launching the mysql client program as root, which is an administrative user. You have to do this because only the administrator can assign permissions. After you've given everybody on your computer permission to access a particular database, you can launch the program without that last bit of typing to work on that database.

Then check your notes and find the IP address for your computer, and type:

```
GRANT all privileges on antiques.* to ""@192.168.123.123;
```

You've just given anybody on your computer permission to access the Antiques database. You did it in two different ways, because different application servers sometimes require different access methods.

5. When you have finished working in MySQL, you quit the program by just typing

```
quit;
```

The program will tell you good-bye, and you're back to the % prompt. Note that this quits only the client program, not the server; and that's the way you want it. The server portion (mysqld) must be up and running as you work on your Dreamweaver files. Unless you specifically shut the server down, it will stay running until you shut down your computer.

Note

You'll need to add permissions like this for every new database you create. If you want to just grant permissions once and for all, instead of specifying **antiques.***, specify ***.***— note that this is a security risk if your computer is on a network or if you're connected to the Internet (especially if you have an always-on connection like such as a cable modem or DSL). Enterprising hackers now have access to even the administrative tables of your MySQL installation.

Restarting the Server

The next time you start up your Mac and are ready to work on some live data pages, you'll need to re-start the server. Do just what you did in step 2: Launch the Terminal and type `~/users/fred/mysql/bin/safe_mysqld --user=fred &`.

Getting Around in MySQL

As long as you never have to edit a database, you don't have to know much more about working in MySQL than what has already been covered in this appendix. However, you might find it handy to know at least the basics of working with databases in the MySQL client program.

MySQL works in the command-line interface. You type in SQL commands to edit the database. (This is actually a great way to learn how to write SQL statements.) After you've got the client program launched in your Command Prompt or Terminal window, and the `mysql>` prompt is showing, you can use some basic commands to examine and edit your database. Table C.1 shows some of these basic commands you can use to examine and edit your database. (The sample code shows the Antiques database being used.)

Table C.1   Commands for Common Operations in MySQL

To Do This:	Type This (Keywords Are Shown in All Caps):
Open a database for use. (Do this before doing anything else.)	`USE antiques;`
See a list of tables in the current database.	`SHOW tables;`
See a list of the columns in a particular table (for instance, the Customers table).	`DESCRIBE customers;`
See all the contents of a table.	`SELECT * FROM customers;`
See the contents of only one column in the table (all customers' last names, for instance).	`SELECT lname FROM customers;`
Find a particular record (or records) meeting a certain criteria, in the table.	`SELECT * FROM customers WHERE fname="Fred";`
Insert a new record (row) into a table. The data supplied must match the number and type of columns in the table.	`INSERT INTO customers VALUES ("George","Flintstone");`
Change a record in a table.	`UPDATE customers SET fname="Fred" WHERE lname="Flintstone";`

A few tips about entering commands into MySQL:

- It's conventional to put keywords in all caps, but it's not necessary; MySQL is not case-sensitive.

- All commands must end with a semicolon (;). If you end a line by pressing Enter/Return, but without typing a semicolon, MySQL thinks you have not finished entering the command and will patiently wait for you to finish. You can take advantage of this to type long command statements on multiple lines, for easier reading.

If you really, really hate command-line interfaces, but still want to use MySQL, a few free GUIs are available at `www.mysql.com`.

Resources and Further Reading

A lot of information is available to you, if you want to learn more about installing and using MySQL. The best place to begin is `http://www.mysql.com/documentation/index.html`—the extensive online documents cover all aspects of the program from installation to command lines, along with a very nice beginner's tutorial to get you started. Mac OS X users can also check out Marc Liyanage's OS X software resources at `http://www.entropy.ch/software/macosx/`. There are also various user forums onMySQL, PHP, and related issues. A good place to begin is `http://www.sourceforge.net/`.

If you like to do your learning from books, try Paul DuBois's excellent *MySQL* (published by New Riders).

Appendix D

What's on the CD-ROM

The accompanying CD-ROM is packed with all sorts of exercise files and products to help you work with this book and with Dreamweaver MX. The following sections contain detailed descriptions of the CD's contents.

For more information about the use of this CD, please review the **ReadMe.txt** file in the root directory. This file includes important disclaimer information, as well as information about installation, system requirements, troubleshooting, and technical support.

Technical Support Issues

If you have any difficulties with this CD, you can access our Web site at http://www.newriders.com.

System Requirements

The CD-ROM was configured for use with systems running Windows 98, Windows 2000, Windows Me, and Windows XP, and with OS 9 (with CarbonLib 1.5 or higher) and OS X for the Macintosh.

Loading the CD Files

To load the files from the CD, insert the disc into your CD-ROM drive. If autoplay is enabled on your machine, the CD-ROM setup program starts automatically the first time you insert the disc. If the CD setup program doesn't start automatically, you can access the files using Windows Explorer/Finder manually. You may copy the files to your hard drive, or use them right off the disc. You may want to copy the files into their own directory on your hard drive; many of the exercises recommend it.

NOTE: This CD-ROM uses long and mixed-case filenames, requiring the use of a protected mode CD-ROM driver.

The Exercise Files

This CD contains all the files you'll need to complete the exercises in *Inside Dreamweaver MX*. These files are for use with the exercises in this book, and are organized by chapter. Please note, however, that you'll not find any folders for chapters 1, 8, 15, 21, 23, 24, 26, 32, 34, and 35; these chapters either do not contain exercises or contain exercises for which you do not need to access any project files.

Read This Before Opening the Software

By opening the CD package, you agree to be bound by the following agreement:

You may not copy or redistribute the entire CD-ROM as a whole. Copying and redistribution of individual software programs on the CD-ROM is governed by terms set by individual copyright holders.

This software is sold as-is, without warranty of any kind, either expressed or implied, including but not limited to the implied warranties of merchantability and fitness for a particular purpose. Neither the publisher nor its dealers or distributors assumes any liability for any alleged or actual damages arising from the use of this program. (Some states do not allow for the exclusion of implied warranties, so the exclusion may not apply to you.)

Index

D

F

VISIT OUR WEB SITE

WWW.NEWRIDERS.COM

On our web site, you'll find information about our other books, authors, tables of contents, and book errata. You will also find information about book registration and how to purchase our books, both domestically and internationally.

EMAIL US

Contact us at: **nrfeedback@newriders.com**

- If you have comments or questions about this book
- To report errors that you have found in this book
- If you have a book proposal to submit or are interested in writing for New Riders
- If you are an expert in a computer topic or technology and are interested in being a technical editor who reviews manuscripts for technical accuracy

Contact us at: **nreducation@newriders.com**

- If you are an instructor from an educational institution who wants to preview New Riders books for classroom use. Email should include your name, title, school, department, address, phone number, office days/hours, text in use, and enrollment, along with your request for desk/examination copies and/or additional information.

Contact us at: **nrmedia@newriders.com**

- If you are a member of the media who is interested in reviewing copies of New Riders books. Send your name, mailing address, and email address, along with the name of the publication or web site you work for.

BULK PURCHASES/CORPORATE SALES

The publisher offers discounts on this book when ordered in quantity for bulk purchases and special sales. For sales within the U.S., please contact: Corporate and Government Sales (800) 382-3419 or **corpsales@pearsontechgroup.com**. Outside of the U.S., please contact: International Sales (317) 581-3793 or **international@pearsontechgroup.com**.

WRITE TO US

New Riders Publishing
201 W. 103rd St.
Indianapolis, IN 46290-1097

CALL/FAX US

Toll-free (800) 571-5840
If outside U.S. (317) 581-3500
Ask for New Riders
FAX: (317) 581-4663

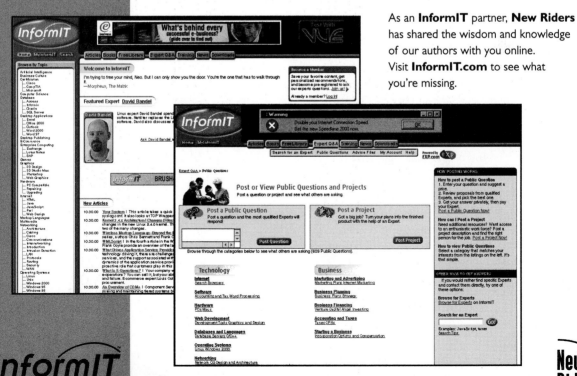

Publishing
the Voices
that Matter

OUR AUTHORS

PRESS ROOM

| web development | design | photoshop | new media | 3-D | server technologies |

EDUCATORS

ABOUT US

CONTACT US

You already know that New Riders brings you the **Voices That Matter**.

But what does that mean? It means that New Riders brings you the

Voices that challenge your assumptions, take your talents to the next

level, or simply help you better understand the complex technical world

we're all navigating.

Visit **www.newriders.com** to find:

▸ **10% discount** and **free shipping** on all book purchases

▸ Never before published chapters

▸ Sample chapters and excerpts

▸ Author bios and interviews

▸ Contests and enter-to-wins

▸ Up-to-date industry event information

▸ Book reviews

▸ Special offers from our friends and partners

▸ Info on how to join our User Group program

▸ Ways to have your Voice heard

WWW.NEWRIDERS.COM

DREAMWEAVER MX

**Dreamweaver MX
Web Development**
0735713081
Drew McLellan
US$45.00

Dreamweaver MX Magic
0735711798
Brad Halstead,
Josh Cavalier, et al.
US$39.99

**Joseph Lowery's Beyond
Dreamweaver**
0735712778
Joseph Lowery
US$45.00

**eLearning with
Dreamweaver MX:
Building Online
Learning Applications**
0735712743
Betsy Bruce
US$45.00

**ColdFusion MX
Applications
with Dreamweaver MX**
0735712719
David Golden
US$49.99

**Dreamweaver MX
Extensions**
0735711828
Laura Gutman
US$39.99

Dreamweaver MX Templates
0735713197
Brad Halstead
Murray Summers
US$29.99
Available October 2002

Dreamweaver MX Killer Tips
0735713022
Joseph Lowery
US$39.99
Available January 2003

New Riders